CW01582938

The Life and Work of St. Paul. Popular Ed

Frederic William Farrar

Nabu Public Domain Reprints:

You are holding a reproduction of an original work published before 1923 that is in the public domain in the United States of America, and possibly other countries. You may freely copy and distribute this work as no entity (individual or corporate) has a copyright on the body of the work. This book may contain prior copyright references, and library stamps (as most of these works were scanned from library copies). These have been scanned and retained as part of the historical artifact.

This book may have occasional imperfections such as missing or blurred pages, poor pictures, errant marks, etc. that were either part of the original artifact, or were introduced by the scanning process. We believe this work is culturally important, and despite the imperfections, have elected to bring it back into print as part of our continuing commitment to the preservation of printed works worldwide. We appreciate your understanding of the imperfections in the preservation process, and hope you enjoy this valuable book.

THE

LIFE AND WORK

OF

ST. PAUL.

THE

LIFE AND WORK

OF

ST. PAUL.

BY

FREDERIC W. FARRAR, D.D., F.R.S.;

LATE FELLOW OF TRINITY COLLEGE, CAMBRIDGE;
ARCHDEACON AND CANON OF WESTMINSTER; AND CHAPLAIN IN ORDINARY
TO THE QUEEN.

Εἰ καὶ Παῦλος ἦν ἀλλ' ἄνθρωπος ἦν.—St. Chrys.

POPULAR EDITION.

CASSELL & COMPANY, Limited:
LONDON, PARIS & NEW YORK.

1884.

[ALL RIGHTS RESERVED.]

1062. e. 6.

BODLEIAN LIBRARY
OXFORD.

TO THE

RIGHT REV. J. B. LIGHTFOOT, D.D.,

LORD BISHOP OF DURHAM,

TO WHOM ALL STUDENTS OF ST. PAUL'S EPISTLES ARE DEEPLY INDEBTED,

AND FROM WHOM FOR THIRTY YEARS I HAVE RECEIVED MANY KINDNESSES,

I Dedicate

THESE STUDIES ON THE LIFE AND WORK

OF

THE APOSTLE OF THE GENTILES.

PREFACE.

In the *Life of Christ* I endeavoured, to the best of my power, to furnish, in the form of a narrative, such a commentary upon the Gospels as should bring to bear the most valuable results of modern research. By studying every line and word of the Evangelists with close and reverent attention; by seeking for the most genuine readings and the most accurate translations; by visiting the scenes in the midst of which our Lord had moved; by endeavouring to form a conception at once true and vivid of the circumstances of the age in which He lived, and the daily conditions of religious thought and national custom by which He was surrounded—I thought that, while calling attention in large to His Divine Nature as the Incarnate Son of God, I might be enabled to set forth in clear outline the teaching and the actions of that human life which He lived for our example, and of that death which He died for us men and for our salvation.

In that work it was no small part of my object to enable readers to study the Gospels with a fuller understanding of their significance, and with a more intense impression of their reality and truth. In the present volume I have undertaken a similar task for the Acts of the Apostles and the thirteen Epistles of St. Paul. My first desire throughout has been to render some assistance towards the study of that large portion of the New Testament which is occupied with the labours and writings of the Apostle of the Gentiles; to show the grandeur of the work and example of one who was indeed a "vessel of election;" and to bring his character and history to bear on the due comprehension of those Epistles, which have bequeathed to all subsequent ages an inestimable legacy of wisdom and knowledge. In order to accomplish this task, I can conscientiously say that I have used my best diligence and care. Circumstances have precluded me from carrying out my original intention of actually visiting the countries in which St. Paul laboured; and to do this was the less necessary because abundant descriptions of them may be found in the works of many recent travellers. This branch of the subject has been amply illustrated in the well-known volumes of Messrs. Conybeare and Howson, and Mr. Thomas Lewin. To those admirable works all students of St. Paul must be largely indebted, and I need not say that my own book is not intended in any way to come into competition with theirs. It has been written in great measure with a different purpose, as well as from a different point of view. My chief object has been to give a definite, accurate, and intelligible impression of St. Paul's teaching; of the controversies in which he was engaged; of the circumstances which educed his statements of doctrine and practice; of the inmost heart of his theology in each of its phases; of his Epistles as a whole, and of each Epistle in particular as complete and perfect in itself. The task is, I think, more necessary than might be generally supposed. In our custom of studying the Bible year after year in separate texts and isolated chapters, we are but too apt to lose sight of what the Bible is as a whole, and even of the special significance of its separate books. I thought, then, that if I could in any degree render each of the Epistles more thoroughly familiar, either in their general aspect or in their special particulars, I should be rendering some service—however humble—to the Church of God.

With this object it would have been useless merely to retranslate the Epistles. To do this, and to append notes to the more difficult expressions, would have been a very old, and a comparatively easy task. But to make the Epistles an integral part of the life—to put the reader in the position of those to whom the Epistles were first read in the infant communities of Macedonia and Proconsular Asia—was a method at once less frequently attempted, and more immediately necessary. I wish above all to make the Epistles comprehensible and real. On this account I have constantly deviated from the English version. Of the merits of that version, its incomparable force and melody, it would be impossible to speak with too much reverence, and it only requires the removal of errors which were inevitable to the age in which it was executed, to make it as nearly perfect as any work of man can be. But our very familiarity with it is often a barrier to our due understanding of many passages; for "words," it has been truly said, "when often repeated, do ossify the very organs of intelligence." My object in translating without reference to the honoured phrases of our English Bible has expressly been, not only to correct where correction was required, but also to brighten the edge of expressions which time has dulled, and to reproduce, as closely as possible, the exact force and form of the original, even in those roughnesses, turns of expression, and unfinished clauses which are rightly modified in versions intended for public reading. To aim in these renderings at rhythm or grace of style has been far from my intention. I have simply tried to adopt the best reading, to give its due force to each expression, tense, and particle, and to represent as exactly as is at all compatible with English idiom what St. Paul meant in the very way in which he said it.

With the same object, I have avoided wearying the reader with those interminable discussions of often unimportant minutiæ—those endless refutations of impossible hypotheses—those exhaustive catalogues of untenable explanations which encumber so many of our Biblical commentaries. Both as to readings, renderings, and explanations, I have given at least a definite conclusion, and indicated as briefly and comprehensively as possible the grounds on which it is formed.

In excluding the enumeration of transient opinions, I have also avoided the embarrassing multiplication of needless references. When any German book has been well translated I have referred to the translation of it by its English title, and I have excluded in every way the mere semblance of research. In this work, as in the *Life of Christ*, I have made large use of illustrations from Hebrew literature. The Talmud is becoming better known every day; the Mishna is open to the study of every scholar in the magnificent work of Surenhusius; and the most important treatises of the Gemara—such as the *Berachôth* and the *Abhôda Zara*—are now accessible to all, in French and German translations of great learning and accuracy. I have diligently searched the works of various Jewish scholars, such as Jost, Grätz, Schwab, Weill, Rabbinowicz, Deutsch, Derenbourg, Munk, and others; but I have had two great advantages—first, in the very full collection of passages from every portion of the Talmud, by Mr. P. J. Herson, in his Talmudic Commentaries on Genesis and Exodus—an English translation of the former of which is now in publication—and, secondly, in the fact that every single Talmudic reference in the following pages has been carefully verified by a learned Jewish clergyman—the Rev. M. Wolkenberg, formerly a missionary to the Jews in Bulgaria. All scholars are aware that references to the Gemara are in general of a most inaccurate and uncertain character, but I have reason to hope that, apart, it may be, from a few accidental errata, every Hebraic reference in the following pages may be received with absolute reliance.

The most pleasant part of my task remains. It is to offer my heartfelt thanks to the many friends who have helped me to revise the following pages, or have given me the benefit of their kind suggestions. To one friend in particular—Mr. C. J. Monro, late Fellow of Trin. Coll., Cambridge—I owe the first expression of my sincerest gratitude. To the Rev. J. Ll. Davies and the Rev. Prof. Plumptre I am indebted for an amount of labour and trouble such as it can be the happiness of few authors to receive from scholars at once so competent and so fully occupied by public and private duties. From the Very Rev. Dean Stanley; from Mr. Walter Leaf, Fell. of Trin. Coll., Cambridge, my friend and former pupil; from the Rev. J. E. Kempe, Rector of St. James's, Piccadilly; from Mr. R. Garnett, of the British Museum; and from my valued colleagues in the parish of St. Margaret's, the Rev. H. H. Montgomery and the Rev. J. S. Northcote, I have received valuable advice, or kind assistance in the laborious task of correcting the proof-sheets. The Bishop of Durham had kindly looked over the first few pages, and but for his elevation to his present high position, I might have derived still further benefit from his wide learning and invariable kindness. If my book fail to achieve the purposes for which it was written, I shall at least have enjoyed the long weeks of labour spent in the closest study of the Word of God, and next to this I shall value the remembrance that I received from so many friends, a self-sacrificing kindness which I had so little right to expect, and am so little able to repay.

I desire also to express my best obligations to my Publishers, and the gentlemen connected with their firm, who have spared no labour in seeing the work through the press.

After having received such ungrudging aid it would be ungrateful to dwell on the disadvantages in the midst of which this book has been written. I have done my best under the circumstances in which a task of such dimensions was alone possible; and though I have fallen far short of my own ideal —though I am deeply conscious of the many necessary imperfections of my work—though it is hardly possible that I should have escaped errors in a book involving so many hundreds of references and necessitating the examination of so many critical and exegetical questions—I still hope that the work will be accepted as furnishing another part of a humble but faithful endeavour to enable those who read them to acquire a more thorough knowledge of a large portion of the Word of God.

F. W. FARRAR.

ST. MARGARET'S RECTORY.
1879.

TABLE OF CONTENTS.

Book I.—THE TRAINING OF THE APOSTLE.

Book II.—ST. STEPHEN AND THE HELLENISTS.

Book III.—THE CONVERSION.

PAGE

Book VIII.—CHRISTIANITY IN ACHAIA.

CHAPTER XXVII.—St. Paul at Athens.

CHAPTER XXVIII.—St. Paul at Corinth.

CHAPTER XXIX.—The First Epistle to the Thessalonians.

CHAPTER XXX.—The Second Epistle to the Thessalonians.

Book IX.—EPHESUS.

CHAPTER XXXI.—Paul at Ephesus.

APPENDIX.

THE

LIFE AND WORK OF ST. PAUL.

Book I.

THE TRAINING OF THE APOSTLE.

CHAPTER I.

INTRODUCTORY.

Σκεῦος ἐκλογῆς μοι ἐστὶν οὗτος.—ACTS ix. 15.

OF the twelve men whom Jesus chose to be His companions and heralds during the brief years of His earthly ministry, two alone can be said to have stamped upon the infant Church the impress of their own individuality. These two were John and Simon. Our Lord Himself, by the titles which He gave them, indicated the distinctions of their character, and the pre-eminence of their gifts. John was called a Son of Thunder; Simon was to be known to all ages as Kephas, or Peter, the Apostle of the Foundation stone.[1] To Peter was granted the honour of authoritatively admitting the first uncircumcised Gentile, on equal terms, into the brotherhood of Christ, and he has ever been regarded as the main pillar of the early Church.[2] John, on the other hand, is the Apostle of Love, the favourite Apostle of the Mystic, the chosen Evangelist of those whose inward adoration rises above the level of outward forms. Peter as the first to recognise the Eternal Christ, John as the chosen friend of the living Jesus, are the two of that first order of Apostles whose names appear to human eyes to shine with the brightest lustre upon those twelve precious stones which are the foundations of the New Jerusalem.[3]

Yet there was another, to whom was entrusted a wider, a more fruitful, a more laborious mission; who was to found more numerous churches, to endure intenser sufferings, to attract to the fold of Christ a vaster multitude of followers. On the broad shoulders of St. Peter rested, at first, the support and defence of the new Society; yet his endurance was not tested so terribly as that of him on whom fell daily the "care of all the churches." St. John was the last survivor of the Apostles, and he barely escaped sharing with his brother the glory of being one of the earliest martyrs; yet even his life of long exile and heavy tribulations was a far less awful trial than that of him who counted it but a light and momentary affliction to "die daily," to be "in deaths oft."[4] A third type of the Apostolate was necessary. Besides the Apostle of Catholicity and the Apostle of Love, the Church of Christ needed also "the Apostle of Progress."

[1] Pet. ii. 4—8. [2] Gal. ii. 9. [3] Rev. xxi. 14.
[4] 1 Cor. xv. 31; 2 Cor. xi. 23.

In truth it is hardly possible to exaggerate the extent, the permanence, the vast importance, of those services which were rendered to Christianity by Paul of Tarsus. It would have been no mean boast for the most heroic worker that he had toiled more abundantly than such toilers as the Apostles. It would have been a sufficient claim to eternal gratitude to have preached from Jerusalem to Illyricum, from Illyricum to Rome, and, it may be, even to Spain, the Gospel which gave new life to a weary and outworn world. Yet these are, perhaps, the least permanent of the benefits which mankind has reaped from his life and genius. For it is in his Epistles—casual as was the origin of some of them—that we find the earliest utterances of that Christian literature to which the world is indebted for its richest treasures of poetry and eloquence, of moral wisdom and spiritual consolation. It is to his intellect, fired by the love and illuminated by the Spirit of his Lord, that we owe the first systematic statement, in their mutual connexion and interdependence, of the great truths of that Mystery of Godliness which had been hidden from the ages, but was revealed in the Gospel of the Christ. It is to his undaunted determination, his clear vision, his moral loftiness, that we are indebted for the emancipation of religion from the intolerable yoke of legal observances—the cutting asunder of the living body of Christianity from the heavy corpse of an abrogated Levitism.[1] It was he alone who was God's appointed instrument to render possible the universal spread of Christianity, and to lay deep in the hearts of European churches the solid bases of Christendom. As the Apostle of the Gentiles he was pre-eminently and necessarily the Apostle of freedom, of culture, of the understanding; yet he has, if possible, a higher glory than all this, in the fact that he too, more than any other, is the Apostle who made clear to the religious consciousness of mankind the "justification by faith" which springs from the mystic union of the soul with Christ—the Apostle who has both brought home to numberless Christians in all ages the sense of their own helplessness, and pointed them most convincingly to the blessedness and the universality of that redemption which their Saviour wrought. And hence whenever the faith of Christ has been most dimmed in the hearts of men, whenever its pure fires have seemed in greatest danger of being stifled, as in the fifteenth century—under the dead ashes of sensuality, or quenched, as in the eighteenth century, by the chilling blasts of scepticism, it is mostly by the influence of his writings that religious life has been revived.[2] It was one of his searching moral precepts—"Let us walk honestly, as in the day; not in rioting and drunkenness, not in chambering and wantonness, not in strife and envying"—which became to St. Augustine a guiding star out of the night of deadly moral aberrations.[3] It was his prevailing doctrine of free deliverance through the merits of Christ which, as it had worked in the spirit of Paul himself to shatter the bonds of Jewish formalism, worked once more in the soul of Luther to

[1] Gal. iv. 9; Rom. viii. 3. (Heb. vii. 18.) [2] See Neander, *Planting*, E.T., p. 78.
[3] Aug. *Confess.* viii. 12—18; Krenkel, *Paulus der Ap. d. Heiden*, p. 1.

burst the gates of brass, and break the bars of iron in sunder with which the Papacy had imprisoned for so many centuries the souls which God made free.

It has happened not unfrequently in the providence of God that the destroyer of a creed or system has been bred and trained in the inmost bosom of the system which he was destined to shake or to destroy. Sakya Mouni had been brought up in Brahminism; Luther had taken the vows of an Augustinian; Pascal had been trained as a Jesuit; Spinoza was a Jew; Wesley and Whitefield were clergymen of the Church of England. It was not otherwise with St. Paul. The victorious enemy of heathen philosophy and heathen worship had passed his boyhood amid the heathen surroundings of a philosophic city. The deadliest antagonist of Judaic exclusiveness was by birth a Hebrew of the Hebrews. The dealer of the death-wound to the spirit of Pharisaism was a Pharisee, a son of Pharisees;[1] had been brought up from his youth at Jerusalem at the feet of Gamaliel;[2] had been taught according to the perfect manner of the law of the fathers; had lived "after the most straitest sect" of the Jewish service.[3] As his work differed in many respects from that of the other Apostles, so his training was wholly unlike theirs. Their earliest years had been spent in the villages of Gennesareth and the fisher-huts on the shores of the Sea of Galilee; his in the crowded ghetto of a Pagan capital. They, with few exceptions, were men neither of commanding genius nor strongly marked characteristics; he was a man of intense individuality and marvellous intellectual power. They were "unlearned and ignorant," untrained in the technicalities, inexperienced in the methods, which passed among the Jews for theologic learning; he had sat as a "disciple of the wise"[4] at the feet of the most eminent of the Rabbis, and had been selected as the inquisitorial agent of Priests and Sanhedrists because he surpassed his contemporaries in burning zeal for the traditions of the schools.[5]

This is the man whose career will best enable us to understand the Dawn of Christianity upon the darkness alike of Jew and Gentile; the man who loosed Christianity from the cerements of Judaism, and inspired the world of Paganism with joy and hope. The study of his life will leave upon our minds a fuller conception of the extreme nobleness of the man, and of the truths which he lived and died to teach. And we must consider that life, as far as possible, without traditional bias, and with the determination to see it as it appeared to his contemporaries, as it appeared to Paul himself. "For if he was a Paul," says St. Chrysostom, "he also was a man,"—nay, more than this, his very infirmities enhanced his greatness. He stands infinitely above the need of indiscriminate panegyric.

[1] Acts xxiii. 6 (Phil. iii. 5). The true reading, υἱὸς Φαρισαίων (א, A, B, C, Syr., Vulg.); he was a Pharisee of the third generation, τριφαρισαῖος.

[2] Acts xxii. 3; xxvi. 4.

[3] Acts xxvi. 5. θρησκεία is rather "cult," "external service," than "religion."

[4] The תלמידי חכם, of whose praises and privileges the Talmud is full.

[5] Gal. i. 14, προέκοπτον ἐν τῷ Ἰουδαϊσμῷ (*i.e.*, in Jewish observances), ὑπὲρ, κ.τ.λ., περισσοτέρως ζηλωτὴς, κ.τ.λ.

If we describe him as exempt from all human weakness—if we look at his actions as though it were irreverence to suppose that they ever fell short of his own ideal—we not only describe an impossible character, but we contradict his own reiterated testimonies. It is not a sinless example which we are now called upon to contemplate, but the life of one who, in deep sincerity, called himself "the chief of sinners;" it is the career of one whose ordinary life (βίος) was human, not divine—human in its impetuosity, human in its sensibilities, human, perhaps, in some of its concessions and accommodations; but whose inner life (ζωή) was truly divine in so far as it manifested the workings of the Spirit, in so far as it was dead to the world, and hid with Christ in God.[1] It is utterly alien to the purpose and manner of Scripture to present to us any of our fellow-men in the light of faultless heroes or unapproachable demi-gods. The notion that it is irreverent to suppose a flaw in the conduct of an Apostle is one of those instances of "false humility" which degrade Scripture under pretence of honouring it, and substitute a dead letter-worship for a living docility. From idealised presentments of the lives of our fellow-servants,[2] there would be but little for us to learn; but we *do* learn the greatest and most important of all lessons when we mark in a struggling soul the triumph of the grace of God—when we see a man, weak like ourselves, tempted like ourselves, erring like ourselves, enabled by the force of a sacred purpose to conquer temptation, to trample on selfishness, to rear even upon sins and failures the superstructure of a great and holy life,—to build (as it were) "the cities of Judah out of the ruined fortresses of Samaria."[3]

It may seem strange if I say that we know the heart of St. Paul to its inmost depths. It is true that, besides a few scattered remnants of ecclesiastical tradition, we have but two sources whence to derive his history—the Acts of the Apostles, and the Epistles of Paul himself; and the day has gone by when we could at once, and without further inquiry, *assume* that both of these sources, in the fullest extent, were absolutely and equally to be relied on. Since Baur wrote his *Paulus*, and Zeller his *Apostelgeschichte*, it has become impossible to make use of the Acts of the Apostles, and the thirteen Epistles commonly attributed to St. Paul, without some justification of the grounds upon which their genuineness is established. To do this exhaustively would require a separate volume, and the work has been already done, and is being done by abler hands than mine. All that is here necessary is to say that I should in no instance make use of any statement in those Epistles of which the genuineness can still be regarded as fairly disputable, if I did not hope to state some of the reasons which appear sufficient to justify my doing so; and that if in any cases the genuineness or proper superscription of any Epistle, or part of an Epistle, seems to me to be a matter of uncertainty, I shall feel no hesitation in expressing such an opinion. Of the Acts of the Apostles I shall have various opportunities to speak incidentally, and, without entering on any

[1] Βίος, *vita quam vivimus*; ζωή, *vita quâ vivimus*. (Gal. ii. 20.)
[2] Rev. xix. 10.
[3] Bossuet (1 Kings xv. 22). Acts xiv. 15.

separate defence of the book against the assaults of modern critics, I will at present only express my conviction that, even if we admit that it was "an ancient Eirenicon," intended to check the strife of parties by showing that there had been no irreconcilable opposition between the views and ordinances of St. Peter and St. Paul;—even if we concede the obvious principle that whenever there appears to be any contradiction between the Acts and the Epistles, the authority of the latter must be considered paramount;—nay, even if we acknowledge that subjective and artificial considerations may have had some influence in the form and construction of the book;—yet the Acts of the Apostles is in all its main outlines a genuine and trustworthy history. Let it be granted that in the Acts we have a picture of essential unity between the followers of the Judaic and the Pauline schools of thought, which we might conjecture from the Epistles to have been less harmonious and less undisturbed; let it be granted that in the Acts we more than once see Paul acting in a way which from the Epistles we should *à priori* have deemed unlikely. Even these concessions are fairly disputable; yet in granting them we only say what is in itself sufficiently obvious, that both records are confessedly fragmentary. They are fragmentary, of course, because neither of them even professes to give us any continuous narrative of the Apostle's life. That life is—roughly speaking—only known to us at intervals during its central and later period, between the years A.D. 36 and A.D. 66. It is like a manuscript of which the beginning and the end are irrecoverably lost. It is like one of those rivers which spring from unknown sources, and sink into the ground before they have reached the sea. But more than this, how incomplete is our knowledge even of that portion of which these records and notices remain! Of this fact we can have no more overwhelming proof than we may derive from reading that "Iliad of woes," the famous passage of the Second Epistle to the Corinthians, where, driven against his will by the calumnies of his enemies to an appearance of boastfulness of which the very notion was abhorrent to him, he is forced to write a summary sketch of what he had done and suffered.[1] That enumeration is given long before the end of his career, and yet of the specific outrages and dangers there mentioned no less than eleven are not once alluded to in the Acts, though many others are there mentioned which were subsequent to that sad enumeration. Not one, for instance, of the five scourgings with Jewish thongs is referred to by St. Luke; one only of the three beatings with Roman rods; not one of the three shipwrecks, though a later one is so elaborately detailed; no allusion to the night and day in the deep; two only of what St. Clement tells us were seven imprisonments.[2] There are even whole classes of perils to which the writer of the Acts, though he was certainly at one time a companion of St. Paul, makes no allusion whatever—as, for instance, the perils of rivers, the perils of robbers, the perils in the wilderness, the perils among false brethren, the hunger, the thirst, the fasting, the cold, the nakedness. And these, which are thus passed over without notice in the

[1] 2 Cor. xi. 24—33, written about A.D. 57, nearly ten years before his death.

[2] ἑπτάκις δεσμὰ φορέσας (Ep. 1 *ad Cor.* 5).

Acts. are in the Epistles mentioned only so cursorily, so generally, so unchronologically, that scarcely one of them can be dwelt upon and assigned with certainty to its due order of succession in St. Paul's biography. If this, then, is the case, who can pretend that in such a life there is not room for a series of events and actions—even for an exhibition of phases of character—in the narrative, which neither did nor could find place in the letters; and for events and features of character in the letters which find no reflection in the narrative? For of those letters how many are preserved? Thirteen only—even if all the thirteen be indisputably genuine—out of a much larger multitude which he must undoubtedly have written.[1] And of these thirteen some are separated from others by great intervals of time; some contain scarcely a single particular which can be made to bear on a consecutive biography; and not one is preserved which gives us the earlier stage of his views and experiences before he had set foot on European soil. It is, then, idle to assume that either of our sources must be rejected as untrustworthy because it presents us with fresh aspects of a myriad-sided character; or that events in the narrative must be condemned as scarcely honest inventions because they present no *primâ facie* accordance with what we might otherwise have expected from brief and scattered letters out of the multiplex correspondence of a varied life. If there were anything in the Acts which appeared to me irreconcilable with the certain indications of the Epistles, I should feel no hesitation in rejecting it. But most, if not all, of the objections urged against the credibility of the Acts appear to me—for reasons to be hereafter given—both frivolous and untenable. If there are any passages in that book which have been represented as throwing a shade of inconsistency over the character of the great Apostle, there is no such instance which, however interpreted, does not find its support and justification in his own undoubted works. If men of great learning, eminence, and acuteness had not assumed the contrary, it might have seemed superfluous to say that the records of history, and the experiences of daily life, furnish us with abundant instances of lives narrated with perfect honesty, though they have been presented from opposite points of view; and of events which appear to be contradictory only because the point of reconcilement between them has been forgotten. Further than this, the points of contact between the Acts and the Epistles are numberless, and it must suffice, once for all, to refer to Paley's *Horæ Paulinæ* in proof that even the undesigned coincidences may be counted by scores. To furnish a separate refutation of all the objections which have been brought against the credibility of the Acts of the Apostles, would be a tedious and interminable task; but the actual narrative of the following pages should exhibit a decisive answer to them, unless it can be shown that it fails to combine the separate *data*, or that the attempt to combine them has led to incongruous and impossible results.

I believe, then, that we have enough, and more than enough, still left to us to show what manner of life Paul lived, and what manner of man he was. A biography sketched in outline is often more true and more useful than one

[1] I do not reckon the Epistle to the Hebrews, believing it to be the work of Apollos.

that occupies itself with minute detail. We do not in reality know more of a great man because we happen to know the petty circumstances which made up his daily existence, or because a mistaken admiration has handed down to posterity the promiscuous commonplaces of his ordinary correspondence. We know a man truly when we know him at his greatest and his best; we realise his significance for ourselves and for the world when we see him in the noblest activity of his career, on the loftiest summit, and in the fullest glory of his life. There are lives which may be instructive from their very littleness, and it may be well that the biographers of such lives should enter into detail. But of the best and greatest it may be emphatically asserted that to know more about them would only be to know less of them. It is quite possible that if, in the case of one so sensitive and so impetuous as St. Paul, a minute and servile record had preserved for us every hasty expression, every fugitive note, every momentary fall below the loftiest standard, the small souls which ever rejoice at seeing the noblest of their race degraded, even for an instant, to the same dead level as themselves, might have found some things over which to glory. That such must have been the result we may infer from the energy and sincerity of self-condemnation with which the Apostle recognises his own imperfections. But such miserable records, even had they been entirely truthful, would only have obscured for us the true Paul —Paul as he stands in the light of history; Paul as he is preserved for us in the records of Christianity; Paul energetic as Peter, and contemplative as John; Paul the hero of unselfishness; Paul the mighty champion of spiritual freedom; Paul a greater preacher than Chrysostom, a greater missionary than Xavier, a greater reformer than Luther, a greater theologian than St. Thomas of Aquinum; Paul the inspired Apostle of the Gentiles, the slave of the Lord Jesus Christ.

CHAPTER II.

BOYHOOD IN A HEATHEN CITY.

Οὐκ ἀσήμου πόλεως πολίτης.—ACTS xxi. 39.

THOUGH we cannot state with perfect accuracy the date either of the birth or death of the great Apostle of the Gentiles, both may be inferred within narrow limits. When he is first mentioned, on the occasion of Stephen's martyrdom, he is called a young man,[1] and when he wrote the Epistle to Philemon he calls himself Paul the aged.[2] Now, although the words *νεανίας*

[1] Acts vii. 58.

[2] Philem., verse 9. It should, indeed, be mentioned that whether we read *πρεσβύτης* or *πρεσβευτής*, the meaning *may* be, "Paul an ambassador, ay, and now even a chained ambassador, of Jesus Christ." Compare the fine antithesis, *ὑπὲρ οὗ πρεσβεύω*

and πρεσβύτης were used vaguely in ancient times, and though the exact limits of "youth" and "age" were as indeterminate then as they have ever been, yet, since we learn that immediately after the death of Stephen, Saul was entrusted with a most important mission, and was, in all probability, a member of the Sanhedrin, he must at that time have been a man of thirty. Now, the martyrdom of Stephen probably took place early in A.D. 37, and the Epistle to Philemon was written about A.D. 63. At the latter period, therefore, he would have been less than sixty years old, and this may seem too young to claim the title of "the aged." But "age" is a very relative term, and one who had been scourged, and lashed, and stoned, and imprisoned, and shipwrecked —one who, for so many years, besides the heavy burden of mental anguish and responsibility, had been "scorched by the heat of Sirius and tossed by the violence of Euroclydon,"[1] might well have felt himself an old and outworn man when he wrote from his Roman prison at the age of threescore years.[2] It is, therefore, tolerably certain that he was born during the first ten years of our era, and probable that he was born about A.D. 3. Since, then, our received Dionysian era is now known to be four years too early, the birth of Christ's greatest follower happened in the same decade as that of our Lord Himself.[3]

But all the circumstances which surrounded the cradle and infancy of the infant Saul were widely different from those amid which his Lord had grown to boyhood. It was in an obscure and lonely village of Palestine, amid surroundings almost exclusively Judaic, that Jesus "grew in wisdom and stature and favour with God and man;" but Saul passed his earliest years in the famous capital of a Roman province, and must have recalled, with his first conscious reminiscences, the language and customs of the Pagan world.

There is no sufficient reason to doubt the entire accuracy of the expression "born in Tarsus," which is attributed to St. Paul in his Hebrew speech to the infuriated multitude from the steps of the Tower of Antonia.[4] To assert that the speeches in the Acts could not have attained to verbal exactness may be true of some of them, but, on the other hand, those who on such grounds as these disparage the work of St. Luke, as a mere "treatise with an object," must bear in mind that it would, in this point of view, have been far more to the purpose if he had made St. Paul assert that he was born in a Jewish town. We must, therefore, reject the curious and twice-repeated assertion of St.

ἐν ἁλύσει, "I am an ambassador in fetters" (Eph. vi. 20). The tone of his later writings is, however, that of an old man.

[1] Jer. Taylor.

[2] Roger Bacon calls himself "senem," apparently at fifty-three, and Sir Walter Scott speaks of himself as a "grey old man" at fifty-five. (See Lightfoot, *Colossians*, p. 404.) According to Philo a man was νεανίας between twenty-one and twenty-eight; but his distinctions are purely artificial. It seems that a man might be called νεανίας and even νεανίσκος till forty. (Xen. *Mem.* i. 2, 35; Krüger, *Vit. Xen.* 12.)

[3] These dates agree fairly with the statement of the Pseudo-Chrysostom (*Orat. Encom. in Pet. et Paul.*, *Opp.* viii., ed. Montfaucon), that he had been for thirty-five years a servant of Christ, and was martyred at the age of sixty-eight.

[4] Acts xxii. 3.

Jerome,[1] that the Apostle was born at Giscala,[2] and had been taken to Tarsus by his parents when they left their native city, in consequence of its devastation by the Romans. The assertion is indeed discredited because it is mixed up with what appears to be a flagrant anachronism as to the date at which Giscala was destroyed.[3] It is, however, worthy of attention. St. Jerome, from his thorough familiarity with the Holy Land, in which he spent so many years of his life, has preserved for us several authentic fragments of tradition, and we may feel sure that he would not arbitrarily have set aside a general belief founded upon a distinct statement in the Acts of the Apostles. If in this matter pure invention had been at work, it is almost inconceivable that any one should have singled out for distinction so insignificant a spot as Giscala, which is not once mentioned in the Bible, and which acquired its sole notoriety from its connexion with the zealot Judas.[4] We may, therefore, fairly assume that the tradition mentioned by St. Jerome is so far true that the parents or grand-parents of St. Paul had been Galilæans, and had, from some cause or other—though it cannot have been the cause which the tradition assigned—been compelled to migrate from Giscala to the busy capital of Pagan Cilicia.

If this be the case, it helps, as St. Jerome himself points out, to explain another difficulty. St. Paul, on every possible occasion, assumes and glories in the title not only of "an Israelite,"[5] which may be regarded as a "name of honour," but also of "a Hebrew"—"a Hebrew of the Hebrews."[6] Now certainly, in its proper and technical sense, the word "Hebrew" is the direct opposite of "Hellenist,"[7] and St. Paul, if brought up at Tarsus, could only strictly be regarded as a Jew of the Dispersion—a Jew of that vast body who, even when they were not ignorant of Hebrew—as even the most learned of them sometimes were—still spoke Greek as their native tongue.[8] It may, of course, be said that St. Paul uses the word Hebrew only in its general sense, and that he meant to imply by it that he was not a Hellenist to the same extent that, for instance, even so learned and eminent a Jew as Philo was, who, with all his great ability, did not know

[1] Jer. *de Viris Illustr.* 5: "De tribu Benjamin et oppido Judaeae Giscalis fuit, quo a Romanis capto, cum parentibus suis Tarsum Ciliciae commigravit." It has been again and again asserted that St. Jerome rejects or discredits this tradition in his Commentary on Philemon (*Opp.* iv. 454), where he says that some understood the term "my fellow-prisoner" to mean that Epaphras had been taken captive at Giscala at the same time as Paul, and had been settled in Colossæ. Even Neander (*Planting*, p. 79) follows this current error, on the ground that Jerome says, "Quis sit Epaphras concaptivus Pauli talem *fabulam* accepimus." But that *fabula* does not here mean "false account," as he translates it, is sufficiently proved by the fact that St. Jerome continues, "Quod si ita EST, possumus et Epaphram illo tempore captum suspicari, quo captus est Paulus," &c.

[2] Giscala, now El-Jish, was the last place in Galilee that held out against the Romans. (Jos. *B. J.* ii. 20, § 6; iv. 2, §§ 1—5.)

[3] It was taken A. D. 67.

[4] Jos. *B. J.* ii. 21, § 1; *Vit.* 10. He calls it Πολίχνη.

[5] John i. 47; Acts xiii. 16; Rom. ix. 4.

[6] 2 Cor. xi. 22; Phil. iii. 5.

[7] See Acts vi. 1, and *infra*, p. 71.

[8] "Parentum conditionem adolescentulum Paulum secutum, et sic posse stare illud, quod de se ipso testatur, 'Hebraei sunt? et ego,' etc., quae illum Judaeum magis indicant, quam Tarsensem" (Jer.).

either the Biblical Hebrew or the Aramaic vernacular, which was still called by that name.[1] Perhaps St. Paul spoke Aramaic with even greater fluency than he spoke Greek itself;[2] and his knowledge of Hebrew may be inferred from his custom of sometimes reverting to the Hebrew scriptures in the original when the LXX. version was less suitable to his purpose. It is an interesting, though undesigned,[3] confirmation of this fact, that the Divine Vision on the road to Damascus spoke to him, at the supreme moment of his life, in the language which was evidently the language of his own inmost thoughts. As one, therefore, to whom the Hebrew of that day was a sort of mother-tongue, and the Hebrew of the Bible an acquired language, St. Paul might call himself a Hebrew, though technically speaking he was also a Hellenist; and the term would be still more precise and cogent if his parents and forefathers had, almost till the time of his birth, been Palestinian Jews.

The Tarsus in which St. Paul was born was very different from the dirty, squalid, and ruinous Mohammedan city which still bears the name and stands upon the site. The natural features of the city, indeed, remain unchanged: the fertile plain still surrounds it; the snowy mountains of the chain of Taurus still look down on it; the bright swift stream of the Cydnus still refreshes it.[4] But with these scenes of beauty and majesty we are the less concerned, because they seem to have had no influence over the mind of the youthful Saul. We can well imagine how, in a nature differently constituted, they would have been like a continual inspiration; how they would have melted into the very imagery of his thoughts; how, again and again, in crowded cities and foul prisons, they would have

> "Flashed upon that inward eye
> Which is the bliss of solitude."

The scenes in which the whole life of David had been spent were far less majestic, as well as far less varied, than many of those in which the lot of St. Paul was cast; yet the Psalms of David are a very handbook of poetic description, while in the Epistles of St. Paul we only breathe the air of cities and synagogues. He alludes, indeed, to the Temple not made with hands, but never to its mountain pillars, and but once to its nightly stars.[5] To David the whole visible universe is but one vast House of God, in which, like angelic ministrants, the fire and hail, snow and vapour, wind and storm, fulfil His word. With St. Paul—though he, too, is well aware that "the invisible things of Him from the creation of the world are clearly visible, being appre-

[1] Philo's ignorance of Hebrew is generally admitted.

[2] Acts xxi. 40: *τῇ Ἑβραΐδι διαλέκτῳ*—*i.e.*, of course, the Syriac. These Jews of Palestine would for the most part be able to understand the Bible, if not in the original Hebrew, at any rate through the aid of a paraphrast.

[3] *E.g.*, in 1 Cor. iii. 19; 2 Cor. viii. 15; 2 Tim. ii. 19. Whether there existed any *Volksbibel* of extracts besides the LXX. I will not discuss. See Hilgenfeld, *Zeitschr.* xviii. (1875), p. 118.

[4] The Cydnus no longer, however, flows *through* Tersoos as it did (Strabo, xiv. 5; Plin. *H. N.* vi. 22; Beaufort's *Karamania*, 271 *sq.*).

[5] Acts xvii. 24; 1 Cor. xv. 41.

hended by the things that He hath made, even His eternal power and divinity"—yet to him this was an indisputable axiom, not a conviction constantly renewed with admiration and delight. There are few writers who, to judge solely from their writings, seem to have been less moved by the beauties of the external world. Though he had sailed again and again across the blue Mediterranean, and must have been familiar with the beauty of those Isles of Greece—

> "Where burning Sappho loved and sung,
> Where grew the arts of war and peace,
> Where Delos rose, and Phœbus sprung;"

though he had again and again traversed the pine-clad gorges of the Asian hills, and seen Ida, and Olympus, and Parnassus, in all their majesty; though his life had been endangered in mountain torrents and stormy waves, and he must have often wandered as a child along the banks of his native stream, to see the place where it roars in cataracts over its rocky course—his soul was so entirely absorbed in the mighty moral and spiritual truths which it was his great mission to proclaim, that not by one verse, scarcely even by a single expression, in all his letters, does he indicate the faintest gleam of delight or wonder in the glories of Nature. There is, indeed, an exquisite passage in his speech at Lystra on the goodness of "the living God, which made heaven and earth, and the sea, and all things that are therein," and "left not Himself without witness, in that He did good, and gave us rain from heaven, and fruitful seasons, filling our hearts with food and gladness."[1] But in this case Barnabas had some share in the address, which even if it do not, as has been conjectured,[2] refer to the fragment of some choral song, is yet, in tone and substance, directly analogous to passages of the Old Testament.[3] And apart from this allusion, I cannot find a single word which shows that Paul had even the smallest susceptibility for the works of Nature. There are souls in which the burning heat of some transfusing purpose calcines every other thought, every other desire, every other admiration; and St. Paul's was one. His life was absorbingly, if not solely and exclusively, the spiritual life—the life which is utterly dead to every other interest of the groaning and travailing creation, the life hid with Christ in God. He sees the universe of God only as it is reflected in the heart and life of man. It is true—as Humboldt has shown in his *Cosmos*—that what is called the sentimental love of Nature is a modern rather than an ancient feeling.[4] In St. Paul, however, this indifference to the

[1] Acts xiv. 17.

[2] By Mr. Humphry, *ad loc.*

[3] Job v. 10; Ps. civ. 15; cxlvii. 8, 9.

[4] Compare the surprise expressed by the Athenian youth at Socrates' description of the lovely scene at the beginning of the *Phaedrus*, § 10, Σὺ δέ γε ὦ θαυμάσιε ἀτοπώτατός τις φαίνει. There is an admirable chapter on this subject in Friedländer, *Sittengesch. Roms*, vii. 5, § 3. The reader will recall the analogous cases of St. Bernard riding all day along the Lake of Geneva, and asking in the evening where it was; of Calvin showing no trace of delight in the beauties of Switzerland; and of Whitefield, who seems not to have borrowed a single impression or illustration from his thirteen voyages across the Atlantic and his travels from Georgia to Boston.

outer world is neither due to his antiquity nor to his Semitic birth, but solely to his individual character. The poetry of the Old Testament is full of the tenderness and life of the pastures of Palestine. In the discourses and conversations of our Lord we find frequent allusions to the loveliness of the flowers, the joyous carelessness of birds, the shifting winds, the red glow of morning and evening clouds. St. Paul's inobservance of these things—for the total absence of the remotest allusión to them by way of even passing illustration amounts to a proof that they did not deeply stir his heart—was doubtless due to the expulsive power and paramount importance of other thoughts. It may, however, have been due also to that early training which made him more familiar with crowded assemblies and thronged bazaars than with the sights and sounds of Nature.[1] It is at any rate remarkable that the only elaborate illustration which he draws from Nature turns not on a natural phenomenon but on an artificial process, and that even this process—if not absolutely unknown to the ancients—was the exact opposite of the one most commonly adopted.[2]

But if St. Paul derived no traceable influence from the scenery with which Tarsus is surrounded, if no voices from the neighbouring mountains or the neighbouring sea mingled with the many and varied tones of his impassioned utterance, other results of this providential training may be easily observed, both in his language and in his life.

The very position of Tarsus made it a centre of commercial enterprise and political power. Situated on a navigable stream, by which it communicated with the easternmost bay of the Mediterranean, and lying on a fruitful plain under that pass over the Taurus which was known as "the Cilician gates," while by the Amanid and Syrian gates it communicated with Syria, it was so necessary as a central emporium that even the error of its having embraced the side of Antony in the civil war hardly disturbed its fame and prosperity.[3]

[1] "For I was bred
In the great city, pent 'mid cloisters dim,
And saw nought lovely save the sky and stars."
Coleridge.

[2] I allude to the famous illustration of the wild olive graft (Rom. xi. 16—25). St. Paul's argument requires that a *wild* slip should have been budded upon a *fruitful* tree—viz., the ἀγριέλαιος of heathendom on the ἐλαία of Judaism. But it is scarcely needful to remark that this is never done, but the reverse—namely, the grafting of a fruitful scion on a wild stock. The olive shoot would be grafted on the oleaster, not the oleaster on the olive (Aug. *in* Ps. lxxii.). It is true that St. Paul here cares solely for the general analogy, and would have been entirely indifferent to its non-accordance with the ordinary method of ἐγκεντρισμός. Indeed, as he says that it is παρὰ φύσιν (xi. 24), it seems needless to show that this kind of grafting was ever really practised. Yet the illustration would, under these circumstances, hardly have been used by a writer more familiar with the facts of Nature. The notion that St. Paul alluded to the much rarer African custom of grafting oleaster (or Ethiopic olive) on olive, *to strengthen the latter* (cf. Plin. *H. N.* xvii. 18; Colum. *De re Rust.* v. 9; Palladius; &c.), is most unlikely, if only for the reason that it destroys the whole force of the truth which he is desiring to inculcate. (*See* Ewbank, ii. 112; Tholuck, *Rom.* 617; Meyer, 343.) He may have known the proverb, ἀκαρπότερον ἀγριελαίου. See, however, a somewhat different view in Thomson, *Land and Book*, p. 53.

[3] Tarsus resisted the party of Brutus and Cassius, but was conquered by Lucius Rufus, B.C. 43, and many Tarsians were sold as slaves to pay the fine of 1,500 talents

It was here that Cleopatra held that famous meeting with the Roman Triumvir which Shakspeare has immortalised, when she rowed up the silver Cydnus, and

> "The barge she sat in like a burnished throne
> Burnt on the water; the poop was beaten gold,
> Purple the sails, and so perfumèd that
> The winds were love-sick with them."

Yet it continued to flourish under the rule of Augustus, and enjoyed the distinction of being both a capital and a free city—*libera* and *immunis*. It was from Tarsus that the vast masses of timber, hewn in the forests of Taurus, were floated down the river to the Mediterranean dockyards; it was here that the vessels were unladen which brought to Asia the treasures of Europe; it was here that much of the wealth of Asia Minor was accumulated before it was despatched to Greece and Italy. On the coins of the city she is represented as seated amid bales of various merchandise. The bright and busy life of the streets and markets must have been the earliest scenes which attracted the notice of the youthful Saul. The dishonesty which he had witnessed in its trade may have suggested to him his metaphors of "huckstering" and "adulterating" the word of life;[1] and he may have borrowed a metaphor from the names and marks of the owners stamped upon the goods which lay upon the quays,[2] and from the earnest-money paid by the purchasers.[3] It may even have been the assembly of the free city which made him more readily adopt from the Septuagint that name of Ecclesia for the Church of Christ's elect of which his Epistles furnish the earliest instances.[4]

It was his birth at Tarsus which also determined the trade in which, during so many days and nights of toil and self-denial, the Apostle earned his daily bread. The staple manufacture of the city was the weaving, first into ropes, then into tent-covers and garments, of the hair which was supplied in boundless quantities by the goat flocks of the Taurus.[5] As the making of these *cilicia* was unskilled labour of the commonest sort, the trade of tentmaker[6] was one both lightly esteemed and miserably paid. It must not,

which he inflicted on the city. (Appian, *Bell. Civ.* iv. 64.) Τάρσος . . πάρ' αὐτοῖς τῶν πόλεων ἀξιολογωτάτη μητρόπολις οὖσα (Jos. *Antt.* i. 6, § 1).

[1] 2 Cor. ii. 17, καπηλεύοντες; iv. 2, δολοῦντες.

[2] Eph. i. 13; iv. 30. ἐσφραγίσθητε.

[3] 2 Cor. i. 22, ἀῤῥαβών.

[4] קָהָל 1 Kings xii. 2 (LXX.) The word "Church," in its more technical modern sense (as in Eph. and Col.), is developed out of the simpler meaning of *congregation* in St. Paul's earlier Epistles.

[5] See Philo, *De Victim.* 836; Plin. *H. N.* v. 32.

[6] σκηνοποιὸς, Acts xviii. 3; σκηνοῤῥάφος, Ps. Chrys. *Orat. Encom.* (*Opp.* viii. 8, Montfauc.). When Chrysostom calls him a σκυτοτόμος, "leather-cutter" (*Hom.* iv. 3, p. 864, on 2 Tim. ii.), this can hardly be correct, because such a trade would not be favoured by strict Pharisees. On the use of *cilicium* for tents see Veget. *Milit.* iv. 6; Serv. ad Virg. *Georg.* iii. 313. It served for many other purposes, as garden rugs, mantelets, shoes, and beds. (Colum. xii. 46; Liv. xxxviii. 7; Mart. xiv. 140; Jer. *Ep.* 108.) To handle the "*olentis barba mariti*" could not have been a pleasant trade. It was "bought from the shepherds of Taurus, and sold to Greek shippers of the Levant." To this day *cilice* means hair-cloth in French.

however, be inferred from this that the family of St. Paul were people of low position. The learning of a trade was a duty enjoined by the Rabbis on the parents of every Jewish boy.[1] The wisdom of the rule became apparent in the case of Paul, as doubtless of hundreds besides, when the changes and chances of life compelled him to earn his own livelihood by manual labour. It is clear, from the education provided for Paul by his parents, that they could little indeed have conjectured how absolutely their son would be reduced to depend on a toil so miserable and so unremunerative.[2] But though we see how much he felt the burden of the wretched labour by which he determined to earn his own bread rather than trespass on the charity of his converts,[3] yet it had one advantage in being so absolutely mechanical as to leave the thoughts entirely free. While he plaited the black, strong-scented goat's hair, he might be soaring in thought to the inmost heaven, or holding high converse with Apollos or Aquila, with Luke or Timothy, on the loftiest themes which can engage the mind of man.

Before considering further the influence exercised by the birthplace on the future fortunes of St. Paul, we must pause to inquire what can be discovered about his immediate family. It must be admitted that we can ascertain but little. Their possession, by whatever means, of the Roman citizenship—the mere fact of their leaving Palestine, perhaps only a short time before Paul's birth, to become units in the vast multitude of the Jews of the Dispersion—the fact, too, that so many of St. Paul's "kinsmen" bear Greek and Latin names,[4] and lived in Rome or in Ephesus,[5] might, at first sight, lead us to suppose that his whole family were of Hellenising tendencies. On the other hand, we know nothing of the reasons which may have compelled them to leave Palestine, and we have only the vaguest conjectures as to their possession of the franchise. Even if it be certain that *συγγενεῖς* means "kinsmen" in our sense of the word, and not, as Olshausen thinks, "fellow-countrymen,"[6] it was so common for Jews to have a second name, which they adopted during their residence in heathen countries, that Andronicus and the others, whom he salutes in the last chapter of the Epistle to the Romans, may all have been genuine Hebrews. The real name of Jason, for instance, may have been Jesus,

[1] On this subject see my *Life of Christ*, i. p. 82, n. Gamaliel himself was the author of the celebrated aphorism, that "learning of any kind (כל תורה, *i.e.*, even the advanced study of the Law) unaccompanied by a trade ends in nothing, and leads to sin" (*Pirke Abhôth*, ii. 2). R. Judah said truly that "labour honours the labourer" (*Nedarim*, f. 49, 2); R. Meir said, "Let a man always teach his son pure and easy trades" (*Toseft.* in *Kidd.* f. 82, 1); R. Judah says, that not to teach one's son a trade is like teaching him robbery (*Kiddushin*, f. 30, 2).

[2] The reason why he was taught this particular trade may have been purely local. Possibly his father had been taught the same trade as a boy. "A man should not change his trade, nor that of his father," says R. Yochanan; for it is said, "Hiram of Tyre was a widow's son, . . . and his father was . . . a worker in brass" (1 Kings vii. 13, 14). (*Erechin*, f. 16, 2.)

[3] 1 Thess. ii. 6, 9; 2 Thess. iii. 8; 1 Cor. ix. 12, 15.

[4] Rom. xvi. 7; Andronicus, Junia, or perhaps Junias (= Junianus); 11, Herodion; 21, Lucius, Jason, Sosipater (*συγγενεῖς*).

[5] See *infra*, *ad loc.*, for the question whether ch. xvi. is a genuine portion of the Epistle to the Romans.

[6] As in Rom. ix. 3.

just as the real name of Paul was Saul.[1] However this may be, the thorough Hebraism of the family appears in many ways. Paul's father and grandfather had been Pharisees,[2] and were, therefore, most strict observers of the Mosaic law. They had so little forgotten their extraction from the tribe of Benjamin —one of the two tribes which had remained faithful to the covenant—that they called their son Saul,[3] partly perhaps because the name, like Theætetus, means "asked" (of God), and partly because it was the name of that unfortunate hero-king of their native tribe, whose sad fate seems for many ages to have rendered his very name unpopular.[4] They sent him, probably not later than the age of thirteen, to be trained at the feet of Gamaliel. They seem to have had a married daughter in Jerusalem, whose son, on one memorable occasion, saved Paul's life.[5] Though they must have ordinarily used the Septuagint version of the Bible, from which the great majority of the Apostle's quotations are taken,[6] and from which nearly his whole theological phraseology is derived, they yet trained him to use Aramaic as his native tongue, and to read the Scriptures—an accomplishment not possessed by many learned Jewish Hellenists—in their own venerable original Hebrew.[7]

That St. Paul was a "Hebraist" in the fullest sense of the word is clear from almost every verse of his Epistles. He reckons time by the Hebrew calendar. He makes constant allusion to Jewish customs, Jewish laws, and Jewish festivals. His metaphors and turns of expression are derived with great frequency from that quiet family life for which the Jews have been in all ages distinguished. Though he writes in Greek, it is not by any means in the Greek of the schools,[8] or the Greek which, in spite of its occasional antitheses and paronomasias, would have been found tolerable by the rhetoricians of his native city. The famous critic Longinus does indeed, if the passage be genuine, praise him as the master of a dogmatic style; but certainly a Tarsian professor or a philosopher of Athens would have been inclined to ridicule his Hebraic peculiarities, awkward anakolutha, harshly-mingled metaphors, strange forms, and irregular constructions.[9] St. Jerome,

[1] When a Greek or Roman name bore any resemblance in sound to a Jewish one, it was obviously convenient for the Jew to make so slight a change. Thus Dosthai became Dositheus; Tarphon, Tryphon; Eliakim, Alkimos, &c.

[2] Acts xxiii. 6.

[3] שָׁאוּל, Shaûl.

[4] It is found as a Hebrew name in the Pentateuch (Gen. xxxvi. 37; xlvi. 10; Ex. vi. 15; Numb. xxvi. 13; but after the death of King Saul it does not occur till the time of the Apostle, and again later in Josephus (*Antt.* xx. 9, § 4; *B. J.* ii. 17, § 4; Krenkel, *Paulus*, p. 217).

[5] Acts xxiii. 16.

[6] There are about 278 quotations from the Old Testament in the New. Of these 53 are identical in the Hebrew, Septuagint, and New Testament; in 10 the Septuagint is correctly altered; in 76 it is altered incorrectly—*i.e.*, into greater divergence from the Hebrew; in 37 it is accepted where it differs from the Hebrew; in 99 all three differ; and there are 3 doubtful allusions. (See Turpie, *The Old Testament in the New*, p. 267, and *passim.*)

[7] *V. supra*, p. 9.

[8] Among numerous explanations of the πηλίκοις γράμμασιν of Gal. vi. 11, one is that his Greek letters were so ill-formed, from want of practice, as to look almost laughable.

[9] See *infra*, Excursus I., "The Style of St. Paul;" and Excursus II., "Rhetoric of St. Paul."

criticising the *οὐ κατενάρκησα ὑμῶν* of 2 Cor. xi. 9, xii. 13—which in our version is rendered, "I was not burdensome to you," but appears to mean literally, "I did not benumb you"—speaks of the numerous *cilicisms* of his style; and it is probable that such there were, though they can hardly be detected with certainty by a modern reader.[1] For though Tarsus was a city of advanced culture, Cilicia was as intellectually barbarous as it was morally despicable. The proper language of Cilicia was a dialect of Phœnician,[2] and the Greek spoken by some of the cities was so faulty as to have originated the term "solecism," which has been perpetuated in all languages to indicate impossible constructions.[3]

The residence of a Jew in a foreign city might, of course, tend to undermine his national religion, and make him indifferent to his hereditary customs. It might, however, produce an effect directly the reverse of this. There had been abundant instances of Hellenistic Jews who Hellenised in matters far more serious than the language which they spoke; but, on the other hand, the Jews, as a nation, have ever shown an almost miraculous vitality, and so far from being denationalised by a home among the heathen, they have only been confirmed in the intensity of their patriotism and their faith. We know that this had been the case with that numerous and important body, the Jews of Tarsus. In this respect they differed considerably from the Jews of Alexandria. They could not have been exempt from that hatred which has through so many ages wronged and dishonoured their noble race, and which was already virulent among the Romans of that day. All that we hear about them shows that the Cilician Jews were as capable as any of their brethren of repaying hate with double hatred, and scorn with double scorn. They would be all the more likely to do so from the condition of things around them. The belief in Paganism was more firmly rooted in the provinces than in Italy, and was specially vigorous in Tarsus—in this respect no unfitting burial-place for Julian the Apostate. No ages are worse, no places more corrupt, than those that draw the iridescent film of an intellectual culture over the deep stagnancy of moral degradation. And this was the condition of Tarsus. The seat of a celebrated school of letters, it was at the same time the metropolis of a province so low in universal estimation that it was counted among the *τρία κάππα κάκιστα*—the three most villainous k's of antiquity, Kappadokia,

[1] "Multa sunt verba, quibus juxta morem urbis et provinciae suae, familiarius Apostolus utitur: e quibus exempli gratiâ pauca ponenda sunt." He refers to *κατενάρκησα* (2 Cor. xi. 9), *ὑπὸ ἀνθρωπίνης ἡμέρας* (1 Cor. iv. 3), and *καταβραβευέτω* (Col. ii. 18); and adds, "Quibus, et aliis multis, usque hodie utuntur Cilices" (Jer. *Ep. ad Algas.* qu. 10). Wetstein, however, adduces *ἀποναρκάω*, from Plut. *De Liber. Educ.* p. 8, and *ναρκάω* occurs in the LXX. (Gen. xxxii. 25, 32; Job xxxiii. 19) and in Jos. *Antt.* viii. 8, § 5; *νάρκη* is the torpedo or *gymnotus*. Since *καταναρκάω* is only found in Hippocrates, Dr. Plumptre thinks it may have been a medical word in vogue in the schools of Tarsus. Gregory of Nyssa, on 1 Cor. xv. 28, quotes *ἐκένωσεν* (Phil. ii. 7), *ὁμειρόμενοι* (1 Thess. ii. 8), *περπερεύεται* (1 Cor. xiii. 4), *ἐριθείας* (Rom. ii. 8), &c., as instances of St. Paul's autocracy over words.

[2] See Hdt. i. 74, vii. 91; Xen. *Anab.* b. ii. 26.

[3] Σολοικισμός. See Strabo, p. 663; Diog. Laert. i. 51. But the derivation from Soli is not certain.

Kilikia, and Krete. What religion there was at this period had chiefly assumed an orgiastic and oriental character, and the popular faith of many even in Rome was a strange mixture of Greek, Roman, Egyptian, Phrygian, Phœnician, and Jewish elements. The wild, fanatical enthusiasms of the Eastern cults shook with new sensations of mad sensuality and weird superstition the feeble and jaded despair of Aryan Paganism. The Tarsian idolatry was composed of these mingled elements. There, in Plutarch's time, a generation after St. Paul, the sword of Apollo, miraculously preserved from decay and rust, was still displayed. Hermes Eriounios, or the luck-bringer, still appears, purse in hand, upon their coins. Æsculapius was still believed to manifest his power and presence in the neighbouring Ægæ.[1] But the traditional founder of the city was the Assyrian, Sardanapalus, whose semi-historical existence was confused, in the then syncretism of Pagan worship, with various representatives of the sun-god—the Asiatic Sandan, the Phœnician Baal, and the Grecian Hercules. The gross allusiveness and origin of this worship, its connexion with the very types and ideals of luxurious effeminacy, unbounded gluttony, and brutal licence, were quite sufficient to awake the indignant loathing of each true-hearted Jew; and these revolts of natural antipathy in the hearts of a people in whom true religion has ever been united with personal purity would be intensified with patriotic disgust when they saw that, at the main festival of this degraded cult the effeminate Sardanapalus and the masculine Semiramis—each equally detestable—were worshipped with rites which externally resembled the pure and thankful rejoicings of the Feast of Tabernacles. St. Paul must have witnessed this festival. He must have seen at Anchiale the most defiant symbol of cynical contentment with all which is merely animal in the statue of Sardanapalus, represented as snapping his fingers while he uttered the sentiment engraved upon the pedestal—

> "Eat, drink, enjoy thyself; the rest is nothing."[2]

The result which such spectacles and such sentiments had left upon his mind had not been one of tolerance, or of blunted sensibility to the horror of evil. They had inspired, on the one hand, an overpowering sense of disgust; on the other, an overwhelming conviction, deepened by subsequent observation, that mental perversity leads to, and is in its turn aggravated by, moral degradation; that error in the intellect involves an ultimate error in the life and in the will; that the darkening of the understanding is inevitably associated with the darkening of the soul and spirit, and that out of such darkness spring the hidden things which degrade immoral lives. He who would know what was the aspect of Paganism to one who had seen it from his childhood upwards in its

[1] *De Def. Orac.* 41; Hausrath, pp. 7—9. See, too, Plutarch, περὶ δεισιδαιμονίας καὶ ἀθεότητος, ii.; Neander, *Ch. Hist.* i. 15, *sq.*

[2] Strabo, xiv. 4; Athen. xii., p. 529; Cic. *Tusc. Disp.* v. 35. Hausrath, p. 7, finds a reminiscence of this in 1 Cor. xv. 32, which may, however, have been quite as probably derived from the wide-spread fable of the Epicurean fly dying in the honey-pot, καὶ βέβρωκα καὶ πέπωκα καὶ λέλουμαι κἂν ἀποθάνω οὐδέν μέλει μοι.

characteristic developments, must read that most terrible passage of all Scripture, in which the full blaze of scorching sunlight burns with its fiercest flame of indignation upon the pollutions of Pagan wickedness. Under that glare of holy wrath we see Paganism in all its unnatural deformity. No halo of imagination surrounds it, no gleam of fancy plays over its glittering corruption. We see it as it was. Far other may be its aspect when the glamour of Hellenic grace is flung over it, when "the lunar beam of Plato's genius" or the meteoric wit of Aristophanes light up, as by enchantment, its revolting sorceries. But he who would truly judge of it—he who would see it as it shall seem when there shall fall on it a ray out of God's eternity, must view it as it appeared to the penetrating glance of a pure and enlightened eye. St. Paul, furnished by inward chastity with a diviner *moly*, a more potent *haemony*, than those of Homer's and Milton's song—unmoved, untempted, unbewitched, unterrified—sees in this painted Circe no laughing maiden, no bright-eyed daughter of the sun, but a foul and baleful harlot; and, seizing her by the hair, stamps deep upon her leprous forehead the burning titles of her shame. Henceforth she may go for all time throughout the world a branded sorceress. All may read that festering stigma; none can henceforth deceive the nations into regrets for the vanished graces of a world which knew not God.[1]

But besides this unmitigated horror inspired by the lowest aspect of heathen life, St. Paul derived from his early insight into its character his deep conviction that earthly knowledge has no necessary connexion with heavenly wisdom. If we may trust the romance of the sophist Philostratus, and if he is not merely appropriating the sentiments which he had derived from Christianity, the youthful Apollonius of Tyana, who was afterwards held up as a kind of heathen parallel to Christ, was studying under the orator Euthydemus at Tarsus at the very time when it must also have been the residence of the youthful Paul;[2] and even Apollonius, at the age of thirteen, was so struck with the contrast between the professed wisdom of the city and its miserable morality, that he obtained leave from his father to remove to Ægæ, and so pursue his studies at a more serious and religious place.[3] The picture drawn, so long afterwards, by Philostratus, of the luxury, buffoonery, the petulance, the dandyism, the gossip, of the life at Tarsus, as a serious boy-philosopher is supposed to have witnessed it, might have no historical value if it were not confirmed in every particular by the sober narrative of the contemporary Strabo. "So great," he says, "is the zeal of the inhabitants for philosophy and all other encyclic training, that they have surpassed even Athens and Alexandria, and every other place one could mention in which philological and philosophical schools have arisen."[4]

[1] *V. infra*, on Rom. i. 18—32.

[2] Philostrat. *Vit. Apoll.* i. 7.

[3] Ὁ δὲ τὸν μὲν διδάσκαλον εἴχετο τὸ δὲ τῆς πόλεως ἦθος ἄτοπόν τε ἡγεῖτο καὶ οὐ χρηστὸν ἐμφιλοσοφῆσαι. τρυφῆς τε γὰρ οὐδαμοῦ μᾶλλον ἅπτονται, σκωπτόλαι τε καὶ ὑβρισταὶ πάντες (Philostr. *Vit. Apollon.*, i., p. 8, chap. 7, ed. Olear. 1709).

[4] Strabo, xiv. 4, pp. 672, 673. See, too, Xen. *Anab.* i. 2, 23; Plin. v. 22; Q. Curt. iii. 5, 1. The Stoics, Athenodorus, tutor of Augustus, and Nestor, tutor of Tiberius, lived at Tarsus: and others are mentioned.

The state of affairs resulting from the social atmosphere which he proceeds to describe is as amusing as it is despicable. It gives us a glimpse of the professorial world in days of Pagan decadence; of a professorial world, not such as it now is, and often has been, in our English and German Universities, where Christian brotherhood and mutual esteem have taken the place of wretched rivalism, and where good and learned men devote their lives to "gazing on the bright countenance of truth in the mild and dewy air of delightful studies," but as it was also in the days of the Poggios, Filelfos, and Politians of the Renaissance—cliques of jealous *savans*, narrow, selfish, unscrupulous, base, sceptical, impure—bursting with gossip, scandal, and spite. "The thrones" of these little "academic gods" were as mutually hostile and as universally degraded as those of the Olympian deities, in which it was, perhaps, a happy thing that they had ceased to believe. One illustrious professor cheated the State by stealing oil; another avenged himself on an opponent by epigrams; another by a nocturnal bespattering of his house; and rhetorical jealousies often ended in bloody quarrels. On this unedifying spectacle of littleness in great places the people in general looked with admiring eyes, and discussed the petty discords of these squabbling sophists as though they were matters of historical importance.[1] We can well imagine how unutterably frivolous this apotheosis of pedantism would appear to a serious-minded and faithful Jew; and it may have been his Tarsian reminiscences which added emphasis to St. Paul's reiterated warnings—that the wise men of heathendom, "alleging themselves to be wise, became fools;" that "they became vain in their disputings, and their unintelligent heart was darkened;"[2] that "the wisdom of this world is folly in the sight of God, for it is written, He who graspeth the wise in their own craftiness." And again, "the Lord knoweth the reasonings of the wise that they are vain."[3] But while he thus confirms his tenet, according to his usual custom, by Scriptural quotations from Job and the Psalms, and elsewhere from Isaiah and Jeremiah,[4] he reiterates again and again from his own experience that the Greeks seek after wisdom and regard the Cross as foolishness, yet that the foolishness of God is wiser than men, and the weakness of God stronger than men, and that God hath chosen the foolish things of the world to confound the wise, and the base things of the world to confound the mighty; and that when, in the wisdom of God, the world by wisdom knew not God, it pleased God by "the foolishness of the proclamation"[5]—for in his strong irony he loves and glories in the antitheses of his opponent's choosing—"by the foolishness of the thing preached" to save them that believe.[6] If the boasted wisdom of the Greek and Roman world was such as the young

[1] *Ποταμός τε αὐτοὺς διαῤῥεῖ Κύδνος, ᾧ παρακάθηνται, κάθαπερ τῶν ὀρνίθων οἱ ὑγροί* (Philostr. *ubi supr.*).

[2] Rom. i. 21, 22.

[3] 1 Cor. iii. 18—20.

[4] Job v. 13; Ps. xciv. 11; Isa. xxix. 14; xxxiii. 18; xliv. 25; Jer. viii. 9; 1 Cor. i. 18—27.

[5] 1 Cor. i. 21, *διὰ τῆς μωρίας τοῦ κηρύγματος*.

[6] 1 Cor. i. 18—25; ii. 14; iii. 19; iv. 10; 2 Cor. xi. 16, 19.

Saul had seen, if their very type of senselessness and foolishness was that which the converted Paul believed, then Paul at least—so he says in his passionate and scornful irony—would choose for ever to be on the side of, to cast in his lot with, to be gladly numbered among, the idiots and the fools.

> "He who hath felt the Spirit of the Highest
> Cannot confound, or doubt Him, or defy;
> Yea, with one voice, O world, though thou deniest,
> Stand thou on that side—for on this am I!"

St. Paul, then, was to the very heart a Jew—a Jew in culture, a Jew in sympathy, a Jew in nationality, a Jew in faith. His temperament was in no sense what we ordinarily regard as a poetic temperament; yet when we remember how all the poetry which existed in the moral depths of his nature was sustained by the rhythms and imagery, as his soul itself was sustained by the thoughts and hopes, of his national literature—when we consider how the star of Abraham had seemed to shine on his cradle in a heathen land, and his boyhood in the dim streets of unhallowed Tarsus to gain freshness and sweetness "from the waving and rustling of the oak of Mamre"[1]—we can understand that though in Christ there is neither Jew nor Greek, neither circumcision nor uncircumcision, but a new creation,[2] yet for no earthly possession would he have bartered his connexion with the chosen race. In his Epistle to the Romans he speaks in almost the very language of the Talmudist: "Israel hath sinned (Josh. vii. 11), but although he hath sinned," said Rabbi Abba bar Zavda, "he is still Israel. Hence the proverb—A myrtle among nettles is still called a myrtle."[3] And when we read the numerous passages in which he vaunts his participation in the hopes of Israel, his claim to be a fruitful branch in the rich olive of Jewish life; when we hear him speak of their adoption, their Shechinah, their covenants, their Law, their worship, their promises, their Fathers, their oracles of God, their claim of kinsmanship with the humanity of Christ,[4] we can understand to the full the intense ejaculation of his patriotic fervour, when—in language which has ever been the stumbling-block of religious selfishness, but which surpasses the noblest utterances of heroic self-devotion—he declares that he could wish himself accursed from Christ[5] for his brethren, his kinsmen, according to the flesh.[6] The valiant spirit of the Jews

[1] Hausrath, p. 20. [2] κτίσις, Gal. vi. 15; iii. 28.

[3] *Sanhedrin*, f. 44, 1. Rom. iii. 2; ix., *passim*.

[4] Rom. ix. 1—5; x. 1; xi. 1. [5] Rom. ix. 3.

[6] Any one who wishes to see the contortions of a narrow exegesis struggling to extricate itself out of a plain meaning, which is too noble for its comprehension, may see specimens of it in commentaries upon this text. This, alas! is only one instance of the spirit which so often makes the reading of an ordinary variorum Pauline commentary one of the most tedious, bewildering, and unprofitable of employments. Strange that, with the example of Christ before their eyes, many erudite Christian commentators should know so little of the sublimity of unselfishness as to force us to look to the parallels of a Moses—nay, even of a Danton—in order that we may be able to conceive of the true nobleness of a Paul! But there are cases in which he who would obtain from the writings of St. Paul their true, and often quite simple and transparent, meaning, must tear away with unsparing hand the accumulated cobwebs of centuries of error.

of Tarsus sent them in hundreds to die, sword in hand, amid the carnage of captured Jerusalem, and to shed their last blood to slake, if might be, the very embers of the conflagration which destroyed the Temple of their love. The same patriotism burned in the spirit, the same blood flowed in the veins, not only of Saul the Pharisee, but of Paul the prisoner of the Lord.

It will be seen from all that we have said that we wholly disagree with those who have made it their favourite thesis to maintain for St. Paul the early acquisition of an advanced Hellenic culture. His style and his dialectic method have been appealed to in order to support this view.[1] His style, however, is that of a man who wrote in a peculiar and provincial Greek, but thought in Syriac; and his dialectical method is purely Rabbinic. As for his deep knowledge of heathen life, we may be sure that it was not derived from books, but from the fatal wickedness of which he had been a daily witness. A Jew in a heathen city needed no books to reveal to him the "depths of Satan." In this respect how startling a revelation to the modern world was the indisputable evidence of the ruins of Pompeii! Who would have expected to find the infamies of the Dead Sea cities paraded with such infinite shamelessness in every street of a little provincial town? What innocent snow could ever hide the guilty front of a life so unspeakably abominable? Could anything short of the earthquake have engulfed it, or of the volcano have burnt it up? And if Pompeii was like this, we may judge, from the works of Aristophanes and Athenæus, of Juvenal and Martial, of Petronius and Apuleius, of Strato and Meleager—which may be regarded as the "*pièces justificatives*" of St. Paul's estimate of heathendom—what Tarsus and Ephesus, what Corinth and Miletus, were likely to have been. In days and countries when the darkness was so deep that the very deeds of darkness did not need to hide themselves—in days and cities where the worst vilenesses of idolatry were trumpeted in its streets, and sculptured in its market-places, and consecrated in its worship, and stamped upon its coins—did Paul need Greek study to tell him the characteristics of a godless civilisation? The notion of Baumgarten that, after his conversion, St. Paul earnestly studied Greek literature at Tarsus, with a view to his mission among the heathen—or that the "books" and parchments which he asked to be sent to him from the house of Carpus at Troas,[2] were of this description—is as precarious as the fancy that his parents sent him to be educated at Jerusalem in order to counteract the commencing sorcery exercised over his imagination by Hellenic studies. Gamaliel, it is true, was one of the few Rabbis who took the liberal and enlightened view about the permissibility of the *Chokmah Jovanith*, or "wisdom of the Greeks"—one of the few who held the desirability of not wholly dissevering the white *tallîth* of Shem from the stained *pallium* of Japhet.[3] But, on the one hand, neither would Gamaliel

[1] See Schaff, *Hist. of Anct. Christianity*, i. 68. [2] 2 Tim. iv. 13.

[3] See *Life of Christ*, Exc. IV. vol. ii. 461. The study of Greek literature by the House of Gamaliel is said to have been connived at by the Rabbis, on the plea that they needed a knowledge of Greek in civil and diplomatic intercourse on behalf of their countrymen (see Etheridge, *Heb. Lit.* p. 45). Rabban Shimon Ben Gamaliel is said to have remarked that there were 1,000 children in his father's house, of whom 500 studied

have had that false toleration which seems to think that "the ointment of the apothecary" is valueless without "the fly which causeth it to stink;" and, on the other hand, if Gamaliel had allowed his pupils to handle such books, or such parts of books, as dwelt on the darker side of Paganism, Paul was not the kind of pupil who would, for a moment, have availed himself of such "ruinous edification."[1] The Jews were so scrupulous, that some of them held concerning books of their own hagiographa—such, for instance, as the Book of Esther—that they were dubious reading. They would not allow their youth even to open the Song of Solomon before the age of twenty-one. Nothing, therefore, can be more certain than that a "Pharisee of Pharisees," even though his boyhood were spent in heathen Tarsus, would not have been allowed to read—barely even allowed to know the existence of—any but the sweetest and soundest portions of Greek letters, if even these.[2] But who that has read St. Paul can believe that he has ever studied Homer, or Æschylus, or Sophocles? If he had done so, would there—in a writer who often "thinks in quotations"—have been no touch or trace of any reminiscence of, or allusion to, epic or tragic poetry in epistles written at Athens and at Corinth, and beside the very tumuli of Ajax and Achilles? Had Paul been a reader of Aristotle, would he have argued in the style which he adopts in the Epistles to the Galatians and the Romans?[3] Had he been a reader of Plato, would the fifteenth chapter of the first Epistle to the Corinthians have carried in it not the most remotely faint allusion to the splendid guesses of the Phaedo? Nothing can be more clear than that he had never been subjected to a classic training. His Greek is not the Greek of the Atticists, nor his rhetoric the rhetoric of the schools, nor his logic the logic of the philosophers. It is doubtful whether the incomparable energy and individuality of his style and of his reasoning would not have been

the law, and 500 the wisdom of the Greeks, and that of these all but two perished [in the rebellion of Bar-cochba?] (*Babha Kama*, f. 83, 1). The author of the celebrated comparison, that "because the two sons of Noah, Shem and Japhet, united to cover with one garment their father's nakedness, Shem obtained the fringed garment (*tallith*), and Japhet the philosopher's garment (*pallium*), which ought to be united again," was R. Jochanan Ben Napuchah (*Midr. Rabbah*, Gen. xxxvi.; Jer. *Sotah*, *ad f.*; Selden, *De Synedr.* ii. 9, 2; Biscoe, p. 60). On the other hand, the narrower Rabbis identified Greek learning with Egyptian thaumaturgy; and when R. Elieser Ben Dama asked his uncle, R. Ismael, whether one might not learn Greek knowledge after having studied the entire law, R. Ismael quoted in reply Josh. i. 8, and said, "Go and find a moment which is neither day nor night, and then abandon yourself in it to Greek knowledge" (*Menachôth*, 99, 2).

[1] 1 Cor. viii. 10, ἡ συνείδησις αὐτοῦ ἀσθενοῦς ὄντος οἰκοδομηθήσεται εἰς τὸ τὰ εἰδωλόθυτα ἐσθίειν. *Ruinosa aedificatio*, Calv. *ad loc.*

[2] See *Sota*, 49, 6; and the strong condemnation of all Gentile books by R. Akibha, Bab. *Sanhedr.* 90, *a.* (Gfrörer, *Jahrh. d. Heils*, i. 114; Philo, ii. 350; Grätz, iii. 502; Derenbourg, *Palest.* 114.) In *Yadayim*, iv. 6, the Sadducees complain of some Pharisees for holding that the Books of Ecclesiastes and Canticles "defile the hands," while "the books of Homeros" do not. The comment appended to this remark shows, however, the most astounding ignorance. The two Rabbis (*in loco*) take "Meros" to be the proper name, preceded by the article, and deriving Meros from *rasas*, to destroy, make the poems of Homer into books which cavil against the Law and are doomed to destruction! Grätz denies that המירס is Homer.

[3] "Melius haec sibi convenissent," says Fritzsche, in alluding to one of St. Paul's antinomies, "si Apostolus Aristotelis non Gamalielis alumnus fuisset."

merely enfeebled and conventionalised if he had gone through any prolonged course of the only training which the Sophists of Tarsus could have given him.[1]

CHAPTER III.

THE SCHOOL OF THE RABBI.

Ἠκούσατε γὰρ τὴν ἐμὴν ἀναστροφήν ποτε ἐν Ἰουδαϊσμῷ, ὅτι . . . προέκοπτον ἐν τῷ Ἰουδαϊσμῷ ὑπὲρ πολλοὺς συνηλικιώτας ἐν τῷ γένει μου.—GAL. i. 13, 14.

"Let thy house be a place of resort for the wise, and cover thyself with the dust of their feet, and drink their words with thirstiness."—*Pirke Abhôth*, i. 4.

"The world was created for the sake of the Thorah."—*Nedarim*, 32, 1.

"Whoever is busied in the law for its own sake is worth the whole world."—PEREK R. MEIR, 1.

So far, then, we have attempted to trace in detail, by the aid of St. Paul's own writings, the degree and the character of those influences which were exercised upon his mind by the early years which he spent at Tarsus, modified or deepened as they must have been by long intercourse with heathens, and with converts from heathendom, in later years. And already we have seen abundant reason to believe that the impressions which he received from Hellenism were comparatively superficial and fugitive, while those of his Hebraic training and nationality worked deep among the very bases of his life. It is this Hebraic side of his character, so important to any understanding of his life and writings, that we must now endeavour to trace and estimate.

That St. Paul was a Roman citizen, that he could go through the world and say in his own defence, when needful or possible, *Civis Romanus sum*, is stated so distinctly, and under circumstances so manifestly probable, that the fact stands above all doubt. There are, indeed, some difficulties about it which induce many German theologians quietly to deny its truth, and attribute the statement to a desire on the part of the author of the Acts "to recommend St. Paul to the Romans as a native Roman," or "to remove the reproach that the originators of Christendom had been enemies of the Roman State." It is true that, if St. Paul was a free-born Roman citizen, his legal rights as established by the Lex Porcia[2] must, according to his own statement, have been eight times violated at the time when he wrote the Second

[1] See Excursus I., "The Style of St. Paul;" Excursus II., "Rhetoric of St. Paul;" and Excursus III., "The Classic Quotations and Allusions of St. Paul." I may sum up the conclusion of these essays by stating that St. Paul had but a slight acquaintance with Greek literature, but that he had very probably attended some elementary classes in Tarsus, in which he had gained a tincture of Greek rhetoric, and possibly even of Stoic principles.

[2] "Porcia lex virgas ab omnium civium Romanorum corpore amovet" (Cic. *pro. Rab.* 3; Liv. x. 9).

Epistle to the Corinthians;[1] while a *ninth* violation of those rights was only prevented by his direct appeal. Five of these, however, were Jewish scourgings; and what we have already said, as well as what we shall say hereafter, may well lead us to suppose that, as against the Jews, St. Paul would have purposely abstained from putting forward a claim which, from the mouth of a Jew, would have been regarded as an odious sign that he was willing to make a personal advantage of his country's subjection. The Jewish authorities possessed the power to scourge, and it is only too sadly probable that Saul himself, when he was their agent, had been the cause of its infliction on other Christians. If so, he would have felt a strong additional reason for abstaining from the plea which would have exempted him from the authority of his countrymen; and we may see in this abstention a fresh and, so far as I am aware, a hitherto unnoticed trait of his natural nobleness. As to the Roman scourgings, it is clear that the author of the Acts, though well aware of the privileges which Roman citizenship entailed, was also aware that, on turbulent occasions and in remote places, the plea might be summarily set aside in the case of those who were too weak or too obscure to support it. If under the full glare of publicity in Sicily, and when the rights of the "*Civitas*" were rare, a Verres could contemptuously ignore them to an extent much more revolting to the Roman sense of dignity than scourging was—then very little difficulty remains in reconciling St. Paul's expression, "Thrice was I beaten with rods," with the claim which he put forth to the prætors of Philippi and to the chiliarch at Jerusalem. How St. Paul's father or grandfather obtained the highly-prized distinction we have no means of ascertaining. It certainly did not belong to any one as a citizen of Tarsus, for, if so, Lysias at Jerusalem, knowing that St. Paul came from Tarsus, would have known that he had also the rights of a Roman. But Tarsus was not a *Colonia* or a *Municipium*, but only an *Urbs Libera;* and this privilege, bestowed upon it by Augustus, did not involve any claim to the *Civitas*. The franchise may either have been purchased by Paul's father, or obtained as a reward for some services of which no trace remains.[2] When Cassius punished Tarsus by a heavy fine for having embraced the side of Antony, it is said that many Tarsians were sold as slaves in order to pay the money; and one conjecture is that St. Paul's father, in his early days, may have been one of these, and may have been first emancipated and then presented with the *Civitas* during a residence at Rome. The conjecture is just possible, but nothing more.

At any rate, this Roman citizenship is not in any way inconsistent with his constant claim to the purest Jewish descent; nor did it appreciably affect his character. The father of Saul may have been glad that he possessed an inalienable right, transmissible to his son, which would protect him in many of those perils which were only too possible in such times; but it made no

[1] When he was about fifty-three years old.

[2] See for such means of acquiring it, Suet. *Aug.* 47; Jos. *B. J.* ii. 14; Acts xxii. 28. The possession of citizenship had to be proved by a "*diploma*," and Claudius punished a false assumption of it with death. (Suet. *Claud.* 25; *Calig.* 28; *Nero*, 12; Epictet. *Dissert.* iii. 24.)

difference in the training which he gave to the young Saul, or in the destiny which he marked out for him. That training, as we can clearly see, was the ordinary training of every Jewish boy. "The prejudices of the Pharisaic house, it has been said, "surrounded his cradle; his Judaism grew like the mustard-tree in the Gospel, and intolerance, fanaticism, national hatred, pride, and other passions, built their nests among its branches."[1] At the age of five he would begin to study the Bible with his parents at home; and even earlier than this he would doubtless have learnt the Shema[2] and the Hallel (Psalms cxiii.—cxviii.) in whole or in part. At six he would go to his "vineyard," as the later Rabbis called their schools. At ten he would begin to study those earlier and simpler developments of the oral law, which were afterwards collected in the Mishna. At thirteen he would, by a sort of "confirmation," become a "Son of the Commandment."[3] At fifteen he would be trained in yet more minute and burdensome *halachôth*, analogous to those which ultimately filled the vast mass of the Gemara. At twenty, or earlier, like every orthodox Jew, he would marry. During many years he would be ranked among the "pupils of the wise,"[4] and be mainly occupied with "the traditions of the Fathers."[5]

It was in studies and habits like these that the young Saul of Tarsus grew up to the age of thirteen, which was the age at which a Jewish boy, if he were destined for the position of a Rabbi, entered the school of some great master. The master among whose pupils Saul was enrolled was the famous Rabban Gamaliel, a son of Rabban Simeon, and a grandson of Hillel, "a doctor of the law had in reputation among all the people."[6] There were only seven of the Rabbis to whom the Jews gave the title of Rabban, and three of these were Gamaliels of this family, who each in turn rose to the high distinction of *Nasî*, or President of the School. Gamaliel I., like his grandfather Hillel, held the somewhat anomalous position of a liberal Pharisee. A Pharisee in heartfelt zeal for the traditions of his fathers,[7] he yet had none of the narrow exclusiveness which characterised Shammai, the rival of his grandfather, and the hard school which Shammai had founded. His liberality of intellect showed itself in the permission of Pagan literature; his largeness of heart in the tolerance which breathes through his speech before the Sanhedrin.

1 Hausrath, p. 19.

2 Strictly Deut. vi. 4—9; but also xi. 13—27; Num. xv. 37—41.

3 *Bar Mitsvah*.

4 *Pirke Abhôth*, v. 21. See too Dr. Ginsburg's excellent article on "Education" in Kitto's *Bibl. Cycl.*

5 *Pirke Abhôth*, i. 1. The two favourite words of the Pharisees were ἀκρίβεια and τὰ πάτρια ἔθη. See Acts xxvi. 5; xxii. 3; Jos. *B. J.* ii. 8, § 14; i. 5, § 2; *Antt.* xiii. 10, § 6; xvii. 2, *ad fin.*

6 Acts v. 34, xxii. 3. See Grätz, *Gesch. d. Juden.* iii. 274.

7 I have noticed farther on (see Excursus V.) the difficulty of being sure which of the Gamaliels is referred to when the name occurs in the Talmud. This, however, is less important, since they were all of the same school, and entirely faithful to Mosaism. We may see the utter change which subsequently took place in St. Paul's views if we compare Rom. xiv. 5, Col. ii. 16, Gal. iv. 10, with the following anecdote:—"Rabban Gamaliel's ass happened to be laden with honey, and it was found dead one Sabbath evening, because he had been unwilling to unload it on that day" (*Shabbath*, f. 154, c. 2).

There is no authority for the tradition that he was a secret Christian,[1] but we see from the numerous notices of him in the Talmud, and from the sayings there ascribed to him, that he was a man of exactly the character which we should infer from the brief notice of him and of his sentiments in the Acts of the Apostles. In both sources alike we see a humane, thoughtful, high-minded, and religious man—a man of sufficient culture to elevate him above vulgar passions, and of sufficient wisdom to see, to state, and to act upon the broad principles that hasty judgments are dangerously liable to error; that there is a strength and majesty in truth which needs no aid from persecution; that a light from heaven falls upon the destinies of man, and that by that light God "shows all things in the slow history of their ripening."

At the feet of this eminent Sanhedrist sat Saul of Tarsus in all probability for many years;[2] and though for a time the burning zeal of his temperament may have carried him to excesses of intolerance in which he was untrue to the best traditions of his school, yet, since the sunlight of the grace of God ripened in his soul the latent seeds of all that was wise and tender, we may believe that some of those germs of charity had been implanted in his heart by his eminent teacher. So far from seeing any improbability in the statement that St. Paul had been a scholar of Gamaliel, it seems to me that it throws a flood of light on the character and opinions of the Apostle. With the exception of Hillel, there is no one of the Jewish Rabbis, so far as we see them in the light of history, whose virtues made him better suited to be a teacher of a Saul, than Hillel's grandson. We must bear in mind that the dark side of Pharisaism which is brought before us in the Gospels—the common and current Pharisaism, half hypocritical, half mechanical, and wholly selfish, which justly incurred the blighting flash of Christ's denunciation—was not the *only* aspect which Pharisaism could wear. When we speak of Pharisaism we mean obedience petrified into formalism, religion degraded into ritual, morals cankered by casuistry; we mean the triumph and perpetuity of all the worst and weakest elements in religious party-spirit. But there were Pharisees and Pharisees. The New Testament furnishes us with a favourable picture of the candour and wisdom of a Nicodemus and a Gamaliel. In the Talmud, among many other stately figures who walk in a peace and righteousness worthy of the race which sprang from Abraham, we see the lovable and noble characters of a Hillel, of a Simeon, of a Chaja, of a Juda "the Holy." It was when he thought of such as these, that, even long after his conversion, Paul could exclaim before the Sanhedrin with no sense of shame or contradiction—"Men and brethren, I am a Pharisee, a son of Pharisees." He would be the more able to make this appeal because, at that moment, he was expressly referring to the

[1] *Recogn. Clem.* i. 65; Phot. *Cod.* 171, p. 199; Thilo, *Cod. Apocr.* p. 501 (Meyer *ad* Acts v. 34).

[2] Acts xxii. 3. The Jewish Rabbis sat on lofty chairs, and their pupils sat at their feet, either on the ground or on benches. There is no sufficient ground for the tradition that up till the time of Gamaliel's death it had been the custom for the pupils to stand. (2 Kings ii. 3; iv. 38; Bab. *Sanhedr.* vii. 2; Biscoe, p. 77.)

resurrection of the dead, which has been too sweepingly characterised as "the one doctrine which Paul the Apostle borrowed from Saul the Pharisee."

It is both interesting, and for the study of St. Paul's Epistles most deeply important, to trace the influence of these years upon his character and intellect. Much that he learnt during early manhood continued to be, till the last, an essential part of his knowledge and experience. To the day of his death he neither denied nor underrated the advantages of the Jew; and first among those advantages he placed the possession of "the oracles of God."[1] He had begun the study of these Scriptures at the age of six, and to them, and the elucidations of them which had been gathered during many centuries in the schools of Judaism, he had devoted the most studious years of his life. The effects of that study are more or less traceable in every Epistle which he wrote; they are specially remarkable in those which, like the Epistle to the Romans, were in whole or in part addressed to Churches in which Jewish converts were numerous or predominant.

His profound knowledge of the Old Testament Scriptures shows how great had been his familiarity with them from earliest childhood. From the Pentateuch, from the Prophets, and above all from the Psalter, he not only quotes repeatedly, advancing at each step of the argument from quotation to quotation, as though without these his argument, which is often in reality quite independent of them, would lack authority; but he also quotes, as is evident, from memory, and often into one brief quotation weaves the verbal reminiscences of several passages.[2] Like all Hellenistic Jews he uses the Greek version of the LXX., but he had an advantage over most Hellenists in that knowledge of the original Hebrew which sometimes stands him in good stead. Yet though he can refer to the original when occasion requires, the LXX. was to him as much "the Bible" as our English version is to us; and, as is the case with many Christian writers, he knew it so well that his sentences are constantly moulded by its rhythm, and his thoughts incessantly coloured by its expressions.

And the controversial use which he makes of it is very remarkable. It often seems at first sight to be wholly independent of the context. It often seems to read between the lines.[3] It often seems to consider the mere words of a writer as of conclusive authority entirely apart from their original application.[4] It seems to regard the word and letter of Scripture as full of divine mysterious oracles, which might not only be cited in matters of doctrine, but even to illustrate the simplest matters of contemporary fact.[5] It attaches consequences of the deepest importance to what an ordinary reader might

[1] Rom. iii. 2.

[2] *E.g.*, Rom. i. 24, iii. 6, iv. 17, ix. 33, x. 18, xi. 8; 1 Cor. vi. 2, ix. 7, xv. 45; &c.

[3] Rom. ii. 24, iii. 10—18, ix. 15; 1 Cor. x. 1—4; Gal. iv. 24—31; &c. This is the essence of the later Kabbala, with its *Pardes*—namely, *Peshat*, "explanation;" *Remes*, "hint;" *Derush*, "homily;" and *Sod*, "mystery." Yet in St. Paul there is not a trace of the methods (*Geneth*) of Gematria, Notarikon, or Themourah, which the Jews applied *very early* to Old Testament exegesis. I have fully explained these terms in a paper on "Rabbinic Exegesis," *Expositor*, May, 1877.

[4] 1 Cor. xiv. 21; Rom. x. 6—9; 1 Cor. xv. 45.

[5] See Rom. x. 15—21.

regard as a mere grammatical expression.[1] But if the general conception of this style of argumentation was due to Paul's long training in Rabbinic principles of exegesis, it should not be forgotten that while these principles often modified the form of his expressions, they cannot in any single instance be said to have furnished the essential matter of his thoughts. It was quite inevitable that one who had undergone the elaborate training of a Rabbi—one who, to full manhood, had never dreamt that any training could be superior to it—would not instantly unlearn the reiterated lessons of so many years. Nor was it in any way necessary to the interests of religious truth that he should do so. The sort of traditional culture in the explanation of Scripture which he learnt at the feet of Gamaliel was not only of extreme value in all his controversies with the Jews, but also enriched his style, and lent fresh vividness to his arguments, without enfeebling his judgment or mystifying his opinions. The ingenuity of the Jewish Rabbi never for one moment overpowers the vigorous sense and illuminated intellect of the Christian teacher. Although St. Paul's method of handling Scripture, undoubtedly, in its general features, resembles and recalls the method which reigns throughout the Talmud, yet the practical force, the inspired wisdom, the clear intuition, of the great Apostle, preserve him from that extravagant abuse of numerical, kabbalistic, esoteric, and impossibly inferential minutiæ which make anything mean anything—from all attempt to emulate the remarkable exegetical feats of those letter-worshipping Rabbis who prided themselves on suspending dogmatic mountains by textual hairs. He shared, doubtless, in the views of the later Jewish schools—the Tanaim and Amoraim—on the nature of inspiration. These views, which we find also in Philo, made the words of Scripture co-extensive and identical with the words of God, and in the clumsy and feeble hands of the more fanatical Talmudists often attached to the dead letter an importance which stifled or destroyed the living sense. But as this extreme and mechanical literalism—this claim to absolute infallibility even in accidental details and passing allusions—this superstitious adoration of the letters and vocables of Scripture as though they were the articulate vocables and immediate autograph of God—finds no encouragement in any part of Scripture, and very direct discouragement in more than one of the utterances of Christ, so there is not a single passage in which any approach to it is dogmatically stated in the writings of St. Paul.[2] Nay, more—the very point of his specific difference from the Judæo-Christians was his denial of the permanent validity of the entire scheme of legislation which it was the immediate object of the Pentateuch to record. If it be asserted that St. Paul deals with the Old Testament in the manner of a Rabbi, let it be said in answer that he uses it to emancipate the souls which Judaism

[1] Gal. iii. 16.

[2] 2 Tim. iii. 16 is no exception; even if θεόπνευστος be there regarded as a predicate, nothing would be more extravagant than to rest on that single adjective the vast hypothesis of literal dictation (see *infra, ad loc.*). On this great subject of inspiration I have stated what I believe to be the Catholic faith fully and clearly in the *Bible Educator*, i. 190 *sq.*

enslaved; and that he deduces from it, not the Kabbala and the Talmud—"a philosophy for dreamers and a code for mummies"[1]—but the main ideas of the Gospel of the grace of God.

It will be easy for any thoughtful and unprejudiced reader of St. Paul's Epistles to verify and illustrate for himself the Apostle's use of Scripture. He adopts the current mode of citation, but he ennobles and enlightens it.[2] That he did not consider the method universally applicable is clear from its omission in those of his Epistles which were intended in the main for Gentile Christians,[3] as also in his speeches to heathen assemblies. But to the Jews he would naturally address a style of argument which was in entire accordance with their own method of dialectics. Many of the truths which he demonstrates by other considerations may have seemed to him to acquire additional authority from their assonance with certain expressions of Scripture. We cannot, indeed, be sure in some instances how far St. Paul meant his quotation for an argument, and how far he used it as a mere illustrative formula. Thus, we feel no hesitation in admitting the cogency of his proof of the fact that both Jews and Gentiles were guilty in God's sight; but we should not consider the language of David about his enemies in the fourteenth and fifty-third Psalms, still less his strong expressions "all" and "no, not one," as adding any great additional force to the general argument. It is probable that a Jew would have done so; and St. Paul, as a Jew trained in this method of Scriptural application, may have done so too. But what has been called his "inspired Targum" of the Old Testament does not bind us to the mystic method of Old Testament commentary. As the Jews were more likely to adopt any conclusion which was expressed for them in the words of Scripture, St. Paul, having undergone the same training, naturally enwove into his style—though only when he wrote to them—this particular method of Scriptural illustration. To them an argument of this kind would be an *argumentum ex concessis*. To us its argumentative force would be much smaller, because it does not appeal to us, as to him and to his readers, with all the force of familiar reasoning. So far from thinking this a subject for regret, we may, on the contrary, be heartily thankful for an insight which could give explicitness to deeply latent truths, and find in an observation of minor importance, like that of Habakkuk, that "the soul of the proud man is not upright, but the just man shall live by his steadfastness"[4]—*i.e.*, that the Chaldeans should enjoy no stable prosperity, but that the Jews, here ideally represented as "the upright man," should, because of their fidelity, live secure—the depth of power and meaning which we attach to that palmary truth of the Pauline theology that "*the just shall live by his faith*."[5]

[1] Reuss, *Théol. Chrét.* i. 268 and 408—421.

[2] See Jowett, *Romans*, i. 353—362.

[3] There are no Scriptural quotations in 1, 2 Thess., Phil., Col.

[4] Hab. ii. 4. (Heb. בֶּאֱמוּנָתוֹ, by his trustworthiness.) See Lightfoot on Gal. iii. 11, and p. 149.

[5] Gal. iii. 11; Rom. i. 17; also in Heb. x. 38. St. Paul omits the μου of the LXX., which is not in the Hebrew.

A similar but more remarkable instance of this apparent subordination of the historic context in the illustrative application of prophetic words is found in 1 Cor. xiv. 21. St. Paul is there speaking of the gift of tongues, and speaking of it with entire disparagement in comparison with the loftier gift of prophecy, *i.e.*, of impassioned and spiritual teaching. In support of this disparaging estimate, and as a proof that the tongues, being mainly meant as a sign to unbelievers, ought only to be used sparingly and under definite limitations in the congregations of the faithful, he quotes from Isaiah xxviii. 11[1] the verse—which he does not in this instance borrow from the LXX. version—"*With men of other tongues and other lips will I speak unto this people, and yet for all that will they not hear me, saith the Lord.*" The whole meaning and context are, in the original, very interesting, and generally misunderstood. The passage implies that since the drunken, shameless priests and prophets chose, in their hiccoughing scorn, to deride the manner and method of the divine instruction which came to them,[2] God should address them in a wholly different way, namely, by the Assyrians, who spake tongues which they could not understand; and yet even to that instruction—the stern and unintelligible utterance of foreign victors—they should continue deaf. This passage, in a manner quite alien from any which would be natural to us, St. Paul embodied in a pre-eminently noble and able argument, as though it illustrated, if it did not prove, his view as to the proper object and limitations of those soliloquies of ecstatic spiritual emotion which were known as Glossolalia, or "the Gift of Tongues."

One more instance, and that, perhaps, the most remarkable of all, will enable us better to understand a peculiarity which was the natural result of years of teaching. In Gal. iii. 16 he says, "Now the promises were spoken to Abraham and to his seed. He saith not, AND TO SEEDS, as applying to many, but, as applying to one, AND TO THY SEED—who is Christ." Certainly at first sight we should say that an argument of immense importance was here founded on the use of the Hebrew word *serâ* in the singular,[3] and its representative the σπέρμα of the LXX.; and that the inference which St. Paul deduces depends solely on the fact that the plural, *zeraîm* (σπέρματα), is not used; and that, therefore, the promise of Gen. xiii. 15 pointed from the first to a special fulfilment in ONE of Abraham's descendants. This *primâ facie* view must, however, be erroneous, because it is inconceivable that St. Paul—a good Hebraist and a master of Hellenistic Greek—was unaware that the plural *zeraîm*, as in 1 Sam. viii. 15, Dan i. 12, and the title of the Talmudic treatise, could not by any possibility have been used in the original promise, because it could only mean "*various kinds of grain*"—exactly in the sense in which he

[1] The quotation is introduced with the formula, "It has been written in *the Law*," a phrase which is sometimes applied to the entire Old Testament.

[2] They ridiculed Isaiah's repetitions by saying they were all "bid and bid, bid and bid, forbid and forbid, forbid and forbid," &c. (*Tsav la-tsav, tsav la-tsav, kav la-kav, kav la-kav*, &c., Heb.). (See an admirable paper on this passage by Rev. S. Cox, *Expositor*, i. p. 101.)

[3] זֶרַע

himself uses *spermata* in 1 Cor. xv. 38—and that the Greek *spermata*, in the sense of "offspring," would be nothing less than an impossible barbarism. The argument, therefore—if it be an argument at all, and not what the Rabbis would have called a *sod*, or "mystery"—does not, and cannot, turn, as has been so unhesitatingly assumed, on the fact that *sperma* is a *singular* noun, but on the fact that it is a *collective* noun, and was deliberately used instead of "sons" or "children;"[1] and St. Paul declares that this *collective* term was meant from the first to apply to Christ, as elsewhere he applies it spiritually to the servants of Christ. In the interpretation, then, of this word, St. Paul reads between the lines of the original, and is enabled to see in it deep meanings which are the true, but not the primary ones. He does not say at once that the promises to Abraham found in Christ—as in the purpose of God it had always been intended that they should find in Christ[2]—their highest and truest fulfilment; but, in a manner belonging peculiarly to the Jewish style of exegesis, he illustrates this high truth by the use of a *collective noun* in which he believes it to have been mystically foreshadowed.[3]

This passage is admirably adapted to throw light on the Apostle's use of the Old Testament. Rabbinic in form, it was free in spirit. Though he does not disdain either Amoraic or Alexandrian methods of dealing with Scripture, St. Paul never falls into the follies or extravagances of either. Treating the letter of Scripture with intense respect, he yet made the literal sense of it bend at will to the service of the spiritual consciousness. On the dead letter of the Urim, which recorded the names of lost tribes, he flashed a mystic ray, which made them gleam forth into divine and hitherto undreamed-of oracles. The actual words of the sacred writers became but as the wheels and wings of the Cherubim, and whithersoever the Spirit went they went. Nothing is more natural, nothing more interesting, in the hands of an inspired teacher nothing is more valuable, than this mode of application. We have not in St. Paul the frigid spirit of Philonian allegory which to a great extent depreciated the original and historic sense of Scripture, and was chiefly bent on educing philosophic mysteries from its living page; nor have we a single instance of Gematria or Notarikon, of Atbash or Albam, of Hillel's *middoth* or Akibha's method of hanging legal decisions on the horns of letters. Into these unreal mysticisms and exegetical frivolities it was impossible that a man should fall who was intensely earnest, and felt, in the vast mass of what he wrote, that he had the Spirit of the Lord. In no single instance does he make one of these general quotations the demonstrative *basis* of the point which he is endeavouring to impress. In every instance

[1] See Lightfoot, *ad loc.*, p. 139.

[2] As in Gen. iii. 15. The Jews could not deny the force of the argument, for they interpreted Gen. iv. 25, &c., of the Messiah. But St. Jerome's remark, "Galatis, quos paulo ante stultos dixerat, factus est stultus," as though the Apostle had purposely used an "accommodation" argument, is founded on wrong principles.

[3] The purely illustrative character of the reference seems to be clear from the different, yet no less spiritualised, sense given to the text in Rom. iv. 13, 16, 18; ix. 8; Gal. iii. 28, 29.

he states the solid argument on which he rests his conclusion, and only adduces Scripture by way of sanction or support. And this is in exact accordance with all that we know of his spiritual history—of the genuineness of which it affords an unsuspected confirmation. He had not arrived at any one of the truths of his special gospel by the road of ratiocination. They came to him with the flash of intuitive conviction at the miracle of his conversion, or in the gradual process of subsequent psychological experience. We hear from his own lips that he had not originally found these truths in Scripture, or been led to them by inductive processes in the course of Scripture study. He received them, as again and again he tells us, by revelation direct from Christ. It was only when God had taught him the truth of them that he became cognisant that they *must* be latent in the writings of the Old Dispensation. When he was thus enlightened to see that they existed in Scripture, he found that all Scripture was full of them. When he knew that the treasure lay hid in the field, he bought the whole field, to become its owner. When God had revealed to him the doctrine of justification by faith, he saw—as we may now see, but as none had seen before him—that it existed implicitly in the trustfulness of Abraham and the "life" and "faith" of Habakkuk. Given the right, nay, the necessity, to spiritualise the meaning of the Scriptures—and given the fact that this right was assumed and practised by every teacher of the schools in which Paul had been trained and to which his countrymen looked up, as it has been practised by every great teacher since—we then possess the key to all such passages as those to which I have referred; and we also see the cogency with which they would come home to the minds of those for whom they were intended. In other words, St. Paul, when speaking to Jews, was happily able to address them, as it were, in their own dialect, and it is a dialect from which Gentiles also have deep lessons to learn.

It is yet another instance of the same method when he points to the two wives of Abraham as types of the Jewish and of the Christian covenant, and in the struggles and jealousies of the two, ending in the ejection of Agar, sees allegorically foreshadowed the triumph of the new covenant over the old. In this allegory, by marvellous interchange, the physical descendants of Sarah become, in a *spiritual* point of view, the descendants of Agar, and those who were Agar's children become Sarah's true spiritual offspring. The inhabitants of the Jerusalem that now is, though descended from Sarah and Abraham, are foreshadowed for rejection under the type of the offspring of Ishmael; and the true children of Abraham and Sarah are those alone who are so *spiritually*, but of whom the vast majority were not of the chosen seed. And the proof of this—if proof be in any case the right word for what perhaps St. Paul himself may only have regarded as allegoric confirmation—is found in Isaiah liv. 1, where the prophet, addressing the New Jerusalem which is to rise out of the ashes of her Babylonian ruin, calls to her as to a barren woman, and bids her to rejoice as having many more children than she that hath a husband. The Jews become metamorphosed into the descendants of Agar, the Gentiles into the seed of Abraham and heirs of the Promise.[1]

This very ranging in corresponding columns of type and antitype, or of the actually existent and its ideal counterpart—this Systoichia in which Agar, Ishmael, the Old Covenant, the earthly Jerusalem, the unconverted Jews, &c., in the one column, are respective counterparts of their spiritual opposites, Sarah, Isaac, the New Covenant, the heavenly Jerusalem, the Christian Church, &c., in the other column—is in itself a Rabbinic method of setting forth a series of conceptions, and is, therefore, another of the many traces of the influence of Rabbinic training upon the mind of St. Paul. A part of the system of the Rabbis was to regard the earth as—

> "But the shadow of heaven, and things therein
> Each to the other like more than on earth is thought."

This notion was especially applied to everything connected with the Holy People, and there was no event in the wanderings of the wilderness which did not stand typically for matters of spiritual experience or heavenly hope.[2] This principle is expressly stated in the First Epistle to the Corinthians,[3] where, in exemplification of it, not only is the manna made the type of the bread of the Lord's Supper, but, by a much more remote analogy, the passing through the waters of the Red Sea, and the being guided by the pillar of cloud by day, is described as "being baptised unto Moses in the cloud and in the sea," and is made a prefigurement of Christian baptism.[4]

But although St. Paul was a Hebrew by virtue of his ancestry, and by virtue of the language which he had learnt as his mother-tongue, and although he would probably have rejected the appellation of "Hellenist," which is indeed never applied to him, yet his very Hebraism had, in one most important respect, and one which has very little attracted the attention of scholars, an Hellenic bias and tinge. This is apparent in the fact which I have already mentioned, that he was, or at any rate that he became, to a marked extent, in the technical language of the Jewish schools, an Hagadist, not an Halachist.[5] It needs but a glance at the Mishna, and still more at the Gemara, to see that

[1] Other specimens of exegesis accordant in result with the known views of the Rabbis may be found in Rom. ix. 33 (compared with Is. viii. 14, xxviii. 16; Luke ii. 34), since the Rabbis applied both the passages referred to—"the rock of offence," and "the corner-stone"—to the Messiah; and in 1 Cor. ix. 9, where by a happy analogy (also found in Philo, *De Victimas Offerentibus*, 1) the prohibition to muzzle the ox that treadeth out the corn is applied to the duty of maintaining ministers (1 Cor. ix. 4, 11; Eph. iv. 8). The expressions in Rom. v. 12; 1 Cor. xi. 10; 2 Cor. xi. 14; Gal. iii. 19, iv. 29, find parallels in the Targums, &c. To these may be added various images and expressions in 1 Cor. xv. 36; 2 Cor. xii. 2; 1 Thess. iv. 16. (See Immer, *Neut. Theol.* 210; Krenkel, p. 218.)

[2] "Quicquid evenit patribus signum filiis," &c. (Wetstein, and Schöttgen *ad* 1 Cor. x. 11). (See Wisd. xi., xvi.—xviii.)

[3] 1 Cor. x. 6, Ταῦτα δὲ τύποι ἡμῶν ἐγενήθησαν. On the manna (= θεῖος λόγος), compare Philo, *De Leg. Alleg.* iv. 56; on the rock (= σοφία τοῦ θεοῦ), *id.* ii. 21.

[4] So Greg. Naz. *Orat.* 39, p. 688, Jer. *Ep. ad Fabiol.* and most commentators, followed by the collect in our baptismal service, "figuring thereby thy holy baptism." But observe that the typology is quite incidental, the moral lesson paramount (1 Cor. x. 6, 11).

[5] See Excursus IV., "St. Paul a Hagadist."

the question which mainly occupied the thoughts and interests of the Palestinian and Babylonian Rabbis, and which almost constituted the entire education of their scholars, was the *Halacha*, or "rule;" and if we compare the Talmud with the Midrashim, we see at once that some Jewish scholars devoted themselves to the Hagada almost exclusively, and others to the Halacha, and that the names frequent in the one region of Jewish literature are rarely found in the other. The two classes of students despised each other. The Hagadist despised the Halachist as a minute pedant, and was despised in turn as an imaginative ignoramus. There was on the part of some Rabbis a jealous dislike of teaching the *Hagadôth* at all to any one who had not gone through the laborious training of the *Halacha*. "I hold from my ancestors," said R. Jonathan, in refusing to teach the *Hagada* to R. Samlaï, "that one ought not to teach the Hagada either to a Babylonian or to a southern Palestinian, because they are arrogant and ignorant." The consequences of the mutual dis-esteem in which each branch of students held the other was that the Hagadists mainly occupied themselves with the Prophets, and the Halachists with the Law. And hence the latter became more and more Judaic, Pharisaic, Rabbinic. The seven rules of Hillel became the thirteen rules of Ishmael,[1] and the thirty-three of Akibha, and by the intervention of these rules almost anything might be added to or subtracted from the veritable Law.[2] The letter of the Law thus lost its comparative simplicity in boundless complications, until the Talmud tells us how Akibha was seen in a vision by the astonished Moses, drawing from every horn of every letter whole bushels of decisions.[3] Meanwhile the Hagadists were deducing from the utterances of the Prophets a spirit which almost amounted to contempt for Levitical minutiæ;[4] were developing the Messianic tradition, and furnishing a powerful though often wholly unintentional assistance to the logic of Christian exegesis. This was because the Hagadists were grasping the spirit, while the Halachists were blindly groping amid the crumbled fragments of the letter. It is not wonderful that the Jews got to be so jealous of the Hagada, as betraying possible tendencies to the heresies of the *minîm*—*i.e.*, the Christians—that they imposed silence upon those who used certain suspected hagadistic expressions, which in themselves were perfectly harmless. "He who profanes holy things," says Rabbi Eliezer of Modin, in the *Pirke Abhôth*, "who slights the festivals, who causes his neighbour to blush in public, who breaks the covenant of Abraham, and discovers explanations of the Law contrary to the Halacha, even if he knew the Law and his works were good, would still lose his share in the life to come."[5]

It is easy to understand from these interesting particulars that if the Hagada and the Halacha were alike taught in the lecture-room of Gamaliel,

[1] See Derenbourg, *Palest.* p. 397.

[2] Even R. Ishmael, who shares with R. Akibha the title of Father of the World, admits to having found three cases in which the Halacha was contrary to the letter of the Pentateuch. It would not be difficult to discover very many more.

[3] *Menachôth*, 29, 2.

[4] Isa. i. 11—15; lviii. 5—7; Jer. vii. 21.

[5] *Pirke Abhôth*, iii. 8; Grätz, iii. 79.

St. Paul, whatever may have been his original respect for and study of the one, carried with him in mature years no trace of such studies, while he by no means despised the best parts of the other, and, illuminated by the Holy Spirit of God, found in the training with which it had furnished him at least an occasional germ, or illustration, of those Christian and Messianic arguments which he addressed with such consummate force alike to the rigid Hebraists and the most bigoted Hellenists in after years.[1]

CHAPTER IV.

SAUL THE PHARISEE.

Ζηλωτὴς ὑπάρχων τῶν πατρικῶν μου παραδόσεων.—GAL. i. 14; ACTS xxii. 3.

Κατὰ τὴν ἀκριβεστάτην αἵρεσιν τῆς ἡμετέρας θρησκείας ἔζησα Φαρισαῖος.—ACTS xxvi. 5.

IF the gathered lore of the years between the ages of thirteen and thirty-three has left, as it must inevitably have left, unmistakable traces on the pages of St. Paul, how much more must this be the case with all the moral struggles, all the spiritual experiences, all those inward battles which are not fought with earthly weapons, through which he must have passed during the long period in which "he lived a Pharisee"?

We know well the kind of life which lies hid behind that expression. We know the minute and intense scrupulosity of Sabbath observance wasting itself in all those *abhôth* and *toldôth*—those primary and derivative rules and prohibitions, and inferences from rules and prohibitions, and combinations of inferences from rules and prohibitions, and cases of casuistry and conscience arising out of the infinite possible variety of circumstances to which those combinations of inference might apply—which had degraded the Sabbath from "a delight, holy of the Lord and honourable," partly into an anxious and pitiless burden, and partly into a network of contrivances hypocritically designed, as it were, in the lowest spirit of heathenism, to cheat the Deity with the mere *semblance* of accurate observance.[2] We know the carefulness about the colour of fringes, and the tying of tassels, and the lawfulness of meats and drinks. We know the tithings, at once troublesome and ludicrous, of mint, anise, and cummin, and the serio-comic questions as to whether in tithing the seed it was obligatory also to tithe the stalk. We know the double fasts of the week, and the triple prayers of the day, and the triple visits to the Temple. We know the elaborate strainings of the water and the wine, that not even the carcase of an animalcula might defeat the energy of Levitical anxiety. We know the constant rinsings and scourings of brazen cups and

[1] See Derenbourg's *Hist. de la Palestine d'après les Thalmuds* (ch. xxi. and xxiii.), which seems to me to throw a flood of light on the views and early training of St. Paul.

[2] See the rules about the mixtures (*Erubhîn*), *Life of Christ*, i. 436, ii. 472.

pots and tables, carried to so absurd an extreme that, on the occasion of washing the golden candelabrum of the Temple, the Sadducees remarked that their Pharisaic rivals would wash the Sun itself if they could get an opportunity. We know the entire and laborious ablutions and bathings of the whole person, with carefully tabulated ceremonies and normal gesticulations, not for the laudable purpose of personal cleanliness, but for the nervously-strained endeavour to avoid every possible and impossible chance of contracting ceremonial uncleanness. We know how this notion of perfect Levitical purity thrust itself with irritating recurrence into every aspect and relation of ordinary life, and led to the scornful avoidance of the very contact and shadow of fellow-beings, who might after all be purer and nobler than those who would not touch them with the tassel of a garment's hem. We know the obtrusive prayers,[1] the ostentatious almsgivings,[2] the broadened phylacteries,[3] the petty ritualisms,[4] the professorial arrogance,[5] the reckless proselytism,[6] the greedy avarice,[7] the haughty assertion of pre-eminence,[8] the ill-concealed hypocrisy,[9] which were often hidden under this venerable assumption of superior holiness. And we know all this quite as much, or more, from the admiring records of the Talmud—which devotes one whole treatise to hand-washings,[10] and another to the proper method of killing a fowl,[11] and another to the stalks of legumes[12]—as from the reiterated "woes" of Christ's denunciation.[13] But we may be sure that these extremes and degeneracies of the Pharisaic aim would be as grievous and displeasing to the youthful Saul as they were to all the noblest Pharisees, and as they were to Christ Himself. Of the seven kinds of Pharisees which the Talmud in various places enumerates, we may be quite sure that Saul of Tarsus would neither be a "bleeding" Pharisee, nor a "mortar" Pharisee, nor a "Shechemite" Pharisee, nor a "timid" Pharisee, nor a "tumbling" Pharisee, nor a "painted" Pharisee at all; but that the only class of Pharisee to which he, as a true and high-minded Israelite, would have borne any shadow of resemblance, and that not in a spirit of self-contentment, but in a spirit of almost morbid and feverish anxiety to do all that was commanded, would be the Tell-me-anything-more-to-do-and-I-will-do-it Pharisee![14]

And this type of character, which bears no remote resemblance to that of many of the devotees of the monastic life—however erroneous it may be, however bitter must be the pain by which it must be accompanied, however deep the dissatisfaction which it must ultimately suffer—is very far from being necessarily ignoble. It is indeed based on the enormous error that man can deserve heaven by care in external practices; that he can win by quantitative goodness his entrance into the kingdom of God; that

[1] Matt. vi. 5. [2] Matt. vi. 2. [3] Matt. xxiii. 5
[4] Mark vii. 4—8. [5] John vii. 49. [6] Matt. xxiii. 15.
[7] Luke xx. 47. [8] Luke xviii. 11. [9] Matt. xxii. 17.
[10] *Yadayim.* [11] *Cholin.* [12] *Ozekin.*
[13] See Schöttgen, *Hor. Hebr.* pp. 7, 160, 204.
[14] *Jer. Berachôth*, ix. 7, &c. See *Life of Christ*, vol. ii. p. 248, where these names are explained.

that kingdom is meat and drink, not righteousness and peace and joy in believing. Occasionally, by some flash of sudden conviction, one or two of the wisest Doctors of the Law seem to have had some glimmering of the truth, that it is *not* by works of righteousness, but only by God's mercy, that man is saved. But the normal and all but universal belief of the religious party among the Jews was that, though of the 248 commands and 365 prohibitions of the Mosaic Law some were "light" and some were "heavy,"[1] yet that to one and all alike—not only in the spirit but in the letter—not only in the actual letter, but in the boundless inferences to which the letter might lead when every grain of sense and meaning had been crushed out of it under mountain loads of "decisions"—a rigidly scrupulous obedience was due. This was what God absolutely required. This, and this only, came up to the true conception of the blameless righteousness of the Law. And how much depended on it! Nothing less than recovered freedom, recovered empire, recovered pre-eminence among the nations; nothing less than the restoration of their national independence in all its perfectness, of their national worship in all its splendour; nothing less than the old fire upon the altar, the holy oil, the sacred ark, the cloud of glory between the wings of the cherubim; nothing less, in short, than the final hopes which for many centuries they and their fathers had most deeply cherished. If but one person could only for one day keep the whole Law and not offend in one point—nay, if but one person could but keep that one point of the Law which affected the due observance of the Sabbath—then (so the Rabbis taught) the troubles of Israel would be ended, and the Messiah at last would come.[2]

And it was at nothing less than this that, with all the intense ardour of his nature, Saul had aimed. It is doubtful whether at this period the utter nullity of the Oral Law could have dawned upon him. It sometimes dawned even on the Rabbis through the dense fogs of sophistry and self-importance, and even on their lips we sometimes find the utterances of the Prophets that humility and justice and mercy are better than sacrifice. "There was a flute in the Temple," says the Talmud, "preserved from the days of Moses; it was smooth, thin, and formed of a reed. At the command of the king it was overlaid with gold, which ruined its sweetness of tone until the gold was taken away. There were also a cymbal and a mortar, which had become injured in course of time, and were mended by workmen of Alexandria summoned by the wise men; but their usefulness was so completely destroyed by this process, that it was necessary to restore them to their former condition."[3] Are not these things an allegory? Do they not imply that by overlaying the written Law with what they called the gold, but what

[1] See *Life of Christ*, ii. 239. All these distinctions were a part of the *Seyyag*, the "hedge of the Law," which it was the one *raison d'être* of Rabbinism to construct. The object of all Jewish learning was to make a *mishmereth* ("ordinance," Lev. xviii. 30) to God's *mishmereth* (*Yebhamôth*, f. 21, 1).

[2] See Acts iii. 19, where ὅπως ἂν is "in order that haply," not "when," as in E. V. (*Shabbath*, f. 118, *b*).

[3] *Eirechin*, f. 10, 2.

was in reality the dross and tinsel of tradition, the Rabbis had destroyed or injured its beauty and usefulness? But probably Saul had not realised this. To him there was no distinction between the relative importance of the Written and Oral, of the moral and ceremonial Law. To every precept—and they were countless—obedience was due. If it *could* be done, he would do it. If on him, on his accuracy of observance, depended the coming of the Messiah, then the Messiah should come. Were others learned in all that concerned legal rectitude? he would be yet more learned. Were others scrupulous? he would be yet more scrupulous. Surely God had left man free?[1] Surely He would not have demanded obedience to the Law if that obedience were not possible! All things pointed to the close of one great *aeon* in the world's history, and the dawn of another which should be the last. The very heathen yearned for some deliverer, and felt that there could be no other end to the physical misery and moral death which had spread itself over their hollow societies.[2] Deep midnight was brooding alike over the chosen people and the Gentile world. From the East should break forth a healing light, a purifying flame. Let Israel be true, and God's promise would not fail.

And we know from his own statements that if external conformity were all—if obedience to the Law did not mean obedience in all kinds of matters which escaped all possibility of attention—if avoidance of its prohibitions did not involve avoidance in matters which evaded the reach of the human senses—then Saul was, touching the righteousness of the Law, *blameless*, having lived in all good conscience towards God.[3] Had *he* put the question to the Great Master, "What shall I do to be saved?" or been bidden to "keep the commandments," it is certain that he would have been able to reply with the youthful ruler, "All these have I kept from my youth," and—he might have added—"very much besides." And yet we trace in his Epistles how bitterly he felt the hollowness of this outward obedience—how awful and how burdensome had been to him "the curse of the Law." Even moral obedience could not silence the voice of the conscience, or satisfy the yearnings of the soul; but these infinitesimal Levitisms, what could they do? Tormenting questions would again and again arise. Of what use was all this? from what did the necessity of it spring? to what did the obedience to it lead? Did God indeed care for the exact size of a strip of parchment, or the particular number of lines in the texts which were upon it, or the way in which the letters were formed, or the shape of the box into which it was put, or the manner in which that box was tied upon the forehead or the arm?[4] Was it, indeed, a very important matter whether "between the two evenings" meant, as the Samaritans

[1] The Rabbis said, "Everything is in the hands of heaven, except the fear of heaven." "All things are ordained by God, but a man's actions are his own." (Barclay, *Talmud*, 18.)

[2] Virg. *Ecl.* iv.; Suet. *Aug.* 94; *Vesp.* 4.

[3] 2 Cor. xi. 22; Rom. xi. 1; Acts xxii. 3, xxiii. 1, 6.

[4] I have adduced abundant illustrations from Rabbinic writers of the extravagant importance attached to minutiæ in the construction of the two phylacteries of the hand (*Tephillin shel Yad*) and of the head (*Teph. shel Rôsh*), in the *Expositor*, 1877, No. xxvii.

believed, between sunset and darkness, or, as the Pharisees asserted, between the beginning and end of sunset? Was it a matter worth the discussion of two schools to decide whether an egg laid on a festival might or might not be eaten?[1] Were all these things indeed, and in themselves, important? And even if they were, would it be errors as to these littlenesses that would really kindle the wrath of a jealous God? How did they contribute to the beauty of holiness? in what way did they tend to fill the soul with the mercy which was better than sacrifice, or to educate it in that justice and humility, that patience and purity, that peace and love, which, as some of the prophets had found grace to see, were dearer to God than thousands of rams and ten thousands of rivers of oil? And behind all these questions lay that yet deeper one which agitated the schools of Jewish thought—the question whether, after all, man could reach, or with all his efforts must inevitably fail to reach, that standard of righteousness which God and the Law required? And if indeed he failed, what more had the Law to say to him than to deliver its sentence of unreprieved condemnation and indiscriminate death?[2]

Moreover, was there not mingled with all this nominal adoration of the Law a deeply-seated hypocrisy, *so* deep that it was in a great measure unconscious? Even before the days of Christ the Rabbis had learnt the art of straining out gnats and swallowing camels. They had long learnt to nullify what they professed to defend. The ingenuity of Hillel was quite capable of getting rid of any Mosaic regulation which had been found practically burdensome. Pharisees and Sadducees alike had managed to set aside in their own favour, by the devices of the "mixtures," all that was disagreeable to themselves in the Sabbath scrupulosity. The fundamental institution of the Sabbatic year had been stultified by the mere legal fiction of the *prosbol*. Teachers who were on the high road to a casuistry which could construct "rules" out of every superfluous particle had found it easy to win credit for ingenuity by elaborating prescriptions to which Moses would have listened in mute astonishment. If there be one thing more definitely laid down in the Law than another it is the uncleanness of creeping things, yet the Talmud assures us that "no one is appointed a member of the Sanhedrin who does not possess sufficient ingenuity to prove from the written Law that a creeping thing is ceremonially clean;"[3] and that there was an unimpeachable disciple at Jabne who could adduce one hundred and fifty arguments in favour of the ceremonial cleanness of creeping things.[4] Sophistry like this was at work even in the days when the young student of Tarsus sat at the feet of Gamaliel; and can we imagine any period of his life when he would not have been wearied by a system at once so meaningless, so stringent, and so insincere? Could he fail to notice that they "hugely violated what they trivially obeyed?"

We may see from St. Paul's own words that these years must have been very troubled years. Under the dignified exterior of the Pharisee lay a wildly-beating heart; an anxious brain throbbed with terrible questionings under the

[1] See *Bitsah*, 1 *ad in.* [2] Rom. x. 5; Gal. iii. 10. [3] *Sanhedr.* f. 17, 1. [4] *Erubhin*, f. 13, 2

broad phylactery. Saul as a Pharisee believed in eternity, he believed in the resurrection, he believed in angel and spirit, in voices and appearances, in dreaming dreams and seeing visions. But in all this struggle to achieve his own righteousness—this struggle so minutely tormenting, so revoltingly burdensome—there seemed to be no hope, no help, no enlightenment, no satisfaction, no nobility—nothing but a possibly mitigated and yet inevitable curse. God seemed silent to him, and heaven closed. No vision dawned on his slumbering senses, no voice sounded in his eager ear. The sense of sin oppressed him; the darkness of mystery hung over him; he was ever falling and falling, and no hand was held out to help him; he strove with all his soul to be obedient, and he was obedient—and yet the Messiah did not come.

The experience of Saul of Tarsus was the heartrending experience of all who have looked for peace elsewhere than in the love of God. All that Luther suffered at Erfurdt Saul must have suffered in Jerusalem; and the record of the early religious agonies and awakenment of the one is the best commentary on the experience of the other. That the life of Saul was free from flagrant transgressions we see from his own bold appeals to his continuous rectitude. He was not a convert from godlessness or profligacy, like John Bunyan or John Newton. He claims integrity when he is speaking of his life in the aspect which it presented to his fellow-men, but he is vehement in self-accusation when he thinks of that life in the aspect which it presented to his God. He found that no external legality could give him a clean heart, or put a right spirit within him. He found that servile obedience inspired no inward peace. He must have yearned for some righteousness, could he but know of it, which would be better than the righteousness of the Scribes and Pharisees. The Jewish doctors had imagined and had directed that if a man did not feel inclined to do this or that, he should force himself to do it by a direct vow. "Vows," says Rabbi Akibha,[1] are the enclosures of holiness." But Saul the Pharisee, long before he became Paul the Apostle, must have proved to the very depth the hollowness of this direction. Vows might be the enclosures of formal practice; they were not, and could not be, the schooling of the disobedient soul; they could not give calm to that place in the human being where meet the two seas of good and evil impulse[2]—to the heart, which is the battle-field on which passionate desire clashes into collision with positive command.

Even when twenty years of weariness, and wandering, and struggle, and suffering, were over, we still catch in the Epistles of St. Paul the mournful echoes of those days of stress and storm—echoes as of the thunder when its fury is over, and it is only sobbing far away among the distant hills. We hear those echoes most of all in the Epistle to the Romans. We hear them when he talks of "the curse of the law." We hear them when, in accents of deep self-pity, he tells us of the struggle between the flesh and the spirit; between the law of sin in his members, and that law of God which, though holy and just and good and ordained to life, he found to be unto death. In

[1] נדרים סייג לפרישות, *Pirke Abhôth*, iii. 10.
[2] The *Yetser tôbh* and the *Yetser ha-râ* of the Talmud.

the days, indeed, when he thus writes, he had at last found peace; he had wrung from the lessons of his life the hard experience that by the works of the law no man can be justified in God's sight, but that, being justified by faith, we have peace with God through our Lord Jesus Christ. And though, gazing on his own personality, and seeing it disintegrated by a miserable dualism, he still found a law within him which warred against that inward delight which he felt in the law of God—though groaning in this body of weakness, he feels like one who is imprisoned in a body of death, he can still, in answer to the question, "Who shall deliver me?" exclaim with a burst of triumph, "I thank God, through Jesus Christ our Lord."[1] But if the Apostle, after he has found Christ, after he has learnt that "there is no condemnation to them that are in Christ Jesus"[2] still felt the power and continuity of the inferior law striving to degrade his life into that captivity to the law of sin from which Christ had set him free, through what hours of mental anguish must he not have passed when he knew of no other dealing of God with his soul than the impossible, unsympathising, deathful commandment, "This *do*, and thou shalt live!" *Could* he "this do"? And, if he could not, what hope, what help? Was there any voice of pity among the thunders of Sinai?[3] Could the mere blood of bulls and goats be any true propitiation for wilful sins?

But though we can see the mental anguish through which Saul passed in his days of Parisaism, yet over the events of that period a complete darkness falls; and there are only two questions, both of them deeply interesting, which it may, perhaps, be in our power to answer.

1. The first is, Did Saul in those days ever see the Lord Jesus Christ?

At first sight we might suppose that the question was answered, and answered affirmatively, in 1 Cor. ix. 1, where he asks, "Am I not an Apostle? Have I not seen Jesus, our Lord?" and still more in 2 Cor. v. 16, where he says, "Yea, though we have known Christ after the flesh, yet now henceforth know we Him no more."[4]

But a little closer examination of these passages will show that they do not necessarily involve any such meaning. In the first of them, St. Paul cannot possibly be alluding to any knowledge of Jesus before His crucifixion, because such mere external sight, from the position of one who disbelieved in Him, so far from being a confirmation of any claim to be an Apostle, would rather have been a reason for rejecting such a claim. It can only apply to the appearance

[1] See Rom. vi., vii., viii., *passim*.

[2] Rom. viii. 1. The rest of this verse in our E. V. is probably a gloss, or a repetition, since it is not found in ℵ, B, C, D, F, G.

[3] "That man that overtook you," said Christian, "was Moses. He spareth none, neither knoweth he how to show mercy to them that transgress his law." (*Pilgrim's Progress.*)

[4] εἰ καὶ ἐγνώκαμεν. It is perfectly true that εἰ καὶ (*quamquam*, "even though," *wenn auch*) in classical writers—though perhaps less markedly in St. Paul—concedes a fact, whereas καὶ εἰ (*etiam si*, "even if,") puts an hypothesis; but the explanation here turns, not on the admitted force of the particles, but on what is meant by "knowing Christ after the flesh"

of Christ to him on the way to Damascus, or to some similar and subsequent revelation.[1] The meaning of the second passage is less obvious. St. Paul has there been explaining the grounds of his Apostolate in the constraining love of Christ for man. He has shown how that love was manifested by His death for all, and how the results of that death and resurrection are intended so utterly to destroy the self-love of His children, so totally to possess and to change their individuality, that "if any man be in Christ he is a new creation." And the Christ of whom he is here speaking is the risen, glorified, triumphant Christ, in whom all things are become new, because He has reconciled man to God. Hence the Apostle will know no man, judge of no man, in his mere human and earthly relations, but only in his union with their risen Lord. The partisans who used, and far more probably abused, the name of James, to thrust their squabbling Judaism even into the intercourse between a Paul and a Peter, and who sowed the seeds of discord among the converts of the Churches which St. Paul had founded, were constantly underrating the Apostolic dignity of Paul, because he had not been an eye-witness of the human life of Christ. The answer of the Apostle always was that he too knew Christ by an immediate revelation, that "it had pleased God *to reveal His Son in him* that he might preach Christ among the Gentiles."[2] The day had been when he had known "Christ according to the flesh"—not indeed by direct personal intercourse with Him in the days of His earthly ministry, but by the view which he and others had taken of Him. In his unconverted days he had regarded Him as a *meeíth*—an impostor who deceived the people, or at the very best as a teacher who deceived himself. And after his conversion he had not perhaps, at first, fully learnt to apprehend the *Plenitude* of the glory of the risen Christ as rising far above the conception of the Jewish Messiah. All this was past. To apprehend by faith the glorified Son of God was a far more blessed privilege than to have known a living Messiah by earthly intercourse. Even if he had known Christ as a living man, that knowledge would have been less near, less immediate, less intimate, less eternal, in its character, than the closeness of community wherewith he now lived and died in Him; and although he had known Him first only by false report, and then only with imperfect realisation as Jesus of Nazareth, the earthly and human conception had now passed away, and been replaced by the true and spiritual belief. The Christ, therefore, whom now he knew was no "Christ after the flesh," no Christ in the days of His flesh, no Christ in any earthly relations, but Christ sitting for ever at the right hand of God. To have seen the Lord Jesus with the eyes was of itself nothing—it was nothing to boast of. Herod had seen Him, and Annas,

[1] Cf. Acts xviii. 9, xxii. 18; 2 Cor. xii. 1. The absence of such *personal* references to Jesus in St. Paul's Epistles as we find in 1 Pet. ii. 21 *sq.*, iii. 18 *sq.*; 1 John i. 1—confirms this view (Ewald, *Gesch.* vi. 389).

[2] Gal. i. 16. I cannot agree with Dr. Lightfoot (following Jerome, Erasmus, &c.) that ἐν ἐμοὶ means "a revelation *made through Paul to others*," as in ver. 24, 1 Tim. i. 16, and 2 Cor. xiii. 3; because, as a friend points out, there is an *exact* parallelism of clauses between i. 11, 12, and 13—17, and ἀποκαλύψαι τὸν υἱὸν αὐτοῦ ἐν ἐμοὶ balances δι' ἀποκαλύψεως Ἰησοῦ Χριστοῦ in ver 12.

and Pilate, and many a coarse Jewish mendicant and many a brutal Roman soldier. But to have seen Him with the eye of Faith—to have spiritually apprehended the glorified Redeemer—that was indeed to be a Christian.

All the other passages which can at all be brought to bear on the question support this view, and lead us to believe that St. Paul had either not seen at all, or at the best barely seen, the Man Christ Jesus. Indeed, the question, "Who art Thou, Lord?"[1] preserved in all three narratives of his conversion, seems distinctly to imply that the appearance of the Lord was unknown to him, and this is a view which is confirmed by the allusion to the risen Christ in 1 Cor. xv. St. Paul there says that to him, the least of the Apostles, and not meet to be called an Apostle, Christ had appeared last of all, as to the abortive-born of the Apostolic family.[2] And, indeed, it is inconceivable that Saul could in any real sense have seen Jesus in His lifetime. That ineffaceable impression produced by His very aspect; that unspeakable personal ascendency, which awed His worst enemies and troubled the hard conscience of His Roman judge; the ineffable charm and power in the words of Him who spake as never man spake, could not have appealed to him in vain. We feel an unalterable conviction, not only that, if Saul had seen Him, Paul would again and again have referred to Him, but also that he would in that case have been saved from the reminiscence which most of all tortured him in after days—the undeniable reproach that he had persecuted the Church of God. If, indeed, we could imagine that Saul had seen Christ, and, having seen Him, had looked on Him only with the bitter hatred and simulated scorn of a Jerusalem Pharisee, then we may be certain that that Holy Face which looked into the troubled dreams of Pilate's wife—that the infinite sorrow in those eyes, of which one glance broke the repentant heart of Peter—would have recurred so often and so heartrendingly to Paul's remembrance, that his sin in persecuting the Christians would have assumed an aspect of tenfold aggravation, from the thought that in destroying and imprisoning them he had yet more openly been crucifying the Son of God afresh, and putting Him to an open shame. The intense impressibility of Paul's mind appears most remarkably in the effect exercised upon him by the dying rapture of St. Stephen. The words of Stephen, though listened to at the time with inward fury, not only lingered in his memory, but produced an unmistakable influence on his writings. If this were so with the speech of the youthful Hellenist, how infinitely more would it have been so with the words which subdued into admiration even the alien disposition of Pharisaic emissaries? Can we for a moment conceive that Paul's Pharisaism would have lasted unconsumed amid the white lightnings of that great and scathing denunciation which Christ uttered in the Temple in the last week of His ministry, and three days before His death? Had St. Paul heard one of these last discourses, had he seen one of those miracles, had he mingled in one of those terrible and tragic scenes to which he must

[1] Acts ix. 5 (xxii. 8, xxvi. 15). There is not the shadow of probability in the notion of Ewald, that St. Paul was the young man clad in a *sindôn*, of Mark xiv. 52.

[2] 1 Cor. xv. 9.

have afterwards looked back as events the most momentous in the entire course of human history, is there any one who can for a moment imagine that no personal reminiscence of such scenes would be visible, even ever so faintly, through the transparent medium of his writings?

We may, then, regard it as certain that when the gloom fell at mid-day over the awful sacrifice of Golgotha, when the people shouted their preference for the murderous brigand, and yelled their execration of the Saviour whose day all the noblest and holiest of their fathers had longed to see, Saul was not at Jerusalem. Where, then, was he? It is impossible to answer the question with any certainty. He may have been at Tarsus, which, even after his conversion, he regarded as his home.[1] Or perhaps the explanation of his absence may be seen in Gal. v. 11. He there represents himself as having once been a preacher of circumcision. Now we know that one of the characteristics of the then Pharisaism was an active zeal in winning proselytes. "Ye compass sea and land," said Christ to them, in burning words, "to make one proselyte; and when he is made, ye make him twofold more the child of Gehenna than yourselves."[2] The conversion which changed Paul's deepest earlier convictions left unchanged the natural impulse of his temperament Why may not the same impetuous zeal, the same restless desire to be always preaching some truth and doing some good work which marked him out as the Apostle of the Gentiles,[3] have worked in him also in these earlier days, and made him, as he seems to imply, a missionary of Pharisaism? If so, he may have been absent on some journey enjoined upon him by the party whose servant, heart and soul, he was, during the brief visits to Jerusalem which marked the three years' ministry of Christ on earth.

2. The other question which arises is, Was Saul married? Had he the support of some loving heart during the fiery struggles of his youth? Amid the to-and-fro contentions of spirit which resulted from an imperfect and unsatisfying creed, was there in the troubled sea of his life one little island home where he could find refuge from incessant thoughts?

Little as we know of his domestic relations, little as he cared to mingle mere private interests with the great spiritual truths which occupy his soul, it seems to me that we must answer this question in the affirmative. St. Paul, who has been very freely charged with egotism, had not one particle of that egotism which consists in attaching any importance to his personal surroundings. The circumstances of his individual life he would have looked on as having no interest for any one but himself. When he speaks of himself he does so always from one of two reasons—from the necessity of maintaining against detraction his apostolic authority, or from the desire to utilise for others his remarkable experience. The things that happened to him, the blessings and privations of his earthly condition, would have seemed matters of supreme indifference, except in so far as they possessed a moral significance, or had any bearing on the lessons which he desired to teach.

[1] Acts ix. 30, xi. 25; Gal. i. 21. [2] Matt. xxiii. 15.
[3] Gal. i. 16. (See Krenkel, p. 18.)

It is, then, only indirectly that we can expect to find an answer to the question as to his marriage. If, indeed, he was a member of the Sanhedrin, it follows that, by the Jewish requirements for that position, he must have been a married man. His official position will be examined hereafter; but, meanwhile, his marriage may be inferred as probable from passages in his Epistles. In 1 Cor. ix. 5 he asks the Corinthians, "Have we not power to lead about a sister, a wife, as well as other Apostles, and as the brethren of the Lord, and Kephas?" This passage is inconclusive, though it asserts his right both to marry, and to take a wife with him in his missionary journeys if he thought it expedient.[1] But from 1 Cor. vii. 8 it seems a distinct inference that he classed himself among *widowers;* for, he says, "I say, therefore, to the *unmarried* and widows, it is good for them if they *abide* (μείνωσιν) even as I." That by "the unmarried" he here means "widowers"—for which there is no special Greek word—seems clear, because he has been already speaking, in the first seven verses of the chapter, to those who have never been married.[2] To them he concedes, far more freely than to the others, the privilege of marrying if they considered it conducive to godliness, though, in the present state of things, he mentions his own personal predilection for celibacy, in the case of all who had the grace of inward purity. And even apart from the interpretation of this passage, the deep and fine insight of Luther had drawn the conclusion that Paul knew by experience what marriage was, from the wisdom and tenderness which characterise his remarks respecting it. One who had never been married could hardly have written on the subject as he has done, nor could he have shown the same profound sympathy with the needs of all, and received from all the same ready confidence. To derive any inference from the loving metaphors which he draws from the nurture of little children[3] would be more precarious. It is hardly possible that Paul ever had a child who lived. Had this been the case, his natural affection could hardly have denied itself some expression of the tender love which flows out so freely towards his spiritual children. Timothy would not have been so exclusively "his own true child" in the faith if he had had son or daughter of his own. If we are right in the assumption that he was married, it seems probable that it was for a short time only, and that his wife had died.

But there is one more ground which has not, I think, been noticed, which seems to me to render it extremely probable that Saul, before the time of his

[1] The notion that the "true yokefellow" (γνήσιε σύζυγε) of Phil. iv. 3 has any bearing on the question is an error as old as Clemens Alexandrinus. (See *Strom.* iii. 7; Ps. Ignat. *ad Philad.* 4, Ὡς Πέτρου καὶ Παύλου καὶ τῶν ἄλλων ἀποστόλων τῶν γάμοις ὁμιλησάντων.)

[2] If so, Chaucer is mistaken when he says, "I wot wel the Apostle was a mayd," *i.e.*, παρθένος, Rev. xiv. 4 (Prologue to *Wife of Bath's Tale*). Ver. 7 does not militate against this view, because there he is alluding, not to his condition, but to the grace of continence. It is not true, as has been said, that early tradition was unanimous in saying that he had never married. Tertullian (*De Monogam.* 3) and Jerome (*Ep.* 22) says so; but Origen is doubtful, and Methodius (*Conviv.* 45), as well as Clemens Alex. and Ps. Ignatius (*v. supra*), says that he was a widower.

[3] 1 Cor. iii. 2, vii. 14, iv. 15; 1 Thess. ii. 7; v. 3.

conversion, had been a married man. It is the extraordinary importance attached by the majority of Jews in all ages to marriage as a moral duty, nay, even a positive command, incumbent on every man.[1] The Mishna fixes the age of marriage at eighteen,[2] and even seventeen was preferred. The Babylonist Jews fixed it as early as fourteen.[3] Marriage is, in fact, the first of the 613 precepts. They derived the duty partly from the command of Gen. i. 28, partly from allusions to early marriage in the Old Testament (Prov. ii. 17; v. 18), and partly from allegorising explanations of passages like Eccl. xi. 6; Job v. 24.[4] The Rabbis in all ages have laid it down as a stringent duty that parents should marry their children young;[5] and the one or two who, like Ben Azai, theoretically placed on a higher level the duty of being more free from incumbrance in order to study the Law, were exceptions to the almost universal rule. But even these theorists were themselves married men. If St. Paul had ever evinced the smallest sympathy with the views of the Therapeutæ and Essenes—if his discountenancing of marriage, under certain immediate conditions, had been tinged by any Gnostic fancies about its essential inferiority—we might have come to a different conclusion. But he held no such views either before or after his conversion;[6] and certainly, if he lived unmarried as a Jerusalem Pharisee, his case was entirely exceptional.

CHAPTER V.

ST. PETER AND THE FIRST PENTECOST.

Ἔκκριτος ἦν τῶν ἀποστόλων, καὶ στόμα τῶν μαθητῶν, καὶ κορυφὴ τοῦ χοροῦ.—CHRYS. *in Joan. Hom.* 88.

Πέτρος ἡ ἀρχὴ τῆς ορθοδοξίας, ὁ μέγας τῆς ἐκκλησίας ἱεροφάντης.—PS. CHRYS. *Orat. Encom.* 9.

WHATEVER may have been the cause of Saul's absence from Jerusalem during the brief period of the ministry of Jesus, it is inevitable that, on his return, he must have heard much respecting it. Yet all that he heard would be exclusively from the point of view of the Pharisees, who had so bitterly opposed His doctrines, and of the Sadducees, who had so basely brought

1 "A Jew who has no wife is not a man" (Gen. v. 2; *Yebhamôth*, f. 63, 1).

2 *Pirke Abhôth*, v. 21.

3 God was supposed to curse all who at twenty were unmarried (*Kiddushin*, 29, 1; 30; *Yebhamôth*, 62, 63). (See Hamburger, *Talmud. Wörterb.* s.v. *Ehe, Verheirathung*; Weill, *La Morale du Judaïsme*, 49, *seq.*) The precept is inferred from "He called *their* name *man* (sing.)," and is found in the Rabbinic digest *Tur-Shulchan Aruch.*

4 See Ecclus. vii. 25; xlii. 9; cf. 1 Cor. vii. 36.

5 Early marriages are to this day the curse of the Jews in Eastern countries. Sometimes girls are married at ten, boys at fourteen (Frankl, *Jews in East*, ii. 18, 84). Not long ago a Jewish girl at Jerusalem, aged fourteen, when asked in school why she was sad, replied that she had been three times divorced.

6 1 Cor. vii. 9 36; 1 Tim. iv. 3; v. 14.

about His death. But he would have abundant opportunities for seeing that the Infant Church had not, as the Jews of Jerusalem had hoped, been extinguished by the murder of its founder. However much the news might fill him with astonishment and indignation, he could not have been many days in Jerusalem without receiving convincing proofs of the energy of what he then regarded as a despicable sect.

Whence came this irresistible energy, this inextinguishable vitality? The answer to that question is the history of the Church and of the world.

For the death of Jesus had been followed by a succession of events, the effects of which will be felt to the end of time—events which, by a spiritual power at once astounding and indisputable, transformed a timid handful of ignorant and terror-stricken Apostles into teachers of unequalled grandeur, who became in God's hands the instruments to regenerate the world.

The Resurrection of Christ had scattered every cloud from their saddened souls. The despair which, for a moment, had followed the intense hope that this was He who would redeem Israel, had been succeeded by a joyous and unshaken conviction that Christ had risen from the dead. In the light of that Resurrection, all Scripture, all history, all that they had seen and heard during the ministry of Jesus, was illuminated and transfigured. And though during the forty days between the Resurrection and the Ascension, the intercourse held with them by their risen Lord was not continuous, but brief and interrupted,[1] yet—as St. Peter himself testifies, appealing, in confirmation of his testimony, to the scattered Jews to whom His Epistle is addressed—God had begotten them again by the Resurrection unto a lively hope, to an inheritance incorruptible, and undefiled, and that fadeth not away.[2] But besides this glorious truth, of which they felt themselves to be the chosen witnesses,[3] their Risen Lord had given them many promises and instructions, and spoken to them about the things which concerned the Kingdom of God. In His last address He had specially bidden them to stay in Jerusalem, and there await the outpouring of the Spirit of which they had already heard.[4] That promise was to be fulfilled to them, not only individually, but as a body, as a Church; and it was to be fulfilled in the same city in which they had witnessed His uttermost humiliation. And they were assured that they should not have long to wait. But though they knew that they should be baptised with the Holy Ghost and with fire "not many days hence," yet, for the exercise of their faith and to keep them watchful, the exact time was not defined.[5]

Then came the last walk towards Bethany, and that solemn parting on the Mount of Olives, when their Lord was taken away from them, and "a cloud

[1] Acts i. 3, δι' ἡμερῶν τεσσαράκοντα ὀπτανόμενος αὐτοῖς. This is the only passage in Scripture which tells us the interval which elapsed between the Resurrection and the Ascension.

[2] 1 Pet. i. 3, 4.

[3] Acts ii. 32; iii. 15; iv. 33; v. 32: x. 40, 41; Luke xxiv. 48, &c. On this fact St. Luke dwells repeatedly and emphatically. (See Meyer on Acts i. 22.)

[4] Acts i. 4; Luke xxiv. 49.

[5] Chrys. *ad loc.* "Numerus dierum non definitus exercebat fidem apostolorum" (Bengel). The reading ἕως τῆς πεντηκοστῆς of D and the Sahidic version is a mere gloss.

received Him out of their sight." But even in His last discourse He had rendered clear to them their position and their duties. When, with lingerings of old Messianic fancies, they had asked Him whether He would at that time re-constitute[1] the kingdom for Israel, He had quenched such material longings by telling them that it was not for them to know "the times or the seasons,"[2] which the Father placed in His own authority.[3] But though these secrets of God were not to be revealed to them or to any living man, there *was* a power which they should receive when the Holy Ghost had fallen upon them—a power to be witnesses to Christ, His sufferings, and His Resurrection, first in the narrow limits of the Holy Land, then to all the world.

From the mountain slopes of Olivet they returned that Sabbath-day's journey[4] to Jerusalem, and at once assembled in the upper chamber,[5] which was so suitable a place for their early gatherings. It was one of those large rooms under the flat roof of Jewish houses, which, for its privacy, was set apart for religious purposes; and in the poverty of these Galilæan Apostles, we can scarcely doubt that it was the same room of which they had already availed themselves for the Last Supper, and for those gatherings on the "first day of the week,"[6] at two of which Jesus had appeared to them. Hallowed by these divine associations, it seems to have been the ordinary place of sojourn of the Apostles during the days of expectation.[7] Here, at stated hours of earnest prayer, they were joined by the mother of Jesus[8] and the other holy women who had attended His ministry; as well as by His brethren, of whom one in particular[9] plays henceforth an important part in the history of the Church. Hitherto these "brethren of the Lord" had scarcely been numbered among those who believed in Christ,[10] or, if they had believed in Him, it had only been in a secondary and material sense, as a human Messiah. But now, as we might naturally conjecture, even apart from tradition, they had been convinced and converted by "the power of His Resurrection." Even in these earliest meetings of the whole Church of Christ at Jerusalem it is interesting to see that, though the Apostles were still Jews in their religion, with no other change as yet beyond the belief in

[1] Acts i. 6, ἀποκαθιστάνεις. [2] Acts i. 7, χρόνους ἢ καιρούς, "periods or crises."

[3] The E.V. passes over the distinction between ἐξουσία here and δύναμις in the next verse, and a neglect of this distinction has led Bengel and others to understand οὐχ ὑμῶν ἐστι in the sense that it was not *yet* their prerogative to know these things ("quæ apostolorum nondum erat nosse"—Beng.), but that it should be so hereafter. That *this*, however, was not the error of our translators appears from their marginal gloss to δύναμις in ver. 8, "the power of the Holy Ghost coming upon you." We shall see hereafter that St. Paul, in common with all the early Christians (1 Thess. iv. 16, 17; 2 Thess. ii. 8; Rom. xiii. 12; 1 Cor. xvi. 22; Phil. iv. 5; 1 Pet. iv. 5; James v. 8; Heb. x. 37), hoped for the near return of Christ to earth.

[4] 2,000 cubits, between five and six furlongs, the distance between the Tabernacle and the farthest part of the camp (cf. Numb. xxxv. 5). This is the only place in which it is alluded to in the N.T.

[5] Not "*an* upper room," as in E.V. It is probably the עֲלִיָּה, or topmost room of the house, which is called ἀνώγεον in Mark xiv. 15.

[6] John xx. 19, 26. [7] Acts i. 13, οὗ ἦσαν καταμένοντες ὅ τε Πέτρος, κ.τ.λ.

[8] Here last mentioned in the N.T. [9] James, the Lord's brother.

[10] Matt. xiii. 46; xii. 55; Mark vi. 3; 1 Cor. xv. 7.

Jesus as the Christ, the Son of the Living God,[1] they yet suffered the women to meet with them in prayer, not in any separate court, as in the Temple services, not with dividing partitions, as in the worship of the synagogue,[2] but in that equality of spiritual communion, which was to develop hereafter into the glorious doctrine that among Christ's redeemed "there is neither Jew nor Greek, there is neither bond nor free, there is neither male and female," but that, in Christ Jesus, all are one.[3]

During the ten days which elapsed between the Ascension and Pentecost, it was among the earliest cares of the Apostles to fill up the vacancy which had been caused in their number by the death of Judas. This was done at a full conclave of the believers in Jerusalem, who, in the absence of many of those five hundred to whom Christ had appeared in Galilee, numbered about one hundred and twenty. The terrible circumstances of the traitor's suicide, of which every varied and shuddering tradition was full of horror, had left upon their minds a deeper faith in God's immediate retribution upon guilt. He had fallen from his high charge by transgression, and had gone to his own place.[4] That his place should be supplied appeared reasonable, both because Jesus Himself had appointed twelve Apostles—the ideal number of the tribes of Israel—and also because Peter, and the Church generally, saw in Judas the antitype of Ahitophel, and applying to him a passage of the 109th Psalm, they wished, now that his habitation was desolate, that another should take his office.[5] The essential qualification for the new Apostle was that he should have been a witness of the Resurrection, and should have companied with the disciples all the time that the Lord Jesus went in and out among them. The means taken for his appointment, being unique in the New Testament, seem to result from the unique position of the Church during the few days between the Ascension and the Descent of the Holy Ghost. As though they felt that the swift power of intuitive discernment was not yet theirs, they selected two, Joseph Barsabbas, who in Gentile circles assumed the common surname of Justus, and Matthias.[6] They then, in accordance

1 "The Church, so to speak, was but half born; the other half was still in the womb of the synagogue. The followers of Jesus were under the guidance of the Apostles, but continued to acknowledge the authority of the chair of Moses in Jerusalem" (Dr. Döllinger, *First Age*, p. 43).

2 Jos. *Antt.* xv. 11, § 5; Philo, ii. 476.

3 Gal. iii. 28.

4 Acts i. 25, εἰς τὸν τόπον τὸν ἴδιον (*al.* δίκαιον). This profound and reverent euphemism is one of the many traces of the reticence with which the early Church spoke of the fate of those who had departed. The reticence is all the more remarkable if the word "place" be meant to bear allusive reference to the same word in the earlier part of the text, where the true reading is τόπον τῆς διακονίας (A, B, C, D), not κλῆρον, as in E.V. The origin of this striking expression may perhaps be the Rabbinic comments on Numb. xxiv. 25, where "Balaam went to his own place" is explained to mean "to Gehenna." Cf. Judg. ix, 55, למקומו, and Targ. Eccles. vi. 6; v. Schöttgen, p. 407; and cf. Clem. Rom. *ad Cor.* i. 5; Polyc. *ad Phil.* 9; Ignat. *ad Magnes.* 5 (Meyer). See too Dan. xii. 13.

5 Ps. xli. 9; cix. 8. The alteration of the LXX. αὐτῶν into αὐτοῦ is a good illustration of the free method of quotation and interpretation of the Old Testament, which is universally adopted in the New. The 109th has been called the Iscariotic Psalm.

6 Of these nothing is known, unless it be true that they were among the Seventy (Euseb. *H. E.* i. 12; Epiphan. *Haer.* i. 20); and that Joseph drank poison unharmed (Papias *ap.* Euseb. *H. E.* iii. 39). On the uncertain derivation of Barsabbas (so in א, A,

with Old Testament analogies[1] and Jewish custom,[2] prayed to God that He would appoint[3] the one whom He chose. The names were written on tablets and dropped into a vessel. The vessel was shaken, and the name of Matthias leapt out. He was accordingly reckoned among the twelve Apostles.[4]

We are told nothing further respecting the events of the ten days which elapsed between the Ascension and Pentecost. With each of those days the yearning hope, the keen expectation, must have grown more and more intense, and most of all when the day of Pentecost had dawned.[5] It was the first day of the week, and the fiftieth day after Nisan 16. The very circumstances of the day would add to the vividness of their feelings. The Pentecost was not only one of the three great yearly feasts, and the Feast of Harvest, but it came to be identified—and quite rightly—in Jewish consciousness with the anniversary of the giving of the Law on Sinai.[6] The mere fact that another solemn festival had come round, and that at the last great festival their Lord had been crucified in the sight of the assembled myriads who thronged to the Passover, would be sufficient on this solemn morning to absorb their minds with that overwhelming anticipation which was a forecast of a change in themselves and in the world's history—of a new and eternal consecration to the service of a new law and the work of a new life.

It was early morning. Before "the third hour of the day" summoned them to the Temple for morning prayer,[7] the believers, some hundred and twenty in number, were gathered once more, according to their custom, in the upper room. It has been imagined by some that the great event of this first Whit-Sunday must have taken place in the Temple. The word rendered

B, E), see Lightfoot, *Hor. Hebr.*, *ad loc.* There is a Judas Barsabbas in Acts xv. 22. Matthias is said to have been martyred (Niceph. ii. 60), and there were apocryphal writings connected with his name (Euseb. *H. E.* iii. 29; Clem. Alex. *Strom.* ii. 163).

[1] Numb. xxvi. 55, 56; Josh. vii. 14; 1 Sam. x. 20; Prov. xvi. 33.

[2] Luke i. 9.

[3] ἀνάδειξον, "appoint," not "show": Luke x. 1, μετὰ δὲ ταῦτα ἀνέδειξεν ὁ Κύριος, ἑτέρους, ἑβδομήκοντα. The word is peculiar in the N.T. to St. Luke. For ἐξελέξω, see Acts i. 2, τοῖς ἀποστόλοις . . . . οὓς ἐξελέξατο. I need hardly notice the strange view that the election of St. Matthias was a sheer mistake made before the gift of the Spirit, and that Paul was in reality the destined twelfth Apostle! (Stier, *Reden d. Apost.* i. 15.)

[4] The method in which the lot was cast (see Lev. xvi. 8; Ezek. xxiv. 6) is not certain, but the expression ἔδωκαν, rather than ἔβαλον κλήρους αὐτοῖς, goes against the notion of their casting dice as in Luke xxiii. 34. "The lot *fell on* Matthias" is a common idiom in all languages (Hom. *Il.* v. 316; *Od. E.* 209; Ps. xxii. 18; Jon. i. 7, &c.; ut cujusque sors exciderat; Liv. xxi. 42). From the use of the word κλῆρος in this passage, in ver. 17 and in viii, 21, xxvi. 18, is probably derived the Latin *clerus* and our *clergy*, clerici, κλῆρος = τὸ σύστημα τῶν διακόνων καὶ πρεσβυτέρων. (Suid.) (Wordsworth, *ad. loc.*)

[5] This is the obvious meaning of συμπληροῦσθαι, not "was drawing near" (cf. Eph. i. 10), or, "had passed."

[6] It is true that this point is not adverted to by either Philo or Josephus. The inference arises, however, so obviously from the comparison of Ex. xii. 2; xix. 1, that we can hardly suppose that it was wholly missed. (See Schöttgen, *ad. loc.*; Jer. *Ep. ad Fabiolam*, xii.; Aug. *c. Faustum*, xxxii. 12; Maimon. *Mor. Nevoch.* iii. 41.) The *Simchath Thorah*, or "Feast of the Joy of the Law," is kept on the last day of the Feast of Tabernacles, when the last Haphtarah from the Pentateuch is read.

[7] *i.e.*, 9 o'clock in the morning (cf. Luke xxiv. 53; Acts ii. 46; iii 1).

"house"[1] might equally mean a "chamber," and is actually used by Josephus of the thirty small chambers which were attached to the sides of Solomon's Temple, with thirty more above them.[2] But it is supremely improbable that the poor and suspected disciples should have been able to command the use of such a room; and further, it is certain that if, in the Herodian temple, these rooms were no larger than those in the Temple of Solomon, the size of even the lower ones would have been wholly inadequate for the accommodation of so large a number. The meeting was probably one of those holy and simple meals which were afterwards known among Christians as the *Agapæ*, or Love feasts. It need hardly be added that any moral significance which might attach to the occurrence of the event in the Temple would be no less striking if we think of the sign of a new era as having hallowed the common street and the common dwelling-place; as the visible inauguration of the days in which neither on Zion nor on Gerizim alone were men to worship the Father, but to worship Him everywhere in spirit and in truth.[3]

It is this inward significance of the event which constitutes its sacredness and importance. Its awfulness consists in its being the solemn beginning of the new and final phase of God's dealings with mankind. To Abraham He gave a promise which was the germ of a religion. When He called His people from Egypt He gave them the Moral Law and that Levitical Law which was to serve as a bulwark for the truths of the theocracy. During the two thousand years of that Mosaic Dispensation the Tabernacle and the Temple had been a visible sign of His presence. Then, for the brief period of the life of Christ on earth, He had tabernacled among men, dwelling in a tent like ours and of the same material.[4] That mortal body of Christ, in a sense far deeper than could be true of any house built with hands, was a Temple of God. Last of all, He who had given to mankind His Son to dwell among them, gave His Spirit into their very hearts. More than this He could not give; nearer than this He could not be. Henceforth His Temple was to be the mortal body of every baptised Christian, and His Spirit was to prefer

> "Before all temples the upright heart and pure."

He who believes this in all the fulness of its meaning, he whose heart and conscience bear witness to its truth, will consider in its true aspect the fulfilment of Christ's promise in the effusion of His Spirit; and regarding the outward wonder as the *least* marvellous part of the Day of Pentecost, will not, as Neander says, be tempted to explain the greater by the less, or "consider it strange that the most wonderful event in the inner life of mankind should be accompanied by extraordinary outward appearances as sensible indications of its existence."[5]

Suddenly, while their hearts burned within them with such ardent zeal, and glowed with such enkindled hope—suddenly on the rapt and expectant

[1] Acts ii. 2, *οἶκον*. [2] Jos. *Antt.* viii. 3, § 2. [3] John iv. 21—23.
[4] Archbishop Leighton, John i. 14, ὁ λόγος σὰρξ ἐγένετο καὶ ἐσκήνωσεν ἐν ἡμῖν.
[5] Neander, p. 3.

assembly came the sign that they had desired—the inspiration of Christ's promised Presence in their hearts—the baptism with the Holy Ghost and with fire—the transforming impulse of a Spirit and a Power from on high—the eternal proof to them, and through them, in unbroken succession, to all who accept their word, that He who had been taken from them into heaven was still with them, and would be with them always to the end of the world.

It came from heaven with the sound as of a rushing mighty wind, filling the whole house where they were sitting, and with a semblance as of infolded flame,[1] which, parting itself in every direction,[2] played like a tongue of lambent light over the head of every one of them. It was not wind, but "a sound as of wind in its rushing violence;" it was not fire, but something which seemed to them like quivering tongues of a flame which gleamed but did not burn—fit symbol of that Holy Spirit which, like the wind, bloweth where it listeth, though we know not whence it cometh or whither it goeth; and, like the kindled fire of love, glowing on the holy altar of every faithful heart, utters, not seldom, even from the stammering lips of ignorance, the burning words of inspiration.

And that this first Pentecost marked an eternal moment in the destiny of mankind, no reader of history will surely deny. Undoubtedly in every age since then the sons of God have, to an extent unknown before, been taught by the Spirit of God. Undoubtedly since then, to an extent unrealised before, we may know that the Spirit of Christ dwelleth in us. Undoubtedly we may enjoy a nearer sense of union with God in Christ than was accorded to the saints of the Old Dispensation, and a thankful certainty that we see the days which kings and prophets desired to see and did not see them, and hear the truths which they desired to hear and did not hear them. And this New Dispensation began henceforth in all its fulness. It was no exclusive consecration to a separated priesthood, no isolated endowment of a narrow Apostolate. It was the consecration of a whole Church—its men, its women, its children—to be all of them "a chosen generation, a royal priesthood, a holy nation, a peculiar people;" it was an endowment, of which the full free offer was meant ultimately to be extended to all mankind. Each one of that hundred and twenty was not the exceptional recipient of a blessing and witness of a revelation, but the forerunner and representative of myriads more. And this miracle was not merely transient, but is continuously renewed. It is not a rushing sound and gleaming light, seen perhaps only for a moment, but it is a living energy and an unceasing inspiration. It is not a visible symbol to a gathered handful of human souls in the upper room of a Jewish house, but a vivifying wind which shall henceforth breathe in all ages of the world's history; a tide of light which is rolling, and shall roll, from

[1] Acts ii. 2, 3, ὥσπερ πνοῆς . . . ὡσεὶ πυρὸς. (Cf. Luke iii. 22, ὡσεὶ περιστερὰν; Ezek. i. 24; xliii. 2; 1 Kings xix. 11.)

[2] γλῶσσαι διαμεριζόμεναι, not "cloven tongues," as in the E.V., though this view of the word is said to have determined the symbolic shape of the episcopal mitre. The expression "tongue of fire" is found also in Isa. v. 24, but there it is a devouring flame.

shore to shore until the earth is full of the knowledge of the Lord as the waters cover the sea.

And if this be the aspect under which it is regarded, the outward symbol sinks into subordinate importance. They who hold the truths on which I have been dwelling will not care to enter into the voluminous controversy as to whether that which is described as audible and visible was so in seeming only—whether the something which sounded like wind, and the something which gleamed like flame,[1] were external realities, or whether they were but subjective impressions, so vivid as to be identified with the things themselves. When the whole soul is filled with a spiritual light and a spiritual fire—when it seems to echo, as in the Jewish legend of the great Lawgiver, with the music of other worlds—when it is caught up into the third heaven and hears words which it is not possible for man to utter—when, to the farthest horizon of its consciousness, it seems as it were filled with the "rush of congregated wings"—when, to borrow the language of St. Augustine, the natural life is dead, and the soul thrills, under the glow of spiritual illumination, with a life which is supernatural—what, to such a soul, is objective and what is subjective? To such questions the only answer it cares to give is, "Whether in the body or out of the body, I cannot tell. God knoweth."[2]

But when from these mysterious phenomena we turn to the effects wrought by them in those for whom they were manifested, we are dealing with things more capable of being defined. Here, however, it is necessary to distinguish between the immediate result and the permanent inspiration. The former astounded a multitude; the latter revived a world. The former led to an immediate conversion; the latter is the power of a holy life. The former was a new and amazing outburst of strange emotion; the latter was the sustaining influence which enables the soul to soar from earth heavenwards in steady flight on the double wings of Faith and Love.

Yet, though there be no manner of comparison between the real importance of the transient phenomenon and the continuous result, it is necessary to a true conception of the age of the Apostles that we should understand what is told us of the former. "And they were all immediately filled," it is said, "with the Holy Spirit, and began to speak with other tongues as the Spirit gave them to utter."[3]

The *primâ facie* aspect of the narrative which follows—apart from the analogy of other Scriptures—has led to the belief that the outpouring of the Holy Spirit at Pentecost was succeeded by an outburst of utterance, in which a body of Galilæans spoke a multitude of languages which they had never learned; and this has led to the inference that throughout their

[1] Acts ii. 2, 3, ὥσπερ . . . ὡσεὶ.

[2] "It did me much harm that I did not then know it was possible to see anything otherwise than with the eyes of the body" (St. Teresa, *Vida*, vii. 11).

[3] Acts ii. 4. λαλεῖν, "to speak," as distinguished from λέγειν, "to say," points rather to the actual articulations than to the thoughts which words convey; ἀποφθέγγεσθαι, *eloqui*, implies a brief forcible utterance. Neither ἕτεραι nor γλῶσσαι throw light on the nature of the phenomena, except as referring to Isa. xxviii. 11.

lives the Apostles possessed the power of speaking languages which they had not acquired.[1]

But if we examine other passages where the same phenomenon is alluded to or discussed, they will show us that this view of the matter is at least questionable. In Mark xvi. 17—waiving all argument as to the genuineness of the passage—the word καινὸς, "new," is omitted in several uncials and versions;[2] but if retained, it goes against the common notion, for it points to strange utterances, not to foreign languages. In the other places of the Acts[3] where the gift of the Spirit is alluded to, no hint is given of the use of unknown languages. In fact, that view of the subject has chiefly been stereotyped in the popular conception by the interpolation of the word "*unknown*" in 1 Cor. xiv.[4] The glossolalia, or "speaking with a tongue," is connected with "prophesying"—that is, exalted preaching—and magnifying God. The sole passage by which we can hope to understand it is the section of the First Epistle to the Corinthians to which I have just alluded.[5] It is impossible for any one to examine that section carefully without being forced to the conclusion that, at Corinth at any rate, the gift of tongues had not the least connexion with foreign languages. Of such a knowledge, if this single passage of the Acts be not an exception, there is not the shadow of a trace in Scripture. That this passage is *not* an exception seems to be clear from the fact that St. Peter, in rebutting the coarse insinuation that the phenomenon was the result of drunkenness, does not so much as make the most passing allusion to an evidence so unparalleled; and that the passage of Joel of which he sees the fulfilment in the outpouring of Pentecost, does not contain the remotest hint of foreign languages. Hence the fancy that *this* was the immediate result of Pentecost is unknown to the first two centuries, and only sprang up when the true tradition had been obscured. The inference that the gift of unlearnt languages was designed to help the Apostles in their future preaching is one that unites a mass of misconceptions. In the first place, such a gift would be quite alien to that law of God's Providence which never bestows on man that which man can acquire by his own unaided efforts. In the second place, owing to the universal dissemination at that time of Greek and Latin, there never was a period in which such a gift

[1] Against this view (which, with the contrast with Babel, &c., is not found, I think, earlier than the Fathers of the fourth and fifth centuries), see Herder, *Die Gabe d. Sprache*; Bunsen, *Hippol.* ii. 12; Ewald, *Gesch. Isr.* vi. 110; Neander, *Planting*, 13, 14; De Wette, *Einleit.* 27—37; Hilgenfeld, *Einleit.* 275; Reuss, *Hist. Apost.* 50—55; Olshausen, *ad loc.*; De Pressensé, *Trois prem. Siècles*, i. 355; and almost every unbiassed modern commentator. Meyer (*ad loc.*) goes so far as to say that "the sudden communication of the gift of speaking in foreign languages is neither logically possible nor psychologically and morally conceivable."

[2] C, L, Δ, Copt., Arm. Apart from these questions, the unlimited universality of the promise leads us to believe that our Lord here, as elsewhere, is using the language of spiritual metaphor. Many a great missionary and preacher has, in the highest sense, spoken "with new tongues" who has yet found insuperable difficulty in the acquisition of foreign languages.

[3] x. 46; xix. 6 (cf. xi. 15). [4] 1 Cor. xiv. 4, 13, 14, 27. [5] 1 Cor. xii.—xiv. 33.

would have been more absolutely needless.[1] In the third place, though all other miracles of the New Testament found their continuance and their analogies, for a time at any rate, after the death of the Apostles, there is no existing allusion, or even early legend, which has presumed the existence of this power.[2] In the fourth place, although Paul 'spoke with a tongue'[3] more than all his converts, it is clear from the narrative of what occurred at Lycaonia, that at a most crucial moment he did not understand the Lycaonian dialect. In the fifth place, early Christian tradition distinctly asserts that the Apostles did *not* possess a supernatural knowledge of foreign tongues, since Papias tells us that Mark accompanied St. Peter as an 'interpreter' (ἑρμηνευτής), and Jerome that Titus was useful to St. Paul from his knowledge of Greek.[4] We are, therefore, forced to look for some other aspect of the utterance of that inspiration which accompanied the heavenly signs of Pentecost. The mistaken explanation of it has sprung from taking too literally St. Luke's dramatic reproduction of the vague murmurs of a throng, who mistook the *nature* of a gift of which they witnessed the *reality*. I do not see how any thoughtful student who has really considered the whole subject can avoid the conclusion of Neander, that "any foreign languages which were spoken on this occasion were only something accidental, and not the essential element of the language of the Spirit."[5]

In ancient times—especially before Origen—there seems to have been an impression that only one language was spoken, but that the miracle consisted in each hearer imagining it to be his own native tongue.[6] The explanation is remarkable as showing an early impression that the passage had been misunderstood. The modern view, developed especially by Schneckenburger (following St. Cyprian and Erasmus), is that the "tongue" was, from its own force and significance, intelligible equally to all who heard it. That such a thing is possible may be readily admitted, and it derives some probability from many analogies in the history of the Church.

[1] For instance, the whole multitude from fifteen countries which heard the Apostles speak "in their own tongues" the wonderful works of God, yet *all* understood the speech which St. Peter addressed to them in Greek. Hence such a power of speaking unlearnt foreign languages would have been a "Luxus-wunder" (Immer, *Neut. Theol.* 195). Far different was it with the true glossolaly, which in its controlled force involved a spiritual power of stirring to its inmost depths the heart of unbelief. (1 Cor. xiv. 22.)

[2] Middleton, *Mirac. Powers*, 120. The passage of Irenæus (*Haer.* v. 6, 1) usually quoted in favour of such a view, tells the other way, since the object of the παντοδαπαὶ γλῶσσαι is there explained to be τὰ κρύφια τῶν ἀνθρώπων εἰς φανερὸν ἄγειν.

[3] 1 Cor. xiv. 18, γλώσσῃ (א, A, D, E, F, G).

[4] Papias, *ap.* Euseb. *H. E.* iii. 39; cf. Iren. iii. 1; interpres. Tert. *adv. Marc.* iv. 5.

[5] *Planting*, 13, 14. I have not touched on any modern analogies to these spiritual manifestations, but agree with the view of Dr. Döllinger, who says that they have occurred "in a lower sphere, and without any miraculous endowment . . . an unusual phenomenon, but one completely within the range of natural operations, which the gift of the Apostolic age came into to exalt and ennoble it" (*First Age of Church*, 315).

[6] Greg. Nyss. *De Spir. Sanct.* Bp. Martensen, *Christl. Dogm.* 381; Overbeck, *App.*, p. 26, and many others. The often-repeated objection of Gregory of Nazianzus (*Orat.* xliv.) that this is to transfer the miracle to the hearers, has no weight whatever. The effect on the hearers was solely due to the power of the new spiritual "tongue."

The stories of St. Bernard, St. Anthony of Padua, St. Vincent Ferrer, St. Louis Bertrand, St. Francis Xavier, and others who are said to have been endowed with the spiritual power of swaying the passions, kindling the enthusiasm, or stirring the penitence of vast multitudes whom they addressed in a language unintelligible to the majority of the hearers, are so far from being inventions, that any one who has been present at the speech of a great orator, though beyond the range of his voice, can readily understand the nature and the intensity of the effect produced.[1] But neither of these theories taken alone seems adequate to account for the language used by St. Peter and St. Paul. Almost all the theories about the glossolalia are too partial. The true view can only be discovered by a combination of them. The belief that languages were used which were unknown, or only partially known, or which had only been previously known to the speaker; that the tongue was a mystic, exalted, poetic, unusual style of phraseology and utterance;[2] that it was a dithyrambic outpouring of strange and rhythmic praise; that it was the impassioned use of ejaculatory words and sentences of Hebrew Scripture; that it was a wild, unintelligible, inarticulate succession of sounds, which either conveyed no impression to the ordinary hearer, or could only be interpreted by one whose special gift it was to understand the rapt and ecstatic strain—none of these views is correct separately, all may have some elements of truth in their combination. This is the meaning of St. Paul's expression "*kinds* of tongues." If we assume, as must be assumed, that the glossolalia at Corinth and elsewhere was identical with the glossolalia at Pentecost, then we must interpret the narrative of St. Luke by the full and earnest discussion of the subject—written, be it remembered, at a far earlier period, and in immediate contact with, and even experience of, the manifestation—by St. Paul. That the glossolaly at Corinth was not a speaking in foreign languages is too clear to need proof. St. Paul in speaking of it uses the analogies of the clanging of a cymbal, the booming of a gong,[3] the indistinct blare of a trumpet,[4] the tuneless strains of flute or harp.[5] We learn that, apart from interpretation, it was not for the edification of any but the speaker;[6] that even the speaker did not always understand it;[7] that it was sporadic in its recurrences;[8] that it was excited, inarticulate,

[1] See *Chapters on Language*, p. 63; Marsh, *Lect. on Lang.* 486—488; Cic. *de Orat.* iii. 216.

[2] Γλῶσσα sometimes means "an unusual expression" (Arist. *Rhet.* iii. 2, 14). Cf. our "gloss," "glossology." See especially Bleek, *Stud. u Krit.* 1829. "Linguam esse cum quis loquatur obscuras et mysticas significationes" (Aug. *de Gen. ad litt.* xii. 8).

[3] 1 Cor. xiii. 1, χαλκὸς ἠχῶν, κύμβαλον ἀλαλάζον.

[4] xiv. 8, ἐὰν ἄδηλον φωνὴν σάλπιγξ δῷ. St. Chrysostom uses language equally disparaging of analogous outbreaks in Constantinople (*Hom. in Ps.* vi. 12; see Dr. Plumptre's interesting article in Smith's *Dict.* iii. 1560).

[5] xiv. 7, ὅμως τὰ ἄψυχα φωνὴν διδόντα, κ.τ.λ., ἐὰν διαστολὴν τοῖς φθόγγοις μὴ δῷ.

[6] xiv. 2, οὐκ ἀνθρώποις λαλεῖ. 4, ἑαυτὸν οἰκοδομεῖ. Cf. 11. The proper meaning of the words λαλεῖν, γλῶσσα, φωνή, all point in this direction. In St. Luke's phraseology the word for a language is not γλῶσσα, but διάλεκτος.

[7] xiv. 19. [8] xiv. 27.

astonishing,[1] intended as a sign to unbelievers rather than as an aid to believers, but even on unbelievers liable, when not under due regulation, to leave an impression of madness;[2] lastly, that, though controllable by all who were truly and nobly under its influence, it often led to spurious and disorderly outbreaks.[3] Any one who fairly ponders these indications can hardly doubt that, when the consciousness of the new power came over the assembled disciples, they did not speak as men ordinarily speak. The voice they uttered was awful in its range, in its tone, in its modulations, in its startling, penetrating, almost appalling power;[4] the words they spoke were exalted, intense, passionate, full of mystic significance; the language they used was not their ordinary and familiar tongue, but was Hebrew, or Greek, or Latin, or Aramaic, or Persian, or Arabic, as some overpowering and unconscious impulse of the moment might direct; the burden of their thoughts was the ejaculation of rapture, of amazement, of thanksgiving, of prayer, of impassioned psalm, of dithyrambic hymn; their utterances were addressed not to each other, but were like an inspired soliloquy of the soul with God. And among these strange sounds of many voices, all simultaneously raised in the accordance of ecstatic devotion,[5] there were some which none could rightly interpret, which rang on the air like the voice of barbarous languages, and which, except to those who uttered them, and who in uttering them felt carried out of themselves, conveyed no definite significance beyond the fact that they were reverberations of one and the same ecstasy—echoes waked in different consciousnesses by the same immense emotion. Such—as we gather from the notices of St. Luke, St. Peter, and St. Paul—was the "Gift of Tongues." And thus regarded, its strict accordance with the known laws of psychology[6] furnishes us with a fresh proof of the truthfulness of the history, and shows us that no sign of the outpouring of the Holy Spirit could have been more natural, more evidential, or more intense.

The city of Jerusalem at that moment was crowded by a miscellaneous multitude of Jews and Proselytes. It was inevitable that the awful sound[7] should arrest the astonished attention, first of one, then of more, lastly of a multitude of the inhabitants and passers-by. The age—an age which was in

[1] xiv. 2. [2] xiv. 23, οὐκ ἐροῦσιν ὅτι μαίνεσθε;

[3] xiv. 9, 11, 17, 20—23, 26—28, 33, 40.

[4] So we infer from St. Paul's allusions, which find illustration in modern analogies. Archd. Stopford describes the "unknown tongue" of the Irish Revivalists in 1859 as "a sound such as I never heard before, unearthly and unaccountable."

[5] This simultaneity of utterance by people under the same impressions is recorded several times in the Acts of the Apostles. It was evidently analogous to, though not perhaps identical with "glossolalia"—the eloquence of religious transport thrilling with rapture and conviction.

[6] Compare in the Old Testament the cases of Saul, &c. (1 Sam. x. 11; xviii. 10; xix. 23, 24). "C'est le langage brûlant et mystérieux de l'extase" (De Pressensé, i. 355).

[7] In Acts ii. 6 the words γενομένης δὲ τῆς φωνῆς ταύτης do not mean (as in the E.V.) "now when this was noised abroad," but "when this sound occurred" (cf. ἦχος, ver. 2; John iii. 8; Rev. vi. 1). It is evidently an allusion to the *Bath-kol*. (See Herzog, *Real-Encycl.*, *s.v.*)

keen expectation of some divine event; the day—the great anniversary of Pentecost and of Sinai; the hour—when people were already beginning to throng the streets on their way to the Temple service—would all tend to swell the numbers, and intensify the feelings of the crowd. Up the steps which led outside the house to the "upper room" they would first begin to make their way in twos and threes, and then to press in larger numbers, until their eagerness, their obtrusion, their exclamations of fear, surprise, admiration, insult, could not fail to break the spell. The Church for the first time found itself face to face with the world—a world loud in its expressions of perplexity, through which broke the open language of hate and scorn. That which fixed the attention of all the better portion of the crowd was the fact that these "Galilæans" were magnifying, in strange tongues, the mercies and power of God. But most of the spectators were filled with contempt at what seemed to them to be a wild fanaticism. "These men," they jeeringly exclaimed, "have been indulging too freely in the festivities of Pentecost.[1] They are drunk with sweet wine."[2]

It was the prevalence of this derisive comment which forced upon the Apostles the necessity of immediate explanation.[3] "The spirits of the prophets," as St. Paul says, with that masculine practical wisdom which in him is found in such rare combination with burning enthusiasm, "are subject unto the prophets."[4] The Apostles were at once able not only to calm their own exaltation, but also, even at this intense moment, to hush into absolute silence the overmastering emotion of their brethren. They saw well that it would be fatal to their position as witnesses to a divine revelation if anything in their worship could, however insultingly, be represented as the orgiastic exhibition of undisciplined fervour. It was a duty to prove from the very first that the Christian disciple offered no analogy to the fanatical fakeer. Clearing the room of all intruders, making a space for themselves at the top of the steps, where they could speak in the name of the brethren to the surging throng who filled the street, the Apostles came forward, and Peter assumed the office of their spokesman. Standing in an attitude, and speaking in a tone, which commanded attention,[5] he first begged for serious attention, and told the crowd that their coarse suspicion was refuted at once by the fact that it was but nine o'clock. He then proceeded to explain to them that this was the fulfilment of the prophecy of Joel that, among other signs and portents of the last days, there should be a special effusion of the Spirit of God, like that of which they had witnessed the manifestations. It was the object of the remainder of his speech to prove that this Spirit had been

[1] See Deut. xvi. 11.

[2] γλεῦκος cannot be "new wine," as in E.V., for Pentecost fell in June, and the vintage was in August.

[3] Acts ii. 15, ὡς ὑμεῖς ὑπολαμβάνετε. There is a slight excuse for this insult, since spiritual emotion may produce effects similar to those which result from intoxication (Eph. v. 18; 1 Sam. x. 10, 11; xviii. 10—Heb., "raved"). Compare the German expression, "Ein Gott-trunkener Mann."

[4] 1 Cor. xiv. 32

[5] Acts ii. 14, σταθεὶς . . . ἐπῆρε τὴν φωνὴν.

outpoured by that same Jesus of Nazareth[1] whom they had nailed to the cross, but whose resurrection and deliverance from the throes of death were foreshadowed in the Psalms of His glorious ancestor.

The power with which this speech came home to the minds of the hearers; the force and fearlessness with which it was delivered by one who, not two months before, had been frightened, by the mere question of a curious girl, into the denial of his Lord; the insight into Scripture which it evinced in men who so recently had shown themselves but 'fools and slow of heart' to believe all that the prophets had spoken concerning Christ;[2] the three thousand who were at once baptised into a profession of the new faith—were themselves the most convincing proofs—proofs even more convincing than rushing wind, and strange tongues, and lambent flames—that now indeed the Promise of the Paraclete had been fulfilled, and that a new *æon* had begun in God's dealings with the world.

CHAPTER VI.

EARLY PERSECUTIONS.

"It fills the Church of God; it fills
The sinful world around;
Only in stubborn hearts and wills
No place for it is found."—KEBLE.

THE life of these early Christians was the poetic childhood of the Church in her earliest innocence. It was marked by simplicity, by gladness, by worship, by brotherhood. At home, and in their place of meeting, their lives were a perpetual prayer, their meals a perpetual love-feast and a perpetual eucharist. In the Temple they attended the public services with unanimous zeal. In the first impulses of fraternal joy many sold their possessions to contribute to a common stock. The numbers of the little community increased daily, and the mass of the people looked on them not only with tolerance, but with admiration and esteem.

The events which followed all tended at first to strengthen their position. The healing of the cripple in Solomon's porch; the bold speech of Peter afterwards; the unshaken constancy with which Peter and John faced the fury of the Sadducees; the manner in which all the disciples accepted and even exulted in persecution, if it came in the fulfilment of their duties;[3] the power

[1] Acts ii. 22, Ναζωραῖος, the Galilæan form of Ναζαραῖος. [2] Luke xxiv. 25.

[3] It is a very interesting fact that on the first summons of Peter and John before the Hierarchs, they were dismissed, with threats, indeed, and warnings, but unpunished, because the Council became convinced (καταλαβόμενοι) that they were "unlearned and ignorant men" (Acts iv. 13). The words, however, convey too contemptuous a notion to English readers. Ἀγράμματοι simply means that their knowledge of Jewish culture was confined to the Holy Scriptures; ἰδιῶται, that they had never studied in rabbinic schools. The word *Hediot* (ἰδιώτης) occurs frequently in the Talmud, and expresses a position far

with which they witnessed to the resurrection of their Lord; the beautiful spectacle of their unanimity; the awful suddenness with which Ananias and Sapphira had been stricken down; the signs and wonders which were wrought by the power of faith; the zeal and devotion which marked their gatherings in Solomon's porch, caused a rapid advance in the numbers and position of the Christian brothers. As their influence increased, the hierarchic clique, which at that time governed the body which still called itself the Sanhedrin, grew more and more alarmed. In spite of the populace, whose sympathy made it dangerous at that time to meddle with the followers of Jesus, they at last summoned the two leading Apostles before a solemn conclave of the Sanhedrin and senate.[1] Probably, as at the earlier session, the whole priestly party were there—the crafty Annas, the worldly Caiaphas,[2] the rich, unscrupulous, money-loving body of Kamhiths, and Phabis, and Kantheras, and Boethusim,[3] the Pharisaic doctors of the law, with Gamaliel at their head; John, perhaps the celebrated Johanan Ben Zakkai;[4] Alexander, perhaps the wealthy brother of the learned Philo;[5] the same body who had been present at those secret, guilty, tumultuous, illegal meetings in which they handed over the Lord Jesus to their Roman executioners—were again assembled, but now with something of misgiving and terror, to make one more supreme effort to stamp out the Galilæan heresy.

The Apostles, when first brought before the Sanhedrin, had been arrested in the evening by the Captain of the Temple, and had been released with strong threats, partly because the Sadducees affected to despise them, but still more because they did not know how to gainsay the miracle of the healing of the cripple. The Apostles had then openly declared that they should be compelled by the law of a higher duty to disregard these threats, and they had continued to teach to increasing thousands that doctrine of the resurrection which filled the Sadducees with the greatest jealousy. It was impossible to leave them unmolested in their career, and by the High Priest's order they were thrust into prison. The Sanhedrin met at dawn to try them; but when they sent for them to the prison they found that the Apostles were not there, but that, delivered by "an angel of the Lord," they were calmly teaching in the Temple. In the deepest perplexity, the Sanhedrists once more despatched

superior to that of the *am-haarets*. The *Hediot* is one who, though not a frequenter of the schools, still pays deference to the authority of the Rabbis; the *am-haarets* is one who hates and despises that authority. Hillel was distinguished for his forbearing condescension towards the ignorance of *Hediots* (*Babha Metzia*, f. 104, 1). Compare John vii. 15, "How knoweth this man letters, *having never learned?*"

1 "Populus sanior quam qui praesunt" (Bengel). The use of the word γερουσία in Acts v. 21 is somewhat perplexing, because we know nothing of any Jewish "senate" apart from the Sanhedrin, and because if γερουσία be taken in an etymological rather than a political sense, the Sanhedrin *included* the elders (iv. 8; xxv. 15). It is impossible, in the obscurity of the subject, to distinguish between the *political* and the *Talmudic* Sanhedrin. See Derenbourg (*Palestine*, 213), who thinks that Agrippa had been the first to introduce Rabbis into the Sanhedrin.

2 Both of these are mentioned as having been at the earlier meeting, and we are probably intended to understand they were also present at this.

3 On these, see *Life of Christ*, ii., pp. 329—342.

4 Lightfoot, *Cent. Chor.* in Matt., *cap.* 15.

5 Jos. *Antt.* xviii. 8, § 1.

the Levitical officer to arrest them, but this time without any violence, which might lead to dangerous results. They offered no resistance, and were once more placed where their Lord had once stood—in the centre of that threatening semicircle of angry judges. In reply to the High Priest's indignant reminder of the warning they had received, St. Peter simply laid down the principle that when our duty to man clashes with our duty to God, it is God that must be obeyed.[1] The High Priest had said, "Ye want to bring upon us the blood of this man." The words are an awful comment on the defiant cry, "His blood be on us, and on our children." *Then* the Sanhedrin had not been afraid of Jesus; now they were trembling at the vengeance which might yet be brought on them by two of the despised disciples. The phrase is also remarkable as furnishing the first instance of that avoidance of the name of Christ which makes the Talmud, in the very same terms, refer to Him most frequently as *Peloni*[2]—"so and so." Peter did not aggravate the Priests' alarm. He made no allusion to the charge of an intended vengeance; he only said that the Apostles, and the Holy Spirit who wrought in them, were witnesses to the resurrection and exaltation of Him whom they had slain. At these words the Sanhedrin ground their teeth with rage, and began to advise another judicial murder, which would, on their own principles, have rendered them execrable to their countrymen, as an assembly given to deeds of blood.[3] This disgrace was averted by the words of one wise man among them. How far the two Apostles were protected by the animosities between the rival sects of Sadducees and Pharisees we do not know, but it was certainly the speech of Gamaliel which saved them from worse results than that scourging by Jewish thongs—those forty stripes save one—which they received, and in which they exulted.[4]

That speech of Gamaliel was not unworthy of a grandson of Hillel—of one of those seven who alone won the supreme title of Rabbanim[5]—of one who subsequently became a President of the Sanhedrin. It has been strangely misunderstood. The supposed anachronism of thirty years in the reference to Theudas has led the school of Baur to deny altogether the genuineness of the speech, but it has yet to be proved that the allusion may not have been perfectly correct. The notion that the speech was due to a secret leaning in favour of Christianity, and the tradition of the Clementine Recognitions, that Gamaliel was in heart a Christian,[6] have no shadow of probability in their favour, since every allusion to him in the Talmud shows that he lived and

[1] Cf. Plat. *Apol.* 29. πείσομαι δὲ Θεῷ μᾶλλον ἢ ὑμῖν. "It were better for me to be called 'fool' all the days of my life, than to be made wicked before *Ha Makom*," *i.e.*, God; literally "the Place" (*Edioth*, ch. v. 6).

[2] In Spanish and Portuguese *fulano* (through the Arabic). The designation *otho hatsh*, "that man," is still more contemptuous. ישו (*Yeshu*) is used as the contraction for ישוע, and is composed of the initial letters of an imprecation.

[3] "The Sanhedrin is not to destroy life, but to save" (*Sanhedr.* 42 *b*). (See *Life of Christ*, ii. 353, and *infra*, Excursus VII.

[4] Deut. xxv. 2.

[5] All the Rabbans except Johanan Ben Zakkai were descendants of Gamaliel.

[6] Thilo, *Cod. Apocr.*, p. 501

died a Pharisee. Nor, again, is there the least ground for Schrader's indignation against his supposed assertion of the principle that the success of a religion is a sufficient test of its truth. We must remember that only the briefest outline of his speech is given, and all that Gamaliel seems to have meant was this—'Let these men alone at present. As far as we can see, they are only the victims of a harmless delusion. There is nothing seditious in their practice, nothing subversive in their doctrines. Even if there were we should have nothing to fear from them, and no need to adopt violent measures of precaution. Fanaticism and imposture are short-lived, even when backed by popular insurrection; but in the views of these men there may be something more than at present appears. Some germ of truth, some gleam of revelation, may inspire their singular enthusiasm, and to fight against this may be to fight against God.' Gamaliel's plea was not so much a plea for systematic tolerance as for temporary caution.[1] The day of open rupture between Judaism and Christianity was indeed very near at hand, but it had not yet arrived. His advice is neither due to the quiescence of Pharisaic fatalism, nor to a 'fallacious *laisser aller* view of the matter, which serves to show how low the Jews had sunk in theology and political sagacity if such was the counsel of their wisest.'[2] There was time, Gamaliel thought, to wait and watch the development of this new fraternity. To interfere with it might only lead to a needless embroilment between the people and the Sanhedrin. A little patience would save trouble, and indicate the course which should be pursued. Gamaliel was sufficiently clear-sighted to have observed that the fire of a foolish fanaticism dies out if it be neglected, and is only kindled into fury by premature opposition. Let those who venture to arraign the principle of the wise Rabbi remember that it is practically identical with the utterance of Christ, "Every plant, which my heavenly Father planted not, shall be plucked up by the roots."[3]

The advice was too sound, and the authority of the speaker too weighty, to be altogether rejected. The Priests and Rabbis, tortured already with guilty anxiety as to the consequences of their judicial murder, renewed their futile command to the Apostles to preach no more in the name of Jesus, and scourging them for disobedience to their former injunctions, let them go. Neither in public nor in private did the Apostles relax their exertions. The gatherings still continued in Solomon's porch; the *agapæ* were still held in the houses of the brethren. So far from being intimidated, the two Apostles only rejoiced that they were counted worthy of the honour of being dishonoured for the name of Him on whom they believed.

[1] Too much has, perhaps, been made of the ἐὰν ᾖ ἐξ ἀνθρώπων as contrasted with εἰ δὲ ἐκ Θεοῦ ἐστιν, vv. 38, 39; cf. Gal. i. 8, 9—(Beng. ἐὰν ᾖ si fit, conditionaliter; εἰ ἔστιν si est, categorice)—as though Gamaliel leaned to the latter view—"wornach der gesetzte *zweite* Fall als der dem Gamaliel wahrscheinlichere erscheint" (Meyer). It merely means—'If it should be from men, as results will show,' and, 'if, a case which I at present suppose, from God.' (See Winer.)

[2] Alford, following Schrader, *Der Apostel Paulus.*

[3] See Matt. xv. 13. It was in this sense that Luther urged the advice of Gamaliel upon the Elector of Trèves.

And here I must pause for a moment to make a remark on the grounds which have led many modern critics to reject the authority of the Acts of the Apostles, and to set it down as a romance, written in the cause of reconciliation between Judaising and Pauline Christians. My object in this volume is not controversial. It has been my endeavour here, as in my *Life of Christ*, to diffuse as widely as I can a clear knowledge of the Dawn of the Christian Faith, and to explain as lucidly as is in my power the bearing of its earliest documents. But I have carefully studied the objections urged against the authenticity and the statements of the New Testament writings; and I cannot forbear the expression of my astonishment at the baselessness of many of the hypotheses which have been accepted in their disparagement. Honesty of course demands that we should admit the existence of an error where such an error can be shown to exist; but the same honesty demands the rejection of all charges against the accuracy of the sacred historian which rest on nothing better than hostile prepossession. It seems to me that writers like Baur and Zeller—in spite of their wide learning and great literary acumen—often prove, by captious objections and by indifference to counter considerations, the fundamental weakness of their own system.[1] Hausrath altogether rejects the

[1] See Baur, *Paul.* i. 35; Zeller, *Die Apostelgesch.*, p. 134. Baur asserts that Gamaliel could not have delivered the speech attributed to him because of "the striking chronological error in the appeal to the example of Theudas." And yet he does not offer any proof either that the Theudas here alluded to is *identical* with the Theudas of Josephus, or that Josephus must *necessarily be right* and St. Luke necessarily wrong. Zeller, while entering more fully into the discussion, seems only to be struck by the resemblance between the two impostors, without allowing for the obvious differences in the accounts of them; and he attaches an extravagant importance to the silence of Josephus about the unimportant movement of the earlier fanatic to whom Gamaliel is supposed to allude; nor does he notice the possibility, admitted even by a Jewish writer (Jost, *Gesch. d. Jud.* ii. 76), that the Theudas of Gamaliel may be the Simon, a slave of Herod, of Jos. *Antt.* xvii. 10, § 6; Tac. *H.* v. 9. On this identification, see Sonntag, *Stud. u. Krit.*, 1837, p. 622; and Hackett, *ad loc.* Again, critics of the Tübingen school point out the supposed absurdity of believing that the Sanhedrin would admit "a notable miracle" and yet punish the men who performed it. But this is to reason from the standpoint of modern times. The Jews have never denied the miracles of Jesus, but they have not on that account believed in His mission. Just as a modern Protestant, familiar with the peculiarities of nervous maladies, might accept the narrative of wonderful cures performed at La Salette, without for a moment admitting the reality of the vision which is supposed to have consecrated the place, so the Jews freely admitted the possibility of inconclusive miracles, which they attributed generally to *kishouf* (*i.e.*, thaumaturgy, miracles wrought by unhallowed influence), or to אחזת עינים, phantasmagoria, or deception of the eyes. (Derenbourg, *Palest.* 106, n. 3; 361, n. 1.) Thus they allowed miraculous power to idols (*Abhôda Zara*, f. 54, 2). There is a Talmudic anecdote (perhaps a sort of allegory on Eccles. x. 8) which exactly illustrates this very point. R. Eliezer ben Dama was bitten by a serpent, and Jacob the *min* (*i.e.*, Christian) *offered to heal him in the name of Jesus.* "Ben Dama, it is forbidden!" said his uncle, R. Ismael. "Let me do it," urged Jacob; "I will prove to you by the Law that it is allowable." Before the argument was over the sick man died. "Happy Ben Dama!" exclaimed his uncle; "thou hast yielded thy soul in purity, without violating a precept of the wise" (*Abhôda Zara*, cf. 27, 6; 55, 1; *Jer. Shabbath*, 14, 4).—When St. Luke makes Gamaliel speak of "Judas of Galilee," whereas Judas was born at Gamala, and commonly known as Judas the Gaulonite (Γαυλανίτης ἀνήρ, Jos. *Antt.* xviii. 1, § 1), this trivial peculiarity would unquestionably have been paraded by German critics as a proof of the unhistorical character of the speech, but for the fortunate accident that Josephus, with reference to the sphere of his activity, thrice calls him ὁ Γαλιλαῖος (*Antt.* xviii. 1, § 6; xx. 5, § 2; *B. J.* ii. 8, § 1).

statement that Paul was "brought up at the feet of Gamaliel," on the ground that Paul calls himself "a zealot" for the traditions of the fathers, and must therefore have belonged far rather to the school of Shammai. He could not, according to this writer, have been trained by a Rabbi who was remarkable for his mildness and laxity. He accordingly assumes that the author of the Acts only invents the relations between St. Paul and Gamaliel in order to confer a sort of distinction upon the former, when the fame of Gamaliel the Second, founder of the school of Jabne, kept alive, in the second century, the fame of his grandfather, Gamaliel the Elder.[1] Now of what value is a criticism which contemptuously, and I may even say calumniously, contradicts a writer whose accuracy, in matters where it can be thoroughly tested, receives striking confirmation from the most opposite sources? It would have been rightly considered a very trivial blot on St. Luke's accuracy if he had fallen into some slight confusion about the enrolment of Quirinus, the tetrarchy of Abilene, the Ethnarch under Aretas, the Asiarchs of Ephesus, the "Prætors" of Philippi, the "Politarchs" of Thessalonica, the "Protos" of Malta, or the question whether "Proprætor" or "Pro-consul" was, in the numerous changes of those days, the exact official title of the Roman Governor of Cyprus or Corinth. On several of these points he has been triumphantly charged with ignorance and error; and on all these points his minute exactitude has been completely vindicated or rendered extremely probable. In every historical allusion—as, for instance, the characters of Gallio, Felix, Festus, Agrippa II., Ananias, the famine in the days of Claudius, the decree to expel Jews from Rome, the death of Agrippa I., the rule of Aretas at Damascus, the Italian band, &c.—he has been shown to be perfectly faithful to facts. Are we to charge him with fraudulent assertions about Paul's relation to Gamaliel on the questionable supposition that, after reaching the age of manhood, the pupil deviated from his teacher's doctrines?[2] Are we, on similar grounds, to charge Diogenes Laertius with falsehood when he tells us that Antisthenes, the Cynic, and Aristippus, the Cyrenaic, were both of them pupils of Socrates? A remarkable anecdote, which will be quoted farther on, has recorded the terrible quarrel between the parties of Rabbi Eliezer and Rabbi Joshua, of whom the former is called a Shammaite, and the latter a Hillelite;[3] and yet both of them were pupils of the same Rabbi, the celebrated Hillelite, R. Johanan Ben Zaccai. Such instances might be indefinitely multiplied. And if so, what becomes of Hausrath's criticism? Like many of the Tübingen theories, it crumbles into dust.[4]

[1] Ha-zaken, as he is usually called.

[2] Turning to Buddæus, *Philos. Hebraeorum* (1720), I find that he answered this objection long ago. An interesting anecdote in *Berachôth*, f. 16, 2, shows that the natural kindness of Gamaliel was too strong for the severity of his own teaching.

[3] *Jer. Shabbath*, i. 7.

[4] See Excursus V., "Gamaliel and the School of Tübingen."

Book II.

ST. STEPHEN AND THE HELLENISTS.

CHAPTER VII.

THE DIASPORA: HEBRAISM AND HELLENISM.

Τόπον οὐκ ἔστι ῥᾳδίως εὑρεῖν τῆς οἰκουμένης ὃς οὐ παραδέδεκται τοῦτο τὸ φῦλον, μηδ' (sic) ἐπικρατεῖται ὑπ' αὐτοῦ.—STRABO, *ap. Jos. Antt.* xiv. 7, § 2. (Cf. Philo, *Leg. ad Gaium*, 36.)

THE gradual change of relation between the Jews and the Christians was an inevitable result of the widening boundaries of the Church. Among the early converts were "Grecians," as well as "Hebrews," and this fact naturally led to most important consequences, on which hinged the historic future of the Christian Faith.

It is not too much to say that any real comprehension of the work of St. Paul, and of the course of events in the days after Christ, must depend entirely on our insight into the difference between these two classes of Jews. And this is a point which has been so cursorily treated that we must here pause while we endeavour to see it in its proper light.

When the successive judgments, first of the Assyrian, then of the Babylonian captivity, had broken all hopes of secular power and all thoughts of secular pride in the hearts of the Jews, a wholly different impulse was given to the current of their life. Settled in the countries to which they had been transplanted, allowed the full rights of citizenship, finding free scope for their individual energies, they rapidly developed that remarkable genius for commerce by which they have been characterised in all succeeding ages. It was only a wretched handful of the nation—compared by the Jewish writers to the chaff of the wheat—who availed themselves of the free permission of Cyrus, and subsequent kings of Persia, to return to their native land.[1] The remainder, although they jealously preserved their nationality and their traditions, made their homes in every land to which they had been drifted by the wave of conquest, and gradually multiplying until, as Josephus tells us,[2] they crowded every corner of the habitable globe, formed that great and remarkable body which continues to be known to this day as "the Jews of the Dispersion."[3]

[1] Of the whole nation only 42,360 returned; and as the separate items of the returning families given by Ezra and Nehemiah only amount to 30,000, it was precariously conjectured by the Jews that the surplus consisted of members of the ten tribes. As a body, however, the ten tribes were finally and absolutely absorbed into the nations—not improbably of Semitic origin—among whom they were scattered (Jos. *Antt.* xi. 5, § 2; 2 Esdr. xiii. 45). Such expressions as τὸ δωδεκάφυλον of James i. 1; Acts xxvi. 7, point rather to past reminiscences, to patriotic yearnings, and to the sacredly-treasured genealogical records of a very few families, than to any demonstrable reality. Of the priestly families only four courses out of the twenty-four returned (Ezra ii. 36—39).

[2] Jos. *Antt.* xiv. 7, § 2.

[3] The word is first found in this sense in Deut. xxviii. 25; Ps. cxlvii. 2, "He shall

This Dispersion of the Chosen People was one of those three vast and world-wide events in which a Christian cannot but see the hand of God so ordering the course of history as to prepare the world for the Revelation of His Son. (i.) The immense field covered by the conquests of Alexander gave to the civilised world a Unity of Language, without which it would have been, humanly speaking, impossible for the earliest preachers to have made known the good tidings in every land which they traversed. (ii.) The rise of the Roman Empire created a Political Unity which reflected in every direction the doctrines of the new faith. (iii.) The dispersion of the Jews prepared vast multitudes of Greeks and Romans for the Unity of a pure Morality and a monotheistic Faith. The Gospel emanated from the capital of Judæa; it was preached in the tongue of Athens; it was diffused through the empire of Rome: the feet of its earliest missionaries traversed, from the Euphrates to the Pillars of Hercules, the solid structure of undeviating roads by which the Roman legionaries—"those massive hammers of the whole earth"[1]—had made straight in the desert a highway for our God. Semite and Aryan had been unconscious instruments in the hands of God for the spread of a religion which, in its first beginnings, both alike detested and despised. The letters of Hebrew and Greek and Latin inscribed above the cross were the prophetic and unconscious testimony of three of the world's noblest languages to the undying claims of Him who suffered to obliterate the animosities of the nations which spoke them, and to unite them all together in the one great Family of God.

This contact of Jew with Greek was fruitful of momentous consequences both to the Aryan and the Semitic race. It is true that the enormous differences between the morals, the habits, the tendencies, the religious systems, the whole tone of mind and view of life in these two great human families, inspired them with feelings of mutual aversion and almost detestation. Out of the chaos of struggling interests which followed the death of Alexander, there gradually emerged two great kingdoms, the Egyptian and the Syrian, ruled respectively by the Ptolemies and the Seleucids. These dynasties had inherited the political conceptions of the great Macedonian conqueror, and desired to produce a fusion of the heterogeneous elements included in their government. Both alike turned their eyes to Palestine, which became the theatre of their incessant contentions, and which passed alternately under the sway of each. The Ptolemies, continuing the policy of Alexander, did their utmost to promote the immigration of Jews into Egypt. The Seleucids, both by force and by various political inducements, settled them as largely as they could in their western cities. Alike the Lagidæ and the Seleucidæ knew the value of the Jews as quiet and order-loving citizens. To the shores of the

gather together the outcasts (נִדְחֵי; LXX., τὰς διασπορὰς) of Israel." It is also found in 2 Macc. i. 27, "Gather together those that are scattered from us, deliver them that serve among the heathen." They were originally called *Benî Galootha* (Ezra vi. 16). In John vii. 35, τὴν διασπορὰν τῶν Ἑλλήνων means the Jews scattered over the Greek world. The only other passages where it occurs in the N.T. are James i. 1; 1 Pet. i. 1.

[1] Shairp, *Mod. Culture.*

Mediterranean flocked an ever-increasing multitude of Greek merchants and Greek colonists. "The torrent of Greek immigration soon met the torrent of Jewish emigration. Like two rivers which poured their differently coloured waves into the same basin without mixing with one another, these two peoples cast themselves on the young Macedonian cities, and there simultaneously established themselves without intermixture, continually separated by the irreconcilable diversity of their beliefs and customs, though continually flung into connexion by community of business and by the uniform legislation which protected their interests."[1]

The effect of this on the Greek was less marked and less memorable than its effect on the Jew. Judaism was more Hellenised by the contact than Hellenism was Judaised. There can be no more striking proof of this fact than the total loss by the "Sons of the Dispersion" of their own mother tongue. That the effects on the Pagan world were less beneficial than might have been anticipated was, in great measure, the fault of the Jews themselves. That sort of obtrusive humility which so often marks a race which has nothing to live on but its memories, was mingled with an invincible prejudice, a rooted self-esteem, an unconcealed antipathy to those of alien race and religion, which, combined as it was with commercial habits by no means always scrupulous, and a success by no means always considerate, alienated into disgust the very sympathies which it should have striven to win. The language in which the Jews are spoken of by the writers of the Empire—a language expressive of detestation mingled with curiosity—sufficiently accounts for the outbreaks of mob violence, from which in so many ages they have been liable to suffer. These outbreaks, if not connived at by the governing authorities, were too often condoned. Yet, in spite of this, the influence insensibly exercised by the Jews over the heathen among whom they lived was full of important consequences for Christianity. "*Victi*," says Seneca, "*victoribus leges dederunt.*" The old Paganism was, in intellectual circles, to a great extent effete. Great Pan was dead. Except in remote country districts, the gods of Olympus were idle names. In Rome the terrors of Tartarus were themes for a schoolboy's laughter. Religion had sunk into a state machinery.[2] The natural consequences followed. Those minds which were too degraded to feel the need of a religion were content to wallow, like natural brute beasts, in the Stygian pool of a hideous immorality. Others became the votaries of low foreign superstitions,[3] or the dupes of every variety of designing charlatans. But not a few were attracted into the shadow of the synagogue, and the majority of these were women,[4] who, restricted as was their influence, yet

[1] Reuss, *Théol. Chrét.* I. i. 93; and in Herzog, *Cyclop. s.v.* "Hellenism." On this isopolity see Jos. *c. Ap.* ii. 4.

[2] See Juv. ii. 149; Boissier, *La Religion Romaine*, i. 374—450 and *contra* Friedländer, *Sittengesch. Roms* (who goes too far).

[3] Because these presented vaguer and more shadowy conceptions of the Divine, more possible to grasp than gross concrete images (see Hausrath, *Neut. Zeitg.* ii. 76), and because Greek religion was too gay for a sick and suffering world (Apul. *Metam.* xi. *passim*). See Cat. x. 26; Ov. *F.* iv. 309; *A. A.* i. 78; Juv. vi. 489, 523; Tac. *Ann.* xvi. 6, &c.

[4] The important part played by these proselytes (who are also called σεβόμενοι, εὐσεβεῖς,

could not fail to draw the attention of their domestic circles to the belief which they had embraced. In every considerable city of the Roman Empire the service of the synagogue was held in Greek, and these services were perfectly open to any one who liked to be present at them. Greek, too, became emphatically the language of Christianity. Multitudes of early converts had been Jewish proselytes before they became Christian disciples. They passed from the synagogue of Hellenists into the Church of Christ.

The influences exercised by the Dispersion on the Jews themselves were, of course, too varied and multitudinous to be summed up under one head; yet we may trace two consequences which, century after century, worked in opposite directions, but each of which was deeply marked. On the one hand they became more faithful to their religion; on the other more cosmopolitan in their views. Although they made their home in the heathen countries to which they had been removed by conquest, or had wandered in pursuit of commerce, it must not be supposed that they were at all ready to forfeit their nationality or abandon their traditions. On the contrary, the great majority of them clung to both with a more desperate tenacity. In the destruction of their independence they had recognised the retribution threatened in that long-neglected series of prophecies which had rebuked them for their idolatries. Of all polytheistic tendencies the Jew was cured for ever, and as though to repair past centuries of rebellion and indifference—as though to earn the fulfilment of that great promise of an Anointed Deliverer which was the centre of all their hopes—they devoted themselves with all the ardour of their self-conscious pride to keep the minutest observances of their Law and ritual. Their faithfulness—a complete contrast to their old apostasies—was due to the work of the *Sopherîm*. or Scribes. It was towards Jerusalem that they worshipped; it was to the Sanhedrin of Jerusalem that they looked for legal decisions; it was from the *Amoraîm* and *Tanaîm* of Jerusalem that they accepted all solutions of casuistical difficulties; it was from Jerusalem that were flashed the fire-signals which announced over many lands the true date of the new moons; it was into the treasury of Jerusalem that they poured, not only the stated Temple-tribute of half a shekel, but gifts far more costly, which told of their unshaken devotion to the church of their fathers. It was in Jerusalem that they maintained a special synagogue, and to Jerusalem that they made incessant pilgrimages.[1] The hatred, the suspicion, the contempt created in many countries by the exclusiveness of their prejudices, the peculiarity of their institutions, the jealousy of their successes, only wedded them more fanatically to the observance of their Levitical rules by giving a tinge of martyrdom to the fulfilment of obligations. It became

εὐλαβεῖς) may be seen in Acts x. 2; xiii. 43; xvi. 14, &c., and *passim*. Owing to the painful and, to Hellenic imagination, revolting rite of circumcision, women were more frequently converted to Judaism than men. Josephus (*B. J.* ii. 20, § 2) tells us that nearly all the women of Damascus had adopted Judaism; and even in the first century three celebrated Rabbis were sons of heathen mothers who had embraced the faith of Moses (Derenbourg, *Palest.*, p. 223).

[1] See Philo, *Legat.* 36; *in Flacc.* 7; Jos. *Antt.* xvi. 6, § 3; xviii. 9, § 1; Cic. *pro Flacc.* 28; *Shekalim*, 7, 4; *Rosh Hashana*, 2, 4.

with them a point of conscience to maintain the institutions which their heathen neighbours attacked with every weapon of raillery and scorn. But these very circumstances tended to produce a marked degeneracy of the religious spirit. The idolatry, which in old days had fastened on the visible symbols of alien deities, only assumed another form when concentrated on the dead-letter of documents, and the minute ritualism of service. Gradually, among vast masses of the Jewish people, religion sank almost into fetichism. It lost all power over the heart and conscience, all its tender love, all its inspiring warmth, all its illuminating light. It bound the nation hand and foot to the corpse of meaningless traditions. Even the ethics of the Mosaic legislation were perverted by a casuistry which was at once timid in violating the letter, and audacious in superseding the spirit. In the place of moral nobleness and genial benevolence, Judaism in its decadence bred only an incapacity for spiritual insight, a self-satisfied orthodoxy, and an offensive pride. It enlisted murder and falsity in defence of ignorant Shibboleths and useless forms. The difference between the ideal Jew of earlier and later times can only be measured by the difference between the moral principles of the Law and the dry precedents of the Mishna—by the difference which separates the Pentateuch from the Talmud, the Book of Exodus from the *Abhôda Zara*.[1]

But while it produced these results in many of the Jewish communities, there were others, and there were special individuals in all communities, in whom the influence of heathen surroundings worked very differently. There were many great and beautiful lessons to be learnt from the better aspects of the heathen world. If there was a grace that radiated from Jerusalem, there were also gifts which brightened Athens. The sense of beauty—the exquisiteness of art—the largeness and clearness of insight—the perfection of literary form which characterised the Greek of the age of Pericles, had left the world an immortal heritage; and Rome had her own lessons to teach of dignity, and law, and endurance, and colonisation, and justice. Commerce is eminently cosmopolitan. The Jewish Captivity, with the events which followed it, made the Jews a commercial people. This innate tendency of the race had been curbed, first by the Mosaic legislation,[2] then by the influence of the prophets. But when these restrictions had been providentially removed, the Jew flung himself with ardour into a career from which he had been hitherto restrained. So far from regarding as identical the notions of "merchant" and "Canaanite,"[3] the Rabbis soon began to sing the praises of

[1] "The author of the Pentateuch and the *Tanaîm* moved in different worlds of ideas" (Kuenen, iii. 291).

[2] Deut. xvi. 16, 17; Lev. xxv.; Ps. cvii. 23. See Jos. *c. Ap.* i. 12. The chapter begins with the remark, ἡμεῖς τοίνυν οὔτε χώραν οἰκοῦμεν παράλιον οὔτ' ἐμπορίαις χαίρομεν, οὐδὲ ταῖς πρὸς ἄλλους διὰ τούτων ἐπιμιξίαις. Munk (*Palest.*, p. 393) makes some excellent remarks on this subject, showing that commerce would not only have encouraged intercourse with the heathen, but would also have disturbed the social equilibrium at which Moses aimed, so that it was impossible as long as the Law was rigidly observed (Hos. xii. 8; Amos viii. 4—6, &c.).

[3] Targum of Jonathan (Zech. xiv. 21).

trade. "There can be no worse occupation than agriculture!" said R. Eleazar. "All the fanning in the world will not make you so remunerative as commerce," said Rabh[1] as he saw a cornfield bowing its golden ears under the summer breeze.[2] So easy is it for a people to get over an archaic legislation if it stands in the way of their interests or inclinations! The Mosaic restrictions upon commerce were, of course, impracticable in dealing with Gentiles, and in material successes the Jews found something, at any rate, to make up to them for the loss of political independence. The busy intercourse of cities wrought a further change in their opinions. They began to see that God never meant the nations of the world to stand to each other in the position of frantic antagonism or jealous isolation. A Jerusalem Rabbi, ignorant of everything in heaven and earth and under the earth, except his own *Halacha*, might talk of all the rest of the world promiscuously as an "elsewhere" of no importance;[3] but an educated Alexandrian Jew would be well aware that the children of heathen lands had received from their Father's tenderness a share in the distribution of His gifts. The silent and imperceptible influences of life are often the most permanent, and no amount of exclusiveness could entirely blind the more intelligent sons of the Dispersion to the merits of a richer civilisation. No Jewish boy familiar with the sights and sounds of Tarsus or Antioch could remain unaware that all wisdom was not exhausted in the trivial discussions of the Rabbis; that there was something valuable to the human race in the Greek science which Jewish nescience denounced as thaumaturgy; that there might be a better practice for the reasoning powers than an interminable application of the *Middôth* of Hillel; in short, that the development of humanity involves larger and diviner duties than a virulent championship of the exclusive privileges of the Jew.[4]

We might naturally have conjectured that these wider sympathies would specially be awakened among those Jews who were for the first time brought into close contact with the great peoples of the Aryan race. That contact was first effected by the conquests of Alexander. He settled 8,000 Jews in the Thebais, and the Jews formed a third of the population of his new city of Alexandria. Large numbers were brought from Palestine by Ptolemy I., and they gradually spread from Egypt, not only over "the parts of Libya about

[1] Rabh was a contemporary of Rabbi (Judah the Holy), and was "Head of the Captivity."

[2] *Yebhamôth*, f. 63, 1.

[3] חוצה לארץ, "outside the land" (Frankl, *Jews in the East*, ii. 34). Something like the French *là-bas*.

[4] Many of the Rabbis regarded the Gentiles as little better than so much fuel for the fires of Gehenna. R. Jose construes Isa. xxxiii. 12, "And the peoples shall be a *burning like* lime." Rabh Bar Shilo explained it "that they should be burnt because of their neglect of the Law, which was written upon lime." (See the curious *Hagadah* in *Sotah*, f. 35, 2.) But the Hellenist would soon learn to feel that—

"All knowledge is not couch'd in Moses' Law,
The Pentateuch, or what the Prophets wrote;
The Gentiles also know, and write, and teach
To admiration, taught by Nature's light."—MILTON, *Par. Reg.* iv. 225.

Cyrene," but along the whole Mediterranean coast of Africa.[1] Seleucus Nicator, after the battle of Ipsus, removed them by thousands from Babylonia, to such cities as Antioch and Seleucia; and, when their progress and prosperity were for a time shaken by the senseless persecutions of Antiochus Epiphanes, they scattered themselves in every direction until there was hardly a seaport or a commercial centre in Asia Minor, Macedonia, Greece, or the Islands of the Ægean, in which Jewish communities were not to be found. The vast majority of these Jewish settlers adopted the Greek language, and forgot that Aramaic dialect which had been since the Captivity the language of their nation.

It is to these Greek-speaking Jews that the term Hellenist mainly and properly refers. In the New Testament there are two words, *Hellen* and *Hellenistes*, of which the first is rendered "Greek," and the second "Grecian." The word "Greek" is used as an antithesis either to "barbarians" or to "Jews." In the first case it means all nations which spoke the Greek language;[2] in the second case it is equivalent to "Gentiles."[3] The meaning of the word Hellenist or "Grecian" is wholly different. As far as the form is concerned, it means, in the first instance, one who "Græcises" in language or mode of life, and it points to a difference of training and of circumstances, not to a difference of race.[4] It is therefore reserved as the proper antithesis, not to "Jews,"—since vast numbers of the Hellenists were Jews by birth,—but to strict "Hebrews." The word occurs but twice in the New Testament,[5] and in both cases is used of Jews who had embraced Christianity but who spoke Greek and used the Septuagint version of the Bible instead of the original Hebrew or the Chaldaic Targum of any Interpreter.[6]

[1] See Philo, *c. Fl.* ii. 523; Jos. *Antt.* xiv. 7, § 2; Dr. Deutsch in Kitto's *Cycl.*, *s.v.* "Dispersion;" and Canon Westcott in Smith's *Bible Dict.*

[2] See Acts xviii. 17; 1 Cor. i. 22, 23; Rom. i. 14. The emissaries of Abgarus—if such they were—who applied to Philip when they wished to see Jesus were "Greeks," not "Grecians" (John xii. 20).

[3] Rom. i. 16; ii. 9; iii. 9; 1 Cor. x. 32; Gal. ii. 3. &c. Thus in 2 Macc. iv. 13, Ἑλληνισμὸς is equivalent to ἀλλοφυλισμός; and in iv. 10, 15; vi. 9, τὰ Ἑλληνικὰ ἤθη means "Paganism;" and in Isa. ix. 12, "Philistines" is rendered by the LXX. Ἕλληνας.

[4] Cf. Xen. *Anab.* vii. 3, 12.

[5] Acts vi. 1; ix. 29. In xi. 20 the true reading is Ἕλληνας.

[6] Some of the Hebraising Hellenists hated even the Septuagint (Geiger, *Urschr.* 419, 439; Zunz, *Gottesd. Vort.* 95). The various classes of Christians may be tabulated as follows:—

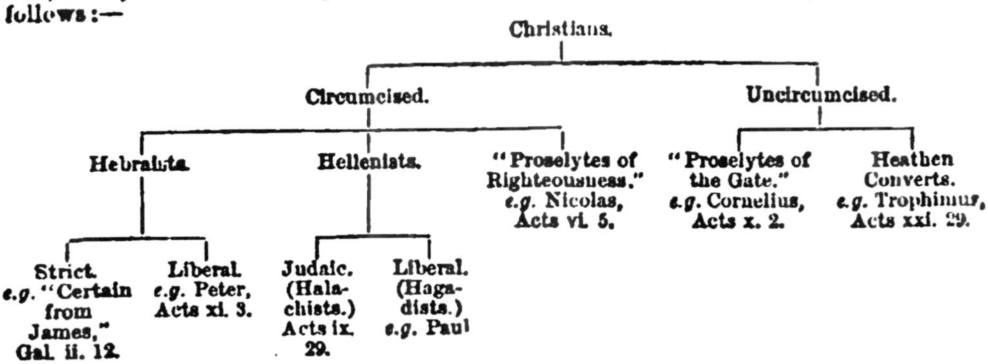

Now this Hellenism expressed many shades of difference, and therefore the exact meaning of the word Hellenist varies with the circumstances under which it is used. The accident of language might make a man, technically speaking, a Hellenist, when politically and theologically he was a Hebrew; and this must have been the condition of those Hellenists who disputed against the arguments of St. Paul in his first visit to Jerusalem.[1] On the other hand, the name might imply that alienation from the system of Judaism, which in some Jews extended into positive apostasy, and into so deep a shame of their Jewish origin, as to induce them, not only in the days of Jason and Menelaus,[2] but even under the Herods, to embrace the practices of the Greeks, and even to obliterate the external sign of their nationality.[3] Others again, like the astute Herodian princes, were hypocrites, who played fast and loose with their religion, content to be scrupulous Jews at Jerusalem, while they could be shameless heathen at Berytus or Cæsarea. But the vast majority of Hellenists lay between these extremes. Contact with the world had widened their intelligence and enabled them so far to raise their heads out of the heavy fog of Jewish scholasticism as to distinguish between that which was of eternal and that which was but of transient significance. Far away from Jerusalem, where alone it was *possible* to observe the Levitical law, it was a natural result that they came to regard outward symbols as merely valuable for the sake of inward truths. To this class belonged the wisest members of the Jewish Dispersion. It is to them that we owe the Septuagint translation, the writings of Philo and Josephus, and a large cycle of historical, poetic, and apocryphal literature. Egypt was the main centre of this Græco-Jewish activity, and many of the Jews of Alexandria distinguished themselves in the art, the learning, and the accomplishments of the Greeks.[4] It is hardly to be wondered at that these more intellectual Jews were not content with an infructuose Rabbinism. It is not astonishing that they desired to represent the facts of their history, and the institutions of their religion, in such an aspect as should least waken the contempt of the nations among whom they lived.[5] But although this might be done with perfect honesty, it tended, no doubt, in some to the adoption of unauthorised additions to their history, and unauthorised explanations of their Scriptures—in one word, to that style of

[1] Acts ix. 29.

[2] See 2 Macc. iv. 13, *seqq.*, "Now such was the height of Greek fashions, and increase of heathenish manners, through the exceeding profaneness of Jason, that ungodly wretch, and no high priest, . . . that the priests, . . . despising the temple, . . . hastened to be partakers of the unlawful allowance in the place of exercise, after the game of Discus called them forth," &c. מלכות יון הרשעה, "the abominable kingdom of Javan," is an expression which stereotypes the hatred for Greek fashions.

[3] ἐπισπασμὸς (1 Cor. vii. 18). The condition of a מָשׁוּךְ (1 Macc. i. 15; Jos. *Antt.* xii. 5, § 1). (On Judaic Hellenism, see Ewald, *Gesch.* v. § ii. 4.)

[4] Thus, an Ezekiel wrote a tragedy on Moses; another, Philo, wrote an Epic on Jerusalem; Theodotus, a tragedy on the Rape of Dina; Demetrius and Eupolemos wrote secular history. The story of Susanna is a novelette. But the feeling of stricter Jews was sternly opposed to these forms of literary activity. In the letter of Aristeas we are told that Theopompus was struck with madness, and Theodektes with blindness, for offences in this direction (Hausrath, *Neut. Zeitg.* ii. 130).

[5] Such was the main object of Josephus in his *Antiquities.*

exegesis which, since it deduced anything out of anything, nullified the real significance of the sacred records.[1] Nor can we be surprised that this Alexandrian theosophy—these allegoric interpretations—this spirit of toleration for the Pagan systems by which they were surrounded—were regarded by the stricter Jews as an incipient revolt from Mosaism thinly disguised under a hybrid phraseology.[2] Hence arose the antagonism between advanced Hellenists and the Hebrews, whose whole patriotic existence had concentrated itself upon the Mosaic and Oral Law. The severance between the two elements became wider and wider as the Jews watched the manner in which Christianity spread in the Gentile world. The consciousness that the rapidity of that diffusion was due, not only to the offer of a nobler faith, but also to the loosening of an intolerable yoke, only made their exclusiveness more obstinate. It was not long before the fall of Jerusalem that there took place in the school of R. Hananiah Ben Hiskiah Ben Garon, that memorable meeting at which eighteen ordinances were resolved upon, of which it was the exclusive object to widen the rift of difference between Jews and Pagans. These ordinances, to which the Mishna only alludes, are found in a *baraïta* ("supplemental addition") of R. Simeon Ben Johai in the second century, and they consist of prohibitions which render impossible any interchange of social relations between Jews and heathen. It was in vain that R. Joshua and the milder Hillelites protested against so dangerous a bigotry. The quarrel passed from words to blows. The followers of Hillel were attacked with swords and lances, and some of them were killed. "That day," says the Jerusalem Talmud, "was as disastrous to Israel as the one on which they made the golden calf;" but it seemed to be a general opinion that the eighteen resolutions could not be rescinded even by Elias himself, because the discussion had been closed by bloodshed; and they were justified to the national conscience by the savage massacres which had befallen the Jews at Beth-shan, Cæsarea, and Damascus.[3] The feelings of Jews towards Pagans were analogous to the hatred of Hebrews to Hellenists. In later days the Christians absorbed the entire fury of that detestation which had once burned in the Jewish heart against Hellenism. When a question arose as to the permissibility of burning the Gospels and other books of the Christians (*Minîm*), considering how frequently

[1] The views of these liberal Hellenists may be seen represented in the works of the pseudo-Aristeas, the pseudo-Aristobulus, and in the verses of Phocylides (Kuenen, *Religion of Israel*, iii. 180). It was the aim of an entire cycle of literature to prove that all Greek wisdom was derived from Jewish sources, and the names of Orpheus and the Sibyl were frequently given to Jewish forgeries and interpolations (Clem. Alex. *Strom.* v. 4; Euseb. *Praep. Evang.* vii. 14; viii. 10; xiii. 12). Bel and the Dragon, the Epistle of Jeremiah, the letter of pseudo-Heraclitus, &c., belong to this class of writings. See too Wisd. of Solomon x.—xii.; Jos. *c. Ap.* ii. 39; Hausrath, *N. Zeitgesch.* ii. 100, *sq.* Josephus says that Pythagoras borrowed from Moses (*c. Ap.* i. 22).

[2] Such Hebraising Hellenists are the author of "the Epistle of Jeremiah," and (on the whole) of Wisdom (see vii. 22, *seq.*, xiii.—xix.). "The Liberal Hellenists spiritualised and volatilised the wall of partition between Jews and Pagans," so that, although Philo said that the wall should still be kept up, it is not surprising to find that his nephew, the Procurator Tiberius Alexander, had abandoned Judaism (Jos. *Antt.* xx. 5, § 2; Kuenen, *Rel. of Israel*, iii.).

[3] *Shabbath*, i. 7; Grätz, iii. 494; Derenbourg, *Palest.*, p. 274.

they contained the name of God, "May I lose my son," exclaimed Rabbi Tarphon, "if I do not fling these books into the fire when they come into my hands, name of God and all. A man chased by a murderer, or threatened by a serpent's bite, ought rather to take refuge in an idol's temple than in the houses of the *Minîm*, for these latter know the truth and deny it, whereas idolaters deny God because they know Him not."[1]

Such, then, being the feelings of the Palestinian Jews with regard to every approach towards idolatry, the antagonism between them and the more liberal Hellenists rose from the very nature of things, and was so deeply rooted that we are not surprised to find a trace of it even in the history of the Church;—for the earliest Christians—the Apostles and disciples of Jesus—were almost exclusively Hebrews and Israelites,[2] the former being a general, and the latter a religious designation. Their feeling towards those who were Hellenists in principles as well as in language would be similar to that of other Jews, however much it might be softened by Christian love. But the jealousies of two sections so widely diverse in their sympathies would be easily kindled; and it is entirely in accordance with the independent records of that period that, "when the number of the disciples was being multiplied," there should have arisen, as a natural consequence, "a murmuring of the Grecians against the Hebrews."

The special ground of complaint was a real or fancied neglect of the widows of Hellenists in the daily ministration of food and assistance. There might be some jealousy because all the offices of the little Church were administered by Hebrews, who would naturally have been more cognisant of the claims of their immediate compatriots. Widows, however, were a class who specially required support. We know how full a discussion St. Paul applies to their general position even at Corinth, and we have already mentioned that some of the wisest regulations attributed to Gamaliel were devoted to ameliorating the sufferings to which they were exposed. In the seclusion to which centuries of custom had devoted the Oriental woman, the lot of a widow, with none to plead her cause, might indeed be bitter. Any inequalities in the treatment of the class would awaken a natural resentment, and the more so because previous to their conversion these widows would have had a claim on the *Corban*, or Temple treasury.[3]

But the Apostles met these complaints in that spirit of candour and generosity which is the best proof how little they were responsible for any partiality which may have been shown to the widows of the Hebrews. Summoning a meeting of the disciples, they pointed out to them that the day had now come in which it was inconvenient for the Apostles to have anything further to do with the apportionment of charity[4]—a routine task which

[1] *Shabbath*, 116 *a*; Derenbourg, p. 380.

[2] The Hellenic names of Philip and Andrew prove nothing, because at this epoch such names were common among the Jews. But they may have had Hellenic connexions. (John xii. 20.)

[3] 2 Macc. iii. 10, "Then the high priest told him (Heliodorus) that there was such money laid up for the relief of widows and fatherless children."

[4] Acts. vi. 2, διακονεῖν τραπέζαις. That τράπεζα has not here its meaning of "bank"

diverted them from more serious and important duties. They therefore bade the meeting elect seven men of blameless character, high spiritual gifts, and practical wisdom, to form what we should call a committee of management, and relieve the Apostles from the burden, in order that they might devote their energies to prayer and pastoral work. The advice was followed, and seven were presented to the Apostles as suitable persons. They were admitted to the duties of their position with prayer and the laying on of hands, which have been thenceforth naturally adopted in every ordination to the office of a deacon.[1]

The seven elected were Stephen, Philip, Prochorus, Nicanor, Timon, Parmenas, and Nicolas, a proselyte of Antioch. The fact that every one of them bears a Greek name has often been appealed to as a proof of the conciliatoriness of the Apostles, as though they had elected every one of their committee from the very body which had found some reason to complain. This, however, would have been hardly just. It would have been to fly into an opposite extreme. The frequency with which the Jews of this time adopted Greek names prevents us from drawing any conclusion as to their nationality. But although we cannot be certain about the conjecture of Gieseler that three of them were Hebrews, three of them Hellenists, and one a proselyte, it is only natural to suppose that the choice of them from different sections of the Church would be adopted as a matter of fairness and common sense. And the fact that a Gentile like Nicolas should thus have been selected to fill an office so honourable and so responsible is one of the many indications which mark the gradual dawn of a new conception respecting the Kingdom of God.

Though two alone[2] of the seven are in any way known to us, yet this

(Jos. *Antt.* xii. 2, § 3: cf. τραπεζίταις, Matt. xxv. 27; τράπεζαν, Luke xix. 23), is clear from the context.

[1] The seven officers were not, however, "deacons" in the modern sense of the word, nor were they mere almoners. The only special title given to any one of them is Evangelist (Acts xxi. 8). Alike their gifts and their functions are loftier than those required for deacons in 1 Tim. iii. Deacons in the modern sense find their nearer prototypes in the νεώτεροι and νεανίσκοι (Acts v. 5, 10; cf. Luke xxii. 26), and in the *Chazzanîm* of the synagogue (Luke iv. 20). The seven, as St. Chrysostom observes, rather had the duties of presbyters, and must be regarded as a body chosen only for a special purpose—τέως εἰς τοῦτο ἐχειροτονήθησαν. Another analogy for this appointment was furnished by the existing institution of three almoners (*Parnasîm*), who undertook the collection and distribution of the "alms of the cup" (see Dr. Ginsburg in Kitto, *s.v.* "Synagogue") and "alms of the box" in the Jewish synagogues; and these were always chosen by the entire congregation of the synagogue, as the Apostles here suggest should be done in the case of the new functionaries.

[2] Nicolas is no exception. If, as early tradition asserted, Luke was himself "a proselyte of Antioch" (Euseb. *H. E.* iii. 4; Jer. *De Virr. Illustr.* 7), this may have suggested the passing reference to him. The evidence which connects him with "the sect of the Nicolaitanes" (Rev. ii. 6, 15), and the story that they adopted both their name and their abominable doctrines from a perversion of his remark that we ought παραχρῆσθαι τῇ σαρκί, are insufficient. παραχρῆσθαι, though used of unrestrained indulgence (Suid.), has also the sense of διαχρῆσθαι, to mortify (Just. M. *Apol.* 49). Irenaeus (*c. Haer.* i. 47), followed by many of the Fathers (Hippolytus, *R. H.* vii. 36; Tertullian, *De Praescr. Haeret.* c. 46), accepts the tradition of his connexion with the sect. Clemens of Alexandria, while defending him from the charge of personal immorality, and admitting that the meaning of his words (which, to say the least, were unfortunately chosen) had been entirely misunderstood (τὴν ἐγκράτειαν τῶν περισπουδάστων ἡδονῶν τὸ "παραχρῆσθαι τῇ

election was a crisis in the history of the Church. At the work of Philip we shall glance hereafter, but we must now follow the career of Stephen, which, brief as it was, marked the beginning of a memorable epoch. For St. Stephen must be regarded as the immediate predecessor of him who took the most prominent part in bringing about his martyrdom; he must be regarded as having been, in a far truer sense than Gamaliel himself, the Teacher of St. Paul. St. Paul has, indeed, been called a "colossal St. Stephen;" but had the life of St. Stephen been prolonged—had he not been summoned, it may be, to yet loftier spheres of activity—we know not to what further heights of moral grandeur he might have attained. We possess but a single speech to show his intellect and inspiration, and we are suffered to catch but one glimpse of his life. His speech influenced the whole career of the greatest of the Apostles, and his death is the earliest martyrdom.

CHAPTER VIII.

WORK AND MARTYRDOM OF ST. STEPHEN.

Παύλου ὁ διδάσκαλος.—BASIL SELEUC. *Orat. de S. Steph.*

Καὶ ἴδοι τις ἂν τὸ λεγόμενον σαφῶς εἰ τὴν σοφίαν τοῦ Στεφάνου, εἰ τὴν Πέτρου γλῶτταν, εἰ τὴν Παύλου ῥυμὴν ἐννοήσειε, πῶς οὐδὲν αὐτοὺς ἔφερεν οὐδὲν ὑφίστατο, οὐ δημῶν θυμὸς, οὐ τυράννων ἐπαναστάσεις, οὐ δαιμόνων ἐπιβουλὴ, οὐ θάνατοι καθημερινοί. ἀλλ' ὥσπερ ποταμοὶ πολλῷ τῷ ῥοίζῳ φερόμενοι οὕτω πάντα παρασύροντες ἀπῄεσαν.—S. CHRYS. *in Joan. Hom.* li. *Opp.* viii. 30.

"This farther only have I to say, my lords, that like as St. Paul was present and consenting to the death of the proto-martyr St. Stephen, and yet they be now twain holy saints in heaven, . . . so I verily trust we may hereafter meet in heaven merrily together, to our everlasting salvation."—*Last Words of Sir T. More to his Judges.*

THE appointment of the Seven, partly because of their zeal and power, and partly because of the greater freedom secured for the Apostles, led to marked successes in the progress of the Church. Not only was the number of disciples in Jerusalem greatly multiplied, but even a large number of the priests[1] became obedient to the faith. Up to this time the acceptance of the

σαρκὶ" ἐδιδάσκει, *Strom.* iii. iv. 26, ed. Pott., p. 523), yet tells a dubious, and probably mistaken, story about his conduct when charged with jealousy of his wife. This story is repeated by Eusebius (*H. E.* iii. 29), and other Fathers. For further information on the subject, and on the identification by Cocceius cf Nicolas with Balaam in Rev. ii., see Giesoler, *Ecc. Hist.* i. 86, E.T.; Mansel, *Gnostic Her.*, p. 72; Derenbourg, p. 363.

[1] Cf. John xii. 42. Commentators have resorted to extraordinary shifts to get rid of this simple statement, which, as I have shown in the text, involves no improbability. Some would adopt the wholly worthless v. l. ἰουδαίων found in a few cursive MSS. and the Philoxenian Syriac. Others accept Beza's conjectural emendation, πολύς τε ὄχλος καὶ ἱερέων (sc. τινες). Others, again, follow Heinsius and Elsner in the suggestion that ὄχλος τῶν ἱερέων means "priests of the common order," "plebeian priests," what the Jews might have called עמי הארץ or "people-of-the-land priests," as distinguished from the *Thalmîdî hachachâmîm*, or "learned priests;" but there is no trace that any such distinction existed, although it is in itself all but certain that none of these converts came

Gospel, so far from involving any rupture with Judaism, was consistent with a most scrupulous devotion to its observances. It must be borne in mind that the priests in Jerusalem, and a few other cities, were a multitudinous body,[1] and that it was only the narrow aristocratic clique of a few alien families who were Sadducees in theology and Herodians in politics. Many of the lower ranks of the priesthood were doubtless Pharisees, and as the Pharisees were devoted to the doctrine of the Resurrection, there was nothing inconsistent with their traditions in admitting the Messiahship of a Risen Saviour. Such a belief would at this time, and indeed long afterwards, have made little difference in their general position, although if they were true believers it would make a vast difference in their inward life. The simplicity, the fervour, the unity, the spiritual gifts of the little company of Galilæans, would be likely to attract the serious and thoughtful. They would be won by these graces far more than by irresistible logic, or by the appeals of powerful eloquence. The mission of the Apostles at this time was, as has been well observed, no mere apostolate of rhetoric, nor would they for a moment pretend to be other than they were—illiterate men, untrained in the schools of technical theology and rabbinic wisdom. Had they been otherwise, the argument for the truth of Christianity, which is derived from the extraordinary rapidity of its dissemination, would have lost half its force. The weapons of the Apostolic warfare were not carnal. Converts were won, not by learning or argument, but by the power of a new testimony and the spirit of a new life.

Up to this period the name of Stephen has not occurred in Christian history, and as the tradition that he had been one of the seventy disciples is valueless,[2] we know nothing of the circumstances of his conversion to Christianity. His recognition, however, of the glorified figure, which he saw in his ecstatic vision, as the figure of Him who on earth had called Himself "the Son of Man," makes it probable that he was one of those who had enjoyed the advantage of hearing the living Jesus, and of drawing from its very fountain-head the river of the water of life.[3] We would fain know more of one who, in so brief a space of time, played a part so nobly wise. But it was with Stephen as it has been with myriads of others whose names have been written in the Book of Life; they have been unknown among men, or known only during one brief epoch, or for one great deed. For a moment, but for a moment only, the First Martyr steps into the full light of history. Our insight into his greatness is derived almost solely from the record of a single speech and a single day—the last speech he ever uttered—the last day of his mortal life.

from the families of the lordly and supercilious Boethusim, Kamhits, &c. But neither here nor in i. 15, ὄχλος ὀνομάτων, has ὄχλος a contemptuous sense.

[1] 4,289 had returned with Ezra (ii. 36—39).

[2] Epiphan. *Haer.* xl., p. 50.

[3] That he was a Hellenist is not merely a precarious inference from the Greek form of his name, which may merely have been a rendering of the Aramaic *Kelil*, but is implied by the narrative itself, and is rendered certain by the character of his speech; but whether he was trained at Alexandria, or was a Roman freedman (Plumptre on Acts vi. 5), and what had brought him to Jerusalem, we cannot tell.

It was the *faith* of Stephen, together with his loving energy and blameless sanctity, which led to the choice of him as one of the Seven. No sooner was he elected than he became the most prominent of them all. The grace which shone in his colleagues shone yet more brightly in him,[1] and he stood on a level with the Apostles in the power of working wonders among the people. Many a man, who would otherwise have died unknown, has revealed to others his inherent greatness on being entrusted with authority. The immense part played by Stephen in the history of the Church was due to the development of powers which might have remained latent but for the duties laid on him by his new position. The distribution of alms seems to have been a part only of the task assigned him. Like Philip, he was an Evangelist as well as a Deacon, and the speech which he delivered before the Sanhedrin, showing as it does the logical force and concentrated fire of a great orator and a practised controversialist, may explain the stir which was caused by his preaching.

The scenes of that preaching were the Hellenistic synagogues of Jerusalem. To an almoner in a city where so many were poor, and to a Hellenist of unusual eloquence, opportunities would constantly recur in which he was not only permitted, but urged, to explain the tenets of the new society. Hitherto that society was in full communion with the Jewish Church. Stephen alone was charged with utterances of a disloyal tendency against the tenets of Pharisaism, and this is a proof how different was his preaching from that of the Twelve, and how much earlier he had arrived at the true appreciation of the words of Jesus respecting the extent and nature of His Kingdom. That which, in the mind of a Peter, was still but a grain of mustard seed, sown in the soil of Judaism, had already grown, in the soul of a Stephen, into a mighty tree. The Twelve were still lingering in the portals of the synagogue. For them the new wine of the kingdom of heaven had not yet burst the old wine-skins. As yet they were only regarded as the heads of a Jewish sect,[2] and although they believed that their faith would soon be the faith of all the world, there is no trace that, up to this time, they ever dreamed of the abrogation of Mosaism, or the free admission of uncircumcised Gentiles into a full equality of spiritual privileges. A proselyte of righteousness—one who, like Nicolas of Antioch, had accepted the sign of circumcision—might, indeed, be held worthy of honour; but one who was only a "proselyte of the gate,"[3] one who held back from the seal of the covenant made to Abraham, would not be regarded as a full Christian any more than he would be regarded as a full Jew.

Hence, up to this time, the Christians were looked on with no disfavour by that Pharisaic party which regarded the Sadducees as intriguing apostates. They were even inclined to make use of the Resurrection which the Christians proclaimed, as a convenient means of harassing their rivals. Nor was it they

[1] χάριτος (ℵ, A, B, D, &c.), not πίστεως, is the true reading in Acts vi. 8.
[2] Acts xxiv. 5; xxviii. 22, αἵρεσις.
[3] The *name* did not arise till later, but is here adopted for convenience' sake.

who had been guilty of the murder of Jesus. They had not, indeed, stirred one finger for His deliverance, and it is probable that many of them—all those hypocrites of whom both Jesus and John had spoken as a viper brood—had looked with satisfaction on the crime by which their political opponents had silenced their common enemy. Yet they did not fear that His blood would be brought on *them*, or that the Apostles would ever hurl on them or their practices His terrible denunciations. Though the Christians had their private meetings on the first day of the week, their special tenets, their sacramental institutions, and their common meal, there was nothing reprehensible in these observances, and there was something attractive even to Pharisees in their faithful simplicity and enthusiastic communism.[1] In all respects they were "devout according to the Law." They would have shrunk with horror from any violation of the rules which separated clean from unclean meats; they not only observed the prescribed feasts of the Pentateuch and its single fast, but even adopted the fasts which had been sanctioned by the tradition of the oral Law; they had their children duly circumcised; they approved and practised the vows of the Nazarites; they never omitted to be on their knees in the Temple, or with their faces turned towards it, at the three stated hours of prayer.[2] It needs but a glance at the symbolism of the Apocalypse to see how dear to them were the names, the reminiscences, the Levitical ceremonial, the Temple worship of their Hebrew fellow-citizens. Not many years later, the "many myriads of Jews who believed were *all* zealous of the Law," and would have thought it a disgrace to do otherwise than "to walk orderly."[3] The position, therefore, which they held was simply that of one synagogue more, in a city which, according to the Rabbis, could already boast that it possessed as many as 480. They might have been called, and it is probable that they were called, by way of geographical distinction, "the Synagogue of the Nazarenes."

But this acceptance with the people could only be temporary and deceptive. If, indeed, the early believers had never advanced beyond this stand-point, Christianity might have been regarded to the last as nothing more than a phase of Pharisaism, heretical for its acceptance of a crucified Messiah, but worthy of honour for the scrupulosity of its religious life. But had Christianity never been more than this, then the olive branch would have died with the oleaster on which it was engrafted. It was as necessary for the Church as for the world that this hollow semblance of unison between religions which, in their distinctive differences, were essentially antagonistic, should be rudely dissipated. It was necessary that all Christians, whether

[1] The Jews would have regarded them at that time as *Chaberîm*, a body of people associated, quite harmlessly, for a particular object.

[2] Called שחרית, *shachrith*, at 9; מנחה, *minchah*, at 3.30; and מעריב, *mearib*, at dark (Acts ii. 1; iii. 1; x. 30).

[3] Acts xxi. 20, 24. See for the facts in the previous paragraphs, Acts x. 9, 14, 30; xiii. 2, 3; xviii. 18, 21; xx. 6, 16; xxii. 3; Rom. xiv. 5; Gal. iv. 10; v. 2; Phil. iii. 2; Rev. ii. 9; iii. 9; vii. 15; xi. 19, &c.; Reuss. *Théol. Chrét.* i. 291, who quotes Sulpic. Sever. ii. 31, "Christum Deum sub legis observatione credebant."

Jews or Gentiles, should see how impossible it was to put a new patch on an old garment.

This truth had been preached by Jesus to His Apostles, but, like many other of His words, it lay long dormant in their minds. After some of His deepest utterances, in full consciousness that He could not at once be understood, He had said, "He that hath ears to hear, let him hear." And as they themselves frankly confess, the Apostles had not always been among those "who had ears to hear." Plain and reiterated as had been the prophecies which He had addressed to them respecting His own crucifixion and resurrection, the first of these events had plunged them into despair and horror, the second had burst upon them with a shock of surprise. He who commanded the light to shine out of darkness had, indeed, shined in their hearts "to give the light of the knowledge of the glory of God in the face of Jesus Christ;"[1] but still they were well aware that they had this treasure "in earthen vessels." To attribute to them an equality of endowments, or an entire unanimity of opinion, is to contradict their plainest statements. To deny that their knowledge gradually widened is to ignore God's method of revelation, and to set aside the evidence of facts. To the last they "knew in part, and they prophesied in part."[2] Why was James the Lord's brother so highly respected by the people as tradition tells us that he was? Why was Paul regarded by them with such deadly hatred? Because St. Paul recognised more fully than St. James the future universal destiny of a Christianity separated from Judaic institutions. The Crucifixion had, in fact, been the protest of the Jew against an isopolity of faith. "From that moment the fate of the nation was decided. Her religion was to kill her. But when the Temple burst into flames, that religion had already spread its wings and gone out to conquer an entire world."[3]

Now, as might have been expected, and as was evidently designed by their Divine Master, the *last* point on which the Galilæan Apostles attained to clearness of view and consistency of action was the fact that the Mosaic Law was to be superseded, even for the Jew, by a wider revelation. It is probable that this truth, in all its fulness, was never finally apprehended by all the Apostles. It is doubtful whether, humanly speaking, it would ever have been grasped by any of them if their powers of insight had not been quickened, in God's appointed method, by the fresh lessons which came to them through the intellect and faith of men who had been brought up in larger views. The obliteration of natural distinctions is no part of the divine method. The inspiration of God never destroys the individuality of those holy souls which it has made into sons of God and prophets. There are, as St. Paul so earnestly tried to impress upon the infant Churches, diversities of gifts, diversities of ministrations, diversities of operations, though it is the same Spirit, the same Lord, the same God, who worketh all things in all.[4] The Hellenistic training of a Stephen and a Saul prepared them for the acceptance

[1] 2 Cor. iv. 6, 7. [2] 1 Cor. xiii. 9. [3] Kuenen, *Rel. of Isr.* iii. 281.
[4] 1 Cor. xii. 4—6

of lessons which nothing short of an express miracle could have made immediately intelligible to a Peter and a James.

Now the relation of the Law to the Gospel had been exactly one of those subjects on which Jesus, in accordance with a divine purpose, had spoken with a certain reserve. His mission had been to found a kingdom, not to promulgate a theology; He had died not to formulate a system, but to redeem a race. His work had been not to construct the dogmas of formal creeds, but to purify the soul of man, by placing him in immediate relation to the Father in Heaven. It required many years for Jewish converts to understand the meaning of the saying that "He came not to destroy the Law but to fulfil." Its meaning could indeed only become clear in the light of other sayings of which they overlooked the force. The Apostles had seen Him obedient to the Law; they had seen Him worship in the Temple and the Synagogues, and had accompanied Him in His journeys to the Feasts. He had never told them in so many words that the glory of the Law, like the light which lingered on the face of Moses, was to be done away. They had failed to comprehend the ultimate tendency and significance of His words and actions respecting the Sabbath,[1] respecting outward observances,[2] respecting divorce,[3] respecting the future universality of spiritual worship.[4] They remembered, doubtless, what He had said about the permanence of every *yod* and horn of a letter in the Law,[5] but they had not remarked that the assertion of the pre-eminence of moral over ceremonial duties is one unknown to the Law itself. Nor had they seen that His fulfilment of the Law had consisted in its spiritualisation; that He had not only extended to infinitude the range of its obligations, but had derived their authority from deeper principles, and surrounded their fulfilment with diviner sanctions. Nor, again, had they observed how much was involved in the emphatic quotation by Christ of that passage of Hosea, "I will have mercy and not sacrifice."[6] They were not yet ripe for the conviction that to attach primary importance to Mosaic regulations after they had been admitted into the kingdom of Heaven, was to fix their eyes upon a waning star while the dawn was gradually broadening into boundless day.

About the early ministry of Stephen we are told comparatively little in the Acts, but its immense importance has become more clear in the light of subsequent history. It is probable that he himself can never have formed the remotest conception of the vast results—results among millions of Christians through centuries of progress—which in God's Providence should arise from the first clear statement of those truths which he was the first to perceive. Had he done so he would have been still more thankful for the ability with which he was inspired to support them, and for the holy courage which prevented him from quailing for an instant under the storm of violence and hatred which his words awoke.

What it was which took him to the synagogues of Jewish Hellenists we do

[1] Mark ii. 27; John v. 17.
[2] Matt. ix. 13; xii. 7.
[3] Matt. xix. 3, 6, 8; v. 32.
[4] John iv. 22.
[5] Matt. v. 18.
[6] Matt. ix. 13; xii. 7.

not know. It may have been the same missionary zeal which afterwards carried to so many regions the young man of Tarsus who at this time was among his ablest opponents. All that we are told is that "there arose some of the synagogue which is called the synagogue of the Libertines and Cyrenians, and Alexandrians, and those of Cilicia and Asia disputing with Stephen." The form of the sentence is so obscure that it is impossible to tell whether we are meant to understand that the opponents of Stephen were the members of *one* synagogue which united these widely-scattered elements; of *five* separate synagogues; of *three* synagogues—namely, that of the Freedmen, that of the African, and that of the Asiatic Hellenists; or of *two* distinct synagogues, of which one was frequented by the Hellenists of Rome, Greece, and Alexandria; the other by those of Cilicia and Proconsular Asia. The number of synagogues in Jerusalem was (as I have already mentioned) so large that there is no difficulty in believing that each of these bodies had their own separate place of religious meeting,[1] just as at this day in Jerusalem there are separate synagogues for the Spanish Sephardim, the Dutch Anshe hod, and the German and Polish Ashkenazim.[2] The freedmen may have been the descendants of those Jews whom Pompey had sent captive to Italy, and Jews were to be counted by myriads in Greece, in Alexandria, and in the cities of Asia. But to us the most interesting of all these Greek-speaking Jews was Saul of Tarsus, who, beyond all reasonable doubt, was a member of the synagogue of the Cilicians,[3] and who in that case must not only have taken his part in the disputes which followed the exhortations of the fervid deacon,[4] but as a scholar of Gamaliel and a zealous Pharisee, must have occupied a prominent position as an uncompromising champion of the traditions of the fathers.

Though the Saul of this period must have differed widely from that Paul, the slave of Jesus Christ, whom we know so well, yet the main features of his personality must have been the same. He could not have failed to recognise the moral beauty, the dauntless courage, the burning passion latent in the tenderness of Stephen's character. The white ashes of a religion which had smouldered into formalism lay thickly scattered over his own heart, but the fire of a genuine sincerity burned below. Trained as he had been for years in Rabbinic minutiæ, he had not yet so far grown old in a deadening system as to mistake the painted cere-cloths of the mummy for the grace and flush of healthy life. While he listened to St. Stephen, he must surely have felt the contrast between a dead theology and a living faith; between a kindling inspiration and a barren exegesis; between a minute analysis of unimportant ceremonials and a preaching that stirred the inmost depths of the troubled heart. Even the

[1] The assertion of the Talmud (cf. *Sanhedr.* f. 58, 1) that there were 480 synagogues in Jerusalem is indeed valueless, because the remarks of the Rabbis about Jerusalem, Bethyr, and indeed Palestine generally, are mere hyperbole; but, as Renan remarks (*Les Apôtres*, p. 109), it does not seem at all impossible to those who are familiar with the innumerable mosques of Mahommedan cities. We are informed in the Talmud that each synagogue had not only a school for the teaching of Scripture, but also for the teaching of traditions (בית תלמוד למשנה, *Megillah*, f. 73, 4).

[2] See Frankl, *Jews in the East*, ii. 21, E. T.

[3] He may have been a *Libertinus* also.

[4] Acts vi. 9, συζητοῦντες.

rage which is often intensified by the unconscious rise of an irresistible conviction could not wholly prevent him from perceiving that these preachers of a gospel which he disdained as an execrable superstition, had found "in Christ" the secret of a light and joy, and love and peace, compared with which his own condition was that of one who was chained indissolubly to a corpse.

We catch but a single glimpse of these furious controversies. Their immediate effect was the signal triumph of St. Stephen in argument. The Hellenists were unable to withstand the wisdom and the spirit with which he spake. Disdainful Rabbinists were at once amazed and disgusted to find that he with whom they now had to deal was no rude provincial, no illiterate *am ha-arets*, no humble *hediot*, like the fishermen and tax-gatherers of Galilee; but one who had been trained in the culture of heathen cities as well as in the learning of Jewish communities—a disputant who could meet them with their own weapons, and speak Greek as fluently as themselves. Steeped in centuries of prejudice, engrained with traditions of which the truth had never been questioned, they must have imagined that they would win an easy victory, and convince a man of intelligence how degrading it was for him to accept a faith on which, from the full height of their own ignorance, they complacently looked down. How great must have been their discomfiture to find that what they had now to face was not a mere personal testimony which they could contemptuously set aside, but arguments based on premisses which they themselves admitted, enforced by methods which they recognised, and illustrated by a learning which they could not surpass! How bitter must have been their rage when they heard doctrines subversive of their most cherished principles maintained with a wisdom which differed not only in degree, but even in kind, from the loftiest attainments of their foremost Rabbis—even of those whose merits had been rewarded by the flattering titles of "Rooters of Mountains" and "Glories of the Law!"

At first the only discussion likely to arise would be as to the Messiahship of Jesus, the meaning of His death, the fact of His Resurrection. These would be points on which the ordinary Jew would have regarded argument as superfluous condescension. To him the stumbling-block of the Cross would have been insurmountable. In all ages the Messianic hope had been prominent in the minds of the most enlightened Jews, but during the Exile and the Restoration it had become the central faith of their religion. It was this belief which, more than any other, kindled their patriotism, consoled their sorrows, and inspired their obedience. If a Shammai used to spend the whole week in meditating how he could most rigidly observe the Sabbath—if the Pharisees regarded it as the main function of their existence to raise a hedge around the Law—the inspiring motive was a belief that if only for one day Israel were entirely faithful, the Messiah would come. And what a coming! How should the Prince of the House of David smite the nations with the sword of his mouth! How should He break them in pieces like a potter's vessel! How should He exalt the children of Israel into kings of the earth, and feed them with the flesh of Behemoth, and Leviathan, and the bird Bar Juchne, and pour at their feet the treasures of the sea! And to say that *Jesus of Nazareth* was the promised Messiah—to suppose that all the splendid prophecies of patriarchs, and seers, and kings, from the Divine Voice which spoke to Adam in Paradise, to the last utterance of the Angel Malachi—all pointed to, all centred in, One who had been the carpenter of Nazareth, and whom they had seen crucified between two brigands—to say that their very Messiah had just been "hung"[1] by Gentile tyrants at the instance of their own priests;—this, to most of the hearers in the synagogue, would have seemed wicked if it had not seemed too absurd. Was there not one sufficient and decisive answer to it all in the one verse of the Law—"Cursed by God is he that hangeth on a tree?"[2]

Yet this was the thesis which such a man as Stephen—no ignorant Galilæan, but a learned Hellenist—undertook to prove, and *did* prove with such power as to produce silence if not assent, and hatred if not conviction. For with all their adoration of the letter, the Rabbis and Pharisees had but half read their Scriptures, or had read them only to use as an engine of religious intolerance, and to pick out the views which most blended with their personal preconceptions. They had laid it down as a principle of interpretation that the entire books of the Canon prophesied of nothing else but the days of the Messiah. How, under these circumstances, they could possibly miss the conception of a *suffering* as well as of a *triumphant* Messiah,[3] might well amaze us, if there had not been proof in all ages that men may entirely overlook the statements and pervert the meaning of their own sacred books, because, when they read those books, the veil of obstinate prejudice is lying upon their hearts. But when the view of ancient prophecy, which proved that it behoved Christ thus to suffer and to enter into His glory,[4] was forcibly presented to them by the insight and eloquence of one who was their equal in learning and their superior in illumination, we can understand the difficulties to which they were reduced. How, for instance, could they elude the force of the 53rd chapter of Isaiah, to which their Rabbis freely accorded a Messianic interpretation? The Messianic application of what is there said about the Servant of Jehovah, and the deep humiliation borne for the sake of others, is not only found in the Targum of Jonathan and in many Rabbinic allusions, down even to the Book Zohar, but seems to have remained entirely undisputed until the mediæval Rabbis found

[1] תָּלוּי.

[2] Deut. xxi. 23, κεκατηραμένος ὑπὸ τοῦ Θεοῦ. The later view of this, "He that is hanged is an insult to God" arose from the fact that Jewish patriots in the Jewish War were crucified by scores. St. Paul, in quoting the verse, omits the ὑπὸ Θεοῦ (Gal. ii. 13; and Lightfoot, p. 133).

[3] Of the notion of a suffering Messiah, Ben Joseph, as distinguished from the triumphant son of David (Rashi on Isa. xxiv. 18; *Succah*, 52, 1, 2, where reference is made to Zech. xii. 10, and Ps. ii., &c.; see Otho, *Lex. Rab.* s. v. Messiah), there is no trace in Jewish literature till long afterwards. St. Paul's witness from Moses and the Prophets—εἰ παθητὸς ὁ Χριστός, Acts xxvi. 23—only woke a sneer from Agrippa II.

[4] Luke xxiv. 26.

themselves inconvenienced by it in their controversies with Christians.[1] Yet this was but an isolated prophecy, and the Christians could refer to passage after passage which, on the very principles of their adversaries, not only justified them in accepting as the Christ One whom the rulers of the Jews had crucified, but even distinctly foreshadowed the mission of His Forerunner; His ministry on the shores of Gennesareth; His humble entry into Jerusalem; His rejection by His own people; the disbelief of His announcements; the treachery of one of His own followers; the mean price paid for His blood; His death as a malefactor; even the bitter and stupefying drinks that had been offered to Him; and the lots cast upon His clothes—no less than His victory over the grave by Resurrection, on the third day, from the dead, and His final exaltation at the right hand of God.[2] How tremendous the cogency of such arguments would be to the hearers of Stephen cannot be shown more strikingly than by the use made of them by St. Paul after the conversion which they doubtless helped to bring about. It must have been from St. Stephen that he heard them first, and they became so convincing to him that he constantly employs the same or analogous arguments in his own reasonings with his unconverted countrymen.[3]

It is clear that, in the course of argument, Stephen was led to adduce some of those deep sayings as to the purpose of the life of Christ which the keen insight of hate had rendered more intelligible to the enemies of our Lord than they had been in the first instance to His friends. Many of those priests and Pharisees who had been baptised into the Church of Christ with the notion that their new belief was compatible with an unchanged loyalty to Judaism, had shown less understanding of the sayings of their Master, and less appreciation of the grandeur of His mission, than the Sadducees whose hatred had handed Him over to the secular arm. It did lie within the natural interpretation of Christ's language that the Law of Moses, which the Jews at once idolised and evaded, was destined to be annulled; not, indeed, those moral sanctions of it which were eternal in obligation, but the complicated system wherein those moral commandments were so deeply imbedded. The Jewish race were right to reverence Moses as an instrument in the hands of God to lay the deepest foundations of a national life. As a Lawgiver whose Decalogue is so comprehensive in its brevity as to transcend all other codes—as the sole Lawgiver who laid his prohibition against the beginnings of evil, by daring to forbid an evil thought—as one who established for his people a monotheistic faith, a significant worship, and an undefinable hope—he deserved the gratitude and reverence of mankind. That this under-official of an obscure sect of

[1] Proofs of this statement may be found in Dr. A. Wünsche's *Die Leiden des Messias*, and several quotations from his book may be found in the *Speaker's Commentary, ad loc.*

[2] See Is. xl. 3; Mark i. 3; Mal. iii. 1; Matt. xi. 10; Is. viii. 14; ix. 1; Matt. iv. 14; Is. lxi. 1; Luke iv. 18; Ps. lxxviii. 2; Matt. xiii. 35; Ps. cxviii. 22; Luke ii. 34; Acts iv. 11; xiii. 41; Ps. xli. 9; Zech. xi. 12; John xiii. 18; Matt. xxvi. 15; xxvii. 9, 10; Zech. xii. 10; John xix. 37; Isa. liii. 9; Ps. xvi. 10; Matt. xii. 40; Acts ii. 27; Ps. cx. 1; Acts ii. 33; Heb. i. 13, &c. (See Davison, *On Prophecy, passim*; Hausrath, p. 112, seqq.)

[3] Eph. ii. 20; Rom. ix. 34; &c.

yesterday should dare to move his tongue against that awful name, and prophesy the abolition of institutions of which some had been delivered to their fathers of old from the burning crags of Sinai, and others had been handed down from the lips of the mighty teacher through the long series of priests and prophets, was to them something worse than folly and presumption—it was a blasphemy and a crime!

And how did he dare to speak one word against, or hint one doubt as to the permanent glory of, the Temple? The glowing descriptions of the Talmud respecting its colossal size and royal splendour are but echoes of the intense love which breathes throughout the Psalms. In the heart of Saul any word which might sound like a slight to "the place where God's honour dwelt" would excite a peculiar indignation. When the conflagration seized its roofs of cedar-wood and melted its golden tables, every Jew in the city was fired with a rage which made him fight with superhuman strength—

> "Through their torn veins reviving fury ran,
> And life's last anger warmed the dying man."

Among those frenzied combatants was a body of Tarsian youths who gladly devoted their lives to the rescue of Jerusalem. What they felt at that supreme moment may show us what such a zealot as Saul of Tarsus would feel, when he heard one who called himself a Jew use language which sounded like disparagement of "the glory of the whole earth."

Foiled in argument, the Hellenists of the synagogues adopted the usual resource of defeated controversialists who have the upper hand. They appealed to violence for the suppression of reason. They first stirred up the people—whose inflammable ignorance made them the ready tools of any agitator—and through them aroused the attention of the Jewish authorities. Their plot was soon ripe. There was no need of the midnight secrecy which had marked the arrest of Jesus. There was no need to secure the services of the Captain of the Temple to arrest Stephen at twilight, as he had arrested Peter and John. There was no need even to suppress all semblance of violence, lest the people should stone them for their unauthorised interference. The circumstances of the day enabled them to assume unwonted boldness, because they were at the moment enjoying a sort of interregnum from Roman authority. The approval of the multitude had been alienated by the first rumour of defective patriotism. When every rank of Jewish society had been stirred to fury by false witnesses whom these Hellenists had suborned, they seized a favourable moment, suddenly came upon Stephen,[1] either while he was teaching in a synagogue, or while he was transacting the duties of an almoner, and led him away—apparently without a moment's pause—into the presence of the assembled Sanhedrin. Everything was ready; everything seemed to point to a foregone conclusion. The false witnesses were at hand, and confronted their victim with the charge of incessant harangues against "this Holy Place"—the expression seems to show that the Sanhedrin were for this time sitting in their

[1] Acts vi. 12, ἐπιστάντες: cf. xvii. 5.

famous "Hall of Squares,"—and against the Law.[1] In support of this general accusation, they testified that they had heard him say that Jesus—"this Nazarene,"[2] as they indignantly add to distinguish Him from others who bore that common name—"shall destroy this place, and shall change the customs which Moses handed down to us." It is evident that these false witnesses made some attempt to base their accusation upon truth. There was good policy in this, as false witnesses in all ages have been cunning enough to see. Half truths are often the most absolute of lies, because

> "A lie which is half a truth is ever the blackest of lies;
> For a lie which is all a lie may be met and fought with outright,
> But a lie which is part a truth is a harder matter to fight."

It is certain that if Stephen had not used the very expressions with which they charged him, he had used others not unlike them. It is his immortal glory to have remembered the words of Jesus, and to have interpreted them aright. Against the moral Law—the great Ten Words of Sinai, or any of those precepts of exquisite humanity and tenderness which lie scattered amid the ceremonial observances—he is not even falsely accused of having uttered a word. But against the permanent validity of the ceremonial Law he may have spoken with freedom; for, as we have seen, its destined abrogation was involved in the very slight importance which Jesus had attached to it. And for the Oral Law it is probable that Stephen, whose training would have rendered impossible any minute fulfilment of its regulations, neither felt nor professed respect. The expression used by the witnesses against him seems to show that it was mainly, though not perhaps exclusively, of this Oral Law that he had been thinking.[3] It was not, perhaps, any doubt as to its authenticity which made him teach that Jesus should change its customs, for in those days the critical spirit was not sufficiently developed to give rise to any challenge of a current assertion; but he had foreseen the future nullity of these "traditions of the fathers," partly from their own inherent worthlessness, and partly because he may have heard, or had repeated to him, the stern denunciation which the worst of these traditions had drawn from the lips of Christ Himself.[4]

But though Stephen must have seen that the witnesses were really false witnesses, because they misrepresented the tone and the true significance of the language which he had used—although, too, he was conscious how dangerous was his position as one accused of blasphemy against Moses, against the Temple, against the traditions, and against God—it never occurred to him to escape his danger by a technicality or a compromise. To throw discredit even upon the Oral Law would not be without danger in the presence of an assembly whose members owed to its traditions no little of the authority which they enjoyed.[5] But Stephen did not at all intend to confine his argument to this narrow range. Rather the conviction

[1] Acts vi. 13, οὐ παύεται ῥήματα λαλῶν.

[2] Acts vi. 14, Ἰησοῦς, ὁ Ναζωραῖος οὗτος.

[3] Acts vi. 14, τὰ ἔθη ἃ παρέδωκεν ἡμῖν Μωϋσῆς. (Cf. Jos. *Antt.* xiii. 10, § 6, and 16, § 2.)

[4] Matt. xv. 2–6; Mark vii. 3, 5, 8, 9, 13.

[5] Maimon. *Pref.* to the *Yad Hachazakah*; McCaul, *Old Paths*, p. 335.

came upon him that now was the time to speak out—that this was the destined moment in which, even if need be to the death, he was to bear witness to the inner meaning of the Kingdom of his Lord. That conviction—an inspiration from on high—gave unwonted grandeur and heavenliness to his look, his words, his attitude. His whole bearing was ennobled, his whole being was transfigured by a consciousness which illuminated his very countenance. It is probable that the unanimous tradition of the Church is correct in representing him as youthful and beautiful; but now there was something about him far more beautiful than youth or beauty could bestow. In the spiritual light which radiated from him he seemed to be overshadowed by the Shechinah, which had so long vanished from between the wings of the Temple cherubim. While the witnesses had been delivering their testimony, no one had observed the sudden brightness which seemed to be stealing over him; but when the charge was finished, and every eye was turned from the accusers to a fixed gaze on the accused,[1] all who were seated in the Sanhedrin—and one of the number, in all probability, was Saul of Tarsus—"saw his face as it had been the face of an angel."

In the sudden hush that followed, the voice of the High Priest Jonathan was heard putting to the accused the customary and formal question—

"Are these things so?"[2]

In reply to that question began the speech which is one of the earliest, as it is one of the most interesting, documents of the Christian Church. Although it was delivered before the Sanhedrin, there can be little doubt that it was delivered in Greek, which, in the bilingual condition of Palestine—and, indeed, of the civilised world in general—at that time, would be perfectly understood by the members of the Sanhedrin, and which was perhaps the only language which Stephen could speak with fluency.[3] The quotations from the Old Testament follow the Septuagint, even where it differs from the Hebrew, and the individuality which characterises almost every sentence of the speech forbids us to look on it as a mere conjectural paraphrase. There is no difficulty in accounting for its preservation. Apart from the fact that two secretaries were always present at the judicial proceedings of the Sanhedrin,[4] there are words and utterances which, at certain times, are branded indelibly upon the memory of their hearers; and since we can trace the deep impression made by this speech on the mind of

[1] Acts vi. 15, ἀτενίσαντες εἰς αὐτὸν ἅπαντες.

[2] St. Chrysostom sees in the apparent mildness of the question an indication that the High Priest and the Sanhedrin were awed by the supernatural brightness of the martyr's look—ὁρᾷς ὡς μετὰ ἐπιεικείας ἡ ἐρώτησις καὶ οὐδὲν τέως φορτικὸν ἔχουσα; (*Homil.* xv. *in Act.*). But the question appears to have been a regular formula of interrogation. It was, in fact, the "Guilty or Not Guilty?" of the Jewish Supreme Court.

[3] Against this view are urged—(1) the unlikelihood that St. Stephen would have pleaded in Greek before the Sanhedrin; (2) the use of the Hebraism οὐρανοὶ in Acts vii. 56. But as to 1, if even Philo knew no Hebrew, Stephen may have known none; and, 2, the word οὐρανοὶ points to a special Jewish belief, independent of language.

[4] See Jahn, *Archaeol. Bibl.* § 248. He quotes no authority, and I at first felt some doubt about the assertion, but I find it so stated in the Mishna, *Sanhedr.* iv. 2.

St. Paul, we find little difficulty in adopting the conjecture that its preservation was due to him. The *Hagadôth* in which it abounds, the variations from historical accuracy, the free citation of passages from the Old Testament, the roughness of style, above all the concentrated force which makes it lend itself so readily to differing interpretations, are characteristics which leave on our minds no shadow of doubt that whoever may have been the reporter, we have here at least an *outline* of Stephen's speech. And this speech marked a crisis in the annals of Christianity. It led to consequences that changed the Church from a Judaic sect at Jerusalem, into the Church of the Gentiles and of the world. It marks the commencing severance of two institutions which had not yet discovered that they were mutually irreconcilable.

Since the charge brought against St. Stephen was partly false and partly true, it was his object to rebut what was false, and justify himself against all blame for what was true. Hence apology and demonstration are subtly blended throughout his appeal, but the apology is only secondary, and the demonstration is mainly meant to rouse the dormant consciences of his hearers. Charged with blasphemous words, he contents himself with the incidental refutation of this charge by the entire tenor of the language which he employs. After his courteous request for attention, his very first words are to speak of God under one of His most awful titles of majesty, as the God of the Shechinah. On the history of Moses he dwells with all the enthusiasm of patriotic admiration. To the Temple he alludes with entire reverence. Of Sinai and the living oracles he uses language as full of solemnity as the most devoted Rabbi could desire. But while he thus shows how impossible it must have been for him to have uttered the language of a blasphemer, he is all the while aiming at the establishment of facts far deeper than the proof of his own innocence. The consummate art of his speech consists in the circumstance that while he seems to be engaged in a calm, historical review, to which any Jewish patriot might listen with delight and pride, he is step by step leading up to conclusions which told with irresistible force against the opinions of his judges. While he only seems to be reviewing the various migrations of Abraham, and the chequered fortunes of the Patriarchs, he is really showing that the covenants of God with His chosen people, having been made in Ur and Haran and Egypt, were all parts of one progressive purpose, which was so little dependent on ceremonials or places as to have been anterior not only to the existence of the Tabernacle and Temple, not only to the possession of the Holy Land, but even to the rite of circumcision itself.[1]

[1] What fruit the argument bore in the mind of St. Paul we may see in the emphasis with which he dwells on "that faith of our father Abraham which he had being yet uncircumcised" (Rom. iv. 12). How necessary it was to point this out will be seen from the opinions of succeeding Rabbis. "Abraham," says Rabbi—as "Juda the Holy," the compiler of the Mishna, is called, κατ' ἐξοχήν—"was not called perfect until he was circumcised, and by the merit of circumcision a covenant was made with him respecting the giving of the land" (*Joreh Deah*, 260, *ap.* McCaul, *Old Paths*, p. 451; *Nedarim*, f. 31, 2) It is superfluous to add that the latter statement is a flat contradiction of Gen. xv. 18.

While sketching the career of Joseph, he is pointing allusively to the similar rejection of a deliverer greater than Joseph. While passing in review the triple periods of forty years which made up the life of Moses, he is again sketching the ministry of Christ, and silently pointing to the fact that the Hebrew race had at every stage been false alike to Moses and to God. This is why he narrates the way in which, on the first appearance of Moses to help his suffering countrymen, they rudely spurned his interference; and how in spite of their rejection he was chosen to lead them out of the house of bondage. In defiance of this special commission—and it is well worth notice how, in order to conciliate their deeper attention, this palmary point in his favour is not triumphantly paraded, but quietly introduced as an incident in his historic summary—Moses had himself taught them to regard his own legislation as provisional, by bidding them listen to a Prophet like unto himself who should come hereafter. But the history of Moses, whom they trusted, was fatal to their pretence of allegiance. Even when he was on Sinai they had been disloyal to him, and spoken of him as "this Moses," and as one who had gone they knew not where.[1] And, false to Moses, they had been yet more false to God. The Levitical sacrifices had been abandoned from the very time of their institution, for sacrifices to the host of heaven; and the tabernacle of Moloch, and the star of Remphan,[2] had been dearer to them than the Tabernacle of Witness and the Shechinah of God. At last a Jesus—for, in order that he might be heard to due purpose, Stephen suppresses the name of that Jesus of whom his thoughts were full—led them and their Tabernacle into the land of which he dispossessed the Gentiles. That Tabernacle, after an obscure and dishonoured history, had passed away, and it may perhaps be intimated that this was due to their indifference and neglect. David—their own David—had indeed desired to replace it by another, but the actual building of the House was carried out by the less faithful Solomon.[3] But even at the very time the House was built it had been implied in the Prayer of David, and in the dedication prayer of Solomon,[4] that "the Most High dwelleth not in temples made with hands." And to guard against the dangerous superstition into which the reverence paid to material places is apt to degenerate—to obviate the trust in lying words which thought it sufficient to exclaim, "The Temple of the Lord, the Temple of the Lord, the Temple of the Lord are these"—the great Prophet had cried, in God's name,[5] "Heaven is my throne, and earth is my footstool; what house will ye build for me, saith the Lord, or what is the place of my abiding? Did not my hand make all these things?"

[1] Perhaps there is a passing allusion to the expression, "Jesus, this Nazarene," which they had just heard from the lips of the false witnesses.

[2] The LXX. reading for the Hebrew *Chiun*.

[3] It must remain doubtful whether any contrast is intended between the σκήνωμα (v. Suid, s.v.) designed by David, and the οἶκος built by Solomon.

[4] 1 Kings viii. 27; 1 Chron. xxix. 11; quoted by St. Paul, Acts xvii. 24.

[5] Isa. lxvi. 1, 2.

The inference from this—that the day *must* come, of which Jesus had prophesied to the woman of Samaria, in which neither in Gerizim nor yet in Jerusalem should men worship the Father, constituted a perfect defence against the charge that anything which he had said could be regarded as a blasphemy against the Temple.

Thus far he had fulfilled all the objects of his speech, and had shown that injurious words had been as far as possible from his thoughts. It had become clear also from his summary of the national story that the principles which he had advocated were in accordance with the teaching of those past ages; that the rejection of Christ by the rulers of His nation was no argument against His claims; that the Temple *could* not have been meant to be the object of an endless honour; lastly, that if he had said that Jesus should change the customs which Moses had delivered, Moses himself had indicated that in God's due time his entire dispensation was destined to pass away. And he had stated the grounds from which these conclusions followed, rather than urged upon them the inferences themselves. He had done this in deference to their passions and prejudices, and in the hope of bringing the truth gently into their hearts. He might have continued the story through centuries of weak or apostate kings, stained with the blood of rejected prophets, down to the great retribution of the exile; and he might have shown how, after the exile, the obsolete idolatry of the gods of wood and stone had only been superseded by the subtler and more self-complacent idolatry of formalism and letter-worship; how the Book had been honoured to the oblivion of the truths which it enshrined; how in the tithing of mint and anise and cummin there had been a forgetfulness of the weightier matters of the Law; how the smoke of dead sacrifices had been thought of more avail than deeds of living mercy; how circumcision and Sabbatism had been elevated above faith and purity; how the long series of crimes against God's messengers had been consummated in the murder of the Lord of glory. A truth which is only suggested, often comes home to the heart with more force than one which is put in words, and it may have been his original design to guide rather than to refute. But if so, the faces of his audience showed that his object had failed. They were listening with stolid self-complacency to a narrative of which the significant incidents only enabled them to glory over their fathers. It was, I think, something in the aspect of his audience—some sudden conviction that to such invincible obstinacy his words were addressed in vain—which made him suddenly stop short in his review of history, and hurl in their faces the gathered thunder of his wrath and scorn.

"Stiff-necked!" he exclaimed, "and uncircumcised in your heart and in your ears, *ye* are ever in conflict with the Holy Spirit; as your fathers, so ye! Which of the prophets did not your fathers persecute? and they killed those who announced before respecting the coming of the Just, of whom ye now proved yourselves betrayers and murderers; ye who received the Law at the ordinance of angels,[1] and kept it not!"[2]

[1] Acts vii. 52; leg. ἐγένεσθε, A, B, C, D, E.

[2] Acts vii. 53, ἐλάβετε τὸν νόμον εἰς διαταγὰς ἀγγέλων; Gal. iii. 19, ὁ νόμος διαταγεὶς δι' ἀγγέλων;

A denunciation so scathing and so fearless, from the lips of a prisoner whose life depended on their will, might well have startled them; and this strong burst of righteous indignation against those whom he had addressed as "brethren and fathers," can only be accounted for by the long-pent feelings of one whose patience has been exhausted. But he could hardly have addressed them in words more calculated to kindle their fury. The very terms in which he characterised their bearing, being borrowed from their own Law and Prophets, added force to the previous epitome of their history;[1] and to call them uncircumcised *in heart and ears* was to reject with scorn the idle fancies that circumcision alone was enough to save them from God's wrath, and that uncircumcision was worse than crime.[2] To convict them of being the true sons of their fathers, and to brand consciences, already ulcerated by a sense of guilt, with a murder worse than the worst murder of the prophets, was not only to sweep away the prestige of an authority which the people so blindly accepted, but it was to arraign his very judges and turn upon them the tables of accusation. And this he did, not only in the matter of their crucifixion of the Messiah, but also in the matter of disobedience to that Law ordained by angels of which they were at that very moment professing to vindicate the sanctity and the permanence.

It would be difficult in the entire range of literature to find a speech more skilful, more pregnant, more convincing; and it becomes truly astonishing when we remember that it seems to have been delivered on the spur of the moment.[3]

But the members of the Sanhedrin were roused to fury by the undaunted audacity of Stephen's final invective. The most excitable of Western nations can hardly imagine the raging passion which maddens a crowd of Eastern fanatics.[4] Barely able to continue the semblance of a judicial procedure, they

Deut. xxxiii. 2; LXX., ἐκ δεξιῶν αὐτοῦ ἄγγελοι μετ' αὐτοῦ; Ps. lxvii. 18; Heb. ii. 2. In Ps. lxviii. 12 they read מלאכי, "angels," for מלכי, "kings." (*Shabbath*, f. 88, 2.)

[1] Deut. ix. 6, 13; x. 16; xxx. 6; Neh. ix. 16; Ezek. xliv. 7; Jer. ix. 26.

[2] Rabbi [Juda the Holy] said "that circumcision is equivalent to all the Commandments which are in the Law" (*Nedarim*, f. 32, 1).

[3] The impression which it made on the heart of St. Paul is nowhere noticed by St. Luke, or by the Apostle himself; but the traces of that impression are a series of coincidences which confirm the genuineness of the speech. In his earliest recorded speech at Antioch he adopts the same historic method so admirably suited to insinuate truth without shocking prejudice; he quotes the same texts in the same striking phraseology and application (compare Acts vii. 48, 51, with Acts xvii. 24, Rom. ii. 29); alludes to the same tradition (Acts vii. 53, Gal. iii. 19); uses the same style of address (Acts vii. 2, xxii. 1); and gives the same marked significance to the faith of Abraham (Rom. iv. 9, Gal. iii. 7), and to God's dealings with him before the covenant of circumcision (Acts vii. 5—8, Rom. iv. 10—19). Nor can we doubt that 2 Tim. iv. 16 was an echo of the last prayer of Stephen, breathed partly on his own behalf. There are at least seven *Hagadôth* in the speech of Stephen—Acts vii. 2 (call of Abraham); 4 (death of Terah); 14 (seventy-five souls); 16 (burial of Patriarchs at Shechem); 22 (Egyptian training of Moses); 23 (forty years); 42 (desert idolatry); 53 (angels at Sinai). As for the slight instances of σφάλμα μνημονικὸν in 6, 7, 14, 16, they are mere "obiter dicta, auctoris aliud agentis." The attempt to square them rigidly with the Old Testament has led to much dishonest exegesis. The speech of St. Stephen has been called "a compendium of the Old Testament drawn up in fragments of the Septuagint" (Greenfield, *Apol. for the LXX.*, 103). "He had regard to the meaning, not to the words" (Jerome).

[4] Acts vii. 54, διεπρίοντο ταῖς καρδίαις αὐτῶν, καὶ ἔβρυχον τοὺς ὀδόντας ἐπ' αὐτόν.

expressed the agony of hatred which was sawing their hearts asunder, by outward signs which are almost unknown to modern civilisation—by that grinding and gnashing of the teeth only possible to human beings in whom "the ape and the tiger" are not yet quite dead. To reason with men whose passions had thus degraded them to the level of wild beasts would have been worse than useless. The flame of holy anger in the breast of Stephen had died away as suddenly as the lightning. It was a righteous anger; it was aimed not at them but at their infatuation; it was intended not to insult but to awaken.[1] But he saw at a glance that it had failed, and that all was now over. In one instant his thoughts had passed away to that heaven from which his inspiration had come. From those hateful faces, rendered demoniac by evil passion, his earnest gaze was turned upward and heavenward. There, in ecstasy of vision, he saw the Shechinah—the Glory of God—the Jesus "standing" as though to aid and receive him "at the right hand of God." Transported beyond all thought of peril by that divine epiphany, he exclaimed as though he wished his enemies to share his vision: "Lo! I behold the heavens parted asunder,[2] and the Son of Man standing at the right hand of God." At such a moment he would not pause to consider, he would not even be able to consider, the words he spoke; but whether it was that he recalled the Messianic title by which Jesus had so often described himself on earth, or that he remembered that this title had been used by the Lord when He had prophesied to this very Sanhedrin that hereafter they should see the Son of Man sitting on the right hand of power—certain it is that this is the only passage of the New Testament where Jesus is called the Son of Man by lips other than His own.[3]

But those high words were too much for the feelings of his audience. Stopping their ears as though to shut out a polluting blasphemy, they rose in a mass from both sides of the semi-circular range in which they sat, and with one wild yell[4] rushed upon Stephen. There was no question any longer of a legal decision. In their rage they took the law into their own hands, and then and there dragged him off to be stoned outside the city gate.[5]

We can judge how fierce must have been the rage which turned a solemn Sanhedrin into a mob of murderers. It was true that they were at this moment under Sadducean influence, and that this influence, as at the Trial of Christ, was mainly wielded by the family of Hanan, who were the most merciless members of that least merciful sect. If, as there is reason to believe, the martyrdom took place A.D. 37, it was most probably during the brief presidency of the High Priest Jonathan, son of Hanan. Unhappy family of the man whom Josephus pronounces to have been so exceptionally blest! The hoary father, and his son-in-law Caiaphas, imbrued their hands in the blood of Jesus; Jonathan during his few months' term of office was the Nasi of the Sanhedrin which murdered Stephen; Theophilus, another son, was the High

[1] "Non fratri irascitur qui peccato fratris irascitur" (Aug.).

[2] Acts vii. 56, leg., διηνοιγμένους, ℵ, A, B, C.

[3] See, however, Rev. i. 13; xiv. 14.

[4] Acts vii. 57, κράξαντες φωνῇ μεγάλῃ.

[5] See Excursus VI., "Capital Punishments."

Priest who, during the utmost virulence of the first persecution gave Saul his inquisitorial commission to Damascus; Matthias, another son, must, from the date of his elevation, have been one of those leading Jews whom Herod Agrippa tried to conciliate by the murder of James the son of Zebedee; and another Hanan, the youngest son of the "viper brood" brought about with illegal violence the murder of James the brother of the Lord.[1] Thus all these judicial murders—so rare at this epoch—were aimed at the followers of Jesus, and all of them directed or sanctioned by the cunning, avaricious, unscrupulous members of a single family of Sadducean priests.[2]

Stephen, then, was hurried away to execution with a total disregard of the ordinary observances. His thoughts were evidently occupied with the sad scene of Calvary; it would come home to him with all the greater vividness because he passed in all probability through that very gate through which Jesus, four short years before, had borne His cross. It was almost in the words of his Master[3] that when the horrid butchery began—for the precautions to render death speedy seem to have been neglected in the blind rage of his murderers—he exclaimed, "Lord Jesus, receive my spirit."[4] And when bruised and bleeding he was just able to drag himself to his knees it was again in the spirit of that Lord that he prayed for his murderers, and even the cry of his anguish rang forth in the forgiving utterance—showing how little malice there had been in the stern words he had used before—"Lord, lay not to their charge this sin."[5] With that cry he passed from the wrath of men to the peace of God. The historian ends the bloody tragedy with one weighty and beautiful word, "He fell asleep."[6]

To fulfil their dreadful task, the witnesses had taken off their garments;[7] and they laid them "at the feet of a young man whose name was Saul."

It is the first allusion in history to a name, destined from that day forward to be memorable for ever in the annals of the world. And how sad an allusion! He stands, not indeed actively engaged in the work of death; but keeping the clothes, consenting to the violence, of those who, in this brutal

[1] Jos. *Antt.* xviii. 4, § 3; 5, § 3; xix. 6, § 2; xx. 9, § 1.

[2] Every epithet I have used is more than justified by what we know of this family from the New Testament, from Josephus, and, above all, from the Talmud. See Excursus VII., "The Power of the Sanhedrin to Inflict Death."

[3] Luke xxiii. 34, 46.

[4] ἐπικαλούμενον means "calling on Jesus." There is no need for the ingenious conjecture of Bentley that Θ̄Ν is lost by homoeoteleuton of the ON.

[5] This—not as in the Received text—is the proper order of the words (ℵ, A, B, C, D). "Saevire videbatur Stephanus: lingua ferox, cor lene" (Aug. *Serm.* 315). "Si Stephanus non orasset ecclesia Paulum non habuisset." With the expression itself comp. Rev. xiv. 13. Perhaps in the word στήσῃς we may see an allusion to the Jewish notion that a man's sins actually followed and stood by him in the world to come (1 Tim. v. 24; *Sotah*, f. 3, 2).

[6] So in a beautiful epigram of the Anthology, we find the lines, ἱερὸν ὕπνον κοιμᾶται· θνήσκειν μὴ λέγε τοὺς ἀγαθούς. It is the *Neshikah* of the Jews (Deut. xxxiv. 8). That the solemn rhythmical epitrite ἐκοιμήθη is not wholly unintentional seems to be clear from the similar weighty ἀκωλύτως with which, as Bishop Wordsworth points out, the Acts of the Apostles ends. St. Luke is evidently fond of paronomasia, as well as St. Paul (cf. κατηξιώθησαν ἀτιμασθῆναι, Acts v. 41). This is the third recorded death in the Christian community: the first had been a suicide, the second a judgment, the third a martyrdom.

[7] This custom is not alluded to in the Mishna or Gemara.

manner, dimmed in blood the light upon a face which had been radiant as that of an angel with faith and love.

Stephen was dead, and it might well have seemed that all the truth which was to be the glory and the strength of Christianity had died with him. But the deliverance of the Gentiles, and their free redemption by the blood of Christ, were truths too glorious to be quenched. The truth may be suppressed for a time, even for a long time, but it always starts up again from its apparent grave. Fra Dolcino was torn to pieces, and Savonarola and Huss were burnt, but the Reformation was not prevented. Stephen sank in his blood, but his place was taken by the young man who stood there to incite his murderers. Four years after Jesus had died upon the cross of infamy, Stephen was stoned for being His disciple and His worshipper; thirty years after the death of Stephen, his deadliest opponent died also for the same holy faith.

Book III.

THE CONVERSION.

CHAPTER IX.

SAUL THE PERSECUTOR.

Ποτὶ κέντρον δέ τοι λακτίζεμεν
τελέθει ὀλίσθηρος οἶμος.—PIND. *Pyth.* ii. 173.

"AT a young man's feet." The expression is vague, but there is good reason to believe that Saul was now not less than thirty years old.[1] The reverence for age, strong among all Orientals, was specially strong among the Jews, and they never entrusted authority to those who had not attained to full years of discretion. We may regard it as certain that even a scholar of Gamaliel, so full of genius and of zeal as Saul, would not have been appointed a commissioner of the Sanhedrin to carry out a responsible inquisition earlier than the age of thirty; and if we attach a literal meaning to the expression, "When they were being condemned to death, I gave a vote against them,"[2] this implies that Saul was a member of the Sanhedrin. If so, he was at this time, by the very condition of that dignity, a married man.[3]

1 Josephus uses *νεανίας* of Agrippa I. when he must have been at least forty (*Antt.* xviii. 6, §7; *v. supra*, p. 7).

2 Acts xxvi. 10, *ἀναιρουμένων τε αὐτῶν κατήνεγκα ψῆφον.*

3 Selden, *De Synedr.* ii. 7, 7. In the Mishna the only qualifications mentioned for membership of the Sanhedrin are that a man must not be a dicer, usurer, pigeon-flyer, or dealer in the produce of the Sabbatical year (*Sanhedr.* iii. 3); but in the Gemara, and in later Jewish writers, we find that, besides the qualification mentioned in Exod. xviii. 21, and Deut. i. 13—16, a candidate must be free from every physical blemish, stainless in character, learned in science, acquainted with more than one language, and with a family

But if the regulation that a Sanhedrist must be a married man was intended to secure the spirit of gentleness,[1] the rule had failed of its purpose in the case of Saul. In the terrible persecution of the Christians which ensued—a persecution far more severe than the former attacks of the Sadducees on the Apostles—he was the heart and soul of the endeavour to stamp out the Christian faith. Not content with the flagging fanaticism of the Sanhedrin, he was at once the prime mover and the chief executor of religious vengeance. The charge which had cost St. Stephen his life must have been partially valid against others of the Hellenistic Christians, and although their views might be more liberal than those of the Galilæan disciples, yet the bonds of affection between the two branches of the Church were still so close that the fate of one section could not be dissevered from that of the other. The Jews were not naturally fond of persecution. The Sanhedrin of this period had incurred the charge of disgraceful laxity. The *Sicarii* were not suppressed; the red heifer was slain no longer;[2] the ordeal of the bitter water had been done away, *because* the crime of adultery had greatly increased.[3] Rabbi Joshua Ben Korcha, when R. Elieser had arrested some thieves, reproached him with the words, "How long will you hand over the people of God to destruction? Leave the thorns to be plucked up by the Lord of the vineyard."[4] But to the seducer (*mesith*), the blasphemer (*megadeph*), and the idolater, there was neither leniency nor compassion.[5] By the unanimous testimony of the Jews themselves, Christians could not be charged with the crime of idolatry;[6] but it was easy to bring them under the penalty of stoning, which was attached to the former crimes. The minor punishments of flagellation and excommunication seem to have been in the power, not only of the Sanhedrin, but even of each local synagogue. Whatever may have been the legal powers of these bodies, whatever licences the temporary relaxation of Roman supervision may have permitted,[7] they were used and abused to the utmost by the youthful zealot. The wisdom of the toleration which Gamaliel himself had recommended appears in the fact that the great persecution, which broke up the Church at Jerusalem, was in every way valuable to the new religion. It dissipated the Judaism which would have endangered the

of his own, because such were supposed to be less inclined to cruelty, and more likely to sympathise with domestic affections. (*Horajoth*, i. 4; *Sanhedr.* f. 17, 1, 36, *b.*; *Menachôth*, f. 65, 1; Maimon. *Sanhedr.* ii.; Otho, *Lex. Rabb.* s. v.) Whatever may be thought of the other qualifications, it is probable that this one, at any rate, was insisted on, and it adds force to our impression that St. Paul had once been a married man (1 Cor. vii. 8; *v. supra*, p. 45, sq. See Ewald, *Sendschr. d. Ap. Paul.* p. 161; *Gesch. d. Apost. Zeitalt.* p. 371).

[1] See Surenhus. *Mishna*, iv. *Praef.*

[2] *Sotah*, f. 47, 1.

[3] Maimon. in *Sotah*, c. 3. They quoted Hos. iv. 14 in favour of this abolition of Num. v. 18. Cf. Matt. xii. 39; xvi. 4.

[4] *Babha Metzia*, f. 82, 2; Otho, *Lex. Rabb.*, s. v. Synedrium.

[5] Deut. xiii. 8, 9; *Sanhedr.* f. 29, 1; 32, 3.

[6] There is not one word about the Christians in the tract *Abhôda Zara*, or on "alien worship."

[7] Marcellus, who was at this time an *ad interim* governor, held the rank, not of Procurator, ἡγεμών, but only of ἐπιμελητής (Jos. *Antt.* xviii. 4, § 2).

spread of Christianity, and showed that the disciples had a loftier mission than to dwindle down into a Galilæan synagogue. The sacred fire, which might have burnt low on the hearth of the upper chamber at Jerusalem, was kindled into fresh heat and splendour when its brands were scattered over all Judæa and Samaria, and uncircumcised Gentiles were admitted by baptism into the fold of Christ.

The solemn burial of Stephen by holy men—whether Hellenist Christians or Jewish proselytes—the beating of the breast, the wringing of the hands with which they lamented him,[1] produced no change in the purpose of Saul. The sight of that dreadful execution, the dying agonies and crushed remains of one who had stood before the Sanhedrin like an angel in the beauty of holiness, could hardly have failed to produce an impression on a heart so naturally tender. But if it was a torture to witness the agony of others, and to be the chief agent in its infliction, then that very torture became a more meritorious service for the Law. If his own blameless scrupulosity in all that affected legal righteousness was beginning to be secretly tainted with heretical uncertainties, he would feel it all the more incumbent on him to wash away those doubts in blood. Like Cardinal Pole, when Paul IV. began to impugn his orthodoxy, he must have felt himself half driven to persecution, in order to prove his soundness in the faith.

The part which he played at this time in the horrid work of persecution has, I fear, been always underrated. It is only when we collect the separate passages—they are no less than eight in number—in which allusion is made to this sad period—it is only when we weigh the terrible significance of the expressions used—that we feel the load of remorse which must have lain upon him, and the taunts to which he was liable from malignant enemies. He "made havoc of"—literally, "he was ravaging"—the Church.[2] No stronger metaphor could well have been used. It occurs nowhere else in the New Testament, but in the Septuagint, and in classical Greek, is applied to the wild boars which uproot a vineyard.[3] Not content with the visitation of the synagogues, he got authority for an inquisitorial visit from house to house, and even from the sacred retirement of the Christian home he dragged not only men, but women, to judgment and to prison.[4] So thorough was his search, and so deadly were its effects, that, in referring to it, the Christians of Damascus can only speak of Saul as "he that *devastated* in Jerusalem them that call on this name,"[5] using the strong word which is strictly applicable to an invading army which scathes a conquered country with fire and sword. So much St. Luke tells us, in giving a reason for the total scattering of the Church, and the subsequent bless-

[1] Acts viii. 2, κοπετὸς μέγας. The word is found in the LXX., Gen. l. 10, &c., but here alone in the New Testament.

[2] Acts viii. 3, ἐλυμαίνετο τὴν ἐκκλησίαν.

[3] Ps. lxxix. 14; Callim. *Hymn. in Dian.* 156, σύες ἔργα σύες φυτὰ λυμαίνονται.

[4] These hostile measures are summed up in the ὅσα κακὰ ἐποίησε τοῖς ἁγίοις of Ananias, who says that the rumour had reached him from many sources (Acts ix. 13).

[5] Acts ix. 21, ὁ πορθήσας.

ings which sprang from their preaching the Word in wider districts. The Apostles, he adds, remained. What was the special reason for this we do not know; but as the Lord's direct permission to the seventy to fly before persecution[1] would have sanctioned their consulting their own safety, it may have been because Jesus had bidden them stay in Jerusalem till the end of twelve years.[2] If, as St. Chrysostom imagines, they stayed to support the courage of others, how was it that the shepherds escaped while the flock was being destroyed? Or are we to infer that the main fury of the persecution fell upon those Hellenists who shared the views of the first martyr, and that the Apostles were saved from molestation by the blameless Mosaism of which one of the leading brethren—no less a person than James, the Lord's brother—was so conspicuous an example? Be that as it may, at any rate they did not fall victims to the rage which was so fatal to many of their companions.

In two of his speeches and four of his letters does St. Paul revert to this crime of an erring obstinacy. Twice to the Galatians does he use the same strong metaphor which was applied to his conduct by the Damascene believers.[3] He tells the Corinthians[4] that he was "the least of the Apostles, not meet to be called an Apostle, because he persecuted the Church of God." He reminds the Philippians[5] that his old Hebraic zeal as a Pharisee had shown itself by his "persecuting the Church." And even when the shadows of a troubled old age were beginning to close around him, keen in the sense that he was utterly forgiven through Him who "came into the world to save sinners, of whom I am chief," he cannot forget the bitter thought that, though in ignorance, he had once been "a blasphemer, and persecutor, and injurious."[6] And when he is speaking to those who knew the worst—in his speech to the raging mob of Jerusalem, as he stood on the steps of the Tower of Antonia—he adds one fact more which casts a lurid light on the annals of the persecution. He shows there that the blood of Stephen was not the only blood that had been shed—not the only blood of which the stains had incarnadined his conscience. He tells the mob not only of the binding and imprisonment of women as well as men, but also that he "persecuted this way *unto the death*."[7] Lastly, in his speech at Cæsarea, he adds what is perhaps the darkest touch of all, for he says that, armed with the High Priest's authority, he not only fulfilled unwittingly the prophecy of Christ[8] by scourging the Christians "often" and "in every synagogue," but that, *when it came to the question of death*, he gave his vote against them, and that he *did his best to compel them to blaspheme*.[9] I say "did his best," because

[1] Matt. x. 23.

[2] *V. infra*, p. 180. A brief visit to Samaria "to confirm the churches" (Acts viii. 14) would not militate against this command.

[3] Gal. i. 13, where he also says that he persecuted them beyond measure (καθ' ὑπερβολήν); and i. 23.

[4] 1 Cor. xv. 9. [5] Phil. iii. 6. [6] 1 Tim. i. 13. [7] Acts xxii. 4.

[8] Matt. x. 17; Mark xiii. 9.

[9] Acts xxvi. 11, ἠνάγκαζον βλασφημεῖν. There is a possibility that in the ἄχρι θανάτου of the previous passage, and the κατήνεγκα ψῆφον of this, St. Paul may allude to his

the tense he uses implies effort, but not necessarily success. Pliny, in a passage of his famous letter to Trajan from Bithynia,[1] says that, in questioning those who, in anonymous letters, were accused of being "Christians," he thought it sufficient to test them by making them offer wine and incense to the statues of the gods and the bust of the emperor, and to blaspheme the name of Christ; and, if they were willing to do this, he dismissed them without further inquiry, because he had been informed that to no one of these things could a genuine Christian ever be impelled.

We do not know that in all the sufferings of the Apostle any attempt was ever made to compel him to blaspheme. With all the other persecutions which he made the Christian suffer he became in his future life too sadly familiar. To the last dregs of lonely and unpitied martyrdom he drank the bitter cup of merciless persecution. Five times—in days when he was no longer the haughty Rabbi, the self-righteous Pharisee, the fierce legate of the Sanhedrin armed with unlimited authority for the suppression of heresy, but was himself the scorned, hunted, hated, half-starved missionary of that which was branded as an apostate sect—five times, from the authority of some ruler of the synagogue, did he receive forty stripes save one. He, too, was stoned, and betrayed, and many times imprisoned, and had the vote of death recorded against him; and in all this he recognised the just and merciful flame that purged away the dross of a once misguided soul—the light affliction which he had deserved, but which was not comparable to the far more eternal weight of glory. In all this he may have even rejoiced that he was bearing for Christ's sake that which he had made others bear, and passing through the same furnace which he had once heated sevenfold for them. But I doubt whether any one of these sufferings, or all of them put together, ever wrung his soul with the same degree of anguish as that which lay in the thought that he had used all the force of his character and all the tyranny of his intolerance to break the bruised reed and to quench the smoking flax—that he had endeavoured, by the infamous power of terror and anguish, to compel some gentle heart to blaspheme its Lord.

The great persecution with which St. Paul was thus identified—and which, from these frequent allusions, as well as from the intensity of the language employed, seems to me to have been more terrible than is usually admitted—did not spend its fury for some months. In Jerusalem it was entirely successful. There were no more preachings or wonders in Solomon's Porch; no more throngs that gathered in the streets to wait the passing shadow of Peter and John; no more assembled multitudes in the house of Mary, the mother of St. Mark. If the Christians met, they met in mournful secrecy and diminished numbers, and the Love-feasts, if held at all, must have been held as in the

own endeavour (cf. Gal. vi. 12) to have them capitally punished, without implying that the vote was carried. I have translated the ἀναιρουμένων so as to admit of this meaning, which, perhaps, acquires a shade of additional probability from Heb. xii. 4, "Ye have not yet resisted unto blood," if that Epistle was specially addressed to Palestinian Jews.

[1] Plin. *Ep.* x. 97 . . . . "praeterea maledicere Christo; *quorum nihil cogi posse dicuntur* qui sunt revera Christiani."

early days before the Ascension, with doors closed, for fear of the Jews. Some of the Christians had suffered cruelly for their religion; the faithless members of the Church had doubtless apostatised; the majority had fled at once before the storm.[1]

It is, perhaps, to indicate the *continuance* of this active hostility that St. Luke here inserts the narrative of Philip's preaching as a fitting prelude to the work of the Apostle of the Gentiles. At this narrative we shall glance hereafter; but now we must follow the career of Saul the Inquisitor, and see the marvellous event which, by one lightning flash, made him "a *fusile* Apostle"—which in one day transformed Saul the persecutor into Paul the slave of Jesus Christ.

His work in Jerusalem was over. The brethren who remained had either eluded his search-warrant, or been rescued from his power. But the young zealot was not the man to do anything by halves. If he had smitten one head of the hydra,[2] it had grown up in new places. If he had torn up the heresy by the roots from the Holy City, the winged seeds had alighted on other fertile ground, and the rank weed was still luxuriant elsewhere; so that, in his outrageous madness—it is his own expression[3]—he began to pursue them even to foreign cities. Damascus, he had heard, was now the worst nest of this hateful delusion, and fortunately in that city he could find scope for action; for the vast multitude of Jews which it contained acknowledged allegiance to the Sanhedrin. To the High Priest, therefore, he went—unsated by all his previous cruelties, and in a frame of mind so hot with rage that again it can only be described by the unparalleled phrase that he was "breathing threats and slaughter against the disciples of the Lord."[4] The High Priest—in all probability Theophilus, who was promoted by Vitellius at the Pentecost of A.D. 37[5]—was a Sadducee, and a son of the hated house of Hanan. Yet it was with Saul, and not with Theophilus, that the demand originated, to pursue the heresy to Damascus.[6] Not sorry to find so thorough an instrument in one who belonged to a different school from his own—not sorry that the guilty responsibility for "this man's blood" should be shared by Sadducees with the followers of Hillel—Theophilus gave the letters which authorised Saul to set up his court at Damascus, and to bring from thence in chains all whom he could find, both men and women, to await such mercy as Stephen's murder might lead them to hope for at the hands of the supreme tribunal.[7] In ordinary

[1] This is implied in the ἐν ἐκείνῃ τῇ ἡμέρᾳ, and in the aorist διεσπάρησαν of Acts viii. 1.

[2] Domitian and Maximin struck medals of Hercules and the Hydra with the inscription "Deletâ religione Christianâ quae orbem turbabat."

[3] Acts xxvi. 11, περισσῶς ἐμμαινόμενος αὐτοῖς.

[4] Acts ix. 1, ἐμπνέων ἀπειλῆς καὶ φόνου.

[5] Jos. *Antt.* xviii. 5, § 3.

[6] Acts ix. 2, "If he should find any of *the way*." The word Χριστιανισμός was invented later (*infra*, p. 167). The Jewish writers similarly speak of the "*derek* ha-Notserim," or "way of the Nazarenes."

[7] The repeated allusions to the punishment of women shows not only the keenness of the search, but also the large part played by Christian women in the spread of that religion which first elevated their condition from the degradation of the harem and the narrowness of the gynaeceum. These women-martyrs of the great persecution were the

times when that Jewish autonomy, which always meant Jewish intolerance, was repressed within stern limits by the Roman government—it would have been impossible to carry out so cruel a commission. This might have been urged as an insuperable difficulty if an incidental expression in 2 Cor. xi. 32 had not furnished a clue in explanation of the circumstances. From this it appears that at this time the city was more or less in the hands of Aretas or Hareth, the powerful Emir of Petra.[1] Now there are notices in the Talmud which prove that Hareth stood in friendly relations to the Jewish High Priest,[2] and we can see how many circumstances thus concurred to create for Saul an exceptional opportunity to bring the Christians of Damascus under the authority of the Sanhedrin. Never again might he find so favourable an opportunity of eradicating the heresy of these hated Nazarenes.

CHAPTER X.

THE CONVERSION OF SAUL.

. . . κατελήφθην ὑπὸ τοῦ Χριστοῦ Ἰησοῦ.—PHIL. iii. 12.

"Opfert freudig aus was ihr besessen
 Was ihr einst gewesen, was ihr seyd;
Und in einem seligen Vergessen
 Schwinde die Vergangenheit."—SCHILLER.

ARMED with his credentials Saul started from Jerusalem for his journey of nearly 150 miles. That journey would probably be performed exactly as it is now performed with horses and mules, which are indispensable to the traveller along those rough, bad roads, and up and down those steep and fatiguing hills. Saul, it must be remembered, was travelling in a manner very different from that of our Lord and his humble followers. They who, in preaching the Gospel to the poor, assumed no higher earthly dignity than that of the carpenter of Nazareth and the fishermen of Galilee, would go on foot with staff and scrip from village to village, like the other "people of the land" whom long-robed Scribes despised. Saul was in a very different position, and the little retinue which was assigned him would treat him with all the deference due to a Pharisee and a Rabbi—a legate *à latere* of Theophilus, the powerful High Priest.

But, however performed, the journey could not occupy less than a week, and even the fiery zeal of the persecutor would scarcely enable him to get rid

true predecessors of those Saints Catherine, and Barbara, and Lucia, and Agnes, and Dorothea, and Caecilia, and Felicitas, who leave the light of their names on the annals of Christian heroism.

[1] See Excursus VIII.: "Damascus under Hareth."

[2] A story is told that on one occasion the High Priest Simeon Ben Kamhith was incapacitated from performing the duties of the Day of Atonement, because, while familiarly talking with Hareth on the previous evening, a drop of the Emir's saliva had fallen on the High Priest's dress (cf. *Niddah*, f. 33, 2.)

of the habitual leisureliness of Eastern travelling. And thus, as they made their way along the difficult and narrow roads, Saul would be doomed to a week of necessary reflection. Hitherto, ever since those hot disputes in the synagogues of Cilician Hellenists, he had been living in a whirl of business which could have left him but little time for quiet thought. That active inquisition, those domiciliary visits, those incessant trials, that perpetual presiding over the scourgings, imprisonments, perhaps even actual stonings of men and women, into which he had been plunged, must have absorbed his whole energies, and left him no inclination to face the difficult questions, or to lay the secret misgivings which had begun to rise in his mind.[1] Pride—the pride of system, the pride of nature, the rank pride of the self-styled theologian, the exclusive national Pharisaic pride in which he had been trained—forbade him to examine seriously whether he might not after all be in the wrong. Without humility there can be no sincerity; without sincerity, no attainment of the truth. Saul felt that he could not and would not let himself be convinced; he could not and would not admit that much of the learning of his thirty years of life was a mass of worthless cobwebs, and that all the righteousness with which he had striven to hasten the coming of the Messiah was as filthy rags. He could not and would not admit the possibility that people like Peter and Stephen could be right, while people like himself and the Sanhedrin could be mistaken; or that the Messiah could be a Nazarene who had been crucified as a malefactor; or that after looking for Him so many generations, and making their whole religious life turn on His expected Advent, Israel should have been found sleeping, and have murdered Him when at last He came. If haunting doubts could for a moment thrust themselves into his thoughts, the vehement self-assertion of contempt would sweep them out, and they would be expiated by fresh zeal against the seductive glamour of the heresy which thus dared to insinuate itself like a serpent into the very hearts of its avengers. What could it be but diabolic influence which made the words and the arguments of these blasphemers of the Law and the Temple fasten involuntarily upon his mind and memory? Never would he too be seduced into the position of a *mesith!* Never would he degrade himself to the ignorant level of people who knew not the Law and were accursed!

[1] See Rom. vii. 8, 9, 10. This picture of St. Paul's mental condition is no mere imaginative touch; from all such, both in this work and in my *Life of Christ*, I have studiously abstained. It springs as a direct and inevitable conclusion from his own epistles and the reproof of Jesus, "It is hard for thee to kick against the goads." These words, following the "Why persecutest thou me?" imply, with inimitable brevity, "Seest thou not that *I* am the pursuer and *thou* the pursued?" What were those goads? There were no conceivable goads for him to resist, except those which were wielded by his own conscience. The stings of conscience, the anguish of a constant misgiving, inflicted wounds which should have told him long before that he was advancing in a wrong path. They were analogous to the warnings, both inward and outward, which "forbade the madness" of the Mesopotamian sorcerer. Balaam, too, was taught by experience how terrible a thing it is to "kick against the pricks." The resisted inward struggles of St. Paul are also implied in the "calling" of Gal. i. 15, preceding the "revelation." See Monod, *Cinq Discours*, p. 168; Stier, *Reden d. Apost.* ii. 299; De Pressensé, *Trois Prem. Siècles*, i. 434.)

But the ghosts of these obstinate questionings would not always be so laid. As long as he had work to do he could crush by passion and energy such obtruding fancies. But when his work was done—when there were in Jerusalem no more Hellenists to persecute—when even the Galilæans had fled or been silenced, or been slain—then such doubts would again thicken round him, and he would hear the approach of them like the sound of a stealthy footfall on the turf. Was it not this that kindled his excessive madness—this that made him still breathe out threats and blood? Was not this a part of the motive which had driven him to the wily Sadducee with the demand for a fresh commission? Would not this work for the Law protect him from the perplexing complications of a will that plunged and struggled to resist the agonising goad-thrusts of a ruinous misgiving?

But now that he was journeying day after day towards Damascus, how could he save himself from his own thoughts? He could not converse with the attendants who were to execute his decisions. They were mere subordinates—mere apparitors of the Sanhedrin—members, perhaps, of the Temple guard—ignorant Levites, whose function it would be to drag with them on his return the miserable gang of trembling heretics. We may be sure that the vacuity of thought in which most men live was for Saul a thing impossible. He could not help meditating as the sages bade the religious Jew to meditate, on the precepts and promises of his own Law. For the first time perhaps since he had encountered Stephen he had the uninterrupted leisure to face the whole question calmly and seriously, in the solitude of thoughts which could no longer be sophisticated by the applause of Pharisaic partisans. He was forced to go up into the dark tribunal of his own conscience, and set himself before himself. More terrible by far was the solemnity, more impartial the judgment of that stern session, than those either of the Jewish Sanhedrin, or of that other Areopagus in which he would one day stand. If there be in the character any seriousness at all; if the cancer of conceit or vice have not eaten out all of the heart that is not frivolous and base, then how many a man's intellectual conclusions, how many a man's moral life has been completely changed—and for how many would they not at this moment be completely changed—by the *necessity* for serious reflection during a few days of unbroken leisure?

And so we may be quite sure that day after day, as he rode on under the morning sunlight or the bright stars of an Eastern night, the thoughts of Saul would be overwhelmingly engaged. They would wander back over the past; they would glance sadly at the future. Those were happy years in Tarsus; happy walks in childhood beside "the silver Cydnus;" happy hours in the school of Gamaliel, where there first dawned upon his soul the glories of Moses and Solomon, of the Law and the Temple, of the Priesthood and the chosen race. Those were golden days when he listened to the promised triumphs of the Messiah, and was told how near was that day when the Holy Land should be exalted as the Lady of kingdoms, and when the vaunted strength of Rome, which now lay so heavy on his subjugated people, should be shattered like a potsherd! But had not something of the splendour faded from these more youthful dreams? What had the righteousness of the Law done for him? He had lived, as far as men were concerned, an honourable life. He had been exceedingly zealous, exceedingly blameless in the traditions of the fathers; but what inward joy had he derived from them?—what enlightenment?—what deliverance from that law of his members, which, do what he would, still worked fatally against the law in his mind? His sins of pride and passion, and frailty—would not a jealous God avenge them? Was there any exemption at all from the Law's curse of "death?" Was there any deliverance at all from this ceaseless trouble of a nature dissatisfied with itself, and therefore wavering like a wave of the troubled sea?

Would the deliverance be secured by the coming of the Messiah? That advent for the nation would be triumph and victory; would it be for the individual also, peace of conscience, justification, release from heavy bondage, forgiveness of past sins, strength in present weakness?

And then it must have flashed across him that these Nazarenes, at any rate, whom he had been hunting and slaying, said that it would. For them the Messiah had come, and certainly they had found peace. It was true that their Messiah was despised and rejected; but was not that the very thing which had been said of the Servant of Jehovah in that prophecy to which they always appealed, and which also said that which his troubled conscience needed most:—

"Surely He hath borne our griefs and carried our sorrows: yet we did esteem Him stricken, smitten of God, and afflicted. But he was wounded for our transgressions, He was bruised for our iniquities: the chastisement of our peace was upon him; and with His stripes we are healed. All we like sheep have gone astray; we have turned every one to his own way; and the Lord hath laid on Him the iniquity of us all."[1]

This passage certainly gave a very different aspect to the conception of the Messiah from any which he had been taught to contemplate. Yet the Rabbis had said that *all* prophecies were Messianic. Jesus had been crucified. A crucified Messiah was a horrible thought; but was it worse than a Messiah who should be a leper? Yet here the ideal servant of Jehovah was called a leper.[2] And if His physical condition turned out to be meaner than Israel had always expected, yet surely the moral conception, the spiritual conception, as he had heard it from these hated Galilæans, was infinitely lovelier! They spoke—and oh, undeniably those were blessed words!—of a Messiah through whom they obtained forgiveness of sins. If this were true, what infinite comfort it brought! how it ended the hopelessness of the weary struggle! The Law, indeed, promised life to perfect obedience.[3] But who ever had attained, who *could* attain, to that perfect obedience?[4] Did he see it in the Gentile world, who, though they had not the Law of Moses had

[1] Isa. liii. 4—6.

[2] Isa. lii. 14, liii. 4, "*stricken*," Heb.; cf. Lev. xiii. 13, *Sanhedr.* f. 98.

[3] Lev xviii. 5; Gal. iii. 12.

[4] Rom. x. 5.

their own law of nature?—Did he see it in the Jewish world?—alas, what a depth of disappointment was involved in the very question! Was Hanan, was Caiaphas, was Theophilus, was Ishmael Ben Phabi a specimen of the righteousness of the Law? And if, as was too true, Israel had not attained—if he himself had not attained—to the law of righteousness, what hope was there?[1] Oh, the blessedness of him whose unrighteousness was forgiven, whose sin was covered! Oh, the blessedness of him to whom the Lord would not impute sin! Oh, to have the infinite God who seemed so far away brought near, and to see His face not darkened by the cloud, not glaring through the pillar of fire, but as a man seeth the face of his friend! Oh, that a Man were a hiding-place from the wind, and a covert from the tempest, as the shadow of a great rock in a weary land![2]

And so, again and again, he would realise with a sense of remorse that he was yearning for, that he was gliding into, the very doctrines which he was persecuting to the death. For to these Nazarenes their Son of Man was indeed the image of the Invisible God. Could he be right in thus striving to stamp out a faith so pure, so ennobling? For whether it was heresy or not, that it was pure and ennobling he could not fail to acknowledge. That face of Stephen which he had seen bathed as with a light from heaven until it had been dimmed in blood, must have haunted him then, as we know it did for long years afterwards. Would the Mosaic law have inspired so heavenly an enthusiasm? would it have breathed into the sufferers so infinite a serenity, so bright a hope? And where in all the Holy Pentateuch could he find utterances so tender, lessons so divine, love so unspeakable, motives which so mastered and entranced the soul, as these had found in the words and in the love of their Lord? Those beatitudes which he had heard them speak of, the deeds of healing tenderness which so many attested, the parables so full of divine illumination—the moral and spiritual truths of a Teacher who, though His nation had crucified Him, had spoken as never man spake—oh, Who was this who had inspired simple fishermen and ignorant publicans with a wisdom unattainable by a Hillel or a Gamaliel? Who was this to whom His followers turned their last gaze and uttered their last prayer in death; who seemed to breathe upon them from the parted heavens a glory as of the Shechinah, a peace that passed all understanding? Who was this who, as they declared, had risen from the dead; whose body certainly had vanished from the rock-hewn sepulchre in which it had been laid; whom these good Galilæans—these men who would rather die than lie—witnessed that they had seen, that they had heard, that He had appeared to them in the garden, in the upper chamber, on the public road, to four of them upon the misty lake, to more than five hundred of them at once upon the Galilæan hill? Could that have been a right path which led him to

[1] Rom. ix. 31. When Rabbi Eleazar was sick, and Akibha rejoiced because he feared that Eleazar had been receiving his good things in this life, "Akibha," exclaimed the sufferer, "is there anything in the whole Law which I have failed to fulfil?" "Rabbi," replied Akibha, "thou hast taught me 'There is not a just man upon earth that doeth good, and sinneth not.'" Eccles. vii. 20. (*Sanhedr.* f. 101, 1.)

[2] Isa. xxxii. 2.

persecute these? could it be God's will which had driven him so fiercely along a road that was stained in blood? could he be required to pass through those scenes of horror in which he had haled the wife and the mother to prison, and seen the coarse menials of the synagogue remorselessly scourge men whose

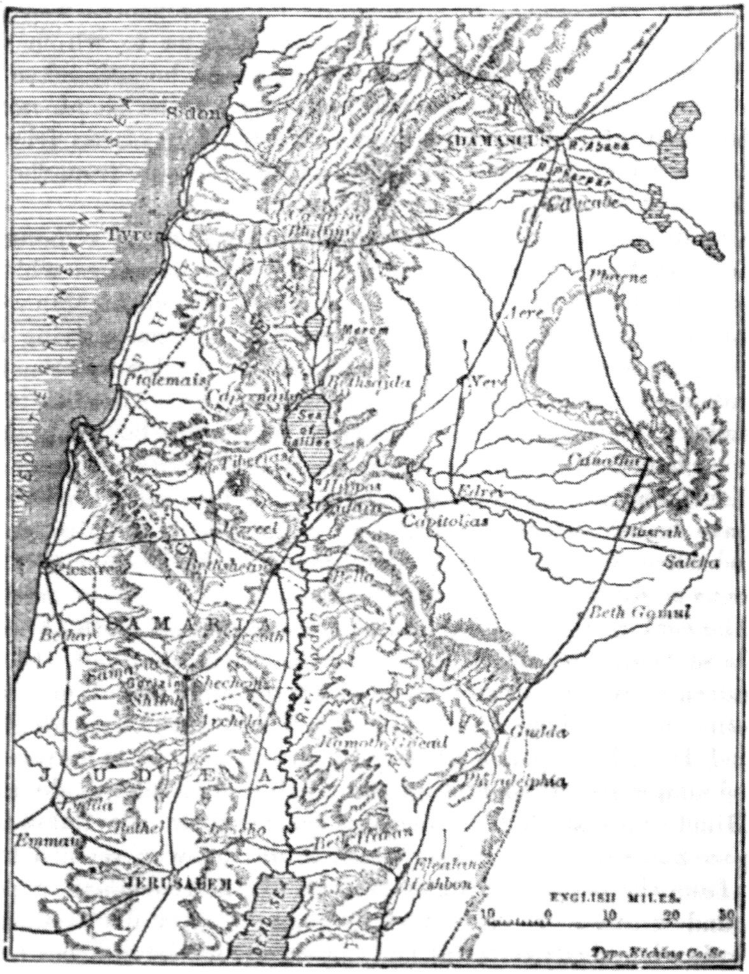

MAP SHOWING THE ROADS FROM JERUSALEM TO DAMASCUS.

life was love and humility and holiness? Had he after all been mistaking pride for faithfulness, and rage for zeal? Had he been murdering the saints that were upon the earth, and them that excelled in virtue? Was Gamaliel right in suggesting the possibility that in meddling with these men they might haply be fighting against God?

So day by day, his mind filled more and more with distracting doubts, his imagination haunted by sights of cruelty which, in spite of all zeal, harrowed up his soul, he journeyed on the road to Damascus. Under ordinary circumstances he might have felt an interest in the towns and scenes through which he passed—in Bethel and Shiloh—in the soft green fields that lie around the base of Mount Gerizim—in Jacob's tomb and Jacob's well—in Bethshean, with its memories of the miserable end of that old king of his tribe whose name he bore—in the blue glimpses of the Lake of Galilee with its numberless memorials of that Prophet of Nazareth whose followers he was trying to destroy. But during these days, if I judge rightly, his one desire was to press on, and by vehement action to get rid of painful thought.

And now the journey was nearly over. Hermon had long been gleaming before them, and the chain of Antilibanus. They had been traversing a bare, bleak, glaring, undulating plain, and had reached the village of Kaukab, or "the Star." At that point a vision of surpassing beauty bursts upon the eye of the weary traveller. Thanks to the "golden Abana" and the winding Pharpar, which flow on either side of the ridge, the wilderness blossoms like the rose. Instead of brown and stony wastes, we begin to pass under the flickering shadows of ancient olive-trees. Below, out of a soft sea of verdure—amid masses of the foliage of walnuts and pomegranates and palms, steeped in the rich haze of sunshine—rise the white terraced roofs and glittering cupolas of the immemorial city of which the beauty has been compared in every age to the beauty of a Paradise of God. There amid its gardens of rose, and groves of delicious fruit, with the gleam of waters that flowed through it, flooded with the gold of breathless morn, lay the eye of the East.[1] To that land of streams, to that city of fountains, to that Paradise of God, Saul was hastening—not on messages of mercy, not to add to the happiness and beauty of the world—but to scourge and to slay and to imprison, those perhaps of all its inhabitants who were the meekest, the gentlest, the most pure of heart. And Saul, with all his tenacity of purpose, was a man of almost emotional tenderness of character.[2] Though zeal and passion might hurry him into acts of cruelty, they could not crush within him the instincts of sympathy, and the horror of suffering and blood. Can we doubt that at the sight of the lovely glittering city—like (if I may again quote the Eastern metaphor) "a handful of pearls in its goblet of emerald"—he felt one more terrible recoil from his unhallowed task, one yet fiercer thrust from the wounding goad of a reproachful conscience?

It was high noon—and in a Syrian noon the sun shines fiercely overhead in an intolerable blaze of boundless light—the cloudless sky glows like molten brass; the white earth under the feet glares like iron in the furnace; the whole air, as we breathe it, seems to quiver as though it were pervaded with subtle flames. That Saul and his comrades should at such a moment have still been pressing forward on their journey would seem to argue a troubled impatience, an impassioned haste. Generally at that time of day the traveller

[1] See Porter's *Syria*, p. 435.
[2] See Adolphe Monod's sermon, *Les Larmes de St. Paul.*

will be resting in his khan, or lying under the shelter of his tent. But it was Saul who would regulate the movements of his little company; and Saul was pressing on.

Then suddenly all was ended—the eager haste, the agonising struggle, the deadly mission, the mad infatuation, the feverish desire to quench doubt in persecution. Round them suddenly from heaven there lightened a great light.[1] It was not Saul alone who was conscious of it. It seemed as though the whole atmosphere had caught fire, and they were suddenly wrapped in sheets of blinding splendour. It might be imagined that nothing can out-dazzle the glare of a Syrian sun at noon; but this light was more vivid than its brightness, more penetrating than its flame. And with the light came to those who journeyed with Saul an awful but unintelligible sound. As though by some universal flash from heaven they were all struck to earth together, and when the others had arisen and had partially recovered from their terror, Saul was still prostrate there. They were conscious that something awful had happened. Had we been able to ask them what it was, it is more than doubtful whether they could have said. Had it been suggested to them that it was some overwhelming sudden burst of thunder, some inexpressibly vivid gleam of electric flame—some blinding, suffocating, maddening breath of the sirocco—some rare phenomenon unexperienced before or since—they might not have known. The vision was not for them. They saw the light above the noonday—they heard, and heard with terror, the unknown sound which shattered the dead hush of noon; but they were not converted by this epiphany. To the Jew the whole earth was full of God's visible ministrants. The winds were His spirits, the flaming fires His messengers; the thunder was the voice of the Lord shaking the cedars, yea, shaking the cedars of Libanus. The *bath-kol* might come to him in sounds which none but he could understand: others might say it thundered when to him an angel spake.[2]

But that which happened was not meant for those who journeyed with Saul:[3] it was meant for him; and of that which he saw and which he heard he confessedly could be the only witness. They could only say that a light had shone from heaven, but to Saul it was a light from Him who is the light of the City of God—a ray from the light which no man can approach unto.[4]

And about that which he saw and heard he never wavered. It was the secret of his inmost being; it was the most unalterable conviction of his soul:

[1] Acts ix. 3, περιήστραψεν, "lightened round." The word is again used in xxii. 6, but is not found in the LXX., and is unknown to classical Greek.

[2] John xii. 29.

[3] Acts ix. 7, εἱστήκεισαν μηδένα θεωροῦντες. Cf. Dan. x. 7, "I Daniel alone saw the vision; for the men that were with me saw not the vision; but a great quaking fell upon them, so that they fled to hide themselves." So in *Shemôth Rabba*, sect. 2, f. 104. 3, it is said that others were with Moses, but that he alone saw the burning bush (Exod. iii. 2). Similarly Rashi, at the beginning of his commentary on Leviticus, says that when God called Moses the voice was heard by him alone.

[4] 1 Tim. vi. 14—16; 2 Cor. xii. 1.

it was the very crisis and most intense moment of his life. Others might hint at explanations or whisper doubt:[1] Saul *knew*. At that instant God had shown him His secret and His covenant. God had found him; had flung him to the ground in the career of victorious outrage, to lead him henceforth in triumph, a willing spectacle to angels and to men.[2] God had spoken to him, had struck him into darkness out of the noonday, only that He might kindle a noon in the midnight of his heart. From that moment Saul was converted. A change total, utter, final had passed over him, had transformed him. God had called him, had revealed His Son in him,[3] had given him grace and power to become an Apostle to the Gentiles, had sent him forth to preach the faith which he had once destroyed, had shone in his heart to give "the light of the knowledge of the glory of God in the face of Jesus Christ."[4]

And the means of this mighty change all lay in this one fact:—at that awful moment *he had seen the Lord Jesus Christ*.[5] To him the persecutor—to him as to the abortive-born of the Apostolic family[6]—the risen, the glorified Jesus had appeared. He had "been apprehended by Christ." On that appearance all his faith was founded; on that pledge of resurrection—of immortality to himself, and to the dead who die in Christ—all his hopes were anchored.[7] If that belief were unsubstantial, then all his life and all his labours were a delusion and a snare—he was a wretch more to be pitied than the wretchedest of the children of the world. But if an angel from heaven preached a different doctrine it was false, for he had been taught by the revelation of Jesus Christ, and if this hope were vain, then to him

> "The pillared firmament was rottenness,
> And earth's base built on stubble."

The strength of this conviction became the leading force in Paul's future life. He tells us that when the blaze of glory lightened round him he was struck to the earth, and there he remained till the voice bade him rise, and when he rose his eyes were blinded;—he opened them on darkness. Had he been asked about the long controversies which have arisen in modern days, as to whether the appearance of the Risen Christ to him was objective or subjective, I am far from sure that he would even have understood them.[8] He uses indeed of this very event the term "vision." "I was not disobedient," he says to King Agrippa, "to the heavenly vision."[9] But the word used for

[1] We trace a sort of hesitating sneer in the Clementine *Homilies*, xvii. 13, "He who believes a vision . . . . may indeed be deceived by an evil demon, ... which really is nothing, and if he asks who it is that appears" [with an allusion to τίς εἶ, Κύριε; (ix. 5)], "it can answer what it will;"—with very much more to the same effect.

[2] 2 Cor. ii. 14.

[3] Acts xxii. 21; xxvi. 17, 18; Gal. i. 15, 16.

[4] 2 Cor. iv. 6.

[5] 1 Cor. ix. 1; xv. 8; *v. supra*, p. 41 *seq.*

[6] 1 Cor. xv. 8.

[7] 1 Cor. xv. 10—29.

[8] See 2 Cor. xii. 1.

[9] Acts xxvi. 19, τῇ οὐρανίῳ ὀπτασίᾳ. When Zacharias came out of the Temple speechless, the people recognised that he had seen an ὀπτασία (Luke i. 22). The women returning from the tomb say they have seen an ὀπτασία ἀγγέλων (Luke xxiv. 23). The word, then, is peculiar to Luke and the Acts, as are so many words. It is, however, the word used in

vision means "a waking vision," and in what conceivable respect could St. Paul have been more overpoweringly convinced that he had in very truth seen, and heard, and received a revelation and a mission from the Risen Christ? Is the essential miracle rendered less miraculous by a questioning of that objectivity to which the language seems decidedly to point? Are the eye and the ear the only organs by which definite certainties can be conveyed to the human soul? are not rather these organs the poorest, the weakest, the most likely to be deceived? To the eyes of St. Paul's companions, God spoke by the blinding light; to their ears by the awful sound; but to the soul of His chosen servant He was visible indeed in the excellent glory, and He spoke in the Hebrew tongue; but whether the vision and the voice came through the dull organs of sense or in presentations infinitely more intense, more vivid, more real, more unutterably convincing to the spirit by which only things spiritual are discerned—this is a question to which those only will attach importance to whom the soul is nothing but the material organism—who know of no indubitable channels of intercourse between man and his Maker save those that come clogged with the imperfections of mortal sense—and who cannot imagine anything real except that which they can grasp with both hands. One fact remains upon any hypothesis—and that is, that the conversion of St. Paul was in the highest sense of the word a miracle, and one of which the spiritual consequences have affected every subsequent age of the history of mankind.[1]

For though there may be trivial variations, obviously reconcilable, and absolutely unimportant, in the thrice-repeated accounts of this event, yet in the narration of the *main* fact there is no shadow of variation, and no possibility of doubt.[2] And the main fact as St. Paul always related and referred to it was this—that, after several days' journey, when they were now near Damascus, some awful incident which impressed them all alike as an infolding fire and a supernatural sound arrested their progress, and in that light, as he lay prostrate on

the passage of the Corinthians just quoted, and the ὀπτασία there leaves him no certainty as to whether it was corporeal or spiritual. The LXX. use it (Dan. ix. 23, &c.) to render מַרְאָה, which is used of a night vision in Gen. xlvi. 2. Phavorinus distinctly says that ὅραμα, whether by day or by night, is distinct from ἐνύπνιον "dream," and it seems as if St. Luke, at any rate, meant by ὀπτασία something more objective than he meant by ὅραμα (Acts ix. 10—12; xi. 5; xii. 9; xvi. 9; xviii. 9) or ἔκστασις (Acts xi. 5; xxii. 17). Ὅρασις, in the N. T., only occurs in Rev. iv. 3; ix. 17; and in a quotation, Acts ii. 17.

[1] At such moments the spirit only lives, and the ψυχὴ, the animal life, is hardly adequate as an ὄργανον ληπτικὸν to apprehend such revelations. See Augustine, *De Genesi ad Litt.* xii. 3. "La chose essentielle est que nous ne perdions pas de vue le grand principe évangélique d'un contact direct de l'esprit de Dieu avec celui de l'homme, contact qui échappe à l'analyse du raisonnement . . . . Le mysticisme évangélique en révélant au sens chrétien un monde de miracles incessants, lui épargne la peine de se préoccuper du petit nombre de ceux qu'analysent contradictoirement le rationalisme critique et le rationalisme orthodoxe" (Reuss, *Hist. Apostolique*, p. 114). "Christ stood before me," said St. Teresa. "*I saw Him with the eyes of the soul more distinctly than I could have seen Him with the eyes of the body*" (*Vida*, vii. 11).

[2] It is superfluous to repeat the reconciliation of these small apparent contradictions, because they are all reconciled and accounted for in the narrative of the text. Had they been of the smallest importance, had they been such as one moment of common sense could fail to solve, a writer so careful as St. Luke would not have left them side by side

the earth, Saul saw a mortal shape[1] and heard a human voice saying to him, "Shaûl, Shaûl"—for it is remarkable how the vividness of that impression is incidentally preserved in each form of the narrative[2]—"why persecutest thou Me? It is hard for thee to kick against the goads."[3] But at that awful moment Saul did not recognise the speaker, whom on earth he had never seen. "Who art Thou, Lord?" he said. And He—"I am Jesus of Nazareth whom thou persecutest."

"Jesus of Nazareth!" Why did the glorified speaker here adopt the name of His obscurity on earth? Why, as St. Chrysostom asks, did He not say, "I am the Son of God; the Word that was in the beginning; He that sitteth at the right hand of the Father; He who is in the form of God; He who stretched out the heaven; He who made the earth; He who levelled the sea; He who created the angels; He who is everywhere and filleth all things; He who was pre-existent and was begotten?" Why did He not utter those awful titles, but "I am Jesus of Nazareth whom thou persecutest"—from the earthly city, from the earthly home? Because His persecutor knew Him not; for had he known Him he would not have persecuted Him. He knew not that He had been begotten of the Father, but that He was from Nazareth he knew. Had He then said to him, "I am the Son of God, the Word that was in the beginning, He who made the heaven," Saul might have said, "That is not He whom I am persecuting." Had He uttered to him those vast, and bright, and lofty titles, Saul might have said, "This is not the crucified." But that he may know that he is persecuting Him who was made flesh,[4] who took the form of a servant, who died, who was buried, naming Himself from the earthly place, He says, "I am Jesus of Nazareth whom thou persecutest." This, then, was the Messiah whom he had hated and despised—this was He who had been the Heavenly Shepherd of his soul;—He who to guide back his wandering footsteps into the straight furrow had held in His hand that unseen goad against which, like some stubborn ox, he had struggled and kicked in vain.

And when the Voice of that speaker from out of the unapproachable

[1] This, though not in the Acts asserted in so many words in the direct narrative, seems to be most obviously implied in the ὤφθην σοι of xxvi. 16, in the contrast of the μηδένα θεωροῦντες of ix. 7, in the Ἰησοῦς ὁ ὀφθείς σοι ἐν τῇ ὁδῷ of ver. 17, in the πῶς ἐν τῇ ὁδῷ εἶδεν τὸν κύριον of verse 27, and in the already quoted references (1 Cor. ix. 1; xv. 8). The remark of Chrysostom, καὶ μὴν οὐκ ὤφθη ἀλλὰ διὰ πραγμάτων ὤφθη, is meant to be perfectly sincere and honest, but when compared with the above passage, seems to show less than the great orator's usual care and discrimination.

[2] Elsewhere he is always called Σαῦλος, but here Σαούλ.

[3] This addition is genuine in Acts xxvi. 14; and ὁ Ναζωραιὸς certainly in xxii. 8. Of the many illustrations quoted by Wetstein, and copied from him by subsequent commentators, the most apposite and interesting are Æsch. *Agam.* 1633, *Prom.* 323, Eur. *Bacch.* 791, Ter. *Phorm.* i. 22, 7. It is, however, remarkable that though ox-goads were commonly used in the East, not one single Eastern or Semitic parallel can be adduced. The reference to Deut. xxxii. 15 is wholly beside the mark, though goads are alluded to in Judg. iii. 31; Ecclus. xxxviii. 25. St. Paul would have been naturally familiar with the common Greek proverbs, and those only will be startled that a Greek proverb should be addressed to him by his glorified Lord, who can never be brought to understand the simple principle that Inspiration must always speak (as even the Rabbis saw) "in the tongue of the sons of men."

[4] Chrysostom adds, τὸν μετ' αὐτοῦ συναναστραφέντα, but this I believe to be a mistake.

brightness had, as it were, smitten him to the very earth with remorse by the sense of this awful truth,—"But rise," it continued, and "stand upon thy feet, and go into the city, and it shall be told thee what thou must do."

This is the form in which the words are, with trivial differences, given in St. Luke's narrative, and in St. Paul's speech from the steps of Antonia. In his speech before Agrippa, it might seem as if more had been spoken then. But in this instance again it may be doubted whether, after the first appalling question, "Shaûl, Shaûl, why persecutest thou Me?" which remained branded so vividly upon his heart, Paul could himself have said how much of the revelation which henceforth transfigured his life was derived from the actual moment when he lay blinded and trembling on the ground, and how much from the subsequent hours of deep external darkness and brightening inward light. In the annals of human lives there have been other spiritual crises analogous to this in their startling suddenness, in their absolute finality. To many the resurrection from the death of sin is a slow and life-long process; but others pass with one thrill of conviction, with one spasm of energy, from death to life, from the power of Satan unto God. Such moments crowd eternity into an hour, and stretch an hour into eternity.

"At such high hours
Of inspiration from the Living God
Thought is not."

When God's awful warnings burn before the soul in letters of flame, it can read them indeed, and know their meaning to the very uttermost, but it does not know, and it does not care, whether it was Perez or Upharsin that was written on the wall. The utterances of the Eternal Sibyl are inscribed on records scattered and multitudinous as are the forest leaves. As the anatomist may dissect every joint and lay bare every nerve of the organism, yet be infinitely distant from any discovery of the principle of life, so the critic and grammarian may decipher the dim syllables and wrangle about the disputed discrepancies, but it is not theirs to interpret. If we would in truth understand such spiritual experiences, the records of them must be read by a light that never was on land or sea.

Saul rose another man: he had fallen in death, he rose in life; he had fallen in the midst of things temporal, he rose in awful consciousness of the things eternal; he had fallen a proud, intolerant, persecuting Jew, he rose a humble, broken-hearted, penitent Christian. In that moment a new element had been added to his being. Henceforth—to use his own deep and dominant expression—he was "in Christ." God had found him; Jesus had spoken to him, and in one flash changed him from a raging Pharisee into a true disciple —from the murderer of the saints into the Apostle of the Gentiles. It was a new birth, a new creation. As we read the story of it, if we have one touch of reverence within our souls, shall we not take off our shoes from off our feet, for the place whereon we stand is holy ground?

Saul rose, and all was dark. The dazzling vision had passed away, and with it also the glittering city, the fragrant gardens, the burning noon. Amazed and startled, his attendants took him by the hand and led him to Damascus. He had meant to enter the city in all the importance of a Commissioner from the Sanhedrin, to be received with distinction, not only as himself a great "pupil of the wise," but even as the representative of all authority which the Jews held most sacred. And he had meant to leave the city, perhaps, amid multitudes of his applauding countrymen, accompanied by a captive train of he knew not how many dejected Nazarenes. How different were his actual entrance and his actual exit! He is led through the city gate, stricken, dejected, trembling, no longer breathing threats and slaughter, but longing only to be the learner and the suppliant, and the lowest brother among those whom he had intended to destroy. He was ignominiously let out of the city, alone, in imminent peril of arrest or assassination, through a window, in a basket, down the wall.

They led him to the house of Judas, in that long street which leads through the city and is still called Straight; and there, in remorse, in blindness, in bodily suffering, in mental agitation, unable or unwilling to eat or drink, the glare of that revealing light ever before his darkened eyes, the sound of that reproachful voice ever in his ringing ears, Saul lay for three days. None can ever tell what things in those three days passed through his soul; what revelations of the past, what lessons for the present, what guidance for the future. His old life, his old self, had been torn up by the very roots, and though now he was a new creature, the crisis can never pass over any one without agonies and energies—without earthquake and eclipse. At last the tumult of his being found relief in prayer; and, in a vision full of peace, he saw one of those brethren for a visit from whom he seems hitherto to have yearned in vain, come to him and heal him. This brother was Ananias, a Christian, but a Christian held in respect by all the Jews, and therefore a fit envoy to come among the Pharisaic adherents by whom we cannot but suppose that Saul was still surrounded. It was not without shrinking that Ananias had been led to make this visit. He had heard of Saul's ravages at Jerusalem, and his fierce designs against the brethren at Damascus; nay, even of the letters of authority from the High Priest which were still in his hand. He had heard, too, of what had befallen him on the way, but it had not wholly conquered his not unnatural distrust. A divine injunction aided the charity of one who, as a Christian, felt the duty of believing all things, and hoping all things. The Lord, appearing to him in a dream, told him that the zeal which had burned so fiercely in the cause of Sadducees should henceforth be a fiery angel of the Cross,—that this pitiless persecutor should be a chosen vessel to carry the name of Christ before Gentiles, kings, and the children of Israel. "For I will show him," said the vision, "how much he must suffer for My name."[1] The good Ananias, hesitated no longer. He entered into the house

[1] "Fortia agere Romanum est; fortia pati Christianum" (Corn. à Lap.).

of Judas, and while his very presence seemed to breathe peace, he addressed the sufferer by the dear title of brother, and laying his hands upon the clouded eyes, bade him rise, and see, and be filled with the Holy Ghost. "Be baptised," he added, "and wash away thy sins, calling on the name of the Lord." The words of blessing and trust were to the troubled nerves and aching heart of the sufferer a healing in themselves. Immediately "there fell from his eyes as it had been scales."[1] He rose, and saw, and took food and was strengthened, and received from the hands of his humble brother that sacrament by which he was admitted into the full privileges of the new faith. He became a member of the Church of Christ, the extirpation of which had been for months the most passionate desire and the most active purpose of his life.

Fruitful indeed must have been the conversation which he held with Ananias, and doubtless with other brethren, in the delicious calm that followed this heart-shaking moment of conviction. In those days Ananias must more and more have confirmed him in the high destiny which the voice of revelation had also marked out to himself. What became of his commission; what he did with the High Priest's letters; how his subordinates demeaned themselves; what alarming reports they took back to Jerusalem; with what eyes he was regarded by the Judaic synagogues of Damascus,—we do not know; but we do know that in those days, whether they were few or many, it became more and more clear to him that "God had chosen him to know His will, and see that Just One, and hear the voice of His mouth, and be His witness unto all men of what he had seen and heard."[2]

And here let me pause to say that it is impossible to exaggerate the importance of St. Paul's conversion as one of the evidences of Christianity. That he should have passed, by one flash of conviction, not only from darkness to light, but from one direction of life to the very opposite, is not only characteristic of the man, but evidential of the power and significance of Christianity. That the same man who, just before, was persecuting Christianity with the most violent hatred, should come all at once to believe in Him whose followers he had been seeking to destroy, and that in this faith he should become a "new creature"—what is this but a victory which Christianity owed to nothing but the spell of its own inherent power? Of all who have been converted to the faith of Christ, there is not one in whose case the Christian principle broke so immediately through everything opposed to it, and asserted so absolutely its triumphant superiority. Henceforth to Paul Christianity was summed up in the one word Christ. And to what does he testify respecting Jesus? To almost every single primarily important fact respecting His Incarnation, Life, Sufferings, Betrayal, Last Supper, Trial, Crucifixion, Resurrection, Ascension, and Heavenly Exaltation.[3] We com-

[1] There is a remarkable parallel in Tob. xi. 13, καὶ ἐλεπίσθη ἀπὸ τῶν κάνθων τῶν ὀφθαλμῶν αὐτοῦ τὰ λευκώματα.

[2] Acts xxii. 14, 15.

[3] See, among other passages, Rom. viii. 3, 11; 1 Tim. iii. 16; Rom. ix. 5; 2 Cor. i. 5; Col. i. 20; xi. 3; 1 Cor. i. 23; ii. 2; v. 7; x. 16; Gal. vi. 19; Eph. ii. 13; Rom. v. 6;

plain that nearly two thousand years have passed away, and that the brightness of historical events is apt to fade, and even their very outline to be obliterated, as they sink into the "dark backward and abysm of time." Well, but are we more keen-sighted, more hostile, more eager to disprove the evidence, than the consummate legalist, the admired rabbi, the commissioner of the Sanhedrin, the leading intellect in the schools—learned as Hillel, patriotic as Judas of Gaulon, burning with zeal for the Law as intense as that of Shammai? He was not separated from the events, as we are, by centuries of time. He was not liable to be blinded, as we are, by the dazzling glamour of a victorious Christendom. He had mingled daily with men who had watched from Bethlehem to Golgotha the life of the Crucified,—not only with His simple-hearted followers, but with His learned and powerful enemies. He had talked with the priests who had consigned Him to the cross; he had put to death the followers who had wept beside His tomb. He had to face the unutterable horror which, to any orthodox Jew, was involved in the thought of a Messiah who "had hung upon a tree." He had heard again and again the proofs which satisfied an Annas and a Gamaliel that Jesus was a deceiver of the people.[1] The events on which the Apostles relied, in proof of His divinity, had taken place in the full blaze of contemporary knowledge. He had not to deal with uncertainties of criticism or assaults on authenticity. He could question, not ancient documents, but living men; he could analyse, not fragmentary records, but existing evidence. He had thousands of means close at hand whereby to test the reality or unreality of the Resurrection in which, up to this time, he had so passionately and contemptuously disbelieved. In accepting this half-crushed and wholly execrated faith he had everything in the world to lose—he had nothing conceivable to gain; and yet, in spite of all—overwhelmed by a conviction which he felt to be irresistible—Saul, the Pharisee, became a witness of the Resurrection, a preacher of the Cross.

CHAPTER XI.

THE RETIREMENT OF ST. PAUL.

> "Thou shalt have joy in sadness soon,
> The pure calm hope be thine,
> That brightens like the eastern moon,
> When day's wild lights decline."—KEBLE.

SAUL was now a "Nazarene," but many a year of thought and training had to elapse before he was prepared for the great mission of his life.

If, indeed, the Acts of the Apostles were our only source of information respecting him, we should have been compelled to suppose that he instantly

vi. 4, 9; viii. 11; xiv. 15; xv. 3; 1 Cor. xv. *passim;* Rom. x. 6; Col. iii. 1; Eph. ii. 6; 1 Tim. iii. 16, &c.

[1] John vii. 12, 47; ix. 16; x. 20.

plunged into the work of teaching. "He was with the disciples in Damascus certain days," says St. Luke; "and immediately in the synagogues he began to preach Jesus, that He is the Son of God;"[1] and he proceeds to narrate the amazement of the Jews, the growing power of Saul's demonstrations, and, after an indefinite period had elapsed, the plot of the Jews against him, and his escape from Damascus.

But St. Luke never gives, nor professes to give, a complete biography. During the time that he was the companion of the Apostle his details, indeed, are numerous and exact; but if even in this later part of his career he never mentions Titus, or once alludes to the fact that St. Paul wrote a single epistle, we cannot be surprised that his notices of the Apostle's earlier career are fragmentary, either because he knew no more, or because, in his brief space, he suppresses all circumstances that did not bear on his immediate purpose.

Accordingly, if we turn to the biographic retrospect in the Epistle to the Galatians, in which St. Paul refers to this period to prove the independence of his apostolate, we find that in the Acts the events of three years have been compressed into as many verses, and that, instead of immediately beginning to preach at Damascus, he immediately retired into Arabia.[2] For "when," he says, "He who separated me from my mother's womb, and called me by His grace, was pleased to reveal His Son in me, that I might preach Him among the Gentiles, immediately I did not communicate with flesh and blood, nor went I up to Jerusalem to those who were Apostles before me, but I went away into Arabia, and again I returned to Damascus."

No one, I think, who reads this passage attentively can deny that it gives the impression of an intentional retirement from human intercourse. A multitude of writers have assumed that St. Paul first preached at Damascus, then retired to Arabia, and then returned, with increased zeal and power, to preach in Damascus once more. Not only is St. Paul's own language unfavourable to such a view, but it seems to exclude it. What would all psychological

[1] Acts ix. 19, 20.

[2] I understand the εὐθέως of Gal. i. 16 as immediately succeeding St. Paul's conversion; the εὐθέως of Acts ix. 20 as immediately succeeding his return to Damascus. The retirement into Arabia must be interpreted as a lacuna either at the middle of Acts ix. 19, or at the end of that verse, or after verse 21. The reasons why I unhesitatingly assume the first of these alternatives are given in the text. There is nothing to be said for supposing with Kuinoel and Olshausen that it was subsequent to the *escape* from Damascus, which seems directly to contradict, or at any rate to render superfluous, the πάλιν of Gal i. 17. We may be quite sure that St. Paul did not talk promiscuously about this period of his life. No man, even with familiar friends, will make the most solemn crises of his life a subject of common conversation; and Paul was by no means a man to wear his heart upon his sleeve. How many hundreds who read this passage will by a moment's thought become aware that apart from written memoranda, and possibly even with their aid, there is no one living who could write his own biography with any approach to accuracy? What reason is there for supposing that it would have been otherwise with St. Paul? What reason is there for the supposition that he entrusted St. Luke with all the important facts which had occurred to him, when we see that what St. Luke was able to record about him neither portrayed one-fourth of his character nor preserved a memorial of one tithe of his sufferings? And it is to be observed that in Acts xxii. 16, 17 where it had no bearing on his immediate subject, St. Paul himself omits all reference to this retirement into Arabia.

considerations lead us to think likely in the case of one circumstanced as Saul of Tarsus was after his sudden and strange conversion? The *least* likely course—the one which would place him at the greatest distance from all deep and earnest spirits who have passed through a similar crisis—would be for him to have plunged at once into the arena of controversy, and to have passed, without pause or breathing-space, from the position of a leading persecutor into that of a prominent champion. In the case of men of shallow nature, or superficial convictions, such a proceeding is possible; but we cannot imagine it of St. Paul. It is not thus with souls which have been arrested in mid-career by the heart-searching voice of God. Just as an eagle which has been drenched and battered by some fierce storm will alight to plume its ruffled wings, so when a great soul has "passed through fire and through water" it needs some safe and quiet place in which to rest. The lifelong convictions of any man may be reversed in an instant, and that sudden reversion often causes a marvellous change; but it is never in an instant that the whole *nature* and *character* of a man are transformed from what they were before. It is difficult to conceive of any change more total, any rift of difference more deep, than that which separated Saul the persecutor from Paul the Apostle; and we are sure that—like Moses, like Elijah, like our Lord Himself, like almost every great soul in ancient or modern times to whom has been entrusted the task of swaying the destinies by moulding the convictions of mankind—like Sakya Mouni, like Mahomet in the cave of Hira, like St. Francis of Assisi in his sickness, like Luther in the monastery of Erfurdt—he would need a quiet period in which to elaborate his thoughts, to still the tumult of his emotions, to commune in secrecy and in silence with his own soul. It was necessary for him to understand the Scriptures; to co-ordinate his old with his new beliefs. It is hardly too much to say that if Saul—ignorant as yet of many essential truths of Christianity, alien as yet from the experience of its deepest power—had begun at once to argue with and to preach to others, he could hardly have done the work he did. To suppose that the truths of which afterwards he became the appointed teacher were all revealed to him as by one flash of light in all their fulness, is to suppose that which is alien to God's dealings with the human soul, and which utterly contradicts the phenomena of that long series of Epistles in which we watch the progress of his thoughts. Even on grounds of historic probability, it seems unlikely that Saul should at once have been able to substitute a propaganda for an inquisition. Under such circumstances it would have been difficult for the brethren to trust, and still more difficult for the Jews to tolerate him. The latter would have treated him as a shameless renegade,[1] the former would have mistrusted him as a secret spy.

We might, perhaps, have expected that Saul would have stayed quietly among the Christians at Damascus, mingling unobtrusively in their meetings, listening to them, learning of them, taking at their love-feasts the humblest place. We can hardly suppose that he cherished, in these first days of his

[1] They would have called him a מומר, one who had abandoned his religious convictions.

Christian career, the developed purpose of preaching an independent Gospel. Assailed, as he subsequently was, on all sides, but thwarted most of all by the espionage of false brethren, and the calumnies of those who desired to throw doubt on his inspired authority, it was indeed a providential circumstance that the events which followed his conversion were such as to separate him as far as possible from the appearance of discipleship to human instructors. As a Pharisee he had sat at the feet of Gamaliel; as a Christian he called no man his master. He asserts, with reiterated earnestness, that his teaching as well as his authority, "his Gospel" no less than his Apostleship, had been received immediately from God. Indeed, the main object of that intensely interesting and characteristic narrative which occupies the two first chapters of the Epistle to the Galatians is to establish the declaration which he felt it necessary to make so strongly, that "the Gospel preached by him was not a human gospel, and that he did not even receive it from any human being, nor was he taught it, but through revelation of Jesus Christ."[1] Had he not been able to assure his converts of this—had he not been able to appeal to visions and revelations of the Lord—he might have furnished another instance of one whose opinions have been crushed and silenced by the empty authority of names. It was from no personal feeling of emulation—a feeling of which a soul so passionately in earnest as his is profoundly incapable—but it was from the duty of ensuring attention to the truths he preached that he felt it to be so necessary to convince the churches which he had founded how deep would be their folly if they allowed themselves to be seduced from the liberty of his Gospel by the retrograde mission of the evangelists of bondage. It was indispensable for the dissemination of the truth that he should be listened to as an Apostle "neither of man, nor by any man, but by Jesus Christ, and God, who raised him from the dead." Had his Apostleship emanated from (ἀπὸ) the Twelve, or been conferred on him by the consecrating act of (διὰ) any one of them,[2] then they might be supposed to have a certain superior commission, a certain coercive power. If, as far as he was concerned, they had no such power, it was because he had received his commission directly from his Lord. And to this independence of knowledge he often refers. He tells the Thessalonians, "by the Word of the Lord,"[3] that those who were still alive at the Second Advent should not be beforehand with—should gain no advantage or priority over—those that slept. He tells the Ephesians[4] that it was by revelation that God "made known to him the mystery which in other generations was not made known to the sons of men—namely, that the Gentiles are co-heirs and co-members and co-partakers[5] of the promise in Christ Jesus, through the Gospel of which he became a minister according to the gift of the grace of God, which was given him according to the mighty working of His power." He tells the Colossians[6] that he became a minister of the Church "in accordance with the stewardship of God given to him for them, that he might fully preach the

[1] Gal. i. 11, 12.
[2] Gal. i. 1, οὐκ ἀπ' ἀνθρώπων οὐδὲ δι' ἀνθρώπου.
[3] 1 Thess. iv. 15, ἐν λόγῳ Κυρίου.
[4] Eph. iii. 3—6.
[5] συγκληρονόμα καὶ σύσσωμα καὶ συμμέτοχα.
[6] Col. i. 25.

Word of God, the mystery hidden from the ages and the generations." From these and from other passages it seems clear that what St. Paul meant to represent as special subjects of the revelation which he had received were partly distinct views of what rule ought to be followed by Christians in special instances, partly great facts about the resurrection,[1] partly the direct vision of a Saviour not only risen from the dead, but exalted at the right hand of God; but especially the central and peculiar fact of his teaching "the mystery of Christ"—the truth once secret, but now revealed—the deliverance which He had wrought, the justification by faith which He had rendered possible, and, most of all, the free offer of this great salvation to the Gentiles, without the necessity of their incurring the yoke of bondage, which even the Jew had found to be heavier than he could bear.[2]

It can hardly, therefore, be doubted that after his recovery from the shock of conviction with which his soul must long have continued to tremble, Paul only spent a few quiet days with Ananias, and any other brethren who would hold out to him the right hand of friendship. He might talk with them of the life which Jesus had lived on earth. He might hear from them those reminiscences of the

"Sinless years
Which breathed beneath the Syrian blue,"

of which the most precious were afterwards recorded by the four Evangelists. In listening to these he would have been fed with "the spiritual guileless milk."[3] Nor can we doubt that in those days more than ever he would refrain his soul and keep it low—that his soul was even as a weaned child. But of the mystery which he was afterwards to preach—of that which emphatically he called "his Gospel"[4]—neither Ananias (who was himself a rigid Jew), nor any of the disciples, could tell him anything. That was taught him by God alone. It came to him by the illuminating power of the Spirit of Christ, in revelations which accompanied each step in that Divine process of education which constituted his life.

But he could not in any case have stayed long in Damascus. His position there was for the present untenable. Alike the terror with which his arrival must have been expected by the brethren, and the expectation which it had aroused among the Jews, would make him the centre of hatred and suspicion, of rumour and curiosity. He may even have been in danger of arrest by the very subordinates to whom his sudden change of purpose must have seemed to delegate his commission. But a stronger motive for retirement than all this would be the yearning for solitude; the intense desire, and even the overpowering necessity, to be for a time alone with God. He was a stricken deer, and was impelled as by a strong instinct to leave the herd. In solitude a man may trace to their hidden source the fatal errors of the past; he may

[1] See 1 Cor. xv. 22; 1 Thess. iv. 15.
[2] See Col. iv. 3; Eph. iii. 3; vi. 19; Rom. xvi. 25.
[3] 1 Pet. ii. 2, τὸ λογικὸν ἄδολον γάλα.
[4] 1 Cor. ix. 17; Gal. ii. 2, 7; 2 Thess. ii. 14; 2 Tim. ii. 8.

pray for that light from heaven—no longer flaming with more than noonday fierceness, but shining quietly in dark places—which shall enable him to understand the many mysteries of life; he may wait the healing of his deep wounds by the same tender hand that in mercy has inflicted them; he may

> "Sit on the desert stone
> Like Elijah at Horeb's cave alone;
> And a gentle voice comes through the wild,
> Like a father consoling his fretful child,
> That banishes bitterness, wrath, and fear,
> Saying, 'MAN IS DISTANT, BUT GOD IS NEAR.'"

And so Saul went to Arabia—a word which must, I think, be understood in its popular and primary sense to mean the Sinaitic peninsula.[1]

He who had been a persecutor in honour of Moses, would henceforth be himself represented as a renegade from Moses. The most zealous of the living servants of Mosaism was to be the man who should prove most convincingly that Mosaism was to vanish away. Was it not natural, then, that he should long to visit the holy ground where the bush had glowed in unconsuming fire, and the granite crags had trembled at the voice which uttered the fiery law? Would the shadow of good things look so much of a shadow if he visited the very spot where the great Lawgiver and the great Prophet had held high communings with God? Could he indeed be sure that he had come unto the Mount Sion, and unto the city of the living God, the heavenly Jerusalem, and to Jesus the Mediator of a new covenant, until he had visited the mount that might be touched and that burned with fire, where amid blackness, and darkness, and tempest, and the sound of a trumpet and the voice of words, Moses himself had exceedingly feared and quaked?

How long he stayed, we do not know. It has usually been assumed that his stay was brief; to me it seems far more probable that it occupied no small portion of those "three years"[2] which he tells us elapsed before he visited Jerusalem. Few have doubted that those "three years" are to be dated from his conversion. It seems clear that after his conversion he stayed but a few days (ἡμέραι τινὲς) with the disciples; that then—at the earliest practicable moment—he retired into Arabia; that after his return he began to preach, and that this ministry in Damascus was interrupted after a certain period (ἡμέραι ἱκαναί) by the conspiracy of the Jews. The latter expression is translated "many days" in the Acts; but though the continuance of his preaching may have occupied days which in comparison with his first brief stay might have been called "many," the phrase itself is so vague that it might be used of almost any period from a fortnight to three years.[3] As to the general correctness of this conclusion I can feel no doubt; the only point which must always remain dubious is whether the phrase "three years" means three complete years, or whether it means one full year, and a part, however short, of two other years. From the chronology of St. Paul's life we can attain no

[1] See Excursus IX., "Saul in Arabia." [2] Gal. i. 18.
[3] It actually is used of three years in 1 Kings ii. 38.

certainty on this point, though such lights as we have are slightly in favour of the longer rather than of the shorter period.

Very much depends upon the question whether physical infirmity, and prostration of health, were in part the cause of this retirement and inactivity. And here again we are on uncertain ground, because this at once opens the often discussed problem as to the nature of the affliction to which St. Paul so pathetically alludes as his "stake in the flesh." I am led to touch upon that question here, because I believe that this dreadful affliction, whatever it may have been, had its origin at this very time.[1] The melancholy through which, like a fire at midnight, his enthusiasm burns its way—the deep despondency which sounds like an undertone even amid the bursts of exultation which triumph over it, seem to me to have been in no small measure due to this. It gave to St. Paul that painful self-consciousness which is in itself a daily trial to any man who, in spite of an innate love for retirement, is thrust against his will into publicity and conflict. It seems to break the wings of his spirit, so that sometimes he drops as it were quite suddenly to the earth, checked and beaten down in the very midst of his loftiest and strongest flights.

No one can even cursorily read St. Paul's Epistles without observing that he was aware of something in his aspect or his personality which distressed him with an agony of humiliation—something which seems to force him, against every natural instinct of his disposition, into language which sounds to himself like a boastfulness which was abhorrent to him, but which he finds to be more necessary to himself than to other men. It is as though he felt that his appearance was against him. Whenever he has ceased to be carried away by the current of some powerful argument, whenever his sorrow at the insidious encroachment of errors against which he had flung the whole force of his character has spent itself in words of immeasurable indignation—whenever he drops the high language of apostolical authority and inspired conviction—we hear a sort of wailing, pleading, appealing tone in his personal addresses to his converts, which would be almost impossible in one whose pride of personal manhood had not been abashed by some external defects, to which he might indeed appeal as marks at once of the service and the protection of his Saviour, but which made him less able to cope face to face with the insults of opponents or the ingratitude of friends. His language leaves on us the impression of one who was acutely sensitive, and whose sensitiveness of temperament has been aggravated by a meanness of presence which is indeed forgotten by the friends who know him, but which raises in strangers a prejudice not always overcome. Many, indeed, of the brethren in the little churches which he founded, had so "grappled him to their souls with hooks of steel," that he could speak in letter after letter of their abounding love and

[1] There is nothing to exclude this in the ἐδόθη μοι of 2 Cor. xii. 7. The affliction might not have arrived at its *full intensity* till that period, which was some years after his conversion, about A.D. 43, when St. Paul was at Antioch or Jerusalem or Tarsus.

tenderness and gratitude towards him[1]—that he can call them "my little children"—that he can assume their intense desire to see him, and can grant that desire as an express favour to *them*;[2] and that he is even forced to soothe those jealousies of affection which were caused by his acceptance of aid from one church which he would not accept from others. But he is also well aware that he is hated with a perfect virulence of hatred, and (which is much more wounding to such a spirit) that with this hatred there is a large mixture of unjust contempt. From this contempt even of the contemptible, from this hatred even of the hateful, he could not but shrink, though he knew that it is often the penalty with which the world rewards service, and the tribute which virtue receives from vice.

It is this which explains the whole style and character of his Epistles.[3] The charges which his enemies made against him have their foundation in facts about his method and address, which made those charges all the more dangerous and the more stinging by giving them a certain plausibility. They were, in fact, yet another instance of those half-truths which are the worst of lies. Thus—adopting the taunts of his adversaries, as he often does—he says that he is in presence "humble" among them,[4] and "rude in speech,"[5] and he quotes their own reproach that "his bodily presence was weak, and his speech contemptible."[6] Being confessedly one who strove for peace and unity, who endeavoured to meet all men half-way, who was ready to be all things to all men if by any means he might save some, he has more than once to vindicate his character from those charges of insincerity, craftiness, dishonesty, guile, man-pleasing and flattery,[7] which are, perhaps, summed up in the general depreciation which he so indignantly rebuts that "he walked according to the flesh,"[8] or in other words that his motives were not spiritual, but low and selfish. He has, too, to defend himself from the insinuation that his self-abasements had been needless and excessive;[9] that even his apparent self-denials had only been assumed as a cloak for ulterior views;[10] and that his intercourse was so marked by levity of purpose, that there was no trusting to his promises.[11] Now how came St. Paul to be made the butt for such calumnies as these? Chiefly, no doubt, because he was, most sorely against his will, the leader of a party, and because there are in all ages souls which delight in lies—men "whose throat is an open sepulchre, and the poison of asps is under their lips;" but partly, also, because he regarded tact, concession, conciliatoriness, as Divine weapons which God had permitted him to use against powerful obstacles; and partly because it was easy to satirise and misrepresent a depression of spirits, a humility of demeanour, which were either the direct results of some bodily affliction, or which the consciousness of this affliction

1 Phil. *passim*.
2 2 Cor. i. 15, 23.
3 See Excursus I.: "The Style of St. Paul as illustrative of his Character."
4 2 Cor. x. 1, 2.
5 2 Cor. xi. 6, ἰδιώτης ἐν λόγῳ.
6 2 Cor. x. 10.
7 2 Cor. ii. 17, iv. 2; 1 Thess. ii. 3—5.
8 2 Cor. x. 2.
9 2 Cor. xi. 7.
10 2 Cor. xii. 16.
11 2 Cor. i. 17.

had rendered habitual. We feel at once that this would be natural to the bowed and weak figure which Albrecht Dürer has represented; but that it would be impossible to the imposing orator whom Raphael has placed on the steps of the Areopagus.[1]

And to this he constantly refers. There is hardly a letter in which he does not allude to his mental trials, his physical sufferings, his persecutions his infirmities. He tells the Corinthians that his intercourse with them had been characterised by physical weakness, fear, and much trembling.[2] He reminds the Galatians that he had preached among them in consequence of an attack of severe sickness.[3] He speaks of the inexorable burden of life, and its unceasing moan.[4] The trouble, the perplexity, the persecution, the prostrations which were invariable conditions of his life, seem to him like a perpetual carrying about with him in his body of the mortification—the putting to death—of Christ;[5] a perpetual betrayal to death for Christ's sake—a perpetual exhibition of the energy of death in his outward life.[6] He died daily, he was in deaths oft;[7] he was being killed all the day long.[8]

And this, too—as well as the fact that he seems to write in Greek and think in Syriac—is the key to the peculiarities of St. Paul's language. The feeling that he was inadequate for the mighty task which God had specially entrusted to him; the dread lest his personal insignificance should lead any of his hearers at once to reject a doctrine announced by a weak, suffering, distressed, overburdened man, who, though an ambassador of Christ, bore in his own aspect so few of the credentials of an embassy; the knowledge that the fiery spirit which "o'erinformed its tenement of clay" was held, like the light of Gideon's pitchers, in a fragile and earthen vessel,[9] seems to be so constantly and so oppressively present with him, as to make all words too weak for the weight of meaning they have to bear. Hence his language, in many passages, bears the traces of almost morbid excitability in its passionate alternations of humility with assertions of the real greatness of his labours,[10] and of scorn and indignation against fickle weaklings and intriguing calumniators with an intense and yearning love.[11] Sometimes his heart beats with such quick emotion, his thoughts rush with such confused impetuosity, that in anakoluthon after anakoluthon, and parenthesis after parenthesis, the whole meaning becomes uncertain.[12] His feeling is so intense that his very words catch a life of their own—they become "living creatures with hands and feet."[13] Sometimes he is almost contemptuous in his assertion of the rectitude which makes him indifferent to vulgar criticism,[14] and keenly bitter in the sarcasm of his self-depreciation.[15] In one or two

1 Hausrath, p. 51. 2 1 Cor. ii. 3. 3 Gal. iv. 13.

4 2 Cor. v. 4, *οἱ ὄντες ἐν τῷ σκήνει στενάζομεν βαρούμενοι.*

5 2 Cor. iv. 8—10, *θλιβόμενοι . . . ἀπορούμενοι . . . διωκόμενοι . . . καταβαλλόμενοι . . . πάντοτε τὴν νέκρωσιν τοῦ Ἰησοῦ ἐν τῷ σώματι περιφέροντες.*

6 *Id.* 11, *ἀεὶ γὰρ ἡμεῖς οἱ ζῶντες, εἰς θάνατον παραδιδόμεθα.*

7 2 Cor. xi. 23; 1 Cor. xv. 31. 8 Rom. viii. 36.

9 2 Cor. iv. 7. 10 1 Cor. xv. 10. 11 Gal. and 2 Cor. *passim.*

12 Gal. iv. 12. 13 Gal. iv. 14; 1 Cor. iv. 13; Phil. iii. 8.

14 1 Cor. iv. 3. 15 1 Cor. iv. 10; x. 15; 2 Cor. xi. 16—19; xii. 11.

instances an enemy might almost apply the word "brutal" to the language in which he ridicules, or denounces, or unmasks the impugners of his gospel;[1] in one or two passages he speaks with a tinge of irony, almost of irritation, about those "accounted to be pillars"—the "out-and-out Apostles," who even if they were Apostles ten times over added nothing to him:[2]—but the storm of passion dies away in a moment; he is sorry even for the most necessary and justly-deserved severity, and all ends in expressions of tenderness and, as it were, with a burst of tears.[3]

Now it is true that we recognise in Saul of Tarsus the restlessness, the vehemence, the impetuous eagerness which we see in Paul the Apostle; but it is hard to imagine in Saul of Tarsus the nervous shrinking, the tremulous sensibility, the profound distrust of his own gifts and powers apart from Divine grace, which are so repeatedly manifest in the language of Paul, the fettered captive of Jesus Christ. It is hard to imagine that such a man as the Apostle became could ever have been the furious inquisitor, the intruder even into the sacred retirement of peaceful homes, the eager candidate for power to suppress a heresy even in distant cities, which Saul was before the vision on the way to Damascus. It is a matter of common experience that some physical humiliation, especially if it take the form of terrible disfigurement, often acts in this very way upon human character.[4] It makes the bold shrink; it makes the arrogant humble; it makes the self-confident timid; it makes those who once loved publicity long to hide themselves from the crowd; it turns every thought of the heart from trust in self to humblest submission to the will of God. Even a dangerous illness is sometimes sufficient to produce results like these; but when the illness leaves its physical marks for life upon the frame, its effects are intensified; it changes a mirthful reveller, like Francis of Assisi, into a squalid ascetic; a favourite of society, like Francis Xavier, into a toilsome missionary; a gay soldier, like Ignatius Loyola, into a rigid devotee.

[1] Gal. iii. 1; iv. 17 (in the Greek).

[2] Gal. ii. 6, *τῶν δοκούντων εἶναί τι,—ὁποῖοί ποτε ἦσαν, οὐδέν μοι διαφέρει*: 9, *οἱ δοκοῦντες στῦλοι εἶναι*: 11, *κατεγνωσμένος ἦν*. 1 Cor. xv. 9; 2 Cor. xi. 5, *τῶν ὑπερλίαν ἀποστόλων*. 2 Cor. xii. 11, *οὐδὲν ὑστέρησα τῶν ὑπερλίαν ἀποστόλων εἰ καὶ οὐδέν εἰμι*.

[3] Gal. iv. 19; 2 Cor. ii. 4; Rom. ix. 1—3. As bearing on this subject, every one will read with interest the verses of Dr. Newman—

> "I dreamed that with a passionate complaint
> I wished me born amid God's deeds of might,
> And envied those who had the presence bright
> Of gifted prophet or strong-hearted saint,
> Whom my heart loves, and fancy strives to paint.
> I turned, when straight a stranger met my sight,
> Came as my guest, and did awhile unite
> His lot with mine, and lived without restraint.
> Courteous he was, and grave; *so meek in mien,*
> *It seemed untrue, or told a purpose weak;*
> *Yet, in the mood, could he with aptness speak*
> *Or with stern force, or show of feeling keen,*
> *Marking deep craft, methought, and hidden pride;*
> Then came a voice, 'St. Paul is at thy side!'"

[4] The *ἐδόθη* of 2 Cor. xii. 7 shows that the "stake in the flesh" was nothing congenital.

What was the nature of this stake in the flesh, we shall examine fully in a separate essay;[1] but that, whatever it may have been, it came to St. Paul as a direct consequence of visions and revelations, and as a direct counteraction to the inflation and self-importance which such exceptional insight might otherwise have caused to such a character as his, he has himself informed us. We are, therefore, naturally led to suppose that the *first* impalement of his health by this wounding splinter accompanied, or resulted from, that greatest of all his revelations, the appearance to him of the risen Christ as he was travelling at noonday nigh unto Damascus. If so, we see yet another reason for a retirement from all exertion and publicity, which was as necessary for his body as for his soul.

CHAPTER XII.

THE BEGINNING OF A LONG MARTYRDOM.

"Be bold as a leopard, swift as an eagle, bounding as a stag, brave as a lion, to do the will of thy Father which is in heaven."—PESACHIM, f. 112, 2.

CALMED by retirement, confirmed, it may be, by fresh revelations of the will of God, clearer in his conceptions of truth and duty, Saul returned to Damascus. We need look for no further motives of his return than such as rose from the conviction that he was now sufficiently prepared to do the work to which Christ had called him.

He did not at once begin his mission to the Gentiles. "To the Jew first" was the understood rule of the Apostolic teaching,[2] and had been involved in the directions given by Christ Himself.[3] Moreover, the Gentiles were so unfamiliar with the institution of preaching, their whole idea of worship was so alien from every form of doctrinal or moral exhortation, that to begin by preaching to them was almost impossible. It was through the Jews that the Gentiles were most easily reached. The proselytes, numerous in every city, were specially numerous at Damascus, and by their agency it was certain that every truth propounded in the Jewish synagogue would, even if only by the agency of female proselytes, be rapidly communicated to the Gentile agora.

It was, therefore, to the synagogues that Saul naturally resorted, and there that he first began to deliver his message. Since the Christians were still in communion with the synagogue and the Temple—since their leader, Ananias, was so devout according to the law as to have won the willing testimony of all the Jews who lived in Damascus[4]—no obstacle would be placed in the way of the youthful Rabbi; and as he had been a scholar in the most

[1] See Excursus X., "St. Paul's 'Stake in the Flesh.'"
[2] Rom. i. 16; Acts iii. 26; xiii. 38, 39, 46; John iv. 22.
[3] Luke xxiv. 47; cf. Isa. ii. 2, 3; xlix. 6; Mic. iv. 2.
[4] Acts xxii. 12.

eminent of Jewish schools, his earliest appearances on the arena of controversy would be awaited with contention and curiosity. We have no reason to suppose that the animosity against the Nazarenes, which Saul himself had kept alive in Jerusalem, had as yet penetrated to Damascus. News is slow to travel in Eastern countries, and those instantaneous waves of opinion which flood our modern civilisation were unknown to ancient times. In the capital of Syria, Jews and Christians were still living together in mutual toleration, if not in mutual esteem. They had been thus living in Jerusalem until the spark of hatred had been struck out by the collision of the Hellenists of the liberal with those of the narrow school—the Christian Hellenists of the *Hagadôth* with the Jewish Hellenists of the *Halacha*. To Saul, if not solely, yet in great measure, this collision had been due; and Saul had been on his way to stir up the same wrath and strife in Damascus, when he had been resistlessly arrested[1] on his unhallowed mission by the vision and the reproach of his ascended Lord.

But the authority, and the letters, had been entrusted to him alone, and none but a few hot zealots really desired that pious and respectable persons like Ananias—children of Abraham, servants of Moses—should be dragged, with a halter round their necks, from peaceful homes, scourged by the people with whom they had lived without any serious disagreement, and haled to Jerusalem by fanatics who would do their best to procure against them the fatal vote which might consign them to the revolting horrors of an almost obsolete execution.

So that each Ruler of a Synagogue over whom Saul might have been domineering with all the pride of superior learning, and all the intemperance of flaming zeal, might be glad enough to see and hear a man who could no longer hold in terror over him the commission of the Sanhedrin, and who had now rendered himself liable to the very penalties which, not long before, he had been so eager to inflict.

And had Saul proved to be but an ordinary disputant, the placidity of Jewish self-esteem would not have been disturbed, nor would he have ruffled the sluggish stream of legal self-satisfaction. He did not speak of circumcision as superfluous; he said nothing about the evanescence of the Temple service, or the substitution for it of a more spiritual worship. He did not breathe a word about turning to the Gentiles. The subject of his preaching was that "Jesus is the Son of God."[2] At first this preaching excited no special indignation. The worshippers in the synagogue only felt a keen astonishment[3] that this was the man who had ravaged in Jerusalem those who called on "this name,"[4] and who had come to Damascus for the express purpose of leading them bound to the High Priest. But when once self-love is seriously wounded, toleration rarely survives. This was the case with the Jews of Damascus. They very soon discovered that it was no mere Ananias

[1] Phil. iii. 12, κατελήφθην ὑπὸ τοῦ Χριστοῦ Ἰησοῦ.
[2] Ἰησοῦν, not Χριστὸν, is here the true reading (א, A, B, C, E).
[3] Acts ix. 21, ἐξίσταντο.
[4] *V. supra*, p. 61.

with whom they had to deal. It was, throughout life, Paul's unhappy fate to kindle the most virulent animosities, because, though conciliatory and courteous by temperament, he yet carried into his arguments that intensity and forth-rightness which awaken dormant opposition. A languid controversialist will always meet with a languid tolerance. But any controversialist whose honest belief in his own doctrines makes him terribly in earnest, may count on a life embittered by the anger of those on whom he has forced the disagreeable task of re-considering their own assumptions. No one likes to be suddenly awakened. The Jews were indignant with one who disturbed the deep slumber of decided opinions. Their accredited teachers did not like to be deposed from the papacy of infallible ignorance. They began at Damascus to feel towards Saul that fierce detestation which dogged him thenceforward to the last day of his life. Out of their own Scriptures, by their own methods of exegesis, in their own style of dialectics, by the interpretation of prophecies of which they did not dispute the validity, he simply confounded them. He could now apply the very same principles which in the mouth of Stephen he had found it impossible to resist. The result was an unanswerable proof that the last *æon* of God's earthly dispensations had now dawned, that old things had passed away, and all things had become new.

If arguments are such as cannot be refuted, and yet if those who hear them will not yield to them, they inevitably excite a bitter rage. It was so with the Jews. Some time had now elapsed since Saul's return from Arabia,[1] and they saw no immediate chance of getting rid of this dangerous intruder. They therefore took refuge in what St. Chrysostom calls "the syllogism of violence." They might at least plead the excuse—and how bitter was the remorse which such a plea would excite in Saul's own conscience—that they were only treating him in the way in which he himself had treated all who held the same opinions. Even-handed justice was thus commending to his own lips the ingredients of that poisoned chalice of intolerance which he had forced on others. It is a far from improbable conjecture that it was at this early period that the Apostle endured one, and perhaps more than one, of those five Jewish scourgings which he tells the Corinthians that he had suffered at the hands of the Jews. For it is hardly likely that they would resort at once to the strongest measures, and the scourgings might be taken as a reminder that worse was yet to come. Indeed, there are few more striking proofs of the severity of that life which the Apostle so cheerfully—nay, even so joyfully—endured, than the fact that in his actual biography not one of these five inflictions, terrible as we know that they must have been, is so much as mentioned, and that in his Epistles they are only recorded, among trials yet more insupportable, in a passing and casual allusion.[2]

But we know from the example of the Apostles at Jerusalem that no such pain or danger would have put a stop to his ministry. Like them, he would have seen an honour in such disgrace. At last, exasperated beyond all en-

[1] Acts ix. 23, ἡμέραι ἱκαναί.

[2] See Excursus XI., "On Jewish Scourgings."

durance at one whom they hated as a renegade, and whom they could not even enjoy the luxury of despising as a heretic, they made a secret plot to kill him.[1] The conspiracy was made known to Saul, and he was on his guard against it. The Jews then took stronger and more open measures. They watched the gates night and day to prevent the possibility of his escape. In this they were assisted by the Ethnarch, who supplied them with the means of doing it. This Ethnarch was either the Arab viceroy of Hareth, or the chief official of the Jews themselves,[2] who well might possess this authority under a friendly prince.

There was thus an imminent danger that Saul would be cut off at the very beginning of his career. But this was not to be. The disciples "took Saul"[3]—another of the expressions which would tend to show that he was exceptionally in need of help—and putting him in a large rope basket,[4] let him down through the window of a house which abutted on the wall.[5] It may be that they chose a favourable moment when the patrol had passed, and had not yet turned round again. At any rate, the escape was full of ignominy; and it may have been this humiliation, or else the fact of its being among the earliest perils which he had undergone, that fixed it so indelibly on the memory of St. Paul. Nearly twenty years afterwards he mentions it to the Corinthians with special emphasis, after agonies and hair-breadth escapes which to us would have seemed far more formidable.[6]

Here, then, closed in shame and danger the first page in this chequered and sad career. How he made his way to Jerusalem must be left to conjecture. Doubtless, as he stole through the dark night alone—above all, as he passed the very spot where Christ had taken hold of him, and into one moment of his life had been crowded a whole eternity—his heart would be full of thoughts too deep for words. It has been supposed, from the expression of which he makes use in his speech to Agrippa, that he may have preached in many synagogues on the days which were occupied on his journey to Jerusalem.[7] But this seems inconsistent with his own statement that he was "unknown by face to the churches of Judæa which were in Christ."[8] It is not, however, unlikely that he may sometimes have availed himself of the guest-chambers which were attached to Jewish synagogues; and if such was the case, he might have taught the first truths of the Gospel to the Jews without being thrown into close contact with Christian communities.

[1] These secret plots were fearfully rife in these days of the Sicarii (Jos. *Antt.* xx. 8, § 5).

[2] 2 Cor. xi. 32, ὁ ἐθνάρχης ἐφρούρει τὴν πόλιν: Acts ix. 24, οἱ Ἰουδαῖοι παρετήρουν τὰς πύλας. Ethnarch, as well as Alabarch, was a title of Jewish governors in heathen cities.

[3] Acts ix. 25. The reading οἱ μαθηταὶ αὐτοῦ, though well attested, can hardly be correct.

[4] On σπυρὶς see my *Life of Christ*, i. 403, 480. In 2 Cor. xi. 33 it is called σαργάνη, which is defined by Hesych. as πλέγμα τι ἐκ σχοινίου.

[5] Such windows are still to be seen at Damascus. For similar escapes, see Josh. ii. 15; 1 Sam. xix. 12.

[6] 2 Cor. xi. 32. St. Paul's conversion was about A.D. 37. The Second Epistle to the Corinthians was written A.D. 57, or early in A.D. 58.

[7] Acts xxvi. 20.

[8] Gal. i. 22.

In any case, his journey could not have been much prolonged, for he tells us that it was his express object to visit Peter, whose recognition must have been invaluable to him, apart from the help and insight which he could not but derive from conversing with one who had long lived in such intimate friendship with the Lord.

CHAPTER XIII.

SAUL'S RECEPTION AT JERUSALEM.

"Cogitemus ipsum Paulum, licet caelesti voce prostratum et instructum, ad hominem tamen missum esse, ut sacramenta perciperet."—AUG. *De Doctr. Christ.*, *Prol.*

To re-visit Jerusalem must have cost the future Apostle no slight effort. How deep must have been his remorse as he neared the spot where he had seen the corpse of Stephen lying crushed under the stones! With what awful interest must he now have looked on the scene of the Crucifixion, and the spot where He who was now risen and glorified had lain in the garden-tomb! How dreadful must have been the revulsion of feeling which rose from the utter change of his present relations towards the priests whose belief he had abandoned, and the Christians whose Gospel he had embraced! He had left Jerusalem a Rabbi, a Pharisee, a fanatic defender of the Oral Law; he was entering it as one who utterly distrusted the value of legal righteousness, who wholly despised the beggarly elements of tradition. The proud man had become unspeakably humble; the savage persecutor unspeakably tender; the self-satisfied Rabbi had abandoned in one moment his pride of nationality, his exclusive scorn, his Pharisaic pre-eminence, to take in exchange for them the beatitude of unjust persecution, and to become the suffering preacher of an execrated faith. What had he to expect from Theophilus, whose letters he had perhaps destroyed? from the Sanhedrists, whose zeal he had fired? from his old fellow-pupils in the lecture-room of Gamaliel, who had seen in Saul of Tarsus one who in learning was the glory of the school of Hillel, and in zeal the rival of the school of Shammai? How would he be treated by these friends of his youth, by these teachers and companions of his life, now that proclaiming his system, his learning, his convictions, his whole life—and therefore theirs no less than his—to have been irremediably wrong, he had become an open adherent of the little Church which he once ravaged and destroyed?

But amid the natural shrinking with which he could not but anticipate an encounter so full of trial, he would doubtless console himself with the thought that he would find a brother's welcome among those sweet and gentle spirits whose faith he had witnessed, whose love for each other he had envied while he hated. How exquisite would be the pleasure of sharing that peace which he had tried to shatter; of urging on others those arguments which had been bringing conviction to his own mind even while he was most passionately resisting them; of hearing again and again from holy and gentle lips the words of Him whom he had once blasphemed! Saul might well have thought that the love, the nobleness, the enthusiasm of his new brethren would more than compensate for the influence and admiration which he had voluntarily forfeited; and that to pluck with them the fair fruit of the Spirit—love, joy, peace, long-suffering, gentleness, goodness, faith, meekness, temperance—would be a bliss for which he might cheerfully abandon the whole world beside. No wonder that "he essayed to join himself to the disciples."[1] His knowledge of human nature might indeed have warned him that "confidence is a plant of slow growth"—that such a reception as he yearned for was hardly possible. It may be that he counted too much on the change wrought in human dispositions by the grace of God. The old Adam is oftentimes too strong for young Melancthon.

For, alas! a new trial awaited him. Peter, indeed, whom he had expressly come to see, at once received him with the large generosity of that impulsive heart, and being a married man, offered him hospitality without grudging.[2] But at first that was all. It speaks no little for the greatness and goodness of Peter—it is quite in accordance with that natural nobleness which we should expect to find in one whom Jesus Himself had loved and blessed—that he was the earliest among the brethren to rise above the influence of suspicion. He was at this time the leader of the Church in Jerusalem. As such he had not been among those who fled before the storm. He must have known that it was at the feet of this young Pharisee that the garments of Stephen's murderers had been laid. He must have feared him, perhaps even have hidden himself from him, when he forced his way into Christian homes. Nay, more, the heart of Peter must have sorely ached when he saw his little congregation slain, scattered, destroyed, and the cœnobitic community, the faith of which had been so bright, the enthusiasm so contagious, the common love so tender and so pure, rudely broken up by the pitiless persecution of a Pupil of the Schools. Yet, with the unquestioning trustfulness of a sunny nature—with that spiritual insight into character by which a Divine charity not only perceives real worth, but even creates worthiness where it did not before exist—Peter opens his door to one whom a meaner man might well have excluded as still too possibly a wolf amid the fold.

But of the other leaders of the Church—if there were any at that time in Jerusalem—not one came near the new convert, not one so much as spoke to him. He was met on every side by cold, distrustful looks. At one stroke he had lost all his old friends; it seemed to be too likely that he would gain no new ones in their place. The brethren regarded him with terror and mistrust; they did not believe that he was a disciple at all.[3] The *facts* which accom-

[1] Acts ix. 26. [2] Gal. i. 18.

[3] Acts ix. 26, ἐπειρᾶτο κολλᾶσθαι τοῖς μαθηταῖς· (the imperfect marks an unsuccessful effort) καὶ πάντες ἐφοβοῦντο αὐτὸν, μὴ πιστεύοντες ὅτι ἐστὶν μαθητής.

panied his alleged conversion they may indeed have heard of; but they had occurred three years before. The news of his recent preaching and recent peril in Damascus was not likely to have reached them; but even if it had, it would have seemed so strange that they might be pardoned for looking with doubt on the persecutor turned brother—for even fearing that the asserted conversion might only be a ruse to enable Saul to learn their secrets, and so entrap them to their final ruin. And thus at first his intercourse with the brethren in the Church of Jerusalem was almost confined to his reception in the house of Peter. "Other of the Apostles saw I none," he writes to the Galatians, "save James the Lord's brother." But though he *saw* James, Paul seems to have had but little communion with him. All that we know of the first Bishop of Jerusalem shows us the immense dissimilarity, the almost antipathetic peculiarities which separated the characters of the two men. Even with the Lord Himself, if we may follow the plain language of the Gospels,[1] the eldest of His brethren seems, during His life on earth, to have had but little communion. He accepted indeed His Messianic claims, but he accepted them in the Judaic sense, and was displeased at that in His life which was most unmistakably Divine. If he be rightly represented by tradition as a Legalist, a Nazarite, almost an Essene, spending his whole life in prayer in the Temple, it was his obedience to Mosaism—scarcely modified in any external particular by his conversion to Christianity—which had gained for him even from the Jews the surname of "the Just." If, as seems almost demonstrable, he be the author of the Epistle which bears his name, we see how slight was the extent to which his spiritual life had been penetrated by those special aspects of the one great truth which were to Paul the very breath and life of Christianity. In that Epistle we find a stern and noble morality which raises it infinitely above the reproach of being "a mere Epistle of straw;"[2] but we nevertheless do not find one direct word about the Incarnation, or the Crucifixion, or the Atonement, or Justification by Faith, or Sanctification by the Spirit, or the Resurrection of the Dead. The notion that it was written to counteract either the teaching of St. Paul, or the dangerous consequences which might sometimes be deduced from that teaching, is indeed most extremely questionable; and all that we can say of that supposition is, that it is not quite so monstrous a chimera as that which has been invented by the German theologians, who see St. Paul and his followers indignantly though covertly denounced in the Balaam and Jezebel of the Churches of Pergamos and Thyatira,[3] and the Nicolaitans of the Church of Ephesus,[4] and the "synagogue of Satan, which say they are Jews, and are not, but do lie," of the Church of Philadelphia.[5] And yet no one can read the Epistle of James side by side with any Epistle of St. Paul's without perceiving how wide were the differences between the two Apostles. St. James was a man eminently inflex-

[1] Matt. xii. 46; Mark iii. 31; Luke viii. 19; John vii. 5.

[2] "Ein recht strohern Epistel, denn sie doch kein evangelisch Art an ihn hat" (Luther, *Praef. N. T.*, 1522); but he afterwards modified his opinion.

[3] Rev. ii. 20. [4] Rev. ii. 6. [5] Rev. iii. 9.

ible; St. Paul knew indeed how to yield, but then the very points which he was least inclined to yield were those which most commanded the sympathy of James. What we know of Peter is exactly in accordance with the kind readiness with which he received the suspected and friendless Hellenist. What we know of James would have led us *à priori* to assume that his relations with Paul would never get beyond the formal character which they wear in the Acts of the Apostles, and still more in the Epistle to the Galatians. But let it not be assumed that because there was little apparent sympathy and co-operation between St. Paul and St. James, and because they dwell on apparently opposite aspects of the truth, we should for one moment be justified in disparaging either the one or the other. The divergences which seem to arise from the analysis of truth by individual minds are merged in the catholicity of a wider synthesis. When St. Paul teaches that we are "justified by faith," he is teaching a truth infinitely precious; and St. James is also teaching a precious truth when, with a different shade of meaning in both words, he says that "by works a man is justified."[1] The truths which these two great Apostles were commissioned to teach were complementary and supplementary, but not contradictory of each other. Of both aspects of truth we are the inheritors. If it be true that they did not cordially sympathise with each other in their life-time, the loss was theirs; but, even in that case, they were not the first instances in the Church of God—nor will they be the last—in which two good men, through the narrowness of one or the vehemence of the other, have been too much beset by the spirit of human infirmity to be able, in all perfectness, to keep the unity of the spirit in the bond of peace.

The man who saved the new convert from this humiliating isolation—an isolation which must at that moment have been doubly painful—was the wise and generous Joseph. He has already been mentioned in the Acts as a Levite of Cyprus who, in spite of the prejudices of his rank, had been among the earliest to join the new community, and to sanction its happy communism by the sale of his own possessions. The dignity and sweetness of his character, no less than the sacrifices which he had made, gave him a deservedly high position among the persecuted brethren; and the power with which he preached the faith had won for him the surname of Barnabas, or "the son of exhortation."[2] His intimate relations with Paul in after-days, his journey all the way to Tarsus from Antioch to invite his assistance, and the unity of their purposes until the sad quarrel finally separated them, would alone render it probable that they had known each other at that earlier period of life during which, for the most part, the closest intimacies are formed. Tradition asserts that Joseph had been a scholar of Gamaliel, and the same feeling which led him to join a school of which one peculiarity was its permission of Greek

[1] James ii. 24. It is hardly a paradox to say that St. James meant by "faith" something analogous to what St. Paul meant by works.

[2] בַּר נְבוּאָה, "son of prophecy." That he had been one of the Seventy is probably a mere guess. (Euseb. *H. E.* i. 12; Clem. Alex. *Strom.* ii. 176.) "Παράκλησις late patet; ubi desides excitat est *hortatio*, ubi tristitiae medetur est *solatium*" (Bengel).

learning, might have led him yet earlier to take a few hours' sail from Cyprus to see what could be learnt in the University of Tarsus. If so, he would naturally have come into contact with the family of Saul, and the friendship thus commenced would be continued at Jerusalem. It had been broken by the conversion of Barnabas, it was now renewed by the conversion of Saul.

Perhaps also it was to this friendship that Saul owed his admission as a guest into Peter's house. There was a close link of union between Barnabas and Peter in the person of Mark, who was the cousin[1] of Barnabas, and whom Peter loved so tenderly that he calls him his son. The very house in which Peter lived may have been the house of Mary, the mother of Mark. It is hardly probable that the poor fisherman of Galilee possessed any dwelling of his own in the Holy City. At any rate, Peter goes to this house immediately after his liberation from prison, and if Peter lived in it, the relation of Barnabas to its owner would have given him some claim to ask that Saul should share its hospitality. Generous as Peter was, it would have required an almost superhuman amount of confidence to receive at once under his roof a man who had tried by the utmost violence to extirpate the very fibres of the Church. But if one so highly honoured as Barnabas was ready to vouch for him, Peter was not the man to stand coldly aloof. Thus it happened that Saul's earliest introduction to the families of those whom he had scattered would be made under the high auspices of the greatest of the Twelve.

The imagination tries in vain to penetrate the veil of two thousand years which hangs between us and the intercourse of the two Apostles. Barnabas, we may be sure, must have been often present in the little circle, and must have held many an earnest conversation with his former friend. Mary, the mother of Mark, would have something to tell.[2] Mark may have been an eye-witness of more than one pathetic scene. But how boundless would be the wealth of spiritual wisdom which Peter must have unfolded! Is it not certain that from those lips St. Paul must have heard about the Divine brightness of the dawning ministry of Jesus during the Galilæan year—about the raising of Jairus' daughter, and the Transfiguration on Hermon, and the discourse in the synagogue of Capernaum, and the awful scenes which had occurred on the day of the Crucifixion? And is it not natural to suppose that such a hearer—a hearer of exceptional culture, and enlightened to an extraordinary degree by the Holy Spirit of God—would grasp many of the words of the Lord with a firmness of grasp, and see into the very inmost heart of their significance with a keenness of insight, from which his informant might, in his turn, be glad to learn?

It must be a dull imagination that does not desire to linger for a moment on the few days during which two such men were inmates together of one obscure house in the city of Jerusalem. But however fruitful their intercourse, it did not at once secure to the new disciple a footing among the

[1] Col. iv. 10.
[2] St. John and other Apostles were probably absent, partly perhaps as a consequence of the very persecution in which Paul had been the prime mover.

brethren whose poverty and persecutions he came to share. Then it was that Barnabas came forward, and saved Saul for the work of the Church. The same discrimination of character, the same charity of insight which afterwards made him prove Mark to be a worthy comrade of their second mission, in spite of his first defection, now made him vouch unhesitatingly for the sincerity of Saul Taking him by the hand, he led him into the presence of the Apostles—the term being here used for Peter,[1] and James the Lord's brother,[2] and the elders of the assembled church—and there narrated to them the circumstances, which either they had never heard, or of the truth of which they had not yet been convinced. He told them of the vision on the road to Damascus, and of the fearlessness with which Saul had vindicated his sincerity in the very city to which he had come as an enemy. The words of Barnabas carried weight, and his confidence was contagious. Saul was admitted among the Christians on a footing of friendship, "going in and out among them." To the generosity and clear-sightedness of Joseph of Cyprus, on this and on a later occasion, the Apostle owed a vast debt of gratitude. Next only to the man who achieves the greatest and most blessed deeds is he who, perhaps himself wholly incapable of such high work, is yet the first to help and encourage the genius of others. We often do more good by our sympathy than by our labours, and render to the world a more lasting service by absence of jealousy, and recognition of merit, than we could ever render by the straining efforts of personal ambition.

No sooner was Saul recognised as a brother, than he renewed the ministry which he had begun at Damascus. It is, however, remarkable that he did not venture to preach to the Hebrew Christians. He sought the synagogues of the Hellenists in which the voice of Stephen had first been heard, and disputed with an energy not inferior to his. It was incumbent on him, though it was a duty which required no little courage, that his voice should be uplifted in the name of the Lord Jesus in the places where it had been heard of old in blasphemy against Him. But this very circumstance increased his danger. His preaching was again cut short by a conspiracy to murder him.[3]

It was useless to continue in a place where to stay was certain death. The little Galilæan community got information of the plot. To do the Jews justice, they showed little skill in keeping the secret of these deadly

[1] Acts ix. 27; Gal. i. 19. The true reading in Gal. i. 18 seems to be "Kephas" (א, A, B, and the most important versions); as also in ii. 9, 11, 14. This Hebrew form of the name also occurs in 1 Cor. ix. 5; xv. 5. Although elsewhere (*e.g.* ii. 7, 8) St. Paul uses "Peter" indifferently with Cephas, as is there shown by the unanimity of the MSS., it seems clear that St. Paul's conception of St. Peter was one which far more identified him with the Judaic Church than with the Church in general. In the eyes of St. Paul, Simon was *specially* the Apostle of the Circumcision.

[2] Gal. i. 19, *ἕτερον δὲ τῶν ἀποστόλων οὐκ εἶδον εἰ μὴ Ἰάκωβον* . . . It is impossible from the form of the words to tell whether James is here regarded as in the *strictest* sense an Apostle or not. The addition of "the Lord's brother"—*τὸ σεμνολόγημα*, as Chrysostom calls it—distinguishes him from James the brother of John, and from James the Less, the son of Alphæus.

[3] Acts ix. 29, *ἐπεχείρουν αὐτὸν ἀνελεῖν*. We know of at least ten such perils of assassination in the life of St. Paul.

combinations. It was natural that the Church should not only desire to save Saul's life, but also to avoid the danger of a fresh outbreak. Yet it was not without a struggle, and a distinct intimation that such was the will of God, that Saul yielded to the solicitations of his brethren. How deeply he felt this compulsory flight may be seen in the bitterness with which he alludes to it[1] even after the lapse of many years. He had scarcely been a fortnight in Jerusalem when the intensity of his prayers and emotions ended in a trance,[2] during which he again saw the Divine figure and heard the Divine voice which had arrested his mad progress towards the gates of Damascus. "Make instant haste, and depart in speed from Jerusalem," said Jesus to him; "for they will not receive thy testimony concerning Me." But to Saul it seemed incredible that his testimony could be resisted. If the vision of the risen Christ by which he had been converted was an argument which, from the nature of the case, could not, alone, be convincing to others, yet it seemed to Saul that, knowing what they did know of his intellectual power, and contrasting his present earnestness with his former persecution, they could not but listen to such a teacher as himself. He longed also to undo, so far as in him lay, the misery and mischief of the past havoc he had wrought. But however deep may have been his yearnings, however ardent his hopes, the answer came, brief and peremptory, "Go! for I will send thee forth afar to the Gentiles."[3]

All reluctance was now at an end; and we can see what at the time must have been utterly dark and mysterious to St. Paul—that the coldness with which he was received at Jerusalem, and the half-apparent desire to precipitate his departure—events so alien to his own plans and wishes, that he pleads even against the Divine voice which enforced the indications of circumstance—were part of a deep providential design. Years afterward, when St. Paul "stood pilloried on infamy's high stage," he was able with one of his strongest asseverations to appeal to the brevity of his stay in Jerusalem, and the paucity of those with whom he had any intercourse, in proof that it was not from the Church of Jerusalem that he had received his commission, and not to the Apostles at Jerusalem that he owed his allegiance. But though at present all this was unforeseen by him, he yielded to the suggestions of his brethren, and scarcely a fortnight after his arrival they —not, perhaps, wholly sorry to part with one whose presence was a source of many embarrassments—conducted him to the coast town of Cæsarea Stratonis[4]

[1] 1 Thess. ii. 15, "who both killed the Lord Jesus, and their own prophets, and *drove us out*" (ἡμᾶς ἐκδιωξάντων).

[2] Acts xxii. 17.

[3] Acts xxii. 17—21. The omission of this vision in the direct narrative of Acts ix. is a proof that silence as to this or that occurrence in the brief narrative of St. Luke must not be taken as a proof that he was unaware of the event which he omits. We may also note, in this passage, the first appearance of the interesting word *μάρτυς*. Here doubtless it has its primary sense of "witness;" but it contains the germ of its later sense of one who testified to Christ by voluntary death.

[4] That he was not sent to Cæsarea *Philippi* is almost too obvious to need argument. Neither *κατήγαγον*, which means a going downwards—*i.e.*, to the coast—nor *ἐξαπέστειλαν*,

to start him on his way to his native Tarsus. Of his movements on this occasion we hear no more in the Acts of the Apostles; but in the Epistle to the Galatians he says that he came into the regions of Syria and Cilicia, but remained a complete stranger to the churches of Judæa that were in Christ, all that they had heard of him being the rumours that their former persecutor was now an evangelist of the faith of which he was once a destroyer; news which gave them occasion to glorify God in him.[1]

Since we next find him at Tarsus, it might have been supposed that he sailed there direct, and there remained. The expression, however, that "he came into the regions of Syria and Cilicia," seems to imply that this was not the case.[2] Syria and Cilicia were at this time politically separated, and there is room for the conjecture that the ship in which the Apostle sailed was destined, not for Tarsus, but for Tyre, or Sidon, or Seleucia, the port of Antioch. The existence of friends and disciples of Saul in the Phœnician towns, and the churches of Syria as well as Cilicia,[3] point, though only with dim uncertainty, to the possibility that he performed part of his journey to Tarsus by land, and preached on the way. There is even nothing impossible in Mr. Lewin's suggestion[4] that his course may have been determined by one of those three shipwrecks which he mentions that he had undergone. But the occasions and circumstances of the three shipwrecks must be left to the merest conjecture. They occurred during the period when St. Luke was not a companion of St. Paul, and he has thought it sufficient to give from his own journal the graphic narrative of that later catastrophe of which he shared the perils. The active ministry in Syria and Cilicia may have occupied the period between Saul's departure in the direction of Tarsus, and his summons to fresh fields of labour in the Syrian Antioch. During this time he may have won over to the faith some of the members of his own family, and may have enjoyed the society of others who were in Christ before him. But all is uncertain, nor can we with the least confidence restore the probabilities of a period of which even the traditions have for centuries been obliterated. The stay of Saul at Tarsus was on any supposition a period mainly of waiting and of preparation, of which the records had no large significance in the history of the Christian faith. The fields in which he was to reap were whitening for the harvest; the arms of the reaper were being strengthened and his heart prepared.

would at all suit the long journey northwards to Cæsarea Philippi; nor is it probable that Saul would go to Tarsus by land, travelling in the direction of the dangerous Damascus, when he could go so much more easily by sea. It is a more interesting inquiry whether, as has been suggested, these words κατήγαγον and ἐξαπέστειλαν, imply a more than ordinary amount of *passivity* in the movements of Paul; and whether in this case the passiveness was due to the attacks of illness which were the sequel of his late vision.

[1] Gal. i. 21—24, ἤμην ἀγνοούμενος . . . ἀκούοντες ἦσαν . . . εὐαγγελίζεται . . . ἐπόρθει.

[2] Gal. i. 21. The expression is not indeed decisive, since Cilicia might easily be regarded as a mere definitive addition to describe the part of Syria to which he went. (Ewald, *Gesch. d. Apost. Zeitalt.* p. 439.)

[3] Acts xxi. 2; xxvii. 3; xv. 23, 41.

[4] *St. Paul*, i. 77.

CHAPTER XIV.

GAIUS AND THE JEWS—PEACE OF THE CHURCH.

"Reliqua ut de monstro narranda sunt."—SUET. *Calig.*

IMMEDIATELY after the hasty flight of Saul from Jerusalem, St. Luke adds,[1] "Then had the church rest throughout the whole of Judæa, and Galilee, and Samaria, being built up, and walking in the fear of the Lord; and by the exhortation of the Holy Spirit was multiplied." At first sight it might almost seem as though this internal peace, which produced such happy growth, was connected in the writer's mind with the absence of one whose conversion stirred up to madness the prominent opponents of the Church. It may be, however, that the turn of his expression is simply meant to resume the broken thread of his narrative. The absence of molestation, which caused the prosperity of the faith, is sufficiently accounted for by the events which were now happening in the Pagan world. The pause in the recorded career of the Apostle enables us also to pause and survey some of the conflicting conditions of Jewish and Gentile life as they were illustrated at this time by prominent events. It need hardly be said that such a survey has an immediate bearing on the conditions of the Days after Christ, and on the work of His great Apostle.

A multitude of concurrent arguments tend to show that Saul was converted early A.D. 37, and this brief stay at Jerusalem must therefore have occurred in the year 39. Now in the March of A.D. 37 Tiberius died, and Gaius—whose nickname of Caligula, or "Bootling," given him in his infancy by the soldiers of his father Germanicus, has been allowed to displace his true name—succeeded to the lordship of the world. Grim as had been the despotism of Tiberius, he extended to the religion of the Jews that contemptuous toleration which was the recognised principle of Roman policy. When Pilate had kindled their fanaticism by hanging the gilt shields in his palace at Jerusalem,[2] Tiberius, on an appeal being made to him, reprimanded the officiousness of his Procurator, and ordered him to remove the shields to Cæsarea. It is true that he allowed four thousand Jews to be deported from Rome to Sardinia, and punished with remorseless severity those who, from dread of violating the Mosiac law, refused to take military service.[3] This severity was not, however, due to any enmity against the race, but only to his indignation against the designing hypocrisy which, under pretence of proselytising, had won the adhesion of Fulvia, a noble Roman lady, to the Jewish religion; and to the detestable rascality with which her teacher and his companions had embezzled the presents of gold and purple which she had entrusted to them as an offering for the Temple at Jerusalem. Even this did

[1] Acts ix. 31, ἡ μὲν οὖν ἐκκλησία (א, A, B, C, and the chief versions). I follow what seems to me to be the best punctuation of the verse.

[2] *Life of Christ*, ii. 362.

[3] Jos. *Antt.* xviii. 3, § 5; Suet. *Tib.* xxxvi.

not prevent him from protecting the Jews as far as he could in their own country; and when Vitellius, the Legate of Syria, had decided that there was *primâ facie* cause for the complaints which had been raised against the Procurator in all three divisions of his district, it is probable that Pilate, who was sent to Rome to answer for his misdemeanours, would have received strict justice from the aged Emperor. But before Pilate arrived Tiberius had ended his long life of disappointment, crime, and gloom.

The accession of Gaius was hailed by the whole Roman world with a burst of rapture,[1] and there were none to whom it seemed more likely to introduce a golden era of prosperity than to the Jews. For if the young Emperor had any living friend, it was Herod Agrippa. That prince, if he could command but little affection as a grandson of Herod the Great, had yet a claim to Jewish loyalty as a son of the murdered Aristobulus, a grandson of the murdered Mariamne, and therefore a direct lineal descendant of that great line of Asmonæan princes whose names recalled the last glories of Jewish independence. Accordingly, when the news reached Jerusalem that Tiberius at last was dead, the Jews heaved a sigh of relief, and not only took with perfect readiness the oath of allegiance to Gaius, which was administered by Vitellius to the myriads who had thronged to the Feast of Pentecost, but offered speedy and willing holocausts for the prosperity of that reign which was to bring them a deeper misery, and a more absolute humiliation, than any which had been inflicted on them during the previous dominion of Rome.[2]

Gaius lost no time in publicly displaying his regard for the Herodian prince, who, with remarkable insight, had courted his friendship, not only before his accession was certain, but even in spite of the distinct recommendation of the former Emperor.[3]

One day, while riding in the same carriage as Gaius, Agrippa was imprudent enough to express his wish for the time when Tiberius would bequeath the Empire to a worthier successor. Such a remark might easily be construed into a crime of high treason, or *laesa majestas*. In a court which abounded with spies, and in which few dared to express above a whisper their real thoughts, it was natural that the obsequious slave who drove the chariot should seek an audience from Tiberius to communicate what he had heard; and when by the influence of Agrippa himself he had gained this opportunity, his report made the old Emperor so indignant, that he ordered the Jewish

[1] Suet. *Calig.* 13, 14.

[2] Compare for this entire narrative Suet. *Caligula;* Philo, *Leg. ad Gaium*, and *in Flaccum;* Jos. *Antt.* xviii. 6—8; *B. J.* ii. 10, § 1; Dion Cass. lix. 8, *seq.;* Grätz, iii. 270—277; Jahn, *Hebr. Commonwealth*, 174.

[3] The adventures of Herod Agrippa I. form one of the numerous romances which give us so clear a glimpse of the state of society during the early Empire. Sent to Rome by his grandfather, he had breathed from early youth the perfumed and intoxicating atmosphere of the Imperial Court as a companion of Drusus, the son of Tiberius. On the death of Drusus he was excluded from Court, and was brought to the verge of suicide by the indigence which followed a course of extravagance. Saved from his purpose by his wife Cypros, he went through a series of debts, disgraces, and escapades, until he was once more admitted to favour by Tiberius at Capreæ.

prince to be instantly arrested. Clothed as he was in royal purple, Agrippa was seized, put in chains, and taken off to a prison, in which he languished for the six remaining months of the life of Tiberius. Almost the first thought of Gaius on his accession was to relieve the friend who had paid him such assiduous court before his fortunes were revealed. Agrippa was at once released from custody. A few days after, Gaius sent for him, put a diadem on his head, conferred on him the tetrarchies of Herod Philip and of Lysanias, and presented him with a golden chain of equal weight with the iron one with which he had been bound.

Now, although Agrippa was a mere unprincipled adventurer, yet he had the one redeeming feature of respect for the external religion of his race. The Edomite admixture in his blood had not quite effaced the more generous instincts of an Asmonæan prince, nor had the sty of Capreæ altogether made him forget that he drew his line from the Priest of Modin. The Jews might well have expected that, under an Emperor with whom their prince was a bosom friend, their interests would be more secure than they had been even under a magnanimous Julius and a liberal Augustus. Their hopes were doomed to the bitterest disappointment; nor did any reign plunge them into more dreadful disasters than the reign of Agrippa's friend.

In August, A.D. 38, Agrippa arrived at Alexandria on his way to his new kingdom. His arrival was so entirely free from ostentation—for, indeed, Alexandria, where his antecedents were not unknown, was the last city in which he would have wished to air his brand-new royalty—that though he came in sight of the Pharos about twilight, he ordered the captain to stay in the offing till dark, that he might land unnoticed.[1] But the presence in the city of one who was at once a Jew, a king, an Idumæan, a Herod, and a favourite of Cæsar, would not be likely to remain long a secret; and if it was some matter of exultation to the Jews, it exasperated beyond all bounds the envy of the Egyptians. Flaccus, the Governor of Alexandria, chose to regard Agrippa's visit as an intentional insult to himself, and by the abuse which he heaped in secret upon the Jewish prince, encouraged the insults in which the mob of Alexandria were only too ready to indulge. Unpopular everywhere, the Jews were regarded in Alexandria with special hatred. Their wealth, their numbers, their usuries, their exclusiveness, the immunities which the two first Cæsars had granted them,[2] filled the worthless populace of a hybrid city with fury and loathing. A Jewish *king* was to them a conception at once ludicrous and offensive. Every street rang with lampoons against him, every theatre and puppet-show echoed with ribald farces composed in his insult, At last the wanton mob seized on a poor naked idiot named Carabbas, who had long been the butt of mischievous boys, and carrying him off to the Gymnasium, clothed him in a door-mat, by way of *tallith*, flattened a

[1] Derenbourg is therefore mistaken (p. 222) that Agrippa "se donna la puérile satisfaction d'étaler son luxe royal dans l'endroit où naguère il avait traîné une si honteuse misère."

[2] Jos. *Antt.* xiv. 7, § 2; xix. 5, § 2, and xiv. 10, *passim* (Decrees of Julius).

papyrus leaf as his diadem, gave him a stalk of papyrus for a sceptre, and surrounding him with a mimic body-guard of youths armed with sticks, proceeded to bow the knee before him, and consult him on state affairs. They ended the derisive pageant by loud shouts of *Maris! Maris!* the Syriac word for "Lord."

Encouraged by impunity and the connivance of the Præfect they then bribed him to acquiesce in more serious outrages. First they raised a cry to erect images of Gaius in the synagogues, hoping thereby to provoke the Jews into a resistance which might be interpreted as treason. This was to set an example which might be fatal to the Jews, not only in Egypt, but in all other countries. Irritated, perhaps, by the determined attitude of the Jews, Flaccus, in spite of the privileges which had long been secured to them by law and charter, published an edict in which he called them "foreigners and aliens," and drove them all into a part of a single quarter of the city in which it was impossible for them to live. The mob then proceeded to break open and plunder the shops of the deserted quarter, blockaded the Jews in their narrow precincts, beat and murdered all who in the pangs of hunger ventured to leave it, and burnt whole families alive, sometimes with green fuel, which added terribly to their tortures. Flaccus, for his part, arrested thirty-eight leading members of their Council, and after having stripped them of all their possessions, had them beaten, not with rods by the lictors, but with scourges by the lowest executioners, with such severity that some of them died in consequence. Their houses were rifled, in the hope of finding arms; but though nothing whatever was found, except common table-knives, men and women were dragged into the theatre, commanded to eat swine's flesh, and tortured if they refused.[1]

But neither these attempts to win popularity among the Gentile inhabitants by letting loose their rage against their Jewish neighbours, nor his ostentatious public loyalty and fulsome private flatteries saved Flaccus from the fate which he deserved. These proceedings had barely been going on for two months, when Gaius sent a centurion with a party of soldiers, who landing after dark, proceeded at once to the house of Stephanion, a freedman of Tiberius, with whom Flaccus happened to be dining, arrested him without difficulty, and brought him to Rome. Here he found that two low demagogues, Isidoras and Lampo, who had hitherto been among his parasites, and who had constantly fomented his hatred of the Jews, were now his chief accusers. He was found guilty. His property was confiscated, and he was banished, first to the miserable rock of Gyara, in the Ægean, and then to Andros. In one of those sleepless nights which were at once a symptom and an aggravation of his madness, Gaius, meditating on the speech of an exile whom he had restored, that during his banishment he used to pray for the death of Tiberius, determined to put an end to the crowd of distinguished criminals which imperial tyranny had collected on the barren islets of the Mediterranean.

[1] There seem to be distinct allusions to these troubles in 3 Macc. (*passim.*).

Flaccus was among the earliest victims, and Philo narrates with too gloating a vindictiveness the horrible manner in which he was hewn to pieces in a ditch by the despot's emissaries.[1]

Gaius had begun his reign with moderation, but the sudden change from the enforced simplicity of his tutelage to the boundless luxuries and lusts of his autocracy—the sudden plunge into all things which, as Philo[2] says, "destroy both soul and body and all the bonds which unite and strengthen the two"—brought on the illness which altered the entire organism of his brain. Up to that time he had been a vile and cruel man; thenceforth he was a mad and sanguinary monster. It was after this illness, and the immediately subsequent murders of Tiberius Gemellus, Macro, and Marcus Silanus, which delivered him from all apprehension of rivalry or restraint, that he began most violently to assert his godhead. His predecessors would have regarded it as far less impious to allow themselves or their fortunes to be regarded as divine, than to arrogate to themselves the actual style and attributes of existing deities.[3] But disdaining all mere demi-gods like Trophonius and Amphiaraus, Gaius began to appear in public, first in the guise of Hercules, or Bacchus, or one of the Dioscuri, and then as Apollo, or Mars, or Mercury, or even Venus (!), and demanded that choruses should be sung in his honour under these attributes; and, lastly, he did not hesitate to assert his perfect equality with Jupiter himself. The majority of the Romans, partly out of abject terror, partly out of contemptuous indifference, would feel little difficulty in humouring these vagaries; but the Jews, to their eternal honour, refused at all costs to sanction this frightful concession of divine honours to the basest of mankind. As there were plenty of parasites in the Court of Gaius who would lose no opportunity of indulging their spite against the Jews, an ingrained hatred of the whole nation soon took possession of his mind. The Alexandrians were not slow to avail themselves of this antipathy. They were well aware that the most acceptable flattery to the Emperor, and the most overwhelming insult to the Jews, was to erect images of Gaius in Jewish synagogues, and they not only did this, but even in the superb and celebrated Chief Synagogue of Alexandria[4] they erected a bronze statue in an old gilt quadriga which had once been dedicated to Cleopatra.

Of all these proceedings Gaius was kept informed, partly by his delighted study of Alexandrian newspapers, which Philo says that he preferred to all other literature, and partly by the incessant insults against the Jews distilled into his ears by Egyptian buffoons like the infamous Helicon.[5]

The sufferings of the Jews in Alexandria at last became so frightful that they despatched the venerable Philo with four others on an embassy to the

[1] It is not impossible that Herod Antipas may have perished in consequence of this same order of Gaius. It is true that Suetonius (*Calig.* 28) only says, "Misit circum *insulas* qui omnes (exsules) trucidarent;" but the *cause* would apply as much to all political exiles, and Dion (lix. 18) distinctly says that he put Antipas to death (κατέσφαξε). The trial of Antipas took place at Puteoli shortly before the Philonian embassy, A.D. 39.

[2] *De Leg.* 2.

[3] See Excursus XII., "Apotheosis of Roman Emperors."

[4] The Diapleuston.

[5] Philo, *Leg.* John *ad Gai.* xxv.

insane youth whom they refused to adore. Philo has left us an account of this embassy, which, though written with his usual rhetorical diffuseness, is intensely interesting as a record of the times. It opens for us a little window into the daily life of the Imperial Court at Rome within ten years of the death of Christ.

The first interview of the ambassadors with Gaius took place while he was walking in his mother's garden on the banks of the Tiber, and the apparent graciousness of his reception deceived all of them except Philo himself. After having been kept waiting for some time, the Jews were ordered to follow him to Puteoli, and there it was that a man with disordered aspect and bloodshot eyes rushed up to them, and with a frame that shivered with agony and in a voice broken with sobs, barely succeeded in giving utterance to the horrible intelligence that Gaius had asserted his intention of erecting a golden colossus of himself with the attributes of Jupiter in the Holy of Holies at Jerusalem. After giving way to their terror and agitation, the ambassadors asked the cause of this diabolical sacrilege, and were informed that it was due to the advice of "that scorpion-like slave," Helicon, who with "a poisonous Ascalonite" named Apelles—a low tragic actor—had made the suggestion during the fit of rage with which Gaius heard that the Jews of Jamnia had torn down a trumpery altar which the Gentiles of the city had erected to his deity with no other intention than that of wounding and insulting them.

So far from this being a transient or idle threat, Gaius wrote to Petronius, the Legate of Syria, and ordered him to carry it out with every precaution and by main force; and though the legate was well aware of the perilous nature of the undertaking, he had been obliged to furnish the necessary materials for the statue to the artists of Sidon.

No sooner had the miserable Jews heard of this threatened abomination of desolation, than they yielded themselves to such a passion of horror as made them forget every other interest. It was no time to be persecuting Christians when the most precious heritage of their religion was at stake. Flocking to Phœnicia in myriads, until they occupied the whole country like a cloud, they divided themselves into six companies of old men, youths, boys, aged women, matrons, and virgins, and rent the air with their howls and supplications, as they lay prostrate on the earth and scattered the dust in handfuls upon their heads. Petronius, a sensible and honourable man, was moved by their abject misery, and with the object of gaining time, ordered the Sidonian artists to make their statue very perfect, intimating not very obscurely that he wished them to be as long over it as possible. Meanwhile, in order to test the Jews, he went from Acre to Tiberias, and there the same scenes were repeated. For forty days, neglecting the sowing of their fields, they lay prostrate on the ground, and when the legate asked them whether they meant to make war against Cæsar, they said, No, but they were ready to die rather than see their temple desecrated, and in proof of their sincerity stretched out their throats. Seeing the obstinacy of their resolution, besieged by the entreaties of Aristobulus and Helcias the elder, afraid, too, that a famine would be caused by the neglect of tillage, Petronius, though at the risk of his own life, promised the Jews that he would write and intercede for them, if they would separate peaceably and attend to their husbandry. It was accepted by both Jews and Gentiles as a sign of the special blessing of God on this brave and humane decision, that no sooner had Petronius finished his speech than, after long drought, the sky grew black with clouds, and there was an abundant rain. He kept his word. He wrote a letter to Gaius, telling him that if the affair of the statue were pressed the Jews would neglect their harvest and there would be great danger lest he should find the whole country in a state of starvation, which might be even dangerous for himself and his suite, if he carried out his intended visit.

Meanwhile, in entire ignorance of all that had taken place, Agrippa had arrived at Rome, and he at once read in the countenance of the Emperor that something had gone wrong. On hearing what it was, he fell down in a fit, and lay for some time in a deep stupor. By the exertion of his whole influence with Gaius he only succeeded in procuring a temporary suspension of the design; and it was not long before the Emperor announced the intention of taking with him from Rome a colossus of gilded bronze—in order to cut off all excuse for delay—and of personally superintending its erection in the Temple, which would henceforth be regarded as dedicated to "the new Jupiter, the illustrious Gaius." Even during his brief period of indecision he was so angry with Petronius for the humanity that he had shown that he wrote him a letter commanding him to commit suicide if he did not want to die by the hands of the executioner.

These events, and the celebrated embassy of Philo to Gaius, of which he has left us so painfully graphic a description, probably took place in the August of the year 40. In the January of the following year the avenging sword of the brave tribune Cassius Chærea rid the world of the intolerable despot.[1] The vessel which had carried to Petronius the command to commit suicide, was fortunately delayed by stormy weather, and only arrived twenty-seven days after intelligence had been received that the tyrant was dead. From Claudius—who owed his throne entirely to the subtle intrigues of Agrippa—the Jews received both kindness and consideration. Petronius was ordered thenceforth to suppress and punish all attempts to insult them [2] in the quiet exercise of their religious duties; and Claudius utterly forbad that prayers should be addressed or sacrifices offered to himself.[3]

[1] The Jews believed that a *Bath-Kôl* from the Holy of Holies had announced his death to the High Priest (Simon the Just), and the anniversary was forbidden to be ever observed as a fast day (*Megillath Taanîth*, § 26; *Sotah*, f. 33, 1; Derenbourg, *Palest.* p. 207).

[2] See the decree of Claudius against the inhabitants of Dor, who had set up his statue in a Jewish synagogue.

[3] Dion Cass. lx. 5.

Book IV.

THE RECOGNITION OF THE GENTILES.

CHAPTER XV.

THE SAMARITANS—THE EUNUCH—THE CENTURION.

"Whenever I look at Peter, my very heart leaps for joy. If I could paint a portrait of Peter I would paint upon every hair of his head 'I believe in the forgiveness of sins.'"—LUTHER.

"Quel Padre vetusto
Di santa chiesa, a cui Cristo le chiavi
Racommandó di questo fior venusto."
DANTE, *Paradiso*, xxxii. 124.

"Blessed is the eunuch, which with his hands hath wrought no iniquity, nor imagined wicked things against God: for unto him shall be given the special gift of faith, and an inheritance in the temple of the Lord more acceptable to his mind. For glorious is the fruit of good labours: and the root of wisdom shall never fall away."—WISD. iii. 14, 15.

THE peace, the progress, the edification, the holiness of the Church, were caused, no doubt, by that rest from persecution which seems to have been due to the absorption of the Jews in the desire to avert the outrageous sacrilege of Gaius. And yet we cannot but ask with surprise whether the Christians looked on with indifference at the awful insult which was being aimed at their national religion. It would mark a state of opinion very different from what we should imagine if they had learnt to regard the unsullied sanctity of Jehovah's Temple as a thing in which they had no longer any immediate concern. Can we for one moment suppose that James the Lord's brother, or Simon the Zealot, were content to enjoy their freedom from molestation, without caring to take part in the despairing efforts of their people to move the compassion of the Legate of Syria? Is it conceivable that they would have stayed quietly at home while the other Jews in tens of thousands were streaming to his headquarters at Cæsarea, or flinging the dust upon their heads as they lay prostrate before him at Tiberias? Or was it their own personal peril which kept them from mingling among masses of fanatics who indignantly rejected their co-operation? Were they forced to confine their energies to the teaching of the infant churches of Palestine because they were not even allowed to participate in the hopes and fears of their compatriots? We may fairly assume that the Jewish Christians abhorred the purposed sacrilege; but if the schools of Hillel and Shammai, and the cliques of Hanan and Herod, hated them only one degree less than they hated the minions of Gaius, it is evident that there could have been nothing for the Apostles to do but to rejoice over their immediate immunity from danger, and to employ the rest thus granted them for the spread of the Kingdom of God. The kings of the earth might rage, and the princes imagine vain things, but *they*, at least, could kiss the Son,[1] and win the blessing of those who trusted in the Lord. It was the darkest midnight of the world's history, but the Goshen of Christ's Church was brightening more and more with the silver dawn.

To this outward peace and inward development was due an event which must continue to have the most memorable importance to the end of time—the admission of Gentiles, as Gentiles, into the Church of Christ. This great event must have seemed inevitable to men like St. Stephen, whose training as Hellenists had emancipated them from the crude spirit of Jewish isolation. But the experience of all history shows how difficult it is for the mind to shake itself free from views which have become rather instinctive than volitional; and though Jesus had uttered words which could only have one logical explanation, the older disciples, even the Apostles themselves, had not yet learnt their full significance. The revelation of God in Christ had been a beam in the darkness. To pour suddenly upon the midnight a full flood of spiritual illumination would have been alien to the method of God's dealings with our race. The dayspring had risen, but many a long year was to elapse before it broadened into the boundless noon.

But the time had now fully come in which those other sheep of which Jesus had spoken—the other sheep which were not of this fold[2]—must be brought to hear His voice. Indirectly, as well as directly, the result was due to St. Paul in a degree immeasurably greater than to any other man. To St. Peter, indeed, as a reward for his great confession, had been entrusted the keys of the Kingdom of Heaven; and, in accordance with this high metaphor, to him was permitted the honour of opening to the Gentiles the doors of the Christian Church. And that this was so ordained is a subject for deep thankfulness. The struggle of St. Paul against the hostility of Judaism from without and the leaven of Judaism from within was severe and lifelong, and even at his death faith alone could have enabled him to see that it had not been in vain. But the glorious effort of his life must have been fruitless had not the principle at stake been publicly conceded—conceded in direct obedience to sanctions which none ventured to dispute—by the most eminent and most authoritative of the Twelve. And yet, though St. Peter was thus set apart by Divine foresight to take the initiative, it was to one whom even the Twelve formally recognised as the Apostle of the Uncircumcision, that the world owes under God the development of Christian faith into a Christian theology, and the emancipation of Christianity from those Judaic limitations which would have been fatal to its universal acceptance.[3] To us, indeed, it is obvious that "it would have been impossible for the Gentiles to adopt the bye-laws of a Ghetto." If the followers of Christ had refused them the right-hand of fellowship on any other conditions, then the world would have gone its own

[1] Ps. ii. 12, נַשְּׁקוּ־בַר, either "kiss the Son," or "worship purely." Which rendering is right has been a disputed point ever since Jerome's day (*Adr. Ruff.* i.). See Perowne, *Psalms*, i. 116.

[2] John x. 16. In this verse it is a pity that the English version makes no distinction between αὐλή, "fold," and ποίμνη, "flock."

[3] Immer, *Neut. Theol.* 206.

way, and Mammon and Belial and Beelzebub would have rejoiced in the undisturbed corruption of a Paganism which was sinking deeper and deeper into the abyss of shame.

And as this deliverance of the Gentiles was due directly to the letters and labours of St. Paul, so the first beginnings of it rose indirectly from the consequences of the persecutions of which he had been the most fiery agent. The Ravager of the Faith was unconsciously proving himself its most powerful propagator. When he was making havoc of the Church, its members, who were thus scattered abroad, went everywhere preaching the word. To the liberal Hellenists this was a golden opportunity, and Philip, who had been a fellow-worker with Stephen, gladly seized it to preach the Gospel to the hated Samaritans. The eye of Jesus had already gazed in that country on fields whitening to the harvests, and the zeal of Philip, aided by high spiritual gifts, not only won a multitude of converts, but even arrested the influence of a powerful *goês*, or sorcerer, named Simon.[1] Justin Martyr calls him Simon of Gitton, and he has been generally identified with Simon Magus, the first heresiarch,[2] and with Simon the Cyprian, whom Felix employed to entrap the wandering affections of the Queen Drusilla. This man, though—as afterwards appeared—with the most interested and unworthy motives, went so far as to receive baptism; and the progress of the faith among his former dupes was so remarkable as to require the immediate presence of the Apostles. St. Peter and St. John went from Jerusalem to confirm the converts, and their presence resulted not only in the public discomfiture of Simon,[3] but also in that outpouring of special manifestations which accompanied the gift of the promised Comforter.

But Philip had the honour of achieving yet another great conversion, destined to prove yet more decisively that the day was at hand when the rules of Judaism were to be regarded as obsolete. Guided by divine impressions and angel voices he had turned his steps southward along the desert road which leads from Eleutheropolis to Gaza,[4] and there had en-

[1] As I have no space to give an account of the strange career and opinions of this "hero of the Romance of Heresy," as given in the Pseudo-Clementine *Homilies* and *Recognitions*, I must content myself by referring to Hippolyt. *Philosoph.* p. 161 *seq.*; Iren. *Haer.* i. 23; Neander, *Ch. Hist.* i. 454; *Planting*, 51—64; Gieseler, *Eccl. Hist.* i. 49; Mansel, *Gnostic Heresies*, 91—94; De Pressensé, i. 396 *seq.* The stories about him are fabulous (Arnob. *Adv. Gent.* 11, 12), and the supposed statue to him (Just. Mart. *Apol.* i. 26, 56; Iren. *Adv. Haer.* i. 23; Tert. *Apol.* 13) is believed, from a tablet found in 1574 on the Insula Tiberina, to have been a statue to the Sabine God *Semo Sancus* (Baronius, *in ann.* 44; Burton, *Bampt. Lect.* 375). A typical impostor of this epoch was Alexander of Abonoteichos (see Lucian, *Pseudo-mantis*, 10—51, and on the general prevalence of magic and theurgy, Döllinger, *Judenth. u. Heidenth.* viii. 2, § 7).

[2] Πάσης αἱρέσεως εὑρετής (Cyril, *Iren. adv. Hær.* i. 27; ii. *praef.*). "Gitton" may very likely be a confusion with Citium, whence "Chittim," &c.

[3] From his endeavour to obtain spiritual functions by a bribe is derived the word *simony*.

[4] The αὕτη ἐστὶν ἔρημος of viii. 26 probably refers to the *road*. Gaza was not destroyed till A.D. 65 (Robinson, *Bibl. Res.* ii. 640). Lange's notion (*Apost. Zeit.* ii. 109) that ἔρημος means "a moral desert" is out of the question. Although paronomasia is so frequent a figure in the N. T., yet I cannot think that there is anything intentional in the εἰς Γάζαν of 26, and the τῆς γάζης of 27.

countered the retinue of a wealthy Ethiopian eunuch, who held the high position of treasurer to the Kandake of Meroe.[1] There seems to be some reason for believing that this region had been to a certain extent converted to Judaism by Jews who penetrated into it from Egypt in the days of Psammetichus, whose descendants still exist under the name of Falâsyán.[2] The eunuch, in pious fulfilment of the duties of a Proselyte of the Gate—and his very condition rendered more than this impossible—had gone up to Jerusalem to worship, and not improbably to be present at one of the great yearly festivals. As he rode in his chariot at the head of his retinue he occupied his time, in accordance with the rules of the Rabbis, in studying the Scriptures, and he happened at the moment to be reading aloud in the LXX. version[3] the prophecy of Isaiah, "He was led as a sheep to slaughter, and as a lamb before his shearer is dumb, so he openeth not his mouth. In his humiliation his judgment was taken away, and his generation who shall declare? for his life is being taken from the earth."[4] Philip asked him whether he understood what he was reading? The eunuch confessed that it was all dark to him, and after having courteously invited Philip to take a seat in his chariot, asked who it was to whom the prophet was referring. Philip was thus enabled to unfold the Christian interpretation of the great scheme of prophecy, and so completely did he command the assent of his listener, that on their reaching a spring of water—possibly that at Bethsoron, not far from Hebron[5]—the eunuch asked to be baptised. The request was addressed to a large-hearted Hellenist, and was instantly granted, though there were reasons which might have made a James or a Simon hesitate. But in spite of the prohibition of Deuteronomy,[6] Philip saw that the Christian Church was to be an infinitely wider and more spiritual communion than that which had been formed by the Mosaic ritual. Recalling, perhaps, the magnificent prediction of Isaiah,[7] which seemed to rise above the Levitical prohibition—recalling, perhaps, also some of the tender words and promises of his Master, Christ—he instantly stepped down with the eunuch into the water. Without any recorded confession of creed or faith—for that which is introduced into Acts viii. 37 is one of the early instances of interpolation[8]—he administered

[1] The title of the Queen of Meroe (Pliny, *H.N.* vi. 35; Dion Cass. liv. 5). (For the "treasure" of Ethiopia see Isa. xlv. 14). Ethiopian tradition gives the eunuch the name of Indich. On the relation of the Jews with Ethiopia see Zeph. iii. 10; Ps. lxviii. 31; and for another faithful Ethiopian eunuch, also a "king's servant" (Ebed-melech), Jer. xxxviii. 7; xxxix. 16.

[2] Renan, *Les Apôtres*, p. 158.

[3] Isa. liii. 7, 8. The quotation in Acts viii. 33 is from the LXX. We might have supposed that the eunuch was reading the ancient Ethiopic version founded on the LXX.; but in that case Philip would not have understood him.

[4] This passage differs in several respects from our Hebrew text.

[5] Josh. xv. 58; Neh. iii. 16; Jer. *Ep.* ciii. The spring is called *Ain edh-Dhirweh.* But Dr. Robinson fixes the site near Tell el-Hasy (*Bibl. Res.* ii. 641). The tradition which fixes it at Ain Haniyeh, near Jerusalem, is much later.

[6] Deut. xxiii. 1. As for the nationality of the Ethiopian it must be borne in mind that even Moses himself had once married an Ethiopian wife (Numb. xii. 1).

[7] Isa. lvi. 3, 8.

[8] It is not found in ℵ, A, B, C, G, H, and the phrase τὸν Ἰησοῦν Χριστόν is unknown to

to one who was not only (as is probable) a Gentile by birth, but a eunuch by condition, the rite of baptism. The law of Deuteronomy forbade him to become a member of the Jewish Church, but Philip admitted him into that Christian communion[1] in which there is neither Jew nor Greek, neither male nor female, neither bond nor free.[2]

The subsequent work of Philip in the towns of Philistia and the sea-coast, as well as during his long subsequent residence at Cæsarea,[3] was doubtless fruitful, but for Christian history the main significance of his life lay in his successful mission to detested Samaritans, and in that bold baptism of the mutilated alien. Deacon though he was, he had not shrunk from putting into effect the Divine intimation which foreshadowed the ultimate obliteration of exclusive privileges. We cannot doubt that it was the fearless initiative of Philip which helped to shape the convictions of St. Peter, just as it was the avowed act of St. Peter which involved a logical concession of all those truths that were dearest to the heart of St. Paul.

In the peaceful visitation of the communities which the undisturbed prosperity of the new faith rendered both possible and desirable, Peter had journeyed westward, and, encouraged by the many conversions caused by the healing of Æneas and the raising of Tabitha, he had fixed his home at Joppa, in order to strengthen the young but flourishing churches on the plain of Sharon. That he lodged in the house of Simon, a tanner, is merely mentioned as one of those incidental circumstances which are never wanting in the narratives of writers familiar with the events which they describe. But we may now see in it a remarkable significance. It shows on the one hand how humble must have been the circumstances of even the chiefest of the Apostles, since nothing but poverty could have induced the choice of such a residence. But it shows further that Peter had already abandoned Rabbinic scrupulosities, for we can scarcely imagine that he would have found it impossible to procure another home,[4] and at the house of a tanner no strict and uncompromising follower of the Oral Law could have been induced to dwell. The daily contact with the hides and carcases of various animals necessitated by this trade, and the materials which it requires, rendered it impure and disgusting in the eyes of all rigid legalists. If a tanner married without mentioning his trade, his wife was permitted to get a divorce.[5] The law of

St. Luke. It is moreover obvious that while there was to some a strong temptation to insert something of the kind, there was no conceivable reason to omit it if it had been genuine.

[1] The significance of the act on those grounds is probably the main if not the sole reason for its narration; and if εὐνοῦχος had merely meant "chamberlain," there would have been no reason to add the word δυνάστης in ver. 27. Dr. Plumptre (*New Testament Commentary, in loc.*) adduces the interesting parallel furnished by the first decree of the first Œcumenical Council (Conc. Nic. *Can.* 1).

[2] Gal. iii. 28. In Iren. *Haer.* iii. 12, Euseb. *H. E.* ii. 1, he is said to have evangelised his own country.

[3] Acts. xxi. 8, 9. Observe the undesigned coincidence in his welcome of the Apostle of the Gentiles. At this point he disappears from Christian history. The Philip who died at Hierapolis (Euseb. *H. E.* iii. 31) is probably Philip the Apostle.

[4] Lydda and Joppa were thoroughly Judaic (Jos. *B. J.* ii. 19, § 1).

[5] *Ketubhôth*, f. 77, 1.

levirate marriage might be set aside if the brother-in-law of the childless widow was a tanner. A tanner's yard must be at least fifty cubits distant from any town,[1] and it must be even further off, said Rabbi Akibha, if built to the west of a town, from which quarter the effluvium is more easily blown. Now, a trade that is looked on with disgust tends to lower the self-respect of all who undertake it, and although Simon's yard may not have been contiguous to his house, yet the choice of his house as a residence not only proves how modest were the only resources which Peter could command, but also that he had learnt to rise superior to prejudice, and to recognise the dignity of honest labour in even the humblest trade.

It is certain that two problems of vast importance must constantly have been present to the mind of Peter at this time: namely, the relation of the Church to the Gentiles, and the relation alike of Jewish and Gentile Christians to the Mosaic, or perhaps it would be more accurate to say—though the distinction was not then realised—to the Levitical law. In the tanner's house at Joppa these difficulties were to meet with their divine and final solution.

They were problems extremely perplexing. As regards the first question, if the Gentiles were now to be admitted to the possession of full and equal privileges, then had God cast off His people? had the olden promises failed? As regards the second question, was not the Law divine? had it not been delivered amid the terrors of Sinai? Could it have been enforced on *one* nation if it had not been intended for all? Had not Jesus himself been obedient to the commandments? If a distinction were to be drawn between commandments ceremonial and moral, where were the traces of any distinction in the legislation itself, or in the words of Christ? Had He not bidden the leper go show himself to the priest, and offer for his cleansing such things as Moses has commanded for a testimony unto them?[2] Had He not said "Think not that I am come to destroy the Law and the Prophets; I am not come to destroy, but to *fulfil?*"[3] Had He not even said, "Till heaven and earth shall pass away, one jot or one tittle shall in no wise pass from the law till all be fulfilled?"[4]

These perplexing scruples had yet to wait for their removal, until, by the experience of missionary labour, God had ripened into its richest maturity the inspired genius of Saul of Tarsus. At that period it is probable that no living man could have accurately defined the future relations between Jew and Gentile, or met the difficulties which rose from these considerations. St. Stephen, who might have enlightened the minds of the Apostles on these great subjects, had passed away. St. Paul was still a suspected novice. The day when, in the great Epistles to the Galatians and the Romans, such problems should be fully solved, was still far distant. There is no hurry in the designs

[1] *Babha Bathra*, f. 25, 1, 16, 2 (where the remark is attributed to Bar Kappara). "No trade," says Rabbi, "will ever pass away from the earth; but happy be he whose parents belong to a respectable trade . . . The world cannot exist without tanners, . . . but woe unto him who is a tanner" (*Kiddushîn*, f. 82, 2).

[2] Matt. viii. 4; Mark i. 44.

[3] Matt. v. 17.

[4] Matt. v. 18; Luke xvi. 17.

of God. It is only when the servitude is at its worst that Moses is called forth. It is only when the perplexity is deepest that Saul enters the arena of controversy. It was only in the fulness of time that Christ was born.

But even at this period St. Peter—especially when he had left Jerusalem—must have been forced to see that the objections of the orthodox Jew to the equal participation of the Gentiles in Gospel privileges could be met by counter objections of serious importance; and that the arguments of Hebraists as to the eternal validity of the Mosaic system were being confronted by the logic of facts with opposing arguments which could not long be set aside.

For if Christ had said that He came to fulfil the Law, had He not also said many things which showed that those words had a deeper meaning than the *primâ facie* application which might be attached to them? Had He not six times vindicated for the Sabbath a larger freedom than the scribes admitted?[1] Had He not poured something like contempt on needless ceremonial ablutions?[2] Had He not Himself abstained from going up thrice yearly to Jerusalem to the three great festivals? Had He not often quoted with approval the words of Hoshea: "I will have mercy and not sacrifice?"[3] Had He not repeatedly said that all the Law and the Prophets hang on two broad and simple commandments?[4] Had He not both by word and action, showed His light estimation of mere ceremonial defilement, to which the Law attached a deep importance?[5] Had He not refused to sanction the stoning of an adulteress? Had He not even gone so far as to say that Moses had conceded some things, which were in themselves undesirable, only because of the hardness of Jewish hearts? Had He not said, "The Law and the Prophets were UNTIL JOHN?"[6]

And, besides all this, was it not clear that He meant His Church to be an Universal Church? Was not this universality of the offered message of mercy and adoption clearly indicated in the language of the Old Testament? Had not the Prophets again and again implied the ultimate calling of the Gentiles?[7] But if the Gentiles were to be admitted into the number of saints and brethren; if, as Jesus Himself had prophesied, there was to be at last one flock and one Shepherd,[8] how could this be if the Mosaic Law was to be considered as of permanent and universal validity? Was it not certain that the Gentiles, as a body, never would accept the whole system of Mosaism, and never would accept, above all, the crucial ordinance of circumcision? Would not such a demand upon them be a certain way of ensuring the refusal of the Gospel message? Or, if they did embrace it, was it conceivable that the Gentiles were never to be anything but mere Proselytes of the Gate, thrust as it were outside the portals of the True Spiritual Temple? If so, were not the most

[1] Luke xiv. 1—6; John v. 10; Mark ii. 23; Matt. xii. 10; John ix. 14; Luke xiii. 14; xvi. 16. (See *Life of Christ*, ii. 114.)
[2] Matt. xv. 20.
[3] Mark xii. 33; Matt. ix. 13; xii. 7.
[4] Matt. xxii. 40.
[5] Matt. xv. 17; Mark vii. 19.
[6] Matt. xix. 8; Mark x. 5—9.
[7] See Rom. xv. 9, 10, 11.
[8] John x. 16, ποίμνη.

primary conceptions of Christianity cut away at the very roots? were not its most beautiful and essential institutions rendered impossible? How could there be love-feasts, how could there be celebrations of the Lord's Supper, how could there be the beautiful spectacle of Christian love and Christian unity, if the Church was to be composed, not of members joined together in equal brotherhood, but of a proletariate of tolerated Gentiles, excluded even from the privilege of eating with an aristocracy of superior Jews? Dim and dwarfed and maimed did such an ideal look beside the grand conception of the redeemed nations of the world coming to Sion, singing, and with everlasting joy upon their heads!

And behind all these uncertainties towered a yet vaster and more eternal question. Christ had died to take away the sins of the world; what need, then, could there be of sacrifices? What significance could there be any more in the shadow, when the substance had been granted?[1] Where was the meaning of types, after they had been fulfilled in the glorious Antitype? What use was left for the lamp of the Tabernacle when the Sun of Righteousness had risen with healing in His wings?

Such thoughts, such problems, such perplexities, pressing for a decided principle which should guide men in their course of action amid daily multiplying difficulties, must inevitably have occupied, at this period, the thoughts of many of the brethren. In the heart of Peter they must have assumed yet more momentous proportions, because on him in many respects the initiative would depend.[2] The destinies of the world during centuries of history—the question whether, ere that brief *aeon* closed, the inestimable benefits of the Life and Death of Christ should be confined to the sectaries of an obsolete covenant and a perishing nationality, or extended freely to all the races of mankind—the question whether weary generations should be forced to accept the peculiarities of a Semitic tribe, or else look for no other refuge than the shrines of Isis or the Stoa of Athens—all depended, humanly speaking, on the line which should be taken by one who claimed no higher earthly intelligence than that of a Jewish fisherman. But God always chooses His own fitting instruments. In the decision of momentous questions rectitude of heart is a far surer guarantee of wisdom than power of intellect. When the unselfish purpose is ready to obey, the supernatural illumination is never wanting. When we desire only to do what is right, it is never long before we hear the voice behind us saying, "This is the way, walk ye in it," however much we might be otherwise inclined to turn aside to the right hand or to the left.

With such uncertainties in his heart, but also with such desire to be guided aright, one day at noon Peter mounted to the flat roof of the tanner's house for his mid-day prayer.[3] It is far from impossible that the house may have

[1] 1 Cor. xiii. 10; Col. ii. 17; Heb. x. i.
[2] "Lo maggior Padre di famiglia" (Dante, *Parad.* xxxii. 136).
[3] Matt. x. 27; xxiv. 17; Luke xvii. 31. House-tops in old days had been the common scenes of idol-worship (Jer. xix. 13; Zeph. i. 5, &c.).

been on the very spot with the one with which it has long been identified. It is at the south-west corner of the little town, and the spring in the courtyard would have been useful to the tanner if he carried on his trade in the place where he lived. A fig-tree now overshadows it, and there may have been one even then to protect the Apostle from the Syrian sun. In any case his eyes must have looked on identically the same scene which we may now witness from that spot: a small Oriental town with the outline of its flat roofs and low square houses relieved by trees and gardens; a line of low dunes and sandy shore; a sea stretching far away to the Isles of the Gentiles—a golden mirror burning under the rays of the Eastern noon in unbroken light, except where it is rippled by the wings of the sea-birds which congregate on the slippery rocks beneath the town, or where its lazy swell breaks over the line of reef which legend has connected with the story of Andromeda. It is a meeting-point of the East and West. Behind us lie Philistia and the Holy Land. Beyond the Jordan, and beyond the purple hills which form the eastern ramparts of its valley, and far away beyond the Euphrates, were the countries of those immemorial and colossal despotisms—the giant forms of empires which had passed long ago "on their way to ruin;" before us—a highway for the nations—are the inland waters of the sea whose shores during long ages of history have been the scene of all that is best and greatest in the progress of mankind. As he gazed dreamily on sea and town did Peter think of that old prophet who, eight centuries before, had been sent by God from that very port to preach repentance to one of those mighty kingdoms of the perishing Gentiles, and whom in strange ways God had taught?[1]

It was high noon, and while he prayed and meditated, the Apostle, who all his life had been familiar with the scanty fare of poverty, became very hungry. But the mid-day meal was not yet ready, and, while he waited, his hunger, his uncertainties, his prayers for guidance, were all moulded by the providence of God, to the fulfilment of His own high ends. There is something inimitably natural in the way in which truths of transcendent importance were brought home to the seeker's thoughts amid the fantastic crudities of mental imagery. The narrative bears upon the face of it the marks of authenticity, and we feel instinctively that it is the closest possible reflection of the form in which divine guidance came to the honest and impetuous Apostle as, in the hungry pause which followed his mid-day supplications, he half-dozed, half-meditated, on the hot flat roof under the blazing sky, with his gaze towards the West and towards the future, over the blazing sea.

A sort of trance came over him.[2]

The heaven seemed to open. Instead of the burning radiance of sky and sea there shone before him something like a great linen sheet,[3] which was being let down to him from heaven to earth by ropes which held it at the four corners.[4] In its vast capacity, as in the hollow of some great ark, he saw

[1] Jonah i. 3. [2] Acts x. 10, ἐγένετο ἐπ' αὐτὸν ἔκστασις (ℵ, A, B, C, E, &c.).
[3] ὀθόνη (cf. John xix. 40).
[4] This seems to be implied in the ἀρχαῖς (see Eur. *Hippol.* 762, and Wetst. *ad loc.*). But

all the four-footed beasts, and reptiles of the earth, and fowls of the air,[1] while a voice said to him, "Rise, Peter, slay and eat." But even in his hunger, kindled yet more keenly by the sight of food, Peter did not forget the habits of his training. Among these animals and creeping things were swine, and camels, and rabbits, and creatures which did not chew the cud or divide the hoof—all of which had been distinctly forbidden by the Law as articles of food. Better die of hunger than violate the rules of the *Kashar*, and eat such things, the very thought of which caused a shudder to a Jew.[2] It seemed strange to Peter that a voice from heaven should bid him, without exception or distinction, to slay and eat creatures among which the unclean were thus mingled with the clean;—nay, the very presence of the unclean among them seemed to defile the entire sheet.[3] Brief as is the narrative of this trance in which bodily sensations assuming the grotesque form of objective images became a medium of spiritual illumination,[4] it is clearly implied that though pure and impure animals were freely mingled in the great white sheet, it was mainly on the latter that the glance of Peter fell, just as it was with "sinners" of the Gentiles, and their admission to the privileges of brotherhood, that his thoughts must have been mainly occupied. Accordingly, with that simple and audacious self-confidence which in his character was so singularly mingled with fits of timidity and depression, he boldly corrects the Voice which orders him, and reminds the Divine Interlocutor that he must, so to speak, have made an oversight.[5]

"By no means, Lord!"—and the reader will immediately recall the scene of the Gospel, in which St. Peter, emboldened by Christ's words of praise, took Him and began to rebuke Him, saying, "Be it far from Thee, Lord,"—

δεδεμένον καὶ are wanting in ℵ, A, B, E. The Vulgate has "quatuor initiis submitti de caelo."

[1] Acts x. 12, πάντα τὰ, "all the," not "all kinds of," which would be παντοῖα. Augustine uses the comparison of the ark (*c. Faust.* xii. 15); omit καὶ τὰ θηρία (ℵ, A, B, &c.).

[2] On the *Kashar*, see *infra*, p. 245. The example of Daniel (i. 8—16) made the Jews more particular. Josephus (*Vit.* 3) tells us that some priests imprisoned at Rome lived only on figs and nuts.

[3] In the Talmud (*Sanhedr.* f. 59, col. 2) there is a curious story about unclean animals supernaturally represented to R. Shimon Ben Chalaphtha, *who slays them for food.* This leads to the remark, "*Nothing unclean comes down from heaven.*" Have we here an oblique argument against the significance of St. Peter's vision? R. Ishmael said that the care of Israel to avoid creeping things would alone have been a reason why God saved them from Egypt (*Babha Metzia*, f. 61, 2). Yet every Sanhedrist must be ingenious enough to prove that a creeping thing is clean (*Sanhedrin*, f. 17, 1).

[4] See some excellent remarks of Neander, *Planting*, i. 73.

[5] Cf. John xiii. 8. Increased familiarity with Jewish writings invariably deepens our conviction that in the New Testament we are dealing with truthful records. Knowing as we do the reverence of the Jews for divine intimations, we might well have supposed that not even in a trance would Peter have raised objections to the mandate of the *bath-Kôl.* And yet we find exactly the same thing in Scripture (1 Kings xix. 14; Jonah iv. 1, 9; Jer. i. 6), in the previous accounts of Peter himself (Matt. xvi. 22); of St. Paul (Acts xxii. 19); and in the Talmudic writings. Few stories of the Talmud convey a more unshaken conviction of the indefeasible obligatoriness of the Law than that of the resistance even to a voice from heaven by the assembled Rabbis, in *Babha Metzia*, f. 59, 2 (I have quoted it in the *Expositor*, 1877). It not only illustrates the point immediately before us, but also shows more clearly than anything else could do the overwhelming forces against which St. Paul had to fight his way.

"for," he added, with a touch of genuine Judaic pride, "I never ate anything profane or unclean." And the Voice spake a second time: "What God cleansed, 'profane' not thou;" or, in the less energetic periphrasis of our Version, "What God hath cleansed, that call not thou common." This was done thrice, and then the vision vanished. The sheet was suddenly drawn up into heaven. The trance was over. Peter was alone with his own thoughts; all was hushed; there came no murmur more from the blazing heaven; at his feet rolled silently the blazing sea.

What did it mean? St. Peter's hunger was absorbed in the perplexity of interpreting the strange symbols by which he felt at once that the Holy Spirit was guiding him to truth—to truth on which he must act, however momentous were the issues, however painful the immediate results. Was that great linen sheet in its whiteness the image of a world washed white,[1] and were its four corners a sign that they who dwelt therein were to be gathered from the east and from the west, from the north and from the south; and were all the animals and creeping things, clean and unclean, the image of all the races which inhabit it? And if so, was the permission—nay, the command—to eat of the unclean no less than of the clean an indication that the Levitical Law was now "ready to vanish away;"[2] and that with it must vanish away, no less inevitably, that horror of any communion with Gentile races which rested mainly upon its provisions? What else could be meant by a command which directly contradicted the command of Moses?[3] Was it really meant that all things were to become new? that even these unclean things were to be regarded as let down from heaven? and that in this new world, this pure world, Gentiles were no longer to be called "dogs," but Jew and Gentile were to meet on a footing of perfect equality, cleansed alike by the blood of Christ?

Nor is the connexion between the symbol and the thing signified quite so distant and arbitrary as has been generally supposed. The distinction between clean and unclean meats was one of the insuperable barriers between the Gentile and the Jew—a barrier which prevented all intercourse between them, because it rendered it impossible for them to meet at the same table or in social life. In the society of a Gentile, a Jew was liable at any moment to those ceremonial defilements which involved all kinds of seclusion and inconvenience; and not only so, but it was mainly by partaking of unclean food that the Gentiles became themselves so unclean in the eyes of the Jews. It is hardly possible to put into words the intensity of horror and revolt with which the Jew regarded swine.[4] They were to him the very ideal and quintessence of all that must be looked upon with an energetic concentration of disgust. He would not even mention a pig by name, but spoke of it as *dabhar acheer*, or "the other thing." When, in the days of Hyrcanus, a pig

[1] So Œcumenius. [2] Heb. viii. 13. [3] Lev. xi. 7; Deut. xiv. 8.

[4] Isa. lxv. 4; lxvi. 3; 2 Macc. vi. 18, 19; Jos. *c. Ap.* ii. 14. The abhorrence was shared by many Eastern nations (Hdt. ii. 47; Pliny, *H. N.* viii. 52; Koran). This was partly due to its filthy habits (2 Pet. ii. 22).

had been surreptitiously put into a box and drawn up the walls of Jerusalem, the Jews declared that a shudder of earthquake had run through four hundred parasangs of the Holy Land.[1] Yet this filthy and atrocious creature, which could hardly even be thought of without pollution, was not only the chief delicacy at Gentile banquets,[2] but was, in one form or other, one of the commonest articles of Gentile consumption. How could a Jew touch or speak to a human being who of deliberate choice had banqueted on swine's flesh, and who might on that very day have partaken of the abomination? The cleansing of all articles of food involved far more immediately than has yet been noticed the acceptance of Gentiles on equal footing to equal privileges.

And doubtless, as such thoughts passed through the soul of Peter, he remembered also that remarkable "parable" of Jesus of which he and his brother disciples had once asked the explanation. Jesus in a few words, but with both of the emphatic formulæ which He adopted to call special attention to any utterance of more than ordinary depth and solemnity—"*Hearken unto me, every one of you, and understand;*" "*If any man hath ears to hear, let him hear,*"[3]—had said, "There is nothing from without a man entering into him which can defile him." What He had proceeded to say—that what truly defiles a man is that which comes out of him—was easy enough to understand, and was a truth of deep meaning; but so difficult had it been to grasp the first half of the clause, that they had asked Him to explain a "parable" which seemed to be in direct contradiction to the Mosaic Law. Expressing His astonishment at their want of insight, He had shown them that what entered into a man from without did but become a part of his material organism, entering, "not into the heart, but into the belly, and so passing into the draught." THIS, HE SAID—as now for the first time, perhaps, flashed with full conviction into the mind of Peter—MAKING ALL MEATS PURE;[4]—as he proceeded afterwards to develop those weighty truths about the inward character of all real pollution, and the genesis of all crime from evil thoughts, which convey so solemn a warning. To me it seems that it was the trance and vision of Joppa which first made Peter realise the true meaning of Christ in one of those few *distinct* utterances in which he had intimated the coming annulment of the Mosaic Law. It is, doubtless, due to the fact that St. Peter, as the informant of St. Mark in writing his Gospel,

[1] *Jer. Berachôth*, iv. 1; Derenbourg, *Palest.* 114; Grätz, iii. 480. (The story is also told in *Babha Kama*, f. 82, 2; *Menachôth*, f. 64, 2; *Sotah*, f. 49, 2.)

[2] *Sumen*, in Plaut. *Curc.* ii. 3, 44; Pers. i. 53; Plin. *H. N.* xi. 37.

[3] Mark vii. 14, 16.

[4] Mark vii. 19. This interpretation, due originally to the early Fathers—being found in Chrysostom, *Hom. in Matt.* li. p. 526, and Gregory Thaumaturgus—was revived, forty years ago, by the Rev. F. Field, in a note of his edition of St. Chrysostom's *Homilies* (iii. 112). (See *Expositor* for 1876, where I have examined the passage at length.) Here, however, it lay unnoticed, till it gained, quite recently, the attention which it deserved. The true reading is certainly καθαρίζων not the καθαρίζον of our edition—a reading due, in all probability, to the impossibility of making καθαρίζων agree with ἀφεδρῶνα. The loss of the true interpretation has been very serious. Now, however, it is happily revived. It has a more direct bearing than any other on the main practical difficulty of the Apostolic age.

and the sole ultimate authority for this vision in the Acts, is the source of *both* narratives, that we owe the hitherto unnoticed circumstance that the two verbs "*cleanse*" and "*profane*"—both in a peculiarly pregnant sense—are the two most prominent words in the narrative of both events.

While Peter thus pondered—perplexed, indeed, but with a new light dawning in his soul—the circumstance occurred which gave to his vision its full significance. Trained, like all Jews, in unquestioning belief of a daily Providence exercised over the minutest no less than over the greatest events of life, Peter would have been exactly in the mood which was prepared to accept any further indication of God's will from whatever source it came. The recognised source of such guidance at this epoch was the utterance of voices apparently accidental which the Jews reckoned as their sole remaining kind of inspired teaching, and to which they gave the name of *Bath-Kol*.[1] The first words heard by Peter after his singular trance were in the voices of Gentiles. In the courtyard below him were three Gentiles, of whom one was in the garb of a soldier. Having asked their way to the house of Simon the Tanner, they were now inquiring whether a certain Simon, who bore the surname of Peter, was lodging there. Instantly there shot through his mind a gleam of heavenly light. He saw the divine connexion between the vision of his trance and the inquiry of these Gentiles, and a Voice within him warned him that these men had come in accordance with an express intimation of God's will, and that he was to go with them without question or hesitation. He instantly obeyed. He descended from the roof, told the messengers he was the person whom they were seeking, and asked their business. They were the bearers of a strange message. "Cornelius," they said, "a centurion, a just man, and a worshipper of God, to whose virtues the entire Jewish nation bore testimony, had received an angelic intimation to send for him, and hear his instructions." Peter at once offered them the free and simple hospitality of the East; and as it was too hot and they were too tired to start at once on their homeward journey, they rested there until the following morning. Further conversation would have made Peter aware that Cornelius was a centurion of the Italian band;[2] that not only he, but all his house, "feared God;" that the generosity of his almsgiving and the earnestness of his prayers were widely known; and that the intimation to send for Peter had been given to him while he was fasting on the previous day at three o'clock. He had acted upon it so immediately that, in spite of the heat and the distance of thirty miles along shore and plain, his messengers had arrived at Joppa by the following noon.

The next morning they all started on the journey which was to involve such momentous issues How deeply alive St. Peter himself was to the consequences which might ensue from his act is significantly shown by his

[1] *Life of Christ*, i. 118.

[2] The Italian cohort was probably one composed of "*Velones*," Italian volunteers. "Cohors militum voluntaria, quae est in Syria" (Gruter, *Inscr.* i. 434; Akerman, *Num. Illustr.* 34). It would be specially required at Cæsarea.

inviting no fewer than six of the brethren at Joppa to accompany him, and to be witnesses of all that should take place.[1]

The journey—since Orientals are leisurely in their movements, and they could only travel during the cool hours—occupied two days. Thus it was not until the fourth day after the vision of Cornelius that, for the first time during two thousand years, the Jew and the Gentile met on the broad grounds of perfect religious equality before God their Father. Struck with the sacredness of the occasion—struck, too, it may be, by something in the appearance of the chief of the Apostles—Cornelius, who had risen to meet Peter on the threshold, prostrated himself at his feet,[2] as we are told that, three hundred years before, Alexander the Great had done at the feet of the High Priest Jaddua,[3] and, six hundred years afterwards, Edwin of Deira did at the feet of Paulinus.[4] Instantly Peter raised the pious soldier, and, to the amazement doubtless of the brethren who accompanied him, perhaps even to his own astonishment, violated all the traditions of a lifetime, as well as the national customs of many centuries, by walking side by side with him in free conversation into the presence of his assembled Gentile relatives. This he did, not from the forgetfulness of an enthusiastic moment, but with the avowal that he was doing that which had been hitherto regarded as irreligious,[5] but doing it in accordance with a divine revelation. Cornelius then related the causes which had led him to send for Peter, and the Apostle began his solemn address to them with the memorable statement that now he perceived with undoubted certainty that "GOD IS NO RESPECTER OF PERSONS, BUT IN EVERY NATION HE THAT FEARETH HIM AND WORKETH RIGHTEOUSNESS IS ACCEPTABLE TO HIM."[6] Never were words more noble uttered. But we must not interpret them to mean the same proposition as that which is so emphatically repudiated by the English Reformers, "That every man shall be saved by the law or sect which he professeth, so that he be diligent to frame his life according to that law and the light of Nature." Had this been the meaning of the Apostle—a meaning which it would be an immense anachronism to attribute to him—it would have been needless for him to preach to Cornelius, as he proceeded to do, the leading doctrines of the Christian faith; it would have been sufficient for him to bid Cornelius continue in prayer and charity without unfolding to him "only the name of Jesus Christ whereby men must be saved." The indifference of nationality was the thought in Peter's mind; not by any means the indifference of

[1] Compare Acts x. 23 with xi. 12.

[2] D and the Syr. have the pragmatic addition, "And when Peter drew near to Cæsarea, one of the slaves running forward gave notice that he had arrived; and Cornelius springing forth, and meeting him, falling at his feet, worshipped him."

[3] See Jos. *Antt.* xi. 8, § 5.

[4] The story is told in Bede, *Eccl. Hist. Angl.* ii. 12.

[5] Acts x. 28, ἀθέμιτον: cf. John xviii. 28. Lightf. *Hor. Hebr. ad Matt.* xviii. 17.

[6] St. Peter's words are the most categorical contradiction of the Rabbinic comments on Prov. xiv. 34, which asserted that any righteous acts done by the Gentiles were sin to them. Such was the thesis maintained even by Hillelites like Gamaliel II. and R. Eliezer of Modin (*Babha Bathra*, f. 10, 2). (*V. infra*, pp. 420, 454.)

religions. All who, to the utmost of the opportunities vouchsafed to them, fear and love God with sincerity of heart, shall be saved by Christ's redemption; some of them—many of them—will He lead to a knowledge of Him in this life; all of them shall see Him and know Him in the life to come.[1]

Accordingly Peter proceeded to recall to these Gentiles all that they had heard[2] of the preaching of peace by Jesus Christ the Lord of all; of His life and ministry after the baptism of John; how God anointed Him with the Holy Spirit and with power; how He went about doing good, and healing all who were under the tyranny of the devil; and then of the Crucifixion and Resurrection from the dead, of which the disciples were the appointed witnesses, commissioned by the Voice of their risen Lord to testify that He is the destined Judge of quick and dead. And while Peter was proceeding to show from the Prophets that all who believed on Him should through His name receive remission of sins, suddenly on these unbaptised Gentiles no less than on the Jews who were present, fell that inspired emotion of superhuman utterance which was the signature of Pentecost. "The Holy Ghost fell upon them." The six brethren who had accompanied Peter from Joppa might well be amazed. Here were men unbaptised, uncircumcised, unclean—men who had been idolaters, dogs of the Gentiles, eaters of the unclean beast, whose touch involved ceremonial pollution—speaking and praising God in the utterances which could only come from hearts stirred by divine influence to their most secret depth. With bold readiness Peter seized the favourable moment. The spectacle which he had witnessed raised him above ignoble prejudices, and the rising tide of conviction swept away the dogmas and habits of his earlier years. Appealing to this proof of the spiritual equality of the Gentile with the Jew, he asked "whether any one could forbid water for their baptism?" No one cared to dispute the cogency of this proof that it was God's will to admit Cornelius and his friends to the privileges of Christian brotherhood. Peter not only commanded them to be baptised in the name of the Lord, but even freely accepted their invitation "to tarry with them certain days."

The news of a revolution so astounding was not long in reaching Jerusalem, and when Peter returned to the Holy City he was met by the sterner zealots who had joined Christianity, by those of whom we shall henceforth hear so often as "those of the circumcision," with the fierce indignant murmur, "*Thou wentest into the house of men uncircumcised, and didst* EAT WITH THEM!"[3] To associate with them, to enter their houses, was not that pollution enough? to touch in familiar intercourse men who had never received the seal of the covenant, to be in daily contact with people who might, no one knew how recently, have had "broth of abominable things in their vessels"—

[1] Cf. Rom. ii. 6, 10, 14, 15.

[2] Acts x. 36. To understand τὸν λόγον here in the Johannine sense seems to me utterly uncritical.

[3] "He who eats with an uncircumcised person, eats, as it were, with a dog; he who touches him, touches, as it were, a dead body; and he who bathes in the same place with him, bathes, as it were, with a leper" (*Pirke Rabbi Eliezer*, 29).

was not this sufficiently horrible? But "*to eat with them*"—to eat food prepared by Gentiles—to taste meat which had been illegally killed by Gentile hands—to neglect the rules of the *Kashar*—to take food from dishes which any sort of unclean insect or animal, nay even "the other thing," might have defiled—was it to be thought of without a shudder?[1]

Thus Peter was met at Jerusalem by something very like an impeachment, but he confronted the storm with perfect courage.[2] What he had done he had not done arbitrarily, but step by step under direct divine guidance. He detailed to them his vision on the roof at Joppa, and the angelic appearance which had suggested the message of Cornelius. Finally he appealed to the outpouring of the Holy Spirit, which had been manifested in those Gentiles by the very same signs as in themselves. Was not this the promised baptism with the Holy Ghost? was it not a proof that God accepted these Gentiles no less fully than He accepted *them?* "What was I that I could withstand God?"

The bold defence silenced for a time the adversaries of an innovation which they regarded as unscriptural and disloyal. They could not dispute facts authenticated by the direct testimony of their six brethren—whom Peter, conscious of the seriousness of the crisis, had very prudently brought with him from Joppa—nor could they deny the apparent approval of heaven. The feeling of the majority was in favour of astonished but grateful acquiescence. Subsequent events prove only too plainly that there was at any rate a displeased minority, who were quite unprepared to sacrifice their monopoly of precedence in the equal kingdom of God. Even in the language of the others[3] we seem to catch a faint echo of reluctance and surprise. Nor would they admit any general principle. The only point which they conceded was—not that the Gentiles were to be admitted, without circumcision, to full communion, still less that Jews would be generally justified in eating with them, as Peter had done—but only that "God had, it seemed, to the Gentiles also granted repentance unto life."

Meanwhile, and, so far as we are aware, in entire independence of these initial movements, the Church had been undergoing a new and vast development in Syria, which transferred the position of the metropolis of Christianity from Jerusalem to Antioch, as completely as it was to be afterwards transferred from Antioch to Rome.

[1] To this day orthodox Jews submit to any inconvenience rather than touch meat killed by a Gentile butcher (McCaul, *Old Paths*, 397, *seq.*). This leads sometimes not only to a monopoly, but even to a downright tyranny on the part of the butcher who has the *kadima* (Frankl, *Jews in the East*, ii.).

[2] Acts xi. 2. διεκρίνοντο πρὸς αὐτόν. Cf. Jud. 9.

[3] Acts xi. 18, ἄραγε καὶ τοῖς ἔθνεσιν.

Book V.

ANTIOCH.

CHAPTER XVI.

THE SECOND CAPITAL OF CHRISTIANITY.

"Quos, per flagitia invisos, vulgus *Christianos* appellabat."—TAC. *Ann.* xv. 44.

Χριστιανός εἰμί.—*Mart. Polyc.* iii.

Εὐχαριστοῦμέν σοι ὅτι τὸ ὄνομα τοῦ Χριστοῦ σου ἐπικέκληται ἐφ ἡμᾶς, καὶ σοὶ προσῳκειώμεθα.—CLEM. ROM.

Οὐκ αὐτοὶ βλασφημοῦσι τὸ καλὸν ὄνομα τὸ ἐπικληθὲν ἐφ' ὑμᾶς;—JAS. ii. 7.

Εἰ ὀνειδίζεσθε ἐν ὀνόματι Χριστοῦ, μακάριοι.—1 PET. iv. 14.

"Nomen . . . quod sicut unguentum diffusum longe lateque redolet."—GAL. *Tyr.* iv. 9.

"Oditur ergo in hominibus innocuis etiam nomen innocuum."—TERT. *Apol.* 3.

THE overruling Providence of God is so clearly marked in the progress of human events that the Christian hardly needs any further proof that "there is a hand that guides." In the events of his own little life the perspective of God's dealings is often hidden from him, but when he watches the story of nations and of religions he can clearly trace the divine purposes, and see the lessons which God's hand has written on every page of history. What seems to be utter ruin is often complete salvation; what was regarded as cruel disaster constantly turns out to be essential blessing.

It was so with the persecution which ensued on the death of Stephen. Had it been less inquisitorial, it would not have accomplished its destined purpose. The Saul who laid in ruins the Church of Jerusalem was unconsciously deepening the foundations of circumstance on which hereafter—the same and not the same—he should rear the superstructure of the Church of God. Saul the persecutor was doing, by opposite means, the same work as Paul the Apostle.

For when the members of the infant Church fled terror-stricken from the Holy City, they carried with them far and wide the good tidings of the Jerusalem above. At first, as was natural, they spoke to Jews alone. It would be long before they would hear how Philip had evangelised Samaria, and how, by his baptism of the eunuch, he had admitted into the Church of Christ one whom Moses had excluded from the congregation of Israel. The baptism of the pious soldier had taken place still later, and the knowledge of it could not at once reach the scattered Christians. In Phœnicia, therefore, and in Cyprus, their preaching was confined at first within the limits of Judaism; nor was it until the wandering Hellenists had reached Antioch that they boldly ventured *TO PREACH TO THE GENTILES.*[1] Whether these

[1] Acts xi. 20. There can be no doubt that Ἕλληνας, and not Ἑλληνιστὰς (which is accepted by our version, and rendered "Grecians") is the true reading. (1) External

Gentiles were such only as had already embraced the "Noachian dispensation," or whether they included others who had in no sense become adherents of the synagogue, we are not told. Greek proselytes were at this period common in every considerable city of the Empire,[1] and it is reasonable to suppose that they furnished a majority, at any rate, of the new converts. However this may have been, the work of these nameless Evangelists was eminently successful. It received the seal of God's blessing, and a large multitude of Greeks turned to the Lord. The fact, so much obscured by the wrong reading followed by our English Version, is nothing less than the beginning, on a large scale, of the *conversion of the Gentiles*. It is one of the great *moments* in the ascensive work begun by Stephen, advanced by Philip, authorised by Peter, and finally culminating in the life, mission, and Epistles of St. Paul.

When the news reached Jerusalem, it excited great attention, and the members of the Church determined to despatch one of their number to watch what was going on. Their choice of an emissary showed that as yet the counsels of the party of moderation prevailed, for they despatched the large-hearted and conciliatory Barnabas. His Levitical descent, and the sacrifice which he had made of his property to the common fund, combined with his sympathetic spirit and liberal culture to give him a natural authority, which he had always used on the side of charity and wisdom.

The arrival of such a man was an especial blessing. This new church, which was so largely composed of Gentiles, was destined to be a fresh starting-point in the career of Christianity. Barnabas saw the grace of God at work, and rejoiced at it, and justified his happy title of "the son of exhortation,"

evidence in favour of Ἕλληνας is indeed defective, since it is only found in A (which also has Ἕλληνας, even in ix. 29, where Ἑλληνιστὰς is the only *possible* reading) and D. ℵ has εὐαγγελιστὰς, which has been altered into Ἕλληνας; but both ℵ and B read καὶ before ἐλάλουν, which indicates a new and important statement. Some of the most important versions are valueless as evidence of reading in this instance, because they have no specific word by which to distinguish Ἑλληνισταὶ and Ἕλληνες. Œcumenius and Theophylact read Ἑλληνιστὰς, and so does Chrysostom in his text, but in his commentary he accepts Ἕλληνας, as does Eusebius. But (2) if we turn to internal evidence it is clear that "Greeks," not "Grecians"—*i.e.*, *Gentiles*, not Greek-speaking Jews—is the only admissible reading; for (i.) Hellenists were, of course, Jews, and as it is perfectly certain that the Ἰουδαίοις of the previous verse cannot mean only Hebraists, this verse 20 would add nothing whatever to the narrative if "Hellenists" were the right reading. (ii.) The statement comes as the sequel and crowning point of narratives, of which it has been the express object to describe the admission of *Gentiles* into the Church. The reading "*Hellenists*" obscures the verse on which the entire narrative of the Acts hinges. (iii.) The conversion of a number of Hellenists at Antioch would have excited no special notice, and required no special mission of inquiry, seeing that the existing Church at Jerusalem itself consisted largely of Hellenists. The entire context, therefore, conclusively proves that Ἕλληνας is the right reading, and it has accordingly been received into the text, in spite of the external evidence against it, by all the best editors—Griesbach, Lachmann, Scholz, Tischendorf, Meyer, Alford, &c. The reason for the corruption of the text seems to have been an assumption that this narrative is retrospective, and that to suppose the admission of Gentiles into the faith before Peter had opened to them the doors of the kingdom would be to derogate from his authority. But this preaching at Antioch may have been subsequent to the conversion of Cornelius; and it was, in any case, the authority of Peter which for the majority of the Church incontrovertibly settled the claim of the Gentiles.

[1] See Acts xiv. 1; xviii. 4; John xii. 20.

by exhorting the believers to cleave to the Lord with purpose of heart. His ministry won over converts in still larger numbers, for, as Luke adds with emphatic commendation, "he was a good man, and full of the Holy Ghost and faith."

The work multiplied in his hands, and needed so much wisdom, knowledge, and energy, that he soon felt the need of a colleague. Doubtless, had he desired it, he could have secured the co-operation of one of the Apostles, or of their trusted adherents. But Barnabas instinctively perceived that a fresher point of view, a clearer insight, a wider culture, a more complete immunity from prejudices were needed for so large and delicate a task. Himself a Grecian, and now called upon to minister not only to Grecians but to Greeks, he longed for the aid of one who would maintain the cause of truth and liberality with superior ability and more unflinching conviction. There was but one man who in any degree met his requirements—it was the delegate of the Sanhedrin, the zealot of the Pharisees, the once persecuting Saul of Tarsus. Since his escape from Jerusalem, Saul had been more or less unnoticed by the leading Apostles. We lose sight of him at Cæsarea, apparently starting on his way to Tarsus, and all that Barnabas now knew about him was that he was living quietly at home, waiting the Lord's call. Accordingly he set out, to seek for him, and the turn of expression seems to imply that it was not without difficulty that he found him. Paul readily accepted the invitation to leave his seclusion, and join his friend in this new work in the great capital of Syria. Thus, twice over, did Barnabas save Saul for the work of Christianity. To his self-effacing nobleness is due the honour of recognising, before they had yet been revealed to others, the fiery vigour, the indomitable energy, the splendid courage, the illuminated and illuminating intellect, which were destined to spend themselves in the high endeavour to ennoble and evangelise the world.

No place could have been more suitable than Antioch for the initial stage of such a ministry. The queen of the East, the third metropolis of the world, the residence of the imperial Legate of Syria, this vast city of perhaps 500,000 souls must not be judged of by the diminished, shrunken, and earthquake-shattered Antakieh of to-day.[1] It was no mere Oriental town, with low flat roofs and dingy narrow streets, but a Greek capital enriched and enlarged by Roman munificence. It is situated at the point of junction between the chains of Lebanon and Taurus. Its natural position on the northern slope of Mount Silpius, with a navigable river, the broad, historic Orontes, flowing at its feet, was at once commanding and beautiful. The windings of the river enriched the whole well-wooded plain, and as the city was but sixteen miles from the shore, the sea-breezes gave it health and coolness. These natural advantages had been largely increased by the lavish genius of ancient art. Built by the Seleucidæ[2] as the royal residence of their dynasty, its wide circuit of many miles was surrounded by walls of astonishing height and thickness, which had

[1] It is now a fifth-rate Turkish town of 6,000 inhabitants. (Porter's *Syria*, p. 568.)
[2] B.C. 301, Apr. 23

been carried across ravines and over mountain summits with such daring magnificence of conception as to give the city the aspect of being defended by its own encircling mountains, as though those gigantic bulwarks were but its natural walls. The palace of the kings of Syria was on an island formed by an artificial channel of the river. Through the entire length of the city, from the Golden or Daphne gate on the west, ran for nearly five miles a fine corso adorned with trees, colonnades, and statues. Originally constructed by Seleucus Nicator, it had been continued by Herod the Great, who, at once to gratify his passion for architecture, and to reward the people of Antioch for their good-will towards the Jews, had paved it for two miles and a half with blocks of white marble.[1] Broad bridges spanned the river and its various affluents; baths, aqueducts, basilicas, villas, theatres, clustered on the level plain, and, overshadowed by picturesque and rugged eminences, gave the city a splendour worthy of its fame as only inferior in grandeur to Alexandria and Rome. Mingled with this splendour were innumerable signs of luxury and comfort. Under the spreading plane-trees that shaded the banks of the river, and among gardens brightened with masses of flowers, sparkled amid groves of laurel and myrtle the gay villas of the wealthier inhabitants, bright with Greek frescoes, and adorned with every refinement which Roman wealth had borrowed from Ionian luxury. Art had lent its aid to enhance the beauties of nature, and one colossal crag of Mount Silpius, which overlooked the city, had been carved into human semblance by the skill of Leïos. In the days of Antiochus Epiphanes, a pestilence had ravaged the kingdom, and to appease the anger of the gods, the king had ordered the sculptor to hew the mountain-mass into one vast statue. The huge grim face, under the rocky semblance of a crown, stared over the Forum of the city, and was known to the Antiochenes as the Charonium, being supposed to represent the head of

"That grim ferryman which poets write of,"

who conveyed the souls of the dead in his dim-gleaming boat across the waters of the Styx.

It was natural that such a city should attract a vast multitude of inhabitants, and those inhabitants were of very various nationalities. The basis of the population was composed of native Syrians, represented to this day by the Maronites;[2] but the Syrian kings had invited many colonists to people their Presidence, and the most important of these were Greeks and Jews. To these, after the conquest of Syria by Pompey, had been added a garrison of Romans.[3] The court of the Legate of Syria, surrounded as it was by military pomp, attracted into its glittering circle, not only a multitude of rapacious and domineering officials, but also that large retinue of flatterers, slaves, artists, literary companions, and general hangers-on, whose presence was deemed

[1] Jos, *Antt.* xvi. 5, § 3.

[2] Renan, *Les Apôtres*, p. 228.

[3] Syria was made a Roman province B.C. 64. M. Æmil. Scaurus went there as *Quaestor pro Praetore* B.C. 62.

essential to the state of an imperial viceroy. The autonomy of the city, and its consequent freedom from the property tax, made it a pleasant place of abode to many others. The soft, yielding, and voluptuous Syrians, the cunning, versatile, and degraded Greeks, added their special contributions to the general corruption engendered by an enervating climate and a frivolous society. Side by side with these—governed, as at Alexandria, by their own Archon and their own mimic Sanhedrin, but owing allegiance to the central government at Jerusalem—lived an immense colony of Jews. Libanius could affirm from personal experience that he who sat in the agora of Antioch might study the customs of the world.

Cities liable to the influx of heterogeneous races are rarely otherwise than immoral and debased. Even Rome, in the decadence of its Cæsarism, could groan to think of the dregs of degradation—the quacks, and pandars, and musicians, and dancing-girls—poured into the Tiber by the Syrian Orontes. Her satirists spoke of this infusion of Orientalism as adding a fresh miasma even to the corruption which the ebbing tide of glory had left upon the naked sands of Grecian life.[1] It seems as though it were a law of human intercourse, that when races are commingled in large masses, the worst qualities of each appear intensified in the general iniquity. The mud and silt of the combining streams pollute any clearness or sweetness they may previously have enjoyed. If the Jews had been less exclusive, less haughtily indifferent to the moral good of any but themselves, they might have checked the tide of immorality. But their disdainful isolation either prevented them from making any efforts to ameliorate the condition of their fellow-citizens, or rendered their efforts nugatory. Their synagogues—one, at least, of which was a building of some pretensions, adorned with brazen spoils which had once belonged to the Temple of Jerusalem,[2] and had been resigned by Antiochus Epiphanes, in a fit of remorse, to the Jews of Antioch—rose in considerable numbers among the radiant temples of the gods of Hellas. But the spirit of those who worshipped in them rendered them an ineffectual witness; and the Jews, absorbed in the conviction that they were the sole favourites of Jehovah, passed with a scowl of contempt, or "spat, devoutly brutal, in the face" of the many statues which no classic beauty could redeem from the disgrace of being "dumb idols." There were doubtless, indeed, other proselytes besides Nicolas and Luke; but those proselytes, whether few or many in number, had, up to this period, exercised no appreciable influence on the gay and guilty city. And if the best Jews despised all attempts at active propagandism, there were sure to be many lewd and wicked Jews who furthered their own interests by a propaganda of iniquity. If the Jewish nationality has produced some of the best and greatest,

[1] "Jam pridem Syrus in Tiberim defluxit Orontes
Et linguam, et mores, et cum tibicine chordas
Obliquas, necnon gentilia tympana secum
Vexit, et ad circum jussas prostare puellas."
Juv. *Sat.* iii. 62–65.

[2] Jos. *B. J.* vii. 3, § 3.

it has also produced some of the basest and vilest of mankind. The Jews at Antioch were of just the same mixed character as the Jews at Alexandria, or Rome, or Paris, or London; and we may be quite sure that there must have been many among them who, instead of witnessing for Jehovah, would only add a tinge of original wickedness to the seething mass of atheism, idolatry, and polluted life.

And thus for the great mass of the population in Antioch there was nothing that could be truly called a religion to serve as a barrier against the ever-rising flood of Roman sensuality and Græco-Syrian suppleness. What religion there was took the form of the crudest nature-worship, or the most imbecile superstition. A few years before the foundation of a Christian Church at Antioch, in the year 37, there had occurred one of those terrible earthquakes to which, in all ages, the city had been liable.[1] It might have seemed at first sight incredible that an intellectual and literary city like Antioch—a city of wits and philosophers, of casuists and rhetoricians, of poets and satirists—should at once have become the dupes of a wretched quack named Debborius, who professed to avert such terrors by talismans as ludicrous as the famous earthquake-pills which so often point an allusion in modern literature. Yet there is in reality nothing strange in such apparent contrasts. History more than once has shown that the border-lands of Atheism reach to the confines of strange credulity.[2]

Into this city of Pagan pleasure—into the midst of a population pauperised by public doles, and polluted by the indulgences which they procured—among the intrigues and ignominies of some of the lowest of the human race at one

[1] Our authorities for the description and condition of Antioch are unusually rich. The chief are Josephus, *B. J.* vii. 3, § 3; *Antt.* xii. 3, § 1; xvi. 5, § 3; *c. Ap.* ii. 4; 1 Macc. iii. 37; xi. 13; 2 Macc. iv. 7—9, 33; v. 21; xi. 36; Philostr. *Vit. Apollon.* iii. 58; Libanius, *Antioch.* pp. 355, 356; Chrysost. *Homil. ad Pop. Antioch.* vii., *in* Matth., *et passim*; Julian, *Misopogon*; Pliny, *H. N.* v. 18; and, above all, the *Chronographia* of John of Antioch, better known by his Syriac surname of Malala, or the Orator. C. O. Müller, in his *Antiquitates Antiochenae* (Gött. 1830), has diligently examined all these and other authorities. Some accounts of modern Antioch, by travellers who have visited it, may be found in Pocock's *Descript. of the East*, ii. 192; Chesney, *Euphrates Expedition*, i. 425, seqq.; Ritter, *Paläst. u. Syria*, iv. 2. Its hopeless decline dates from 1268, when it was reconquered by the Mohammedans.

[2] The state of the city has been described by a master-hand. "It was," says M. Renan—rendered still more graphic in his description by familiarity with modern Paris—"an unheard-of collection of jugglers, charlatans, pantomimists, magicians, thaumaturgists, sorcerers, and priestly impostors; a city of races, of games, of dances, of processions, of festivals, of bacchanalia, of unchecked luxury; all the extravagances of the East, the most unhealthy superstitions, the fanaticism of orgies. In turns servile and ungrateful, worthless and insolent, the Antiochenes were the finished model of those crowds devoted to Cæsarism, without country, without nationality, without family honour, without a name to preserve. The great Corso which traversed the city was like a theatre, in which all day long rolled the waves of a population empty, frivolous, fickle, turbulent, sometimes witty, absorbed in songs, parodies, pleasantries, and impertinences of every description. It was," he continues, after describing certain dances and swimming-races, which, if we would understand the depravity of Gentile morals, we are forced to mention, "like an intoxication, a dream of Sardanapalus, in which all pleasures, all debaucheries, unfolded themselves in strange confusion, without excluding certain delicacies and refinements" (*Les Apôtres*, p. 221). The Orontes never flowed with fouler mud than when there began to spring up upon its banks the sweet fountain of the river of the water of life.

of the lowest periods of human history[1]—passed the eager spirit of Saul of Tarsus. On his way, five miles from the city, he must have seen upon the river-bank at least the fringe of laurels, cypresses, and myrtles that marked

"——— that sweet grove
Of Daphne by Orontes,"[2]

and caught sight, perhaps, of its colossal statue of Apollo,[3] reared by Seleucus Nicator. But it was sweet no longer, except in its natural and ineffaceable beauty, and it is certain that a faithful Jew would not willingly have entered its polluted precincts. Those precincts, being endowed with the right of asylum, were, like all the asylums of ancient and modern days, far more a protection to outrageous villany than to persecuted innocence;[4] and those umbrageous groves were the dark haunts of every foulness. For their scenic loveliness, their rich foliage, their fragrant herbage, their perennial fountains, the fiery-hearted convert had little taste. He could only have recalled with a sense of disgust how that grove had given its title to a proverb which expressed the superfluity of naughtiness,[5] and how its evil haunts had flung away the one rare chance of sheltering virtue from persecution, when the good Onias was tempted from it to be murdered by the governor of its protecting city.[6]

Such was the place where, in the street Singon, Saul began to preach. He may have entered it by the gate which was afterwards called the Gate of the Cherubim, because twenty-seven years later[7] it was surmounted by those colossal gilded ornaments which Titus had taken from the Temple of Jerusalem. It was a populous quarter, in close proximity to the Senate House, the Forum, and the Amphitheatre; and every time that during his sermon he raised his eyes to the lower crags of Mount Silpius, he would be confronted by the stern visage and rocky crown of the choleric ferryman of Hades. But the soil was prepared for his teaching. It is darkest just before the dawn. When mankind has sunk into hopeless scepticism, the help of God is often very nigh at hand. "Bitter with weariness, and sick with sin," there were many at any rate, even among the giddy and voluptuous Antiochenes, who, in despair of all sweetness and nobleness, were ready to hail with rapture the preaching of a new faith which promised forgiveness for the past, and brought ennoblement to the present. The work grew and prospered, and for a whole year the Apostles laboured in brotherly union and amid constant encouragement. The success of their labours was most decisively marked by

[1] Ausonius says of Antioch and Alexandria,
"Turbida vulgo
Utraque et amentis populi malesana tumultu" (*Ordo Nob. Urb.* iii.).

[2] See the celebrated passage in Gibbon's *Decline and Fall*, ch. xxiii.

[3] Now *Beit-al-Ma'a*—a secluded glen. A few dilapidated mills mark a spot where the shrine of Apollo once gleamed with gold and gems. When Julian the Apostate paid it a solemn visit, he found there a solitary goose! The Bab Bolos, or "Gate of Paul," is on the Aleppo road. The town still bears a bad name for licentiousness, and only contains a few hundred Christians. (See Carne's *Syria*, i. 5, &c.)

[4] 2 Macc. iv. 33.

[5] "Daphnici mores."

[6] Jos. *Antt.* xii. 5, § 1.

[7] A.D. 70.

the coinage of a new word, destined to a glorious immortality;—the disciples were first called CHRISTIANS at Antioch.

It is always interesting to notice the rise of a new and memorable word, but not a few of those which have met with universal acceptance have started into accidental life. It is not so with the word "Christian." It indicates a decisive epoch, and was the coinage rather of a society than of any single man. More, perhaps, than any word which was ever invented, it marks, if I may use the expression, the watershed of all human history. It signalises the emergence of a true faith among the Gentiles, and the separation of that faith from the tenets of the Jews. All former ages, nations, and religions contribute to it. The conception which lies at the base of it is Semitic, and sums up centuries of expectation and of prophecy in the historic person of One who was anointed to be for all mankind a Prophet, Priest, and King. But this Hebrew conception is translated by a Greek word, showing that the great religious thoughts of which hitherto the Jewish race had been the appointed guardians, were henceforth to be the common glory of mankind, and were, therefore, to be expressed in a language which enshrined the world's most perfect literature, and which had been imposed on all civilised countries by the nation which had played by far the most splendid part in the secular annals of the past. And this Greek rendering of a Hebrew idea was stamped with a Roman form by receiving a Latin termination,[1] as though to foreshadow that the new name should be co-extensive with the vast dominion which swayed the present destinies of the world. And if the word was thus pregnant with all the deepest and mightiest associations of the past and of the present, how divine was to be its future history! Henceforth it was needed to describe the peculiarity, to indicate the essence, of all that was morally the greatest and ideally the most lovely in the condition of mankind. From the day when the roar of the wild beast in the Amphitheatre was interrupted by the proud utterance, *Christianus sum*—from the days when the martyrs, like "a host of Scævolas," upheld their courage by this name as they bathed their hands without a shudder in the bickering fire—the idea of all patience, of all heroic constancy, of all missionary enterprise, of all philanthropic effort, of all cheerful self-sacrifice for the common benefit of mankind is in that name. How little thought the *canaille* at Antioch, who first hit on what was to them a convenient nickname, that thenceforward their whole city should be chiefly famous for its "Christian" associations; that the fame of Seleucus Nicator and Antiochus Epiphanes should be lost in that of Ignatius and Chrysostom; and that long after the power of the imperial legates had been as utterly

[1] The Greek adjective from Χριστὸς would have been Χριστεῖος. It is true that ηνὸς and ινὸς are Greek terminations, but *anus* is mainly Roman, and there can be little doubt that it is due—not to the Doric dialect!—but to the prevalence of Roman terminology at Antioch, even if it be admitted that the spread of the Empire had by this time made *anus* a familiar termination throughout the East (cf. Mariani, Pompeiani, &c.). "Christianity" (Χριστιανισμὸς) first occurs in Ignatius (*ad Philad.* 6), as was natural in a Bishop of *Antioch;* and probably "Catholic" (Ignat. *ad Smyrn.* 8) was invented in the same city (*id.* 78). See Bingham, *Antt.* II. i. § 4.

crumbled into the dust of oblivion as the glittering palace of the Seleucidae in which they dwelt, the world would linger with unwearied interest on every detail of the life of the obscure Cypriot, and the afflicted Tarsian, whose preaching only evoked their wit and laughter! How much less could they have conceived it possible that thenceforward all the greatest art, all the greatest literature, all the greatest government, all the greatest philosophy, all the greatest eloquence, all the greatest science, all the greatest colonisation —and more even than this—all of what is best, truest, purest, and loveliest in the possible achievements of man, should be capable of no designation so distinctive as that furnished by the connotation of what was intended for an impertinent *sobriquet!* The secret of the wisdom of the Greek, and the fervour of the Latin fathers, and the eloquence of both, is in that word; and the isolation of the hermits, and the devotion of the monks, and the self-denial of the missionaries, and the learning of the schoolmen, and the grand designs of the Catholic statesmen, and the chivalry of the knights, and the courage of the reformers, and the love of the philanthropists, and the sweetness and purity of northern homes, and everything of divine and noble which marks—from the squalor of its catacombs to the splendour of its cathedrals—the story of the Christian Church. And why does all this lie involved in this one word? Because it is the standing witness that the world's Faith is centred not in formulæ, but in historic realities—not in a dead system, but in the living Person of its Lord. An ironic inscription on the Cross of Christ had been written in letters of Greek, of Latin, and of Hebrew; and that Cross, implement as it was of shame and torture, became the symbol of the national ruin of the Jew, of the willing allegiance of the Greeks and Romans, of the dearest hopes and intensest gratitude of the world of civilisation. An hybrid and insulting designation was invented in the frivolous streets of Antioch, and around it clustered for ever the deepest faith and the purest glory of mankind.

I have assumed that the name was given by Gentiles, and given more or less in sport. It could not have been given by the Jews, who preferred the scornful name of "Galilæan,"[1] and who would not in any case have dragged through the mire of apostasy—for so it would have seemed to them—the word in which centred their most cherished hopes. Nor was it in all probability a term invented by the Christians themselves. In the New Testament, as is well known, it occurs but thrice; once in the historical notice of its origin, and only in two other places as a name used by enemies. It was employed by Agrippa the Second in his half-sneering, half-complimentary interpellation to St. Paul;[2] and it is used by St. Peter as the name of a charge under which the brethren were likely to be persecuted and impeached.[3] But during the

[1] Or, Nazarine. Acts xxiv. 5 (cf. John i. 46; Luke xiii. 2). Cyril, *Catech.* x.

[2] Acts xxvi. 28. This (which was twenty years later) is the first subsequent allusion to the name. Epiphanius (*Haer.* 29, n. 4) says that an earlier name for Christian was Ἰεσσαῖοι.

[3] 1 Pet. iv. 16.

life-time of the Apostles it does not seem to have acquired any currency among the Christians themselves,[1] and they preferred those vague and loving appellations of "the brethren,"[2] "the disciples,"[3] "the believers,"[4] "the saints,"[5] "the Church of Christ,"[6] "those of the way,"[7] "the elect,"[8] "the faithful,"[9] which had been sweetened to them by so much tender and hallowed intercourse during so many heavy trials and persecutions. Afterwards, indeed, when the name Christian had acquired a charm so potent that the very sound of it was formidable, Julian tried to forbid its use by edict,[10] and to substitute for it the more ignominious term of "Nazarene," which is still universal in the East. A tradition naturally sprang up that the name had been invented by Evodius, the first Bishop of Antioch, and even adopted at a general synod.[11] But what makes it nearly certain that this is an error, is that up to this time "Christ" was not used, or at any rate was barely beginning to be used, as a proper name; and the currency of a designation which marked adherence to Jesus as though Christ were His *name* and not His title, seems to be due only to the ignorance and carelessness of Gentiles, who without further inquiry caught up the first prominent word with which Christian preaching had made them familiar.[12] And even this word, in the prevalent itacism, was often corrupted into the shape *Chrestiani*, as though it came from the Greek *Chrêstos*, "excellent," and not from *Christos*, "anointed."[13] The latter term—arising from customs and conceptions which up to this time were almost exclusively Judaic—would convey little or no meaning to Greek or Roman ears. We may therefore regard it as certain that the most famous of all noble words was invented by the wit for which the Antiochenes were famous in antiquity, and which often displayed itself in happy appellations.[14] But whatever may have been the spirit in which the name was given, the disciples would not be long in welcoming so convenient a term. Bestowed as a stigma, they accepted it as a distinction. They who afterwards gloried in the contemptuous re-

[1] The allusion to it in Jas. ii. 7 is, to say the least, dubious.
[2] Acts xv. 1; 1 Cor. vii. 12.
[3] Acts ix. 26; xi. 29.
[4] Acts v. 14.
[5] Rom. viii. 27; xv. 25.
[6] Eph. v. 25.
[7] Acts xix. 9, 23. Compare the name *Methodist*.
[8] 2 Tim. ii. 10, &c.
[9] Eph. i. 1, &c. Later names like *pisciculi*, &c., had some vogue also.
[10] Greg. Naz. *Orat.* iii. 81; Julian, *Epp.* vii., ix.; Gibbon, v. 312, ed. Milman; Renan, *Les Apôtres*, 235.
[11] Suid. ii. 3930 *a*, ed. Gaisford; Malala, *Chronogr.* 10, p. 318, ed. Mill. Dr. Plumptre (*Paul in Asia*, 74) conjectures that Evodius and Ignatius may have been contemporary presbyter-episcopi of the Judaic and Hellenist communities at Antioch. Babylas the martyr and Paul of Samosata, the heresiarchs, were both Bishops of Antioch, as was Meletius, who baptised St. Chrysostom.
[12] "Christus non proprium nomen est, sed nuncupatio potestatis et regni" (Lact. *Div. Instt.* iv. 7; see *Life of Christ*, i. 287, n.). The name "Christian" expressed contemptuous indifference, not definite hatred. Tacitus uses it with dislike—"quos *vulgus* Christianos appellabat" (*Ann.* xv. 44).
[13] In 1 Pet. ii. 3, some have seen a sort of allusion to "the Lord" being both χρίστὸς and χρηστός, just as there seems to be a play on ἰᾶται and Ἰησοῦς in Acts ix. 34; x. 38.
[14] See Julian, *Misopogon* (an answer to their insults about his beard); Zosim. iii. 11; Procop. *B. P.* ii. 8, γελοίοις τε καὶ ἀταξίᾳ ἱκανῶς ἔχονται. Philostr. *Vit. Apollon.* iii. 16; Conyb. and Hows. i. 130.

proaches which branded them as *sarmenticii* and *semaxii*,[1] from the fagots to which they were tied and the stakes to which they were bound, would not be likely to blush at a name which was indeed their robe of victory, their triumphal chariot.[2] They gloried in it all the more because even the ignorant mispronunciations of it which I have just mentioned were a happy *nomen et omen*. If the Greeks and Romans spoke correctly of *Christus*, they gave unwilling testimony to the Universal King; if they ignorantly said *Chrestus*, they bore witness to the Sinless One. If they said *Christiani*, they showed that the new Faith centred not in a dogma, but in a Person; if they said *Chrestiani*, they used a word which spoke of sweetness and kindliness.[3] And beyond all this, to the Christians themselves the name was all the dearer because it constantly reminded them that they too were God's *anointed ones*—a holy generation, a royal priesthood; that they had an unction from the Holy One which brought all truth to their remembrance.[4]

The name marks a most important advance in the progress of the Faith. Hitherto, the Christians had been solely looked upon as the obscure sectarians of Judaism. The Greeks in their frivolity, the Romans in their superficial disdain for all "execrable" and "foreign superstitions," never troubled themselves to learn the difference which divided the Jew from the Christian, but idly attributed the internal disturbances which seemed to be agitating the peace of these detested fanaticisms to the instigations of some unknown person named Chrêstus.[5] But meanwhile, here at Antioch, the inhabitants of the third city in the Empire had seen that there was between the two systems an irreconcilable divergence, and had brought that fact prominently home to the minds of the Christians themselves by imposing on them a designation which seized upon, and stereotyped for ever, the very central belief which separated them from the religion in which they had been born and bred.

[1] Tert. *Apol.* 50.

[2] 1 Pet. iv. 16, εἰ δὲ ὡς Χριστιανός, μὴ αἰσχυνέσθω, δοξαζέτω δὲ τὸν Θεὸν ἐπὶ τῷ ὀνόματι (A, B, &c., not μέρει as in E. V.) τούτῳ. The mere name became a crime. Διώκουσι τοίνυν ἡμᾶς οὐκ ἀδίκους εἶναι καταλαβόντες ἀλλ' αὐτῷ μόνῳ τῷ Χριστιανοὺς εἶναι τὸν βίον ἀδικεῖν ὑπολαμβάνοντες, κ. τ. λ. (Clem. Alex. *Strom.* iv. 11, § 81).

[3] "Sed quum et perperam Chrestiani nuncupamur a vobis (nam nec nominis certa est notitia penes vos) *de suavitate et benignitate compositum est*" (Tert. *Apol.* 3). Οἱ εἰς Χριστὸν πεπιστευκότες χρηστοί τε εἰσὶ καὶ λέγονται (Clem. Alex. *Strom.* ii. 4, § 18). See Just. Mart. *Apol.* 2.

[4] This was a beautiful after-thought. τούτου ἕνεκεν καλούμεθα Χριστιανοὶ ὅτι χριόμεθα ἔλαιον Θεοῦ. (Theoph. *ad Autol.* i. 12; Tert. *Apol.* 3.) Compare the German *Christen* (Jer. Taylor, *Disc. of Confirm.*, § 3). There are similar allusions in Ambr. *De Obit. Valent.*, and Jerome *on Ps.* cv. 15 ("Nolite tangere Christos meos"). See Pearson, *On the Creed*, Art. ii.

[5] Even in Epictetus (*Dissert.* iv. 7, 6) and Marcus Aurelius (xi. 3), Renan (*Les Apôtres*, 232) thinks that "Christians" means *sicarii*. This seems to me very doubtful. Sulpicius Severus (ii. 30) preserves a phrase in which Tacitus says of Christianity and Judaism, "Has superstitiones, licet contrarias sibi, 'iisdem tamen auctoribus profectas.' Christianos a Judaeis exstitisse" (Bernays, *Ueber die Chronik Sulp. Sev.*, p. 57). See Spartianus, *Sept. Sever.* 16; *Caracalla*, 1; Lampridius, *Alex. Sev.* 22—45, 51. Vopiscus, *Saturn.* 8. The confusion was most unfortunate, and peaceful Christians were constantly persecuted while turbulent Jews were protected. (Tert. *Apol.* 2, 3; *Ad Nat.* i. 3; Justin, *Apol.* i. 4—7, n.)

The necessity for such a name marks clearly the success which attended the mission work of those early Evangelists. They could not have tilled a soil which was more likely to be fruitful. With what a burst of joy must the more large-hearted even of the Jews have hailed the proclamation of a Gospel which made them no longer a hated colony living at drawn daggers with the heathen life that surrounded them! How ardently must the Gentile whose heart had once been touched, whose eyes had once been enlightened have exulted in the divine illumination, the illimitable hope! How must his heart have been stirred by the emotions which marked the outpouring of the Spirit and accompanied the grace of baptism! How with the new life tingling through the dry bones of the valley of vision must he have turned away—with abhorrence for his former self, and a divine pity for his former companions—from the poisoned grapes of Heathendom, to pluck the fair fruits which grow upon the Tree of Life in the Paradise of God! How, in one word, must his heart have thrilled, his soul have dilated, at high words like these:—"Such things *were* some of you; but ye washed yourselves, but ye are sanctified, but ye are justified, by the name of the Lord Jesus, and by the Spirit of our God."[1]

CHAPTER XVII.

A MARTYRDOM AND A RETRIBUTION.

"O great Apostle! rightly now
 Thou readest all thy Saviour meant,
What time His grave yet gentle brow
 In sweet reproof on thee was bent."—KEBLE.

THUS it was that at Antioch the Church of Christ was enlarged, and the views of its members indefinitely widened. For a whole year—and it may well have been the happiest year in the life of Saul—he worked here with his beloved companion. The calm and conciliatory tact of Barnabas tempered and was inspirited by the fervour of Saul. Each contributed his own high gifts to clear away the myriad obstacles which still impeded the free flow of the river of God's grace. In the glory and delight of a ministry so richly successful, it is far from impossible that Saul may have enjoyed that rapturous revelation which he describes in the Epistle to the Corinthians, during which he was caught up into Paradise as far as the third heaven,[2] and heard unspeakable words which man neither could nor ought to utter. It was one of those ecstasies which the Jews themselves regarded as the

[1] 1 Cor. vi. 11, ταῦτά τινες ἦτε ἀλλ' ἀπελούσασθε, κ.τ.λ.

[2] The "third heaven" is called "Zevul" by Rashi (cf. *Chagigah*, f. 12, 2). In such visions the soul "hath no eyes to see, nor ears to hear, yet sees and hears, and is all eye, all ear." St. Teresa, in describing her visions as *indescribable*, says, "The restless little butterfly of the memory has its wings burnt now, and it cannot fly." (*Vida*, xviii. 18.)

highest form of revelation—one of those moments of inspiration in which the soul, like Moses on Sinai, sees God face to face and does not die. St. Paul, it must be remembered, had a work to perform which required more absolute self-sacrifice, more unwavering faith, more undaunted courage, more unclouded insight, more glorious superiority to immemorial prejudices, than any man who ever lived. It needed moments like this to sustain the nameless agonies, to kindle the inspiring flame of such a life. The light upon the countenance of Moses might die away, like the radiance of a mountain peak which has caught the colour of the dawn, but the glow in the heart of Paul could never fade. The utterance of the unspeakable words might cease to vibrate in the soul, but no after-influence could obliterate the impression of the eternal message. Amid seas and storms, amid agonies and energies, even when all earthly hopes had ceased, we may be sure that the voice of God still rang in his heart, the vision of God was still bright before his spiritual eye.

The only recorded incident of this year of service is the visit of certain brethren from Jerusalem, of whom one, named Agabus, prophesied the near occurrence of a general famine. The warning note which he sounded was not in vain. It quickened the sympathies of the Christians at Antioch, and enabled the earliest of the Gentile Churches to give expression to their reverence for those venerable sufferers in the Mother Church of Jerusalem who "had seen and heard, and whose hands had handled the Word of Life."[1] A contribution was made for the brethren of Judæa. The inhabitants of that country, and more especially of the Holy City, have been accustomed in all ages, as they are in this, to rely largely on the *chaluka*,[2] or alms, which are willingly contributed to their poverty by Jews living in other countries. The vast sums collected for the Temple tribute flowed into the bursting coffers of the *Benî Hanan*—much as they now do, though in dwindled rills, into those of a few of the leading *Ashkenazim* and *Ansche hod.* But there would be little chance that any of these treasures would help to alleviate the hunger of the struggling disciples. Priests who starved their own coadjutors[3] would hardly be inclined to subsidise their impoverished opponents. The Gentiles, who had been blessed by the spiritual wealth of Jewish Christians, cheerfully returned the benefit by subscribing to the supply of their temporal needs.[4] The sums thus gathered were entrusted by the Church to Barnabas and Saul.

The exact month in which these two messengers of mercy arrived to assist their famine-stricken brethren cannot be ascertained, but there can be but little doubt that it was in the year 44. On their arrival they found the Church in strange distress from a new persecution. It is not impossible that the fury of the onslaught may once more have scattered the chief Apostles, for we hear nothing of any intercourse between them and the two great

[1] 1 John i. 1.

[2] According to Dr. Frankl (*Jews in the East*, ii. 31) a sum of 818,000 piastres finds its way annually to Jerusalem, for a Jewish population of some 5,700 souls. It is distributed partly as *chaluka*—*i.e.*, at so much per head, without distinction of age or sex—and partly as *kadima*, according to the rank of the recipient.

[3] Derenbourg, p. 232, *seq.*

[4] Rom. xv. 26, 27.

leaders of the Church of Antioch. Indeed, it is said that the alms were handed over, not to the Apostles, but to the Elders. It is true that Elders may include Apostles, but the rapid and purely monetary character of the visit, and the complete silence as to further details, seem to imply that this was not the case.

The Church of Antioch was not the sole contributor to the distresses of Jerusalem. If they helped their Christian brethren, the Jews found benefactors in the members of an interesting household, the royal family of Adiabene, whose history is much mingled at this time with that of Judæa, and sheds instructive light on the annals of early Christianity.

Adiabene, once a province of Assyria, now forms part of the modern Kurdistan. Monobazus, the king of this district, had married his sister Helena, and by that marriage had two sons, of whom the younger, Izates, was the favourite of his parents.[1] To save him from the jealousy of his other brothers, the king and queen sent him to the court of Abennerig, king of the Charax-Spasini, who gave him his daughter in marriage. While he was living in this sort of honourable exile, a Jewish merchant, named Hananiah, managed to find admission into the harem of Abennerig, and to convert some of his wives to the Jewish faith. In this way he was introduced to Izates, of whom he also made a proselyte. Izates was recalled by his father before his death, and endowed with the princedom of Charrae; and when Monobazus died, Helena summoned the leading men of Adiabene, and informed them that Izates had been appointed successor to the crown. These satraps accepted the decision, but advised Helena to make her elder son, Monobazus, a temporary sovereign until the arrival of his brother, and to put the other brothers in bonds preparatory to their assassination in accordance with the common fashion of Oriental despotism.[2] Izates, however, on his arrival, was cheerfully acknowledged by his elder brother, and set all his other brothers free, though he sent them as hostages to Rome and various neighbouring courts. I shall subsequently relate the very remarkable circumstances which led to his circumcision.[3] At present I need only mention that his reign was long and prosperous, and that he was able to render such important services to Artabanus, the nineteenth Arsacid, that he received from him the kingdom of Nisibis, as well as the right to wear the peak of his tiara upright, and to sleep in a golden bed—privileges usually reserved for the kings of Persia. Even before these events, Helena had been so much struck with the prosperity and piety of her son, that she too had embraced Judaism, and at this very period was living in Jerusalem. Being extremely wealthy, and a profound admirer of Jewish institutions, she took energetic measures to alleviate the severity of the famine; and by importing large quantities of corn from Alexandria, and of dried figs from Cyprus, she was happily able to save many lives. Her

[1] Josephus (*Antt.* xx. 2, § 1) attributes this partiality to a prophetic dream.

[2] Hence we are told that "'King' Mumbaz made golden handles for the vessels used in the Temple on the Day of Atonement" (*Yoma*, 37 *a*).

[3] *Infra*, p. 429.

royal bounty was largely aided by the liberality of Izates,[1] whose contributions continued to be of service to the Jews long after the arrival of Saul and Barnabas with the alms which they had brought from Antioch for their suffering brethren.

It is clear that they arrived shortly before the Passover, or towards the end of March; for St. Luke fixes their visit about the time of Herod's persecution, which began just before, and would, but for God's Providence, have been consummated just after, that great feast. Indeed, it was *à priori* probable that the Apostles would time their visit by the feast, both from a natural desire to be present at these great annual celebrations, and also because that was the very time at which the vast concourse of visitors would render their aid most timely and indispensable.

They arrived, therefore, at a period of extreme peril to the little Church at Jerusalem, which had now enjoyed some five years of unbroken peace.[2]

Herod Agrippa I., of whom we have already had some glimpses, was one of those singular characters who combine external devotion with moral laxity. I have elsewhere told the strange story of the part which on one memorable day he played in Roman history,[3] and how his supple address and determination saved Rome from a revolution, and placed the uncouth Claudius on his nephew's throne. Claudius, who with all his pedantic and uxorious eccentricity was not devoid either of kindness or rectitude, was not slow to recognise that he owed to the Jewish prince both his life and his empire. It was probably due, in part at least, to the influence of Agrippa that shortly after his accession he abolished the law of "Impiety" on which Gaius had so vehemently insisted,[4] and which attached the severest penalties to any neglect of the imperial cult. But the further extension of the power of Agrippa was fraught with disastrous consequences to the Church of Christ. For the Jews were restored to the fullest privileges which they had ever enjoyed, and Agrippa set sail for Palestine in the flood-tide of imperial favour and with the splendid additions of Judæa and Samaria, Abilene, and the district of Lebanon[5] to Herod Philip's tetrarchy of Trachonitis, which he had received at the accession of Gaius.[6]

It is natural that a prince of Asmonæan blood,[7] who thus found himself in

[1] Oros. vii. 6; Jos. *Antt.* xx. 2, § 5. Helena is also said to have given to the Temple a golden candlestick, and a golden tablet inscribed with the "trial of jealousy" (*Yoma*, 37 *a*).

[2] Caligula's order to place his statue in the Temple was given in A.D. 39. Herod Agrippa died in A.D. 44.

[3] *Seekers after God*, p. 76.

[4] Dion, lx. 3, 5.

[5] Jos. *Antt.* xix. 5, §§ 2, 3.

[6] *Id.* xviii. 5, § 4.

[7] Agrippa I. was the grandson of Herod the Great and Mariamne. Mariamne was the granddaughter of Hyrcanus II., who was a grandson of Hyrcanus I., who was a son of Simon, the elder brother of Judas Maccabæus. Some of the Rabbis were, however, anxious to deny any drop of Asmonæan blood to the Herodian family. They relate that Herod the Great had been a slave to one of the Asmonæans, and one day heard a Bath-Kol saying, "Every slave that now rebels will succeed." Accordingly, he murdered all the family, except one young maiden, whom he reserved for marriage. But she mounted to the roof, cried out that "any one who asserted himself to be of the Asmonæan house

possession of a dominion as extensive as that of his grandfather Herod the Great, should try to win the favour of the people whom he was sent to govern. Apart from the subtle policy of facing both ways so as to please the Jews while he dazzled the Romans, and to enjoy his life in the midst of Gentile luxuries while he affected the reputation of a devoted Pharisee, Agrippa seems to have been sincere in his desire to be—at any rate at Jerusalem—an observer of the Mosaic Law. St. Luke, though his allusions to him are so brief and incidental, shows remarkable fidelity to historic facts in presenting him to us in both these aspects. In carrying out his policy, Agrippa paid studious court to the Jews, and especially to the Pharisees. He omitted nothing which could win their confidence or flatter their pride, and his wife, Cypros,[1] seems also to have been as much attached to the party as her kinswoman, Salome, sister of Herod the Great.[2]

It is clear that such a king—a king who wished to foster the sense of Jewish nationality,[3] to satisfy the Sadducees, to be supported by the Pharisees, and to be popular with the multitude—could not have lived long in Jerusalem, which was his usual place of residence,[4] without hearing many complaints about the Christians. At this time they had become equally distasteful to every section of the Jews, being regarded not only as fanatics, but as apostates, some of whom sat loosely to the covenant which God had made with their fathers. To extirpate the Christians would, as Agrippa was well aware, be the cheapest possible way to win general popularity. It was accordingly about the very time of the visit of the two Apostles to the Passover, as delegates from Antioch, that "he laid hands on certain of the Church to injure them; and he slew James, the brother of John, with the sword; and seeing that it was pleasing to the Jews, proceeded to arrest Peter also."[5] Thus in a single touch does St. Luke strike the keynote of Agrippa's policy, which was an unscrupulous desire for such popularity as could be earned by identifying himself with Jewish prejudices. In the High Priests of the day he would find willing coadjutors. The priest for the time being was probably Elionæus, whom Josephus calls a son of Kanthera, but whom the Talmud calls a son of Caiaphas.[6] If so, he would have been animated with an hereditary fury

henceforth would be a slave, for that she alone of that house was left;" and flinging herself down was killed. Some say that for seven years Herod preserved her body in honey, to make people believe that he was married to an Asmonæan princess. Angry with the Rabbis, who insisted on Deut. xvii. 15, he killed them all, except the Babha Ben Buta (whom he blinded by binding up his eyes with the skin of a hedgehog), that he might have one counsellor left. Having disguised himself, and tried in vain to tempt Babha Ben Buta to say something evil of him, he revealed himself, and asked what he ought to do by way of expiation. The blind man answered, "Thou hast extinguished the light of the world (see Matt. v. 14); rekindle it by building the Temple" (*Babha Bathra*, f. 3, 2, *seqq.*).

1 Cypros was the name of the wife of Antipater and mother of Herod the Great. She was descended from a Nabathean family; her name, which is probably connected with כפר (*Kepher*), was borne by several Herodian Princesses (Derenbourg, *Palest.*, p. 210).

2 See Excursus XXIV., "The Herods in the Acts."

3 Jos. *Antt.* xx. 1, § 1.

4 *Id.* xix. 7, § 3.

5 Acts xii. 1—3.

6 Jos. *B. J.* xix. 8, § 1; *Para*, iii. 5; *Ben Hakkaïph*; Derenbourg, p. 215.

against the followers of Christ, and would have been an eager instrument in the hands of Herod. When such allies were in unison, and Agrippa in the very plenitude of his power, it was easy to strike a deadly blow at the Nazarenes. It was no bold Hellenist who was now singled out as a victim, no spirited opponent of Jewish exclusiveness. James, as the elder brother of the beloved disciple, perhaps as a kinsman of Christ Himself, as one of the earliest and one of the most favoured Apostles, as one not only of the Twelve, but of the Three, as the son of a father apparently of higher social position than the rest of the little band, seems to have had a sort of precedence at Jerusalem; and for this reason alone—not, so far as we are aware, from being personally obnoxious—he was so suddenly seized and martyred that no single detail or circumstance of his martyrdom has been preserved. Two words[1] are all the space devoted to recount the death of the first Apostle by the historian who had narrated at such length the martyrdom of Stephen. It may be merely due to a sense of inadequacy in this brief record that Christian tradition told how the constancy and the harangues of James converted his accuser, and caused him to become a voluntary sharer of his death.[2] But perhaps we are meant to see a spiritual fitness in this lonely and unrecorded end of the son of Thunder. He had stood by Jesus at the bedside of the daughter of Jairus, and on the holy mount, and in the agony of the garden; had once wished to call down fire from heaven on those who treated his Lord with incivility; had helped to urge the claim that he might sit in closest proximity to His throne of judgment. There is a deep lesson in the circumstance that he should, meekly and silently, in utter self-renouncement, with no visible consolation, with no elaborate eulogy, amid no pomp of circumstance, with not even a recorded burial, perish first of the faithful few who had forsaken all to follow Christ, and so be the first to fulfil the warning prophecy that he should drink of His bitter cup, and be baptised with His fiery baptism.

It was before the Passover that James had been doomed to feel the tyrant's sword. The universal approbation of the fact by the Jews—an approbation which would be all the more conspicuous from the presence of the vast throngs who came to Jerusalem to celebrate the Passover—stimulated the king, to whom no incense was so sweet as the voice of popular applause, to inflict a blow yet more terrible by seizing the most prominent of all the Apostles. Peter was accordingly arrested, and since there was no time to finish his trial before the Passover, and the Jews were not inclined to inflict death by their own act during the Feast, he was kept in prison till the seven sacred days had elapsed that he might then be put to death with the most ostentatious publicity.[3] Day after day the Apostle remained in close custody, bound by either arm to two soldiers, and guarded by two others. Aware how irreparable would be the loss of one so brave, so true, so gifted with spiritual fervour and wisdom,

[1] Acts xii. 2, ἀνεῖλε . . . μαχαίρᾳ.

[2] Clem. Alex. *ap.* Euseb. *H. E.* ii. 9. The Apostle, it is said, looked at him for a little time, and then kissed him, with the words, "Peace be with you," just before they both were killed.

[3] Acts xii. 4, ἀνάγειν.

the Christians of Jerusalem poured out their hearts and souls in prayer for his deliverance. But it seemed as if all would be in vain. The last night of the Feast had come; the dawn of the morning would see Peter brought forth to the mockery of trial, and the certainty of death. It seemed as if the day had already come when, as his Lord had told him, another should gird him, and carry him whither he would not. But in that last extremity God had not forsaken His Apostle or His Church. On that last night, by a divine deliverance, so sudden, mysterious, and bewildering, that to Peter, until he woke to the sober certainty of his rescue, it seemed like a vision,[1] the great Apostle was snatched from his persecutors. After briefly narrating the circumstances of his deliverance to the brethren assembled in the house of Mary, the mother of John Mark the Evangelist, he entrusted them with the duty of bearing the same message to James, the Lord's brother, and to the other Christians who were not present, and withdrew for a time to safe retirement, while Herod was left to wreak his impotent vengeance on the unconscious quaternion of soldiers.

It might well seem as though the blood of martyrdom brought its own retribution on the heads of those who cause it to be spilt. We have seen Agrippa in the insolent plenitude of his tyranny; the next scene exhibits him in the horrible anguish of his end. It was at the beginning of April, A.D. 44, that he had slain James and arrested Peter; it was probably the very same month which ended his brief and guilty splendour, and cut him off in the flower of his life.

Versatile and cosmopolitan as was natural in an adventurer whose youth and manhood had experienced every variety of fortune, Agrippa could play the heathen at Cæsarea with as much zeal as he could play the Pharisee at Jerusalem. The ordinary herd of Rabbis and hierarchs had winked at this phase of his royalty, and had managed to disintegrate in their imaginations the Herod who offered holocausts in the Temple from the Herod who presided in amphitheatres at Berytus; the Herod who wept, because he was only half a Jew, in the Temple at the Passover, and the Herod who presided at Pagan spectacles at Cæsarean jubilees.[2] One bold Pharisee—Simon by name—did indeed venture for a time to display the courage of his opinions. During an absence of Agrippa from Jerusalem, he summoned an assembly, and declared the king's actions to be so illegal that, on this ground, as well as on the ground of his Idumæan origin, he ought to be excluded from the Temple. As it was not Agrippa's object to break with the Pharisees, he merely sent for Simon to Cæsarea, made him sit by his side in the theatre, and then asked him, gently, "whether he saw anything there which contradicted the law of Moses?" Simon either was or pretended to be convinced that there was no overt infraction of Mosaic regulations, and after begging the king's pardon was dismissed with a small present.

It was in that same theatre that Agrippa met his end. Severe troubles had arisen in the relations between Judæa and the Phœnician cities of Tyre

[1] Acts xii. 9.

[2] Jos. *Antt.* xix. 7, § 4.

and Sidon, and since that maritime strip of coast depends entirely for its subsistence on the harvests of Palestine, it was of the extremest importance to the inhabitants of the merchant cities that they should keep on good terms with the little autocrat.[1] The pressure of the famine, which would fall on them with peculiar severity, made them still more anxious to bring about a reconciliation, and the visit of Agrippa to Cæsarea on a joyful occasion furnished them with the requisite opportunity.

That occasion was the news that Claudius had returned in safety from his expedition to Britain, and had been welcomed at Rome with an outburst of flattery, in which the interested princelings of the provinces thought it politic to bear their part.[2] Agrippa was always glad of any excuse which enabled him to indulge his passion for gladiatorial exhibitions and the cruel vanities of Roman dissipation. Accordingly he hurried to Cæsarea, which was the Roman capital of Palestine, and ordered every preparation to be made for a splendid festival. To this town came the deputies of Tyre and Sidon, taking care to secure a friend at court in the person of Blastus, the king's groom of the bedchamber.[3]

It was on the second morning of the festival, at the early dawn of a burning day in the Syrian spring, that Agrippa gave audience to the Phœnician embassy. It was exactly the time and place and occasion in which he would be glad to display his magnificence and wealth. Accordingly he entered the theatre with his royal retinue in an entire robe of tissued silver, and taking his seat on the *bêma*, made to the Tyrians and Sidonians a set harangue. As he sat there the sun blazed on his glittering robe, and seemed to wrap him in a sheet of splendour. The theatre was thronged with his creatures, his subjects, the idle mob whose amusement he was supplying with profuse liberality, and the people whose prosperity depended on his royal favour. Here and there among the crowd a voice began to be heard shouting that it was a god who was speaking to them,[4] a god whose radiant epiphany was manifested before their eyes. In the prime of life, and of the manly beauty for which his race was remarkable, at the zenith of his power, in the seventh year of his reign, in the plenitude of his wealth,[5] an autocrat by his own position, and an autocrat rendered all but irresistible by the support of the strange being whom his supple address had saved from the dagger to seat him on the imperial throne—surrounded, too, at this moment by flatterers and parasites, and seated in the very midst of the stately buildings which Jews and Gentiles alike knew to have been conferred upon the city by the architectural extravagance of his race—the feeble intellect of Agrippa was turned by this intoxicating incense. He thought himself to be the god whom they declared.

[1] Cf. 1 Kings v. 9; Ezek. xxvii. 17; Ezra iii. 7.

[2] Dion Cass. lx. 23; Suet. *Claud.* 17; Philo, *Leg.* 45. See Lewin, *Fasti Sacri*, §§ 1668, 1674; and *contra* Wieseler, *Chron. d. Apost. Zeit.* 130.

[3] *ἐπὶ τοῦ κοιτῶνος*, *cubicularius*, praefectus cubiculi.

[4] See Jos. *Antt.* xix. 8, § 2, which closely confirms the narrative of Acts xii.

[5] His revenue is stated to have been 12,000,000 of drachmæ, or more than £425,000 a year.

Why should not *he* accept the apotheosis so abjectly obtruded on a Caligula or a Claudius? He accepted the blasphemous adulation, which, as a King of the Jews, he ought to have rejected with indignant horror. At that very moment his doom was sealed. It was a fresh instance of that irony of heaven which often seems to place men in positions of superlative gorgeousness at the very moment when the fiat is uttered which consigns them to the most pitiable and irrecoverable fall.[1]

There was no visible intervention. No awful voice sounded in the ears of the trembling listeners. No awful hand wrote fiery letters upon the wall. St. Luke says merely that the angel of God smote him. Josephus introduces the grotesque incident of an owl seated above him on one of the cords which ran across the theatre, which Agrippa saw, and recognised in it the predicted omen of impending death.[2] Whether he saw an owl or not, he was carried from the theatre to his palace a stricken man—stricken by the hand of God. In five days from that time—five days of internal anguish and vain despair,[3] in the fifty-fourth year of his age, and the fourth of his reign over the entire dominion of his grandfather—Agrippa died. And whatever may be the extent to which he had won the goodwill of the Jews by his lavish benefactions, the Gentiles hated him all the more because he was not only a Jew but an apostate. A consistent Jew they could in some measure tolerate, even while they hated him; but for these hybrid renegades they always express an unmitigated contempt. The news of Agrippa's death was received by the population, and especially by the soldiers, both at Cæsarea and Sebaste with feastings, carousals, and every indication of indecent joy. Not content with crowning themselves with garlands, and pouring libations to the ferryman of the Styx, they tore down from the palace the statues of Agrippa's daughters, and subjected them to the most infamous indignities. The foolish inertness of Claudius left the insult unpunished, and these violent and dissolute soldiers contributed in no small degree to the evils which not many years afterwards burst over Judæa with a storm of fire and sword.[4]

[1] See Bishop Thirlwall's *Essay on the Irony of Sophocles*.

[2] He says that an owl was sitting on a tree on the day of Agrippa's arrest at Capreae, and that a German soothsayer had foretold that he should become a king, but should be near his death when he saw that owl again. See also Euseb. *H. E.* ii. 10, who substitutes the angel for the owl.

[3] Jos. *Antt.* xix. 8, § 2, γαστρὸς ἀλγήμασι διεργασθείς: Acts xii. 23, σκωληκόβρωτος ἀπέθανεν. Whether there be any disease which can strictly be described as the phthiriasis, *morbus pedicularis*, is, as I have mentioned in my *Life of Christ*, i. 47, more than doubtful. The death of Herod Agrippa, like that of his grandfather, has been so called, but not by the sacred historians. It is, however, an historic fact that many cruel tyrants have died of ulcerous maladies, which the popular rumour described much as Lactantius describes them in his tract *De Mortibus persecutorum*. Instances are—Pheretima (Herod. iv. 205, εὐλέων ἐξέζεσεν, where the retributive appropriateness of the disease is first pointed out); Antiochus Epiphanes (2 Macc. v. 9); Herod the Great (Jos. *Antt.* xvii. 6, § 5, *B. J.* i. 33, §§ 8, 9); Maximius Galerius (Euseb. *H. E.* viii. 16); Maximin (*id.* ix. 10, 11; Lact. *De Mort. persec.* xxxiii.); Claudius Lucius Herminianus (Tertull. *ad Scap.* iii. cum vivus vermibus ebulliisset "Nemo sciat" dicebat, "ne gaudeant Christiani"); Duke of Alva; &c.

[4] Jos. *Antt.* xix. 9, § 1.

Of these scenes Saul and Barnabas may have been eye-witnesses on their return journey from Jerusalem to Antioch. The order of events in St. Luke may indeed be guided by the convenience of narrating consecutively all that he had to say about Herod Agrippa, and above all of showing how the sudden onslaught on the Church, which seemed to threaten it with nothing short of extermination, was checked by the deliverance of Peter, and arrested by the retribution of God. This would be the more natural if, as there seems to be good reason to believe, the ghastly death of Herod took place in the very same month in which, by shedding the blood of the innocent in mere pursuit of popularity, he had consummated his crimes.[1] If Saul and Barnabas were at Jerusalem during Peter's imprisonment, they may have been present at the prayer meeting at the house of Mary, the mother of Mark, and the kinswoman of Barnabas. If so we can at once account for the vivid minuteness of the details furnished to St. Luke respecting the events of that memorable time.[2]

In any case, they must have heard the death of Agrippa discussed a thousand times, and must have recognised in it a fresh proof of the immediate governance of God. But this was to them a truth of the most elementary character. Their alleged indifference to public questions simply arose from their absorption in other interests. Their minds were full of deeper concerns than the pride and fall of kings; and their visit to Jerusalem was so purely an episode in the work of St. Paul that in the Epistle to the Galatians he passes it over without a single allusion.[3] There is nothing surprising in the omission. It is the object of the Apostle to show his absolute independence of the Twelve. This second visit to Jerusalem had, therefore, no bearing on the subject with which he was dealing. More than eleven years had already elapsed since the Crucifixion, and a very ancient tradition says that twelve years (which to the Jews would mean anything above eleven years) was the period fixed by our Lord for the stay of the Apostles in the Holy City.[4] Even if we attach no importance to the tradition, it is certain that it approximates to known facts, and we may therefore assume that, about this time, the Apostles began to be scattered in various directions. St. Paul passes over this eleemosynary visit, either because in this connexion it did not occur to his memory, or because the mention of it was wholly unimportant for his purpose.

Yet there was one circumstance of this visit which was fraught with

[1] Saul and Barnabas seem to have started from Antioch with the intention of arriving at Jerusalem for the Passover of April 1, A.D. 44. The martyrdom of James immediately preceded the Passover, and the imprisonment of Peter took place during the Paschal week (Acts xii. 3—6). It was immediately afterwards that Herod started for Cæsarea; and if the object of his visit was to celebrate the return of Claudius from Britain, it must have been in this very month. For Claudius returned early in A.D. 44, and it would take some little time for the news to reach Jerusalem. Further, Josephus says that Agrippa reigned seven years (*Antt.* xix. 8, § 2), and as he was appointed in April, A.D. 37, these seven years would end in April, A.D. 44. See the question fully examined in Lewin, *Fasti Sacri*, p. 280.

[2] In D is mentioned even the number of steps from Peter's prison to the street.

[3] Gal. ii. 1.

[4] See Apollon. *ap.* Euseb. *H. E.* v. 18; Clem. Alex. *Strom.* vi. p. 762, ed. Potter.

future consequences full of sadness to both the Apostles. Barnabas, as we have seen, was nearly related to John Mark, son[1] of that Mary in whose house was the upper room. It would be most natural that he, and therefore that Saul, should, during their short visit, be guests in Mary's house, and the enthusiasm of her son may well have been kindled by the glowing spirit of his cousin and the yet more fiery ardour of his great companion. The danger of further persecution seemed to be over, but Peter, Mark's close friend and teacher, was no longer in Jerusalem, and, in spite of any natural anxieties which the prevalent famine may have caused, the Christian mother consented to part with her son, and he left Jerusalem in the company of the Apostle of the Gentiles.

CHAPTER XVIII.

JUDAISM AND HEATHENISM.

"Whoso breaketh a hedge [applied by the Rabbis to their *Seyyag la Thorah*, or 'hedge for the Law'], a serpent shall bite him."—ECCLES. x. 8.

"'Gods of Hellas! Gods of Hellas!'
Said the old Hellenic tongue;
Said the hero-oaths, as well as
Poets' songs the sweetest sung!
'Have ye grown deaf in a day?
Can ye speak not yea or nay—
Since Pan is dead?'"—E. BARRETT BROWNING.

"Die Götter sanken vom Himmelsthron
Es stürtzten die herrlichen Saülen,
Und geboren wurde der Jungfrau Sohn
Die Gebrechen der Erde zu heilen;
Verbannt ward er Sinne flüchtige Lust
Und der Mensch griff denkend in seine Brust."
SCHILLER.

WHEN Barnabas and Saul returned to Antioch they found the Church still animated by the spirit of happy activity. It was evidently destined to eclipse the importance of the Holy City as a centre and stronghold of the Faith. In the Church of Jerusalem there were many sources of weakness which were wanting at Antioch. It was hampered by depressing poverty. It had to bear the brunt of the earliest persecutions. Its lot was cast in the very furnace of Jewish hatred; and yet the views of its most influential elders were so much identified with their old Judaic training that they would naturally feel less interest in any attempt to proselytise the Gentiles.

At Antioch all was different. There the prejudices of the Jews wore an aspect more extravagant, and the claims of the Gentiles assumed a more overwhelming importance. At Jerusalem the Christians had been at the

[1] Col. iv. 10, ὁ ἀνέψιος means "cousin," not "sister's son," which would be ἀδελφιδοῦς.

mercy of a petty Jewish despot. At Antioch the Jews were forced to meet the Christians on terms of perfect equality, under the impartial rule of Roman law.[1]

Of the constitution of the early Church at Antioch nothing is said, but we are told of a little group of prophets and teachers[2] who occupied a prominent position in their religious services. These were Barnabas, Simeon (surnamed, for distinction's sake, Niger, and possibly, therefore, like Lucius, a native of Cyrene), Manaen, and Saul. Of Simeon and Lucius nothing whatever is known, since the suggestion that Lucius may be the same person as Luke the Evangelist is too foundationless to deserve a refutation. Of Manaen, or, to give him his proper Jewish name, Menahem, we are told the interesting circumstance that he was the foster-brother of Herod Antipas. It has, therefore, been conjectured that he may have been a son of the Essene who lent to Herod the Great the influence of his high authority,[3] and who, when Herod was a boy at school, had patted him on the back and told him he should one day be king.[4] If so, Menahem must have been one of the few early converts who came from wealthy positions; but there is nothing to prove that he was thus connected with the celebrated Essene, and in any case he can hardly have been his son.[5]

It was during a period of special service, accompanied by fasting, that the Holy Spirit brought home to their souls the strong conviction of the new work which lay before the Church, and of the special commission of Barnabas and Saul.[6] The language in which this Divine intimation is expressed seems to imply a sudden conviction following upon anxious deliberation; and that special prayer and fasting[7] had been undertaken by these prophets and teachers in order that they might receive guidance to decide about a course which had been already indicated to the two Apostles.

[1] "Eruditissimis hominibus liberalissimisque studiis affluens" (Cic. *pro Archiâ*, iii.).

[2] The accurate distinction between "prophets" and "teachers" is nowhere laid down, but it is clear that in the Apostolic age it was well understood (1 Cor. xii. 28; Eph. iv. 11). But the question naturally arises whether it is meant that Barnabas and Saul were "prophets" or "teachers"—or whether they were both. The latter, perhaps, is the correct view. The prophet stood higher than the teacher, was more immediately inspired, spoke with a loftier authority; but the teacher, whose functions were of a gentler and humbler nature, might, at great moments, and under strong influences, rise to the power of prophecy, while the prophet also might on ordinary occasions fulfil the functions of a teacher. (See Neander, *Planting*, p. 133, *seqq.*)

[3] Jos. *Antt.* xv. 10, § 5.

[4] Incidents of this kind are also told of Galba (Tac. *Ann.* vi. 20; Suet. *Galb.* 4; Jos. *Antt.* xviii. 6, § 9), of Henry VII., and of Louis Philippe.

[5] Because Manaen the Essene must have attained middle age when Herod the Great was a boy, and since we have now reached A.D. 45, this Manaen could only have been born when the other was in extreme old age.

[6] Acts xiii. 2, 'Αφορίσατε δή, "Come, set apart at once." The meaning of the λειτουργούντων (hence our word "liturgy") is probably general. Chrysostom explains it by κηρυττόντων. For other instances of the word, see Luke i. 23; Rom. xv. 16; 2 Cor. ix. 12; Phil. ii. 30. The ὃ προσκέκλημαι αὐτοὺς implies, of course, that Barnabas and Saul had already received a summons to the work (cf. Acts ix. 15; xxii. 21; Rom. i. 1; Gal. i. 1). Hooker thinks that Paul was made an Apostle because James could not leave Jerusalem; and Barnabas to supply the place of James the brother of John (*Eccl. Pol.* VII. iv. 2).

[7] On fasting in Ember weeks see Bingham xxi. ch. 2.

St. Paul, indeed, must long have yearned for the day in which the Lord should see fit to carry out His own promise "to send him far hence to the Gentiles."[1] The more deeply he thought over his predicted mission, the more would he realise that it had been predestined in the councils of God. Gentiles worshipped idols, but so had their own fathers done when they dwelt beyond Euphrates. Jewish Rabbis had admitted that, after all, Abraham himself was but the earliest of the proselytes.[2] If, as legend told, Terah had been a maker of idols, and if Abraham had received his first call, as Stephen had said, while yet living in Ur of the Chaldees, why should not thousands of the heathen be yet numbered among the elect of God? Had not God made of one blood all the nations upon earth? Had not the aged Simeon prophesied that the infant Jesus should be a light to lighten the Gentiles, no less than the glory of His people Israel? And were there not to be reckoned among His human ancestors Rahab, the harlot of Jericho, and Ruth, the loving woman of the accursed race of Moab? Had not Hadassah been a sultana in the seraglio of Xerxes? Had not Moses himself married a woman of Ethiopia?[3] And among the great doctors of recent days was it not asserted that Shammai was descended from Haman the Amalekite?[4] And, however necessary had been the active hostility to mixed marriages, and all other close intercourse with the heathen in the reforming period of Ezra and Nehemiah, had not Zephaniah declared in the voice of prophecy that "men should worship Jehovah every one from his place, even all the isles of the heathen?"[5] Nay, did no deeper significance than was suggested in the vulgar exegesis lie in the ancient promise to Abraham, that "in him all families of the earth should be blessed?"[6] Did the prophecy that all the ends of the earth should see the salvation of our God[7] merely mean that they should see it as excluded aliens, or as wanderers doomed to perish? If the Gentiles were to come to the light of Zion, and kings to the brightness of her dawn—if the isles were to wait for God, and the ships of Tarshish[8]—did this merely mean that the nations were but to be distant admirers and tolerated servants, admitted only to the exoteric doctrines and the less peculiar blessings, and tolerated only as dubious worshippers in the Temple's outmost courts? Would not this be to them a blessing like the blessing of Esau, which was almost like a curse, that their dwelling should be away from the fatness of the earth, and away from the dew of blessing from above?[9] Or, after all, if such reasonings were inconclusive—if, however con-

[1] Acts ix. 15, 16.

[2] Josh. xxiv. 2. The apologue of the gazelle feeding among a flock of sheep, found in the Talmud, and attributed to Hillel, beautifully expresses the toleration of the wiser and more enlightened Rabbis; but the proselytism contemplated is, of course, that purchased by absolute conformity to Jewish precepts.

[3] The Rabbis, to get over this startling fact, interpreted *koosith* ("Ethiopian woman") by *Gematria*, and made it mean "fair of face;" since *koosith* = 736 = the Hebrew words for "fair of eyes."

[4] Similarly it was said that Akibha descended from Sisera.

[5] Zeph. ii. 11.

[6] Gen. xii. 3; Gal. iii. 14.

[6] Isa. lii. 10.

[8] Isa. lx. 3, 9.

[7] Gen. xxvii. 39, "Behold, *without* the fatness of the earth shall be thy dwelling, and *without* the dew of heaven from above" (v. Kalisch, *in loc.*).

clusive, they were still inadequate to break down that barrier of prejudice which was an obstacle more difficult to surmount than the middle wall of partition—was any argument needful, when they had heard so recently the *command* of their Lord that they were *to go into all the world and preach the Gospel to every creature*,[1] and the *prophecy* that they should be witnesses unto the uttermost parts of the earth?[2]

Such convictions may have been in the heart of Paul long before he could persuade others to join in giving effect to them. It is matter of daily experience that the amount of reasoning which ought to be sufficient to produce immediate action is often insufficient to procure even a languid assent. But the purpose of the Apostle was happily aided by the open-hearted candour of Barnabas, the intellectual freshness of the Church of Antioch, and the immense effect produced by the example of Peter, who had won even from the Church of Jerusalem a reluctant acquiescence in the baptism of Cornelius.

And apart from the all but ineradicable dislike towards the heathen which must have existed in the minds of Jews and Jewish Christians, as a legacy of six centuries of intolerance—even supposing this dislike to be removed from *within*—yet the attempt to win over to the new faith the vast opposing forces of Judaism and heathenism *without* the fold might well have seemed fantastic and impossible. Could any but those whose hearts were lit with a zeal which consumed every difficulty, and dilated with a faith to which it seemed easy to remove mountains, listen without a smile to the proposal of evangelising the world which was then being advanced by two poor Jews—Jews who, as Jews by birth, were objects of scorn to the Gentiles, and as Jews who sat loose to what had come to be regarded as the essence of Judaism, were objects of detestation to Jews themselves? Is it possible to imagine two emissaries less likely to preach with acceptance "to the Jew first, and afterwards to the Greek?" And if the acceptance of such a mission required nothing short of the religious genius and ardent faith of Paul, surely nothing short of the immediate aid of the Holy Spirit of God could have given to that mission so grand and eternal a success.

For even had the mission been to the Jews exclusively, the difficulties which it presented might well have seemed insuperable. It must utterly fail unless the Jew could be persuaded of two things, of which one would be most abhorrent to his pride, the other most opposed to his convictions, and both most alien to his deepest prejudices. To become a Christian he would be forced to admit that all his cherished conceptions of the Messiah had been carnal and erroneous, and that when, after awaiting His advent for twenty centuries, that Lord had come suddenly to His Temple, the Jews had not only rejected but actually crucified Him, and thereby filled up the guilt which their fathers had incurred by shedding the blood of the Prophets. Further, he would have to acknowledge that not only his "hereditary customs," but even the Law—the awful fiery Law which he believed to have been delivered by God Himself from the

[1] Mark xvi. 15.

[2] Acts i. 8.

shrouded summit of Sinai—was destined, in all the facts which he regarded as most distinctive, to be superseded by the loftier and more spiritual revelation of this crucified Messiah. Lastly, he would have to resign without a murmur those exclusive privileges, that religious haughtiness by which he avenged himself on the insults of his adversaries, while he regarded God as being "a respecter of persons," and himself as the special favourite of Heaven.

And fear would be mingled with hatred. Under certain conditions, in the secrecy of Oriental seraglios, in the back-stairs intercourse of courts and *gynæcea*, in safe places like the harem of Abennerig and the audience-room of Helen of Adiabene, with Mary of Palmyra, or Fulvia, the wife of Saturninus, or Poppæa in the Golden House,[1] a Jew was glad enough to gain the ear of an influential proselyte, and the more moderate Jews were fully content in such cases with general conformity. They found it easy to devour widows' houses and make long prayers. But they were well aware that every widely successful attempt to induce Gentile proselytes to practise the outward ceremonies of their religion would be fraught with the extremest peril to their communities,[2] and would lead in every city of the Empire to a renewal of such scenes as those of which Alexandria had lately been the witness. It is probable that they would have checked any impolitic zeal on the part of even an orthodox Rabbi; but it filled them with fury to see it displayed by one who, as a schismatic, incurred a deadlier odium than the most corrupted of the heathen. To them a Paul was even more hateful than a Flaccus, and Paul was all the more hateful because he had once been Saul. And that this audacious pervert should not only preach, but preach to the heathen; and preach to the heathen a doctrine which proposed to place him on a level with the Jew; and, worse still, to place him on this level without any acceptance on his part of the customs without which a Jew could hardly be regarded as a Jew at all—this thought filled them with a rage which year after year was all but fatal to the life of Paul, as for long years together it was entirely fatal to his happiness and peace.[3]

Yet even supposing these obstacles to be surmounted, supposing that the missionaries were successful in converting their own countrymen, and so were enabled, by means of the "Proselytes of the Gate," to obtain their first point of contact through the synagogue with the heathen world, might it not seem after all as if their difficulties had then first begun? What hopes could they possibly entertain of making even the slightest impression on that vast weltering mass of idolatry and corruption? Now and then, perhaps, they might win the heart of some gentle woman, sick to death of the cruelty and depravity of

[1] Jos. *Antt.* xiii. 9, § 1; 11, § 3; 15, § 4; xviii. 3, § 5; xx. 2, § 4; *B. J.* ii. 17, § 10; *c. Ap.* ii 39; Tac. *Ann.* ii. 85; *H.* v. 5; Hor. *Sat.* I. iv. 142; Dion Cass. xxxvii. 17, &c.; Juv. *Sat.* vi. 546. See too Derenbourg, *Palestine*, p. 223, *seq.*

[2] As early as B.C. 139 Jews had been expelled from Rome for admitting proselytes to the Sabbath (Mommsen, *Röm. Gesch.* ii. 429). On the wider spread of Sabbatism even among heathens, see Jos. *c. Ap.* ii. 11, § 29. There appear to be some traces of the Jews taking pains annually to secure *one* proselyte (ἕνα προσήλυτον, Matt. xxiii. 15), to *typify* the salvability of the Gentiles (Taylor, *Pirke Abhôth*, p. 36).

[3] See Excursus XIII., "Burdens laid on Proselytes."

which she was forced to be a daily witness; here and there, perhaps, of some slave, oppressed and ignorant, and eager to find a refuge from the intolerable indignities of ancient servitude;—but even if they could hope for this, how far had they then advanced in the conversion of Heathendom, with all its splendid worldliness and glittering fascination?

For to the mass of the heathen, as I have said, their very persons were hateful from the mere fact that they were Jews.[1] And so far from escaping this hatred, the missionaries were certain to be doubly hated as Christian Jews. For during the first century of Christianity, the ancients never condescended to inquire what was the distinction between a Jew and a Christian.[2] To them a Christian was only a more dangerous, a more superstitious, a more outrageously intolerable Jew, who added to the follies of the Jew the yet more inexplicable folly of adoring a crucified malefactor. It is to the supposed turbulence of One whom he ignorantly calls Chrestus, and imagines to have been still living, that Suetonius attributes the riots which cost the Jews their expulsion from Rome. The stolid endurance of agony by the Christians under persecution woke a sort of astonished admiration;[3] but even Pliny, though his candid account of the Christians in Bithynia refutes his own epithets, could only call Christianity "a distorted and outrageous superstition;" and Tacitus and Suetonius, using the substantive, only qualify it by the severer epithets of "deadly," "pernicious," and "new."[4]

The heathen world into which, "as lambs among wolves," the Apostles were going forth, was at that moment in its worse condition. The western regions, towards which the course of missions took its way, were prevalently Greek and Roman; but it was a conquered Greece and a corrupted Rome. It was a Greece which had lost its genius and retained its falsity, a Rome which had lost its simplicity and retained its coarseness. It was Greece in her lowest stage of seducer and parasite; it was Rome at the epoch of her most gorgeous gluttonies and her most gilded rottenness. The heart of the Roman Empire under the Cæsars was "a fen of stagnant waters." Cæsarism has found its modern defenders, and even a Tiberius has had his eulogists among the admirers of despotic power; but no defence can silence the damning evidence of patent facts. No advocacy can silence the awful indictment which St. Paul writes to the inhabitants of the imperial city.[5] If such things were done in the green tree, what was done in the dry? What was the condition of the thistles, if this was the code of the forest-trees? If St. John in the Apocalypse describes Rome as the harlot city which had made the nations drunk with the cup of the wine of her fornications, he uses

[1] See Excursus XIV., "Hatred of the Jews in Classical Antiquity."

[2] In Dio (lxvii. 12—14) the Christian (?) martyr Acilius Glabrio is called a Jew.

[3] Marc. Aurel. xi. 3; Mart. x. 25; Epict. *Dissert.* iv. 8.

[4] Plin. *Ep.* x. 97, "superstitionem pravam et immodicam;" Tac. *Ann.* xv. 44, "exitiabilis superstitio;" Suet. *Nero*, 16, "novae et maleficae superstitionis." See Excursus XV., "Judgments of Early Pagan Writers on Christianity."

[5] See Friedländer, *Sittengesch. Roms*, B. v. Denis, *Idées Morales dans l'Antiquité*, ii. 218—236.

language no whit severer than that of Seneca, who speaks of Rome as a cesspool of iniquity;[1] or than that of Juvenal, who pictures her as a filthy sewer, into which have flowed the abominable dregs of every Achæan and Syrian stream.[2] Crushed under the ignominies inflicted on her by the despotism of madmen and monsters;[3] corrupted by the pollutions of the stage, and hardened by the cruelties of the amphitheatre; swarming with parasites, impostors, prisoners, and the vilest slaves; without any serious religion; without any public education; terrorised by insolent soldiers and pauperised mobs, the world's capital presents at this period a picture unparalleled for shame and misery in the annals of the world. But, reduced as it was to torpor under the night-mare of an absolutism which it neither could nor would shake off, the Roman world had sought its solace in superstition, in sensuality, or in Stoicism. The superstition mainly consisted in the adoption of cunning systems of priestcraft, impassioned rituals, horrible expiations borrowed from the degrading mythologies of Egypt or from the sensual religions of Galatia and Phrygia.[4] So rife were these, and so dangerous to morality and order, that long before this age the Senate had vainly attempted the suppression of the rites offered to Sabazius, to Isis, and to Serapis.[5] The jingling of sistra, and the cracked voices of beardless Galli, were familiar in every Roman town.[6] The sensuality was probably more shameful, and more shameless, than has ever been heard of in history. And amid this seething corruption, it was the few alone who retained the virtue and simplicity of the old family life and worship. The Stoicism in which the greater and more suffering spirits of the epoch—a Cremutius Cordus, a Thrasea Paetus, an Helvidius Priscus, an Annaeus Cornutus, a Musonius Rufus, a Barea Soranus—found refuge, was noble and heroic, but hard and unnatural. He who would estimate the reaction of man's nobler instincts against the profligacy of Pagan life—he who would judge to what heights the Spirit of God can aid those who unconsciously seek Him, and to what depths the powers of evil can degrade their willing votaries—must bridge over the gulf which separates a Petronius and an Appuleius from the sweetness and dignity of "minds naturally Christian," like those of an Epictetus and an Aurelius. He who would further estimate the priceless services which Christianity can still render even to souls the most naturally exalted, must once more compare the chill, the sadness, the painful tension, the haughty

[1] Cf. Sall. *Cat.* xxxvii. 5, "Hi Romam sicut in *sentinam* confluxerunt."

[2] Juv. iii. 62; Tac. *Ann.* xv. 44.

[3] Cf. Tac. *Ann.* ii. 85; iv. 55, 56; Suet. *Tib.* 35; Ov. *Fast.* ii. 497, *seq.*

[4] Such were the taurobolies and kriobolies—hideous blood baths.

[5] Valerius Maximus (I. iii. 3) relates that when the Senate had ordered the demolition of a Serapeum at Rome (A.U.C. 535), no workman could be induced to obey the order, and the Consul had himself to burst open the door with an axe (see, too, Liv. xxxix. 8—18; Cic. *De Legg.* ii. 8; Dion. Halic. ii. 20; Dion Cass. xl. 47; Tert. *Apol.* 6; *Adv. Nat.* i. 10, quoted by Renan, *Les Apôtres*, p. 316, and for Isis worship, Appul. *Metam.* xi.).

[6] Firmicius Maternus, in the days of Constantine, did not think it worth while to refute Greek and Roman mythology (*De Errore Profanæ Relig.*) but only the rites of Isis, Mithras, Cybele, &c.

exclusiveness, the despairing pride of Stoicism with the warmth, the glow, the radiant hope, the unbounded tenderness, the free natural emotion, the active charities, the peaceful, infinite contentment of Christianity as it shines forth with all its living and breathing sympathies in the Epistles of St. Paul.

And this difference between Stoicism and Christianity is reflected in the lives of their disciples. While the last genuine representatives of Roman statesmanship and Roman virtue were thinking it a grand thing to hold aloof from the flatteries into which the other senators plunged with such headlong baseness—while they were being regarded as models of heroism for such acts as rising and walking out of the senate when some more than usually contemptible flattery was being proposed—while they were thus eating away their own hearts in the consciousness of an ineffectual protest, and finding it difficult to keep even their own souls from "the contagion of the world's slow stain"—two Jews of obscure name, of no position, without rank, without wealth, without influence, without either literary, political, or military genius, without any culture but such as a Roman noble would have despised as useless and grotesque—but mighty in the strength of a sacred cause, and irresistible in the zeal of a conscious inspiration—set forth unnoticed on the first of those journeys which were destined to convert the world. For He who made and loved the world, and knew the needs of the world which He died to save, had sent them forth; and if He had sent them forth without any apparent means for the fulfilment of His great design, it was because He willed to choose "the foolish things of the world to confound the wise, and the weak things to confound the mighty, and things which are not to bring to nought things which are, that no flesh should glory in His presence."[1]

Vast, then, as was the task before them, and hedged around by apparently insuperable difficulties, the elders of the Church of Antioch were convinced that Barnabas and Saul had indeed been summoned on a Divine mission, and that they dared no longer delay the distinct manifestation of the will of the Spirit. They held one more special prayer and fast,[2] laid on the heads of their two great brethren the hands of consecration, and sent them on their way. Already, in his vision, Paul had been predestined to be an Apostle of the Gentiles;[3] henceforth, after this solemn ordination, he receives the title of an Apostle in its more special significance.[4] For a time, as in his Epistles to the Thessalonians, he modestly abstains from himself adopting it; but when his name was vilified, when his teaching was thwarted, when his authority was impugned, he not only adopted it,[5] but maintained his independent position as a teacher, and his right to be regarded as in nowise inferior to the very chiefest of the Twelve.

[1] 1 Cor. i. 27, 28.
[2] Acts xiii. 3, νηστεύσαντες . . . προσευξάμενοι.
[3] Acts xxvi. 17, ἐξαιρούμενός σε ἐκ τοῦ λαοῦ καὶ τῶν ἐθνῶν εἰς οὓς ἐγὼ σὲ ἀποστέλλω.
[4] Acts xiv. 4, 14 (cf. John xvii. 18; Heb. iii. 1).
[5] Except in the few purely private lines which he wrote to Philemon, and in the letter to his beloved Philippians who needed no assertion of his claim.

Book VI.

THE FIRST MISSIONARY JOURNEY.

CHAPTER XIX.

CYPRUS.

Τί λέγεις; καὶ Παῦλος ἐφοβεῖτο κινδύνους; Ἐφοβεῖτο καὶ σφόδρα ἐδεδοίκει. Εἰ γὰρ καὶ Παῦλος ἦν ἀλλ' ἄνθρωπος ἦν . . . Εἰ γὰρ οὐκ ἐφοβεῖτο ποία καρτερία τὸ τοὺς κινδύνους φέρειν; Ἐγὼ γὰρ καὶ διὰ τοῦτο αὐτὸν θαυμάζω ὅτι φοβούμενος καὶ οὐχ ἁπλῶς φοβούμενος ἀλλὰ καὶ τρέμων τοὺς κινδύνους διὰ παντὸς ἔδραμε στεφανούμενος καὶ πανταχοῦ τὸ κήρυγμα σπείρων.—CHRYSOST. *Opp.* x. 44, *ed.* Montfaucon.

"The travelled ambassador of Christ, who snatched Christianity from the hands of a local faction, and turned it to a universal faith, whose powerful word shook all the gods from Cyprus to Gibraltar, who turned the tide of history and thought, giving us the organisation of Christendom for the legions of Rome, and for Zeno and Epicurus, Augustine, Eckhart, and Luther."—MARTINEAU, *Hours of Thought*, p. 88.

"SENT forth by the Holy Spirit"—more conscious instruments, perhaps, of God's will than has ever been the case before or since, and starting on a journey more memorable in its issues than any which had ever been undertaken by man—Saul and Barnabas, accompanied by their more youthful attendant, John Mark, started on their way. What thoughts were in their minds as they turned their backs on the street Singôn, where they had preached with such acceptance and success? There were myriads of heathen and thousands of Jews in that gay voluptuous city who had not accepted Christianity; but the two Apostles were summoned to other work. They passed between the theatre and the amphitheatre,[1] crossed the main thoroughfare of the city with its trees and statues and colonnades, passed the Roman sentries who guarded the residence of the Legate of Syria in the old palace of the Seleucidæ, crossed the bridge over the Orontes, and leaving the grove of Daphne on their right upon the further bank of the river, made their way, through the oleanders and other flowering shrubs which form a gorgeous border to its purple rocks, along the sixteen miles which separated them from the port of Seleucia. History has contemptuously obliterated from her annals the names of countless kings who have set forth from their capitals for the scourge or conquest of nations at the head of armies, and with all the pomp and circumstance of glorious war; but centuries after those conquerors are in their turn forgotten whom she still deigns to commemorate, she will preserve in the grateful memory of mankind the names of these two poor Jews, who started on foot, staff in hand, with little, perhaps, or nothing in their scrip but the few dates that suffice to satisfy the hunger of the Eastern traveller.

From Antioch they might have made their way to Tarsus. But Paul had

1 See the elaborate plans and pictures of ancient and modern Antioch in Mr. Lewin's *St. Paul*, i., pp. 92—95.

in all probability preached already in his native Cilicia,[1] and as Barnabas was by birth a Cypriote, they bent their voyage thitherward. It was towards the west, towards Chittim and the Isles of the Gentiles, that the course of missions naturally tended. All land routes were more or less dangerous and difficult. Roads were, with few exceptions, bad; vehicles were cumbrous and expensive; robbers were numerous and insolent. But the total suppression of piracy by Pompey had rendered the Mediterranean safe, and in the growth of navigation it had become "the marriage-ring of nations."[2] Along the eastern coast of Asia Minor the Jews had long been scattered in numbers far exceeding those to be found there at the present day; and while the extension of the Greek language furnished an easy means of communication, the power of Roman law, which dominated over the remotest provinces of the Empire, afforded the missionaries a free scope and a fair protection. Accordingly they descended the rocky stairs which led down to the port of Seleucia,[3] and from one of its two piers embarked on a vessel which was bound for Cyprus. And thus began "the great Christian Odyssey."[4] The Apostolic barque has spread her sails; the wind breathes low, and only aspires to bear upon its wings the words of Jesus. If Rome has but too good reason to complain of the dregs of moral contamination which the Syrian Orontes poured forth to mingle with her yellow Tiber, on this occasion, at any rate, the Syrian river made ample amends by speeding on their way with its seaward current these messengers of peace and love.

As they sail south-westward over the hundred miles of that blue sea which one of them was destined so many times to traverse—the sea which four times wrecked him with its unregardful storms, and tossed him for a night and a day on its restless billows; as they sit at the prow and cast their wistful gaze towards the hills which overshadow the scene of their future labours,—or, resting at the stern, not without a glance of disgust at its heathen images, look back on the rocky cone of Mount Casius, "on which three centuries later smoked the last pagan sacrifice,"[5] they must have felt a deep emotion at the thought that now for the first time the Faith, on which depended the hopes of the world, was starting for fresh regions from its native Syria. Little did St. Paul know how trying in its apparent failures, how terrible in its real hardships, was the future which lay before him! That future—the fire of the furnace in which the fine gold of his heroic spirit was to be purged from every speck of dross—was mercifully hidden from him, though in its broad

[1] Gal. i. 21; Acts ix. 30; xi. 25. That there were churches in Cilicia appears from Acts xv. 41.

[2] See some good remarks in Renan, *Les Apôtres*, p. 280, *seq.*; and for an exhaustive treatment, Herzfeld, *Gesch. d. jüdischen Handels.*

[3] Polyb. v. 59.

[4] Renan, *Les Apôtres*, p. 386; cf. *St. Paul*, p. 13, "Ce fut la seconde poésie du Christianisme. Le lac de Tibériade et les barques de pêcheurs avaient fourni la première. Maintenant un souffle plus puissant des aspirations vers les terres plus lointaines nous entraîne en haute mer."

[5] El Djebel el Akrâ, "the *bald* mountain" (Chesney, *Euphrat.* i. 386; Amm. Marcell. xxii. 14, § 8; Julian, *Misop.* 361).

outlines he must have been but too well able to conjecture something of its trials. But had he foreseen *all* that was before him—had he foreseen the scourgings, the flagellations, the stoning, the shipwrecks,[1] the incessant toilings on foot along intolerable and dangerous roads, the dangers from swollen rivers and rushing watercourses, the dangers from mountain brigands, the dangers from Jews, from Gentiles, from false Christians in city and wilderness and sea,—the frantic crowds that nearly tore him to pieces, the weary nights, the chill, naked, thirsty, famine-stricken days, the incessant wearing responsibility, the chronic disease and weakness,—all the outrages, all the insults, all the agitating bursts of indignation against those who put stumbling-blocks in the paths of the weak,[2] the severe imprisonments, the incessant death, and all ended by desertion, failure, loneliness, chains, condemnation, the chilly dungeon,[3] the nameless martyrdom—had he foreseen all this, could he have borne it? His human spirit might indeed have shrunk at all the efforts and the agonies which lay before him—greater probably than have ever fallen to the lot of man; yet even at this early phase of his missionary career I doubt not that the hero's heart would have boldly uttered, "I hold not my life dear unto myself," and the faith of the Christian would have enabled him to say, "I can do all things through Christ that strengtheneth me."

Yet to all human judgment how ill qualified, physically, was the Apostle for the vast and perilous work which lay before him. The strongest athlete might well have quailed as he thought of the toil, the sleeplessness, the manual labour, the mental anxiety. The most imposing orator might have trembled at the thought of facing so many hostile potentates and raging crowds. The finest moral courage might have entreated to be spared the combined opposition alike of false friends and furious enemies. But Paul was no Milo, no Demosthenes, no Scipio Africanus; he was physically infirm, constitutionally nervous, painfully sensitive. His bodily presence was weak, his speech despised, his mind often overwhelmed with with fear. But over the feeble body and shrinking soul dominated a spirit so dauntless that he was ready all his life long to brave torture, to confront mobs, to harangue tribunals, to quail as little before frowning tyrants as before stormy seas. He might have addressed his ailing body in the words of the great hero as he rode into the thick of battle, "Aha, you tremble! but you would tremble far more if you knew whither I meant to take you to-day."[4]

The concurrent testimony of tradition, and the oldest attempts at representation, enable us to summon up before us the aspect of the man. A modern writer, who cannot conceal the bitter dislike which mingles with his unwilling admiration, is probably not far wrong in characterising him as a small and ugly Jew.[5] You looked on a man who was buffeted by an

[1] 2 Cor. xi. 23—33. [2] 2 Cor. xi. 29, τίς σκανδαλίζεται, καὶ οὐκ ἐγὼ πυροῦμαι.
[3] Clem. Rom. *Ep. ad loc.* i. 5. [4] Marshal Turenne.
[5] Even Luther described St. Paul as "ein armes dürres Männlein wie unser Philippus" (Melancthon).

angel of Satan. And yet when you spoke to him; when the prejudice inspired by his look and manner had been overcome; when, at moments of inspiring passion or yearning tenderness, the soul beamed out of that pale, distressful countenance; when with kindling enthusiasm the man forgot his appearance and his infirmity, and revealed himself in all the grandeur of his heroic force; when triumphing over weakness he scathed his enemies with terrible invective, or rose as it were upon the wings of prophecy to inspire with consolation the souls of those he loved—then, indeed, you saw what manner of man he was. It was Paul seated, as it were, on sunlit heights, and pouring forth the glorious paean in honour of Christian love; it was Paul withstanding Peter to the face because he was condemned; it was Paul delivering to Satan the insolent offender of Corinth; it was Paul exposing with sharp yet polished irony the inflated pretensions of a would-be wisdom; it was Paul rolling over the subterranean plots of Judaisers the thunders of his moral indignation; it was Paul blinding Elymas with the terror of his passionate reproof; it was Paul taking command, as it were, of the two hundred and seventy souls in the driven dismantled hulk, and by the simple authority of natural pre-eminence laying his injunctions on the centurion and the Roman soldiers whose captive he was; it was Paul swaying the mob with the motion of his hand on the steps of Antonia; it was Paul making even a Felix tremble; it was Paul exchanging high courtesies in tones of equality with governors and kings; it was Paul "fighting with wild beasts" at Ephesus, and facing "the lion" alone at Rome. When you saw him and heard him, then you forgot that the treasure was hid in an earthen vessel; out of the shattered pitcher there blazed upon the darkness a hidden lamp which flashed terror upon his enemies and shone like a guiding star to friends.

So that, if ugliness, and fear and trembling, and ill-health,[1] and the knowledge that he belonged to a hated sect, and was preaching a despised foolishness—if these were terrible drawbacks, they were yet more than counterbalanced by the possession of unequalled gifts. Among his slighter outward advantages were a thorough training in the culture of his own nation, a good mastery of Greek, the knowledge of a trade by which he could support himself, and familiarity with the habits of men of every class and nation, derived from long residence both in Jewish and Gentile cities. As widower and childless, he was unencumbered by any domestic ties, and could only suffer an individual anguish without risking those who depended on him. Lastly, the possession of the Roman citizenship, though inadequate to protect him against provincial tumults, and though he probably waived the appeal to it among his own countrymen, yet stood him in good stead in more than one dangerous crisis. But these would have been less than nothing without the possession of other and far higher gifts. Such were the astonishing endurance which no trials could exhaust, and which enabled the most physically weak of the Apostles[2] to become the most ceaselessly active; the

[1] See 2 Cor. x. 10; Gal. iv. 13; 1 Cor. ii. 3; 2 Cor. iv. 7; vii. 5; xi. 6; xii. *passim*.
[2] Ἀσθενὴς is the key-note of 2 Cor. xiii. 3—9.

high conviction that God had called him to a special Apostolate "to make the Gentiles obedient by word and deed;"[1] the enthusiasm of humanity," which made him ready to associate, for their souls' sake, whether with men who had once been thieves and drunkards, or with sweet, innocent, and gentle women;[2] the courtesy which made him equally at home among slaves and among kings; the power of style which rose or fell with the occasion, sometimes condescending to the humblest colloquialism, sometimes rising to the most impassioned eloquence; the clearness of insight which always kept one end in view, and sacrificed all minor points to attain it;[3] the total emancipation from that slavery to trifles which is the characteristic of small minds, and is ever petrifying religion into formulæ, or frittering it away into ceremonial; the spirit of concession; the tact of management; the willingness to bear and forbear, descend and condescend; the tolerance of men's prejudices; the contented acceptance of less than was his due.—And there were in the soul of Paul qualities more precious for his life's work than even these. There was the tenderness for his converts which makes his words ever sound as though he were ready to break into sobs as he thinks on the one hand of their affection, on the other of their ingratitude;[4] there was the conviction which makes him anticipate the very fiat of the throne of judgment,[5] and vehemently to exclaim that if an angel were to preach a different gospel it would be false;[6] there was the missionary restlessness so often found in the great pioneers of salvation, which drives him from city to city and continent to continent in the cause of God; there was the ardent and imaginative impulse which made it the very poetry of his life to found churches among the Gentiles as the first messenger of the Gospel of peace;[7] and last, but perhaps most important of all, there was the perfect faith, the absolute self-sacrifice, self-obliteration, self-annihilation, which rendered him willing, nay glad, to pour out his whole life as a libation—to be led in triumph from city to city as a slave and a captive at the chariot-wheels of Christ.

The immense personal ascendency of St. Paul has almost effaced the recollection of the fellow-workers to whose co-operation he owed so much; but we must not forget that throughout the perilous initiatives of this great work, he had Barnabas ever at his side, to guide him by his calm wisdom, and support him by his steady dignity. Barnabas, the friend of his youth, perhaps the school-fellow of his studies,—who had taken him by the hand; who had drawn him from his obscure retirement; who had laboured with him at Antioch; who had been his fellow-almoner at Jerusalem—was still sharing his difficulties, and never envied or murmured when he saw himself being gradually subjugated by the powerful individuality of a younger convert. To us Barnabas must always be a less memorable figure than Paul, but let us not forget that up to this time he had held a higher rank, and wielded a more authoritative

[1] Rom. xv. 18. [2] 1 Cor. vi. 9—11. [3] 1 Cor. ix. 19.
[4] 1 Thess. ii. 7, 11; Gal. iv. 19; 1 Cor. iv. 15; Philem. 10.
[5] Rom. ii. 16. [6] Gal. i. 8.
[7] Rom. x. 18; xv. 18; Gal. i. 16; 1 Cor. i. 1; iii. 10; ix. 16; 2 Cor. xi. 2.

influence. As a Levite, as a prophet, as one who for the needs of the community had cheerfully sacrificed his earthly goods, as one who enjoyed to a very high degree the confidence of the Apostles, Barnabas, in these early days, was enabled to lend to St. Paul's conceptions a weight which they could hardly otherwise have won. It is only when the work has actually begun that Barnabas seems naturally to sink to a subordinate position. No sooner have they left Salamis than the very order of the names is altered. Sergius Paulus sends for "Barnabas and Saul," but it is Saul who instantly comes to the front to meet the opposition of Elymas; it is "Paul and his company" who sail from Paphos to Perga; it is Paul who answers the appeal to speak at Antioch in Pisidia; it is Paul who is stoned at Lystra; and thenceforth, it is "Paul and Barnabas" throughout the rest of the history, except in the circular missive from James and the Church at Jerusalem.[1]

Nor must we altogether lose sight of the younger of the three voyagers—John, whose surname was Mark, who went with them in the capacity of their minister, corresponding, perhaps, in part to our notion of a deacon.[2] The presence of an active attendant, who could make all arrangements and inquiries, would be almost necessary to a sufferer like Paul. If Barnabas shared with Paul the reluctance to administer in person the rite of baptism,[3] we may suppose that this was one of the functions in which Mark would help them. Nor was it an unimportant circumstance to both of them that Mark, as the avowed friend and *protégé* of Peter, would have been unlikely to share in any mission which did not command the entire approval of his illustrious leader. In this and many other ways, now as at the close of his life, Paul doubtless felt that Mark was, or could be, "profitable to him for ministry." His nature imperiously demanded the solace of companionship; without this he found his work intolerable, and himself the victim of paralysing depression.[4] The principles which he adopted, his determination that under no circumstances would he be oppressive to his converts, the missionary boldness which constantly led him into such scenes of danger as none but a man could face, deprived him of that resource of female society—a sister, a wife—which other Apostles enjoyed, and which has been found so conducive to the usefulness of even such devoted missionaries as Adoniram Judson or Charles Mackenzie. But Paul was a missionary of the type which has been reproduced in Francis Xavier or Coleridge Patteson; and whatever he may have been in the past, he was now, at any rate, a lonely man.

Such were the three humble Christian emissaries whose barque, bending its prow to the south-west, sailed towards the mountains of Cyprus, and, leaving

[1] Acts xv. 25; and Acts xiv. 14, where Barnabas is taken for the superior deity.

[2] Acts xiii. 5, ὑπηρέτης. In Luke iv. 20 the ὑπηρέτης is the *Chazzan* of the Synagogue. Mark, like Barnabas, may have been connected with the tribe of Levi; on the name κολοβοδάκτυλος and traditions about him, see Ewald, *Gesch.* vi. 445.

[3] 1 Cor. i. 13—

[4] 1 Thess. iii. 1; 2 Cor. ii. 13; Phil. ii. 19, 20; 2 Tim. iv. 11. It has been said that St. Paul "had a thousand friends, and loved each as his own soul, and seemed to live a thousand lives in them, and to die a thousand deaths when he must quit them."

the long promontory of Dinaretum on the right, sailed into the bay of Salamis. The scene must have been very familiar to Barnabas. Before them lay the flourishing commercial town, conspicuous for its temple of the Salaminian Jupiter, which tradition assigned to Teucer, son of Telamon. Beyond the temple there stretched away to the circle of enclosing hills a rich plain, watered by the abundant streams of the Pediaeus. The site of the town, which our recent acquisition of the island has rendered so familiar, is now marked by a few ruins about four miles to the north of the modern Famagosta. The ancient town never entirely recovered the frightful injuries which it underwent, first from an insurrection of the Jews in the reign of Trajan, and afterwards from an earthquake. But when the Apostles stepped ashore, upon one of the ancient piers of which the ruins are still visible, it was a busy and important place, and we cannot doubt that Barnabas would find many to greet him in his old home. Doubtless, too, there would be some to whom their visit was peculiarly welcome, because, ever since the persecution of Stephen, Cyprus had been connected with the spread of Christianity.[1]

That Barnabas had had a considerable voice in thus repaying to his native island the service which it had rendered to Antioch,[2] may be conjectured from the fact that subsequently, when he had parted from Paul, he and Mark once more chose it as the scene of their missionary labours. After this first visit, Paul, often as he passed in sight of it, seems never to have landed there, disliking, perhaps, to build on other men's foundations; nor does he allude to Cyprus or to other Cypriotes in any of his Epistles. Whether there be any truth or not in the legend which says that Barnabas was martyred in the reign of Nero, and buried near Salamis, it is quite fitting that the church and grotto near it should be dedicated to him.

But apart from any facilities which may have been derived from his connexion with the island, it was without doubt an excellent place to form a starting-point for the evangelisation of the world. One of the largest islands in the Mediterranean, possessed of a fertile soil, varied in physical formation, and within easy reach of the three great continents, it had been marked out by nature as a convenient centre for extensive traffic. The trade in natural products—chiefly metals and wine—together with the fact that Augustus had farmed the copper-mines to Herod the Great, had attracted a large Jewish population. So vast, indeed, were their numbers, that in the reign of Trajan (A.D. 116) they rose upon the native inhabitants, under a certain Artemio, and slew 240,000 of them in one terrible massacre. The revolt was suppressed by Hadrian with awful severity, and after that time no Jew might set foot upon the shore of Cyprus on pain of death.[3]

Of their work at Salamis we are told nothing, except that "they continued

[1] Acts xxi. 16. [2] Acts xi. 20.

[3] Strabo, xiv. 682; Tac. *H.* ii. 2, 4; Jos. *Antt.* xiii. 10, § 4; xvi. 4, § 5; xvii. 12, §§ 1, 2; *B. J.* ii. 7, § 2; Philo, *Leg.*, p. 587; Milman, *Hist. of Jews*, iii. 111. For its ancient history see Meursius, *Opp.* iii.; for its modern condition, now so interesting to us, see General Cesnola's *Cyprus.*

preaching the word of God in the synagogues of the Jews."[1] It appears from this that Salamis was one of the towns where the Jews' quarter was sufficiently populous to maintain several synagogues; and if the Apostles came in contact with the heathen at all, it would only be with proselytes. But the notices of this part of their journey are scant, nor is any indication given of the length of their stay in Cyprus. Any work among the Gentiles was doubtless hindered by the apotheosis of sensuality for which the island was noted. The contact of Greeks with Phœnicians had caused a fusion between the subtle voluptuousness of the Hellenic race and the more burning passion of the Phœnicians and other Orientals; and the maritime population who touched at the island from every civilised country were ready learners in the school of degradation. Venus was the presiding goddess; and as she received from this fact her name of Cypris, so she was most commonly alluded to in the poets as the Paphian, Amathusian, or Idalian, from her temples in various parts of the island. She was

> "Idalian Aphrodite, beautiful,
> Fresh as the foam, new bathed in Paphian wells."

It was hitherward that she came as Aphrodite Anadyomene, when

> "From the sea
> She rose and floated in her pearly shell,
> A laughing girl."

It was by these "purple island sides" that she first

> "Fleeted a double light in air and wave."

Yet in the Paphian temple, where no blood was offered, where her immemorial shrine, famous even in the days of Homer,[2] breathed from a hundred altars the odour of perpetual incense,[3] and where kings and emperors turned aside to do her homage, the image which was enshrined in her *adytum* was no exquisite female figure sculptured by the hand of a Phidias or a Scopas, but a coarse truncated cone of white marble[4]—a sort of Asherah—such as might naturally serve as the phallic symbol of the Assyrian and Sidonian deity from whom this form of nature-worship was derived.[5] And as her temples had the right of asylum—a right which was certain to crowd their vicinity with criminals of every variety—we might have conjectured, apart from direct testimony, that the worship was to the last degree debasing; that the Paphian

[1] Acts xiii. 5, κατήγγελλον. [2] Hom. *Od.* 8, 362. [3] Virg. *Æn.* i. 417.

[4] As it was white (τὸ δε ἄγαλμα οὐκ ἂν εἰκάσαις ἄλλῳ τῳ ἢ πυραμίδι λευκῇ) there cannot be much doubt that it was of marble, though Maximus Tyr. adds ἡ δὲ ὕλη ἀγνοεῖται (*Diss.* 8, 8). "Apud Cyprios Venus in modum umbilici, vel ut quidam volunt, *Metae*, colitur" (Serv. *ad Æn.* i. 724).

[5] Tac. *H.* ii. 3; Strabo, xiv. 683; Athen. xv. 18. The crescent and star represented on coins as adorning the front of the Temple are perhaps a trace of the Phœnician origin of the worship, and of the connexion between the Paphian Venus and the Phœnician Asherah (Mövers, *Phön.* 607). The sun, at Emesa, had a similar κονοειδὲς σχῆμα (Herodian. v. 3), a sort of βαιτύλιον διïπετές. Models of it were sold (ἀγαλμάτιον σπιθαμιαῖον. Athen. xv. 18).

divinity was no Aphrodite Ourania,[1] but the lowest kind of Aphrodite Pandemos; that her worship was simply the prostitution of religion to the excuse of lust. Nor is it strange that under such circumstances there should be deadly opposition between the Jews and the Greek or Phœnician inhabitants, such as existed of old between the Jews and Canaanites. The mutual hatred thus engendered culminated in the internecine war which so soon broke out between the rival populations; it may have been one of the reasons why in Cyprus we read of no preaching to the heathen.

After their residence in Salamis the three missionaries traversed the whole island.[2] It is about a hundred miles in length from Salamis to New Paphos; and they probably followed a main road along the coast, diverging to places like Citium, the birthplace of Zeno the Stoic; Amathus, one of the shrines of Venus; and any towns where they would find the little Ghettos, whose conversion to the faith was their prime object. But not one incident of their journey is preserved for us until they reached the town of Paphos. By this name is intended, as the narrative shows, not the old and famous Paphos, the modern Kuklia, to which wanton pilgrimages were yearly made in honour of the old shrine so "famous-infamous" for many ages, but Nea-Paphos,[3] the modern Baffa, now a decayed and mouldering village, but then a bustling haven, and the residence of the Roman Proconsul Sergius Paulus.[4]

It does not in any way impugn the claim of Sergius Paulus to be regarded as a person of intelligence that he had with him, apparently residing in his house, a Jewish impostor named Bar-Jesus, who had arrogated to himself the complimentary title of Elymas, the Ulemah, or Wizard.[5] A notorious infidel like Philippe Égalité, though in other respects a man of ability, could yet try to presage his fate by the sort of cup-augury involved in examining the grounds of coffee (Κυλικομάντεια; cf. Gen. xliv. 5). A belief in some personal Power, the arbiter of man's destiny, above and beyond himself, is a primary necessity of the human mind. Mankind can never dispense with this belief, however superfluous, in certain cases, and for a time, it may seem to be to the individual. The noble Romans who had lost all firm hold on the national religion, felt themselves driven by a kind of instinctive necessity to get such a connexion with the unseen world as could be furnished them by the mysticism of Oriental quacks. A Marius had resorted to the prognostications of the Jewess Martha. At this particular epoch augurs, haruspices, Babylonians,

[1] The Virgin Mary is adored by Cypriotes under the name *Aphroditissa!* (Löhber, *Cyprus*, p. 105.)

[2] Acts xiii. 6, διελθόντες δὲ ὅλην τὴν νῆσον ℵ, A, B, C, D, E. In omitting ὅλην our version follows G, H.

[3] "The dance, music, and song of the sacred processions of 3,000 years ago have been replaced by the *coo-coo-vaie* of the owl, and wild cries of other night-birds, and the piteous bark of famished dogs, left behind by no less famished masters, to roam the Oriental village in search of carrion. This is the Paphos of to-day" (Cesnola's *Cyprus*, p. 216).

[4] See Excursus XVI., "The Proconsulate of Sergius Paulus."

[5] Renan, however, says, "Élim ou sage . . . . mot arabe dont le pluriel est *ouléma*. Le mot n'existe ni en hébreu ni en araméen; ce qui rend fort douteuse cette étymologie d'Élymas" (*St. Paul*, p. 15). Ewald thinks he was a Nabathaean (*Gesch.* vi. 453).

mathematici, astrologers, magians, soothsayers, casters of horoscopes, fortune-tellers, ventriloquists, dream-interpreters,[1] flocked to Rome in such multitudes, and acquired such vogue, as to attract the indignant notice of both satirists and historians. A few of them—like Apollonius of Tyana, and at a later period, Alexander of Abonoteichos, and the cynic Peregrinus—attracted universal attention. There was scarcely a Roman family that did not keep or consult its own foreteller of the future; and Juvenal describes the Emperor Tiberius as seated "with a herd of Chaldæans" on his rock at Capri.[2] Nothing would be more natural than that an intelligent and inquiring Roman, in the *ennui* of the smallest of the provinces, and finding himself amid a mixed population, half of Phœnician origin, and devoted to strange forms of religion, should have amused his leisure by inquiries into the bizarre superstitions by which he was surrounded.[3] The prevalence of earthquakes in Cyprus would be likely to give to the minds of the residents that gloomy and credulous tinge which is often found in countries liable to such terrible inflictions; and New Paphos had been devastated by an earthquake sufficiently recent[4] to have left a deep impression. Perhaps from this, perhaps from other causes, Bar-Jesus had acquired unusual influence; but it is an additional confirmation of the accuracy of St. Luke—one of those remote and incidental, and therefore unsuspected confirmations, which so often occur to establish the veracity of the sacred writers—that we find Cyprus to have been specially famous for its schools of religious imposture, of which one was professedly Jewish. Simon Magus was in all probability an inhabitant of Citium.[5] There is a most singular passage of Pliny, which, when we combine it with his reference to a Sergius Paulus, may be regarded as a confused echo in the mind of the Roman littérateur of these very events, heard from the very Proconsul about whom we are at present reading. He tells us that there were at Paphos two schools of soothsayers, one of which professed connexion with Moses, Jamnes, and Jotapes, who were Jews, and a much more recent Cyprian one.[6] To this school Bar-Jesus must have belonged, and Pliny's allusion throws once more a singular light on the fidelity of the careful Evangelist.[7]

The same feelings which had induced Sergius Paulus to domicile the Jewish sorcerer in the proconsular residence would naturally induce him to send for the new teachers, whose mission had evidently attracted attention by that loving earnestness which differed so widely from the contemptuous neutrality

[1] Juv. iii. 27. "Augur, schoenobates, medicus, magus."

[2] Tac. *H.* v. 3; Hor. *Sat.* I. ii. 1; *Od.* I. xi. 2; Juv. *Sat.* iii. 42, 60; vi. 543, 553, 562; x. 93; Suet. *Tib.* 36, 69; Aul. Gell. i. 9; Jos. *Antt.* viii. 2; xx. 5, § 1; *B. J.* vi. 5, § 1. Compare Matt. xxiv. 23, 24; Acts viii. 9; xvi. 16; xix. 19; 2 Tim. iii. 13 (γόητες); Rev. xix. 20.

[3] See Jos. *Antt.* xx. 7, § 2.

[4] In the reign of Augustus (Dion Cass. liv. 23).

[5] *Supra*, p. 146.

[6] Tac. *H.* v. 3. Plin. *H. N.* xxx. 2, 6, "Est et alia factio a Mose et Jamne et Jotape Judaeis pendens, sed multis millibus post Zoroastrem. *Tanto recentior est Cypria.*" In Jamnes and Jotapes there seems to be some dim confusion of supposed Jews with the traditional Egyptian magicians Jannes and Jambres (2 Tim. iii. 8).

[7] Luke i. 3, ἀκριβῶς παρηκολουθηκότι.

of the synagogue. But the position of soothsayer to a Roman Proconsul—even though it could only last a year[1]—was too distinguished and too lucrative to abandon without a struggle. Elymas met the Apostles in open controversy, and spared neither argument nor insult in his endeavour to persuade Sergius of the absurdity of the new faith. Instantly Saul—and this is the moment seized by the historian to tell us that he was also called by the name of Paul, which henceforth he exclusively uses—came to the front to bear the full force of the sorcerer's opposition. A less convinced or a less courageous man might well have shrunk from individual collision with a personage who evidently occupied a position of high consideration in the immediate household of the noble Roman. But to a spirit like St. Paul's, while there could be infinite compassion for ignorance, infinite sympathy with infirmity, infinite tenderness towards penitence, there could, on the other hand, be no compromise with imposture, no tolerance for cupidity, no truce with Canaan. He stood up, as it were, in a flame of fire, his soul burning with inspired indignation, against a man whose cowardice, greed, and worthlessness he saw and wished to expose. Fixing on the false prophet and sorcerer that earnest gaze which was perhaps rendered more conspicuous by his imperfect sight,[2] he exclaimed, "O full of all guile and all villainy, thou son of the devil,[3] thou foe of all righteousness, cease, wilt thou, thy perversion of the Lord's straight paths." And then, perceiving the terror produced on the mind of the unmasked hypocrite by this bold and blighting invective, he suddenly added, "And now, see, the Lord's hand is upon thee, and thou shalt be blind, not seeing the sun for a time."[4] The denunciation instantly took effect; the sorcerer felt in a moment that his impostures were annihilated, that he stood in the presence of an avenging justice. A mist swam before his eyes, followed by total darkness, and groping with outstretched hands he began to seek for some one to lead and guide him.

Nor was it strange that a display of spiritual power so startling and so irresistible should produce a strong conviction on the mind of the Proconsul.[5] How far his consequent belief was deep-seated or otherwise we have no evidence which would enable us to judge. But the silence of St. Luke would seem to indicate that he was not baptised, and we can hardly look on him as a deep and lifelong convert, since otherwise we should, in the rarity of great men in the Christian community, have as certainly heard of him in their records as we

[1] Dion Cassius tells us that these senatorial appointments were ἐπετήσιοι καὶ κληρωτοί (liii. 13).

[2] Cf. Acts xxiii. 1.

[3] Possibly in allusion to his name Bar-Jesus—as though he had said, "called the son of the salvation of Jehovah, but really the son of the devil, and the enemy of all righteousness." For διάβολος cf. John viii. 44. The reading of the Peshito *Bar-Shûma*, "son of a wound" or "son of a name," is hard to account for, unless it be by euphemism (Castell, *Lex. Syr.* s. v.).

[4] Acts xiii. 11, ἄχρι καιροῦ, literally, "until an opportunity," or, as we should say, "for the present." "Sciebat Apostolus, sui memor exempli, de tenebris oculorum, mentis posse resurgere ad lucem;" Bede,—following the hint of St. Chrysostom that οὐ κολάζοντος ἦν τὸ ῥῆμα ἀλλ' ἐπιστρέφοντος.

[5] Acts xiii. 12.

hear of the very few who at this period—like Flavius Clemens of Flavia Domitilla—joined the Church from the ranks of the noble or the mighty.

The question has been often asked why it is at this point in the narrative that the name Saul is finally replaced by the name Paul.[1] The old answer supplied by St. Jerome, that he took the name as a trophy of his conversion of Sergius Paulus, has long and deservedly been abandoned; there would have been in it an element of vulgarity impossible to St. Paul. Nor is there anything to urge in favour of the fancy that he took the name as a token of his humility, to signify that he was "the least of the Apostles."[2] It is much more probable that he had either possessed from the first an alternative name for facility of intercourse among the heathen, or that this Roman designation may point to his possession of the Roman franchise, and perhaps to some bond of association between his father or grandfather and the Æmilian family, who bore the cognomen of Paulus. If he adopted the name on the present occasion it may have been because it was to a slight extent alliterative with his Hebrew name *Shaûl*, which would, in its Grecised form, be represented by *Saulos;* but that was a form which he could not use in intercourse with the Greeks, owing to the fact that the word in Greek would be a sort of slang term for "uppish," or wanton. The mere changing of his name was so little unusual that it had been from the earliest ages a custom among his countrymen. Joseph had been known to the Egyptians as Zaphnath Paaneah; Daniel to the Assyrians as Belteshazzar; Hadassah to the Persians as Esther; Jesus, Hillel, Onias, Joseph, Tarpho to the Greeks as Jason, Pollio, Menelas, Hegesippus, and Trypho. When not assonant the name was sometimes a translation, as Peter is of Cephas, and Didymus of Thomas. Sometimes, however, this name for use among the Gentiles was due to accidental relations, as when Josephus took the praenomem of Flavius in honour of Vespasian. Of this we have other instances, in the Acts of the Apostles, in the persons of John and Joses, who were known by the Latin designations of Marcus and Justus. In Paul's case, however, as ancient Christian writers have pointed out, the change of name marks also a total change in all the conditions of his life. "Paul suffers what Saul had inflicted; Saul stoned, and Paul was stoned; Saul inflicted scourgings on Christians, and Paul five times received forty stripes save one; Saul hunted the Church of God, Paul was let down in a basket; Saul bound, Paul was bound."[3]

[1] "A primo ecclesiae spolio Proc. Serg. Paulo victoriae suae trophaea retulit, erexitque vexillum ut Paulus a Saulo vocaretur" (Jer. *ad Philem.* 1). In the *Toldôth Jeshu* the name is connected with פעל, "he worked." If so, both words being passive participles, the change would be like a change from "sought" to "wrought;" and I cannot help thinking that the true explanation may lie here. Heinrichs explains Σαῦλος δὲ, ὁ καὶ Παῦλος, "der *auch, so wie der Proconsul*, ebenfalls Paulus hiess."

[2] Paulus, a contraction of Pauxillus, means "least." "Paulus enim parvus" (Aug. *Serm.* clxix.). "Non ob aliud, quantum mihi videtur hoc nomen elegit nisi ut se ostenderet tamquam minimum Apostolorum" (Aug. *De Spir. et Lit.* xii.). With his usual exuberance of fancy he contrasts the "little" Saul of Benjamin, with the tall persecuting king. But in *Conf.* viii. 4 he leans to the other theory, "Ipse minimus Apostolorum tuorum, &c. . . . Paulus vocari amavit ob tam magnae insigne victoriae."

[3] *Ap.* Aug. *Append. Serm.* 204.

CHAPTER XX.

ANTIOCH IN PISIDIA.

"Respondebit tibi Evangelica tuba, Doctor Gentium, vas aureum in toto orbe resplendens."—JER. *Adv. Pelag.* Dial. iii., p. 545.

HAVING now traversed Cyprus, "Paul and his company"—to use the expression by which St. Luke so briefly intimates that the whole force of the mission was now identified with one man—weighed anchor from Paphos for Perga in Pamphylia. Whether they chose Perga as their destination in accordance with any preconceived plan, or whether it was a part of "God's unseen Providence by men nicknamed chance," we do not know. It was not easy for an ancient traveller to go exactly in what direction he liked, and he was obliged, in the circumscribed navigation of those days, to be guided in his movements by the accident of finding vessels which were bound for particular ports.[1] Now between Paphos, the political capital of Cyprus, and Perga, the capital of Pamphylia, there was in that day a constant intercourse, as would probably still be the case between Satalia and the western port of Cyprus but for the dangerous character of the now neglected harbour of Baffa. For Perga then, the missionaries embarked. They sailed into the deep bight of Attaleia, and up the broad, and in those days navigable, stream of the Cestrus, and anchored under the cliffs, which were crowned by the acropolis of the bright Greek city and the marble pillars of its celebrated Temple of Artemis.

But at Perga they made no stay, and their visit was only marked by a single but disheartening incident. This was the desertion by John Mark of the mission cause; "separating from them, he returned to Jerusalem." The causes which led him thus to look back after he had put his hand to the plough are not mentioned, but it is evident that to the ardent soul of Paul, at any rate, they appeared blameworthy, for we shall see that he subsequently refused the companionship of one who had shown such deficient resolution.[2] It is, however, but too easy to conjecture the mixed motives by which Mark was actuated. He was young. The novelty of the work had worn off. Its hardships, even under the favourable circumstances in Cyprus, had not been slight. His mother was at Jerusalem, perhaps alone, perhaps exposed to persecution. It may be, too, that the young man saw and resented the growing ascendency of Paul over his cousin Barnabas. And besides all this, Mark, bred up in the very bosom of the Church at Jerusalem, may have felt serious misgivings about the tendency of that liberal theology, that broad universalism of proffered admission into the Church, which seemed to throw into the background the immemorial sanctity, not only of the oral but even of the written Law. Such may have been the yearnings, the misgivings, the half-unconscious jealousies and resentments which filled his mind, and

[1] See the chapter on ancient modes of travel in Friedländer, *Sittengesch. Roms.*

[2] Acts xv. 38.

whatever may have been the qualms of conscience which might otherwise have troubled his desertion of the sacred task, these excuses and arguments for doing so must have met with a powerful ally in the circumstances which were evidently before them.

For as Mark gazed on the mighty chain of Taurus, and remembered that they were now about to penetrate countries of shifting languages, of unsettled government, of semi-barbarous populations, of strangely mingled worships, the brigand fastnesses of Pamphylians, Selgenses, Pisidians, Lycaonians, Isaurians, Cilicians, Cliti, Homodanenses,[1] he may not have been sorry to conceal dislike to the task on which he had entered under the plea of filial duty. At the time his defection must have been to Paul, even more than to Barnabas, a positive misfortune. Barnabas, though he clung to his friend and fellow-labourer with entire whole-heartedness, must yet have missed the genial brightness, the graphic utterance, the quick spirit of observation with which his cousin relieved the sombre absorption of Paul in his immediate purpose; and Paul, who ever loved the personal services of younger companions, must have been a little embittered, as daily worries became more trying in the absence of a vigorous comrade. There must have been in his heart a feeling of indignation against one who forsook them at the very moment when he could least be replaced, and when the difficulties which he could so greatly have lightened began to assume their most formidable shape.

So Mark left them, and the Apostles at once made their way towards the interior. Although we are not told of any synagogue at Perga, yet, since they preached there on their return journey, there must have been some special reason for their now leaving the place. This reason has been found in the probability that they reached the town towards the middle of spring,[2] when the entire population of the cities on the plain and sea-coast are in the habit of moving inland to the *yailahs*, or, as they would be called in Switzerland, "*alps*," or mountain pastures, which enable them to escape the fierce and malarious heat of the lower regions.[3] It would be useless to preach in Perga at the very time that its main population were deserting it; and any of the numerous caravans or family-migrations, which were filling the roads and passes with mules and camels and herds of cattle, would furnish the Apostles with company and protection. Without such escort it would have been imprudent, if not impossible, for them to make their way by those dangerous roads where it is probable that the snow-drifts still lay in many places, and they might often find the bridges shattered and swept away by the sudden spates of rushing streams.

The few modern travellers who have visited these parts of Asia Minor

[1] Strabo, xii. 6, 7. See Lewin, i. 130, *sqq.*

[2] Con. and Howson, i. 177, who quote Spratt and Forbes, *Travels in Lycia*, i. 48, 242, 248; Fellowes, *Lycia*, 238.

[3] A striking description of such a migration among the Kirghis Tartars may be found in Mr. Atkinson's Travels.

have furnished us with minute and picturesque descriptions of the abrupt stone-paved ascents; the sarcophagi and sculptured tombs among the projecting rocks; the narrowing valleys through which the rivers descend, and over which frown precipices perforated with many caves; the sudden bursts of magnificent prospect in which you gaze "from the rocky steps of the throne of winter upon the rich and verdant plain of summer, with the blue sea in the distance;" the constant changes of climate; the zones of vegetation through which the traveller ascends; the gleam of numberless cascades caught here and there amid the dark pine groves that clothe the lower slopes; the thickets of pomegranate and oleander that mantle the river-beds; the wild flowers that enamel the grass with their rich inlay; the countless flocks of cattle grazing over pastures whose interminable expanses are only broken by the goat's-hair huts of the shepherd, made to this day of the same material as that by the manufacture of which St. Paul earned his daily bread. And when the traveller has emerged on the vast central plateau of Asia Minor they describe the enchanting beauty of the fresh and salt water lakes by which the road often runs for miles; the tortoises that sun themselves in the shallow pools; the flights of wild swans which now fill the air with rushing wings, and now "ruffle their pure cold plumes" upon the waters; the storks that stand for hours patiently fishing in the swampy pools. Such must have been the sights which everywhere greeted the eyes of Paul and Barnabas as they made their way from Perga to the Pisidian Antioch. They would have filled a modern missionary with rapture, and the feelings of gratitude and adoration with which a Martyn or a Heber would have "climbed by these sunbeams to the Father of Lights" would have gone far to help them in the endurance of their hard and perilous journeys. Mungo Park, in a touching passage, has described how his soul, fainting within him to the very point of death, was revived by seeing amid the scant herbage of the desert a single tuft of emerald moss, with its delicate filaments and amber spores; and the journals of those whose feet in recent days have been beautiful upon the mountains over which they carried the message of peace, abound in passages delightfully descriptive of the scenes through which they passed, and which they regarded as aisle after aisle in the magnificent temple of the one true God. But, as we have already noticed, of no such feeling is there a single trace in the writings of the Apostle or of his historian. The love of natural scenery, which to moderns is a source of delight so continuous and so intense, was little known to the ancients in general, and in spite of a few poetic exceptions, was known perhaps to the Semites of that age least of all.[1] How often did Paul climb the mountain passes of the Taurus; how often had he seen Olympus

"Soaring snow-clad through its native sky;"

how often had he passed on foot by "the great rivers that move like God's

[1] St. Paul was eminently a *homo desideriorum;* a man who, like all the best Jews, lived in the hopes of the future (Rom. viii. 24; xv. 4; Tit. ii. 13, &c.).

eternity;" how often had his barque furrowed the blue waters of the Ægean, among those

> "Sprinkled isles,
> Lily on lily, which o'erlace the sea,
> And laugh their pride when the light wave lisps Greece!"

But all these scenes of glory and loveliness left no impression upon his mind, or have at least left no trace upon his page.[1] We might pity the loss which he thus suffered, and regret the ineffectualness of a source of consolation which would otherwise have been ever at hand, were it not that to St. Paul such consolations were needless. The soul that lived in heaven,[2] the thoughts which were full of immortality, the conviction that the Lord was at hand, the yearning for the souls for which Christ died—made up to him for all besides. God would have granted all other consolations had he needed them; but the steps which were ever on the golden streets of the New Jerusalem trod heedlessly over the volcanic soil of a world treasured up with the stores of fire which should hereafter reduce it to ashes.[3] The goblet which was full of the new wine of the kingdom of heaven had no room in it for the fruit of the vine of even those earthly pleasures which are of all others the most innocent, the most universal, and the most blest.

Nor must we fail to see that there was an advantage as well as a disadvantage in this absorption. If St. Paul never alludes to the transcendent beauties of the lands through which he travelled, so neither does one word escape him about the recurrent annoyances, the perpetual minor discomforts and vexations of travel. The journals of modern wanderers tell us of the drenching rains, the glaring heats, the terrible fatigues, the incessant publicity, the stings of insects, the blinding storms of dust, the trying changes of season, the scarcity and badness of provisions. But to Paul all these trivial burdens, which often, nevertheless, require more heroism for their patient endurance than those more serious perils which summon up all our fortitude for their conquest or resistance, were as nothing. He felt the tedium and the miseries of travel as little as he cared for its rewards. All these things had no bearing on his main purpose; they belonged to the indifferent things of life.

And so the Apostles made their way up the valley of the Cestrus, passed along the eastern shore of the large and beautiful lake Eyerdir, and after a journey of some forty leagues, which probably occupied about a week, they arrived at the flourishing commercial town of Antioch in Pisidia, or Antiochia Cæsarea. We learn from Strabo that it had been founded by the Magnetes, re-founded by Seleucus, and subsequently made a Roman colony, with free municipal government, by Augustus. The centrality of its position on roads

[1] There are some excellent remarks on this subject in Friedländer, *Sittengesch. Roms*, vii. 5, 3. He shows that the ancients rather noticed details than general effects. They never allude to twilight colours, or the blue of distant hills, or aërial perspective. Landscape painting, the culture of exotic plants, and the poetry of natural history have developed those feelings in the moderns (Humboldt's *Cosmos*, ii.).

[2] Phil. iii. 20; Eph. ii. 6, &c.

[3] 2 Pet. iii. 7.

which communicated southwards with Perga and Attaleia, westwards with Apamea, northwards with the great towns of Galatia, and eastwards with Iconium and the Cilician gates, made it a great commercial emporium for the trade of Asia Minor in wood, oil, skins, goat's hair, and Angola wool. Its true position—for it had long been confused with Ak-sher, the ancient Philomelium—was discovered by Mr. Arundell in 1833.[1] Conspicuous among its ruins are the remains of a noble aqueduct, which shows its former importance. Its coins are chiefly remarkable for the prominence given on the one hand to its colonial privileges, and on the other to its very ancient worship of the moon as a masculine divinity under the title of Mēn Archaios. This worship had in former days been very flourishing, and the temple of Mēn had been thronged with Hieroduli, who lived on its estates and revenues. Strabo tells us that, some seventy years before this time, on the death of King Amyntas, to whom Pisidia had been assigned by Mark Antony, this temple had been abolished; but though the worship may have been entirely shorn of its ancient splendour, it probably still lingered among the ignorant and aboriginal population.

But the message of the Apostles was not in the first instance addressed to the native Pisidians, nor to the Greeks, who formed the second stratum of the population, nor to the Romans, who were the latest occupants, but primarily to the Jews who had come thither with the stream of Latin immigration, which secured them equal privileges with the other inhabitants. Doubtless the first care of the Apostles—and this was the work in which Mark might have been specially useful—was to repair to the "strangers' rooms" attached to the synagogue, and then to find convenient lodgings in the Jews' quarter, and to provide means of securing a sale for the *cilicium*, by the weaving of which Paul honourably lived. The trade only occupied his hands, without interrupting either his meditations or his speech, and we may reasonably suppose that not a few of the converts who loved him best, were won rather by the teaching and conversations of the quiet rooms where he sat busily at work, than by the more tumultuous and interrupted harangues in the public synagogues.

But the mission of Paul and Barnabas was not meant for the few alone. They always made a point of visiting the synagogue on the Sabbath Day, and seizing any opportunity that offered itself to address the congregation. The visit to Antioch in Pisidia is rendered interesting by the scenes which led to the first sermon of St. Paul of which the record has been preserved.

The town possessed but a single synagogue, which must, therefore, have been a large one. The arrangements were no doubt almost identical with those which exist in the present day throughout the East. As they entered the low, square, unadorned building, differing from Gentile places of worship by its total absence of interior sculpture, they would see on one side the lattice-work partition, behind which sat a crowd of veiled and silent women. In front of these would be the reader's desk, and in its immediate neighbourhood,

[1] It is near the insignificant modern town of Jalobatz, and its identity is rendered certain by coins and inscriptions. (See Arundell, *Asia Minor*, ch. xii.; Hamilton, *Researches in Asia Minor*, i., ch. xxvii.; in Con. and Hows. i. 182.)

facing the rest of the congregation, those chief seats which Rabbis and Pharisees were so eager to secure. The *Kibleh*, or sacred direction towards which all prayer was offered, was Jerusalem; and on that side would be the curtain, behind which was the ark containing the sacred rolls.[1] Paul, as a former Sanhedrist, and Barnabas, as a Levite, and both of them as men of superior Jewish education, might fairly have claimed to sit in the chairs or benches set apart for the elders. But perhaps they had been told what their Lord had said on the subject, and took their seats among the ordinary worshippers.[2]

Each as he entered covered his head with his *tallith*, and the prayers began. They were read by the *Sheliach* or "apostle of the congregation,[3] who stood among the standing congregation. The language employed was probably Greek. Hebrew had long been to the Jews a learned language, understood only by the few, and in remote places, like Antioch of Pisidia, known possibly to only one or two. In spite of the stiff conservatism of a few Rabbis, the Jews as a nation had the good sense to see that it would be useless to utter prayers unless they were "understanded of the people." [4] After the prayers followed the First Lesson, or *Parashah*, and this, owing to the sanctity which the Jews attached to the very sounds and letters of Scripture, was read in Hebrew, but was translated or paraphrased verse by verse by the *Meturgeman*, or interpreter. The *Chazzân*, or clerk of the synagogue, took the *Thorah*-roll from the ark, and handed it to the reader. By the side of the reader stood the interpreter, unless he performed that function for himself, as could be easily done, since the Septuagint version was now universally disseminated. After the *Parashah*, was read the short *Haphtarah*, or what we should call the Second Lesson, from the Prophets, the translation into the vernacular being given at the end of every three verses. After this followed the *Midrash*, the exposition or sermon. It was not delivered by one set minister, but, as at the present day any distinguished stranger who happens to be present is asked by way of compliment to read the *Thorah*, so in those days the *Rosh ha-Kenéseth* might ask any one to preach who seemed likely to do so with profit to the worshippers.[5]

Accordingly on this occasion when the *Haphtarah* and *Parashah* were ended, the *Batlanîm*—the "men of leisure" who managed the affairs of the synagogue, and corresponded to our churchwardens—sent the *Chazzân* to ask the strangers if they had any word of exhortation to the people. Some rumour that they were preachers of a new and remarkable doctrine must already have spread in the little Jewish community, and it was evidently

[1] תיבה.

[2] Matt. xxiii. 6, πρωτοκαθεδρίαι, קתדרין. Philo makes frequent allusions to the order and arrangements of synagogue-worship at this period.

[3] שליח צבור.

[4] *Berachôth*, f. 3, 1; *Sota*, f. 21, 1.

[5] προελθὼν δὲ ὁ πρεσβύτατος καὶ τῶν δογμάτων ἐμπειρότατος διαλέγεται (Philo, *Quod Omn. Prob.* 12). Dr. Frankl, in his *Jews in the East*, tells us that he was constantly called upon to perform this function. Full details of synagogue worship may be found in Maimonides, *Jad Hachezaka* (*Hilch. Tephil.* viii. 10—12), and s. v. *Haphtarah* and *Synagogue* in Kitto's *Cyclopædia*, by Dr. Ginsburg.

expected that they would be called upon. Paul instantly accepted the invitation.[1] Usually a Jewish preacher sat down during the delivery of his sermon,[2] as is freely done by Roman Catholics abroad; but Paul, instead of going to the pulpit, seems merely to have risen in his place, and with uplifted arm and beckoning finger[3]—in the attitude of one who, however much he may sometimes have been oppressed by nervous hesitancy, is proved by the addresses which have been preserved to us, to have been in moments of emotion and excitement a bold orator—he spoke to the expectant throng.

The sermon in most instances, as in the case of our Lord's address at Nazareth, would naturally take the form of a *Midrash* on what the congregation had just heard in one or other of the two lessons. Such seems to have been the line taken by St. Paul in this his first recorded sermon. The occurrence of two words in this brief address, of which one is a most unusual form,[4] and the other is employed in a most unusual meaning,[5] and the fact that these two words are found respectively in the first of Deuteronomy and the first of Isaiah, combined with the circumstance that the historical part of St. Paul's sermon turns on the subject alluded to in the first of these chapters, and the promise of free remission is directly suggested by the other, would make it extremely probable that those were the two chapters which he had just heard read. His sermon in fact, or rather the heads of it, which can alone be given in the brief summary of St. Luke,[6] is exactly the kind of masterly combination and application of these two Scripture lessons of the day which we should expect from such a preacher. And when turning to the Jewish Lectionary, and bearing in mind its extreme antiquity, we find that these two very lessons are combined as the *Parashah* and *Haphtarah* of the same Sabbath, we see an almost convincing proof that those were the two lessons which had been read on that Sabbath Day in the synagogue of Antioch more than 1,800 years ago.[7] Here again we find another minute and most unsuspected trace of the close faithfulness of St. Luke's narrative, as well as an incidental proof that St. Paul spoke in Greek. The latter point, however, hardly needs proof. Greek was at that time the language of the civilised world to an extent far greater than

[1] We can hardly imagine that he showed the feigned reluctance inculcated by the rabbis (*Berachôth*, 34, 1).

[2] Luke iv. 20.

[3] Cf. Acts xii. 17; xxi. 40; xxvi. 1.

[4] Acts xiii. 18, ἐτροφοφόρησεν (A, C, E), "carried them as a man carries his little son." LXX., Deut. i. 31; cf. Ex. xix. 4; Isa. lxiii. 9; Am. ii. 10, &c. He is not here reproaching them, but only speaking of God's mercy to them. The word also occurs in 2 Macc. vii. 27.

[5] Acts xiii. 17, ὕψωσεν, in the sense of "he brought them up" (Isa. i. 2); whereas elsewhere it means "elevated" or "raised up" (Luke i. 52; 2 Cor. xi. 7). In verse 19 he uses κατεκληρονόμησεν (ℵ, A, B, C, D, E, G, H, &c.) in the rare sense of "divided as an inheritance" (where our text follows the correction, κατεκληροδότησεν), as in Deut. i. 38.

[6] It should not be forgotten that no single address of St. Paul in the Acts would take more than five minutes in delivery.

[7] They are read on the Sabbath which, from the first word of the chapter in Isaiah, is called the Sabbath *Hazon*. In the present list of Jewish lessons, Deut. i.—iii. 22 and Isa. i. 1—22, stand forty-fourth in order under the Masoretic title of דברים. This brilliant conjecture is due to Bengel.

French is the common language of the Continent. It is quite certain that all the Jews would have understood it; it is very doubtful whether more than a few of them would have understood the Pisidian dialect; it is to the last degree improbable that Paul knew anything of Pisidian; and that he suddenly acquired it by the gift of tongues, can only be regarded as an exploded fancy due to an erroneous interpretation.

St. Paul's sermon is not only interesting as a sign of the more or less extemporaneous tact with which he utilised the scriptural impressions which were last and freshest in the minds of his audience, but far more as a specimen of the facts and arguments which he urged in his first addresses to mixed congregations of Jews and Proselytes. The numerous and exclusively Pauline expressions[1] in which it abounds, show that either notes of it must have been preserved by some Antiochene Christian, or that he must himself have furnished an outline of it to St. Luke.[2] It is further important as an indication that even at this early period of his career Paul had been led by the Spirit of God, if not to the full comprehension, at least to the germ, of those truths which he afterwards developed with such magnificent force and overwhelming earnestness. The doctrine of justification by faith, and of the inutility of the works of the law to procure remission of sins, lie clearly involved in this brief but striking sermon, which also gives us some insight into Paul's method of applying Scripture; into his adoption of the current chronology of his nation;[3] and, lastly, into the effects which had been pro-

[1] See (in the Greek) Acts xiii. 25 compared with xx. 24, 2 Tim. iv. 7; 26 with xx. 32; 27 with xxiv. 21; 39 with Rom. vi. 7; 39 with Rom. v. 9, Gal. iii. 11, and others, in Alford's references. Compare, too, the thoughts and expressions of 33, 34 with Rom. i. 4, vi. 9; and 39 with Rom. viii. 3, Gal. iii. 11.

[2] Perhaps a better hypothesis is that in general outline the three main sections of it (Acts xiii. 16—22, 23—31, 32—41) may have been often repeated. (Ewald, vi. 658.)

[3] For instance, in verse 20 he makes the period of the Judges last 450 years. It is true that here the best uncial MSS. transpose the ἔτεσι τετρακοσίοις καὶ πεντήκοντα to the previous verse (א, A, B, C, and the Coptic, Sahidic, and Armenian versions). But this is exactly one of the instances in which the "paradiplomatic" evidence entirely outweighs that of the MSS. For the reading of the text is found in E, G, H, and many other MSS.; and while we see an obvious reason why it should have been altered, we see none why the other reading should have been tampered with. The case stands thus. The chronology which gives a period of 450 years to the Judges is in direct contradiction to 1 Kings vi. 1, which makes the fourth year of Solomon's reign fall in the 480th year after the Exodus. Why, then, do modern editors adopt it in spite of the oldest uncials? Not, as Bishop Wordsworth says, out of "arbitrary caprice," or "to gratify a morbid appetite of scepticism by contradictions invented by itself, and imputed to Holy Writ," or "an inordinate love of discovering discrepancies in Holy Scripture;" but for reasons, of which he must surely have been aware—viz., because (1) the same erroneous chronology is also found in Josephus (*Antt.* viii. 3, § 1, and potentially in xx. 10, § 1), and is, therefore, obviously the current one among the Jews; and was current (2) because it is the exact period given *by the addition of the vague and often synchronous periods given in the Book of Judges itself.* And (3) even if we accept the corrected reading—which can only be done in the teeth of the rule, "Faciliori lectioni praestat ardua"—we only create fresh chronological difficulties. On such subjects the knowledge of St. Paul and the Apostles never professes to be more than the knowledge of their time. To attribute to them a miraculous superiority to the notions of their day in subjects within the reach of man's unaided research, is an error which all the greatest modern theologians have rightly repudiated as pregnant with mischief. Similarly, in verse 33, ἐν τῷ πρώτῳ ψαλμῷ, though only found in D, is un-

duced upon his mind by the speeches he had heard from St. Peter and from St. Stephen. From the latter of these he borrows his use of what may be called the historic method; from the former, the remarkable Messianic argument for the Resurrection which he founds on a passage in the Second Psalm.[1]

Beginning with a courteous address to the Jews and Proselytes, and bespeaking their earnest attention, he touched first on that providence of God in the history of Israel of which they had just been reminded in the Haphtarah. He had chosen them, had nurtured them in Egypt, had delivered them from its bondage, had carried them like a nursing father in the wilderness, had driven out seven nations of Canaan before them, had governed them by judges for 450 years, and then for forty years, as tradition said, had granted them for their king one whom—with an allusion to his own name and tribe which is inimitably natural—he calls "Saul, the son of Kish, of the tribe of Benjamin." Then fusing three separate passages of scriptural encomium on David into one general quotation (13-22) he announces the central truth which it was his mission to preach: that, of David's seed, God had raised up according to His promise One who, as His very name signified, was a Saviour, and to whom the great acknowledged prophet, John the Baptist, had borne direct witness. It was true that the rulers of Jerusalem—and on this painful side of the subject he dwells but lightly—had, less from deliberate wickedness than from ignorance, put Him to death, thereby fulfilling the direct prophecies of Scripture. But—and this was the great fact on which he relied to remove the terrible offence of the Cross—GOD HAD RAISED HIM FROM THE DEAD (23-31). This was an historic objective fact, to which, as a fact tested by their living senses, many could bear witness. And lest they should hesitate about this testimony, he proceeded to show that it was in accordance with all those prophecies which had been for centuries the most inspiring part of their nation's faith. The Resurrection to which they testified was the highest fulfilment of the Psalm in which God had addressed David as His son. And there were two special passages which foreshadowed this great truth. One was in Isaiah, where the Prophet had promised to God's true children the holy, the sure, mercies of David; the other was that on which St. Peter had dwelt in his speech at Pentecost—the confident hope expressed in that *Michtam* or "Golden Psalm"—that God would not leave his soul in hell, or suffer His holy one to see corruption. More must have been involved in that yearning conviction than could possibly affect David himself. He had died, he had seen corruption; but He of the seed of David whom God had raised—of Him alone was it true that His soul was not left in the unseen world, and His flesh had not seen corruption. What they had to preach, then, was forgiveness of sins

doubtedly the right reading, as against δευτέρῳ, which is found in א and the other uncials, which is simply a correction, because the quotation is from Psalm ii. 7; and it was overlooked that among the Jews in St. Paul's time the *Second* Psalm was regarded as the First, the First being "an introduction to the Psalter."

[1] Compare Acts xiii. 35—37 with St. Peter's speech in Acts ii. 27.

through Him. In the Mosaic Law—and once more Paul touched but lightly, and in language least likely to cause offence, upon this dangerous ground—remission of sins was not to be found; but there was not only remission, but *justification*, for all who believed in Jesus. A quotation from Habakkuk formed the striking conclusion of a sermon which had been thus weighted with awful truths and startling testimony. It warned them that however startling that testimony might be, yet if they disbelieved it as their fathers had disbelieved the threat of Chaldean retribution, the contempt of insolent derision might be followed by the astonishment of annihilating doom (32-41).[1]

Thus, from the standpoint of those who heard him—commenting on the passages which had just sounded in their ears—appealing to the prophecies in which they believed—quoting, or alluding to, the Scriptures which they held so sacred—relying on the history to which they clung with such fond affection, and pouring his flood of light on those "dark speeches upon the harp" which had hitherto wanted their true explanation—thus mingling courtesy and warning, the promises of the past and their fulfilment in the present—thus drowning the dark horror which lay in the thought of a crucified Messiah in the dawning light of His resurrection—did St. Paul weave together argument, appeal, and testimony to convince them of the new and mighty hope which he proffered, and to foreshadow that which was so difficult for them to accept—the doing away of the old as that which, having received its divine fulfilment, must now be regarded as ineffectual symbol and obsolete shadow, that in Christ all things might become new.[2]

It was not surprising that a discourse so powerful should produce a deep effect. Even the Jews were profoundly impressed. As they streamed out of the synagogue, Jew and Gentile alike[3] begged that the same topics might be dwelt on in the discourse of the next Sabbath;[4] and after the entire breaking up of the congregation, many both of the Jews and of the Proselytes of the Gate followed Paul and Barnabas for the purpose of further inquiry and conversation. Both at that time and during the week the Apostles did all they could to widen the knowledge of these inquirers, and to confirm their nascent faith.[5] Meanwhile the tidings of the great sermon spread through the city.

[1] Acts xiii. 41, "ye despisers" corresponds to "among the heathen" in the original of Hab. i. 5, because the LXX. which St. Paul here quotes seems to have read בֹּגְדִים (*bogĕdîm*), "arrogantes," for בַגּוֹיִם (*baggoim*), by one of the numberless instances of variant readings in the Hebrew of which the Greek version affords so striking a proof.

[2] Paul speaks slightingly of his own eloquence; but we see by the recorded specimens of his sermons to barbarians in Pisidia, to philosophers at Athens, and to Jews at Jerusalem, how powerful was his method; and we are sure that there must also have been the "vividus vultus, vividae manus, vividi oculi, denique omnia vivida."

[3] Acts xiii. 42. The E. V. has "the Gentiles besought;" but τὰ ἔθνη is an idle gloss, not found in ℵ, A, B, C, D, E, &c.

[4] εἰς τὸ μεταξὺ σάββατον. The use of μεταξὺ for "next following" has puzzled commentators, and led them to such erroneous renderings as "for the intervening week;" but it is found in late Greek (Jos. *B. J.* v. 4, § 2; *c. Ap.* i. 21; Plut. *Inst. Lac.* 42), and is a mere extension of the classical Greek idiom. (See my *Brief Greek Syntax*, § 82, iv.)

[5] Acts xiii. 43, "urged them to abide by the grace of God;" cf. xx. 24. The expression is thoroughly Pauline. (1 Cor. xv. 10; 2 Cor. vi. 1, &c.)

On the following Sabbath a vast crowd, of all ranks, nationalities, and classes, thronged the doors of the synagogue. Immediately the haughty exclusiveness of the Jews took the alarm. They were jealous that a single address of this dubious stranger, with his suspicious innovations, should have produced a greater effect than their years of proselytism. They were indignant that one who seemed to have suddenly dropped down among them from the snows of Taurus with an astonishing gospel should, at a touch, thrill every heart with the electric sympathy of love, and achieve more by one message of free salvation than they had achieved in a century by raising a prickly hedge around the exclusive sanctity of their Law. Paul—again the chief speaker—no longer met with attentive and eager listeners; he was interrupted again and again by flat contradiction and injurious taunts.[1] At last both the Apostles saw that the time was come to put an end to the scene, and to cease a form of ministration which only led to excited recriminations. Summoning up all their courage—and few acts are more courageous than the unflinching announcement of a most distasteful intention to an infuriated audience—they exclaimed that now they had done their duty, and discharged their consciences towards their own countrymen. They had made to them the offer of eternal life, and that offer had been disdainfully repudiated.[2] "Lo! you may be astonished and indignant, but now we turn to the Gentiles. In doing so we do but fulfil the prophecy of Isaiah, who said of our Lord that He was ordained for a Light of the Gentiles, and for salvation to the ends of the earth."

Gladly and gratefully did the Gentiles welcome the mission which now to them exclusively made free offer of all, and more than all, the blessings of Judaism without its burdens. All who, by the grace of God, decided to range themselves in the ranks of those who desired eternal life[3] accepted the faith. More and more widely[4] the word of the Lord began to spread. But the Jews were too powerful to be easily defeated. They counted among their proselytes a large number of women, of whom some were of high rank.[5] Their commercial ability had also secured them friends among the leading people of the city, who were the municipal Roman authorities. Tolerant of every legalised religion, the Romans had a profound distaste for religious embroilments, and so long as the Jews behaved peaceably, were quite willing to afford them protection. Knowing that all had gone smoothly

[1] Acts xiii. 45, ἀντέλεγον.

[2] Acts xiii. 46, οὐκ ἀξίους κρίνετε ἑαυτοὺς τῆς αἰωνίου ζωῆς.

[3] ὅσοι ἦσαν τεταγμένοι εἰς ζ. αἰ. Those only will find in this expression a hard Calvinism who overlook the half-middle usage of the participle which is found in xx. 13 (cf. ii. 47) and in Philo. In a Calvinistic sense, moreover, the words are in direct antinomy with xiii. 46. The E.V. followed Tyndale, but the Rhemish "pre-ordained" is even stronger. The close juxtaposition of the two phrases shows the danger of building unscriptural systems on the altered perspective of isolated expressions.

[4] Acts xiii. 49, διεφέρετο.

[5] Jos. *B. J.* ii. 20, § 2; cf. Strab. vii. 2, ἅπαντες τῆς δεισιδαιμονίας ἀρχηγοὺς οἴονται τὰς γυναῖκας: cf. Juv. *Sat.* vi. 542. In Ps. lxviii. 11, "The Lord gave the word: great was the company of the preachers" (lit. "the female messengers," εὐαγγελιστρίαι, LXX.), fantastic commentators of the literalist type find in the fact that הַמְבַשְּׂרוֹת is feminine, an indication of the prominent agency of women in the spread of the Gospel.

till these new-comers had appeared, they were readily induced to look on them with dislike, especially since they were viewed with disfavour by the ladies of their families.[1] They joined in the clamour against the Apostles, and succeeded in getting them banished out of their boundaries. The Apostles shook off their feet the deep dust of the parched roads in testimony against them,[2] and passed on to Iconium, where they would be under a different jurisdiction.[3] But the departure did not destroy the infant Church which they had founded. It might have been expected that they would leave gloom and despondency among their discouraged converts; but it was not so. They left behind them the joy of a new hope, the inspiration of a new faith, the outpouring of the Holy Spirit in the hearts of those who had learnt of the heavenly promise.

CHAPTER XXI.

THE CLOSE OF THE JOURNEY.

Ἄπιστοι γὰρ Λυκάονες ὡς καὶ Ἀριστοτέλης μαρτυρεῖ.—SCHOL. *in Hom. Il.* iv. 88.

"WHEN they persecute you in this city, flee ye to another," our Lord had said to His twelve Apostles when He sent them forth as lambs among wolves.[4] Expelled from Antioch,[5] the Apostles obeyed this injunction. They might have crossed the Paroreian range to Philomelium, and so have made their way westwards to Synnada and the Phrygian cities, or to Colossæ and Laodicea. What circumstances determined their course we cannot tell, but they kept to the south of the Paroreia, and, following a well-traversed road, made their way to the pleasant city of Iconium. For a distance of about sixty miles the road runs south-eastwards over bleak plains, scoured by wild asses and grazed by countless herds of sheep, until it reaches the green oasis on which stands the city of Iconium.[6] It is the city so famous through the Middle Ages, under the name of Konieh, as the capital of the Sultans of Roum, and the scene of the romantic siege by Godfrey of Bouillon. Here, on the edge of an interminable steppe, and nearly encircled by snow-clad hills, they had entered the district of Lycaonia, and found themselves in the capital city of an independent tetrarchy. The diversity of political governments which at this time prevailed in Asia Minor was so far an advantage to the Apostles,

[1] αὐταὶ δὲ καὶ τοὺς ἄνδρας προκαλοῦνται (Strabo, *l.c.*). For the indulgence of the Romans towards the Jews in the provinces, Renan refers to Jos. *Antt.* xiv. 10, § 11; xvi. 6, §§ 2, 4, 6, 7; Cic. *pro Flacco*, 28, &c.

[2] Matt. x. 14.

[3] Antioch was a Roman colony, under the general jurisdiction of the Propraetor of Galatia. Iconium was under a local tetrarch. (Plin. *H. N.* v. 27.)

[4] Matt. x. 25.

[5] Acts xiii. 51, ἐξέβαλον αὐτούς.

[6] Strabo, xii. 6. Mentioned in Xen. *Anab.* i. 2, 19; Cic. *ad Fam.* iii. 8; v. 20; xv. 4, as lying at the intersection of important roads between Ephesus and Tarsus, &c.

that it rendered them more able to escape from one jurisdiction to another. Their ejection from Antioch must have received the sanction of the colonial authorities, who were under the Propraetor of Galatia; but at Iconium they were beyond the Propraetor's province, in a district which, in the reign of Augustus, belonged to the robber-chief Amyntas, and was still an independent tetrarchy of fourteen towns.[1]

Doubtless, as at Antioch, their first care would be to secure a lodging among their fellow-countrymen, and the means of earning their daily subsistence. On the Sabbath they entered as usual the one synagogue which sufficed the Jewish population. Invitations to speak were at first never wanting, and they preached with a fervour which won many converts both among Jews and proselytes. The *Batlanîm*, indeed, and the Ruler of the Synagogue appear to have been against them, but at first their opposition was in some way obviated.[2] Some of the Jews, however, stirred up the minds of the Gentiles against them.[3] Over the Proselytes of the Gate the Apostles would be likely to gain a strong influence. It would not be easy to shake their interest in such teaching, or their gratitude to those who were sacrificing all that made life dear to their desire to proclaim it. But when Jewish indignation was kindled, when the synagogue became the weekly scene of furious contentions,[4] it would be easy enough to persuade the Gentile inhabitants of the city that these emissaries, who had already been ejected from Antioch, were dangerous incendiaries, who everywhere disturbed the peace of cities. In spite, however, of these gathering storms the Apostles held their ground, and their courage was supported by the evident blessing which was attending their labour. So long as they were able not only to sway the souls of their auditors, but to testify the power of their

[1] Plin. *N.H.* v. 25. Some doubt seems to rest on this, from the existence of a coin of the reign of Nero in which it is called Claudiconium, and of a coin of Gallienus in which it is called a colony; but the adoption of the name of Claudius may have been gratuitous flattery, and the privilege conceded long afterwards.

[2] Although not authentic, there may be some basis of tradition in the reading of D and (in part) Syr. marg., οἱ δὲ ἀρχισυνάγωγοι τῶν Ἰουδαίων καὶ οἱ ἄρχοντες τῆς συναγωγῆς ἐπήγαγον αὐτοῖς διωγμὸν κατὰ τῶν δικαίων . . . . ὁ δὲ κύριος ἔδωκεν ταχὺ εἰρήνην.

[3] This seems to be suggested by the contrast of Ἑλλήνων in verse 1 with ἐθνῶν in verse 2.

[4] Renan compares the journey of the Apostles from Ghetto to Ghetto to those of the Arab Ibn Batoutah, and the mediæval traveller Benjamin of Tudela. A more recent analogy may be found in Dr. Frankl's *Jews in the East*. The reception of these Christian teachers by remote communities of Jews has been exactly reproduced in modern times by the bursts of infuriated curses, excommunications, mobs, and stone-throwings with which modern Jews have received missionaries in some of their larger Moldavian communities. Here is the description of one such scene by a missionary:—"Fearful excommunications were issued in the synagogue, pronouncing most terrible judgments on any Jew holding communication with us; or who, on receiving any of our publications, did not at once consign them to the flames. The stir and commotion were so great that I and my brother missionaries were obliged to hold a consultation, whether we should face the opposition or fly from the town. We resolved to remain and face the danger in the name of God, and the next day being Saturday, the Jewish Sabbath, we went out with a stock of our publications. When we got near the synagogue we were driven away by a yelling, cursing, blaspheming crowd, who literally darkened the air with the stones they threw at us. We were in the greatest danger of being killed. Ultimately, however, we faced them, and by dint of argument and remonstrance gained a hearing." (*Speech of the Rev. M. Wolkenberg at Salisbury*, August 8, 1876.)

mission by signs and wonders, they felt that it was not the time to yield to opposition. Their stay, therefore, was prolonged, and the whole population of the city was split into two factions—the one consisting of their enemies, the other of their supporters. At length the spirit of faction grew so hot that the leaders of the hostile party of Jews and Gentiles made a plot to murder the Apostles.[1] Of this they got timely notice, and once more took flight. Leaving the tetrarchy of Iconium, they still pursued the great main road, and made their way some forty miles into the district of Antiochus IV., King of Commagene, and to the little town of Lystra in Lycaonia.

The site of Lystra has never been made out with perfect certainty, but there is good reason to believe that it was at a place now known as Bin Bir Kilisseh, or the Thousand and One Churches,—once the see of a bishop, and crowded with the ruins of sacred buildings. It lies in the northern hollows of the huge isolated mass of an extinct volcano, "rising like a giant from a plain level as the sea."[2] It is called the Kara Dagh, or Black Mountain, and is still the haunt of dangerous robbers.

Both at Lystra and in the neighbouring hamlets the Apostles seem to have preached with success, and to have stayed for some little time. On one occasion Paul noticed among his auditors a man who had been a cripple from his birth. His evident eagerness[3] marked him out to the quick insight of the Apostle as one on whom a work of power could be wrought. It is evident on the face of the narrative that it was not every cripple or every sufferer that Paul would have attempted to heal; it was only such as, so to speak, met half-way the exertion of spiritual power by their own ardent faith. Fixing his eyes on him, Paul raised his voice to its full compass, and cried—"Rise on thy feet upright." Thrilled with a divine power, the man sprang up; he began to walk. The crowd who were present at the preachings, which seem on this occasion to have been in the open air, were witnesses of the miracle, and reverting in their excitement, perhaps from a sense of awe, to their rude native Lycaonian dialect[4]—just as a Welsh crowd, after being excited to an overpowering degree by the English discourse of some great Methodist, might express its emotions in Welsh—they cried: 'The gods have come down to us in the likeness of men. The tall and venerable one is Zeus; the other, the younger and shorter one, who speaks so powerfully, is Hermes.'[5] Ignorant

[1] The *Acta Pauli et Theclae*, of which the scene is laid at Iconium, are so purely apocryphal as hardly to deserve notice. They are printed in Grabe, *Spicileg.* 1; Tischendorf, *Acta Apost. Apocr.* p. 40. Tertullian says that a presbyter in Asia was deposed for having forged the story out of love for Paul (*De Bapt.* 17); St. Jerome adds that it was St. John who deposed him.

[2] Kinneir, *Travels in Karamania*, p. 212.

[3] Acts xiv. 9, ἤκουε τοῦ Παύλου λαλοῦντος.

[4] Jablonski, in his monograph *De Linguâ Lycaoniâ*, concluded that it was a corrupt Assyrian, and therefore Semitic dialect; Guhling, that it was Greek, corrupted with Syriac. The only Lycaonian word we know is δέλβεια, which means "a juniper," as we find in Steph. Byzant.

[5] It is hardly worth while to produce classical quotation to show that Hermes was the god of eloquence (Hor. *Od.* i. 10; Macrob. *Saturn.* i. 8). Hence his epithet Λόγιος (*Orph. Hymn.* xxvii. 6). "Quo didicit culte lingua favente loqui" (Ov. *F.* v. 668).

of the native dialect, the Apostles did not know what the crowd were saying,[1] and withdrew to their lodging. But meanwhile the startling rumour had spread. Lycaonia was a remote region where still lingered the simple faith in the old mythologies.[2] Not only were there points of resemblance in Central Asia between their own legends and the beliefs of the Jews,[3] but this region was rendered famous as the scene of more than one legendary Epiphany, of which the most celebrated—recorded in the beautiful tale of Philemon and Baucis[4]—was said to have occurred in this very neighbourhood. Unsophisticated by the prevalent disbelief, giving ready credence to all tales of marvel, and showing intense respect for any who seemed invested with special sacredness,[5] the Lycaonians eagerly accepted the suggestion that they were once more favoured by a visit from the old gods, to whom in a faithless age they had still been faithful. And this being so, *they* at least would not be guilty either of the impious scepticism which had ended in the transformation into a wolf of their eponymous prince Lycaon, or of the inhospitable carelessness which for all except one aged couple had forfeited what might have been a source of boundless blessings. Before the gate of the town was a Temple of Zeus, their guardian deity. The Priest of Zeus rose to the occasion. While the Apostles remained in entire ignorance of his proceedings he had procured bulls and garlands, and now, accompanied by festive crowds, came to the gates to do them sacrifice.[6] Paul and Barnabas were the last to hear that they were about to be the centres of an idolatrous worship, but when they did hear it they, with their sensitive conceptions of the awful majesty of the one true God, were horror-stricken to an extent which a Gentile could hardly have understood.[7] Rending their garments, they sprang out with loud cries among the multitude, expostulating with them, imploring them to believe that they were but ordinary mortals like themselves, and that it was the very object of their mission to turn them from these empty idolatries to the one living and true God, who made the heaven, and the earth, and the sea, and all that in them is. And so, as they gradually gained more of the ear of the multitude, they explained that during past generations God had, as it were, suffered all the heathen to walk in their own ways,[8] and had not given them special

[1] See Chrysost. *Hom.* xxx. The notion of St. Jerome, that the power of the Apostles to speak to the Lycaonians in their own language was one of the reasons why the people took them for gods, is utterly baseless.

[2] Some remarkable proofs are given by Döllinger (*Judenth. u. Heidenth.* bk. viii. 2, § 5).

[3] For instance, the sort of dim tradition of the Deluge at Apamea Kibôtos.

[4] Ov. *Met.* viii. 626, *seq.*; *Fast.* v. 495; Dio. Chrysost. *Orat.* xxxiii. 408. On the common notion of these epiphanies, see Hom. *Od.* xvi. 484; Hes. *Opp. et D.* 247; Cat. lxv. 384.

[5] Tyana, the birthplace of the contemporary thaumaturge, Apollonius, who was everywhere received with so deep a reverence, is not far to the east of Lystra and Derbe.

[6] Probably the gates of the house, cf. xii. 13, Jul. Poll. *Onomast.* i. 8, 77 (cf. Virg. *Ecl.* iii. 487; Tert. *De Cor. Mil.* x.).

[7] Menexenus, the physician of Alexander, claimed to be a god, as did Alexander of Abonoteichus, to say nothing of the *Divi Cæsares.*—Ἐξεπήδησαν, ℵ, A, B, C, D, E, &c. Barnabas is put first because he is most reverenced as *Zeus Poliouchos.* In the story of Baucis and Philemon the miracle at once led to a sacrifice.

[8] Acts xiv. 16, πάντα τὰ ἔθνη.

revelations: and yet even in those days He had not left Himself without witness by the mercies which He then sent, as He sends them now, "by giving us from heaven rains and fruitful seasons, by filling our hearts with food and gladness."

Such was the strong yet kindly and sympathetic protest uttered by the Apostles against the frank superstition of these simple Lycaonians. It was no time now, in the urgency of the moment, to preach Christ to them, the sole object being to divert them from an idolatrous sacrifice, and to show the futile character of the polytheism of which such sacrifices formed a part. Paul, who was evidently the chief speaker, does this with that inspired tact which can always vary its utterances with the needs of the moment. No one can read the speech without once more perceiving its subtle and inimitable coincidence with his thoughts and expressions.[1] The rhythmic conclusion is not unaccordant with the style of his most elevated moods; and besides the appropriate appeal to God's natural gifts in a town not in itself unhappily situated, but surrounded by a waterless and treeless plain, we may naturally suppose that the "filling our hearts with food and gladness" was suggested by the garlands and festive pomp which accompanied the bulls on which the people would afterwards have made their common banquet. Nor do I think it impossible that the words may be an echo of lyric songs[2] sung as the procession made its way to the gates. To use them in a truer and loftier connexion would be in exact accord with the happy power of seizing an argument which St. Paul showed when he turned into the text of his sermon at Athens the vague inscription to the Unknown God.

But the Lystrenians did not like to be baulked of their holiday and of their banquet; and those who had been most prominent in proclaiming the new epiphany of Zeus and Hermes were probably not a little ashamed. M. Renan is right in the remark that the ancient heathen had no conception of a miracle as the evidence of a doctrine. If, then, the Apostles could work a miracle, and yet indisputably disclaim all notion of being gods in disguise, what were they, and what became of their miracle? The Lycaonians, in the sulky revulsion of their feelings, and with a somewhat uneasy sense that they had put themselves into a ridiculous position, were inclined to avenge their error on those who had innocently caused it. They were a faithless and fickle race, liable, beyond the common wont of mobs, to sudden gusts of feeling

[1] Compare xiv. 15, ἀπὸ τούτων τῶν ματαίων ἐπιστρέφειν ἐπὶ Θεὸν ζῶντα with 1 Thess. i. 9, ἐπεστρέψατε πρὸς τὸν Θεὸν ἀπὸ τῶν εἰδώλων, κ.τ.λ., and the anarthrous Θεὸν ζῶντα with Rom. ix. 26, &c. Compare too the very remarkable expression and thought of ver. 16 with the speech at Athens, xvii. 30, Rom. i. 20, ii. 15, &c., and ver. 17 with Rom. i. 19, 20. The readings "us" and "*our* hearts" (ἡμῖν and ἡμῶν, A, B, G, H, and the Coptic and Ethiopian versions) are not certain, since these are exactly points in which diplomatic evidence can hardly be decisive; but they are surely much more in St. Paul's manner, and illustrate the large sympathy with which he was always ready to become all things to all men, and therefore to Gentiles to speak as though he too were a Gentile.

[2] Mr. Humphry *in loc.* not unnaturally took this for the fragment of some lyric song, and though most editors have rejected his conjecture, I think that its apparent improbability may partly be removed by the suggestion in the text (*infra*, Excursus III., p. 696).

and impulse.[1] In their disappointment they would be inclined to assume that if these two mysterious strangers were not gods they were despicable Jews; and if their miracle was not a sign of their divinity, it belonged to the malefic arts of which they may well have heard from Roman visitors. And on the arrival of the Jews of Antioch and Iconium at Lystra, with the express purpose of buzzing their envenomed slanders into the ears of these country people, the mob were only too ripe for a tumult. They stoned Paul, and, when they thought he was dead, dragged him outside their city gates, leaving him, perhaps, in front of the very Temple of Jupiter to which they had been about to conduct him as an incarnation of their patron deity. But Paul was not dead. This had not been a Jewish stoning, conducted with fatal deliberateness, but a sudden riot, in which the mode of attack may have been due to accident. Paul, liable at all times to the swoons which accompany nervous organisations, had been stunned, but not killed; and while the disciples stood in an agonised group around what they thought to be his corpse, he recovered his consciousness, and raised himself from the ground. The mob meanwhile had dispersed; and perhaps in disguise, or under cover of evening—for all these details were as nothing to Paul, and are not preserved by his biographer—he re-entered the little city.

Was it in the house of Eunice and Lois that he found the sweet repose and tender ministrations which he would need more than ever after an experience so frightful? If Lystra was thus the scene of one of his intensest sufferings, and one which, lightly as it is dwelt upon, probably left on his already enfeebled constitution its lifelong traces, it also brought him, by the merciful providence of God, its own immense compensation. For it was at Lystra that he converted the son of Eunice, then perhaps a boy of fifteen,[2] for whom he conceived that deep affection which breathes through every line of the Epistles addressed to him. This was the Timotheus whom he chose as the companion of his future journeys, whom he sent on his most confidential messages, to whom he entrusted the oversight of his most important churches, whom he summoned as the consolation of his last imprisonment, whom he always regarded as the son in the faith who was nearest and dearest to his heart. If Luke had been with St. Paul in this his first journey, he would probably have mentioned a circumstance which the Apostle doubtless regarded as one of God's best blessings, and as one which would help to obliterate in a feeling of thankfulness even the bitter memories of Lystra.[3] But we who, from scattered allusions, can see that it was here and now that St. Paul first met with the gentlest and dearest of all his converts, may dwell with pleasure on the thought that Timotheus stood weeping in that group of disciples who

[1] Commenting on the treachery of Pandarus, in *Il.* iv. 88—92, the Scholiast quotes the testimony of Aristotle to the untrustworthy character of the Lycaonians; and see Cic. *Epp. ad Att.* v. 21, &c., who speaks of the natives of these regions with great contempt.

[2] This can hardly be regarded as in any way doubtful if we compare 1 Tim. i. 2, 18 and 2 Tim. ii. 1 with Acts xvi. 1.

[3] 2 Tim. iii. 11.

surrounded the bleeding missionary, whose hearts glowed with amazement and thankfulness when they saw him recover, who perhaps helped to convey him secretly to his mother's house, and there, it may be, not only bound his wounds, but also read to him in the dark and suffering hours some of the precious words of those Scriptures in which from a child he had been trained.

But after so severe a warning it was scarcely safe to linger even for a single day in a town where they had suffered such brutal violence. Even if the passion of the mob had exhausted itself, the malignity of the Jews was not so likely to be appeased. Once more the only safety seemed to be in flight; once more they took refuge in another province. From Lystra in Lycaonia they started, under the grey shades of morning, while the city was yet asleep, for the town of Derbe,[1] which was twenty miles distant, in the district of Isaurica. It is grievous to think of one who had been so cruelly treated forced to make his way for twenty miles with his life in his hand, and still all battered and bleeding from the horrible attack of the day before. But if the dark and rocky summit of Kara Dagh, the white distant snows of Mount Ægaeus,[2] and the silver expanse of the White Lake had little power to delight his wearied eyes, or calm his agitated spirit, we may be sure that He was with him whom once he had persecuted, but for whose sake he was now ready to suffer all; and that from hour to hour, as he toiled feebly and wearily along from the cruel and fickle city, "God's consolations increased upon his soul with the gentleness of a sea that caresses the shore it covers."

At Derbe they were suffered to rest unmolested. It may be that the Jews were ignorant that Paul was yet alive. That secret, pregnant with danger to the safety of the Apostle, would be profoundly kept by the little band of Lystrenian disciples. At any rate, to Derbe the Jews did not follow him with their interminable hate. The name of Derbe is omitted from the mention of places where he reminds Timothy that he had suffered afflictions and persecutions. His work seems to have been happy and successful, crowned with the conversion of those disciples whom he ever regarded as "his hope and joy and crown of rejoicing." Here, too, he gained one more friend in Gaius of Derbe, who afterwards accompanied him on his last visit to Jerusalem.[3]

And now that they were so near to Cybistra (the modern Eregli), through

[1] It appears from the evidence of coins compared with Dio Cass. lix. 8, that both Derbe and Lystra were under Antiochus IV. of Commagene (Eckhel, iii. 255; Lewin, *Fasti Sacri*, p. 250). If the inference be correct they could not, even in a political sense, be called "Churches of Galatia."

[2] The site of Derbe is still doubtful. Strabo (xii. 6) calls it a φρούριον Ἰσαυρίας καὶ λιμήν, where it has long been seen that the true reading must be λίμνη, and if so the lake must be Ak Ghieul, or the "White Lake." Near this place Hamilton found a place called Divlé, which would be an easy metathesis for the name Δελβεία, by which the town was sometimes called; but another site much more to the north, where he found the ruins of an Acropolis, seems more likely. This, which is the site marked in Kiepert's map, answers the requirements of Strabo, xii. 6, since it is on the confines of Isaurica and Cappadocia, on a lake, and not far from Laranda (Karawan). See Lewin, i. 151.

[3] Acts xx. 4. The Gaius of xix. 29 was a Macedonian, and of Rom. xvi. 23 and 1 Cor. i. 14 a Corinthian.

which a few stages would have brought them to the Cilician gates, and so through Tarsus to Antioch, it might have been assumed that this would have been the route of their return. Why did they not take it? There may be truth in the ingenious suggestion of Mr. Lewin,[1] "that the road—as is sometimes still the case—had been rendered impassable by the waters of Ak Ghieul, swollen by the melting of the winter snows, and that the way through the mountains was too uncertain and insecure."[2] But they may have had no other reason than their sense of what was needed by the infant Churches which they had founded. Accordingly they went back, over the wild and dusty plain, the twenty miles from Derbe to Lystra, the forty miles from Lystra to Iconium, the sixty miles from Iconium to Antioch. It may well be supposed that it needed no slight heroism to face once more the dangers that might befall them. But they had learnt the meaning of their Lord's saying, "He who is near Me is near the fire." Precautions of secrecy they doubtless took, and cheerfully faced the degrading necessity of guarded movements, and of entering cities, perhaps in disguise, perhaps only at late nightfall and early dawn. The Christians had early to learn those secret trysts and midnight gatherings and private watchwords by which alone they could elude the fury of their enemies. But the Apostles accomplished their purpose. They made their way back in safety, everywhere confirming the disciples, exhorting them to constancy, preparing them for the certainty and convincing them of the blessing of the tribulations through which we must enter the kingdom of God.[3] And as some organisation was necessary to secure the guidance and unity of these little bodies of converts, they held solemn meetings, at which, with prayer and fasting, they appointed elders,[4] before they bestowed on them a last blessing and farewell. In this manner they passed through Lycaonia, Iconium, and Pisidia, and so into Pamphylia; and since on their first journey they had been unable to preach in Perga, they did so now. Possibly they found no ship ready to sail down the Cestrus to their destination. They therefore made their way sixteen miles overland to the flourishing seaport of Attaleia, at the mouth of the Katarrhaktes, which at that time found its way to the sea over a range of cliffs in floods of foaming waterfall; and from thence—for they never seem to have lingered among the fleeting and mongrel populations of these seaport towns—they took ship to Seleucia, saw once more the steep cone of Mount Casius, climbed the slopes of Coryphæus, and made their way under the pleasant shade of ilex, and myrtle, and arbutus, on the banks of the Orontes, until once more they crossed the well-known bridge, and saw the grim head of Charon staring over the street Singôn, in which neighbourhood the little Christian community were prepared to welcome them with keen interest and unbounded love.

[1] Referring to Hamilton (*Researches*, ii. 313), who found the road from Eregli impassable from this cause.

[2] Strabo, XII. vi. 2—5; Tac. *Ann.* iii. 48; xii. 55; Cic. *ad Att.* v. 20, 5, &c.

[3] Acts xiv. 22. The ἡμᾶς may imply a general Christian sentiment. It cannot in this connexion be relied on as showing the presence of St. Luke.

[4] Acts xiv. 23, χειροτονήσαντες is perfectly general, as in 2 Cor. viii. 19.

So ended the first mission journey of the Apostle Paul—the first flight as it were of the eagle, which was soon to soar with yet bolder wing, in yet wider circles, among yet more raging storms. We have followed him by the brief notices of St. Luke, but we have no means of deciding either the exact date of the journey, or its exact duration. It is only when the crises in the history of the early Church synchronise with events of secular history, that we can ever with certainty ascertain the date to which they should be assigned.[1] We have seen that Paul and Barnabas visited Jerusalem about the time of Herod Agrippa's death, and this took place in April A.D. 44. After this they returned to Antioch, and the next thing we are told about them is their obedience to the spiritual intimation which marked them out as Evangelists to the heathen. It is reasonable to believe, therefore, that they spent about a year at Antioch, since they could not easily find vessels to convey them from place to place except in the months during which the sea was regarded as open. Now navigation with the ancients began with the rising of the Pleiades, that is, in the month of March; and we may assume with fair probability that March, A.D. 45, is the date at which they began their evangelising labours. Beyond this all must be conjecture. They do not seem to have spent more than a month or two in Cyprus;[2] at Antioch in Pisidia their stay was certainly brief. At Iconium they remained "a considerable tmie;" but at Lystra again, and at Derbe, and on their return tour, and at Perga and Attaleia, the narrative implies no long residence. Taking into account the time consumed in travelling, we are hardly at liberty to suppose that the first circuit occupied much more than a year, and they may have returned to the Syrian Antioch in the late spring of A.D. 46.[3]

[1] See Chronological Excursus, *infra*, p. 753.

[2] Acts xiv. 3, ἱκανὸν χρόνον. This may mean anything, from a month or two, up to a year or more. It is a phrase of frequent occurrence in St. Luke (see Acts viii. 11; xxvii. 9; Luke viii. 27; xx. 9).

[3] That Antioch in Pisidia, Iconium, Derbe, and Lystra were *not* the churches of Galatia, as has been suggested by Böttger (*Beiträge*, i. 28, *sq.*), Renan, Hausrath, and others, is surely demonstrable. Galatia had two meanings—the first ethnographical, the second political. The ethnographic use was the popular and the all but universal one. It meant that small central district of Asia Minor, about 200 miles in length, which was occupied by the three Gallic tribes—the Trocmi, the Tolistobogii, the Tectosages—with the three capitals, Tavium, Pessinus, and Ancyra. Politically it meant a "department," an "administrative group," a mere agglomeration of districts thrown into loose cohesion by political accidents. In this political meaning the Roman province of Galatia was based on the kingdom of Amyntas (Dion Cass. liii. 26), a wealthy grazier and freebooter, who had received from Mark Antony the kingdom of Pisidia, and by subsequent additions had become possessed of Galatia Proper, Lycaonia, parts of Pamphylia, and Cilicia Aspera. On his death various changes occurred, but when Paul and Barnabas were on their first journey Pamphylia was under a propraetor; Iconium was a separate tetrarchy; Lystra and Derbe belonged to Antiochus IV. of Commagene. Galatia, Pisidia north of the Paroreia, and the greater part of Lycaonia formed the Roman province of Galatia. But even if we grant that St. Paul and St. Luke might have used the word Galatia in its artificial sense, even then Antioch in Pisidia appears to be the only town mentioned in this circuit which is actually in the Roman province. This alone seems sufficient to disprove the hypothesis that in the first journey we have a narrative of the founding of the Galatian Church. Further, as far as St. Luke is concerned, it would be a confused method, unlike his careful accuracy, to use the words Pisidia, Lycaonia, Pamphylia, and later in his narrative Mysia, and other districts in their geographical sense, and then

But brief as was the period occupied, the consequences were immense. For though Paul returned from this journey a shattered man—though twenty years afterwards, through a vista of severe afflictions, he still looks back, as though they had happened but yesterday, to the "persecutions, afflictions, which came upon him at Antioch, at Iconium, at Lystra; what persecutions he endured, and yet from all the Lord delivered him"[1]—though the journeyings and violence, and incessant menace to life, which has tried even men of such iron nerves as Oliver Cromwell, had rendered him more liable than ever to fits of acute suffering and intense depression,[2] yet, in spite of all, he returned with the mission-hunger in his heart; with the determination more strongly formed than ever to preach the word, and be instant in season and out of season; with the fixed conviction that the work and destiny in life to which God had specially called him was to be the Apostle of the heathen.[3]

That conviction had been brought unalterably home to his soul by the experience of every town at which they had preached. Up to a certain point, and that point not very far within the threshold of his subject, the Jews were willing to give him a hearing; but when they began to perceive that the Gospel was universal—that it preached a God to whom a son of Abraham was no whit dearer than any one in any nation who feared Him and loved righteousness—that it gave, in fact, to the title of "son of Abraham" a significance so purely metaphorical as to ignore all special privilege of blood—their anger burnt like flame. It was the scorn and indignation of the elder brother against the returning prodigal, and his refusal to enjoy privileges which henceforth he must share with others.[4] The deep-seated pride of the

suddenly, without any notice, to use Galatia in Acts xvi. in its political sense, especially as this political sense was shifting and meaningless. It can hardly be supposed that since he must hundreds of times have heard St. Paul mention the churches of Galatia, he should, if *these* were the churches of Galatia, never drop a hint of the fact, and, ignoring the Roman province altogether, talk of Antioch "of Pisidia," and Lystra and Derbe, "cities of Lycaonia." I should be quite content to rest an absolute rejection of the hypothesis on these considerations, as well as on the confusion which it introduces into the chronology of St. Paul's life. The few arguments advanced in favour of this view —*e.g.*, the allusion to Barnabas in Galatians ii. 1—are wholly inadequate to support it against the many counter improbabilities. Indeed, almost the only serious consideration urged in its favour—namely, the very cursory mention in Acts xvi. 6 of what we learn from the Epistle was the founding of a most important body of churches—is nullified by the certainty which meets us at every step that the Acts does not furnish us with a complete biography. In other instances also—as in the case of the churches in Syria and Cilicia—he leaves us in doubt about the time and manner of their first evangelisation. The other form of this theory, which sees the founding of the Galatian churches in the words καὶ τὴν περίχωρον (Acts xiv. 6), escapes some of these objections, but offers far greater difficulties than the common belief which sees the evangelisation of Galatia in the cursory allusion of Acts xvi. 6.

[1] 2 Tim. iii. 11.

[2] Gal. i. 10; vi. 17.

[3] 1 Cor. ix. 21; Gal. v. 11; Rom. xv. 16; Eph. iii. 6, &c.

[4] The Rabbis who spoke in truer and more liberal tones were rare. We find, indeed, in *Berachôth*, f. 34, 2, a remarkable explanation of the verse "Peace, peace to him that is far off, and to him that is near," which amounts to an admission that penitents and prodigals are dearer to God (as being here addressed first) than Pharisees and elder brothers; but it is the penitents of *Israel* who are contemplated, just as some of the Fathers held out hopes to Catholics and Christians (merely on the ground of that privilege) which they denied to others. (Jer. *in* Isa. lxvi. 16, *in* Eph. iv. 12, &c.)

Jews rose in arms. Who were these obscure innovators who dared to run counter to the cherished hopes and traditional glories of well-nigh twenty centuries? Who were these daring heretics, who, in the name of a faith which all the Rabbis had rejected, were thus proclaiming to the Gentiles the abandonment of all exclusive claim to every promise and every privilege which generations of their fathers had held most dear?

But this was not all. To abandon privileges was unpatriotic enough; but what true Jew, what observer of the *Halachah*, could estimate the atrocity of apostatising from principles? Had not Jews done enough, by freely admitting into their synagogues the Proselytes of the Gate? Did they not even offer to regard as a son of Israel every Gentile who would accept the covenant rite of circumcision, and promise full allegiance to the Written and Oral Law? But the new teachers, especially Paul, seemed to use language which, pressed to its logical conclusion, could only be interpreted as an utterly slighting estimate of the old traditions, nay, even of the sacred rite of circumcision. It is true, perhaps, that they had never openly recommended the suppression of this rite; but it was clear that it occupied a subordinate place in their minds, and that they were disinclined to make between their Jewish and Gentile converts the immensity of difference which separated a Proselyte of Righteousness from a Proselyte of the Gate.

It is very possible that it was only the events of this journey which finally matured the views of St. Paul on this important subject. The ordinary laws of nature had not been reversed in his case, and as he grew in grace and in the knowledge of our Lord Jesus Christ, so his own Epistles,[1] though each has its own divine purpose, undoubtedly display the kind of difference in his way of developing the truth which we should ordinarily attribute to growth of mind. And it is observable that St. Paul, when taunted by his opponents with having once been a preacher of circumcision, does not meet the taunt by a denial, but merely by saying that at any rate his persecutions are a sign that *now* that time is over. In fact, he simply thrusts aside the allusion to the past by language which should render impossible any doubts as to his sentiments in the present. In the same way, in an earlier part of his Epistle,[2] he anticipates the charge of being a time-server—a charge which he knew to be false in spirit, while yet the malignity of slander might find some justification of it in his broad indifference to trifles—not by any attempt to explain his former line of action, but by an outburst of strong denunciation which none could mistake for men-pleasing or over-persuasiveness. Indeed, in the second chapter of the Galatians, St. Paul seems distinctly to imply two things. The one is that it was the treacherous espionage of false brethren that first made him regard the question as one of capital importance; the other that his views on the subject were at that time so far from being final, that it was with a certain amount of misgiving as to the practical decision that he went up to the

[1] 2 Cor. v. 16; 1 Cor. xiii. 9—12. Bengel says that when the Epistles are arranged chronologically, "*incrementum apostoli spirituale cognoscitur*" (p. 583).
[2] Gal. i. 10

consultation at Jerusalem. It was the result of this interview—the discovery that James and Kephas had nothing to contribute to any further solution of the subject—which first made him determined to resist to the utmost the imposition of the yoke on Gentiles, and to follow the line which he had generally taken. But he had learnt from this journey that nothing but the wisdom of God annihilating human foolishness, nothing but the gracious Spirit of God breaking the iron sinew in the neck of carnal obstinacy, could lead the Jews to accept the truths he preached. Paul saw that the husbandmen in charge of the vineyard would never be brought to confess that they had slain the Heir as they had slain well-nigh all who went before Him. Though He had come first to His own possessions, His own people refused to receive Him.[1] Israel after the flesh would not condescend from their haughty self-satisfaction to accept the free gift of eternal life.

And, therefore, he was now more than ever convinced that his work would lie mainly among the Gentiles. It may be that the fury and contempt of the Jews kindled in him too dangerously for the natural man—kindled in him in spite of all tender yearnings and relentings—too strong an indignation, too fiery a resentment. It may be that he felt how much more adapted others were than himself to deal with these; others whose affinities with them were stronger, whose insight into the inevitable future was less clear. The Gentiles were evidently prepared to receive the Gospel. For these other sheep of God evidently the fulness of time had come. To those among them who were disposed for eternal life the doctrine of a free salvation through the Son of God was infinitely acceptable. Not a few of them had found in the Jewish teaching at least an approach to ease.[2] But the acceptance of Judaism could only be accomplished at the cost of a heavy sacrifice. Even to become a "Proselyte of the Gate" subjected a man to much that was distasteful; but to become a Proselyte of the Gate was nothing. It was represented by all the sterner bigots of Judaism as a step so insignificant as to be nearly worthless. And yet how could any man stoop to that which could alone make him a Proselyte of Righteousness, and by elevating him to this rank, place on him a load of observances which were dead both in the spirit and in the letter, and which yet would most effectually make his life a burden, and separate him—not morally, but externally—from all which he had loved and valued most?[3] The sacrifices which an African convert has to make by abandoning polygamy—which a Brahmin has to make by sacrificing caste—are but a small measure of what a Gentile had to suffer if he made himself a Jew. How

[1] John i. 11, εἰς τὰ ἴδια . . . οἱ ἴδιοι.

[2] Further than the outermost pale of Judaism they could not approach. Religious thoughtfulness in a Gentile was a crime, "A Gentile who studies the Law (beyond the seven Noachian precepts) is guilty of death;" for it is said (Deut. xxxiii. 4) "Moses commanded *us* a Law, even the inheritance of the congregation of Jacob;" but not of Gentiles (and, therefore, Rashi adds it is *robbery* for a Gentile to study the Law) (*Sanhedrin*, f. 59, 1.) This is embodied by Maimonides, *Dig. Hilchoth Menachin*, x. 9.

[3] "A Gentile who offers to submit to all the words of the Law *except* one is not received." Rabbi Jose Ben Rabbi Jehudah said, "Even if he rejects one of the *Halachôth* of the Scribes" (*Benchorôth*, f. 30, 2).

eagerly then would such an inquirer embrace a faith which, while it offered him a purer morality, and a richer hope for the future, and a greater strength for the present, and a more absolute remission for the past, offered him these priceless boons unaccompanied by the degradation of circumcision and the hourly worry of distinctions between meats! Stoicism might confront him with the barren inefficiency of "the categorical imperative;" the Gospel offered him, as a force which needed no supplement, the Spirit of the living Christ. Yes, St. Paul felt that the Gentiles could not refuse the proffered salvation. He himself might only live to see the green blade, or at best to gather a few weak ears, but hereafter he was confident that the full harvest would be reaped. Henceforth he knew himself to be essentially the Apostle of the Gentiles, and to that high calling he was glad to sacrifice his life.

CHAPTER XXII.

THE CONSULTATION AT JERUSALEM.

Ἐλεύθερος ὢν ἐκ πάντων, πᾶσιν ἐμαυτὸν ἘΔΟΥΛΩΣΑ, *ἵνα τοὺς πλείονας κερδήσω.*—1 Cor. ix. 19.

The first step of Paul and Barnabas on their arrival at Antioch had been to summon a meeting of the Church, and give a report of their mission and its success, dwelling specially on the proof which it afforded that God had now opened to the Gentiles "a door of faith." God Himself had, by His direct blessing, shown that the dauntless experiment of a mission to the heathen was in accordance with His will.

For some time the two Apostles continued to rest from their toils and perils amid the peaceful ministrations of the new metropolis of Christianity. But it is not intended that unbroken peace should ever in this world continue for long to be the lot of man. The Church soon began to be troubled by a controversy which was not only of pressing importance, but which seemed likely to endanger the entire destiny of the Christian faith.

Jewish and Gentile converts were living side by side at Antioch, waiving the differences of view and habit which sprang from their previous training, and united heart and soul in the bonds of a common love for their common Lord. Had they entered into doubtful disputations,[1] they would soon have found themselves face to face with problems which it was difficult to solve; but they preferred to dwell only on those infinite and spiritual privileges of which regarded themselves as equal sharers.

Into this bright fraternal community came the stealthy sidelong intrusion of certain personages from Judæa,[2] who, for a time, profoundly disturbed the peace of the Church. Pharisees scarcely emancipated from their Pharisaism

[1] Rom. xiv. 1, *μὴ εἰς διακρίσεις διαλογισμῶν.*

[2] Gal. ii. 4, *παρεισῆλθον*: cf. Jude 4, *παρεισέδυσαν*, "sneaked in."

—Jews still in bondage to their narrowest preconceptions—brethren to whom the sacred name of brethren could barely be conceded[1]—they insinuated themselves into the Church in the petty spirit of jealousy and espionage,[2] not with any high aims, but with the object of betraying the citadel of liberty, and reducing the free Christians of Antioch to their own bondage. St. Luke, true to his conciliatory purpose, merely speaks of them as "certain from Judæa;" but St. Paul, in the heat of indignant controversy, and writing under a more intense impression of their mischievous influence, vehemently calls them "the false brethren secretly introduced."[3] But though, throughout their allusions to this most memorable episode in the history of early Christianity, the Apostle and the Evangelist are writing from different points of view, they are in complete accordance as regards the main facts. The combination of the details which they separately furnish enables us to reproduce the most important circumstances of a contest which decided for ever the future of the Gentile Church.[4]

These brethren in name, but aliens in heart, came with a hard, plausible, ready-made dogma—one of those shibboleths in which formalists delight, and which usually involve the death-blow of spiritual religion. It demanded obedience to the Law of Moses, especially the immediate acceptance of circumcision[5] as its most typical rite; and it denied the possibility of salvation on any other terms. It is possible that hitherto St. Paul may have regarded circumcision as a rule for Jews, and a charitable concession on the part of Gentiles. On these aspects of the question he was waiting for the light of God, which came to him in the rapid course of circumstances, as it came to the whole world in the fall of Jerusalem. But even among the Jews of the day, the more sensible and the more enlightened had seen that for a pious Gentile a mere external mutilation could not possibly be *essential*. Ananias, who had the honour of converting the royal family of Adiabene, had distinctly advised Izates that it was not desirable to risk his crown by external compliance to a needless rite.[6] It was only when men like Eleazar—fierce and

[1] This is expressly stated in the margin of the later Syriac version, and in two cursive MSS. 8, 137. Epiphanius says that "their leaders were Cerinthus, the subsequent Gnostic opponent of St. John, and 'Ebion'" (*Haer.* 28, 30). But Ebion is a mere "mythical eponymus" (Mansel, *Gnostic Her.* 125; Tert. *De praescr. Haeret.* 33). Ebionite is an epithet (Epiphan. *Haer.* xxx.), and means "poor" (Orig. *c. Cels.* ii. 1; Neander, *Ch. Hist.* ii. 14).

[2] Gal. ii. 4, κατασκοπῆσαι. I suppose that the title מומחה (*moomhah*)—one authorised by a diploma to give decisions—would have been technically claimed by these visitors.

[3] Gal. ii. 4, τοὺς παρεισάκτους ψευδαδέλφους, "falsos et superinducticios fratres" (Tert. *adv. Marc.* v. 3). The strongly indignant meaning of παρεισάγειν may be seen in 2 Pet. ii. 1, "false teachers who shall privily bring in (παρεισάξουσιν) heresies of perdition."

[4] The addition in D and the margin of the Syriac, καὶ τῷ ἔθει Μωυσέως περιπατῆτε, and in the *Constitutiones Apostolicae*, καὶ τοῖς ἔθεσιν οἷς διετάξατο, though not genuine, yet show what was felt to be implied.

[5] Acts xv. 1, περιτμηθῆτε, "be *once* circumcised;" ℵ, A, B, C, D. Even Josephus (see next note) seems to think that the horrible death of Apion was a punishment in kind for his *ridicule* of circumcision (*c. Ap.* ii. 14). From this anecdote we can measure the courage of St. Paul, and the intense hatred which his views excited.

[6] Josephus, as a liberal Pharisee, held the same view (*Antt.* xx. 2, § 4; *Vit.* 23, 31). The Talmud mentions a certain Akiles (whom some identify with Aquila, the Greek translator

narrow literalists of the school of Shammai—intervened, that Proselytes of the Gate were taught that their faith and their holiness were valueless unless they assumed the badge of Proselytes of Righteousness.[1] Izates and Monobazus, as was sure to be the case with timid and superstitious natures, had risked all to meet the views of these uncompromising zealots, just as from baser motives Aziz, King of Emesa, and Polemo of Cilicia had yielded in order to win the hands of the wealthy and beautiful princesses of the house of Herod.[2] But it was quite certain that such an acceptance of Messaism would continue to be, as it always had been, extremely exceptional; and Paul saw that if Christianity was to be degraded into the mere superimposition of a belief in Christ as the Jewish Messiah upon the self-satisfaction of Shammaite fanaticism,[3] or even on the mere menace of the Law, it was not possible, it was not even desirable, that it should continne to exist. The force of habit might, in one who had been born a Jew, freshen with the new wine of the Gospel the old ceremonialism which had run to the lees of Rabbinic tradition. In Jerusalem a Christian might not be sensible of the loss he suffered by chaining his new life to the corpse of meaningless *halachôth*; but in Antioch, at any rate, and still more in the new missionfields of Asia, such bondage could never be allowed.

We can imagine the indignant grief with which St. Paul watched this continuous, this systematic[4] attempt to undo all that had been done, and to render impossible all further progress. Was the living and life-giving spirit to be thus sacrificed to the dead letter? Were these new Pharisees to compass sea and land to make one proselyte, only that they might add the pride of the Jew to the vice of the Gentile, and make him ten times more narrow than themselves? Was the superstitious adoration of dead ordinances to dominate over the heaven-sent liberty of the children of God? If Moses had, under Divine guidance, imposed upon a nation of sensual and stiff-necked slaves not only a moral law of which Christ Himself had indefinitely deepened the obligation, but also the crushing yoke of "*statutes which were*

of the Bible) as having submitted to circumcision, and also a Roman senator (*Abhôda Zara*, 10; Hamburger, *s.v.* "Beschneidung"). The Roman Metilius saved his life by accepting circumcision (Jos. *B. J.* ii. 17, § 10). Antoninus *forbade* it in the case of Gentile proselytes (Gieseler, i., § 38).

[1] "So great is circumcision," said Rabbi [Jehuda Hakkadosh], "that but for it the Holy One, blessed be He, would not have created the world; for it is said (Jer. xxxiii. 25), 'But for My covenant [*i.e.*, circumcision] I would not have made day and night, and the ordinance of heaven and earth'" (*Nedarim*, f. 31, 2). "Abraham was not called 'perfect' till he was circumcised. It is as great as all the other commandments" (Exod. xxxiv. 27), (*Id.* f. 32, 1). It was one of the laws in the case of which the Jews preferred death to disobedience (*Shabbath*, f. 130, 1). The "good king" in *Pseudo-Baruch* (§§ 61, 66) is one who does not allow the existence of an uncircumcised person on the earth.

[2] Izates and Monobazus would have been called "lion-proselytes," and Aziz and Polemo "Shechemite proselytes."

[3] "How many laws have you?" asked a Gentile of Shammai. "Two," said Shammai, "the written and the oral." "I believe the former," said the Gentile, "not the latter; accept me as a proselyte on condition of learning the written law only." Shammai ejected him with a curse (*Shabbath*, f. 31, 1).

[4] Acts xv. 1 ἐδίδασκον.

not good, and ordinances whereby they could not live,"[1] was this yoke—now that it had been abolished, now that it had become partly impossible and mostly meaningless—to be disastrously imposed on necks for which its only effect would be to madden or to gall?[2] Was a Titus, young, and manly, and free, and pure, with the love of Christ burning like a fire on the altar of his soul, to be held at arm's length by some unregenerate Pharisee, who while he wore broad *tephillin*, and *tsitsith* with exactly the right number of threads and knots, was yet an utter stranger to the love of Christ, and ignorant as a child of His free salvation? Were Christians, who were all brethren, all a chosen generation and a royal priesthood, to be treated by Jews, who had no merit beyond the very dubious merit of being Jews, as though they were unclean creatures with whom it was not even fit to eat? The Jews freely indulged in language of contemptuous superiority towards the proselytes, but was such language to be for one moment tolerated in the brotherhood of Christ?[3]

It is easy to understand in what a flame of fire Paul must often have stood up to urge these questions during the passionate debates which immediately arose.[4] It may be imagined with what eager interest the Gentile proselytes would await the result of a controversy which was to decide whether it was enough that they should bring forth the fruits of the Spirit—love, joy, peace, long-suffering, gentleness, goodness, faith, meekness, temperance—or whether they must also stick up *mezuzôth* on their houses, and submit to a concision, and abstain from the free purchases of the market, and not touch perfectly harmless kinds of food, and petrify one day out of every seven with a rigidity of small and conventionalised observances. To us it may seem amazing that the utterances of the prophets were not sufficient to show that the essence of religion is *faith*, not outward service; and that so far from requiring petty accuracies of posture, and dress, and food, what the Lord requires of us is that we should do justice, and love mercy, and walk humbly with our God.[5] But the Judaisers had tradition, authority, and the Pentateuch on their side, and the paralysis of custom rendered many Jewish converts incapable of resisting conclusions which yet they felt to be false. So far as they were true Christians at all, they could not but feel that the end of the commandment was love out of a good heart and a pure conscience, and faith unfeigned; but when their opponents flourished in their faces the Thorah-rolls, and asked them whether they dared to despise the immemorial sanctities of Sinai, or diminish the obligation of laws uttered by Moses amid its burning glow, the ordinary Jew

[1] Ezek. xx. 25.

[2] "Circumcidere genitalia instituere *ut diversitate noscantur,*" says Tacitus (*Hist.* v 5), and adds as an aggravation "Transgressi in morem eorum idem usurpant."

[3] Here is a specimen of the language of Jewish Rabbis towards proselytes: "Proselytes and those who sport with children [the meaning is dubious] delay the coming of the Messiah. As for proselytes, it is explained by Rabh Chelbo's remark, that they are as injurious to Israel as a scab (since in Isa. xiv. 1 it is said, 'strangers' *will be joined* to them (ונספחו), and ספחת means 'a scab'); because, says Rashi, they are not up to the precepts, and cause calamities to Israel" (*Niddah*, f. 13, 2).

[4] Acts xv. 2.

[5] Mic. vi. 8; Deut. x. 12; Hos. vi. 6; 1 Sam. xv. 22.

and the ordinary Gentile were perplexed. On these points the words of Jesus had been but a beam in the darkness, certain indeed to grow, but as yet only shining amid deep midnight. They did not yet understand that Christ's fulfilment of the Law was its abrogation, and that to maintain the type in the presence of the antitype was to hold up superfluous candles to the sun. From this imminent peril of absorption in exclusive ritual one man saved the Church, and that man was Paul. With all the force of his argument, with all the weight of his authority, he affirmed and insisted that the Gentile converts should remain in the free conditions under which they had first accepted the faith of Christ.[1]

When there appeared likely to be no end to the dispute,[2] it became necessary to refer it to the decision of the Church at Jerusalem, and especially of those Apostles who had lived with the living Jesus. It is far from improbable that this plan was urged—nay, demanded—by the Judaisers themselves,[3] who must have been well aware that the majority of that Church looked with alarm and suspicion on what they regarded as anti-Judaic innovations. There may even have been a certain insolence (which accounts for the almost irritable language of St. Paul long afterwards) in their manner of parading their immensely superior authority of living witnesses of the life of Jesus like James and Kephas. They doubtless represented the deputation to Jerusalem as a necessary act of submission, a going up of Paul and Barnabas to be judged by the Jerusalem synod.[4] At this period Paul would not openly repudiate the paraded superiority of the Twelve Apostles. When he says to the Galatians that "he consulted them about the Gospel he was preaching, lest he might be, or had been, running to no purpose," he shows that at this period he had not arrived at the quite unshaken conviction, which made him subsequently say that "whether he or an angel from heaven preached any other gospel, let him be anathema."[5] In point of fact it was at this interview that

[1] Comp. MS. D, ἔλεγεν γὰρ ὁ Παῦλος μένειν οὕτως κάθως ἐπίστευσαν διϊσχυριζόμενος.

[2] The expressions of Acts xv. 2, γενομένης οὖν στάσεως καὶ συζητήσεως οὐκ ὀλίγης, κ.τ.λ., are very strong. Στάσις is "insurrection" (Mark xv. 7; Luke xxiii. 19). For συζήτησις see Acts vi. 9; xxviii. 29; Mark ix. 14.

[3] As is again asserted in D, παρήγγειλαν αὐτοῖς τῷ Παύλῳ καὶ τῷ Βαρνάβᾳ καὶ τισιν ἄλλοις ἀναβαίνειν πρὸς τοὺς ἀποστόλους, κ.τ.λ., ὅπως κριθῶσιν ἐπ' αὐτοῖς περὶ τοῦ ζητήματος τούτου.

[4] See the previous extract from D.

[5] I have here assumed without hesitation that the visit to Jerusalem of Gal. ii. 1—10, though there mentioned as though it were a *second* visit, was identical with that of Acts xv., and therefore was in reality his *third* visit. There are in the Acts of the Apostles *five* visits of St. Paul to Jerusalem—viz., (1) after his conversion (ix. 26); (2) with the Antiochene contribution (xi. 30); (3) to consult the Apostles about the necessity of circumcision for the Gentiles (xv. 2); (4) after his second missionary journey (xviii. 22); (5) before his imprisonment at Cæsarea (xxi.). Now this visit of Gal. ii. could not possibly have been the *first;* nor, as is proved by Gal. ii. 7, as well as by the whole chronology of his life, could it have been the *second;* nor, as we see from the presence of Barnabas (comp. Gal. ii. 1 with Acts xv. 39), could it have been the *fourth;* for no one can assume that it was without accusing St. Paul of disingenuous suppression when he spoke to the Galatians of this sole intercourse which he had had with the Apostles; and that it was not the *fifth* is quite decisively proved by Gal. ii. 11. By the exhaustive method, therefore, we see that the visit dwelt on in Gal. ii. must have been the *third.* It would, indeed, be conceivable that it was some visit not recorded by the author of the

he learnt that his own insight and authority were fully equal to those of the Apostles who were in Christ before him; that they had nothing to tell him and nothing to add to him; that, on the contrary, there were spheres of work which belonged rather to him than to them, and in which they stood to him in the position of learners;[1] that Jesus had fulfilled His own promise that it was *better* for His children that He should go away, because His communion with them by the gift of His Holy Spirit was closer and more absolute than by His actual presence. But even now Paul must have chafed to submit the decision of truths which he felt to be true to any human authority. But for one circumstance he must have felt like an able Roman Catholic bishop—a Strossmeyer or a Dupanloup—who has to await a decision respecting tenets which he deems irrefragable, from a Pope in all respects his inferior in ability and in enlightenment. That circumstance was the inward voice, the spiritual intimation which revealed to him that this course was wise and necessary. St. Luke, of course, tells the external side of the event, which was that Paul went by desire of the Church of Antioch; but St. Paul himself, omitting this as irrelevant to his purpose, or regarding it as an expression of the will of Heaven, tells his converts that he went up "by revelation." From Paul also we learn the interesting circumstance that among those who accompanied himself and Barnabas was Titus, perhaps a Cretan Gentile whom he had converted at Cyprus during his first journey.[2] Paul took him as a Gentile representative of his own converts, a living pledge and witness that uncircumcised Greeks, seeing that they were equal partakers of the gift of the Holy Ghost, were not to be treated as dogs and outcasts. The declared approval of God was not to be set aside for the fantastic demands of man, and the supercilious tolerance or undisguised contempt of Jews for proselytes was at once a crime and an ignorance when displayed towards a brother in the faith.

Acts if there were any reason whatever for such a supposition; but when we consider how impossible it was that such a visit should have occurred without the knowledge of St. Luke, and how eminently the facts of it accorded with the views which he wished to further, and how difficult it is to find any other occasion on which such a visit would have been natural, we have no valid reason for adopting such an hypothesis. Nor, indeed, can anything be much clearer than the identity of circumstances in the visits thus described. In the two narratives the same people go up at the same time, from the same place, for the same object, in consequence of the same interference by the same agitators, and with the same results. Against the absolute certainty of the conclusion that the visits described were one and the same there is nothing whatever to set but trivial differences of detail, every one of which is accounted for in the text. As for St. Paul's non-allusion to the so-called "decree," it is sufficiently explained by its local, partial, temporary—and, so far as principles were concerned, indecisive—character; by the fact that the Galatians were *not asking for concessions*, but seeking bondage; and by the Apostle's determination not to settle such questions by subordinating his Apostolic independence to any authority which could be described as either "of man or by man," by anything, in short, except the principles revealed by the Spirit of God Himself. Prof. Jowett (*Gal.* i. 253) speaks of the unbroken image of harmony presented by the narrative of the Acts contrasted with the tone of Gal. ii. 2–6; but "an unbroken image of harmony" is not very accordant with the πολλὴ συζήτησις of Acts xv. 7, which is an obvious continuation of the στάσις καὶ ζήτησις οὐκ ὀλίγη of ver. 2. The *extent* to which the Acts "casts the veil of time over the differences of the Apostles" seems to me to be often exaggerated.

[1] Gal. ii. 7—9.

[2] Ewald, *Gesch.* vi. 456.

Alike the commencement and the course of their overland journey were cheered by open sympathy with their views. From Antioch they were honourably escorted on their way; and as they passed through Berytus, Tyre, Sidon, and Samaria, narrating to the Churches the conversion of the Gentiles, they—like Luther on his way to the Diet of Worms—were encouraged by unanimous expressions of approval and joy. On arriving at Jerusalem they were received by the Apostles and elders, and narrated to them the story of their preaching and its results, together with the inevitable question to which it had given rise. It was on this occasion apparently that some of the Christian Pharisees at once got up, and broadly insisted on the moral necessity of Mosaism and circumcision, implying, therefore, a direct censure of the principles on which Paul and Barnabas had conducted their mission.[1] The question thus stated by the opposing parties was far too grave to be decided by any immediate vote; the deliberate judgment of the Church on so momentous a problem could only be pronounced at a subsequent meeting. Paul used the interval with his usual sagacity and power. Knowing how liable to a thousand varying accidents are the decisions arrived at by promiscuous assemblies—fearing lest the voice of a mixed gathering might only express the collective incapacity or the collective prejudice—he endeavoured to win over the leaders of the Church by a private statement of the Gospel which he preached. Those leaders were, he tells us, at this time, James,[2] who is mentioned first because of his position as head of the Church at Jerusalem, and Peter and John. These he so entirely succeeded in gaining over to his cause—he showed to them with such unanswerable force that they could not insist on making Gentile Christians into orthodox Jews without incurring the tremendous responsibility of damming up for ever the free river of the grace of God—that they resigned to his judgment the mission to the Gentiles. Eminent as they were in their own spheres, great as was their force of character, marked as was their individuality, they could not resist the personal ascendency of Paul.[3] In the presence of one whose whole nature evinced the intensity of his inspired conviction, they felt that they could not assume the position of superiors or guides.[4] Whatever may have been their original prejudices, these noble-hearted men allowed neither their private predilections nor any fibre of natural jealousy to deter their acknowledgment of their great fellow-workers. They gave to Paul and Barnabas the right hands of fellowship, and acknowledged them as Apostles to the Gentiles. One touching request alone they made. The Church of Jerusalem had been plunged from the first in abject poverty. It had suffered perhaps from the temporary experiment of communism; it had

[1] The παρεδέχθησαν ὑπὸ τῆς ἐκκλησίας of Acts xv. 4 implies a preliminary meeting distinct from the συνήχθησάν τε of ver. 6.

[2] Not here characterised as "the Lord's brother," because James, the son of Zebedee, was dead, and James, the son of Alphæus, was an Apostle of whom nothing is known.

[3] See John xvi. 7.

[4] Gal. ii. 7, ἰδόντες: 9, γνόντες.

suffered certainly from the humble rank of its first converts, the persecutions which they had endured, and the chronic famine to which their city was liable. Paul and Barnabas were working in wealthy Antioch, and were likely to travel among Gentiles, who, if not rich, were amply supplied with the means of livelihood. Would they forget Jerusalem? Would they suffer those to starve who had walked with Jesus by the Lake of Galilee, and sat beside His feet when He preached the Sermon on the Mount? Already once they had brought from Antioch the deeply acceptable *Chaluka*,[1] which in the fiercest moment of famine and persecution had as much relieved the brethren as the royal bounties of Helena had sustained the Jews. Surely they would not let religious differences prevent them from aiding the hunger-bitten Church? It might be that they had been treated by Jerusalem Christians of the Pharisaic party with surreptitious opposition and undisguised dislike, but surely this would not weigh with them for a moment. The three heads of the afflicted Church begged the missionaries to the luxurious world "that they would remember the poor." It was a request in every respect agreeable to the tender and sympathetic heart of Paul.[2] Apart from all urging, he had already shown spontaneous earnestness[3] in his holy work of compassion, and now that it came to him as a sort of request, by way of acknowledging the full recognition which was being conceded to him, he was only too glad to have such means of showing that, while he would not yield an inch of essential truth, he would make any amount of sacrifice in the cause of charity. Thenceforth Paul threw himself into the plan of collecting alms for the poor saints at Jerusalem with characteristic eagerness. There was scarcely a Church or a nation that he visited which he did not press for contributions, and the Galatians themselves could recall the systematic plan of collection which he had urged upon their notice.[4] In the very hottest moment of displeasure against those who at any rate *represented themselves* as emissaries of James, he never once relaxed his kindly efforts to prove to the Church, which more than all others suspected and thwarted him, that even theological differences, with all their exasperating bitterness, had not dulled the generous sensibility of a heart which, by many a daily affliction, had learnt to throb with sympathy for the afflicted.

One part, then, of his mission to Jerusalem was fulfilled when the Lord's brother, and he to whom He had assigned "the keys of the kingdom of heaven," and he who had leaned his head at the Last Supper upon His breast, had yielded to him their friendly acknowledgment. It is on this that he chiefly dwells to the Galatians. In their Churches brawling Judaisers had dared to impugn his commission and disparage his teaching, on the asserted

[1] חֲלוּקָה

[2] Gal. ii. 10. ὃ καὶ ἐσπούδασα αὐτὸ τοῦτο ποιῆσαι; *lit.*, "which also I was eager to do at once that very thing." "*Quod* etiam sollicitus fui *hoc* ipsum facere." (Vulg.)

[3] Acts xi. 29.

[4] 1 Cor. xvi. 3; cf. 2 Cor. viii., ix.; Rom. xv. 27. Even many years after we find St. Paul still most heartily fulfilling this part of the mutual compact (Acts xxiv. 17). Phrygia alone seems to have contributed nothing.

authority of the mother Church and its bishop. It was Paul's object to prove to them that his sacred independence had been acknowledged by the very men who were now thrust into antagonism with his sentiments. There may be in his language a little sense of wrong; but, on the other hand, no candid reader can fail to see that a fair summary of the antagonism to which he alludes is this—"Separation, not opposition; antagonism of the followers rather than of the leaders; personal antipathy of the Judaisers to St. Paul rather than of St. Paul to the Twelve."[1]

But St. Luke is dealing with another side of this visit. To him the authority of Paul was not a subject of doubt, nor was it seriously questioned by those for whom he wrote; but with the *teaching* of Paul it was far different, and it was Luke's object to show that the main principles involved, so far from being dangerous, had received the formal sanction of the older Apostles. That there was a severe struggle he does not attempt to conceal, but he quotes an authentic document to prove that it ended triumphantly in favour of the Apostle of the Gentiles.

A concrete form was given to this debate by the presence of Titus as one of Paul's companions. Around this young man arose, it is evident, a wild clamour of controversy. The Judaisers insisted that he should be circumcised. So long as he remained uncircumcised they refused to eat with him, or to regard him as in any true sense a brother. They may even have been indignant with Paul for his free companionship with this Gentile, as they had previously been with Peter for sharing the hospitality of Cornelius. The Agapæ were disturbed with these contentions, and with them the celebration of the Holy Communion. Alike Titus and Paul must have had a troubled time amid this storm of conflicting opinions, urged with the rancorous intensity which Jews always display when their religious fanaticism is aroused. Even after the lapse of five or six years[2] St. Paul cannot speak of this episode in his life without an agitation which affects his language to so extraordinary a degree as to render uncertain to us the result, of which doubtless the Galatians were aware, but about which we should be glad to have more complete certainty. The question is, did Paul, in this particular instance, yield or not? In other words, was Titus circumcised? In the case of Timothy, Paul avowedly took into account his Jewish parentage on the mother's side, and therefore circumcised him as a Jew, and not as a Gentile, because otherwise it would have been impossible to secure his admission among Jews. Even this might be enough to give rise to the charges of inconsistency with which we know him to have been assailed. But if he had indeed bowed to the storm in the case of Titus—if he, the firmest champion of Christian uncircumcision, the foremost preacher of the truth that in Christ Jesus neither circumcision was anything nor uncircumcision, but faith which worketh by love, had still allowed

[1] Jowett, *Romans*, &c., i. 326. In this essay, and that of Dr. Lightfoot on "St. Paul and the Three" (Gal. 276—346), the reader will find the facts fairly appreciated and carefully stated.

[2] The date of the "Council" at Jerusalem is about A.D. 51; that of the Epistle to the Galatians about A.D. 58.

an adult Gentile convert to submit to a Jewish rite which had no meaning except as an acknowledgment that he was bound to keep the Mosaic Law—then, indeed, he might be charged with having sacrificed the very point at issue. He might of course urge that he had only done it for the moment by way of peace, because otherwise the very life of Titus would have been endangered, or because his presence in the Holy City might otherwise have caused false rumours and terrible riots,[1] as the presence of Trophimus did in later years. He might say, "I circumcised Titus only because there was no other chance of getting the question reasonably discussed;" but if he yielded at all, however noble and charitable may have been his motives, he gave to his opponents a handle against him which assuredly they did not fail to use.

Now that he was most vehemently urged to take this step is clear, and perhaps the extraordinary convulsiveness of his expressions is only due to the memory of all that he must have undergone in that bitter struggle.[2] In holding out to the last he had, doubtless, been forced to encounter the pressure of nearly the whole body of the Church at Jerusalem, including almost certainly all who were living of the twelve Apostles, and their three leaders. Perhaps even Barnabas himself might, as afterwards, have lost all firm grasp of truths which seemed sufficiently clear when he was working with Paul alone on the wild uplands of Lycaonia. Certainly St. Paul's moral courage triumphed over the severest test, if he had the firmness and fortitude to hold out against this mass of influence. It would have been far bolder than Whitefield standing before a conclave of Bishops, or Luther pleading his cause at Rome. As far as courage was concerned, it is certain that no fear would ever have induced him to give way; but might he not have yielded *ad interim*, and as a charitable concession, in order to secure a permanent result?

Let us consider, in all its roughness, his own language. "Then," he says, "fourteen years after,[3] I again went up to Jerusalem with Barnabas, taking

[1] This element of the decision has been universally overlooked. Gentiles of course there were in Jerusalem, but for a Jew deliberately to introduce an uncircumcised Gentile *as a full partaker of all religious rites in a Judæo-Christian community* was a terribly dangerous experiment. If all the power and influence of Josephus *could hardly save from massacre two illustrious and highly-connected Gentiles who had fled to him for refuge*—although there was no pretence of extending to them any religious privileges—because the multitude said that "they ought not to be suffered to live if they would not change their religion to the religion of those to whom they fled for safety" (*Vit.* 31), *how could Paul answer for the life of Titus?*

[2] This is the view of Dr. Lightfoot (*Gal.* p. 102), who says, "The counsels of the Apostles of the circumcision are the hidden rock on which the grammar of the sentence is wrecked;" and "the sensible undercurrent of feeling, the broken grammar of the sentence, the obvious tenour of particular phrases, all convey the impression that, though the final victory was complete, it was not attained without a struggle, in which St. Paul maintained, at one time almost single-handed, the cause of Gentile freedom." I give my reason afterwards for adopting a different conclusion. The sense of a complete victory contemplated years afterwards would hardly produce all this agitation. It would have been alluded to with the calm modesty of conscious strength. Not so an error of judgment involving serious consequences though actuated by the best motives. *If Titus was not circumcised, why does not Paul plainly say so?*

[3] Gal. ii. 1—6. Fourteen years after his first visit.

with me also Titus.[1] Now, I went up in accordance with a revelation, and I referred to them[2] the Gospel which I am preaching among the Gentiles—privately, however, to those of repute, lest perchance I am now running,[3] or even had run, to no purpose.[4] But not even Titus, who was with me, Greek though he was, was *obliged* to be circumcised; but [he was only circumcised?] because of the stealthily-introduced false brethren—people who came secretly in to spy out our liberty which we have in Christ Jesus, in order that they shall[5] utterly enslave us, [(to whom) not even][6] for an hour did we yield *by way of submission*—in order that the truth of the Gospel may remain entirely with you;[7] from those, however, who are reputed[8] to be something—whatever they were[9] makes no matter to me—God accepts no man's face—well, to me

[1] And some others, whom, however, he could hardly be said to "take with him" (Acts xv. 2).

[2] ἀνεθέμην αὐτοῖς, "communicated" or "referred to them"—not "placed in their hands" (cf. Acts xxv. 14). Tertullian says "*ad patrocinium Petri, &c.*," which is too strong.

[3] I take τρέχω as an *indic.*, but it may be the subjunctive, as in 1 Thess. iii. 5, and for the metaphor Phil. ii. 16.

[4] Dr. Lightfoot takes this to mean "that my past and present labours might not be thwarted by opposition or misunderstanding." So Theophylact, *ad loc.*, ἵνα μὴ στάσις γένηται καὶ ἵνα ἀρθῇ τὸ σκάνδαλον. The context seems to me to show that it implies a desire on St. Paul's part to know *whether anything valid could be urged against* his own personal conviction. And so Tert. *adv. Marc.* i. 20; v. 3; iv. 2. The admission of the possibility of a misgiving as to the *practical* issue only adds strength to the subsequent confirmation. To St. Paul's uncertainty or momentary hesitation I would compare that of St. John the Baptist (Matt. xi. 3).

[5] καταδουλώσουσι (א, A, B, C, D, E). I have literally translated the bold solecism, which was not unknown to Hellenistic Greek, and by which it gains in vividness (cf. iv. 17, ἵνα ζηλοῦτε).

[6] In the insertion, omission, or variation of these two words οἷς οὐδὲ the MSS. and quotations become as agitated and uncertain as the style of the writer. If we could believe that the word οὐδὲ—"not even"—was spurious it would then, I think, be obvious that St. Paul meant to say, "Owing to these false brethren *I did*, it is true, *make a temporary concession* (πρὸς ὥραν), but only with a view of ultimately securing for you *a permanent liberty*" (διαμείνῃ πρὸς ὑμᾶς); "ostendens," as Tertullian says, *propter quid fecerit* quod nec fecisset nec ostendisset, si illud propter quod fecit non accidisset" (*adv. Marc.* v. 3). But admittedly the evidence of the manuscripts is in favour of retaining the negative, though it is omitted in Irenæus, is absent from many Latin copies, is declared on the doubtful authority of Victorinus to have been absent from the *majority* of Latin and Greek manuscripts, and is asserted by Tertullian to have been fraudulently introduced by the heretic Marcion. Surely the uncertainty which attaches to it, joined to the fact that *even its retention* by no means excludes the supposition that Paul, to his own great subsequent regret, had given way under protest while the debate was pending, are arguments in favour of this having been the case. If this view be right it would give a far deeper significance to such passages as Gal. i. 10; iv. 11. In that case his vacillation was an error of policy, which we have no more reason to believe was impossible in his case than a moral error was in that of St. Peter at Antioch; but it would have been an error of practical judgment, not of unsettled principle; an error of noble self-abnegation, not of timid complaisance. And surely St. Paul would have been the very last of men to claim immunity from the possibility of error. "The fulness of divine gifts," says Dr. Newman, "did not tend to destroy what is human in him, but to spiritualise and perfect it."

[7] διαμείνῃ.

[8] δοκοῦντες, "seem," not "seemed," as in E.V.

[9] Renan and others see in this a covert allusion to the former disbelief of James; this is utterly unlikely, seeing that the reference is also to Peter and John. It means, rather, "however great their former privilege in nearness to the living Christ" (cf. 2 Cor. vi. 16). Indeed, it is better to join the ποτε to the ὁποῖοι, "*qualescunque.*"

those in repute added nothing." Such is a literal translation of his actual words in this extraordinary sentence; and he then proceeds to narrate the acknowledgment of the Three, that his authority was in no sense disparate with theirs; nay, that in dealing with the Gentiles he was to be regarded as specially endowed with Divine guidance.

But does he mean that, "I never for a moment yielded and circumcised Titus, in spite of the enormous pressure which was put upon me"? or does he mean, "I admit—grieved as I am to admit it—that in the case of Titus I *did* yield. Titus *was* circumcised, but not *under compulsion*. I yielded, but not out of *submission*. The concession which I made—vast as it was, mistaken as it may have been—was not an abandonment of principle, but a stretch of charity"?

It must be remembered that Paul "cared for *ideas*, not for forms;" the fact that circumcision was a matter in itself indifferent—the admitted truth that men could be saved by the grace of our Lord Jesus Christ, and by that alone—may have induced him, under strong pressure,[1] to concede that the rite should be performed—with the same kind of half-contemptuous indifference to the exaggeration of trifles which makes him say to the Galatians in a burst of bitter irony, "I wish that, while they are about it, these Judaisers, who make so much of circumcision, would go a little farther still and make themselves altogether like your priests of Agdistis."[2] When Paul took on him the Nazarite vow, when he circumcised Timothy,[3] he did it out of a generous desire to remove all needless causes of offence, and not to let his work be hindered by a stiff refusal to give way in things unimportant. We know that it was his avowed principle to become all things to all men, if so be he might win some. His soul was too large to stickle about matters of no moment. Can we not imagine that in the wild strife of tongues which made Jerusalem hateful so long as the uncircumcised Titus was moving among the members of the Church, Paul might have got up and said, "I have come here to secure a decision about a matter of vast moment. If the presence of Titus looks to you like an offensive assertion of foregone conclusions—well, it is only an individual instance—and while the question is still undecided, I will have him circumcised, and we shall then be able to proceed more calmly to the consideration of the general question"? Might he not have regarded this as a case in which it was advisable "*reculer pour mieux sauter*"? and to his own friends who shared his sentiments might he not have said, "What does it matter in this particular instance? It *can* mean nothing. Titus himself is generous enough to wish it for the sake of peace; he fully understands that he is merely yielding to a violent prejudice. It may be most useful to him in securing future admission to Jewish assemblies. To him, to us, it will be regarded as 'concision,' not 'circumcision;' an outward observance submitted to from voluntary good nature; not by any means a solemn precedent, or a significant rite"? And would not Titus have also urged the Apostle not to be deterred

[1] Acts xv. 10. [2] Gal. v. 12 (in the Greek). [3] Acts xvi. 3.

by any consideration for him? Might he not naturally have said, "I am grieved that there should be all this uproar and heart-burning on my account, and I am quite willing to allay it by becoming a proselyte of righteousness"? If Titus took this generous line, Paul's reluctance to take advantage of his generosity might have been increased, and yet an additional argument would have been supplied to his opponents. "Moses," they would have said, "commanded circumcision; we cannot let this Gentile sit at our Agapæ without it; he is himself, much to his credit, quite ready to consent to it; why do you persist in troubling our Israel by your refusal to consent?"

For whatever may be urged against this view, I cannot imagine why, if Paul did *not* yield, he should use language so ambiguous, so involved, that *whether we retain the negative or not* his language has still led many—as it did in the earliest ages of the Church—to believe that he did the very thing which he is generally supposed to be denying. Nothing could have been easier or pleasanter than to say, "I did *not* circumcise Titus, though every possible effort was made to force me to do so. My not doing so—even at Jerusalem, even at the beginning of the whole controversy, even at the head-quarters of the Judæo-Christian tyranny, even in the face of the evident wish of the Apostles—proves, once for all, both my independence and my consistency." But it was immensely more difficult to explain why he *really had given way* in that important instance. It may be that Titus was by his side while he penned this very paragraph, and, if so, it would be to Paul a yet more bitter reminder of a concession which, more than aught else, had been quoted to prove his subjection and his insincerity. He is therefore so anxious to show *why* he did it, and what were *not* his motives, that ultimately he unconsciously omits to say it in so many words at all.[1] And if, after the decision of the meeting, and the battle which he had fought, Paul still thought it *advisable* to circumcise Timothy merely to avoid offending the Jews whom he was about to visit, would not the same motives work with him at this earlier period when he saw how the presence of Titus threw the whole Church into confusion? If the false inferences which might be deduced from the concession were greater in the case of a pure-blooded Gentile, on the other hand the necessity for diminishing offence was also more pressing, and the obligatoriness of circumcision had at that time been less seriously impugned. And it is even doubtful whether such a course was not overruled for good. But for this step would it, for instance, have been possible for Titus to be overseer of the Church of Crete? Would any circumcised Jew have tolerated at this epoch the "episcopate" of an uncircumcised Gentile? I have dwelt long

[1] "Cette transaction coûta beaucoup à Paul, et la phrase dans laquelle il en parle est une des plus originales qu'il ait écrites. Le mot qui lui coûte semble ne pouvoir couler de sa plume. La phrase au premier coup d'œil paraît dire que Titus ne fut pas circoncis, tandis qu'elle implique qu'il le fut" (Renan, *St. Paul*, p. 92). It need hardly be said that there is no question of *suppression* here, because I assume that the fact was perfectly well known. We find a similar characteristic of style and character in Rom. ix. Baur, on the other hand (but on very insufficient grounds), thinks that "nothing can be more absurd." Yet it was the view of Tertullian (*c. Marc.* v. 3), and Baur equally disbelieves the expressly asserted circumcision of Timothy.

upon this incident because, if I am right, there are few events in the biography of St. Paul more illustrative alike of his own character and of the circumstances of his day. He would rather have died, would rather have suffered a schism between the Church of Jerusalem and the Churches of her Gentile converts, than admit that there could be no salvation out of the pale of Mosaism. In this or that instance he was ready enough—perhaps, in the largeness of his heart, too ready for his own peace—to go almost any length rather than bring himself and, what was infinitely more dear to him, the Gospel with which he had been entrusted, into collision with the adamantine walls of Pharisaic bigotry. But he always let it be understood that his *principle* remained intact—that Christ had in every sense abolished the curse of the Law—that, except in its universal moral precepts, it was no longer binding on the Gentiles—that the "traditions of the fathers" had for them no further significance. He intended at all costs, by almost unlimited concession in the case of individuals, by unflinching resistance when principles were endangered, to establish, as far at any rate as the Gentiles were concerned, the truth that Christ had obliterated the handwriting in force against us, and taken it out of the way, nailing the torn fragments of its decrees to His cross.[1]

And so the great debate came on. The Apostles—at any rate, their leaders—had to a great extent been won over in private conferences; the opponents had been partially silenced by a personal concession. Paul must have looked forward with breathless interest to the result of the meeting which should decide whether Jerusalem was still to be the metropolis of the Faith, or whether she was to be abandoned to the isolation of unprogressive literalism, while the Gospel of Christ started on a new career from Antioch and from the West. One thing only must not be. She must not swathe the daily-strengthening youth of Christianity in the dusty cerements of an abolished system; she must not make Christianity a religion of washings and cleansings, of times and seasons, of meats and drinks, but a religion of holiness and of the heart—a religion in which men might eat or not as they pleased, and might regard every day as alike sacred, so that they strove with all their power to reveal in their lives a love to man springing out of the root of love to God.

We are not surprised to hear that there was much eager and passionate debate.[2] Doubtless, as in all similar gatherings of the Church to settle disputed questions, there were mutual recriminations and misunderstandings, instances of untenable argument, of inaccurate language, of confused conceptions. The Holy Spirit, indeed, was among them then, as now, in all gatherings of faithful Christian men: He was with them to guide and to inspire. But neither then nor now—as we see by the clearest evidence of the New Testament then, and as we see by daily experience now—did His influence work to the miraculous extinction of human differences, or obliteration of human

[1] Col. ii. 14.

[2] See on this dissension Hooker, *Eccl. Pol.* IV. xi. 4.

imperfections. Those who supported the cause of Paul rendered themselves liable to those charges, so terrible to a Jew, of laxness, of irreligion, of apostasy, of unpatriotism, of not being believers in revealed truth. Was not Moses inspired? Was the Sacred Pentateuch to be reduced to a dead letter? Were all the curses of Ebal to be braved? Were the Thorah-rolls to be flung contemptuously into the Dead Sea? On the other hand, those who maintained the necessity of circumcision and of obedience to the Law, laid themselves open to the fatal question, "If the Law is essential to salvation, what, then, has been the work of Christ?"

But when the subject had been amply discussed, Peter arose.[1] Which side he would take could be hardly doubtful. He had, in fact, already braved and overborne the brunt of a similar opposition. But an exceptional instance was felt to be a very different thing from a universal rule. It was true that Peter did not now stand alone, but found the moral support, which was so necessary to him, in the calm dignity of Barnabas and the fervid genius of Paul. But in all other respects his task was even more difficult than it had been before, and, rising to the occasion, he spoke with corresponding boldness and force.[2] His speech was in accordance with the practical, forthright, non-argumentative turn of his mind. Filled with energetic conviction by the logic of facts, he reminded them how, long ago,[3] the question had been practically settled. God had selected him to win over the first little body of converts from the Gentile world; and the gift of the Spirit to them had showed that they were cleansed by faith. To lay on them the burden of the Law—a burden to the daily life which it surrounded with unpractical and often all but impracticable observances—a burden to the conscience because it created a sense of obligation of which it could neither inspire the fulfilment nor remedy the shortcoming—a burden which had therefore been found intolerable both by their fathers and themselves[4]—was simply to tempt God by hindering His manifest purposes, and resisting His manifest will. In one doctrine all present were agreed;[5] it was that alike the Jews and the Gentile converts should be saved only by the grace of the Lord Jesus Christ. The inference then was obvious, that they were not and could not be saved by the works of the Law. In the observance of those works the Jews, on whom they were originally enjoined, might naturally persevere till fresh light came; but these hereditary customs had never been addressed to the Gentiles, and, since they were unnecessary to salvation, they must

[1] On the views of St. John, see Excursus XVII., "St. John and St. Paul."

[2] Acts xv. 7—11. Again we have to notice the interesting circumstance that in this brief speech the language is distinctly Petrine. Such minute marks of authenticity are wholly beyond the reach of a forger.

[3] The expression ἀφ' ἡμερῶν ἀρχαίων would naturally refer to the ἀρχὴ of the Gospel (cf. xi. 15; xxi. 16; Phil. iv. 15). But if the conversion of Cornelius took place during the "rest" procured for the Church by the absorption of the Jews in their attempt to rebut the mad impiety of Gaius, A.D. 40, that was not twelve years before this time.

[4] Gal. v. 3. The Law was a ζυγὸς δουλείας, the Gospel a ζυγὸς χρηστός, a φορτίον ἐλαφρόν (Matt. xi. 29, 30).

[5] Cf. Acts xi. 17.

obviously be to the Gentiles not burdensome only, but a positive stumbling-block.

The weight of Peter's dignity had produced silence in the assembly. The excitement was now so far calmed that Paul and Barnabas were at least listened to without interruptions. Barnabas—who, in the Jewish Church, still retained his precedence, and who was as acceptable to the audience from his past liberality as Paul was unacceptable from his former persecutions—spoke first; but both he and Paul seem to have abstained from *arguing* the question. All the arguments had been urged at private conferences when words could be deliberately considered. They were not there to impress their own views, but to hear those of the Apostles and of the Church they governed. Barnabas never seems to have been prominent in debate, and Paul was too wise to discuss theological differences before a promiscuous audience. They confined themselves, therefore, to a simple history of their mission, dwelling especially on those "signs and wonders" wrought by their hands among the Gentiles, which were a convincing proof that, though they might not win the approval of man, they had all along enjoyed the blessing of God.

Then rose James. Every one present must have felt that the practical decision of the Church—Paul must have felt that, humanly speaking, the future of Christianity—depended on his words. A sense of awe clung about him and all he said and did. Clothed with a mysterious and indefinable dignity as "the brother of the Lord," that dignity and mystery were enhanced by his bearing, dress, manner of life, and entire appearance. Tradition, as embodied in an Ebionite romance, and derived from thence by Hegesippus,[1] represents him as wearing no wool, but clothed in fine white linen from head to foot, and—either from some priestly element in his genealogy, or to symbolise his "episcopate" at Jerusalem—as wearing on his forehead the *petalon*, or golden plate of High-priesthood.[2] It is said that he was so holy, and so highly esteemed by the whole Jewish people, that he alone was allowed, like the High Priest, to enter the Holy Place; that he lived a celibate[3] and ascetic life; that he spent long hours alone in the Temple praying for the people, till his knees became hard and callous as those of the camel; that he had the power of working miracles; that the rain fell in accordance with his prayers; that it was owing to his merits that God's impending wrath was averted from the Jewish nation; that he received the title of "the Just" and *Obliam*, or "Rampart of the People; and that he was shadowed forth in the images of

1 "The Ascent of James." The narrative of Hegesippus is quoted at length by Eusebius, *H. E.* ii. 23. Other passages which relate to him are Epiphan. *Haer.* lxxviii. 7, 13, 14; Jer. *De Virr. Illustr.* 2; *Comm.* in Gal. i. 19.

2 Epiphan. *Haer.* xxix. 4. The same story is told of St. John, on the authority of Polycrates, Bishop of Ephesus (Euseb. *H. E.* iii. 31; v. 24). Either Polycrates has taken literally some metaphorical allusion, or John really did sometimes adopt a symbol of Christian High-priesthood. The former seems the more probable supposition.

3 This is rendered doubtful by 1 Cor. ix. 5, unless he was an exception to the other *Desposyni*.

the prophets.[1] Some of these details must be purely imaginative; but legends, as has well been said, are like the clouds that gather upon the mountain summits, and show the height and take the shapes of the peaks about which they cling. We may readily believe that he was a Nazarite, perhaps even an ascetic—one who, by the past affinities of his character, was bound rather to Banus, and John Baptist, and the strict communities of the Essenes, than to the disciples of One who came eating and drinking, pouring on social life the brightness of His holy joy, attending the banquet of the Pharisee at Capernaum, and the feast of the bridegroom at Cana, not shrinking from the tears with which Mary of Magdala or the perfumes with which Mary of Bethany embathed his feet.

Such was the man who now rose to speak, with the long locks of the Nazarite streaming over his white robe, and with all the sternness of aspect which can hardly have failed to characterise one who was so rigid in his convictions, so uncompromising in his judgments, so incisive in his speech. The importance of his opinion lay in the certainty that it could hardly fail to be, at least nominally, adopted by the multitude, among whom he exercised an authority, purely local indeed and limited, but within those limits superior even to that of Peter. The most fanatical of bigots could hardly refuse to be bound by the judgment of one who was to the very depth of his being a loyal Jew; to whom even unconverted Jews looked up with reverence; to whom the "Law," which neither St. Peter nor St. John so much as mention in their Epistles, was so entirely the most prominent conception that he does not once mention the Gospel, and only alludes to it under the aspect of a law, though as "the perfect law of liberty."[2]

His speech—which, as in so many other instances, bears internal marks of authenticity[3]—was thoroughly Judaic in tone, and yet showed that the private arguments of the Apostles of the Gentiles had not been thrown away on a mind which, if in comparison with the mind of a Paul, and even of a Peter, it was somewhat stern and narrow, was yet the mind of a remarkable and holy man who would not struggle against the guidance of the Holy Spirit of God. Peter, in one of those impetuous outbursts of generous conviction which carried him beyond his ordinary self, had dauntlessly laid down broad principles which are, perhaps, the echo of thoughts which Paul had impressed upon his mind. It would have been too much to expect that James would speak with equal breadth and boldness. Had he done so, we should have felt at once that he was using language unlike himself, unlike all that we know of

[1] Dan. i. 8, 12; Tob. i. 11, 12. ὡς οἱ προφῆται δηλοῦσι περὶ αὐτοῦ (Heges. *ubi supr.*). This, perhaps, refers to Isa. iii. 10. If he be the Jacob of Kephar Sechaniah he is indeed regarded as a *Min*, yet he is represented as having various dealings with orthodox Rabbis (Grätz, *Gnostic. u. Judaism.* p. 25). The name Oblias, חוּבְלְיָה, is explained by Hausrath to mean "Jehovah my chain," with allusion to the Nazarite vow. Hitzig. (*Kl. Propheten*) thinks the name may refer to the staff called "bands" in Zech. xi. 7. Is it possible the name may be some confusion of *Abh leam*, "father of the people"?

[2] James i. 25; ii. 12.

[3] *E.g.*, "on whom my name has been called;" cf. James ii. 7.

him, unlike the language of his own Epistle. But though his speech is as different from St. Peter's as possible—though it proposed restrictions where *he* had indicated liberty—it yet went farther than could have been hoped; farther than bigots either liked or cordially accepted; and, above all, it conceded the main point at issue in implying that circumcision and the ceremonial law were, as a whole, non-essential for the Gentiles.

Requesting their attention, he reminded them that Symeon[1]—as, using the Hebrew form of the name, he characteristically calls his brother Apostle—had narrated to them the Divine intimations which led to the call of the Gentiles, and this he shows was in accordance with ancient prophecy, and, therefore, with Divine fore-ordination.[2] But obviously—this was patent to all Jews alike—the Gentiles would never accept the whole Mosaic Law. His authoritative decision,[3] therefore, took the form of "a concession and a reserve." He proposed to release the converted Gentiles from all but four restrictions—which belonged to what was called the Noachian dispensation[4]—abstinence, namely, from things polluted by being offered to idols,[5] and from fornication, and from anything strangled, and from blood.[6] "For," he adds, in words which are pregnant with more than one significance, "Moses from of old hath preachers in the synagogues in every city, being read every Sabbath day." By this addition he probably meant to imply that since Moses was universally read in synagogues attended both by Jews and by Gentile converts, we will tell the Gentiles that this Law which they hear read is not universally binding on them, but only so far as charity to the Jew requires; and we will tell the Jews that we have no desire to abrogate *for them* that Law to whose ordinances they bear a weekly witness.

One of the most remarkable points in this speech is the argument deduced from the prophecy of Amos, which was primarily meant as a prophecy of the restoration of Israel from captivity, but which St. James, with a large insight into the ever-widening horizons of prophecy, applies to the ideal restoration, the reception of Jehovah as their common Father by the great family of man. In the rebuilding of the ruined tabernacle of David he sees the upraising of the Church of Christ as an ideal temple to which the Gentiles also shall be joined. Nor is it a little striking that in adducing this prophecy he quotes, not the Hebrew, but mainly the Septuagint.[7] The Greek differs

[1] As in 2 Peter i. 1. This is the last mention of Peter in the Acts.

[2] Amos ix. 11, 12. The true reading here, among numberless divergences, seems to be γνωστὰ ἀπ' αἰῶνος (ℵ, B, C), "it has been known of old." James affirms what Amos prophesied, but his speech is not free from difficulties. (See Baur, *Paul.* i. 124.)

[3] ἐγὼ κρίνω, but he was only *primus inter pares*. (See Acts xv. 6; xxi. 25.)

[4] See Gen. ix. 4.

[5] Acts xv. 20, ἀλισγήματα τῶν εἰδώλων = εἰδωλόθυτα (ver. 29; xxi. 25) Ἀλισγέω = *gâal*, "to redeem with blood" (Dan. i. 8; Mal. i. 7). We are told that the Jews in the days of Antiochus were ready to die rather than εἰδωλοθύτων ἀπογεύεσθαι.

[6] These two restrictions are practically identical, the πνικτὰ being only forbidden because they necessarily involved the eating of the blood. Αἷμα cannot mean "the shedding of blood"—homicide, as some of the Fathers supposed. On "things strangled" and "blood" see Tert. *Apol.* ix.; Schöttgen, *Hor. Hebr. in loc.*; Kalisch on Gen. ix. 4.

[7] παρενοχλεῖν (ver. 19) occurs only in the LXX.

essentially from the Hebrew, and differs from it in the essence of the interpretation, which lies not only in the ideal transference from the Temple to the Church, but in direct reference to the Gentiles—viz.:

"*That the residue of men might seek after the Lord*, and all the Gentiles upon whom My name is called, saith the Lord."

But the Hebrew says, much less appositely to the purpose of the speaker,

"*That they may possess the remnant of Edom*, and of all the heathen upon whom My name is called, saith the Lord."

The difference is due to one of those numberless and often extraordinary variations of the original text of which the Septuagint is so decisive a proof, and which makes that version so interesting a study.[1] This application of James may be regarded as implicitly involved even in the Hebrew, and is yet more directly supported by other passages;[2] but the fact that here and elsewhere the New Testament writers quote and argue from the undeniably variant renderings of the Septuagint, quoting them from memory, and often differing in actual words *both* from these and from the Hebrew, shows how utterly removed was their deep reverence for Scripture from any superstition about the literal dictation of mere words or letters.

The debate was now at an end, for all the leaders had spoken. The objections had been silenced; the voice of the chief elder had pronounced the authoritative conclusion. It only remained to make that conclusion known to those who were immediately concerned. The Apostles and Elders and the whole Church therefore ratified the decision, and selected two of their own body, men of high repute—Judas Barsabas and Silas[3]—to accompany the emissaries from the Church of Antioch on their return, and to be pledges for the genuineness of their written communication. The letter which they sent embodied their resolutions, and ran as follows:—"The Apostles and Elders[4] and brethren to the brethren from the Gentiles in Antioch and Syria

[1] The LXX. seems clearly to have read אָדָם (*adâm*), "man," for אֱדוֹם (*edôm*). Dr. Davidson, *Sacr. Hermen.* p. 462, goes so far as to suppose that the Jews have here altered the Hebrew text.

[2] *E.g.*, Ps. lxxxvi. 9; xxii. 31; cii. 18; Isa. xliii. 7.

[3] The Silas of Acts is, of course, the Silvanus—the name being Romanised for convenience—of the Epistles (1 Thess. i. 1; 2 Thess. i. 1), and perhaps of 1 Pet. v. 12. He is not mentioned in the Acts after the first visit of St. Paul to Corinth, and in undesigned coincidence with this his name disappears in the superscription of the Epistles after that time. (See Wordsworth, Phil. i. 1.)

[4] Although καὶ οἱ is omitted (א, A, B, C, the Vulgate and Armenian versions, Irenæus, and Origen, and the καὶ by D), I still believe them to be genuine. The diplomatic evidence seems indeed to be against them, the weight of the above Uncials, &c., being superior to that of E, G, H, the majority of Cursives, and the Syriac, Coptic, and Æthiopic versions. But objection to the apparent parity assigned to the brethren might have led, even in early days, to their omission, while if not genuine it is not easy to see why they should have been inserted. They also agree better with ver. 22, "with the whole Church," and ver. 24, "going out *from among us*." The importance of the reading is shown by its bearing on such debates as the admission of laymen into ecclesiastical conferences, &c. Wordsworth quotes from Beveridge, *Codex Canonum Vindicatus*, p. 20, the rule "*Laici ad judicium de doctrina aut disciplina Ecclesiastica ferendum nunquam admissi sunt.*"

and Cilicia, greeting.[1] Since we heard that some who went out from among us troubled you with statements, subverting[2] your souls, who received no injunction from us,[3] we met together, and decided to select men and send them to you with our beloved Barnabas and Paul,[4] persons[5] who have given up their lives for the name of our Lord Jesus Christ.[6] We have therefore commissioned Judas and Silas to make in person the same announcement to you by word of mouth—namely, that it is our decision, under the guidance of the Holy Ghost,[7] to lay no further burden[8] upon you beyond these necessary things: to abstain from things offered to idols, and from blood, and from strangled, and from fornication, in keeping yourselves from which it shall be well with you. Farewell."[9]

It will be observed that throughout this account I have avoided the terms "Council" and "decree." It is only by an unwarrantable extension of terms that the meeting of the Church at Jerusalem can be called a "Council," and the word connotes a totally different order of conceptions to those that were prevalent at that early time. The so-called Council of Jerusalem in no way resembled the General Councils of the Church, either in its history, its constitution, or its object. It was not a convention of ordained delegates, but a meeting of the entire Church of Jerusalem to receive a deputation from the Church of Antioch. Even Paul and Barnabas seem to have had no vote in the decision, though the votes of a promiscuous body could certainly not be more enlightened than theirs, nor was their allegiance due in any way to James. The Church of Jerusalem might out of respect be consulted, but it had no claim to superiority, no abstract prerogative to bind its decisions on the free Church of God.[10] The "decree" of the "Council" was little more than the wise recommendation of a single synod, addressed to a particular dis-

[1] χαίρειν, lit. "rejoice." It is a curious circumstance that the *Greek* salutation—for the Hebrew salutation would be שָׁלוֹם, "Peace"—is only found in the letter of a Gentile, Claudius Lysias (xxiii. 26), and in the letter of him who must have taken a main part in drawing up this letter (James i. 1).

[2] ἀνασκευάζοντες, lit., "digging up from the foundations" (Thuc. iv. 116).

[3] This disavowal is complete, and yet whole romances about counter-missions in direct opposition to St. Paul, and organised by James, are securely built on the expression in Gal. ii. 12, τινὰς ἀπὸ Ἰακώβου, though it is very little stronger than the τινὲς κατελθόντες ἀπὸ τῆς Ἰουδαίας of xv. 1, and not so strong as the τινὲς ἐξ ἡμῶν ἐξελθόντες here.

[4] In order, of course, that no possible suspicion might attach to the letter as an expression of their real sentiments.

[5] I have expressed the difference of ἄνδρας and ἀνθρώπους, but the only difference intended is that the latter expression is more generic.

[6] They were martyrs at least in will (Alf.).

[7] Cf. Ex. xiv. 31; 1 Sam. xii. 18. Hence the "Sancto Spiritu suggerente," commonly prefixed to decrees of Councils.

[8] This word (cf. ver. 10) seems to show the hand of Peter (cf. Rev. ii. 24).

[9] D, followed by some versions, and many Cursives, has the curious addition, "and whatsoever ye do not wish to be done to yourselves, do not to another. Farewell, walking in the Holy Spirit." With these *minimum* requirements, intended to put Gentiles on the footing of Proselytes of the Gate, compare Lev. xvii. 8—16; xviii. 26.

[10] See Article xxi. Pope Benedict XIV. says, "*Speciem* quandam et *imaginem Synodi* in praedicta congregatione eminere" (*De Synod.* i. 1—5; *ap.* Denton, Acts ii. 82).

trict, and possessing only a temporary validity.[1] It was, in fact, a local *concordat*. Little or no attention has been paid by the universal Church to two of its restrictions; a third, not many years after, was twice discussed and settled by Paul, on the same general principles, but with a by no means identical conclusion.[2] The concession which it made to the Gentiles, in not insisting on the necessity of circumcision, was equally treated as a dead letter by the Judaising party, and cost Paul the severest battle of his lifetime to maintain. If this circular letter is to be regarded as a binding and final decree, and if the meeting of a single Church, not by delegates but in the person of all its members, is to be regarded as a Council, never was the decision of a Council less appealed to, and never was a decree regarded as so entirely inoperative alike by those who repudiated the validity of its concessions,[3] and by those who discussed, as though they were still an open question, no less than three of its four restrictions.[4]

The letter came to the Churches like a message of peace. Its very limitation was, at the time, the best proof of its inspired wisdom. Considering the then state of the Church, no decision could have more clearly evinced the guidance of the Holy Spirit of God.[5] It was all the more valuable because there were so many questions which it left unsolved. The heads of the Church admitted—and that was something—that circumcision was *non-essential* to Gentiles, and they may seem to have indulged in an extreme liberality in not pressing the distinction between clean and unclean meats, and, above all, in not insisting on the abstinence from the flesh of swine. By these concessions they undoubtedly removed great difficulties from the path of Gentile converts. But, after all, a multitude of most pressing questions remained, and left an opening for each party to hold almost exactly the same opinions as before. A Gentile was not to be *compelled* to circumcision and Mosaism. Good; but might it not be infinitely *better* for him to accept them? Might there not have been in the minds of Jewish Christians, as in those of later Rabbis, a belief that "even if Gentiles observe the seven Noachian precepts, they do not receive the same reward as Israelites?"[6] It is, at any rate, clear that neither now nor afterwards did the Judaisers admit Paul's dogmatic principles, as subsequently stated to the Galatians and Romans. Probably

[1] Hooker, *Eccl. Pol.* IV. xi. 5.

[2] Rom. xiv.; 1 Cor. viii.

[3] Gal. iii. 1; v. 2, and *passim*. It is astonishing to find that even Justin declares the eating of εἰδωλόθυτα to be as bad as idolatry, and will hold no intercourse with those who do it (*Dial. c. Tryph.* 35); but the reason was that by that time (as in the days of the Maccabees) it had been adopted by the heathen as a *test* of apostasy. And compare 1 Cor. x. 20, 21. (Ritschl, *Alt. Kath. Kirch.* 310, 2nd ed.)

[4] St. Paul discusses the question of meats offered to idols without the remotest reference to this decree, and the Western Church have never held themselves bound to abstain "from things strangled," and from blood (Aug. *c. Faust.* xxxii. 13). St. Paul's silence about the decree when he writes to the Romans perhaps rises from its provisional and partial character. It was only addressed to the Gentile converts of "Antioch, Syria, and Cilicia."

[5] "Ils virent que le seul moyen d'échapper aux grands questions est de ne pas les résoudre . . . de laisser les problèmes s'user et mourir faute de raison d'être" (Renan, *St. P.* 93)

[6] *Abhôda Zara*, f. 3, 1.

they regarded him, at the best, as the Ananias for future Eleazers.[1] Above all, the burning question of social relations remained untouched. Titus had been circumcised as the only condition on which the members of the Church at Jerusalem would let him move on an equal footing among themselves. It was all very well for them to decide with more or less indifference about "*choots learets*," "the outer world," "people elsewhere," "those afar,"[2] as though they could much more easily contemplate the toleration of uncircumcised Christians, provided that they were out of sight and out of mind in distant cities; but a Jew was a Jew, even if he lived in the wilds of Isauria or the burnt plains of Phrygia; and how did this decision at Jerusalem help him to face the practical question, "Am I, or am I not, to share a common table with, to submit to the daily contact of people that eat freely of that which no true Jew can think of without a thrill of horror—the unclean beast?"

These were the questions which, after all, could only be left to the solution of time. The prejudices of fifteen centuries could not be removed in a day. Alike the more enlightened and the more bigoted of Jews and Gentiles continued to think very much as they had thought before, until the darkness of prejudice was scattered by the broadening light of history and of reason.

The *genuineness* of this cyclical letter is evinced by its extreme naturalness. A religious romancist could not possibly have invented anything which left so much unsolved. And this genuineness also accounts for the startling appearance of a grave moral crime among things so purely ceremonial as particular kinds of food. There is probably no other period in the history of the world at which the Apostles would have found it needful to tell their Gentile converts to abstain from fornication, as well as from things offered to idols, things strangled, and blood. The first of these four prohibitions was perfectly intelligible, because it must have been often necessary for a Gentile Christian to prove to his Jewish brethren that he had no hankering after the "abominable idolatries" which he had so recently abandoned. The two next prohibitions were desirable as a concession to the indefinable horror with which the Jews and many other Eastern races regarded the eating of the blood, which they considered to be "the very life."[3] But only at such a period as this could a moral pollution have been placed on even apparently the same footing as matters of purely national prejudice. That the reading is correct,[4] and that

[1] See Pfleiderer, ii. 13.

[2] Acts ii. 39, οἱ εἰς μακράν; Col. iv. 5, οἱ ἔξω.

[3] Gen. ix. 4; Lev. xvii. 14. So too Koran, Sur. v. 4. See Bähr, *Symbolik*, ii. 207. On the other hand, "the blood" was a special delicacy to the heathen (Hom. *Od.* iii. 470; xviii. 44; Ov. *Met.* xii. 154); and hence "things strangled" were with them a common article of food. Rutilius calls the Jew, "Humanis animal dissociale cibis" (*It.* i. 384). Even this restriction involved a most inconvenient necessity for never eating any meat but *kosher*, *i.e.*, meat prepared by Jewish butchers in special accordance with the laws of slaughtering (שחיטה). It would more or less necessitate what would be, to a Gentile at any rate, most repellent—the "cophinus foenumque supellex" (Juv. *Sat.* iii. 14), which were, for these reasons, the peculiarity of the Jew (Sidon. *Ep.* vii. 6).

[4] There is not the faintest atom of probability in Bentley's conjecture of πορκεία. At the same time, it must be noted as an extraordinary stretch of liberality on the part of the Judaisers not to require the abstention from swine's flesh by their Gentile brethre

the thing forbidden is the sin of fornication,[1] not idolatry, or mixed marriages, or marriages between blood relations (1 Cor. v. 1), or second marriages (1 Tim. iii. 2), or any of the other explanations in which an astonished exegesis has taken refuge, must be regarded as certain. How, then, can the fact be accounted for? Only by the boundless profligacy of heathendom; only by the stern purity of Christian morals. The Jews, as a nation, were probably the purest among all the races of mankind; yet even they did not regard this sin as being the moral crime which Christianity teaches us to consider it;[2] and they lived in the midst of a world which regarded it as so completely a matter of indifference that Socrates has no censure for it,[3] and Cicero declares that no Pagan moralist had ever dreamt of meeting it with an absolute prohibition.[4] What is it that has made the difference in the aspect which sensuality wears to the ancient and to the modern conscience? I have no hesitation in answering that the reason is to be found in the purity which every page of the New Testament breathes and inspires, and specially in the words of our Blessed Lord, and in the arguments of St. Paul. If the blush of modesty on youthful cheeks is a holy thing, if it be fatal alike to individuals and to nations "to burn away in mad waste" the most precious gifts of life, if debauchery be a curse and stain which more than any other has eaten into the heart of human happiness, then the saintly benefactor to whose spirituality we owe the inestimable boon of having impressed these truths upon the youth of every Christian land is he who—taught by the Spirit of the Lord—showed more clearly, more calmly, more convincingly than any human being has ever shown, the true heinousness, the debasing tendency, the infusive virulence of sins which, through the body, strike their venom and infix their cancer into

(Ἰουδαῖος θᾶττον ἂν ἀποθάνοι ἢ χοιρεῖον φάγοι, Sext. Emp.; see Tac. *H.* v. 4; Sen. *Ep.* 108, 22; Macrob. *Sat.* ii. 4). This abstinence was common in the East (Dion Cass. lxxix. 11).

[1] The notion that πορνεία can mean things *sold* (πέρνημι) in the market after idol feasts is also utterly untenable. See the question examined by Baur, *Paul.* i. 146, *seq.* Besides, the four prohibitions correspond to those attributed to Peter in Ps. Clem. *Hom.* vii. 4, where μὴ ἀκαθάρτως βιοῦν = πορνεία.

[2] In point of fact the Jews probably regarded the other three things with infinitely *greater* horror than this. The practice even of their own Rabbis, though veiled under certain decent forms, was far looser than it should have been, as is proved by passages in the Talmud (*Gittin*, f. 90; *Joma*, f. 18, 2; Selden, *Ux. Hebr.* iii. 17).

[3] Xen. *Mem.* iii. 13.

[4] This passage is remarkable as coming from one of the purest of all ancient writers (Cic. *pro Cael.* xx.; cf. Ter. *Adelph.* i. 2, 21). The elder Cato was regarded as a model of stern Roman virtue, yet what would be thought in Christian days of a man who spoke and acted as he did? (Hor. *Sat.* i. 2, 31.) If Cato could so regard the sin, what must have been the vulgar estimate of it? Nor must it be forgotten that the letter was addressed to Jews and Gentiles alike familiar with an epoch in which, as indeed for many previous centuries, this crime, and crimes yet more heinous, formed a recognised part of the *religious worship* of certain divinities (cf. Baruch vi. 43; Strabo, viii. 6); and in which the pages of writers who reek with stains like these formed a part of the current literature. Few circumstances can show more clearly the change which Christianity has wrought. But to every reader of the letter the immediate link of connexion between εἰδωλόθυτα and πορνεία would be but too obvious. Further, it should be steadily observed that the allusions—stern yet tender, uncompromising yet merciful—of St. Paul's own Epistles to the prevalence of this sin, show most decidedly that if conversion at once revealed to Christians its true heinousness, it often failed to shield them against temptation to its commission.

the soul; of sins which have this peculiar sinfulness—that they not only destroy the peace and endanger the salvation of the soul which is responsible for itself, but also the souls of others, which, in consequence of the sinner's guilty influence, may remain impenitent, yet for the sake of which, no less than for his own, Christ died.

CHAPTER XXIII.

ST. PETER AND ST. PAUL AT ANTIOCH.

"Separati epulis, discreti cubilibus."—TAC. *H.* v. 5.

"At ais Ecclesia est sancta, Patres sunt sancti. Bene; sed Ecclesia quamlibet sancta tamen cogitur dicere Remitte nobis peccata nostra. Sic Patres quamlibet sancti per remissionem peccatorum salvati sunt."—LUTHER, *Comm. on Galat.* i.

SUCH, then, was the result of the appeal upon which the Judaisers had insisted; and so far as the main issue was concerned the Judaisers had been defeated. The Apostles, in almost indignantly repudiating the claim of those men to express their opinions, had given them a rebuff. They had intimated their dislike that the peace of Churches should be thus agitated, and had declared that circumcision was not to be demanded from the Gentiles. It needed but a small power of logic to see that, Christianity being what it was, the decision at least *implied* that converts, whether Jews or Gentiles, were to bear and forbear, and to meet together as equals in all religious and social gatherings. The return of the delegates was therefore hailed with joy in Antioch, and the presence of able and enlightened teachers like Judas and Silas, who really were what the Pharisaic party had falsely claimed to be—the direct exponents of the views of the Apostles—diffused a general sense of unity and confidence. After a brief stay, these two emissaries returned to Jerusalem.[1] On Silas, however, the spell of Paul's greatness had been so powerfully exercised that he came back to Antioch, and threw in his lot for some time with the great Apostle of the Gentiles[2].

Paul, in fact, by the intensity of his convictions, the enlightenment of his understanding, the singleness of his purpose, had made himself completely master of the situation. He had come to the very forefront in the guidance of the Church. The future of Christianity rested with the Gentiles, and to the Gentiles the acts and writings of Paul were to be of greater importance than those of all the other Apostles. His Apostolate had been decisively recognised. He had met Peter and John, and even the awe-inspiring brother

[1] The true reading is not πρὸς τοὺς Ἀποστόλους, as in our version, but "to those who sent them" (πρὸς τοὺς ἀποστείλαντας αὐτούς—ℵ, A, B, C, D).

[2] The reading of our version, ver. 34, "Notwithstanding it pleased Silas to abide there still," is the pragmatic gloss of a few MSS., to which D adds μόνος δὲ Ἰούδας ἐπορεύθη. It is not found in ℵ, A, B, G, E, H. Of course, either this fact or the return of Silas is implied by ver. 40, but the separate insertion of it is exactly one of those trivialities which ancient writers are far less apt than moderns to record.

of the Lord, in conference, and found himself so completely their equal in the gifts of the Holy Ghost, that it was impossible for them to resist his credentials. He had greatly enlarged their horizon, and they had added nothing to him. He had returned from Jerusalem more than ever conscious of himself, conscious of his own power, clear in his future purposes. He inspired into the Church of Antioch his own convictions with a force which no one could resist.

But since the letter from Jerusalem suggested so many inquiries, and laid down no universal principle, it was inevitable that serious complications should subsequently arise. A scene shortly occurred which tested to the extremest degree the intellectual firmness and moral courage of St. Paul. St. Peter seems about this time to have begun that course of wider journeys which, little as we know of them, carried him in some way or other to his final martyrdom at Rome. We do not again hear of his presence at Jerusalem. John continued there in all probability for many years, and Peter may have felt his presence needless; nor is it unlikely that, as Peter dwelt on the wider views which he had learnt from intercourse with his brother Apostle, he may have found himself less able to sympathise with the more Judaic Christianity of James. At any rate, we find him not long after this period at Antioch, and there so frankly adopting the views of St. Paul, that he not only extended to all Gentiles the free intercourse which he had long ago interchanged with Cornelius, but seems in other and more marked ways to have laid aside the burden of Judaism.[1] Paul could not but have rejoiced at this public proof that the views of the Apostle of the circumcision were, on this momentous subject, identical with his own. But this happiness was destined to be seriously disturbed. As the peace of the Church of Antioch had been previously troubled by "certain which came down from Jerusalem," so it was now broken by the arrival of "certain from James." Up to this time, in the Agapæ of Antioch, the distinction of Jew and Gentile had been merged in a common Christianity, and this equal brotherhood had been countenanced by the presence of the Apostle who had lived from earliest discipleship in the closest intercourse with Christ. But now a cloud suddenly came over this frank intercourse.[2] Under the influence of timidity, the plastic nature of Peter, susceptible as it always was to the impress of the moment, began to assume a new aspect. His attitude to the Gentile converts was altered. "He began to draw away and separate himself," in order not to offend the rigid adherents of the Lord's brother.[3] It is not said that they claimed any direct authority, or were armed with any express commission; but they were strict Jews, who, however much they might tolerate the non-observance of the Law by Gentiles, looked with suspicion—perhaps almost with horror—on any Jew

[1] Gal. ii. 14, ἐθνικῶς καὶ οὐχ Ἰουδαϊκῶς ζῇς. Nothing definite can be made of the tradition that St. Peter was first Bishop of Antioch.

[2] If the reading ἦλθεν in Gal. ii. 12 were right it could only point to James himself; but this would have been a fact which tradition could not have forgotten, and James seems never to have left Jerusalem.

[3] Gal. ii. 12, ὑπέστελλεν καὶ ἀφώριζεν ἑαυτόν.

who repudiated obligations which, for *him* at any rate, they regarded as stringent and sacred.[1] A false shame, a fear of what these men might say, dislike to face a censure which would acquire force from those accumulated years of habit which the vision of Joppa had modified, but not neutralised—perhaps too a bitter recollection of all he had gone through on a former occasion when he "had gone in unto men uncircumcised and eaten with them"—led Peter into downright hypocrisy.[2] Without any acknowledged change of view, without a word of public explanation, he suddenly changed his course of life, and it was almost inevitable that the other Jewish Christians should follow this weak and vacillating example. The Apostle who "seemed to be a pillar" proved to be a "reed shaken with the wind."[3] To the grief and shame of Paul, even Barnabas—Barnabas, his fellow-worker in the Churches of the Gentiles—even Barnabas, who had stood side by side with him to plead for the liberty of the Gentiles at Jerusalem, was swept away by the flood of inconsistency, and in remembering that he was a Levite forgot that he was a Christian. In fact, a strong Jewish reaction set in. There was no question of charity here, but a question of principle. To eat with the Gentiles, to live as do the Gentiles, was for a Jew either right or wrong. Interpreted in the light of those truths which lay at the very bases of the Gospel, it was right; and if the Church was to be one and indivisible, the agreement that the Gentiles were not to put on the yoke of Mosaism seemed to imply that they were not to lose status by declining to do so. But to shilly-shally on the matter, to act in one way to-day and in a different way to-morrow, to let the question of friendly intercourse depend on the presence or absence of people who were supposed to represent the stern personality of James, could not under *any* circumstances be right. It was monstrous that the uncircumcised Gentile convert was at one time to be treated as a brother, and at another to be shunned as though he were a Pariah. This was an uncertain, underhand sort of procedure, which St. Paul could not for a moment sanction. He could not stand by to see the triumph of the Pharisaic party over the indecision of men like Peter and Barnabas. For the moral weakness which succumbs to impulse he had the deepest tenderness, but he never permitted himself to maintain a truce with the interested selfishness which, at a moment's notice, would sacrifice a duty to avoid an inconvenience. Paul saw at a glance that Kephas[4] (and the Hebrew name seemed best to suit the Hebraic defection) was wrong—wrong

[1] How anxious James was to conciliate the inflammable multitude who were "zealous for the Law" is apparent from Acts xxi. 24.

[2] The forger of the letter of Peter to James, printed at the head of the Clementine *Homilies*, deeply resents the expression, § 2. But St. Peter's "hypocrisy" consisted in "having implied an objection which he did not really feel, or which his previous custom did not justify" (Jowett, *Gal.* i. 245). It is idle to say that this shows the non-existence of the "decree;" that, as I have shown, left the question of intercourse with the Gentiles entirely undefined.

[3] See Hausrath, p. 252. "Boldness and timidity—first boldness, then timidity—were the characteristics of his nature" (Jowett, i. 243). See also Excursus XVII., "St. John and St. Paul."

[4] Gal. ii. 11, Κηφᾶς (א, A, B, C).

intellectually, if not morally—and that he was mainly responsible for the wrong into which the others had been betrayed by his example. He did not, therefore, hesitate to withstand him to the face. It was no occasion for private remonstrance; the reproof must be as public as the wrong, or the whole cause might be permanently imperilled. Perhaps few things demand a firmer resolution than the open blame of those who in age and position are superior to ourselves. For one who had been a fierce persecutor of Christians to rebuke one who had lived in daily intercourse with Christ was a very hard task. It was still more painful to involve Barnabas and other friends in the same censure; but that was what duty demanded, and duty was a thing from which Paul never shrank.

Rising at some public gathering of the Church, at which both Jews and Gentiles were present, he pointedly addressed Peter in language well calculated to show him that he stood condemned.[1] "If thou," he said before them all, "being a born Jew, art living Gentile fashion and not Jew fashion, how[2] canst thou try[3] to compel the Gentiles to Judaise?"[4] So far his language complained of his brother Apostle's inconsistency rather than of his present conduct. It was intended to reveal the inconsistency which Peter had wished to hide. It directly charged him with having done the very thing which his present withdrawal from Gentile communion was meant to veil. "You have been living as a Gentile Christian in the midst of Gentile Christians; you may alter your line at this moment, but such has been your deliberate conduct. Now, if it is unnecessary for you, a born Jew, to keep the Law, how can it be necessary, even as a counsel of perfection, that the Gentiles should do so? Yet it must be necessary, or at least desirable, if, short of this, you do not even consider the Gentiles worthy of your daily intercourse. If your present separation means that you consider it to be a contamination to eat with them, you are practically forcing them to be like you in all respects. Be it so, if such is your view; but let that view be clearly understood. The Church must not be deceived as to what your example *has* been. If indeed that conduct was wrong, then say so, and let us know your reasons; but if that conduct was *not* wrong, then it concedes the entire equality and liberty which in the name of Christ we claim for our Gentile brethren, and you have left yourself no further right to cast a doubt on this by your present behaviour." It has been the opinion of some that St. Paul's actual speech to Peter ended with this question, and that the rest of the chapter is an argument addressed to the Galatians. But though, in his eager writing, St. Paul may unconsciously pass from what he

[1] Gal. ii. 11, κατεγνωσμένος ἦν. This is the word which gives such bitter offence to the forger of the Clementine *Homilies*, xvii. 18, 19. "Thou didst withstand me as an opponent (ἐνάντιος ἀνθέστηκάς μοι) . . . If thou callest me condemned (κατεγνωσμένον) thou accusest God who revealed Christ to me," &c., and much more to the same effect.

[2] πῶς.

[3] Gal. ii. 14. The wrong aspirate in οὐχ Ἰουδαϊκῶς may be a Cilicism. But surely the editors should give us ἰουδαϊκῶς. The ἐφ' ἐλπίδι of the best MSS. in 1 Cor. ix. 10 is supported by the occurrence of ἐλπίς in inscriptions.

[4] ἀναγκάζεις, "are by your present conduct practically obliging." "He was half a Gentile, and wanted to make the Gentiles altogether Jews" (Jowett, *Galat.* i. 244).

said in the assembly at Antioch to the argument which he addressed to apostatising converts in Galatia, yet he can hardly have thrown away the opportunity of impressing his clear convictions on this subject upon Peter and the Church of Antioch. He wished to drive home the sole legitimate and logical consequence of the points already established; and we can scarcely doubt that he used on this occasion some of those striking arguments which we shall subsequently examine in the Epistle to the Galatians.[1]

They all turn on the great truth over which the Holy Spirit had now given him so firm a grasp—the truth of Justification by Faith alone. If no man could see salvation save by means of faith, and on account of Christ's mercy, then even for the Jew the Law was superfluous. The Jew, however, might, on grounds of national patriotism, blamelessly continue the observances which were ancient and venerable,[2] provided that he did not trust in them. But the Gentile was in no way bound by them, and to treat him as an inferior because of this immunity was to act in contradiction to the first principles of Christian faith. The contrasted views of St. Paul and of the Judaists were here brought into distinct collision, and thereby into the full light on which depended their solution. Faith without the Law, said the Judaists, means a state of Gentile "sinfulness." Faith with the Law, replied St. Paul, means that Christ has died in vain.[3] Among good and holy men love would still be the girdle of perfectness; but when the controversy waxed fierce between

[1] See on Gal. ii. 15—21, *infra*, p. 436.

[2] See some admirable remarks on the subject in Augustine, *Ep.* lxxxii. He argues that, after the revelation of faith in Christ, the ordinances of the Law had lost their life: but that just as the bodies of the dead ought to be honourably conducted, with no feigned honour, but with real solemnity to the tomb, and not to be at once deserted to the abuse of enemies or the attacks of dogs—so there was need that the respect for the Mosaic Law should not be instantly or rudely flung aside. But, he says, that even for a Jewish Christian to observe what could still be observed of the Law after it had been abrogated by God's own purpose in the destruction of Jerusalem, would be to act the part, not of one who honours the dead, but of one who tears out of their resting-places the buried ashes of the slain.

[3] Holstein, *Protestantenbibel*, 729. This dissension—if dissension it could be called—between the two great Apostles will shock those only who, in defiance of all Scripture, persist in regarding the Apostles as specimens of supernatural perfection. Of course, the errors of good men, even if they be mere errors of timidity on one side and vehemence on the other, will always expose them to the taunts of infidels. But when Celsus talks of the Apostles "inveighing against each other so shamefully in their quarrels," he is guilty—so far as the New Testament account of the Apostles is concerned—of gross calumny (*ap.* Orig. *c. Cels.* v. 64). The "blot of error," of which Porphyry accused St. Peter, shows only that he was human, and neither Gospels nor Epistles attempt to conceal his weaknesses. The "petulance of language" with which he charges St. Paul finds no justification in the stern and solemn tone of this rebuke; and to deduce from this dispute "the lie of a pretended decree" is a mere abuse of argument. We may set aside at once, not without a feeling of shame and sorrow, the suggestion (Clem. Alex. *ap.* Euseb. *H. E.* i. 12) that this Kephas was not St. Peter, but one of the Seventy; and the monstrous fancy—monstrous, though stated by no less a man than Origen (*ap.* Jer. *Ep.* cxii.), and adopted by no less a man than Chrysostom (*ad loc.*), and for a time by Jerome—that the whole was a scene acted between the two Apostles for a doctrinal purpose! As if such dissimulation would not have been infinitely more discreditable to them than a temporary disagreement in conduct! The way in which St. Peter bore the rebuke, and forgave and loved him who administered it, is ten-thousandfold more to his honour than the momentary inconsistency is to his disgrace.

inspired conviction on the one side, and designing particularism on the other, hard terms were used. "Your principle is a nullification of Moses, of inspiration, of religion itself," said the Judaists; "it is downright rationalism; it is rank apostasy." "Your Gospel," replied the Apostle, "is no Gospel at all; it is the abnegation of the Gospel; it is a bondage to carnal rudiments; it is a denial of Christ."

A reproof is intolerable when it is administered out of pride or hatred, but the wounds of a friend are better at all times than the precious balms of an enemy that break the head. We are not told the immediate effect of Paul's words upon Peter and Barnabas, and in the case of the latter we may fear that, even if unconsciously, they may have tended, since human nature is very frail and weak, to exasperate the subsequent quarrel by a sense of previous difference. But if Peter's weakness was in exact accordance with all we know of his character, so too would be the rebound of a noble nature which restored him at once to strength. The needle of the compass may tremble and be deflected, but yet it is its nature to point true to the north; and if Peter was sometimes swept aside from perfectness by gusts of impulse and temptation; if after being the first to confess Christ's divinity he is the first to treat Him with presumption; if at one moment he becomes His disciple, and at another bids Him depart because he is himself a sinful man; if now he plunges into the sea all faith, and now sinks into the waves all fear; if now single-handed he draws the sword for His Master against a multitude, and now denies Him with curses at the question of a servant-maid—we are not surprised to find that one who on occasion could be the boldest champion of Gentile equality was suddenly tempted by fear of man to betray the cause which he had helped to win.[1] But the best proof that he regretted his weakness, and was too noble-hearted to bear any grudge, is seen in the terms of honour and affection in which he speaks of Paul and his Epistles.[2] It is still more clearly shown by his adopting the very thoughts and arguments of Paul, and in his reference, while writing among others to the Galatians, to the very words of the Epistle in which his own conduct stood so strongly condemned.[3] The legend which is commemorated in the little Church of "*Domine quo vadis*" near Rome, is another interesting proof either that this tendency to vacillation in Peter's actions was well understood in Christian antiquity, or that he continued to the last to be the same Peter—"consistently inconsistent," as he has most happily been called—liable to weakness and error, but ever ready to confess himself in the wrong, and to repent, and to amend:—

"And as the water-lily starts and slides
Upon the level in little puffs of wind,
Though anchored to the bottom—such was he."

[1] At such an epoch of transition it was inevitable that charges of inconsistency should be freely bandied about on both sides, and with a certain amount of plausibility. Cf. Gal. vi. 13.

[2] 2 Pet. iii. 15.

[3] Comp. 1 Pet. ii. 16, 17 with Gal. v. 1, 13, 14, and 1 Pet. ii. 24 with a passage of this very remonstrance (Gal. ii. 20).

But while to a simple and lofty soul like that of Peter there might almost be something of joy in the frank acknowledgment of error and the crushing down of all anger against the younger, and, at that period, far less celebrated man who had publicly denounced him, such was by no means the case with the many adherents who chose to elevate him into the head of a faction.[1] What may have been the particular tenets of the Kephas-party at Corinth, we have no means for deciding, and the only thing which we can imagine likely was that their views were identical with those of the least heretical Ebionites, who held the Mosaic Law to be binding in its entirety on all Jews. Whatever may have been the action of James, or of those who assumed his authority,[2] neither in the New Testament, nor in the earliest Christian writings, is there any trace of enmity between Paul and Peter, or of radical opposition between their views.[3] The notion that there was, has simply grown up from the pernicious habit of an over-ingenious criticism which "neglects plain facts and dwells on doubtful allusions." Critics of this school have eagerly seized upon the Clementines—a malignant and cowardly Ebionite forgery of uncertain date—as furnishing the real clue to the New Testament history, while they deliberately ignore and set aside authority incomparably more weighty. Thus the silence[4] of Justin Martyr about the name and writings of St. Paul is interpreted into direct hostility, while the allusions of the *genuine* Clement, which indicate the unanimity between the Apostles, are sacrificed to the covert attacks of the forger who assumes his name. But St. Paul's whole argument turns, not on the supposition that he is setting up a counter-gospel to the other Apostles, but on Peter's temporary treason to *his own* faith, *his own* convictions, *his own* habitual professions;[5] and all subsequent facts prove that the two Apostles held each other in the highest mutual

[1] "And I of Kephas;" but when Paul again refers to the parties, with the delicate consideration of true nobleness, he omits the name of Kephas.

[2] The minute accounts of a counter-mission *inaugurated by James* are nothing more or less than an immense romance built on a single slight expression (τινας ἀπὸ Ἰακώβου), applicable only with any certainty to the one occasion to which it is referred. In Gal. ii. 12; iv. 16; 1 Cor. i. 12; ix. 1, 3, 7; 2 Cor. iii. 1; x. 7; Phil. i. 15, 17, we see the traces of a continuous opposition to St. Paul by a party which, in the nature of things, must have had its head-quarters in Jerusalem; and of course the leaders at Jerusalem could not remain wholly uninfluenced by the tone of thought around them, and the views which were in the very atmosphere which they daily breathed. Yet they publicly disavowed the obtrusive members of their community (Acts xv. 24), and towards St. Paul personally they always, as far as we know, showed the most perfect courtesy and kindness, and to them personally he never utters one single disrespectful or unfraternal word. There is not a trace of that stern or bitter tone of controversy between them and him which we find interchanged by Bernard and Abelard, Luther and Erasmus, Fénélon and Bossuet, Wesley and Whitefield. He always speaks of them with gentleness and respect (1 Cor. ix. 5; Eph. iii. 5, &c.).

[3] Even the *Praedicatio Pauli* (preserved in Cyprian, *De Rebaptismate*) implies that they were reconciled at Rome before their martyrdom, "postremo in urbe, quasi tunc primum, invicem sibi esse cognitos."

[4] On the explanation of this silence, which does not, however, exclude apparent allusions, see Westcott, *Canon*, p. 135; Lightfoot, *Gal.*, p. 310. Who can suppose that Justin's γίνεσθε ὡς ἐγὼ ὅτι κἀγὼ ἤμην ὡς ὑμεῖς (*Cohort. ad Graec.*, p. 40) bears only an accidental resemblance to Gal. iv. 12?

[5] Maurice, *Unity*, 497.

esteem; they were lovely and pleasant in their lives, and in death they were not divided.[1]

Thus, then, thanks to St. Paul, the battle was again won, and the Judaisers, who were so anxious to steer the little ship of the Church to certain wreck and ruin on the rocks of national bigotry, could no longer claim the sanction of the relapsing Peter. But no sooner was all smooth in the Church of Antioch than the old mission-hunger seized the heart of Paul, and urged him with noble restlessness from the semblance of inactivity. Going to his former comrade Barnabas, he said, "Come, let us re-traverse our old ground, and see for ourselves how our brethren are in every city in which we preached the word of the Lord." Barnabas readily acceded to the proposal, but suggested that they should take with them his cousin Mark.[2] But to this Paul at once objected. The young man who had suddenly gone away home from Pamphylia, and left them, when it was too late to get any other companion, to face the difficulties and dangers of the journey alone, Paul did not think it right to take with them. Neither would give way; neither put in practice the exquisite and humble Christian lesson of putting up with less than his due. A quarrel rose between these two faithful servants of God as bitter as it was deplorable,[3] and the only hope of peace under such circumstances lay in mutual separation. They parted, and they suffered for their common fault. They parted to forgive each other indeed, and to love and honour each other, and speak of each other hereafter with affection and respect, but never to work together again; never to help each other and the cause of God by the union of their several gifts; never to share with one another in the glory of Churches won to Christ from the heathen; and in all probability to rue, in the regret of lifelong memories, the self-will, the want of mutual concession, the unspoken soft answer which turneth away wrath, which, in a few bitter moments, too late repented of, robbed them both of the inestimable solace of a friend.

Which was right? which was wrong? We are not careful to apportion between them the sad measure of blame,[4] or to dwell on the weaknesses which marred the perfection of men who have left the legacy of bright examples to all the world. In the mere matter of judgment each was partly right, each partly wrong;[5] their error lay in the persistency which did not

[1] See Excursus XVIII., "The Attacks on St. Paul in the Clementines." In the Romish Church the commemoration of St. Paul is *never separated* from that of St. Peter. On the feast-days set apart to each saint, the other is invariably honoured in the most prominent way.

[2] The true reading of Acts xv. 37 is ἐβούλετο, ℵ, A, B, C, E, Syr., Copt., Æth., &c. (Vulg. *volebat*). The word is characteristically mild compared with the equally characteristic vehemence of the ἠξίου . . . μὴ of St. Paul.

[3] Notice the emphatic tone of the original in Acts xv. 39. The word παροξυσμὸς (= "*exacerbatio*," "provocation") implies the interchange of sharp language; but it also implies a temporary ebullition, not a permanent quarrel. Elsewhere it only occurs in Heb. x. 24; Deut. xxix. 28 (LXX.).

[4] "Viderint ii qui de Apostolis judicant; mihi non tam bene est, immo non tam malè est, ut Apostolos committam" (Tert. *De Praescr.* 24).

[5] Paulus severior, Barnabas clementior; uterque in suo sensu abundat; et tamen dissensio habet aliquid humanae fragilitatis" (Jer. *Adv. Pelag.* ii. 522).

admit of mutual accommodation. Each was like himself. St. Barnabas may have suffered himself too strongly to be influenced by partiality for a relative; St. Paul by the memory of personal indignation. Barnabas may have erred on the side of leniency; Paul on the side of sternness. St. Paul's was so far the worst fault, yet the very fault may have risen from his loftier ideal.[1] There was a "severe earnestness" about him, a sort of intense whole-heartedness, which could make no allowance whatever for one who, at the very point at which dangers began to thicken, deserted a great and sacred work. Mark had put his hand to the plough, and had looked back; and, conscious of the serious hindrance which would arise from a second defection, conscious of the lofty qualities which were essential to any one who was honoured with such Divine responsibilities, St. Paul might fairly have argued that a cause must not be risked out of tenderness for a person.[2] Barnabas, on the other hand, might have urged that it was most unlikely that one who was now willing to face the work again should again voluntarily abandon it, and he might fairly have asked whether one failure was to stamp a lifetime. Both persisted, and both suffered. Paul went his way, and many a time, in the stormy and agitated days which followed, must he have sorely missed, amid the provoking of all men and the strife of tongues, the repose and generosity which breathed through the life and character of the Son of Exhortation. Barnabas went his way, and, dissevered from the grandeur and vehemence of Paul, passed into comparative obscurity, in which, so far from sharing the immortal gratitude which embalms the memory of his colleague, his name is never heard again, except in the isolated allusions of the letters of his friend.

For their friendship was not broken. Barnabas did not become a Judaiser, or in any way discountenance the work of Paul. The Epistle which passed by his name is spurious,[3] but its tendency is anti-Judaic, which would not have been the case if, after the dispute at Antioch, he had permanently sided with the anti-Pauline faction. In the Acts of the Apostles he is not again mentioned. Whether he confined his mission-work to his native island, whither he almost immediately sailed with Mark, or whether, as seems to be implied by the allusion in the Epistle to the Corinthians, he extended it more widely, he certainly continued to work on the same principles as before, taking with him no female companion, and accepting nothing from the Churches to which he preached.[4]

And though, so far as they erred, the Apostles suffered for their error,

[1] Ὁ Παῦλος ἐζήτει τὸ δίκαιον, ὁ Βαρνάβας τὸ φιλάνθρωπον (Chrys.). [2] Prov. xxv. 19.

[3] It is examined and rejected, among others, by Hefele, *Das Sendschr. d. Ap. Barnabas* (Tübingen, 1840).

[4] 1 Cor. ix. 6; Gal. ii. 9. It has been inferred from the mention of Mark as known to the Churches of Bithynia, Pontus, Cappadocia, Galatia (1 Pet. i. 1; v. 13), and Colossae (Col. iv. 10), and his presence long afterwards in Asia Minor (2 Tim. iv. 11), that, if he continued to accompany his cousin Barnabas, Asia Minor, and especially its eastern parts, may have been the scene of their labours (Lewin, i. 165). The allusion in Col. iv. 10 has been taken to imply that by that time (A.D. 63) Barnabas was no longer living. Nothing certain is known about the place, manner, or time of his death. The *Acta et Passio Barnabae in Cypro* is apocryphal. St. Mark is said to have been martyred at Alexandria.

God overruled evil for good. Henceforth they were engaged in two spheres of mission action instead of one, and henceforth also the bearing and the views of Paul were more free and vigorous, less shackled by associations, less liable to reaction. Hitherto his position in the Church of Jerusalem had depended much upon the countenance of Barnabas. Henceforth he had to stand alone, to depend solely on himself and his own Apostolic dignity, and to rely on no favourable reception for his views, except such as he won by the force of right and reason, and by the large benefits which accrued to the Church of Jerusalem from the alms which he collected from Gentile Churches.

And Mark also profited by the difference of which he was the unhappy cause. If the lenient partiality of one Apostle still kept open for him the missionary career, the stern judgment of the other must have helped to make him a more earnest man. All that we henceforth know of him shows alike his great gifts and his self-denying energy. In his Gospel he has reflected for us with admirable vividness the knowledge and experience of his friend and master St. Peter, to whom, in his later years, he stood in the same relation that Timothy occupied towards St. Paul.[1] But even St. Paul saw good cause not only to modify his unfavourable opinion, but to invite him again as a fellow-labourer.[2] He urges the Colossians to give him a kindly welcome,[3] and even writes to Timothy an express request that he would bring him to Rome to solace his last imprisonment, because he had found him—that which he had once failed to be—"profitable to him for ministry."[4]

CHAPTER XXIV.

BEGINNING OF THE SECOND MISSIONARY JOURNEY: PAUL IN GALATIA.

"Come, let us get up early to the vineyards; let us see if the vines flourish."—CANT. vii. 12.

THE significant silence as to any public sympathy for Barnabas and Mark, together with the prominent mention of it in the case of Paul, seems to show that the Church of Antioch in general considered that St. Paul was in the right. Another indication of the same fact is that Silas consented to become his companion. Hitherto Silas had been so closely identified with the Church of Jerusalem that he had been one of the emissaries chosen to confirm the genuineness of the circular letter, and in the last notice of him which occurs in Scripture we find him still in the company of St. Peter, who sends him from Babylon with a letter to some of the very Churches which he had visited with St. Paul.[5] His adhesion to the principles of St. Paul, in spite of the

[1] 1 Pet. v. 13.
[2] Philem. 24.
[3] Col. iv. 10.
[4] 2 Tim. iv. 11, εἰς διακονίαν.
[5] 1 Pet. v. 12. The identity cannot, however, be regarded as certain.

close bonds which united him with the Jewish Christians, is a sufficient proof that he was a man of large nature; and as a recognised prophet of Jerusalem and Antioch, his companionship went far to fill up the void left in the mission by the departure of Barnabas. His name Silvanus,[1] and the fact that he, too, seems to have been a Roman citizen,[2] may perhaps show that he had some connexion with the Gentile world, to which, therefore, he would be a more acceptable Evangelist. In every respect it was a happy Providence which provided St. Paul with so valuable a companion. And as they started on a second great journey, carrying with them the hopes and fortunes of Christianity, they were specially commended by the brethren to the grace of God.

St. Paul's first object was to confirm the Churches which he had already founded. Such a confirmation of proselytes was an ordinary Jewish conception,[3] and after the vacillations of opinion which had occurred even at Antioch, Paul would be naturally anxious to know whether the infant communities continued to prosper, though they were harassed by persecutions from without, and liable to perversion from within. Accordingly he began his mission by visiting the Churches of Syria and Cilicia. It is probable that he passed along the eastern coast of the Gulf of Issus, and through the Syrian and Amanid Gates to the towns of Alexandria and Issus.[4] There the road turned westward, and led through Mopsuestia and Adana to Tarsus. From Tarsus three routes were open to him—one running along the shore of the Mediterranean to the Cilician Seleucia, and then turning inland through the Lycaonian Laranda to Derbe; the other a narrow and unfrequented path through the mountains of Isauria; the third, which in all probability he chose as the safest, the most frequented and the most expeditious, through the famous Cilician Gates,[5] which led direct to Tyana, and then turning southwestward ran to Cybistra, and so to Derbe, along the southern shore of Lake Ak Ghieul.[6] And if, indeed, Paul and Silas took this route and passed through the narrow gorge under its frowning cliffs of limestone, clothed here and there with pine and cedar, which to the Crusaders presented an appearance so terrible that they christened it the Gates of Judas, how far must they have been from imagining, in their wildest dreams, that their footsteps—the footsteps of two obscure and persecuted Jews—would lead to the traversing of that pass centuries afterwards by kings and their armies. How little did they dream that those warriors, representing the haughtiest chivalry of Europe, would hold the name of Jews in utter execration, but would be sworn to rescue the traditional tomb of that Christ whom they acknowledged as their Saviour,

[1] Silas may be of Semitic origin. Josephus mentions four Orientals of the name (Krenkel, p. 78).

[2] Acts xvi. 20, 37.

[3] See Schleusner, *s.v.* στηρίζω.

[4] The Syrian gates are now called the Pass of Beylan; the Amanid Gates are the Kara-Kapu.

[5] Now the Külek-Boghaz.

[6] For further geographical details, see Con. and Howson, ch. viii., and Lewin, ch. x. It is humiliating to think that the roads in St. Paul's day were incomparably better, and better kept, than they are at this moment, when the mere *débris* of them suffice for peoples languishing under the withering atrophy of Turkish rule.

from the hands of a mighty people who also recognised Him as a Prophet, though they did not believe Him to be Divine!

Whatever road was taken by Paul and Silas, they must have been their own messengers, and announced their own arrival. And we can well imagine the surprise, the emotion, the delight of the Christians in the little Isauric town, when they suddenly recognised the well-known figure of the missionary, who, arriving in the opposite direction, with the wounds of the cruel stonings fresh upon him, had first taught them the faith of Christ. Can we not also imagine the uneasiness which, during this visitation of the Churches which he loved so well, must often have invaded the heart of Paul, when almost the first question with which he must have been greeted on all sides would be, "And where is Barnabas?" For Barnabas was a man born to be respected

THE COUNTRY ROUND TARSUS.

and loved; and since Silas—great as may have been his gifts of utterance, and high as were his credentials[1]—would come among them as a perfect stranger, whom they could not welcome with equal heartiness, we may be sure that if Paul erred in that sad dissension, he must have been reminded of it, and have had cause to regret it at every turn.

From Derbe once more they passed to Lystra. Only one incident of their visit is told us, but it happily affected all the future of the great Apostle. In his former visit he had converted the young Timotheus, and it was in the house of the boy's mother Eunice,[2] and his grandmother Lois, that he and Silas were probably received. These two pious women were Jewesses who had now accepted the Christian faith. The marriage of Eunice with a Greek,[3]

[1] προφῆται (Acts xv. 32).

[2] The name Eunice being purely Greek might seem to indicate previous association with Gentiles.

[3] At the same time, mixed marriages were far less strictly forbidden to women than

and the non-circumcision of her son, indicate an absence of strict Judaism which, since it was not inconsistent with "unfeigned faith," must have made them more ready to receive the Gospel; and Paul himself bears witness to their earnest sincerity, and to the careful training in the Scriptures which they had given to their child.

We are led to suppose that Eunice was a widow, and if so she showed a beautiful spirit of self-sacrifice in parting with her only son. The youthful Timothy is one of the best known and most lovable of that little circle of companions and followers—chiefly Gentile converts—who are henceforth associated with the wanderings of St. Paul. Of the many whom Paul loved, none were dearer to him than the young disciple of Lystra. Himself without wife or child, he adopted Timothy, and regarded him as a son in all affectionate nearness. "To Timothy, my son;" "my true son in the faith"—such are the terms in which he addresses him;[1] and he reminds the Philippians how well they knew "that, as a son with a father, he had slaved with him for the Gospel."[2] And slight as are the touches which enable us to realise the character of the young Lystrenian, they are all wonderfully graphic and consistent. He was so blameless in character that both in his native Lystra and in Iconium the brethren bore warm and willing testimony to his worth.[3] In spite of a shyness and timidity which were increased by his youthfulness,[4] he was so entirely united in heart and soul with the Apostle that among his numerous friends and companions he found no one so genuine, so entirely unselfish, so sincerely devoted to the furtherance of the cause of Christ.[5] He was, in fact, more than any other the *alter ego* of the Apostle. Their knowledge of each other was mutual;[6] and one whose yearning and often lacerated heart had such deep need of a kindred spirit on which to lean for sympathy, and whose distressing infirmities rendered necessary to him the personal services of some affectionate companion, must have regarded the devoted tenderness of Timothy as a special gift of God to save him from being crushed by overmuch sorrow. And yet, much as Paul loved him, he loved his Churches more; and if any Church needs warning or guidance, or Paul himself desires to know how it prospers, Timothy is required to overcome his

to men. Drusilla and Berenice married Gentile princes, but compelled them first to accept circumcision. The omission of the covenant rite in the case of Timothy may have been owing to the veto of the child's Greek father.

[1] 1 Tim. i. 2, 18; 2 Tim. ii. 2.

[2] Phil. ii. 22, ἐδούλευσεν εἰς τὸ εὐαγγέλιον.

[3] Whether Timothy belonged to Lystra or to Derbe is a matter of small importance, but that in point of fact he did belong to Lystra seems so clear from a comparison of Acts xvi. 1, 2; xx. 4; and 2 Tim. iii. 11, that it is strange there should have been so much useless controversy on the subject. The notion that "Gaius" in Acts xx. 4 could not be "of Derbe," because there is a Gaius of Macedonia in xix. 29 (who may or may not be the Gaius of Rom. xvi. 23; 1 Cor. i. 14), is like arguing that there could not be a Mr. Smith of Monmouth and another Mr. Smith of Yorkshire; and the transference on this ground of the epithet Δερβαῖος to Τιμόθεος in the absence of all evidence of MSS. is mere frivolity.

[4] Acts xvi. 2.

[5] Phil. ii. 20, οὐδένα γὰρ ἔχω ἰσόψυχον, ὅστις γνησίως τὰ περὶ ὑμῶν μεριμνήσει· οἱ πάντες γὰρ τὰ ἑαυτῶν ζητοῦσιν, οὐ τὰ Ἰησοῦ Χριστοῦ.

[6] 2 Tim. iii. 10, Σὺ δὲ παρηκολούθηκάς μου τῇ διδασκαλίᾳ τῇ ἀγωγῇ, κ.τ.λ.

shrinking modesty,[1] to console the persecuted Churches of Macedonia,[2] or face the conceited turbulence of Corinth,[3] or to be the overseer of the Church of Ephesus,[4] with its many troubles from without and from within. In fact, no name is so closely associated with St. Paul's as that of Timothy. Not only were two Epistles addressed to him, but he is associated with St. Paul in the superscription of five;[5] he was with the Apostle during great part of his second missionary journey;[6] he was with him at Ephesus;[7] he accompanied him in his last voyage to Jerusalem;[8] he helped to comfort his first imprisonment at Rome;[9] he is urged, in the Second Epistle addressed to him, to hasten from Ephesus, to bring with him the cloak, books, and parchments which St. Paul had left with Carpus at Troas, and to join him in his second imprisonment before it is too late to see him alive.[10] Some sixteen years had elapsed between the days when Paul took Timothy as his companion at Lystra,[11] and the days when, in the weary desolation of his imprisoned age, he writes once more to this beloved disciple.[12] Yet even at this latter date St. Paul addresses him as though he were the same youth who had first accompanied him to the hallowed work. "To him," says Hausrath, "as to the Christian Achilles, the Timotheus-legend attributes eternal youth;" this being, according to the writer, one of the signs that the two pastoral Epistles addressed to Timothy were the work of a writer in the second century.[13] But surely it is obvious that if Timothy, when St. Paul first won him over to the faith of Christ, was not more than sixteen or seventeen years old, he would be still far short of the prime of life when the Second Epistle was addressed to him; and that, even if he were older, there is no more familiar experience than an old man's momentary forgetfulness that those whom he has known as boys have grown up to full manhood.[14]

This was the youth whose companionship Paul now secured. Young as he was, the quick eye of Paul saw in him the spirit of loving and fearful duty—read the indications of one of those simple, faithful natures which combine the glow of courage with the bloom of modesty. When Jesus had sent forth His disciples He had sent them forth two and two; but this was only in their native land. It was a very different thing to travel in all weathers, through the blinding dust and burning heat of the plains of Lycaonia, and over the black volcanic crags and shelterless mountain ranges of Asia. He had suffered from the departure of Mark in Pisidia, and hence-

[1] 1 Cor. iv. 17; xvi. 10, ἀφόβως.
[2] Acts xix. 22; 1 Thess. iii. 2; Phil. ii. 18—20.
[3] 1 Cor. xvi. 10.
[4] 1 Tim. i. 3.
[5] 1, 2 Thess., 2 Cor., Phil., Col.
[6] Acts xvi. 3; xvii. 14; xviii. 5.
[7] 1 Cor. iv. 17; xvi. 10.
[8] Acts xx. 4.
[9] Phil. ii. 18—20.
[10] 2 Tim. iv. 9, 13.
[11] *Circ.* A.D. 51.
[12] *Circ.* A.D. 66.
[13] Hausrath, p. 259. He admits that they "contain important historic indications."
[14] It has always been recognised as a most natural touch in Tennyson's poem, "The Grandmother," that she speaks of her old sons as though they were still lads. But even if Timotheus had reached the age of forty by the time he was appointed "Bishop" of Ephesus, there would be nothing incongruous in saying to him, Μηδείς σου τῆς νεότητος καταφρονείτω (1 Tim. iv. 12), or τὰς δὲ νεωτερικὰς ἐπιθυμίας φεῦγε (2 Tim. ii. 22), especially as these were written not many years after the μή τις οὖν αὐτὸν ἐξουθενήσῃ of 1 Cor. xvi. 11.

forth we never find him without at least two associates—at this time Silas and Timothy; afterwards Titus and Timothy in Macedonia and Achaia, and Luke and Aristarchus in his journey to Rome.

It may surprise us that the first step he took was to circumcise Timothy; and that since the rite might be performed by any Israelite, he did it with his own hands.[1] We have, indeed, seen that he was in all probability driven to circumcise the Gentile Titus; but we are not told of any pressure put upon him to perform the same rite for Timothy, who, though the son of a Jewess, had grown up without it. Nothing is more certain than that, in St. Paul's opinion, circumcision was valueless. His conduct, therefore, can only be regarded as a second concession to, or rather a prevention and anticipation of, prejudices so strong that they might otherwise have rendered his work impossible. St. Luke says that it was done "on account of the Jews in those regions; for they all knew that his father was a Greek." Now, if this was generally known, whereas it was not so widely known that his mother was a Jewess, St. Paul felt that Timothy would everywhere be looked upon as an uncircumcised Gentile, and as such no Jew would eat with him, and it would be hopeless to attempt to employ him as a preacher of the Messiah in the synagogues, which they always visited as the beginning of their labours. If, on the other hand, it were known that he was by birth a Jewish boy—since the rule was that nationality went by the mother's side[2]—an uncircumcised Jew would be in every Ghetto an object of execration. If, then, Timothy was to be ordained to the work of the ministry, his circumcision was indispensable to his usefulness, and his Jewish parentage was sufficient to deprive the act of the dangerous significance which might much more easily be attached to it in the case of Titus. Obviously, too, it was better that Paul should do it spontaneously than that it should receive a factitious importance by being once more extorted from him in spite of protest. He did it, not in order to please himself, but that he might condescend to the infirmities of the weak.[3]

The circumcision was followed by a formal ordination. The whole Church was assembled; the youth made the public profession of his faith;[4] the elders and Paul himself solemnly laid their hands upon his head;[5] the prophetic voices which had marked him out for a great work[6] were confirmed by those who now charged him with the high duties which lay before him, and at the same time warned him of the dangers which those duties

[1] By none, however, *except* an Israelite (*Abhôda Zara*, f. 27, 1).

[2] "Partus sequitur ventrem" is the rule of the Talmud (*Bechoroth*, 1, 4, &c.; Wetst. *ad loc.*). If the Jews knew that his mother was a Jewess, and yet that he had not received the "seal of the covenant," they would have treated him as a *mamser*. (See Ewald, *Alterth.* 257.)

[3] Rom. xv. 1; 1 Cor. ix. 20.

[4] 1 Tim. vi. 12, ὡμολόγησας τὴν καλὴν ὁμολογίαν ἐνώπιον πολλῶν μαρτύρων.

[5] 1 Tim. iv. 14, τὸ χάρισμα ὃ ἐδόθη σοι διὰ προφητείας μετὰ ἐπιθέσεως τῶν χειρῶν τοῦ πρεσβυτερίου. 2 Tim. i. 6, διὰ τῆς ἐπιθέσεως τῶν χειρῶν μου.

[6] 1 Tim. i. 18, κατὰ τὰς προαγούσας ἐπὶ σὲ προφητείας. Compare the happy prognostications of Staupitz about the work of Luther.

involved;[1] the grace of the Holy Spirit descended like a flame into his heart,[2] and the gentle boy of Lystra was henceforth the consecrated companion of toils and wanderings, of which the issue was the destined conversion of the world.

The mission opened with every circumstance of encouragement. The threefold cord of this ministry was not quickly broken. At each city which they visited they announced the decisions arrived at by the Apostles and elders at Jerusalem,[3] and the Churches were strengthened in the faith, and grew in number daily.

In this way they traversed "the Phrygian and Galatian district."[4] There has been much speculation as to the towns of Phrygia at which they rested, but in the absolute silence of St. Luke, and in the extreme looseness of the term "Phrygian," we cannot be sure that St. Paul preached in a single town of the region which is usually included under that term. That he did not found any church seems clear from the absence of allusion to any Phrygian community in the New Testament. The conjecture that he travelled on this occasion to the far distant Colossæ is most improbable, even if it be not excluded by the obvious inference from his own language.[5] All that we can reasonably suppose is that after leaving Iconium he proceeded to Antioch in Pisidia—since there could be no reason why he should neglect to confirm the Church which he had founded there—and then crossed the ridge of the Paroreia to Philomelium, from which it would have been possible for him either to take the main road to the great Phrygian town of Synnada, and then turn north-eastwards to Pessinus, or else to enter Galatia by a shorter and less frequented route which did not run through any Phrygian town of the slightest importance. It does not seem to have been any part of St. Paul's plan to evangelise Phrygia. Perhaps he may have originally intended to make his way by the road through Apamea, to Colossæ and Laodicea, and to go down the valley of the Mæander to Ephesus. But if so, this intention was hindered by the guidance of the Holy Spirit.[6] Such providential hindrances to a course which seemed so obvious may well have been mysterious to St. Paul; but they appear less so to us when, viewing them in the light of history,

[1] 1 Tim. i. 18, ἵνα στρατεύῃ ἐν αὐταῖς τὴν καλὴν στρατείαν; cf. iv. 14; vi. 12.

[2] 2 Tim. i. 6, ἀναζωπυρεῖν (= "to fan into fresh flame," κυρίως τοὺς ἄνθρακας φυσᾶν, Suid.; σφοδρότερον τὸ πῦρ ἐργάζεσθαι, Theophyl.) τὸ χάρισμα τοῦ Θεοῦ, ὅ ἐστιν ἐν σοὶ, κ.τ.λ.

[3] In a loose way even Antioch and Iconium might be regarded as Churches of Cilicia, Tarsus (as appears from coins, Lewin, i. 171) being regarded as a capital of Lycaonia, Isauria, and even of Caria. Further, the circular letter had been drawn up with more or less express reference to what had taken place in these Churches (Acts xv. 12).

[4] The true reading is τὴν Φρυγίαν καὶ Γαλατικὴν χώραν (א, A, B, C, D).

[5] Col. i. 4, 6, 7; ii. 1.

[6] It will be seen that I take the clause κωλυθέντες, κ.τ.λ. (Acts xvi. 6) retrospectively—*i.e.*, as the reason assigned for their divergence into the Phrygian and Galatian district. If they entertained the design of preaching in Asia—*i.e.*, in Lydia—the natural road to it would have been from Antioch of Pisidia, and it is hardly likely that they would have *intentionally* turned aside to the semi-barbarous regions of Phrygia and Galatia first; indeed, we have St. Paul's own express admission (Gal. iv. 13) that his evangelisation of Galatia was the result of an accidental sickness. The permission to preach in Asia was only *delayed* (Acts xix. 10).

we see that otherwise the Epistle to the Galatians might never have been written, and that thus the whole course of Christian theology might have been entirely changed.

Of any work in Phrygia, therefore, there was nothing to narrate;[1] but we may well deplore St. Luke's non-acquaintance with the details of that visit to Galatia, which were deeply interesting and important, and of which we are now left to discover the incidents by piecing the fragmentary notices and allusions of the Epistle.

We may suppose that on finding it impossible to preach at this time in the great cities of Lydian Asia,[2] St. Paul and his companions next determined to make their way to the numerous Jewish communities on the shores of the Euxine. They seem to have had no intention to preach among a people so new to them, and apparently so little promising, as the Galatians. But God had other designs for them; they were detained in Galatia, and their stay was attended with very memorable results.

St. Luke, who uses the ordinary geographical term, must undoubtedly have meant by the term Galatia that central district of the Asian peninsula[3] which was inhabited by a people known to the ancient world under the names of Celts, Galatians, Gauls, and (more recently) Gallo-Greeks. Their history was briefly this. When the vast tide of Aryan migration began to set to the westward from the valleys of the Oxus and the plains of Turkestan, the Celtic family was among the earliest that streamed away from their native seats.[4] They gradually occupied a great part of the centre and west of Europe, and various tribes of the family were swept hither and thither by different currents, as they met with special obstacles to their unimpeded progress. One of their Brennuses,[5] four centuries before the Christian era, inflicted on Rome its deepest humiliation. Another, one hundred and eleven years later,[6] filled Northern Greece with terror and rapine, and when his hordes were driven back by the storms and portents which seconded the determined stand of the Greeks at Delphi, they joined another body under Leonnorius and Lutarius,[7]

[1] That *some* converts were made is implied by Acts xviii. 23. The absence of a definite Phrygian Church is seen in the silence about any collection there.

[2] "Asia" in the Acts (cf. Catull. xlvi. 5) seems always to mean the region round the old "Asian meadow" of Homer (*Il.* ii. 461)—*i.e.*, the entire valley and plain of the Cayster—*i.e.*, Lydia. Every one of "the seven churches which are in Asia" (Rev. i.—iii.) is Lydian.

[3] The term Asia Minor is first used by Orosius in the fourth century (Oros. i. 2).

[4] On the Celtic migrations, see the author's *Families of Speech*, 2nd ed. (reprinted in *Language and Languages*), p. 329.

[5] B.C. 390. The word Brennus is a Latinised form of the title which is preserved in the Welsh *brenin*, "king."

[6] B.C. 279.

[7] Liv. xxxviii. 16. These names—Celtic words of obscure origin with Latin terminations—are eagerly seized on by German travellers and commentators, and identified with Leonard and Lothair (Luther), in order to prove that the people of Galatia were not Celts, but Teutons. Why both French and Germans should be so eager to claim affinities with these not very creditable Galatians I cannot say; but meanwhile it must be regarded as certain that the Galatæ were Celts, and not only Celts, but Cymric Celts. The only other arguments, besides these two names, adduced by Wieseler and other German writers are—(1) The name *Germanopolis*—a late and hideous hybrid which, at the best,

struggled across the Hellespont in the best way they could, and triumphantly established themselves in the western regions of Asia Minor. But their exactions soon roused an opposition which led to an effectual curbing of their power, and they were gradually confined in the central region which is partly traversed by the valleys of the Sangarius and the Halys. Here we find them in three tribes, each of which had its own capital. Bordering on Phrygia were the Tolistobogii, with their capital Pessinus; in the centre the Tectosages, with their capital Ancyra; and to the eastward, bordering on Pontus, were the Trocmi, with their capital Tavium.[1] Originally the three tribes were each divided into four tetrarchies, but at length they were united (B.C. 65) under Deiotarus, tetrarch of the Tolistobogii, the Egbert of Galatian history.[2] The Romans under Cn. Manlius Vulso had conquered them in B.C. 189,[3] but had left them nominally independent; and in B.C. 36 Mark Antony made Amyntas king. On his death, in B.C. 25, Galatia was joined to Lycaonia and part of Pisidia, and made a Roman province; and since it was one of the Imperial provinces, it was governed by a Propraetor. This was its political condition when Paul entered Pessinus, which, though one of the capitals, lies on the extreme frontier, and at that time called itself Sebaste of the Tolistobogii.[4]

The providential cause which led to St. Paul's stay in the country was, as he himself tells us, a severe attack of illness: and the manner in which he alludes to it gives us reason to infer that it was a fresh access of agony from that "stake in the flesh" which I believe to have been acute ophthalmia, accompanied, as it often is, by violent cerebral disturbance.[5] In his letter to his Galatian converts he makes a touching appeal, which in modern phraseology might run as follows:[6]—"Become as I am, brethren, I beseech you" (*i.e.*, free

only points to the settlement of some Teutonic community among the Gauls; (2) the tribe of Teutobodiaci, about whom we know too little to say what the name means; and (3) the assertion of St. Jerome that the Galatians (whom he had personally visited) spoke a language like the people of Trèves (Jer. in *Ep. Gal.* ii. *praef.*). This argument, however, tells precisely in the opposite direction, since the expressions of Cæsar and Tacitus decisively prove that the Treveri were Gauls (Tac. *Ann.* i. 43, *H.* iv. 71; Cæs. *B. G.* ii. 4, &c.), though they aped Teutonic peculiarities (Cæs. *B. G.* viii. 25; Tac. *Germ.* 28). Every trait of their character, every certain phenomenon of their language, every proved fact of their history, shows beyond the shadow of a doubt that the Galatæ, or Gauls, were not Slavs, nor Teutons, but Celts; and it is most probable that the names Galatæ and Celtæ are etymologically identical. The ingenuity which elaborately sets itself to overthrow accepted and demonstrated conclusions leads to endless waste of time and space. Any who are curious to see more on the subject will find it in the Excursus of Dr. Lightfoot's *Galatians*, pp. 229—240.

[1] Tolistobogii, or Tolosatobogii, seems to combine the elements of Tolosa (Toulouse) and Boii. The etymologies of Tectosages (who also occur in Aquitaine, Cæs. *B. G.* vi. 24; Strabo, p. 187) and Trocmi are uncertain. Other towns of the Galatæ were Abrostola, Amorium, Tolosochorion, towns of the Tolistobogii; Corbeus and Aspona, of the Tectosages; Mithradatium and Danala, of the Trocmi.

[2] Strabo, p. 567.

[3] Liv. xxxviii. 12. "Hi jam degeneres sunt; mixti et Gallograeci vere, quod appellantur."

[4] It is now a mere heap of ruins.

[5] On this subject see *infra*, Excursus X., "The Stake in the Flesh."

[6] Gal. iv. 12—14. This passage may serve to illustrate the necessity of a new English version founded on better readings. Thus in verse 12, the "*be*" of our version should be

from the yoke of external and useless ordinances), "for I, too, made myself as you are.[1] Jew that I was, I placed myself on the level of you Gentiles, and now I want you to stand with me on that same level, instead of trying to make yourselves Jews. I do not wish to speak by way of complaint about you. You never did *me* any personal wrong.[2] Nay, you know that when I preached the Gospel among you, on my first visit, it was in consequence of an attack of sickness, which detained me in the midst of a journey; you could not, therefore, feel any gratitude to me as though I had come with the express purpose of preaching to you; and besides, at that time weak, agonised with pain, liable to fits of delirium, with my eyes red and ulcerated by that disease by which it pleases God to let Satan buffet me, you might well have been tempted to regard me as a deplorable object. My whole appearance must have been a trial to you—a temptation to you to reject me. But you did not; you were very kind to me. You might have treated me with contemptuous indifference;[3] you might have regarded me with positive loathing;[4] but instead of this you honoured, you loved me, you received me as though I was an angel—nay, even as though I were the Lord of angels, as though I were even He whom I preached unto you. How glad you were to see me! How eagerly you congratulated yourselves and me on the blessed accident—nay, rather, on the blessed providence of God, which had detained me amongst you![5] So generous, so affectionate were you towards me, that I bear you witness that to aid me as I sat in misery in the darkened rooms, unable to bear even a ray of light without excruciating pain, you would,

rendered "become;" and the "*I am* as you are" should be "I became;" the "*have* not injured" should be "*did* not injure," since the tense is an aorist, not a perfect, and the allusion is to some fact which we do not know. In verse 13 the δὲ ought not to be left unnoticed; "through infirmity of the flesh" is a positive mistake (since this would require δι' ἀσθενείας, *per*) for "on account of an attack of illness," as in Thuc. vi. 102; τὸ πρότερον probably means "the former time," not "at the first." In verse 14 the best reading is not τὸν πειρασμόν μου, but τὸν π. ὑμῶν (ℵ, A, B, C, D, F, G, &c., and "faciliori lectioni praestat ardua"); and ἐξεπτύσατε is stronger than "rejected." In verse 15, ποῦ, not τίς, is probably the right reading, and ἦν should certainly be omitted—and the meaning is not "where is *the blessedness ye spake of*," but "your self-congratulation on my arrival among you;" the ἂν should certainly be omitted with ἐξωρύξατε, as it makes the Greek idiom far more vivid, although inadmissible in English (cf. John xv. 22; xix. 11). In verse 16 the ὥστε draws a conclusion, "so that," which is suddenly and delicately changed into a question, "have I?" instead of "I have." It is only by studying the intensely characteristic Greek of St. Paul that we are able, as it were, to lay our hands on his breast and feel every beat of his heart.

[1] Gal. ii. 17; 1 Cor. ix. 21.

[2] Cf. 2 Cor. ii. 5, οὐκ ἐμὲ λελύπηκεν.

[3] Cf. 2 Cor. x. 10. His bodily presence is ἀσθενής, and his speech ἐξουθενημένος.

[4] Lit., "Ye did not despise nor loathe your temptation in my flesh;" one of the nobly careless expressions of a writer who is swayed by emotion, not by grammar. It means "You did not loathe," &c., "me, though my bodily aspect was a temptation to you." "Grandis tentatio discipulis, si magister infirmetur" (Primas.). On the possible connexion of ἐξεπτύσατε with epilepsy see *infra*, p. 713. It would be most accurately explained by ophthalmia.

[5] The sufferings of St. Paul from travels when in a prostrate condition of body have been aptly compared by Dean Howson to those of St. Chrysostom and Henry Martyn in Pontus. They both lie buried at Tocat (Comana). (C. and H. i. 295.)

if that could have helped me, have plucked out your eyes and given them to me."[1]

Nothing is more natural than that the traversing of vast distances over the burning plains and freezing mountain passes of Asia Minor—the constant changes of climate, the severe bodily fatigue, the storms of fine and blinding dust, the bites and stings of insects, the coarseness and scantness of daily fare—should have brought on a return of his malady to one whose health was so shattered as that of Paul. And doubtless it was the anguish and despair arising from the contemplation of his own heartrending condition, which added to his teaching that intensity, that victorious earnestness, which made it so all-prevailing with the warm-hearted Gauls.[2] If they were ready to receive him as Christ Jesus, it was because Christ Jesus was the Alpha and the Omega, the beginning and the end of all his teaching to them. And hence, in his appeal to their sense of shame, he uses one of his own inimitably picturesque words to say, "Senseless Galatians, what evil eye bewitched you?[3] before whose eyes, to avert them from such evil glances, I painted as it were visibly and large the picture of Jesus Christ crucified."[4]

But the zealous readiness of the Galatians, their impulsive affection, the demonstrative delight with which they accepted the new teaching, was not solely due to the pity which mingled with the admiration inspired by the new teacher. It may have been due, in some small measure, to the affinities presented by the new religion to the loftiest and noblest parts of their old beliefs; and at any rate, being naturally of a religious turn of mind,[5] they may have been in the first instance attracted by the hearing of a doctrine which promised atonement in consequence of a shedding of blood. But far more than this, the quick conversion of the Galatians was due to the mighty out-

[1] No one disputes that this in itself may be a metaphorical expression for any severe sacrifice, as in Cat. lxxxii. :—

"Quinti si tibi vis oculos debere Catullum,
Aut aliud si quid carius est oculis."

But how incomparably more vivid and striking, and how much more germane to the occasion, does the expression become if it was an attack of ophthalmia from which Paul was suffering!

[2] No doubt the Galatians with whom he had to deal were not the Gallic peasants who were despised and ignorant ("paene servorum loco habentur," Cæs. *B. G.* vi. 13); but the Gallo-græci, the more cultivated and Hellenised Galli of the towns. (Long in *Dict. Geogr. s.v.*)

[3] Gal. iii. 1. Omit τῇ ἀληθείᾳ μὴ πείθεσθαι with א, A, B, D, E, F, G, &c., and ἐν ὑμῖν with א, A, B, C.

[4] Gal. iii. 1, οἷς κατ' ὀφθαλμοὺς Ἰησοῦς Χριστὸς προεγράφη ἐσταυρωμένος. It is true that προγράφειν is elsewhere always used in the sense of "to write before" (Rom. xv. 5; Eph. iii. 3), and not "to post" or "placard" (Ar. *Av.* 450), even in Hellenistic and late Greek (1 Macc. x. 36; Jude 4; Justin, *Apol.* ii. 52, B); but the sense and the context here seem to show that St. Paul used it—as we often find modern compounds used—in a different sense (προσζωγραφήθη). The large picture of Jesus Christ crucified was set up before the mental vision of these spiritual children of Galatia ("Dicitur fascinus proprie *infantibus* nocere"—Primas.) to avert their wandering glances from the dangerous witchery (τίς ὑμᾶς ἐβάσκανεν) of the evil eye (רַע עָיִן, Prov. xxiii. 6; Ecclus. xiv. 6, &c.; βάσκανοι, Ælian. *H. A.* i. 53). We may be reminded of the huge emblazoned banner with which Augustine and his monks caught the eye of Ethelbert at Canterbury.

[5] "Natio est omnis Gallorum admodum dedita religionibus" (Cæs. *B. G.* vi. 16).

pouring of the Spirit which followed Paul's preaching, and to the new powers[1] which were wrought in his converts by their admission into the Church. But while these were the results among the truer converts, there must have also been many whose ready adhesion was due to that quick restlessness, that eager longing for change, which characterised them,[2] as it characterised the kindred family of Greeks with which they were at this time largely mingled. It was the too quick springing of the good seed on poor and shallow soil; it was the sudden flaming of fire among natures as light, as brittle, as inflammable as straw. The modification of an old religion, the hearty adoption of a new one, the combination of an antique worship with one which was absolutely recent, and as unlike it as is possible to conceive, had already been illustrated in Galatian history. As Celts they had brought with them into Asia their old Druidism, with its haughty priestcraft, and cruel expiations.[3] Yet they had already incorporated with this the wild nature-worship of Agdistis or Cybele, the mother of the gods. They believed that the black stone which had fallen from heaven was her image, and for centuries after it had been carried off to Rome[4] they continued to revere her venerable temple, to give alms to her raving eunuchs, to tell of the vengeance which she had inflicted on the hapless Atys, and to regard the pine groves of Dindymus with awe.[5] But yet, while this Phrygian cult was flourishing at Pessinus, and commanding the services of its hosts of mutilated priests, and while at Tavium the main object of worship was a colossal bronze Zeus of the ordinary Greek type,[6] at Ancyra, on the other hand, was established the Roman deification of the Emperor Augustus, to whom a temple of white marble, still existing in ruins, had been built by the common contributions of Asia.[7] Paul must have seen, still fresh and unbroken, the celebrated *Monumentum Ancyranum*, the will of Augustus engraved on the marble of

[1] Gal. iii. 5, ὁ ἐπιχορηγῶν (=abundantly supplying; cf. Phil. i. 19; 2 Pet. i. 5) ὑμῖν τὸ πνεῦμα καὶ ἐνεργῶν δυνάμεις ἐν ὑμῖν. The latter clause may undoubtedly mean "working miracles among you;" but the parallels of 1 Cor. xii. 10; Matt. xiv. 2, seem to show that it means "working powers *in* you." See, too, Isa. xxvi. 12; Heb. xiii. 21. ἐνέργημα means, as Bishop Andrewes says, "a work inwrought in us." In 1 Cor. xii. 10 the "operations of *powers*" are distinguished from the "gifts of *healings*."

[2] Cæsar complains of their "mobilitas," "levitas," and "infirmitas animi," and says, "in consiliis capiendis mobiles et novis plerumque rebus studentes" (*B. G.* ii. 1; iv. 5; iii. 10; and Liv. x. 28).

[3] Strabo, xii. 5, p. 567, who tells us that they met in council at Drynemetum, or "Oak-shrine" (*drw* cf. δρῦς, and *nemed*, "temple"), as Vernemetum = "Great-shrine" (Venant. Fortun. i. 9), and Augustonemetum = "Augustus-shrine."

[4] B.C. 204. See Liv. xxix. 10, 11. The name of the town was dubiously connected with Πεσεῖν. (Herodian. i. 11.)

[5] Liv. xxxviii. 18: Strabo, p. 489; Diod. Sic. iii. 58. Julian found the worship of Cybele still languishing on at Pessinus in A.D. 363, and made a futile attempt to galvanise it into life (Amm. Marc. xxii. 9). The lucrative features in the worship of Cybele—the sale of oracles and collection of alms—may have had their attraction for the avaricious Gauls.

[6] Strabo, xii. 5. The very site of Tavium is unknown.

[7] Ancyra—then called Sebaste Tectosagum, in honour of Augustus—is now the flourishing commercial town of Angora. The Baulos-Dagh—Paul-Mountain—near Angora still reminds the traveller of St. Paul's visit to these cities, which is also rendered more probable by their having been early episcopal sees.

the temple, and copied from the inscription set up by his own command upon bronze tablets in front of his mausoleum; but while he may have glanced at it with interest, and read with still deeper pleasure on one of the pillars the decree in which the Emperor had rewarded the friendliness of the Jews by a grant of religious immunity,[1] he must have thought with some pity and indignation of the frivolity of spirit which could thus readily combine the oldest and the newest of idolatrous aberrations—the sincere and savage orgies of Dindymene with the debasing flattery of an astute intriguer—the passionate abandonment to maddening religious impulse, and the calculating adoration of political success. In point of fact, the three capitals of the three tribes furnished data for an epitome of their history, and of their character. In passing from Pessinus to Ancyra and Tavium the Apostle saw specimens of cults curiously obsolete side by side with others which were ridiculously new. He passed from Phrygian nature-worship through Greek mythology to Roman conventionalism. He could not but have regarded this as a bad sign, and he would have seen a sad illustration of the poorer qualities which led to his own enthusiastic reception, if he could have read the description in a Greek rhetorician long afterwards of the Galatians being so eager to seize upon what was new, that if they did but get a glimpse of the cloak of a philosopher, they caught hold of and clung to it at once, as steel filings do to a magnet.[2] In fact, as he had bitter cause to learn afterwards, the religious views of the Gauls were more or less a reflex of the impressions of the moment, and their favourite sentiments the echo of the language used by the last comer. But on his first visit their faults all seemed to be in the background. Their tendencies to revelries and rivalries, to drunkenness and avarice, to vanity and boasting, to cabals and fits of rage, were in abeyance,[3]—checked if not mastered by the powerful influence of their new faith, and in some instances, we may hope, cured altogether by the grace of the Holy Spirit of God. All that he saw was their eagerness and affection, their absence of prejudice, and willingness to learn—all that vivacity and warmheartedness which were redeeming points in their Celtic character.[4]

How long he was detained among them by his illness we are not told, but it was long enough to found several churches, one perhaps in each of the three capitals, and it may be in some of the minor towns. His success was clearly

[1] Jos. *Antt.* xvi. 6, § 2. On Cæsar-worship see Tac. *Ann.* iv. 55, 56.

[2] Themistius, *Or.* xxiii., p. 299; *ap.* Wetstein in Gal. i. 6. καὶ τριβωνίου παραφανέντος ἐκκρέμανται εὐθὺς ὥσπερ τῆς λίθου τὰ σιδήρια.

[3] Gal. v. 7, 15, 21, 26. Diodorus Siculus says that they were so excessively drunken (κάτοινοι καθ' ὑπερβολήν) that they drenched themselves with the raw wine imported by merchants, and drank with such violent eagerness as either to stupefy themselves to sleep or enrage themselves to madness (v. 26; cf. Ammian. Marc. xv. 12). He also calls them "extravagantly avaricious" (v. 27; Liv. xxxviii. 27) and testifies to their disorderly and gesticulative fits of rage (v. 31; Ammian. Marc. *l.c.*).

[4] The vitality of traits of character in many races is extraordinary, and every one will recognise some of these Celtic peculiarities in the Welsh, and others in the Irish. Ancient testimonies to their weaknesses and vices have often been collected, but the brighter features which existed then, as they do still, are chiefly witnessed to by St. Paul.

among the Gauls; and in the absence of all personal salutations in his Epistle, we cannot tell whether any of the aboriginal Phrygians or Greek settlers, or of the Roman governing class, embraced the faith. But though he is avowedly writing to those who had been Gentiles and idolators,[1] there must have been a considerable number of converts from the large Jewish population[2] which had been attracted to Galatia by its fertility, its thriving commerce, and the privileges which secured them the free exercise of their religion. These Jews, and their visitors from Jerusalem, as we shall see hereafter, proved to be a dangerous element in the infant Church.

The success of this unintended mission may have detained St. Paul for a little time even after his convalescence; and as he retraced his journey from Tavium to Pessinus he would have had the opportunity which he always desired of confirming his recent converts in the faith. From Pessinus the missionaries went towards Mysia, and laid their plans to pass on to the numerous and wealthy cities of western Bithynia, at that time a senatorial province. But once more their plans, in some way unknown to us, were divinely overruled. The "Spirit of Jesus"[3] did not suffer them to enter a country which was destined indeed to be early converted, but not by them, and which plays a prominent part in the history of early Christianity.[4] Once more divinely thwarted in the fulfilment of their designs, they made no attempt to preach in Mysia,[5] which in its bleak and thinly populated uplands offered but few opportunities for evangelisation, but pressed on directly to Troas, where an event awaited them of immense importance, which was sufficient to explain the purpose of Him who had shaped the ends which they themselves had so differently rough-hewn.

From the slopes of Ida,[6] Paul and Silvanus with their young attendant

[1] Gal. iv. 8; v. 2; vi. 12, &c. On the other hand, iv. 9 has been quoted (Jowett, i. 187) as "an almost explicit statement that they were Jews;" this is not, however, necessarily the case. Doubtless, writing to a church in which there were both Jews and Gentiles, St. Paul may use expressions which are sometimes more appropriate to one class, sometimes to the other, but "the weak and beggarly elements" to which the converts are *returning* may include Gentile as well as Jewish ritualisms; and some of them may have passed through both phases.

[2] St. Peter in addressing the Diaspora of Galatia and other districts (1 Pet. i. 1) must have had Jews as well as Gentiles in view. The frequency of Old Testament quotations and illustrations in the Epistle to the Galatians is perhaps a proof that not a few of the converts had been originally proselytes. Otherwise it would be impossible to account for the fact that "in none of St. Paul's Epistles has the cast of the reasoning a more Jewish character" (Jowett, i. 186). Gal. iii. 27, 28 may allude to the existence of converts from both classes.

[3] Acts xvi. 7. This ἅπαξ λεγόμενον, which is the undoubtedly correct reading (א, A, B, C², D, E, and many versions and Fathers), perhaps indicates that St. Luke is here using some document which furnished him with brief notes of this part of Paul's journeys. The remarkable fact that in the *Filioque* controversy neither side appealed to this expression shows how early the text had been altered by the copyists.

[4] See Pliny's letter to Trajan (x. 97), when he was Proconsul of Bithynia, asking advice how to deal with the Christians.

[5] This must be the meaning of παρελθόντες (=ἀφέντες, "neglecting"). It cannot be *translated* "passing through," which would be διελθόντες, though a glance at the map will show that they *must* have passed through Mysia without stopping. The absence of synagogues and the remote, unknown character of the region account for this.

[6] Acts xvi. 8, κατέβησαν.

descended the ravine which separated the mountain from the port and colony. They were on classic ground. Every step they took revealed scenes to which the best and brightest poetry of Greece had given an immortal interest. As they emerged from the pine groves of the many-fountained hill, with its exquisite legend of Œnone and her love, they saw beneath them the

> "Ringing plains of windy Troy,"

where the great heroes of early legend had so often

> "Drunk delight of battle with their peers."

But if they had ever heard of

> "The face that launched a thousand ships,
> Or sacked the topmost towers of Ilion,"

or looked with any interest on the Simois and the Scamander, and the huge barrows of Ajax and Achilles, they do not allude to them. Their minds were full of other thoughts.

The town at which they now arrived had been founded by the successors of Alexander, and had been elevated into a colony with the *Jus Italicum*. This privilege had been granted to the inhabitants solely because of the romantic interest which the Romans took in the legendary cradle of their greatness, an interest which almost induced Constantine to fix there, instead of at Byzantium, the capital of the Eastern Empire. Of any preaching in Alexandria Troas nothing is told us. On three separate occasions at least St. Paul visited it.[1] It was there that Carpus lived, who was probably his host, and he found it a place peculiarly adapted for the favourable reception of the Gospel.[2] On this occasion, however, his stay was very short,[3] because he was divinely commanded to other work.

St. Paul had now been labouring for many years among Syrians, Cilicians, and the mingled races of Asia Minor; but during that missionary activity he had been at Roman colonies like Antioch in Pisidia, and must have been thrown very frequently into the society of Greeks and Latins. He was himself a Roman citizen, and the constant allusions of his Epistles show that he, like St. Luke, must have been struck with admiration for the order, the discipline, the dignity, the reverence for law which characterised the Romans, and especially for the bravery, the determination, the hardy spirit of self-denial which actuated the Roman soldier.[4] He tells us, later in his life, how frequently his thoughts had turned towards Rome itself,[5] and as he brooded

[1] Acts xx. 1, 2, compared with 2 Cor. ii. 12; 1 Cor. xvi. 5—9; and Acts xx. 6; and 2 Tim. iv. 13.

[2] 2 Cor. ii. 12.

[3] Acts xvi. 10, εὐθέως ἐζητήσαμεν implies that they took the first ship which they could find for a voyage to Macedonia.

[4] This is shown by the many military and agonistic metaphors in his Epistles.

[5] Acts xix. 21; cf. Rom. i. 13—"Oftentimes I purposed to come to you;" xv. 23—"I have had a great desire these many years to come to you." These passages were written from Achaia—probably from Corinth—six or seven years after this date.

on the divinely indicated future of Christianity, we cannot doubt that while wandering round the then busy but now land-locked and desolate harbour of Troas, he had thrown many a wistful glance towards the hills of Imbros and Samothrace; and perhaps when on some clear evening the colossal peak of Athos was visible, it seemed like some vast angel who beckoned him to carry the good tidings to the west. The Spirit of Jesus had guided him hitherto in his journey, had prevented him from preaching in the old and famous cities of Asia, had forbidden him to enter Bithynia, had driven the stake deeper into his flesh, that he might preach the word among the Gauls. Anxiously must he have awaited further guidance;—and it came. In the night a Macedonian soldier[1] stood before him, exhorting him with these words, "Cross over into Macedonia and help us." When morning dawned, Paul narrated the vision to his companions,[2] "and immediately we sought," says the narrator, who here, for the first time, appears as the companion of the Apostle, "to go forth into Macedonia, inferring that the Lord has called us to preach the Gospel to them." With such brevity and simplicity is the incident related which of all others was the most important in introducing the Gospel of Christ to the most advanced and active races of the world, and among them to those races in whose hands its future destinies must inevitably rest.

The other incident of this visit to the Troas is the meeting of Paul with Luke, the author of the Acts of the Apostles and the Gospel. This meeting is indicated with profound modesty by the sudden use of the pronoun "we;" but even without this the vivid accuracy of detail in the narrative which immediately ensues, is in such striking contrast with the meagreness of much that has gone before, that we should have been driven to conjecture the presence of the writer on board the little vessel that now slipped its hawsers from one of the granite columns which we still see lying prostrate on the lonely shores of the harbour of Troas.

And this meeting was a happy one for Paul; for, of all the fellow-workers with whom he was thrown, Timotheus alone was dearer to him than Luke. From the appearance and disappearance of the first personal pronoun in the subsequent chapters of the Acts,[3] we see that he accompanied St. Paul to Philippi, and rejoined him there some seven years afterwards, never again to part with him so long as we are able to pursue his history. How deeply St. Paul was attached to him appears in the title "the beloved physician;" how entire was his fidelity is seen in the touching notice, "Only Luke is with me."

[1] The ἀνὴρ and the ἑστὼς, and the instant recognition that it was a Macedonian, perhaps imply this. It is called an ὅραμα, which is used of impressions more distinct than those of dreams. Acts x. 3, ἐν ὁράματι φανερῶς. Matt. xvii. 9 (the Transfiguration).

[2] D, διεγερθεὶς οὖν διηγήσατο τὸ ὅραμα ἡμῖν (Acts xvi. 10).

[3] The "we" begins in Acts xvi. 10; it ends when Paul leaves Philippi, xvii. 1. It is resumed at Philippi at the close of the third missionary journey, xx. 5, and continues till the arrival at Jerusalem, xxi. 18. It again appears in xxvii. 1, and continues throughout the journey to Rome. Luke was also with the Apostle during his first (Col. iv. 14; Philem. 24) and second imprisonments (2 Tim. iv. 11). It is far from certain that 2 Cor. viii. 18 refers to him.

He shared his journeys, his dangers, his shipwreck; he shared and cheered his long imprisonments, first at Cæsarea, then at Rome. More than all, he became the biographer of the Great Apostle, and to his allegiance, to his ability, to his accurate preservation of facts, is due nearly all that we know of one who laboured more abundantly than all the Apostles, and to whom, more than to any of them, the cause of Christ is indebted for its stability and its dissemination.

Of Luke himself, beyond what we learn of his movements and of his character from his own writings, we know but little. There is no reason to reject the unanimous tradition that he was by birth an Antiochene,[1] and it is clear from St. Paul's allusions that he was a Gentile convert, and that he had not been circumcised.[2] That he was a close observer, a careful narrator, a man of cultivated intellect, and possessed of a good Greek style,[3] we see from his two books; and they also reveal to us a character gentle and manly, sympathetic and self-denying. The incidental allusion of St. Paul shows us that he was a physician, and this allusion is singularly confirmed by his own turns of phrase.[4] The rank of a physician in those days was not in any respect so high as now it is, and does not at all exclude the possibility that St. Luke may have been a freedman; but on this and all else which concerns him Scripture and tradition leave us entirely uninformed. That he was familiar with naval matters is strikingly shown in his account of the shipwreck, and it has even been conjectured that he exercised his art in the huge and crowded merchant vessels which were incessantly coasting from point to point of the Mediterranean.[5] Two inferences, at any rate, arise from the way in which his name is introduced: one that he had already made the acquaintance of St. Paul, perhaps at Antioch; the other that, though he had some special connexion with Philippi and Troas, his subsequent close attachment to the Apostle in his

[1] Euseb. *H. E.* iii. 4; Jer. *De Virr. Illustr.* Such allusions as "Nicolas, a proselyte of Antioch," and the mention of Christians important there, but otherwise unknown, lend probability to this tradition (cf. xi. 20; xiii. 1, &c.). If we could attach any importance to the reading of D in Acts xi. 28 (συνεστραμμένων δὲ ἡμῶν), it would show that Luke had been at Antioch during the year when Paul and Barnabas were working there before the famine. The name Lucas is an abbreviation of Lucanus, as Silas of Silvanus; but the notion that they were the same person is preposterous.

[2] Col. iv. 10, 11, 14.

[3] As an incidental confirmation that he was a Gentile, Bishop Wordsworth (on 1 Thess. ii. 9) notices that he says "day and night" (Acts ix. 24), whereas when he is reporting the speeches of St. Paul (Acts xx. 31; xxvi. 7, in the *Greek*) he, like St. Paul himself (1 Thess. iii. 10; 2 Thess. iii. 8; 1 Tim. v. 5, &c.), always says "night and day," in accordance with the Jewish notion that the night preceded the day. A more decisive indication that Luke was a Gentile is Acts i. 19, τῇ ἰδίᾳ διαλέκτῳ αὐτῶν, slipped into St. Peter's speech. "Lucas, medicus Antiochensis, ut scripta ejus indicant" (Jer.).

[4] See a highly ingenious paper by Dr. Plumptre on St. Luke and St. Paul (*The Expositor*, No. xx., Aug., 1876). He quotes the following indications of medical knowledge:—The combination of feverish attacks with dysentery (Acts xxviii. 8), and the use of τιμὴ in the sense (?) of *honorarium*; βάσεις and σφυρὰ in Acts iii. 7 (cf. Hippocrates, p. 637); the incrustation caused by ophthalmia (Acts ix. 18); ἔκστασις (Acts x. 9, 10); σκωληκόβρωτος (Acts xii. 23); "Physician, heal thyself," only in Luke iv. 23; θρόμβοι (Luke xxii. 44), &c.

[5] Smith, *Voy. and Shipwreck*, p. 15, who shows that St. Luke's nautical knowledge is at once *accurate* and *unprofessional*.

journeys and imprisonments may have arisen from a desire to give him the benefit of medical skill and attention in his frequent attacks of sickness.[1] The lingering remains of that illness which prostrated St. Paul in Galatia may have furnished the first reason why it became necessary for Luke to accompany him, and so to begin the fraternal companionship which must have been one of the richest blessings of a sorely troubled life.

Book VII.

CHRISTIANITY IN MACEDONIA.

CHAPTER XXV.

PHILIPPI.

"The day is short; the work abundant; the labourers are remiss; the reward is great; the master presses."—PIRKE ABHÔTH, ii.

So with their hearts full of the high hopes inspired by the consciousness that they were being led by the Spirit of God, the two Apostles, with Luke and Timotheus, set sail from the port of Troas. As the south wind sped them fast upon their destined course, they may have seen a fresh sign that He was with them who causes the east wind to blow in the heavens, and by His power brings in the south wind.[2] Owing to this favourable breeze, they traversed in two days the distance which occupied five days when they returned.[3] On the first day they ran past Tenedos and Imbros straight for Samothrace, and anchored for the night to leeward of it. Did Paul as he gazed by starlight, or at early dawn, on the towering peak which overshadows that ancient island, think at all of its immemorial mysteries, or talk to his companions about the Cabiri, or question any of the Greek or Roman sailors about the strange names of Axiocheros, Axiochersos, and Axiochersa? We would gladly know, but we have no data to help us, and it is strongly probable that to all such secondary incidents he was habitually indifferent.

[1] Dr. Plumptre (*ubi supra*) tries to show that the intercourse of Luke, the Physician, left its traces on St. Paul's own language and tone of thought—*e.g.*, the frequent use of ὑγιαίνω (1 Tim. i. 10; vi. 3, &c., in eight places), which is found three times in St. Luke, and not in the other Gospels; νοσῶ (1 Tim. vi. 4); γάγγραινα (2 Tim. ii. 17); τυφόω (1 Tim. iii. 6; vi. 4, &c.); κεκαυτηριασμένοι (1 Tim. iv. 2); κνηθόμενοι (2 Tim. iv. 3); Hippocr., p. 444; γυμνασία (1 Tim. iv. 8); στόμαχος (1 Tim. v. 23); the anti-ascetic advice of Col. ii. 23 (which means that "ascetic rules have no value in relation to bodily fulness"—*i.e.*, are no remedy against its consequences in disordered passions); κατατομή (Phil. iii. 2); σκύβαλα (Phil. iii. 8, &c.). The facts are curious and noticeable, even if they will not fully bear out the inference.

[2] See Con. and Hows. i. 305. The description of the voyage by St. Luke, however brief, is, as usual, demonstrably accurate in the minutest particulars.

[3] Acts xx. 6.

On the next day, still scudding before the wind,[1] they passed the mouth of the famous Nestus; sailed northward of Thasos amid the scenes so full to us of the memory of Thucydides; gazed for the first time on the "gold-veined crags" of Pangaeus; saw a rocky promontory, and on it a busy seaport, over which towered the marble Maiden Chamber of Diana; and so, anchoring in the roadstead, set foot—three of them for the first time—on European soil. The town was Neapolis, in Thrace—the modern Kavala—which served as the port of the Macedonian Philippi. Here St. Paul did not linger. As at Seleucia, and Attaleia, and Perga, and Peiraeus, and Cenchreæ, he seemed to regard the port as being merely a starting-point for the inland town.[2] Accordingly, he at once left Neapolis by the western gate and took the Egnatian road, which, after skirting the shore for a short distance, turns northward over a narrow pass of Mount Pangaeus, and so winds down into a green delicious plain,—with a marsh on one side where herds of large-horned buffaloes wallowed among the reeds, and with meadows on the other side, which repaid the snows of Hæmus, gathered in the freshening waters of the Zygactes, with the bloom and odour of the hundred-petal rose. At a distance of about seven miles they would begin to pass through the tombs that bordered the roadsides in the neighbourhood of all ancient cities, and one mile further brought them to Philippi, whose Acropolis had long been visible on the summit of its precipitous and towering hill.[3]

The city of Philippi was a monumental record of two vast empires. It had once been an obscure place, called Krenides from its streams and springs; but Philip, the father of Alexander, had made it a frontier town, to protect Macedonia from the Thracians, and had helped to establish his power by the extremely profitable working of its neighbouring gold mines. Augustus, proud of the victory over Brutus and Cassius,—won at the foot of the hill on which it stands, and on the summit of which Cassius had committed suicide,—elevated it to the rank of a colony, which made it, as St. Luke calls it, if not the first yet certainly "a first city of that district of Macedonia."[4] And this, probably, was why St. Paul went directly to it. When Perseus, the last successor of Alexander, had been routed at Pydna (June 22, B.C. 168), Macedonia had been reduced to a Roman province in four divisions. These, in accordance

[1] St. Luke most accurately omits εὐθυδρομήσαμεν of the *second* day's voyage; a S.S.E. wind—and such are prevalent at times in this part of the Ægean—would speed them direct to Samothrace, but not quite in so straight a course from Samothrace to Neapolis.

[2] *V. supra*, p. 219.

[3] Appian, iv. 105. On the site of it is a small Turkish village, called Filibedjik.

[4] The full title, "Colonia Augusta Julia Victrix Philippensium," is found on inscriptions (*Miss. Archéol.*, p. 18). A great deal has been written about ἥτις ἐστὶ πρώτη τῆς μερίδος τῆς Μακεδονίας πόλις κολωνία. A favourite explanation is that it means "the first city of Macedonia they came to," regarding Neapolis as being technically in Thrace. Both parts of the explanation are most improbable: if πρώτη only meant "the first they came to," it would be a frivolous remark, and would require the article and the imperfect tense; and Neapolis, as the port of Philippi, was certainly regarded as a Macedonian town. Πρώτη is justifiable politically—for Philippi, though not the capital of Macedonia Prima, was certainly more important than Amphipolis. Bp. Wordsworth makes it mean "the chief city of *the frontier* of Macedonia" (cf. Ezek. xlv. 7).

with the astute and machiavellic policy of Rome, were kept distinct from each other by differences of privilege and isolation of interests which tended to foster mutual jealousies. Beginning eastwards at the river Nestus, Macedonia Prima reached to the Strymon; Macedonia Secunda, to the Axius; Macedonia Tertia, to the Peneus; and Macedonia Quarta, to Illyricum and Epirus.[1] The capitals of these divisions respectively were Amphipolis, Thessalonica,—at which the Proconsul of the entire province fixed his residence,—Pella, and Pelagonia. It is a very reasonable conjecture that Paul, in answer to the appeal of the Vision, had originally intended to visit—as, perhaps, he ultimately did visit—all four capitals. But Amphipolis, in spite of its historic celebrity had sunk into comparative insignificance, and the proud colonial privileges of Philippi made it in reality the more important town.

On the insignia of Roman citizenship which here met his gaze on every side—the S.P.Q.R., the far-famed legionary eagles, the panoply of the Roman soldiers which he was hereafter so closely to describe, the two statues of Augustus, one in the paludament of an Imperator, one in the semi-nude cincture of a divinity—Paul could not have failed to gaze with curiosity; and as they passed up the Egnatian road which divided the city, they must have looked at the figures of tutelary deities rudely scratched upon the rock, which showed that the old mythology was still nominally accepted. Can we suppose that they were elevated so far above the sense of humour as not to smile with their comrade Silvanus as they passed the temple dedicated to the rustic god whose name he bore, and saw the images of the old man,

"So surfeit-swollen, so old, and so profane,"

whom the rural population of Italy, from whom these colonists had been drawn, worshipped with offerings of fruit and wine?

They had arrived in the middle of the week, and their first care, as usual, was to provide for their own lodging and independent maintenance, to which Luke would doubtless be able to contribute by the exercise of his art. They might have expected to find a Jewish community sheltering itself under the wings of the Roman eagle; but if so they were disappointed. Philippi was a military and agricultural, not a commercial town, and the Jews were so few that they did not even possess a synagogue. If during those days they made any attempt to preach, it could only have been in the privacy of their rooms, for when the Sabbath came they were not even sure that the town could boast of a *proseucha*, or prayer-house.[2] They knew enough, however, of the habits of the Jews to feel sure that if there were one, it would be on the river-bank, outside the city. So they made their way through the gate[3] along the ancient causeway which led directly to the Gangites,[4] and under the triumphal arch

[1] Liv. xlv. 18—29. We cannot be sure that these divisions were still retained.

[2] Acts xvi. 13. This is the sense which I extract from the various readings of ℵ, A, B (?), C, D, and from the versions.

[3] Acts xvi. 13, πύλης, ℵ, A, B, C, D, &c.

[4] Perhaps from the same root as Ganges (Renan, p. 145).

which commemorated the great victory of Philippi ninety-four years before.[1] That victory had finally decided the prevalence of the imperial system, which was fraught with such vast consequences for the world. In passing to the banks of the river the missionaries were on the very ground on which the battle had been fought, and near which the camps of Brutus and Cassius had stood, separated by the river from the army of Octavianus and Antony.

But when they reached the poor open-air *proseucha*,[2] strange to say, they only found a few women assembled there. It was clearly no time for formal orations. They simply sat down, and entered into conversation with the little group.[3] Their words were blessed. Among the women sat a Lydian proselytess, a native of the city of Thyatira, who had there belonged to the guild of dyers.[4] The luxurious extravagance of the age created a large demand for purple in the market of Rome, and Lydia found room for her profitable trade among the citizens of Philippi. As she sat listening, the arrow of conviction pierced her heart. She accepted the faith, and was baptised with her slaves and children.[5] One happy fruit her conversion at once bore, for she used hospitality without grudging. "If you have judged me," she said, "to be faithful to the Lord, come to my house, and stay there." To accede to the request, modestly as it was urged, was not in accordance with the principles which the great Apostle had laid down to guide his conduct. Fully acknowledging the right of every missionary of the faith to be maintained by those to whom he ministered, and even to travel about with a wife, or an attendant deaconess, he had yet not only foregone this right, but begged as a personal favour that it might not be pressed upon him, because he valued that proof of his sincerity which was furnished by the gratuitous character of his ministry. Lydia, however, would not be refused, and she was so evidently one of those generous natures who have learnt how far more blessed it is to give than to receive, that Paul did not feel it right to persist in his refusal. The trade of Lydia was a profitable one, and in her wealth, joined to the affection which he cherished for the Church of Philippi beyond all other Churches, we see the probable reason why he made other Churches jealous by accepting pecuniary aid from his Philippian converts, and from them alone.[6]

There is some evidence that, among the Macedonians, women occupied a more independent position, and were held in higher honour, than in other

[1] Called Kiemer (*Miss. Archéol.*, p. 118).

[2] *Proseuchae* were circular-shaped enclosures open to the air (Epiphan. *Haer*. lxxx. 1), often built on the sea-shore or by rivers (Phil. *in Flacc.* 14; Jos. *Antt.* xiv. 10, § 23; Tert. *ad Nat.* i. 13; Juv. *Sat.* iii. 12), for the facility of the frequent ablutions which Jewish worship required.

[3] Acts xvi. 13, ἐλαλοῦμεν ;- 14, ταῖς λαλουμένοις.

[4] The province of Lydia was famous for the art of dyeing in purple (Hom. *Il.* vi. 141; Claud. *Rapt. Proserp.* i. 270; Strabo, xiii. 4, 14). Sir G. Wheler found an inscription at Thyatira mentioning "the dyers" (οἱ βαφεῖς).

[5] Acts xvi. 14, ἤκουεν . . . διήνοιξεν. How unlike invention is the narrative that, summoned by a vision to Macedonia, his first and most important convert is a woman of the Asia in which the Spirit had forbidden him to preach!

[6] 1 Thess. ii. 5, 7, 9; twice in Thessalonica, Phil. iv. 16; once in Athens, 2 Cor. xi. 9; once in Rome, Phil. iv. 10.

parts of the world.[1] In his Epistle to the Philippians St. Paul makes prominent mention of two ladies, Euodia and Syntyche, who were well known in the Christian community, although unhappily they could not agree with each other.[2] The part that women played in the dissemination of the Gospel can hardly be exaggerated, and unless it was a mere accident that only women were assembled in the *proseucha* on the first Sabbath at Philippi, we must suppose that not a few of the male converts mentioned shortly afterwards[3] were originally won over by their influence. The only converts who are mentioned by name are Epaphroditus, for whom both Paul and the Philippian Church seem to have felt a deep regard; Clemens, and Syzygus, or "yokefellow,"[4] whom Paul addresses in a playful paronomasia, and entreats him to help the evangelising toils—the joint wrestlings for the Gospel—of Euodia and Syntyche. But besides these there were other unnamed fellow-workers to whom St. Paul bears the high testimony that "their names were in the book of life."

Very encouraging and very happy must these weeks at Philippi have been, resulting, as they did, in the founding of a Church, to whose members he finds it needful to give but few warnings, and against whom he does not utter a word of blame. The almost total absence of Jews meant an almost total absence of persecution. The Philippians were heart-whole in their Christian faith. St. Paul's entire Epistle to them breathes of joy, affection, and gratitude. He seems to remember that he is writing to a colony, and a military colony—a colony of Roman "athletes." He reminds them of a citizenship loftier and more ennobling than that of Rome;[5] he calls Epaphroditus not only his fellow-worker, but also his fellow-soldier, one who had stood shoulder to shoulder with him in the new Macedonian phalanx, which was to join as of old in an advance to the conquest of the world. He derives his metaphorical expressions from the wrestling-ground and the race.[6] Alike St. Paul and St. Luke seem to rejoice in the strong, manly Roman nature of these converts, of whom many were slaves and freedmen, but of whom a large number had been soldiers, drawn from various parts of Italy in the civil wars—men of the hardy Marsian and Pelignian stock—trained in the stern, strong discipline of the Roman legions, and unsophisticated by the debilitating Hellenism of a mongrel population. St. Paul loved them more and honoured them more than he did the dreamy, superstitious Ephesians, the fickle, impulsive Gauls, or the conceited, factious Achaians. In writing to Thessalonica and Philippi he had to deal with men of a larger mould and manlier mind—more true and more tender than the men

[1] See Lightfoot, *Philip.*, p. 55. [2] Phil. iv. 2. [3] Acts xvi. 40.

[4] It is true that the name does not occur elsewhere, but I cannot for a moment believe with Clemens Alex. (*Strom.* iii. 6, § 53) and Epiphanius (*H. E.* iii. 30) that the word Σύζυγε means "wife." Lydia is not mentioned in the Epistle, unless the name of this Lydian lady was Euodia or Syntyche. She may have died, or have returned to her native city in the intervening years. She most assuredly would have been named if the Epistle had been a forgery.

[5] Phil. i. 27, πολιτεύεσθε: iii. 20, πολίτευμα.

[6] Phil. i. 27, στήκετε: iii. 12, διώκω: 14, ἐπὶ τὸ βραβεῖον: iv. 3, συνήθλησαν: i. 27, συναθλοῦντες: iii. 16, τῷ αὐτῷ στοιχεῖν.

of Corinth, with their boastful ignorance which took itself for knowledge, or the men of Asia, with their voluptuous mysticisms and ceremonial pettiness. He was now thrown for the first time among a race which has been called the soundest part of the ancient world,[1] a race which shone forth like torches in narrow and winding streets, like stars that beamed their light and life in the dark firmament—blameless children of God amid the dwarfed and tortuous meanness of a degenerate race.[2]

Their stay in this fruitful field of labour was cut short by an unforeseen circumstance, which thwarted the greed of a few interested persons, and enlisted against Paul and Silas the passions of the mob. For there is this characteristic difference between the persecutions of Jews and Gentiles—that the former were always stirred up by religious fanaticism, the latter by personal and political interests which were accidentally involved in religious questions. Hitherto the Apostles had laboured without interruption, chiefly because the Jews in the place, if there were any at all, were few and uninfluential; but one day, as they were on their way to the *proseucha*, they were met by a slave-girl, who, having that excitable, perhaps epileptic diathesis which was the qualification of the Pythonesses of Delphi, was announced to be possessed by a Python spirit.[3] Nothing was less understood in antiquity than these obscure phases of mental excitation, and the strange flashes of sense, and even sometimes of genius, out of the gloom of a perturbed intellect, were regarded as inspired and prophetic utterances. As a fortune-teller and diviner, this poor girl was held in high esteem by the credulous vulgar of the town.[4] A slave could possess no property, except such *peculium* as his master allowed him, and the fee for consulting this unofficial Pythoness was a lucrative source of income to the people who owned her. To a poor afflicted girl like this, whose infirmities had encircled her with superstitious reverence, more freedom would be allowed than would have been granted, even in Philippi, to ordinary females in the little town; and she would be likely—especially if she were of Jewish birth—to hear fragments of information about

[1] See the excellent remarks of Hausrath, p. 281, *seqq.*

[2] Phil. ii. 15.

[3] Acts xvi. 16, πνεῦμα Πύθωνα (א, A, B, C, D, &c.). The corresponding Old Testament expression is אוֹב *obh* (Lev. xx. 6). It points to the use of ventriloquism, as I have shown, s.v. "Divination," in Smith, *Bibl. Dict.* At this period, and long before, people of this class—usually women—were regarded as prophetesses, inspired by the Pythian Apollo (πυθόληπτοι). Hence they were called Πύθωνες, and Εὐρυκλεῖς, from an ancient soothsayer named Eurycles and ἐγγαστρίμυθοι, from the convulsive heavings, and the speaking as out of the depths of the stomach, which accompanied their fits (Sophocles, *Fr.* στερνόμαντις). See Plutarch, *De Defect. Orac.* 9; Galen, *Gloss. Hippocr.* (Ἐγγαστρίμυθοι· οἱ κεκλεισμένου τοῦ στόματος φθεγγόμενοι διὰ το δοκεῖν ἐκ τῆς γαστρὸς φθέγγεσθαι). Hesych. s.v. Schol. *ad Ar. Vesp.* 1019, and Tertullian, *Apol.* 23, who distinctly defines them as people "qui de Deo pati existimantur, *qui anhelando praefantur.*" Neander quotes from Ellis the interesting fact that the priest of Obo, in the Society Isles, found himself unable to reproduce his former convulsive ecstasies of supposed inspiration, after his conversion to Christianity (*Planty.*, p. 176).

[4] We know that "an idol is nothing in the world," and therefore the expression that this girl had "a Python spirit" is only an adoption of the current Pagan phraseology about her. Hippocrates attributed epileptic diseases to possession by Apollo, Cybele, Poseidon, &c., *De Morbo Sacr.* (C. and H. i. 321).

Paul and his teaching. They impressed themselves on her imagination, and on meeting the men of whom she had heard such solemn things, she turned round[1] and followed them towards the river, repeatedly calling out—perhaps in the very phrases which she had heard used of them—"These people are slaves of the Most High God, and they are announcing to us the way of salvation."[2] This might be tolerated once or twice, but at last it became too serious a hindrance of their sacred duties to be any longer endured in silence.

In an outburst of pity and indignation[3]—pity for the sufferer, indignation at this daily annoyance—Paul suddenly turned round, and addressing the Pytho by whom the girl was believed to be possessed, said, "I enjoin thee, in the name of Jesus Christ, to go out of her." The effect was instantaneous. The calm authoritative exorcism restored the broken harmony of her being. No more paroxysms could be expected of her; nor the wild unnatural screaming utterances, so shrill and unearthly that they might very naturally be taken for Sibylline frensies. Her masters ceased to expect anything from her oracles. Their hope of further gain "went out" with the spirit.[4] A piece of property so rare that it could only be possessed by a sort of joint ownership was rendered entirely valueless.

Thus the slave-masters were touched in their pockets, and it filled them with fury. They could hardly, indeed, go before the magistrates and tell them that Paul by a single word had exorcised a powerful demon; but they were determined to have vengeance somehow or other, and, in a Roman colony composed originally of discharged Antonian soldiers, and now occupied partly by their descendants, partly by enfranchised freedmen from Italy,[5] it was easy to raise a clamour against one or two isolated Jews. It was the more easy because the Philippians might have heard the news of disturbances and riots at Rome, which provoked the decree of Claudius banishing all Jews from the city.[6] They determined to seize this opportunity, and avail themselves of a similar plea.[7] They suddenly arrested Paul and Silas, and dragged them before the sitting magistrates.[8] These seem to have relegated the matter to the *duumviri*,[9] who were the chief authorities of the

[1] Acts xvi. 16, ἀπαντῆσαι: 17, κατακολουθήσασα.

[2] Slaves; cf. Acts iv. 29; Rom. i. 1; Tit. i. 1.

[3] Acts xvi. 18, διαπονηθείς. The same word is used of the strong threats of the priests at the teaching of the Apostles in Jerusalem (Acts iv. 2).

[4] Acts xvi. 19, ἐξῆλθεν ἡ ἐλπὶς τῆς ἐργασίας αὐτῶν. The use of the same word after the ἐξῆλθεν (τὸ πνεῦμα) αὐτῇ τῇ ὥρᾳ is perhaps intentional.

[5] This is proved by the inscriptions found at Philippi, which record the donors to the Temple of Silvanus, nearly all of whom are slaves or freedmen (*Miss. Archéol.*, p. 75).

[6] Acts xviii. 2; Suet. *Claud.* 25. See Ewald, vi. 488.

[7] Judaism was a *religio licita*, but anything like active proselytism was liable to stern suppression. See Paul. *Sentent.*, 21; Serv. Virg. *Æn.* viii. 187: and the remarkable advice of Mæcenas to Augustus to dislike and punish all religious innovators (τοὺς δὲ ξενίζοντάς τι περὶ αὐτὸ [τὸ θεῖον] καὶ μίσει καὶ κόλαζε. Dio. Cass. vii. 36). "Quoties," says Livy, "hoc patrum avorumque aetate negotium est ut sacra externa fieri vetarent, sacrificulos vatesque foro, circo, urbe prohiberent" (Liv. xxxix. 16).

[8] Possibly the aediles (*Miss. Archéol.*, p. 71).

[9] Acts xvi. 19, εἵλκυσαν πρὸς τὴν ἀγορὰν ἐπὶ τοὺς ἄρχοντας: 20, καὶ προσαγαγόντες αὐτοὺς τοῖς στρατηγοῖς. The different verbs—of which the second is so much milder—and the different titles surely imply what is said in the text.

colony, and who, aping the manners and the titles of Imperial Rome, had the impertinence to call themselves "Prætors."[1] Leading their prisoners into the presence of these "Prætors," they exclaimed, "These fellows are utterly troubling our city, being mere Jews; and they are preaching customs which it is not lawful for us, who are Romans, to accept or to practise."[2] The mob knew the real state of the case, and sympathised with the owners of the slave girl, feeling much as the Gadarenes felt towards One whose healing of a demoniac had interfered with *their* gains. In the minds of the Greeks and Romans there was always, as we have seen, a latent spark of abhorrence against the Jews. These sweepings of the Agora vehemently sided with the accusers, and the provincial duumvirs, all the more dangerous from being pranked out in the usurped peacock-plumes of "prætorian" dignity, assumed that the mob must be right, or at any rate that people who were Jews must be so far wrong as to deserve whatever they might get. They were not sorry at so cheap a cost to gratify the Roman conceit of a city which could boast that its citizens belonged to the Voltinian tribe.[3] It was another proof that—

> "Man, proud man,
> Dressed in a little brief authority,
> Plays such fantastic tricks before high heaven
> As makes the angels weep, who, with our spleens,
> Would all themselves laugh mortal."

Paul and Silas had not here to do with the haughty impartiality and supercilious knowledge which guided the decisions of a Gallio, but with the "justice's justice" of the Vibiuses and Floruses who at this time fretted their little hour on the narrow stage of Philippi. Conscious of their Roman citizenship, they could not have expected so astounding a result of their act of mercy, as that their political franchise should be ignored, and they themselves, after condemnation without trial, ignominiously hurried off into the punishments reserved for the very meanest malefactors.[4] Such, however, was the issue of the hearing. Their Prætorships would imitate the divine Claudius, and wreak on these wandering Israelites a share of the punishment which the

[1] Acts xvi. 20. στρατηγὸς is the Greek version of the originally military title "Prætor;" and it was also a Greek title in vogue for the chief magistrates in little cities (Ar. *Polit.* vii. 8). The fashion seems to have been set in Italy, where Cicero, a hundred years before this time, notices with amusement the "cupiditas" which had led the Capuan Duumviri to arrogate to themselves the title of "Prætors," and he supposes that they will soon have the impudence to call themselves "Consuls." He notices also that their "lictors" carried not mere staves (*bacilli*), but actual bundles of rods with axes inside them (*fasces*) as at Rome (*De Leg. Agrar.* 34). The name *stradigo* lingered on in some cities till modern days (Wetst. *in loc.*).

[2] Acts xvi. 20, Ἰουδαῖοι ὑπάρχοντες: 21, Ρωμαίοις οὖσι. Since neither "exorcism" nor "Judaism" (though they regarded Judæa as a "suspiciosa et maledica civitas," Cic. *pro Flacc.* 28, and generally *teterrima*, Tac. *H.* v. 8) were cognisable offences, the slave-owners have to take refuge in an undefined charge of innovating proselytism.

[3] *Miss. Archéol.*, p. 40.

[4] The Jews, who were so infamously treated by Flaccus, felt this, as Paul himself did (1 Thess. ii. 2, ὑβρισθέντες, ὡς οἴδατε, ἐν Φιλίπποις), to be a severe aggravation of their sufferings (Philo, *in Flacc.* 10, αἰκισθῆναι μάστιξιν αἷς ἔθος τοὺς κακούργων πονηροτάτους προπηλακίζεσθαι).

misdeeds of their countrymen had brought upon them at Rome. As the proceedings were doubtless in Latin, with which Paul and Silas had little or no acquaintance, and in legal formulæ and procedures of which they were ignorant, they either had no time to plead their citizenship until they were actually in the hands of the lictors,[1] or, if they had, their voices were drowned in the cries of the colonists. Before they could utter one word in their own defence, the sentence—"*summovete, lictores, despoliate, verberate*"—was uttered; the Apostles were seized; their garments were rudely torn off their backs;[2] they were hurried off and tied by their hands to the *palus*, or whipping-post in the forum; and whether they vainly called out in Greek to their infuriated enemies, "We are Roman citizens," or, which is far more likely, bore their frightful punishment in that grand silence which, in moments of high spiritual rapture, makes pain itself seem painless[3]—in that forum of which ruins still remain, in the sight of the lowest dregs of a provincial outpost, and of their own pitying friends, they endured, at the hands of these low lictors, those outrages, blows, strokes, weals, the pangs and butchery, the extreme disgrace and infamy, the unjust infliction of which even a hard-headed and hard-hearted Gentile could not describe without something of pathos and indignation.[4] It was the first of three such scourgings with the rods of Roman lictors which Paul endured, and it is needless to dwell even for one moment on its dangerous and lacerating anguish. We, in these modern days, cannot read without a shudder even of the flogging of some brutal garotter, and our blood would run cold with unspeakable horror if one such incident, or anything which remotely resembled it, had occurred in the life of a Henry Martyn or a Coleridge Patteson. But such horrors occurred eight times at least in the story of one whose frame was more frail with years of suffering than that of our English missionaries, and in whose life these pangs were but such a drop in the ocean of his endurance, that, of the eight occasions on which he underwent these horrible scourgings, this alone has been deemed worthy of even passing commemoration.[5]

[1] Perhaps Paul's language in verse 37 is generic. If so he would be most unlikely to plead a privilege which would protect himself alone.

[2] On this tearing off of the garments see Liv. viii. 32; Tac. *H.* iv. 27; Val. Max. ii. 7, 8; Dion. Halic. ix. 39. The verbs used are *scindere*, *spoliare*, *lacerare* (also the technical word for the laceration of the back by the rods), περικαταῤῥῆξαι, showing that it was done with violence and contumely.

[3] A much lower exaltation than that of the Apostle's would rob anguish of half its sting (cf. Cic. *in Verr.* ii. v. 62, "Hâc se commemoratione civitatis omnia verbera depulsurum, cruciatumque a corpore dejecturum arbitrabatur").

[4] Cato *ap.* Aul. Gell. x. 3.

[5] The five *Jewish* scourgings were probably submitted to without any protest (*v. supra*, p. 24). From a fourth nearly consummated beating with thongs (?) he did protect himself by his political privilege (Acts xxii. 25). Both that case and this show how easily, in the midst of a tumult, a Roman citizen might fail to make his claim heard or understood; and the instance mentioned by Cicero, who tells how remorselessly Verres scourged a citizen of Messana, though "inter dolorem crepitumque plagarum," he kept exclaiming "*Civis Romanus sum*," shows that in the provinces the insolence of power would sometimes deride the claim of those who were little likely to find an opportunity of enforcing it (Cic. *in Verr.* i. 47; v. 62, &c.). Moreover, the reverence for the privilege must have been

Nor was this all. After seeing that a scourging of extreme severity had been inflicted, the duumvirs, with the same monstrous violation of all law, flung Paul and Silas into prison, and gave the jailer special orders to keep them safely. Impressed by this injunction with the belief that his prisoners must have been guilty of something very heinous, and determined to make assurance doubly sure, the jailer not only thrust them into the dank, dark, loathsome recesses of the inner prison, but also secured their feet into "the wood." "The wood" was an instrument of torture used in many countries, and resembling our "stocks," or rather the happily obsolete "pillory," in having five holes—four for the wrists and ankles, and one for the neck.[1] The jailer in this instance only secured their feet; but we cannot be surprised that the memory of this suffering lingered long years afterwards in the mind of St. Paul, when we try to imagine what a poor sufferer, with the rankling sense of gross injustice in his soul, would feel who—having but recently recovered from a trying sickness—after receiving a long and frightful flagellation as the sequel of a violent and agitated scene, was thrust away out of the jeers of the mob into a stifling and lightless prison, and sat there through the long hours of the night with his feet in such durance as to render it impossible except in some constrained position to find sleep on the foul bare floor.[2]

Yet over all this complication of miseries the souls of Paul and Silas rose in triumph. With heroic cheerfulness they solaced the long black hours of midnight with prayer and hymns.[3] To every Jew as to every Christian, the Psalms of David furnished an inexhaustible storehouse of sacred song. That night the prison was wakeful. It may be that, as is usually the case, there was some awful hush and heat in the air—a premonition of the coming catastrophe; but, be that as it may, the criminals of the Philippian prison were listening to the sacred songs of the two among them, who deserving nothing had suffered most. "The prison," it has been said, "became an Odeum;"

much weakened by the shameless sale of it to freedmen and others by the infamous Messalina (Dion Cass. lx. 676). Further than this, it would be quite easy to stretch the law so far as to make it appear that they had forfeited the privilege by crime. At any rate it is certain that under the Empire not citizens only, but even senators, were scourged, tortured, and put to death, without the slightest protection from the Porcian and Valerian laws (Tac. *H.* i. 6; ii. 10, &c.). And although Paul willingly—nay, gladly—endured the inevitable trials which came before him in the performance of duty (2 Cor. xi. 23), I do not believe that he would have accepted anguish or injustice which he had a perfect right to escape.

[1] Acts xvi. 24, *ξύλον* or *ποδοκάκη* (cf. Job xiii. 27). In Latin *nervus*. It had five holes, and is hence called *πεντεσύριγγον* (Schol. Ar. *Eq.* 1046; cf. Poll. viii. 72; Plaut. *Capt.* iii. 79; Euseb. *H. E.* vi. 39; Job xiii. 27; xxxiii. 11; Jer. xxix. 26).

[2] If by the *Tullianum* at Rome we may judge of other prisons—and it seems that the name was generic for the lowest or inmost prison, even of provincial towns (Appul. *Met.* ix. 183; C. and H. i. 326)—there is reason to fear that it must have been a very horrible place. And, indeed, what must ancient Pagan provincial prisons have been at the best, when we bear in mind what English and Christian and London prisons were not fifty years ago?

[3] "The leg feels nothing in the stocks," says Tertullian, "when the soul is in heaven; though the body is held fast, to the spirit all is open." Christian endurance was sneered at as "sheer obstinacy." In a Pagan it would have been extolled as magnificent heroism.

and the guilty listened with envy and admiration to the "songs in the night" with which God inspired the innocent. Never, probably, had such a scene occurred before in the world's history, and this perfect triumph of the spirit of peace and joy over shame and agony was an omen of what Christianity would afterwards effect. And while they sang, and while the prisoners listened, perhaps to verses which "out of the deeps" called on Jehovah, or "fled to Him before the morning watch," or sang—

> "The plowers plowed upon my back and made long furrows,
> But the righteous Lord hath hewn the snares of the ungodly in pieces"—

or triumphantly told how God had "burst the gates of brass, and smitten the bars of iron in sunder"—suddenly there was felt a great shock of earthquake, which rocked the very foundations of the prison. The prison doors were burst open; the prisoners' chains were loosed from the staples in the wall.[1] Startled from sleep, and catching sight of the prison doors standing open, the jailer instantly drew his sword, and was on the point of killing himself, thinking that his prisoners had escaped, and knowing that he would have to answer for their production with his life.[2] Suicide was the common refuge of the day against disaster, and might have been regarded at Philippi as an act not only natural but heroic.[3] Paul, however, observed his purpose, and, always perfectly self-possessed even in the midst of danger, called out to him in a loud voice, "Do thyself no harm, for we are all here." The entire combination of circumstances—the earthquake, the shock of sudden terror, the revulsion of joy, which diverted his intention of suicide, the serene endurance and calm forgiveness of his prisoners—all melted the man's heart. Demanding lights, he sprang into the inner prison, and flung himself, in a tremor of agitation, at the feet of Paul and Silas. Then, releasing their feet from the stocks, and leading them out of their dark recess, he exclaimed, "Lords (Κύριοι), what must I do to be saved?" His mode of address showed deep reverence. His question echoed the expression of the demoniac.[4] And the Apostles answered him partly in the terms which he had used. "Believe," they said, "on the Lord (Κύριον) Jesus Christ, and thou shalt be saved, and thy house." Deeply impressed, the man at once assembled his household in a little congregation, and, worn and weary and suffering as they were, Paul and Silas spoke to them of Him by whom they were to find salvation.[5] Then the jailer, pitying their condition, washed their bruised backs, and immediately afterwards was, with his whole house, baptised in the faith.[6] All this seems to have taken place in

[1] Acts xvi. 26.
[2] See the Dig. *De custodia et exhibitione reorum*, xlviii., iii. 12 and 16.
[3] Sen. *De Prov.* ii. 6; *Ep.* 58; Diog. Laert. vii. 130; Cic. *De Fin.* i. 15, &c.
[4] Acts xvi. 17, ὁδὸν σωτηρίας: ver. 30, ἵνα σωθῶ.
[5] Acts xvi. 33, ἐν ἐκείνῃ τῇ ὥρᾳ.
[6] Ἔλουσεν καὶ ἐλούθη, "he washed and was washed," says Chrysostom. For the bearing of the expression οἱ αὐτοῦ πάντες (Acts xvi. 33), and ὁ οἶκος αὐτῆς (ver. 15), cf. xviii. 8; 1 Cor. i. 16. On infant baptism, see Coleridge, *Aids to Reflection.* The Church of England wisely makes no direct use of this argument in Art. xxvii. But though Bengel's remark,

the prison precincts. Not till then did they think of food or rest. Leading them upstairs into his house, he set a table before them, and in that high hour of visitation from the Living God, though he had but heard words and been told of a hope to come, he and his whole house felt that flow of elevated joy which sprang naturally from a new and inspiring faith.[1]

Day dawned, and the duumvirs were troubled. Whether they had felt the earthquake,[2] and been alarmed lest these "slaves of the Most High God" should be something more than the poor Jewish wanderers that they seemed to be, or whether the startling events of the night had reached their ears—they had at any rate become heartily ashamed of their tumultuary injustice. They felt it incumbent on them to hush up the whole matter, and get rid as quickly as possible of these awkward prisoners. Accordingly, they sent their lictors, no longer to use their rods in outrageous violation of justice, but to "set those people free." The jailer hurried to Paul with the message of peaceful liberation, which no doubt he thought would be heartily welcomed. But Paul felt that at least some reparation must be offered for an intolerable wrong, and that, for the sake of others if not for his own, these provincial justices must be taught a lesson not to be so ready to prostitute their authority at the howling of a mob. Sending for the lictors themselves, he sternly said, in a sentence of which every word was telling, "After beating us publicly uncondemned, Romans though we are by right, they flung us into prison; and now they are for casting us out secretly. No such thing. Let them come in person, and conduct us out."[3] The lictors took back the message to the "Prætors," and it filled them with no small alarm. They had been hurried by ignorance, prejudice, and pride of office into glaring offences against the Roman law.[4] They had condemned two Roman citizens without giving them their chartered right to a fair trial;[5] and, on condemning them, had further outraged the birthright and privilege of citizenship by having them bound and scourged; and they had thus violated the Porcian law[6] in the presence of the entire mob of the forum, and in sight of some at least who would be perfectly able to take the matter up and report their conduct in high quarters. Their worships had simply flagellated in public the law

"Quis credat in tot familiis nullum fuisse infantem?" is not decisive, the rest of his observation, "Et Judaeos circumcidendis, Gentiles lustrandis illis assuetos, non etiam obtulisse illos baptismo?" has much weight.

[1] Acts xvi. 34, ἠγαλλιᾶτο, impf. C, D various versions, &c. καίτοι οὐδὲν ἦν ἀλλὰ ῥήματα μόνον καὶ ἐλπίδες χρησταί.

[2] In Acts xvi. 35, D adds ἀναμνησθέντες τὸν σεισμὸν τὸν γεγονότα.

[3] Acts xvi. 37. The Ῥωμαίους ὑπάρχοντας is perhaps an allusion to the insolent Ἰουδαῖοι ὑπάρχοντες and Ῥωμαίοις οὖσιν of the accusers (ver. 21). See the Lex Cornelia, *Dict. of Antt.*, p. 638; Paulus, *Instt.*, let. iv.; *De incuriis*, § 8.

[4] Zeller starts (*Hilgenfeld's Zeitsch.* 1864, p. 103) the amazing theory that this is a reproduction of the story found in Lucian's *Toxaris* (27—34), about a Greek medical student named Antiphilus, who is imprisoned in Egypt with his servant on a false charge of theft from a temple. Krenkel (p. 221) characterises it as "a subtle conjecture" that the narrative of the Acts is an imitation of this story. And this is criticism!

[5] Cic. *in Verr.* ii. 1, 9; Plaut. *Curcul.* v. 3, 16; Tac. *H.* i. 6.

[6] Cic. *pro Rabir.* 3.

and majesty of Rome.[1] They did not at all like the notion of being themselves summoned before the Proconsul's court to answer for their flagrant illegality; so, trusting to the placability of the Jewish character as regards mere personal wrongs, they came in person, accompanied, says one manuscript, by many friends.[2] Entreating the pardon of their prisoners, they urged them, with reiterated requests, to leave the city, excusing themselves on the plea that they had mistaken their true character, and pleading that, if they stayed, there might be another ebullition of public anger.[3] Paul and Silas, however, were courageous men, and had no intention to give any colour of justice to the treatment they had received by sneaking out of the city. From the prison they went straight to the house of Lydia; nor was it till they had seen the assembled brethren, and given them their last exhortation, that they turned their backs on the beautiful scenes where a hopeful work had been rudely ended by their first experience of Gentile persecution. But, in accordance with a frequent custom of St. Paul,[4] they left Luke behind them.[5] Perhaps at Philippi he had found favourable opportunities for the exercise of his art, and he could at the same time guide and strengthen the little band of Philippian converts, before whom days and years of bitter persecution were still in store.[6]

CHAPTER XXVI.

THESSALONICA AND BERŒA.

Μνημονεύετε γὰρ ἀδελφοὶ τόν κόπον ἡμῶν καὶ τὸν μόχθον.—1 Thess. ii. 9.

"In oppidum devium Beroeam profugisti."—Cic. *in Pis.* 36.

Leaving Philippi, with its mingled memories of suffering and happiness, Paul and Silvanus and Timotheus took an easy day's journey of about three-and-thirty miles to the beautiful town of Amphipolis. It lies to the south of a splendid lake, under sheltering hills, three miles from the sea, and on the edge of a plain of boundless fertility. The strength of its natural position,

1 "Facinus est vinciri civem Romanum, *scelus* verberari," Cic. *in Verr.* v. 66.

2 Acts xvi. 39, D, *παραγενόμενοι μετὰ φίλων πολλῶν εἰς τὴν φυλακήν.*

3 All this is intrinsically probable, otherwise I would not, of course, insert it on the sole and fantastic authority of D, *εἰπόντες Ἠγνοήσαμεν τὰ καθ᾽ ὑμᾶς ὅτι ἐστε ἄνδρες δίκαιοι*, &c., and *μήποτε πάλιν συστραφῶσιν ἡμῖν ἐπικράζοντες καθ᾽ ὑμῶν.*

4 Cf. xvii. 14; xviii. 19; Titus i. 5; 2 Tim. iv. 20.

5 The third person is resumed in Acts xvii. 1, and the first person only recurs in Acts xx. 5.

6 Phil. i. 28—30. Although here and there the Apostles won a convert of higher rank, it was their glory that their followers were mainly the babes and sucklings of human intellect—not many wise, not many noble, not many rich, but the weak things of the world. "Philosophy," says Voltaire, "was never meant for the people. The *canaille* of to-day resembles in everything the *canaille* of the last 4,000 years. *We have never cared to enlighten cobblers and maid-servants. That is the work of Apostles.*" Yes; and it was the work of Christ.

nearly encircled by a great bend of the river, the mines which were near it, and the neighbouring forests, which furnished to the Athenian navy so many pines, fit

"To be the mast
Of some great ammiral,"

made it a position of high importance during the Peloponnesian wars. If St. Paul had ever read Herodotus he may have thought with horror of the human sacrifice of Xerxes[1]—the burial alive at this place of nine youths and nine maidens; and if he had read Thucydides—which is excessively doubtful, in spite of a certain analogy between their forms of expression—he would have gazed with peculiar interest on the sepulchral mound of Brasidas, and the hollowing of the stones in the way-worn city street which showed the feet of men and horses under the gate, and warned Kleon that a sally was intended.[2] If he could read Livy, which is by no means probable, he would recall the fact that in this town Paulus Æmilius[3]—one of the family from whom his own father or grandfather may have derived his name—had here proclaimed, in the name of Rome, that Macedonia should be free. But all this was little or nothing to the Jewish missionaries. At Amphipolis there was no synagogue, and therefore no ready means of addressing either Jews or Gentiles.[4] They therefore proceeded the next day thirty miles farther, through scenery of surpassing loveliness, along the Strymonic Gulf, through the wooded pass of Aulon, where St. Paul may have looked at the tomb of Euripides, and along the shores of Lake Bolbe to Apollonia. Here again they rested for a night, and the next day, pursuing their journey across the neck of the promontory of Chalcidice, and leaving Olynthus and Potidæa, with their heart-stirring memories, far to the south, they advanced nearly forty miles farther to the far-famed town of Thessalonica, the capital of all Macedonia, and though a free city,[5] the residence of the Roman Proconsul.

Its position on the Egnatian road, commanding the entrance to two great inland districts, and at the head of the Thermaic Gulf, had made it an important seat of commerce. Since the days when Cassander had re-founded it, and changed its name from Therma to Thessalonica in honour of his wife, who was a daughter of Philip of Macedon, it had always been a flourishing city, with many historic associations. Here Cicero had spent his days of melancholy exile.[6] Here a triumphal arch, still standing, commemorates the victory of Octavianus and Antony at Philippi. From hence, as with the blast of a trumpet, not only in St. Paul's days,[7] but for centuries afterwards, the Word of God sounded forth among the neighbouring tribes. Here Theodosius was guilty of that cruel massacre, for which St. Ambrose, with heroic faithfulness, kept him for eight months from the cathedral of Milan. Here its good and learned Bishop Eustathius wrote those *scholia* on Homer, which

[1] Hdt. vii. 114. [2] Thuc. iv. 103—107, v. 6—11. [3] Liv. xlv. 30.
[4] The town had become so insignificant that Strabo does not even mention it.
[5] Plin. *H. N.* iv. 17. [6] Cic. *Pro. Planc.* 41. [7] 1 Thess. i. 8, ἐξήχηται.

place him in the first rank of ancient commentators. It received the title of "the orthodox city," because it was for centuries a bulwark of Christendom, but it was taken by Amurath II. in 1430. Saloniki is still a great commercial port of 70,000 inhabitants, of whom nearly one-third are Jews; and the outrage of Mohammedan fanaticism which has brought its name into recent prominence is but the beginning of events which will yet change the map and the destinies of Southern Europe.

At this city—blighted now by the curse of Islam, but still beautiful on the slopes of its vine-clad hills, with Pelion and Olympus full in view—the missionaries rested, for here was the one Jewish synagogue which sufficed for the entire district.[1] After securing the means of earning their daily bread, which was no easy matter, they found a lodging in the house of a Jew, who had Græcised the common name of Jesus into Jason.[2] Even if their quarters were gratuitously allowed them, St. Paul, accepting no further aid, was forced to daily and nightly labour of the severest description[3] to provide himself with the small pittance which alone sufficed his wants. Even this was not sufficient. Poor as he was—for if he ever possessed any private means he had now lost them all[4]—the expenses of the journey from Philippi had probably left him and his companions nearly penniless, and but for the timely liberality of the Philippians it would have fared hardly with the Apostle, and he might even have been left without means to pursue his further journeys.[5] There is no contradiction between the two contributions from Philippi and the Apostle's account of his manual labours; for there is nothing to show that he only stayed in Thessalonica a little more than three weeks.[6] In addition to the fact that the second contribution would be partly wanted for his new journeys, we find that at this time a famine was raging, which caused the price of wheat to rise to six times its usual rate.[7] However much this famine may have enhanced the difficulties of St. Paul and his companions, it must have confirmed him in the purpose of placing the motives of his ministry above suspicion by making it absolutely gratuitous. Such disinterestedness added much to the strength of his position, especially in the "deep poverty" which must have prevailed in such times among the low-born proselytes of a despised religion. If St. Paul did not refuse the contributions from Philippi, it was because they came spontaneously, at an hour of bitter need, from those who could spare the money, and who, as he well knew, would be pained by any refusal of their

[1] Acts xvii. 1. ἡ συναγωγὴ is probably the right reading, though the ἡ is wanting in ℵ, A, B, D. In any case it is evidently meant that there was but one synagogue, and tradition still points out the mosque—once the Church of St. Demetrius, which is supposed to stand upon its site. There are now nearly forty Jewish synagogues in Saloniki.

[2] Rom. xvi. 21.

[3] 1 Thess. ii. 9, νυκτὸς γὰρ καὶ ἡμέρας ἐργαζόμενοι, πρὸς τὸ μὴ ἐπιβαρῆσαί τινα ὑμῶν, κ.τ.λ.

[4] Phil. iii. 8, τὰ πάντα ἐζημιώθην.

[5] Phil. iv. 15, 16.

[6] He can hardly have failed to stay much longer, for Philippi was a hundred miles from Thessalonica, and it would take time for news to travel and the to-and-fro journey to be made.

[7] Pointed out by Mr. Lewin, *Fasti Sacri*, p. 290; *St. Paul*, i. 231.

proffered aid. Yet all who knew him knew well that the aid came unsought, and that, as far as Paul's own personal life was concerned, he was utterly indifferent to privations, and set the example of an unflinching endurance rendered easy by a perfect trust in God.[1]

For three Sabbaths in succession he went to the synagogue, and argued with the Jews. It might well have been that the outrage at Philippi, and its still lingering effects, would have damped his zeal, and made him shrink from another persecution. But, fresh as he was from such pain and peril, he carried on his discussions with undiminished force and courage,[2] explaining the prophecies, and proving from them that the Messiah was to suffer, and to rise from the dead, and that "this is the Messiah, Jesus, whom I am preaching to you."[3] The synagogue audience was mainly composed of Jews, and of these some were convinced and joined the Church.[4] Conspicuous among them for his subsequent devotion, and all the more conspicuous as being almost the only warmly-attached convert whom St. Paul won from the ranks of "the circumcision," was Aristarchus, the sharer of St. Paul's perils[5] from mob-violence at Ephesus, of his visit to Jerusalem, of his voyage and shipwreck, and of his last imprisonment. A larger number, however, of proselytes and of Greeks accepted the faith,[6] and not a few women, of whom some were in a leading position. This inveterate obstinacy of the Jews, contrasting sadly with the ready conversion of the Gentiles, and especially of women, who in all ages have been more remarkable than men for religious earnestness, is a phenomenon which constantly recurs in the early history of Christianity. Nor is this wholly to be wondered at. The Jew was at least in possession of a religion, which had raised him to a height of moral superiority above his Gentile contemporaries; but the Gentile of this day had no religion at all worth speaking of. If the Jew had more and more mistaken the shell of ceremonialism for the precious truths of which that ceremonialism was but the integument, he was at least conscious that there *were* deep truths which lay enshrined behind the rites and observances which he so fanatically cherished. But on what deep truths could the Greek woman rest, if her life were pure, and if her thoughts had been elevated above the ignorant domesticism which was the only recognised virtue of her sex? What comfort was there for her in the cold grey eyes of Athene, or the stereotyped smile of the voluptuous Aphrodite? And when the Thessalonian Greek raised his eyes to the

[1] Phil. iv. 11, 12.

[2] 1 Thess. ii. 2, ἐπαῤῥησιασάμεθα: Acts xvii. 2, διελέγετο αὐτοῖς. The teaching of the synagogue admitted of discussions and replies (John vi. 25, &c.); as it does to this day in the Rabbinic synagogues.

[3] Acts xvii. 3, διανοίγων καὶ παρατιθέμενος.

[4] One of these was Secundus (Acts xx. 4), and, perhaps, a Gaius (xix. 29). The names are common enough, but it is a curious coincidence to find them, as well as the name Sosipater, inscribed among the Politarchs on the triumphal arch of Thessalonica.

[5] Acts xix. 29; xx. 4; Col. iv. 10, συναιχμάλωτος: Philem. 24.

[6] In Acts xvii. 4, even if there be insufficient MSS. evidence in favour of the reading τῶν τε σεβομένων καὶ Ἑλλήνων (A, D, Vulg., Copt.), yet the Epistles prove decidedly that Gentiles predominated among the converts.

dispeopled heaven of the Olympus, which towered over the blue gulf on which his city stood—when his imagination could no longer place the throne of Zeus, and the session of his mighty deities, on that dazzling summit where Cicero had remarked with pathetic irony that he saw nothing but snow and ice—what compensation could he find for the void left in his heart by a dead religion?[1] By adopting circumcision he might become, as it were, a Helot of Judaism; and to such a sacrifice he was not tempted. But the Gospel which Paul preached had no esoteric doctrines, and no supercilious exclusions, and no repellent ceremonials; it came with a Divine Example and a free gift to all, and that free gift involved all that was most precious to the troubled and despondent soul. No wonder, then, that the Church of Thessalonica was mainly Gentile, as is proved by the distinct language of St. Paul,[2] and the total absence of any Old Testament allusion in the two Epistles. In the three weeks of synagogue preaching, St. Paul had confined his argument to Scripture; but to Gentile converts of only a few months' standing such arguments would have been unintelligible, and they were needless to those who had believed on the personal testimony to a risen Christ.

After mentioning the first three Sabbaths, St. Luke furnishes us with no further details of the stay at Thessalonica. But we can trace several interesting facts about their further residence from the personal allusions of St. Paul's Epistles. The First Epistle to the Thessalonians—the earliest of all his letters which have come down to us—was written within a month or two of his departure. We trace in it the tone of sadness and the yearning for a brighter future which were natural to one whose habitual life at this time was that of a hated and hunted outcast. We see that the infant Church was remarkable for a faithfulness, love, and patience which made it famous as a model church in all Macedonia and Achaia.[3] It shone all the more brightly from the fierce afflictions which from the first encompassed the brethren, but failed either to quench their constancy or dim their joy.[4] St. Paul dwells much on his own bearing and example among them; the boldness which he showed in spite of present opposition and past persecutions; the total absence of all delusive promises in a teaching which plainly warned them that to be near Christ was to be near the fire;[5] the conviction wrought by the present power of the Holy Spirit testifying to his words;[6] the simplicity and sincerity which enabled him to appeal to them as witnesses that his Gospel was not stained by the faintest touch of deceitful flattery, or guilty motive, or vain-glorious self-seeking;[7] the independence which he had maintained;[8] the self-sacrificing tenderness which he had showed; the incessant severity of his industry;[9] the blameless purity of his life; the individual solicitude of his

[1] "Subversae Deorum arae, lares a quibusdam in publicum abjecti" (Suet. *Calig.* 5). "Plures nusquam jam Deos ullos interpretabantur" (Plin. *Epp.* vi. 20; *supra*, p.17).

[2] 1 Thess. i. 9; ii. 14.

[3] 1 Thess. i. 2, 3, 6—8.

[4] 2 Thess. i. 4, 5; 1 Thess. ii. 14; i. 6.

[5] 1 Thess. iii. 4, "We told you before that we should suffer tribulation.' ὁ ἐγγύς μου ἐγγὺς τοῦ πυρός (saying of our Lord. Orig. *Hom. in Jerem.* iii. 778).

[6] *Id.* ii. 1, 2. [7] *Id.* i. 5. [8] *Id.* ii. 3—6. [9] *Id.* ii. 6; 2 Thess. iii. 8—10.

instructions.[1] And this high example had produced its natural effects, for they had embraced his teaching with passionate whole-heartedness as a divine message,[2] and inspired him with an affection which made their image ever present to his imagination, though untoward hindrances had foiled a twice-repeated attempt to visit them again.

The Epistle also throws light on that special feature of St. Paul's teaching which was ultimately made the ground for the attack upon him. His sufferings had naturally turned his thoughts to the future; the cruelty of man had tended to fix his faith yet more fervently on the help of God; the wickedness of earthly rulers, and the prevalence of earthly wrongs, had combined with circumstances on which we shall touch hereafter, to fill his teaching with the hopes and prophecies of a new kingdom and a returning King. His expectation of the rapid revelation of that Second Advent had been a theme of encouragement under incessant afflictions.

Few indeed were the untroubled periods of ministry in the life of St. Paul. The jealousy and hatred which had chased him from city to city of Pisidia and Lycaonia pursued him here. The Jews from first to last—the Jews for whom he felt in his inmost heart so tender an affection—were destined to be the plague and misery of his suffering life. At Antioch and Jerusalem, Jews nominally within the fold of Christ opposed his teaching and embittered his days; in all other cities it was the Jews who contradicted and blasphemed the holy name which he was preaching. In the planting of his Churches he had to fear their deadly opposition; in the watering of them, their yet more deadly fraternity. The Jews who hated Christ sought his life; the Jews who professed to love Him undermined his efforts. The one faction endangered his existence, the other ruined his peace. Never, till death released him, was he wholly free from their violent conspiracies or their insidious calumnies. Without, they sprang upon him at every opportunity like a pack of wolves; within, they hid themselves in sheep's clothing to worry and tear his flocks. And at Thessalonica he had yet a new form of persecution against which to contend. It was not purely Jewish as in Palestine, or purely Gentile as at Philippi, or combined as at Iconium, but was simply a brutal assault of the mob, hounded on by Jews in the background. Jealous,[3] as usual, that the abhorred preaching of a crucified Messiah should in a few weeks have won a greater multitude of adherents than they had won during many years to the doctrines of Moses—furious, above all, to see themselves deprived of the resources, the reverence, and the adhesion of leading women—they formed an unholy alliance with the lowest dregs of the Thessalonian populace. Owing to the dishonour in which manual pursuits were held in ancient days,[4] every large city had a superfluous population of worthless idlers—clients who lived on the doles of the wealthy, flatterers who

[1] 1 Thess. ii. 9. [2] *Id.* ii. 13.

[3] This is sufficiently obvious, whether we read ζηλώσαντες in Acts xvii. 5 (A, B, E, and many versions) or not.

[4] "Illiberales autem et sordidi quaestus mercenariorum omniumque quorum operae non artes sunt; est enim ipsa merces auctoramentum servitutis" (Cic. *De Off.* i. 42).

fawned at the feet of the influential, the lazzaroni of streets, mere loafers and loiterers, the hangers-on of forum,[1] the claqueurs of law-courts, the scum that gathered about the shallowest outmost waves of civilisation. Hiring the assistance of these roughs and scoundrels,[2] the Jews disturbed the peace of the city by a fanatical riot, and incited the mob to attack the house of Jason, in order to bring the Apostles before the popular Assembly. But Paul had received timely warning, and he and his companions were in safe concealment. Foiled in this object, they seized Jason and one or two others whom they recognised as Christians, and dragged them before the Politarchs,[3] or presiding magistrates of the free city of Thessalonica. "These fellows," they shouted, "these seditious agitators of the civilised world[4] have found their way here also. Jason has received them. The whole set of them ought to be punished on a *crimen majestatis*, for they go in the teeth of Cæsar's decrees, and say that there is a different king, namely Jesus."[5] But the mob did not altogether succeed in carrying their point. In dealing with the seven Politarchs, under the very shadow of the proconsular residence, they were dealing with people of much higher position, and much more imbued with the Roman sense of law, than the provincial *duumviri* of Philippi. Neither the magistrates nor the general multitude of the city liked the aspect of affairs. It was on the face of it too ludicrous to suppose that hard-working artisans like Jason and his friends could be seriously contemplating revolutionary measures, or could be really guilty of *laesa majestas*.[6] A very short hearing sufficed to show them that this was some religious opinion entertained by a few poor people, and so far from taking strong measures or inflicting any punishment, they contented themselves with making Jason and the others give some pecuniary security[7] that they would keep the peace, and so dismissed

[1] *Subrostrani* (Cic. *Epp. Fam.* viii. 1, 2), *Subbasilicani* (*Plant. Capt.* iv. 2, 35), *turba forensis*. "Lewd" (A.S. *læwede*) means (1) lay, (2) ignorant, (3) bad.

[2] Acts xvii. 5, τῶν αγοραίων ἄνδρας τινὰς πονηρούς. Cf. Ar. *Eq.* 181; Sen. *De Benef.* 7.

[3] This name is unknown to classical literature. It would have furnished fine scope for the suspicious ingenuity of Baur and Zeller, had it not been fortunately preserved as the title of the Thessalonian magistrates on a still legible inscription over the triumphal arch at Thessalonica, known as the Vardár gate (Böckh. *Inscr.* 1967). This arch was recently destroyed, but the fragments were saved by our Consul, and were brought to the British Museum in 1876. There are *seven*, and among them the names of Sosipater, Gaius, and Secundus. There are no *soi-disant* στρατηγοὶ or ῥαβδοῦχοι in the *Urbs Libera* Thessalonica, as there were at the colony Philippi, but there was a δῆμος and πολιτάρχαι.

[4] The expression shows how widely Christianity was spreading, and perhaps alludes to the recent events at Rome, which may have been a sufficient reason for the Jews themselves to keep rather in the background, and incite the Gentiles to get the Apostles expelled.

[5] The half truth, which made this accusation all the more of a lie, is seen in St. Paul's preaching of the Second Advent (1, 2 Thess. *passim*) and the kingdom of Christ (1 Thess. ii. 12; 2 Thess. i. 5), and not impossibly in some distortion of what he had told them of ὁ κατέχων and τὸ κατέχον (2 Thess. ii. 6, 7). The "*nec Caesaribus honor*" is one of the complaints of Tacitus against the Jews (*Hist.* v. 5).

[6] We see in the pages of Tacitus that it was the endless elasticity of this charge—the *crimen majestatis*—which made it so terrible an engine of tyranny (*Ann.* iii. 38). The facts here mentioned strikingly illustrate this. Any one who chose to turn *delator* might thus crush an obscure Jew as easily as he could crush a powerful noble.

[7] Acts xvii. 9, λαβόντες τὸ ἱκανὸν sounds like a translation of the Latin phrase "Satis-

them. But this was a sufficient sign that for the present further mission work would be impossible. No magistrates like the presence of even an innocently disturbing element in their jurisdiction, and if Paul and Silas were brought in person before them, they might not escape so easily. Nor, in the defective police regulations of antiquity, was it at all certain that the moderation of the magistrates would be an efficient protection to two poor Jews from the hatred and violence of a mob. In any case it is probable that they would be unwilling to run the risk of impoverishing Jason and their other friends by causing a forfeiture of the scant and much-needed earnings which they had been obliged to pledge. The brethren, therefore, devised means to secure the escape of Paul and Silas by night. It is not impossible that Timotheus stayed among them for a time, to teach and organise the Church, and to add those last exhortations which should nerve them to bear up against the persecutions of many years.[1] For in the Church of the Thessalonians, which was in some respects the fairest gain of his mission, St. Paul felt an intense solicitude, manifested by the watchful care with which he guarded its interests.[2]

When night had fallen over the tumult which had been surging through the streets of Thessalonica, news of the issue of the trial before the Politarchs was brought to Paul and Silas in their concealment. The dawn might easily witness a still more dangerous outbreak, and they therefore planned an immediate escape. They gathered together their few poor possessions, and under the cover of darkness stole through the silent and deserted streets under the triumphal Arch of Augustus, and through the western gate. Whither should they now turn? From Philippi, the virtual capital of Macedonia Prima, they had been driven to Thessalonica, the capital of Macedonia Secunda. An accidental collision with Gentile interests had cost them flagellation, outrage, and imprisonment in the colony; the fury of Jewish hatred had imperilled their lives, and caused trouble and loss to their friends in the free city. Should they now make their way to Pella, the famous birthplace of the young Greek who had subdued the world, and whose genius had left an indelible impress on the social and political conditions which they everywhere encountered? To do this would be obviously useless. The Jewish synagogues of the dispersion were in close connexion with each other, and the watchword would now be evidently given to hound the fugitives from place to place, and especially to silence Paul as the arch-apostate who was persuading all men everywhere, as they calumniously asserted, to forsake the Law of Moses. Another and less frequented road would lead them to a comparatively unimportant town, which lay off the main route, in which their pre-

datione acceptâ." Cf. Lev. xxv. 26 (LXX.). It was the Jewish sense that the Romans loved justice which made them all the more readily accept their yoke (Jos. *Antt.* xvii. 9, § 4, and 13, § 2; *B. J.* vi. 6, § 2; Dion Cass. xxxvi. 37). Titus upbraided them with all the generous favours which they had received from Rome (Jos. *B. J.* vi. 2, § 4).

[1] I agree with Alford in thinking that the mention of Timothy in the superscription of both Epistles, and his mission to them from Athens, prove that he was with St. Paul during this visit.

[2] Thess. ii. 18.

sence might, for a time at any rate, remain unsuspected. Striking off from the great Via Egnatia to one which took a more southerly direction, the two fugitives made their way through the darkness. A night escape of at least fifty miles, along an unknown road, involving the dangers of pursuit and the crossing of large and frequently flooded rivers like the Axius, the Echidorus, the Lydias, and some of the numerous affluents of the Haliacmon, is passed over with a single word. Can we wonder at the absence of all allusion to the beauties, delights, and associations of travel in the case of one whose travels were not only the laborious journeys, beset with incessant hardships, of a sickly Jewish artisan, but also those of one whose life in its endless trials was a spectacle unto the universe, to angels and to men?[1]

The town which they had in view as a place of refuge was Berœa,[2] and their motive in going there receives striking and unexpected illustration from a passage of Cicero. In his passionate philippic against Piso he says to him that after his gross maladministration of Macedonia, he was so unpopular that he had to slink into Thessalonica incognito, and by night;[3] and that from thence, unable to bear the concert of wailers, and the hurricane of complaints, he left the main road and fled to the out-of-the-way town of Berœa. We cannot doubt that this comparatively secluded position was the reason why Paul and Silas chose it as safer than the more famous and frequented Pella.

And as they traversed the pleasant streets of the town—"dewy," like those of Tivoli, "with twinkling rivulets"—it must have been with sinking hearts, in spite of all their courage and constancy, that Paul and Silas once more made their way, as their first duty, into the synagogue of the Jews. But if the life of the Christian missionary has its own breadths of gloom, it also has its lights, and after all the storms which they had encountered they were cheered in their heaviness by a most encouraging reception. The Jews of this synagogue were less obstinate, less sophisticated, than those whom St. Paul ever found elsewhere. When he had urged upon them those arguments from the Psalms, and from Isaiah, and from Habakkuk, about a Messiah who was to die, and suffer, and rise again, and about faith as the sole means of justification, the Jews, instead of turning upon him as soon as they understood the full scope and logical conclusions of his arguments, proved themselves to be "nobler"[4] than those of Thessalonica—more generous, more simple, more sincere and truth-loving. Instead of angrily rejecting this new Gospel, they daily and diligently searched the Scriptures to judge Paul's arguments and references by the word and the testimony. The result was that many Jews believed, as well as Greeks—men and women of the more respectable classes. They must have spent some weeks of calm among these

[1] 1 Cor. iv. 9.

[2] Berœa is perhaps a Macedonian corruption for Pherœa (cf. Βίλιππος for Φίλιππος). It is now called Kara Pheria.

[3] Cic. *in Pis.* 36. Adduced by Wetstein *ad loc.*

[4] Acts xvii. 11, εὐγενέστεροι. The expression is interesting as an instance of εὐγενής, used (as in modern times) in a secondary and moral sense. The best comment on it is the "Nobilitas sola est atque unica virtus."

open-minded Berœans, for twice during the stay St. Paul conceived the design of going back to his beloved Thessalonians. Untoward obstacles prevented this,[1] and so heavily did the interests of the persecuted Church rest on his mind that either from Berœa, or subsequently from Athens, he sent Timothy to inquire into and report their state. One permanent friend, both to St. Paul and to Christianity, was gained in the person of Sopater, of Berœa.

But it would have been too much to hope that all should be thus open to conviction, and the news was soon unfavourably reported to the Synagogue of Thessalonica. The hated name of Paul acted like a spark on their inflammable rage, and they instantly despatched emissaries to stir up storms among the mob of Berœa.[2] Once more Paul received timely notice from some faithful friend. It was impossible to face this persistent and organised outburst of hatred which was now pursuing him from city to city. And since it was clear that Paul, and not Silas, was the main object of persecution, it was arranged that, while Paul made good his escape, Silas and Timothy—who may have joined his companions during their residence at Berœa—should stay to set in order all that was wanting, and water the good seed which had begun to spring.

And so—once more in his normal condition of a fugitive—St. Paul left Berœa. He was not alone, and either from the weakness of his eyesight or from his liability to epilepsy, all his movements were guided by others. "The brethren" sent him away to go seawards,[3] and there can be little doubt that they led him sixteen miles to the colony of Dium,[4] whence he sailed fro Athens. That he did not proceed by land seems certain. It was the longer, the more expensive, the more dangerous, and the more fatiguing route. If St. Paul was so little able to make his way alone that, even by the sea route, some of the Berœan brethren were obliged to accompany him till they left him safe in lodgings at Athens, it is clear that by the land route their difficulties, to say nothing of the danger of pursuit, would have been much increased. The silence of St. Luke as to any single town visited on the journey is conclusive,[5] and we must suppose that some time in autumn, St. Paul embarked on the stormy waves of the Mediterranean, and saw the multitudinous and snowy peaks of Olympus melt into the distant blue. He sailed along shores of which every hill and promontory is voiceful with heroic memories; past Ossa and Pelion, past the coast of Thermopylæ, along the shores of Eubœa,[6]

[1] 1 Thess. ii. 18.

[2] Acts xvii. 13, σαλεύοντες τοὺς ὄχλους.

[3] Acts xvii. 14, ὡς ἐπὶ τὴν θάλασσαν is a mere pleonastic phrase for "in the direction of the sea" (Strabo, xvi. 2, &c.). Ἕως, the reading of ℵ, A, B, F, and other variations of the text, seem to have arisen from the comparative rarity of the expression. The notion that he only made a feint of going to the sea, and then turned landwards to foil pursuit, arises from an erroneous interpretation of the phrase.

[4] Perhaps to Alorus or Methone. (Renan, *St. Paul*, p. 166, quoting Strabo, vii., pp. 20, 22; Leake, iii. 435.)

[5] The addition of D, παρῆλθεν δὲ τὴν Θεσσαλίαν ἐκωλύθη γὰρ εἰς αὐτοὺς κηρύξαι τὸν λόγον, throws no light on the question.

[6] Whether St. Paul sailed down the Euripus or to the east of Eubœa is uncertain. The former route was the more common.

round the "marbled steep" of Sunium, where the white Temple still stood entire, until his eye caught the well-known glimpse of the crest and spear-head of Athene Promachos on the Acropolis,[1]—the helm was turned, and, entering a lovely harbour, his ship dropped anchor in full sight of the Parthenon and the Propylæa.

Book VIII.

CHRISTIANITY IN ACHAIA.

Ὦ ταὶ λιπαραὶ καὶ ἰοστέφανοι καὶ ἀοίδιμοι
Ἑλλάδος ἔρεισμα, κλειναὶ Ἀθᾶναι, δαιμόνιον πτολίεθρον.—PIND. *Fr.* 47.

Τοιοῦτον αὐτοῖς Ἄρεος εὔβουλον πάγον
ἐγὼ συνῄδη χθόνιον ὄνθ', ὃς οὐκ ἐᾷ
Τοιοῦσδ' ἀλήτας τῇδ' ὁμοῦ ναίειν πόλει.—SOPH. *Œd. Col.* 947.

Ποῦ νῦν τῆς Ἑλλάδος ὁ τῦφος; ποῦ τῶν Ἀθηνῶν τὸ ὄνομα; ποῦ τῶν φιλοσόφων ὁ λῆρος; ὁ ἀπὸ Γαλιλαίας, ὁ ἀπὸ Βηθσαΐδα, ὁ ἄγροικος πάντων ἐκείνων περιεγένετο.
CHRYS. *Hom.* iv. *in Act.* iii. (*Opp.* ix. 38, *ed.* Montfaucon).

CHAPTER XXVII.

ST. PAUL AT ATHENS.

"Immortal Greece, dear land of glorious lays,
Lo, here the Unknown God of thine unconscious praise."—KEBLE.

ATHENS!—with what a thrill of delight has many a modern traveller been filled as, for the first time, he stepped upon that classic land! With what an eager gaze has he scanned the scenery and outline of that city

——————"on the Ægean shore,
Built nobly, pure the air, and light the soil,
Athens, the eye of Greece, mother of arts
And eloquence."

As he approached the Acropolis what a throng of brilliant scenes has passed across his memory; what processions of grand and heroic and beautiful figures have swept across the stage of his imagination! As he treads upon Attic ground he is in "the Holy Land of the Ideal;" he has reached the most sacred shrine of the "fair humanities" of Paganism. It was at Athens that the human form, sedulously trained, attained its most exquisite and winning beauty; there that human freedom put forth its most splendid power; there that human intellect displayed its utmost subtlety and grace; there that Art reached to its most consummate perfection; there that Poetry uttered alike its sweetest and its sublimest strains; there that Philosophy attuned to the most

[1] Pausan. *Attic.* i. 28, 2; Herod. v. 77.

perfect music of human expression its loftiest and deepest thoughts. Had it been possible for the world by its own wisdom to know God; had it been in the power of man to turn into bread the stones of the wilderness; had permanent happiness lain within the grasp of sense, or been among the rewards of culture; had it been granted to man's unaided power to win salvation by the gifts and qualities of his own nature, and to make for himself a new Paradise in lieu of that lost Eden, before whose gate still waves the fiery sword of the Cherubim,—then such ends would have been achieved at Athens in the day of her glory. No one who has been nurtured in the glorious lore of that gay and radiant city, and has owed some of his best training to the hours spent in reading the history and mastering the literature of its many noble sons, can ever visit it without deep emotions of gratitude, interest, and love.[1]

And St. Paul must have known at least something of the city in whose language he spoke, and with whose writers he was not wholly unfamiliar. The notion that he was a finished classical scholar is, indeed, as we have shown already, a mere delusion; and the absence from his Epistles of every historical reference proves that, like the vast mass of his countrymen, he was indifferent to the history of the heathen, though profoundly versed in the history of Israel. He was, indeed, no less liberal and cosmopolitan—nay, in the best sense, far more so—than the most advanced Hellenist, the most cultivated Hagadist of his day. Yet he looked at "the wisdom of Javan" as something altogether evanescent and subsidiary—an outcome of very partial enlightenment, far from pure, and yet graciously conceded to the ages of ignorance. It was with no thrill of rapture, no loyal recognition of grace and greatness, that Paul landed at Phalerum or Peiræus, and saw the crowning edifices of the Acropolis, as it towered over the wilderness of meaner temples, stand out in their white lustre against the clear blue sky. On the contrary, a feeling of depression, a fainting of the heart, an inward unrest and agitation, seems at once to have taken possession of his susceptible and ardent temperament; above all, a sense of loneliness which imperiously claimed the solace of that beloved companionship which alone rendered his labours possible, or sustained him amid the daily infirmities of his troubled life. As he bade farewell to the faithful Berœan brethren who had watched over his journey, and had been to him in the place of eyes, the one message that he impresses on them is urgently to enjoin Silas and Timotheus to come to him at once with all possible speed. In the words of St. Luke we still seem to catch an echo of the yearning earnestness which shows us that solitude[2]—and above all solitude in such a place—was the one trial which he found it the most difficult to bear.

But even if his two friends were able instantly to set out for Athens, a full week must, at the lowest computation, inevitably elapse before Silas could reach

[1] We read the sentiments of Cicero, Sulpicius, Germanicus, Pliny, Apollonius, &c., in Cic. *Ep. ad Quint. fratr.* i. 1; *Epp. Fam.* iv. 5; *ad Att.* v. 10; vi. 1; Tac. *Ann.* ii. 53; Plin. *Ep.* viii. 24; Philostr. *Vit. Apoll.* v. 41; Renan, *St. Paul*, 167; but, as he adds, "Paul belonged to another world; his Holy Land was elsewhere."

[2] Acts xvii. 15, λαβόντες ἐντολὴν πρὸς τὸν Σίλαν καὶ τὸν Τιμόθεον ἵνα ὡς τάχιστα ἔλθωσιν πρὸς αὐτόν.

him from Berœa, and a still longer period before Timothy could come from Thessalonica; and during those days of weary and restless longing there was little that he could do. It is probable that, when first he was guided by his friends to his humble lodging, he would have had little heart to notice the sights and sounds of those heathen streets, though, as he walked through the ruins of the long walls of Themistocles to the Peiraic gate, one of the brethren, more quick-eyed than himself, may have pointed out to him the altars bearing the inscription, 'ΑΓΝΩΣΤΟΙΣ ΘΕΟΙΣ,[1] which about the same time attracted the notice of Apollonius of Tyana, and were observed fifty years afterwards by the traveller Pausanias, as he followed the same road.[2] But when the brethren had left him—having no opportunity during that brief stay to labour with his own hands—he relieved his melancholy tedium by wandering hither and thither, with a curiosity[3] largely mingled with grief and indignation.[4]

The country had been desolated by the Roman dominion, but the city still retained some of its ancient glories. No Secundus Carinas had as yet laid his greedy and tainted hand on the unrivalled statues of the Athens of Phidias. It was the multitude of these statues in a city where, as Petronius says,[5] it was more easy to meet a god than a man, which chiefly absorbed St. Paul's attention. He might glance with passing interest at the long colonnades of shops glittering with wares from every port in the Ægean; but similar scenes had not been unfamiliar to him in Tarsus, and Antioch, and Thessalonica. He might stroll into the Stoa Pœcile, and there peer at the paintings, still bright and fresh, of Homeric councils of which he probably knew nothing, and of those Athenian battles about which, not even excepting Marathon,[6] there is no evidence that he felt any interest. The vast enlargement of his *spiritual* horizon would not have brought with it any increase of secular knowledge, and if Paul stood in these respects on the level of even the Gamaliels of his day, he knew little or nothing of Hellenic story.[7] And for the same reason he would have been indifferent to the innumerable busts of Greeks of every degree of eminence, from Solon and Epimenides down to recent Sophists and Cosmetae,

[1] Pausan. I. i. 4; Hesych. *s. v.*, 'Αγνῶτες θεοί: *v. infra*, p. 301).

[2] They lay on the road between the Phaleric port and the city, and St. Paul may possibly have landed at Phalerum, the nearest though not the most frequented harbour for vessels sailing from Macedonia.

[3] Acts xvii. 23, διερχόμενος καὶ ἀναθεωρῶν τὰ σεβάσματα ὑμῶν.

[4] *Id.* 16, παρωξύνετο τὸ πνεῦμα αὐτοῦ. Cf. 1 Cor. xiii. 5, οὐ παροξύνεται, "is not exasperated."

[5] Petron. *Sat.* 17.

[6] Mr. Martineau, after remarking that modern lives of St. Paul have been too much of the nature of "illustrative guide-books, so instructive, that by far the greatest part of their information would have been new to St. Paul himself," adds that "in the vicinity of Salamis or Marathon he would probably recall the past no more than a Brahmin would in travelling over the fields of Edgehill or Marston Moor" (*Studies in Christianity* p. 417).

[7] Nothing in the Talmud is more amazing than the total absence of the geographic, chronological, and historic spirit. A genuine Jew of that Pharisaic class in the midst of which St. Paul had been trained, cared more for some pedantically minute *halacha*, about the threads in a *tsitsith*, than for all the Pagan history in the world.

and still more indifferent to the venal intrusions which Athenian servility had conceded to Roman self-importance. A glance would have been more than enough for Greek statues decapitated to furnish figures for Roman heads, or pedestals from which the original hero had been displaced to make room for the portly bulk and bloated physiognomy of some modern Proconsul. Some Jew might take a certain pride in pointing out to him the statues of Hyrcanus, the Asmonæan High Priest, and of that beautiful Berenice before whom he little thought that he should one day plead his cause.[1] But his chief notice would be directed to the bewildering multiplicity of temples, and to the numberless "idols" which rose on every side. Athens was the city of statues. There were statues by Phidias, and Myron, and Lysicles, and statues without number of the tasteless and mechanical copyists of that dead period of the Empire; statues of antiquity as venerable as the olive-wood Athênê which had fallen from heaven, and statues of yesterday; statues colossal and diminutive; statues equestrian, and erect, and seated; statues agonistic and contemplative, solitary and combined, plain and coloured; statues of wood, and earthenware, and stone, and marble, and bronze, and ivory, and gold, in every attitude, and in all possible combinations; statues starting from every cave, and standing like lines of sentinels in every street.[2] There were more statues in Athens, says Pausanias, than in all the rest of Greece put together, and their number would be all the more startling, and even shocking, to St. Paul, because, during the long youthful years of his study at Jerusalem, he had never seen so much as one representation of the human form, and had been trained to regard it as apostasy to give the faintest sanction to such violations of God's express command. His earlier Hellenistic training, his natural large-heartedness, his subsequent familiarity with Gentile life, above all, the entire change of his views respecting the universality and permanence of the Mosaic Law, had indeed indefinitely widened for him the shrunken horizon of Jewish intolerance. But any sense of the dignity and beauty of Pagan art was impossible to one who had been trained in the schools of the Rabbis.[3] There was nothing in his education which enabled him to admire the simple grandeur of the Propylæa, the severe beauty of the Parthenon, the massive proportions of the Theseum, the exquisite elegance of the Temple of the Wingless Victory. From the nude grace and sinewy strength of the youthful processions portrayed on frieze or entablature, he would have turned away with something of impatience, if not with something even of disgust. When the tutor of Charles the Fifth, the good Cardinal of Tortosa, ascended the Papal throne under the title of Adrian the Sixth, and his attendants conducted him to the Vatican to show him its splendid treasures of matchless statuary, his sole

[1] Jos. *Antt.* xix. 8, § 5.

[2] "Athenae simulacra Deorum hominumque habentes omni genere et materiae et artium insignia" (Liv. xlv. 27).

[3] The reader will recall the censure passed on Gamaliel for having merely entered a bath in which was a statue of Aphrodite (*infra*, p. 705).

remark, in those uncouth accents which excited so much hatred and ridicule in his worthless subjects, was

"SUNT IDOLA ANTIQUORUM!"[1]

It was made a scoff and a jest against him, and doubtless, in a Pontiff of the sixteenth century, it shows an intensity of the Hebraising spirit singularly unsoftened by any tinge of Hellenic culture. But, as has been admitted even by writers of the most refined æsthetic sympathies, the old German Pope was more than half right. At any rate, the sort of repugnance which dictated his disparaging remark would have been not only natural, but inevitable, in a Pharisee in the capital of Judaism and under the very shadow of the Temple of the Most High. We who have learnt to see God in all that is refined and beautiful; whom His love has lifted above the perils of an extinct paganism; whom His own word has taught to recognise sunbeams from the Fountain of Light in every grace of true art and every glow of poetic inspiration, may thankfully admire the exquisite creations of ancient genius;—but had Paul done so he could not have been the Paul he was. "The prejudices of the iconoclastic Jew," says Renan, with bitter injustice, "blinded him; he took these incomparable images for idols. 'His spirit,' says his biographer, 'was embittered within him when he saw the city *filled with idols.*' Ah, beautiful and chaste images; true gods and true goddesses, tremble! See the man who will raise the hammer against you. The fatal word has been pronounced: you are *idols.* The mistake of this ugly little Jew will be your death-warrant."[2]

Yes, their death-warrant as false gods and false goddesses, as "gods of the heathen" which "are but idols,"[3] but not their death-warrant to us as works of art; not their death-warrant as the imaginative creations of a divinely-given faculty; not their death-warrant as echoes from within of that outward beauty which is a gift of God; not in any sense their death-warrant as standing for anything which is valuable to mankind. Christianity only discouraged Art so long as Art was the handmaid of idolatry and vice; the moment this danger ceased she inspired and ennobled Art. It is all very well for sentimentalists to sigh over "the glory that was Greece, and the grandeur that was Rome;" but Paganism had a very ragged edge, and it was *this* that Paul daily witnessed. Paganism, at its *best*, was a form assumed by natural religion, and had a power and life of its own; but, alas! it had not in it enough salt of solid morality to save its own power and life from corruption. St. Paul needed no mere historical induction to convince him that the loftiest heights of culture are compatible with the lowest abysses of depravity, and that a shrine of consummate beauty could be a sink of utter infamy. Nay, more, he

[1] He walled up, and never entered, the Belvedere (Symonds, *Renaissance*, p. 377).

[2] *St. Paul*, p. 172. The word κατείδωλον is, however, St. Luke's, not St. Paul's.

[3] "The pagan worship of beauty . . . had ennobled art and corrupted nature; extracted wonders from the quarries of Pentelicus, and horrors from the populace of Rome and Corinth; perfected the marbles of the temple, and degraded the humanity of the worshipper. Heathenism had wrought into monstrous combination physical beauty and moral deformity" (Martineau, *Hours of Thought*, p. 306).

knew by personal observation, what we may only be led to conjecture by thoughtful comparison, that there was no slight connexion between the superficial brightness and the hidden putrescence; that the flowers which yielded the intoxicating honey of ancient art were poisoned flowers; that the perfectness of sculpture might have been impossible without the nude athleticism which ministered to vice. For one who placed the sublime of manhood in perfect obedience to the moral law, for one to whom purity and self-control were elements of the only supreme ideal, it was, in that age, impossible to love, impossible to regard even with complacence, an Art which was avowedly the handmaid of Idolatry, and covertly the patroness of shame. Our regret for the extinguished brilliancy of Athens will be less keen when we bear in mind that, more than any other city, she has been the corruptress of the world. She kindled the altars of her genius with unhallowed incense, and fed them with strange fires. Better by far the sacred Philistinism—if Philistinism it were—for which this beautiful harlot had no interest, and no charm, than the veiled apostasy which longs to recall her witchcraft and to replenish the cup of her abomination. Better the uncompromising Hebraism which asks what concord hath Christ with Belial and the Temple of God with idols, than the corrupt Hellenism which, under pretence of artistic sensibility or archæological information, has left its deep taint on modern literature, and seems to be never happy unless it is raking amid the embers of forgotten lusts.

Nor was Paul likely to be overpowered by the sense of Athenian greatness. Even if his knowledge of past history were more profound than we imagine it to have been, yet the Greece that he now saw was but a shadow and a corpse—"Greece, but living Greece no more."[1] She was but trading on the memory of achievements not her own; she was but repeating with dead lips the echo of old philosophies which had never been sufficient to satisfy the yearnings of the world. Her splendour was no longer an innate effulgence, but a lingering reflex. Centuries had elapsed since all that was grand and heroic in her history had "gone glimmering down the dream of things that were;" and now she was the weak and contemptuously tolerated dependent of an alien barbarism,[2] puffed up by the empty recollection of a fame to which she contributed nothing, and retaining no heritage of the past except its monuments, its decrepitude, and its corruption. Among the things which he saw at Athens there were few which Paul could naturally admire. He would

[1] See Apollonius, *Ep.* lxx. (*ubi supr.*). Ἕλληνες οἴεσθε δεῖν ὀνομάζεσθαι . . . ἀλλ' ὑμῶν γε οὐδὲ τὰ ὀνόματα μένει τοῖς πολλοῖς, ἀλλ' ὑπὸ νέας ταύτης εὐδαιμονίας (the patronage of Rome), ἀπολωλέκασι τὰ τῶν προγόνων σύμβολα.

[2] The nominal freedom of Athens had been spared by successive conquerors. Though she had always been on the defeated side with Mithridates, Pompey, Brutus and Cassius, and Anthony, yet the Roman Emperors left her the contemptuous boon of an unfettered loquacity. This was her lowest period. "She was no longer the city of Theseus; she was not yet the city of Hadrian" (Renan, p. 178). About this very time the city was visited by the thaumaturgist Apollonius, and, according to Philostratus, the estimate which he formed of the city was most unfavourable . . . οὐ μένοντες Ἕλληνες ὅπως δὲ οὐ μένοντες ἐγὼ φράσω, Γέρων σοφὸς οὐδεὶς Ἀθηναῖος . . . ὁ κόλαξ παρὰ ταῖς πύλαις, ὁ συκοφάντης πρὸ τῶν πυλῶν, ὁ μαστροπὸς πρὸ τῶν μακρῶν τειχῶν, ὁ παράσιτος πρὸ τῆς Μουνυχίας καὶ πρὸ τοῦ Πειραιοῦ, ἡ θεὸς δὲ οὐδὲ Σούνιον ἔχει (*Opp. Philostr*, ed. Olear. ii. 406).

indeed have read with interest the moral inscriptions on the Hermæ which were presented to her citizens by the tyrant Hipparchus,[1] and would have looked with something of sympathy on such altars as those to Modesty and to Piety. But, among the many altars visible in every street, there was one by which he lingered with special attention, and of which he read with the deepest emotion the ancient inscription—

ΑΓΝΩΣΤΩΙΘΕΩΙ.
"To the unknown God."[2]

The better-known altars, of which the inscriptions were in the plural, and which merely bore witness to the catholicity of Paganism, would have had less interest for him. It is merely one of the self-confident assertions which are too characteristic of Jerome[3] that St. Paul misquoted the singular for the plural. The inscription to which he called attention on the Areopagus was evidently an ancient one, and one which he had observed on a single altar.[4] Whether that altar was one of those which Epimenides had advised the Athenians to build to whatever god it might be—τῷ προσήκοντι θεῷ—wherever the black and white sheep lay down, which he told them to loose from the Areopagus; or one dedicated to some god whose name had in course of time become obliterated and forgotten;[5] or one which the Athenians had erected under some visitation of which they could not identify the source[6]—was to St. Paul a matter of indifference. It is not in the least likely that he supposed the altar to have been intended as a recognition of that Jehovah[7] who seemed so mysterious to the Gentile world. He regarded it as a proof of the confessed inadequacy, the unsatisfied aspirations, of heathendom. He saw in it, or liked to read *into* it, the acknowledgment of some divinity after whom they yearned, but to the knowledge of whom they had been unable to attain; and this was He whom he felt it to be his own mission to make known. It was with this thought that he consoled his restless loneliness in that uncongenial city; it was this thought which rekindled his natural ardour as he wandered through its idol-crowded streets.[8]

[1] Such as Μνῆμα τόδ' Ἱππάρχου· στεῖχε δίκαια φρονῶν, or Μνῆμα τόδ' Ἱππάρχου· μὴ φίλον ἐξαπάτα.

[2] This, and not "to *an* unknown God," is the right rendering.

[3] "Inscriptio arae *non ita erat ut Paulus asseruit* Ignoto Dei; sed ita; Diis Asiae et Europae et Africae, Diis ignotis et peregrinis. Verum quia Paulus non pluribus Diis ignotis indigebat sed uno tantum ignoto Deo, singulari verbo usus est." Jer. *ad Tit.* i. 12 (see Biscoe, p. 210).

[4] Acts xvii. 23, βωμὸν ᾧ ἐπεγέγραπτο. The fact that Pausanias (*Attic.* i. 1), Philostratus (*Vit. Apollon.* vi. 3), and others (Diog. Laert. i. x. 100, &c.), mentions altars, ἀγνώστων δαιμόνων, does not of course prove that there was no altar with the singular inscription; nor, indeed, is it certain that these words may not mean altars on *each* of which was an inscription, Ἀγνώστῳ θεῷ, as Winer understands them. Dr. Plumptre favours the view that it means "to the Unknowable God;" and compares it with the famous inscription on the veil of Isis, and the Mithraic inscription found on an altar at Ostia, "*Signum indeprehensibilis Dei*," and 1 Cor. i. 21.

[5] Eichhorn.

[6] Chrysostom.

[7] Called by the Gentiles ὁ πάγκρυφος (Just. Mart. *Paraenet ad. Graecos*, 38; *Apol.* ii. 10; Philo, *Leg.* § 44).

[8] Acts xvii. 16. And yet his high originality was shown in the fact that he did not, like his race in general, vent his indignation in insults, "Gens contumelia numinum insignis" (Plin. *H. N.* xiii. 9; Cic. *p. Flacc.* 67). Claudius, in confirming their privi-

His work among the Jews was slight. He discoursed,[1] indeed, not unfrequently with them and their proselytes in the synagogue or meeting-room[2] which they frequented; but it is probable that they were few in number, and we find no traces either of the teaching which he addressed to them or of the manner in which they received it. It was in the market-place of Athens—the very Agora in which Socrates had adopted the same conversational method of instruction four centuries[3] before him—that he displayed his chief activity in a manner which he seems nowhere else to have adopted, by conversing daily and publicly with all comers. His presence and his message soon attracted attention. Athens had been in all ages a city of idlers, and even in her prime her citizens had been nicknamed Gapenians,[4] from the mixture of eager curiosity and inveterate loquacity which even then had been their conspicuous characteristics. Their greatest orator had hurled at them the reproach that, instead of flinging themselves into timely and vigorous action in defence of their endangered liberties, they were for ever gadding about asking for the very latest news;[5] and St. Luke—every incidental allusion of whose brief narrative bears the mark of truthfulness and knowledge—repeats the same characteristic under the altered circumstances of their present adversity. Even the foreign residents caught the infection, and the Agora buzzed with inquiring chatter at this late and decadent epoch no less loudly than in the days of Pericles or of Plato.

Among the throng of curious listeners, some of the Athenian philosophers were sure, sooner or later, to be seen. The Stoa Pœcile, which Zeno had made his school, and from which the Stoics derived their name, ran along one side of the Agora, and not far distant were the gardens of Epicurus. Besides the adherents of these two philosophical schools, there were Academics who followed Plato, and Peripatetics who claimed the authority of Aristotle, and Eclectics of every shade.[6] The whole city, indeed, was not unlike one of our

leges, warned them, μὴ τὰς τῶν ἄλλων ἐθνῶν δεισιδαιμονίας ἐξουθενίζειν (Jos. *Antt.* xix. 5, § 3). κατείδωλον means "full of idols," not as in the E. V., "wholly given to idolatry;" "non *simulacris dedita*, sed *simulacris referta*" (*Herm. ad Vig.* p. 638) cf. κατάμπελος, κατάδενδρος. The word receives most interesting illustration from Wetstein, from whom all succeeding commentators have freely borrowed.

[1] Acts xvii. 17, διελέγετο, not "disputed," but "conversed."

[2] No trace of any building which could have been a synagogue has been found at Athens. It has been inferred from passages in the Talmud that Jews were numerous in Athens; but these passages apply to a much later period, and in any case the Talmud is perfectly worthless as a direct historic guide.

[3] Socrates died B.C. 399.

[4] Κεχηναῖοι, Ar. *Eq.*, 1262. Demades said that the crest of Athens ought to be a great tongue. "Alexander qui quod cuique optimum est eripuit Lacedaemona *servire* jubet, Athenas *tacere*" (Sen. *Ep.* 94; see Demosth. *Phil.* iv.) τὴν πόλιν ἅπαντες τῶν Ἑλλήνων ὑπολαμβάνουσιν ὡς φιλόλογός τε ἐστιν καὶ πολύλογος (Plat. *Legg.* i. 11).

[5] καινότερον (cf. Matt. xiii. 52). "Nova statim sordebant, *noviora* quaerebantur" (Bengel). Gill says that a similar question מה הדוא was common in the Rabbinic schools (*Bammidbar Rabba*, f. 212, 4).

[6] "From whose mouth issued forth
Mellifluous streams that watered all the schools
Of Academics old and new, with those
Surnamed Peripatetics, and the school
Epicurean, and the Stoic severe." (Milton, *Par. Reg.*)

University towns at the deadest and least productive epochs of their past. It was full of professors, rhetors, tutors, arguers, discoursers, lecturers, grammarians, pedagogues, and gymnasts of every description; and among all these Sophists and Sophronists there was not one who displayed the least particle of originality or force. Conforming sceptics lived in hypocritical union with atheist priests, and there was not even sufficient earnestness to arouse any antagonism between the empty negations of a verbal philosophy and the hollow professions of a dead religion.[1] And of this undistinguished throng of dilettanti pretenders to wisdom, not a single name emerges out of the obscurity. Their so-called philosophy had become little better than a jingle of phrases[2]—the languid repetition of effete watchwords—the unintelligent echo of empty formulæ. It was in a condition of even deeper decadence than it had been when Cicero, on visiting Athens, declared its philosophy to be all a mere chaos—ἄνω κάτω—upside down.[3] Epicureans there were, still maintaining the dictum of their master that the highest good was pleasure; and Stoics asserting that the highest good was virtue; but of these Epicureans some had forgotten the belief that the best source of pleasure lay in virtue, and of these Stoics some contented themselves with their theoretic opinion with little care for its practical illustration. With the better side of both systems Paul would have felt much sympathy, but the defects and degeneracies of the two systems rose from the two evil sources to which all man's sins and miseries are mainly due—namely, sensuality and pride. It is true indeed that—

> "When Epicurus to the world had taught
> That pleasure was the chiefest good,
> His life he to his doctrines brought,
> And in a garden's shade that sovran pleasure sought;
> Whoever a true Epicure would be,
> May there find cheap and virtuous luxury."

But the famous garden where Epicurus himself lived in modest abstinence[4] soon degenerated into a scene of profligacy, and his definition of pleasure, as consisting in the absence of physical pain or mental perturbation (ἀταραξία), had led to an ideal of life which was at once effeminate and selfish. He had misplaced the centre of gravity of the moral system, and his degenerate followers,

[1] See Renan, *St. Paul*, p. 186, who refers to Cic. *ad Fam.* xvi. 21; Lucian, *Dial. Mort.* xx. 5; Philostr. *Apollon.* iv. 17.

[2] Φιλοσοφία Ἑλλήνων λόγων ψόφος. Tertullian asks, "Quid simile philosophus et Christianus?" (Tert. *Apol.* 46); but Paul, catholic and liberal to all truth, would have hailed the truths which it was given to Greek philosophers to see (Clem. Alex. *Strom.* vi. 8, § 65, and *passim*). χρησίμη πρὸς θεοσέβειαν γίνεται προπαιδεία τις οὖσα (*Id.* i. 5, § 28; Aug. *De Civ. Dei*, ii. 7).

[3] We can the better estimate this after reading such a book as Schneider's *Christliche Klänge aus dem Griech. und Rom. Classikern* (1865). The independence, cheerfulness, royalty, wealth of the true Christian recall the Stoic "kingliness," αὐτάρκεια—the very word which St. Paul often uses (2 Cor. ix. 8; Phil. iv. 11—18; 1 Cor. iv. 8—10, &c., compared with Cic. *De Fin.* iii. 22; Hor. *Sat.* I. iii. 124—136; Sen. *Ep. Mor.* ix.). But what a difference is there between these apparent resemblances when we look at the Stoic and Christian doctrines—i. in their real significance; and ii. in their surroundings.

[4] Juv. *Sat.* xiii. 172; xiv. 319.

while they agreed with him in avowing that pleasure should be the aim of mortal existence, selected the nearer and coarser pleasures of the senses in preference to the pleasures of the intellect or the approval of the conscience. The sterner and loftier Epicureans of the type of Lucretius and Cassius were rare; the school was more commonly represented by the base and vulgar Hedonists who took as their motto, "Let us eat and drink, for to-morrow we die."[1] On the other hand, their great Stoic rivals had little reason to boast the efficacy of their nobler theory. Aiming at the attainment of a complete supremacy not only over their passions, but even over their circumstances —professing fictitious indifference to every influence of pain or sorrow,[2] standing proudly alone in their unaided independence and self-asserted strength, the Stoics, with their vaunted apathy, had stretched the power of the will until it cracked and shrivelled under the unnatural strain; and this gave to their lives a consciousness of insincerity which, in the worse sort of them, degraded their philosophy into a cloak for every form of ambition and iniquity, and which made the nobler souls among them melancholy with a morbid egotism and an intense despair. In their worst degeneracies Stoicism became the apotheosis of suicide, and Epicureanism the glorification of lust.[3]

How Paul dealt with the views and arguments of these rival sects—respectively the Pharisees and the Sadducees of the pagan world[4]—we do not know. Perhaps these philosophers considered it useless to discuss philosophical distinctions with one whose formal logic was as unlike that of Aristotle as it is possible to imagine—who had not the least acquaintance with the technicalities of philosophy, and whom they would despise as a mere barbarous and untrained Jew. Perhaps he was himself so eager to introduce to their notice the good news of the Kingdom of Heaven, that with him all questions as to the moral standpoint were subordinate to the religious truth from which he was convinced that morality alone could spring. They may have wanted to argue about the *summum bonum*; but he wanted to preach Christ. At any rate, when he came to address them he makes no allusion to the more popularly known points of contrast between the schools of philosophy, but is entirely occupied with the differences between their views and his own as to the nature and attributes of the Divine. Even to the philosophers who

[1] Cf. Eccles. v. 18; Wisd. ii. 7—9.

[2] "For there was never yet philosopher
That could endure the toothache patiently." (Shakespeare.)

[3] The ancient philosophers in the days of the Roman Empire (ἐκ πώγωνος σοφοί, Phoenicides *ap.* Meineke, *Com. Fr.* iv. 511; Lucian, *Eun.* 8; Lact. *Instt.* iii. 25; *Bactroperitae*, Jer. in Matt. xi. 10, &c.) had as a body sunk to much the same position as the lazy monks and begging friars of the Middle Ages (see Sen. *Ep. Mor.* v. 1, 2; Tac. *Ann.* xvi. 32; Juv. iii. 116; Hor. *Sat.* i. 3, 35, 133). The reproaches addressed to them by the Roman satirists bear a close resemblance to those with which Chaucer lashed the mendicant preachers, and Ulric von Hutten scathed the degenerate monks.

[4] Josephus evidently saw the analogy between the Pharisees and the Stoics (Jos. *Antt.* xiii. 1, § 5; xviii. 1, § 2; *B. J.* ii. 8, §§ 2—14); and "Epicureans" is a constant name for heretics, &c., in the Talmud.

talked with him in the market-place[1] the subject-matter of his conversation had been neither pleasure nor virtue, but Jesus and the Resurrection.[2] The only result had been to create a certain amount of curiosity—a desire to hear a more connected statement of what he had to say. But this curiosity barely emerged beyond the stage of contempt. To some he was "apparently a proclaimer of strange deities;"[3] to others he was a mere "sparrow," a mere "seed-pecker"[4]—"a picker-up of learning's crumbs," a victim of unoriginal hallucinations, a retailer of second-hand scraps. The view of the majority of these frivolous sciolists respecting one whose significance for the world transcended that of all their schools would have coincided nearly with that of

"Cleon the poet from the sprinkled isles,"

which our poet gives in the following words:—

"And for the rest
I cannot tell thy messenger aright,
Where to deliver what he bears of thine,
To one called Paulus—we have heard his fame
Indeed, if Christus be not one with him—
I know not nor am troubled much to know.
Thou canst not think a mere barbarian Jew,
As Paulus proves to be, one circumcised,
Hath access to a secret shut from us?
Thou wrongest our philosophy, O King,
In stooping to inquire of such an one,
As if his answer could impose at all.
He writeth, doth he? well, and he may write!
O, the Jew findeth scholars! certain slaves,
Who touched on this same isle, preached him and Christ;
And (as I gathered from a bystander)
Their doctrines could be held by no sane man."[5]

[1] When Apollonius landed at the Peiraeus he is represented as finding Athens very crowded and intensely hot. On his way to the city he met many philosophers, some reading, some perorating, and some arguing, all of whom greeted him. παρῄει δὲ οὐδεὶς αὐτὸν, ἀλλὰ τεκμηράμενοι πάντες ὡς εἴη Ἀπολλώνιος συνανεστρέφοντό τε καὶ ἠσπάζοντο χαίροντες (Philostr. *Vit.* iv. 17).

[2] Acts xvii. 18. The word "virtue" occurs but once in St. Paul (Phil. iv. 8), and ἡδονή, in the classic sense only in Tit. iii. 3. The notion that the philosophers took "the Resurrection" to be a new goddess Anastasis, though adopted by Chrysostom, Theophylact, Œcumenius, &c., and even in modern times by Renan ("Plusieurs à ce qu'il paraît, prirent *Anastasis* pour un nom de déesse, et crurent que Jésus et Anastasis étaient quelque nouveau couple divin que ces rêveurs orientaux venaient prêcher," *St. Paul*, p. 190), seems to me almost absurd. It would argue, as has been well said, either utter obscurity in the preaching of St. Paul, or the most incredible stupidity in his hearers.

[3] It is almost impossible to suppose that St. Luke is not mentally referring to the charge against Socrates, ἀδικεῖ Σωκράτης . . . καινὰ δαιμόνια εἰσφέρων (Xen. *Mem.* I. i.).

[4] Σπερμολόγος, a seed-pecking bird, applied as a contemptuous nickname to Athenian shoplifters and area sneaks (Eustath. *ad Od.* v. 490), and then to babblers who talked of things which they did not understand. It was the very opprobrium which Demosthenes had launched against Æschines (*Pro Coronâ*, p. 269, *ed Reiske*). Compare the terms gobemouche, engoulevent, &c.

[5] Browning, *Men and Women.*

With some hearers, however, amusement and curiosity won the day. So far as they could understand him he seemed to be announcing a new religion. The crowd on the level space of the Agora rendered it difficult for all to hear him, and as the Areopagus would both furnish a convenient area for an harangue, and as it was there that the court met which had the cognizance of all matters affecting the State religion, it was perhaps with some sense of burlesque that they led him up the rock-hewn steps—which still exist—to the level summit, and placed him on the "Stone of Impudence," from which the defendants before the Areopagus were wont to plead their cause.[1] Then, with a politeness that sounds ironical, and was, perhaps, meant by the volatile ring-leaders of the scene as a sort of parody of the judicial preliminaries, they began to question him as in old days their ancestors had tried and condemned Anaxagoras, Diagoras, Protagoras, and Socrates, on similar accusations.[2] They said to him, "May we ascertain from you what is this new doctrine about which you have been talking? You are introducing some strange topic to our hearing. We should like, then, to ascertain what these things might mean?" And so the audience, keenly curious, but brimming over with ill-suppressed contempt and mirth, arranged themselves on the stone steps, and wherever they could best hear what sort of novelties could be announced by this strange preacher of a new faith.

But it was in no answering mood of levity that St. Paul met their light inquiries. The "ugly little Jew," who was the noblest of all Jews, was, perhaps, standing on the very stone where had once stood the ugly Greek who was the noblest of all Greeks, and was answering the very same charge. And Socrates could jest even in immediate peril of his life; but St. Paul, though secure in the tolerance of indifference, had all the solemnity of his race, and was little inclined to share in any jest. His was one of those temperaments which are too sad and too serious for light humour; one of those characters which are always and overwhelmingly in earnest. To meet badinage by badinage was for him a thing impossible. A modern writer is probably correct when he says that in ordinary society St. Paul would certainly not have been regarded as an interesting companion. On the other hand, he was too deeply convinced of his own position as one to which he had been called by the very voice and vision of his Saviour to be in the least wounded by frivolous innuendos or disdainful sneers. He was not overawed by the dignity of his judicial listeners, or by the reputation of his philosophic critics, or by the stern associations of the scene in the midst of which he stood.

[1] Acts xvii. 19, ἐπιλαβόμενοι αὐτοῦ. It is quite a mistake to suppose that any violence is intended. Cf. ix. 27. Pausanias (*Attic.* i. 28, 5) is our authority for the λίθος Ἀναιδείας.

[2] It was the express function of the Areopagus to take cognizance of the introduction of ἐπίθετα ἱερά. Many writers hold that this was a judicial proceeding, and Wordsworth that it might have been an *Anakrisis*; and our translators, from their marginal note, "it was the highest court in Athens," probably shared the same view. The narrative, however, gives a very different impression. The Athenians were far less in earnest about their religion than Anytus and Meletus had been in the days of Socrates, and if this was meant for a trial it could only have been by way of conscious parody, as I have suggested.

Above him, to the height of one hundred feet, towered the rock of the Acropolis like the vast altar of Hellas—that Acropolis which was to the Greek what Mount Sion was to the Hebrew, the splendid boss of the shield ringed by the concentric circles of Athens, Attica, Hellas, and the world.[1] Beneath him was that temple of the awful goddesses whose presence was specially supposed to overshadow this solemn spot, and the dread of whose name had been sufficient to prevent Nero, stained as he was with the guilt of matricide, from setting foot within the famous city.[2] But Paul was as little daunted by the terrors and splendour of Polytheism in the seat of its grandest memorials and the court of its most imposing jurisdiction, as he was by the fame of the intellectual philosophy by whose living representatives he was encompassed. He knew, and his listeners knew, that their faith in these gay idolatries had vanished.[3] He knew, and his listeners knew, that their yearning after the unseen was not to be satisfied either by the foreign superstitions which looked for their votaries in the ignorance of the gynæceum, or by those hollow systems which wholly failed to give peace even to the few. He was standing under the blue dome of heaven,[4] a vaster and diviner temple than any which man could rear. And, therefore, it was with the deepest seriousness, as well as with the most undaunted composure, that he addressed them: "Athenians!"[5] he said, standing forth amongst them, with the earnest gaze and outstretched hand which was his attitude when addressing a multitude, "I observe that in every respect you are unusually religious."[6] Their attention would naturally be won, and even a certain amount of personal kindliness towards the orator be enlisted, by an exordium so courteous and so entirely in accordance with the favourable testimony which many writers had borne to their city as the common altar and shrine of Greece.[7] "For," he continued,

[1] Aristid. *Panathen.* i. 99; C. and H. i. 383.

[2] The Semnae, or Eumenides. (Suet. *Ner.* 34.)

[3] It is hard to conceive the reality of a devotion which laughed at the infamous gibes of Aristophanes against the national religion (*Lysistr.* 750).

[4] Ὑπαίθριοι ἐδικάζοντο (Pollux, viii. 118).

[5] Ἄνδρες Ἀθηναῖοι, &c. It was the ordinary mode of beginning a speech, and it seems to be strangely regarded by the author of *Supernatural Religion*, iii. 82, as a sign that these speeches are not genuine.

[6] Acts xvii. 22, δεισιδαιμονεστέρους. "Quasi superstitiores," Vulg.; "someway religious," Hooker; "very devout," Lardner; "very much disposed to the worship of divine Beings," Whateley; "Le plus religieux des peuples," Renan; "exceedingly scrupulous in your religion," Humphry. The word is used five times by Josephus, and always in a respectful sense, as it is in Acts xxv. 19. Of the many unfortunate translations in this chapter "too superstitious" (*allzu aberglaubisch*, Luth.) is the most to be regretted. It at once alters the key-note of the speech, which is one of entire conciliatoriness. The value of it as a model for courteous polemics—a model quite as necessary in these days as at any past period—is greatly impaired in the E. V. It is possible to be "uncompromising" in opinions, without being violent in language or uncharitable in temper. St. Paul, however, would not have been likely to act contrary to the caution which struck Apollonius as necessary—σωφρονέστερον καὶ τὸ περὶ πάντων Θεῶν εὖ λέγειν καὶ τοῦτο Ἀθήνησι οὗ καὶ ἀγνώστων δαιμόνων βωμοὶ ἵδρυνται (Philostr. *Vit.* vi. 3).

[7] ὅλη βωμὸς, ὅλη θῦμα Θεοῖς καὶ ἀνάθημα (Xen. *De Rep. Athen.*; *Alcib.* ii. p. 97; Pausan. *Attic.* 24). τοὺς εὐσεβεστάτους τῶν Ἑλλήνων (Jos. *c. Ap.* ii. 12; Isocr. *Paneg.* 33; Thuc. ii. 38; Ælian, *Var. Hist.* v. 17; Pausan. xxiv. 8). When Apollonius landed at Athens Philostratus says, τὴν μὲν δὴ πρώτην διάλεξιν ἐπειδὴ φιλοθύτας τοὺς Ἀθηναίους εἶδεν, ὑπὲρ ἱερῶν διελέξατο (*Vit.* vi. 2). φιλόθεοι μάλιστα πάντων εἰσί (Jul. *Misopogon*).

"in wandering through your city, and gazing about me on the objects of your devotion,[1] I found among them[2] an altar on which had been carved an inscription, "TO THE UNKNOWN GOD."[3] That, then, which ye unconsciously[4] adore, that am I declaring unto you. The God who made the universe and all things in it, He being the natural[5] Lord of heaven and earth, dwelleth not in temples made with hands,[6] nor is He in need of anything[7] so as to receive service[8] from human hands, seeing that He is Himself the giver to all of life and breath and all things; and He made of one blood[9] every nation of men to dwell on the whole face of the earth, ordaining the immutable limits to the times and extents of their habitation,[10] inspiring them thereby to seek God, if after all they might grope in their darkness[11] and find Him, though, in reality,[12] He is not far from each one of us; for in Him we live, and move, and *are*, as some[13] also of your own poets have said—

"(We need Him all,)
For we are e'en His offspring."

[1] Not, as in E.V., "your devotions" (cf. Philostr. *Vit. Apollon.* iv. 19, p. 156).

[2] καὶ. For ἀναθεωρῶν D reads διϊστορῶν, perspiciens, *d*. The ἐπεγέγραπτο implies permanence, and perhaps antiquity.

[3] ὃ . . . τοῦτο, ℵ, A, B, D, with Origen and Jerome. Cf. Hor. *Epod.* v. 1. "At O Deorum quicquid in caelo regit;" and the frequent piacular inscription, "Sei Deo Sei Deae." The vague expression "the Divine" is common in Greek writers.

[4] Ver. 23, ἀγνοοῦντες, not "ignorantly," which would have been unlike Paul's urbanity, but "*without knowing Who He is*," with reference to ἀγνώστῳ (cf. Rom. i. 20). The word εὐσεβεῖτε also implies genuine piety.

[5] ὑπάρχων.

[6] An obvious reminiscence of the speech of Stephen (vii. 48; cf. Eurip. *Fragm. ap.* Clem. Alex. *Strom.* V. ii. 76).

[7] A proposition to which the Epicureans would heartily assent.

[8] θεραπεύεται, "is served," not "is worshipped," which is meaningless when applied to "hands." It means by offerings at the altar, &c. (cf. *Il.* i. 39, εἴ ποτέ τοι χαρίεντ' ἐπὶ νηὸν ἔρεψα).

[9] αἵματος is, to say the least, dubious, being omitted in ℵ, A, B, the Coptic, and Sahidic versions, &c. On the other hand, as Meyer truly observes, ἀνθρώπου would have been a more natural gloss than αἵματος; and the Jews used to say that Adam was רמא של עלם, "the blood of the world."

[10] Job xii. 23.

[11] ψηλαφᾶν, to fumble, like a blind man, or one in the dark (Arist. *Pax,* 691; Gen. xxvii. 21; Isa. lix. 10; cf. Rom. i. 21, x. 6—8):—

"I stretch lame hands of faith, and *grope*
And gather dust and chaff, and call
To what I feel is Lord of all,
And faintly trust the larger hope."—*Tennyson.*

[12] He means to imply that the necessity for this groping was their own fault—was due to *their* withdrawal to a distance from God, not His withdrawal from them.

[13] The poet actually quoted is Aratus of Cilicia, perhaps of Tarsus, and the line comes from the beginning of his Φαινόμενα:—

πάντῃ δὲ Διὸς κεχρήμεθα πάντες
Τοῦ γὰρ καὶ γένος ἐσμέν.

But he says τινες, because the same sentiment, in almost the same words, is found in Kleanthes, *Hymn. in Jov.* 5, ἐκ σοῦ γὰρ γένος ἐσμέν, and it was, not improbably, a noble common-place of other sacred and liturgical poems. Cf. Virg. *Georg.* iv. 221—225. Bentley remarked that this chapter alone proves "that St. Paul was a great master in all the learning of the Greeks" (*Boyle Lectures*, iii.). This is a very great exaggeration. See Excursus III., p. 696, *seq.*

Since, then, we are the offspring of God, we ought not to think that the Divine is like gold or silver or brass, the graving of art and of man's genius."[1]

Condensed as this speech evidently is, let us pause for an instant, before we give its conclusion, to notice the consummate skill with which it was framed, the pregnant meanings infused into its noble and powerful sentences. Such skill was eminently necessary in addressing an audience which attached a primary importance to rhetoric, nor was it less necessary to utilise every moment during which he could hope to retain the fugitive attention of that versatile and superficial mob. To plunge into any statements of the peculiar doctrines of Christianity, or to deal in that sort of defiance which is the weapon of ignorant fanaticism, would have been to ensure instant failure; and since his sole desire was to win his listeners by reason and love, he aims at becoming as a heathen to the heathen, as one without law to them without law, and speaks at once with a large-hearted liberality which would have horrified the Jews, and a classic grace which charmed the Gentiles. In expressions markedly courteous, and with arguments exquisitely conciliatory, recognising their piety towards their gods, and enforcing his views by an appeal to their own poets, he yet manages, with the readiest power of adaptation, to indicate the fundamental errors of every class of his listeners. While seeming to dwell only on points of agreement, he yet practically rebukes in every direction their natural and intellectual self-complacency.[2] The happy Providence—others, but not St. Paul, might have said the happy *accident*[3]—which had called his attention to the inscription on the nameless altar, enabled him at once to claim them as at least partial sharers in the opinions which he was striving to ennunciate. His Epicurean auditors believed that the universe had resulted from a chance combination of atoms; he tells them that it was their Unknown God who by His fiat had created the universe and all therein. They believed that there were many gods, but that they sat far away beside their thunder, careless of mankind; he told them that there was but one God, Lord of heaven and earth. Around them arose a circle of temples as purely beautiful as hands could make them—yet there, under the very shadow of the Propylæa and the Parthenon, and with all those shrines of a hundred divinities in full view with their pillared vestibules and their Pentelic marble, he tells the multitude that this God who was One, not

[1] "Judaea gens Deum sine simulacro colit" (Varro, *Fr.* p. 229). Hence the "Nil praeter nubes et caeli numen adorat" of Juv. xiv. 97 and "Dedita sacris Incerti Judaea Dei" of Luc. ii. 592; Tac. *H.* v. 6.

[2] Paul had that beautiful spirit of charity which sees the soul of good even in things evil. Hostile as he was to selfish hedonism, and to hard "apathy," he may yet have seen that there was a good side to the philosophy both of Epicurus and Zeno, in so far as Epicurus taught "the happiness of a cultivated and self-contented mind," and Zeno contributed to diffuse a lofty morality. "Encore que les philosophes soient les protecteurs de l'erreur toutefois ils ont frappé à la porte de la vérité. (Veritatis fores pulsant. Tert.) S'ils ne sont pas entrés dans son sanctuaire, s'ils n'ont pas eu le bonheur de la voir et de l'adorer dans son temple, ils se sont quelquefois présentés à ses portiques, et lui ont rendu de loin quelque hommage" (Bossuet, *Panég. de Ste. Cathérine*).

[3] The word τύχη does not occur in the N.T.

many, dwelt not in their toil-wrought temples,[1] but in the eternal temple of His own creation.—But while he thus denies the Polytheism of the multitude, his words tell with equal force against the Pantheism of the Stoic, and the practical Atheism of the Epicurean. While he thus de-consecrated, as it were, the countless temples, the Stoics would go thoroughly with him;[2] when he said that God needeth not our ritualisms, the Epicurean would almost recognise the language of his own school;[3] but, on the other hand, he laid the axe at the root of their most cherished convictions when he added that Matter was no eternal entity, and God no impersonal abstraction, and Providence no mere stream of tendency without us, which, like a flow of atoms, makes for this or that; but that He was at once the Creator and the Preserver, the living and loving Lord of the material universe, and of all His children in the great family of man, and of all the nations, alike Jew and Gentile, alike Greek and barbarian, which had received from His decrees the limits of their endurance and of their domains. In this one pregnant sentence he also showed the falsity of all autochthonous pretensions, and national self-glorifications, at the expense of others, as well as of all ancient notions about the local limitations of special deities. The afflicted Jew at whom they were scoffing belonged to a race as dear to Him as the beautiful Greek; and the barbarian was equally His care, as from His throne He beholds all the dwellers upon earth. And when he told them that God had given them the power to find Him, and that they had but dimly groped after Him in the darkness—and when he clenched by the well-known hemistich of Aratus and Cleanthes (perhaps familiar to them at their solemn festivals) the truth that we are near and dear to Him, the people of His pasture and the sheep of His hand, they would be prepared for the conclusion that all these cunning effigies—at which he pointed as he spoke—all these carved and molten and fictile images, were not and could not be semblances of Him, and ought not to be worshipped[4] were they even as venerable as the "heaven-fallen image"—the Διοπετὲς ἄγαλμα—of their patron-goddess, or glorious as the chryselephantine statue on which Phidias had expended his best genius and Athens her richest gifts.

Thus far, then, with a considerateness which avoided all offence, and a power of reasoning and eloquence to which they could not be insensible, he had demonstrated the errors of his listeners mainly by contrasting them with the counter-truths which it was his mission to announce.[5] But lest the mere

[1] 2 Chron. vi. 32, 33. ποῖος δ' ἂν οἶκος τεκτόνων πλασθεὶς ὕπο Δέμας τὸ θεῖον περιβάλοι τοίχων πτυχαῖς; (Eur. *ap.* Clem. Alex. *Strom.* V. xi. 76).

[2] Seneca, *ap.* Lact. *Instt.* vi. 25, and *Ep. Mor.* xxxi. 11.

[3] "Omnis enim per se Divom natura necesse est
Immortali aevo summâ cum pace fruatur . . .
Ipsa suis pollens opibus, nihil indiga nostri."—Lucr. ii. 650.

Cf. Sen. *Ep.* 95, 47. St. Paul, however, more probably derived the sentiment, if from any source, from 2 Macc. xiv. 35, or from Ps. l. 11, 12; Job xli. 11.

[4] See for the Pagan view Cic. *de Nat. Deor.* i. 18.

[5] The Epicurean notion of happiness as the result of coarser atoms was as material as Paley's, who considers it to be "a certain state of the nervous system in that part of the system in which we feel joy and grief . . . which may be the upper region of the stomach or the fine net-work lining the whole region of the *praecordia*" (*Moral Philos.* ch. vi.).

demonstration of error should end only in indifference or despair, he desired to teach the Stoic to substitute sympathy for apathy, and humility for pride, and the confession of a weakness that relied on God for the assertion of a self-dependence which denied all need of Him; and to lead the Epicurean to prefer a spiritual peace to a sensual pleasure, and a living Saviour to distant and indifferent gods. He proceeded, therefore, to tell them that during long centuries of their history God had overlooked or condoned[1] this ignorance, but that now the kingdom of heaven had come to them—now He called them to repentance—now the day of judgment was proclaimed, a day in which the world should be judged in righteousness by One whom God had thereto appointed, even by that Jesus to whose work God had set His seal by raising Him from the dead——

That was enough. A burst of coarse derision interrupted his words.[2] The Greeks, the philosophers themselves, could listen with pleasure, even with something of conviction, while he demonstrated the nullity of those gods of the Acropolis, at which even their fathers, four centuries earlier, had not been afraid to jeer. But now that he had got to a point at which he mixed up mere Jewish matters and miracles with his predication—now that he began to tell them of that Cross which was to them foolishness, and of that Resurrection from the dead which was inconceivably alien to their habits of belief—all interest was for them at an end. It was as when a lunatic suddenly introduces a wild delusion into the midst of otherwise sane and sensible remarks. The "strange gods" whom they fancied that he was preaching became too fantastic even to justify any further inquiry. They did not deign to waste on such a topic the leisure which was important for less extraordinary gossip.[3] They were not nearly serious enough in their own belief, nor did they consider this feeble wanderer a sufficiently important person to make them care to enforce against St. Paul that decree of the Areopagus which had brought Socrates to the hemlock draught in the prison almost in sight of them; but they instantly offered to the great missionary a contemptuous toleration more fatal to progress than any antagonism. As they began to stream away, some broke into open mockery, while others, with polite irony, feeling that such a

[1] Ver. 30, ὑπεριδών. "Winked at" is a somewhat unhappy colloquialism of the E. V. (cf. Rom. i. 24). It also occurs in Ecclus. xxx. 11. "Times of ignorance" is a half-technical term, like the Arabic *jahilujya* for the time before Mahomet.

[2] Acts xvii. 32. "The moment they heard the words 'resurrection of the dead,' some began to jeer." Ἐχλεύαζον, which occurs here only in the N.T., is a very strong word. It means the expression of contempt by the lips, as μυκτηρίζω by the nostrils. It is used by Aquila in Prov. xiv. 9, for "Fools *make a mock* at sin." Not that the ancients found anything ludicrous in the notion of the resurrection of the *soul;* it was the resurrection of the body which seemed so childish to them. See Plin. *N. H.* vii. 55; Lucian, *De Mort. Peregr.* 13. The heathen Caecilius in Minucius Felix (*Oct.* 11, 34) says, "Oraculis fabulas adstruunt. Renasci se ferunt *post mortem et cineres et favillas*, et *nescio quâ fiduciâ mendaciis* invicem credunt." See Orig. c. *Cels.* v. 14; Arnob. ii. 13; Athenag. *De Resurr.* iii. 4; Tert. *De Carn. Christi*, 15; &c.

[3] There is a sort of happy play of words in the εὐκαίρουν of Acts xvii. 21. It is not a classical word, but implies that they were too busy to spare time from the important occupation of gossiping.

speaker deserved at least a show of urbanity, said to him, "Enough for one day. Perhaps some other time we will listen to you again about *Him*." But even if they were in earnest, the convenient season for their curiosity recurred no more to them than it did afterwards to Felix.[1] On that hill of Ares, before that throng, Paul spoke no more. He went from the midst of them, sorry, it may be, for their jeers, seeing through their spiritual incapacity, but conscious that in that city his public work, at least, was over. He could brave opposition; he was discouraged by indifference. One dignified adherent, indeed, he found—but one only[2]—in Dionysius the Areopagite;[3] and one more in a woman—possibly a Jewess—whose very name is uncertain:[4] but at Athens he founded no church, to Athens he wrote no epistle, and in Athens, often as he passed its neighbourhood, he never set foot again. St. Luke has no pompous falsehoods to tell us. St. Paul was despised and ridiculed, and he does not for a moment attempt to represent it otherwise; St. Paul's speech, so far as any immediate effects were concerned, was an all but total failure, and St. Luke does not conceal its ineffectiveness.[5] He shows us that the Apostle was exposed to the ridicule of indifferentism, no less than to the persecutions of exasperated bigotry.

And yet his visit was not in vain. It had been to him a very sad one. Even when Timotheus had come to cheer his depression and brighten his solitude, he felt so deep a yearning for his true and tried converts at Thessalonica, that, since they were still obliged to face the storm of persecution, he had sacrificed his own feelings, and sent him back to support and comfort that struggling Church.[6] He left Athens as he had lived in it, a despised and lonely man. And yet, as I have said, his visit was not in vain. Many a deep thought in the Epistle to the Romans may have risen from the Apostle's reflections over the apparent failure at Athens. The wave is flung back, and streams away in broken foam, but the tide advances with irresistible majesty and might. Little did those philosophers, in their self-satisfied superiority, suppose that the trivial incident in which they had condescended to take part was for them the beginning of the end.[7] Xerxes and his Persians

[1] Acts xxiv. 25.

[2] "Le pédagogue est le moins convertissable des hommes" (Renan, p. 199). "C'est qu'il faut plus d'un miracle pour convertir à l'humilité de la croix un sage du siècle" (Quesnel).

[3] Christian tradition makes him a bishop and martyr (Euseb. *H.E.* iii. 4; iv. 23; Niceph. iii. 11), and he is gradually developed into St. Denys of France. The books attributed to him, *On the Heavenly Hierarchy*, *On the Divine Names*, &c., are not earlier than the fifth century.

[4] Δάμαλις, "heifer," would be a name analogous to Dorcas, &c.; Damaris occurs nowhere else, and is probably a mere difference of pronunciation. It can have nothing to do with δάμαρ, and has led to the conjecture that she was a Syrian metic. Absolutely nothing is known about her.

[5] Yet we are constantly asked to believe, by the very acute and impartial criticism of sceptics, that St. Luke is given to inventing the names of illustrious converts to do credit to St. Paul. If any one will compare Philostratus's *Life of Apollonius* with the Acts of the Apostles he will soon learn to appreciate the difference between the cloudy romance of a panegyrist and the plain narrative of a truthful biographer.

[6] As may be inferred from 1 Thess. iii. 2. Did Silas also join him at Athens, and was he also sent back (to Beroea)? The ἡμεῖς is in favour of the supposition, the μόνοι is against it.

[7] Renan alludes to the Edict of Justinian suppressing the Athenian chair of Philosophy 474 years after.

had encamped on the Areopagus, and devoted to the flames the temples on the Acropolis on the very grounds urged by St. Paul, "that the gods could not be shut within walls, and that the whole universe was their home and temple."[1] Yet the sword and fire of Xerxes, and all the millions of his vast host, have been utterly impotent in their effects, if we compare them to the results which followed from the apparent failure of this poor and insulted tent-maker. Of all who visit Athens, myriads connect it with the name of Paul who never so much as remember that, since the epoch of its glory, it has been trodden by the feet of poets and conquerors and kings. They think not of Cicero, or Virgil, or Germanicus, but of the wandering tent-maker. In *all* his seeming defeats lay the hidden germ of certain victory. He founded no church at Athens, but there—it may be under the fostering charge of the converted Areopagite—a church grew up. In the next century it furnished to the cause of Christianity its martyr bishops and its eloquent apologists.[2] In the third century it flourished in peace and purity. In the fourth century it was represented at Nicaea, and the noble rhetoric of the two great Christian friends St. Basil and St. Gregory of Nazianzus was trained in its Christian schools. Nor were many centuries to elapse ere, unable to confront the pierced hands which held a wooden Cross, its myriads of deities had fled into the dimness of outworn creeds, and its tutelary goddess, in spite of the flashing eyes which Homer had commemorated, and the mighty spear which had been moulded out of the trophies of Marathon, resigned her maiden chamber to the honour of that meek Galilæan maiden who had lived under the roof of the carpenter of Nazareth—the virgin mother of the Lord.[3]

CHAPTER XXVIII.

ST. PAUL AT CORINTH.

"Men, women, rich and poor, in the cool hours
Shuffled their feet along the pavement white,
Companioned or alone; while many a light
Flared here and there from wealthy festivals,
And threw their moving shadows on the walls,
Or found them clustered in the corniced shade
Of some arched temple-door or dusky colonnade."

KEATS, *Lamia*.

"*Ecclesia Dei in Corintho:* laetum et ingens paradoxon."

BENGEL, in 1 Cor. i. 2.

UNNOTICED as he had entered it—nay, even more unnoticed, for he was now alone—St. Paul left Athens. So little had this visit impressed him, that he only once alludes to it, and though from the Acrocorinthus he might often

[1] Cic. *Legg.* ii. 10.

[2] Publius, A.D. 179; Quadratus, Euseb. *H. E.* iv. 23; Aristides, A.D. 126; Athenagoras, *circ.* A.D. 177.

[3] It was probably in the sixth century, when Justinian closed the schools of philosophy, that the Parthenon was dedicated to the Virgin Mary, and the Theseum to St. George of Cappadocia.

have beheld its famed Acropolis, he never felt the smallest inclination to enter it again. This was his only recorded experience of intercourse with the Gentile Pharisaism of a pompous philosophy. There was more hope of raging Jews, more hope of ignorant barbarians, more hope of degraded slaves, than of those who had become fools because in their own conceit they were exceptionally wise; who were alienated by a spiritual ignorance born of moral blindness; who, because conscience had lost its power over them, had become vain in their imaginations, and their foolish heart was darkened.

He sailed to Corinth, the then capital of Southern Greece, which formed the Roman province of Achaia. The poverty of his condition, the desire to waste no time, the greatness of his own infirmities, render it nearly certain that he did not make his way over those forty miles of road which separate Athens from Corinth, and which would have led him through Eleusis and Megara, but that he sailed direct, in about five hours, across the Saronic bay, and dropped anchor under the low green hills and pine-woods of Cenchreæ. Thence he made his way on foot along the valley of Hexamili, a distance of some eight miles, to the city nestling under the huge mass of its rocky citadel. Under the shadow of that Acrocorinthus, which darkened alternately its double seas,[1] it was destined that St. Paul should spend nearly two busy years of his eventful life.

It was not the ancient Corinth—the Corinth of Periander, or of Thucydides, or of Timoleon—that he was now entering, but Colonia Julia, or Laus Juli Corinthus, which had risen out of the desolate ruins of the older city. When the Hegemony had passed from Sparta and Athens, Corinth occupied their place, and as the leader of the Achæan league she was regarded as the light and glory of Greece. Flamininus, when the battle of Cynoscephalae had destroyed the hopes of Philip, proclaimed at Corinth the independence of Hellas.[2] But when the city was taken by L. Mummius, B.C. 146, its inhabitants had been massacred, its treasures carried off to adorn the triumph of the conqueror, and the city itself devastated and destroyed. For a hundred years it lay in total ruin, and then Julius Cæsar, keenly alive to the beauty and importance of its position, and desiring to call attention to the goddess for whose worship it had been famous, and whose descendant he professed to be, rebuilt it from its foundations, and peopled it with a colony of veterans and freedmen.[3]

It sprang almost instantly into fame and wealth. Standing on the bridge of the double sea, its two harbours—Lechæum on the Corinthian and Cenchreæ on the Saronic Gulf—instantly attracted the commerce of the east and west. The Diolkos, or land-channel, over which ships could be dragged across the Isthmus, was in constant use, because it saved voyagers from the circumnavigation of the dreaded promontory of Malea.[4] Jews with a keen eye to

[1] Stat. *Theb.* vii. 106.

[2] B.C. 196.

[3] B.C. 44. Pausan. ii. 1, 3; Plut. *Caes.* 57; Strabo, viii. 6.

[4] Cape Matapan. The Greeks had a proverb, Μαλέας περιπλέων ἐπιλάθου τῶν οἴκαδε—as we might say, "Before sailing round Malea, make your will" (Strab. viii. p. 368). "Formidatum Maleae caput" (Stat. *Theb.* ii. 33).

the profits of merchandise, Greeks attracted by the reputation of the site and the glory of the great Isthmian games, flocked to the protection of the Roman colony. The classic antiquities found amid the *débris* of the conflagration, and the successful imitations to which they led, were among the earliest branches of the trade of the town. Splendid buildings, enriched with ancient pillars of marble and porphyry, and adorned with gold and silver, soon began to rise side by side with the wretched huts of wood and straw which sheltered the mass of the poorer population.[1] Commerce became more and more active. Objects of luxury soon found their way to the marts, which were visited by every nation of the civilised world—Arabian balsam, Egyptian papyrus, Phœnician dates, Libyan ivory, Babylonian carpets, Cilician goats'-hair, Lycaonian wool, Phrygian slaves. With riches came superficial refinement and literary tastes. The life of the wealthier inhabitants was marked by self-indulgence and intellectual restlessness, and the mass of the people, even down to the slaves, were more or less affected by the prevailing tendency. Corinth was the Vanity Fair of the Roman Empire, at once the London and the Paris of the first century after Christ.

It was into the midst of this mongrel and heterogeneous population of Greek adventurers and Roman bourgeois, with a tainting infusion of Phœnicians—this mass of Jews, ex-soldiers, philosophers, merchants, sailors, freedmen,[2] slaves, tradespeople, hucksters, and agents of every form of vice—a colony "without aristocracy, without traditions, without well-established citizens"—that the toil-worn Jewish wanderer made his way. He entered it as he had entered Athens—a stricken and lonely worker; but here he was lost even more entirely in the low and careless crowd. Yet this was the city from which and to whose inhabitants he was to write those memorable letters which were to influence the latest history of the world. How little we understand what is going on around us! How little did the wealthy magnates of Corinth suspect that the main historic significance of their city during this epoch would be centred in the disputes conducted in a petty synagogue, and the thoughts written in a tent-maker's cell by that bent and weary Jew, so solitary and so wretched, so stained with the dust of travel, so worn with the attacks of sickness and persecution! How true it is that the living world often knows nothing of its greatest men!

For when we turn to the Epistles to the Thessalonians and Corinthians, and trace the emotions which during this period agitated the mind of the Apostle, we find him still suffering from weakness[3] and anxiety, from outward opposition and inward agonies. He reminds the Thessalonians that he had prepared them for his tribulations and their own, and speaks touchingly of the comfort which he had received from the news of their faith in the midst of his afflictions.[4] Had he possessed the modern temperament he might often have been helped to peace and calm as he climbed the steep Acrocorinthus and gazed

[1] 1 Cor. iii. 12; Hausrath, p. 317.

[2] Ἐποίκους τοῦ ἀπελευθερικοῦ γένους πλείστους (Strab. viii. 6).

[3] Probably another attack of his malady (1 Cor. ii. 3).

[4] 1 Thess. iii. 4, 7.

from its lofty summit on the two seas studded with the white sails of many lands, or watched the glow of sunset bathing in its soft lustre the widespread pageant of islands and mountains, and groves of cypress and pine. But all his interest lay in those crowded streets where his Lord had much people, and in the varied human surroundings of his daily life. How deeply he was impressed by these may be seen in the Corinthian Epistles. His illustrations are there chiefly drawn from Gentile customs—the wild-beast fights,[1] which Athens would never admit while she had an Altar to Pity; the lovely stadium, in which he had looked with sympathy on the grace and strength and swiftness of many a youthful athlete; the race[2] and the boxing-matches,[3] the insulting vanity of Roman triumph,[4] the long hair of effeminate dandies,[5] the tribunal of the Proconsul,[6] the shows of the theatre,[7] the fading garland of Isthmian pine.[8]

But there was one characteristic of heathen life which would come home to him at Corinth with overwhelming force, and fill his pure soul with infinite pain. It was the gross immorality of a city conspicuous for its depravity even amid the depraved cities of a dying heathenism.[9] Its very name had become a synonym for reckless debauchery. This abysmal profligacy of Corinth was due partly to the influx of sailors, who made it a trysting-place for the vices of every land, and partly to the vast numerical superiority of the slaves, of which, two centuries later, the city was said to contain many myriads.[10] And so far from acting as a check upon this headlong immorality, religion had there taken under its immediate protection the very pollutions which it was its highest function to suppress. A thousand Hierodouloi were consecrated to the service of Impurity in the infamous Temple of Aphrodite Pandemos. The Lais of old days, whose tomb at Corinth had been marked by a sphinx with a human head between her claws, had many shameless and rapacious representatives. East and west mingled their dregs of foulness in the new Gomorrah of classic culture,[11] and the orgies of the Paphian goddess were as notorious as those of Isis or of Asherah. It was from this city and amid its abandoned proletariate that the Apostle dictated his frightful sketch of Paganism.[12] It was to the converts of this city that he addressed most frequently, and with most solemn warning and burning indignation, his stern prohibitions of sensual crime.[13] It was to converts drawn from the reeking

[1] 1 Cor. xv. 32; Lucian, *Demonax*, 57; Philostr. *Apollon.* iv. 22.
[2] 1 Cor. ix. 24.
[3] *Id.* ver. 27.
[4] 2 Cor. ii. 14—16.
[5] 1 Cor. xi. 14.
[6] 2 Cor. v. 10.
[7] 1 Cor. iv. 9.
[8] 1 Cor. ix. 25.
[9] Hesych. s. v. Κορινθιάζεσθαι. Wetstein (the great source of classical quotations in illustration of the New Testament, whose stores have been freely rifled by later authors) and others refer to Ar. *Plut.* 149; Hor. *Epp.* I. xvii. 36; Athen. vii. 13; xiii. 21, 32, 54; Strabo, viii. 6, 20—21; xii. 3, 36; Cic. *De Rep.* ii. 4; and Aristid. *Or.* III., p. 39, &c.
[10] On the numbers of slaves in ancient days, see Athenæus vi. p. 275 (ed. Casaubon).
[11] Juv. viii. 112; Hor. *Ep.* I. xvii. 36; Strabo, viii. 6; Athen. xiii. p. 573, ed. Casaubon. A reference to the immorality of the city may still be heard in the use of the word "Corinthians" for profligate idlers.
[12] Rom. i. 21—32.
[13] 1 Cor. v. 1; vi. 9—20; x. 7, 8; 2 Cor. vi. 14; vii. 1.

haunts of its slaves and artisans that he writes that they too had once been sunk in the lowest depths of sin and shame.[1] It is of this city that we hear the sorrowful admission that in the world of heathendom a pure life and an honest life was a thing well-nigh unknown.[2] All sins are bound together by subtle links of affinity. Impurity was by no means the only vice for which Corinth was notorious. It was a city of drunkards;[3] it was a city of extortioners and cheats. But the worse the city, the deeper was the need for his labours, and the greater was the probability that many in it would be yearning for delivery from the bondage of corruption into the glorious liberty of the children of God.

In such a place it was more than ever necessary that St. Paul should not only set an example absolutely blameless, but that he should even abstain from things which were perfectly admissible, if they should furnish a handle to the enemies of Christ. And therefore, lest these covetous shopkeepers and traders should be able to charge him with seeking his own gain, he determined to accept nothing at their hands. There seemed to be a fair chance that he would be able to earn his bread by tent-making in a port so universally frequented. In this respect he was unusually fortunate. He found a Jew of Pontus, named Aquila,[4] who worked at this trade with his wife Priscilla. As nothing is said either of their baptism or their conversion, it is probable that they were already Christians, and Paul formed with them a lifelong friendship, to which he owed many happy hours. This excellent couple were at present living in Corinth in consequence of the decree of Claudius, expelling all Jews from Rome.[5] Tyrannous as the measure was, it soon became a dead letter, and probably caused but little inconvenience to these exiles, because

[1] 1 Cor. vi. 9—11; 2 Cor. xii. 21. [2] 1 Cor. v. 9, 10.

[3] Corinthians were usually introduced drunk on the stage (Ælian. *V. H.* iii. 15; Athen. x. 438, iv. 137; 1 Cor. xi. 21; Hausrath, p. 323).

[4] The Aquila, a Jew of Pontus, who translated the Old Testament into Greek more literally than the LXX., lived more than half a century later, and may conceivably have been a grandson of this Aquila. Pontius Aquila was a noble Roman name (Cic. *ad Fam.* x. 33; Suet. *Jul.* 78); but that Aquila may have been a freedman of that house, and that Luke has made a mistake in connecting him with Pontus, is without the shadow of probability (cf. Acts ii. 9; 1 Pet. i. 1). His real name *may* have been *Onkelos* (Deutsch, *Lit. Rem.*, p. 336), Hebraised from Ἀκύλας, or may have been עכו, Latinised into Aquila; but these are mere valueless conjectures. He was a tent-maker, married to an active and kindly wife, who lived sometimes at Rome, sometimes at Corinth, and sometimes at Ephesus (Acts xviii. 26; 1 Cor. xvi. 19; Rom. xvi. 3; 2 Tim. iv. 19); and they were much beloved by St. Paul, and rendered extraordinary services to the cause of Christianity. Priscilla was probably the more energetic of the two, or she would not be mentioned first in Acts xviii. 18, 26; Rom. xvi. 3; 2 Tim. iv. 19. (Ewald, vi., p. 489; Plumptre, *Bibl. Studies*, p. 417.)

[5] In A.D. 52 the relations of Judæa to Rome began to be extremely unsettled (Tac. *Ann.* xii. 54), and just as the Gauls and Celts were expelled from Rome (A.D. 9) on receipt of the news about the loss of Varus and his legions, so the Jews were now ordered to quit Rome. Suetonius says, "Judaeos impulsore Chresto assidue tumultuantes Româ expulit" (*Claud.* 25). Whether Chrestos was some unknown ringleader of tumult among the immense Jewish population of Rome—so immense, that from their Ghetto across the Tiber no less than 8,000 had petitioned against the succession of Archelaus (Jos. *Antt.* xvii. 11, § 1)—or an ignorant misreading of the name of Christ, cannot be ascertained. We know that Christianity was very early introduced into Rome (Rom. xvi. 7; Acts xxviii. 14), and we know that wherever it was introduced, Jewish tumults followed (Acts xvii. 13; xiv. 19; xiii. 50), and that the Romans never

the nature of their trade seems to have made it desirable for them to move from place to place. At Corinth, as subsequently at Ephesus, Paul worked in their employ, and shared in their profits. These profits, unhappily, were scanty. It was a time of general pressure, and though the Apostle toiled night and day, all his exertions were unable to keep the wolf from the door.[1] He knew what it was to suffer, even from the pangs of hunger, but not even when he was thus starving would he accept assistance from his Achaian converts. He had come to an absolute determination that, while willing to receive necessary aid from churches which loved him, and which he loved, he would forego at Corinth the support which he considered to be the plain right of an Apostle, lest any should say that he too, like the mass of traffickers around him, did but seek his own gain.[2] Contentedly, therefore—nay, even gladly, did he become a fellow-labourer with the worthy pair who were both compatriots and brethren; and even when he was working hardest, he could still be giving instruction to all who sought him. But now, as ever, the rest of the Sabbath furnished him with his chief opportunity. On that day he was always to be found in the Jewish synagogue, and his weekly discourses produced a deep impression both on Jews and Greeks.

But when the period of his solitude was ended by the arrival of Silas from Berœa, and Timotheus from Thessalonica, he was enabled to employ a yet more intense activity. Not only did he find their presence a support, but they also cheered him by favourable intelligence, and brought him a contribution from the Philippians,[3] which alleviated his most pressing needs. Accordingly, their arrival was followed by a fresh outburst of missionary zeal, and he bore witness with a yet more impassioned earnestness to his Master's cause.[4] At this period his preaching was mainly addressed to the Jews, and the one object of it was to prove from Scripture the Messiahship of Jesus.[5] But with them

took the trouble to draw any distinction between Jews and Christians. It is, therefore, quite possible that these incessant riots may have arisen in disputes about the Messiah. Dion Cassius, indeed, corrects Suetonius, and says that the Jews were so numerous that they *could not be expelled* without danger, and that Claudius therefore contented himself with closing their synagogues (Dion, lx. 6). Perhaps the decree was passed, but never really enforced; and Aquila may have been one of the Jews who obeyed it without difficulty for the reasons suggested in the text. Nay, more, he may have been selected for special banishment as a ringleader in the agitation, if, as some suppose, he and his wife were the founders of Christianity at Rome. In any case its operation was brief, for shortly afterwards we again find the Jews in vast numbers at Rome (Rom. xvi. 3; Acts xxviii. 17). It is not at all impossible that the edict may have been identical with, or a part of, that *De Mathematicis Italiâ pellendis* which Tacitus mentions as *atrox et irritum*. Certainly that decree was passed at this very period (Tac. *Ann.* xii. 52), and many of the Jews, addicted as they were to all kinds of iniquities (Jos. *Antt.* i. 1), may easily have been classed with the Mathematici. (See Lewin, *Fasti Sacri*, 1774, 5.)

[1] 2 Cor. xi. 9; 1 Cor. iv. 11, 12; ix. 4.

[2] See Acts xx. 34; 1 Cor. ix. 12; 2 Cor. vii. 2; 1 Thess. ii. 9; 2 Thess. iii. 8.

[3] Phil iv. 15; 2 Cor. xi. 9.

[4] The undoubted reading of Acts xviii. 5 is συνείχετο τῷ λόγῳ, "was being constrained by the word" (א, A, B, D, E, G), not τῷ πνεύματι, as in E. V., "was pressed *in spirit.*" Cf. for the word συνείχετο, Luke xii. 50; 2 Cor. v. 14. De Wette, &c., make it mean "was engrossed" (Vulg., *instabat verbo*), but less correctly. "Sensus est, majore vehementiâ fuisse impulsum ut libere palamque de Christo dissereret" (Calvin).

[5] 1 Cor. xv. 3.

he made no fu[illegible]er progress. Crispus, indeed, the governor of the synagogue, had been converted with all his house; and—perhaps during the absence of his companions—Paul abandoned his usual rule by baptising him with his own hands.[1] But, as a body, the Jews met him with an opposition which at last found expression in the sort of language of which the Talmud furnishes some terrible specimens.[2] No further object could be served by endeavouring to convince them, and at last he shook off the dust of his garments, and calling them to witness that he was innocent of their blood,[3] he announced that from that day forth he should preach only to the Gentiles.

Already he had converted some Gentiles of humble and probably of slavish origin, the first among these being the household of Stephanas.[4] With Crispus and these faithful converts, he migrated from the synagogue to a room close by, which was placed at his disposal by a proselyte of the name of Justus.[5] In this room he continued to preach for many months. The entire numbers of the Corinthian converts were probably small—to be counted rather by scores than by hundreds. This is certain, because otherwise they could not have met in a single room in the small houses of the ancients, nor could they have been all present at common meals. The minute regulations about married women, widows, and virgins seem to show that the female element of the little congregation was large in proportion to the men, and it was even necessary to lay down the rule that women were not to teach or preach among them, though Priscilla and Phœbe had been conspicuous for their services.[6] And yet, small as was the congregation, low as was the position of most of them, vile as had been the antecedents of some, the method and the topics of the Apostle's preaching had been adopted with much anxiety. He was by no means at home among these eager, intellectual, disputatious, rhetoric-loving, sophisticated Greeks. They had none of the frank simplicity of his Thessalonians, none of the tender sympathy of his Philippians, none of the emotional susceptibility of his Galatian converts. They were more like the scoffing and self-satisfied Athenians. At Athens he had adopted a poetic and finished style, and it had almost wholly failed to make any deep impression. At Corinth, accordingly, he adopted a wholly different method. Ill and timid, and so nervous that he sometimes trembled while addressing them[7]—conscious that his bodily presence was mean in the judgment of these connoisseurs in beauty,

[1] 1 Cor. i. 14.

[2] Acts xviii. 6, ἀντιτασσομένων . . . καὶ βλασφημούντων. See "Life of Christ," ii. 452.

[3] Ezek. xxxiii. 4.

[4] 1 Cor. xvi. 15, "the firstfruits of Achaia" (in Rom. xvi. 5 the true reading is "of *Asia*"). Fortunatus and Achaicus were probably slaves or freedmen, as were "Chloe's household"; Tertius—who had the high honour of being the amanuensis of the Epistle to the Romans—and Quartus were probably descendants of the Roman veterans who were the first colonists, and may have been younger brothers of Secundus. Lucius, Jason, and Sosipater were Jews (Rom. xvi. 21).

[5] There is no sufficient ground for calling him Titius Justus on the strength of E and one or two versions; it seems to be simply due to the homœoteleuton in ὀνόματι. There is still less ground for identifying him with Titus.

[6] Rom. xvi. 1, 2.

[7] 1 Cor. ii. 3.

and his speech contemptible in the estimation of these judges of eloquence[1]—thinking, too, that he had little in the way of earthly endowment, unless it were in his infirmities,[2] he yet deliberately decided not to avoid, as he had done at Athens, the topic of the Cross.[3] From Corinth he could see the snowy summits of Parnassus and Helicon; but he determined never again to adorn his teaching with poetic quotations or persuasive words of human wisdom,[4] but to trust solely to the simple and unadorned grandeur of his message, and to the outpouring of the Spirit by which he was sure that it would be accompanied. There was, indeed, a wisdom in his words, but it was not the wisdom of this world, nor the kind of wisdom after which the Greeks sought. It was a spiritual wisdom of which he could merely reveal to them the elements—not strong meat for the perfect, but milk as for babes in Christ. He aimed at nothing but the clear, simple enunciation of the doctrine of Christ crucified.[5] But what was lacking in formal syllogism or powerful declamation was more than supplied by power from on high. Paul had determined that, if converts were won, they should be won, not by human eloquence, but by Divine love. Nor was he disappointed in thus trusting in God alone. Amid all the sufferings which marked his stay among the Achaians, he appeals to their personal knowledge that, whatever they may have thought or said among themselves about the weakness of his words, they could not at least deny the "signs, and wonders, and powers"[6] which, by the aid of the Spirit, were conspicuous in his acts. They must have recalled many a scene in which, under the humble roof of Justus, the fountains of the great deep of religious feeling were broken up, the strange accents of "the tongues" echoed through the thrilled assembly, and deeds were wrought which showed to that little gathering of believers that a Power higher than that of man was visibly at work to convince and comfort them. And thus many Corinthians—the Gentiles largely exceeding the Jews in number—were admitted by baptism into the Church.[7] The majority of them were of the lowest rank, yet they could number among them some of the wealthier inhabitants, such as Gaius, and perhaps Chloe, and even Erastus, the chamberlain of the city. Nor was it in Corinth only that Christians began to be converted. Paul, like Wesley, "regarded all the world as his parish," and it is little likely that his restless zeal would have made him stay for nearly two years within the city walls. We know that there was a church at Cenchreæ, whose deaconess afterwards "carried under the folds of her robe the whole future of Christian theology;"[8] and saints were scattered in small communities throughout all Achaia.[9]

And yet, though God was thus giving the increase, it must have required

[1] 2 Cor. x. 1, 10. Luther, who seems to have entered into the very life of St. Paul, calls him "Ein armes dürres Männlein wie unser Philippus" (Melancthon).

[2] 2 Cor. xii. 5, 9.

[3] 1 Cor. i. 23; ii. 2.

[4] 1 Cor. ii. 1—5. ἀνθρωπίνης is a good explanatory gloss of A, C, J, &c.

[5] 1 Cor. i. 17; ii. 2; 2 Cor. i. 18.

[6] 2 Cor. xii. 12.

[7] Acts xviii. 8.

[8] Renan, p. 219.

[9] 2 Cor. i. 1; Rom. xvi. 1. The nearest Achaian towns would be Lechæum, Schœnus, Cenchreæ, Crommyon, Sicyon, Argos.

no small courage in such a city to preach such a doctrine, and the very vicinity of the synagogue to the house of Justus must have caused frequent and painful collisions between the Jews and the little Christian community. Among all the sorrows to which St. Paul alludes whenever he refers to this long stay at Corinth, there is none that finds more bitter expression than his complaint of his fellow-countrymen. He speaks of them to the Thessalonians in words of unusual exasperation, saying that they pleased not God, and were contrary to all men, and that by their attempts to hinder the preaching to the Gentiles of the Christ whom they had murdered, they had now filled up the measure of their sins.[1] The rupture was open and decisive. If they had excommunicated him, and he was filled with such anger and despair when he thought of them, it is certain that the struggle between them must have been a constant source of anxiety and peril. This might even have ended in Paul's withdrawal to new fields of labour in utter despondency but for the support which again, as often at his utmost need, he received from a heavenly vision. The Lord whom he had seen on the road to Damascus appeared to him at night, and said to him: "Fear not, but speak, and hold not thy peace; for I am with thee, and no man shall set on thee to hurt thee; for I have much people in this city."

But at last the contest between the Jews and the Christians came to a head. The Proconsul of Achaia[2] ended his term of office, and the Proconsul appointed by the emperor was Marcus Annæus Novatus, who, having been adopted by the friendly rhetorician Lucius Junius Gallio, had taken the name of Lucius Junius Annæus Gallio, by which he is generally known. Very different was the estimate of Gallio by his contemporaries from the mistaken one which has made his name proverbial for indifferentism in the Christian world. To the friends among whom he habitually moved he was the most genial, the most lovable of men. The brother of Seneca, and the uncle of Lucan, he was the most universally popular member of that distinguished family. He was pre-eminently endowed with that light and sweetness which are signs of the utmost refinement, and "the sweet Gallio" is the epithet by which he alone of the ancients is constantly designated.[3] "No mortal man is so sweet to any single person as he is to all mankind,"[4] wrote Seneca of him.

[1] 1 Thess. ii. 14—16.

[2] The term Proconsul is historically exact. The Government of Achaia had been so incessantly changed that a mistake would have been excusable. Achaia had been Proconsular under Augustus; imperial, for a time, under Tiberius (Tac. *Ann.* i. 76); Proconsular, after A.D. 44, under Claudius (Suet. *Claud.* xxv.); free under Nero (Suet. *Ner.* 24); and again Proconsular under Vespasian (Suet. *Vesp.* viii.). See *supra*, p. 197, and Excursus XVI.

[3] "Dulcis Gallio" (Stat. *Sylv.* ii. 7, 32). See *Seekers after God*, 16—21. I need not here recur to the foolish notion that Gallio sent some of St. Paul's writings to his brother Seneca. On this see Aubertin, *Sénèque et St. Paul*, p. 117. Nor need I recur to the resemblance between the Roman philosopher and the Apostle, which I have examined in *Seekers after God*, 174—183, and which is fully treated by Dr. Lightfoot (*Phil.* pp. 268—331).

[4] "Nemo mortalium uni tam dulcis est quam hic omnibus" (Sen. *Quaest. Nat.* iv. *praef.* § 11). He dedicates to him his *De Irâ* and *De Vitâ Beatâ*, and alludes to him in *Ep.* civ. *Consol. ad Helv.* 16.

"Even those who love my brother Gallio to the very utmost of their power yet do not love him enough,"[1] he says in another place. He was the very flower of pagan courtesy and pagan culture—a Roman with all a Roman's dignity[2] and seriousness, and yet with all the grace and versatility of a polished Greek.[3]

Such was the man on whose decision the fortunes of Paul were to depend. Whoever the former Proconsul had been, he had not been one with whom the Jews could venture to trifle, nor had they once attempted to get rid of their opponent by handing him over to the secular arm. But now that a new Proconsul had arrived, who was perhaps unfamiliar with the duties of his office, and whose desire for popularity at the beginning of his government might have made him complaisant to prosperous Jews, they thought that they could with impunity excite a tumult. They rose in a body, seized Paul, and dragged him before the tesselated pavement on which was set the curule chair of the Proconsul. It was evident that they had presumed on his probable inexperience, and on his reputation for mildness; and, with all the turbulent clamour of their race, they charged Paul with "persuading men to worship God contrary to the Law." Though Claudius had expelled them from Rome, their religion was a *religio licita—i.e.*, it was licensed by the State; but the religion of "this fellow," they urged, though it might pass itself off under the name of Judaism, was not Judaism at all—it was a spurious counterfeit of Judaism, which had become a *religio illicita* by running counter to its Mosaic Law.[4] Such was the charge urged by a hubbub of voices, and, as soon as it had become intelligible, Paul was on the point of making his defence. But Gallio was not going to trouble himself by listening to any defence. He took no notice whatever of Paul, and, disregarding him as completely as though he had been non-existent, replied to the Jews by a contemptuous dismissal of them and their charge. With a thorough knowledge of, and respect for, the established laws, but with a genuinely Roman indifference for conciliatory language, and a more than Roman haughtiness of demeanour towards a people whom, like his brother, he probably despised and detested, he stopped the proceedings with the remark that their accusation against St. Paul, as a violator of any law, Mosaic or otherwise, which he could recognise, was utterly baseless. "Had this been a matter of civil wrong or moral outrage[5] it would have been but right for me to put up with you, and listen to these charges of yours; but if it be a number of questions[6] about an opinion, and

[1] "Gallionem, fratrem meum, quem nemo non parum amat etiam qui amare plus non potest" (*Nat. Qu.* iv. *praef.* § 10).

[2] Seneca (*Ep.* 104), in allusion to his high rank, playfully calls him "my Lord Gallio." He committed suicide after the ruin of his family in the plot against Nero, though his life had been spared (Tac. *Ann.* xv. 73; Dion Cass. lxii. 25; Euseb. *Chron. ad A.U.C.* 818).

[3] Dion Cass. lx. 35.

[4] Hence though παρὰ τὸν νόμον, ver. 13, means "contrary to the Jewish law" (cf. ver. 15), it might in this way come under the cognisance of the Roman law.

[5] Ver. 14, ἀδίκημα, a legal injury; ῥᾳδιούργημα, a moral offence.

[6] ζητήματα *infr.* A, B, D[2], E, Coptic, Sahidic, Armenian, &c. "My lord's" Roman disdain for the *gens sceleratissima* is heard in every accent.

about mere names, and *your* law, see to it yourselves; for a judge of these matters I do not choose to be.' Having thus, as we should say, quashed the indictment, "my Lord Gallio" ordered his lictors to clear the court. We may be sure they made short work of ejecting the frustrated but muttering mob, on whose disappointed malignity, if his countenance at all reflected the feelings expressed by his words, he must have been looking down from his lofty tribunal with undisguised contempt.[1] It took the Romans nearly two centuries to learn that Christianity was something infinitely more important than the Jewish sect which they mistook it to be. It would have been better for them and for the world if they had tried to get rid of this disdain, and to learn wherein lay the secret power of a religion which they could neither eradicate nor suppress. But while we regret this unphilosophic disregard, let us at least do justice to Roman impartiality. In Gallio, in Lysias, in Felix, in Festus, in the centurion Julius, even in Pilate,[2] different as were their degrees of rectitude, we cannot but admire the trained judicial insight with which they at once saw through the subterranean injustice and virulent animosity of the Jews in bringing false charges against innocent men. Deep as was his ignorance of the issues which were at stake, the conduct of Gallio was in accordance with the strictest justice when "he drave them from his judgment-seat."

But the scene did not end here. The volatile Greeks,[3] though they had not dared to interfere until the decision of the Proconsul had been announced, were now keenly delighted to see how completely the malice of the Jews had been foiled; and since the highest authority had pronounced the charge against St. Paul to be frivolous, they seized the opportunity of executing a little Lynch law. The ringleader of the Jewish faction had been a certain Sosthenes, who may have succeeded Crispus in the function of Ruler of the Synagogue, and whose zeal may have been all the more violently stimulated by the defection of his predecessor.[4] Whether the Corinthians knew that St. Paul was a Roman citizen or not, they must at least have been aware that he had separated from the synagogue, and that

[1] Perhaps no passage of the ancient authors, full as they are of dislike to the Jews (see *infra*, Excursus XIV.), expresses so undisguised a bitterness, or is so thoroughly expressive of the way in which the Romans regarded this singular people, as that in which Tacitus relates how Tiberius banished 4,000 freedmen "infected with that superstition" into Sardinia, to keep down the brigands of that island, with the distinct hope that the unhealthy climate might help to get rid of them—"et si, ob gravitatem caeli interissent, vile damnum" (*Ann.* ii. 85). Suetonius tells us, with yet more brutal indifference, that Tiberius, on pretext of military service, scattered them among all the unhealthiest provinces, banishing the rest on pain of being reduced to slavery (Suet. *Tib.* 36; Jos. *Antt.* xviii. 3, § 5).

[2] Acts xxiii. 29; xxv. 19. The ignorant provincialism of the justices at Philippi was of too low a type to understand Roman law.

[3] Acts xviii. 17, πάντες. The οἱ Ἕλληνες of D, E is a gloss, though a correct one. If this Sosthenes is identical with the Sosthenes of 1 Cor. i. 1, he must have been subsequently converted; but the name is a common one, and it is hardly likely that two rulers of the synagogue would be converted in succession.

[4] I give the view which seems to me the most probable, passing over masses of idle conjectures.

many Gentiles espoused his views. They thought it intolerable that Jews should try to trump up charges against one who in some measure belonged to themselves. The opportunity to show these Jews what they thought of them, and give them a lesson as to the way in which they should behave in the future, was too tempting. Accordingly they seized Sosthenes, and gave him a beating in the actual basilica in front of the tribunal, and under the very eyes of the Proconsul. An ancient gloss says that he pretended not to see what they were doing,[1] but the text implies that he looked on at the entire proceeding with unfeigned indifference. So long as they were not guilty of any serious infraction of the peace, it was nothing to him how they amused themselves. He had been familiar with similar disturbances in Rome. The Jews were everywhere a turbulent, fanatical race. What was it to him if the Greek *gamins* liked to inflict a little richly-deserved castigation? It would be so much the better if they taught this Sosthenes and any number more of these Jews a severe lesson. They would be more likely (he thought) to keep order in future, and less likely to trouble him again with their meanness and their malevolence, their riots and their rancours.[2]

There is one thing that we cannot but deeply regret. It is that Gallio's impatient sense of justice has deprived us of another speech by St. Paul which, delivered under such circumstances, and before such a judge, would have been of the deepest interest. But Gallio dismissed the whole scene from his mind as supremely unimportant. Had he ever thought it worth alluding to, in any letter to his brother Seneca, it would have been in some such terms as these:—"I had scarcely arrived when the Jews tried to play on my inexperience by dragging before me one Paulus, who seems to be an adherent of Chrestus, or Christus, of whom we heard something at Rome. I was not going to be troubled with their malefic superstitions, and ordered them to be turned out. The Greeks accordingly, who were favourable to Paulus, beat one of the Jews in revenge for their malice. You would have smiled, if you had been present, at these follies of the *turba forensis*. *Sed haec hactenus.*"

But the superficiality which judges only by externals always brings its own retribution. It adores the mortal and scorns the divinity; it welcomes the impostor and turns the angel from its door. It forms its judgment on trivial accidents, and ignores eternal realities. The haughty, distinguished, and cultivated Gallio, brother of Seneca, Proconsul of Achaia, the most popular man and the most eminent littérateur of his day, would have been to the last degree amazed had any one told him that so paltry an occurrence would be for ever recorded in history; that it would be the only scene in his life in which posterity would feel a moment's interest; that he would owe

[1] "Tunc Gallio fingebat enim non videre" (MS. *d*).

[2] Paley (*Hor. Paul.*) points out the honesty with which St. Luke narrates the supercilious indifference of great men to the circumstances which affected the life of the Apostle. The "things," however, for which Gallio "did not care" were not "the things of the kingdom of heaven," but the beating of a Jew by Greeks.

to it any immortality he possesses; that he would for all time be mainly judged of by the glimpse we get of him on that particular morning; that he had flung away the greatest opportunity of his life when he closed the lips of the haggard Jewish prisoner whom his decision rescued from the clutches of his countrymen; that a correspondence between that Jew Shaûl, or Paulus, and his great brother Seneca, would be forged and would go down to posterity;[1] that it would be believed for centuries that that wretched prisoner had converted the splendid philosopher to his own "execrable superstition," and that Seneca had borrowed from him the finest sentiments of his writings; that for all future ages that bent, ophthalmic, nervous, unknown Jew, against whom all other Jews seemed for some inconceivably foolish reason to be so infuriated, would be regarded as transcendently more important than his deified Emperors and immortal Stoics; that the "parcel of questions" about a mere opinion, and names, and a matter of Jewish law, which he had so disdainfully refused to hear, should hereafter become the most prominent of all questions to the whole civilised world.

And Paul may have suspected many of these facts as little as "the sweet Gallio" did. Sick at heart with this fresh outrage, and perhaps musing sadly on the utterance of his Master that He came not to send peace on earth but a sword, he made his way back from the *bêma* of the great Proconsul to the little congregation in the room of Justus, or to his lodging in the squalid shop of Aquila and Priscilla.

CHAPTER XXIX.

THE FIRST EPISTLE TO THE THESSALONIANS.

"Ergo latet ultimus dies ut observentur omnes dies."—AUG.

AT some period during his stay in Corinth, and probably before his arrest by the Jews early in the year 53, or at the close of A.D. 52, an event had taken place of immense significance in the life of the Apostle and in the history of the Christian faith. He had written to the Thessalonians a letter which may possibly have been the first he wrote to any Christian church,[2] and which

[1] No one in these days doubts that the letters of St. Paul and Seneca (Fleury, *St. Paul and Sénèque*, ii. 300; Aubertin, *Sénèque et St. Paul*, 409; Lightfoot, *Phil.* 327; Boissier, *La Religion Romaine*, ii. 52—104) are spurious. On the real explanation of the resemblances between the two, see *Seekers after God*, p. 270, *sq.*, and *passim.* It will there be seen how small ground there is for Tertullian's expression "Seneca *saepe noster*."

[2] I only put this as a possibility. It will be seen hereafter (see 1 Cor. v. 9; 2 Cor. x. 9) that I regard it as certain that St. Paul wrote other letters, of which some—perhaps many—have perished; and it is difficult to believe that (for instance) he wrote no word of thanks to the Philippians for the contributions which they had twice sent to him at Thessalonica, or that he wrote nothing to the Thessalonians themselves when he sent Timothy to them from Athens. Does not the whole style of these Epistles show that they could not have been the first specimens of their kind? We cannot be surprised that,

certainly is the earliest of those that have come down to us. He had begun, therefore, that new form of activity which has produced effects so memorable to all generations of the Christian world.

We have already seen that Paul had left Timotheus in Macedonia, had been joined by him in Athens, and had once more parted from him, though with deep reluctance and at great self-sacrifice, because his heart yearned for his Thessalonian converts, and he had been twice prevented from carrying out his earnest desire to visit them once more. After doing all that he could to comfort and support them in their many trials, Timotheus had returned, in company with Silas, to Corinth, and doubtless there the Apostle had talked with them long and earnestly about the friends and brethren who had been won to Christ in the Macedonian city. There was deep cause for thankfulness in their general condition, but there was some need for advice and consolation. Paul could not send Timothy again. There was other work to be done. Other Churches required his own personal services. Nor could he spare the companions of his toils in the midst of a city which demanded his whole energy and strength. But since he could neither come to the Thessalonians himself, nor send them back his truest and dearest fellow-workers, he would at least write to them, and let his letter supply, as far as possible, the void created by his absence. It was a very happy Providence which inspired him with this thought. It would come quite naturally to him, because it had been a custom in all ages for Jewish communities to correspond with each other by means of travelling deputations, and because the prodigious development of intercourse between the chief cities of Italy, Greece, and Asia rendered it easy to send one or other of the brethren as the bearer of his missives. And epistolary correspondence was the very form which was of all others the best adapted to the Apostle's individuality. It suited the impetuosity of emotion which could not have been fettered down to the composition of formal treatises. It could be taken up or dropped according to the necessities of the occasion or the feelings of the writer. It permitted of a freedom of expression which was far more intense and far more natural to the Apostle than the regular syllogisms and rounded periods of a book. It admitted something of the tenderness and something of the familiarity of personal intercourse. Into no other literary form could he have infused that intensity which made a Christian scholar truly say of him that he alone of writers seems to have written, not with fingers and pen and ink, but with his very heart, his very feelings, the unbared palpitations of his inmost being;[1] which made Jerome say that in his writings the words were all so many thunders;[2] which made Luther say that his expressions were like living creatures with hands and feet. The theological importance of this consideration is immense, and has, to the deep injury of the Church, been

amid the disorders of the times, letters written on fugitive materials should have perished, especially as many of them may have been wholly undoctrinal. In 2 Thess. iii. 17 could St. Paul say ὅ ἐστι σημεῖον ἐν πάσῃ ἐπιστολῇ, if he had only written *one!*

[1] Casaubon, *Adversaria ap. Wolf.*, p. 135. [2] Jer. *ad Pammach.* Ep. 48.

too much neglected. Theologians have treated the language of St. Paul as though he wrote every word with the accuracy of a dialectician, with the scrupulous precision of a school-man, with the rigid formality of a philosophic dogmatist. His Epistles as a whole, with their insoluble antinomies, resist this impossible and injurious method of dealing with them as absolutely as does the Sermon on the Mount. The epistolary form is eminently spontaneous, personal, flexible, emotional. A dictated epistle is like a conversation taken down in shorthand. In one word, it best enabled Paul to be himself, and to recall most vividly to the minds of his spiritual children the tender, suffering, inspired, desponding, terrible, impassioned, humble, uncompromising teacher, who had first won them to become imitators[1] of himself and of the Lord, and to turn from hollow ritualisms or dead idols to serve the living and true God, and to wait for His Son from heaven, whom He raised from the dead, even Jesus who delivereth us from the coming wrath.

And one cause of this vivid freshness of style which he imparted to his Epistles was the fact that they were, with few if any exceptions, not deeply premeditated, not scholastically regular, but that they came fresh and burning from the heart in all the passionate sincerity of its most immediate feelings. He would even write a letter in the glow of excited feeling, and then wait with intense anxiety for news of the manner of its reception, half regretting, or more than half regretting, that he had ever sent it.[2] Had he written more formally he would never have moved as he *has* moved the heart of the world. Take away from the Epistles of St. Paul the traces of passion, the invective, the yearning affection, the wrathful denunciation, the bitter sarcasm, the distressful boasting, the rapid interrogatives, the affectionate entreaties, the frank colloquialisms, the personal details—those marks of his own personality on every page which have been ignorantly and absurdly characterised as intense egotism—and they would never have been, as they are, next to the Psalms of David, the dearest treasures of Christian devotion;—next to the four Gospels the most cherished text-books of Christian faith. We cannot but love a man whose absolute sincerity enables us to feel the very beatings of his heart; who knows not how to wear that mask of reticence and Pharisaism which enables others to use speech only to conceal their thoughts; who, if he smites under the fifth rib, will smite openly and without a deceitful kiss; who has fair blows but no precious balms that break the head; who has the feelings of a man, the language of a man, the love, the hate, the scorn, the indignation of a man; who is no envious cynic, no calumnious detractor, no ingenious polisher of plausible hypocrisies, no mechanical repeater of worn-out shibboleths, but who will, if need be, seize his pen with a burst of tears to speak out the very thing he thinks;[3] who, in the accents of utter truthfulness alike to friend and to enemy, can argue, and denounce, and expose, and plead, and pity, and forgive; to whose triumphant faith and transcendent influence has been due

[1] 1 Thess. i. 6, μιμηταὶ, not "followers," as in E.V. See Excursus I., on "The Style of St. Paul as Illustrative of his Character.

[2] 2 Cor. vii. 8.

[3] 2 Cor. ii. 4.

in no small measure that fearless and glad enthusiasm which pervaded the life of the early Church.

And thus, when Timothy had told him all that he had observed among the brethren of Thessalonica, we may feel quite sure that, while his heart was full of fresh solicitude, he would write to guide and comfort them,[1] and that many days would not elapse before he had dictated the opening words:—

"Paul, and Silvanus, and Timotheus to the Church [2] of the Thessalonians in God the Father and our Lord Jesus Christ, grace to you, and peace [from God our Father and the Lord Jesus Christ [3]]."

This opening address is in itself an interesting illustration of St. Paul's character. Though his letters are absolutely his own, yet with that shrinking from personal prominence which we often trace in him, he associates with himself in the introduction not only the dignified Silas,[4] but even the youthful Timothy;[5] and in these his earlier, though not in his later Epistles, constantly uses "we" for "I." By "we" he does not mean to imply that the words are conjointly those of his two fellow-labourers, since he adopts the expression even when he can only be speaking of his individual self;[6] but he is actuated by that sort of modesty, traceable in the language and literature of all nations, which dislikes the needlessly frequent prominence of the first personal pronoun.[7] In his letters to all other Churches, except to the Philippians, to whom the designation was needless, he calls himself Paul an Apostle, but he does not use the

[1] That the external evidence to the genuineness of the Epistles to the Thessalonians is amply sufficient may be seen in Alford, iii., *Prolegom.*; Davidson, *Introduct.* i. 19—28; Westcott, *On the Canon*, 68, n., 168, &c. The internal evidence derived from style, &c., is overwhelming (Jowett, i. 15—26). The counter-arguments of Kern, Schrader, Baur, &c., founded, as usual, alike on divergences and coincidences, on real similarities and supposed discrepancies, on asserted references and imaginary contradictions to the Acts, are silently met in the text. They carry no conviction with them, and have found few followers; Baur (*Paul*, ii. 85—97), to a great extent, furnishing positive arguments against his own conclusion. (See Lünemann, *Br. an die Thessal.* 10—15.) Grotius, Ewald, Baur, Bunsen, Davidson, &c., consider that the First Epistle is really the second; but the hypothesis is against external and internal evidence, is wholly needless, and creates obvious difficulties. It would require many volumes to enter into all these discussions for every Epistle; but though I have no space for that here, I have respectfully and impartially considered the difficulties raised, and in many cases shown incidentally my grounds for disregarding them. One most inimitable mark of genuineness is the general resemblance of tone between the Epistle and that written ten years later to the other chief Macedonian Church—Philippi. (See Lightfoot in Smith's *Bibl. Dict.*)

[2] So in 1, 2 Thess., 1, 2 Cor., and Gal. But in the other Epistles τοῖς ἁγίοις.

[3] This addition is probably spurious. It belongs to 2 Thess. i. 2, and was added because the greeting is so short. As we have now reached St. Paul's first Epistle I must refer the reader to the Excursus which gives the Uncial Manuscripts of the Epistles, *infra*, Excursus XX.

[4] Acts xv. 22, 32, 34.

[5] Silas and Timothy are associated with him in 2 Thess.; Sosthenes in 1 Cor.; Timothy in 2 Cor., Phil., Col., and Philem. Paul writes in his own name only to the Romans and Laodiceans, which Churches he had not personally visited. Origen says that the concurrence of Paul and Silas flashed out the lightning of these Epistles (*Hom.* v. *in Jerem.* 588 *b*).

[6] In 1 Thess. iii. 2, 6, and in Phil. ii. 19, Timothy is spoken of, though associated with Paul in the greeting. 1 Thess. ii. 18, "we . . even I Paul."

[7] "We" is chiefly characteristic of 1, 2 Thess. In 2 Thess. the only passage which relapses into "I" is ii. 5.

title directly[1] to the Thessalonians, because his claim to it in its more special sense had not yet been challenged by insidious Judaisers.[2] In his five earlier Epistles he always addresses "the Church;" in his later Epistles "the Saints," and the reason for this is not clear;[3] but to all Churches alike he repeats this opening salutation, "Grace and peace."[4] It is a beautiful and remarkable blending of the salutations of the Jew and the Greek, the East and the West, with their predominant ideals of calm and brightness. The solemn greeting of the Jew was SHALÔM, "Peace be to you;" the lighter greeting of the Greek was χαίρειν, "Rejoice;" the Church of Christ—possessed of a joy that defied tribulation, heir to a peace that passeth understanding—not only combined the two salutations, but infused into both a deeper and more spiritual significance.[5]

After this salutation[6] he opens his letter with that expression of thankfulness on their behalf which he addresses even to the Corinthians, whose deeds were so sad a contrast to their ideal title of saints, and which is never wanting, except in the burning letter to the apostatising Galatians. So invariable is this characteristic of his mind and style that it has acquired a technical description, and German writers call it the *Danksagung* of the Epistles.[7] It was no mere insincere compliment or rhetorical artifice. Those to whom he wrote, however much they might sink below their true ideal, were still converts, were a Church, were saints, were brethren. There might be weak, there might

[1] See 1 Thess. ii. 6.

[2] It would have been inappropriate in the private note to Philemon.

[3] Another slight peculiarity is that in his first two Epistles he says "the Church of the Thessalonians;" whereas in the next three he prefers the expression "the Church in" such and such a city. This may be a mere trifle.

[4] In his Pastoral Epistles he adds the word ἔλεος, "mercy." We may thus sum up the peculiarities of the salutations:—i. "An Apostle," in all except Philem. and Phil. ii. "To the Church," in 1, 2 Thess., 1, 2 Cor., Gal. iii. "To the *Church of* the," 1, 2 Thess.; but "to the Church which is *in*," 1, 2 Cor., Gal. In all other Epistles "To the *saints*." iv. "Grace and peace," in all but the Pastoral Epistles, which have "Grace, *mercy*, and peace."

[5] Χάρις, quae est principium omnis boni; εἰρήνη, quae est finale bonorum omnium (Tho. Aquin.).

[6] The Epistle, which is mainly personal and practical, may be analysed as follows:—I. i.—iii. Historical; II. iv., v. Hortatory; each ending with a prayer. (I.) i. 1. Brief greeting. i. 2—10. Thanksgiving for their conversion and holiness. ii. 1—12. Appeal to them as to the character of his ministry. ii. 13—16. Renewed expression of thanksgiving for their constancy under persecutions, and bitter complaint of the Jews. ii. 17—iii. 10. His personal feelings towards them, and the visit of Timothy. iii. 11—13. His prayer for them. (II.) iv. 1—8. Warning against impurity. iv. 9, 10. Exhortation to brotherly love; and 11, 12, honourable diligence. iv. 13—v. 11. The only doctrinal part of the Epistle. iv. 13—18. Consolation about the dead. v. 1—11. Duty of watchfulness, since the Lord's advent is near, and the time uncertain. v. 12—15. Their duties to one another. 16—22. Spiritual exhortations. 23, 24. His prayer for them. 25—28. Last words and blessing. The Epistle is characterised by simplicity of style, and the absence of controversy and of developed doctrine. Its keynote is "hope," as the keynote of the Epistle to the Philippians is "joy."

[7] Ewald, *Die Sendschreiben des Ap. Paulus*, 19,39, &c. It may perhaps be urged that some of these peculiarities may be due to the ordinary stereotyped formula of correspondence in the humbler classes. Thus, in papyrus rolls of the British Museum (edited for the Trustees by J. Forshall), we find such phrases as εἴη ἂν ὡς τοῖς θεοῖς εὐχομένη διατελῶ, and even, apparently, σοῦ διὰ παντὸς μνείαν ποιούμενοι. But St. Paul's incessant variations show how little he was inclined to mere formulæ.

be false, there might be sinful members among them, but as a body they were washed and sanctified and justified, and the life of even those who were unworthy of their high vocation yet presented a favourable contrast to the lives of the heathen around them. But the expression of thankfulness on behalf of the Thessalonians is peculiarly full and earnest. It is an overflow of heartfelt gratitude, as indeed the special characteristic of the letter is its sweetness.[1] St. Paul tells them that he is always giving thanks to God for them all, mentioning them in his prayers, filled with the ever-present memory of the activity of their faith, the energy of their love, the patience of their hope.[2] He reminds them of the power and fulness and spiritual unction which had accompanied his preaching of the Gospel, and how they had become[3] imitators[4] of him and of Christ with such spiritual gladness in the midst of such deep affliction[5] that they had become models to all the Churches of Northern and Southern Greece, and their faith had been as a trumpet-blast[6] through all the Mediterranean coasts. So universally was their belief in God known and spread abroad, that there was no need for St. Paul or his companions to tell how they had worked at Thessalonica, because every one had heard of their conversion from idolatry to belief in the very and living God,[7] and to the waiting for the return of that risen Saviour who delivereth us from the coming wrath.[8]

He appeals to them, therefore, as to unimpeachable witnesses of the earnestness of his visit to them, and of the boldness with which he had faced the dangers of Thessalonica, after such recent and painful experience of the

[1] "Habet haec Epistola meram quandam dulcedinem" (Bengel).

[2] Cf. Gal. v. 6. Thus in the very first lines which we possess from his pen we meet with his fundamental trilogy of Christian virtues—faith, hope, love. Cf. v. 8; Col. i. 4; Eph. i. 15, 18; iii. 17, 18, 20, &c. See Reuss, *Théol. Chrét.* ii. 240.

[3] St. Paul, like many emotional and impressible writers, is constantly haunted by the same word, which he then repeats again and again—ἤτις ἀκουόντεσσι νεωτάτη ἀμφιπέληται ἀκουόντεσσι. He uses the verb γίνομαι no less than eight times, although, as Bishop Ellicott points out, it only occurs twelve times in all the rest of the New Testament, except in quotations from the LXX. "Un mot l'obsède, il le ramène dans une page à tout propos. Ce n'est pas de la stérilité: c'est de la contention de l'esprit et une complète insouciance de la correction du style" (Renan, p. 233).

[4] μιμηταὶ, E.V. "followers."

[5] i. 6. The reader will notice the exquisite originality of conception in the words ἐν θλίψει πολλῇ μετὰ χαρᾶς Πνεύματος Ἁγίου. It is no rhetorical oxymoron, but the sign of a new *aeon* in the world's history.

[6] i. 8, ἐξήχηται. ὡσ ἐπὶ σάλπιγγος λαμπρὸν ἠχούσης (Theoph.). Admitting for the warmth of feeling which dictated the expression, it suggests no difficulty when we remember that a year may have elapsed since his visit, and that Thessalonica was "posita in gremio imperii Romani" (Cic.), and stood "on a level with Corinth and Ephesus in its share of the commerce of the Levant."

[7] i. 10, Ἀληθινῷ (1 John v. 20). Ζῶντι as contrasted with dead men and idols (Wisd. xiv. 15; Gal. iv. 8), which are mere *elîlîm*, "nullities" (Lev. xix. 4), and *habhâlîm*, "vapours." The expression shows that the Thessalonian Church was mainly composed of Gentiles, which accords with Acts xvii. 4, if we read καὶ Ἑλλήνων (*supra*, p. 288). If we omit καὶ there is still no contradiction, for obviously many Gentiles, especially women, were converted, and even the proselytes had once been idolaters.

[8] Not as in E. V., "who *delivered* (ῥυόμενον) us from the wrath *to come*" (ἐρχομένης, not μελλούσης). The deliverance is continuous ("Christus nos semel ἐλυτρώσατο semper ῥύεται"—Bengel); the wrath works as a normal law (i. 1—10).

outrages of Philippi. It has been evident, even through these opening sentences of thanksgiving, that there is in his words an undercurrent of allusion to some who would, if they could, have given a very different account of his conduct and motives.[1] These appeals to their knowledge of the life and character and behaviour of Paul and his two fellow-missionaries would have been needless if they had never been impugned. But it is easy to understand that alike the Jews in their eagerness to win back the few members of the synagogue who had joined the brethren, and the Gentiles vexed at the silent rebuke against their own sins, would whisper calumnies about the new teachers, and try to infuse into others their own suspicions. The cities of that age swarmed with every kind and denomination of quack and impostor. Might not these three poor Jews—that silent and dignified elder, the shy, gentle youth, and the short enthusiast of mean aspect—might they not be only a new variety of the genus *goês*—like the wandering Galli and worshippers of Isis, or Chaldaei, or Mathematici, or priests of Mithras?[2] Were they not a somewhat suspicious-looking trio? What was their secret object? Was it with sinister motives that they gathered into their communities these widows and maidens? Were they not surreptitiously trying to get hold of money? or might it not be their own exaltation at which they were aiming?—Now there were some charges and attacks which, in after days, as we shall see, filled Paul with bitter indignation; but insinuations of this nature he can afford to answer very calmly. Such calumnies were too preposterous to be harmful; such innuendos too malevolent to be believed. In order to disprove them he had but to appeal at once to notorious facts; and, indeed, *no* elaborate disproof was needed, for his Thessalonian friends *knew*, and God was witness,[3] that there had been no deceit, no uncleanness, no base motives, no secret avarice, no desire to win favour, no fawning flattery in the exhortations of the missionaries. They had come, not for selfishness, but for sacrifice; not for glory, but to pour out their hearts' tenderness, and spend their very lives for the sake of their converts,[4] cherishing them as tenderly[5] as a nursing mother fosters her children in her warm bosom,[6] yet waiving their own rights, and taking nothing whatever from them, nor laying the smallest burden upon them.[7] The brethren knew that while they were preaching they regarded

[1] 1 Thess. ii. 5, 9. These phrases are not accounted for by contrast with *heathen* deceptions. The ὑμῖν τοῖς πιστεύουσιν of verse 10 means "though *others* did not so regard our conduct."

[2] Hausrath, p. 300; μάγοι καὶ γόητες (Theoph.); ii. 3, ἐν δόλῳ (2 Cor. ii. 17; iv. 2; xi. 13). ἀκαθαρσία *may* only mean "impure motives" (*e.g.*, covetousness; cf. 2 Cor. xi. 8; 1 Tim. iii. 8; Titus i. 7); "Unlauterkeit, Beimischung menschlicher Begehrnisse" (Ewald); verse 5, πλεονεξία (Acts xx. 33; 1 Cor. ix. 15; 2 Cor. xii. 14).

[3] 1 Thess. ii. 5.

[4] ii. 8, *leg.* ὁμειρόμενοι, ℵ, A, B, C, D, E, F, G, "clinging to you;" προσδεδεμένοι (Theoph.); ἀντεχόμενοι ὑμῶν (Œcumen.).

[5] ii. 7, ἤπιοι, found also in 2 Tim. ii. 24. The νήπιοι of ℵ, B, C, D, F, G, is an obvious instance of mere homoeoteleuton.

[6] ii. 7, θάλπῃ.

[7] ἐν βάρει εἶναι, "oneri esse" (Vulg.). It may mean to be dictatorial (πολλῆς ἀπολαῦσαι τιμῆς, Chrys.), but see verse 9; 2 Cor. xi. 9; xii. 16; 2 Thess. iii. 8.

their mission as a glorious privilege;[1] and because their one desire was to please God, they endured and laboured[2] night and day[3] to win their own bread, setting blameless examples of holiness towards God, and righteousness towards men, and all the while exhorting their followers one by one[4] to live lives worthy of God and of the kingdom of His Christ.[5]

And this was why, thank God, the Thessalonians had accepted their preaching for what it was—a divine and not a human message; and had borne suffering at the hands of their Gentile neighbours with the same exemplary courage as the Churches of Judæa, who in like manner had been persecuted by the Jews. And here Paul, as he so constantly does, "*goes off at a word.*" The mere incidental mention of Jews makes him digress to denounce them, writing as he did in the very heat of those conflicts which ended in his indignant withdrawal from their synagogue at Corinth, and recalling the manner in which these murderers of the Lord and of the Prophets,[6] displeasing[7] to God and the common enemies of man,[8] chased him from city to city, and tried to prevent his mission to the Gentiles. And it is thus, he says, that they are always filling up the measure of guilt, and the wrath came upon them to the end—potentially overtook them—in that sudden consummation of their sins. Their very sin, he seems to say, in hindering the proclamation of the Gospel, was itself their punishment; their wrath against Christ was God's wrath against them; their dementation would be, and was, their doom.[9]

And having been thus diverted by his feeling of indignation against them

[1] ii. 4, *δεδοκιμάσμεθα*. [2] ii. 9, *κόπος*, "active toil;" *μόχθος*, "steady endurance of toil."

[3] St. Paul uses the ordinary Hebrew expression (iii. 10; 2 Thess. iii. 8, &c.), which arose from the notion, found in an old border oath, that "God made the earth in six days and seven nights." Hence too the term *νυχθήμερον*. St. Luke, writing in his own person, says, "day and night" (Acts ix. 24). The fact that there were wealthy and distinguished women among the proselytes (Acts xvii. 4) made this self-denial the more striking.

[4] ii. 11, *ἕνα ἕκαστον ὑμῶν*. Chrysostom says, *βάβαι ἐν τοσούτῳ πλήθει μηδένα παραλιπεῖν*; but probably the Christians in Thessalonica would have made an exceedingly small modern parish.

[5] ii. 1—12.

[6] Omit *ἰδίους*, ℵ A, B, D, &c. "*Suos* adjectio est haeretici" (*i.e.*, of Marcion)—Tert. *adv.* Marc. v. 15.

[7] *μὴ ἀρεσκόντων*. The *μὴ*, though "the prevailing New Testament combination with the participle" (Ellicott), is slightly less severe than if he had used *οὐκ*.

[8] The momentary exacerbation against the Jews in the mind of St. Paul must have been unusually intense to wring from him such words as these. We almost seem to catch the echo of the strong condemnation uttered against them by Gentiles as a God-detested race, who hated all men ("*odium generis humani*"—Tac. *H.* v. 5; Juv. *Sat.* xiv. 100), and such a view of them (which Lünemann here fails to overthrow) must have caused a deep pang to one who remained at heart a genuine patriot. (See Rom. ix. 1—5.) But the triumph of the Jews over the impious attempts of Caligula had caused a great recrudescence of fanaticism among them.

[9] ii. 14—16. Baur, in arguing that this could only have been written after the destruction of Jerusalem, makes a double mistake. First, he takes *ἔφθασεν* in the sense of *ἔφθακεν* (like the E. V. "*has* come"), which is the erroneous gloss of B, D; and secondly, he does not see the ethical conception which I have here tried to bring out. The wrath of God found its full consummation in the fulness of their criminality (Matt. xxvii. 25); the fiat of their doom had then gone forth. It was not finally consummated till the fall of Jerusalem, eighteen years later, but signs were already obvious that its execution would not long be delayed. To the prescient eye of St. Paul the commencing troubles in Palestine—and the recent expulsion of the Jews from Rome—would be ample to

from the topic of self-defence—on which, indeed, nothing more was necessary to be said—he goes on to tell them that regarding them as his glory and joy and crown of boasting[1] at the coming of Christ—feeling, in his absence from them, like a father bereaved of his children[2]—he had twice purposed to come to them, and had twice been hindered by Satan.[3] He had, however, done the next best thing he could. He had parted from Timothy in Athens, and sent him to prevent them from succumbing[4] to those fierce afflictions, of the certainty of which they had been faithfully forewarned; and to ascertain their faith, as shown by the dubious result of too definite temptations.[5] When Timothy rejoined him at Corinth, the news which he had brought back was so reassuring—he was able to give so good an account of their faith, and love, and steadfastness, and affection—that it had cheered the Apostle in the midst of his own heavy afflictions, and been to him like a fresh spring of life. No thanks to God could be too hearty for this blessing, and it added intensity to his prayer that God would yet enable him to come and see them, and to perfect all deficiencies of their faith. He concludes this historic or personal section of his Epistle with the fervent prayer that God would deepen the spirit of love which already prevailed among them, and so enable them to stand before Him in blameless holiness at the coming of our Lord Jesus with all His saints.[6]

From these earnest and loving messages he turns to the practical part of his letter. He beseeches[7] and exhorts them not to be stationary, but to advance more and more in that Christian course which he had marked out for them. And then he enters on those special injunctions which he knew to be most needful. First and foremost he puts the high virtue of purity.

justify his expression. In the true prophetic spirit he regards the *inevitable* as the *actual*. It is possible, too, that St. Paul may be alluding to the great discourse of Christ (Matt. xxiii. 37—39; xxiv. 6, 16. Cf. Rom. i. 18; Dan. ix. 24).

[1] Ezek. xvi. 12 (LXX.).

[2] ii. 17, ἀπορφανισθέντες ἀφ' ὑμῶν.

[3] Once apparently at Berœa, once at Athens. The Satanic hindrance may have been in Berœa Jewish persecutions, in Athens feeble health. (Cf. Rom. xv. 22.) He is writing to Gentile converts, to whom it will be observed that he does not adduce, in either Epistle, a single quotation from the Old Testament, with which they could have been as yet but little familiar; but the immediate reference of trials, sickness, and hindrances to Satan is found to this day in all Oriental forms of speech. Even in the Bible the term Satan is sometimes applied to "any adversary" or "opposing influence" (cf. 1 Chron. xxi. 1 with 2 Sam. xxiv. 1). "The devil," ὁ διάβολος, as distinguished from unclean spirits, δαιμόνια, is only used by St. Paul in Eph. iv. 27; vi. 11; and three times in the letters to Timothy. Where he regarded the hindrance as Satanic he carries out his purpose another time, but where it is a divine prohibition (Acts xvi. 6, 7) he finally gives it up. Acts xxi. 4 is only an apparent exception.

[4] He here uses the metaphor σαίνεσθαι, derived from the fawning cowardice of frightened animals; elsewhere he uses the metaphor στέλλεσθαι, "to furl the sails in a high wind." He calls Timothy "a fellow-worker with God" (συνεργὸν τοῦ Θεοῦ, D), an expression only altered in the MSS. because of its boldness (1 Cor. iii. 9; 2 Cor. vi. 1).

[5] iii. 5, μή πως ἐπείρασεν . . . καὶ εἰς κενὸν γένηται.

[6] ii. 17—iii. 13. *Parousia* occurs six times in these two Epistles, and only besides in 1 Cor. xv. 23. The word "advent" is said to occur first in Tert. *De Resurrect.* 24. The "saints" seems to be a reference, not to angels (Ps. lxxxix. 7; Matt. xvi. 27; Jude 14, &c.), because St. Paul does not use this term of angels (*kedoshim*, Ps. cxxxix. 7), but to those mentioned in iv. 16; 1 Cor. vi. 2.

[7] ἐρωτῶμεν, as in v. 12; 2 Thess. ii. 1; only elsewhere to his other Macedonian Church (Phil. iv. 3).

These converts had but recently been called out of a heathenism which looked very lightly on the sins of the flesh. The mastery over lifelong habits of corruption was not to be won in a day. They were still in danger of relapsing into sensual crime. It was necessary to remind them that, however small might be the censure which Gentiles attached to fornication,[1] and even to yet darker and deadlier sins,[2] they were in direct opposition to the command, and would immediately deserve the retribution of that God whose will was their sanctification, and who laid on them the duty, however difficult, of acquiring a secure and tranquil mastery over their body and its lusts.[3] If then any one among them professed to despise these precepts as though they were merely those of the Apostle, he must now be reminded that he was thereby despising, not any human teacher, but God, who called them, not for uncleanliness, but in sanctification,[4] and by giving them His Holy Spirit, not only deepened the duty, but also inspired them with the power to sanctify His Temple in their hearts.[5]

The next Christian virtue of which he speaks is brotherly love. He feels it unnecessary to do so,[6] for God Himself had taught them both to recognise that duty and to put it in practice, not only towards the members of their own church, but towards all Macedonian Christians (vs. 9, 10).

Further, they should make it their ambition to be quiet,[7] working with

[1] Cic. *pro Caelio*, 48; Hor. *Sat.* I. ii. 32; Ter. *Adelph.* I. ii. 21; Jer. *Ep.* 77; Aug. *De Civ. Dei*, xiv. 18.

[2] Ver. 7, οὐ . . . ἐπὶ ἀκαθαρσίᾳ ἀλλ' ἐν ἁγιασμῷ.

[3] iv. 4. The exact meaning of εἰδέναι ἕκαστον ὑμῶν τὸ ἑαυτοῦ σκεῦος κτᾶσθαι, κ.τ.λ., must remain uncertain. It is wrongly translated in the E.V. "that every one of you should know how to *possess* his vessel," &c., for κτᾶσθαι is "to *acquire*." I have given what would be a very fine and forcible meaning of the words, but it cannot be regarded as *certain* that σκεῦος means "body" (cf. 2 Cor. iv. 7, Chrys., Theoph., Œcumen., Theod., Tert., and most modern writers). I regard it, however, as by far the most probable interpretation (cf. 1 Sam. xxi. 5; 2 Cor. iv. 7). So ἀγγεῖον is used for "body" in Philo, and *vas* in Latin writers (see Cic. *T. Disp.*, i. 22; Lucr, iii. 44). Theodore of Mopsuestia and Augustine make it mean "his own wife;" and then it would be a recommendation to the spirit of chastity at once preserved and continued in a holy marriage (Heb. iii. 4). This view has been recently adopted by De Wette, Schott, &c., as it was by Aquinas and Estius. In favour of it are the Hebrew כְּלִי for wife (see Rabbinic instances in Schoettgen, *Hor. Hebr.*, *ad loc.*), and the phrase κτᾶσθαι γυναῖκα (Ecclus. xxxvi. 29. Cf. Eph. v. 28; 1 Cor. vii. 2; 1 Pet. iii. 7). But would the Thessalonians, whose women held a much higher and freer position than Oriental women, have been aware of this somewhat repulsive Orientalism? Would the use of it have been worthy of St. Paul's refinement? and is he not, as Theodoret observes, speaking to celibates and to women as well as to men?

[4] *Leg.* διδόντα, ℵ, B, D, E, F, G.

[5] iv. 1—8. The dark warning of iv. 6 is lost in the E. V., because, though it would be but too intelligible to Pagan converts, St. Paul veils it under the delicate euphemisms, the *honesta aposiopesis*, familiar to his sensitive refinement (cf. 1 Cor. v. 1, 2; 2 Cor. vii. 11, &c.; Eph. v. 3, 12). At any rate, the Greek commentators, who would here be most likely to see his meaning, take him to mean not only adultery, but yet deeper abysses of wickedness. It cannot be "business," which would be τοῖς πράγμασιν. (See Döllinger, *Judenth. u. Heidenth.*)

[6] This sort of παράλειψις (or praeteritio), noticed here by Theophylact, is a rhetorical figure characteristic of St. Paul's kindliness (see v. 1; 2 Cor. ix. 1; Philem. 19). But the phrase also implies that it is *easier* to teach Christian virtue than to eradicate habitual vice.

[7] One of St. Paul's happy turns of expression (*oxymoron*, Rom. xii. 11; cf. Isa. xxx. 7).

their own hands,[1] and not to meddle with others, and not to rely on the assistance of others, but to present to the outer world a spectacle of honourable and active independence (vs. 11, 12).

And now, by these moral exhortations, by thus recalling them from over-eschatological excitement to the quiet fulfilment of the personal duties which lay nearest at hand, he has prepared the way for the removal of a serious doubt which had troubled some of them. Since he left them there had been deaths in the little community, and these deaths had been regarded by some of the survivors with a peculiar despondency. They had been taught again and again to hope for, to look unto, the coming of Christ. That blessed Presence was to be for them the solution of all perplexities, the righting of all wrongs, the consolation for all sufferings. What the hopes of the birth of the Messiah had been to the Jew, that the hope of His return with all His saints was to the early Christian. And it was natural that such a topic should be prominent in the addresses to a church which, from its very foundation, had been, and for years continued to be, peculiarly afflicted.[2] What, then, was to be said about those who had died, and therefore had not seen the promise of Christ's coming? What could be said of those whose life had ended like the common life of men—no wrongs righted, no miseries consoled? Had not they been beguiled of their promise, disappointed in their hope, deceived, even, as to the event on which they had fixed their faith? And if *they*, why not *others?* If the dead were thus frustrated in their expectation, why might not the living be? St. Paul has already given them the advice which would prevent them from brooding too much on that one uncertain moment of Christ's coming. He has bidden them be pure, and loving, and diligent, and live their daily lives in simple honour and faithfulness. He would have eminently approved the quiet good sense of that president of the Puritan assembly, who, when a dense darkness came on, and some one proposed that they should adjourn because it might be the beginning of the Day of Judgment, proposed rather that candles should be lighted, because if it *was* to be the Day of Judgment, they could not be found better employed than in the quiet transaction of duty. But Paul does not leave his converts in their perplexity about their departed friends. He tells them, in words which have comforted millions of mourners since, not to sorrow as those that have no hope,[3] for that "if we believe that Jesus died and

[1] This shows that the Thessalonian converts were mainly artisans.

[2] 2 Cor. vii. 5.

[3] That the Gentiles were at this time, as a rule, despondent in their views of death, in spite of dim hopes and splendid guesses, is certain. "Mortuus nec ad Deos, nec ad homines acceptus est" (*Corp. Inscr.* i. 118; Boissier, *La Rel. Rom.* i. 304, *seq.*). See, for the more ancient Greek view, *Æsch. Eumen.* 648, &c. The shade of Achilles says to Ulysses in Hades:

> "'Talk not of reigning in this dolorous gloom,
> Nor think vain words,' he cried, 'can ease my doom;
> Better by far laboriously to bear
> A weight of woes, and breathe the vital air
> Slave to the meanest hind that begs his bread,
> Than reign the sceptred monarch of the dead.'"

rose again, even so them also which had been laid asleep by Jesus will God bring with Him."[1] He even enters into details. He tells them "by the word of the Lord"[2] that death would practically make no difference whatever between the living and the dead, for that in the tremendous "NOW" of the Day of Judgment[3] the Lord Himself should descend from heaven with a cry of summons, with the voice of the archangel,[4] and with the trump of God,[5] and that then the dead in Christ should rise first, and we who are alive and remain[6] be caught up to meet the Lord in the air, and so be for ever with Him. "Wherefore," he says, "comfort one another with these words."[7]

But *when* should this be?—after what period, at what critical moment?[8] That was a question which he need not answer, because they themselves knew precisely[9] the only answer which could be given, which was that the day of the Lord should come as a thief in the night, overwhelming those that chose darkness with sudden destruction. But *they* were not of the darkness, but children of light; so that, however suddenly it came, that day could not find them unprepared.[10] For which purpose let them be sober and vigilant, like soldiers, armed with faith and love for a breastplate, and the hope of salvation for a helmet;[11] since God had not appointed them for wrath, but to obtain salvation through Him who had died in order that they, whether in life or in death, might live with Him for ever.[12] The Thessalonians are bidden to continue edifying and comforting one another with these words. Did none of them ask, "But what will become of the Jews? of the heathen? of the sinners and backsliders among ourselves?" Possibly they did. But here, and in the Romans, and in the Corinthians, St. Paul either did not anticipate such questions, or refused to answer them. Perhaps he had heard the admirable Hebrew apophthegm, "Learn to say, '*I do not know.*'" This at least is certain, that with him the idea of the resurrection is so closely connected with that of faith, and hope, and moral regeneration, that when he speaks of it he will speak of it mainly, indeed all but exclusively, in connexion with the resurrection of the saints.[13]

[1] iv. 14. If the διὰ τοῦ Ἰησοῦ be taken with κοιμηθέντας, "laid asleep by Jesus." Cf. Acts iii. 16; Rom. i. 8; v. 11; 2 Cor. i. 5, &c.

[2] "Quasi Eo ipso loquente" (Beza). As this can hardly be referred to Matt. xxiv. 31, and must be compared with the Hebrew phrase (1 Kings xx. 35, &c.), we can only understand it either of a traditional utterance of Christ or a special revelation to the Apostle. Ewald, however, says (*Sendschr.* 48), "Aus Christusworten die ihnen gewiss auch schriftlich vorlagen."

[3] Luther.

[4] Archangel only here and in Jud. 9.

[5] The imagery is borrowed from Ex. xix. 16.

[6] These words will be explained *infra*.

[7] iv. 13—18. These verses furnish one leading *motive* of the Epistle.

[8] v. 1, περὶ δὲ τῶν χρόνων καὶ τῶν καιρῶν.

[9] v. 2, ἀκριβῶς.

[10] v. 4, A, B, read κλέπτας, which would be a slight change of metaphor. "Weil der Dieb nur in und mit der Nacht kommt, vom Tage aber überrascht wird" (Ewald). Cf. Matt. xxiv. 37; Rom. xiii. 11—14.

[11] The germ of the powerful and beautiful figure of the Christian's panoply which is elaborated in Eph. vi. 13—17; Rom. xiii. 12. (Cf. Wisd. v. 18; Baruch v. 12.)

[12] v. 1—11.

[13] Pfleiderer, i. 275; Rom. vi. 23; 1 Cor. xv. 22, &c. See Reuss, *Théol. Chrét.* ii. 214.

To the thoughts suggested by St. Paul's treatment of this weighty topic we shall revert immediately. He ends the Epistle with moral exhortations—all, doubtless, suggested by the needs of the Church—of extraordinary freshness, force, and beauty. There were traces of *insubordination* among them, and he bids them duly respect and love, for their work's sake, the spiritual labourers and leaders of their community,[1] and to be at peace among themselves. He further tells them—perhaps in these last verses especially addressing the presbyters—to warn those unruly brethren who would not obey. There was *despondency* at work among them, and he bids them "comfort the feeble-minded, take the weak by the hand, be patient towards all men." They were to avoid all retaliations, and seek after all kindness[2] (vers. 12—15). Then follow little arrow-flights of inestimably precious exhortation. Was depression stealing into their hearts? Let them meet it by remembering that God's will for them in Christ Jesus was perpetual joy, unceasing prayer, universal thanksgiving. Had there been any collisions of practice, and differences of opinion, among the excited enthusiasts whose absorption in the expected return of Christ left them neither energy nor wish to do their daily duties, while it made them also set very little store by the calmer utterances of moral exhortation? Then, besides the exhortation to peace, and the noble general rule to avoid every kind of evil,[3] he warns them that they should neither quench the Spirit nor despise prophesyings—that is, neither to stifle an impassioned inspiration nor to undervalue a calm address[4]—but to test all that was said to them, and hold fast what was good.[5]

Then, once more, with the affirmation that God's faithfulness would grant the prayer, he prays that God would sanctify them wholly, and preserve their bodies, their wills and affections, their inmost souls,[6] blamelessly till that coming of the Lord to which he has so often alluded. He asks their prayers for himself; bids them salute all the brethren with a holy kiss;[7] adjures them by the Lord[8] that his letter be read to the entire community; and so

[1] These vague terms seem to show that the ecclesiastical organisation of the Church was as yet very flexible.

[2] v. 15, contrast this with Soph. *Philoct.* 679.

[3] Not "every appearance of evil" (E.V.), grand as such an exhortation undoubtedly is. It may perhaps be "from every evil appearance," everything which has an ill look: possibly it refers to bad γένη of spiritual teaching.

[4] 1 Cor. xiv. 39.

[5] Vers. 16—21. What they needed was the διάκρισις πνευμάτων (1 Cor. xii. 10; Heb. v. 14), and to be δόκιμοι τραπεζῖται.

[6] v. 23, σῶμα, "body;" ψυχὴ, the entire human life and faculties; πνεῦμα, the divinely imbreathed spirit, the highest region of life. ὁλοτελεῖς, ὁλόκληροι (James i. 4). (Trench, *Synon*, p. 70.)

[7] The τοὺς ἀδελφοὺς πάντας must mean "one another," as in Rom. xvi. 16; 1 Cor. xvi. 20; 2 Cor. xiii. 12; 1 Pet. v. 14, unless these few concluding lines are addressed specially to the elders. On the "kiss of charity"—an Oriental custom—see Bingham, *Antiq.* iii. 3, 3; Hooker, *Pref.* iv. 4.

[8] The very strong adjuration may have been rendered necessary by some of the differences between the converts and the leading members of the community, at which the Apostle hints in v. 12—15. Some influential persons, to whom the letter was first handed, might be inclined to suppress any parts of it with which they disagreed, or which seemed to condemn their views or conduct. Timothy may have brought the news that

concludes with his usual ending, "The grace of our Lord Jesus Christ be with you. Amen."[1] These last three verses were probably written in his own hand.

It may easily be imagined with what rapture the arrival of such a letter would be hailed by a young, persecuted, and perplexed community; how many griefs it would console; how many doubts it would resolve; how much joy, and hope, and fresh enthusiasm it would inspire. It could not but have been delightful in any case to be comforted amid the storm of outward opposition, and to be inspirited amid the misgivings of inward faithlessness, by the words of the beloved teacher whose gospel had changed the whole current of their lives. It was much to feel that, though absent from them in person, he was present with them in heart,[2] praying for them, yearning over them, himself cheered by the tidings of their constancy; but it was even more to receive words which would tend to heal the incipient disagreements of that small and loving, but inexperienced, and as yet but half-organised community, and to hear the divinely authoritative teaching which silenced their worst fears. And further than this, if the words of St. Paul shine so brightly to us through the indurated dust of our long familiarity, how must they have sparkled for them in their fresh originality, and with heaven's own light shining on those oracular gems! "Having received the word *in much affliction with joy of the Holy Ghost*;"[3]—that was no mere artificial *oxymoron*, but an utterance which came from a new world, of which they were the happy lords. "Jesus which delivereth us from the coming wrath;"[4] "God who called you unto His kingdom and glory;"[5] "This is the will of God, even your sanctification;"[6] "So shall we ever be with the Lord;"[7] "Ye are all the children of the light and the children of the day;"[8] "See that none render evil for evil unto any;"[9] "Rejoice evermore."[10] What illimitable hopes, what holy obligations, what golden promises, what glorious responsibilities, what lofty ideals, what

some previous letter of the Apostle to this, or other churches, had not properly been made known. How easily such an interference was possible we see from 3 John 9, "I wrote to the Church, but Diotrephes, who loveth to have the pre-eminence among them, receiveth us not" (see Ewald, *Sendschr*, p. 51). Dionysius of Corinth deplores the falsification of his own letters (Euseb. *H. E.* iv. 23). St. Paul generally asked for a prayer himself towards the close of a letter (Eph. vi. 19; Col. iv. 3; 2 Thess. iii. 1).

[1] This γνώρισμα or badge of cognisance is found, with slight variations, at the close of all St. Paul's Epistles. Thus:—

(α) In 1 Thess. v. 28; 1 Cor. xvi. 23 we have, "The grace of our Lord Jesus Christ be with you," to which the word "all" is added in 2 Thess. iii. 18; Rom. xvi. 24; Phil. iv. 23.

(β) In Philem. 25; Gal. vi. 18 we have, "The grace of our Lord Jesus Christ be with your spirit" ("brethren," Gal.).

(γ) In Col. iv. 18; 1 Tim. vi. 21; 2 Tim. iv. 22 we have the shortest form, "Grace be with you" (thee), to which Titus iii. 15 adds "all."

(δ) In Eph. vi. 24 we have the variation, "Grace be with all them that love the Lord Jesus Christ in sincerity," and in 2 Cor. xiii. 14 alone the full "Apostolic benediction."

The *subscriptions* added to the Epistles at a much later period are mostly valueless (see Paley, *Horae Paulinae*, chap. xv.).

[2] 1 Thess. ii. 17.

[3] i. 6. [4] i. 10. [5] ii. 12. [6] iv. 3.

[7] iv. 17. [8] v. 5. [9] v. 15. [10] v. 16.

reaches of morality beyond any which their greatest writers had attained, what strange renovation of the whole spirit and meaning of life, lay hidden for them in those simple words![1] The brief Epistle brought home to them the glad truth that they could use, for their daily wear, that glory of thought which had only been attained by the fewest and greatest spirits of their nation at their rarest moments of inspiration; and therewith that grandeur of life which, in its perfect innocence towards God and man, was even to these unknown.

It is a remarkable fact that in this Epistle St. Paul alludes no less than four times to the coming of Christ,[2] and uses, to describe it, the word *parousia*—"presence"—which also occurs in this sense in the second Epistle,[3] but in only one other passage of all his other Epistles.[4] Whether, after the erroneous conclusions which the Thessalonians drew from this letter, and the injurious effects which this incessant prominence of eschatology produced in their characters, he subsequently made it a less salient feature of his own teaching, we cannot tell. Certain, however, it is that the misinterpretation of his first letter, and the reprehensible excitement and restlessness which that misinterpretation produced,[5] necessitated the writing of a second very shortly after he had received tidings of these results.[6] It is equally certain that, from this time forward, the visible personal return of Christ and the nearness of the end, which are the predominant topics in the First Epistle to the Thessalonians, sink into a far more subordinate topic of reference; and that, although St. Paul's language in the letter was misunderstood, yet the misunderstanding was not a wilful but a perfectly natural one; and that in his later letters he anticipates his own death, rather than the second Advent, as his mode of meeting Christ. The divine and steady light of history first made clear to the Church that our Lord's prophetic warnings as to His return applied primarily to the close of the Jewish dispensation, and the winding up of all the past, and the inauguration of the last great æon of God's dealings with mankind.

[1] Baur (*Paul.* ii.), Kern (*Tüb. Zeitschr.* 1839), Van der Vaier (*Die beiden Briefen aan de Thessal.*), De Wette (*Einleit.*), Volkmar, Zeller, &c., and the Tübingen school generally, except Hilgenfeld (*Die Thessalonicherbriefe*), reject both Epistles to the Thessalonians as ungenuine, and Baur calls the First Epistle a "mattes Nachwerk." I have carefully studied their arguments, but they seem to me so slight as to be scarcely deserving of serious refutation. The difficulties which would be created by rejecting these Epistles are ten times as formidable as any which they suggest. If an unbiassed scholar, familiar with the subject, cannot *feel* the heart of St. Paul throbbing through every sentence of these Epistles, it is hardly likely that argument will convince him. External evidence (Iren. *Haer.* v. 6, 1; Clem. Alex. *Paedag.* i., p. 109, ed. Potter; Tert. *De Resurrect. Carnis*, cap. 24), though sufficiently strong, is scarcely even required. Not only Bunsen, Ewald, &c., but even Hilgenfeld (*l.c.*), Holtzmann (Thessalon. in Schenkel, *Bibel-lexikon*), Pfleiderer (*Paulinism.* 29), Hausrath, Weisse, Schmidt, &c., accept the first.

[2] ii. 19; iii. 13; iv. 15; v. 23. [3] 2 Thess. ii. 1, 8. [4] 1 Cor. xv. 23.

[5] We find in St. Paul's own words abundant proof that his teaching was distorted and slandered, and St. Peter gives us direct positive assurance that such was the case (2 Pet. iii. 16).

[6] Tradition should have some weight, and πρὸς Θεσσαλονικεῖς β΄ is the reading of A, B, D, E, F, G. The internal evidences also, to some of which I have called attention, seem to me decisive.

CHAPTER XXX.

THE SECOND EPISTLE TO THE THESSALONIANS.

Δεῖ γὰρ ταῦτα γενέσθαι πρῶτον, ἀλλ' οὐκ εὐθέως τὸ τέλος.—LUKE xxi. 9.

MANY months could not have elapsed before the Apostle heard that the Thessalonians, with all their merits and virtues, were still, and even more than previously, hindered in moral growth by eschatological enthusiasms. When he wrote to them before, they were tempted to despond about the death of friends, whom they supposed likely to be thus deprived of part at least of the precious hopes which were their main, almost their sole, support in the fiery furnace of affliction. The Apostle's clear assurance seems to have removed all anxiety on this topic, but now they regarded the immediate coming of Christ as a thing so certain that some of them were tempted to neglect his exhortations, and to spend their lives in aimless religious excitement.[1] St. Paul felt how fatal would be such a temperament to all Christian progress, and the main object of his second letter was to control into calm, and shame into diligence, the gossiping enthusiasm which fatally tended towards irregularity and sloth. They were not to desert the hard road of the present for the mirage which seemed to bring so close to them the green Edens of the future; they were not to sacrifice the sacredness of immediate duty for the dreamy sweetness of unrealised expectations. The Advent of Christ might be near at hand; but it was not so instant as they had been led to imagine from an erroneous view of what he had said, and by mistaken reports—possibly even by written forgeries—which ascribed to him words which he had never used, and opinions which he had never held.

The expression on which the Apocalyptic fanaticism of the less sensible Thessalonians seems to have fastened was that which occurs in 1 Thess. iv. 15—"WE, which are alive and remain to the presence of the Lord, shall certainly not anticipate those that have fallen asleep." It was not unnatural that they should interpret this to mean that their teacher himself expected to survive until the Epiphany of their Lord's presence.[2] If so, it must be very close at hand; and again, if so, of what use were the petty details of daily routine, the petty energies of daily effort? Was it not enough to keep themselves alive *anyhow* until the dawn of that near day, or the shadows of that rapidly approaching night, which might be any day or any night, on which all earthly interests should be dissipated for ever as soon as the voice of God and the trumpet of the dead should sound?

Now, we ask, had this been the real meaning of the words of St. Paul?

[1] The reader will be struck with the close analogy of this temptation to that which did so much mischief among the Anabaptists and other sects in the days of the Reformation. The Thessalonian Church may have had its Carlstadts whom St. Paul felt it necessary to warn, just as Luther fought, with all the force of his manly sense, against the crudities of the religious errors which had derived their impulse from a perversion of his own teaching.

[2] Ἐπιφάνεια τῆς παρουσίας.

The question has been voluminously and angrily debated. It has been made, in fact (and very needlessly), the battle-ground as to the question of verbal inspiration. Some have tried to maintain the desperate and scarcely honest position that neither St. Paul nor the Apostles generally had any expectation of the near visible advent of Christ; others that they were absolutely convinced that it would take place in their own generation, and even in their own lifetime.

Not in the interests of controversy, but in those of truth, I will endeavour to prove that neither of these extreme theses can be maintained. If the view of the Thessalonians had been *absolutely* groundless, it would have been easy for St. Paul to say to them, as modern commentators have said for him, "You mistook my general expression for a specific and individual one. When I said '*we* which are alive and remain' at the presence of Christ, I did not mean either myself, or you, in particular, but merely 'the living'—the class to which we at present belong—as opposed to the dead, about whose case I was speaking to you.[1] You are mistaken in supposing that I meant to imply a conviction that before my own death the Lord would reappear." Now, he does not say this at all;[2] he only tells them not to be drifted from their moorings, not, as he expresses it, to be tossed from their sound sense[3] by the supposition that he had spoken of the actual instancy[4] of the day of the Lord. He tells them plainly that certain events must occur before that day came; and these as certainly are events which precluded all possibility of the Second Advent taking place for them to-morrow or the next day. But, on the other hand, he does *not* tell them that the day of the Lord was not *near* (ἐγγύς). If he had done so he would have robbed of their meaning the exhortations which had formed the staple of his preaching at Thessalonica, as they constituted the only prominent doctrinal statement of his First Epistle.[5] If we are to judge of St. Paul's views by his own language, and not by the preconceptions of scholasticism, we can divine what would have been his answer to the plain question, "Do you personally expect to live till the return of Christ?" At *this* period of his life his answer would have been, "I cannot speak positively on the matter. I see clearly that, before His return, certain things must take place; but, on the whole, I do expect it." But at a later period of his life he would have said in substance, "It may be so; I cannot tell. On the whole, however, I no longer hope to survive till that day; nor does it seem to me of any importance whether I do or not. At that day the quick will have no advantage over the dead. What I now look forward to, what I sometimes even yearn for, is my own death. I know that when I die I shall be with Christ,

[1] 1 Thess. iv. 15. ἡμεῖς . . . οὐ περὶ ἑαυτοῦ φησίν—ἀλλὰ τοὺς πιστοὺς λέγει (Chrys.).

[2] It is never his method to explain away his views because they have been perverted, but merely to bring them out in their full and proper meaning.

[3] μὴ ταχέως σαλευθῆναι ἀπὸ τοῦ νοὸς (2 Thess. ii. 2).

[4] ἐνέστηκεν.

[5] As Baur rightly observes (*Paulus*, ii. 94): but to assume that therefore the Epistle cannot be St. Paul's is to the last degree uncritical. Moreover, though there are no other "dogmatic ideas" brought forward with very special prominence, there are "dogmatic ideas" *assumed* in every line.

and it is for that pathway into His presence that I am now watching. In the earlier years of my conversion we all anticipated a speedier development of Antichrist, a speedier removal of the restraining power, a speedier brightening of the clouds about the flaming feet of our Saviour. That for which I now look is far more the spiritual union with my Lord than His visible manifestation. It may be, too, that He cometh in many ways. If we ever mistook the nearer for the farther horizons of His prophecy, it is but a part of that ignorance which, as He Himself warned us, should, as regards the details of this subject, be absolute and final. For said He not when He was yet with us, '*Of that day and that hour knoweth no man; no, not the angels which are in heaven, neither the Son, but the Father*'? But whether He come so soon as we have expected, or not, yet in one form or another assuredly now and ever 'the Lord is at hand;' and the lesson of His coming is that which He also taught us, and which we have taught from Him—'Take ye heed, watch and pray, for *ye know not when* the time is.'"

That these were the views of St. Paul and of other Apostles on "the crises and the periods" respecting which, if they ventured to hold any definite opinion at all, they could not but, according to their Lord's own warning, be liable to be mistaken, will, I think, be evident to all who will candidly weigh and compare with themselves the passages to which I here refer.[1]

Now so far as the fall of Jerusalem and the passing of doom upon the Jewish race was "a day of the Lord," so far even the most literal acceptation of their words is in close accordance with the actual results. Nor should this remarkable coincidence be overlooked. On December 19th, A.D. 69, the Capitoline Temple was burnt down in the war between Vitellius and Vespasian, which Tacitus calls the saddest and most shameful blow, and a sign of the anger of the gods. On August 10, A.D. 70, a Roman soldier flung a brand within the Temple of Jerusalem. "Thus," says Döllinger,[2] "within a few months the national sanctuary of Rome and the Temple of God, the two most important places of worship in the old world, owed their destruction to Roman soldiers—thoughtless instruments of the decrees and judgment of a higher power. Ground was to be cleared for the worship of God in spirit and in truth. The heirs of the two temples, the Capitoline and the Jewish—a handful of artisans, beggars, slaves, and women—were dwelling at the time in some of the obscure lanes and alleys of Rome; and only two years before,

[1] Allusions to a near Advent, 1 Thess. i. 9, 10, "ye turned to God . . . . to wait for His Son from heaven;" 1 Cor. i. 7, "To wait for the coming of the Lord Jesus" (cf. 2 Thess. iii. 5); 1 Cor. xv. 51, "We shall not all sleep, but we shall all be changed" (cf. 1 Thess. iv. 15—17); James v. 8, 9, "The coming of the Lord draweth nigh . . . The judge standeth before the door;" 1 Pet. iv. 7, "The end of all things is at hand;" 1 John ii. 18, "Even now are there many antichrists, whereby we know that it is the last time;" Rev. xxii. 20, "Surely I come quickly." On the sayings of our Lord, on which the expectation was perhaps founded (Matt. xxiv. 29, 30, 34), see my *Life of Christ*, ii. 257, *sq.* On the other hand, if St. Paul contemplated the possibility of being alive at the Day of the Lord, he also was aware that though *near*, it would not be *immediate* (2 Cor. iv. 14; 2 Thess. ii.; Rom. xi. 24—27), and at a later period looked forward to his own death (Phil. i. 20—23).

[2] *Judenth. u. Heidenth.* ix. *ad. f.*

when they had first drawn public attention to themselves, a number of them were sentenced to be burnt alive in the imperial gardens, and others to be torn in pieces by wild beasts."

We may, then, say briefly that the object of the Second Epistle to the Thessalonians was partly to assure them that, though St. Paul believed the day of the Lord to be near—though he did not at all exclude the possibility of their living to witness it—yet it was not so instantaneous as in the least to justify a disruption of the ordinary duties of life.[1] He had as little meant positively to assert that he would survive to the Advent when he said "*we* that are alive," than he meant positively to assert that he should die before it occurred, when, years afterwards, he wrote, "He which raised up the Lord Jesus shall raise up *us* also by Jesus."[2] That the "we" in these instances was generic is obvious from the fact that he uses it of the dead and of the living in the same Epistle, saying in one place, "*We* shall not all sleep,"[3] and in another, "God will also raise up *us* by His own power."[4]

On the nearness of the final Messianic Advent, the Jewish and the Christian world were at one; and even the Heathen were in a state of restless anticipation. The trials of the Apostle had naturally led him to dwell on this topic both in his preaching at Thessalonica, and in his earlier Epistle. His Second Epistle follows the general outlines of the First, which indeed formed a model for all the others. Nothing is more remarkable than the way in which the Epistles combine a singular uniformity of method with a rich exuberance of detail.[5] In this respect they are the reflex of a life infinitely varied in its adventures, yet swayed by one simple and supremely dominant idea. Except when special circumstances, as in the Epistles to the Corinthians, modify his ordinary plan, his letters consist, as a rule, of six parts, viz.:—i. a solemn salutation; ii. an expression of thankfulness to God for His work among those to whom he is writing; iii. a section devoted to religious doctrine; iv. a section

[1] The dread of some imminent world-catastrophe, preluded by prodigies, was at this time universal (Tac. *Ann.* vi. 28; xii. 43, 64; xiv. 12, 22; xv. 22; *Hist.* i. 3; Suet. *Nero*, 36, 39; Dion Cass. lx. 35; lxi. 16—18, &c.). Hausrath, *N. Zeitgesch.* ii. 108. Renan *L'Antechrist*, p. 35: "On ne parlait que de prodiges et de malheurs."

[2] 2 Cor. iv. 14.

[3] 1 Cor. xv. 51, on the reading, *v. infra*, p. 399.

[4] 1 Cor. vi. 14. Here, as in so many cases, a passage of the Talmud throws most valuable light on the opinions of St. Paul, which, on such a subject—where all special illumination was deliberately withdrawn—were inevitably coloured by the tone of opinion prevalent in his own nation:—"'When will Messiah come?' asked R. Joshua Ben Laive of Elijah the Tishbite. 'Go and ask Himself.' 'Where is He?' 'At the gateway of Rome.' 'How shall I know Him?' 'He sits among the diseased poor.' (Rashi quotes Isa. liii. 5.) 'All the others change the bandages of their sores simultaneously, but He changes them successively, lest, if called, His coming should be delayed.' R. Joshua Ben Laive went to Him, and saluted Him with the words 'Peace be to thee, my Rabbi, my teacher.' 'Peace be unto thee, Son of Laive,' was the answer of Messiah. 'When will the Master come?' asked the Rabbi. 'TO-DAY,' was the answer. By the time the Rabbi had finished telling the story to Elijah, the sun had set. 'How?' said the Rabbi; 'He has not come! Has He lied unto me?' 'No,' said Elijah, '*He meant* "TO-DAY, IF YE WILL HEAR HIS VOICE"' (Ps. xcv. 7)." (*Sanhedrin*, f. 98, 1.) This involves the same truth as the famous remark of St. Augustine, "Ergo latet ultimus dies, ut observentur omnes dies," which was also said by R. Eliezer.

[5] See Reuss, *Théol. Chrét.* ii. 11.

devoted to practical exhortation; v. a section composed of personal details and greetings; and, vi. the final autograph benediction which served to mark the authenticity of the Epistle. We have already noticed that this is the general structure of the First Epistle, and it will be observed no less in the subjoined outline of the Second.[1]

After the greeting, in which, as in the last Epistle, he associates Silas and Timothy with himself,[2] he thanks God once more for the exceeding increase[3] of their faith, and the abounding love which united them with one another, which enabled him as well as others[4] to hold them up in the Churches of God[5] as a model of faith and patience, and that, too, under special tribulations. Those tribulations, he tells them, are an evidence that the present state of things cannot be final; that a time is coming when their persecutors will be punished, and themselves have relaxation from endurance[6]—which time will be at the Epiphany, in Sinaitic splendour,[7] of the Lord Jesus with His mighty angels, to inflict retribution on the Gentile ignorance which will not know God, and the disobedient obstinacy which rejects the Gospel. That retribution shall be eternal cutting off from the presence and glorious power of Christ[8] when He shall come to be glorified in His saints and to be wondered

[1] i. The greeting, 2 Thess. i. 1, 2. ii. The thanksgiving, or Eucharistic section, mingled with topics of consolation derived from the coming of Christ, i. 3—12. iii. The dogmatic portion, which, in this instance, is the remarkable and indeed unique section about the Man of Sin, ii. 1—12; the thanksgiving renewed with exhortations and ending in a prayer, ii. 13—17. iv. The practical part, consisting of a request for their prayers (iii. 1—5). v. Exhortations, and messages, also ended by a prayer, iii. 6—16. vi. The autograph conclusion and benediction, iii. 17, 18. These divisions, however, are not rigid and formal; one section flows naturally into another, with no marked separation. Each of the prayers (ii. 16; iii. 16) begins with the same words, Αὐτὸς δὲ ὁ Κύριος.

[2] This accurately marks the date of the letter, as having been written at Corinth shortly after the former. Silas ceases to be a fellow-worker with Paul, and apparently joins Peter, after the visit to Jerusalem at the close of the two years' sojourn at Corinth. It is probable that the mental and religious affinities of Silas were more closely in accordance with the old Apostles who had sent him to Antioch than with St. Paul.

[3] ὑπεραυξάνει. It is a part of St. Paul's emphatic style that he delights in compounds of ὑπὲρ, as ὑπεροχή, ὑπερλίαν, ὑπερβάλλω, ὑπερεκπερισσοῦ, &c.

[4] 2 Thess. i. 4, ἡμᾶς αὐτούς.

[5] This is a strong argument against Ewald's view that the Epistle was written from Berœa; but it does not prove, as Chrysostom says, that a considerable time must have elapsed. Writing from Corinth, there were Churches both in Macedonia and Achaia to which St. Paul alludes. There can be little doubt that the Epistle was written late in A.D. 53 or early in A.D. 54.

[6] ἄνεσιν.

[7] Ex. iii. 2; xix. 18; xxiv. 17; 2 Chr. vii. 1, &c. ℵ, A, K, L, have πυρὶ φλογός. The comma should be after *fire*, not, as in E.V., after "angels."

[8] i. 9. It is clear that ἀπὸ here means "separation from," *not* "immediately after," or "by." This is the only passage in all St. Paul's Epistles where his eschatology even seems to touch on the future of the impenitent. When Chrysostom triumphantly asks, "Where, then, are the Origenists? He calls the destruction αἰώνιον;" his own remarks in other places show that he could hardly have been unaware that this rhetoric of "œconomy" might sound convincing to the ignorant and the superficial, but had no bearing whatever on the serious views of Origen. Observe, i. διδόναι ἐκδίκησιν (cf. 2 Sam. xxii. 48, LXX.) does not mean "take vengeance." ii. The fire is not penal fire, but is the Shechinah-glory of Advent (Dan. vii. 9; Ex. iii. 2). iii. Those spoken of are not sinners in general, but wilful enemies and persecutors. iv. The retribution is not "destruction," but "destruction-from-the-Presence of the Lord," *i.e.*, a cutting off from

at in all that believed in Him.[1] And that they may attain to this glory, he prayed that God may count them worthy of their calling, and bring to fulfilment the goodness in which they delight,[2] and the activity of their faith, both to the glory of their Lord and to their own glory, as granted by His grace.[3]

Then follows the most remarkable section of the letter, and the one for the sake of which it was evidently written. He had, in his first letter, urged them to calmness and diligence, but the eagerness of expectation, unwittingly increased by his own words, had prevailed over his exhortations, and it was now his wish to give them further and more definite instruction on this great subject. This was rendered more necessary by the fact that their hopes had been fanned into vivid glow, partly by prophecies which claimed to be inspired, and partly by words or letters which professed to be stamped with his authority. He writes, therefore, in language of which I have attempted to preserve something of the obvious mystery and reticence.[4]

"Now we beseech you, brethren, touching[5] the presence of our Lord Jesus Christ and our gathering[6] to meet Him, that ye be not quickly tossed from your state of mind,[7] nor even be troubled either by spirit,[8] or by word, or by letter purporting to come from us,[9] as though the day of the Lord is here.[10] Let no one deceive you in *any* way, because[11]—unless the apostasy[12] come first, and the man of sin

Beatific Vision. v. The "æonian exclusion" of this passage takes place at Christ's First Advent, not at the final Judgment Day.

[1] They will inspire wonder, because they will in that day reflect His brightness.

[2] i. 11, πληρώσῃ εὐδοκίαν ἀγαθωσύνης. Not as in E.V., "fulfil all the good pleasure of *his* goodness," but "honestatis dulcedinem"—*i.e.*, "honestatem, quâ recreemini." Εὐδοκία, indeed, is often referred to God (Eph. i. 5, 9, &c.); but ἀγαθωσύνη, used four times in St. Paul, is "moral and human goodness," the classic χρηστότης. It is borrowed from the LXX. (See Eccl. ix. 18.)

[3] 2 Thess. i. 3—12.

[4] Neither this nor any other passage which I translate apart from the E.V. is intended as a specimen of desirable translation. I merely try to translate in such terms as shall most easily explain themselves to the modern reader, while they reproduce as closely as possible the *form* of the original.

[5] ὑπέρ, not an adjuration in the New Testament, yet a little stronger than περί.

[6] An obvious allusion to 1 Thess. iv. 17. The substantive ἐπισυναγωγή only occurs in Heb. x. 25, but the verb in Matt. xxiii. 37; xxiv. 31, "as a hen gathereth her chickens under her wings" (cf. John xi. 52).

[7] "Fro youre witte" (Wicl.); "from your sense" (Rhemish version).

[8] *i.e.*, by utterance professing to be inspired. The "discerning of spirits," or testing of what utterances were, and what were not, inspired, was one of the most important χαρίσματα in the early Church.

[9] The commentators from Chrysostom and Theodoret downwards are almost unanimous in taking this to mean that a letter on these subjects had been forged in St. Paul's name, and had increased the excitement of the Thessalonians. It seems to me that the requirements of the expression are fulfilled if we make the surely more probable supposition that some letter had been circulated among them—perhaps anonymous, perhaps with perfectly honest intentions—which professed to report his exact opinions, while in reality it misunderstood them.

[10] This, rather than "is immediately imminent," seems to be the meaning of ἐνέστηκεν (Rom. viii. 38; Gal. i. 4, &c.). τινὲς γὰρ προφητείαν ὑποκρινόμενοι ἐπλάνων τὸν λαὸν ὡς ἤδη παρόντος τοῦ Κυρίου (Theod.). At any rate, the word implies the closest possible proximity. τὰ ἐνεστῶτα means "things present." (See Rom. viii. 38; 1 Cor. iii. 22).

[11] He purposely suppresses the discouraging words "The Lord will not come."

[12] Certainly not "the revolt of the Jews."

be revealed,[1] the son of destruction,[2] who opposeth,[3] and exalteth himself above and against every one who is called God,[4] or is an object of worship, so that he enters and seats himself in the shrine of God,[5] displaying himself that he is God. Do you not recall that, while I was still with you, I used to tell you this? And now the restraining power—you know what it is—which prevents his appearing—that he may appear in his own due time [and not before]. For the mystery of the lawlessness is already working, only he who restrains now—until he be got out of the way.[6] And then shall be revealed the lawless one, whom the Lord Jesus shall destroy with the breath of His mouth, and shall annihilate with the Epiphany of His presence;[7] whose presence is in accordance with the energy of Satan in all power, and signs, and prodigies of falsehood, and in all deceitfulness of iniquity for the ruin of those who are perishing,[8] because they received not the love of the truth that they might be saved. And, because of this, God is sending[9] them an energy of error, so that they should believe the lie[10] that all may be judged who believed not the truth, but took pleasure in unrighteousness.[11]

Of this strange but unquestionably genuine passage, which is nevertheless so unlike anything else in St. Paul's Epistles, I shall speak immediately. He proceeds to tell them that *their* case, thank God, was very different from that of these doomed dupes of Antichrist, seeing that God had chosen and called them from the beginning[12] to sanctification and salvation and glory.[13] He exhorts them therefore, to stand fast, and hold the teaching which they had received from his words and his genuine letter, and prays that our Lord Jesus Christ and God our Father may comfort them and stablish them in all goodness.[14]

[1] The apocalypse of the Antichrist.

[2] Whose end is destruction (Phil. iii. 19; John xvii. 12).

[3] A human Satan or adversary (Renan, p. 255).

[4] ὑπεραιρόμενος . . . ἐπί, perhaps "*exceedingly* exalteth himself against." Dan. xi. 36, speaking of Antiochus Epiphanes.

[5] καθίσαι . . . εἰς. A *constructio praegnans*. (See my *Brief Greek Syntax*, § 89). Omit ὡς θεόν, ℵ, A, B, D, &c. ναὸν stronger than ἱερόν, and could only be naturally understood of the Jewish Temple.

[6] "Tantum qui nunc tenet (teneat) donec de medio fiat" (Tert. *De Resur. Carn.* 25). I have attempted to preserve the unfinished clauses (*anakolutha*) of the original, which are full of meaning. The ὁ κατέχων may, however, be merely misplaced by hyperbaton.

[7] Isa. xi. 4; Wisd. xi. 20, 21. A rabbinic expression. "Prima adventus ipsius emicatio" (Bengel).

[8] I so render τοῖς ἀπολλυμένοις because it is the dative of "disadvantage." The ἐν is probably spurious, being omitted in ℵ, A, B, D, F, G.

[9] *Leg.* πέμπει, ℵ, A, B, D, F, G. The "strong delusion" of the E.V. is a happy expression; it is penal blindness, judicial infatuation, the dementation before doom.

[10] 1 Tim. iv. 1, 2.

[11] 2 Thess. ii. 1—12. In the E.V. there are the following five or six obvious errors, which I have corrected:—Ver. 1, ὑπὲρ τῆς παρουσίας, "by the coming;" ver. 2, ἀπὸ τοῦ νοὸς, "in mind;" ἐνέστηκε, "is at hand" (which is not strong enough, and contradicts "Maranatha," ὁ κύριος ἐγγὺς); ver. 3, ἡ ἀποστασία, "*a* falling away;" ver. 4, ἐπὶ πάντα, κ. τ. λ., "*above* all, &c.," instead of "against every one," though this is perhaps defensible—ὡς Θεὸν, "as God," is probably spurious, not being found in ℵ, A, B, D; ver. 5, ἔλεγον, "I told;" ver. 11, τῷ ψεύδει, "*a* lie;" ver. 12, κριθῶσι, "be damned." There are also minor inaccuracies. But while calling attention to these, let me not be supposed to speak with any feeling but admiration and gratitude of our English version. It needs the revision which it is receiving, but it is magnificent with all its defects; and while those defects are far fewer than might have been reasonably expected, there is incomparable merit in its incessant felicity and noble rhythm.

[12] ἀπ' ἀρχῆς (Eph. i. 4). B, F, G have ἀπαρχήν, "as a firstfruit;" but this was not a fact (Acts. xvi.).

[13] εἰς περιποίησιν δόξης, "to the obtaining of glory;" cf. 1 Thess. v. 9; Heb. x. 39.

[14] 2 Thess. ii. 13—17.

Beginning the practical section of the Epistle, he asks their prayers that the Gospel may have free course among others as among them, and that he may be delivered from perverse and wicked men;[1] and expressing his trust in God, and his confidence in them, prays that the Lord may guide their hearts into the love of God and the patience of Christ.[2] That patience was lacking to some of them who, he had been told, were walking disorderly, not following the precepts he had given, or the example he had set. The rule he had given was that a man who would not work had no right to eat, and the example he had set, as they well knew, had been one of order, manly self-dependence, strenuous diligence, in that he had voluntarily abandoned even the plain right of maintenance at their hands.[3]

He therefore commands and exhorts[4] in the name of Christ those who were irregular, and whose sole business was to be busybodies,[5] to be quiet and diligent, and earn their own living; and if, after the receipt of this letter, any one refused obedience to his advice, they were to mark that man by avoiding his company that he might be ashamed; not, however, considering him as an enemy, but admonishing him as a brother. As for the rest, let them not be weary in fair-doing;[6] and he again concludes with a prayer that the Lord of Peace Himself may give them peace perpetually, and in every way. The Lord be with them all![7]

And having dictated so far—probably to his faithful Timothy—the Apostle himself takes the pen, for the use of which his weak sight so little fitted him, and bending over the papyrus, writes:—

"The salutation of me Paul with my own hand, which autograph salutation is the proof of genuineness in every Epistle.[8] This is how I write. The Grace of our Lord Jesus Christ be with you all."[9]

[1] An allusion to his struggles with the Jews at Corinth. "Synagogas Judaeorum fontes persecutionum" (Tert. *Scorp.* 10). ἄτοπος only in Luke xxiii. 41, and Acts. xxviii. 6.

[2] *i.e.*, a patience like His patience. The "patient *waiting for* Christ," of the E.V., though partially sanctioned by Chrysostom and Theophylact, can hardly be tenable, and they prefer the meaning here given.

[3] iii. 1—11.

[4] These injunctions are more emphatic, authoritative, and precise than those of the First Epistle; another sign that this followed it. παραγγέλλω, so much stronger than ἐρωτῶ, occurs four times in this Epistle (iii. 4, 6, 10, 12), and only elsewhere, of his Epistles, in 1 Thess. iv. 11; 1 Tim. vi. 13; 1 Cor. vii. 10; xi. 17.

[5] 2 Thess. iii. 11, οὐκ ἐργαζομένους ἀλλὰ περιεργαζομένους (see *infra*, p. 695, "The Rhetoric of St. Paul").

[6] Καλοποιοῦντες, "beautiful conduct;" not exactly ἀγαθοπ., "well-doing" (cf. 2 Cor. viii. 21).

[7] iii. 12—16.

[8] iii. 17, 18. This emphatic autograph signature, not necessary in the first letter, had been rendered necessary since that letter was written by the credence given to the unauthorised communication alluded to in ii. 2. The "*every* Epistle" shows that St. Paul meant henceforth to write to Churches not unfrequently. Of course, Epistles sent by accredited messengers (*e.g.*, 2 Cor. and Phil.) would not need authentication. The ordinary conclusion of letters was ἔρρωσθε, "farewell." On this authenticating signature see Cic. *ad Att.* viii. 1; Suet. *Tib.* 21, 32.

[9] The "all" is only found in 2 Cor., Rom., and Tit. (cf. Eph. vi. 24 and Heb. xiii. 25), but was peculiarly impressive here, because his last words have been mainly those of censure.

Valuable to us, and to all time, as are the practical exhortations of this brief Epistle, the distinctive cause for its being written was the desire to dispel delusions about the instantaneous appearance of Christ, which prevented the weak and excitable from a due performance of their duties, and so tended to diminish that respect for them among the heathen which the blamelessness of the early Christians was well calculated to inspire. To the Thessalonians the paragraph on this subject would have had the profoundest interest. To us it is less immediately profitable, because no one has yet discovered, or ever will discover, what was St. Paul's precise meaning; or, in other words, because neither in his time, nor since, have any events as yet occurred which Christians have unanimously been able to regard as fulfilling the conditions which he lays down. We need not, however, be distressed if this passage must be ranked with the very few others in the New Testament which must remain to us in the condition of insoluble enigmas. It was most important for the Thessalonians to know that they did not need to get up every morning with the awe-inspiring expectation that the sun might be darkened before it set, and the air shattered by the archangelic trumpet, and all earthly interests smitten into indistinguishable ruin. So far St. Paul's assurance was perfectly distinct. Nor, indeed, is there any want of clearness in his language. The difficulties of the passage arise exclusively from our inability to explain it by subsequent events. But these one or two obscure passages in no wise affect the value of St. Paul's writings.[1] Since his one object is always edification, we may be sure that subjects which are with him purely incidental, which are obscurely hinted at, or only partially worked out, and to which he scarcely ever afterwards recurs, are non-essential parts of the central truths, to the dissemination of which he devoted his life. To the Messianic surroundings of a Second personal Advent he barely again alludes. He dwells more and more on the mystic oneness with Christ, less and less on His personal return. He speaks repeatedly of the indwelling presence of Christ, and the believer's incorporation with Him, and hardly at all of that visible meeting in the air which at this epoch was most prominent in his thoughts.[2]

We may assume it as a canon of ordinary criticism that a writer intends to be understood,[3] and, as a rule, so writes as to be actually understood by those whom he addresses. We have no difficulty in seeing that what St. Paul here says to the Thessalonians is that Christ's return, however near, was not so instantaneous as they thought, because, before it could occur, there must come "the apostasy," which will find its personal and final development in the apocalypse of "the man of sin"—a human Satan who thrust himself into the temple of God and into rivalry with Him. Then, with an air of mystery and secrecy which reminds us of the Book of Daniel and the Revelation of St.

[1] See Reuss, *Théol. Chrét.* ii., p. 10.

[2] 1 Cor. viii. 6; Gal. iii. 28; Eph. iv. 6, &c.

[3] "No man writes unintelligibly on purpose" (Paley, *Hor. Paulinae*). He acutely points out how the very obscurity of this passage furnishes one strong argument for the genuineness of the Epistle, which I note by way of curiosity that Hilgenfeld regards as "a little Pauline Apocalypse of the last year of Trajan" (*Einleit.* 642).

John,[1] and with a certain involved embarrassment of language, he reminds them of his repeated oral teachings about something, and some person,[2] whose power must first be removed before this mystery of iniquity could achieve its personal and final development. They knew, he says, what was "the check" to the full development of this opposing iniquity, which was already working, and would work, until the removal of "the checker." After that removal, with power and lying portents winning the adherence of those who were doomed to penal delusion, the Lawless One should be manifested in a power which the breath and brightness of Christ's Presence should utterly annihilate. Between the saved, therefore, and the Second Advent there lay two events—"the removal of the restrainer," and the appearance of the Lawless One. The destruction of the latter would be simultaneous with the event which they had so often been bidden to await with longing expectation.

This is what St. Paul plainly says; but how is it to be explained? and why is it so enigmatically expressed?

The second question is easily answered. It is enigmatically expressed for two reasons—first, because all that is enigmatical in it for us had been orally explained to the Thessalonians, who would therefore clearly understand it; and secondly, because there was some obvious danger in committing it to writing. This is in itself a sufficient proof that he is referring to the Roman Empire and Emperor. The tone of St. Paul is exactly the same as that of Josephus, when he explains the prophecy of Daniel. All Jews regarded the Fourth Empire as the Roman; but when Josephus comes to the stone which is to dash the image to pieces, he stops short, and says that "he does not think proper to explain it,"[3]—for the obvious reason that it would have been politically dangerous for him to do so.

Now this reason for reticence at once does away with the conjecture that "the check," or "the checker," was some distant power or person which did not for centuries come on the horizon, even if we could otherwise adopt the notion that St. Paul was uttering some far-off vaticination of events which, though they might find their fulfilment in distant centuries, could have no meaning for the Thessalonians to whom he wrote. When a few Roman Catholic commentators say that the Reformation was the Apostasy, and Luther the Man of Sin, and the German Empire "the check;" or when a mass of Protestant writers unhesitatingly identify the Pope with the Man of Sin—one can only ask whether, apart from traditional exegesis, they have really brought themselves to hold such a view? If, as we have seen, St. Paul undoubtedly held that the day of the Lord was *at hand*, though not

[1] These secrets and dim allusions (cf. Dan. xii. 10) current among the early Christians (like the greeting and symbol ἰχθύς), and the riddles of the number of the beast (666 = נרון קסר, Nero Cæsar: cf. Jos. *B. J.* vi. 5, §1; Suet. *Ner.* 40, *Vesp.* 4; Tac. *H.* v. 13) in Rev. xiii. 18, and in the Sibylline books, were necessitated by the dangers which surrounded them on every side. The years which elapsed between the Epistle and the Apocalypse had made the views of the Christians as to Antichrist much more definite (Renan, *L'Antechrist*, p. 157, &c.).

[2] 2 Thess. ii. 6, 7, ὁ κατέχων—τὸ κατέχον.

[3] See the instructive passage, Jos. *Antt.* x. 10, § 4.

immediate, do they really suppose, on the one hand, that St. Paul had any conception of Luther? or, on the other, that the main development of lawlessness, the main human representative of the power of Satan, is the succession of the Popes? Can any sane man of competent education seriously argue that it is the Papacy which pre-eminently arrays itself in *superiority to, and antagonism against,* every one who is called God, or every object of worship?[1] that its essential characteristic marks are lawlessness, lying wonders, and blasphemous self-exaltation? or that the annihilation of the Papacy —which has long been so physically and politically weak—"by the breath of His mouth and the brightness of His coming," is to be one main result of Christ's return? Again, do they suppose that St. Paul had, during his first visit, *repeatedly revealed* anything analogous to the development of the Papacy—an event which, in their sense of the word, can only be regarded as having taken place many centuries afterwards—to the Thessalonians who believed that the coming of Christ might take place on any day, and who required two epistles to undeceive them in the notion? If these suppositions do not sink under the weight of their own *intrinsic* unreasonableness, let them in the name of calm sense and Christian charity be consigned henceforth to the vast limbo of hypotheses which time, by accumulated proofs, has shown to be utterly untenable.[2]

To that vast limbo of exploded exegesis—the vastest and the dreariest that human imagination has conceived—I have no intention of adding a fresh conjecture. That "the check" was the Roman Empire, and "the checker" the Roman Emperor, may be regarded as reasonably certain; beyond this, all is uncertain conjecture. In the Excursus I shall merely mention, in the briefest possible manner, as altogether doubtful, and most of them as utterly valueless, the attempts hitherto made to furnish a definite explanation of the expressions used; and shall then content myself with pointing out, no less briefly, the

[1] St. Paul's "Lawless One," and "Man of Sin," who is to be destroyed by the advent of Christ must have some chronological analogy to St. John's Antichrist. Now St. John's Antichrist in the Epistles is mainly Gnostic heresy ("omnis haereticus Antichristus"—Luther), and the denial that Jesus Christ is come in the flesh (1 John iv. 3). In the Apocalypse it is Nero. In the Old Testament Antichrist is Antiochus Epiphanes. What has this to do either with the Papacy or with the Reformation?

[2] If it be urged that this was the view of Jewell and Hooker, Andrewes and Sanderson, &c., the answer is that the knowledge of the Church is not stationary or stereotyped. The Spirit of God is with her, and is ever leading her to wider and fuller knowledge of the truth. Had those great men been living now, they too would have enlarged many of their views in accordance with the advance now made in the interpretation of the Scripture. Few can have less sympathy than I have with the distinctive specialities of the Church of Rome; but in spite of what we hold to be her many and most serious errors she is, by the free acknowledgment of our own formularies, a Church, and a Christian Church, and has been pre-eminently a mother of saints, and many of her Popes have been good, and noble, and holy men, and vast benefactors of the world, and splendid maintainers of the Faith of Christ; and I refuse to regard them as "sons of perdition," or representatives of blasphemy and lawlessness, or to consider the destruction of their line with everlasting destruction from the presence of the Lord as the one thing to be looked forward to with joy at the coming of Him who we believe will welcome many of them, and myriads of those who accept their rule, into the blessed company of His redeemed.

regions in which we must look for illustrations to threw such light as is possible on the meaning of St. Paul.[1] As to the precise details, considering the utter want of unanimity among Christian interpreters, I am content to say, with St. Augustine, "I confess that I am entirely ignorant what the Apostle meant."

Book IX.

EPHESUS.

CHAPTER XXXI.

PAUL AT EPHESUS.

"They say this town is full of cozenage;
As, nimbling jugglers that deceive the eye,
Disguised cheaters, prating mountebanks,
And many such-like liberties of sin."

SHAKSP. *Comedy of Errors.*

"Diana Ephesia; cujus nomen unicum . . . . totus veneratur orbis."

APPUL. *Metam.*

THE justice of Gallio had secured for St. Paul an unmolested residence in Corinth, such as had been promised by the vision which had encouraged him amid his earlier difficulties. He availed himself of this pause in the storm of opposition by preaching for many days—perhaps for some months—and then determined to revisit Jerusalem, from which he had now been absent for nearly three years. It may be that he had collected something for the poor; but in any case he felt the importance of maintaining amicable relations with the other Apostles and with the mother church. He wished also to be present at the approaching feast—in all probability the Pentecost—and thereby to show that, in spite of his active work in heathen cities, and the freedom which he claimed for Gentile converts, in spite, too, of that deadly opposition of many synagogues which had already cost him so dear, he was still at heart a loyal although a liberal Jew. Accordingly, he bade farewell to the friends whom he had converted, and, accompanied by Priscilla and Aquila, set out for Cenchreæ. At that busy seaport, where a little church had been already formed, of which Phœbe was a deaconess, he gave yet another proof of his allegiance to the Mosaic law. In thanksgiving for some deliverance[2]—perhaps from an attack of sickness, perhaps from the Jewish riot—he had taken upon him the vow of the temporary Nazarite. In accordance with this, he abstained

[1] See *infra*, Excursus XIX., "The Man of Sin." For the symbols employed, see Ezek. xxxviii. 16, 17; Dan. vii. 19, 11, 23—26; xi. 31, 36.

[2] See Jos. *B. J.* ii. 15, § 1, and the Mishna treatise *Nazir*, ii. 3. Spencer (*De Leg. Hebr.* iii. 6, § 1) thinks, most improbably, that it was done to obtain a fair voyage. Cf. Juv. *Sat.* xii. 81.

from wine, and let his hair grow long. At the legal purification which formed the termination of the vow, the head could only be shaved at Jerusalem; but as it was often impossible for a foreign Jew to reach the Holy City at the exact time when the period of his vow concluded, it seems to have been permitted to the Nazarite to cut his hair,[1] provided that he kept the shorn locks until he offered the burnt-offering, the sin-offering, and the peace-offering in the Temple, at which time his head was shaved, and all the hair burnt in the fire under the sacrifice of the peace-offerings. Accordingly, Paul cut his hair at Cenchreæ, and set sail for Ephesus. The mention of the fact is not by any means trivial or otiose. The vow which St. Paul undertook is highly significant as a proof of his *personal* allegiance to the Levitic institutions, and his desire to adopt a policy of conciliation towards the Jewish Christians of the Holy City.[2]

A few days' sail, if the weather was ordinarily propitious, would enable his vessel to anchor in the famous haven of Panormus, which was then a forest of masts at the centre of all the Mediterranean trade, but is now a reedy swamp in a region of desolation. His arrival coincided either with the eve of a Sabbath, or of one of the three weekly meetings of the synagogue, and at once, with his usual ardour and self-forgetfulness, he presented himself among the Ephesian Jews. They were a numerous and important body, actively engaged in the commerce of the city, and had obtained some special privileges from the Roman Emperors.[3] Not only was their religion authorised, but their youth were exempted from military service. One of their number, the "Chaldean" or "astrologer" Balbillus, had at this period availed himself of the deepening superstition which always accompanies a decadent belief, and had managed to insinuate himself into the upper circles of Roman society until he ultimately became the confidant of Nero.[4] Accustomed in that seething metropolis to meet with opinions of every description, the Jews at first offered no opposition to the arguments of the wandering Rabbi who preached a crucified Messiah. Nay, they even begged him to stay longer with them. His desire to reach Jerusalem and pay his vow rendered this impossible; but in bidding them farewell he promised that, God willing,[5] he would soon

[1] The word used is κειράμενος, "polling," not ξυρησάμενος, "shaving," or as in E. V. "having shaved" (see 1 Cor. xi. 14; St. Paul dislikes long hair). The notion that it was Aquila and not Paul who made the vow may be finally dismissed; it merely arose from the fact that Aquila is mentioned after his wife; but this, as we have seen, is also the case in 2 Tim. iv. 19; Rom. xvi. 3, and is an undesigned coincidence, probably due to her greater zeal.

[2] "He that makes a vow builds, as it were, a private altar, and if he keeps it, offers, as it were, a sacrifice upon it" (*Yebhamoth*, f. 109, 2; *Nedarim*, f. 59, 1). The views of the Rabbis about vows may be found in *Erubhin*, f. 64, 2; *Chagigah*, f. 10, 1; *Rosh Hashanah*, f. 10, 1; *Nedarim*, f. 2, 1; f. 30, 2, &c. They have been collected by Mr. P. J. Hershon in his Hebrew commentary on Genesis exclusively drawn from the Talmud, in the synoptical note on Gen. xxviii. 20. They throw very little light on St. Paul's vow. The rule is that all votive terms, whether *corban*, *conem*, *cones*, or *conech*, are equally binding (*Nedarim*, f. 2, 1). Perhaps Paul liked the *temporary* ascetic element in the vow (1 Cor. ix. 25; Jos. *B. J.* ii. 15, § 1).

[3] Jos. *Antt.* xiv. 10.

[4] Suet. *Nero*, 40; Dion Cass xvi. 9.

[5] James iv. 15.

return. Once more, therefore, he weighed anchor, and sailed to Cæsarea. From thence he hastened to Jerusalem, which he was now visiting for the fourth time after his conversion. He had entered it once a changed man;[1] he had entered it a second time with a timely contribution from the Church of Antioch to the famine-stricken poor;[2] a third time he had come to obtain a decision of the loud disputes between the Judaic and the liberal Christians which threatened, even thus early, to rend asunder the seamless robe of Christ.[3] Four years had now elapsed, and he came once more, a weak and persecuted missionary, to seek the sympathy of the early converts,[4] to confirm his faithful spirit of unity with them, to tell them the momentous tidings of churches founded during this his second journey, not only in Asia, but for the first time in Europe also, and even at places so important as Philippi, Thessalonica, and Corinth. Had James, and the circle of which he was the centre, only understood how vast for the future of Christianity would be the issues of these perilous and toilsome journeys—had they but seen how insignificant, compared with the labours of St. Paul, would be the part which they themselves were playing in furthering the universality of the Church of Christ—with what affection and admiration would they have welcomed him! How would they have striven, by every form of kindness, of encouragement, of honour, of heartfelt prayer, to arm and strengthen him, and to fire into yet brighter lustre his grand enthusiasm, so as to prepare him in the future for sacrifices yet more heroic, for efforts yet more immense! Had anything of the kind occurred, St. Luke, in the interests of his great Christian Eirenicon—St. Paul himself, in his account to the Galatians of his relations to the twelve—could hardly have failed to tell us about it. So far from this, St. Luke hurries over the brief visit in the three words that "he saluted the Church,"[5] not even pausing to inform us that he fulfilled his vow, or whether any favourable impression as to his Judaic orthodoxy was created by the fact that he had undertaken it. There is too much reason to fear that his reception was cold and ungracious; that even if James received him with courtesy, the Judaic Christians who surrounded "the Lord's brother" did not; and even that a jealous dislike of that free position towards the Law which he established amongst his Gentile converts, led to that determination on the part of some of them to follow in his track and to undermine his influence, which, to the intense embitterment of his latter days, was so fatally successful. It must have been with a sad heart, with something even of indignation at this unsympathetic coldness, that St. Paul hurriedly terminated his visit. But none of these things moved him. He did but share them with his Lord, whom the Pharisees had hated and the Sadducees had slain. He did but share them with every great prophet and every true thinker before and since. Not holding even his life dear unto himself, it is not likely that the peevishness of unprogressive tradition, or the non-appreciation of suspicious narrowness, should make him swerve from his divinely appointed

[1] About A.D. 37. [2] A.D. 44. [3] About A.D. 50. [4] About A.D. 54.

[5] St. Luke does not so much as mention the word Jerusalem, but the word ἀναβὰς disproves the fancy that Paul went no further than Cæsarea.

course. God had counted him worthy of being entrusted with a sacred cause. He had a work to do; he had a Gospel to preach. If in obeying this call of God he met with human sympathy and kindness, well; if not, it was no great matter. Life might be bitter, but life was short, and the light affliction which was but for a moment was nothing to the exceeding and eternal weight of glory. Once more he set forth for a new, and, as it turned out, for the most brilliantly energetic, for the most eternally fruitful, for the most overwhelmingly afflictive period of his life of toil.

From Jerusalem he went to Antioch, where we can well imagine that a warmer and kindlier greeting awaited him. In that more cordial environment he rested for some little time; and thence, amid many a day of weariness and struggle, but cheered in all probability by the companionship of Timothy and Titus, and perhaps also of Gaius, Aristarchus, and Erastus, he passed once more through the famous Cilician gates of Taurus,[1] and travelled overland through the eastern region of Asia Minor,[2] confirming on his way the Churches of Galatia and Phrygia. In Galatia he ordered collections to be made for the poor at Jerusalem by a weekly offertory every Sunday.[3] He also found it necessary to give them some very serious warnings; and although, as yet, there had been no direct apostasy from the doctrines which he had taught, he could trace a perceptible diminution of the affectionate fervour with which he had been at first received by that bright but fickle population.[4] Having thus endeavoured to secure the foundations which he had laid in the past, he descended from the Phrygian uplands, and caught a fresh glimpse of the Marseilles of the Ægean, the hostelry and emporium of east and west,[5] the great capital of Proconsular Asia. Very memorable were the results of his visit. Ephesus was the third capital and starting-point of Christianity. At Jerusalem, Christianity was born in the cradle of Judaism; Antioch had been the starting-point of the Church of the Gentiles; Ephesus was to witness its full development, and the final amalgamation of its unconsolidated elements in the work of John, the Apostle of Love. It lay one mile from the Icarian Sea, in the fair Asian meadow where myriads of swans and other waterfowl disported themselves amid the windings of Cayster.[6] Its buildings were clustered under the protecting shadows of Coressus and Prion, and in the delightful neighbourhood of the Ortygian Groves. Its haven, which had once been among the most sheltered and commodious in the Mediterranean, had been partly silted up by a mistake in engineering, but was still thronged with vessels from every part of the civilised world. It lay at the meeting-point of great roads, which led northwards to Sardis and Troas, southwards to Magnesia and Antioch, and thus commanded easy access to the great river-valleys of the Hermus and Mæander, and the whole interior continent. Its seas and rivers

[1] From Antioch to the Cilician gates, through Tarsus, is 412 miles.
[2] ἀνωτερικὰ is practically equivalent to ἀνατολικά.
[3] 1 Cor. xvi. 1, 2. But the collection does not seem to have been sent with that of the Grecian churches (Rom. xv. 25, 26). Perhaps the Judaic emissaries got hold of it.
[4] Gal. iv. 16; v. 21.
[5] Renan, p. 337.
[6] Now the Kutschuk Meadere, or Little Mæander.

were rich with fish; its air was salubrious; its position unrivalled; its population multifarious and immense. Its markets, glittering with the produce of the world's art, were the Vanity Fair of Asia. They furnished to the exile of Patmos the local colouring of those pages of the Apocalypse in which he speaks of "the merchandise of gold, and silver, and precious stones, and of pearls, and fine linen, and purple, and silk, and scarlet, and all thyine wood, and all manner vessels of ivory, and all manner vessels of most precious wood, and of brass, and iron, and marble, and cinnamon, and odours, and ointment and frankincense, and wine, and oil, and fine flour, and wheat, and beasts, and sheep, and horses, and chariots, and slaves, *and souls of men*."[1]

And Ephesus was no less famous than it was vast and wealthy. Perhaps no region of the world has been the scene of so many memorable events in ancient history as the shores of Asia Minor. The whole coast was in all respects the home of the best Hellenic culture, and Herodotus declares that it was the finest site for cities in the world of his day.[2] It was from Lesbos, and Smyrna, and Ephesus, and Halicarnassus that lyric poetry, and epic poetry, and philosophy, and history took their rise, nor was any name more splendidly emblazoned in the annals of human culture than that of the great capital of Ionia.[3] It was here that Anacreon had sung the light songs which so thoroughly suited the soft temperament of the Greek colonists in that luxurious air; here that Mimnermos had written his elegies; here that Thales had given the first impulse to philosophy; here that Anaximander and Anaximenes had learnt to interest themselves in those cosmogonic theories which shocked the simple beliefs of the Athenian burghers; here that the deepest of all Greek thinkers, "Heracleitus the Dark," had meditated on those truths which he uttered in language of such incomparable force; here that his friend Hermodorus had paid the penalty of virtue by being exiled from a city which felt that its vices were rebuked by his mere silent presence;[4] here that Hipponax had infused into his satire such deadly venom;[5] here that Parrhasius and Apelles had studied their immortal art. And it was still essentially a Greek city. It was true that since Attalus, King of Pergamos, nearly two hundred years before, had made the Romans heirs to his kingdom, their power had gradually extended itself in every direction, until they were absolute masters of Phrygia, Mysia, Caria, Lydia,[6] and all the adjacent isles of Greece, and that now the splendour of Ephesus was materially increased by its being the residence of the Roman Proconsul. But while the presence of a few noble Romans and their suites added to the gaiety and power of the city, it did not affect the prevailing Hellenic cast of its civilisation, which was far more deeply imbued with Oriental than with Western influences. The Ephesians crawled at the feet of the Emperors, flattered them with abject servility, built temples

[1] Rev. xviii. 12, 13.
[2] *Hist.* i. 142. For full accounts of Ephesus see Guhl's *Ephesiaca* (Berl. 1843).
[3] See Hausrath, p. 339, *seqq.*
[4] See Strabo, xiv., p. 642.
[5] Cic. *ad Fam.* vii. 24.
[6] Cic. *pro Flacco*, 27; Plin. *H. N.* v. 28; *ap.* Hausrath, *l.c.*

to their crime or their feebleness, deified them on their inscriptions and coins.[1] Even the poor simulacrum of the Senate came in for a share of their fulsomeness, and received its apotheosis from their complaisance.[2] The Romans, seeing that they had nothing to fear from these degenerate Ionians, helped them with subsidies when they had suffered from earthquakes, flung them titles of honour, which were in themselves a degradation, left them a nominal autonomy, and let them live without interference the bacchanalian lives which passed in a round of Panionic, Ephesian, Artemisian, and Lucullian games. Such then was the city in which St. Paul found a sphere of work unlike any in which he had hitherto laboured. It was more Hellenic than Antioch, more Oriental than Corinth, more populous than Athens, more wealthy and more refined than Thessalonica, more sceptical and more superstitious than Ancyra or Pessinus. It was, with the single exception of Rome, by far the most important scene of all his toils, and was destined, in after-years, to become not only the first of the Seven Churches of Asia, but the seat of one of those great Œcumenical Councils which defined the faith of the Christian world.

The character of the Ephesians was then in very bad repute. Ephesus was the head-quarters of many defunct superstitions, which owed their maintenance to the self-interest of various priestly bodies. South of the city, and brightened by the waters of the Cenchrius, was the olive and cypress grove of Leto,[3] where the ancient olive-tree was still shown to which the goddess had clung when she brought forth her glorious "twin-born progeny."[4] Here was the hill on which Hermes had proclaimed their birth; here the Curetes, with clashing spears and shields, had protected their infancy from wild beasts; here Apollo himself had taken refuge from the wrath of Zeus after he had slain the Cyclopes; here Bacchus had conquered and spared the Amazons during his progress through the East. Such were the arguments which the Ephesian ambassadors had urged before the Roman Senate in arrest of a determination to limit their rights of asylum. That right was mainly attached to the great world-renowned Temple of Artemis, of which Ephesus gloried in calling herself the sacristan.[5] Nor did they see that it was a right which was ruinous to the morals and well-being of the city. Just as the mediæval sanctuaries attracted all the scum and villainy, all the cheats and debtors and murderers of the country round, and inevitably pauperised and degraded the entire vicinity[6]—just as the squalor of the lower purlieus of Westminster to this day is accounted for by its direct affiliation to the crime and wretchedness which sheltered itself from punishment or persecution under the shadow of the Abbey—so the vicinity of the great Temple at Ephesus reeked with the congregated pollutions of Asia. Legend told how, when the temple was

[1] See the *Corpus Inscr. Gr.* 2957, 2961, &c. (Renan, p. 338, who also quotes Plut. *Vit. Anton.* 24). Chandler, *Travels*, i. 25; Falkener, *Ephesus*, p. 111; φιλοσέβαστος and φιλόκαισαρ are common in Ephesian inscriptions.

[2] Θεὸς or ἱερὰ Συγκλητός on coins, &c. (Renan, p. 352).

[3] Strabo, xiv., p. 947.

[4] Tac. *Ann.* iii. 61.

[5] Acts xix. 35, νεωκόρος.

[6] I have already pointed out this fact in speaking of Daphne and Paphos, *supra*, pp. 166, 196. This was why Tiberius tried to abolish all "asyla" (Suet. *Tib.* 37).

finished, Mithridates stood on its summit and declared that the right of asylum should extend in a circle round it as far as he could shoot an arrow, and the arrow miraculously flew a furlong's distance. The consequence was that Ephesus, vitiated by the influences which affect all great sea-side commercial cities, had within herself a special source of danger and contagion.[1] Ionia had been the corruptress of Greece,[2] Ephesus was the corruptress of Ionia—the favourite scene of her most voluptuous love-tales, the lighted theatre of her most ostentatious sins.

The temple, which was the chief glory of the city and one of the wonders of the world,[3] stood in full view of the crowded haven. Ephesus was the most magnificent of what Ovid calls "the magnificent cities of Asia,"[4] and the temple was its most splendid ornament. The *ancient* temple had been burnt down by Herostratus—an Ephesian fanatic who wished his name to be recorded in history—on the night of the birth of Alexander the Great. It had been rebuilt with ungrudging magnificence out of contributions furnished by all Asia—the very women contributing to it their jewels, as the Jewish women had done of old for the Tabernacle of the Wilderness. To avoid the danger of earthquakes, its foundations were built at vast cost on artificial foundations of skin and charcoal laid over the marsh.[5] It gleamed far off with a star-like radiance.[6] Its peristyle consisted of one hundred and twenty pillars of the Ionic order hewn out of Parian marble. Its doors of carved cypress-wood were surmounted by transoms so vast and solid that the aid of miracles was invoked to account for their elevation. The staircase which led to the roof was said to have been cut out of a single vine of Cyprus. Some of the pillars were carved with designs of exquisite beauty.[7] Within were the masterpieces of Praxiteles and Phidias, and Scopas and Polycletus. Paintings by the greatest of Greek artists, of which one—the likeness of Alexander the Great by Apelles— had been bought for a sum said to be equal in value to £5,000 of modern money, adorned the inner walls. The roof of the temple itself was of cedar-wood, supported by columns of jasper on bases of Parian marble.[8] On these pillars hung gifts of priceless value, the votive offerings of grateful superstition. At the end of it stood the great altar adorned by the bas-relief

[1] This is pointed out by Philostratus in the person of Apollonius. He praises them for their banquets and ritual, and adds μεμπτοὶ δε σύνοικοι τῇ θεῷ νύκτας τε καὶ ἡμέρας ἢ οὐκ ἂν ὁ κλέπτης τε καὶ λῃστὴς καὶ ἀνδραποδιστὴς καὶ πᾶς εἴ τις ἄδικος ἢ ἱερόσυλος ἦν ὁρμώμενος αὐτόθεν. τὸ γὰρ τῶν ἀποστερούντων τεῖχός ἐστιν. See, too, Strabo, xiv. 1, 23.

[2] Hence the proverb "Ionian effeminacy." On their gorgeous apparel, see Athen. p. 525. "Taught by the soft Ionians" (Dyer, *Ruins of Rome*).

[3] Philo, Byzant. *De Sept. orbis miraculis*, 7, μόνος ἐστὶ θεῶν οἶκος. Falkener's *Ephesus*, pp. 210—346.

[4] Ov. *Pont.* II. x. 21.

[5] See Plin. *H. N.* xxxvi. 21; Diog. Laert. ii. 8; Aug. *De Civ. Dei*, xxi. 4. Old London Bridge was built, not "on woolsacks," but out of the proceeds of a tax on wool. The anecdote of the discovery of the white marble by Pisidorus is given in Vitruv. x. 7.

[6] μετεωροφανές.

[7] One splendid example of the drum of one of these "columnae caelatae" (Plin.) is now in the British Museum. For a complete and admirable account of the temple and its excavation, see Wood's *Ephesus*, p. 267, *seq.*

[8] Now in the mosque of St. Sophia.

of Praxiteles. behind which fell the vast folds of a purple curtain. Behind this curtain was the dark and awful adytum in which stood the most sacred idol of classic heathendom; and again, behind the adytum was the room which, inviolable under divine protection, was regarded as the wealthiest and securest bank in the ancient world.

The image for which had been reared this incomparable shrine was so ancient that it shared with the Athene of the Acropolis, the Artemis of Tauris, the Demeter of Sicily, the Aphrodite of Paphos, and the Cybele of Pessinus, the honour of being regarded as a Διοπετὲς Ἄγαλμα—"an image that fell from heaven."[1] The very substance of which it was made was a matter of dispute; some said it was of vine-wood, some of ebony, some of cedar, and some of stone.[2] It was not a shapeless meteorite like the Kaaba at Mecca, or the Hercules of Hyettus,[3] or the black-stone of Pessinus; nor a phallic cone like the Phœnician Aphrodite of Paphos;[4] nor a mere lump of wood like the Cadmean Bacchus;[5] but neither must we be misled by the name Artemis to suppose that it in any way resembled the quivered "huntress chaste and fair" of Greek and Roman mythology. It was freely idealised in many of the current representations,[6] but was in reality a hideous fetish, originally meant for a symbol of fertility and the productive power of nature. She was represented on coins—which, as they bear the heads of Claudius and Agrippina, must have been current at this very time, and may have easily passed through the hands of Paul—as a figure swathed like a mummy, covered with monstrous breasts,[7] and holding in one hand a trident and in the other a club. The very ugliness and uncouthness of the idol added to the superstitious awe which it inspired, and just as the miraculous Madonnas and images of Romanism are never the masterpieces of Raphael or Bernardino Luini, but for the most part blackened Byzantine paintings, or hideous dolls like the Bambino, so the statue of the Ephesian Artemis was regarded as far more awful than the Athene of Phidias or the Jupiter of the Capitol. The Jewish feelings of St. Paul—though he abstained from "blaspheming" the goddess[8]—would have made him regard it as pollution to enter her temple; but many a time on coins, and paintings, and in direct copies, he must have seen the strange image of the great Artemis of the Ephesians, whose worship, like that of so many fairer and more human idols, his preaching would doom to swift oblivion.[9]

[1] Pliny (*H. N.* xvi. 79) and Athenagoras (*Pro Christ.* 14) say it was made by Endaeus, the pupil of Daedalus.

[2] Vitruv. ii. 9; Callim. *Hymn Dian.* 239. [3] Pausan. ix. 24. [4] *V. supra*, p. 196.

[5] Pausan. ix. 12. See Guhl, *Ephesiaca*, p. 185; Falkener, *Ephesus*, 287. The Chaeronean Zeus was a sceptre (Pausan. ix. 40); the Cimmerian Mars, a scimitar (Hdt. iv. 62).

[6] *E.g.*, in the statue preserved in the Museo Borbonico at Naples, which, if we may judge from coins, is a very unreal representative of the venerable ugliness of the actual statue.

[7] πολύμαστος, multimamma; "omnium bestiarum et viventium nutrix" (Jer. *Procem. in Ep. ad Eph.*).

[8] Acts xix. 37, οὔ ε βλασφημοῦντας τὴν θεὰν ὑμῶν.

[9] "What is become of the Temple of Diana? Can a wonder of the earth be vanished

Though the Greeks had vied with the Persians in lavish contributions for the re-erection of the temple, the worship of this venerable relic was essentially Oriental. The priests were amply supported by the proceeds of wide domains and valuable fisheries, and these priests, of Megabyzi, as well as the "Essen,"[1] who was at the head of them, were the miserable Persian or Phrygian eunuchs who, with the Melissae, or virgin-priestesses, and crowds of idle slaves, were alone suffered to conduct the worship of the Mother of the Gods. Many a time, in the open spaces and environs of Ephesus, must Paul have seen with sorrow and indignation the bloated and beardless hideousness of these coryphaei of iniquity.[2] Many a time must he have heard from the Jewish quarter the piercing shrillness of their flutes, and the harsh jangling of their timbrels; many a time have caught glimpses of their detestable dances and corybantic processions, as with streaming hair, and wild cries, and shaken torches of pine, they strove to madden the multitudes into sympathy with that orgiastic worship, which was but too closely connected with the vilest debaucheries.[3] Even the Greeks, little as they were liable to be swept away by these bursts of religious frenzy, seem to have caught the tone of these disgraceful fanatics. At no other city would they have assembled in the theatre in their thousands to yell the same cry over and over again for "about the space of two hours," as though they had been so many Persian dervishes or Indian yogis. This senseless reiteration was an echo of the screaming ululatus which was one of the characteristics of the cult of Dindymene and Pessinus.[4]

We are not surprised to find that under the shadow of such a worship superstition was rampant. Ephesus differed from other cities which Paul had visited mainly in this respect, that it was pre-eminently the city of astrology, sorcery, incantations, amulets, exorcisms, and every form of magical imposture. On the statue of the goddess, or rather, perhaps, on the inverted pyramid which formed the basis for her swathed and shapeless feet, were inscribed certain mystic formulæ to which was assigned a magic efficacy. This led to the manufacture and the celebrity of those "Ephesian writings,"

like a phantom, without leaving a trace behind? We now seek the temple in vain; the city is prostrate and the goddess gone" (Chandler; see *Sibyll. Orac.* v. 293—305). The wonder is deepened after seeing the massiveness of the superb fragments in the British Museum. That the Turkish name Aïa Solouk is a corruption of Ἁγία Θεολόγου, and therefore a reminiscence of St. John, is proved by the discovery of coins bearing this inscription, and struck at Ayasaluk (Wood, p. 183). Perhaps St. John originally received the name by way of contrast with the *Theologi* of the Temple.

[1] The resemblance of the word and character to the "Essenes" is accidental. It means "a king (queen) bee."

[2] Quint. v. 12. What sort of wretches these were may be seen in Juv. vi. 512; Prop. ii. 18, 15; Appuleius, *Metamorph.*

[3] Apollonius, in his first address to the Ephesians, delivered from the platform of the temple, urged them to abandon their idleness, folly, and feasting, and turn to the study of philosophy. He speaks of these dances, and says αὐλῶν μὲν πάντα μεστὰ ἦν, μεστὰ δὲ ἀνδρογύνων, μεστὰ δὲ κτύπων, κ.τ.λ (Philostr. *Vit. Apoll.* iv. 2, p. 141). He praises them, however, for their philosophic interests, &c. (viii. 8, p. 339). Incense-burners, flute-players, and trumpeters are mentioned in an inscription found by Chandler (*Inscr. Ant.*, p. 11).

[4] Hausrath, p. 342.

which were eagerly supplied by greedy imposture to gaping credulity. Among them were the words *askion*, *kataskion*, *lix*, *tetras*, *damnameneus*, and *aisia*,[1] which for sense and efficiency were about on a par with the *daries*, *derdaries*, *astataries*, or *ista*, *pista*, *sista*, which Cato the elder held to be a sovereign remedy for a sprain,[2] or the *shavriri*, *vriri*, *iriri*, *riri*, *iri*, *ri*, accompanied with knockings on the lid of a jug, which the Rabbis taught as an efficacious expulsion of the demon of blindness.[3]

Stories, which elsewhere would have been received with ridicule, at Ephesus found ready credence. About the very time of St. Paul's visit it is probable that the city was visited by Apollonius of Tyana; and it is here that his biographer Philostratus places the scene of some of his exploits. One of these is all the more interesting because it is said to have taken place in that very theatre into which St. Paul, though in imminent peril of being torn to pieces, could scarcely be persuaded not to enter. During his visit to Ephesus, the thaumaturge of Tyana found the plague raging there, and in consequence invited the population to meet him in the theatre. When they were assembled, he rose and pointed out to them a miserable and tattered old man as the cause of the prevailing pestilence. Instantly the multitude seized stones and, in spite of the old man's remonstrances, stoned him to death. When the heaped stones were removed, they found the carcase of a Molossian hound, into which the demon had transformed himself;[4] and on this spot they reared a statue of Herakles Apotropaios! Philostratus did not write his romance till A.D. 218, and his hero Apollonius has been put forth by modern infidels as a sort of Pagan rival to the Jesus of the Gospels. Let any one read this wretched production, and judge! The Pagan sophist, with all his vaunted culture and irritating euphuism, abounds in anecdotes which would have been regarded as pitiably foolish if they had been narrated by the unlettered fisherman of Galilee, strangers as they were to all cultivation, and writing as they did a century and a half before.

Another and a far darker glimpse of the Ephesus of this day may be obtained from the letter of the pseudo-Heraclitus. Some cultivated and able Jew,[5] adopting the pseudonym of the great ancient philosopher, wrote some letters in which he is supposed to explain the reason why he was called "the weeping philosopher," and why he was never seen to laugh. In these he fully justifies his traditional remark that the whole Ephesian population deserved to be throttled man by man. He here asks how it is that their state flourishes in spite of its wickedness; and, in the inmost spirit of the Old Testament, he sees in that prosperity the irony and the curse of Heaven. For Artemis and

[1] Clem. Alex. *Strom.* v. 46.

[2] Cato, *De Re Rustica Fr.* 160 (see Donaldson, *Varron.*, p. 234).

[3] *Abhoda Zara*, f. 12, 2.

[4] *Vit. Apoll.* iv. 10, p. 147. Alexander of Abonoteichos, a much more objectionable imposter than Apollonius, lived till old age on the wealth got out of his dupes, and seriously persuaded the world that the mother of his daughter was the goddess of the moon!

[5] The theory of Bernays is that the letters were written by a Pagan, but interpolated by a Jew.

her worship he has no scorn too intense. The dim twilight of her adytum is symbolical of a vileness that hateth the light. He supposes that her image is "stonen" in the contemptuous sense in which the word is used by Homer —*i.e.*, idiotic and brutish. He ridicules the inverted pyramid on which she stands. He says that the morals which flourish under her protection are worse than those of beasts, seeing that even hounds do not mutilate each other, as her Megabyzus has to be mutilated, because she is too modest to be served by a man. But instead of extolling her modesty, her priests ought rather to curse her for lewdness, which rendered it unsafe otherwise to approach her, and which had cost them so dear. As for the orgies, and the torch festivals, and the antique rituals, he has nothing to say of them, except that they are the cloak for every abomination. These things had rendered him a lonely man. This was the reason why he could not laugh. How could he laugh when he heard the noises of these infamous vagabond priests, and was a witness of all the nameless iniquities which flourished so rankly in consequence of their malpractices—the murder, and waste, and lust, and gluttony, and drunkenness? And then he proceeds to moral and religious exhortations, which show that we are reading the work of some Jewish and unconverted Apollos, who is yet an earnest and eloquent proclaimer of the one God and the Noachian law.

In this city St. Paul saw that "a great door and effectual was open to him," though there were "many adversaries."[1] During his absence an event had happened which was to be of deep significance for the future. Among the myriads whom business or pleasure, or what is commonly called accident, had brought to Ephesus, was a Jew of Alexandria named Apollonius,[2] or Apollos, who not only shared the culture for which the Jews of that city were famous in the age of Philo, but who had a profound knowledge of Scripture, and a special gift of fervid eloquence.[3] He was only so far a Christian that he knew and had accepted the baptism of John; but though thus imperfectly acquainted with the doctrines of Christianity, he yet spoke and argued in the synagogue with a power and courage which attracted the attention of the Jewish tent-makers Priscilla and Aquila. They invited him to their house, and showed him the purely initial character of John's teaching. It may have been the accounts of the Corinthian Church which he had heard from them that made him desirous to visit Achaia, and perceiving how useful such a ministry as his might be among the subtle and intellectual Greeks, they not only encouraged his wish,[4] but wrote for him "letters of commendation"[5] to the Corinthian elders. At Corinth his eloquence produced a great sensation, and he became a pillar of strength to the brethren. He had so thoroughly profited by that reflection of St. Paul's teaching which he had caught from Priscilla and Aquila, that in his public disputations with the hostile Jews he proved from their own Scriptures, with an irresistible cogency, the

[1] 1 Cor. xvi. 9.
[2] So in D.
[3] Acts xviii. 25, ζέων τῷ πνεύματι (cf. Rom. xii. 11).
[4] προτρεψάμενοι, sc. αὐτόν (Acts xviii. 27).
[5] συστατικὴ ἐπιστολή (2 Cor. iii. 1).

Messiahship of Christ, and thus was as acceptable to the Christians as he was formidable to the Jews. He watered what Paul had planted.[1]

By the time of St. Paul's arrival, Apollos had already started for Corinth. He had, however, returned to Ephesus before St. Paul's departure, and the Apostle must have gazed with curiosity and interest on this fervid and gifted convert. A meaner soul might have been jealous of his gifts, and all the more so because, while less valuable, they were more immediately dazzling and impressive than his own. St. Paul was of too noble a spirit to leave room for the slightest trace of a feeling so common, yet so ignoble. Apollos had unwittingly stolen from him the allegiance of some of his Corinthian converts; his name had become, in that disorderly church, a watchword of faction. Yet St. Paul never speaks of him without warm sympathy and admiration,[2] and evidently appreciated the high-minded delicacy which made him refuse to revisit Corinth,[3] in spite of pressing invitations, from the obvious desire to give no encouragement to the admiring partisans who had elevated him into unworthy rivalry with one so much greater than himself.

Ephesus, amid its vast population, contained specimens of every form of belief, and Apollos was not the only convert to an imperfect and half-developed form of Christianity. Paul found there, on his arrival, a strange backwater of religious opinion in the persons of some twelve men who, like Apollos, and being perhaps in some way connected with him, were still disciples of the Baptist. Although there were some in our Lord's time who stayed with their old teacher till his execution, and though the early fame of his preaching had won him many followers, of whom some continued to linger on in obscure sects,[4] it was impossible for any reasonable man to stop short at this position except through ignorance. St. Paul accordingly questioned them, and upon finding that they knew little or nothing of the final phase of John's teaching, or of the revelation of Christ, and were even ignorant of the very name of the Holy Spirit, he gave them further instruction until they were fitted to receive baptism, and exhibited those gifts of the Spirit—the speaking with tongues and prophecy—which were the accepted proofs of full and faithful initiation into the Church of Christ.[5]

For three months, in accordance with his usual plan, he was a constant visitor at the synagogue, and used every effort of persuasion and argument to ripen into conviction the favourable impressions he had at first created. St. Luke passes briefly over the circumstances, but there must have been many

[1] 1 Cor. iii 6. There can be little reasonable doubt that Apollos was the author of the Epistle to the Hebrews. In reading that Epistle (which cannot be dealt with in this volume) it is easy to see that, essentially Pauline as is much of its phraseology, the main method is original, and would probably be more pleasing and convincing to *Jews* than any which St. Paul was led to adopt. Some have seen a distinction between his pupils and St. Paul's in Titus iii. 14, οἱ ἡμέτεροι, but see *infra*, *ad loc.*

[2] Tit. iii. 13,

[3] 1 Cor. xvi. 12.

[4] Sabaeans, Mendaeans, &c. (Neander, *Ch. Hist.* ii. 57). We find from the Clementine Recognitions that there were some of John's disciples who continued to preach him as the Messiah.

[5] Cf. Heb. vi. 4—6.

an anxious hour, many a bitter struggle, many an exciting debate, before the Jews finally adopted a tone not only of decided rejection, but even of so fierce an opposition, that St. Paul was forced once more, as at Corinth, openly to secede from their communion. We do not sufficiently estimate the pain which such circumstances must have caused to him. His life was so beset with trials, that each trial, however heavy in itself, is passed over amid a multitude that were still more grievous. But we must remember that St. Paul, though a Christian, still regarded himself as a true Israelite, and he must have felt, at least as severely as a Luther or a Whitefield, this involuntary alienation from the religious communion of his childhood. We must conjecture, too, that it was amid these early struggles that he once more voluntarily submitted to the recognised authority of synagogues, and endured some of those five beatings by the Jews, any one of which would have been regarded as a terrible episode in an ordinary life.

As long as opposition confined itself to legitimate methods, St. Paul was glad to be a worshipper in the synagogue, and to deliver the customary Midrash; but when the Jews not only rejected and reviled him, but even endeavoured to thwart all chance of his usefulness amid their Gentile neighbours, he saw that it was time to withdraw his disciples from among them;[1] and, as their number was now considerable, he hired the school of Tyrannus—some heathen sophist of that not very uncommon name.[2] It was one of those schools of rhetoric and philosophy which were common in a city like Ephesus, where there were many who prided themselves on intellectual pursuits. This new place of worship gave him the advantage of being able to meet the brethren daily, whereas in the synagogue this was only possible three times a week. His labours and his preaching were not unblessed. For two full years longer he continued to make Ephesus the centre of his missionary activity, and, as the fame of his Gospel began to spread, there can be little doubt that he himself took short journeys to various neighbouring places, until, in the strong expression of St. Luke, "all they that dwelt in Asia heard the word of the Lord Jesus, both Jews and Greeks."[3] In Ephesus itself his reputation reached an extraordinary height, in consequence of the unusual works of power which God wrought by his hands.[4] On this subject he is himself silent even by way of allusion, and though he speaks to the Ephesian elders[5] of his tears, and trials, and dangers, he does not say a word as

[1] Epænetus (Rom. xvi. 5, *leg.* Ἀσίας) was his first convert.

[2] Jos. *B. J.* i. 26, § 3; 2 Macc. iv. 40. It is very unlikely that this was a Beth Midrash (Meyer), as it was St. Paul's object to withdraw from the Jews. There was a Sophist Tyrannus mentioned by Suidas. The τινος is spurious (ℵ, A, B), which shows that this Tyrannus was known in Ephesus (see Heinsen, *Paulus*, 218).

[3] Hence forty years later, in Bithynia, Pliny (*Ep.* 96) writes, "Neque enim civitates tantum, sed vicos etiam atque agros superstitionis istius contagio pervagata est.'

[4] Acts xix. 11, δυνάμεις οὐ τὰς τυχούσας.

[5] The "Epistle to the Ephesians," being a circular letter, naturally contains but few specific allusions—which, if intelligible to one Christian community, would not have been so to another. We should have expected such allusions in his speech; but "omittit Doctor gentium narrare miracula, narrat labores, narrat aerumnas, narrat

to the signs and wonders which in writing to the Corinthians he distinctly claims. Although St. Paul believed that God, for the furtherance of the Gospel, did allow him to work "powers" beyond the range of human experience, and in which he humbly recognised the work of the Spirit granted to faith and prayer, yet he by no means frequently exercised these gifts, and never for his own relief or during the sickness of his dearest friends. But it was a common thing in Ephesus to use all kinds of magic remedies and curious arts. We are not, therefore, surprised to hear that articles of dress which had belonged to Paul, handkerchiefs which he had used, and aprons with which he had been girded in the pursuit of his trade,[1] were assumed by the Ephesians to have caught a magic efficacy, and were carried about to sick people and demoniacs. St. Luke was not with the Apostle at Ephesus, and enters into no details; but it is clear that his informant, whoever he was, had abstained from saying that this was done by St. Paul's sanction. But since Ephesus was the head-quarters of diabolism and sorcery, the use of St. Paul's handkerchiefs or aprons, whether authorised by him or not, was so far overruled to beneficial results of healing as to prove the superiority of the Christian faith in the acropolis of Paganism, and to prepare the way for holy worship in the stronghold of Eastern fanaticism and Grecian vice. He who "followed not Jesus," and yet was enabled to cast out devils in His name, could hardly fail to be the prototype of others who, though they acted without sanction, were yet, for good purposes, and in that unsearched borderland which lies between the natural and the supernatural, enabled by God's providence to achieve results which tended to the furtherance of truth.

But lest any sanction should be given to false and superstitious notions, we can hardly fail to see in the next anecdote which St. Luke has preserved for us a direct rebuke of mechanical thaumaturgy. Exorcism was a practice which had long been prevalent among the Jews, and it was often connected with the grossest credulity and the most flagrant imposture.[2] Now there was a Jewish priest of some distinction of the name of Sceva,[3] whose seven sons wandered about from place to place professing to eject demons; and on learning the reputation of St. Paul, and hearing doubtless of the cures effected by the application of his handkerchiefs, they thought that by combining his name with that of Jesus, they could effect cures in the most virulent cases, which defeated even the ring and root of Solomon.[4] Encouraged possibly by some apparent initial success—so at least the story seems to imply—two of these

tribulationes quae Paulo Paulique imitatoribus ipsis miraculis sunt clariores" (Novarinus).

[1] σουδάρια, *sudaria*; ἡμικίνθια, *semicincta*.

[2] Jos. *Antt.* viii. 2, § 5. For this ridiculous jugglery, which seems to have deceived Vespasian, see my *Life of Christ*, i. 237. The prevalence of Jewish exorcists is attested by Justin Martyr, *Dial.* 85.

[3] Acts xix. 14, ἀρχιερέως—a general expression; perhaps a head of one of the twenty-four courses.

[4] Jos. *Antt. l.c.* We find many traces of this kind of superstition in the Talmudic writings: *e.g.*, the belief that the *Minim* could cure the bites of serpents by the name of Jesus (*v. supra*, p. 63). In the *Toldôth Jeshu*, the miracles of our Lord are ex-

seven itinerant impostors[1] visited a man who was evidently a raving maniac, but who had those sufficiently lucid perceptions of certain subjects which many madmen still retain. Addressing the evil demon, they exclaimed, "We exorcise you by Jesus, whom Paul preacheth." In this instance, however, the adjuration proved to be a humiliating failure. The maniac astutely replied, "Jesus I recognise, and Paul I know;[2] but who are you?" and then leaping upon them with the superhuman strength of madness, he tore their clothes off their backs, and inflicted upon them such violent injuries that they were glad to escape out of the house stripped and wounded.

So remarkable a story could not remain unknown. It spread like wildfire among the gossiping Ephesians, and produced a remarkable feeling of dread and astonishment. One result of it was most beneficial. We have had repeated occasion to observe that the early Christians who had been redeemed from heathendom, either in the coarsenesses of slave-life or in the refined abominations of the higher classes, required a terrible struggle to deliver themselves by the aid of God's Holy Spirit from the thraldom of past corruption. The sternly solemn emphasis of St. Paul's repeated warnings—the actual facts which occurred in the history of the early churches—show conclusively that the early converts required to be treated with extreme forbearance, while, at the same time, they were watched over by their spiritual rulers with incessant vigilance. The stir produced by the discomfiture of the Beni Sceva revealed the startling fact that some of the brethren in embracing Christianity had not abandoned magic. Stricken in conscience, these secret dealers in the superstitious trumpery of "curious arts" now came forward in the midst of the community and confessed their secret malpractices. Nor was it only the dupes who acknowledged the error. Even the deceivers came forward, and gave the most decisive proof of their sincerity by rendering impossible any future chicanery. They brought the cabalistic and expensive books[3] which had been the instruments of their trade, and publicly burned

plained by an unutterably silly story as to the means by which He possessed himself of the *Shemhamephoresh* or sacred name. Witchcraft had in all ages been prevalent among the Jews (Ex. xxii. 18; 1 Sam. xxviii. 3, 9; Mic. v. 12); it continued to be so at the Christian era, and it was necessary even to warn converts against any addiction to it (Gal. v. 20; 2 Tim. iii. 13, γόητες).

[1] In verse 16 the reading ἀμφοτέρων of א, A, B, D, is almost certainly correct. They were actuated by exactly the same motives as Simon Magus, but had shown less cunning in trying to carry them out.

[2] Acts xix. 15, Τὸν Ἰησοῦν γιγνώσκω καὶ τὸν Παῦλον ἐπίσταμαι; Vulg., "Jesum *novi* et Paulum *scio*."

[3] On these Ἐφέσια γράμματα see the illustrations adduced by Wetstein. Some of them were copies of the mystic words and names engraved in enigmatic formulæ (αἰνιγματώδεις—Eustath. in *Od.* xiv. p. 1864) on the crown, girdle, and feet of the statue of Artemis. Whole treatises were written in explanation of them, which resemble certain Chinese treatises. An addiction to magic, therefore, assumed almost necessarily a secret belief in idolatry. One of the titles of Artemis was *Magos*. Balbillus (Suet. *Ner.* 36) and Maximus (Gibbon, ii. 291, ed. Milman) were both Ephesian astrologers. Eustathius (*l.c.*—cf. Philostr. *Vit. Apol.* vii. 39) tells us that Crœsus was saved by reciting them on the pyre, and that in a wrestling bout a Milesian, who could not throw an Ephesian, found that he had Ephesian incantations engraved on a die. When this was taken from him the Milesian threw him thirty times in succession.

them. It was like the *Monte della Pietà* reared by the repentant Florentines at the bidding of Savonarola; and so extensive had been this secret evil-doing, that the value of the books destroyed by the culprits in this fit of penitence was no less than fifty thousand drachms of silver, or, in our reckoning, about £2,030.[1] This bonfire, which must have lasted some time,[2] was so striking a protest against the prevalent credulity, that it was doubtless one of the circumstances which gave to St. Paul's preaching so wide a celebrity throughout all Asia.

This little handful of incidents is all that St. Luke was enabled to preserve for us of this great Ephesian visit, which Paul himself tells us occupied a period of three years.[3] Had we nothing else to go by, we might suppose that until the final outbreak it was a period of almost unbroken success and prosperity. Such, however, as we find from the Epistles[4] and from the Apostle's speech to the Ephesian elders,[5] was very far from being the case. It was indeed an earnest, incessant, laborious, house-to-house ministry, which carried its exhortations to each individual member of the church. But it was a ministry of many tears; and though greatly blessed, it was a time of such overwhelming trial, sickness, persecution, and misery, that it probably surpassed in sorrow any other period of St. Paul's life. We must suppose that during its course happened not a few of those perils which he recounts with such passionate brevity of allusion in his Second Epistle to the Corinthians. Neither from Jews, nor from Pagans, nor from nominal Christians was he safe. He had suffered alike at the hands of lawless banditti and stately magistrates; he had been stoned by the simple provincials of Lystra, beaten by the Roman colonists of Philippi, hunted by the Greek mob at Ephesus, seized by the furious Jews at Corinth, maligned and thwarted by the Pharisaic professors of Jerusalem. Robbers he may well have encountered in the environs,[6] as tradition tells us that St. John the Evangelist did in later days, as well as in the interior, when he travelled to lay the foundation of various churches.[7] Perils among his own countrymen we know befell him there, for he reminds the elders of Ephesus of what he had suffered from the ambuscades of the Jews.[8] To perils by the heathen and in the city he must have

Hence the Ἐφέσια γράμματα were sometimes engraved on seals (Athen. xii. 584). Renan says (p. 345) that the names of the "seven sleepers of Ephesus" are still a common incantation in the East.

[1] On the almost certain supposition that the "pieces of silver" were Attic drachms of the value of about 9¾d. If they were Roman denarii the value would be £1,770. Classic parallels to this public abjuration of magic are quoted from Liv. xl. 29; Suet. *Aug.* 31; Tac. *Ann.* xiii. 50; *Agric.* 2.

[2] κατέκαιον, impf.

[3] Acts xx. 31; but owing to the Jewish method of reckoning any *part* of time to the whole, the period did not *necessarily* much exceed two years.

[4] Chiefly those to the Corinthians. On the Epistle to "the Ephesians" see *infra.*

[5] Acts xx. 18—35.

[6] 2 Cor. xi. 26.

[7] He had not, however, visited Laodicea or Colossæ, where churches were founded by Philemon and Epaphras (Col. i. 7; iv. 12—16). But he may well have made journeys to Smyrna, Pergamos, Thyatira, Sardis, Philadelphia, &c. (See 1 Cor. xvi. 19.)

[8] Acts xx. 19; which again shows the fragmentary nature of the narrative as regards all particulars of personal suffering.

often been liable in the narrow streets. Of his perils among false brethren, like Phygellus, and Hermogenes, and Alexander, we may see a specimen in the slanders against his person, and the internecine opposition to his doctrine, of which we shall meet with future proofs. Perils in the wilderness and in the sea were the inevitable lot of one who travelled over vast districts in those days, when navigation was so imperfect and intercourse so unprotected. It was very shortly after his departure from Ephesus that he wrote of all these dangers, and if, as is possible, he took more than one voyage from the haven of Ephesus to various places on the shores of the Levant, it may have been at this time that he suffered that specially perilous shipwreck, in the escape from which he floated a day and a night upon the stormy waves.[1] And all this time, with a heart that trembled with sympathy or burned with indignation,[2] he was carrying out the duties of a laborious and pastoral ministry,[3] and bearing the anxious burden of all the churches, of which some, like the churches of Corinth and Galatia, caused him the most acute distress. Nor were physical cares and burdens wanting. True to his principle of refusing to eat the bread of dependence,[4] he had toiled incessantly at Ephesus to support, not himself only, but even Aristarchus and the others who were with him; and not even all his weariness, and painfulness, and sleepless nights of mingled toil and danger,[5] had saved him from cold, and nakedness, and the constant pangs of hunger during compulsory or voluntary fasts.[6] And while he was taking his place like a general on a battle-field, with his eye on every weak or endangered point; while his heart was constantly rent by news of the defection of those for whom he would gladly have laid down his life; while a new, powerful, and organised opposition was working against him in the very churches which he had founded with such peril and toil;[7] while he was being constantly scourged, and mobbed, and maltreated, and at the same time suffering from repeated attacks of sickness and depression; while he was at once fighting a hand-to-hand battle and directing the entire campaign;—he yet found time to travel for the foundation or confirming of other churches, and to write, as with his very heart's blood, the letters which should rivet the attention of thousands of the foremost intellects, eighteen centuries after he himself had been laid in the nameless grave. In these we find that at the very hour of apparent success he was in the midst of foolishness, weakness, shame—"pilloried," as it were, "on infamy's high stage," the sentence of death hanging ever over his head, cast down, perplexed, persecuted, troubled on every side, homeless, buffeted, ill-provided with food and clothes, abused,

[1] Whether a brief and unsatisfactory visit to Corinth was among these journeys is a disputed point, which depends on the interpretation given to 2 Cor. i. 15, 16; xiii. 1, and which will never be finally settled. A multitude of authorities may be quoted on both sides, and fortunately the question is not one of great importance.

[2] 2 Cor. xi. 29. [3] Acts xx. 20, 31. [4] Acts xx. 34. [5] 2 Cor. xi. 27.

[6] And that, too, although the tents made at Ephesus had a special reputation, and were therefore probably in some demand (Plut. *Alcib.* 12; Athen. xii. 47).

[7] Perhaps the Judaic Christians were more content to leave him alone while he was working in Europe, and were only aroused to opposition by his resumption of work in Asia (Krenkel, *Paulus*, p. 183).

persecuted, slandered, made as it were the dung and filth of all the world.[1] Nay, more, he was in jeopardy not only every day, but every hour; humanly speaking, he had fought with wild beasts in the great voluptuous Ionic city; he was living every day a living death. He tells us that he was branded like some guilty slave with the stigmata of the Lord Jesus;[2] that he was being "killed all the day long;[3] that he was "in deaths oft;"[4] that he was constantly carrying about with him the deadness of the crucified Christ;[5] his life an endless mortification, his story an inscription on a cross. What wonder if, amid these afflictions, there were times when the heroic soul gave way? What wonder if he speaks of tears, and trembling, and desolation of heart, and utter restlessness; of being pressed out of measure, above strength, despairing of life itself,[6] tried almost beyond the extreme of human endurance —without fightings, within fears? What wonder if he is driven to declare that if *this* is all the life belonging to our hope in Christ, he would be of all men the most miserable?[7] And yet, in the strength of the Saviour, how triumphantly he stemmed the overwhelming tide of these afflictions; in the panoply of God how dauntlessly he continued to fling himself into the never-ending battle of a warfare which had no discharge.[8] Indomitable spirit! flung down to earth, chained like a captive to the chariot-wheels of his Lord's triumph,[9] haled as it were from city to city, amid bonds and afflictions,[10] as a deplorable spectacle, amid the incense which breathed through the streets in token of the victor's might—he yet thanks God that he is thus a captive, and glories in his many infirmities. Incomparable and heroic soul! many saints of God have toiled, and suffered, and travelled, and preached, and been execrated, and tortured, and imprisoned, and martyred, in the cause of Christ. Singly they tower above the vulgar herd of selfish and comfortable men; but yet the collective labours of some of their greatest would not equal, nor would their collective sufferings furnish a parallel to those of Paul, and very few of them have been what he was—a great original thinker, as well as a devoted practical worker for his Lord.

But of this period we learn from the Acts only one closing scene,[11] and it is doubtful whether even this is painted for us in colours half so terrible as the reality. Certain it is that some of the allusions which we have been noticing must bear reference to this crowning peril, and that, accustomed though he was to the daily aspect of danger in its worst forms, this particular danger and the circumstances attending it, which are rather hinted at than detailed, had made a most intense impression upon the Apostle's mind.

At the close of about two years, his restless fervour made him feel that he could stay no longer in the school of Tyrannus. He formed the plan of starting after Pentecost, and visiting once more the churches of Macedonia

[1] 1 Cor. iv. 8—13; 2 Cor. iv. 8, 9.
[2] Gal. vi. 17.
[3] Rom. viii. 36.
[4] 2 Cor. xi. 23.
[5] 2 Cor. iv. 10.
[6] 2 Cor. i. 8.
[7] 1 Cor. xv. 19.
[8] See Greg. Naz. *Orat.* ii. 38—40.
[9] 2 Cor. ii. 14—16.
[10] Acts xx. 23.
[11] There are further hints in the farewell speech to the Ephesian elders (Acts xx. 18—35).

and Achaia, which he had founded in his second journey, and of sailing from Corinth to pay a fifth visit to Jerusalem, after which he hoped to see Rome, the great capital of the civilisation of the world.[1] In furtherance of this purpose he had already despatched two of his little band of fellow-workers, Timothy and Erastus, to Macedonia with orders that they were to rejoin him at Corinth. Erastus[2]—if this be the chamberlain of the city—was a person of influence, and would have been well suited both to provide for the Apostle's reception and to superintend the management of the weekly offertory, about which St. Paul was at present greatly interested. The visit to Jerusalem was rendered necessary by the contribution for the distressed Christians of that city, which he had been collecting from the Gentile churches, and which he naturally desired to present in person, as the best possible token of forgiveness and brotherhood, to the pillars of the unfriendly community. This had not been his original plan.[3] He had originally intended, and indeed had announced his intention, in a letter no longer extant,[4] to sail straight from Ephesus to Corinth, make his way thence by land to the churches of Macedonia, sail back from thence to Corinth, and so sail once more from Corinth to Jerusalem. Weighty reasons, which we shall see hereafter, had compelled the abandonment of this design. The ill news respecting the condition of the Corinthian churches which he had received from the slaves of Chloe compelled him to write his first extant letter to the Corinthians, in which he tacitly abandons his original intention, but sends Titus, and with him "the brother," to regulate to the best of their power the gross disorders that had arisen.[5] Probably at the same time he sent a message to Timothy—uncertain, however, whether it would reach him in time—not to go to Corinth, but either to return to him or to wait for him in Macedonia. The first Epistle to the Corinthians was written about the time of the Passover in April, and probably in the very next month an event occurred which, at the last moment, endangered his stay and precipitated his departure.

It was now the month of May, and nothing seemed likely to interfere with the peaceful close of a troubled ministry. But this month was specially dedicated to the goddess of Ephesus, and was called from her the Artemisian.[6] During the month was held the great fair—called Ephesia—which attracted an immense concourse of people from all parts of Asia, and was kept with all possible splendour and revelry. The proceedings resembled the Christmas festivities of the middle ages, with their boy bishops and abbots of misrule. The gods were personated by chosen representatives, who received throughout the month a sort of mock adoration. There was an Alytarch, who represented Zeus; a Grammateus, who played the part of Apollo; an Amphithales, who per-

[1] Cf. Rom. i. 15; xv. 23—28; Acts xix. 21.

[2] Rom. xvi. 23; 2 Tim. iv. 20, but there is no certainty in the matter. The name was common.

[3] 2 Cor. i. 16—23.

[4] *V. infra*, p. 383.

[5] 1 Cor. xvi. 5—7.

[6] The decree dedicating the entire month to Artemis has been found by Chandler on a slab of white marble near the aqueduct, and is given by Boeck, *Corp. Inscr.* 2954. It is nearly contemporary with the time of St. Paul.

sonated Hermes; and in the numberless processions and litanies, and sacrifices, they paced the streets, and were elevated in public places, arrayed in robes of pure white or of tissued gold, and wearing crowns which were set with carbuncles and pearls. The theatre and stadium were densely crowded by festive throngs to listen to the musical contests, to watch the horse-races, and the athletic exhibitions, or to look on with thrills of fiercer emotion at the horrible combats of men and beasts. The vast expense of these prolonged festivities and superb spectacles was entirely borne by the College of the ten Asiarchs, who thus fulfilled the same functions as those of the Curule Ædiles at Rome. They were men of high distinction, chosen annually from the wealthiest citizens of the chief cities of Asia, and it was their duty to preside over the games, and to keep order in the theatre. The heavy pecuniary burden of the office was repaid in honorary privileges and social distinctions. Their names were recorded on coins and in public inscriptions, and the garlands and purple robes which distinguished them during the continuance of the feast were the external marks of the popular gratitude.[1]

During the sacred month the city rang with every sort of joyous sounds; gay processions were constantly sweeping to the famous temple; drunkenness and debauchery were rife; even through the soft night of spring the Agora hummed with the busy throngs of idlers and revellers.[2] It was inevitable that at such a time there should be a recrudescence of fanaticism, and it is far from improbable that the worthless and frivolous mob, incited by the Eunuch priests and Hierodules of Artemis, may have marked out for insult the little congregation which met in the school of Tyrannus, and their well-known teacher. This year there was a perceptible diminution in the fast and furious mirth of the Artemisian season, and the cause of this falling off was perfectly notorious.[3] Not only in Ephesus, but in all the chief cities of Proconsular Asia, deep interest had been excited by the preaching of a certain Paulus, who, in the very metropolis of idolatry, was known to be quietly preaching that they were no gods which were made with hands. Many people had been persuaded to adopt his views; many more had so far at least been influenced by them as to feel a growing indifference for mummeries and incantations, and even for temples and idols. Consequently there arose in Ephesus "no small stir about that way." Paul and his preaching, the brethren and their assemblages, were in all men's mouths, and many a muttered curse was aimed at them by Megabyzos and Melissae, and the hundreds of hangers-on which gather around every great institution. At last this ill-concealed exasperation came to a head. The chief sufferer from the diminished interest in the goddess and her

[1] These particulars are mainly derived from the account of Malalas.

[2] Achill. Tat. 5.

[3] No one will be astonished at this who reads Pliny's account of the utter neglect into which heathen institutions had fallen half a century after this time, in the neighbouring province of Bithynia, as a direct consequence of Christian teaching, and that though the Christians were a persecuted sect. There, also, complaints came from the priests, the purveyors of the sacrifices, and other people pecuniarily interested. They had the sagacity to see that their peril from Christianity lay in its universality.

Hieromenia, had been a certain silversmith, named Demetrius, who sold to the pilgrims little silver shrines and images in memorial of their visits to Ephesus[1] and her temple. They were analogous to the little copies in alabaster or silver of the shrine of Loretto, and other famous buildings of Italy; nor was it only at Ephesus, but at every celebrated centre of Pagan worship, that the demand for such memorials created the supply. Demetrius found that his trade was beginning to be paralysed, and since the emasculate throng of sacred slaves and musicians dared not strike a blow for the worship which fed their lazy vice, he determined, as far as he could, to stop the mischief. Calling together a trades-union meeting of all the skilled artisans and ordinary workmen who were employed in this craft,[2] he made them a speech, in which he first stirred up their passions by warning them of the impending ruin of their interests,[3] and then appealed to their latent fanaticism to avenge the despised greatness of their temple, and the waning magnificence of the goddess whom all Asia and the world worshipped.[4] The speech was like a spark on inflammable materials. Their interests were suffering,[5] and their superstition was being endangered; and the rage which might have been despised if it had only sprung from greed, looked more respectable when it assumed the cloak of fanaticism. The answer to the speech of Demetrius was a unanimous shout of the watchword of Ephesus, "Great is Artemis of the Ephesians!" So large a meeting of the workmen created much excitement. Crowds came flocking from every portico, and agora, and gymnasium, and street. The whole city was thrown into a state of riot, and a rush was made for the Jewish quarter and the shop of Aquila. What took place we are not exactly told, except that the life of the Apostle was in extremest danger. The mob was, however, balked of its intended prey. Paul, as in the similar peril at Thessalonica, was either not in the house at the time, or had been successfully concealed by Priscilla and her husband, who themselves ran great risk of being killed in their efforts to protect him.[6] Since, however, the rioters could

[1] Called ἀμφιδρύματα ναΐδια, aediculae. Chrysostom says ἴσως ὡς κιβώρια μικρά. Similar images and shrines are mentioned in Ar. *Nub.* 598; Dio. Sic. i. 15; xv. 49; Dion Cass. xxxix. 20; Dion. Hal. ii. 22; Amm. Marcell. xxii. 13; Petron. 29. The custom is an extremely ancient one. "The tabernacle of Moloch, and the star of your god Remphan," which the Israelites took up in the wilderness, were of the same description. Little images of Pallas (παλλάδια περιαυτόφορα) Demeter, &c., were in special request, and an interesting earthenware aedicula of Cybele found at Athens is engraved in Lewin, i. 414. Appuleius (*Metam.* xi.) says that at the end of the festival small silver images of Artemis were placed on the temple steps for people to kiss.

[2] We learn from numerous inscriptions that guilds and trades-unions (συνεργασίαι, συμβιώσεις) were common in Ionia (see Renan, p. 355). "τεχνῖται, artifices nobiliores, ἐργάται, *operarii*" (Bengel).

[3] Cf. Acts xvi. 19.

[4] "Diana Ephesia, cujus nomen unicum, multiformi specie, ritu vario, nomine multijugo, *totus veneratur orbis*" (Appul. *Metam.* ii.). Pliny calls the temple "orbis terrarum miraculum" (*H. N.* xxxvi. 14); and the image and temple are found on the coins of many neighbouring cities.

[5] Compare the case of the Philippians (Acts xvi. 19). They were, as Calvin says, fighting for their "hearths" quite as much as their "altars," "ut scilicet *culinam* habeant bene calentem."

[6] Rom. xvi. 4.

not find the chief object of their search, they seized two of his companions—Gaius of Macedonia,[1] and the faithful Aristarchus.[2] With these two men in their custody, the crowd rushed wildly into the vast space of the theatre,[3] which stood ever open, and of which the still visible ruins—"a wreck of immense grandeur"—show that it was one of the largest in the world, and could easily have accommodated 30,000 spectators.[4] Paul, wherever he lay hidden, was within reach of communication from the disciples. Full of anxiety for the unknown fate of his two companions, he eagerly desired to make his way into the theatre and there address the rioters. There is, perhaps, no courage greater than that which is required from one who, in imminent danger of being torn to pieces, dares to face the furious insults and raging passions of an exasperated crowd. But the powers and the spirit of the Apostle always rose to a great occasion, and though he was so sensitive that he could not write a severe letter without floods of tears, and so nervous that he could scarcely endure to be left for even a few days alone, he was quite capable of this act of supreme heroism. He always wished to be in the fore-front of battle for his Master's cause. But his friends better appreciated the magnitude of the danger. Gaius and Aristarchus were too subordinate to be made scapegoats for the vengeance of the crowd; but they were sure that the mere appearance of that bent figure and worn and wasted face, which had become so familiar to many of the cities of Asia, would be the instant signal for a terrible outbreak. Their opposition was confirmed by a friendly message from some of the Asiarchs,[5] who rightly conjectured the chivalrous impulse which would lead the Apostle to confront the storm. Anxious to prevent bloodshed, and save the life of one whose gifts and greatness they had learnt to admire, and well aware of the excitability of an Ephesian mob, they sent Paul an express warning not to trust himself into the theatre.

The riot, therefore, spent itself in idle noise. The workmen had, indeed, got hold of Gaius and Aristarchus; but as the crowd did not require these poor Greeks, whose aspect did not necessarily connect them with what was generally regarded as a mere Jewish sect, they did not know what to do with them. The majority of that promiscuous assemblage, unable to make anything of the discordant shouts which were rising on every side, could only guess why they were there at all. There was, perhaps, a dim impression that some one or other was going to be thrown to the wild beasts, and doubtless among those varying clamours voices were not wanting like those with which the theatre of Smyrna rang not many years afterwards—at the martyrdom of Polycarp—of "Paul to the lions!" "The Christians to the lions!"[6] One

[1] Not Gaius of Derbe (xx. 4) or "mine host" (Rom. xvi. 23).

[2] Aristarchus of Thessalonica is mentioned in xx. 4; xxvii. 2; Col. iv. 10; Philem. 24.

[3] Cf. Acts xii. 21; Tac. *H.* ii. 80; Cic. *ad Fam.* viii. 2; Corn. Nep. *Timol.* iv. 2; Jos. *B. J.* vii. 3, § 3. The theatre was the ordinary scene of such gatherings.

[4] Fellowes, *Asia Minor*, p. 274. Wood says 25,000 (*Ephes.* p. 68).

[5] It was the Asiarch Philip at Smyrna, who resisted the cry of the mob, ἵνα ἐπαφῇ Πολυκάρπῳ λέοντα (Euseb. *H. E.* iv. 15).

[6] See 1 Cor. iv. 9; 1 Cor. xv. 32; *Act. Mart. Polycarp.* 12. The stadium where the Bestiarii fought was near the theatre, and the Temple of Artemis was in full view of it.

thing, however, was generally known, which was, that the people whose proceedings were the cause for the tumult were of Jewish extraction, and a Greek mob was never behindhand in expressing its detestation for the Jewish race. The Jews, on the other hand, felt it hard that they, who had long been living side by side with the Ephesians in the amicable relations of commerce, should share the unpopularity of a sect which they hated quite as much as the Greeks could do. They were anxious to explain to the Greeks and Romans a lesson which they could not get them to learn—namely, that the Jews were not Christians, though the Christians might be Jews. Accordingly they urged Alexander to speak for them, and explain how matters really stood. This man was perhaps the coppersmith who, afterwards also, did Paul much evil, and who would be likely to gain the hearing of Demetrius and his workmen from similarity of trade. This attempt to shift the odium on the shoulders of the Christians entirely failed. Alexander succeeded in struggling somewhere to the front, and stood before the mob with outstretched hand in the attempt to win an audience for his oration. But no sooner had the mob recognised the well-known traits of Jewish physiognomy than they vented their hate in a shout of "Great is Artemis[1] of the Ephesians!" which was caught up from lip to lip until it was reverberated on every side by the rocks of Prion and Coressus, and drowned all others in its one familiar and unanimous roar.

For two hours, as though they had been howling dervishes, did this mongrel Greek crowd continue incessantly their senseless yell.[2] By that time they were sufficiently exhausted to render it possible to get a hearing. Hitherto the authorities, afraid that these proceedings might end in awakening Roman jealousy to a serious curtailment of their privileges, had vainly endeavoured to stem the torrent of excitement; but now, availing himself of a momentary lull, the Recorder of the city—either the mock officer of that name, who was chosen by the Senate and people for the Artemisia, or more probably the permanent city official—succeeded in restoring order.[3] It may have been all

It is, however, very unlikely that St. Paul actually fought with wild beasts. The expression was recognised as a metaphorical one (2 Tim. iv. 17), ἀπὸ Συρίας μέχρι Ῥώμης θηριομαχῶ (Ignat. *Rom.* c. 5); οἵοις θηρίοις μαχόμεθα (Appian, *Bell. Civ.* p. 273). A legend naturally attached itself to the expression (Niceph. *H. E.* ii. 25). The pseudo-Heraclitus (Ep. vii.), writing about this time, says of the Ephesians, ἐξ ἀνθρώπων θηρία γεγονότες. Moreover, St. Paul uses the expression in a letter written *before* this wild scene at Ephesus had taken place.

[1] I preserve the Greek name because their Asian idol, who was really Cybele, had still less to do with Diana than with Artemis.

[2] They probably were so far corrupted by the contact with Oriental worship as to regard their "vain repetitions in the light of a religious function" (see 1 Kings xviii. 26; Matt. vi. 7). Moreover, they distinctly believed that the glory, happiness, and perpetuity of Ephesus was connected with the maintenance of a splendid ritual. On the discovered inscription of the decree which dedicated the entire month of May to the Artemisian Paneguris, are these concluding words:—οὕτω γὰρ ἐπὶ τὸ ἄμεινον τῆς θρησκείας γινομένης ἡ πόλις ἡμῖν ἐνδοξοτέρα τε καὶ εὐδαίμων εἰς τὸν πάντα διαμενεῖ χρόνον (Boeckh, 2,954). It is probable that St. Paul may have read this very inscription, which seems to be of the age of Tiberius.

[3] The Proconsul of Asia was practically autocratic, being only restrained by the dread of being ultimately brought to law. Subject to his authority the chief towns of Asia were autonomous, managing their domestic affairs by the decisions of a Boulé and

the more easy for him, because one who was capable of making so admirably skilful and sensible a speech could hardly fail to have won a permanent respect, which enhanced the dignity of his position. "Ephesians!" he exclaimed, "what human being is there who is unaware that the city of the Ephesians is a sacristan[1] of the great Artemis, and the Heaven-fallen? Since, then, this is quite indisputable, your duty is to maintain your usual calm, and not to act in the precipitate way in which you have acted,[2] by dragging here these men, who are neither temple-robbers,[3] nor blasphemers of your goddess.[4] If Demetrius and his fellow-artisans have any complaint to lodge against any one, the sessions are going on,[5] and there are proconsuls;[6] let them settle the matter between them at law. But if you are making any further inquisition about any other matter, it shall be disposed of in the regular meeting of the Assembly.[7] For, indeed, this business renders us liable to a charge of sedition, since we shall be entirely unable to give any reasonable account of this mass meeting."

The effect of this speech was instantaneous.

"He called
Across the tumult, and the tumult fell."

The sensible appeal of the "*vir pietate gravis*" made the crowd repent of their unreasoning uproar, and afraid of its possible consequences, as the Recorder alternately flattered, intimidated, argued, and soothed. It reminded

Ekklesia. The Recorder acted as Speaker, and held a very important position. The historic accuracy of St. Luke cannot be more strikingly illustrated than it is by one of the Ephesian inscriptions in Boeckh, No. 2,960, which records how the "*Augustus-loving*" (φιλοσέβαστος) senate of the Ephesians, and its *temple-adorning* (νεωκόρος) Demos consecrated a building in the *Proconsulship* (ἐπὶ ἀνθυπάτου) of Peduceus Priscinus, and by the decree of Tiberius Claudius Italicus, the "*Recorder*" (γραμματεὺς) of the Demos.

[1] νεωκόρον, "temple-sweeper." It was an honorary title granted by the Emperor to various cities in Asia, and often recorded on coins.

[2] Acts xix. 36, κατεσταλμένους ὑπάρχειν καὶ μηδὲν προπετὲς ποιεῖν. Cicero (*pro Flacco*) gives a striking picture of the rash and unjust legislation of Asiatic cities, "quum in theatro imperiti homines rerum omnium rudes ignarique considerant" (cf. Tac. *H.* ii. 80).

[3] Wood, p. 14. This, strange to say, was a common charge against Jews (see on Rom. ii. 22).

[4] Another striking indication that St. Paul's method as a missionary was not to shock the prejudices of idolaters. Chrysostom most unjustly accuses the Recorder of here making a false and claptrap statement.

[5] ἀγόραιοι ἄγονται, "Conventûs peraguntur"—not as in E.V., "the law is open." Every province was divided into districts (διοικήσεις, conventûs), which met at some assize town. "Ephesum vero, alterum lumen Asiæ, remotiores conveniunt" (Plin. *H. N.* v. 31).

[6] There was under ordinary circumstances only one Proconsul in any province. The plural may be generic, or may mean the Proconsul and his assessors (*consiliarii*), as ἡγεμόνες means "the Procurator or his assessors" in Jos. *B. J.* ii. 16, § 1. But Basnage has ingeniously conjectured that the allusion may be to the joint authority of the Imperial Procurators, the knight P. Celer, and the freedman Helius. In the first year of Nero, A.D. 54, they had, at the instigation of Agrippina, poisoned Junius Silanus, Proconsul of Asia, whose gentle nature did not preserve him from the peril of his royal blood (Tac. *Ann.* xiii. 1). As P. Celer at any rate did not return to Rome till the year A.D. 57, it is conjectured that he and Helius may have been allowed to be Vice-Proconsuls till this period by way of rewarding them for their crimes (Lewin, *Fasti Sacri*, 1806, 1838; Biscoe, *On the Acts*, pp. 282—285).

[7] There were three regular meetings of the Assembly (ἔννομοι ἐκκλήσιαι) every month (and see Wood, p. 50).

them very forcibly that, since Asia was a senatorial, not an imperial province, and was therefore governed by a Proconsul with a few officials, not by a Proprætor with a legion, they were responsible for good order, and would most certainly be held accountable for any breach of the peace. A day of disorder might forfeit the privileges of years. The Recorder's speech, it has been said, is the model of a popular harangue. Such excitement on the part of the Ephesians was *undignified*, as the grandeur of their worship was unimpeached; it was *unjustifiable*, as they could prove nothing against the men; it was *unnecessary*, as other means of redress were open; and, finally, if neither pride nor justice availed anything, fear of the Roman power[1] should restrain them. They felt thoroughly ashamed, and the Recorder was now able to dismiss them from the theatre.

It is not, however, likely that the danger to St. Paul's person ceased, in a month of which he had spoiled the festivity, and in a city which was thronged, as this was, with aggrieved interests and outraged superstitions. Whether he was thrown into prison, or what were the dangers to which he alludes, or in what way God delivered him "from so great a death,"[2] we cannot tell. At any rate, it became impossible for him to carry out his design of staying at Ephesus till Pentecost.[3] All that we are further told is that, when the hubbub had ceased, he called the disciples together, and, after comforting them,[4] bade the Church farewell—certainly for many years, perhaps for ever.[5] He set out, whether by sea or by land we do not know, on his way to Macedonia. From Silas he had finally parted at Jerusalem. Timothy, Titus, Luke, Erastus, were all elsewhere; but Gaius and Aristarchus, saved from their perilous position in the theatre, were still with them, and he was now joined by the two Ephesians, Tychicus and Trophimus, who remained faithful to him till the very close of his career.

The Church which he had founded became the eminent Christian metropolis of a line of Bishops, and there, four centuries afterwards, was held the great Œcumenical Council which deposed Nestorius, the heretical Patriarch of Constantinople.[6] But "its candlestick" has been for centuries "removed out of his place;"[7] the squalid Mohammedan village which is nearest to its site does not count one Christian in its insignificant population;[8] its temple is a

[1] Hackett, p. 246. There was nothing on which the Romans looked with such jealousy as a tumultuous meeting, "Qui coetum et concentum fecerit *capitale sit*" (Sen. *Controv.* iii. 8). The hint would not be likely to be lost on Demetrius.

[2] 2 Cor. i. 10.

[3] The period of his stay at Ephesus was τριετίαν ὅλην (Acts xx. 31). The ruin called "the prison of St. Paul" may point to a true tradition that he was for a time confined, and those who see in Rom. xvi. 3–20, the fragment of a letter to Ephesus, suppose that his imprisonment was shared by his kinsmen Andronicus and Junias, who were "of note among the Apostles," and earlier converts than himself.

[4] Acts xx. 1, παρακαλέσας (A, B, D, E).

[5] It was only the elders whom he saw at Miletus.

[6] A.D. 431.

[7] Rev. ii. 5.

[8] *V. supra*, p. 358. See, for the present condition of Ephesus, Arundell, *Seven Churches of Asia*, p. 27; Fellowes, *Asia Minor*, p. 274; Falkener, *Ephesus and the Temple of Diana;* and especially Mr. J. T. Wood's *Discoveries at Ephesus*. The site of the temple has first been established with certainty by Mr. Wood's excavations.

mass of shapeless ruins; its harbour is a reedy pool; the bittern booms amid its pestilent and stagnant marshes; and malaria and oblivion reign supreme over the place where the wealth of ancient civilisation gathered around the scenes of its grossest superstitions and its most degraded sins. "A noisy flight of crows," says a modern traveller, "seemed to insult its silence; we heard the partridge call in the area of the theatre and the Stadium."[1]

CHAPTER XXXII.

CONDITION OF THE CHURCH AT CORINTH.

> "Hopes have precarious life;
> They are oft blighted, withered, snapt sheer off;—
> But faithfulness can feed on suffering,
> And knows no disappointment."—*Spanish Gipsy.*

No one can realise the trials and anxieties which beset the life of the great Apostle during his stay at Ephesus, without bearing in mind how grave were the causes of concern from which he was suffering, in consequence of the aberrations of other converts. The First Epistle to the Corinthians was written during the latter part of his three years' residence at the Ionian metropolis;[2] and it reveals to us a state of things which must have rent his heart in twain. Any one who has been privileged to feel a deep personal responsibility for some great and beloved institution, will best appreciate how wave after wave of affliction must have swept across his sea of troubles as he heard from time to time those dark rumours from Galatia and Corinth, which showed how densely the tares of the enemy had sprung up amid the good wheat which he had sown.

Apollos, on his return to Ephesus, must have told him some very unfavourable particulars. St. Paul had now been absent from the Corinthians for nearly three years, and they may well have longed—as we see that they did long—for his presence with an earnestness which even made them unjust towards him. The little band of converts—mostly of low position, and some of them of despicable antecedents—not a few of them slaves, and some of them slaves of the most degraded rank—were left in the midst of a heathendom which presented itself at Corinth under the gayest and most alluring aspects. It is not in a day that the habits of a life can be thrown aside. Even those among them whose conversion was most sincere had yet a terrible battle to fight against two temptations: the temptation to dishonesty, which had mingled with their means of gaining a livelihood; and the temptation to sensuality, which was interwoven with the very fibres of their being. With Christianity awoke conscience. Sins to which they had once lightly yielded

[1] See Chandler, pp. 109—137.

[2] Probably about April, A.D. 57.

as matters of perfect indifference, now required an intense effort to resist and overcome, and every failure, so far from being at the worst a venial weakness, involved the agonies of remorse and shame. And when they remembered the superficially brighter and easier lives which they had spent while they were yet pagans;[1] when they daily witnessed how much sin there might be with so little apparent sorrow; when they felt the burdens of their life doubled, and those earthly pleasures which they had once regarded as its only alleviations rendered impossible or wrong—while as yet they were unable to realise the exquisite consolation of Christian joy and Christian hope—they were tempted either to relapse altogether, or to listen with avidity to any teacher whose doctrines, if logically developed, might help to relax the stringency of their sacred obligations. While Paul was with them they were comparatively safe. The noble tyranny of his personal influence acted on them like a spell; and with his presence to elevate, his words to inspire, his example to encourage them, they felt it more easy to fling away all that was lower and viler, because they could realise their right to what was higher and holier. But when he had been so long away—when they were daily living in the great wicked streets, among the cunning, crowded merchants, in sight and hearing of everything which could quench spiritual aspirations and kindle carnal desires; when the gay, common life went on around them, and the chariot-wheels of the Lord were still afar—it was hardly wonderful if the splendid vision began to fade. The lustral water of Baptism had been sprinkled on their foreheads; they fed on the Sacrament of the Body and Blood of Christ; but, alas! Corinth was not heaven, and the prose of daily life followed on the poetry of their first enthusiasm, and it was difficult to realise that, for them, those living streets might be daily brightened with manna dews. Their condition was like the pause and sigh of Lot's wife, as, amid the sulphurous storm, she gazed back on the voluptuous ease of the City of the Plain. Might they no longer taste of the plentiful *Syssitia* on some festive day? Might they not walk at twilight in the laughing bridal procession, and listen to the mirthful jest? Might they not watch the Hieroduli dance at some lovely festival in the Temples of Acrocorinth? Was all life to be hedged in for them with thorny scruples? Were they to gaze henceforth in dreaming phantasy, not upon bright faces of youthful deities, garlanded with rose and hyacinth, but on the marred visage of One who was crowned with thorns? Oh, it was hard to choose the kingdom of God; hard to remember that now they were delivered out of the land of Egypt; hard for their enervation to breathe the eager and difficult air of the pure wilderness. It was hard to give up the coarse and near for the immaterial and the far; hard not to lust after the reeking flesh-pots, and not to loathe the light angel food; hard to give up the purple wine in the brimming goblet for the cold water from the spiritual rock; hard to

[1] "In the young pagan world
Men deified the beautiful, the glad,
The strong, the boastful, and it came to nought;
We have raised pain and sorrow into heaven" (Athelwold).

curb and crucify passions which once they had consecrated under guise of religion; hard not to think all these temptations irresistible, and to see the way of escape which God had appointed them for each; hard to be bidden to rejoice, and not to be suffered even to murmur at all these hardnesses of life. And the voice which had taught them the things of God had now for so long been silent; for three years they had not seen the hand which pointed them to Heaven. It was with some of them as with Israel, when Moses was on Sinai: they sat down to eat and to drink, and rose up to play. Many, very many—some in shame and secrecy, others openly justifying their relapse by the devil-doctrines of perverted truth—had plunged once more into the impurity, the drunkenness, and the selfishness, as though they had never heard the heavenly calling, or tasted the eternal gift.

So much even Apollos must have told the Apostle; and when he had occasion, in a letter now lost[1]—probably because it was merely a brief and businesslike memorandum—to write and inform them of his intended, but subsequently abandoned, plan of paying them a double visit, and to bid them contribute to the collection for the poor saints at Jerusalem, he had, in a message which required subsequent explanation, briefly but emphatically bidden them not to keep company with fornicators.[2]

And now a letter had come from Corinth. So far from dwelling on the ruinous disorders into which many members of the Church had fallen, it was entirely self-complacent in tone; and yet it proved the existence of much doctrinal perplexity, and, in asking advice about a number of practical subjects, had touched upon questions which betrayed some of the moral and intellectual errors which the Church, in writing the letter, had so disingenuously concealed.[3]

1. After greeting him, and answering him, in words which he quotes, that "they remembered him in all things, and kept the ordinances as he delivered them,"[4] they had asked him a whole series of questions about celibacy and marriage, which had evidently been warmly discussed in the Church, and decided in very different senses. Was married life in itself wrong, or if not wrong, yet undesirable? or, if not even undesirable, still a lower and less worthy condition than celibacy? When persons were already married, was it their duty, or, at any rate, would it be saintlier to live together as though they were unmarried? Might widows and widowers marry a second time? Were mixed marriages between Christians and heathens to be tolerated, or ought a Christian husband to repudiate a heathen wife, and a Christian wife to leave a heathen husband? and ought fathers to seek marriages for their daughters, or let them grow up as virgins?

2. Again, what were they to do about meats offered to idols? They had

[1] The spurious letter of the Corinthians to St. Paul, and his answer, preserved in Armenian, are perfectly valueless.

[2] See 1 Cor. x. 1—14.

[3] The interchange of such letters (אִגְּרוֹת) on disputed points of doctrine between the synagogues was common.

[4] 1 Cor. xi. 2.

prefaced their inquiry on this subject with the conceited remark that "they all had knowledge,"[1] and had perhaps indicated their own opinion by the argument that an idol was nothing in the world, and that all things were lawful to their Christian freedom. Still, they wished to know whether they might ever attend any of the idol festivals? The question was an important one for the poor, to whom a *visceratio*[2] was no small help and indulgence. Was it lawful to buy meat in the open market, which, without their knowing it, might have been offered to idols? Might they go as guests to their heathen friends and relations, and run the risk of partaking of that which had been part of a sacrifice?[3]

3. Then, too, a dispute had risen among them about the rule to be observed in assemblies. Was it the duty of men to cover their heads? Might women appear with their heads uncovered? And might they speak and teach in public?

4. They had difficulties, also, about spiritual gifts. Which was the more important, speaking with tongues or preaching? When two or three began at the same time to preach or speak with tongues, what were they to do?

5. Further, some among them had been perplexed by great doubts about the Resurrection. There were even some who maintained that by the Resurrection was meant something purely spiritual, and that it was past already. This view had arisen from the immense material difficulties which surrounded the whole subject of a resurrection of the body. Would Paul give them his solution of some of their difficulties?

6. He had asked them to make a collection for the poor in Judæa: they would be glad to hear something more about this. What plans would he recommend to them?

7. Lastly, they were very anxious to receive Apollos once more among them. They had enjoyed his eloquence, and profited by his knowledge. Would Paul try to induce him to come, as well as pay them his own promised visit?

Such, we gather from the First Epistle to the Corinthians, were the inquiries of a letter which had been brought to the Apostle at Ephesus by Stephanas, Fortunatus, and Achaicus. It was inevitable that St. Paul should talk to these worthy slaves about the Church of which they were the delegates. There was quite enough in the letter itself to create a certain misgiving in

[1] 1 Cor. viii. 1.

[2] Public feasts at funerals or idol festivals, &c., Cic. *Off.* ii. 16; Liv. viii. 32, &c. They played a large part in the joy and plenty of ancient life. Arist. *Eth.* viii. 9, 5; Thuc. ii. 38.

[3] The Jews had strong feelings on this subject (cf. Num. xxv. 2; Ps. cvi. 28; Tob. i. 10—14); but it is monstrous to say that St. Paul here teaches the violation of such scruples, or that he is referred to in Rev. ii. 14. On the contrary, he says, "Even if you as Gentiles think nothing of it, still *do not do it*, for the sake of others; only the concession to the weak need not become a tormenting scrupulosity." It is doubtful whether even St. Peter and St. John would not have gone quite as far as this. So strict were Judaic notions on the subject that, in the case of wine, for instance, not only did a cask of it become undrinkable to a Jew if a single heathen libation had been poured from it, but "even a touch with the presumed intention of pouring away a little to the gods is enough to render it unlawful." This is called the law of נסך.

his mind, and some of its queries were sufficient to betray an excited state of opinion. But when he came to talk with these visitants from Chloe's household, and they told him the simple truth, he stood aghast with horror, and was at the same time overwhelmed with grief. Reluctantly, bit by bit, in answer to his questionings, they revealed a state of things which added darkness to the night of his distress.

8. First of all, he learnt from them that the Church which he had founded was split up into deplorable factions.

It was the result of visits from various teachers who had followed in the wake of Paul, and built upon his foundations very dubious materials by way of superstructure. "Many teachers, much strife," had been one of the wise and pregnant sayings of the great Hillel, and it had been fully exemplified at Corinth, where, in the impatient expression of St. Paul, they had had "ten thousand pedagogues." The great end of edification had been lost sight of in the violences of faction, and all deep spirituality had been evaporated in disputatious talk. He heard sad rumours of "strifes, heartburnings, rages, dissensions, backbitings, whisperings, inflations, disorderliness."[1]

i. It became clear that even the visit and teaching of Apollos had done harm—harm which he certainly had not intended to do, and which, as a loyal friend and follower of Paul, he was the first to regret. Paul's own preaching to these Corinthians had been designedly simple, dealing with the great broad fact of a Redeemer crucified for sin, and couched in language which made no pretence to oratorical ornament. But Apollos, who had followed him, though an able man, was an inexperienced Christian, and not only by the natural charm of his impassioned oratory, but also by the way in which he had entered into the subtle refinements so familiar to the Alexandrian intellect, had unintentionally led them first of all to despise the unsophisticated simplicity of St. Paul's teaching, and next to give the rein to all the sceptical fancies with which their faith was overlaid. Both the manner and the matter of the fervid convert had so delighted them that, with entire opposition to his own wishes, they had elevated him into the head of a party, and had perverted his views into dangerous extravagances. These Apollonians were so puffed up with the conceit of knowledge, so filled with the importance of their own intellectual emancipation, that they had also begun to claim a fatal moral liberty. They had distracted the Sunday gatherings with the egotisms of rival oratory; had shown a contemptuous disregard for the scruples of weaker brethren; had encouraged women to harangue in the public assemblies as the equals of men; were guilty of conduct which laid them open to the charge of the grossest inconsistency; and even threw the cloak of sophistical excuse over one crime so heinous that the very heathen were ready to cry shame on the offender. In the accounts brought to him of this Apollos-party, St. Paul could not but see the most extravagant exaggeration of his own doctrines—the half-truths, which are ever the most dangerous of errors. If it was pos-

[1] 2 Cor. xii. 20.

sible to wrest the truths which he himself had taught into the heretical notions which were afterwards promulgated by Marcion, his keen eye could detect in the perversions of the Alexandrian eloquence of Apollos the deadly germs of what would afterwards develop into Antinomian Gnosticism.

ii. But Apollos was not the only teacher who had visited Corinth. Some Judaic Christians had come, who had been as acceptable to the Jewish members of the Church as Apollos was to the Greeks.[1] Armed with commendatory letters from some of the twelve at Jerusalem, they claimed the authority of Peter, or, as they preferred to call him, of Kephas. They did not, indeed, teach the necessity of circumcision, as others of their party did in Galatia. There the local circumstances would give some chance of success to teaching which in Corinth would have been rejected with contempt; and perhaps these particular emissaries felt at least some respect for the compact at Jerusalem. But yet their influence had been very disastrous, and had caused the emergence of a Petrine party in the Church. This party—the ecclesiastical ancestors of those who subsequently vented their hatred of Paul in the Pseudo-Clementines—openly and secretly disclaimed his authority, and insinuated disparagement of his doctrines. Kephas, they said, was the real head of the Apostles, and therefore of the Christians. Into his hands had Christ entrusted the keys of the kingdom; on the rock of his confession was the Church of the Messiah to be built. Paul was a presumptuous interloper, whose conduct to Kephas at Antioch had been most unbecoming. For who was Paul? not an Apostle at all, but an unauthorised innovator. He had been a persecuting Sanhedrist, and he was an apostate Jew. What had he been at Corinth? A preaching tent-maker, nothing more. Kephas, and other Apostles, and the brethren of the Lord, when they travelled about, were accompanied by their wives or by ministering women, and claimed the honour and support to which they were entitled. Why had not Paul done the same? Obviously because he felt the insecurity of his own position. And as for his coming again, a weak, vacillating, unaccredited pretender, such as he was, would take care not to come again. And these preachings of his were heretical, especially in their pronounced indifference to the Levitic law. Was he not breaking down that hedge about the law, the thickening of which had been the life-long task of centuries of eminent Rabbis? Very different had been the scene after Peter's preaching at Pentecost! It was the speaking with tongues—not mere dubious doctrinal exhortation—which was the true sign of spirituality. We are more than sure that the strong, and tender, and noble nature of St. Peter would as little have sanctioned this subterranean counter-working against the Apostle of the Gentiles, as Apollos discountenanced the impious audacities which sheltered themselves under his name.

[1] The circumstances of Corinth were very similar when Clement wrote them his first Epistle. He had still to complain of that "strange and alien, and, for the elect of God, detestable and unholy spirit of faction, which a few rash and self-willed persons (πρόσωπα) kindled to such a pitch of dementation, that their holy and famous reputation, so worthy of all men's love, was greatly blasphemed" (*Ep. ad Cor.* i.).

iii. And then had come another set of Judaisers—one man in particular—to whom the name of even Kephas was unsatisfactory. He apparently was—or, what is a very different thing, he professed to be—an adherent of James,[1] and to him even Peter was not altogether sound. He called himself a follower of Christ, and disdained any other name. Perhaps he was one of the Desposyni. At any rate, he prided himself on having seen Christ, and known Christ in the flesh. Now the Lord Jesus had not married, and James, the Bishop of Jerusalem, was unmarried; and this teacher evidently shared the Essene abhorrence of marriage. He it was who had started all the subtle refinements of questions respecting celibacy and the married life. He it was who gathered around him a few Jews of Ebionite proclivities, who degraded into a party watchword even the sacred name of Christ.[2]

9. Thus, as St. Paul now learnt fully for the first time, the Church of Corinth was a scene of quarrels, disputes, partisanships, which, in rending asunder its unity, ruined its strength. On all these subjects the Corinthians, in their self-satisfied letter, had maintained a prudent but hardly creditable silence. Nor was this all that they had concealed. They had asked questions about spiritual gifts; but it was left for the household of Chloe to break to St. Paul the disquieting news that the assemblies of the Church had degenerated into scenes so noisy, so wild, so disorderly, that there were times when any heathen who dropped in could only say that they were all mad. Sometimes half a dozen enthusiasts were on their legs at once, all pouring forth wild series of sounds which no human being present could understand, except that sometimes, amid these unseemly—and might they not at times, with some of these Syrian emissaries, be these half-simulated—ecstasies, there were heard words that made the blood run cold with shuddering horror.[3] At other times, two or three preachers would interrupt each other in the attempt to gain the ear of the congregation all at the same moment. Women rose to give their opinions, and that without a veil on their heads, as though they were not ashamed to be mistaken for the Hetairæ, who alone assumed such an unblushing privilege. So far from being a scene of peace, the Sunday services had become stormy, heated, egotistic, meaningless, unprofitable.

10. And there was worse behind. It might at least have been supposed that the Agapæ would bear some faint traditional resemblance to their name, and be means of reunion and blessedness worthy of their connexion with the Eucharistic feast! Far from it! The deadly leaven of selfishness—display-

[1] We cannot for a moment believe that Peter and James really approved of the methods of these men, because to do so would have been a flagrant breach of their own compact (Gal. ii. 9). But it is matter of daily experience that the rank and file of parties are infinitely less wise and noble than their leaders.

[2] About the Christ party there have been three main views:—(1) That they were adherents of James (Storr, &c.); (2) that they were neutrals, who held aloof from all parties (Eichhorn, &c.); (3) that they were a very slight modification of the Peter-party (Baur, *Paul.* i. 272—292). It is remarkable that to this day there is in England and America a sect, which, professing to disdain human authority, usurps the exclusive name of "Christians" (see Schaff. *Apost. Ch.* i. 339).

[3] 1 Cor. xii. 3 (cf. 1 John ii. 22; iv. 1—3); Ἀνάθεμα Ἰησοῦν.

ing itself in its two forms of sensuality and pride—had insinuated itself even into these once simple and charitable gatherings. The kiss of peace could hardly be other than a hypocritical form between brethren, who at the very moment might be impleading one another at law before the tribunal of a heathen Praetor about some matter of common honesty. The rich brought their luxurious provisions, and greedily devoured them, without waiting for any one; while the poor, hungry-eyed Lazaruses—half-starved slaves, who had no contributions of their own to bring—watched them with hate and envy as they sat famishing and unrelieved by their full-fed brethren. Greediness and egotism had thus thrust themselves into the most sacred unions; and the besetting Corinthian sin of intoxication had been so little restrained that men had been seen to stretch drunken hands to the very chalice of the Lord!

11. Last and worst, not only had uncleanness found its open defenders, so that Christians were not ashamed to be seen sitting at meat amid the lascivious surroundings of heathen temples, but one prominent member of the Church was living in notorious crime with his own stepmother during the lifetime of his father; and, though the very Pagans execrated this atrocity, yet he had not been expelled from the Christian communion, not even made to do penance in it, but had found brethren ready, not merely to palliate his offence, but actually to plume themselves upon leaving it unpunished. This man seems to have been a person of distinction and influence, whom it was advantageous to a Church largely composed of slaves and women to count among them. Doubtless this had facilitated his condonation, which may have been founded on some antinonian plea of Christian liberty; or on some Rabbinic notion that old ties were rendered non-existent by the new conditions of a proselyte; or by peculiarities of circumstance unknown to us. But though this person was the most notorious, he was by no means the only offender, and there were Corinthian Christians—even many of them—who were impenitently guilty of uncleanness, fornication, and lasciviousness.[1] In none of his writings are the Apostle's warnings against this sin—the besetting sin of Corinth—more numerous, more solemn, or more emphatic.[2]

Truly, as he heard this catalogue of iniquities—while he listened to the dark tale of the shipwreck of all his fond hopes which he had learnt to entertain during the missionary labour of eighteen months—the heart of St. Paul must have sunk within him. He might well have folded his hands in utter despair. He might well have pronounced his life and his preaching a melancholy failure. He might well have fled like Elijah into utter solitude, and prayed, "Now, O Lord, take away my life, for I am not better than my fathers." But it was not thus that the news affected this indomitable man. His heart, indeed, throbbed with anguish, his eyes were streaming with tears, as, having heard to the bitter end all that the slaves of Chloe had to tell him, he proceeded to make his plans. First, of course, his intended brief immediate

[1] 2 Cor. xii. 21.

[2] 1 Cor. v. 11; vi. 15–18; x. 8; xv. 33, 34.

visit to Corinth must be given up. Neither he nor they were yet in a mood in which their meeting could be otherwise than infinitely painful. He must at once despatch Titus to Corinth to inform them of his change of plan, to arrange about the collection, and to do what little he could, before rejoining him at Troas. He must also despatch a messenger to Timothy to tell him not to proceed to Corinth at present. And then he *might* have written an apocalyptic letter, full of burning denunciation and fulminated anathemas; he might have blighted these conceited, and lascivious, and quarrelsome disgracers of the name of Christian with withering invectives, and rolled over their trembling consciences thunders as loud as those of Sinai. Not such, however, was the tone he adopted, or the spirit in which he wrote. In deep agitation, which he yet managed almost entirely to suppress, summoning all the courage of his nature, forgetting all the dangers and trials which surrounded him at Ephesus, asking God for the wisdom and guidance which he so sorely needed, crushing down deep within him all personal indignations, every possible feeling of resentment or egotism at the humiliations to which he had personally been subjected, he called Sosthenes to his side, and flinging his whole heart into the task immediately before him, began to dictate to him one of the most astonishing and eloquent of all his letters, the first extant Epistle to the Corinthians. Varied as are the topics with which it deals, profound as were the difficulties which had been suggested to him, novel as were the questions which he had to face, alienated as were many of the converts to whom he had to appeal, we see at once that the Epistle was no laborious or long-polished composition. Enlightened by the Spirit of God, St. Paul was in possession of that insight which sees at once into the heart of every moral difficulty. He was as capable of dealing with Greek culture and Greek sensuality as with Judaic narrowness and Judaic Pharisaism. He shows himself as great a master when he is applying the principles of Christianity to the concrete and complicated realities of life, as when he is moving in the sphere of dogmatic theology. The phase of Jewish opposition with which he has here to deal has been modified by contact with Hellenism, but it still rests on grounds of externalism, and must be equally met by spiritual truths. Problems however dark, details however intricate, become lucid and orderly at once in the light of external distinctions. In teaching his converts St. Paul had no need to burn the midnight oil in long studies. Even his most elaborate Epistles were in reality not elaborate. They leapt like vivid sparks from a heart in which the fire of love to God burnt until death with an ever brighter and brighter flame.

1. His very greeting shows the fulness of his heart. As his authority had been impugned, he calls himself "an Apostle of Jesus Christ by the will of God," and addresses them as a Church, as sanctified in Christ Jesus, and called to be saints, uniting with them in the prayer for grace and peace all who, whatever their differing shades of opinion or their place of abode, call upon the name of our Lord Jesus Christ, both theirs and ours.[1] Thus, in his very address to them, he strikes the

[1] "Est enim haec periculosa tentatio nullam Ecclesiam putare ubi non appareat perfecta puritas" (Calvin). The absence of fixed ecclesiastical organisation is clear, as he addresses the

key-note of his own claim to authority, and of the unity and holiness which they so deeply needed. "Observe, too," says St. Chrysostom, "how he ever nails them down to the name of Christ, not mentioning any man—either Apostle or teacher—but continually mentioning Him for whom they yearn, as men preparing to awaken those who are drowsy after a debauch. For nowhere in any other Epistle is the name of Christ so continuously introduced; here, however, it is introduced frequently, and by means of it he weaves together almost his whole exordium."[1]

2. Although he has united Sosthenes[2] with him in the superscription, he continues at once in the first person to tell them that he thanks God always for the grace given them in Christ Jesus, for the eloquence and knowledge with which they were enriched in Him, so that in waiting for the Apocalypse of Christ, they were behindhand in no spiritual gift; and as the testimony of Christ was confirmed among them, so should Christ confirm them to be blameless unto the end, since God was faithful, who had called them unto the communion of His Son Jesus Christ our Lord.[3]

3. That communion leads him at once to one of the subjects of which his heart is full. He has heard on indisputable authority, and not from one person only, of schisms and strifes among them, and he implores them by the name of Christ to strive after greater unity in thought and action.[4] They were saying, "I am of Paul, and I of Apollos, and I of Kephas, and I of Christ." What! has Christ been parcelled into fragments?[5] Some of them called themselves *his* party; but had *he* been crucified for them? had they been baptised into *his* name? It may be that Apollos, fresh from his discipleship to John's baptism, had dwelt very prominently on the importance of that initial rite; but so liable were men to attach importance to the mere human minister, that Paul, like his Master, had purposely abstained from administering it, and except Crispus and Gaius—and, as he afterwards recalls, Stephanas and his household—he cannot remember that he has baptised any of them. Christ had sent him not to baptise, but to preach; and that not in wisdom of utterance, that Christ's cross might not be rendered void. The mention of preaching brings him to the aberrations of the Apollonian party. They had attached immense importance to eloquence, logic, something which they called and exalted as wisdom. He shows them that they were on a wholly mistaken track. Such human wisdom, such ear-flattering eloquence, such superficial and plausible enticements, he had deliberately rejected. Of human wisdom he thought little. It lay under the ban of revelation.[6] It had not led the world to the knowledge of God. It had not saved the world from the crucifixion of Christ. And, therefore, he had not preached to them about the Logos, or about Æons, or in Philonian allegories, or with philosophical refinements. He had offered neither a sign to the Jews, nor wisdom to the Greeks. What he had to preach was regarded by the world as abject foolishness—it was the Cross—it was the doctrine of a crucified Messiah, which was to the Jews revolting; of a crucified Saviour, which was to the Greeks ridiculous; but it pleased

entire community, and holds no "bishops" responsible for the disorders, and for carrying out the excommunication.

[1] 1 Cor. i. 1—3. The name of Christ occurs no less than nine times in the first nine verses.

[2] Whether the Sosthenes of Acts xviii. 17, who may have been subsequently converted (Wetst. ii. 576), or an unknown brother, we do not know. He may have been one of the bearers of the Corinthian letter to Ephesus; "one of the seventy, and afterwards Bishop of Colophon" (Euseb. *H. E.* i. 12).

[3] i. 4—9. Observe the perfect sincerity of the Apostle. He desires, as always, to thank God on behalf of his converts; here, however, he has no *moral* praise to imply. The Corinthians have received rich spiritual blessings and endowments, but he cannot speak of them as he does of the Thessalonians or Philippians.

[4] Ver. 10, *νοῒ καὶ . . . γνώμῃ*. "intus in credendis, et sententiâ prolatâ in agendis" (Bengel).

[5] It is deeply instructive to observe that St. Paul here refuses to enter into the differences of view from which the parties sprang. He does not care to decide which section of wrangling "theologians" or "churchmen" is right and which is wrong. He denounces the *spirit* of party as a sin and a shame where unity between Christians is the first of duties and the greatest of advantages.

[6] i. 20, *ποῦ συζητητὴς, κ. τ. λ.*, but in Isa. xxxiii. 18 (cf. Ps. xlviii. 12), "*where is he who counteth the towers?*"

God to save believers by the foolishness (in the world's view) of the thing preached,[1] and it was to those who were in the way of salvation the wisdom and the power of God. They were not the wise, and the mighty, and the noble of the world, but, as a rule, the foolish, and the weak, and the despised.[2] It was not with the world's power, but with its impotences; not with its strength, but with its feebleness; not with its knowledge, but with its ignorance; not with its rank, but its ignobleness; not with kings and philosophers, but with slaves and women, that its divine forces were allied; and with them did God so purpose to reveal His power that no glory could accrue to man, save from the utter abasement of *human* glory. That was why Paul had come to them, not with rhetoric, but with the simple doctrine of Christ crucified;[3] not with oratoric dignity, but in weakness, fear, and trembling; not with winning elocution, but with spiritual demonstration and spiritual power—so that man might be utterly lost in God, and they might feel the origin of their faith to be not human but divine.[4]

4. Yet they must not be misled by his impassioned paradox into the notion that the matter and method of his teaching was really folly. On the contrary, it was wisdom of the deepest and loftiest kind—only it was a wisdom of God hidden from the wise of the world; a wisdom of insight into things which eye hath not seen nor ear heard, and which had never set foot on human heart,[5] but which were revealed to him by that Spirit which alone searcheth the depths of God,[6] and which he had taught in words not learnt from wisdom, but from that same Spirit of God, combining spirituals with spirituals.[7] And this spiritual wisdom was, to the natural man,[8] folly, because it could be only discerned by a spiritual faculty of which the natural man was absolutely devoid. It was to him what painting is to the blind, or music to the deaf.[9] But the spiritual man possesses the requisite discernment, and, sharing the mind of Christ, is thereby elevated above the reach of merely natural judgment.

5. And then, with wholesome irony, he adds that this divine condition, which was earthly folly, he could only teach them in its merest elements; in its perfection it was only for the perfect, but they, who thought themselves so wise and learned, were in spiritual wisdom fleshen babes, needing milk such as he had given them, not meat, which they—being fleshly—were still too feeble to digest.[10] These might seem hard words, but while there were envy, and strife, and divisions among them, how could they be regarded as anything but fleshy and unspiritual? Paul and Apollos! who were Paul and Apollos but mere human ministers? Paul planting, Apollos watering—neither of them anything in himself, but each of them one in their ministry, and each responsible for his own share in it. God only gave the harvest. "God's fellow-workers are we; God's acre, God's building are ye." Paul,

[1] i. 21, διὰ τῆς μωρίας τοῦ κηρύγματος, not "the foolishness of preaching" (κηρύξεως). In 23, 24 "cross," "stumblingblock," "folly," "power" would be respectively *seccel*, *miscol*, *mashcal*, *secel*, and some see in it a sign that St. Paul had in his thoughts a Syriac paronomasia (Winer, *N. T. Gramm.*, E. T., p. 658).

[2] A needful warning to "Corinthios non minus lasciviâ, quam *opulentiâ, et philosophiae* studio insignes" (Cic. *De Leg. Agr.* ii. 32).

[3] All the more remarkable because "a Corinthian style" meant "a polished style" (Wetst. *ad loc.*).

[4] i. 19; ii. 5; cf. Jer. ix. 23, 24; Isa. xxxiii. 18, is freely cited from the LXX.

[5] Possibly a vague echo of Isa. lxiv. 4 (cf. lii. 15, and lxv. 17); or from some lost book (Chrys.) like the "Revelation of Elias," ἐπὶ καρδίαν ἀνέβη, עָלָה עַל לֵב. *Both* explanations are possible, for the lost book may have echoed Isaiah. A modern theory regards the words as liturgical.

[6] Ver. 10. The attempt to make Rev. ii. 24 an ironical reference to this is most baseless.

[7] Ver. 13, πνευματικοῖς πνευματικὰ συγκρίνοντες, others render it "explaining spiritual things to spiritual men" (Gen. xl. 8; Dan. v. 12; LXX.) or "in spiritual words."

[8] Ver. 14, ψυχικὸς, "homines solius animae et carnis" (Tert. *De jejun.* 17).

[9] ii. 6—16. He refutes the Alexandrian teaching by accepting its very terms and principle—"mystery," "initiated," "spiritual man," &c., but showing that it is an eternal universal reality, not some apprehension of particular men (see Maurice, *Unity*, p. 408).

[10] iii. 2, σαρκινοὶ; 4, σαρκικοῖς. A severe blow at Alexandrian conceit. He has to treat them not as adepts but as novices, not as hierophants but as uninitiated, not as "theologians," but as catechumens, *for the very reason* that they thought so much of themselves (cf. the exactly analogous language of our Lord in John ix. 41).

as a wise master-builder, has laid the foundation; others were building on it all sorts of superstructures. But the foundation was and could be only one—namely, Christ—and the gold, silver, precious marbles, logs, hay, stubble, built on it should be made manifest in its true quality in God's ever-revealing fire,[1] and if worthless, should be destroyed, however sincere the builder might be. If his superstructure was sound, he would be rewarded; if perishable, it would be burnt in the consuming flame, and he should suffer loss, though he himself, since he had built on the true foundation, would be saved as by fire.[2] Did they not know then that they were a temple, a holy temple for the spirit of God? If any man destroy God's temple, God shall destroy him. And human wisdom might destroy it, for before God human wisdom was folly. The mere human wisdom of this or that favourite teacher has nothing to do with the real building. If a man wanted Divine wisdom, let him gain it by the humble paths of what was regarded as human folly. How unworthy, then, to be boasting about mere human teachers—how unworthy was it of their own immense privilege and hope—when all things were theirs—Paul, Apollos, Kephas, the universe, life, death, the immediate present, the far future—all theirs, and they Christ's, and Christ God's. Their party leaders were but poor weak creatures at the best, of whom was required one thing only—faithfulness. As for himself he regarded it as a matter utterly trivial whether he were judged by their tentative opinions or by man's insignificant feeble transient day;[3] nay, he even judged not himself. He was conscious indeed of no sin as regards his ministry;[4] but even on that he did not rely as his justification, depending only on the judgment of the Lord. "So then be not ye judging anything before the due time until the Lord come, who shall both illuminate the crypts of darkness and reveal the counsels of the heart." Then, and not till then, shall the praise which he deserves, and no other praise, accrue to each from God.[5]

6. He had, with generous delicacy, designedly put into prominence his own name and that of Apollos (instead of those of Kephas or the Jerusalem emissary) as unwilling leaders of factions which they utterly deprecated, that the Corinthians might learn in their case not to estimate them above the warrant of their actual words,[6] and might see that he was actuated by no mere jealousy of others, when he denounced their inflated exasperation amongst themselves in the rival display of what after all, even when they existed, were not intrinsic merits, but gifts of God.[7] And what swelling self-appreciation they showed in all this party spirit! For them the hunger, and the poverty, and the struggle, are all over. What plentitude and satiety of satisfaction you have gained; how rich you are; what thrones you sit on; and all without us. Ah, would it were really so, that we might at least share your royal elevation! For the position of us poor Apostles is very different. "God, I think, displayed us last as condemned criminals,[8] a theatric spectacle to the universe, both angels and men. We are fools for Christ's sake, but ye are wise in Christ; we weak, but ye strong; ye glorious, but we dishonoured. Up to this very

[1] iii. 13, ἀποκαλύπτεται. By calling this a *praesens futurascens*, and not recognising the normal, unceasing operation of the moral laws of God, commentators have missed a great truth (cf. Matt. iii. 10; Col. iii. 6; Eph. v. 6).

[2] St. Paul does not care to make his metaphor "run on all fours." The general application is sufficient for him. (See Reuss, *Les Epîtres*, i. 169.)

[3] iv. 3, ἀνακριθῶ. An *anakrisis* was an examination preliminary to trial. ἡμέρας, this forcible expression has been explained as a Hebraism (Jer. xvii. 16), a *Cilicism* (Jer. *ad Algas.* 10), and a Latinism (*diem dicere*, &c., Grot.).

[4] Ver. 4. οὐδὲν . . . ἐμαυτῷ σύνοιδα, "I am conscious of no guilt" ("Nil conscire sibi," Hor. *Ep.* I. i. 61). "I know nothing by myself," in this sense is old English. "I am sorry that each fault can be proved by the queen" (Cranmer, *Letter to Henry VIII.*).

[5] iv. 1—4.

[6] iv. 6. The word φρονεῖν is omitted by the chief Uncials. I take μὴ ὑπὲρ ὃ γέγραπται to be a sort of proverb, like "keep to your written evidence." Throughout this section St. Paul's mind is full of the word "inflation" (φυσιοῦσθε; ver. 18, ἐφυσιώθησαν: 19, πεφυσιωμένων: v. 2, πεφυσιωμένοι; viii. 1, ἡ γνῶσις φυσιοῖ; xiii. 4, ἡ ἀγάπη οὐ φυσιοῦται). This is because when St. Paul comes to them, he is afraid of finding this vice of a conceited theology. 2 Cor. xii. 20, φυσιώσεις. Elsewhere the word only occurs in Col. ii. 18.

[7] iv. 7, τίς γάρ σε διακρίνει;

[8] iv. 9, ὡς ἐπιθανατίους, "veluti *bestiarios*" (Tert. *De Pudic.* 14).

hour we both hunger and thirst, and are ill-clad,[1] and are buffeted, and are hustled from place to place, and toil, working with our own hands; being abused, we bless; being persecuted, we endure; being reviled, we entreat; as refuse of the universe[2] are we become, the offscouring of all things till now." These are bitter and ironical words of contrast between you and us, I know; but I write not as shaming you. I am only warning you as my beloved children. For, after all, you *are* my children. Plenty of teachers, I know, have followed me; but (and here comes one of his characteristic impetuosities of expression) even if you have a myriad pedagogues[3] in Christ—however numerous, or stern, or authoritative—you have not many fathers. It was I who begot you through the Gospel in Christ Jesus, and I therefore entreat you to follow my example; and on this account I sent you my beloved and faithful son Timothy, to remind you of my invariable practice and teaching.[4] Do not think, however, that I am afraid to confront in person the inflated opposition of some who say that I do not really mean to come myself. Come I will, and that soon, if the Lord will; and will ascertain not what these inflated critics *say*, but what they *are;* not their power of talk, but of action. "But what will ye? Am I to come to you with a rod, or in love and the spirit of gentleness?"[5]

7. One thing at least needs the rod. A case of incest—of a son taking his father's wife—so gross, that it does not exist even among the heathen,[6] is absolutely notorious among you, and instead of expelling the offender with mourning and shame, you—oh! strange mystery of the invariable connexion between sensuality and pride—have been inflated with sophistical excuses about the matter.[7] "I, at any rate, absent in body, but present in spirit, have already judged as though actually present the man who acted thus in this thing, in the name of our Lord Jesus Christ—you being assembled together, and my spirit which is present with you, though my body is absent—with the power of our Lord Jesus Christ, to hand over such a man to Satan, for destruction of the flesh, that the spirit may be saved in the day of the Lord Jesus Christ."[8] If any passage of the letter was written with sobs, which are echoed in his very words, as Sosthenes wrote them down from his lips, it is this. He summons up the scene and sentence of excommunication. He is absent, yet he is there; and there, with the power of Christ, he pronounces the awful sentence which hands over the offender to Satan in terrible mercy, that by destruction of his flesh he may be saved in the spirit. And then he adds, "The subject of your self-glorification is hideous.[9] Know ye not that a little leaven leaveneth the whole lump? Purge out then at once the old leaven, that ye may be a new lump, as ye are (ideally) unleavened.[10] For indeed our Passover is slain[11]—

[1] Cf. 2 Cor. xi. 27.

[2] περικάθαρματα, *purgamenta*, "things vile, and worthless, and to be flung away," not "placular offerings," περίψημα. The Scholiast on Ar. *Plut.* 456, says, that in famines and plagues it was an ancient Greek and Roman custom to *wipe off* guilt by throwing wretches into the sea, with the words "*Become our peripsema.*" The reference here is probably less specific, but cf. Prov. xxi. 18; כֹּפֶר (LXX.), Tob. v. 18. ἐγώ περίψημά σου became (from this view) a common Christian expression (Wordsworth, *ad loc.*).

[3] iv. 15, παιδαγωγούς.

[4] St. Paul had already sent him, before the necessity had arisen for the more immediate despatch of Titus; but he seems to have countermanded the order, uncertain, however, whether the messenger would reach him in time, and rather expecting that Timothy would arrive among them before himself ("*if* Timotheus come," xvi. 10). In any case the Corinthians would have heard that Timothy had been sent to come to them through Macedonia, and Paul's enemies drew very unfavourable inferences from this.

[5] iv. 6—21.

[6] The ὀνομάζεται, "is named," of our text is spurious, being omitted in א, A, B, C, D, E, F, G. As to the fact illustrated by the almost local tragedy of Hippolytus, see Cic. *pro Cluent.* 5, "O mulieris scelus incredibile et praeter hanc unam in omni vitâ inauditum" (Wetst. *ad loc.*).

[7] This might seem inconceivable; but *v. supra*, p. 383.

[8] It was the last awful, reluctant declaration, "that a man who has wilfully chosen an evil master, shall feel the bondage that he may loathe it, and so turn to his true Lord" (Maurice, *Unity*, p. 414). On the comparative leniency of excommunication see Hooker, *Eccl. Pol.* iii. 1, 13.

[9] v. 6, οὐ καλὸν (litotes), τὸ καύχημα ὑμῶν (not καύχησις).

[10] St. Paul was writing near the time of the Passover; but the allusions are spiritual.

[11] v. 7, ἐτύθη, "slain" (Matt. xxii. 4; Acts x. 13). The "for us," ὑπὲρ ἡμῶν is a doctrinal gloss not found in A, B, C, D, E, F, G.

Christ. Let us, then, keep the feast, not with the old leaven, neither with leaven of vice and wickedness, but with unleavenedness of sincerity and truth."[1]

And here he pauses to explain a clause in his last Epistle which had excited surprise. In it he had forbidden them to associate with fornicators. This had led them to ask the astonished question[2] whether it was really their duty to go out of the world altogether? His meaning was, as he now tells them, that if any *Christian* were notoriously guilty, either of fornication or any other deadly sin,[3] with such they were not to associate,—not even to sit at table with them. They really need not have mistaken his meaning on this point. What had he, what had they, to do with judging the outer world? This passage reads like a marginal addition, and he adds the brief, uncompromising order, "Put away at once that wicked man from among yourselves."[4]

8. The allusion to judging naturally leads him to another point. Dare they, the destined judges of the world and of angels, go to law about mere earthly trifles, and that before the heathen? Why did they not rather set up the very humblest members of the Church to act as judges in such matters? Shame on them! So wise and yet no one of them wise enough to be umpire in mere trade disputes? Better by far have no quarrels among themselves, but suffer wrong and loss; but, alas! instead of this some of them inflicted wrong and loss, and that on their own brethren. Then follows a stern warning—the unjust should not inherit the kingdom of God—"Be not deceived"—the formula by which he always introduces his most solemn passages—neither sensual sinners in all their hideous varieties, nor thieves, nor over-reachers, nor drunkards, nor revilers, nor extortioners, shall inherit the kingdom of God. "And these abject things some of you were;[5] but ye washed yourselves, but ye were sanctified, but ye were justified in the name of the Lord Jesus, and the Spirit of our God." It is evident that some of them were *liable* to be deceived; that they liked to be deceived on this point, and they seem to have boldly said that the Christian is free, that "all things are lawful" to him because he is no longer under the law, but under grace. "All things are lawful to me." Yes, says St. Paul, but all things are not expedient. "All things are lawful to me." Yes, but I will not become the slave of the fatal tyranny of anything. The case of meats, which perhaps they adduced to show that they might do as they liked, irrespective of the Mosaic law, was not a case in point. They were ἀδιάφορα—matters of indifference about which each man might do as he liked; they, and the belly which assimilated them, were transient things, destined to be done away with. Not so the body; *that* was not created for fornication, but for the Lord, and as God had raised Christ so should He raise the bodies of Christ's saints. And then—thus casually as it were in this mere passing reference—he lays down for all time the eternal principles which underlie the sacred duty of chastity. He tells them that their bodies, their members, are not their own, but Christ's;—that the union with Christ is destroyed by unions of uncleanness;—that sensuality is a sin against a man's own body; that a Christian's body is not his own, but a temple of the indwelling Spirit, and that he is not his own, but bought with a price. "Therefore," he says, feeling that he had now laid down truths which should be impregnable against all scepticism, "glorify God in your body."[6]

9. This paragraph, touching as it has done on the three topics of chastity, meats offered to idols, and the resurrection, introduces very naturally his answers to their inquiries on these subjects, and nobly wise they are in their charity, their wisdom, their large-heartedness. He is not speaking of marriage in the abstract, but of

[1] v. 1—9.

[2] v. 10, ἐπεὶ ὀφείλετε ἄρα, κ. τ. λ.

[3] Ver. 11, "or an idolater." Evidently as in x. 7; Col. iii. 5; otherwise how could he be a Christian? Unless he is thinking of some hybrid Christian of the type of Constantine, who "bowed in the house of Rimmon."

[4] v. 9—13, Ἐξάρατε. The καὶ (omitted in א, A, B, C, F, G) is spurious, and spoils the characteristic abruptness.

[5] vi. 11, ταῦτά τινες ἦτε.

[6] vi. 1—20. The words which follow in our version, καὶ ἐν τῷ πνεύματι ὑμῶν, ἅτινά ἐστι τοῦ Θεοῦ, are omitted in א, A, B, C, D, E, F, G.

marriage regarded with reference to the near advent of Christ, and relating to the circumstances and conditions of the most corrupt city of ancient Greece. The Corinthian letter seems to have been written by those members of the Church who, partly it may be in indignant revolt against the views of the small faction which had adopted Antinomian opinions, seem to have regarded celibacy as the only perfect form of life. In the abstract, somewhat hesitatingly, and with the confession that here he is not sure of his ground, and is therefore offering no authoritative decision, St. Paul on the whole agrees with them.[1] "He quotes, with something of approval, their dictum that the maiden life is the best,[2] and utters the wish that all had the same spiritual grace[3]—the *charisma* of continence—as he himself. But since this was not the case, as a permitted remedy against the universal prevalence of unchastity, he recommended (but not by way of distinct injunction) that Christians should live together, and with no long ascetic separations, in the married state.[4] As regards widowers[5] and widows their celibacy for the rest of their lives would be an honourable state, but immediate marriage would be better than long-continued desires.[6] Divorce had been discouraged by Christ himself, and on that analogy he pronounced against any voluntary dissolution of unions already existing between Pagans and Christians, since the children of such unions were holy, and therefore the unions holy, and since the believing wife or husband might win to the faith the unbelieving partner. The general rule which he wished all Christians to observe was that they should abide in the state in which they were called, whether circumcised or uncircumcised, since "circumcision is nothing, and uncircumcision is nothing, but keeping of the commandments of God."[7] Even if a Christian were a slave and might obtain his freedom, it would be better for him to brook slavery,[8] seeing that earthly relations were utterly insignificant

[1] "If we compare the letter of Gregory the Great to Augustine (in Bede), in answer to inquiries not altogether dissimilar, respecting the Anglo-Saxon converts, we see at once how immeasurably more decisive and minute the Pope is than the Apostle" (Maurice, *Unity*, p. 423). The chapter is the best manual for the *ductor dubitantium*, because it teaches him "that he must not give himself airs of certainty on points where certainty is not to be had" (*id.* 429). See Kuenen, *Profeten*, ii. 67 *sq.*, and Lord Lyttelton in *Contemp. Rev.* xxi. p. 917.

[2] vii. 1, καλὸν ἀνθρώπῳ γυναικὸς μὴ ἅπτεσθαι. St. Jerome's characteristic comment is that "if it is good for a man not to touch a woman, it must be bad to do so, and therefore marriage is, to say the least, inferior to celibacy." St. Paul's own distinct permission, and in some cases injunction, to marry, might have shown him how false and dangerous are the results which spring from the undue pressure of incidental words (Eph. v. 24; 1 Tim. ii. 15, &c.) St. Paul does not say "good" (ἀγαθὸν), but "fair" (which he afterwards limits by the present need, ver. 20), as we might say, "there is in holy celibacy a certain moral beauty." Hence Jerome's "Suspecta est mihi bonitas rei quam magnitudo alterius mali malum cogit esse inferius" (*adv. Jovin.* i. 9) is a mistake. Celibacy is *καλόν*, but there are *some* for whom marriage is even κάλλιον. See for the use of *καλός* Matt. xviii. 8, xxvi. 24; 1 Tim. i. 8. It is curious to see the ascetic tendency at work in vii. 3 (ὀφειλομένην εὔνοιαν, and 5, τῇ νηστείᾳ καὶ, and σχολάσητε and συνέρχησθε for ἦτε). The true readings are found in א, A, B, C, D, F, though not followed in our version.

[3] vii. 7, θέλω, but in later years his deliberate decision (βούλομαι) was that younger widows should marry (1 Tim. v. 14).

[4] vii. 1—7.

[5] τοῖς ἀγάμοις, *v. supra*, pp. 45, 46.

[6] Ver. 9, γαμῆσαι (aor.), ἢ πυροῦσθαι (pres.).

[7] 1 Cor. vii. 18, 19. The μὴ ἐπισπάσθω refers to a method of obliterating the sign of the covenant adopted by apostate Jews in times of persecution (1 Macc. i. 15; Jos. *Antt.* xii. 5, § 1), and which a Christian might be tempted to adopt to save him from that ridicule which the manners of ancient life brought upon Jews (Mart. xvii. 29). The Rabbis decided that one who had done this must be re-circumcised. R. Jehudah denied this, because of the danger; but the wise men replied that it had been frequently done with no injurious results in the days of Bar-Cosiba (*Yebhamóth*, f. 72, 1; Buxtorf, *Lex. Chald.*, s. v. משך, *meshookim* = *recutiti*).

[8] 1 Cor. vii. 21, ἀλλ' εἰ καὶ δύνασαι ἐλεύθερος γενέσθαι, μᾶλλον χρῆσαι. I have taken δουλείᾳ as the word to be understood with Chrysostom, Theodoret, Luther, Bengel, De Wette, Meyer, &c.; cf. 1 Tim. vi. 2. I take this view—i. Because the whole argument turns on the desirability of *staying in the present condition*, whatever it is, with a view to the nearness of the day of the Lord. ii. Because this was the view arrived at also by the lofty Stoic moralists who, like Epictetus, knew that even a slave could live a noble life (Epictet. *Dissert.* iii. 26; Ench. x., xxxii.). Earthly conditions were but a χρῆσις φαντασιῶν; cf. Col. iii. 22. iii. Because St. Paul may have been thinking at the moment of the Christian slaves of Christian masters who would be treated as brothers. iv. Because χρῆσθαι, rather implies the continuance of an existing than the acceptance of a new condition. Otherwise we can hardly imagine his giving such advice, since "a man is to abide in his calling if it

when regarded from the spiritual standpoint.[1] As to virgins he could only give his opinion that, considering the present distress, and the nearness of the end, and the affliction which marriage at such a period brought inevitably in its train, it was better for them not to marry. Marriage, indeed, he told them distinctly, was no sin, but he wished to spare them the tribulation it involved; he did not wish them, now that the time was contracted,[2] and the fleeting show of the world was passing away, to bear the distracting burden of transient earthly and human cares, or to use the world to the full,[3] but to let their sole care be fixed on God.[4] If then a father determined not to give his maiden daughter in marriage, he did well; but if a lover sought her hand, and circumstances pointed that way, he was not doing wrong in letting them marry.[5] Widows might re-marry if they liked, but in accordance with the principles which he had been laying down, he thought they would be happier if they did not. It was but his wish and advice; he asserted no Divine authority for it; yet in giving it he thought that he too had—as other teachers had claimed to have—the spirit of God.[6]

10. As to the pressing question—a question which bore on their daily life[7]—about meats offered to idols, he quotes, but only by way of refutation, their self-satisfied remark that they "all had knowledge"—knowledge at the best was a much smaller thing than charity, and the very claim to possess it was a proof of spiritual pride and ignorance. If they knew that an idol was nothing in the world, and their conscience as to this matter was quite clear and strong, it was no sin for them personally to eat of these sacrifices; but if others, whose consciences were weak, saw them feasting in idol temples, and were led by this ostentatious display of absence of scruple[8] to do by way of imitation what they themselves thought wrong, then this knowledge and liberty of theirs became a stumbling-block, an edification of ruin,[9] a source of death to the conscience of a brother; and since thus to smite the sick conscience of a brother was a sin against Christ, he for one would never touch flesh again while the world lasted rather than be guilty of putting a fatal difficulty in a brother's path.[10]

be not hurtful to faith and morals" (Aug. *ad Gal.* ii. 11); but that could hardly be said of slavery. "Impudicitia . . . in servo necessitas" (Sen. *Controv.* iv., *Praef.*). "Enfants, ils grandissaient en désordre; vieillards, ils mouraient souvent dans la misère" (Wallon, *De l'Esclavage*, i. 332).

[1] vii. 10—24. Verses 17—24 are a little digression on the general principle that it is best to remain contentedly in our present lot. In ver. 23 he says, with a fine play on words, "You *are* slaves in one sense; do not *become* so in another."

[2] Ver. 29, *συνεσταλμένος*.

[3] Ver. 31, *καταχρώμενοι*; cf. ix. 12, 18. *μεριμνᾷ, εὐπάρεδρον, ἀπερισπάστως*; cf. Luke x. 41.

[4] Alone of nations the Jews implied the sanctity of marriage by every name that they gave it. *Kiddushin* from *kadosh*, "to sanctify;" *mekadesh*, "a bridegroom," &c. The phrase *Hare ath mekoodesheth li*, "Behold thou art sanctified for me," is still addressed by the bridegroom to the bride (Rabbinowicz, *Législat. Criminelle du Talmud*, p. 227).

[5] vii. 25. On the rights of Jewish fathers over their unmarried daughters see *Ketubhôth*, f. 46, 2. They were so absolute that he might even *sell* his daughter (*Kiddushin*, 3 *b*; *Ketubhôth*, 46 *b*). When however she reached the "flower of her age," she might refuse any husband given her before she was really *nubilis*. Her refusal was technically called *miôn* מיאון (*Yebhamôth*, 107 *b*). She might even be married while yet a *ketanah*—*i.e.*, not yet twelve. When she reached that age she was called *naarah* (נערה), and six months later was held to have reached her full maturity, and become a *bagreth*, בוגרת. See the Talmudic authorities in Rabbinowicz, *Trad. des Traités Synhedrin*, &c., *Législation Criminelle du Talmud*, p. 214; Weill, *La Femme Juive*, pp. 11—14. On the care for widows, *id.* p. 72.

[6] vii. 1—40.

[7] To this day the Jewish slaughterer, who must pass a course of study, practically decides what is clean (*thor*) and unclean (*tâmê*). When he has discovered that an animal has no legal blemish he attaches to it a leaden seal with the word "lawful" (*kâshêr*) on it; (D'Israeli, *Genius of Judaism*, 156; *Dict. Bibl.* s. v. *Pharisees*; McCaul, *Old Paths*, 380—386, 396—402; *v. supra*, p. 245.

[8] Ver. 10. Such feasts were often in temples:

> "Hoc illis curia templum,
> Hae sacris sedes epulis; hic ariete caeso
> Perpetuis soliti Patres considere mensis." (*Æn.* vii. 174.)

Cf. Hdt. i. 31; Judg. ix. 27; 2 Kings xix. 37.

[9] Tert. *De Praescr. Haer.* 8.

[10] viii. 1—13. Here, as usual, St. Paul shows himself transcendently superior to the Rabbis. In *Abhôda Zara* f. 8, 1, R. Ishmael lays down the rule that if Israelites "outside the land" are

11. And at this point begins a remarkable digression, which, though a digression, indirectly supported the position which some of his adversaries had impugned, and though personal in its details, is, in Paul's invariable manner, made subservient to eternal truths. They might object that by what he had said he was curtailing their liberty, and making the conscience of the weak a fetter upon the intelligence of the strong. Well, without putting their objection in so many words, he would show them that he practised what he taught. He, too, was free, and an Apostle, *their* Apostle at any rate, and had every right to do as the other Apostles did—the Desposyni, and Kephas himself—in expecting Churches to support them and their wives.[1] That right he even defends at some length, both by earthly analogies of the soldier, husbandman, and shepherd,[2] and by a happy Rabbinic midrash on the non-muzzling of the ox that treadeth out the corn;[3] and by the ordinary rules of gratitude for benefits received;[4] and by the ordinance of the Jewish Temple,[5] and the rule of Christ;[6] yet plain as the right was, and strenuously as he maintained it, he had never availed himself of it, and, whatever his enemies might say, he never would. He *must* preach the Gospel; he could not help himself; his one reward would be the power to boast that he had not claimed his rights to the full, but had made the Gospel free, and so removed a possible source of hindrance. Free, then, as he was, he had made himself a slave (as in one small particular he was asking them to do) for the sake of others; a slave to all, that he might gain the more; putting himself in their place, meeting their sympathies, and even their prejudices, half way; becoming a Jew to the Jews, a legalist to legalists, without law to those without law (never, however, forgetting his real allegiance to the law of Christ),[7] weak to the weak, all things to all men in order by all means to save some. And if he thus denied himself, should not they also deny themselves?[8] In their Isthmian games each strove to gain the crown, and what toil and temperance they endured to win that fading wreath of pine! Paul did the same. He ran straight to the goal. He aimed straight blows, and not in feint, at the enemy;[9] nay, he even blackened his body with blows, and led it about as a slave,[10] lest in any way after acting as herald to others he himself should be rejected from the lists.[11]

If *he* had to strive so hard, could *they* afford to take things so easily? The Israelites had not found it so in the wilderness; they, too, were in a sense baptised unto Moses in the cloudy pillar and the Red Sea waves;[12] they, too, in a sense partook of the Eucharist in eating the heavenly manna, and drinking of the symbolic following rock;[13] yet how many[14] of them fell because of gluttony, and idolatry, and

asked to a Gentile funeral they "eat of the sacrifices of the dead," even if they take with them their own food and are waited on by their own servants. In confirmation of which hard and bigoted decision he refers to Ex. xxxiv. 15, from which he inferred that the acceptance of the invitation was equivalent to eating the sacrifice. R. Jochanan the Choronite would not eat *moist* olives, even in a time of famine, if handled by an *am haarets*, because they might have absorbed water, and so become unclean (*Yebhamoth*, f. 15, 2).

[1] I have here endeavoured to make clear the by no means obvious connexion of thought which runs through these chapters. Possibly there may have been some accidental transposition. Those who consider 2 Cor. vi. 14—vii. 1, to be misplaced, find an apt space for it here.

[2] ix. 7. [3] ix. 8—10. [4] 11, 12. [5] 13. [6] 14.

[7] He describes the concessions (*συγκατάβασις*) of love. "Paulus non fuit anomus, nedum antinomus" (Bengel). "The Lawless" is the name by which he is covertly calumniated in the spurious letter of Peter to James (*Clementines*, ch. ii.).

[8] In these paragraphs exhortations to the general duty of self-denial are closely mingled with the arguments in favour of the particular self-denial—concession to the weak—which he is urging throughout this section. "In the one party faith was not strong enough to beget a liberalising knowledge, not strong enough in the other to produce a brotherly love" (Kling).

[9] His was no sham fight (*σκιαμαχία*); he struck anything rather than the air (*ὡς οὐκ ἀέρα δέρων*). The E.V. renders as though it were *οὐχ ὡς ἀέρα δέρων*. Cf. *Æn.* v. 446, and Wetst. *ad loc.*

[10] *ὑπωπιάζω*; lit., "blacken with blows under the eyes, as in a fight." "*Lividum facio* corpus meum et in servitutem redigo" (Iren. iv. 7).

[11] ix. 1—27; *κηρύξας*, the Christian herald of the laws of the contest, is also a candidate in it.

[12] Fiduciâ verbi Mosis commiserant se aquis (Melancthon).

[13] x. 4—xi. 1. The division of chapters here stops a verse too short. On St. Paul's spiritualisation and practical application of Old Testament history, see *supra*, pp. 27—28. For other instances see v. 7; Gal. iv. 22; Heb. vii. &c.)

[14] x. 8. "Twenty-*three* thousand." Perhaps a *σφάλμα μνημονικὸν* for 24,000 (Num. xxv. 9).

lust, and rebellion, and murmuring, and were awful warnings against overweening self-confidence! Yes, the path of duty was difficult, but not impossible, and no temptation was beyond human power to resist, because with the temptation God provided also *the* escape. Let them beware, then, of all this scornful indifference about idolatry. As the Eucharist united them in closest communion with Christ, and with one another, so that by all partaking of the one bread they became one body and one bread, so the partaking of Gentile sacrifices was a communion with demons.[1] The idol was nothing, as they had urged, but it *represented* an evil spirit;[2] and fellowship with demons was a frightful admixture with their fellowship in Christ, a dangerous trifling with their allegiance to God. He repeats once more that what is lawful is not always either expedient or edifying. Let sympathy, not selfishness, be their guiding principle. Over-scrupulosity was not required of them. They might buy in the market, they might eat, at the private tables of the heathen, what they would, and ask no questions; but if their attention was prominently drawn to the fact that any dish was part of an idol-offering, then—though they might urge that "the earth was the Lord's, and the fulness thereof," and that it was hard for them to be judged, or their liberty abridged in a purely indifferent act, which they might even perform in a religious spirit—still let them imitate Paul's own example, which he had just fully explained to them, which was, indeed, Christ's example, and consisted in being absolutely unselfish, and giving no wilful offence either to Jews or Gentiles, or the Church of God.

In this noble section of the Epistle, so remarkable for its tender consideration and its robust good sense, it is quite clear that the whole sympathies of St. Paul are theoretically with the strong, though he seems to feel a sort of *practical* leaning to the ascetic side. He does not, indeed, approve, under any circumstances, of an ostentatious, defiant, insulting liberalism. To a certain extent the prejudices—even the absurd and bigoted prejudices—of the weak ought to be respected, and it was selfish and wrong needlessly to wound them. It was above all wrong to lead them by example to do violence to their own conscientious scruples. But when these scruples, and this bigotry of the weak, became in their turn aggressive, then St. Paul quite sees that they must be discouraged and suppressed, lest weakness should lay down the law for strength. To tolerate the weak was one thing; to let them tyrannise was quite another. Their ignorance was not to be a limit to real knowledge; their purblind gaze was not to bar up the horizon against true insight; their slavish superstition was not to fetter the freedom of Christ. In matters where a little considerateness and self-denial would save offence, there the strong should give up, and do less than they might; but in matters which affected every day of every year, like the purchase of meat in the open market, or the acceptance of ordinary invitations, then the weak must not attempt to be obtrusive or to domineer. Some, doubtless, would use hard words about these concessions. They might charge St. Paul, as they had charged St. Peter, with violating the awful and fiery law. They might call him "the lawless one," or any other ugly nick-name they liked; he was not a man to be "feared with bugs," or to give up a clear and certain principle to avoid an impertinent and senseless clamour. Had he been charged with controver-

[1] Cf. 2 Cor. vi. 14 *seq.* Evil spirits occupied a large part of the thoughts and teaching of Jewish Rabbis; *e.g.*, Lilith, Adam's first wife, was by him the mother of all demons (*Psachim*, f. 112, 2). As the Lord's Supper puts the Christian in mystical union with Christ, so partaking of idol feasts puts the partaker into symbolic allegiance to devils. Pfleiderer compares the Greek legend that by eating a fruit of the nether world a man is given over to it (*Paulinism*, i. 239).

[2] The heathen gods as idols were *εἴδωλα*, *Elilim*, supposititious, unreal, imaginary; but in another aspect they were demons. The Rabbis, in the same way, regard idols from two points of view—viz., as dead material things, and as demons. "Callest thou an idol a dog?" said "a philosopher" to Rabban Gamaliel. "An idol is really something." "What is it?" asked Gamaliel. "There was once a conflagration in our town," said the philosopher, "and the temple of the idol remained intact when every house was burnt down." At this remark the Rabban is silent (*Abhôda Zara*, f. 54, 2). Almost in the very words of St. Paul, Zonan once said to R. Akibha, "Both thou and I know that an idol hath nothing in it;" but he proceeds to ask how it is that miracles of healing are undoubtedly wrought at idol shrines? Akibha makes the healing a mere accidental coincidence with the time when the chastisements would naturally have been withdrawn (*Abhôda Zara*, f. 55, 1).

ting the wise and generous but local and temporary agreement which has been exalted into "the decree of the Council of Jerusalem," he would have quietly answered that that was but a recommendation addressed to a few predominantly Jewish Churches; that it did not profess to have any universal or permanent authority; and that he was now arguing the case on its own merits, and laying down principles applicable to every Church in which, as at Corinth, the Gentiles formed the most numerous element.

12. A minor point next claimed his attention. Some men, it appears, had sat with covered heads at their assemblies, and some women with uncovered heads, and they had asked his opinion on the matter. Thanking them for their kind expressions of respect for his rules and wishes, he at once decides the question on the highest principles. As to men it might well have seemed perplexing, since the Jewish and the Roman custom was to pray with covered, and the Greek custom to to pray with uncovered, heads. St. Paul decides for the Greek custom. Christ is the head of the man, and man might therefore stand with unveiled head before God, and if he veiled his head he did it needless dishonour, because he abnegated the high glory which had been bestowed on him by Christ's incarnation. Not so with the woman. The head of the woman is the man, and therefore in holy worship, in the presence of the Lord of her lord, she ought to appear with veiled head.[1] Nature itself taught that this was the right decision, giving to the woman her veil of hair, and teaching the instinctive lesson that a shorn head was a disgrace to a woman, as long hair, the sign of effeminacy, was a disgrace to a man. The unveiled head of the man was also the sign of his primeval superiority, and the woman having been the first to sin, and being liable to be seduced to sin, ought to wear "power on her head because of the angels."[2] Man and woman were indeed one in Christ, but for that very reason these distinctions of apparel should be observed. At any rate, St. Paul did not mean to enter into any dispute on the subject. If nature did not teach them that he had decided rightly, he could only refer them to the authority of custom, and that ought to be decisive, except to those who loved contentiousness.[3]

13. Then follows a stern rebuke—all the sterner for the self-restraint of its twice-repeated "I praise you not"—for the shameful selfishness and disorder which they had allowed to creep into the love-feasts which accompanied the Supper of the Lord—especially the gluttony, drunkenness, and ostentation of the wealthier members of the community, and the contemptuous indifference which they displayed to the needs and sensibilities of their poorer neighbours. The simple narrative of the institution and objects of the Supper of the Lord, which he had received from the Lord and delivered unto them, and the solemn warning of the danger which attended its profanation, and which was already exhibited in the sickness, feebleness, and deaths of many among them, is meant to serve as a remedy against their gross disorders. He tells them that the absence of a discrimination (*διάκρισις*) in their own hearts had rendered necessary a judgment (*κρίμα*) which was mercifully meant as a training

[1] For *exousian*, see Stanley, Corinth. *ad loc.* The attempts to read *exiousa*, &c., are absurd. The word may be a mere colloquialism, and if so we may go far astray in trying to discover the explanation of it. If St. Paul invented it, it may be a Hebraism, or be meant to imply her own true power, which rests in accepting the sign of her husband's power over her. Chardin says that in Persia a veil is the sign that married women "are under subjection." Compare Milton's—

"She as a veil down to the slender waist
Her unadornèd golden tresses wore . . .
As the vine waves its tendrils, which *implied*
Subjection, but required with gentle sway,
And by her yielded, by him best received."

See Tert. *De Vel. Virg.* 7, 17; and in illustration of Chrysostom's view there alluded to, see Tob. xii. 12; Ps. cxxxviii. 1 (LXX.); Eph. iii. 10.

[2] For the explanation of this allusion *v. infra*, Excursus IV.

[3] xi. 1—17. The last phrase—interesting as showing St. Paul's dislike to needless and disturbing innovations—is like the Rabbinic phrase, "Our Halacha is otherwise;" your custom is a *Thekunah*, or novelty, a חדוש (*Babha Metsia*, f. 112).

(*παιδευόμεθα*) to save them from final condemnation (*κατάκριμα*).[1] All minor matters about which they may have asked him, though they kept back the confession of this their shame, are left by the Apostle to be regulated by himself personally on his arrival.[2]

14. The next three chapters—of which the thirteenth, containing the description of charity, is the most glorious gem, even in the writings of St. Paul—are occupied with the answer to their inquiries about spiritual gifts. Amid the wild disorders which we have been witnessing we are hardly surprised to find that the Glossolalia had been terribly abused. Some, we gather—either because they had given the reins to the most uncontrollable excitement, and were therefore the impotent victims of any blasphemous thought which happened for the moment to sweep across the troubled horizon of their souls; or from some darkening philosophical confusion, which endeavoured to distinguish between the Logos and Him that was crucified, between the Man Jesus and the Lord Christ; or perhaps again from some yet unsolved Jewish difficulty about the verse "Cursed is he that hangeth on a tree;"[3]—amid their unintelligible utterances, had been heard to exclaim, *Anathema Iesous*, "Jesus is accursed;" and, having as yet very vague notions as to the true nature of the "gift of tongues," the Corinthians had asked Paul in great perplexity what they were to think of this? His direct answer is emphatic. When they were the ignorant worshippers of dumb idols they may have been accustomed to the false inspiration of the Pythia, or the Sibyl—the possessing mastery by a spiritual influence which expressed itself in the broken utterance, and streaming hair, and foaming lip, and which they might take to be the spirit of Python, or Trophonius, or Dis. But now he lays down the great principles of that "discernment of spirits," which should enable them to distinguish the rapt utterance of divine emotion from the mechanical and self-induced frenzy of feminine feebleness or hypocritical superstition. Whatever might be the external phenomena, the utterances of the Spirit were one in import. No man truly inspired by Him could say, "Anathema is Jesus;"[4] or uninspired by Him could say from the heart, "Jesus is the Lord." The *charismata*, or gifts, were different; the "administrations" of them, or channels of their working, were different; the operations, energies, or effects of them were different; but the source of them was One—one Holy Ghost, from whom they are all derived; one Lord, by whom all true ministries of them are authorised; one God, who worketh all their issues in all who possess them.[5] And this diverse manifestation of one Spirit, whether practical wisdom or scientific knowledge; whether the heroism of faith with its resultant gifts of healing, or energies of power, or impassioned utterance, or the ability to distinguish between true and false spiritual manifestations; or, again, kinds of tongues, or the interpretation of tongues,[6] were all subordinated to one sole end—edification. And, therefore, to indulge in any conflict between gifts, any rivalry in their display, was to rend asunder the unity which reigned supreme through this rich multiplicity; to throw doubt on the unity of their origin, to ruin the unity of their action. The gifts, whether healings, helps, governments, or tongues, occurred separately in different individuals; but each of these—whether

[1] These distinctions, so essential to the right understanding of the passage, are hopelessly obliterated in the E.V., which also swerves from its usual rectitude by rendering ἢ "*and*" instead of "*or*" in ver. 27, that it might not seem to sanction "communion in one kind." The "unworthily" in ver. 29 is perhaps a gloss, though a correct one. The *κλώμενον*, "broken," of ver. 24 seems to have been tampered with from dogmatic reasons. It is omitted in ℵ, A, B, C, and D reads *θρυπτόμενον*, perhaps because of John xix. 36.

[2] xi. 17—34.

[3] Deut. xxi. 23.

[4] Perhaps a gross and fearful abuse of the *principle* involved in 2 Cor. v. 16, as though people of spiritual intuitions were emancipated from the mere acknowledgment of Jesus. One could easily expect this from what we know of the "everlasting Gospel" in the thirteenth century, and of similar movements in different times of the Church (Maurice, *Unity*, 445). How startling to these *illuminati* to be told that the *highest* operation of the Spirit was to acknowledge Jesus!

[5] James i. 17.

[6] xii. 8—10. I have indicated, without dwelling on, the possible classification hinted at by the ἑτέρῳ (9, 10), as contrasted with the ᾧ μὲν and ἄλλῳ. "Knowledge (γνῶσις) as distinguished from "wisdom," deals with "mysteries" (xiii. 2; xv. 51; viii. *passim*).

Apostle, or prophet, or teacher—was but a baptised member of the one body of Christ; and by a fresh application of the old classic fable of Menenius Agrippa, he once more illustrates the fatal results which must ever spring from any strife between the body and its members.[1] Let them covet the better gifts—and tongues, in which they gloried most, he has studiously set last—and yet he is now about to point out to them a path more transcendent than any gifts. And then, rising on the wings of inspired utterance, he pours forth, as from the sunlit mountain heights, his glorious hymn to CHRISTIAN LOVE. Without it a man may speak with human, aye, and even angelic tongues, and yet have become but as booming gong or clanging cymbal.[2] Without it, whatever be his unction, or insight, or knowledge, or mountain-moving faith, a man is nothing. Without it he may dole away all his possessions, and give his body to be burned, yet is profited nothing. Then follows that description of love, which should be written in letters of gold on every Christian's heart—its patience, its kindliness; its freedom from envy, vaunting self-assertion,[3] inflated arrogance, vulgar indecorum; its superiority to self-seeking; its calm control of temper; its oblivion of wrong;[4] its absence of joy at the wrongs of others; its sympathy with the truth; its gracious tolerance; its trustfulness; its hope; its endurance.[5] Preaching, and tongues, and knowledge, are but partial, and shall be done away when the perfect has come; but love is a flower whose petals never fall off.[6] Those are but as the lispings, and emotions, and reasonings of a child; but this belongs to the perfect manhood, when we shall see God, not as in the dim reflection of a mirror, but face to face, and know him, not in part, but fully, even as now we are fully known. Faith, and hope, and love, are all three, not transient gifts, but abiding graces; but the greatest of these—the greatest because it is the root of the other two; the greatest because they are for ourselves, but love is for others; the greatest because neither in faith nor in hope is the entire and present fruition of heaven, but only in the transcendent and illimitable blessedness of "faith working by love;" the greatest because faith and hope are human, but love is essentially divine—the greatest of these is love.[7]

15. On such a basis, so divine, so permanent, it was easy to build the decision about the inter-relation of spiritual gifts; easy to see that preaching was superior to glossolaly; because the one was an introspective and mostly unintelligible exercise, the other a source of general advantage. The speaker with tongues, unless he could also interpret, or unless another could interpret for him his inarticulate ecstacies, did but utter indistinct sounds, like the uncertain blaring of a trumpet or the confused discordances of a harp or flute. Apart from interpretation "tongues" were a mere talking into air. They were as valueless, as completely without significance, as the jargon of a barbarian. Since they were so proud of these displays, let them pray for ability to interpret their rhapsodies. The prayer, the song of the spirit, should be accompanied by the assent of the understanding, otherwise the "tongue" was useless to any ordinary worshipper, nor could they claim a share in what was said by adding their Amen[8] to the voice of Eucharist. Paul, too—and he thanked

[1] xii. 1—31. See a noble passage in Maurice, *Unity*, 469. *seq.*, contrasting this conception with the *artificial* view of society in Hobbes' *Leviathan*. The absolute unity of Jews and Gentiles (ver. 13) exhibited in baptism and the Lord's Supper,—whence it resulted that the Jews wortd henceforth be but "a dwindling majority in the Messianic kingdom,"—was, with the Cross, the chief stumbling-block to the Jews.

[2] "Ephyreïa aera" (Virg. *Georg.* ii. 464); Corinthian brass (Plin. *H. N.* 34, 2, 3).

[3] Ver. 4, *οὐ περπερεύεται*. *Perperus*, "a braggart." "Heavens! how I *showed* off (*ἐνεπερπερευσάμην*) before my new auditor, Pompeius!" (Cic. *ad Att.* i. 14).

[4] xiii. 5, "does not reckon the wrong." The opposite of "all his faults observed, *set in a note-book.*"

[5] Ver. 7, *στέγει* means "bears," "endures." Its classic meaning is "holds water;" and this is also true of love with its gracious reticences and suppressions, *οὐδὲν βάναυσον ἐν ἀγάπῃ* (Clem. *Rom.*).

[6] Ver. 8, *οὐδέποτε ἐκπίπτει*. So we may understand the metaphor, as in Jaines i. 11, *ἐξέπεσε* (Isa. xxviii. 4); others prefer the classic sense, "is never hissed off the stage;" has its part to play on the stage of eternity.

[7] xii. 31—xiii. 13.

[8] xiv. 16, *πῶς ἐρεῖ τὸ Ἀμήν*. "He who says Amen is greater than he who blesses" (*Berachôth*, viii. 3).

God that he was capable of this deep spiritual emotion—was more liable to the impulse of glossolaly than any of them;[1] yet so little did he value it—we may even say so completely did he disparage it as a part of public worship—that after telling them that he had rather speak five intelligible words to teach others than ten thousand words in "a tongue,"[2] he bids them not to be little children in intelligence, but to be babes in vice, and quotes to them, in accordance with that style of adaptation with which his Jewish converts would have been familiar, a passage of Isaiah,[3] in which Jehovah threatens the drunken priests of Jerusalem that since they would not listen to the simple preaching of the prophet, he would teach them—and that, too, ineffectually—by conquerors who spoke a tongue which they did not understand. From this he argues that "tongues" are not meant for the Church at all, but are a sign to unbelievers; and that, if exercised in the promiscuous way which was coming into vogue at Corinth, would only awaken, even in unbelievers, the contemptuous remark that they were a set of insane fanatics, whereas the effect of preaching might be intense conviction, prostrate worship, and an acknowledgment of the presence of God among them.[4]

16. The disorders, then, in the Corinthian Church had sprung from the selfish struggle of each to show off his own special gift, whether tongue, or psalm, or teaching, or revelation. If they would bear in mind that edification was the object of worship, such scenes would not occur. Only a few at a time, therefore, were to speak with tongues, and only in case some one could interpret, otherwise they were to suppress the impulse. Nor were two people ever to be preaching at the same time. If the rivalry of unmeaning sounds among the glossolalists had been fostered by some Syrian enthusiast, the less intolerable but still highly objectionable disorder of rival preachers absorbed in the "egotism of oratory" was an abuse introduced by the admirers of Apollos. In order to remedy this, he lays down the rule that if one preacher was speaking, and another felt irresistibly impelled to say something, the first was to cease. It was idle to plead that they could not control themselves. The spirits which inspire the true prophet are under the prophet's due control, and God is the author, not of confusion but of peace. Women were not to speak in church at all; and if they wanted any explanations they must ask their husbands at home. This was the rule of all Churches, and who were they that they should alter these wise and good regulations? Were they the earliest Church? Were they the only Church? A true preacher, a man truly spiritual, would at once recognise that these were the commands of the Lord; and to invincible bigotry and obstinate ignorance Paul has no more to say. The special conclusion is that preaching is to be encouraged, and glossolaly not forbidden, provided that it did not interfere with the general rule that everything is to be done in decency and order. It is, however, extremely probable that the almost contemptuous language of the Apostle towards "the tongues"—a manifestation at first both sacred and impressive, but liable to easy simulation and grave abuse, and no longer adapted to serve any useful function—tended to suppress the display of emotion which he thus disparaged. Certain it is that from this time forward we hear little or nothing of "the gift of tongues." It—or something which on a lower level closely resembled it—has re-appeared again and again at different places and epochs in the history of the Christian Church. It seems, indeed, to be a natural consequence of fresh and overpowering religious emotion. But it can be so easily imitated by the symptoms of hysteria, and it leads to consequences so disorderly and deplorable, that except as a rare and isolated phenomenon it has been generally discountenanced by that sense of the necessity

[1] Why does he thank God for a gift which he is rating so low as an element of worship? Because the highest value of it was *subjective*. He who was capable of it was, at any rate, not dead: his heart was not petrified; he was not past feeling; he could feel the direct influence of the Spirit of God upon *his* spirit.

[2] "Rather half of ten of the edifying sort than a thousand times ten of the other" (Bosser).

[3] xiv. 21, ἐν τῷ νόμῳ. So Ps. lxxxii. 6 is quoted as "the Law" in John x. 34. On this passage *v. supra*, p. 30.

[4] xiv. 1—26.

for decency and order which the Apostle here lays down, and which has been thoroughly recognised by the calm wisdom of the Christian Church. The control and suppression of the impassioned emotion which expressed itself in glossolaly is practically its extinction, though this in no way involves the necessary extinction of the inspiring convictions from which it sprang.[1]

17. Then follows the immortal chapter in which he confirms their faith in the resurrection, and removes their difficulties respecting it. If they would not nullify their acceptance of the Gospel in which they stood, and by which they were saved, they must hold fast the truths which he again declares to them, that Christ died for our sins, was buried, and had been raised the third day. He enumerates His appearances to Kephas, to the Twelve, to more than five hundred at once of whom the majority were yet living, to James, to all the Apostles; last, as though to the abortive-born, even to himself.[2] "For I am the least of the Apostles, who am not adequate to be called an Apostle, because I persecuted the Church of God. Yet by the grace of God I am what I am, and His grace towards me has not proved in vain, but more abundantly than all of them I laboured—yet not I, but the grace of God which was with me; whether, then, it be I or they, so we preach, and so ye believed."[3]

If, then, Christ had risen, whence came the monstrous doctrine of some of them that there was no resurrection of the dead? The two truths stood or fell together. If Christ had not risen, their faith was after all a chimera, their sins were unforgiven, their dead had perished; and if their hope in Christ only was a hope undestined to fruition, they were the most pitiable of men. But since Christ had risen, we also shall rise, and as all men share the death brought in by Adam, so all shall be quickened unto life in Christ.[4] But each in his own rank. The firstfruits Christ; then His redeemed at His appearing, when even death, the last enemy, shall be reduced to impotence; then the end, when Christ shall give up His mediatorial kingdom, and God shall be all in all. And if there were no resurrection, what became of their practice of getting themselves baptised for the dead?[5] And why did the Apostles brave the hourly peril of death? By his boast of them in Christ he asseverates that his life is a daily dying. And if, humanly speaking, he fought beasts at Ephesus,[6] what would be the gain to him if the dead rise not? The Epicureans would then have some excuse for their base sad maxim, "Let us eat and drink, for to-morrow we die." Was it intercourse with the heathen that produced their dangerous unbelief? Oh, let them not be deceived! let them beware of this dangerous leaven! "Base associations destroy excellent characters." Let them awake at once to righteousness out of their drunken dream of disbelief, and break off the sinful habits which it engendered! Its very existence among them was an ignorance of God, for which they ought to blush.[7]

[1] xiv. 26—40.

[2] xv. 8, τῷ ἐκτρώματι (cf. Num. xii. 12, LXX.; see also Ps. lviii. 8).

[3] xv. 1—12 (cf. Epict. Diss. iii. 1, 36).

[4] "Even so *in Christ* shall *all* be made alive." Here is one of the antinomies which St. Paul leaves side by side. On the one hand, "life in Christ" is co-extensive with "death in Adam;" on the other, only those who are "in Christ" shall be made alive. Life here can hardly mean less than salvation. But it is asserted of all universally, and Adam and Christ are contrasted as death and life. Certainly in this and other places the Apostle's language suggests the natural conclusion that "the principle which has come to actuality in Christ is of sufficient energy to quicken all men for the resurrection to the blessed life" (Baur, *Paul.* ii. 219). But if we desire to arrive at a rigid eschatological doctrine we must compare one passage with another. See Excursus XXI., "Theology and Antinomies of St. Paul."

[5] Perhaps this is only a passing *argumentum ad hominem*; if so it shows St. Paul's large tolerance that he does not here pause to rebuke so superstitious a practice. It needs no proof that "baptism for the dead" *means* "baptism for the dead," and not the meanings which commentators put into it, who go to Scripture to support tradition, not to seek for truth.

[6] Of course metaphorically, or he would have mentioned it in 2 Cor. xi. His three points in 29—34 are—if there be no resurrection (1) why do some of you get yourselves baptised to benefit your relatives who have died unbaptised?—(2) Why do we live in such self-sacrifice? (3) What possibility would there be of resisting Epicurean views of life among men in general?

[7] xv. 12—35.

And as for material difficulties, Paul does not merely fling them aside with a "Senseless one!" but says that the body dies as the seed dies, and our resurrection bodies shall differ as the grain differs with the nature of the sown seed, or as one star differs from another in glory. The corruption, the indignity, the strengthlessness of the mortal body, into which at birth the soul is sown, shall be replaced by the incorruption, glory, power of the risen body. The spiritual shall follow the natural; the heavenly image of Christ's quickening spirit replace the earthly image of Adam, the mere living soul.[1] Thus in a few simple words does St. Paul sweep away the errors of Christians about the physical identity of the resurrection-body with the actual corpse, which have given rise to so many scornful materialist objections. St. Paul does not say with Prudentius—

"Me nec dente, nec ungue
Fraudatum redimet patefacti fossa sepulcri;"

but that "flesh and blood" cannot enter into the kingdom of God; that at Christ's coming the body of the living Christian will pass by transition, that of the dead Christian by resurrection, into a heavenly, spiritual, and glorious body.[2]

The body, then, was not the same, but a spiritual body; so that all coarse material difficulties were idle and beside the point. In one moment, whether quick or dead, at the sounding of the last trumpet, we should be changed from the corruptible to incorruption, from the mortal to immortality. "Then shall be fulfilled the promise that is written, Death is swallowed up into victory. Where, O death, is thy sting? where, O death, thy victory?[3] The sting of death is sin, the power of sin is the law. But thanks be to God, who is giving us the victory through our Lord Jesus Christ. Therefore, my brethren beloved, prove yourselves steadfast, immovable, abounding in the work of the Lord always, knowing that your toil is not fruitless in the Lord."[4]

So ends this glorious chapter—the hope of millions of the living, the consolation for the loss of millions of the dead. And if, as we have seen, Paul was the most tried, in this life the most to be pitied of men, yet what a glorious privilege to him in his trouble, what a glorious reward to him for all his labours and sufferings, that he should have been so gifted and enlightened by the Holy Spirit as to be enabled thus, incidentally as it were, to pour forth words which rise to a region far above all difficulties and objections, and which teach us to recognise in death, not the curse, but the coronation, not the defeat, but the victory, not the venomous serpent,

[1] xv. 35—50. In this chapter there is the nearest approach to *natural* (as apart from *architectural* and *agonistic*) metaphors. Dean Howson (*Charact. of St. P.* 6) points out that there is more imagery from natural phenomena in the single Epistle of St. James than in all St. Paul's Epistles put together.

[2] Ver. 52. "The *dead* shall be raised, *we* (the living) shall be changed." Into the question of the intermediate state St. Paul, expecting a near coming of Christ, scarcely enters. Death was κοιμᾶσθαι, resurrection was συνδοξασθῆναι. Did he hold that there was an intermediate provisional building of God's which awaited us in heaven after the stripping off of our earthly tent? The nearest allusion to the question may be found in 2 Cor. v.; 1—4 (Pfleiderer, i. 261).

[3] θάνατε (not ᾅδη), ℵ A, B, C, D, E, F, G.

[4] xv. 50—58. "It is very evident that the Apostle here regards the whole history of the world and men as the scene of the conflict of two principles, one of which has sway at first, but is then attacked and conquered, and finally destroyed by the other. The first of these principles is death; the history of the world begins with this, and comes to a close when death, and with death the dualism of which history is the development, has entirely disappeared from it" (Baur, *Paul.* ii. 225). In this chapter the only resurrection definitely spoken of is a resurrection "in Christ." On the *final* destiny of those who are now perishing (ἀπολλύμενοι) St. Paul never touches with any definiteness. But he speaks of the final conquest of death, the last enemy—where "death" seems to be used in its deeper spiritual and scriptural sense; he says (Rom. viii. 19—23) that "the whole creation (πᾶσα ἡ κτίσις) shall be delivered from the bondage of corruption into the glorious liberty of the children of God;" he contrasts the universality of man's disobedience with the universality of God's mercy; he says where sin abounded there grace did *much more* abound (Rom. v. 20); he speaks of God's *will* to bestow universal favour commensurate with universal sin (Rom. xi. 32); he dwells on the solution of dualism in unity and the tending of all things into God (εἰς αὐτὸν τὰ πάντα, Rom. xi. 30—36); his whole splendid philosophy of history consists in showing (Rom. Gal. *passim*) that each lower and sadder stage and moment of man's condition is a necessary means of achieving the higher; and he says that God, at last, "shall be all in all." Whatever antinomies may be left unsolved, let Christians duly weigh these truths.

but the veiled angel, not the worst enemy, but the greatest birthright of mankind. Not by denunciation of unorthodoxy, not by impatient crushing of discussion, not by the stunning blows of indignant authority, does he meet an unbelief even so strange, and so closely affecting the very fundamental truths of Christianity, as a denial of the resurrection; but by personal appeals, by helpful analogies, by calm and lofty reasoning, by fervent exhortations, by the glowing eloquence of inspired convictions. Anathema would have been worse than useless; at excommunication he does not so much as hint; but the refutation of perilous error by the presentation of ennobling truth has won, in the confirmation of the faith, in the brightening of the hope of centuries, its high and permanent reward.

Let us also observe that St. Paul's inspired conviction of the Resurrection rests, like all his theology, on the thought that the life of the Christian is a life "in Christ." On Plato's fancies about our reminiscence of a previous state of being he does not touch; but for the unfulfilled ideas on which Plato builds he offers the fulfilled ideal of Christ. He founds no arguments, as Kant does, on the failure of mankind to obey the "categorical imperative" of duty; but he points to the Sinless Man. He does not follow the ancients in dwelling on false analogies like the butterfly; nor is he misled like his very ablest contemporaries and successors by the then prevalent fable of the Phœnix. He does not argue from the law of continuity, or the indestructibility of atoms, or the permanence of force, or the general belief of mankind. But his main thought, his main argument is—Ye are Christ's, and Christ is risen; if ye died with him to sin, ye shall also live with him to righteousness here, and therefore to glory hereafter. The life ye now live is lived in the faith of the Son of God, and being eternal in its very nature, contains in itself the pledge of its own inextinguishable vitality. He teaches us alike in the phenomena of human sin and of human sanctity to see the truth of the Resurrection. For the forgiveness of sin Christ died; for the reward and the hope and the support of holiness he lives at the right hand of God. He does not so much *argue in favour of* the Resurrection as *represent* it, and make us feel its force. The Christian's resurrection from the death of sin to the life of righteousness transcends and involves the lesser miracle of his resurrection from the sleep of death to the life of heaven.

18. The Epistle closes with practical directions and salutations. He establishes a weekly offertory, as he had done in Galatia, for the saints at Jerusalem. He tells them that he will either—should it be worth while—take it himself to Jerusalem, or entrust it with commendatory letters from them, to any delegates whom they might approve. He announces without comment his altered intention of not taking them *en route* as he went to Macedonia, as well as on his return, and so giving them a double visit, but tells them that he should come to them by way of Macedonia, and probably spend the winter with them, that they might help him on his further journey; and that he means to remain in Ephesus till Pentecost, because a great door is open to him, and there are many adversaries.

Timothy will perhaps come to them. If so they are not to despise his youth, or alarm his timidity by opposition, but to aid his holy work, and to help him peacefully on his way to the Apostle with those who accompanied him. They had asked that Apollos might visit them. St. Paul had done his best to second their wishes, but Apollos—though holding out hopes of a future visit—declined to come at present, actuated in all probability by a generous feeling that, under present circumstances, his visit would do more harm than good.[1]

Then a brief vivid exhortation. "Watch! stand in the faith! be men! be strong! let all your affairs be in love."

Then a few words of kindly eulogy of Stephanas, Fortunatus, and Achaicus—of whom Stephanas had been the earliest Achaian convert—who devoted themselves to ministry to the saints, and by their visit had consoled *him* for his absence from them, and *them* by eliciting this Epistle. He urges them to pay due regard and deference to all such true labourers. It is not impossible that these few words may have been

[1] xvi. 12, θέλημα does not mean "Apollos' will," but (probably) "God's will."

added by an afterthought, lest the Corinthians should suppose that it was from those—especially if they were of Chloe's household—that St. Paul had heard such distressing accounts of the Church, and so should be inclined to receive them badly on their return. Then the final autograph salutation:—

"The salutation of me, Paul, with my own hand;" but before he can pen the final benediction, there is one more outburst of strong and indignant feeling. "If any one loveth not the Lord, let him be Anathema;[1] Maranatha, the Lord is near. The grace of our Lord Jesus Christ be with you." That would have been the natural ending, but he had had so much to reprobate, so many severe things to say, that to show how unabated, in spite of all, was his affection for them, he makes the unusual addition, "My love be with you all in Christ Jesus. Amen."[2] So ends the longest and, in some respects, the grandest and most characteristic of his Epistles. He had suppressed indeed all signs of the deep emotion with which it had been written; but when it was despatched he dreaded the results it might produce—dreaded whether he should have said too much; dreaded the possible alienation, by any over-severity, of those whom he had only desired to win. His own soul was all quivering with its half-stifled thunder, and he was afraid lest the flash which he had sent forth should scathe too deeply the souls at which it had been hurled. He would even have given much to recall it,[3] and awaited with trembling anxiety the earliest tidings of the manner in which it would be received. But God overruled all for good; and, indeed, the very writings which spring most naturally and spontaneously from a noble and sincere emotion, are often those that produce the deepest impression upon the world, and are less likely to be resented—at any rate, are more likely to be useful—than the tutored and polished utterances which are carefully tamed down into the limits of correct conventionality. Not only the Church of Corinth, but the whole world, has gained from the intensity of the Apostle's feelings, and the impetuous spontaneity of the language in which they were expressed.

CHAPTER XXXIII.

SECOND EPISTLE TO THE CORINTHIANS.

"There are three crowns: the crown of the Law, the crown of the Priesthood, and the crown of Royalty: but the crown of a good name mounts above them all."—*Pirke Abhôth*, iv. 19.

When St. Paul left Ephesus he went straight to Troas, with the same high motive by which he was always actuated—that of preaching the Gospel of Christ.[4] He had visited the town before, but his stay there had been shortened by the imploring vision of the man of Macedon, which had decided his great intention to carry the Gospel into Europe. But though his preach-

[1] I cannot pretend to understand what St. Paul exactly meant by this. Commentators call it an "imprecation;" but such an "imprecation" does not seem to me like St. Paul. Anathema is the Hebrew *cherem* of Lev. xxvii. 29; Num. xxi. 2, 3 (*Hormah*); Josh. vi. 17. But the later Jews used it for "excommunication," whether of the temporary sort (*nidui*) or the severe. The severest form was called *Shematha*. The Fathers mostly take it to mean "excommunication" here, and in Gal. i. 8, 9, and some see in *Maranatha* an allusion to *Shem atha* (the name cometh). But probably these are after-thoughts. It is a sudden expression of deep feeling; and that it is less terrible than it sounds we may hope from 1 Cor. v. 5; 1 Tim. i. 20, where the object is amendment, not wrath. For "anathematise" see Matt. xxvi. 74; Acts xxiii. 12.

[2] The subscription is, as usual, spurious. It arose from a mistaken inference from xvi. 5. The letter itself shows that it was written in Ephesus (xvi. 8), and though Stephanas, Fortunatus, and Achaicus may have been its bearers, Timotheus could not have been.

[3] 2 Cor. vii. 8.

[4] 2 Cor. ii. 12, 13.

ing was now successful, and "a door was opened for him in the Lord,"[1] he could not stay there from extreme anxiety. "He had no rest for his spirit, because he found not Titus his brother." Titus had been told to rejoin him at Troas; but perhaps the precipitation of St. Paul's departure from Ephesus had brought him to that town earlier than Titus had expected, and, in the uncertain navigation of those days, delays may easily have occurred. At any rate, he did not come, and Paul grew more and more uneasy, until in that intolerable oppression of spirit he felt that he could no longer continue his work, and left Troas for Macedonia. There, at last, he met Titus, who relieved his painful tension of mind by intelligence from Corinth, which, although chequered, was yet on the main point favourable. From Titus he learnt that his change of plan about the visit had given ground for unfavourable criticism,[2] and that many injurious remarks on his character and mode of action had been industriously disseminated, especially by one Jewish teacher.[3] Still, the effect of the first Epistle had been satisfactory. It had caused grief, but the grief had been salutary, and had issued in an outburst of yearning affection, lamentation, and zeal.[4] Titus himself had been received cordially, yet with fear and trembling.[5] The offender denounced in his letter had been promptly and even severely dealt with,[6] and all that St. Paul had said to Titus in praise of the Church had been justified by what he saw.[7] Accordingly, he again sent Titus to them,[8] to finish the good work which he had begun, and with him he sent the tried and faithful brother "whose praise is in the Gospel through all the Churches;"[9] and this time Titus was not only ready but even anxious to go.[10]

In what town of Macedonia St. Paul had met with Titus, and also with Timothy, we do not know. Great uncertainty hangs over the details of their movements, and indeed all the events of this part of the journey are left in obscurity: we can only conjecture that during it St. Paul had even travelled as far as Illyricum.[11] At some point in the journey, but probably not at Philippi, as the subscription to the Epistle says—because, as is evident from the Epistle itself, he had visited most of the Churches of Macedonia,[12]—he wrote his Second Epistle to the Corinthians. From it we learn that, whatever may have been in this region the special nature of his affliction—whether grievous sickness, or external persecutions, or inward anxieties, or apparently all of these combined—his stay in Macedonia had suffered from the same overwhelming distress which had marked the close of his residence in Ephesus,

[1] The use of this expression by St. Luke is one of the many interesting traces of his personal intercourse with St. Paul. (See 1 Cor. xvi. 9.)

[2] 2 Cor. i. 17.

[3] iii. 1; v. 11; vii. 2, 3; x. 10; xi. 18—20.

[4] vii. 6—11.

[5] vii. 13, 15.

[6] ii. 5—10.

[7] vii. 14.

[8] viii. 6.

[9] viii. 18, 23.

[10] viii. 17. That there was a slight unwillingness the first time seems to be shown by the way in which St. Paul felt himself obliged to encourage him in his mission.

[11] Rom. xv. 19.

[12] 2 Cor. viii. 1; ix. 2. Philippi, on the other hand, would be the first city which he would reach.

and which had driven him out of Troas.[1] The Churches were themselves in a state of affliction, which Paul had naturally to share,[2] and he describes his condition as one of mental and physical prostration: "Our flesh had no rest, but we are troubled on every side; from without fightings, from within fears."[3] And this helps to explain to us the actual phenomena of the letter written amid such circumstances. If HOPE is the key-note of the Epistle to the Thessalonians, JOY of that to the Philippians, FAITH of that to the Romans, and HEAVENLY THINGS of that to the Ephesians, AFFLICTION is the one predominent word in the Second Epistle to the Corinthians.[4] The Epistles to the Thessalonians contain his views on the Second Advent; the Epistle to the Galatians is his trumpet-note of indignant defiance to retrograding Judaisers; the Epistle to the Romans is the systematic and, so to speak, scientific statement of his views on what may be called, in modern language, the scheme of salvation; the Epistle to the Philippians is his outpouring of tender and gladdened affection to his most beloved converts; the First Epistle to the Corinthians shows us how he applied the principles of Christianity to daily life in dealing with the flagrant aberrations of a most unsatisfactory Church; his Second Epistle to the Corinthians opens a window into the very emotions of his heart, and is the agitated self-defence of a wounded and loving spirit to ungrateful and erring, yet not wholly lost or wholly incorrigible souls."[5]

And this self-defence was not unnecessary. In this Epistle we find St. Paul for the first time openly confronting the Judaising reaction which assumed such formidable dimensions, and threatened to obliterate every distinctive feature of the Gospel which he preached. It is clear that in some of the Churches which he had founded there sprang up a Judaic party, whose hands were strengthened by commendatory letters from Jerusalem, and who not only combated his opinions, but also grossly abused his character and motives. By dim allusions and oblique intimations we trace their insidious action, and in this Epistle we find ourselves face to face with them and their unscrupulous opposition. It differs greatly from the one that preceded it. St. Paul is no longer combating the folly of fancied wisdom, or the abuse of true liberty. He is no longer occupied with the rectification of practical disorders and theoretical heresies. He is contrasting his own claims with those of his opponents, and maintaining an authority which had been most rudely and openly impugned.

It is not impossible that the attack had been suggested by St. Paul's

1 viii. 2. 2 iv. 8—12. 3 vii. 5.

4 θλίψις, θλίβομαι (2 Cor. i. 4, 6, 8; ii. 4; iv. 8; viii. 13).

5 "The Apostle pours out his heart to them, and beseeches them, in return, not for a cold, dry, critical appreciation of his eloquence, or a comparison of his with other doctrines, but the sympathy of churchmen, if not the affection of children." Parts of the Epistle, taken alone, might seem to be "almost painfully personal," and we "might have thought that the man had got the better of the ambassador. But when we learn how essentially the man and the ambassador are inseparable, then the 'folly,' the boasting, the shame, are not mere revelations of character, but revelations of the close bonds by which one man is related to another" (Maurice, *Unity*, 488).

sentence on the incestuous offender.[1] His case seems to have originated a quarrel among the Corinthian Christians, of whom some sided with him and some with his father. It is clear upon the face of things that we do not know all the circumstances of the case, since it is all but inconceivable that, had there been no extenuating fact, he should have found defenders for a crime which excited the horror of the very heathen. Even those who placed sensuality on the same level as eating meats offered to idols, and therefore regarded it as a matter of indifference—whose view St. Paul so nobly refutes in his first Epistle—could not have sided with this person if there were no palliating element in his offence. And, indeed, if this had not been the case, he would scarcely have ventured to continue in Church membership, and to be, with his injured father, a frequenter of their love-feasts and partaker in their sacraments. It may be quite true, and indeed the allusions to him in the Second Epistle show, that he was weak rather than wicked. But even this would have been no protection to him in a wrong on which Gallio himself would have passed a sentence of death or banishment, and which the Mosaic law had punished with excision from the congregation.[2] There must therefore have been something which could be urged against the heinousness of his transgression, and St. Paul had distinctly to tell the Corinthians that there was no personal feeling mixed up with his decision.[3] His words had evidently implied that the Church was to be assembled, and there, with his spirit present with them, to hand him over to Satan, so that judgment might come on his body for the salvation of his soul. That is what he practically tells the Church to do. Did they do it? It seems to be at least doubtful. That they withdrew from his communion is certain; and the very threat of excommunication which hung over him—accompanied, as he and the Church thought that it would be, with supernatural judgments—was sufficient to plunge him into the depths of misery and penitence. Sickness and death were at this time very prevalent among the Corinthian converts, and St. Paul told them that this was a direct punishment of their profanation of the Lord's Supper. It is clear that the offender was not contumacious, and in his Second Epistle St. Paul openly forgives him, and remits his sentence, apparently on the ground that the Corinthians had already done so. In fact, since the desired end of the man's repentance, and the purging of the Church from all complicity with or immoral acquiescence in his crime had been attained without resorting to extreme measures, St. Paul even exhorts the Corinthians to console and forgive the man, and, in fact, restore him to full Church membership. Still, it does seem as if they had not exactly followed the Apostle's

[1] The theory that the offender of the second Epistle is an entirely different person, alluded to in some lost intermediate letter, seems to me untenable, in spite of the consensus of eminent critics (De Wette, Bleek, Credner, Olshausen, Neander, Ewald, &c.), who, in some form or other, adopt such a hypothesis. I see nothing inconsistent with the older view either in the tone of 1 Cor., or the effect it produced, or in St. Paul's excitement, or in the movements of Titus, or in the language about the offence. But I have not space to enter more fully into the controversy.

[2] Lev. xvii. 8; xx. 11; Deut. xxvii. 20.

[3] 2 Cor. vii. 11, 12.

advice, and as if the party opposed to him had, so to speak, turned upon him and repudiated his authority. They said that he had not come, and he would not come. It was all very well to write stern and threatening letters, but it was not by letters, but by the exercise of miraculous power, that Kephas had avenged the wrongs of the Church and of the Spirit on Ananias and Sapphira, and on Simon Magus. Paul could not do this. How could it be expected of a man so mean of aspect, so vacillating in purpose, so inefficient in speech? It was not Paul who had been chosen as the twelfth Apostle, nor was he an Apostle at all. As the abuses among his followers showed that his teaching was dangerous, so his inability to rectify them was a proof that his authority was a delusion. The very fact that he had claimed no support from his converts only marked how insecure he felt his position to be. What the Church really wanted was the old stringency of the Mosaic Law; some one from Jerusalem; some true Apostle, with his wife, who would rule them with a real supremacy, or at least some emissary from James and the brethren of the Lord, to preach "another Gospel," more accordant with the will of Jesus Himself.[1] Paul, they implied, had never known Jesus, and misrepresented Him altogether;[2] for He had said that no jot or tittle of the law should pass, and that the children's bread should not be cast to dogs. Paul preached himself,[3] and indeed seemed to be hardly responsible for what he did preach. He was half demented; and yet there was some method in his madness, which showed itself partly in self-importance and partly in avarice, both of which were very injurious to the interests of his followers.[4] What, for instance, could be more guileful and crafty than his entire conduct about this collection which he was so suspiciously eager to set on foot?[5] He had ordered them to get up a subscription in his first letter;[6] had, in answer to their inquiries,[7] directed that it should be gathered, as in the Galatian Churches, by a weekly offertory, and had, since this, sent Titus to stimulate zeal in the matter. Now certainly a better emissary could not possibly have been chosen, for Titus was himself a Greek, and therefore well fitted to manage matters among Greeks; and yet had visited Jerusalem, so that he could speak from ocular testimony of the distress which was prevalent among the poorer brethren; and had further been present at the great meeting in Jerusalem at which Paul and Barnabas had received the special request to be mindful of the poor. Yet even this admirably judicious appointment, and the transparent independence and delicacy of mind which had made Paul—with an insight into their character which, as events showed, was but too prescient—entirely to refuse all support from them, was unable to protect him from the coarse insinuation that this was only a cunning device to hide his real intentions, and give him a securer grasp over their money. Such

[1] See Hausrath, p. 420. [2] 2 Cor. xi. 4. [3] 2 Cor. xii. 5.

[4] v. 13, εἴτε γὰρ ἐξέστημεν· xi. 1, ὄφελον ἠνείχεσθέ μου μικρόν τι τῆς ἀφροσύνης· 16, μή τίς με δόξῃ ἄφρονα εἶναι (cf. xii. 6).

[5] xii. 16, ὑπάρχων πανοῦργος δόλῳ ὑμᾶς ἔλαβον. Evidently the quotation of a slander, which he proceeds to refute.

[6] The one no longer extant. [7] 1 Cor. xvi. 1—4.

were the base and miserable innuendoes against which even a Paul had deliberately to defend himself! Slander, like some vile adder, has rustled in the dry leaves of fallen and withered hearts since the world began. Even the good are not always wholly free from it, and the early Christian Church, so far from being the pure ideal bride of the Lord Jesus which we often imagine her to be, was (as is proved by all the Epistles) in many respects as little and in some respects even less pure than ours. The chrisom-robe of baptism was not preserved immaculate either in that or in any other age. The Church to which St. Paul was writing was, we must remember, a community of men and women of whom the majority had been familiar from the cradle with the meanness and the vice of the poorest ranks of heathenism in the corruptest city of heathendom. Their ignorance and weakness, their past training and their present poverty, made them naturally suspicious; and though we cannot doubt that they were morally the best of the class to which they belonged, though there may have been among them many a voiceless Epictetus—a slave, but dear to the immortals—and though their very reception of Christianity proved an aspiring heart, a tender conscience, an enduring spirit, yet many of them had not got beyond the inveteracy of life-long habits, and it was easy for any pagan or Judaic sophister to lime their "wild hearts and feeble wings." But God's mercy overrules evil for good, and we owe to the worthless malice of obscure Judaic calumniators the lessons which we may learn from most of St. Paul's Epistles.[1] A trivial characteristic will often show better than anything else the general drift of any work, and as we have already pointed out the prominence in this Epistle of the thought of "tribulation," so we may now notice that, though "boasting" was of all things the most alien to St. Paul's genuine modesty, the most repugnant to his sensitive humility, yet the boasts of his unscrupulous opponents so completely drove him into the attitude of self-defence, that the word "boasting" occurs no less than twenty-nine times in these few chapters, while it is only found twenty-six times in all the rest of St. Paul's writings.[2]

The Second Epistle to the Corinthians, and those to the Galatians and Romans, represent the three chief phases of his controversy with Judaism. In the Epistle to the Galatians he overthrew for ever the repellent demand that the Gentiles should be circumcised; in the Epistle to the Romans he established for ever the thesis that Jews and Gentiles were equally guilty, and could be justified only by faith, and not by works. In both these Epistles he establishes, from different points of view, the secondary and purely disciplinary functions of the law as a preparatory stage for the dispensation of free grace. In both Epistles he shows conclusively that instead of the false

[1] The authenticity of the letter has never been questioned. The three main divisions are: i.—vii. Hortatory and retrospective, with an under-current of apology. viii., ix. Directions about the contribution. x.—xiii. Defence of his Apostolic position. The more minute analysis will be seen as we proceed. But it is the least systematic, as the First is the most systematic of all his writings.

[2] Especially in 2 Cor. x., xi., xii. This finds its illustration in the prominence of "*inflation*" in 1 Cor. *passim*; but only elsewhere in Col. ii. 18.

assertion that "it is in vain to be a Christian without being a Jew," should be substituted the very opposite statement, that it is in vain to be a Christian if, as a Christian, one relies on being a Jew as well. But, however irresistible his arguments might be, they would be useless if the Judaists succeeded in impugning his Apostolic authority, and proving that he had no right to be regarded as a teacher. The defence of his claims was, therefore, very far from being a mere personal matter; it involved nothing less than a defence of the truth of his Gospel. Yet this defence against an attack so deeply wounding, and so injurious to his cause, was a matter of insuperable difficulty. His opponents could produce their "commendatory letters," and, at least, claimed to possess the delegated authority of the Apostles who had lived with Jesus (2 Cor. iii. 1—18). This was a thing which Paul could not and would not do. He had *not* derived his authority from the Twelve. His intercourse with them had been but slight. His Apostolate was conferred on him, not mediately by them, but immediately by Christ. He had, indeed, "seen the Lord" (1 Cor. ix. 1), but on this he would not dwell, partly because his direct intercourse with Christ had been incomparably smaller than that of a Peter or a James; and partly because he clearly saw, and wished his converts to see, that spiritual union was a thing far closer and more important than personal companionship. To two things only could he appeal: to the visions and revelations which he had received from the Lord, above all, his miraculous conversion; and to the success, the activity, the spiritual power, which set a seal of supernatural approval to his unparalleled ministry.[1] But the first of these claims was deliberately set aside as subjective, both in his own lifetime and a century afterwards.[2] The difficulty of convincing his opponents on this subject reflects itself in his passion, a passion which rose in part because it forced upon him the odious semblance of self-assertion. His sole irresistible weapon was "the sword of the Spirit, which is the word of God."

I will now proceed to give an outline of this remarkable letter, which, from the extreme tension of mind with which it was written, and the constant struggle between the emotions of thankfulness and indignation,[3] is more difficult in its expressions and in its causal connections than any other. The labouring style,—the interchange of bitter irony with pathetic sincerity,—the manner in which word after word—now "tribulation," now "consolation," now "boasting," now "weakness,"—now "simplicity," now "manifestation," takes possession of the Apostle's mind—serve only to throw into relief the

[1] 2 Cor. ii. 14; iii. 2; x. 20—23; 1 Cor. ix. 1; xv. 10, &c.

[2] Pr. Clement. *Hom.* xvii. 13, *seq.* πῶς δέ σοι καὶ πιστεύσομεν αὐτό . . . ; πῶς δέ σοι καὶ ὤφθη ὁπότε αὐτοῦ τὰ ἐνάντια τῇ διδασκαλίᾳ φρονεῖς;

[3] But, as Dean Stanley observes (*Cor.*, p. 348), "the thankfulness of the first part is darkened by the indignation of the third, and even the directions about the business of the contribution are coloured by the reflections both of his joy and of his grief. And in all those portions, though in themselves strictly personal, the Apostle is borne away into the higher region in which he habitually lived, so that this Epistle becomes the most striking instance of what is the case more or less with all his writings, a new philosophy of life poured forth not through systematic treatises, but through occasional bursts of human feeling."

frequent bursts of impassioned eloquence. The depth of tenderness which is here revealed towards all who were noble and true, may serve as a measure for the insolence and wrong which provoked in the concluding chapters so stern an indignation. Of all the Epistles it is the one which enables us to look deepest into the Apostle's heart.

Another characteristic of the letter has been observed by the quick insight of Bengel. "The whole letter," he says, "reminds us of an itinerary, but interwoven with the noblest precepts." "The very stages of his journey are impressed upon it," says Dean Stanley, "the troubles at Ephesus, the anxiety of Troas, the consolations of Macedonia, the prospect of moving to Corinth."[1]

After the greeting, in which he associates Timothy—who was probably his amanuensis—with himself, and with brief emphasis styles himself an "Apostle of Jesus Christ by the will of God," he begins the usual expression of thankfulness, in which the words "tribulation" and "consolation" are inextricably intertwined, and in which he claims for the Corinthians a union with him in both.

"Blessed be the God and Father of our Lord Jesus Christ, the Father of mercies, and God of all consolation, who consoleth us in all our tribulation, that we may be able to console those in all tribulation, by the consolation wherewith we are ourselves consoled by God. For as the sufferings of Christ abound towards us, so by Christ aboundeth also our consolation. But whether we are troubled, it is for your consolation and salvation which worketh in the endurance of the same sufferings which we also suffer, and our hope is sure on your behalf;[2] or whether we are consoled, it is for your consolation and salvation, knowing that as ye are partakers of the sufferings, so also of the consolation."[3]

He then alludes to the fearful tribulation, excessive and beyond his strength, whether caused by outward enemies or by sickness, through which he has just passed in Asia, which has brought him to the verge of despair and of the grave, in order that he may trust solely in Him who raiseth the dead. "Who from such a death rescued us, and will rescue, on whom we have hoped that even yet will He rescue." And as it was the supplication of many which had won for him this great charism, he asks that their thanksgivings may be added to those of many, and that their prayers may still be continued in his behalf.[4]

For however vile might be the insinuations against him, he is proudly conscious of the simplicity[5] and sincerity of his relations to all men, and especially to them, "not in carnal wisdom, but in the grace of God." Some had suspected him of writing private letters and secret messages, of intriguing in fact with individual members of his congregation; but he tells them that he wrote nothing except what they are now reading, and fully recognise, as he hopes they will continue to recognise, and even more fully than heretofore, even as some of them[6] already recognised, that they and he are a mutual subject of boasting in the day of the Lord. *This* was the reason why he had originally intended to pay them two visits instead of one. Had he then been guilty of the levity, the fickleness, the caprice

[1] The thread of the Epistle is historical, but it is interwoven with digressions. The broken threads of narrative will be found in i. 8, 15; ii. 1, 12, 13; vii. 5; viii. 1; ix. 2; xiii. 1.

[2] Verse 6. This is the position of these words in most uncials.

[3] "Communio sanctorum," Phil. ii. 26 (Bengel).

[4] i. 1–11; i. 8. *ὥστε ἐξαπορηθῆναι*, though generally he was *ἀπορούμενος οὐκ ἐξαπορούμενος*, iv. 8. *ἀπόκριμα τοῦ θανάτου* to the question, "How will it all end?" the only answer seemed to be "Death." *καθ' ὑπερβολήν*, iv. 17; Rom. vii. 13; 1 Cor. xii. 31; Gal. i. 13.

[5] i. 12. *ἁπλότης*, in answer to the charge of duplicity, is a characteristic word of this Epistle (viii. 2; ix. 11, 13; xi. 3); but here, א, A, B, C, K, read *ἁγιότητι*.

[6] i. 14, *ἀπὸ μέρους*.

with which he had been charged in changing his plan? Did the "Yes, yes" of his purposes mean much the same thing as "No, no," like the mere shifting feebleness of an aimless man?[1] Well, if they chose to say this of him *as a man*, at any rate, there was *one* emphatic "Yes," one unalterable fixity and affirmation about him, and that was his preaching of Christ. Jesus Christ, the Son of God, preached by him and Silvanus and Timotheus, had proved Himself to be not "Yes" and "No;" but in Him was God's infinite "Yes," and therefore also the Christian's everlasting Amen to all God's promises.[2] He who confirmed all of them alike into the Anointed (εἰς χριστον), and anointed them (χρίσας), was God, who also set His seal on them, and gave them in their hearts the earnest of His Spirit.[3] He called God to witness upon his own soul that it was with a desire to spare them that he no longer came[4] to Corinth. And then, conscious that jealous eyes would dwell on every phrase of his letter, and if possible twist its meaning against him, he tells them that by using the expression "sparing them," he does not imply any claim to lord it over their *faith*, for faith is free and by it they stand; but that he is speaking as a fellow-worker of their joy, and therefore he had decided that his second visit to them should not be in grief.[5] Was it natural that he should like to grieve those who caused him joy, or be grieved by those from whom he ought to receive joy? His joy, he felt sure, was theirs also, and therefore he had written to them instead of coming; and that previous letter—sad as were its contents—had not been written to grieve them, but had been written in much tribulation and compression of heart and many tears, that they might recognise how more abundantly he loved them. Grief, indeed, there had been, and it had fallen on him, but it had not come on him only, but partly on them, and he did not wish to press heavily on them all.[6] And the sinner who had caused that common grief had been sufficiently censured by the reprobation of the majority of them;[7] so that now, on the contrary, they should forgive and comfort him, that a person such as he was—guilty, disgraced, but now sincerely penitent—may not be swallowed up by his excessive grief. Let them now assure him of their love. The object of the former letter had been fulfilled in testing their obedience. If *they* forgave (as they had partially done already, in not strictly carrying out his decision), so did he; "and what I have forgiven, if

[1] I have never been even approximately satisfied with any explanation of this passage. St. Chrysostom makes it mean, "Did I show levity, or do I plan after the flesh that the yea with me must be always yea, and the nay always nay, as it is with a man of the world who makes his plans independently of God's over-ruling of them?" As there are no emphatic affirmations in the case, Matt. v. 37, James v. 12, throw no light on the passage, unless some such words had been quoted against him in the perverted sense that when once you have said a thing you must at all costs do it, however completely circumstances have changed.

[2] Compare the Ἀμὴν ἀμὴν ("Verily, verily") of which the Gospels are so full. I read διὸ καὶ δι' αὐτοῦ, with ℵ, A, B, C, D, F, G.

[3] ἀῤῥαβὼν, earnest-money, part-payment, προκαταβολή; an ancient (עֵרָבוֹן, Gen. xxxviii. 17, 18; *arrhabo*—Plaut. *Rud. Prol.* 46) and modern word (Fr. *arrhes*) made current by Semitic commerce. (Cf. ἀπαρχὴ, Rom. viii. 23.)

[4] i. 23. Here, and as, I believe, in ii. 1 and xiii. 1, he speaks of his *intended* visit as a real one. The E. V. mistakes οὐκέτι, "no longer," for οὔπω, "not yet;" but the expression really illustrates the much-disputed verses to which I have referred, and inclines me to the opinion that St. Paul had not visited Corinth more than once when this letter was written. But the question is one of very small importance, though so much has been written on it.

[5] Lit., "not again to come to you in grief," as he would be doing *if* he had visited them once in grief, and were then obliged to come a second time in the same spirit. No doubt the words literally imply that he had *already once* visited them in grief, and that expression would hardly be correct for his *first* visit; but he merely uses it in his vivid way as though his *intended* visit—which, had he carried it out, *would* have been in grief—had been a real visit. The πάλιν is even omitted in D, E, F, G. Theodoret, who ought to know what Greek means, takes πάλιν ἐλθεῖν merely in the sense of "re-visit," separating it from ἐν λύπῃ altogether.

[6] This is another of those ambiguous expressions—due to the emotion of the writer and the delicacy of the subjects of which he is treating, and his desire to be kind and just though there was so much to blame—about which it is impossible to feel any certainty of the exact explanation. I have partly followed the view of St. Chrysostom.

[7] *Some* had evidently been recalcitrant. In ii. 6 the word for "punishment" is ἐπιτιμία, not κόλασις or τιμωρία; but the general meaning is that of punishment (Wisd. iii. 10. Philo, περὶ ἄθλων καὶ ἐπιτιμιῶν, "on rewards and punishments."

I have forgiven anything,[1] is for your sakes, in the presence[2] of Christ, that we may not be over-reached by Satan, for we are not ignorant of his devices."[3]

Well, he did *not* come to them, and he *did* write, and what was the consequence? His anxiety to know the effect produced by his letter and change of plan was so intense, that it almost killed him. Successful as was the opening which he found for the Gospel of Christ at Troas, he abandoned his work there, because he could not endure the disappointment and anguish of heart which the non-arrival of Titus caused him. He therefore went to Macedonia. There at last he met Titus, but he omits to say so in his eagerness to thank God, who thus drags him in triumph in the service of Christ. Everywhere the incense of that triumph was burnt; to some it was a sweet savour that told of life, to others a sign of imminent death. St. Paul is so possessed by the metaphor that he does not even pause to disentangle it. He is at once the conquered enemy dragged in triumph, and the incense burned in sign of the victor's glory. The burning incense is a sign to some of life ever-renewed in fresh exultation; to others of defeat ever deepening into death. To himself, at once the captive and the sharer in the triumph, it is a sign of death, and of daily death, and yet the pledge of a life beyond life itself.[4] And who is sufficient for such ministry? For he is not like the majority[5]—the hucksters, the adulterators, the fraudulent retailers of the Word of God,—but as of sincerity, but as of God—in the presence of God he speaks in union with Christ.[6]

Is this self-commendation to them? Does he need letters of introduction to them?[7] And here, again, follows one of the strangely mingled yet powerful metaphors so peculiar to the greatest and most sensitive imaginations. "Ye are our Epistle," says St. Paul, "written on our hearts, recognised and read by all men, being manifestly an Epistle of Christ, ministered by us, written not with ink, but with the spirit of the living God; not on stonen tablets, but on fleshen tablets—hearts."[8] He does not need a commendatory letter to them; they are themselves his commendatory letter to all men; it is a letter of Christ, of which he is only the writer and carrier;[9] and it is not engraved on granite like the Laws of Moses, but on their hearts. Thus they are at once the commendatory letter written on Paul's heart, and they have a letter of Christ written on their own hearts by the Spirit, and of that letter Paul has been the human agent.[10]

It was a bold expression, but one which sprang from a confidence which Christ inspired, and had reference to a work for God. That work was the ministry of the New Covenant—not of the slaying letter but of the vivifying spirit,[11] for which

[1] ii. 10. The best reading seems to be ὃ κεχάρισμαι, εἴ τι κεχάρισμαι, ℵ, A, B, C, F, G Evidently we are here in the dark about many circumstances; but we infer that St. Paul's sentence of excommunication, as ordered in his former letter, had *not* been carried out, partly because some opposed it, but also in part because the man repented in consequence of his exclusion from the communion of the majority of the Church. St. Paul might have been angry that his plain order had been disobeyed by the Church as such; but, on the contrary, he is satisfied with their partial obedience, and withdraws his order, which timely repentance had rendered needless.

[2] Cf. Prov. viii. 30, LXX.

[3] i. 12—ii. 11.

[4] On this metaphor, *v. infra*, Excursus III. The last great triumph at Rome had been that of Claudius, when Caradoc was among the captives.

[5] ii. 17. οἱ πολλοὶ is a strong expression, but οἱ λοιποὶ, "the rest," the reading of D, E, F, G, J, is still more impassioned. It is possible that this may have been softened into the other reading, just as οἱ πολλοὶ has been softened into πολλοί. We must remember how many and diverse were the elements of error at Corinth—conceit, faction, Pharisaism, licence, self-assertion; and St. Paul (Rom. v.) seems to use οἱ πολλοὶ peculiarly.

[6] ii. 12—17 (cf. Isa. i. 22, LXX.).

[7] iii. 1. It is astonishing to find Ebionite hatred still burning against St. Paul in the second century, and covertly slandering him because *he* had no ἐπιστολαὶ συστατικαὶ from James. All who came without such letters were to be regarded as false prophets, false apostles, &c. (Cf. 2 Cor. xi. 13; Gal. ii. 12.) (Ps. Clem. *Recogn.* iv. 34; *Hom.* xi. 35.)

[8] Read καρδίαις, ℵ, A, B, C, D, E, G. For the metaphor compare Prov. iii. 3; vii. 3; Ezek. xi. 19; Ex. xviii. 18.

[9] Compare the identification of the seed sown and the hearts that receive it in Mark iv. 16.

[10] iii. 1—3.

[11] iii. 6, ἀποκτείνει; Rom. iv. 15; vii. 6, 7, 10, 11; Gal. iii. 10; John vi. 63. ζωοποιεῖ, Rom. vi. 4, 11; viii. 2, 10; Gal. v. 2.

God gave the sufficiency. And what a glorious ministry! If the ministry of the Law—tending in itself to death, written in earthly letters, graven on granite slabs, —yet displayed itself in such glory that the children of Israel could not gaze on the face of Moses because of the glory of his countenance, which was rapidly fading away,[1] how much more glorious was the Ministry of Life, of Righteousness, of the Spirit, which by comparison outdazzles that other glory into mere darkness,[2] and is not transitory (διὰ δόξης) but permanent (ἐν δόξῃ). It was the sense of being entrusted with that ministry which gave him confidence. Moses used to put a veil over his face that the children of Israel might not see the evanescence of the transient; and the veil which *he* wore on his bright countenance when he spoke to them reminds him of the veil which *they* yet wore on their hardened understandings when his Law was read to them, which should only begin to be removed the moment they turned from Moses to Christ,[3] from the letter to the spirit, from slavery to freedom. But he and all the ministers of Christ gazed with no veil upon their faces upon *His* glory reflected in the mirror of His Gospel; and in their turn seeing that image as in a mirror,[4] caught that ever-brightening glory as from the Lord, the Spirit. How could one entrusted with such a ministry grow faint-hearted? How could he—as Paul's enemies charged him with doing—descend into "the crypts of shame?" Utterly false[5] were such insinuations. He walked not in craftiness; he did not adulterate the pure Word of God; but his commendatory letter, the only one he needed, was to manifest the truth to all consciences in God's sight. There was no veil over the truths he preached; if veil there was, it was only in the darkened understandings of the perishing, so darkened into unbelief by the god of the present world,[6] that the brightness of the gospel of the glory of Christ could not illuminate them. He it is—Christ Jesus the Lord, the image of God—He it is, and not ourselves, whom Paul and all true Apostles preached. He had been accused of self-seeking and self-assertion. Such sins were *impossible* to one who estimated as he did the glory of His message. All that he could preach of himself was that Christ was Lord, and that he was their slave for Christ's sake. For God had shone in the hearts of His ministers only in order that the bright knowledge which they had caught from gazing, with no intervening veil, on the glory of Christ, might glow for the illumination of the world.[7]

A glorious ministry; but what weak ministers! Like the torches hid in Gideon's pitchers, their treasure of light was in earthen vessels,[8] that the glory of their victory over the world and the world's idolatries might be God's, not theirs. This was why they were at once weak and strong—weak in themselves, strong in God—"in everything being troubled, yet not crushed; perplexed, but not in despair; persecuted, but not forsaken; flung down, but not destroyed; always carrying about in our body the putting to death of the Lord Jesus Christ, in order that also the life of Jesus may be manifested in our body. For we, living as we are, are ever being handed over to death for Jesus' sake, in order that the life of Jesus also may be manifested in our mortal flesh. So that death is working in us—seeing that for Christ's sake and for your sakes we die daily—but life in you. The trials are mainly ours; the blessings yours. Yet we know that this daily death of ours shall be followed by a resurrection. He who raised Christ shall also raise us from the daily death of our

[1] iii. 7. The word "*till*" in the E.V. of Ex. xxxiv. 33 seems to be a mistake for "when." He put on the veil, not to dim the splendour while he spoke, but (so St. Paul here implies) to veil the evanescence when he had ended his words—καταργοῦμαι (1 Cor. i. 28; ii. 6; vi. 13; xiii. 8, 11; xv. 24—twenty-two times in this group of Epistles).

[2] iii. 10, 11, οὐ δεδόξασται τὸ δεδοξασμένον ἐν τούτῳ τῷ μέρει.

[3] iii. 16, ἐπιστρέψῃ . . . περιαιρεῖται.

[4] iii. 18, κατοπτριζόμενοι. Chrysostom, &c., make it mean "reflecting," but there seems to be no instance of that sense.

[5] iv. 2. Cf. 1 Cor. iv. 5. Hence the prominence of the word φανερόω in this Epistle (ii. 14; iii. 3; iv. 10; v. 10, 11; vii. 12; xi. 6).

[6] Cf. John xiv. 30; Eph. ii. 2. "Grandis sed horribilis descriptio Satanae" (Bengel).

[7] iii. 4—iv. 6.

[8] He was a σκεῦος ἐκλογῆς (Acts ix. 15), but the σκεῦος was itself ὀστράκινον. "Lo vas d' elezione" (Dante, *Inf.* ii. 28).

afflicted lives[1] and from the death in which they end, and shall present us, with you, to God's glory, by the increase of grace and more abundant increase of thanksgiving. For this reason *we* do not play the coward, but even if our outward man is being destroyed, yet the inward man is being renewed day by day. For the lightness of our immediate affliction is working out for us, in increasing excess, an eternal weight of glory, since our eyes are fixed not on the visible, but on the invisible; for the things visible are transient, but the things invisible are eternal.[2] The tents of our earthly bodies shall be done away, but then we shall have an eternal building. We groan, we are burdened in this tent of flesh,[3] we long to put on over it, as a robe, our house from heaven—if, as I assume, we shall not indeed be found bodiless[4]—that the mortal may be swallowed up by life.[5] And God, who wrought us for this end, has given us the earnest of His Spirit that it shall be so. Hence, since we walk by faith, death itself has for us lost all terrors; it will be but an admission into the nearer presence of our Lord. To please Him is our sole ambition, because we shall each stand before His tribunal to receive the things done by the body;—to be paid in kind for our good and evil, not by arbitrary infliction, but by natural result.[6] This is our awful belief, and we strive to make it yours.[7] To God our sincerity is manifest already, and we hope that it will be to your consciences, since we tell you all this not by way of commending ourselves, but that you may have something of which to boast about us against those whose boasts are but of superficial things. They call us mad,[8]—well, if so, it is for God; or if we be sober-minded, it is for you.[9] Our one constraining motive is Christ's love. Since He died for all, all in His death died to sin, and therefore the reason of His death was that we may not live to ourselves, but to Him who died and rose again for us. From henceforth, then, we recognise no relation to Him which is not purely spiritual. Your Jerusalem emissaries boast that they knew the living Christ; and in consequence maintain their superiority to us. If we ever recognised any such claim—if we ever relied on having seen the living Christ—we renounce all such views from this moment.[10] 'He who is in Christ is a new creation; the old things are passed away; lo! all things have become new.' It is the spiritual Christ, the glorified Christ—whom God made to be sin for us—in

[1] "God exhibits death in the living, life in the dying" (Alford).

[2] Cf. Plat. *Phaedo*, 79.

[3] Wisd. ix. 15, "the earthly tabernacle (γεῶδες σκῆνος) weigheth down the mind."

[4] v. 3. So I understand this difficult clause. It seems to imply some condition which is *not* that of disembodied spirits, between the death of the mortal and the reception of the resurrection body (cf. Hdt. v. 92; Thuc. iii. 58).

[5] Again, notice the strange confusion of metaphors. It is only the very greatest writers who can venture to write thus; only those whose thoughts are like a flame, that cracks the enclosing lamp of language that it may emit more heat and light.

[6] It is not easy to see the exact correlation between the judicial process of result according to good and evil conduct—even as regards saints—and that free absolute justification by faith in Christ, that complete forgiveness of sins, and tearing up of the bond which is against us, on which St. Paul dwells in v. 19, 21; Rom. iii. 25; Col. ii. 14. But faith is as little troubled by unsolved antinomies in the kingdom of grace as in that of nature (see *infra*, Excursus XXI., p. 732).

[7] v. 11. So Chrysostom, &c., but it is one of the many verses in this Epistle about which no absolute certainty is attainable. It *may* mean "knowing that the fear of God (*timorem Domini*, Vulg.) is the principle of my own life, I try to persuade you of this truth; that it *is* so God knows already.

[8] Cf. Acts xxvi. 24.

[9] "My revelations, ecstacies, glossolaly, are phases of intercourse of my soul with God; my practical sense and tact are for you."

[10] 2 Cor. v. 16, ἀπὸ τοῦ νῦν. In Gal. i. 15, 16, St. Paul has said that "it pleased God to reveal His Son in him," and in his view "the entire, absolute importance of Christianity resided in the person of Christ. God had disclosed to him as the Son of God that Jesus whom he had opposed as a false Messiah. But the resurrection had elevated his historic Christ far above a Jewish Messiah (1 Cor. xv. 8). The death of Christ had severed His connexion with mere national elements, and He was then manifested in the universal and spiritual sphere in which all absolute importance of Judaism was obliterated. St. Paul here says that since he began to live for Christ, who died and rose, Jesus is no longer for him a Messiah after the flesh. *That* conception of Him is now purged of all sensuous, Judaic, personal limitations, and Christ becomes not only one who lived and died in Judæa, but who lives and reigns in the heart of every Christian on the absolute principle of the spiritual life." (Baur, *Paul.* ii. 126.) When Paul had once shaken himself free, first from his unconverted Pharisaism, then from the Judæo-Christian stage of his earlier convictions, he grasped the truth that the risen and ascended Lord of all dwarfed and shamed the notion of all mere local, and family, and national restrictions.

whom God reconciled the world unto Himself, not imputing their trespasses unto them—whom we preach; and our ministry is the Ministry of Reconciliation which God entrusted to us, and in virtue of which we, as ambassadors on Christ's behalf, entreat you to be reconciled to God. 'Him who knew not sin He made sin on our behalf, that we may become the righteousness of God in Him.'[1] As His fellow-workers we entreat you, then, not to render null the acceptance of His grace in this the day of salvation, and that this our ministry may not be blamed, we give no legitimate cause of offence in anything, but in everything commend ourselves[2] as ministers of God "in much endurance, in tribulations, in necessities, in pressure of circumstance, in blows, in prisons, in tumults, in toils, in spells of sleeplessness, in fastings, in pureness, in knowledge, in long-suffering, in kindness, in the Holy Spirit, in love unfeigned, in the word of truth, in the power of God, by the arms of righteousness on the right and left, by glory and dishonour, by ill report and good report; as deceivers and yet true, as being ignored and yet recognised, as dying and behold we live, as being chastened yet not being slain, as being grieved and yet rejoicing, as paupers yet enriching many, as having nothing yet as having all things in full possession."[3]

He may well appeal to this outburst of impassioned eloquence as a proof that his mouth is open and his heart enlarged towards them, and as the ground of entreaty that, instead of their narrow jealousies and suspicions, they would, as sons, love him with the same large-heartedness, and so repay him in kind, and separate themselves from their incongruous yoke-fellowship with unbelief[4]—the unnatural participations, symphonies, agreements of righteousness and light with lawlessness and darkness, of Christ with worthlessness,[5] of God's temple with idols, which forfeited the glorious promises of God.[6] Let them cleanse themselves from these corruptions from within and from without. And then, to clench all that he has said, and for the present to conclude the subject, he cries, 'Receive us! we wronged nobody, ruined nobody, defrauded nobody—such charges against us are simply false. I do not allude to them to condemn you. I have said already that you are in my heart to die together and live together. I speak thus boldly because of the consolation and superabundant joy—in the midst of all the tribulations—which came on me in Macedonia with overwhelming intensity—without, battles; within, fears. But God, who consoleth the humble,[7] consoled us by the coming of Titus, and the good news about your reception of my letter, and the yearning for me, and the lamentation, and the zeal which it awoke on my behalf. At one time I regretted that I had written it, but, though it pained you, I regret it no longer, because the pain was a holy and a healing pain, which awoke earnestness in you—self-defence and indignation against wrong, and a fear and yearning towards me, and zeal for God, and punishment of the offender. It was not to take either one side or the other in the quarrel that I wrote to you, but that your allegiance and love to me might be manifested to yourselves[8] before God. I did not care for those people—their offence and quarrel. I cared only for you. And you stood the test. You justified all that I had boasted to Titus about you, and the respect and submission with which you received him have inspired me with

[1] The meaning of this verse will be brought out *infra*, p. 472, *seq.*

[2] The reader will observe how much the mention of the *συστατικαὶ ἐπιστολαί* has dominated throughout this majestic self-defence. The statement of the nature and method of His ministry is the only commendatory letter which to them, at least, Paul will deign to use. Yet in making a self-defence so utterly distasteful to him, observe how noble and eternal are the thoughts on which he dwells, and the principles upon which he insists.

[3] iv. 7—vi. 10.

[4] An allusion to the "diverse kinds," and ox and ass ploughing together (Lev. xix. 19; Deut. xxii. 10). I am unable to see so strongly as others the digressive and parenthetic character of vi. 14—vii. 1.

[5] vi. 15, *βελίαρ*. Belial is not originally a proper name (Prov. vi. 12, "a naughty person" is Adam belial); and this is why there was no worship of Belial.

[6] These are given (vi. 18) in "a mosaic of citations" from 2 Sam. vii. 14, 8; Is. xliii. 6 (Plumptre); perhaps, however, St. Paul had in his mind also Jer. xxxi. 3—33; Ezek. xxxvi. 28.

[7] Cf. x. 1. He touchingly accepts the term applied to him.

[8] vii. 12. The reading seems to be *τὴν σπουδὴν ὑμῶν τὴν ὑπὲρ ἡμῶν πρὸς ὑμᾶς.* (C, E, J, K.)

deep joy on his account, and him with a deep affection for you. I rejoice, then, that in everything I am in good heart about you.'[1]

He proceeds to give them a proof of it. The churches of Macedonia he tells them, poor as they are,[2] afflicted as they are, yet with a spontaneous liberality, absolute self-devotion, and affectionate enthusiasm for his wishes, giving themselves first to God beyond his hopes, had not only subscribed largely to the collection for the saints, but had entreated him to take part in its management. Encouraged by this, he had asked Titus to finish the arrangement of this matter with the rest of his good work among them. As they abounded in so many gifts and graces, let them abound in this. He did not want to order them, he only told them what others had done, and asked (not on his own behalf) a proof of their love, even as Christ had set them the example of enriching others by His own poverty. They had begun the collection first, but Macedonia had finished it. They need not give more than they could afford, for God looked not to the gift, but to the spirit of the giver. Nor did he wish to pauperise them in order to set others at ease, but only to establish between Jewish and Gentile churches a reciprocity of aid in time of need. Titus had gladly accepted the commission, and with him he sent the brother, whose praise in the Gospel is known in all the churches, and who has been specially elected by the churches to this office; since so great was Paul's determination to give not the slightest handle to mean insinuations, that he would have nothing to do with the money himself.[3] With Titus and this brother he sent a third, whose earnestness had been often tested in many circumstances, and who was now specially stimulated by his confidence in the Corinthians. If they wanted to know anything about these three visitors, Titus was his partner and fellow-worker towards them; the other two brethren were delegates of the churches,[4] the glory of Christ. Let the Corinthians give a proof of their love, and a justification to all churches of his boasting about them. As to the general desirability of the collection he surely need say nothing. He had been boasting of their zeal, and had told the Macedonian churches that the Achaians had been ready a year ago. In this there was some reason to fear that he had been in error, having mistaken their ready professions for actual accomplishment. He had therefore sent on these brethren, lest, if Macedonians came with him on his arrival, and found them unprepared, he—to say nothing of them—should be ashamed of a boast which would turn out to be false. He exhorts them, therefore, to willing liberality, trusting that God would reward them. Let them give beneficently, not grudgingly. "But (notice) this—He who soweth sparingly, sparingly also shall reap, and he who soweth with blessings, with blessings."[5] "And God is able to make all grace abound towards you, that in everything, always, having all sufficiency, ye may abound to every good work." And this collection was not only for the aid of the saints, but also for the glory of God by the thanksgiving to Him, and prayer for them which it called forth. The recipients would glorify God for it as a sign of genuine religion, and would yearn towards them in love, because of the grace of God abounding in them. "Thanks," he says, identifying himself with the feelings of the grateful recipients—"thanks to God for His unspeakable gift."[6]

At this point the whole tone of the Epistle changes—changes so completely that, in this section of it (x. i.—xiii. 10), many have not only seen an entirely separate letter, but have even with much plausibility identified it

[1] vi. 11—vii. 16.

[2] Dean Stanley refers to Arnold, *Rom. Commonwealth*, ii. 382.

[3] viii. 20 (cf. Prov. iii. 3, LXX.), ἁδρότης, *lit.* "ripeness." These *hapax legomena* occur freely in Paul's unquestioned Epistles. He readily took up new words. He may, for instance, have picked up the word ἐπιχορηγῶν (first used in ix. 10, and then in Gal. iii. 5; Col. ii. 19; Eph. iv. 16) at Athens. It is unknown to the LXX. of the Old Testament, and only found in Ecclus. xxv. 22.

[4] Lit. "apostles," but here in its untechnical sense of "authorised delegates." Who these two brethren were is quite uncertain;—perhaps Luke and Trophimus.

[5] ix. 6, ἐπ' εὐλογίαις, *i.e.*, in a large, gracious, liberal spirit (Prov. xi. 24; xxii. 9).

[6] viii. 1—ix. 15.

with that stern missive alluded to in vii. 8—12, which caused the Corinthians so much pain, and stirred them up to such vigorous exertion, which is usually identified with the first extant Epistle.[1] It is difficult to accept any such hypothesis in the teeth of the evidence of all manuscripts; and when we remember the perpetual interchange of news between different Churches, it is a much simpler and more natural supposition that, as the first part of the letter had been written while he was in anxiety about them, and the second after his mind had been relieved by the arrival of Titus, so this third part of the letter was written after the arrival of some other messenger, who bore the disastrous tidings that some teacher had come from Jerusalem whose opposition to St. Paul had been more marked and more unscrupulous than any with which he had yet been obliged to deal. However that may be, certain it is that these chapters are written in a very different mood from the former.[2] There is in them none of the tender effusiveness and earnest praise which we have been hearing, but a tone of suppressed indignation, in which tenderness, struggling with bitter irony, in some places renders the language laboured and obscure,[3] like the words of one who with difficulty restrains himself from saying all that his emotion might suggest. Yet it is deeply interesting to observe that "the meekness and gentleness of Christ" reigns throughout all this irony, and he utters no word of malediction like those of the Psalmists. And there is also a tone of commanding authority, which the writer is driven to assume as a last resource, since all forbearance has been so grievously misunderstood. Some among them—one person in particular[4]—had been passing their censures and criticisms on St. Paul very freely, saying that his person was mean;[5] that he was untutored in speech;[6] that he was only bold in letters, and at a distance; that he walked "according to the flesh;"[7] that he was certainly a weakling, and probably a madman.[8] They had been urging their own near connexion with Christ as a subject of self-commendation;[9] had been preaching another Jesus, and a different Gospel, and imparting a different spirit;[10] had been boasting immeasurably of their superiority, though they were thrusting themselves into

[1] If such a supposition were at all probable, we should rather infer from xii. 18 that this section was an Epistle written *after* the mission of Titus and the brother alluded to in viii. 18. But the suggestion in the text seems to me to meet most of the difficulties.

[2] A change of tone of an analogous character—from a more distant and respectful to a more stern and authoritative style—is observable in Rom. xiv., xv. (*v. infra*, p. 450). So there is a wide difference between the apologetic and the aggressive part of Demosthenes, *De Coronâ* (Hug). Semler was the first to suggest that this Epistle was an amalgamation of three, which is also the view of Weisse. The Αὐτὸς δὲ ἐγὼ Παῦλος of x. 1 (cf. Gal. v. 2; Eph. iii. 1; Philem. 19) at once marks the change.

[3] Theodoret says of x. 12—18 that St. Paul wrote it obscurely (ἀσαφῶς) from a desire not to expose the offenders too plainly.

[4] x. 2, τινας: 7, εἴ τις πέποιθεν ἑαυτῷ: 10, φησι, "says he:" 11, ὁ τοιοῦτος: 12, τισι: 18, ὁ ἑαυτὸν συνιστῶν: xi. 4, ὁ ἐρχόμενος.

[5] x. 1, 10.

[6] xi. 6.

[7] x. 2, κατὰ σάρκα, *i.e.*, with mere earthly motives; that he was timid, complaisant, inconsistent, self-seeking.

[8] xi. 16, 17, 19. Compare the blunt "Thou art mad, Paul!" of Festus.

[9] x. 7.

[10] xi. 4, ἄλλον Ἰησοῦν . . . ἕτερον πνεῦμα . . . εὐαγγέλιον ἕτερον.

spheres of work in which they had not laboured;[1] and by whispered seductions had been beguiling the Corinthians from the simplicity of their original faith.[2] In contrast to the self-supporting toils and forbearance of St. Paul, these men and their coryphaeus had maintained their claim to Apostolic authority by an insolence, rapacity, and violence,[3] which made Paul ironically remark that his weakness in having any consideration for his converts, instead of lording it over them, had been a disgrace to him. And, strange to say, the ministry and doctrine of this person and his clique had awakened a distinct echo in the hearts of the unstable Corinthians. They had taken them at their own estimate; had been dazzled by their outrageous pretensions; benumbed by the "torpedo-touch" of their avarice; and confirmed in a bold disregard for the wishes and regulations of their true Teacher.[4]

It is at these intruders that St. Paul hurls his indignant, ironical, unanswerable apology. "Mean as he was of aspect,"[5] he entreats them by the gentleness and mildness of Christ that when he came he might not be forced to show that if "he walked after the flesh," at any rate the weapons he wielded were not after the flesh, but strong enough to humble insolence, and punish disobedience, and rase the strongholds of opposition, and take captive every thought into the obedience of Christ. Did they judge by outward appearance? They should find that he was as near to Christ as any member of the party that used His name. They should find that his personal action, founded on a power of which he well might boast, but which God had given him for their edification, not for destruction, could be as weighty and powerful, as calculated to terrify them, as his letters.[6] He would not, indeed, venture to enter with them into the mean arena of personal comparisons,[7] which proved the unwisdom of his opponents; nor would he imitate them in stretching his boasts to an illimitable extent. He would confine these boasts to the range of the measuring-line which God had given him, and which was quite large enough without any over-straining to reach to them, even as His Gospel had first reached them; for, unlike his opponents, he was not exercising these boasts in spheres of labour not his own, but had hope that, as their faith enlarged, he would be still more highly esteemed, and the limit of his work extended to yet wider and untried regions. Let the boaster then boast in the Lord, since the test of a right to boast was not in self-commendation, but in the commendation of the Lord.[8]

He entreats them to bear with him, just a little, in this folly—nay, he is sure they do so.[9] He feels for them a godly jealousy, desiring to present them as a chaste virgin to Christ, but fearful lest they should be seduced from their simplicity as the serpent beguiled Eve. It would have been easy for them (it appears) to tolerate this new preacher[10] if he is preaching another Jesus, a different spirit, a different gospel; but he professes to preach the *same*, and such being the case he had no more

[1] x. 15. [2] xi. 3. [3] xi. 20, 21. [4] x. 18; xi. 8, 20; xii. 13, 14.

[5] Many of these expressions, as St. Chrysostom saw, are quotations of the sneers of his opponents—*κατ' εἰρωνείαν φησὶ τὰ ἐκείνων φθεγγόμενος*. For traces of similar irony, see 1 Cor. iv. 8—11; vi. 3—8; ix. 1—16; xv. 6.

[6] x. 1—11. This comparison of his letters and his personal conduct (ver. 10) is quoted from the Jerusalem emissary (*φησιν*, "he says;" 7, *τις*; 11, *τοιοῦτος*).

[7] x. 12, *ἐγκρῖναι ἢ συγκρῖναι*, an untranslatable paronomasia.

[8] x. 12—18. The haunting word is, as in so many parts of the Epistle, "boast" and "commendation" (iii. 1; iv. 2; v. 12; x. 12, 16, 17, 18; xi. 10, 12, 18, 30; xii. 1, 5, 6, 11), with especial reference to the commendatory letters. It was an easy thing, he hints, for these Judaisers to come comfortably with "letters" from Jerusalem to Corinth, and there be supported by admiring adherents whom *his* toils had converted; a very different thing to traverse the world as a friendless missionary, and sow the seed of the Gospel in virgin soil.

[9] xi. 1, *μικρόν τι . . . ἀλλὰ καί*. This Epistle is characterised by haunting words, and the key-words of this chapter are *ἀνέχομαι* (1, 4, 19, 20) and *ἄφρων* (1, 16, 17, 19, 21; xii. 6, 11). Dr. Plumptre sees in this the echo of some taunt which Titus had reported—"His folly is becoming intolerable."

[10] xi. 4, *ὁ ἐρχόμενος*.

authority than Paul, who claimed that he had in no respect fallen short of the most super-apostolic Apostles.[1] A mere laic in eloquence he might be, but there was at any rate no defect in his knowledge; and the proof of this as regards *them* was obvious in everything among all men,[2] unless, indeed, he had transgressed by humiliating himself for their exaltation by preaching to them gratuitously. Other Churches he plundered, preaching to the Corinthian, and being paid his wages by others. And though he was in positive want while among them, he did not benumb them with his exactions, as though he were some gymnotus, but was helped by Macedonians, and kept and would keep himself from laying any burden whatever on them. That boast no one should obstruct,[3] not (God knows) because he did not love them, but because he would cut off the handle from those who wanted a handle, and that, in this topic of boasting, he and his opponents might be on equal grounds. The last remark is a keen sarcasm, since, if they charged Paul with taking money, they charged him with the very thing which he did *not* do, and which they *did*.[4] "For such," he adds with passionate severity, "are false Apostles, deceitful workers, transforming themselves into Apostles of Christ; nor is this to be wondered at, for Satan himself transforms himself into an angel of light.[5] It is no great thing then, if also His ministers transform themselves as ministers of righteousness, whose end shall be according to their works. Again I say, Let no one think me a fool; or, if you do, receive me even as you would receive a fool, that I too, as well as they, may boast a little." He claims nothing lofty or sacred or spiritual for this determined boasting. It was a folly, but not one of his own choosing. Since many adopted this worldly style of boasting, he would meet them with their own weapons; and the Corinthians, since they were so wise, would, he was sure, gladly tolerate mere harmless fools, seeing that they tolerated people much more objectionable—people who enslaved, devoured,[6] took them in—people who assumed the most arrogant pretensions—people who smote them in the face.[7] "Of course all this is to my discredit, it shows how weak I was in not adopting a similar line of conduct. Yet, speaking in this foolish way, I possess every qualification which inspires them with this audacity. I, like them, am a Hebrew, an Israelite, of the seed of Abraham;[8] I am not only, as they claim to be, a minister of Christ, but (I am speaking in downright madness) something more." And then follows the most marvellous fragment ever written of any biography; a fragment beside which the most imperilled lives of the most suffering saints shrink into insignificance, and which shows us how fractional at the best is our knowledge of the details of St. Paul's life—"in toils more abundantly, in stripes above measure, in prisons more abundantly, in deaths oft; of the Jews five times received I forty stripes save one; thrice was I beaten with rods; once was I stoned; thrice I suffered shipwreck; a night and day have I spent in the deep;[9] in journeyings often; in perils of rivers, in perils of robbers, in perils

[1] xi. 5, τῶν ὑπερλίαν Ἀποστόλων, literally "the extra-super Apostles." There is undoubtedly a sense of indignation in the use, twice over, of this strange colloquialism; but it is aimed, not at the Twelve, with whom St. Paul's relations were always courteous and respectful, but at the extravagant and purely human claims (mere superiority, κατὰ σάρκα) asserted for them by these emissaries. He compares himself with them in knowledge (xi. 5), in self-denial about support (xi. 6—21), in privileges of birth (22), in labours and perils (23—33), in the fact that his weakness resulted from pre-eminent revelations (xii. 1—10), and in the supernatural signs of Apostleship (xii. 11, 12).

[2] xi. 6. If φανερώσαντες (ℵ, B, F, G) be the right reading, it means "manifesting it (*i.e.*, *knowledge*) to you in everything among all."

[3] xi. 10. *leg.* φραγήσεται.

[4] How long this vile calumny continued may be seen in the identification of him with Simon Magus in the Clementines.

[5] This incidentally alludes to a Hagadah respecting Job i. 6, or the angel who wrestled with Jacob (Eisenmenger, *Entd. Judenth.* i. 845).

[6] It is very probable that the Claudian famine had made many needy Jewish Christians from Jerusalem go the round of the Churches, *demanding* and receiving the *Chaluka*.

[7] Cf. 1 Kings xxii. 24; Matt. v. 39; Luke xxii. 64; Acts xxiii. 2. Even teachers could act thus. 1 Tim. iii. 3; Titus i. 7.

[8] We can hardly imagine that the Ebionite lie that St. Paul was a Gentile, who had got himself circumcised in order to marry the High Priest's daughter, had as yet been invented; yet the Tarsian birth and Roman franchise may have led to whispered insinuations.

[9] Ex. xv. 5 (LXX.). Theophylact makes it mean "in Bythos," a place near Lystra, after the stoning.

from my own race, in perils from Gentiles, in perils in the city, in perils in the wilderness, in perils in the sea, in perils among false brethren; in toil and weariness, in sleeplessness often, in hunger and thirst, in fastings often; besides the things additional to all these, the care which daily besets me,[1] my anxiety for all the Churches. Who is weak, and I share not his weakness? who is made to stumble, and I do not burn with indignation? If I *must* boast, I will boast of this, the weakness to which I alluded. The God and Father of our Lord Jesus Christ, who is blessed for evermore, knoweth that I am not lying. In Damascus the ethnarch of Aretas the king was guarding the city of the Damascenes, wishing to seize me; and through a window in a large basket, I was let down through the wall, and escaped his hands."[2]

Such had been his "preparation of feebleness," without which he could neither have been what he was, nor have done what he did. Such is one glimpse of a life never since equalled in self-devotion, as it was also "previously without precedent in the history of the world." Here he breaks off that part of the subject. Did he intend similarly to detail a series of other hair-breadth escapes? or glancing retrospectively at his perils, does he end with the earliest and most ignominious? Or was it never his intention to enter into such a narrative, and did he merely mention the instance of ignominious escape at Damascus, so revolting to the natural dignity of an Oriental and a Rabbi, as a climax of the disgraces he had borne? We cannot tell. At that point, either because he was interrupted, or because his mood changed, or because it occurred to him that he had already shown his ample superiority in the "weakness" of voluntary humiliation to even the most "super-apostolic Apostles," he here stops short, and so deprives us of a tale inestimably precious, which the whole world might have read with breathless interest, and from which it might have learnt invaluable lessons. However that may be, he suddenly exclaims, "Of course it is not expedient for me to boast.[3] I will come to visions and revelations of the Lord." I know a man in Christ fourteen years ago (whether in the body or out of the body[4] I know not, God knows) snatched such an one as far as the third heaven.[5] And I know such a man (whether in the body or apart from the body I know not, God knows) that he was snatched into Paradise, and heard unspeakable utterances which it is not lawful for man to speak. Of such an one I will boast—but of myself I will not boast except in these weaknesses; for even should I wish to boast I shall not be a fool; for I will speak the truth. But I forbear lest any one should estimate about me above what he sees me to be, or hears at all from me. And to prevent my over-exaltation by the excess of the revelation, there was given me a stake in the flesh,[6] a messenger of Satan to buffet me, that I may not be over-exalted. About this I thrice besought the Lord that it (or he) may stand off from me. And He has said to me, 'My grace sufficeth thee; for my power is perfected in weakness.' Most gladly then will I rather boast in my weaknesses that the power of Christ may spread a tent over me.[7] *That* is why I boast in weaknesses, insults, necessities, persecutions, distresses, for Christ's sake. For when I am weak, then I am mighty. I have become a fool in boasting. You compelled me. For I ought to be 'commended' by *you*. For in no respect was I behind the 'out and out' Apostles,[8] even though I am nothing. Certainly the signs of an Apostle were

[1] xi. 28, *ἐπίστασις* (ℵ, B, D, E, F, G).

[2] xi. 1—33. On the escape from Damascus, see *supra*, p. 128.

[3] δὴ is the most forcible and natural reading, and here the MSS. variations δὲ (ℵ, D) and δεῖ (B, E, F, G) are probably due to itacism or misapprehension. The δὴ implies, "You will see from the humiliating escape to which I have just so solemnly testified that in my case boasting is not expedient." If the following "for" (D) be correct, it is due to counter-currents of feeling; but it is omitted in A, B, G.

[4] xii. 3. *leg.* χωρὶς, B, D, E. The physical condition was probably identical with that to which Hindu psychologists give the name of *Túrya*,—a fourth state, besides those of waking, dreaming, and slumber. The Hindu yogis call it *Vidéha sthiti*, and dwell rapturously on it in their mystic writings and songs.

[5] The "third heaven" occurs here only. For paradise, see Luke xxiii. 43.

[6] On this "stake in the flesh," *v. infra*, Excursus X. *κολαφίζῃ*, lit. "should slap in the face."

[7] xii. 9, *ἐπισκηνώσῃ ἐπ' ἐμὲ*.

[8] xii. 1—11. The colloquialism closely reproduces that of St. Paul.

wrought among you in all patience, by signs, and portents, and powers. The single fact that I did not benumb you with exactions is your sole point of inferiority to other Churches. Forgive me this *injustice!* See, a third time I am ready to come to you, and I will not benumb you, for I seek not yours but you. Children ought to treasure up for their parents, but so far from receiving from you, I will very gladly spend and be utterly spent for your souls, even though the more exceedingly I love you, the less I am loved. But stop! though I did not burden you, yet 'being a cunning person I caught you by guile.' Under the pretext of a collection I got money out of you by my confederates! I ask you, is that a fact? Did Titus or the brother whom I have sent with him over-reach you in any respect? Did not they behave exactly as I have done? You have long been fancying that all this is by way of self-defence to you.[1] Do not think it! *You* are no judges of mine. My appeal is being made in the presence of God in Christ; yet, beloved, it has all been for your edification. It was not said to defend myself, but to save us from a miserable meeting, lest we mutually find each other what we should not wish; lest I find you buzzing with quarrels, party spirit, outbreaks of rage, self-seekings, slanders, whisperings, inflations, turbulences; and lest, on my return to you, my God humble me in my relation to you, and I shall mourn over many of those who have sinned before and not repented for the uncleanness, fornication, and wantonness which they practised. It is the third time that I am intending to visit you;[2] it will be like the confirming evidence of two or three witnesses. I have forewarned, and I now warn these persons once more that, if I come, I will not spare. Since you want a proof that Christ speaks in me, ye shall have it. He was crucified in weakness; we share His death and His weakness, but we shall also share His life and power. Prove *yourselves*, test *yourselves*. Is Christ in you, or are you spurious Christians, unable to abide the test? You will, I hope, be forced to recognise that *I* am not spurious; but my prayer is that *you* may do no evil, not that *my* genuineness may be manifested; that *you* may do what is noble, even if therewith *we* be regarded as spurious. Against the truth, against genuine faithfulness, I have no power, but only *for* it. Be true to the Gospel, and I shall be powerless; and you will be mighty, and I shall rejoice at the result. I ever pray for this, for your perfection. That is why I write while still absent, in order that when present I may have no need to exercise against you with abrupt severity[3] the power which the Lord gave me, and gave me for building up, not for rasing to the ground."[4]

He would not end with words in which such uncompromising sternness mingled with his immense and self-sacrificing forbearance. He adds, therefore, in his own hand—"Finally, brethren, farewell; be perfect, be comforted, be united, be at peace; then shall the God of love and peace be with you. Salute one another with a holy kiss. All the saints salute you." And then follows the fullest of his Apostolic benedictions, "thence adopted by the Church in all ages as the final blessing of her services"—"The grace of our Lord Jesus Christ, and the love of God, and the fellowship of the Holy Ghost be with you all."[5]

[1] πάλαι (ℵ, A, B, F, G, Vulg.).

[2] xii. 14. He has been at Corinth once; is now going a second time (πάλιν); and had once intended to go. This is like a thing attested by two or three witnesses, and will certainly be fulfilled. I agree with Baur in saying, "Let us give up the fiction of a *journey* for which we can find no reasonable grounds" (*Paul.* ii. 320).

[3] ἀποτόμως only in Titus i. 13, not in LXX. The metaphor is either "by way of amputation" or "precipitately," as in Wisd. v. 23; ἀποτομία (Rom. xi. 22).

[4] xii. 13—xiii. 10.

[5] xiii. 11—13. As these are the last extant words of St. Paul to the Corinthians, it is interesting to see what was the condition of the Church when St. Clement of Rome wrote to them thirty-five years later. We find that they were still somewhat turbulent, somewhat disunited, somewhat sceptical, and St. Clement has to recall to them the examples of St. Peter and St. Paul. On the whole, however, we can see that the appeals and arguments of the Apostle in these two letters have not been in vain. About A.D 135 the Church was visited by Hegesippus (Euseb. *H.E.* iv. 22), who spoke favourably of their obedience and liberality. Their Bishop Dionysius was exercising a wide-spread influence. In speaking of the Resurrection, St. Clement alludes to the Phœnix (*ad* Rom. i. 24, 25), which in that age excited much interest (Tac. *Ann.* vi. 28; Plin. *H.N.* x. 2). Can any one fail to see a "grace of superintendency" in the absence of such illustrations from the page of the Apostles?

CHAPTER XXXIV.

THE SECOND VISIT TO CORINTH.

Διδακτικὸν, ἀνεξίκακον.—2 TIM. ii. 24.

ST. LUKE passes over with the extremest brevity the second sojourn of St. Paul in Macedonia. The reason for his silence may have been that the period was not marked by any special events sufficiently prominent to find room in his pages. It was no part of his plan to dwell on the sources of inward sorrow which weighed so heavily upon the mind of St. Paul, or to detail the afflictions which formed the very groundwork of his ordinary life. It was the experience of St. Paul, more perhaps than that of any man who has ever lived—even if we select those who have made their lives a sacrifice to some great cause of God—that life was a tissue of minor trials, diversified by greater and heavier ones. But St. Luke—not to speak of the special purposes which seem to have guided his sketch—only gives us full accounts of the events which he personally witnessed,[1] or of those which he regarded of capital importance, and about which he could obtain information which he knew to be trustworthy. It is one of the many indications of the scantiness of his biography that he does not even once mention a partner and fellow-worker of St. Paul so dear to him, so able, so energetic, and so deeply trusted as the Greek Titus, of whose activity and enthusiasm the Apostle made so much use in furthering the Offertory, and in the yet more delicate task of dealing with the Christian Corinthians at this most unsatisfactory crisis of their troubled history.

St. Luke accordingly, passing over the distress of mind and the outward persecution which St. Paul tells us he had at this time encountered, says nothing about the many agitations of which we are able from the Epistles to supply the outline. All that he tells us is that Paul passed through these regions, and encouraged them with much exhortation. He does not even mention the interesting circumstance that having preached during his second journey at Philippi, Thessalonica, and Berœa, the capitals respectively of Macedonia Prima, Secunda, and Tertia, he now utilised the intentional postponement of his visit to Corinth by going through Macedonia Quarta as far as Illyricum. Whether he only went to the borders of Illyricum, or whether he entered it and reached as far as Dyrrachium, and even as Nicopolis, and whether by Illyricum is meant the Greek district or the Roman province[2] that went by that name, we cannot tell; but at any rate St. Paul mentions this country as marking the circumference of the outermost circle of those missionary journeys of which Jerusalem was the centre.

That the Offertory greatly occupied his time and thoughts is clear from

[1] So the Muratorian Canon: "acta autē omniū apostolorum sub uno libro scribta sunt lucas optime theofile comprindit quia sub praesentia ejus singula gerebantur."

[2] "Titus unto Dalmatia," 2 Tim. iv. 10.

his own repeated allusions and the prominence which he gives to this subject in the Epistles to the Corinthians. It must have been one of his trials to be perpetually pleading for pecuniary contributions, among little bodies of converts of whom the majority were not only plunged in poverty, but who had already made the most conspicuous sacrifices on behalf of their Christian faith. It was clear to him that this fact would be unscrupulously used as a handle against him. However careful and businesslike his arrangements might be—however strongly he might insist on having no personal share in the distribution, or even the treasurership of these funds—persons would not be wanting to whisper the base insinuation that Paul found his own account in them by means of accomplices, and that even the laborious diligence with which he worked day and night at his trade, and failed even thus to ward off the pains of want, was only the cloak for a deep-laid scheme of avarice and self-aggrandisement. It was still worse when these charges came from the emissaries of the very Church for the sake of whose poor he was facing this disagreeable work of begging.[1] But never was there any man in this world —however innocent, however saintly—who has escaped malice and slander; indeed, the virulence of this malice and the persistency of this slander are often proportionate to the courage wherewith he confronts the baseness of the world. St. Paul did not profess to be indifferent to these stings of hatred and calumny; he made no secret of the agony which they caused him. He was, on the contrary, acutely sensible of their gross injustice, and of the hindrance which they caused to the great work of his life; and the irony and passion with which, on fitting occasions, he rebuts them is a measure of the suffering which they caused. But, as a rule, he left them unnoticed, and forgave those by whom they were perpetrated:—

> "Assailed by slander and the tongue of strife
> His only answer was a blameless life;
> And he that forged and he that flung the dart,
> Had each a brother's interest in his heart."

For he was not the man to neglect a duty because it was disagreeable, or because his motives in undertaking it might be misinterpreted. And the motives by which he was actuated in this matter were peculiarly sacred. In the first place, the leading Apostles at Jerusalem had bound him by a special promise to take care of their poor, almost as a part of the hard-wrung compact by which their Church had consented to waive, in the case of Gentile converts, the full acceptance of legal obligations. In the second place, the need really existed, and was even urgent; and it was entirely in consonance with St. Paul's own feelings to give them practical proof of that brotherly love which he regarded as the loftiest of Christian virtues. Then, further, in his early days, his ignorant zeal had inflicted on the Church of Jerusalem a deadly injury, and he would fain show the sincerity and agony of his repentance by

[1] To this day the Chaluka and Kadima at Jerusalem are the source of endless heart-burnings and jealousies, and cause no particle of gratitude, but are accepted by the Jews as a testimonial to the high desert of living in the Holy City.

doing all he could, again and again, to repair it. Lastly, he had a hope—sometimes strong and sometimes weak—that so striking a proof of disinterested generosity on the part of the Gentile Churches which he had founded would surely touch the hearts of the Pharisaic section of the mother Church, and if it could not cement the differences between the Christians of Judæa and Heathendom, would at least prevent the needless widening of the rift which separated them. At moments of deeper discouragement, writing from Corinth to Rome,[1] while he recognises the ideal fitness of an effort on the part of Gentile Christians to show, by help in temporal matters, their sense of obligation for the spiritual blessings which had radiated to them from the Holy City, and while he looks on the contribution as a harvest gathering to prove to Jewish Christians the genuineness of the seed sown among the heathen, he yet has obvious misgivings about the spirit in which even this offering may be accepted, and most earnestly entreats the Romans not only to agonise with him in their prayers to God that he may be delivered from Jewish violence in Judæa, but also that the bounty of which he was the chief minister might be graciously received. It may be that by that time experiences of conflict with the Judaisers in Corinth may have somewhat damped the fervour of his hopes; for *before* his arrival there,[2] he gives expression to glowing anticipations that their charitable gifts would not only relieve undeserved distress, but would be a proof of sincere allegiance to the Gospel of Christ, and would call forth deep thankfulness to God.[3] Alas! these glowing anticipations were doomed—there is too much reason to fear—to utter disappointment.

Having finished his work in the whole of Macedonia, and finding no more opportunity for usefulness in those parts,[4] he at last set out on his way to Corinth. It was probably towards the close of the year 57, but whether Paul travelled by sea or land, and from what point he started, we do not know. After his journey into Macedonia Quarta, he perhaps returned to Thessalonica, which was a convenient place of rendezvous for the various brethren who now accompanied him. The number of his associates makes it most probable that he chose the less expensive, though, at that late season of the year, more dangerous mode of transit, and took ship from Thessalonica to Cenchreae. The care of the money, and his own determination to have nothing to do with it, rendered it necessary for the treasurers appointed by the scattered communities to accompany his movements. The society of these fellow-travellers must have been a source of deep happiness to the over-tried and over-wearied Apostle, and the sympathy of such devoted friends must have fallen like dew upon his soul. There was the young and quiet Timothy, the beloved companion of his life; there was Tychicus, who had been won in the school of Tyrannus, and remained faithful to him to the very last;[5] there was Gaius of Derbe, a living memorial of the good work done in his earliest missionary

[1] Rom. xv. 25—32. [2] 2 Cor. viii. 24; ix. 12—15.
[3] 2 Cor. ix. 14. [4] Rom. xv. 23, μηκέτι τόπον ἔχων ἐν τοῖς κλίμασι τούτοις.
[5] 2 Tim. iv. 12.

journey. Thessalonica had contributed no less than three to the little band—Jason, his fellow-countryman, if not his kinsman, whose house at St. Paul's first visit had been assaulted by a raging mob, which, failing to find his guest, had dragged him before the Politarchs; Aristarchus, who had shared with him the perils of Ephesus, as he subsequently shared his voyage and shipwreck; and Secundus, of whom no particulars are known. Besides these, Beroea had despatched Sopater, a Jewish convert, who is one of those who sends his greetings to the Roman Christians.[1] In Corinth itself he was again looking forward to a meeting with some of his dearest friends—with Titus, whose courage and good sense rendered him so invaluable; with Luke the beloved physician, who was in all probability the delegate of Philippi; with Trophimus, an Ephesian Greek, the fatal but innocent cause of St. Paul's arrest at Jerusalem, destined long afterwards to start with him on his voyage as a prisoner, but prevented from sharing his last sufferings by an illness with which he was seized at Miletus;[2] and with the many Corinthian Christians—Justus, Sosthenes, Erastus, Tertius, Quartus, Stephanas, Fortunatus, Achaicus, and lastly Gaius of Corinth, with whom St. Paul intended to stay, and whose open house and Christian hospitality were highly valued by the Church.

The gathering of so many Christian hearts could not fail to be a bright point in the cloudy calendar of the Apostle's life. What happy evenings they must have enjoyed, while the toil of his hands in no way impeded the outpouring of his soul! what gay and genial intercourse, such as is possible in its highest degree only to pure and holy souls! what interchange of thoughts and hopes on the deepest of all topics! what hours of mutual consolation amid deepening troubles; what delightful Agapæ; what blessed partaking of the Holy Sacrament; what outpourings of fervent prayer! For three months St. Paul stayed at Corinth, and during these three months he wrote, in all probability, the Epistle to the Galatians, and certainly the Epistle to the Romans—two of the most profound and memorable of all his writings.[3] And since it was but rarely that he was his own amanuensis—

[1] Rom. xvi. 21. The exact sense which St. Paul attributed to συγγενὴς is uncertain.

[2] 2 Tim. iv. 20.

[3] The subtle indications that the Epistle to the Galatians was written nearly at the same time as the Second Epistle to the Corinthians consist of casual reflections of the same expression and pre-occupation with the same order of thought. The tone, feeling, style, and mode of argument show the greatest similarity. Compare, for instance—

2 CORINTHIANS.	GALATIANS.	2 CORINTHIANS.	GALATIANS.
i. 1	i. 1.	xi. 2	iv. 17.
xi. 4	i. 6.	xi. 20	v. 15.
v. 11	i. 10.	xii. 20, 21	v. 20, 21.
xii. 11	ii. 6.	ii. 7	vi. 1.
v. 15	ii. 20.	xiii. 5	vi. 4.
viii. 6	iii. 3.	ix. 6	vi. 8.
v. 21	iii. 13.	v. 17	vi. 15.

These are but specimens of coincidence in thought and expression, which might be almost indefinitely multiplied. To dwell on the close resemblance between Galatians and Romans is needless. It was noticed a thousand years ago. The Epistle to the Galatians is the rough sketch, that to the Romans the finished picture. The former is an impassioned controversial personal statement of the relation of Gentile Christians mainly to one legal obligation—circumcision; the latter is a calm, systematic, general treatise

since it is his custom to associate one or more and sometimes the whole body of his fellow-travellers with himself in the superscriptions of his letters, as well as to send greetings from them—may we not regard it as certain that those letters were read aloud to the little knot of friends, and formed fruitful topics of long and earnest discussion? Did even St. Paul anticipate that those few rolls of papyrus would be regarded to the latest ages of the world as a priceless treasure?

But what was the state of things which the Apostle found when he stepped out of the house of Gaius into the house of Justus? It was St. Luke's object to show the fundamental unity which existed among Christians, and not to dwell upon the temporary differences which unhappily divided them. He does not, indeed, conceal the existence of discordant elements, but his wish seems to have been to indicate the essential harmony which these discords might disturb, but not destroy. He has not, therefore, told us a single detail of St. Paul's encounter with the false Apostles, the deceitful workers who had huckstered and adulterated the Word of God, or with that one insolent and overbearing emissary, who with his stately presence, trained utterance, and immense pretensions, backed with credentials from Jerusalem and possibly with the prestige of a direct knowledge of Christ, had denied St. Paul's Apostleship, and omitted no opportunity of blackening his character. Did this man face St. Paul? Did his followers abide by the defiance which they had expressed towards him? Was there a crisis in which it was decisively tested on which side the true power lay? Did he after all come with a rod, or in the spirit of meekness? was the proof of his Apostleship given by the exercise of discipline, and the utterance of excommunications which struck terror into flagrant apostates, or did the returning allegiance of the erring flock, and the increase of holiness among them, render it unnecessary to resort to stringent measures? To all these questions we can return no certain answer. We may imagine the hush of awful expectation with which the little community gathered in the room of Justus would receive the first entrance and the first utterances of one whose love they had so terribly tried, and against whose person they had levelled such unworthy sarcasms. Personal questions would, however, weigh least with him. They knew well that it was not for party opposition but for moral contumacy that his thunders would be reserved. Since many of them were heinous offenders, since many had not even repented after serious warnings, how must they have shuddered with dread, how must their guilty consciences have made cowards of them all, when at last, after more than three years, they stood face to face with one who could hand them too over to Satan with all the fearful consequences which that sentence entailed! Over all these scenes the veil of oblivion has fallen. The one pen that might have recorded them has written nothing, nor do we hear a single rumour from any other source.

on the relations of the Gospel to the Law. An instructive comparison of Gal. iii. 6—29 with Rom. iv., &c., will be found in Lightfoot's *Galatians*, pp. 44—46.

But that for the time the Apostle triumphed—that whether in consequence of an actual exertion of power, or of a genuine repentance on the part of his opponents, his authority was once more firmly established—we may infer from his hint that until the Corinthian difficulties were removed he could take no other task in hand, and that in the Epistles which he wrote during these three months of his residence at the Achaian capital he contemplates yet wider missions and freely yields himself to new activities.[1]

Yet, amid our ignorance of facts, we do possess the means of reading the inmost thoughts which were passing through the soul of St. Paul. The two Epistles which he despatched during those three months were in many respects the most important that he ever wrote, and it inspires us with the highest estimate of his intellectual power to know that, within a period so short and so much occupied with other duties and agitations, he yet found time to dictate the Letter to the Galatians, which marks an epoch in the history of the Church, and the Letter to the Romans, which may well be regarded as the most important of all contributions to the system of its theology.

CHAPTER XXXV.

IMPORTANCE OF THE EPISTLE TO THE GALATIANS.

"In Ex. xxxii. 16, for *charuth*, 'graven,' read *cheruth*, 'freedom,' for thou wilt find no freeman but him who is engaged in the Thorah."—R. MEIR (*Perek.* 2).

"He is a freeman whom THE TRUTH makes free,
And all are slaves beside."

. . . . παρακύψας εἰς νόμον τέλειον τὸν τῆς ἐλευθερίας . . . (JAMES i. 25).

WE have already seen that in his brief second visit to the Churches of Galatia, on his road to Ephesus, St. Paul seems to have missed the bright enthusiasm which welcomed his first preaching. His keen eye marked the germs of coming danger, and the warnings which he uttered weakened the warmth of his earlier relationship towards them. But he could hardly have expected the painful tidings that converts once so dear and so loving had relapsed from everything which was distinctive in his teaching into the shallowest ceremonialism of his Judaising opponents. Already, whoever sanctioned them, these men had spoilt his best work, and troubled his happy disciples at Antioch and at Corinth, and they had their eye also on Ephesus. Thus to intrude themselves into other men's labours—thus to let him bear the brunt of all dangers and labours while they tried to monopolise the result—to watch indifferently and unsympathetically while the sower bore forth his good

[1] Rom. i. 13; xv. 24, 32.

seed, weeping, and then securely to thrust their blunt and greedy sickles into the ripening grain—to dog the footsteps of the bold, self-sacrificing missionary with easy, well-to-do men-pleasers, who, with no personal risk, stole in his absence into the folds which he had constructed, in order to worry with privy paws his defenceless sheep—to trouble with their petty formalisms and artificial orthodoxies the crystal water of Christian simplicity and Christian happiness—to endanger thus the whole future of Christianity by trying to turn it from the freedom of a universal Gospel into the bondage of a Judaic law—to construct a hedge which, except at the cost of a cutting in the flesh, should exclude the noblest of the Gentiles while it admitted the vilest of the Jews—all this, to the clear vision of St. Paul, seemed bad enough. But thus to thrust themselves among the little communities of his Galatian converts—to take advantage of their warm affections and weak intellects—to play on the vacillating frivolity of purpose which made them such easy victims, especially to those who offered them an external cult far more easy than spiritual religion, and bearing a fascinating resemblance to their old ceremonial paganism—this to St. Paul seemed intolerably base.

Vexed at this Galatian fickleness, and stung with righteous indignation at those who had taken advantage of it, he seized his pen to express in the most unmistakable language his opinion of the falsity and worthlessness of the limits into which these Christian Pharisees wished to compress the principles of Christianity—the worn-out and burst condition of the old bottles in which they strove to store the rich, fresh, fermenting wine. It was no time to pause for nice inquiries into motives, or careful balancing of elements, or vague compromise, or polished deference to real or assumed authority. It was true that this class of men came from Jerusalem, and that they belonged to the very Church of Jerusalem for whose poorer members he was making such large exertions. It was true that, in one flagrant instance at any rate, they had, or professed to have, the authority of James. Could it be that James, in the bigotry of lifelong habit, had so wholly failed to add understanding and knowledge to his scrupulous holiness, that he was lending the sanction of his name to a work which St. Paul saw to be utterly ruinous to the wider hopes of Christianity? If so, it could not be helped. James was but a man—a holy man indeed, and a man inspired with the knowledge of great and ennobling truths—but no more faultless or infallible than Peter or than Paul himself. If Peter, more than once, had memorably wavered, James also might waver; and if so, James in this instance was indubitably in the wrong. But St. Paul, at least, never says so; nor does he use a word of disrespect to "the Lord's brother." The Church of Jerusalem had, on a previous occasion, *expressly repudiated* others who professed to speak in their name; nor is there any proof that they had ever sanctioned this sort of counter-mission of espionage, which was subversive of all progress, of all liberty, and even of all morals. For, whoever may have been these Judaic teachers, vanity, party spirit, sensuality, had followed in their wake. They must be tested by their fruits, and those fruits were bitter and poisonous.

Some of them, at least, were bad men, anxious to stand well with everybody, and to substitute an outward observance for a true religion. Greed, self-importance, externalism, were everything to them; the Cross was nothing. If they had not been bad men they would not have been so grossly inconsistent as to manipulate and evade the Law to which they professed allegiance. If they had not been bad men they would not have made the free use they did of the vilest of controversial weapons—surreptitious sneers and personal slanders. Yet by such base means as these they had persistently tried to undermine the influence of their great opponent. They systematically disparaged his authority. He was, they said, no Apostle whatever; he was certainly not one of the Twelve; he had never seen Jesus except in a vision, and therefore lacked one essential of the Apostolate; all that he knew of Christianity he had learnt at Jerusalem, and that he had wilfully perverted; his Gospel was not the real Gospel; such authority as he had was simply derived from the heads of the Church at Jerusalem, to whom his doctrines must be referred. Many of his present developments of teaching were all but blasphemous. They were a daring apostasy from the oral and even from the written Law; a revolt against the traditions of the fathers, and even against Moses himself. Was not his preaching a denial of all inspiration? Could they not marshal against him an array of innumerable texts? Was not well-nigh every line of the five books of Moses against him? Who was this Paul, this renegade from the Rabbis, who, for motives best known to himself, had become a nominal Christian from a savage persecutor? Who was he that he should set himself against the Great Lawgiver?[1] If he argued that the Law was abrogated, how could he prove it? Christ had never said so. On the contrary, He had said that not a fraction of a letter of the Law should pass till all was fulfilled. To that the Twelve could bear witness. They kept the Law. They were living at peace with their Jewish brethren who yet did not recognise Jesus as the Messiah. Must not Paul's opinions be antagonistic to theirs, if he was the only Christian who could not show his face at Jerusalem without exciting the danger of a tumult? Besides, he was really not to be trusted. He was always shifting about, now saying one thing and now another, with the obvious intention of pleasing men. What could be more inconsistent than his teaching and conduct with regard to circumcision? He had told the Galatians that they need not be circumcised, and yet he himself had once preached circumcision—aye, and more than preached it, he had practised it! Would he answer these two significant questions—Who circumcised Timothy? Who circumcised Titus?

St. Paul saw that it was time to speak out, and he did speak out. The matter at issue was one of vital importance. The very essence of the Gospel

[1] The elements of the above paragraph are drawn partly from the "Galatians," partly from the "Corinthians." For the Ebionite slanders against St. Paul, see Iren. *Adv. Haer.* i. 26; Euseb. *H. E.* iii. 27; Epiphan. *Haer.* xxx. 25; Ps. Clem. *Hom.* ii. 17—19. "Totius mundi odio me oneravi," says Luther, "qui olim eram tutissimus. Ministerium Ecclesiae omnibus periculis expositum est, Diaboli insultationibus, mundi ingratitudini, sectarum blasphemiis" (*Colloq.* i. 18).

—the very liberty which Christ had given—the very redemption for which He had died—was at stake. The fate of the battle hung apparently upon his single arm. He alone was the Apostle of the Gentiles. To him alone had it been granted to see the full bearings of this question. A new faith must not be choked at its birth by the past prejudices of its nominal adherents. Its grave-clothes must not thus be made out of its swaddling-bands. The hour had come when concession was impossible, and there must be no facing both ways in the character of his conciliatoriness. Accordingly he flung all reticence and all compromise to the winds. Hot with righteous anger, he wrote the Epistle to the Galatians. It was his gage of battle to the incompetence of traditional authority—his trumpet-note of defiance to all the Pharisees of Christianity, and it gave no uncertain sound.[1]

Happily, he could give distinctness to his argument by bringing it to bear on one definite point. In recovering the lost outwork of Galatia he would carry the war into the camp of Jerusalem. The new teachers asserted, as at Antioch, the necessity of circumcision for Gentile Christians. If Paul could storm that bastion of Judaising Christianity, he knew that the whole citadel must fall. Circumcision was the very badge of Jewish nationality—the very nucleus of Jewish ceremonialism; the earliest, the most peculiar, the most ineffaceable of Jewish rites. Adam, Noah, Jacob, Joseph, Moses, Balaam, had all been born circumcised.[2] So completely was it the seal of the Covenant, that it had been given not even to Moses, but to Abraham. Joseph had seen that it was duly performed in Egypt. Moses had insisted upon it at all risks in Midian. Joshua had renewed it in Canaan; and so sacred was it deemed to be that the stone knives with which it had been performed were buried in his grave at Timnath Serah. Was there a king or prophet who had not been circumcised? Had not Jesus Himself submitted to circumcision? Was not Elias supposed to be always present, though unseen, to witness its due performance? Was not the mechanical effacement of it regarded as the most despicable of Hellenising apostasies? It was true that in the temporary and local letter which the Apostles had sanctioned they had said that it was not *indispensable* for Gentile converts; but a thing might not be indispensable, and yet might be pre-eminently *desirable*. Let them judge for themselves. Did they not hear the Law read? Was not the Law inspired? If so, how could they arbitrarily set it aside?[3]

[1] "It was necessary that the particularisms of Judaism, which opposed to the heathen world so repellent a demeanour and such offensive claims, should be uprooted, and the baselessness of its prejudices and pretensions fully exposed to the world's eye. This was the service which the Apostle achieved for mankind by his magnificent dialectic" (Baur, *First Three Centuries*, i. 73).

[2] *Abhôth* of Rabbi Nathan, ch. ii.

[3] "But for circumcision, heaven and earth could not exist; for it is said, 'Save for (the sign of) my covenant, I should not have made day and night the ordinances of heaven and earth'" (*Nedarim*, f. 32, col. 1, referring to Jerem. xxxiii. 25). The same remark is made about the whole Law. Rabbi (Juda Hakkadosh) says how great is circumcision, since it is equivalent to all the commandments of the Law, for it is said, "Behold the *blood* of the covenant which the Lord hath made with you, concerning all (Heb., *above* all) these words" (Ex. xxiv. 8).—*Nedarim*, f. 32, 1. Angels so detest an

It was ever thus that Judaism worked, beginning with the Psalms and pure Monotheism, and then proceeding to the knife of circumcision, and the yoke of the Levitic Law, in which they entangled and crushed their slaves.[1] It was ever thus that they compassed sea and land to make one proselyte, and when they had got him, made him ten times more the child of Gehenna than themselves. There was nothing at which the Jew gloried so much as thus leaving his mark on the very body of the despised and hated heathen—hardly less despised and hated, almost even more so, if he had hoped to equal them and their privileges by consenting to become a Jew. It was thus that they had got into their net the royal family of Adiabene. Helena, the amiable queen who fed the paupers of Jerusalem with dried figs and grapes in the famine of Claudius, and who now lies interred with some of her children in the Tombs of the Kings, had taken upon her the vow of the Nazarite for seven years. Just before the completion of the vow at Jerusalem, she had—was it accidentally, or by some trickery?—touched a corpse, and therefore had to continue the vow for seven years more. Once more at the conclusion of this term she had again incurred some trivial pollution, and had again to renew it for yet seven years more. Ananias, a Jewish merchant, in pursuance of his avocations, had got access to the seraglio of King Abennerig, and there had made a proselyte of the queen, and, through her influence, of her two sons, Izates and Monobazus. But he had had the good sense and large-heartedness to tell them that the essence of the Law was love to God and love to man. He was probably a Hagadist, who valued chiefly the great broad truths of which the outward observances of Mosaism were but the temporary casket; and he had the insight to know that for the sake of an outward rite, which could not affect the heart, it was not worth while to disturb a people and imperil a dynasty. His advice must not be confused with the cynical and immoral indifference which made Henri IV. observe that "Paris was well worth a mass." It was, on the contrary, an enlightenment which would not confound the shadow with the substance.[2] It was the conviction that the inscription on the *Chêl* should be obliterated, and the *Chêl* itself broken down.[3] But on the steps of the enlightened Ananias came a narrow bigot, the Rabbi Eliezer of Galilee, and he employed to the facile weakness of the young princes the very argument which the Judaising teacher, whoever he was, employed to the Galatians: "My king, you are sinning against the Law, and therefore against God. It is not enough to read the Law; you must do the Law. Read for yourself what it says about circumcision, and you will see

uncircumcised person that, when God spoke to Abraham before circumcision, He spoke in Aramaic, which, it appears, the angels do not understand (*Yalkuth Chadash*, f. 117, 3).

[1] See Hausrath, p. 263.

[2] Josephus had the good sense to take the same line when "two great men" came to him from Trachonitis; but though for the time he succeeded in persuading the Jews not to force circumcision upon them, yet afterwards these fugitives were nearly massacred by a fanatical mob, and could only secure their lives by a hasty flight. See the very instructive passage in *Vit. Jos.* 23, 31.

[3] Eph. ii. 14.

how wrong you are."[1] Prince Izates was so much struck with this "uncompromising orthodoxy" that he secretly withdrew into another chamber, and there had the rite performed by his physician. Not long after he and his brother were reading the Pentateuch, and came to the passage about circumcision in Ex. xii. 48. Monobazus looked up at his brother, and said, "I am sorry for you, my brother," and Izates made the same remark to him. This led to a conversation, and the brothers confessed, first to each other, and then to Queen Helena, that they had both been secretly circumcised. The queen was naturally alarmed and anxious, and dangerous consequences ensued. But these were nothing to the Jewish fanatic. They would only be a fresh source of publicity, and therefore of glorifying in the flesh of his proselyte. Again, we read in the Talmud that Rabbi[2] was a great friend of "the Emperor Antoninus." On one occasion the Emperor asked him, "Wilt thou give me a piece of Leviathan in the world to come?"—since the flesh of Leviathan and of the bird Barjuchneh are to be the banquet of the blessed hereafter. "Yes," answered Rabbi. "But why dost thou not allow me to partake of the Paschal Lamb?" "How can I," answered Rabbi, "when it is written that 'no uncircumcised person shall eat thereof'?" Upon hearing this Antoninus submitted to the rite of circumcision, and embraced Judaism. The imagination of Rabbis and Pharisees was flattered by the thought that even emperors were not too great to accept their *Halacheth*. What would be their feelings towards one who offered the utmost blessings of the Chosen People without a single Judaic observance to the meanest slave?

Self-interest was an additional and a powerful inducement with these retrogressive intruders. Although Christian, they, like the Twelve, like even Paul himself, were still Jews. At Jerusalem they continued regularly to attend the services at the Temple and the gatherings of their synagogue. To be excommunicated from the synagogue in little Jewish communities like those that were congregated in Ancyra and Pessinus was a very serious matter indeed. It was infinitely more pleasant for them to be on good terms with the Jews, by making proselytes of righteousness out of St. Paul's converts. Thus circumcision was only the thin end of the wedge.[3] It obviated the painful liability to persecution. It would naturally lead to the adoption of all the observances, which the converts would constantly hear read to them in the Jewish service. But, if not, it did not much matter. It was not really necessary for them to keep the whole Law. A sort of decent external conformity was enough. So long as they made "a fair show

[1] Jos. *Antt.* xx. 2, § 4. This interesting royal family had a house in Jerusalem (Jos. *B. J.* v. 6, § 1; vi. 6, § 3).

[2] Rabbi Juda Hakkadosh is thus called κατ ἐξοχήν. The anecdote is from *Jer. Megillah*, cap. i. For another wild story about their intercourse, see *Abhôda Zara*, f. 10, 2. The Talmud being the most utterly unhistorical and unchronological of books, it is difficult to say which Emperor is the one alluded to in this and a multitude of similar fables about his supposed intercourse with Rabbi. It cannot be Antoninus Pius, who never left Rome; nor M. Aurelius, who was unfavourable both to Jews and Christians. Possibly the worthless Caracalla may be alluded to, since he once visited Palestine. Heliogabalus appears to be alluded to in some passages of the Talmud as "the younger Antoninus," and he, too, is said to have accepted circumcision.

[3] Gal. v. 3, 6, 12—14.

in the flesh," they might in reality do pretty much as they liked. It was against all this hypocrisy, this retrogression, this cowardice, this mummery of the outward, this reliance on the mechanical, that Paul used words which were half battles. There should be no further doubt as to what he really meant and taught. He would leap ashore among his enemies, and burn his ships behind him. He would draw his sword against this false gospel, and fling away the scabbard. What Luther did when he nailed his Theses to the door of the Cathedral of Wittenberg, that St. Paul did when he wrote the Epistle to the Galatians. It was the manifesto of emancipation. It marked an epoch in history. It was for the early days of Christianity what would have been for Protestantism the Confession of Augsburg and the Protest of Spires combined; but it was these "expressed in dithyrambs, and written in jets of flame;" and it was these largely intermingled with an intense personality and impassioned polemics. It was a De Corona, a Westminster Confession, and an Apologia in one. If we wish to find its nearest parallel in vehemence, effectiveness, and depth of conviction, we must look forward for sixteen centuries, and read Luther's famous treatise, *De Captivitate Babylonica*, in which he realised his saying "that there ought to be set aside for this Popish battle, a tongue of which every word is a thunderbolt."[1] To the Churches of Galatia he never came again; but the words scrawled on those few sheets of papyrus, whether they failed or not of their immediate effect, were to wake echoes which should "roll from soul to soul, and live for ever and for ever."

CHAPTER XXXVI.

THE EPISTLE TO THE GALATIANS.

"The Epistle to the Galatians is my Epistle; I have betrothed myself to it: it is my wife."—LUTHER.

"Principalis adversus Judaismum Epistola."—TERT. *adv. Marc.* v. 2.

"Discrimen Legis et Evangelii est depictum in hoc dicto 'posteriora me a videbitis, faciem meam non videbitis.'

Lex	Dorsum Ira Peccatum Infirmitas	Evangelium	Facies Gratia Donum Perfectio."

LUTHER, *Colloq.* i., p. 20, ed. 1571.

"Judaism was the narrowest (*i.e.* the most special) of religions, Christianity the most human and comprehensive. In a few years the latter was evolved out of the former, taking all its intensity and durability without resort to any of its limitations. . . . In St. Paul's Epistles we see the general direction in which thought and events must have advanced: otherwise the change would seem as violent and inconceivable as a convulsion which should mingle the Jordan and the Tiber."—MARTINEAU, *Studies of Christianity*, p. 420.

IN the very first line of the Apostle's greeting a part of his object—the vin-

[1] Luther, *Tisch-Reden*, 249. But though Luther constantly defends his polemical ferocity by the example of St. Paul, St. Paul never (not even in Gal. v. 12) shows the violence and coarseness which deface the style of Luther.

dication of his Apostolic authority—becomes manifest.[1] In the Epistles to the Thessalonians he had adopted no title of authority; but since those Epistles had been written, the Judaists had developed a tendency to limit the term Apostle almost exclusively to the Twelve, and overshadow all others with their immense authority. The word had two technical senses. In the lower sense it merely meant a messenger or worker in the cause of the Gospel, and as an equivalent to the common Jewish title of *Sheliach*, was freely bestowed on comparatively unknown Christians, like Andronicus and Junias.[2] Now Paul claimed the title in the highest sense, not from vanity or self-assertion, but because it was necessary for the good of his converts. He had the primary qualification of an Apostle in that he had seen Christ, though for reasons which he explained in the last Epistle he declined to press it. He had the yet further qualification that his Apostolate and that of Barnabas had been publicly recognised by the Church of Jerusalem. But this claim also he wished to waive as unreal and even misleading; for his Apostolate was derived from no merely human authority. Writing to the Corinthians, some of whom had impugned his rights, he had intentionally designated himself as "a called Apostle of Jesus Christ by the will of God." Writing to these weak and apostatising Galatians it was necessary to be still more explicit, and consequently he addresses them with his fullest greeting, in which he speaks both of his own authority and of the work of Christ. By impugning the first they were setting temporary relations above spiritual insight; by errors respecting the latter they were nullifying the doctrine of the Cross.

"Paul, an Apostle, not from men, nor by the instrumentality of any man, but by Jesus Christ and God our Father, who raised Him from the dead, and all the brethren with me,[3] to the Churches of Galatia. Grace to you and Peace from God the Father and our Lord Jesus Christ, who gave Himself for our sins that He may

[1] The general outline of the Epistle is as follows:—It falls into three divisions—1. Personal (an element which recurs throughout); 2. Dogmatic; 3. Practical. In the first part (i., ii.) he vindicates his personal independence (α) *negatively*, by showing that he was an Apostle before any intercourse with the Twelve (i. 17, 18); and (β) *positively*, since he had secured from the Apostles the triumphant recognition of his own special principles on three occasions, viz., (i.) in an association on perfectly equal terms with Peter (18, 19); (ii.) when they were compelled by facts to recognise his equal mission (ii. 9, 10); and (iii.) when he convinced Peter at Antioch that he was thoroughly in the wrong (ii. 11—21). 2. Passing naturally to the dogmatic defence of justification by faith, he proves it (α) by the Christian consciousness (iii. 1—5), and (β) from the Old Testament (iii. 6—18). This leads him to the question as to the true position of the Law, which he shows to be entirely secondary, (α) *objectively*, by the very nature of Christianity (iii. 19—29); and (β) *subjectively*, by the free spiritual life of Christians (iv. 1—11). After affectionate warnings to them about those who had led them away (iv. 11—30), he passes to—3. The practical exhortation to Christian freedom (v. 1—12), and warnings, both general (13—18) and special (v. 16—vi. 10), against its misuse. Then follows the closing summary and blessing (vi. 11—18).

[2] Rom. xvi. 7; cf. Phil. ii. 25; 2 Cor. viii. 23. Similarly the title Imperator was used by Cicero and other Romans down to Junius Blæsus, long after its special sense had been isolated to connote the absolute head of the state.

[3] At this time he was accompanied by a larger number of brethren than at any other. This is one of the minute circumstances which support the all-but-certain inference that the Epistle was written at this particular period, during St. Paul's three months' stay at Corinth, towards the close of A.D. 57.

deliver us from this present evil state of the world, according to the will of our God and Father, to whom is His due glory[1] for ever and ever. Amen."[2]

This greeting is remarkable, not only for the emphatic assertion of his independent Apostleship, and for the skill with which he combines with this subject of his Epistle the great theologic truth of our free deliverance[3] by the death of Christ, but also for the stern brevity of the terms with which he greets those to whom he is writing. A sense of wrong breathes through the fulness of his personal designation, and the scantiness of the address to his converts. He had addressed the Thessalonians as "the Church of the Thessalonians in God our Father and the Lord Jesus Christ." He had written "to the Church of God which is in Corinth, to the sanctified in Christ Jesus, called to be saints." About this very time he wrote to the Romans as "beloved of God, called to be saints." To the Philippians, Ephesians, Colossians, he adds the words "saints in Christ Jesus," and "saints and faithful brethren;" but to these Galatians alone, in his impetuous desire to deal at once with their errors, he uses only the brief, plain address, "To the Churches of Galatia."

And then without one word of that thanksgiving for their holiness, or their gifts, or the grace of God bestowed on them, which is found in every one of his other general Epistles, he bursts at once into the subject of which his mind is so indignantly full.

"I am amazed that you are so quickly shifting from him who called you in the grace of Christ into a *different* Gospel, which is not merely *another*,[4] only there are some who are troubling you, and wanting to reverse the Gospel of Christ. But even though we, or an angel from heaven, should preach contrary to what we preached to you, *let him be accursed*.[5] As we have said before, so now again I say deliberately, If any one is preaching to you anything contrary to what ye received, LET HIM BE ACCURSED.[6] Well, am I NOW trying to be plausible to men, or to conciliate God Himself? Had I still been trying to be a man-pleaser, I should not have been what I am—a slave of Christ."[7]

Such was the startling abruptness, such the passionate plainness with which he showed them that the time for conciliation was past. Their Jewish teachers said that Paul was shifty and complaisant, and that he did not preach the real Gospel. He tells them that it is they who are perverters of the Gospel, and that if they, or any one of them, or any one else, even an angel, preaches

[1] ἡ δόξα, sub. ἐστιν. Matt. vi. 13; 1 Pet. iv. 11. [2] i. 1—5.

[3] i. 4, ἐξέληται. "*Deliver* strikes the key-note of the Epistle" (Lightfoot). ἐνεστῶτος, "present," Rom. viii. 38.

[4] If μετατίθεσθε is really a mental pun (as Jerome thought) on *Galatae* and גלל, we might almost render it *galatising*. For ἕτερον, "different," and ἄλλο, "another," see 2 Cor. xi. 4. Hence ἕτερος came to mean "bad;" θάτερον is the opposite to "good."

[5] i. 8, ἀνάθεμα; the meaning "excommunicated" is later, and would not suit ἄγγελος.

[6] There is a sort of *syllepsis* in this, and the τὸν Θεὸν is more emphatic than the ἀνθρώπους. Probably Paul had been accused of emancipating the Gentiles from Judaism out of mere complaisance.

[7] i. 1—10, ἔτι, "after all I have endured;" v. 11; vi. 17; 1 Cor. xv. 30–32.

contrary to what he has preached, let the ban—the cherem—fall on him. He has said this before, and to show them that it is not a mere angry phrase, he repeats it more emphatically now, and appeals to it as a triumphant proof that whatever they could charge him with having done and said before, now, at any rate, his language should be unmistakably plain.

"Now I declare to you, brethren, as to the Gospel preached by me that it is not a mere human Gospel. For neither did I myself receive it from man, nor was I taught it, but by revelation from Jesus Christ. For you heard my manner of life formerly in Judaism, that I extravagantly[1] persecuted the Church of God, and ravaged it, and was making advance in Judaism above many my equals in age in my own race, being to an unusual degree a zealot for the traditions of my fathers. But when He who set me apart even from my mother's womb and called me by His grace thought good to reveal His Son in me that I should preach Him among the Gentiles, immediately I did not confer with mere human teachers, nor did I go away to Jerusalem to those who were Apostles before me, but I went away into Arabia, and again returned to Damascus.

"Next, after three years, I went up to Jerusalem to visit Kephas, and I stayed at his house fifteen days: but not a single other Apostle did I see, except James, the Lord's brother.[2] Now in what I am writing to you, see, before God, I am not lying.[3]

"Next I came into the regions of Syria and Cilicia; and was quite unknown by person to the Churches of Judæa which were in Christ, only they were constantly being told that our former persecutor is now a preacher of the faith which once he ravaged. And they glorified God in me.[4]

"Next, after fourteen years, I again went up to Jerusalem with Barnabas, taking with me Titus also.[5] And I went up by revelation, and referred to them the Gospel which I preach among the Gentiles,[6] privately however to those of repute, lest perchance I might be running, or even ran, to no purpose.[7] But not even Titus, who was with me, being a Greek, was *compelled* to be circumcised—but because of the false brethren secretly introduced, who slank in to spy out our liberty which we have in Christ Jesus that they might utterly enslave us—[to whom not even (?)] for an hour we yielded *by way of the subjection they wanted*, in order that the truth of the Gospel may permanently remain with you.[8] From, those, however, who are reputed to be something—whatever they once were, makes no matter to me, God cares for no man's person[9]—for to me those in repute contributed nothing, but, on the contrary, seeing that I have been entrusted with the Gospel of the uncircumcision, as Peter of the circumcision—for He who worked for Peter for the Apostolate of the circumcision, worked also for me towards the Gentiles—and recognising the grace granted

[1] i. 13, *καθ' ὑπερβολήν*, *à outrance*.

[2] Who in one sense was, and in another was not, an Apostle, not being one of the Twelve.

[3] *V. supra*, pp. 131 — 134. As I have already examined many of the details of this Epistle for biographical purposes, I content myself with referring to the passages. The strong appeal in i. 20 shows that Paul's truthfulness had been questioned. (Cf. 1 Thess. v. 27.)

[4] i. 11—24.

[5] *V. supra*, pp. 232 — 237. Paul's purpose here is not the tedious pedantry of chronological exactitude.

[6] ii. 2, ἀνεθέμην, not to submit to their decision, but with the strong belief that he could win their concurrence. (Cf. Acts xxv. 14.)

[7] Phil. ii. 16. I have already explained the probable meaning of this—"that I might feel *quite* sure of the truth and *practicability* of my views." Even Luther admits, "Sathan saepe mihi dixit, quid si falsum esset dogma tuum?" (*Colloq*. ii. 12.)

[8] *V. supra*, p. 234.

[9] ii. 6, Θεὸς ἀνθρώπου. The position is emphatic. This seems to glance at the absurdity of founding *spiritual* authority on mere *family* or *external* claims. (See Martineau, *Studies in Christianity*, p. 428.)

to me, James, and Kephas, and John, who are in repute as pillars, gave right hands of fellowship to me and Barnabas, that we to the Gentiles, and they to the circumcision—only that we should bear in mind the poor, which very thing I was of my own accord even eager to do.[1]

"But when Kephas came to Antioch I withstood him to the face, because he was a condemned man.[2] For before the arrival of certain from James[3] he used to eat with the Gentiles; but on their arrival[4] he began to withdraw and separate himself, being afraid of these Jewish converts. And the rest of the Jews joined in this hypocrisy, so that even Barnabas was swept away by their hypocrisy.[5] But when I perceived that they were not walking in the straight truth of the Gospel, I said to Kephas, before them all, If you, a born Jew, are living Gentile-wise and not Judaically, how can you try to compel the Gentiles to Judaise? We, Jews by birth and not 'sinners' of the Gentiles,[6] but well aware that no man is justified as a result of the works of the Law, but only by means of faith in Jesus Christ—even *we* believed on Jesus Christ that we may be justified as a result of faith in Christ, and not of the works of Law; for from works of Law 'no flesh shall be justified.'[7] But (you will object) if, while seeking to be justified in Christ, we turn out to be even ourselves 'sinners' (men no better than the Gentiles), is then Christ a minister of sin?[8] Away with the thought! For if I rebuild the very things I destroyed, *then* I prove myself to be not only a 'sinner' but a transgressor." The very rebuilding (he means) would prove that the previous destruction was guilty; "but it was not so," he continues to argue, "for it was by Law that I died to Law;" in other words, it was the Law itself which led me to see its own nullity, and thereby caused my death to it that I might live to God.[9] "I have been crucified with Christ;" my old sins are nailed to His cross, no less than my old Jewish

[1] ii. 1—10. It was, as Tertullian says, a *distributio officii*, not a *separatio evangelii* (*De Praescr. Haer.* 28). He had already shown his care for the poor (Acts xi. 30).

[2] ii. 11, κατεγν. Manifestly and flagrantly in the wrong. Cf. Rom. xiv. 23. To make κατὰ πρόσωπον mean "by way of mask," and treat the scene as one got up (κατὰ σχῆμα) between the Apostles—as Origen and Chrysostom do—or to assume that Kephas does not mean Peter—as Clemens of Alexandria does—is a deplorable specimen of the power of dogmatic prejudice to blind men to obvious fact. St. Peter's weakness bore other bitter fruit. It was one ultimate cause of Ebionite attacks on St. Paul, and of Gnostic attacks on Judaism, and of Porphyry's slanders of the Apostles, and of Jerome's quarrel with Augustine. (See Lightfoot, pp. 123—126.)

[3] Cf. Acts xv. 24.

[4] ii. 12, ἦλθεν (א, B, D, F, G), if St. Paul really wrote it, could only mean "when *James* came;" and so Origen understood it (*c. Cels.* ii. 1).

[5] We can scarcely even imagine the deadly offence caused by this boldness, an offence felt a century afterwards (Iren. *Haer.* i. 26; Euseb. *H. E.* iii. 27; Epiphan. *Haer.* xxx. 16; Baur, *Ch. Hist.* 89, 98). Even when the Pseudo-Clementine Homilies were written the Jewish Christians had not forgiven the word κατεγνωσμένος. Εἰ κατεγνωσμένον με λέγεις Θεοῦ ἀποκαλύψαντός μοι τὸν Χριστὸν κατηγορεῖς (Clem. Hom. xvii. 19). And yet, however bitter against unscrupulous Judaism, St. Paul is always courteous and respectful when he speaks of the Twelve. The *Praedicatio Petri* (in Cyprian, *De Rebapt.*) says that Peter and Paul remained unreconciled till death.

[6] Cf. Rom. ix. 30, ἔθνη τὰ μὴ διώκοντα δικαιοσύνην; Luke vi. 32, 33; Matt. v. 47; ix. 10, 11.

[7] Ps. cxliii. 2. St. Paul's *addition* ἔργοις νόμου is an obvious inference. The accentuation of meaning on *ritual* or *moral* observance must depend on the context. Here the latter is *mainly* in question (Neander, *Planting*, i. 211).

[8] It is impossible to say how much of this argument was actually addressed to Peter. μὴ γένοιτο, חָלִילָה; cf. Gen. xliv. 7, 17.

[9] The Latin fathers and Luther understand it "by the law (of Christ) I am dead to the law (of Moses)." The best commentary is Rom. vii. 1—11. Expressions like this led to the charge of antinomianism, which St. Paul sets aside in 1 Cor. ix. 21. Celsus taunts the Apostles with the use of such language while yet they could denounce each other (*ap.* Orig. v. 64). But they did not profess to have attained their own *ideal* (Phil. iii. 13).

obligations; yet this death is life—not mine, however, but the life of Christ in me; and so far as I now live in the flesh, I live in faith on the Son of God who loved me, and gave Himself up for me. I am not, therefore, setting at nought the grace of God by proclaiming my freedom from the Levitical Law; *you* are doing that, not I; "for had righteousness been at all possible by Law, then it seems Christ's death was superfluous."[1]

He has now sufficiently vindicated his independent Apostleship, and since this nullification of the death of Christ was the practical issue of the Galatian retrogression into Jewish ritualism, he passes naturally to the doctrinal truth on which he had also touched in his greeting, and he does so with a second burst of surprise and indignation:—

"Dull Galatians![2] who bewitched you with his evil eye,—you before whose eyes Jesus Christ crucified was conspicuously painted?[3] This is the only thing I want to learn of you;—received ye the Spirit as a result of works of Law, or of faithful hearing? Are ye so utterly dull? After beginning the sacred rite spiritually, will ye complete it carnally? Did ye go through so many experiences in vain?[4] if it be indeed in vain. He then that abundantly supplieth to you the Spirit, and worketh powers in you, does he do so as a result of works of Law or of faithful hearing? Of faith surely—just as 'Abraham believed God and it was accounted to him for righteousness.' Recognise then that they who start from faith, *they* are sons of Abraham. And the Scripture foreseeing[5] that God justifies the Gentiles as a result of faith,[6] preached to Abraham as an anticipation of the Gospel, 'In thee shall all the Gentiles be blessed.' So they who start from faith are blessed with the faithful Abraham. For as many as start from works of law are under a curse. For it stands written, 'Cursed is every one who does not abide by all the things written in the book of the Law to do them.' But that by Law no man is justified with God is clear because 'The just shall live by faith.' But the Law is not of faith, but (of works, for its formula is) he that *doth* these things shall live by them. Christ ransomed us from the curse of the Law,—becoming on our behalf a curse, since it is written, 'Cursed is every one who hangeth on a tree'[7]—that the blessing of Abraham may by Christ Jesus accrue to the Gentiles, that we may receive the promise of the Spirit by means of faith."[8]

Then came some of the famous arguments by which he establishes these weighty doctrines—arguments incomparably adapted to convince those to

[1] ii. 11—21. For an examination of this paragraph, *v. supra*, pp. 250, 251.

[2] iii. 1, ἀνόητοι, as in Luke xxiv. 25. So far from being dull in things not spiritual, Themistius calls them ὀξεῖς καὶ ἀγχίνοι καὶ εὐμαθέστεροι τῶν ἄγαν Ἑλλήνων (*Plat.* 23).

[3] If προγράφω has here the same sense as in Rom. xv. 4, Eph. iii. 3, Jude 4, it must mean "prophesied of;" but this gives a far weaker turn to the clause.

[4] iii. 4, ἐπάθετε seems here to have its more general sense, as in Mark v. 26; if the common sense "suffered" be retained, it must allude to troubles caused by Judaisers.

[5] A Hebraic personification. "What saw the Scripture?" is a Rabbinic formula Schöttg. *ad loc.*). The passages on which the argument is founded are Gen. xv. 6; (xii. 3; Deut. xxvii. 26; xxi. 23; Lev. xviii. 5; Hab. ii. 4. The reasoning will be better understood from 2 Cor. v. 15—21; Rom. vi. 3—23.

[6] ἐκ πίστεως, "*from* faith" as a cause; or διὰ τῆς πίστεως, *per fidem*, "by means of faith as an instrument;" never διὰ πίστιν, *propter fidem*, "on account of faith" as a merit.

[7] The original reference is to the exposure of the body on a stake after death (Deut. xxi. 23; Josh. x. 26). St. Paul omits the words "of God" after "cursed," which would have required long explanation, for the notion that it meant "a curse, or insult, against God" is a later gloss. Hence the Talmud speaks of Christ as "the hung" (תָּלוּי.)

[8] iii. 1—14.

whom he wrote, because they were deduced from their own principles, and grounded on their own methods, however startling was the originality of the conclusions to which they lead. Merely to translate them without brief explanatory comment would add very little to the reader's advantage. I will endeavour, therefore, to throw them into a form which shall supply what is necessary to render them intelligible.

"Brethren," he says, "I will give you an every-day illustration.[1] No one annuls, or vitiates by additions, even a mere human covenant when it has been once ratified. Now the Promises were uttered to Abraham 'and to his seed.' The word employed is neither plural in form nor in significance. A plural word might have been used had *many* been referred to; the reason for the use of a collective term is pre-eminently indicated, and that one person is Christ.[2] What I mean is this: God made and ratified a covenant with Abraham; and the Law which came four hundred and thirty years afterwards[3] cannot possibly nullify the covenant or abrogate the promise. Now God has bestowed the gift on Abraham by promise, and therefore clearly it was not bestowed as a result of obedience to a law.[4]

"Why, then, was the Law? you ask; of what use was it?" Very briefly St. Paul gives them the answer, which in the Epistle to the Romans he elaborates with so much more fulness.

Practically, the answer may be summed up by saying that the Law was damnatory, temporary, mediate, educational.[5] It was added to create in the soul the sense of sin, and so lead to the Saviour, who in due time should come to render it no more necessary;[6] and it was given by the ministry of angels[7] and a human mediator. It was not, therefore, a promise, but a contract; and a promise direct from God is far superior to a contract made by the agency of a human mediator between God and man.[8] The Law, therefore, was but "supplementary, parenthetical, provisional,

[1] iii. 15. κατὰ ἄνθρωπον, *i.e.*, ἐξ ἀνθρωπίνων παραδειγμάτων (Chrys.).

[2] *V. supra*, pp. 30, 31.

[3] In Gen. xv. 13, Acts vii. 6, &c., the period in Egypt seems to count from Abraham's visit.

[4] iii. 15—18.

[5] iii. 15, ἐπιδιατάσσεται; 19, προσετέθη; Rom. v. 20, παρεισῆλθεν. The Law was (1) τῶν παραβάσεων χάριν, restricted and conditioned; (2) ἄχρις οὗ, κ.τ.λ., temporary and provisional; (3) διαταγεὶς, κ.τ.λ., mediately (but not immediately) given by God; (4) ἐν χειρὶ μεσ., mediately (not immediately) received from God (Bp. Ellicott, *ad loc.*). The Law is a harsh, imperious incident in a necessary divine training.

[6] iii. 19, παραβάσεων χάριν means "to bring transgression to a head." See Rom. v. 20; 1 Cor. xv. 56. The fact is here stated in all its harshness, but in Rom. vii. 7, 13, the Apostle shows by a masterly psychological analysis in what way this was true—namely, because (i.) law actually tends to provoke disobedience, and (ii.) it gives the sting to the disobedience by making us fully conscious of its heinousness. The Law thus brought the disease of sin to a head, that it might then be cured. We might not be able to follow these pregnant allusions of the Epistle if we did not possess the Epistle to the Romans as a commentary upon it. The Galatians could only have understood it by the reminiscences of Paul's oral teaching.

[7] Jos. *Antt.* xv. 5, § 3; Acts vii. 53; Deut. xxxiii. 2. These angels at Sinai are often alluded to in the Talmud. R. Joshua Ben Levi rendered Psalm lxviii. 12, "The Angels (מלאכי) of hosts kept moving" the Children of Israel nearer to Sinai when they retired from it (*Shabbath*, f. 88, 2).

[8] iii. 19, 20. A "mediator" in Jewish language meant one who stands in the middle position between two parties.

"The voice of God
To mortal ear is dreadful. They beseech
That Moses might repeat to them His will,
And terror cease." (Milton, *P. L.* xii. 235.)

Moses receives the Law direct from God (ἐν χειρὶ), and hands it to man (Ex. xx. 19). He therefore was not one of the contracting parties; but God is one, *i.e.*, He is no mediator,

manuductory." How startling would such arguments be to those who had, from their earliest childhood, been taught to regard the Law as the one divine, inspired, perfect, and eternal thing on earth; the one thing which alone it was worth the labour of long lives to study, and the labour of long generations to interpret and to defend! And how splendid the originality which could thus burst the bonds of immemorial prejudice, and the courage which could thus face the wrath of outraged conviction! It was the enlightenment and inspiration of the Holy Spirit of God; yes, but the Spirit works by the human instruments that are fitted to receive His indwelling power; and, in the admirable saying of the Chinese philosopher, "The light of heaven cannot shine into an inverted bowl." To many a thoughtful and candid Jew it must have come like a flash of new insight into the history of his nation, and of mankind, that he had elevated the Law to too exclusive a position; that the promise to Abraham was an event of far deeper significance than the legislation of Sinai; that the Promise, not the Law, was the *primary* and *original* element of Judaism; and that therefore to fall back from Christianity of Judaism was to fall back from the spirit to the letter—an unnatural reversion of what God had ordained.

But he proceeds, "Is there any opposition between the Law and the Promise? Away with the thought! In God's œconomy of salvation both are united, and the Law is a *relative* purpose of God which is taken up into His *absolute* purpose as a means.[1] For had a Law been given such as could give life, righteousness would in reality have been a result of law; but the Scripture shut up all things under sin, that the promise which springs from faith in Jesus Christ may be given to all who believe. For before the faith came we were under watch and ward of Law, till the faith which was to be revealed. So the Law became our tutor unto Christ, the stern slave guiding us from boyish immaturity to perfect Christian manhood,[2] in order that we may be justified as a result of faith. But when the faith came we are no longer under a tutor. For by the faith ye are all sons of God in Jesus Christ. For as many of you as were baptised into Christ, put on Christ. There is no room for Jew or Greek, no room for slave or free, no room for male or female; for ye are all one man in Christ Jesus;[3] and if ye are of Christ then it seems ye are Abraham's seed, heirs according to promise.[4]

"Now, what I mean is, that so long as the heir is an infant he differs in no

but one of the parties to the covenant (διαθήκη). It is only under a *different* aspect that Christ is a mediator (1 Tim. ii. 5). The passage has no reference to the eternal unity of God, which is not at all in question, but to the fact that He stands by Himself as one of the contracting parties. The "Law," then, has the same subordinate position as the "Mediator" Moses. The Promise stands above it as a "covenant," in which God stands alone—"is one"—and in which no mediator is concerned. Such seems to be the clear and simple meaning of this endlessly-disputed passage. (See Baur, *Paul*, ii. 198.) Obviously, (1) the Promise had a wider and nobler scope than the Law; (2) the Law was provisional, the Promise permanent; (3) the Law was given directly by angels, the Promise directly by God; but, while he leaves these three points of contrast to be inferred, he adds the fourth and most important, that (4) the Promise was given, without any mediating human agency, from God to man. On the sources of the (perfectly needless) "three hundred explanations" of a passage by no means unintelligible, see Reuss, *Les Epîtres*, i. 109.

[1] iii. 19, 20. Holsten, *Inhalt des Briefs an die Galater*, p. 30.

[2] iii. 24, παιδαγωγὸς εἰς Χριστόν. The παιδαγωγὸς was often the most valueless of the slaves. Perikles appointed the aged Zopyrus as the παιδαγωγὸς of Alkibiades. This fact can, however, hardly have entered into St. Paul's meaning. The world, until Christ came, was in its pupilage, and the Law was given to hold it under discipline, till a new period of spiritual freedom dawned. The more inward relation between Law and sin, and its power to bring sin more to our conscience, and so bring about the possibility of its removal, are, as we shall see, worked out in the Epistle to the Romans.

[3] Contrast this with the Jewish morning prayer, in which in three benedictions a man blesses God who has not made him a Gentile, a slave, or a woman.

[4] iii. 21—29.

respect from a slave, though he is lord of all, but is under tutors and stewards till the term fixed by his father. So we, too, when we were infants, were enslaved under elements of material teaching; but when the fulness of time came God sent forth His Son—born of a woman, that we may receive the adoption of sons;[1] born under Law, that He may ransom those under Law. But because ye are sons, God sent forth the Spirit of His Son into our hearts crying, Abba, our Father! So thou art no longer a slave but a son, and if a son, an heir also by God's means. Well, in past time not knowing God ye were slaves to those who by nature are not gods, but now after recognising God—nay, rather being recognised by God—how can ye turn back again to the weak and beggarly rudiments,[2] to which again from the beginning ye want to be slaves? Ye are anxiously keeping days and months and seasons and years. I fear for you that I have perhaps toiled for you in vain."[3]

In this clause the boldness of thought and utterance is even more striking. He not only urges the superiority of the Christian covenant, but speaks of the Jewish as mere legal infancy and actual serfdom; nay, more, he speaks of the ceremonial observances of the Levitical Law as "weak and beggarly rudiments;" and, worse than all, he incidentally compares them to the ritualisms of heathendom, implying that there is no essential difference between observing the full moon in the synagogue and observing it in the Temple of Mên; between living in leafy booths in autumn, or striking up the wail for Altis in spring; nay, even between circumcision and the yet ghastlier mutilations of the priests of Cybele.[4] Eighteen hundred years have passed since this brief letter was written, and it has so permeated all the veins of Christian thought that in these days we accept its principles as a matter of course; yet it needs no very violent effort of the imagination to conceive how savage would be the wrath which would be kindled in the minds of the Jews—aye, and even of the Jewish Christians—by words which not only spoke with scorn of the little distinctive observances which were to them as the very breath of their nostrils, but wounded to the quick their natural pride, by placing their cherished formalities, and even the antique and highly-valued badge of their nationality, on a level with the pagan customs which they had ever regarded with hatred and contempt. Yet it was with no desire to waken infuriated prejudice that St. Paul thus wrote. The ritualisms of heathen worship, so far as they enshrined or kept alive any spark of genuine devotion, were not objectionable—had a useful function; in this respect they stood on a level with those of Judaism. The infinite superiority of the Judaic ritual arose from its being the shadow of good things to come. It had fulfilled its task,

[1] iv. 4, 5. Notice the chiasmus of the original which would not suit the English idiom. Notice, too, the importance of the passage as showing that men did not *begin* to be sons of God, when they were *declared* sons of God, just as the Roman act of emancipation did not *cause* sons to be sons, but merely put them in possession of their rights (Maurice, *Unity*, p. 504).

[2] iv. 3, στοιχεῖα τοῦ κόσμου; 9, ἀσθενῆ καὶ πτωχὰ στοιχεῖα, physical elements of religion, symbols, ceremonies (cf. Col. ii. 8), &c., which invest the natural with religious significance. Both in Judaism and heathenism religion was so much bound up with the material and the sensuous as to place men in bondage. In neither was God recognised as a Spirit (Baur, *New Test. Theol.*, p. 171). Or the notion may be that ritualism is only the elementary teaching, the A B C of religion.

[3] iv. 1—11. Cf. Col. ii. 16.

[4] Hausrath, p. 268.

and ought now to be suffered to drop away. It is not for the sake of the calyx, but for the sake of the corolla, that we cultivate the flower, and the calyx may drop away when the flower is fully blown. To cling to the shadow when it had been superseded by the substance was to reverse the order of God.

Then comes a strong and tender appeal.

"Become as I, because I too became as you, brethren, I beseech you.[1] It is not I whom you wronged at all, by your aberrations. Nay, to me you were always kind. You know that the former time it was in consequence of a sickness that I preached to you; and though my personal condition might well have been a trial to you, ye despised me not, nor loathed me,[2] but as an angel of God ye received me, as Christ Jesus. What, then, has become of your self-felicitation? for I bear you witness that, if possible, ye dug out your very eyes and gave them me. So, have I become your enemy by speaking the truth to you?[3]

"Mere alien teachers are paying court to you assiduously, but not honourably; nay, they want to wall you up from every one else, that you may pay court to them.[4] Now, to have court paid to you is honourable in an honourable cause always, and not only when I am with you,[5] my little children whom again I travail with, until Christ be formed in you. But I could have wished to be with you now, and to change my voice to you,[6] for I am quite at a loss about you."[7]

Then, returning as it were to the attack, he addresses to them the curious allegory of the two wives of Abraham, Sarah and Hagar, and their sons Ishmael and Isaac.[8]

Those are types of the two covenants—Hagar represents Sinai, corresponds to, or is under the same head with bondage, with the Law, with the Old Covenant, and therefore with the earthly Jerusalem, which is in bondage under the Law; but Sarah corresponds to freedom, and the promise, and therefore to the New Covenant, and to the New Jerusalem which is the free mother of us all. There must be antagonism between the two, as there was between the brother-sons of the slave and the free-woman; but this ended in the son of the slave-woman being cast out. So it is now; the unbelieving Jews, the natural descendants of the real Sarah, are the spiritual descendants of Hagar, the ejected bondwoman of the Sinaitic wilderness, and they persecute the Gentiles, who are the prophesied descendants of the spiritual Sarah. The spiritual descendants of Sarah shall inherit the blessing of which those Jews who are descended physically from her should have no share. Isaac, the supernatural child of promise, represents the spiritual seed of Abraham,—that is Christ, and all who, whether Jew or Gentile, are in Him. "Therefore, brethren, we," he adds—identifying himself far more entirely with Gentiles than with Jews, "are not children of a slave-woman, but of the free. In the freedom wherewith Christ freed us, stand then, and be not again enyoked with the yoke of slavery."

[1] *i.e.*, free from the bondage of Judaism.

[2] iv. 14, ἐξεπτύσατε—lit., "spat out," Krenkel (*v. infra*, Excursus X.) explains this of the "spitting" to avert epilepsy. "Despuimus comitiales morbos" (Plin. xxviii. 4, 7; Plaut. *Capt.* iii. 4, 18, 21).

[3] iv. 12—16. On this passage, *v. infra*, Excursus X.

[4] iv. 17, ἵνα—ζηλοῦτε (ind.), but probably *meant* for a subjunctive; the apparent solecism is probably due to the difficulty of remembering the inflexions of the contract verb; cf. 1 Cor. iv. 6.

[5] He seems to mean, "I do not blame zealous attachment, provided it be (as mine to you was) from noble motives, and provided it be not terminated (as yours to me was) by a temporary separation."

[6] *i.e.*, to speak to you in gentler tones.

[7] iv. 17—20.

[8] On this allegory see *supra*, p. 32.

Again, how strange and how enraging to the Jews would be such an allegory! It was Philonian, Rabbinic; but it was more admirable than any allegory in Philo, because it did not simply merge the historical in the metaphorical; and more full of ability and insight than any in the Rabbis.[1] This was, indeed, "to steal a feather from the spicy nest of the Phœnix" in order to wing the shaft which should pierce her breast. The Jews, the descendants of Sarah, by the irresistible logic of their own most cherished method, here find themselves identified with the descendants of the despised and hated Hagar, just as before they had heard the proof that not they but the converted Gentiles were truly Abraham's seed![2]

And the Galatians must be under no mistake; they cannot serve two masters; they cannot combine the Law and the Gospel. Nor must they fancy that they could escape persecution by getting circumcised and stop at that point. "See," he says, "I, Paul—who, as they tell you, once preached circumcision—I, Paul, tell you that, if you hanker after reliance on circumcision, Christ shall profit you nothing. Nay, I protest again to every person who gets himself circumcised, that he is a debtor to keep the whole Law. Ye are nullified from Christ, ye who seek justification in Law, ye are banished from His grace; for we spiritually, as a consequence of faith, earnestly await the hope of righteousness. For in Christ neither circumcision availeth anything, nor uncircumcision, but faith working by means of love."[3] "In these," as Bengel says, "stands all Christianity."

"Ye were running bravely. Who broke up your path to prevent your obeying truth? This persuasion is not from Him who calleth you. It is an alien intrusion —it comes only from one or two—yet beware of it. A little leaven leaveneth the whole lump. *I* feel confident with respect to you[4] in the Lord that you will adopt my views; and he who troubles you shall bear the burden of his judgment, be he who he may. And as for me, if I am still preaching circumcision, why am I still an object of persecution? The stumbling-block of the cross has been done away with, it appears! *They* are not persecuted,—just because they preach circumcision; why then should *I* be, if as they say I preach it too? Would that these turners of you upside down would go a little further than circumcision, and make themselves like the priests of Cybele![5]

"I cannot help this strong language; for *ye* were called for freedom, brethren; only, not freedom for a handle to the flesh, but by love be slaves to one another.[6] For the whole Law is absolutely fulfilled[7] in one word in the 'Thou shalt love thy neighbour as thyself.' But if ye are biting and devouring one another, take heed that ye be not consumed by one another.[8]

[1] It was no mere pretty application of a story. It was the detection in one particular case of a divine law, which might be traced through every fact of the divine history (Maurice, *Unity*, 508). How different from Philo's allegory, in which Charran is the senses; Abraham, the soul; Sarah, divine wisdom; Isaac, human wisdom; Ishmael, sophistry; &c.

[2] iv. 21—31. [3] v. 1—6. [4] v. 10, ἐγὼ πέποιθα εἰς ὑμᾶς.

[5] v. 7—12, ἀποκόψονται; cf. ἀποκεκομμένοι, Deut. xxiii. 1. I have given the only admissible meaning. Reuss calls it "une phrase affreuse, qui révolte notre sentiment." This is to judge a writer by the standard of two millenniums later. Accustomed to Paul's manner and temperament it would have been read as a touch of rough humour, yet with a deep meaning in it—viz., that circumcision to Gentiles was mere *concision* (Phil. iii. 2, 3), and if as such it had any virtue in it, there was something to be said for the priests at Pessinus.

[6] 1 Peter ii. 16.

[7] v. 14, πεπλήρωται, has been fulfilled; Matt. xxii. 40; Rom. xiii. 8 (Lev. xix. 18).

[8] v. 13—15. To a great extent the Apostle's warning was fulfilled. Julian, *Ep.* 52, speaks of their internecine dissensions. Galatia became not only the stronghold of Montanism, but the headquarters of Ophites, Manichees, Passalorynchites, Ascodrogites, Artotyrites, Borborites, and other

"Gorgons and hydras, and chimæras dire;"

and St. Jerome speaks of Ancyra as *Schismatibus dilaccrata, dogmatum varietatibus constuprata* (Lightfoot, *Gal.*, p. 31).

"I mean then, walk spiritually, and there is no fear of your fulfilling the lusts of the flesh. The flesh and the spirit are mutually opposing principles, and their opposition prevents your fulfilling your highest will. But if ye are led by the spirit ye are not under Law. Now the deeds of the flesh are manifest; such are fornication, uncleanness, wantonness, idolatry, witchcrafts,[1]—enmities, discord, rivalry, wraths, cabals, party-factions, envies, murders,[2]—drunkennesses, revellings,[3] and things like these; as to which I warn you now, as I warned you before, that all who do such things shall not inherit the kingdom of God. But the fruit of the Spirit[4] is love, joy, peace, longsuffering, kindness, beneficence, faith, gentleness, self-control. Against such things as these there is no law. But they that are of Christ Jesus crucified the flesh with its passions and desires. If we are living spiritually, spiritually also let us walk. Let us not become vainglorious, provoking one another, envying one another."[5]

At this point there is a break. It may be that some circumstance at Corinth had powerfully affected him. Another lapse into immorality may have taken place in that unstable church, or something may have strongly reminded St. Paul of the overwhelming effect which had been produced by the sentence on the particular offender whom he had decided to hand over to Satan. However this may be, he says with peculiar solemnity:

"Brethren, even though a man be surprised in a transgression, ye the spiritual restore such an one in a spirit of meekness, considering thyself lest even thou shouldst be tempted. Bear ye the burdens of one another's cares,[6] and so shall ye fulfil the law of Christ. But if any man believes himself to be something when he is nothing, he is deceiving himself. But let each man test his own work, and then he shall have his ground of boasting with reference to himself, and not to his neighbour. For each one shall bear his own appointed load.[7]

"Let then him who is taught the word communicate with the teacher in all good things.[8] Be not deceived, God is not mocked. Whatsoever a man soweth, that also he shall reap. For he that soweth to his flesh, from his flesh shall reap corruption; but he that soweth to the Spirit, from the Spirit shall reap life eternal. [That is the general principle; apply it to the special instance of the contribution for which I have asked you.] Let us not lose heart in doing right, for at the due time we shall reap if we faint not. Well, then, as we have opportunity, let us do good to all men, but especially to those who are of the family of the faith.[9]

"Look ye with what large letters I write to you with my own hand.[10] As many as want to make fair show in the flesh, want to compel you to get yourselves circumcised, only that they may not be persecuted for the cross of Christ. For not even the circumcision party themselves keep the law, yet they want to get you circumcised that they may boast in your flesh. But far be it from me to boast except in the cross of our Lord Jesus Christ, by whom the world has been crucified to me, and I to the world. For neither circumcision is anything nor uncircumcision, but a new creation.[11] And as many as shall walk by this rule, peace on them

[1] Sins *with others* against God.
[2] Sins against our neighbour.
[3] Personal sins (Bengel).
[4] *Deeds* of the flesh, because they spring from ourselves; *fruit* of the spirit, because they need the help of God's grace (Chrys.).
[5] v. 16—26.
[6] vi. 2, βαρη, weaknesses, sufferings, even sins.
[7] vi. 1—5. vi. 5, φορτιον of responsibility and moral consequence.
[8] 1 Cor. ix.; Rom. xii. 13; 1 Thess. v. 12.
[9] vi. 6—10.
[10] Theodore of Mopsuetia, believing that only the conclusion of the letter was autograph, makes the size of the letters a sort of sign that the Apostle does not blush for anything he has said. But the style of the letter seems to show that it was not dictated to an amanuensis.
[11] It will be seen that in those two clauses he has resumed both the polemical (12,

and mercy, and on the Israel of God." And then, as though by a sudden afterthought, we have the "Henceforth let no man trouble me, for I bear in triumph on my body the brands of Jesus."[1]

"The grace of our Lord Jesus Christ be with your spirit, brethren. Amen."[2]

Such was the Epistle to the Galatians; nor can we without some knowledge of what Judaism then was, and what it was daily becoming, form any adequate conception of the daring courage, the splendid originality—let us rather say the inspired and inspiring faith—which enabled the Apostle thus to throw off the yoke of immemorial traditions, and to defy the hatred of those among whom he had been trained as a Hebrew and a Pharisee. We must remember that at this very time the schools of Rabbinism were fencing the Law with a jealous exclusiveness which yearly increased in its intensity; and that while St. Paul was freely flinging open all, and more than all, of the most cherished hopes and exalted privileges of Judaism, without one of its burdens, the Rabbis and Rabbans were on the high road to the conclusion that any Gentile who dared to get beyond the seven Noachian precepts—any Gentile, for instance, who had the audacity to keep the Sabbath as a day of rest—without becoming a proselyte of righteousness, and so accepting the entire yoke of Levitism, "neither adding to it nor diminishing from it," deserved to be beaten and punished, and to be informed that he thereby legally incurred the penalty of death.[3] What was the effect of the Epistle on the Churches of Galatia we cannot tell; but for the Church of Christ the work was done. By this letter Gentiles were freed for ever from the peril of having their Christianity subjected to impossible and carnal conditions. In the Epistle to the Romans circumcision does not occur as a practical question. Judaism continued, indeed, for some time to exercise over Christianity a powerful influence, but in the Epistle of Barnabas circumcision is treated with contempt, and even attributed to the deception of an evil angel;[4] in the Epistle of Ignatius, St. Paul's distinction of the true and false circumcision is absolutely accepted;[5] and even in the Clementine Homilies, Judaistic as they are, not a word is said of the necessity of circumcision, but he who desires to be un-Hellenised must be so by baptism and the new birth.[6]

13) and the dogmatic theses (14, 16) of the letter; and that the personal (17) as well as the doctrinal truth (18) on which he has been dwelling recur in the last two verses. Thus, from first to last, the Epistle is characterised by remarkable unity.

[1] Hence, as one marked with the brands of his master, in his next Epistle (Rom. i. 1) he for the first time calls himself "a slave of Jesus Christ." Stigmata were usually a punishment, so that in classic Greek, *stigmatias* is "a rascal." Whether St. Paul's metaphor turns on his having been a deserter from Christ's service before his conversion, or on his being a Hierodoulos (Hdt. ii. 113), is doubtful. There seem, too, to be traces of the branding of *recruits* (Rönsch. *Das N. T. Tertullian's*, p. 700). The use of "stigmata" for the "five wounds" has had an effect analogous to the notion of "unknown" tongues.

[2] vi. 11—18. The one unusual last word, "brethren," beautifully tempers the general severity of tone.

[3] See *Sanhedrin*, f. 58, c. 2; and Maimonides, *Yad Hachezakah* (*Hilchoth Melachim*, § 10, *Hal.* 9).

[4] Ep. Ps. Barnab. ix.

[5] Ep. ad Philad. 6, ὁ τῆς κάτω περιτομῆς ψευδοιουδαῖος.

[6] ἀφελληνισθῆναι (Ps. Clem. *Hom.* iii. 9).

The Epistle to the Galatians was quickly followed by that to the Romans, which was at once singularly like and singularly unlike its immediate predecessor. No violent external opposition, no deep inward sorrow was at that particular moment absorbing the Apostle's soul. It was a little pause in his troubled life. The period of his winter stay at Corinth was drawing to a close. He was already contemplating a yet wider circle for his next missionary tour. The tide of his thoughts was turning wholly towards the West. He wished to see Rome, and, without making any prolonged visit, to confirm the Gospel in the capital of the world. He did not contemplate a long stay among the Roman Christians, because it was his invariable principle not to build on other men's foundations. But he wished to be helped by them—with facilities which a great capital alone can offer—on his journey to Spain, where as yet the Gospel had been unpreached. His heart was yearning towards the shores whose vessels he saw in the ports of Lechæum and Cenchreæ, and whose swarthy sailors he may have often met in the crowded streets.

But before he could come to them he determined to carry out his long-planned visit to Jerusalem. Whether the members of that church loved or whether they hated him—whether they would give to his converts the right hand of fellowship or hold them at arm's-length—he at least would repay evil with good; he would effectually aid their mass of struggling pauperism; he would accompany the delegates who carried to them a proof of Gentile love and generosity, and would himself hand over to the Apostles the sums—which must by this time have reached a considerable amount—which had been collected solely by his incessant endeavours. How earnestly and even solemnly had he brought this duty before the Galatians, both orally and by letter! how carefully had he recommended the Corinthians to prevent all uncertainty in the contributions by presenting them in the form of a weekly offering! how had he stimulated the Macedonians by the forwardness of the Achaians, and the Achaians by the liberality of the Macedonians! And after all this trouble, forethought, and persistence, and all the gross insinuations which he had braved to bring it to a successful issue, it was but natural that one so warm-hearted should wish to reap some small earthly reward for his exertions by witnessing the pleasure which the subscription afforded to the mother church, and the relief which it furnished to its humbler members. But he did not conceal from himself that this visit to Jerusalem would be accompanied by great dangers. He was thrusting his head into the lion's den of Judaism, and from all his past experience it was but too clear that in such a place, and amid the deepened fanaticism of one of the yearly feasts, perils among his own countrymen and perils among false brethren would beset every step of his path. Whether he would escape those perils was known to God alone. Paul was a man who cherished no illusions. He had studied too deeply the books of Scripture and the book of experience to be ignorant of the manner in which God deals with His saints. He knew how Elijah, how Isaiah, how Jeremiah, how Ezekiel, how Daniel, how John the Baptist, how the Lord Jesus Himself, had lived and died. He knew that devotion to God's work involved no protection from earthly miseries and trials, and he quoted without a murmur the sad words of the Psalmist, "For Thy sake are we killed all the day long; we are accounted as sheep appointed to be slain."[1] But whether it was God's will that he should escape or not, at any rate it would be well to write to the Roman Christians, and answer all objections, and remove all doubts respecting the real nature of his teaching, by a systematic statement of his beliefs as to the true relations between Jews and Gentiles, between the Law and the Gospel, as viewed in the light of the great Christian revelation that we are justified through faith in Christ. This, if anything, might save him from those Judaic counter-efforts on the part of nominal Christians, which had undone half his work, and threatened to render of no effect the cross of Christ. He therefore availed himself of the earliest opportunity to write and to despatch the greatest of all his Epistles—one of the greatest and deepest and most memorably influential of all compositions ever written by human pen—the Epistle to the Romans.

CHAPTER XXXVII.

THE EPISTLE TO THE ROMANS, AND THE THEOLOGY OF ST. PAUL.

Πῶς γὰρ ἔσται βροτὸς δίκαιος ἔναντι κυρίου;—JOB XXV. 4 (LXX.).

"But to the cross He nails thy enemies,
The Law that is against thee, and the sins
Of all mankind; with Him these are crucified,
Never to hurt them more who rightly trust
In this His satisfaction."

MILTON, *Par. Lost*, xii. 415.

Παῦλος ὁ μέγας τῆς ἀληθείας κῆρυξ, τὸ καύχημα τῆς ἐκκλησίας, ὁ ἐν οὐρανοῖ ἄνθρωπος.—PS. CHRYS. *Orat. Encom.*

I.—INTRODUCTORY.

BEFORE we enter on the examination of the Epistle to the Romans, it will be necessary to understand, as far as we can, the special objects which the Apostle had in view, and the conditions of the church to which it was addressed.

The first conqueror who had introduced the Jews in any numbers into Rome was the great Pompeius, who treated the nation with extreme indignity.[2] In the capital of the world they showed that strong self-reliance by which they have ever been distinguished. From the peculiarities of their religious

[1] Rom. viii. 36.
[2] Jos. *Antt.* xiv. 4, §§1–5; *B. J.* i. 7; Florus. iii. 5; Tac. *H.* v. 9; Cic. *pro Flac.* xxvii., &c.

conviction, they were useless and troublesome as ordinary slaves, but they displayed in every direction the adaptability to external conditions which, together with their amazing patience, has secured them an ever-strengthening position throughout the world. They soon, therefore, won their emancipation, and began to multiply and flourish. The close relations of friendship which existed between Augustus and Herod the Great improved their condition; and at the dawn of the Christian era, they were so completely recognised as an integral section of the population, with rights and a religion of their own, that the politic Emperor assigned to them that quarter beyond the Tiber which they have occupied for ages since.[1] From these dim purlieus, where they sold sulphur matches, and old clothes, and broken glass, and went to beg and tell fortunes on the Cestian or Fabrician bridge,[2] 8,000 of them swarmed forth to escort fifty deputies who came from Jerusalem with a petition to Augustus.[3] It was doubtless the danger caused by their growing numbers which led to that fierce attempt of Sejanus to get rid of them which Tacitus records, not only without one touch of pity, but even with concentrated scorn.[4] The subsequent, but less atrocious decree of Claudius,[5] brought about St. Paul's friendship with Aquila and Priscilla, and is probably identical with the measure alluded to by Suetonius in the famous passage about the "*Impulsor Chrestus.*"[6] If so, it is almost certain that Christians must have been confounded with Jews in the common misfortune caused by their Messianic differences.[7] But, as Tacitus confesses in speaking of the attempt to expel astrologers from Italy, these measures were usually as futile as they were severe.[8] We find that those Jews who had left Rome under immediate pressure began soon to return.[9] Their subterranean proselytism,[10] as far back as the days of Nero, acquired proportions so formidable that Seneca,[11] while he characterised the Jews as a nation steeped in wickedness (*gens sceleratissima*), testifies to their immense diffusion. It is therefore certain that when St. Paul first arrived in Rome (A.D. 61), and even at the time when he wrote this letter (A.D. 58), the Jews, in spite of the unrepealed

[1] I have described this quarter of Rome in *Seekers after God*, p. 168.

[2] Mart. *Ep.* i. 42, 109; vi. 93; x. 3, 5; xii. 57; Juv. xiv. 134, 186, 201; Stat. *Silv.* i., vi. 72. They continued here for many centuries, but were also to be found in other parts of Rome. On their mendicancy see Juv. iii. 14, 296; vi. 542. On their *faithfulness to the Law*, see Hor. *Sat.* i., ix. 69; Suet. *Aug.* 76; Juv. xiv. 96; Pers. v. 184; &c.

[3] Jos. *Antt.* xvii. 1.

[4] Tac. *Ann.* ii. 85; Sueton. *Tib.* 36; Jos. *Antt.* xviii. 3, 5.

[5] Acts xviii. 2.

[6] *V. supra*, p. 279; *infra*, p. 720. Since *Christus* would be meaningless to classic ears, the word was *surfrappé* (see my *Families of Speech*, p. 119). *Chrestianus* is common in inscriptions; Renan, *St. Paul*, 101.

[7] And perhaps by the commencing troubles in Judæa, early in A.D. 52.

[8] Tac. *Ann.* xii. 52, "atrox et irritum." It is not impossible that these may be one and the same decree, for the Mathematici, and impostors closely akin to them, were frequently Jews.

[9] Dion Cass. (lx. 6), who is probably alluding to this decree, says that the Jews were not expelled, but only forbidden to meet in public assemblies. Aquila, however, as a leading Christian, would be naturally one of those who was compelled to leave.

[10] Hor. *Sat.* I. ix. 70; Pers. *Sat.* v. 180; Ovid, *A. A.* i. 76; Juv. vi. 542; Suet. *Aug.* 76; Merivale, vi. 257, *seq.*, &c.

[11] Ap. Aug. *De Civ. Dei*, vi. 11; *v. infra*, Excursus XIV.

decree of Claudius, which had been passed only six years before, formed a large community, sufficiently powerful to be an object of alarm and jealousy to the Imperial Government.

Of this Jewish community we can form no conjecture how many were Christians; nor have we a single *datum* to guide us in forming an estimate of the numbers of the Christian Church in Rome, except the vague assertion of Tacitus, that a "vast multitude" of its innocent members were butchered by Nero in the persecution by which he strove to hide his guilty share in the conflagration of July 19, A.D. 64.[1] Even the salutations which crowd the last chapter of the Epistle to the Romans do not help us. Twenty-six people are greeted by name, besides "the Church in the house" of Aquila and Priscilla, some of the "households" of Aristobulus and Narcissus,[2] the "brethren," with Asyncritus and others, and the "saints" with Olympas and others.[3] All that we could gather from these notices, if we could be sure that the sixteenth chapter was really addressed to Rome, is that the Roman Christians possessed as yet no common place of meeting, but were separated into at least three communities grouped around different centres, assembling in different places of worship, and with no perceptible trace of ecclesiastical organisation. But there is nothing whatever to show whether these communities were large or small, and we shall see that the sixteenth chapter, though unquestionably Pauline, was probably addressed to the Ephesian and not to the Roman Church.

Assuming, however, that the Christians were numerous, as Tacitus expressly informs us, two questions remain, of which both are involved in deep obscurity. The one is, "When and how was Christianity introduced into Rome?" The other is, "Was the Roman Church predominantly Jewish or predominantly Gentile?"

1. Tradition answers the first question by telling us that St. Peter was the founder of Latin Christianity, and this answer is almost demonstrably false. It is first found in a work, at once malignant and spurious, written late in the second century, to support a particular party. That work is the forged Clementines,[4] in which we are told that Peter was the first Bishop of Rome. Tradition, gathering fresh particulars as it proceeds, gradually began to assert,

[1] Tac. *Ann.* xv. 40, 41; Suet. *Nero*, 38.

[2] The mention of these two names has been regarded as an argument that the sixteenth chapter really belongs to the Roman letter, since Aristobulus, the son of Herod, and other Herodian princes of that time, had been educated in Rome, whose slaves and freedmen these might be. Again, although Narcissus, the celebrated freedman of Claudius, had been put to death in A.D 54 (Tac. *Ann.* xiii. 1), four years before the date of this letter, "they of the household of Narcissus" may have been some of his slaves. On the other hand, neither of these names was uncommon, and it is less intrinsically improbable that there should have been a Narcissus and an Aristobulus at Ephesus, than that there should have been so many Asiatic intimates and Jewish kinsmen of St. Paul at Rome. Muratori (No. 1328) and Orelli (No. 720) give an inscription found at Ferrara from a tablet erected by *Tib. Claud. Narcissus*, to the *manes* of his wife, *Dicæosune* (Righteousness). See an interesting note on this in Plumptre, *Bibl. Stud.*, p. 428.

[3] Rom. xvi. 5, 14, 15.

[4] *Recognit.* i. 6.

with more or less confidence, that he came to Rome in the second year of Claudius (A.D. 42); that he met and confounded Simon Magus; that he continued Bishop of Rome for twenty-five years; that he was ultimately martyred by being crucified, head downwards, at his own humble desire; and that this took place on June 29th, the same day as the execution of St. Paul. In attestation of their martyrdom, Gaius refers to their "trophies" near the city.[1] The lateness of these details, the errors with which they are mingled, and the obvious party reasons for their invention, forbid our attaching to them any historic value. It is not at all probable that St. Peter arrived at the city till the year of his death. This at least is certain—that, in the New Testament, the sole asserted trace of his presence in Rome is to be found in the highly disputable allusion, "They of Babylon salute you."[2] He may have died in Rome; he may even have preached in Rome; he may even have been accepted by the Jewish section of Roman Christians as their nominal "Bishop;" but that he was not, and could not have been, in any true sense the *original founder* of the Roman Church is freely admitted even by Roman Catholics themselves.

At what time the chance seeds of Christianity had been wafted to the shores of Italy[3] we are utterly unable to say. That this took place in our Lord's lifetime is improbable, nor is it worth while to do more than allude to the fiction which ascribes to the Emperor Tiberius a favourable opinion respecting the divinity of Christ.[4] All that we can safely assert is the likelihood that the good tidings may first have been conveyed by some of those Jews and proselytes from Rome who heard the speech of St. Peter at Pentecost;[5] or by others who, like St. Paul himself, received their first impressions from the close reasoning and fiery eloquence of St. Stephen as they sat among chance visitors in the synagogue of the Libertini.[6]

2. If this conjecture be correct, we see that, from the first, the Church of Rome must have contained both Jewish and Gentile elements. The mere probabilities of the case will not enable us to decide which of the two elements preponderated, and if we turn to the Epistle we are met by

[1] Euseb. *H. E.* ii. 14, 25 (quoting Dionysius of Corinth); Id. *Dem. Ev.* iii. 3; Origen (*ap. Euseb.* iii. 1); Justin Martyr, *Apolog.* ii. 26; Tert. *De Praescr. Haer.* 36; *c. Marc.* iv. 5; Gaius *ap. Euseb.* ii. 25. Justin, and perhaps others, were misled by the inscription to the Sabine deity Semo Sancus, which they read *Simoni Sancto*. Peter is also associated with Paul in the founding of Christianity at Rome by Clemens, *Ep. ad Cor.* 5; by the Κήρυγμα Πέτρου; by Lactant. *Instt. Div.* iv. 21; by Iren. *Haer.* iii. 3; by Epiphan. *Haer.* i. 27; Oros. vii. 7; *Constt. Apost.* vii. 46; &c. &c.

[2] The Acts prove that St. Peter was at Jerusalem about A.D. 49 (Acts xv.); and in Antioch about A.D. 53 (Gal. ii. 11); and the Epistles with the Acts prove all but conclusively that he was not at Rome during the first or second imprisonment of St. Paul. If "Babylon" in 1 Pet. v. 13, means Babylon and not Rome—a question which cannot be *positively* decided—then St. Peter was in Babylon ten years later than this. (See Baur, *Paul*, ii. 291 *seqq.*) Spanheim, in his celebrated *Dissertatio* (1679), dwells much on Gal. ii. 9 as a strong argument against the likelihood of Peter's visiting Rome. Ellendorf (a Roman Catholic writer) admits that it cannot be *proved*; but even Neander and Gieseler admit it to be probable.

[3] Acts xxviii. 14.

[4] Tert. *Apolog.* 5, 21 (Just. Mart. *Apolog.* i. 35, 48).

[5] Acts ii. 9.

[6] Acts vi. 9.

indications so dubious that critics have arrived at the most opposite conclusions.[1] Baur cannot even imagine how it is possible for any one to avoid the conclusion that the Apostle has Jewish Christians in view throughout. Olshausen, on the other hand, pronounces with equal confidence on the prominence of Gentiles. Each can refer to distinct appeals to both classes. If, at the very outset of the Epistle, St. Paul seems to address the whole Church as Gentiles, and in xi. 13 says, "I speak unto you Gentiles," and in xv. 15, 16, writes in the exclusive character of Apostle of the Gentiles,[2] and in x. 1 speaks of the Jews in the third person;[3] yet, on the other hand, in iv. 1 he speaks of "Abraham *our* father," and says that he is writing to those who "know the Law," and have once been under its servitude. If, again, the multitude of quotations from the Jewish scriptures[4] might be supposed to have most weight with Jews (though we find the same phenomenon in the Epistle to the Galatians), yet, on the other hand, in the apologetic section (ix.—xi.) the argument is rather *about* the Jews than addressed *to* them,[5] and the moral precepts of the practical chapters seem to have in view the liberal Gentiles far more than the Ebionising Jews. The views of the latter are not directly combated, while the former are bidden to waive their personal liberty rather than cause any personal offence.

Of these apparent contradictions the solution most commonly accepted is that suggested by Professor Jowett,[6] that even the Gentile converts had been mainly drawn from the ranks of proselytes, who at Rome were particularly numerous,[7] so that "the Roman Church appeared to be at once Jewish and Gentile—Jewish in feeling, Gentile in origin; Jewish, for the Apostle everywhere argues with them as Jews; Gentile, for he expressly addresses them as Gentiles." This, no doubt, was the condition of other Churches, and may have been that of the Church at Rome. But as this hypothesis by no means solves all the difficulties, it seems to me a preferable supposition that St. Paul

[1] Neander, Meyer, De Wette, Olshausen, Tholuck, Reuss, &c., are confident that it was mainly intended for Gentiles; Baur, Schwegler, Thiersch, Davidson, Wordsworth, &c., for Jews.

[2] i. 13. "Among you, as among other Gentiles" (cf. 5, 6).

[3] x. 1, "My heart's desire and prayer for them" (ὑπὲρ αὐτῶν—א, A, B, D, E, F, G—not ὑπὲρ τοῦ Ἰσραήλ).

[4] The phrase καθὼς γέγραπται occurs no less than *nineteen* times in this single Epistle, as it does on almost every page of the Talmud.

[5] ix. 1; x. 1; xi., *passim*.

[6] Jowett, *Romans*, vol. ii. 23.

[7] Tac. *H.* v. 5; Cic. *pro Flacco*, 28, &c. We read of Jewish slaves in the noblest houses. There was an Acme in the household of Livia; a Samaritan named Thallus was a freedman of Tiberius; Aliturus was a favourite mime of Nero, &c. The Judaic faithfulness of these Jews is proved by the inscriptions on their graves; Garucci, *Cimitero*, 4; Grätz, iv. 123, 506; and by the allusions of classic writers. Suet. *Aug.* 57, 76, &c. It is remarkable that among Jewish proselytes are found such names as Fulvia, Flavia, Valeria, &c., while the Christians were mainly Tryphænas and Tryphosas, slave names ("Luxurious," "wanton") which no human being would voluntarily bear. It appears from inscriptions given by Gruter and Orelli that there were many Jewish synagogues in Rome, *e.g.*, *Synagoga Campi*, *Augusti*, *Agrippae*, *Suburrae*, *Oleae*. The titles φιλέντολος and φιλόλαος on their tombs significantly indicate their orthodoxy and patriotism. (See too Hor. *Sat.* II. iii. 288.)

is not so much addressing a special body as purposely arguing out a fundamental problem, and treating it in an ideal and dramatic manner. To the Roman Christians as a body he was avowedly a stranger, but he knew that Jews and Gentiles, each with their special difficulties and prejudices, existed side by side in every Church which he had visited, and he wished once for all to lay down, not only for the Roman Christians, but for all who might read his letter, the principles which were to guide their mutual relations. He is stating the truths which could alone secure the perfect unity of that Church of the future in which the distinctions between Jew and Greek were to be no more. It was natural that before he visited a strange Church, and one so important as the Church of Rome, he should desire plainly to state to them the Gospel which he meant to preach. But surely it is hardly probable that he would wish the benefits of this consummate effort to be confined to a single Church. The hypothesis that several copies of the letter were made, and that with appropriate conclusions, it was sent in whole or in part to other Churches beside that of Rome, is not only intrinsically reasonable, but also accounts for some of the peculiar phenomena presented by the manuscripts, and especially by the structure of the concluding chapters.[1]

[1] (i.) The mission of Phœbe to Ephesus is more probable than a mission to Rome, which was nearly three times more distant; nor could Paul well have addressed a *strange* Church in language of such urgent request on the subject of her visit (Rom. xvi. 1, 2). (ii.) It is strange that St. Paul should salute twenty-six people at a Church which he had never visited, and address them in terms of peculiar intimacy and affection, when he only salutes one or two, or none at all, in Churches which he had founded. (iii.) Aquila and Priscilla were at Ephesus when St. Paul wrote 1 Cor. xvi. 19, and again at Ephesus when he wrote 2 Tim. iv. 19. It is strange to find them settled at Rome with a Church in their house between these two dates. ("Quoi ! toute l'Eglise d'Ephèse s'était donc donné rendesvous in Rome?" Renan, *St. Paul*, lxviii.) (iv.) How is it that there are *no* salutations to Eubulus, Pudens, Linus, Claudia (2 Tim. iv. 21)? (v.) How comes it that "Epænetus, the first-fruits of Asia," is at Rome? and that so many others are there who have—*in other places*, of which, from the nature of the case, Ephesus is the one which most prominently suggests itself—toiled so much, and suffered so much for Paul, and even shared his frequent prisons (xvi. 7, 9, 12, 13)? (vi.) If so many were at Rome who deserve to be specially signalised as "beloved," and "approved," and "elect," and "kinsmen," and "toilers," how is it that they all deserted him at the hour of need (2 Tim. iv. 16)? Was the Church at Rome so mere a sand-cloud that all these had been scattered from Rome? or had they all been put to death in the persecution of A.D. 64? How is it that not one of these exemplary twenty-six are among the three Jewish friends who are alone faithful to him, even before the Neronian persecutions began, and only a few years after this letter was despatched (Col. iv. 10, 11)? (vii.) Again, how comes it that the severe yet fraternal reproachfulness of xvi. 17—20 is so unlike the apologetic and distant politeness of xv. 15—20? (viii.) How came Timothy and St. Paul's other friends, whose salutations to Thessalonica or to Ephesus would be natural, to send them so freely to distant and unvisited Rome? (ix.) Even if these considerations were unimportant, how is it that they are so well supported by the apparently different terminations of the Epistle at xv. 33, and xvi. 20 and 24, as well as xvi. 27? Why is the concluding doxology missing in F, G, and some MSS. mentioned by Jerome? Why is it placed after xiv. 23 in L, in most cursives, in Greek Lectionaries, in Chrysostom, Theodoret, &c.? Why is it found twice in Codex A (xiv. 24 and xvi. 25)? Why did Marcion, with no apparent dogmatic reason, omit the two last chapters altogether? Why, lastly, does so important a manuscript as G, founded as it is on a very ancient manuscript, omit the words ἐν Ῥώμῃ in i. 7, 15? No fair critic will, I think, assert that these difficulties are collectively unimportant; and they find a perfectly simple and adequate solution if, without accepting the entire details of Renan's theory, we suppose with him (*St. Paul*, lxiii.—lxxv.) that the main body of the Epistle was sent

3. We come, then, to the question, What is the main object of the Epistle to the Romans? And here we must not be surprised if we meet with different answers. The highest works of genius, in all writings, whether sacred or secular, are essentially many-sided. Who will pretend to give in a few words the central conception of the "Prometheus Vinctus" or of "Hamlet"? Who will profess to unite all suffrages in describing the main purpose of Ecclesiastes or of Job? Yet, although the purpose of the Epistle has been differently interpreted, from our ignorance of its origin, and of the exact condition of the Church to which it was written, it is impossible so to state it as not to express one or other of its essential meanings.

The first question which meets us affects the general character of the Epistle. Is it didactic or polemical? Is it general or special? The divergent views of commentators may here be easily reconciled. It is only indirectly and secondarily polemical; the treatment is general even if the immediate motive was special. Its tone has nothing of the passionate intensity which the Apostle always betrays when engaged in controversy with direct antagonists. It has been supposed by some that he desired to vindicate to the Roman Church his Apostolic authority. Undoubtedly such a vindication is implicitly involved in the masterly arguments of the Epistle; yet how different is his style from the vehemence with which he speaks in the Epistles to the Corinthians! Bishop Wordsworth says that it is "an apology for the Gospel against Judaism;" but where is the burning invective and indignant eloquence of the Epistle to the Galatians? We have no trace here of the ultra-liberalism of Corinth, or the dreamy asceticisms of Colossæ, or the servile Pharisaisms of Galatia. Clearly he is not here dealing with any *special* dissensions, heresies, or attacks on his authority.[1] The very value of the Epistle, as a systematic exposition of "the Gospel of Protestantism," depends on the calmness and

not only to Rome, but also to Ephesus, Thessalonica, and possibly some other Church, *with differing conclusions*, which are all preserved in the present form of the Epistle. On the other side may be set the remark of Strabo (xiv. 5), that many Tarsians were at Rome, and that Rome swarmed with Asiatics (Friedländer, *Sittengesch. Roms.* i. 59); the certainty that even in the days of Scipio, and much more in each succeeding generation, the majority of the inhabitants of Rome—the *faex populi*—were but "stepsons of Italy" (Sen. *ad Helv.*, *Cons.* 6, "Non possum ferre Quirites *Graecam* urban," Juv. *Sat.* iii. 61, 73, *seq.*, "St. ! tacete quibus nec pater nec mater est") and predominantly Greek (see Lightfoot, *Philippians*, p. 20); and that the names of Amplias, Urbanus, Stachys, Apelles, Nereus, Hermes, Hermas, are all found, as Dr. Lightfoot has shown (*ib.* 172—175), in the inscriptions of the *Columbaria* among the slaves in the households of various Cæsarian families; and not only these, but the rarer names Tryphæna, Tryphosa, Patrobas, and even Philologus and Julia *in connexion*, which is at least a curious coincidence. But when we remember the many hundreds of slaves in each great Roman household; and the extreme commonness of the names by which they were mostly called; and the fact that Garucci found that Latin names were twice as numerous as the Greek in the old Jewish cemetery at Rome,—we must still consider it more likely that chap. xvi., in whole or in part, was addressed to Ephesus as a personal termination to the copy of the Roman Epistle, which could hardly fail to be sent to so important a Church. (See Schulz, *Stud. u. Krit.* 1829; Ewald, *Sendschr.* 428; Reuss, *Les Epîtres*, ii. 19.) Of all theories, that of Baur, that the chapter was forged to show how intimate were the relations of Paul with the Roman Church, seems to me the most wanton and arbitrary.

[1] Reuss, *Les Epîtres*, ii. 11.

lucidity with which the Apostle appeals to an ideal public to follow him in the discussion of abstract truths. We seem already to be indefinitely removed from the narrow fanaticism of those who insisted on the impossibility of salvation apart from circumcision. The Hellenistic Judaism of a great city, however ignorant and however stereotyped, was incapable of so gross an absurdity, and in the wider and deeper questions which were naturally arising between the Jew and the Gentile Christian, there was as yet nothing sufficiently definite to exasperate the Apostle with a sense of ruinous antagonism. The day indeed was not far distant when, in the very city to which he was writing, some would preach Christ even of contention, hoping to add affliction to his bonds.[1] But this lay as yet in the unknown future. He wrote during one of those little interspaces of repose and hope which occur in even the most persecuted lives. The troubles at Corinth had been temporarily appeased, and his authority established. He was looking forward with the deepest interest to fresh missions, and although he could not deliberately preach at Rome, because he had made it a rule not to build on another man's foundation, he hoped to have his heart cheered by a kindly welcome in the imperial city before he started to plant the Cross on the virgin soil of Spain. And the Church of Rome stood high in general estimation. It was composed of Jews and Gentiles, of whom, not long afterwards, the former seem to have ranged themselves in uncompromising hostility to the Gospel; but he could as little foresee this as he could be aware that, in the second century, the Ebionism of this section of the Church would lead to a malignant attack on his character. At this time there do not seem to have been any open divisions or bitter animosities.[2] Differences of opinion there were between "the weak," who attached importance to distinctions of meats and drinks, and "the strong," who somewhat scornfully discarded them; but it seems as though, on the whole, the Jews were forbearing and the Gentiles moderate. Perhaps the two parties owed their immunity from dissensions to the passage of the Gentiles into the Church through the portals of the synagogue; or perhaps still more to the plasticity of ecclesiastical organisation which enabled the foreign and Græco-Roman converts to worship undisturbed in their own little congregations which met under the roof of an Aquila or an Olympas. If the Jewish and Gentile communities were separated by a marked division, collisions between the two sections would have been less likely to occur.

Be this as it may, it is evident that it was in a peaceful mood that the Apostle dictated to Tertius the great truths which he had never before so thoroughly contemplated as a logical whole.[3] The broad didactic character

[1] Phil. i. 16. These were evidently Judaisers (iii. 2; Col. iv. 11).

[2] The only trace of these is in xvi. 17—20; τὰς διχοστασίας, τὰ σκάνδαλα. But this furnishes one of the arguments against that chapter as part of the Epistle to the *Romans*.

[3] See the much more tender tone towards the Jews, and also towards the Law, in Rom. iv. 16, xi. 26, &c., compared with Gal. iv. 3, 2 Cor. iii. 6, &c. In the "not only—but also" of iv. 16 is reflected the whole conciliatory character of the Epistle to the Romans (Pfleiderer, ii. 45).

of the Epistle, its freedom from those outbursts of emotion which we find in others of his writings, is perfectly consistent with its having originated in historic circumstances; in other words, with its having been called forth, as was every one of the other Epistles, by passing events. St. Paul was on his way to Jerusalem, and his misgivings as to the results of the visit were tempered by the hope that the alms which he had collected would smooth the way for his favourable reception. Rome was the next place of importance which he intended to visit. How would he be received by the Christians of the great city? Would they have heard rumours from the Pharisees of Jerusalem that he was a godless and dangerous apostate, who defied all authority and abandoned all truth? It was at any rate probable that, even if he had not been represented to them in the most unfavourable light, he would have been spoken of as one who was prepared to abandon not only the peculiarities, but even the exclusive hopes and promises of Judaism. To a great extent this was true; and, if true, how serious, nay, how startling, were the consequences which such a belief entailed! They were views so contrary to centuries of past conviction, that they at least deserved the most careful statement, the most impregnable defence, the most ample justification, from the ancient scriptures. Such a defence, after deep meditation on the truths which God's Spirit had revealed to his inmost soul, he was prepared to offer in language the most conciliatory, the most tender—in language which betrayed how little the unalterable fixity of his conviction had quenched the fire of his patriotism, or deadened the quickness of his sensibility.[1] He expresses an inextinguishable love for his countrymen, and a deep sense of their glorious privileges, at the very moment that he is explaining why those countrymen have been temporarily rejected, and showing that those privileges have been inexorably annulled.[2] He declares his readiness to be even "anathema from Christ" for the sake of Israel, in the very verses in which he is showing, to the horrified indignation of his Jewish readers, that not the physical, but the spiritual seed of Abraham, are alone the true Israel of God.[3]

[1] "We see," says Dr. Davidson, "a constant conflict between his convictions and feelings; the former too deep to be changed, the latter too strong to be repressed, too ardent to be quenched by opposition of the persons he loved" (*Introdn.* i. 127).

[2] We can judge what the Jewish estimate of these privileges was by such passages of the Talmud as *Yebhamôth*, f. 47, 2; *supra*, p. 227.

[3] There can be no more striking contrast to the whole argument of the Epistle to the Romans than the following very remarkable passage in the *Abhôda Zara* (f. 3, col. 1—3), which will serve to show to what infinite heights above the ordinary Rabbinism of his nation St. Paul had soared. I appeal to any candid and learned Jew which is noblest, truest, divinest, manliest—the tone and the reasoning of the Epistle to the Romans, or the bigotry and frivolity of the following passage:—

"In the days of the Messiah, the Holy One, blessed be He, holding the roll of the Law in His bosom, will call upon those who have studied it to come forward and receive their reward. Instantly the idolatrous nations will appear in a body (Isa. xliii. 9), but will be told to present themselves separately with their Scribes at their head, that they may understand the answers severally addressed to them. The Romans, as the most renowned of all, will enter first. 'What has been your occupation?' will be demanded of them. They will point to their baths and forums, and the gold and silver with which they enriched the world, adding, 'All this we *have done that Israel may have leisure for*

If the current feelings of the Jews towards the Gentiles were much embittered—if they habitually regarded them in the spirit of hostile arrogance—it is very possible that the section respecting the relative position of the Jews and Gentiles (ix.—xi.) may be, as Baur argues, the kernel of the whole Epistle, in the sense that these were the first thoughts which had suggested themselves to the mind of the Apostle. Yet it is not correct to say that "the whole dogmatic treatment of the Epistle can be considered as nothing but the most radical and thorough-going refutation of Judaism and Jewish Christianity."[1] In his reaction against the purely dogmatic view which regards the Epistle as "a compendium of Pauline dogma in the form of an apostolic letter,"[2] Baur was led into a view too purely historical; and in his unwillingness to regard the central section as a mere *carollary* from the doctrines

the study of the Law.' 'Fools!' will be the stern answer: 'have you not done all this for your own pleasure, the market-places, and the baths alike, to pamper your own self-indulgence? and as for the gold and silver, it is Mine (Hagg. ii. 8). Who among you can declare this Law?' (Isa. xliii. 9).

"The Romans retire crestfallen, and then the Persians enter. They too will urge that they built bridges, took cities, waged wars to give Israel leisure to study the Law; but receiving the same rebuke as the Romans, they too will retire in dejection.

"Similarly all other nations, in the order of their rank, will come in to hear their doom; the wonder is that they will not be deterred by the failure of the others, but will still cling to their vain pleas. But then the Persians will argue that they built the Temple, whereas the Romans destroyed it; and the other nations will think that since they, unlike the Romans and Persians, never oppressed the Jews, they may expect more lenience.

"The nations will then argue, 'When has the Law been offered to us, and we refused it?' In answer it is inferred from Deut. xxxiii. 2 and Hab. iii. 3 that the Law had been offered to each in turn, but that they would not have it. Then they will ask, 'Why didst Thou not place us also underneath the mount (Ex. xix. 17) as Thou didst Israel, bidding us accept the Law, or be crushed by the mountain?' To whom Jehovah will reply, 'Let us hear the first things (Isa. xliii. 9). Have you kept the Noachic precepts?' They answer, 'Have the Jews kept the Law though they received it?' God answers, 'Yes; I Myself bear them witness that they have.' 'But is not Israel thy firstborn, and is it fair to admit the testimony of a Father?' 'The heaven and earth shall bear them witness.' 'But are not they interested witnesses?'* 'Well, then, you yourselves shall testify;' and accordingly Nimrod has to testify for Abraham, Laban for Jacob, Potiphar's wife for Joseph, Nebuchadnezzar for the three children, Darius for Daniel, Job's friends for Job. Then the nations entreat, 'Give us *now* the Law, and we will keep it.' 'Fools! do ye want to enjoy the Sabbath without having prepared for it? However, I will give you one easy precept—keep the Feast of Tabernacles' (Zech. xiv. 16). Then they will all hurry off to make booths on the roofs of their houses. But the Holy One, blessed be He, will make the sun blaze with midsummer heat, and they will desert the booths with the scornful exclamation, 'Let us break His bands asunder, and fling away His cords from us' (Ps. ii. 3). Then the Lord, sitting in the heavens, shall laugh at them. The only occasion on which He laughs *at* His creatures," though He does so *with* His creatures, notably with Leviathan, every day.

[1] Baur, *Paul.* i. 349; Olshausen, *Romans*, Introd. § 5. Philippi calls it "a connected doctrinal statement of the specifically Pauline Gospel."

[2] In any case this statement would be far too broad. If the Epistle to the Romans be a complete statement of what may be called the Apostle's "Soteriology," it contains little or none of the Eschatology which distinguishes these Epistles to the Thessalonians, or the Christology of the Epistle to the Colossians, or the Ecclesiology of the Epistle to the Ephesians. It is hardly worth while to notice the opinions that it is a mere defence of his Apostolate (Mangold), or a description and vindication of the Pauline system of missionary labours (Schott.). See Lange's *Romans*, p. 38, E. T.

* Because they only exist for the sake of the Law (*Nedarim*, f. 32, col. 1).

enunciated in the first eight chapters, he goes too far in calling them the heart and pith of the whole, to which everything else is only an addition. These chapters may have been first in the order of thought, without being first in the order of importance; they may have formed the original motive of the Epistle, and yet may have been completely thrown into subordination by the grandeur of the conceptions to which they led.

May we not well suppose that the Epistle originated as follows? The Apostle, intending to start for Jerusalem, and afterwards to open a new mission in the West, thought that he would utilise an interval of calm by writing to the Roman Church, in which, though not founded by himself, he could not but feel the deepest interest. He knows that, whatever might be the number of the Gentile Christians, the nucleus of the Church had been composed of Jews and proselytes, who would find it very hard to accept the lesson that God was no respecter of persons. Yet this was the truth which he was commissioned to teach; and if the Jews could not receive it without a shock—if even the most thoughtful among them could not but find it hard to admit that their promised Messiah—the Messiah for whom they had yearned through afflicted centuries—was after all to be even more the Messiah of the Gentiles than of the Jews—then it was pre-eminently necessary for him to set this truth so clearly, and yet so sympathetically, before them, as to soften the inevitable blow to their deepest prejudices. It was all the more necessary because, in writing to the more liberal Judaisers, he had not to deal with the ignorant malignity of those who had seduced his simple Galatians. In writing to the Churches of Galatia, and smiting down with one shattering blow their serpent-head of Pharisaism, he had freed his soul from the storm of passion by which it had been shaken. He could now write with perfect composure on the larger questions of the position of the Christian in reference to the Law, and of the relations of Judaism to Heathenism, and of both to Christianity. That the Gentiles were in no respect inferior to the Jews in spiritual privileges—nay, more, that the Gentiles were actually superseding the Jews by pressing with more eagerness into the Church of Christ[1]—was a fact which no Jewish Christian could overlook. Was God, then, rejecting Israel? The central section of the Epistle (ix.—xi.) deals with this grave scruple: and the Apostle there strives to show that (1) spiritual sonship does not depend on natural descent, since the only justification possible to man—namely, justification by faith—was equally open to Jews and Gentiles (ix.); that (2), so far as the Jews are losing their precedence in the divine favour, this is due to their own rejection of a free offer which it was perfectly open to them to have embraced (x.); and that (3) this apparent rejection is softened by the double consideration that (α) it is partial, not absolute, since there was "a remnant of the true Israelites according to the election of grace"; and (β) it is temporary, not final, since, when the full blessing of the Gentiles has

[1] Just as in the days of Christ the publicans and harlots were admitted before the Pharisees into the kingdom of God (Matt. xxi. 31, 32).

been secured, there still remains the glorious hope that all Israel would at last be saved.[1]

But was it not inevitable that from this point his thoughts should work backwards, and that the truths to which now, for the first time, he gave full and formal expression should assume an importance which left but subordinate interest to the minor problem? From the *relative* his thoughts had been led on to the absolute. From the question as to the extinction of the exclusive privileges of the Jews, he had ascended to the question of God's appointed plan for the salvation of mankind—its nature, its world-wide freedom, its necessity. That plan the Apostle sums up in the one formula, JUSTIFICATION BY FAITH, and in order to establish and explain it he had to prove the universality of human sin; the inability alike of Jew and Gentile to attain salvation by any law of works; the consequent "subordinate, relative, negative" significance of the Law; the utter and final evanescence of all difference between circumcision and uncircumcision in the light of a dispensation now first revealed. And thus the real basis of this, as of every other Epistle, is "Christ as the common foundation on which Jew and Gentile could stand, the bond of human society, the root of human righteousness."[2] It may be quite true that throughout all these high reasonings, and the many questions to which they give rise, there runs an undertone of controversy, and that the Apostle never lost sight of the fact that he was endeavouring to prove for the Roman Christians, and through them to the entire Church, the new and startling doctrine that, since the annihilation of sin was rendered possible by faith, and faith alone, all claims founded on Jewish particularism were reduced to nothingness. This is the main point; but even the practical questions which receive a brief decision at the close of the Epistle, are handled in strict accordance with the great principles which he has thus established of the Universality of Sin, and the Universality of Grace.[3]

Such seems to me to be the origin and the idea of the Epistle to the Romans, of which Luther says that "it is the masterpiece of the New Testament, and the purest gospel, which can never be too much read or studied, and the more it is handled, the more precious it becomes;" on which Melancthon founded the doctrinal system of the Reformed Church; which Coleridge called "the most profound work in existence;" in which Tholuck, who wrote the first really important and original commentary upon it in recent times, saw "a Christian philosophy of universal history." Its general outline may be given as follows:—After a full and solemn greeting, he passes, in the simplest and most natural manner, to state his fundamental thesis of justi-

[1] See Baur, *Paul.* ii. 328.

[2] Maurice, *Unity*, p. 477.

[3] If we were to choose one phrase as expressing most of the idea of the Epistle, it would be, "As in Adam all die, even so in Christ shall all be made alive" (1 Cor. xv. 22). "Its precepts naturally arise from its doctrinal assertions, that (1) all are guilty before God; that (2) all need a Saviour; that (3) Christ died for all; that (4) we are all one body in Him" (Bp. Wordsworth's *Epistles*, p. 200).

fication by faith,[1] which he illustrates and supports by quoting the Septuagint version of Hab. ii. 4. The necessity for this mode of salvation rests in the universality of sin—a fact taught, indeed, by human experience, but too apt to be overlooked, and therefore needing to be argumentatively enforced. Thus Jews and Gentiles are reduced to the same level, and the exceptional privileges of the Jew do but add to his condemnation (i. 16—iii. 20). Consequently by the works of the Law—whether the natural or the Mosaic Law—no flesh can be justified, and justification can only be obtained by the faith of man accepting the redemption of Christ, so that all alike are dependent on the free will of God (iii. 21—30).[2] Aware of the extreme novelty of these conclusions, he illustrates them by Scripture (iii. 31—iv. 25), and then dwells on the blessed consequences of this justification (v. 1—11). These consequences are foreshadowed in the whole moral and religious history of mankind as summed up in the two periods represented by Adam and by Christ (v. 12—21). Having thus completed the statement of his great doctrine, he meets the objections which may be urged against it. So far from diminishing the heinousness, or tending to the multiplication of sin, he shows that it involves the radical annihilation of sin (vi.). If any were startled at the close juxtaposition of the Law and sin, he points out that while the Law in itself is holy, just, and good, on the other hand what he has said of it, relatively to mankind, is demonstrated by its psychological effects, and that in point of fact the Law is, for the changed nature of the believer, superseded by a new principle of life—by the Spirit of God quickening the heart of man (vii. 1—viii. 11). This naturally leads him to a serious appeal to his readers to live worthily of this changed nature, and to a magnificent outburst of thanksgiving, which rises at last into a climax of impassioned eloquence (viii. 12—39).

At this point he finds himself face to face with the question from which his thoughts probably started—the relations of Judaism to Heathenism, and of Christianity to both. In an episode of immense importance, especially to the age in which he wrote, he shows that God's promises to Israel, when rightly understood, both *had* been, and *should* be, fulfilled, and that—so far as they seemed for the moment to have been made void—the failure was due to the obstinate hardness of the chosen people (ix.—xi.). The remainder of the Epistle is more practical and popular. He urges the duties of holiness, humility, unity, the faithful use of opportunities, hope, and above all love, on which he dwells earnestly and at length (xii.). Then, perhaps with special reference to the theocratic prejudices of Jewish Christians, he enforces the duty of obedience to civil authority, and reverts once more to love as the chief of Christian graces; enforcing these practical exhortations by the thought that the night of sin and ignorance was now far spent, and the day was

[1] ὁ δὲ δίκαιος ἐκ πίστεώς [μου] ζήσεται. The *μου* is omitted by St. Paul, and, indeed, by many MSS. of the LXX. (see *supra* on Gal. iii. 11).

[2] This passage contains the very quintessence of Pauline theology. See it admirably explained and developed by Reuss, *Théol. Chrét.* ii. 18—107.

near (xiii.). He then points out the necessity for mutual forbearance and mutual charity between the strong and the weak—that is, between those who considered themselves bound by legal prescriptions, and those who realised that from such elements they were emancipated by the glorious liberty of the children of God; mingling with these exhortations some reference to the views which he had already expressed about the mutual relation of Jews and Christians (xiv.—xv. 13). The remainder of the Epistle is chiefly personal. He first offers an earnest and graceful apology for having thus ventured to address a strange Church—an apology based on his apostolic mission (xv. 14—21)—and then sketches the outline of his future plans, specially entreating their prayers for the good success of his approaching visit to Jerusalem. In the last chapter, which I have given reasons for believing to have been addressed, at any rate in part, not to Romans, but to Ephesians, he recommends Phœbe to the kindly care of the Church (1, 2); sends affectionate salutations to six-and-twenty of the brethren (3—16); gives a severe warning against those who fostered divisions, which concludes with a promise and a benediction (17—20); repeats the benediction after a few salutations from the friends who were with him (21—24); and ends with an elaborate and comprehensive doxology, in which some have seen "a liturgical antiphony in conformity with the fundamental thought of the Epistle."[1]

II.

GENERAL THESIS OF THE EPISTLE.

Ὦ τοῦ ἰδιώτου τὸ θαῦμα ὢ τοῦ ἀγραμμάτου ἡ σοφία.—Ps. Chrys. *Orat. Encom.* (Opp. viii. 10).

"Such we are in the sight of God the Father, as is the very Son of God Himself. Let it be counted folly, or frenzy, or fury, or whatsoever. It is our wisdom and our comfort; we care for no knowledge in the world but this, that man hath sinned, and God hath suffered; that God hath made Himself the Son of men, and men are made the righteousness of God."—Hooker, *Serm.* ii. 6.

"It breaketh the window that it may let in the light; it breaketh the shell that we may eat the kernel; it putteth aside the curtain that we may enter into the most Holy Place: it removeth the cover of the well that we may come by the water."—*Pref. to Authorised Version.*

We must now look more closely at this great outline of one of the most essential factors of Christian theology; and I must ask my readers, Bible in hand, to follow step by step its solemn truths as they gradually expand themselves before our view.

The Salutation, which occupies the first seven verses, is remarkable as

[1] *v.* Lange, *ad loc.*

being the longest and most solemnly emphatic of those found in any of his Epistles. Had he adopted the ordinary method of his day, he would have simply headed his letter with the words, "Paul, an Apostle of Jesus Christ, to the Roman Christians, greeting."[1] But he had discovered an original method of giving to his first salutation a more significant and less conventional turn, and of making it the vehicle for truths to which he desired from the first to arrest attention. Thus, in one grand single sentence, of which the unity is not lost in spite of digressions, amplifications, and parentheses, he tells the Roman Christians of his solemn setting apart,[2] by grace, to the Apostolate; of the object and universality of that Apostolate; of the truth that the Gospel is no daring novelty, but the preordained fulfilment of a dispensation prophesied in Scripture;[3] of Christ's descent from David, according to the flesh, and of his establishment with power as the Son of God according to the spirit of holiness[4] by the resurrection of the dead.[5]

We ask, as we read the sentence, whether any one has ever compressed more thoughts into fewer words, and whether any letter was ever written which swept so vast an horizon in its few opening lines?[6]

He passes on to his customary thanksgiving "by Jesus Christ" for the widely-rumoured faith of the Christians at Rome;[7] and solemnly assures them how, in his unceasing prayers on their behalf, he supplicates God that he may be enabled to visit them, because he yearns to see them, and impart to them, for their stability, some spiritual gift.[8] Then, with infinite delicacy, correcting an expression which, to strangers, might seem to savour of assumed authority, he explains that what he longs for is an *interchange* between them of mutual encouragement;[9] for he wishes them to know[10] that, though hindered hitherto, he has often planned to come to them, that he might reap among them, as among all other Gentiles, some of the fruit of his ministry. The Gospel has been entrusted to him, and he regards it as something due from him, a debt which he has to pay to all Gentiles alike, whether Greeks or non-Greeks, whether civilised or uncivilised. He is therefore eager, so far as

[1] This is the earliest letter which he addresses to "the saints." His former letters were all addressed "to the Church" or "Churches" (1, 2 Thess., 1, 2 Cor., Gal.). It is also the first in which he calls himself "a slave of Jesus Christ."

[2] ἀφωρισμένος. Cf. Acts xiii. 2, ἀφορίσατε.

[3] γραφαὶ ἅγιαι, not "sacred writings," but like ἱερὰ γράμματα, a proper name for the Scriptures, and therefore anarthrous.

[4] The form of expression is of course antithetical, but it seems to me that Dr. Forbes, in his *Analytical Commentary*, pushes this antithesis to most extravagant lengths.

[5] 1—7. In ver. 4, ἀνάστασις νεκρῶν, is not "from" (ἐκ), but "of" the dead, regarded as accomplished in Christ. The notions of χάρις and εἰρήνη are united in Num. vi. 25, 26.

[6] "Epistola tota sic methodica est, ut ipsum quoque exordium ad rationem artis compositum sit" (Calvin).

[7] The ἐν ὅλῳ τῷ κόσμῳ of course only means among the humble and scattered Christian communities, and therefore furnishes no argument against the truth of Acts xxviii. 21, 22.

[8] The expressions in these verses (ἐπιποθῶ, 11; συμπαρακληθῆναι, 12; προεθέμην, ἐκωλύθην, καρπὸν, 13; ὀφειλέτης, 14) are closely analogous to those in xv. (ἐνεκοπτόμην, 22; ἐπιποθίαν, 23; ὀφειλέται, 27; συναναπαύσωμαι, 32).

[9] Cf. xv. 24. Erasmus goes too far in calling this a "*sancta adulatio.*"

[10] οὐ θέλω δὲ ὑμᾶς ἀγνοεῖν, xi. 25; 1 Thess. iv. 13; 1 Cor. x. 1, xii. 1; 2 Cor. i. 8.

it depends on him, to preach the Gospel even in the world's capital, even in imperial Rome.[1]

This leads him to the fundamental theme, which he intends to treat. Many are ashamed of that Gospel; he is not;[2] *"for it is the power of God unto salvation to every one that believeth, to the Jew first,[3] and also to the Greek. For in it God's righteousness is being revealed from faith to faith, even as it is written, 'But the just shall live by faith.'"*[4]

How easy are these words to read! Yet they require the whole Epistle for their adequate explanation, and many volumes have been written to elucidate their meaning. Rome is the very centre of human culture, the seat of the widest, haughtiest despotism which the world has ever seen, and he is well aware that to the world's culture the Cross is foolishness, and feebleness to the world's power. Yet he is not ashamed of the Gospel of that Cross, for to all who will believe it, whether the Jew to whom it was first offered or the Greek to whom it is now proclaimed, it is the display of God's power in order to secure their salvation. Even those few words "to the Jew first, and *also to the Greek*" are the sign that a new aeon has dawned upon the world; and having thus indicated in two lines the source (God's power), the effect (salvation), and the universality of the Gospel (to Jew and Gentile), he proceeds to sum up its essence. "In it," he says, "God's righteousness is being revealed from faith to faith."

We repeat the familiar words, but what meaning should we attach to them? It would take a lifetime to read all that has been written about them in interminable pages of dreary exegesis, drearier metaphysics, and dreariest controversy. Traducianist and Pelagian, Calvinist and Arminian, Sublapsarian and Supralapsarian, Solifidian and Gospeller, Legalist and Antinomian, Methodist and Baptist, have wrangled about them for centuries, and strewn the field of polemical theology with the scattered and cumbering *débris* of technicalities and anathemas. From St. Augustine to St. Thomas of Aquinum, and from St. Thomas to Whitefield, men have—

"Reasoned high
Of providence, foreknowledge, will, and fate,
Fixed fate, free-will, foreknowledge absolute,
And found no end in wandering mazes lost;"

and their controversies have mainly turned on these words. Does it not seem presumptuous to endeavour to express in one simple sentence what they appear to state?[5] Not if we distinguish between "ideas of the head" and "feelings

[1] i. 8—15.

[2] What cause he might have had to be tempted to shame by the feelings of the lordlier and more cultivated Gentiles may be seen in the remark of Tacitus (*Ann.* xv. 44), who classes Christianity among the "cuncta atrocia aut pudenda" which flow together into the vortex of Roman life.

[3] πρῶτον, precedence, genetic and historical (John iv. 22; Acts i. 8).

[4] i. 16, 17.

[5] It will be observed that the true explanation of the *meaning of the words* is one thing, and one which may be regarded as approximately certain; the adequate explana-

of the heart." Not if we bear in mind that these controversies arise mainly from "the afterthoughts of theology." We can only understand St. Paul's views in the light of his own repeated elucidations, comments, and varied modes of expression; yet with this guidance we should sum up the results of endless discussions, prolonged for a thousand years, by interpreting his words to mean that *In the Gospel is being made known*[1] *to the world that inherent righteousness of God, which, by a judgment of acquittal pronounced once for all in the expiatory death of Christ, He imputes to guilty man, and which beginning for each individual, with his trustful acceptance of this reconciliation of himself to God in Christ, ends in that mystical union with Christ whereby Christ becomes to each man a new nature, a quickening spirit.*

It is impossible, I think, in fewer words to give the full interpretation of this pregnant thesis. The end and aim of the Gospel of God is the salvation of man. Man is sinful, and cannot by any power of his own attain to holiness. Yet without holiness no man can see the Lord. Therefore, without holiness no man can be saved. How, then, is holiness to be attained? The Gospel is the answer to that question, and this Epistle is the fullest and most consecutive exposition of this divine dispensation. The essence of the answer is summed up in the one phrase "JUSTIFICATION BY FAITH." In this verse it is expressed as "the righteousness and justice of God" which "is being revealed in the Gospel from faith to faith." The word for "righteousness" is also rendered "justification." But neither of this word, nor of the word "faith," has St. Paul ever given a formal definition. It is only from his constantly-varied phrases, and from the reasonings by which he supports, and the quotations by which he illustrates them, that we can ascertain his meaning. Many writers have maintained that this meaning is vague and general, incapable of being reduced to rigid and logical expression, impossible to tesselate into any formal scheme of salvation. We must not overlook the one element of truth which underlies these assertions. Undoubtedly there is a vast gulf between the large impassioned utterances of mystic fervour and the cold analytic reasonings of technical theology; between emotional expressions and elaborate systems; between Orientalism and scholasticism; between St. Paul and St. Thomas of Aquinum. Speculative metaphysics, *doctrines* of sin, *theories* of imputation, transcendental ontology—these in the course of time were inevitable; but these are not the foundation, not the essence, not the really important element of Christianity. This has been too much forgotten. Yet there is all the difference in the world between understanding what Paul meant to express, and pretending to have fathomed to their utmost depths the Eternal Truths which lie behind his doctrine; and it is perfectly possible for us to comprehend God's scheme, so far as it affects our actions and our hopes, without

tion of the *doctrine* is quite another thing, and all attempt to do it lands us at once in the region of insoluble mysteries. "We cannot measure the arm of God with the finger of man."

[1] ἀποκαλύπτεται—"progressive revelation," but ἐφανερώθη, it has been once for all manifested; or rather πεφανέρωται (iii. 21) has been manifested *now and for ever*.

attempting to arrange in the pigeon-holes of our logical formulæ the incomprehensible mysteries encircling that part of it which has alone been opened for our learning.

1. We may, then, pronounce with reasonable certainty that in this memorable thesis of the Epistle, "*God's righteousness*," which, in the first instance, means a quality of God, is an expression which St. Paul uses to express the imputation of this righteousness by free bestowal upon man, so that man can regard it as a thing given to himself—a righteousness which proceeds from God and constitutes a new relation of man towards Him—a justification of man, a declaration of man's innocence—an acquittal from guilt through Christ given by free grace—the principle, ordained by God himself, which determines the religious character of the race, and by which the religious consciousness of the individual is conditioned.[1]

2. And when St. Paul says that this "righteousness of God" springs "*from faith*," he does not mean that faith is in any way the meritorious *cause* of it, for he shows that man is justified by free grace, and that this justification has its *ground* in the spontaneous favour of God, and its *cause* in the redemptive work of Christ;[2] but what he means is that faith is the receptive instrument[3] of it—the personal appropriation of the reconciling love of God, which has once for all been carried into effect for the race by the death of Christ.

3. Lastly, when he says that this righteousness of God is being revealed in the Gospel "from faith *to faith*," he implies the truth, which finds frequent illustration in his writings, that there are ascensive degrees and qualities of Christian faith.[4] Leaving out of sight the dead faith (*fides informis*) of the schoolmen, its lowest stage (i.) is the being theoretically persuaded of God's favour to us in Christ on higher grounds than those of sensuous perception and ordinary experience, namely, because we have confidence in God (*assensus fiducia*). In a higher stage (ii.) it has touched the inmost emotions of the

[1] Pfleiderer, *Paulinism*, i. 178. "The acceptance wherewith God receives us into His favour as if we were righteous—it consists in the forgiveness of sins and the imputation of the righteousness of Christ" (Calvin). "Faith taketh hold of Christ, and hath Him enclosed, as the ring doth the precious stone. And whosoever shall be found having this confidence in Christ apprehended in the heart, him will God accept for righteous" (Luther). [See, too, the twelve ancient authorities quoted in the Homily on the salvation of mankind.] "The righteousness wherewith we shall be clothed in the world to come is both perfect and inherent; that whereby here we are justified is perfect, but not inherent—that whereby we are sanctified, inherent, but not perfect" (Hooker, Serm. ii. 3). "The righteousness which God gives and which he approves" (Hodges). "The very righteousness of God Himself . . . imputed and imparted to men in Jesus Christ (Jer. xxiii. 6; xxxiii. 16) . . . who . . . is made righteousness to us (1 Cor. i. 30) . . . so that we may be not only acquitted by God, but may become the righteous of God in Him (2 Cor. v. 21)" (Bishop Wordsworth).

[2] The Tridentine decree speaks of God's glory and eternal life as the *final*, of God as the *efficient*, of Christ as the *meritorious*, of baptism as the *instrumental*, and of God's righteousness as the *formal* cause of justification.

[3] ὄργανον ληπτικόν. We are justified *per*, not *propter* fidem (Acts x. 1, 2).

[4] "From faith to faith," *i.e.*, "which begins in faith and ends in faith, of which faith is the beginning, middle, and end" (Baur, who compares ὀσμὴ ζωῆς εἰς ζωήν, 2 Cor. ii. 16). In the first stage the *Glaube* passes into *Treue*.

heart, and has become a trustful acceptance of the gift of favour by God, "a *self-surrender of the heart* to the favourable will of God as it presents itself to us in the word of reconciliation." But it has a higher stage (iii.) even than this, in which it attains a mystical depth, and becomes a mystical *incorporation with Christ* (*unio mystica*) in a unity of love and life—a practical acquaintance with Christ, which completes itself by personal appropriation of His life and death. In its final and richest development (iv.) it has risen from the passive attitude of receptivity into a spontaneous active force—"*a living impulse and power of good in every phase of personal life.*"[1] In this last stage it becomes so closely allied to *spirit*, that what is said of the one may be said of the other, and that which regarded from without is "faith," regarded from within is "spirit." Faith, in this full range of its Pauline meaning, is both a single act and a progressive principle. As a *single act*, it is the self-surrender of the soul to God, the laying hold of Christ, the sole means whereby we appropriate this reconciling love, in which point of view it may be regarded as the root of the new relation of man to God in justification and adoption. As a *progressive principle* it is the renewal of the personal life in sanctification[2]—a preservation of the "righteousness of God" *objectively*

[1] For these ascensive uses of the word faith see (i.) Rom. iv. 18, Heb. xi. 1; (ii.) Rom. x. 9, Phil. iii. 7; (iii.) Phil. i. 21, Gal. ii. 20; (iv.) 1 Cor. vi. 17. (Baur, *N. Test. Theol.* 176.) It should be observed that in his earlier Epistles St. Paul does not use the word at all in the modern sense of "a body of doctrine," though this meaning of the word begins to appear in the Pastoral Epistles. From the lowest stage of the word, in which it merely means "belief" and "faithfulness," he rises at once to the deeper sense of "fast attachment to an unseen power of goodness," and then gradually mounts to that meaning of the word in which it is peculiar to himself, namely, mystic union, absolute incorporation, with Christ.

[2] Rom. xii. 3; 2 Cor. x. 15. "Faith," says Luther (*Preface to Romans*), "is a divine work in us, which changes us, and creates us anew in God." "Oh es ist ein lebendig, geschäftig, thätig, mächtig Ding um den Glauben, dass es unmächtig ist dass er nicht ohne Unterlass, sollte Gutes wirken. Er fragt auch nicht ob gute Werke zu thun sind, sondern ehe man fragt hat er sie gethan, und ist immer im Thun. . . . Also dass unmöglich ist Werke vom Glauben zu scheiden: ja so unmöglich als brennen und leuchten vom Feuer mag geschieden werden." Coming from hearing (ἀκοὴ πίστεως, Gal. iii., 2), it is primarily a belief of the Gospel (π. τοῦ εὐαγγελίο). As Christ is the essence of the Gospel, it becomes π. τοῦ Χριστοῦ (Gal. ii. 16, iii. 26), the faith which has its principle in Christ. It is further defined as "faith in His Blood" (Rom. iii. 24, 25), and thus is narrowed stage by stage in proportion as it grows more intense and inward, passing from theoretical assent to certainty of conviction (Baur, *Paul.* ii. 149). The antithesis of faith and works is only one of abstract thought; it is at once reconciled in the simple moral truth of such passages as 1 Cor. iii. 13, ix. 17, Gal. vi. 7, &c. I cannot here enter on the supposed contradiction between St. Paul and St. James. It will be sufficient to remark that they were dealing with entirely different provinces of religious life, and were using every one of the three words, "faith," "works," and "justification," in wholly different senses. By "faith" St. James (who knew nothing of its Pauline meaning), only meant outward profession of dead Jewish religiosity. By "works" Paul meant Levitism and even moral actions regarded as external; whereas James meant the *reality* of a moral and religious life. Their meeting-point may be clearly seen in 2 Cor. v. 10; Rom. ii.; 1 Cor. xiii. 1. And in the superficial contrast lies a real coincidence. "The regal law of St. James (i. 25, ii. 8) is the law of liberty in the Epistle to the Galatians. Both are confuting Jewish vanity and Pharisaism. Only the work of St. James was to confute the Pharisee by showing what was the true service of God, and that of St. Paul to show what foundation had been laid for a spiritual and universal economy after the Jewish ceremonial had crumbled" (Maurice, *Unity*, 511). See Wordsworth, *Epistles*, p. 205; Hooker, *Eccl. Pol.* I. xi. 6.

bestowed upon us, in the inward and ever-deepening righteousness of our own life; it is, in fact, a new and spiritual life, lived in the faith of the Son of God, who loved us, and gave Himself for us.[1] And hence will be seen at once the absurdity of any radical antithesis between Christian faith and Christian works, since they can no more exist apart from each other than the tree which is severed from the root, or, to use the illustration of Luther, than fire can exist apart from light and heat. "Justification and sanctification," says Calvin, "cohere, but they are not one and the same. It is faith alone which justifies, and yet the faith which justifies is not alone; just as it is the heat alone of the sun which warms the earth, and yet in the sun it is not alone, because it is always conjoined with light."

In accordance with his usual manner when he is enunciating a new truth, St. Paul seeks to support it by the Old Testament Scriptures, and reads the deeper meaning which he has now developed into the words, "The just shall live by faith," which Habakkuk had used in the far simpler sense of "the just shall be delivered by his fidelity." But St. Paul reads these simple words by the light of his own spiritual illumination, which, like the fabled splendour on the graven gems of the Urim, makes them flash into yet diviner oracles. Into the words "faith" and "life" he infuses a significance which he had learnt from revelation, and, as has been truly said, where Habakkuk ends, Paul begins. And, in fact, his very phrase, "justification by faith," marks the meeting-point of two dispensations. The conception of "justification" has its roots in Judaism; the conception of "faith" is peculiarly Christian. The latter word so completely dominates over the former, that δικαιοσύνη from its first meaning of "righteousness," a quality of God, comes to mean subjectively "justification" as a condition of man—the adequate relation in which man has to stand towards God. Man's appropriation of God's reconciling love in Christ has issued in a change in man's personal life: justification has become sanctification, which is the earnest of future glory.

III.

UNIVERSALITY OF SIN.

"Ruit in vetitum, damni secura, libido."—CLAUD.

HAVING thus endeavoured to render clear the one subject which underlies the entire system of St. Paul's theology, we can proceed more rapidly in trying to catch his line of thought through the remainder of the Epistle.

[1] See the two very valuable sections on Faith and Justification in Pfleiderer's *Paulinisium*, § v. Other explanations of "from faith to faith" are—1, "from the Old to the New Testament" (Origen, Chrys., &c.); 2, "Ex fide legis in fidem evangelii" (Tert.); 3, "from faith *to the believer*" (iii. 22; Olshausen, &c.); 4, "from weak to strong faith" (cf. 2 Cor. iii. 18; Ps. lxxxiv. 7; Luther, &c.); 5, "An intensive expression = *mera fides;* faith the *prora et puppis* (Bengel, &c.); 6, From Divine faithfulness to human faith (Ewald). Cf. Heb. xii. 2, "the *author* and *finisher* of our faith" (Lange, *ad loc.*).

i. Now, since the Apostle had already dwelt on the universality of the Gospel, it was necessary to show that it applied equally to Jews and Pagans; that the universality of free grace was necessitated by the universality of wilful sin. Righteousness and sin, soteriology and hamartiology, are the fundamental thoughts in St. Paul's theological system. The first is a theoretic consequence of our conception of God's nature; the second an historic fact deducible from experience and conscience.

As there is a righteousness of God which is being revealed in the Gospel, so, too, there is a wrath of God against sin which is ever being revealed from heaven, by the inevitable working of God's own appointed laws, against all godlessness and unrighteousness of those who in their unrighteousness suppress the truth.[1] And since the world is mainly Gentile, he speaks of the Gentiles first. Some might imagine that their ignorance of God made them excusable. Not so. The facts which render them inexcusable[2] are (i.) that God did in reality manifest Himself to them, and the invisibilities of His eternal power and Godhead were clearly visible in His works;[3] and (ii.) that though they knew God, yet by denying Him the due glory and gratitude, they suffered themselves to plunge into the penal darkness of ignorant speculation, and the penal folly of self-asserted wisdom, and the self-convicted boast of a degraded culture, until they sank to such depths of spiritual imbecility as to end even in the idolatry of reptiles;[4] and (iii.) because mental infatuation, both as its natural result and as its fearful punishment, issued in moral crime. Their sin was inexcusable, because it was the outcome and the retribution, and the natural child, of sin. Because they guiltily abandoned God, God abandoned them to their own guiltiness.[5] The conscious lie of idolatry became the conscious infamy of uncleanness. Those "passions of dishonour" to which God abandoned them rotted the heart of manhood with their retributive corruption, and affected even women with their execrable stain.[6] Pagan society, in its hideous disintegration, became one foul disease of unnatural depravity. The cancer of it ate into the heart; the miasma of it tainted the air. Even the moralists of Paganism were infected with its vileness.[7] God scourged their moral ignorance by suffering it to become a deeper ignorance. He punished their contempt by letting them make themselves utterly contemptible. The mere consequence of this abandonment of them was a natural Nemesis, a justice in kind, beginning even in this life, whereby their unwillingness to discern *Him* became an *incapacity* to discern[8] the most elementary

[1] κατεχόντων (τὴν ἀλήθειαν), i. 18. In 19, τὸ γνωστὸν is "that which *is* known," not "which *may* be known." Ἀποκαλύπτεται, is being revealed. "The modes of the New Testament converge towards the present moment" (Jowett).

[2] In verse 20, obviously εἰς τὸ εἶναι, κ. τ. λ., expresses rather a *consequence* than a *purpose*.

[3] ἀόρατα καθορᾶται, "*Invisibilia videntur*" an admirable oxymoron. "Deum non vides, tamen Deum agnoscis ex ejus operibus" (Cic. *Q. T.* i. 29. Cf. *De Div.* ii. 72). The world was to the Gentiles a θεογνωσίας παιδευτήριον (Basil). On this point see Humboldt, *Cosmos*, ii. 16.

[4] As in Egypt. Egyptian worship was now spreading in Italy:—

> "Nos in templa tuam Romana recepimus Isim
> Semideosque canes" (Luc. *Phars.* viii. 83).

[5] Verse 24, παρέδωκε, "non *permissivè*, nec ἐκβατικῶς sed δικαστικῶς"—*i.e.*, not as a mere result, but as a judgment in kind.

[6] This is the period of which Seneca says that women counted their years by the number of their divorced husbands (*De Benef.* iii. 15).

[7] There are only too awful and only too exhaustive proofs of all this, and (if possible), worse than all this, in Döllinger, *Heidenthum und Judenthum*, 684. But "Ostendi debent *scelera* dum puniuntur *abscondi flagitia*."

[8] i. 28, καθὼς οὐκ ἐδοκίμασαν . . . παρέδωκεν . . . εἰς ἀδόκιμον νοῦν, "As they

distinctions between nobleness and shame. Therefore, their hearts became surcharged with every element of vileness;—with impurity in its most abysmal degradations, with hatred alike in its meanest and its most virulent developments, with insolence culminating in the deliberate search for fresh forms of evil,[1] with cruelty and falsity in their most repulsive features. And the last worst crime of all—beyond which crime itself could go no further—was the awfully *defiant* attitude of moral evil, which led them—while they were fully aware of God's sentence of death,[2] pronounced on willing guilt—not only to incur it themselves, but, with a devilish delight in human depravity and human ruin, to take a positive pleasure in those who practise the same. Sin, as has been truly said, reaches its climax in wicked *maxims* and wicked *principles*. It is no longer Vice the result of moral weakness, or the outcome of an evil education, but Vice deliberately accepted with all its consequences, Vice assuming the airs of self-justification, Vice in act becoming Vice in elaborate theory—the unblushing shamelessness of Sodom in horrible aggravation of its polluting sin.[3]

Thus did Paul brand the insolent brow of Pagan life. It is well for the world—it is above all well for the world in those ages of transition and decay, when there is ever an undercurrent or tendency towards Pagan ideals—to know what Paganism was, and ever tended to become. It is well for the world that it should have been made to see, once for all, what features lurked under the smiling mask, what a heart of agony, rank with hatred, charred with self-indulgence,[4] lay throbbing under the purple robe. And in St. Paul's description not one accusation is too terrible, not one colour is too dark. He does but make known to us what heathen writers unblushingly reveal in those passages in which, like waves of a troubled sea, they foam out their own mire and dirt.[5] It is false to say that Christianity has added to the gloom of the world. It is false that it has weakened its literature, or cramped its art. It has been wilfully perverted; it has been ignorantly misunderstood. Rightly interpreted it does not sanction a single doctrine, or utter a single precept, which is meant to extinguish one happy impulse, or dim one innocent delight.

refused . . . God gave them to a *refuse* mind" (Vaughan, *ad loc.*). St. Paul was deeply impressed (24, 26, 28) with the ethic retributive law of the punishment of sin with sin. It was recognised both by Jews and Gentiles (*Pirke Abhôth*, iv. 2; Sen. *Ep.* 16).

[1] i. 30, ἐφευρετὰς κακῶν (2 Macc. vii. 31). Pliny (*H. N.* xv. 5) applies this very expression to the Greeks. *Some* of these words occur in speaking of corruptions *within* the Church (2 Tim. iii. 2); "of so little avail is *nominal* Christianity" (Vaughan); εὑρετὴς ἀγαθῶν (Prov. xvi. 20).

[2] i. 32, τὸ δικαίωμα, "the just decree;" ποιοῦσιν, "single acts;" πράσσουσιν, "habitual condition." Possibly an οὐκ has dropped out before ἐπιγνόντες ("they did *not fully* know"), of which some readings show a trace.

[3] i. 16—32. The Apostle is fond of these accumulative lists (συναθροισμὸς) of good and evil (2 Cor. xii. 20; Gal. v. 19; Eph. v. 3, 4; 1 Tim. i. 9; 2 Tim. iii. 2). No satisfactory classification of the order can be made. Bengel says, "Per membra *novem*, in affectibus; *duo* in sermone; *tria* respectu Dei et sui, et proximi; *duo* in rebus gerendis; *sex* respectu necessitudinum." On verses 27, 28, the best comment is to be found in Aristophanes, Juvenal, and Suetonius; on 29—31, in Thuc. iii. 82—84. See the contemporary testimony of Sen. *De Irâ*, ii. 8, "Omnia sceleribus ac vitiis plena sunt . . . nec furtiva jam scelera sunt." The special horror of the age is reflected in Tac. *H.* i. 2, and *passim*. "Le premier siècle de notre ère a un cachet infernal qui n'appartient qu'à lui; le siècle des Borgia peut seul lui être comparé en fait de scélératesse" (Renan, *Mélanges*, p. 167).

[4] i. 27, ἐξεκαύθησαν.

[5] Jud. 13; Isa. lvii. 20.

What it does is to warn us against seeking and following the lowest and most short-lived pleasures as a final end. This was the fatal error of the popular Hedonism. St. Paul's sketch of its moral dissolution and the misery and shame which it inevitably involved, is but another illustration of the truth that

> "Who follows pleasure, pleasure slays,
> God's wrath upon himself he wreaks;
> But all delights attend his days
> Who takes with thanks but never seeks."

ii. Having thus accomplished his task of proving the guilt of the Gentiles, he turns to the Jews. But he does so with consummate tact. He does not at once startle them into antagonism, by shocking all their prejudices, but begins with the perfectly general statement, "Therefore[1] thou art inexcusable, O man—*every one* who judgest." The "therefore" impetuously anticipates the reason why he who judges others is, in this instance, inexcusable—namely, because he does the same things himself. He does not at once say, as he might have done, "You who are Jews are as inexcusable as the Gentiles, because in judging them you are condemning yourselves, and though you habitually call them 'sinners' you are no less sinners yourselves."[2] This is the conclusion at which he points, but he wishes the Jew to be led step by step into self-condemnation, less hollow than vague generalities.[3] He is of course speaking alike of Jews and of Pagans *generically*, and not implying that there were no exceptions. But he has to introduce the argument against the Jews carefully and gradually, because, blinded by their own privileges, they were apt to take a very different view of their own character. But they were less excusable because more enlightened. He therefore begins, "O man," and not "O Jew," and asks the imaginary person to whom he is appealing whether he thinks that God will in his case make an individual exception to His own inflexible decrees? or whether he intends to despise the riches of God's endurance, by ignoring[4] that its sole intention is to lead him to repentance—and so to heap up against himself a horrible treasury of final ruin? God's law is rigid, universal, absolute. It is that God will repay every man all to his works.[5] This law is illustrated by a twofold amplification, which, beginning and ending with the reward of goodness, and inserting twice over in the

[1] This Διὸ of ii. 1 is clearly *proleptic*.

[2] Gal. ii. 15, ἡμεῖς φύσει Ἰουδαῖοι, καὶ οὐκ ἐξ ἐθνῶν ἁμαρτωλοί. Meyer truly says this judging of the Gentiles (which they little dreamt would be pointed out to them as self-condemnation, by one of themselves) was a characteristic of the Jews.

[3] Thus the High-priest said over the scapegoat, "Thy people have failed, sinned, and transgressed before Thee" (*Yoma*, 66 *a*).

[4] Ver. 4, ἀγνοῶν. Ἄγει, "Deus ducit *volentem* duci . . . non cogit necessitate" (Bengel).

[5] The apparent contradiction to the fundamental theme of the Epistle is due to his speaking here of ordinary morality. "The divine valuation placed on men apart from redemption" (Tholuck). Fritzsche's comment that "the Apostle is here inconsistent, and opens a *semita per honestatem* near the *via regia* of justification" is very off-hand and valueless.

middle clause the punishment of sin,[1] expresses the thought that this rule applies to *all*, by twice repeating that it applies to the Jew first and also to the Greek; but to the Jew *first*, only because of his fuller knowledge and, therefore, deeper responsibility. And having thus introduced the name of the Jew, he lays down with a firm hand the eternal principle—so infinitely blessed, yet so startlingly new to the prejudices of a nation which for more than a thousand years had been intoxicating itself with the incense of spiritual pride—that *there is no respect of persons with God*. Each section of humanity shall be judged in accordance with its condition.

"As many as sinned without the Law, shall also without the Law perish; and as many as sinned in the Law, shall be condemned by the Law." Righteousness before God depends, not on *possession* of the Law, but on *obedience* to it. Gentiles as well as Jews had a law; Jews the Mosaic law, Gentiles a natural law written on their hearts, and sufficiently clear to secure, at the day of judgment,[2] their acquittal or condemnation before the prophetic session of their own consciences, in accordance with the decision of Christ the Judge.[3] Jew, then, and Gentile stand before God equally guilty, because equally condemned of failure to fulfil the moral law which God had laid down to guide their lives. The word "*ALL*," as has been truly observed, is the governing word of the entire Epistle. *All*—for whatever may be the modifications which may be thought necessary, St. Paul does not himself make them—*all* are equally guilty, *all* are equally redeemed. All have been temporarily rejected, all shall be ultimately received. All shall be finally brought into living harmony with that God who is above all, and through all, and in all,—by whom, and from whom, and unto whom, all things are, and all things tend.[4]

And then Paul turns upon the self-satisfied Jew, who has been thus insensibly entrapped (as it were) into the mental admission of his own culpability, and after painting in a few touches his self-satisfied pretensions to spiritual, moral, and intellectual superiority, and then leaving his sentence unfinished, bursts into a question of indignant eloquence, in which there is no longer any masked sarcasm, but terribly serious denunciation of undeniable sins. He does not use one word of open raillery, or give offence by painting in too glaring colours the weaknesses, follies, and hypocrisies of the Pharisee, yet the picture which stands out from phrases in themselves perfectly polished, and even apparently complimentary, is the picture of the full-blown religionist

[1] The figure of speech is called *Chiasmus*, or introverse parallelism. "Glory and honour, and immortality—precious pearls; eternal life—the goodly pearl, Matt. xiii. 46" (Lange).

[2] ii. 16, *leg.* κρίνει, "is judging," not κρινεῖ, "shall judge."

[3] ii. 1—16. St. Paul adds κατὰ τὸ εὐαγγέλιόν μου. "Suum appellat ratione ministerii" (Calv.). It means, of course, the Gospel of free grace which he preached to Gentiles (Gal. ii. 7). In verse 14, "Do by nature the things of the law." St. Paul (who is not here speaking with theologic precision, but dealing with general external facts) recognises even in heathens the existence of the nobler nature and its better impulses. See the remarkable expression of Aristotle, ὁ ἐλευθέριος οὕτως ἕξει οἷον νόμος ὢν ἑαυτῷ (*Eth. Nic.* iv. 14, 9). It is strange to see so great a commentator as Bengel joining φύσει with τὰ μὴ νόμον ἔχοντα, and interpreting it to mean "do the same things that the Law does," *i.e.*, commanding, condemning, punishing, &c.! Nothing would have been more amazing to St. Paul than the notion that he discouraged good works. The phrase occurs no less than fourteen times in his three last short Epistles.

[4] See Rom. v. 15—20; x. 12; 1 Cor. xv. 28; Col. iii. 11; 2 Cor. v. 15; Heb. ii. 8; &c.

in all his assumed infallibility, and the very air of the "Stand aside, for I am holier than thou."

"But if"[1] (so we may draw out the splendid rhetoric), "if thou vauntest the proud name of Jew,[2] and makest the Law the pillow of thy confidence,[3] and boastest thy monopoly in God, and art the only one who canst recognise His will, and discriminatest the transcendent[4] in niceties of moral excellence, being trained in the Law from infancy,—if thou art quite convinced that thou art a Leader of the blind, a Light of those in darkness, one who can train the foolishness, and instruct the infancy of all the world besides, possessing as thou dost the very form and body of knowledge and of truth in the Law—*thou then that teachest another, dost thou not teach thyself?* thou that preachest against theft, art thou a thief? thou that forbiddest adultery, art thou an adulterer?[5] loather of idols, dost thou rob temples?[6] boaster in the Law, by violation of the Law dost thou dishonour God? For"—and here he drops the interrogative to pronounce upon them the categorical condemnation which was as true then as in the days of the Prophet—"for on your account the name of God is being blasphemed among the Gentiles."[7] They had relied on sacrifices and offerings, on tithes and phylacteries, on ablutions and *mezuzoth*,—but "*omnia vanitas praeter amare Deum et illi soli servire*,"—"all things are emptiness save to love God, and serve Him only,"—and this weightier matter of the Law they had utterly neglected in scrupulous attention to its most insignificant minutiæ. In fact, the difference between Heathenism and Judaism before God was the difference between Vice and Sin. The Jews were guilty of the sin of violating express commands; the heathens sank into an actual degradation of nature. The heathens had been punished for an unnatural transposition of the true order of the universe by being suffered to pervert all natural relations, and so to sink into moral self-debasement; but the Jews had been "admitted into a holier sanctuary," and so were "guilty of a deeper sacrilege."[8]

[1] ii. 17, εἰ δὲ, and not ἴδε, is almost unquestionably the true reading, ℵ, A, B, D, K, "oratio vehemens et splendida" (Est.).

[2] ἐπονομάζῃ.

[3] Verse 17, ἐπαναπαύῃ.

[4] Verse 18, δοκιμάζεις τὰ διαφέροντα. See Heb. v. 14. The διαστολὴ ἁγίων καὶ βεβήλων (Philo) was the very function of a Rabbi; and the Pharisee was a Separatist, because of his scrupulosity in these distinctions.

[5] Verse 21, on the morality of the Pharisees and Rabbis, see Surenhusius, *Mishna*, ii. 290—293, and cf. Jas. iv. 4—13; v. 1—6; Matt. xix. 8; xxiii. 13—25. Josephus calls his own generation the most ungodly of all, and says that earthquake and lightning must have destroyed them if the Romans had not come. *B. J.* iv. 3, § 3; v. 9, § 4; 10, § 5; 13, § 6. Take the single fact that the "ordeal of jealousy" had been abolished, because of the prevalence of adultery, by R. Johanan ben Zaccai quoting Hos. iv. 14 (*Sotah*, f. 47, 1).

[6] Verse 22, ὁ βδελυσσόμενος. They called idols תּוֹעֵבָה, βδελύγματα, 2 Kings xxiii. 13, &c. LXX. ἱεροσυλεῖς. The reference is not clear, but see Deut. vii. 25; Acts xix. 36, 37; Jos. *Antt.* iv. 8, § 10; xx. 9, § 2. Or does it refer to defrauding their own Temple? (Mal. i. 8; iii. 8—10.) σπήλαιον λῃστῶν (Matt. xxi. 13). Josephus quotes a Greek historian, Lysimachus, who said that from the conduct of the Jews in robbing the Temples of their charms that city was called *Hierosyla* (*Temple-plunder*) and afterwards changed to Hierosolyma; a story which he angrily rejects (*c. Ap.* i. 34).

[7] ii. 17—24. In verse 24 the *words* of Isa. lii. 5 are curiously combined with the *sense* of Ezek. xxxvi. 21—23.

[8] The needfulness of this demonstration may be seen from the fact that some of the Talmudists regarded perfection as possible. They denied the sinfulness of *evil thoughts* by interpreting Ps. lxvi. 18 to mean—"If I contemplate iniquity in my heart, the *Lord does not notice it*" (*Kiddushin*, f. 40, 1). R. Jehoshua Ben Levi, admitted to Paradise without dying, is asked if the rainbow has appeared in his days, and answers "Yes." "Then," said they, "thou art not the son of Levi, for the rainbow never appears when there is one perfectly righteous man in the world." "The fact was that no rainbow *had* appeared, but he was too modest to say so"! (*Kiddushin*, f. 40, 1).

From this impassioned strain he descends—in a manner very characteristic of his style—into a calmer tone. "But"—some Jew might urge, in accordance with the stubborn prejudices of theological assumption, which by dint of assertion, has passed into invincible belief—"but *we* are *circumcised!* Surely you would not put *us* on a level with the uncircumcised—the dogs and sinners of the Gentiles?" To such an implied objection, touching as it does on a point wholly secondary, however primary might be the importance which the Jew attached to it, St. Paul can now give a very decisive answer, because with wonderful power he has already stripped them of all genuine precedence, and involved them in a common condemnation. He therefore replies in words which, however calm and grave, would have sounded to a Jerusalem Pharisee like stinging paradox.

"Circumcision is indeed an advantage if thou keepest the Law; but if thou art—as I have generically shown that thou art—a violator of the Law, then *thy circumcision has become uncircumcision.*[1] If, then, the circumcision of the disobedient Jew is really uncircumcision, is it not conversely plain that the 'uncircumcision of the obedient Gentile is virtually circumcision,'[2] and is even in a position to pass judgment upon Jewish circumcision? God (strange and heretical as you may think it) loves the man who does his duty more than the man who bears a cutting in his flesh. You praise literal circumcision; God praises the unseen circumcision of the heart. Offensive as the antithesis may sound to you, the faithless Jew is but a Gentile; the faithful Gentile is, in God's sight, an honoured Jew! Though none may have told you this truth before—though you denounce it as blasphemous, and dangerous, and contrary to Scripture—yet, for all that, the mere national Judaism is a spiritual nonentity; the Judaism of moral faithfulness alone is dear to God."[3]

IV.

OBJECTIONS AND CONFIRMATIONS.

"The stars of morn shall see Him rise
Out of His grave, fresh as the dawning light;
Thy ransom paid, which man from death redeems,
His death for man, as many as offered life
Neglect not, and the benefit embrace
Of faith, not void of works."—MILTON, *Par. Lost*, xii. 422.

So far then, both by fact and by theory, he has shown that Jews and Gentiles are equal before God; equally guilty, equally redeemed. But here a Jew might exclaim in horror, "Has the Jew then no superiority? Is circumcision wholly without advantage?" Here St. Paul makes a willing concession, and

[1] This is reluctantly admitted even in the Talmud. The Rabbis hold generally that "no circumcised man can see hell" (*Midr. Tillin*, 7, 2); but they get over the moral danger of the doctrine by saying that when a guilty Jew comes to Gehenna, an angel makes his περιτομή into ἀκροβυστία (*Shem. Rabbah*, 138, 13; cf. 1 Macc. i. 15; Jos. *Antt.* xii. 6, § 2), and they even entered into minute particulars to show how it was done.

[2] Ford quotes an imitation from Tillotson—if we walk contrary to the Gospel "*our baptism is no baptism*, and *our Christianity is heathenism*" (Sermon on 2 Tim. ii. 19).

[3] ii. 25—29.

replies, "Much advantage every way. First, because they were entrusted with the oracles of God." The result of that advantage was that the Jew stood at a higher stage of religious consciousness than the Gentile. Judaism was the religion of revelation, and therefore the religion of the promise; and therefore the religion which typically and symbolically contained the elements of Christianity; and the religion of the idea which in Christianity was realised. Christianity was, indeed, *spiritualised* Judaism, an advance from servitude to freedom, from nonage to majority, from childhood to maturity, from the flesh to the spirit; yet even in this view Judaism had been, by virtue of its treasure of revelation, preparatory to the absolute religion.[1] This was its first advantage. What he might have added as his secondly and thirdly, we may conjecture from a subsequent allusion,[2] but at this point he is led into a digression by his eagerness to show that his previous arguments involved no abandonment on God's part of His own promises. This might be urged as an objection to what he has been saying. He answers it in one word:—

Some of the Jews had been unfaithful; shall their unfaithfulness nullify God's faith? Away with the thought![3] Alike Scripture and reason insist on God's truthfulness, though every man were thereby proved a liar. The horror with which he rejects the notion that God has proved false, interferes with the clearness of his actual reply. It lies in the word "*some.*" God's promises were true; true to the nation as a nation; for *some* they had been nullified by the moral disobedience which has its root in unbelief, but for all true Jews the promises were true.[4]

A still bolder objection might be urged—"All men, you say, are guilty. In their guilt lies the Divine necessity for God's scheme of justification. Must not God, then, be unjust in inflicting wrath?" In the very middle of the objection the Apostle stops short—first to apologise for even formulating a thought so blasphemous—"I am speaking as men speak;"[5] "these thoughts are not my own;"—then to repudiate it with horror, "Away with the thought!"—lastly, to refute it by anticipation, "If it were so, how shall God judge the world?"[6] Thus fortified, as it were, by the *reductio ad absurdum*, and purified by the moral justification, he follows this impious logic to its conclusion—"God's truth, it seems, abounded in my falseness; why, then, am I still being judged as a sinner? and why"—"such [he pauses to remark] is the blasphemous language attributed to *me!*"—"why may we not do evil that good may come?" To this monstrous perversion of his teaching he deigns no further immediate reply. There are in theology, as in nature, admitted antinomies. The relative truth of doctrines, their truth as regards mankind, is not affected by pushing them into the regions of the absolute, and showing that they involve contradictions if thrown into syllogisms. We may not push the truths of the finite and the temporal into the regions of the infinite and the eternal. Syllogistically stated, the existence of evil might be held to *demonstrate* either the weakness or the cruelty of God; but such syllogisms, without the faintest attempt to answer them, are flung aside as valueless and irrelevant by the faith and conscience of mankind. The mere *statement* of some objections is their most effective re-

[1] iii. 2. "In vetere Testamento Novum latet, in Novo Testamento vetus patet."

[2] ix. 4, 5.

[3] *Ten* times in this Epistle (iii. 4, 6, 31; vi. 2, 15; vii. 7, 13; ix. 14; xi. 1, 11), and in 1 Cor. vi. 15; Gal. ii. 17; iii. 21.

[4] iii. 1—4.

[5] iii. 5. There is an interesting reading, κατὰ ἀνθρώπων. "Is God unjust who inflicts His anger against men?" (MSS. mentioned by Rufinus). τί ἐροῦμεν; cf. vi. 1; vii. 7; ix. 14, 30. It is found in no other Epistle.

[6] For similar instances of entangled objection and reply, Tholuck refers to vii. and Gal. iii. See, too, Excursus XXI., "On the Antinomies of St. Paul."

futation. It shows that they involve an absurdity easily recognisable. However logically correct, they are so morally repulsive, so spiritually false, that silence is the only answer of which they are worthy. Such an objection is the one which Paul has just stated. It is sufficient to toss it away with the sense of shuddering repulsion—the *horror naturalis*—involved in a *μὴ γένοιτο*. It is enough to bid it avaunt, as we might avert with a formula an evil omen. People say that Paul has taught the hideous lie that we may sin to get experience—or sin to add to Christ's redeeming glory—or that the end justifies the means; or that we may do evil that good may come. "*They say—— What say they? Let them say!*" All that Paul has to say to them is merely that "their judgment is just."[1]

What further, then, can the Jew allege?[2] Absolutely nothing! In spite of every objection, Jew and Gentile are all proved to be under sin. Here this section of the proof might close, and on a demonstrated fact of human history Paul might have based his Gospel theology. But neither to himself nor to his readers would the proof have seemed complete without Old Testament sanction. He therefore proceeds to quote a number of fragmentary passages from the fifth, tenth, fourteenth, and hundred-and-fortieth Psalms, and from the fifty-ninth of Isaiah, the validity of which, in this connexion, he rests upon their use of the word "all," which implies Jews as well as Gentiles. The Law (which here means the Old Testament generally) must *include* the Jews, because it is specially *addressed* to Jews. The intention, then, of the Law "is that *every* mouth may be stopped, and *all the world* be recognised as guilty before God;" guilty because[3] by the works of the Law[4]—seeing that, as a fact, neither Jew nor Gentile has obeyed it—no flesh shall be justified before God. Half, then, of his task is done. For before he could prove the thesis of i. 17, that in the Gospel was being revealed a justification by faith—it was necessary for him to demonstrate that *by no other means* could justification be attained. "For"—and here he introduces an anticipative thought, which later on in his epistle he will have seriously to prove—"by the Law is the full knowledge of sin."[5]

V.

JUSTIFICATION BY FAITH.

"1. Paedagogica (Caerimoniae) } illae sunt necessariae sed non justificant.
Justitia 2. Civilis (Decalogus) }
3. Dei et fidei, coram Deo justificat."

LUTHER, *Colloqu.* i. 30.

---

iii. "But now," he says, and this introduces one of the fullest and weightiest passages in all his writings, "without the Law"—which all have failed to keep—

[1] iii. 5—8.

[2] iii. 9, προεχόμεθα properly means "use as a pretext;" the reading προκατέχομεν περισσόν of D, G, Syr. is a gloss to give the meaning of προέχομεν, "do we excel?" which suits the sense far better. Wetstein renders it "are we (the Jews) surpassed by the Gentiles?" But as the Greek Fathers made it mean "have we the advantage?" (Vulg. *praecellimus*), perhaps the sense is admissible here.

[3] iii. 19. λέγει speaks, λαλεῖ utters: cf. John viii. 43, λαλίαν, λόγον. This is the only place in the New Testament where our translators have rendered διότι by "therefore," though it occurs twenty-two times. Everywhere else they render it "for" or "because." It may mean "therefore" in classical Greek, but διὸ is the usual New Testament word in this sense. If rendered "because," a comma only should be placed after Θεῷ.

[4] ἔργα νόμου, the works of *any* law, whether ritual, Mosaic, or general, and whether as to the works *prescribed* by it, or those *produced* by it.

[5] iii. 9—20.—ἐπίγνωσις ἁμαρτίας, and therefore the Law cannot justify, since, as Calvin says, "Ex eadem scatebrâ non prodeunt vita et mors."

"the righteousness of God," both in itself and as an objective gift of justification to man, "has been manifested, being witnessed to by the Law and the Prophets." The nature of that witness he will show later on; at present he pauses to give a fuller, and indeed an exhaustive, definition of what he means by "the righteousness of God." "I mean the righteousness of God accepted by means of faith in Jesus Christ, coming to and upon *all* believers—*all*, for there is no difference. For all sinned, and are failing to attain the glory of God, being justified freely by His grace, by means of the redemption which is in Christ Jesus, whom God set forth as a propitiation,[1] by means of faith in His blood, for the manifestation of His own righteousness"—which righteousness might otherwise have been doubted or misunderstood—"because of the prætermission of past sins in God's forbearance; with a view (I say) to the manifestation of this righteousness at this present epoch, that He might, by a divine paradox, and by a new and divinely predestined righteousness, be just and the justifier of him whose life springs from faith in Jesus."[2]

Let us pause to enumerate the separate elements of this great statement. It brings before us in one view—

1. *Justification*,—the new relation of reconcilement between man and God.

2. *Faith*,—man's trustful acceptance of God's gift, rising to absolute self-surrender, culminating in personal union with Christ, working within him as a spirit of new life.

3. The *universality* of this justification by faith,—a possibility offered to, because needed by, all.

4. This means of salvation *given*, not earned, nor to be earned; a free gift due to the free favour or grace of God.

5. The object of this faith, the source of this possibility of salvation, *the life and death of Christ*, as being (i.) a redemption—that is, a ransom of mankind from the triple bondage of the law, of sin, and of punishment; (ii.) a propitiatory victim,[3]—not (except by a rude, imperfect, and most mis-

[1] Ver. 25. This verse is "the Acropolis of the Christian faith" (Olshausen). Ἀπολύτρωσις (not in LXX.) implies—i., bondage; ii., ransom; iii., deliverance (Eph. i. 7). Many most eminent theologians (Origen, Theodoret, Theophylact, Augustine, Erasmus, Luther, Calvin, Grotius, Calovius, Olshausen, Tholuck, &c.) make ἱλαστήριον mean "mercy-seat," since ἱλαστήριον is the *invariable* word for the *capporeth* in the LXX. (Ex. xxv., *passim*, &c.), which *never* uses it for an expiatory sacrifice (θῦμα). Philo also (*Vit. Mos.*, p. 668; cf. Jos. *Antt.* iii. 6, § 5) calls the mercy-seat a symbol, ἵλεω δυνάμεως. It is, therefore, difficult to suppose how Hellenist readers of this Epistle could attach any other meaning to it. The *capporeth* between the Shekinah and the Tables of the Law, sprinkled with atoning blood by the High Priest as he stood behind the rising incense, is a striking image of Christ (Heb. ix. 25). I quite agree with Lange in calling Fritzsche's remark, "Valeat *absurda explicatio*," an "ignorantly contemptuous one;" but as Christ is *nowhere else* in the New Testament compared to the mercy-seat, and the comparison would here be confined to the *single word*, I cannot help thinking that the word, though ambiguous, must here bear an analogous meaning to ἱλασμὸς, also rendered "a propitiation" in 1 John iv. 10.

[2] iii. 22—27. Bengel points out the grandeur of this evangelic paradox. In the Law God is just and condemns; in the Gospel He is just and forgives. God's judicial righteousness both condemns and pardons. On God's "prætermission" of past sins (iii. 25, πάρεσις, *praetermissio*, not ἄφεσις, *remissio*) compare Ps. lxxxi. 12; Acts xiv. 16; xvii. 30; Lev. xvi. 10. Tholuck calls the Atonement "the divine theodicy for the past history of the world."

[3] "Here is a foundation for the Anselmic theory of satisfaction, but not for its grossly anthropopathic execution." Schaff, *ad loc.* (Lange's *Romans*, 2—7). And this is only the *external* aspect of the death of Christ, the merely judicial aspect pertaining to

leading anthropomorphism) *as regards God*, but from the finite and imperfect standpoint of man; and therefore the Apostle adds that Christ becomes such *to us* by means of faith in His blood.

6. The *reason* for this,—the manifestation of God's righteousness, which might otherwise have been called in question, because of the prætermission of past sins.

7. The *end* to be attained,—that, in perfect consistency with justice, God might justify all whose new life had its root in faith.

Boasting then is impossible, since merit is non-existent. By *works* it is unattainable; by the very conception of *faith* it is excluded. This holds true alike for Jew and Pagan, and Justification is God's free gift to man as man,[1] because He is One, and the God alike of Jews and Gentiles. To the Jew faith is the source, to the Gentile the instrument of this justification.[2]

But here another objection has to be combated. The Jew might say, "By this faith of yours you are nullifying the Law"—meaning by the Law the whole Mosaic dispensation, and generally the Old Testament as containing the history of the covenant people. On the contrary, St. Paul replies, I am establishing it on a firmer basis;[3] for I am exhibiting it in its true position, manifesting it in its true relations; showing it to be the divinely-necessary part of a greater system; adding to the depth of its spirituality, rendering possible the cheerful obedience to its requirements; indicating its divine fulfilment. I am showing that the consciousness of sin which came by the Law is the indispensable preparation for the reception of grace. Let us begin at the very beginning. Let us go back from Moses even to Abraham. What did he, our father, gain by works?[4] By his works he gained nothing before God, as St. Paul proves by the verse that "He *believed* God, and it was *imputed* to him for righteousness."[5] That word "*imputed*" repeated eleven

the sphere of Law. The inward motive—the element in which God's essential nature is revealed, is the grace of God (Rom. iii. 24).

[1] Ver. 28, "Therefore [but γὰρ, ℵ, A] we reckon that a man is justified by faith without the works of the Law." This is the verse in which Luther interpolated the word "alone"—"Vox SOLA tot clamoribus lapidata" (Erasm.). Hence the name Solifidian. It was a legitimate *inference*, and was already existing in the Nuremberg Bible (1483) and the Genoese (1476), but was an unfortunate apparent contradiction of οὐκ ἐκ πίστεως μόνον (James ii. 24). But Luther's famous preface shows sufficiently that he recognised the necessity of works in the same sense as St. James (see Art. xi., xii.). Luther was not guilty of the foolish error which identifies faith with mere belief; and yet, perhaps, his mode of dealing with this verse led to his rash remark as to the impossibility of reconciling the two Apostles (*Colloqu.* ii. 203).

[2] iii. 27—30, περιτομὴν ἐκ πίστεως . . . ἀκροβυστίαν διὰ τῆς πίστεως seems to imply some real difference in the Apostle's view, though Meyer (usually such a purist) here denies it. Calvin sees a shade of irony in it—"*This* is the grand difference: the Jew is saved *ex* fide, the Gentile *per* fidem!" Bengel is probably right when he says that it implies the priority of the Jews, and the acceptance of the Gospel from them by the Gentiles;—the Jews as an outgrowth of faith, the Gentiles by the means of *the* faith. (see Gal. iii. 22—26).

[3] iii. 31. See chap. vi.; viii. 4; xiii. 10.

[4] iv. 1. If we do not omit εὑρηκέναι (with B), κατὰ σάρκα must go with εὑρηκέναι, not as in A. V. with πατέρα. It means, "What did he obtain by purely human efforts?" *e.g.*, by circumcision (Baur); *propriis viribus* (Grot.); *Nach rein menschlicher Weise* (De Wette). St. Paul here attacks a position which afterwards became a stronghold of Talmudists.

[5] St. Paul here follows the LXX., which changes the active into the passive. The faith of Abraham was a common subject of discussion in Jewish schools. See some remarkable parallels in 1 Macc. ii. 52; Philo's eulogy of faith, *De Abrahamo*, ii. 39; *De*

times in the chapter, is the keynote of the entire passage, and is one of very primary importance in the argument with the Jews, who held that Abraham obeyed the Law before it was given.[1] To us, perhaps, it is of secondary importance, since the Apostle did not *derive* his views from these considerations, but discovered the truths revealed to him in passages which, until he thus applied them, would not have been seen to involve this deeper significance. It required, as De Wette says, no small penetration thus to unite the *climax* of religious development with the historic point at which the series of religious developments began. To a worker, he argues, the pay is not "*imputed*" as a favour, but *paid* as a debt; but Abraham's faith was "*imputed*" to him for righteousness, just as it is to all who believe on Him who justifies the ungodly. This truth David also indicates when he speaks of the blessedness of the man to whom God *imputeth* righteousness, or, which comes to the same thing, "does not impute sin." Now this imputation can have nothing to do with circumcision, because the phrase is used at a time before Abraham was circumcised, and circumcision was only a *sign*[2] of the righteousness imputed to him because of his faith, that he might be regarded as "the father of the faithful," whether they be circumcised or uncircumcised. Had the great promise to Abraham, on which all Jews relied, come to him by the Law? Not so, for two reasons. First, because the promise was long prior to the Law, and would have been nullified if it were made to depend on a subsequent law; and, secondly, because the Law causes the sense of wrongdoing,[3] and so works wrath, not promise. Hence, it was the strength of Abraham's faith looking to God's promise in spite of his own and Sarah's age,[4] which won him the imputed righteousness; and this was recorded for us because the faith, and the promise, and the paternity, are no mere historic circumstances, but have all of them a spiritual significance, full of blessedness for all who "believe on Him who raised Jesus our Lord from the dead, who was delivered up for our sins, and raised for our justification."[5]

This, then, is the proof that the doctrine of Justification is not contrary to Scripture, and does not vilipend, but really establishes the Law; and into the last verse are skilfully introduced the new conceptions of Christ's death for our sin, and His resurrection to procure our imputed righteousness, which are further developed in the subsequent chapters.

But first, having proved his point, he dwells on its blessed consequences, which may be summed up in the two words Peace and Hope.

These are treated together. We have Peace,[6] because through Christ we have our access into the free favour of God, and can exult not only in the hope of the

Mut. Nom. i. 586. Nay, since the plural "laws" is used in Gen. xxvi. 5, Rabh held that he kept both the written and the oral law (*Yoma*, f. 28, 2).

[1] *Kiddushin*, f. 82, 1.

[2] iv. 11. The word "seal" (אות) occurs in the formula of circumcision (*Berachoth*, xiii. 1). A circumcised child was called "an espoused of blood" &c., to God (Ex. iv. 26).

[3] See vii. 7, *seqq.*

[4] In iv. 19 the οὐ should be omitted (א, A, B, C, Syr., &c.). He *did* perceive and consider the weakness of his own body, but *yet* had faith. In fact, "not considering his own body" contradicts Gen. xvii. 17.

[5] iv. 1—25. In verse 25 the first διὰ is retrospective, the second is prospective; διὰ τὰ παραπτώματα, "on account of our transgressions;" διὰ τὴν δικαίωσιν, "to secure our being justified." Luther calls this verse "a little covenant, in which all Christianity is comprehended."

[6] v. 1, ἔχωμεν is the better supported reading (א, A, B, C, D, K, L); but ἔχομεν gives by far the better sense, and the other reading may be due to the Pietistic tendency of the Lectionaries to make sentences hortative,—which apparently began to work very early. For a defence of ἔχωμεν, I may refer to the Rev. J. A. Beet's able commentary on the Epistle, which reached me too late for use.

future, but even in the afflictions of the present, which tend to hope because first they work endurance, then approved firmness.[1] The certainty of our Hope is due to the love of God poured into our hearts by His Holy Spirit, and unmistakable to us, since, by a stretch of self-sacrifice unknown to humanity,[2] Christ died for us, not because of any justice, much less any goodness of ours, but while we were yet sinners and enemies. And since we have been reconciled to God by His death, much more shall we be saved by His life, so that our hope—founded on this reconciliation to God—may even acquire a tinge of exultation.[3] Our Peace, then, is an immediate sentiment which requires no external proof; and our Hope is founded on the love of God assured to us in three ways—namely, by Christ's death for us while we were yet enemies to God; on the strength to endure afflictions and see their blessed issue; and above all on union with Christ in death and life.[4]

And this universality of Sin, and universality of Justification, leads Paul to one of his great sketches of the religious history of humanity. To him that history was summed up in three great moments connected with the lives of Adam, Moses, and Christ, of which the mission of Moses was the least important. Those three names corresponded to three stages in the world's religious history—Promise, Law, and Faith—of which the third is the realisation of the first. Adam was a type of Christ, and each stood as it were at the head of long lines of representatives. Each represents the principle of a whole æon. Adam's first sin developed a *principle* from which none of his posterity could be free; and Christ introduced the possibility of a new and saving principle, the necessity for which had been made manifest by the dispensation of Moses. Here, however, as so often, the logical statement is incomplete and entangled, owing to the rush of the Apostle's thoughts.[5]

"So then, *as* by one man sin entered into the world, and by sin death, and so death extended to all men on the ground that all sinned,"[6] he probably meant to

[1] Matt. v. 10—12; Acts v. 41; 1 Pet. iv. 13, 14; 2 Cor. xii. 10, 11.

[2] v. 7, Chrysostom, Theodoret, Erasmus, Calvin, Meyer, &c., make no difference between ἀγαθὸς, "good," and δίκαιος, "just," as though St. Paul meant "one would scarcely die for a good man, though possibly one *might*." It is, however, more probable that St. Paul meant "one would not die merely for a man of ordinary integrity, but for a *truly good* man one might even dare to die" (cf. Cic. *De Off.* iii. 15).

[3] v. 11, ἀλλὰ καὶ καυχώμενοι.

[4] Verses 1—12.

[5] 1 Cor. xv. 45. The difference between Adam and Eve (1 Tim. ii. 14) was a smaller matter, and one which had little or no bearing on the destiny of the human being, whether male or female.

[6] Pages and almost volumes of controversy have been written on verse 12. ἐφ' ᾧ πάντες ἥμαρτον. Many make the ᾧ *masc.*, and, referring it to Adam, render it "in whom (Aug.), or, "by whose means" (Grot.), or "on whose account" (Chrys.). There can, however, be no doubt that ᾧ is neuter (cf. 2 Cor. v. 4; Phil. iii. 12, iv. 10), and that it means neither "unto which (death)," as a *final cause*, nor any variation on this meaning, but "inasmuch as." Since, however, the argument of St. Paul seems simply to be that sin was universal, and that the universality of death was *a proof of this*, it certainly seems admissible to understand ἐφ' ᾧ in the universal sense of "in accordance with the fact that." It is here used in a larger and looser causal connexion than usual. Sin and death are universal, and are inseparably linked together; it might be supposed that where there was no law there was no sin; it is true that sin is not *fully imputed* where there is no law; but death entered the world through sin, and so death passed upon all men, "which shows that—which involves the presupposition that—all sinned." This is Baur's view, and if it be tenable, the discussions about "original sin," "inherent total depravity," &c., are irrelevant to this passage (Baur, *Paul.* ii. 183—186). Let us, at any

add as the second half of the parallel, "*so, too*, by one man came justification, and so life was offered to all." The conclusion of the sentence was, however, displaced by the desire to meet a difficulty. He had said, "all sinned," but some one might object, "How so? you have already told us that where there is no law there is no transgression; how, then, could men sin between Adam and Moses?" The answer is far from clear to understand. St. Paul might perhaps have referred to the law of nature, the transgression of which involved sin; but what he says is that "till the law, sin was in the world, but sin is not imputed when there is no law." If he had said, "sin is not brought into prominent self-consciousness," his meaning would have been both clear and consistent, but the verb used (ἐλλογεῖται) does not admit of this sense. Perhaps we may take the word popularly to imply that "it is not *so fully* reckoned or imputed," a view which may find its illustration in our Lord's remark that the sin of Sodom and Gomorrah was less unpardonable than that of Chorazin and Bethsaida. It seems as if he meant to imply a distinction between "*sin*" in general, and the "*transgression*" of some special law or laws in particular.[1] "Every sin," as St. Thomas Aquinas says, "may be called a transgression in so far as it transgresses a natural law; but it is a more serious thing to transgress a law both natural and written. And so, when the law was given, transgression increased and deserved greater anger." But the only proof which St. Paul offers that there *was* sin during this period is that, throughout it, death also reigned.[2] When, however, he passes from this somewhat obscure reply (13, 14), to show how Adam was a type of Christ, his meaning again becomes clear. He dwells first on the points of difference (15—18), and then on those of resemblanc (18, 19). The differences between the results caused by Adam and Christ are differences both qualitative and quantitative—both in degree and kind.

i. By Adam's one transgression the many died, but the free grace of Christ abounded to the many in a far greater degree.[3]

rate, imitate St. Paul in dwelling rather on the positive than the negative side, rather on Christ than Adam, rather on the superabundance of grace than the origin of sin.

[1] So most of the commentators. "*Sine lege potest esse quis iniquus sed non praevaricator*" (Augustine). Luther explains ἐλλογεῖται, "sin is not minded"—"*man achtet ihrer nicht.*"

[2] Ver. 14, "Even over those who had not sinned after the similitude of Adam's transgression"—*i.e.*, who had broken no positive direct command—whose ἁμαρτία was not a definite παράβασις. Dr. Schaff (Lange's *Romans*, p. 191, E.T.) gives a useful sketch of the theories about original sin and imputation. 1. The PANTHEISTIC and Necessitarian makes sin inherent in our finite constitution, the necessary result of matter. 2. The PELAGIAN treats Adam's sin as a mere *bad example*. 3. The PRÆ-ADAMIC explains sin by antenatal existence, metempsychosis, &c. 4. The AUGUSTINIAN—all men sinned in Adam (cf. Heb. vii. 9, 10). "*Persona corrumpit naturam, natura corrumpit personam*"—*i.e.*, Adam's sin caused a sinful nature, and sinful nature causes individual sin. This has many subdivisions according as the imputation of Adam's sin was regarded as (α) Immediate; (β) Mediate; or (γ) Antecedent. 5. The FEDERAL—vicarious representation of mankind in Adam, in virtue of a one-sided (μονόπλευρον) contract of God with man (*foedus operum*, or *naturae*); with subdivisions of (α) The Augustino-federal; (β) The purely federal or forensic. 6. The NEW ENGLAND CALVINISTS, who deny imputation and distinguish between *natural ability* and *moral inability* to keep innocence. 7. The ARMINIAN, which regards hereditary corruption not as sin or guilt, but as infirmity, a maladive condition, &c. I ask, would Paul have been willing to enter into all these questions? Have they in any way helped the cause of Christianity or deepened vital religion? Can they be of primary importance, since the traces of them in Scripture are so slight that scarcely any two theologians entirely agree about them? Do they tend to humility and charity and edification, or to "vain word-battlings"?

[3] The contrast is between *plurality* and *unity*; the phrase "*the many*" (not "many," as in Luther and the E.V.) does not for a moment imply any exception (*e.g.*, Enoch, or Elijah). It is merely due to the fact that "all" may sometimes be "a few" (Aug.). "Adamus et Christus," says Bengel, "secundum rationes contrarias, conveniunt in positivo, differunt in comparativo." See Bentley, Sermon upon Popery. *Opp.* iii. 244. Observe the parallel between the κρῖμα, κατάκριμα, χάρισμα, δικαίωμα, of verse 16 and the

ii. The condemnation of the race to death sprang from the *single* transgression of one; the sentence of acquittal was freely passed in spite of *many* transgressions.

iii. By the transgression of Adam began the reign of *death;* far more shall all who are receiving the superabundance of grace of the gift of righteousness reign in life by the One, Jesus Christ. But with these differences there is also a parallel of deeper resemblance. One transgression (Adam's sin), and one sentence of condemnation on all; one act of righteousness (Christ's death), and one justification which gives life to all;—by the disobedience of the one,[1] the many were made sinners;[2] by the obedience of the one, the many shall be made righteous.[3] Thus St. Paul states the origin of sin in this passage; but however he might have solved the antinomy of its *generic* necessity and *individual* origin, which he leaves unsolved, he would certainly have been ready to say with Pseudo-Baruch that "every one of us is the Adam to his own soul."

But here once more the question recurs, What then of the Law? Is that divine revelation to go for nothing? To that question St. Paul has already given one answer in the Epistle to the Galatians: he now gives another, which till explained might well have caused a shock. To the Galatians he had explained that the ante-Messianic period was the *tirocinium* of the world, and that during this period the Law was necessary as a pædagogic discipline. To the Romans he presents a new point of view, and shows that the Law was not merely a corrective system thrust in between the promise and its fulfilment,, but an essential factor in the religious development of the world. It appears in the new aspect of a "power of sin," in order that by creating the knowledge of sin it may mediate between sin and grace. The Law, he says, came in (the word he uses has an almost disparaging sound,[4] which probably, however, he did not intend) "that transgression might multiply." A terrible purpose indeed, and one which he subseqnently explained (chap. vii.): but even here he at once hastens to add that where sin multiplied, grace super-

παράπτωμα, κατάκριμα, δικαίωμα, and δικαίωσις of verse 18. The distinction between these words seems to be as follows:—1. δικαίωμα, *actio justificativa*, *Rechtsfertigungsthat*, the act which declares us just. 2. δικαίωσις, the process of justification. 3. δικαιοσύνη, the condition of being justified. Rothe quotes Arist., *Eth. Nic.*, v. 10, where δικαίωμα is defined as τὸ ἐπανόρθωμα τοῦ ἀδικήματος. In verse 16, D, E, F, G, read ἁμαρτήματος.

[1] Adam, says Luther, stuck his tooth, not into an *apple*, but into a *stachel*, namely, the Divine command. Pelagius, in his commentary on Romans (preserved in Augustine's works), renders δι' ἑνὸς ἀνθρώπου, "*per unum hominem, Evam!*" Philo's views about the Fall may be seen in his *Legg. Alleg.* ii. 73—106. He regards gluttony and lust as the source of all evil, and considers that all men are born in sin, *i.e.*, under the dominion of sensuality (*De Mundi Opif.* 37; *Vit. Mos.* iii. 675). "God made not death, but ungodly men with their works called it to them" (Wisd. i. 13—16).

[2] *In what way* they were made sinners St. Paul nowhere defines. There is no distinctive Pelagianism, or Traducianism, here. To say with Meyer, "men were placed in the category of sinners because they sinned in and with Adam's fall," is, as Lange remarks, not exegesis, but Augustinian dogmatics. St. Paul simply accepted the universal fact of death as a proof of the universal fact of sin, and regards death and sin as beginning with Adam. Beza, Bengel, Reuss, &c., understand κατεστάθησαν and κατασταθήσονται in an imputative sense—"*regarded* as sinners"—which is a defensible translation, and makes the parallel more complete.

[3] Vs. 12—20.

[4] v. 20, παρεισῆλθεν, Vulg. *Subintravit*, "supervened," "came in besides," cf. προσετέθη, Gal. iii. 19. In Gal. ii. 4 the surreptitious notion of παρὰ is derived from the context. The notion of "between," "*medio tempore subingressa est*," is not in the word itself.

abounded, that as sin reigned in death, so also grace might reign through righteousness into life eternal, by Jesus Christ our Lord.[1]

The next chapter (vi.) is of vast importance as stating an objection which might well be regarded as deadly, and as showing us how best to deal with an apparent paradox. If grace superabounds over sin, why should we not continue in sin? After first throwing from him the hateful inference with a "Perish the thought!" he proceeds in this chapter to prove, first in a mystic (vi. 1—15), and then in a more popular exposition (15—23), the moral consequences of his doctrine. In the first half of this chapter he uses the metaphor of death, in the latter the metaphor of *emancipation*, to illustrate the utter severance between the Christian and sin.

Ideally, theoretically, it should be needless to tell the Christian not to sin; he is *dead* to sin; the very name of "elect" or "saint" excludes the entire conception of sin, because the Christian is "IN CHRIST." Those two words express the very quintessence of all that is most distinctive in St. Paul's theology, and yet they are identical with the leading conception of St. John, who (we are asked to believe) rails at him in the Apocalypse as Balaam and Jezebel, a sham Jew, and a false apostle! That the two words "in Christ" sum up the distinctive secret, the revealed mystery of the Christian life, especially as taught by St. Paul and by St. John, will be obvious to any thoughtful reader. If this mystic union, to which both Apostles again and again recur, is expressed by St. Paul in the metaphors of stones in a temple of which Christ is the foundation,[2] of members of a body of which Christ is the head,[3] St. John records, and St. Paul alludes to, the metaphor of the branches and the vine,[4] and both Apostles without any image again and again declare that the Christian life is a spiritual life, a supernatural life, and one which we can only live by faith in, by union with, by partaking of the life of the Son of God.[5] With both Apostles Christ is our life, and apart from Him we have no true life.[6] St. Paul, again, is fond of the metaphor of wearing Christ as a garment, putting on Christ, putting on the new man,[7] reflecting Him with ever-brightening splendour.[8] In fact, the words "in Christ" and "with Christ" are his most constantly recurrent phrases. We work for Him, we live in Him, we die in Him, we rise with Him, we are justified by Him. We are His sheep, His scholars, His soldiers, His servants.

[1] v. 20, 21. The old Protestant divines thus stated the uses of the Law:—1. *Usus primus*, civil or political—to govern states. 2. *Usus secundus*, convictive or pædagogic—to convince us of sin. 3. *Usus tertius*, didactic or formative—to guide the life of a believer (*Formula Concordiae*, p. 594). Dr. Schaff, in his useful additions to the translation of Lange's *Romans*, points out that these three correspond to the German sentence that the Law is a *Zügel* (1, a restraint); a *Spiegel* (2, a mirror); and a *Riegel* (3, a rod). The Law multiplies transgressions because—i. "Nitimur in vetitum semper, cupimus que negata." "Ignoti nulla cupido." ii. "Because desires suppressed forcibly from without increase in virulence" (St. Thomas). iii. "Because suppressive rules kindle anger against God" (Luther). But the real end of the Law was not the multiplication of transgressions *per se*, but that the precipitation of sin might lead to its expulsion; that the culmination of sin might be the introduction of grace. "Non crudeliter hoc fecit Deus sed ratione medicinae—augebatur morbus, crescit malitia, quaeritur medicus, et totum sanatur" (Aug. in Ps. cii.).

[2] Eph. ii. 19—22 (1 Pet. ii. 5; Isa. xxviii. 16).

[3] Rom. xii. 5; Eph. iv. 16; 1 Cor. xii. 12, 13, 27; Col. i. 18.

[4] John xv. 5; Rom. vi. 5; Phil. i. 11.

[5] 2 Cor. v. 17; Rom. vi. 8; Gal. ii. 20; Eph. iii. 6; Col. iii. 3; John x. 28; xiv. 19; xv. 4—10; 1 John v. 20; ii. 24, &c.

[6] John iii. 27; v. 24; xi. 25; xiv. 20; Gal. ii. 20; Col. iii. 4; 1 John i. 1; v. 12, &c.

[7] Gal. iii. 27; Rom. xiii. 14; Eph. iv. 24; Col. iii. 10.

[8] 2 Cor. iii. 18.

The life of the Christian being hid with Christ in God, his death with Christ is a death to sin, his resurrection with Christ is a resurrection to life. The dipping under the waters of baptism is his union with Christ's death; his rising out of the waters of baptism is a resurrection with Christ, and the birth to a new life. "What baptism is for the individual," it has been said, "Christ's death is for the race." If the Christian has become *coalescent* with Christ in His death, he shall also in His resurrection.[1] The old sin-enslaved humanity is crucified with Christ, and the new man has been justified from sin, because he is dead to it, and lives in Christ. This is the ideal. Live up to it. Dethrone the sin that would rule over your frail nature. "Be not ever presenting your members as weapons of unrighteousness, but present yourselves once for all,[2] to God as alive from the dead, and your members as instruments of righteousness to God. For sin shall not lord it over you; for ye are not under the Law, but under grace."[3] Die to sin, die to lust, die to your old vulgar, enslaved. corrupted self, die to the impulses of animal passion, and the self-assertion of worldly desire; for Christ too died, and you are one with him in death, that you may be one in life. But these words, again, raise the ghost of the old objection. "Shall we then *sin*, since we are not under the Law, but under grace?" and this objection St. Paul again refutes by the same argument, clothed in a more obvious and less mystic illustration, in which he amplifies the proverb of Jesus, "Ye cannot serve two masters." A man must either be a slave of sin unto death, or of obedience unto righteousness.[4] Thank God, from that old past slavery of sin you were freed, when you submitted to the form of doctrine to which you were handed over by God's providence; and then—if in condescension to your human weakness I may use an imperfect expression—you were enslaved to righteousness.[5] The fruit of that former slavery was shame and misery; its end was death. This new enslavement to God is perfect freedom; its fruit is sanctification, its end eternal life. "For the wages of sin is death; but the free gift of God is eternal life in Christ Jesus our Lord."[6]

iv. At this point of his argument the Apostle felt it imperative to define more clearly, and establish more decisively, his view as to the position of the Law in the scheme of salvation. Apart from his discussion of this question in the Epistle to the Galatians, he has already, in this Epistle, made three incidental remarks on the subject, which might well horrify those Jews and Jewish Christians who were unfamiliar with his views. He has said—

1. That "by the works of the Law shall no flesh be justified before God: for by the Law is the full knowledge of sin" (iii. 20).

2. That "the Law came in as an addition that transgression might abound" (v. 20).

3. That the Christian "is not under the Law, but under grace," and that *therefore* sin is not to lord it over him (vi. 14).

[1] vi. 5, σύμφυτοι. The Vulg. "*complantati*" is too strong. It is from φύω, not φυτεύω.
[2] vi. 13, παριστάνετε . . . παραστήσατε. In the New Testament ὅπλα is always "weapons." Cf. Rom. xiii. 12; 2 Cor. vi. 7.
[3] vi. 1—15.
[4] vi. 16. The phrase "a slave of obedience" is strange. Perhaps he used ὑπακοῆς instead of δικαιοσύνης, because of the two senses of the word, "righteousness" and "justification."
[5] vi. 18, Ἐδουλώθητε. "Deo servire vera libertas est" (Aug.). "Whose *service* is perfect freedom." Ἀνθρώπινον λέγω—Calvin, following Origen and Chrysostom, renders this clause, "I require nothing which your fleshly weakness could not do."
[6] vi. 15—23.

Such statements as these, if left unsupported and unexplained, might well turn every Jewish reader from respectful inquiry into incredulous disgust; and he therefore proceeds to the difficult task of justifying his views.

The task was difficult because he has to prove scripturally and dialectically the truths at which he had arrived by a wholly different method. The central point of his own conviction was that which runs through the Epistle to the Galatians,[1] that if salvation was to be earned by "*doing*"—if the Law was sufficient for justification—then Christ's death was needless and vain. If he were right in his absolute conviction that only by faith in the blood of Christ are we accounted righteous before God, then clearly the Law stood condemned of incapacity to produce this result. Now by the Law St. Paul meant the *whole* Mosaic Law, and there is not in him a single trace of any distinction between the degree of sacredness in the ceremonial and the moral portion of it. If there had been, he might perhaps have adopted the luminous principle of the author of the Epistle to the Hebrews, and shown that the Law was only abrogated by the completeness of its fulfilment; that its inefficiency only proves its typical character; and that the type disappeared in the fulness of the antitype, as a star is lost in the brightness of the sun. This method of allegory was by no means unfamiliar to St. Paul; he not only adopts it freely,[2] but must have learnt it as no small element of his Rabbinic training in the school of Gamaliel. But, on the one hand, this attribution of a spiritual depth and mystery to every part of the ceremonial Law would have only tended to its glorification in the minds of Judaisers who had not yet learnt its abrogation; and, on the other hand, it was not in this way that the relation of the Law to the Gospel had specially presented itself to the mind of Paul. The typical relation of the one to the other was real, and to dwell upon it would, no doubt, have made St. Paul's arguments "less abrupt and less oppressive to the consciousness of the Jews;"[3] but it would also have made them less effective for the emancipation of the Church and the world. The Law must be deposed, as it were, from its long primacy in the minds of the Jews, into that negative, supplementary, secondary, inefficient position which alone belonged to it, before it could with any prudence be reinstalled into a position of reflected honour. It had only a subordinate, provisional importance; it was only introduced *per accidens*. Its object was pædagogic, not final. St. Paul's reasoning might inflict pain, but the pain which he inflicted was necessary and healing; and it was well for the Jews and for the world that, while he strove to make his arguments acceptable by stating them in a tone as conciliatory as possible, he did not strive to break the shock of them by any unfaithful weakening of their intrinsic force.

i. His first statement had been that the Law could not justify.[4] That

[1] Gal. ii. 21; iii. 21.

[2] The muzzled ox, 1 Cor. ix. 9; Sarah and Hagar, Gal. iv. 24; the evanescence of the light on the face of Moses, 2 Cor. iii. 7—13; the following rock, 1 Cor. x. 4; the cloud and sea, 1 Cor. x. 1, 2.

[3] Pfleiderer, *Paulinismus*, i. 73, E. T.

[4] Rom. iii. 20.

it could not justify he saw at once, because had it been adequate to do so, then the death of Christ would have been superfluous. But *why* was it that the Law was thus inefficacious? St. Paul rather indicates than clearly states the reason in the next chapter (viii.). It is because the Law, as regards its form, is external; it is a command from without; it is a letter which denounces sentence of death on its violators;[1] it has no sympathy wherewith to touch the heart; it has no power whereby to sway the will. "Spiritual" in one sense it is, because it is "holy, just, and good;" but it is in no sense a "quickening spirit," and therefore can impart no life. And why? Simply because it is met, opposed, defeated by a strong counter-principle of man's being—the dominion of sin in the flesh. It was "weak through the flesh"—that is, through the sensuous principle which dominates the whole man in body and soul.[2] In the human *spirit*, Paul perceived a moral spontaneity to good; in the *flesh*, a moral spontaneity to evil; and from these different elements results "the dualism of antagonistic moral principles."[3] Man's natural self-will resists the Divine determination; the subjective will is too strong for the objective command. Even if man could obey a part of the Law he could not be justified, because the Law laid a curse on him who did not meet *all* its requirements, which the moral consciousness knew that it could not do.[4]

ii. But St. Paul's second proposition—that the Law multiplied transgressions[5]—sounded almost terribly offensive. "The Law," he had already said in the Galatians, was added until the coming of the promised seed, "*for the sake of transgressions.*"[6] To interpret this as meaning "a *safeguard* against transgressions"—though from another point of view, and in another order of relations, this might be true[7]—is in this place an absurdity, because St. Paul is proving the inability of the Law to perform this function at all effectually. It would, moreover, entirely contradict what he says—namely, that the object of the Law was the *multiplication* of transgressions. Apart from the Law, there may indeed be "sin" (ἁμαρτία), although, not being brought into the light of self-consciousness, man is not aware of it (Rom. v. 13; vii. 7); but he has already told us that there is not "transgression" (iv. 15), and there is not "imputation" (v. 13), and man lives in a state of relative innocence, little pained by the existence of objective evil.[8] It was,

[1] 2 Cor. iii. 6.

[2] The σάρξ is not only the material body, but an active inherent principle, which influences not only the ψυχὴ or natural life, but even the νοῦς or human spirit (Baur, *Paul.* ii. 140).

[3] Gal. v. 17; Pfleiderer, i. 54. To this writer I am much indebted, as well as to Baur and Reuss, among many others, for my views of Pauline theology. I must content myself with this large general acknowledgment, because they write from a standpoint widely different from my own, and because I find in the pages of all three writers very much with which I entirely disagree.

[4] Gal. iii. 10; James ii. 10.

[5] Rom. v. 20.

[6] Gal. iii. 19, χάριν παραβάσεων προσετέθη.

[7] The *usus primus* or *politicus* of the Law—*v. supra*, p. 479. It is a safeguard against acts which, when the law is uttered, become transgressions.

[8] To be "naked and not ashamed" is, in the first instance, the prerogative of innocence; but it becomes ultimately the culmination of guilt.

therefore, St. Paul's painful and difficult task to sever the Law finally from all *direct* connexion with salvation, by showing that, theologically considered—and this was the point which to the Jew would sound so paradoxical and so wounding—God had expressly designed it, not for the prevention of sin, and the affecting of righteousness, but for the *increase of sin*, and the *working of wrath*.[1] It *multiplied sin*, because, by a psychological fact, which we cannot explain, but which St. Paul here exhibits with marvellous insight into human nature, the very existence of a commandment acts as an incitement to its violation ("Permissum fit vile nefas"); and it *worked wrath* by forcing all sin into prominent self-consciousness,[2] and thus making it the source of acute misery; by bringing home to the conscience that sense of guilt which is the feeling of disharmony with God; by darkening life with the shadows of dread and self-contempt; by creating the sense of moral death, and by giving to physical death its deadliest sting.[3]

iii. The third proposition—that "we are not under the Law, but under grace"[4]—has been already sufficiently illustrated; and it must be borne in mind that the object of St. Paul throughout has been to show that the true theological position of the Law—its true position, that is, in the Divine œconomy of salvation—is to come in between sin and grace, to be an impulse in the process of salvation. He has already shown this, historically and exegetically, in the fifth chapter, as also in Gal. iii., by insisting on the fact that the Law, as a supplementary ordinance,[5] cannot disannul a free promise which was prior to it by 430 years, and which had been sanctioned by an oath. The Law, then, shows (1) the impossibility of any *other* way of obtaining the fulfilment of the promise, except that of free favour; and (2) the impossibility of regarding this promise as a *debt* (ὀφείλημα) when it was a free gift. In this point of view the Law fulfils the function of driving man to seek that justification which is possible by faith alone. *Objectively* and historically, therefore, the history of man may be regarded in four phases—Sin, Promise, Law, Grace—Adam, Abraham, Moses, Christ; *subjectively* and individually, also in four phases—relative innocence, awakened consciousness, imputable transgression, free justification. The one is the Divine, the other is the human side of one and the same process; and both find their illustration, though each independently of the other, in the theology of St. Paul.[6]

[1] Pfleiderer, i. 81. "Whoever separates himself from the words of the Law is consumed by fire" (*Babha Bathra*, f. 79, 1).

[2] "The strength of sin is the Law" (1 Cor. xv. 56), because it is what it is essentially through man's consciousness of it. It strengthens the perception of sin, and weakens the consciousness of any power in the will to resist it.

> "And therefore Law was given them to *evince*
> *Their natural pravity*, by stirring up
> Sin against Law to fight; that when they see
> Law can discover sin, but not remove,
> Save by those shadowy expiations weak,
> The blood of bulls and goats, they may conclude
> Some blood more precious must be paid for man."—Milton, *P. L.* xii. 285.

The last three lines express the argument in the Epistle to the Hebrews.

[3] Rom. iv. 15; vii. 10—13. [4] Rom. vi. 14. [5] Gal. iii.

[6] Rom. v., vii., xi.; Gal. iii., iv.

And if it be asserted, by way of modern objection to this theology, and to St. Paul's methods of argument and exegesis, that they suggest multitudes of difficulties; that they pour new wine into old wine-skins, which burst under its fermentation; that they involve a mysticising idealisation of 1,500 years of history and of the plain literal intention of large portions of the Old and New Testament Scriptures; that Moses would have been as horrified to be told by St. Paul that the object of his Law was only to multiply transgression, and intensify the felt heinousness of sin, as he is said to have been when in vision he saw Rabbi Akhibha imputing to him a thousand rules which he had never sanctioned; that the Law was obviously given with the intention that it should be obeyed, not with the intention that it should be broken; that St. Paul himself has spoken in this very Epistle of "doers of the Law being justified," and of "works of the Law," and of "working good," and of a recompense for it,[1] and of "reaping what we have sown;"[2] that he has in every one of his Epistles urged the necessity of moral duties, not as an *inevitable result* of that union with Christ which is the Christian's life, but as things after which Christians should *strive*, and for the fulfilment of which they should train themselves with severe effort;[3] and that in his Pastoral Epistles these moral considerations, as in the Epistles of St. Peter and St. James, seem to have come into the foreground,[4] while the high theological verities seem to have melted farther into the distance—if these objections be urged, as they often have been urged, the answers to them are likewise manifold. We have not the smallest temptation to ignore the difficulties, though it would be easy by separate examination to show that to state them thus is to shift their true perspective. As regards St. Paul's style of argument, those who see in it a falsification of Scripture, a treacherous dealing with the Word of God, which St. Paul expressly repudiates,[5] should consider whether they too may not be intellectually darkened by suspicious narrowness and ignorant prepossessions.[6] St. Paul regarded the Scripture as the irrefragable Word of God, and yet, even when he seems to be attaching to mere words and sounds a "talismanic value," he never allows the letter of Scripture to becloud the illumination (φωτισμὸς) of spiritual enlightenment.[7] Even when he seemed to have the whole Pentateuch against him, he never suffered the outward expression to enthral the emancipated idea. He knew well that one word of God cannot contradict another, and his allegorising and spiritualising methods—(which, in one form or other, are absolutely essential, since the Law speaks in the tongue of the sons of men, and human language is at the best but an asymptote to thought)—are not made the vehicle of mechanical inference or individual caprice, but are used in support of formative truths, of fruitful ideas, of spiritual convictions, of direct revelations, which are as the Eternal

[1] Rom. ii. 6—13; iv. 4.
[2] Gal. vi. 7; 2 Thess. iii. 13; 1 Cor. xv. 58.
[3] 1 Cor. ix. 25—27; Phil. iii. 14.
[4] Mic. vi. 12; 1 Tim. iv. 7, 8; ii. 3; Tit. iii. 8; ii. 14; 2 Pet. i. 10, 11; James ii. 17, 24.
[5] 2 Cor. ii. 17, οὐ καπηλεύοντες; 2 Cor. iv. 2, μηδὲ δολοῦντες.
[6] 2 Cor. iv. 1—7.
[7] 2 Cor. iv. 4.

Temple, built within the temporary scaffolding of abrogated dispensations. In this way of dealing with Scripture he was indeed regarded as a blasphemer by a Pharisaism which was at once unenlightened and unloving; but he was a direct successor of the Prophets, who dealt in a spirit of sacred independence with earlier revelations,[1] and with their mantle he had caught a double portion of their spirit. He felt that the truths his opponents characterised as "temerities" and "blasphemies" were as holy as the Trisagion of the Seraphim; that his "apostasy from Moses"[2] was due to a reverence for him far deeper than that of his upholders, and that there was an immemorial, nay, even an eternal validity, in the most extreme of his asserted innovations.

And as for apparent contradictions, St. Paul, like all great thinkers, was very careless of them. It is even doubtful whether they were distinctly present to his mind. He knew that the predestinations of the Infinite cannot be thrust away—as though they were ponderable dust inurned in the Columbaria—in the systems of the finite. He knew that in Divine as well as in human truths there are certain *antinomies*, irreconcilable by the mere understanding, and yet perfectly capable of being fused into unity by the divinely enlightened reason, or, as he would have phrased it, by the spirit of man which has been mystically united with the Spirit of Christ. As a scheme, as a system, as a theory of salvation—abstractly considered, ideally treated—he knew that his line of argument was true, and that his exposition of the Divine purpose was irrefragable, because he knew that he had received it neither from man, nor by any man,[3] but by the will of God. But there is a difference between the ideal and the actual—between the same truths regarded in their theological bearing as parts of one vast philosophy of the plan of salvation, and stated in everyday language in their immediate bearing upon the common facts of life. In the language of strict and accurate theology, to talk of the "merit" of works, and the "reward" of works, or even the possibility of "good" works, was erroneous; but yet—without any of such Protestant after-thoughts as that these works are the fruits of unconscious faith, or that without this faith they cannot in any sense be good, and without dreaming of any collision with what he says elsewhere, and untroubled by any attempt to reconcile his statements with the doctrine of original sin—he could and did talk quite freely about "Gentiles doing *by nature* the things of the Law," and says that "the doer of the Law shall be justified," and that God will render to every man *according to his works*.[4] St. Paul would probably have treated with contempt, as a mere carping criticism, which allowed no room for common sense in dealing

[1] Jer. xxxi. 29. Ezek. xviii. 2; xx. 25, "Wherefore I gave them also statutes that were not good, and judgments whereby they should not live." Hos. vi. 6, "I desired mercy and not sacrifice; and the knowledge of God more than burnt offering." Jer. vii. 22, 23, "I spake not unto your fathers concerning burnt offerings or sacrifices, but this thing commanded I them, saying, Obey my voice."

[2] Acts xxi. 21, "They have been indoctrinated with the view that you teach apostasy from Moses."

[3] Gal. i. 1, οὐκ ἀπ' ἀνθρώπων, οὐδὲ δι' ἀνθρώπου.

[4] Rom. ii. 13, 14; xiv. 10. See, too, 2 Cor. v. 10; Gal. vi. 7; Eph. vi. 8; Col. iii. 24, 25.

with the truths of revelation, any attempt to show that in such passages—both on this and on other subjects—he appears to contradict himself.[1] He would very briefly, and with profound indifference, have contented himself with saying that his remarks in these passages are not *in pari materiâ.*[2] He is not there speaking or thinking at all of the doctrine of redemption. He is there talking about "the justification of the Law," which is a very different thing from "the justification by faith." He is there using general language, altogether irrespective of the Gospel. Protestant commentators with all their elaborate and varying theories—that in these works faith is included as the highest work;[3] that they are perfected in faith;[4] that "works will be adduced in the day of judgment, not as meriting salvation, but as proofs and results of faith;"[5] that "the imperfect works of the sanctified will be rewarded, not on the ground of the Law, but on the ground of grace;"[6] that he was mentally referring to a "prevenient grace" over the Gentile world, and so on—are doubtless dogmatically right, but they are far more anxious to save St. Paul's orthodoxy and consistency than he would have been himself. It is at least doubtful whether such considerations were consciously present to his mind. He would have held it enough to reply that, in these passages, he was only applying the current language of morality to the concrete relations of actual life;[7] and that "the doctrine of justification cannot conflict with the doctrine of God's righteousness by virtue of which He will reward every man according to his works."[8] When St. Paul was using the language of accurate theology, he would have shown the nullity of righteousness by works. But, in any case, he would have thought far more highly of the possibility of such righteousness than of the righteousness of dogmatic orthodoxy, or the righteousness of the letter; the righteousness of the jealous heresy-hunter, or the righteousness of the religious partisan.[9]

Lastly, it will be seen how little St. Paul is troubled by the apparent paradoxes which result from the doctrines which he enforces. By those who manipulated truth to suit their own parties and purposes; by those who huckstered the Word of Life; by those who pushed truths into extravagant inferences, and then condemned them on the ground of their possible misapplication—his doctrines were denounced as "dangerous;" and we know as a fact that, even in his own lifetime, what he taught was made a handle for evil doctrine,[10] and was subjected to perilous perversions.[11] When such arguments as these were urged against him, St. Paul treated them with entire disdain. Truth

[1] For these antinomies, which exist in theology as they exist in nature, and are complementary truths of which the harmony is to be found in the Infinite, see Excursus XXI.

[2] "Haec descriptio justitiae legis, quae nihil impedit alia dicta de justitia fidei" (Melancthon in Rom. ii. 13). He is here "laying down those general principles of justice, according to which, irrespective of the Gospel, all men are to be judged" (Hodge on Rom. ii. 6).

[3] Limborch. [4] Luthardt. [5] Gerhard. [6] Stuart.

[7] Baur, *N. Test. Theol.* 181; Pfleiderer, i. 78. [8] Lange on Rom. ii. 6—10.

[9] Lehrgerechtigkeit; Buchstabende Echtigkeit, Negationsgerechtigkeit, Parteigerechtigkeit (Lange, *ubi supra*).

[10] Rom. iii. 8. [11] 2 Pet. iii. 16, στρεβλοῦσιν . . . πρὸς τὴν ἰδίαν αὐτῶν ἀπώλειαν.

may be wrested, truth may be distorted, truth may be made an instrument of self-destruction—but truth is truth, and can take care of itself, and needs no "lying for God" to serve as its buttress.[1] The doctrine of free grace might be, and was, quoted in the cause of antinomianism, and degraded into a justification of sensuality. The predominance of grace over sin was twisted into a reason for doing evil that good might come. The hope of future forgiveness was pleaded as a ground for continuing in sin. Well, let it be so. The ocean of truth did not cease to be an ocean because here and there a muddy river of error flowed stealthily in its tides. In answer to the moral perversity which abused truth into an occasion of wickedness, St. Paul thought it sufficient to appeal to the right feeling of mankind. If a man chooses to pervert a Divine and gracious doctrine into a "dangerous downfall," he does so at his own peril. Evil inferences St. Paul merely repudiates with a "God forbid!"[2]—of malignant misinterpreters he thought it enough to say that "their condemnation was just!"[3]

After these preliminary considerations we are in a position to proceed uninterruptedly with our sketch of the Epistle, since we are now in possession of its main conceptions. Proceeding then to a further expansion of his views respecting the Law, and speaking (chap. vii.) to those who know it, the Apostle further enforces the metaphor that the Christian is dead to his past moral condition, and has arisen to a new one. A woman whose husband is dead is free to marry again; we are dead to the Law, and are therefore free to be united to Christ. Obviously the mere passing illustration must not be pressed, because if used as *more* than an illustration it is doubly incomplete—incomplete because the word "dead" is here used in two quite different senses; and because, to make the analogy at all perfect, the Law ought to have died to us, and not we to the Law. But St. Paul merely makes a cursory use of the illustration to indicate that the new life of the Christian involves totally new relationships;[4] that death naturally ends all legal obligations; and that our connexion with the risen Christ is so close that it may be compared to a conjugal union. Hence our whole past condition, alike in its character and its results, is changed, and a new Law has risen from the dead with our new life—a Law which we must serve in the newness of the spirit, not in the oldness of the letter. He who is dead to sin is dead to the Law, because the Law can only reign so long as sin reigns, and because Christ in His crucified body has destroyed the body of sin.[5]

But St. Paul is conscious that in more than one passage he has placed the Law and Sin in a juxtaposition which would well cause the very deepest

[1] Job xiii. 7, 8.
[2] Rom. iii. 4, 6, 31; vi. 2, 15; vii. 7, &c.; Gal. ii. 17; iii. 21; vi. 14; 1 Cor. vi. 15.
[3] Rom. iii. 8.
[4] 2 Cor. xi. 2; Eph. v. 25.
[5] vii. 1—6. The very harshness of the construction ἀποθανόντες ἐν ᾧ ("by dying to that in which we were held fast") seems to make it more probable than the τοῦ θανάτου of D, E, F, G. The E.V. renders ἀποθανόντος, the unsupported conjecture of Beza, or Erasmus.

offence. To show his meaning he enters on a psychological study, of which the extreme value has always been recognised entirely apart from its place in the scheme of theology. Here he writes as it were with his very heart's blood; he dips his pen in his inmost experience. He is not here dealing with the ideal or the abstract, but with the sternest facts of actual daily life. There have been endless discussions as to whether he is speaking of himself or of others; whether he has in view the regenerate or the unregenerate man. Let even good men look into their own hearts and answer. Ideally, the Christian is absolutely one with Christ, and dead to sin; in reality, as again and again St. Paul implies even of himself, his life is a warfare in which there is no discharge. There is an Adam and a Christ in each of us. "The angel has us by the hand, and the serpent by the heart." The old Adam is too strong for young Melancthon.[1] Here, then, he explains, from a knowledge of his own heart, confirmed by the knowledge of *every* heart, that the Law, though not the *cause* of sin, is yet the *occasion* of it; and that there are in every human being *two* laws—that is, two opposing tendencies—which sway him from time to time, and in greater or less degree in opposite directions. And in this way he wrote an epitome of the soul's progress. When we have once realised that the "I" of the passage is used in different senses—sometimes of the flesh, the lower nature, in the contemplation of which St. Paul could speak of himself as the chief of sinners; sometimes of the higher nature, which can rise to those full heights of spiritual life which he has been recently contemplating; sometimes generically of himself as a member of the human race—it is then easy to follow his history of the soul.

The Law is not sin—Heaven forbid!—but it provokes disobedience,[2] and it creates the *consciousness* of sin. Without it there is sin indeed, but it is dead; in other words, it is latent and unrecognised. That is the age of fancied innocence, of animal irreflective life, of a nakedness which is not ashamed. But it is a condition of "immoral tranquillity" which cannot be permanent; of misplaced confidence which causes many an aberration from duty. When the blind tendency of wrong becomes conscious of itself by collision with a direct command, then sin acquires fresh life at the expense of that misery and shame which is spiritual death.[3] Thus sin, like Satan, disguises itself under the form of an angel of light, and seizes the opportunity furnished by the command which in itself is holy, just, and good,[4] to utterly deceive and to slay me.[5]

[1] "Our little lives are kept in equipoise
By struggles of two opposite desires:
The struggle of the instinct that enjoys,
And the more noble instinct that aspires."

[2] Of this thought there are many interesting classical parallels. Liv. xxxiv. 4: "Parricidae cum lege coeperunt, et illis facinus poena monstravit." Sen. *De Clem.* i. 23: "Gens humana ruit per vetitum et nefas." Hor. *Carm.* i. 3, 26: "Quod licet ingratum est, quod non licet acrius urit." Ov. *Amor.* ii. 19, &c.: "The Law produces reflection on the forbidden object, curiosity, doubt, distrust, imagination, lust, susceptibility of the seed of temptation and of seduction, and finally rebellion—the παράβασις" (Lange).

[3] "Mors peccati vita est hominis; vita peccati mors hominis" (Calvin). "By the *jetser ha-rá*" (the evil impulse), says Rabbi Simeon Ben Lakish, "is meant the angel of death" (Tholuck).

[4] Holy in its origin, just in its requirements, good in its purpose.

[5] vii. 7—12.

"What?" one may ask, "did that which is *good* become *death* to me?" Nay, but sin *by means of* that which was good effected my death, because by means of the commandment sin's exceeding sinfulness was dragged into recognition. How came this? It came out of the struggle of the higher and the lower elements of our being; out of the contest between my fleshen and servile nature [1] and the Law's spirituality of origin,—the result of which is that I am two men in one, and live two lives in one, not doing what I desire, and doing what I detest. In me—that is, in my flesh—dwelleth no good thing; but I am not my flesh. I identify my own individuality with that higher nature which *wills* what is noble, but is too often defeated by the indwelling impulses of sin.[2] My true self, my inward man,[3] delights in the law of God; but my spirit, my intellect and my reason are in constant warfare with another law—a sensual impulse of my fleshy nature—which often reduces me into the bondage of its prison-house. Wretched duality of condition which makes my life a constant inconsistency! Wretched enchainment of a healthy, living organism to a decaying corpse! Who shall rescue me from these struggles of a disintegrated individuality?

"Thanks to God through Jesus Christ our Lord!" It is a sign of the intensity of feeling with which he is writing that he characteristically omits to mention the very thing for which he thanks God. But the words "through Jesus Christ our Lord" sufficiently show that his gratitude is kindled by the conviction that the deliverance is possible—that the deliverance has been achieved.[4] I, my very self—the human being within me[5]—serve with my mind the law of God. Through my weakness, my inconsistency, my imperfect faith, my imperfect union with Christ, I still serve with my flesh the law of sin;[6] but that servitude is largely weakened, is practically broken. There is no condemnation for those who by personal union with Christ[7] live in accordance with the Spirit. Sin is slavery and death; the Spirit is freedom and life. The Law was rendered impotent by the flesh, but God, by sending His own Son in the form of sinful flesh[8] and as a sin-offering,[9] con-

[1] vii. 14. σαρκινὸς, "fleshen," *carneus;* σαρκικὸς, "fleshly," *carnalis*. The former is here the true reading, and involves (of course) less subjection to the flesh than the latter.

[2] The most commonly-quoted of the classic parallels is Ovid's "Video meliora proboque, Deteriora sequor" (*Met.* vii. 19). The nearest is ὃ μὲν θέλει (ὁ ἁμαρτάνων) οὐ ποιεῖ καὶ ὃ μὴ θέλει ποιεῖ. Δύο γὰρ σαφῶς ἔχω ψυχάς (Xen. *Cyr.* vi. 1). Chrysostom calls ver. 21 ἀσαφὲς εἰρημένον, but the obscurity is only caused by the trajection of ὅτι, which involves the repetition of ἐμοί. It means "I find, then, the law that evil is close at hand to me when my will is to do good."

[3] Cf. 1 Pet. iii. 4. ὁ κρυπτὸς τῆς καρδίας ἄνθρωπος. German writers speak of the "pseudo-plasmatic man" with his νοῦς τῆς σαρκὸς, φρόνημα τῆς σαρκὸς, σῶμα τῆς ἁμαρτιας, νόμος ἐν τοῖς μέλεσι, σάρξ, &c. Schuh. *Pathologie und Therapie des Pseudo-plasmen*, 18. "This double personality is a dethronement of the ἐγὼ in favour of the ἁμαρτία."

[4] Instead of "I thank God" (εὐχαριστῶ), the easier, and therefore less probable reading, of D, E, F, G is ἡ χάρις τοῦ Θεοῦ, or Κυρίου. More probable is the χάρις τῷ θεῷ of B and the Sahidic.

[5] vii. 25, αὐτὸς ἐγώ. I believe this to be the true meaning, though many reject it. St. Paul is speaking in his own person, not by μετασχηματισμός (see 1 Cor. iv. 6). An "infection of nature" remains even in the regenerate (Art. ix.).

[6] There is a determining power in the "flesh" which Paul calls "a law in the members," and which by its predominance becomes "a law of sin." This is opposed by the rational principle, the νοῦς or human πνεῦμα—the ἔσω ἄνθρωπος—the higher spiritual consciousness, which can however never, by itself, invade and conquer the flesh. Its power is rather potential than actual. Reason is the *better* principle in man, but the flesh is the stronger. It is not the Divine πνεῦμα. Nothing but union with Christ can secure to the νοῦς the victory over the σάρξ (Baur, *Paul.* ii. 146).

[7] viii. 1. "Christus in homine, ubi fides in corde" (Aug.). The true reading is, "There is, then, *now* no condemnation to those in Christ Jesus." The rest of the verse is a gloss.

[8] *Lit.*, "in a flesh-likeness of sin."

[9] περὶ ἁμαρτίας "as a sin-offering" חַטָּאת, *chattath*. Lev. xvi. 5: λήψεται δύο χιμάρους

demned to death[1] the victorious power of sin in the flesh, and so enabled us, by a spiritual life, to meet the otherwise impossible requirements of the Law. Our life is no longer under the dominion of the flesh, which obeys the law of sin, but of the spirit.[2] The death of Christ has, so to speak, shifted the centre of gravity of our will. If Christ be in us, the body indeed is still liable to death because of sin, but the spirit—our own spiritual life—(he does not say merely '*contains* the elements of life,' but in his forcible manner)—*is* life, because of the righteousness implanted by the sanctifying Spirit of God. If that Spirit which raised Jesus from the dead dwell in us, He who raised Christ from the dead will also quicken us to full life, partially but progressively here, but triumphantly and finally beyond the grave.[3] And even here, in a measure, we attain to the "life of the spirit." Never, indeed, can we fulfil the *whole* Law (Gal. iii. 10); but for the quantitative is substituted a qualitative fulfilment, and the "totality of the disposition contains in itself the totality of the Law." In that stage life becomes life indeed. The "law of the spirit" is the "*law of the spirit of life in Christ Jesus.*"

This, then, shows us the true law, and the final issue of our lives. If we are led by the Spirit of God we are the sons of God, and the spirit of fear becomes the spirit of sonship, and the cry of slavery the cry of confident appeal to a Father in heaven. Thus we become joint-heirs with Christ; and, therefore, to share His glory we must share His sufferings. The full glory of that sonship is to be ours beyond the grave, and in comparison with it the sufferings of this life are nothing. The life of all creation is now in anguish, in bondage, in corruption, yearning for a freedom which shall be revealed when we too have entered on the full glory of our inheritance as the children of God. We, though we have the first-fruits of the spirit, share in the groaning misery of nature, as it too shares in inarticulate sympathy with our impatient aspirations. We live, we are saved BY HOPE, and the very idea of Hope is the antithesis of present realisation.[4]

Hope is not possession, is not reality; it can but imply *future* fruition; it is Faith in Christ directed to the future. But we have something more and better than Hope. We have the help in weakness, the intercession even in prayer that can find no utterance, of the Holy Spirit Himself. We know, too, that *all things* work together for good to all them that love God and are called according to His purpose. He ends the Divine work that He begins. Election—predestination to conformity and brotherhood with Christ—vocation—justification—these four steps all follow, all must inevitably follow each other, and must end in glorification. So certain is this glorification, this entrance into the final fulness of sonship and salvation, that St. Paul—with one of those splendid flashes of rhetoric which, like all true rhetoric, come directly from the intensities of emotion, and have nothing to do with the technicalities of art—speaks of it in the same past tense which he has employed for every other stage in the process. Those whom He foreknew,[5] predestined, called, justified —them He also *glorified*.[6]

"What shall we then say to these things?" What, but that magnificent burst

περὶ ἁμαρτίας. Ps. xl. 7: περὶ ἁμαρτίας οὐκ ᾔτησας (Heb. x. 8). Lev. iv. 25: ἀπὸ τοῦ αἵματος τοῦ τῆς ἁμαρτίας.

[1] κατέκρινεν, "condemned to execution" (Matt. xxvii. 13).

[2] Ver. 6. On the φρόνημα τῆς σαρκὸς, see Art. ix. Philo also dwells strongly on the impotence of man apart from Divine grace (*Legg. Alleg.* i. 48, 55, 101).

[3] vii. 13—viii. 11. The change from τοῦ ἐγείραντος Ἰησοῦν to ὁ ἐγείρας τὸν Χριστὸν is remarkable. "Appellatio Jesu spectat ad ipsum, Christi refertur ad nos" (Bengel, viii. 11) partly resumes the subject of v. 11 after the separate points handled in v. 12—21; vi. 1—23; vii. 1—6, 7—25.

[4] viii. 18—25.

[5] There are four explanations of "foreknew," and each is claimed alike by Calvinists and Arminians! (Tholuck.) But, "in the interpretation of Scripture, if we would feel as St. Paul felt, or think as he thought, we must go back to that age in which the water of life was still a running stream."

[6] viii. 26—30.

of confidence and rapture[1] which we will not degrade by the name of peroration, because in St. Paul no such mere artificiality of construction is conceivable, but which fitly closes this long and intricate discussion, in which he has enunciated truths never formulated since the origin of the world, but never to be forgotten till its final conflagration. The subtleties of dialectic, the difficulties of polemical argument, the novelties of spiritualising exegesis, are concluded; and, firm in his own revealed conviction, he has urged upon the conviction of the world, and fixed in the conviction of Christians for ever, the deepest truths of the Gospel entrusted to his charge. What remains but to give full utterance to his sense of exultation in spite of earthly sufferings, and "to reduce doubt to absurdity" by a series of rapid, eager, triumphant questions, which force on the minds of his hearers but one irresistible answer? In spite of all the anguish that persecution can inflict, in spite of all the struggles which the rebellious flesh may cause, "we are more than conquerors through Him that loved us. For I am convinced that neither death nor life, nor angels nor principalities, nor things present, nor things to come, nor height nor depth, nor any other created thing, shall be able to separate us for a moment[2] from God's love manifested towards us in Christ Jesus our Lord." In spite of failure, in spite of imperfection, our life is united with the life of Christ, our spirit quickened by the Spirit of Christ, and what have we to fear if all time, and all space, and all nature, and all the angels of heaven, and all the demons of hell, are utterly powerless to do us harm?[3]

CHAPTER XXXVIII.

PREDESTINATION AND FREE WILL.

"Everything is foreseen, and free will is given. And the world is judged by grace, and everything is according to work."—R. AKHIBHA in *Pirke Abhôth*, iii. 24.

Ὁρᾷς ὅτι οὐ φύσεως οὐδὲ ὑλικῆς ἀνάγκης ἐστὶ τὸ εἶναι χρυσοῦν ἢ ὀστράκινον ἀλλὰ τῆς ἡμετέρας προαιρέσεως.—CHRYS. *ad* 2 Tim. ii. 21.

"Reasoned high
Of Providence, foreknowledge, will and fate,
Fixed fate, free will, foreknowledge absolute,
And found no end in wandering mazes lost."
MILTON, *Paradise Lost*, ii. 558.

"Soll ich dir die Gegend zeigen
Musst du erst das Dach besteigen."—GÖTHE.

WE now come to the three memorable chapters (ix., x., xi.) in which St. Paul faces the question which had, perhaps, led him to state to the Jews and Gentiles of Rome the very essence of his theology. He has told them "his Gospel"—that revealed message which he had to preach, and by virtue of

[1] Compare the outburst in 1 Cor. xv. 54. "In fact, as verses 19—23 may be called a sacred elegy, so we may term 31—39 a sacred ode; that is as tender and fervent as this is bold and exalted—that, an amplification of "we do groan being burdened" (2 Cor. v. 4); this, a commentary on "this is the victory that overcometh the world" (1 John v. 4). Philippi, *ad loc.*

[2] viii. 39, χωρίσαι.

[3] Compare this rapture of faith and hope with the aching despair of materialism. "To modern philosophical unbelief the beginning of the world, as well as its end, is sunk in mist and night, because to it the centre of the world—the historical Christ—is sunk in mist and night" (Lange). The time was ripe for the recognition of a deliverer. Plato and Seneca had clearly realised and distinctly stated that man was powerless to help himself from his own misery and sin. (Sen. *Ep.* 53. Cf. Tac. *Ann.* iii. 18; Cic. *De Off.* ii. 4, 18.)

which he was the Apostle of the Gentiles. He has shown that Jews and Gentiles were equally guilty, equally redeemed. The Redemption was achieved; but only by faith, in that sense of the word which he has so fully explained, could its blessings be appropriated. Alas! it was but too plain that while the Gentiles were accepting this great salvation, and pressing into the Kingdom of Heaven, the Jews were proudly holding aloof, and fatally relying on a system now abrogated, on privileges no longer exclusive. Their national hopes, their individual hopes, were alike based on a false foundation, which it has been the Apostle's duty inexorably to overthrow. Their natural exclusiveness he meets by the unflinching principle that there is no favouritism with our Heavenly Father; he meets their attempts after a legal righteousness by proving to them that they, like the Gentiles, are sinners, that they cannot attain a legal righteousness, and that no such endeavour can make them just before God. Obviously he was thus brought face to face with a tragic fact and a terrible problem. The *fact* was that the Jews were being rejected, that the Gentiles were being received. Even thus early in the history of Christianity it had become but too plain that the Church of the future would be mainly a Church of Gentiles, that the Jewish element within it would become more and more insignificant, and could only exist by losing its Judaic distinctiveness. The *problem* was, how could this be, in the face of those immemorial promises, in the light of that splendid history? Was God breaking His promises? Was God forgetting that they were "the seed of Abraham His servant, the children of Jacob whom He had chosen?"[1] To this grave question there was (1) a theologic answer, and (2) an historic answer. (1) The theologic answer was—that acceptance and rejection are God's absolute will, and in accordance with His predestined election to grace or wrath. (2) The historic answer was—that the rejection of the Jews was the natural result of their own obstinacy and hardness. The two answers might seem mutually irreconcilable; but St. Paul, strong in faith, in inspiration, in sincerity, never shrinks from the seeming oppositions of an eternal paradox. He often gives statements of truth regarded from different aspects, without any attempt to show that they are, to a higher reason than that of man, complementary, not (as they appear) contradictory, of each other. Predestination is a certain truth of reason and of revelation; free will is a certain truth of revelation and of experience. They are both true, yet they seem mutually exclusive, mutually contradictory. The differences between Supralapsarians and Sublapsarians do not really touch the question; God's foreknowledge is always recognised, but in no way does it solve the difficulty of the absolute decree. If we say that St. Paul is here mainly arguing about great masses of men, about men in nations, and the difference between Jews and Gentiles, that is partially true; but he most

[1] "Who hath not known passion, cross, and travail of death, cannot treat of foreknowledge without injury and inward enmity towards God. Wherefore, take heed that thou drink not wine while thou art yet a sucking babe" (Luther). He also said, "The *ninth* chapter of the Epistle to the Romans *is* the ninth. Learn first the eight chapters which precede it."

definitely recognises the case of individuals also, and God is the God not only of nations, but of individuals. In any case, this sacrifice of the individual to the interests of the mass would be but a thrusting of the difficulty a little further back. The thought that many, though Edomites, will be saved, and many, though of Israel, will be lost, may make the antenatal predilection for Israel and detestation of Esau less startling to us, and it is quite legitimate exegetically to soften, by the known peculiarities of Semitic idiom, the painful harshness of the latter term. But even then we are confronted with the predestined hardening of Pharaoh's heart. St. Paul recognises—all Scripture recognises—the naturalness of the cry of the human soul; but the remorseless logic of a theology which is forced to reason at all about the Divine prescience can only smite down the pride of finite arguments with the iron rod of revealed mysteries. Man is but clay in the potter's hands. God is omnipotent; God is omniscient; yet evil exists, and there is sin, and there is death, and after death the judgment; and sin is freely forgiven, and yet we shall receive the things done in the body, and be judged according to our works. All things end in a mystery, and all mysteries resolve themselves into one—the existence of evil. But, happily, this mystery need in no way oppress us, for it is lost in the Plenitude of God. The explanation of it has practically nothing to do with us. It lies in a region wholly apart from the facts of common life. When St. Paul tells us "that it is not of him that willeth, nor of him that runneth," he is dealing with one order of transcendental ideas; but when he comes to the common facts of Christian life, he bids us will, and he bids us run, and he bids us work out our own salvation with fear and trembling; exactly as he tells us that justification is of faith alone, and not of works, and yet constantly urges us to good works, and tells us that God will reward every man according to his works.[1] Beyond this we cannot get. "Decretum horribile fateor," said Calvin, "at tamen verum." Theology must illustrate by crushing analogies its irreversible decrees, but it cannot touch the sphere of practical experience, or weaken the exhortations of Christian morality. God predestines; man is free. How this is we cannot say; but *so* it is. St. Paul makes no attempt to reconcile the two positions. "Neither here nor anywhere else does he feel called upon to deal with speculative extremes. And in whatever way the question be speculatively adjusted, absolute dependence and moral self-determination are *both* involved in the immediate Christian self-consciousness."[2] The finite cannot reduce the infinite to conditions, or express by syllogisms the mutual relations of the two. The truths must be stated, when there is need to state them, although each of them belongs to separate orders of ideas. Since they cannot be reconciled, they must be left side by side. It is an inevitable necessity, implied throughout all Scripture, that, as regards such questions, the sphere of dogma and the sphere of homily should often be regarded as though they were practically separate from each other,

[1] ἀποδιδόναι (Rom. ii. 6; 2 Tim. iv. 8); ἀνταπόδοσις (Col. iii. 24); μισθὸς (1 Cor. iii. 8; ix. 17), &c.
[2] Baur, *Paul.* ii. 259.

though in reality they intersect each other. And the reason of this is that both are enclosed in the circumference of a sphere by far more vast—that sphere of the Divine, of which for us the centre is everywhere, and the circumference, not indeed "nowhere," but immeasurably beyond our ken.[1] This is one comfort. And again, just as St. Paul refuses to find the substantial essence of morality anywhere but in the inmost disposition, so he does away with the *individual ego* by raising it to the *universal ego*—to that humanity which is present, and is identified with itself, in every separate individual.[2] It is unquestionable that he *categorically asserts*, and that without limitations, the redemption of the universe and of the race.[3] In that thought, and in the thought of God's infinite love, lies the gleam of light in the saddest destinies or the most perplexed enigmas of the individual. The logical conclusions of an exaggerated dogmatism are rectified by the unchangeable certainties of moral conviction, and the inspired hopes of a child-like love.

"Ah, truly," says Reuss,[4] "if the last word of the Christian revelation is contained in the image of the potter and the clay, it is a bitter derision of all the deep needs and legitimate desires of a soul aspiring towards its God. This would be at once a satire of reason upon herself, and the suicide of revelation." But it is neither the *last* word, nor the *only* word; nor has it any immediate observable bearing on the concrete development of our lives. It is not the *only* word, because in nine-tenths of Scripture it is as wholly excluded from the sphere of revelation as though it had been never revealed at all; and it is not the *last* word, because throughout the whole of Scripture, and nowhere more than in the writings of the very Apostle who has faced this problem with the most heroic inflexibility, we see bright glimpses of something beyond. How little we were intended to draw logical conclusions from the metaphor, is shown by the fact that we are living souls, not dead clay; and St. Paul elsewhere recognised a power, both within and without our beings, by which, as by an omnipotent alchemy, mean vessels can become precious, and vessels of earthenware be transmuted into vessels of gold.[5] Vessels fitted for destruction may be borne with much long-suffering. Apparent loss is made the immediate instrument of wider gain. Partial rejection is to pave the way for universal acceptance. God wills the salvation of all.[6] Where sin abounds, there grace superabounds.[7] God giveth freely to all, and freely calleth all, and His gifts and calling are without repentance. Israel is rejected, Israel in part is hardened, yet "all Israel shall be saved."[8] "God shut up all into

[1] The Rabbis, to avoid even the most distant semblance of irreverent anthropomorphism, often spoke of God as *Ha-Makôm*, "the place;" and it is one of their grand sayings that "the Universe is not the place of God, but God is the Place of the Universe."

[2] Baur, *Three Centuries*, p. 32.

[3] See Rom. viii. 19—24; xi. 32; 1 Tim. ii. 3—6 (Acts iii. 21; Rev. xxi. 4; xxii. 3).

[4] *Théol. Chrét.* ii. 115.

[5] 2 Tim. ii. 21.

[6] 1 Tim. ii. 4; Tit. ii. 11; 2 Pet. iii. 9.

[7] Rom. v. 20, 21.

[8] Rom. xi. 26.

disobedience, that He might pity all."[1] The duality of election resolves itself into the higher unity of an all-embracing counsel of favour; and the sin of man, even through the long Divine œconomy of the *æons*, is seen to be but a moment in the process towards that absolute end of salvation, which is described as the time when God shall be "all things in all things," and therefore in all men; and when the whole groaning and travailing creation shall be emancipated into "the freedom of the glory of the children of God."[2] If disobedience has been universal, so too is mercy; and Divine mercy is stronger and wider, and more infinite and more eternal, than human sin. Here, too, there is an antinomy. St. Paul recognises such a thing as "perdition;" there are beings who are called "the perishing."[3] There are warnings of terrible significance in Scripture and in experience. But may we not follow the example of St. Paul, who quite incontestably dwells by preference upon the wide prospect of infinite felicity; who seems always lost in the contemplation of the final triumph of all good? However awful may be the future retribution of sinful lives, we still cannot set aside—what true Christian would wish to set aside?—the Scriptures, which say that "as in Adam all die, even so in Christ shall all be made alive;" that all things tend "unto God," as all things are from Him and by Him;[4] that Christ shall reign until He hath put all enemies under His feet, and that the last which shall be destroyed is death.[5]

Let us, then, see more in detail how the Apostle deals with a fact so shocking to every Jew as the deliberate rejection of Israel from every shadow of special privilege in the kingdom of God; let us see how he proves a doctrine against which, at first sight, it might well have seemed that the greater part of the Old Testament and 1,500 years of history were alike arrayed.

It should be observed that in his most impassioned polemic he always unites a perfect conciliatoriness of tone with an absolute rigidity of statement. If he must give offence, he is ready to give offence to any extent, so far as the offence must inevitably spring from the truth which it is his sacred duty to proclaim. Doubtless, too, much that he said might be perverted to evil results; be it so. There are some who abuse to evil purposes God's own sunlight, and who turn the doctrine of forgiveness into a curse. Are we to quench His sunlight? are we to say that He does not forgive? Some Jews were, doubtless, dangerously shaken in all their convictions by the proclamation of the Gospel, as some Romanists were by the truths of the Reformation. Is error to be immortal because its eradication is painful? Is the mandrake to grow, because its roots shriek when they are torn out of the ground? Or is it not better, as St. Gregory the Great said, that a scandal should be created than that truth should be suppressed? There is no style of

[1] Rom. xi. 32.

[2] 1 Cor. xv. 22; Rom. xi. 15—36; viii. 19—23. See Baur, *First Three Centuries*, p. 72; Pfleiderer, ii. 256, 272—275; Reuss, *Théol. Chrét.* ii. 23, *seqq.*

[3] Ἀπολλύμενοι. This word does not mean "the lost," a phrase which does not exist in Scripture, but "the perishing."

[4] Rom. xi. 36; 1 Cor. viii. 6; Col. i. 16, 17.

[5] 1 Cor. xv. 25—28; Eph. i. 20—22; 2 Tim. i. 10 (Matt. xi. 27; Heb. ii. 8, 14).

objection to the proclamation of a new or a forgotten truth which is so false, so faithless, and so futile, as the plea that it is "dangerous." But one duty is incumbent on all who teach what they believe to be the truths of God. It is that they should state them with all possible candour, courtesy, forbearance, considerateness. The controversial method of St. Paul furnishes the most striking contrast to that of religious controversy in almost every age. It is as different as anything can be from the reckless invective of a Jerome or of a Luther. It bears no relation at all to the unscrupulousness of a worldly ecclesiasticism. It is removed by the very utmost extreme of distance from the malice of a party criticism, and the Pharisaism of a loveless creed.

Thus, though he knows that what he has to enforce will be most unpalatable to the Jews, and though he knows how virulently they hate him, how continuously they have thwarted his teaching and persecuted his life, he begins with an expression of love to them so tender and so intense, that theologians little accustomed to an illimitable unselfishness felt it incumbent upon them to explain it away.

"I say the truth in Christ, I lie not, my conscience bearing me witness in the Holy Spirit, that I have great grief and incessant anguish in my heart;" and then, in the intensity of his emotion, he omits to state the cause of his grief, because it is sufficiently explained by what follows and what has gone before. It is grief at the thought that Israel should be hardening their hearts against the Gospel. "For I could have wished my own self to be anathema from Christ[1] on behalf of my brethren, my kinsmen according to the flesh, seeing that they are Israelites, whose is the adoption,[2] and the Shechinah,[3] and the covenants, and the legislation, and the ritual, and the promises, whose are the fathers, and of whom is Christ, according to the flesh, who is over all—God blessed for ever. Amen."[4] On his solemn appeal to the fact of his readiness even to abandon all hopes of salvation if thereby he could save his brethren, I think it only necessary to say that the very form in which it is

[1] חֵרֶם, Deut. vii. 46; Zech. xiv. 11; Gal. i., 8, 9; 1 Cor. xii. 3; xvi. 22. Strong natures have ever been capable of braving even the utmost loss for a great end. "If not, blot me, I pray thee, out of the book which Thou hast written" (Ex. xxxii. 32). "Que mon nom soit flétri," said Danton, "pourvu que la France soit libre." "Let the name of George Whitefield perish if God be glorified."

[2] 2 Cor. vi. 18.

[3] Ex. xvi. 10; 1 Sam. iv. 22, &c. (LXX.)

[4] Rom. ix. 1—5. On the punctuation of this last verse a great controversy has arisen. Many editors since the days of Erasmus (and among them Lachmann, Tischendorf, Rückert, Meyer, Fritzsche) put the stop at "flesh;" others at "all" (Locke, Baumgarten, Crusius); and regard the concluding words as a doxology to God for the grandest of the privileges of Israel. In favour of this punctuation is the fact that Paul, even in his grandest Christological passages, yet nowhere calls Christ, "*God over all*," nor ever applies to Him the word εὐλογητός. (See i. 25; 1 Cor. iii. 23; viii. 6; 2 Cor. i. 3; xi. 31; Eph. i. 17; iv. 6; 1 Tim. ii. 5, &c.) But, on the other hand, a doctrinal ἅπαξ λεγόμενον may, as Lange says, mark a culminating point; and having regard (i.) to the language which Paul uses (Phil. ii. 6; Col. i. 15; ii. 9; 1 Cor. viii. 6; 2 Cor. iv. 4), and (ii.) to the grammatical structure of the sentence, and (iii.) to the *position* of εὐλογητὸς (which in doxologies in the New Testament stands always first), and (iv.) to the unanimity of all ancient commentators, and (v.) to the fact that the clause probably alludes to Ps. lxvii. 19 (LXX.), and in Eph. iv. 8, St. Paul quotes the *previous* verse of this Psalm, and applies it to Christ,—the punctuation of our received text can hardly be rejected. Yet there is weight in Baur's remark that κατὰ σάρκα is added to show that it is as only "after the flesh" that the Jews could claim the birth of the Messiah, and that the "God over all blessed for ever" would have been allowing too much to Jewish particularism. (Cf. Gal. iv. 4, γενόμενος ἐκ γυναικὸς.) For a full examination of the question, I may refer to my papers on the text in the *Expositor*, 1879.

expressed shows his sense that such a wish is by the very nature of things impossible. Further explanation is superfluous to those who feel how natural, how possible, is the desire for even this vast self-sacrifice to the great heart of a Moses or a Paul.

"Not, however, as though the Word of God has failed."[1] This is the point which St. Paul has to prove, and he does it by showing that God's gifts are matters of such free choice that the Jew cannot put forward any exclusive claim to their monopoly.

In fact, all who are Jews naturally are not Jews spiritually—are not, therefore, in any true sense heirs of the promise. To be of the seed of Abraham is nothing in itself. Abraham had many sons, but only one of them, the son of Sarah, was recognised in the promise.[2]

Not only so, but even of the two sons of the son of promise one was utterly rejected; and so completely was this a matter of choice, and so entirely was it independent of merit, that before there could be any question of merit, even in the womb, the elder was rejected to servitude, the younger chosen for dominion. And this is stated in the strongest way by the prophet Malachi—"Jacob I loved, but Esau I hated."[3]

"Is God unjust then?" To a natural logic the question might seem very excusable, but St. Paul simply puts it aside as irrelevant and impossible, while he re-states the fact which suggests it by quoting as decisive two passages of Scripture.[4] God has an absolute right to *love* whom He will; for He says to Moses, "Whomsoever I pity, him I will pity; and whomsoever I compassionate, him I will compassionate;" so that pity is independent of human will or effort. And God has an absolute right to *hate* whom He will; for Scripture says to Pharaoh, "For this very purpose I raised thee up, to display in thee my power, and that my name may be proclaimed in all the earth."[5]

So then God pities, and God hardens, whom He will.

Again, the natural question presents itself—"Why does He then blame? If wickedness be the result of Divine Will, what becomes of moral responsibility?"

In the first place, Paul implies that the question is absurd. Who are you, that you can call God to account? No matter what becomes of moral responsibility, it does not at any rate affect God's decree. Man is but passive clay in the Potter's hands; He can mould it as He will.[6]

1 ἐκπέπτωκεν, "fallen like a flower," Job xiv. 2; but see 1 Cor. xiii. 8; James i. 11.

2 ix. 6—9; comp. *Nedarim*, f. 31, 1. "Is not Ishmael an alien, and yet of the seed of Abraham?" It is written, "In *Isaac* shall thy seed be called." "But is not Esau an alien, and yet of the seed of Isaac?" "No. 'In Isaac,' but *not all Isaac*."

3 Mal. i. 2, 3. Hated = "loved less" (Gen. xxix. 31; Matt. vi. 24; x. 37, compared with Luke xiv. 26); and the next verse shows that *temporal* position is alluded to.

4 "These arguments of the Apostle are founded on two assumptions. The first is that the Scriptures are the word of God; and the second, that what God actually does cannot be unrighteous" (Hodge). At the same time it is most necessary, as Bishop Wordsworth says, "not to allow the mind to dwell exclusively or mainly on single expressions occurring here or there, but to consider their relation to the context, to the whole scope of the Epistle, to the other Epistles of St. Paul, and to the general teachings of Holy Writ" (*Epistles*, p. 201).

5 ix. 14—18. "Satis habet," says Calvin, "Scripturae testimoniis *impuros latratus* compescere;" but the "impure barkings" (a phrase which St. Paul would never have used) shows the difference between the Apostle of the Gentiles and the Genevan Reformer. Σκληρύνει, however, in ver. 18, cannot mean "treats hardly." Calovius says that God does not harden ἐνεργητικῶς, "by direct action," but συγχωρητικῶς (permissively), ἀφορμητικῶς (by the course of events), ἐγκαταλειπτικῶς (by abandonment), and παραδοτικῶς (by handing men over to their worst selves). It may be said that this chapter contradicts the next, and Fritzsche goes so far as to say that "Paul would have better agreed with himself if he had been the pupil of Aristotle, not of Gamaliel;" but the contradiction, or rather the antinomy, is not in any of St. Paul's arguments, but in the very nature of things.

6 ix. 19—22. It was a common metaphor (Jer. xviii. 6; Isa. xlv. 9; Wisd. xv. 7; Sirach xxxiii. 13).

But Paul would not thus *merely* smite down the timid questioning of sinners by the arbitrary irresponsibility of Infinite Power. He gives a gleam of hope; he sheds over the ultimate Divine purposes a flash of insight. He asks a question which implies a large and glorious answer, and the very form of the question shows how little he desires to dwell on the unpractical insoluble mysteries of Divine reprobation.[1]

What if God, willing to display His wrath, and to make known His power—(he will not say, "created vessels of wrath," or "prepared them for destruction," but, swerving from a conclusion too terrible for the wisest)—"*endured in much longsuffering* vessels of wrath fitted for destruction . . . ? And what if He did this that He might also make known the riches of His glory towards the vessels of mercy which He before prepared for glory . . . ?" What if even those decrees which seemed the harshest were but steps towards an ultimate good? . . By that blessed purpose *we* profit, whom God called both out of the Jews and out of the Gentiles. This calling is illustrated by the language of two passages of Hosea,[2] in which the prophet calls his son and daughter Lo-ammi and Lo-ruhamah (Not-my-people and Not-pitied) because of the rejection of Israel, but at the same time prophesies the day when they shall again be His people, and He their God:—and by two passages of Isaiah[3] in which he at once prophesies the rejection of the mass of Israel and the preservation of a remnant.[4]

Having thus established the fact on Scriptural authority, what is the conclusion? Must it not be that—so entirely is election a matter of God's free grace—the Gentiles, though they did not pursue righteousness, yet laid hold of justification by faith; and that the Jews, though they did pursue a legal righteousness, have not attained to justification? How can such a strange anomaly be explained? Whatever may be the working of Divine election, humanly speaking, their rejection is the fault of the Jews. They chose to aim at an impossible justification by works, and rejected the justification by faith. Again St. Paul refers to Isaiah in support of his views.[5] They stumbled at Christ. To them, as to all believers, He might have been a firm rock of foundation; they made Him a stone of offence.[6] The desire of his heart, his prayer to God, is for their salvation. But their religious zeal has taken an ignorant direction. They are aiming at justification by works, and therefore will not accept God's method, which is justification by faith.[7]

In the path of works they cannot succeed, for the Law finds its sole end, and aim, and fulfilment in Christ,[8] and through Him alone is justification possible. Even these truths the Apostle finds in Scripture, or illustrates by Scriptural quotations. He contrasts the statement of Moses, that he who obeyed the ordinances of

[1] When we read such passages as Rom. viii. 22—24; 2 Cor. v. 18; Acts iii. 19, 21, we think that St. Paul would have seen a phase of truth in the lines—

"Safe in the hands of one disposing power,
Or in the natal or the mortal hour;
All Nature is but Art, unknown to thee;
All Chance, Direction which thou canst not see;
All Discord, Harmony not understood;
All partial evil, universal good."

[2] Hos. i. 9, 10; ii. 23.

[3] Isa. x. 22; i. 9.

[4] ix. 22—30. Ver. 28 is an exegetical translation which St. Paul adopts from the LXX. As the form of quotation has only an indirect bearing on the argument, the reader must refer to special commentaries for its elucidation.

[5] Isa. viii. 14; xxviii. 16.

[6] In ix. 33, the "be ashamed" of the LXX., followed by St. Paul, is an exegetical translation of "make haste" or "flee hastily."

[7] ix. 30—x. 4.

[8] x. 4, τέλος—*i.e.*, the righteousness at which the Law aims is accomplished in Christ, and the Law leads to Him; He is its fulfilment and its termination. Its glory is done away, but He remains, because His eternal brightness is the τέλος τοῦ καταργουμένου (Gal.)

the Law should live by them,[1] with those other words which he puts into the mouth of Justification personified, "Say not in thine heart who shall ascend into heaven, or who shall descend into the abyss, but the word is very nigh thee in thy mouth and in thy heart," which (being used originally of the Law) he explains of the nearness and accessibility of the Gospel which was now being preached, and which was summed up in the confession and belief in Him as a risen Saviour. This is again supported by two quotations in almost the same words—one from Isaiah (xxviii. 16), "Every one that believeth on Him shall not be ashamed;" and one from Joel (ii. 32), "Every one that calleth on the name of the Lord shall be saved"—and the "every one" of course includes the Gentile no less than the Jew.[3]

But had the Jews enjoyed a real opportunity of hearing the Gospel? In a series of questions, subordinated to each other by great rhetorical beauty, St. Paul shows that each necessary step has been fulfilled—the hearing, the preachers, the mission of those whose feet were beautiful upon the mountains, and who preach the glad tidings of peace; but, alas! the *faith* had been wanting, and, therefore, also the calling upon God. For all had not hearkened to the Gospel. It was not for want of hearing, for in accordance with prophecy (Ps. xix. 4) the words of the preachers had gone out to all the world; but it was for want of faith, and this, too, had been prophesied, since Isaiah said, "Who believed our preaching?" Nor, again, was it for want of warning. Moses (Deut. xxxii. 21) had told them ages ago that God would stir up their jealousy and kindle their anger by means of those Gentiles whom in their exclusive arrogance they despised as "no nation;" and Isaiah (lxv. 1, 2) says with daring energy, "I was found by such as sought me not, I became manifest to such as inquired not after me," whereas to Israel he saith, "The whole day long I outspread my hands to a disobedient and antagonistic people."[2]

Thus, with quotation after quotation—there are nine in this chapter alone, drawn chiefly from Deuteronomy, Isaiah, and the Psalms—does St. Paul state his conviction as to the present rejection of the Gospel by his own nation; while he tries to soften the bitter rage which it was calculated to arouse both against himself and against his doctrine, by stating it in words which would add tenfold authority to the dialectical arguments into which they are enwoven. But having thus established two very painful, and at first sight opposing truths—namely, that the Jews were being deprived of all exclusive privileges by the decree of God (ix.), and that this forfeiture was due to their own culpable disbelief (x.)—he now enters on the gladder and nobler task of explaining how these sad truths are robbed of their worst sting, when we recognise that they are but the partial and transient phenomena incidental to the evolution of a blessed, universal, and eternal scheme.

"I ask, then, did God reject His people? Away with the thought! for at worst the rejection is but partial." Of this he offers himself as a proof, being as he is "an Israelite, of the seed of Abraham, of the tribe of Benjamin;" and he then quotes the analogy of the 7,000 whom God "reserved for Himself," who in the days of Elijah had not bowed the knee to Baal. On this he pauses to remark that the very phrase, "I reserved for myself," implies that this remnant was saved by faith, and not by works. But how came it that the majority had missed the end for which they sought? Because, he answers, they were hardened; God (as

[1] א, A, B, ἐν αὐτῇ.

[2] x. 4—12. It is remarkable that in verse 11 the important word πᾶς is found neither in the Hebrew nor in the LXX. Cf. ix. 33.

[3] x. 14—21.

Isaiah prophesied) had sent them a spirit of stupor which finds its illustration in the phrase, "let their eyes be darkened," amid David's prayer for the humiliation and bewilderment of his enemies.[1]

But then another awful question occurs: is this hardening, this spiritual blindness, to be final? "Did they stumble that they may utterly fall?" Again Paul exclaims, Perish the thought! Their very fall was meant for salvation to the Gentiles, and to stimulate their own hearts to better things. And here his readers could not but feel that he was explaining facts which were taking place under their very eyes. In every instance the Gospel had been offered first to the Jew; in every instance the Jew had rejected it; and it was through this very obstinacy that it had now been offered everywhere to the Gentile. The Messiah rejected by the Jew was daily being glorified as the Redeemer of the Gentile. The Church of the Christ was now securely founded, but even already Antioch, and Rome, and Ephesus, and Thessalonica were far more its capitals than the Holy City. But this fact revealed a glorious anticipation. If their *deficiency* was thus the wealth of the Gentiles, how much more would their replenishment! It was his grand mission to preach this to the Gentiles, and thereby, if possible, to stir the Jews to emulation, for if their rejection be the world's reconciliation, what will be their acceptance but life from the dead?

And that there will be this restoration of Israel he illustrates by a double metaphor.

i. When the heave-offering was offered, the whole lump of dough acquired sacredness from the fact that a portion of it was sanctified to the Lord. So with Israel. Their first-fruits—Abraham and their patriarchal fathers—were holy, and their holiness was ideally attributable to all the race.

ii. The second metaphor has a wider applicability. The root of the olive-tree is the source of its fruitfulness; but if some of its branches lose their fruitfulness and become withered, they are lopped off and are replaced by grafts of the wild olive, which then shares the richness of the tree. Such withered branches were the present unbelieving majority of Israel. That they should be lopped off is a part of God's just and necessary severity. To explain this truth—to bring it home to the pained and angry consciousness of his people—has been one of his objects in this great Epistle, and he has carried it out, at whatever cost, with a most unflinching sincerity. But meanwhile, if the Gentiles in their turn were tempted to assume the airs of particularism with which the Jews had so long gloried over them, what a warning should be conveyed to them by the state of things here shadowed forth! And how much consolation might the Jew find in this metaphor to revive the fainting hopes of his patriotism, and to alleviate his wounded pride of nationality by gentler and holier thoughts! For Christ, after all, was a rod of the stem of Jesse, and a branch out of his roots. The Gentiles were admitted into the Church through the vestibule of the Temple. With the Jews had remained till this moment the oracles of God. In Judaism—its privileges, its promises, its prophecies—were the germs of Christianity. The new rich fruitfulness of the Gentiles was drawn from the tree into which they had been grafted. Little cause had they to boast against the natural branches. Deep cause had they to take warning by the fate which those branches had undergone. They, in their turn, might be lopped off, and—though here the metaphor as such breaks down—the old branches might be grafted into their proper place once more.[2] Let them remember that faith was the source of their new privileges, as the want of it had caused the ruin of those whom they replaced; let them not be high-minded, but fear.[3]

[1] xi. 1—11.

[2] This of course was, physically, an impossible method of *ἐγκεντρισμός*: the other, if adopted at all, was most rare. (*V. supra*, p. 12.)

[3] xi. 16—24.

The concluding words of this section of the Epistle open a glorious perspective of ultimate hope for all whose hearts are sufficiently large and loving to accept it. He calls on the brethren not to ignore the mystery that the partial hardening of Israel should only last till the fulness of the Gentiles should come in; and he appeals to Scripture (Isa. lix. 20) to support his prophecy that "all Israel shall be saved," beloved as they are for the sake of their fathers as regards the election of grace, though now alienated for the blessing of the Gentiles as regards the Gospel.

For God's gifts and calling admit of no revocation; once given, they are given for ever.[1] Once themselves disobedient, the Gentiles were now pitied in consequence of the disobedience of the Jews; so the Jews were now disobedient, but when the pity shown to the Gentiles had achieved their full redemption, the Jews in turn should share in it.[2] "For"—such is the grand conclusion of this sustained exposition of the Divine purposes—"God shut up all into disobedience,[3] that He might show mercy unto all."—Many are anxious, in accordance with their theological views, to weaken or explain away the meaning of these words; to show that "all" does not really mean "all" in the glad, though it does in the gloomy clause; or to show that "having mercy upon all" is quite consistent with the final ruin of the vast majority. Be that as it may, the Apostle, as he contemplates the universality of free redeeming grace, bursts into a pæan of praise and prophecy: "O the depth of the riches, and wisdom, and knowledge of God! how unsearchable are His judgments, and untrackable His ways! For who ever fathomed the mind of the Lord, or who ever became His counsellor? Or who gave Him first, and it shall be repaid to him? For from Him, and through Him, and unto Him are all things. To Him be glory for ever. Amen."

CHAPTER XXXIX.

FRUITS OF FAITH.

"La foi justifie quand il opère, mais il n'opère que par la charité" (Quesnel).

"Not that God doth require nothing unto happiness at the hands of man save only a naked belief (for hope and charity we may not exclude), but that without belief all other things are as nothing; and it is the ground of those other divine virtues" (Hooker, *Eccl. Pol.* I. xi. 6).

"Faith doth not shut out repentance, hope, love, dread, and the fear of God, to be joined with faith in every man that is justified; but it shutteth them out from the office of justifying" (*Homily of Salvation*, pt. i.).

[It is needless to point out that the sense of the word "faith" in these passages is by no means the Pauline sense of the word."]

At this point there is a marked break in the letter, and we feel that the writer has now accomplished the main object for which he wrote. But to

[1] Hos. xiii. 14, "I will redeem them from death . . . repentance shall be hid from mine eyes."

[2] xi. 41. If, as in this explanation, the comma is placed after ἠπείθησαν, the connexion of τῷ ὑμετέρῳ ἐλέει is very awkward, and almost unparalleled. On the other hand, the antithesis is spoiled if we place the comma after ἐλέει, and render it, "So they too now disbelieved (or disobeyed) the pity shown to you."

[3] In the declaratory sense.

this, as to all his letters, he adds those noble practical exhortations, which are thus made to rest, not on their own force and beauty, but on the securer basis of the principles which he lays down in the doctrinal portion. No one felt more deeply than St. Paul that it requires great principles to secure our faithfulness to little duties, and that every duty, however apparently insignificant, acquires a real grandeur when it is regarded in the light of those principles from which its fulfilment springs. Since, then, the mercy and pity of God, as being the source of His free grace, have been dwelt upon throughout the Epistle, St. Paul begins the practical part of it—"I exhort you therefore, brethren, by the compassions of God"—for these, and not the difficult doctrines of election and reprobation, are prominent in his mind—"to present your bodies, not like the dead offerings of Heathenism or Judaism, but "a *living* sacrifice, holy, well-pleasing to God—your reasonable service, and not to be conformed to this world, but to be transformed[1] in the renewing of your mind, that ye may discriminate what is the will of God, good and acceptable to Him, and perfect."

This general exhortation is then carried into details, unsystematically indeed, and even unsyntactically, but with an evident rush and glow of feeling which gives to the language a perfection transcending that of conscious art.[2] The prevalent thought is the duty of love:—to the brethren, love without dissimulation; to the Church, love without struggling self-assertion; to the civil power, love without fear; to the world, love without despising its rights or mingling with its immoralities.[3] First, by the grace given to him, he urges them "not to be high-minded above what they ought to be minded, but to mind to be soberminded,[4] each in porportion to their God-apportioned receptivity of faith;" and he illustrates and enforces this duty of modest simplicity in the fulfilment of their mutual ministries,[5] by touching once more on the apologue of the body and the members,[6] which he has already applied in his Letter to the Corinthians. The moral of the metaphor is that "Diversity without unity is disorder; unity without diversity is death."[7] Then with a free interchange of participles, infinitives, and imperatives, and with a mixture of general and special exhortations, he urges them to love, kindliness, zeal, hope, patience, prayer, generosity, forgiveness, sympathy, mutual esteem, self-

[1] Ver. 2, συσχηματίζεσθε, "*fashioned* in accordance;" μεταμορφοῦσθε, "trans-*formed*." Σχῆμα, as in Phil. ii. 8, is the outward, transitory fashion; μορφή, the abiding and substantial form.

[2] Ver. 3, μὴ ὑπερφρονεῖν παρ' ὃ δεῖ φρονεῖν, ἀλλὰ φρονεῖν εἰς τὸ σωφρονεῖν.

[3] Lange *ad loc.*

[4] xii. 3.

[5] In ver. 6 the "prophecy [*i.e.*, high Christian teaching] according to the proportion of faith" (κατὰ τὴν ἀναλογίαν τῆς πίστεως) means that the Christian teacher is to keep within the limits of his gift assigned him by his individuality (Tholuck), *i.e.*, not to push his χάρισμα as a preacher into disproportionate prominence (Deut. xviii. 18). The objective sense of πίστις as a body of doctrines is later. Hence the common rule of explaining Scripture, "according to the analogy of faith," though most true and necessary, is a misapplication of the original meaning of the phrase.

[6] 1 Cor. xii. 12—27.

[7] Lange. The conception of Christian fellowship involves both unity and variety. "The Spirit resolves the variety into unity, introduces variety into the unity, and reconciles unity to itself through variety" (Baur).

restraint, the steady love of God, the steady loathing of evil, the deliberate victory of virtue over vice. It is clear that the dangers which he most apprehended among the Roman Christians were those exacerbations which spring from an unloving and over-bearing self-confidence; but he gives a general form to all his precepts, and the chapter stands unrivalled as a spontaneous sketch of the fairest graces which can adorn the Christian life.[1]

The first part of the thirteenth chapter has a more obviously special bearing. It is occupied by a very earnest exhortation to obedience towards the civil power, based on the repeated statements that it is ordained of God; that its aim is the necessary suppression of evil; that it was not, under ordinary circumstances, any source of terror to a blameless life; and that it should be obeyed and respected, not of unwilling compulsion, but as a matter of right and conscience.[2] This was, indeed, the reason why they paid taxes,[3] and why the payment of them should be regarded as a duty to God.[4]

The warmth with which St. Paul speaks thus of the functions of civil governors may, at first sight, seem surprising, when we remember that a Helius was in the Præfecture, a Tigellinus in the Prætorium, a Gessius Florus in the provinces, and a Nero on the throne. On the other hand, it must be borne in mind that the Neronian persecution had not yet broken out; and that the iniquities of individual emperors and individual governors, while it had free rein in every question which affected their greed, their ambition, or their lust, had not as yet by any means destroyed the magnificent ideal of Roman Law. If there were bad rulers, there were also good ones. A Cicero as well

[1] xii. 1—21. As regards special expressions in this chapter, we may notice—ver. 9, ἀποστυγοῦντες "loathing;" κολλώμενοι, "bridal intimacy with." Ver. 10, τῇ φιλαδελφίᾳ φιλόστοργοι, "love your brethren in the faith as though they were brethren in blood;" προηγούμενοι, Vulg. *invicem praevenientes*," "anticipating one another, and going before one another as guides in giving honour" (ver. 11). The evidence between the readings, καιρῷ, "serving the opportunity," and Κυρίῳ, "the Lord," is very nicely balanced, but probably rose from the abbreviation κρῳ. The other clause is, "In zealous work not slothful; boiling in spirit" (cf. the נָבִיא, "a prophet"). In ver. 13, μνείαις, "memories," can hardly be the true reading. In ver. 14, the διώκοντες, "pursuing hospitality," may have suggested the thought of διώκοντας, "persecutors;" ver. 16, τοῖς ταπεινοῖς συναπαγόμενοι is either "modestissimorum exempla sectantes" (Grot.), "letting the lowly lead you with them by the hand" (*masc.*), or "humilibus rebus obsecundantes," "going along with lowly things" (*neut.*). Ver. 19, δότε τόπον τῇ ὀργῇ, either (1) "Give place for the divine wrath to work" (Chrys., Aug., &c.); or (2), "Give room to your own anger"—*i.e.*, defer its outbreak—this, however, would be a Latinism, "irae spatium dare (cf. Virg. *Æn.* iv. 433); or (3) "Give place to, yield before, the wrath of your enemy." The first is right. Ver. 20, "coals of fire" (Prov. xxv. 21, 22) to melt him to penitence and beneficent shame. The chapter is full of beautiful trilogies of expression.

[2] xiii. 5, ἀνάγκη (7, 8, Aug.) ὑποτάσσεσθε (D, E, F, G, Vulg., Luther), "Yield to necessity." "Pray for the established Government," said Rabbi Chaneena, "for without it men would eat one another" (*Abhôda Zara*, f. 4, 1). Josephus calls Judas the Gaulonite "the author of the fourth sect of Jewish philosophy," who have "an inviolable attachment to liberty," and say that God is to be the only Ruler (*Antt.* xviii. 1, § 6).

[3] xiii. 6, τελεῖτε is the indicative; not, as in the A.V., an imperative (Matt. xvii. 21). In ver. 4 the μάχαιρα refers to the *jus gladii*. A provincial governor on starting was presented with a dagger by the Emperor. Trajan, in giving it, used the words—*Pro me; si merear, in me.*"

[4] xiii. 1—7.

as a Verres had once been provincial governors; a Barea Soranus as well as a Felix. The Roman government, corrupt as it often was in special instances, was yet the one grand power which held in check the anarchic forces which but for its control were "nursing the impatient earthquake." If now and then it broke down in minor matters, and more rarely on a large scale, yet the total area of legal prescriptions was kept unravaged by mischievous injustice. St. Paul had himself suffered from local tyranny at Philippi, but on the whole, up to this time, he had some reason to be grateful to the impartiality of Roman law. At Corinth he had been protected by the disdainful justice of Gallio, at Ephesus by the sensible appeal of the public secretary; and not long afterwards he owed his life to the soldier-like energy of a Lysias, and the impartial protection of a Festus, and even of a Felix. Nay, even at his first trial his undefended innocence prevailed not only over all the public authority which could be arrayed against him by Sadducean priests and a hostile Sanhedrin, but even over the secret influence of an Aliturus and a Poppæa. Nor had the Jews any reason to be fretful and insubordinate. If the ferocity of Sejanus and the alarm of Claudius had caused them much suffering at Rome, yet, on the other hand, they had been protected by a Julius and an Augustus, and they were in possession of legal immunities which gave to their religion the recognised dignity of a *religio licita.* It may safely be said that, in many a great city, it was to the inviolable strength and grandeur of Roman law that they owed their very existence; because, had it not been for the protection thus afforded to them, they might have been liable to perish by the exterminating fury of Pagan populations by whom they were at once envied and disliked.[1]

No doubt the force of these considerations would be fully felt by those Jews who had profited by Hellenistic culture. It is obvious, however, that St. Paul is here dealing with religious rather than with political or even theocratic prejudices. The early Church was deeply affected by Essene and Ebionitic elements, and St. Paul's enforcement of the truth that the civil power derives its authority from God, points to the antithesis that it was *not* the mere vassalage of the devil. It was not likely that at Rome there should be any of that zealot fanaticism which held it unlawful for a Jew to recognise any other earthly ruler besides God, and looked on the payment of tribute as a sort of apostasy.[2] It is far more likely that the Apostle is striving to counteract the restless insubordination which might spring from tha prevalence of chiliastic notions such as those which we find in the Clementine Homilies, that "the present world with all its earthly powers is the kingdom of the devil," and that so far from regarding the civil governor as "the minister of God for good," the child of the future could only look upon him as the embodied representative of a spiritual enemy. This unpractical and dualistic view might even claim on its side certain phrases alluding to the

[1] Thus the later Rabbis found it necessary to say, with Shemuel, "The law of the Gentile kingdom is valid" (*Babha Kama,* f. 113, 1).
[2] Matt. xxii. 17.

moral wickedness of the world, which had a wholly different application;[1] and therefore Paul, with his usual firmness, lays down in unmistakable terms the rule which, humanly speaking, could alone save the rising Church from utter extinction—the rule, namely, of holding aloof from political disturbances. On the whole, both Jews and Christians had learnt the lesson well, and it was, therefore, the more necessary that the good effects of that faithful fulfilment of the duties of citizenship, to which both Jewish historians and Christian Fathers constantly appeal, should not be obliterated by the fanatical theories of incipient Manichees.

The question as to the payment of civil dues leads St. Paul naturally to speak of the payment of other dues. The one debt which the Christian owes to all men is the debt of love—that love which prevents us from all wrong-doing, and is therefore the fulfilment of the law. To this love he invites them in a powerful appeal, founded on the depth of the night and the nearness of the dawn, so that it was high time to put away the works of darkness and put on the arms of light[2]—nay, more, to put on, as a close-fitting robe, by close spiritual communion, the Lord Jesus Christ Himself.[3]

The fourteenth chapter again reveals the existence of Ebionitic elements in the Roman Church. In a strange city, and especially if he were ont free, a scrupulous Jew, uninfluenced by Hellenism, would find it so impossible to fulfil the requirements of the Law respecting clean and unclean meats, and still more the many minute additions which Rabbinic Pharisaism had made to those requirements, that he would be forced either to sacrifice his convictions, or to reduce his diet to the simplest elements. As St. Paul does not allude to the Law, it is probable that he is here dealing with scruples even more deeply seated. His object is to reconcile the antagonistic feelings of two classes of Christians, whom he calls respectively the "strong" and the "weak." The "strong" regarded all days as equally sacred, or, as the "weak" would have said, as equally profane; whereas the "weak" surrounded the Sabbath and the Jewish festivals with regulations intended to secure their rigid observance.[4] Again, the "strong" ate food of every description without the smallest scruple, whereas the "weak" looked on all animal food with such disgust and suspicion that they would eat nothing but herbs.[5] It is obvious that in adopting so severe a course they went far beyond the requirements of Levit-

[1] John xii. 31, ὁ ἄρχων τοῦ κόσμου τούτου: Eph. ii. 2, τὸν ἄρχοντα τῆς ἐξουσίας τοῦ ἀέρος.

[2] xiii. 12, or "the deeds of light" (ἔργα, A, D, E).

[3] Cf. Gal. iii. 27, Χριστὸν ἐνεδύσασθε.

[4] Rom. xiv. 6. The words, "and he who regardeth not the day, to the Lord he doth not regard it," are omitted by ℵ, A, B, C, D, E, F, G, Vet., It., Vulg., Copt. On the other hand, the Syriac has it, and the omission may be due to the *homœoteleuton* of φρονεῖ, or to doctrinal prejudices, which regarded the clause as dangerous. The clause is far too liberal to have been inserted by a second century scribe; but even if it be omitted, the principle which it involves is clearly implied in the first half of the verse, and in the previous verse.

[5] Seneca tells us that in his youth he had adopted from his Pythagorean teacher Sotion the practice of vegetarianism, but his father made him give it up because it rendered him liable to the suspicion of foreign superstitions (probably Judaism). See *Seekers after God*, p. 15.

ism, and when we find the very same views and practices existing in Rome during the next century,[1] it is hardly possible to avoid the suspicion that the Judaic Christianity of these "weak" brethren was tinged with those Essene, Phrygian, or Pythagorean elements which led them to look on the material and the sensuous as something intrinsically dangerous, if not as positively evil. Epiphanius says that Ebion visited Rome;[2] and although it is more than doubtful whether there ever was such a person, yet the statement shows the prevalence of such views. Now one of the Ebionitic principles was that all meat is impure,[3] and in the Clementine Homilies the eating of meat is attributed to impure demons and bloodthirsty giants; and the Apostle Peter is made to say to Clement that "he makes use only of bread and olives and (sparingly) of other vegetables"[4]—a tradition which we also find attached by Clemens of Alexandria to the names of St. Matthew and James the Lord's brother, and the latter we are told drank no wine or strong drink.[5] It is very possible that St. Paul did not see the necessity of formally warning the Roman Christians against the tendency to dualism. This might be the subterranean origin of wrong notions long before it had risen into clear consciousness. What St. Paul *did* see was the danger that if "the weak" prevailed, Christianity might be frittered away into a troublesome and censorious externalism; or that the "strong" might treat their weaker brethren with a rough and self-exalting contempt which would either put force on tender consciences, or create a permanent disruption between the different members of the Church.[6]

He treats the difficulty in the same masterly manner—broad yet sympathetic, inflexible in convictions yet considerate towards prejudices—which he had already displayed in dealing with a similar question in his Epistle to the Corinthians. But the difference between the tone adopted in this chapter and that in the Epistle to the Galatians is very remarkable, and shows the admirable tact and versatility of the Apostle. He is there establishing the rights of Christian freedom against the encroachments of Pharisaism, so that the assertion of the liberty of the Gentiles was a matter of essential importance. He therefore speaks, as it was a duty to speak, with an almost rough contempt of attaching any vital importance to "beggarly elements." Here his tone is altogether different, because his object is altogether different, as also were his readers. The *right* to enjoy our liberty he can here in the most absolute manner assume. As to the merit of the particular scrupulosities which were in vogue among the weak, he has no occasion to do more than imply his own indifference. What is here necessary is to warn the "strong" not to be arrogant in their condemnations, and the "weak" not to be supercilious in their self-esteem. He has shown the universality of guilt, and the universality of grace, and he has now to show the sacred duty of unanimity among these thus universally

[1] The Ebionites regarded the Sabbath as the holiest command of the Jewish religion.
[2] *Haer.* xxx. 18.
[3] Epiphan. *Haer.* xxx. 15.
[4] *Hom.* xii. 6.
[5] *Paedag.* ii. 1; Euseb. *H. E.* ii. 23; Baur, *Paul.* i. 358.
[6] Gal. iii.; v. 1—9; vi. 12, 13.

called, defending this unanimity against censoriousness on the one hand, and against disdain on the other.

He does not attempt to conceal the bent of his own sympathies; he declares himself quite unambiguously on the side of the "strong." The life of the Christian is a life in Christ, and rises transcendently above the minutiæ of ritual, or the self-torments of asceticism. "The kingdom of God"—such is the great axiom which he lays down for the decision of all such questions—"is not meat and drink; but righteousness, and peace, and joy in the Holy Ghost." The "strong," therefore, in St. Paul's judgment, were in the right. But, for this very reason, it was necessary to warn them against the contemptuous assertion of their superior wisdom.

i. Let each party follow their own course if they believe it to be the best, but let each abstain from the guilt and folly of condemning the other. God, not man, is the judge, by whose judgment each man stands or falls. Nay, he shall stand, for God is able to make him stand. Conceited illuminism is as deep an offence against charity as saintly self-satisfaction. The first counsel, then, on which he strongly insists is mutual forbearance, the careful avoidance of arguments and discussions about disputed points. Let there be no intolerant scrupulosity, and no uncharitable disdain, but an avoidance of dispute and a reciprocal recognition of honest convictions. These differences are not about essentials, and it is not for any man to adopt a violently dogmatic or uncharitably contemptuous tone towards those who differ from himself respecting them. The party-spirit of religious bodies too often finds the fuel for its burning questions in mere weeds and straw.[1]

ii. The second counsel is the cultivation of careful consideration which shall not shock tender consciences; it is, in short, condescendence towards the weakness of others, a willingness to take less than our due, and a readiness to waive our own rights,[2] and enjoy as a private possession between ourselves and God the confidence of our faith. His own positive and sacred conviction is that these rules about food are unessential; that no food is intrinsically unclean. But if by acting on this conviction we lead others to do the same, in spite of the protest of their consciences, then for a paltry self-gratification we are undoing God's work, and slaying a soul for which Christ died.[3] Rather than do this, rather than place a needless stumbling-block in any Christian's path, it were well neither to eat meat nor to drink wine, because Christian love is a thing more precious than even Christian liberty.[4]

iii. His third counsel is the obedience to clear convictions.[5] Happy the man who has no scruples as to things intrinsically harmless. But if another cannot

[1] xiv. 1—12, προσλαμβάνεσθε, "take by the hand;" μὴ εἰς διακρίσεις διαλογισμῶν, "not by way of criticising for them their scrupulous niceties" (Tholuck).

[2] Συγκατάβασις (see Rom. xv. 1), ἐλαττοῦσθαι (John iii. 30), ὑστερεῖσθαι (Phil. iv. 12; 1 Cor. vi. 7); three great Christian conceptions which have in the practice of "religious" parties become perilously obsolete.

[3] 1 Cor. viii. 13.

[4] xiv. 13—21

[5] Augustine's "Omnis infidelium vita, peccatum est" is an instance of the many extravagant inferences which are the curse of theology, and which arise from recklessly tearing words from the context, and pushing them beyond their legitimate significance. We have no right to apply the text apart from the circumstances to which it immediately refers. As a universal principle it is only applicable to the party of which the Apostle is speaking. When applied analogically, "faith" can here only be taken to mean "the moral conviction of the rectitude of a mode of action" (Chrys., De Wette, Meyer, &c.). To pervert the meaning of texts, as is done so universally, is to make a bad play upon words. Our Art. XIII. does not in the least exclude the possibility of *gratia praeveniens* even in heathens (see Rom. ii. 6—15). If Augustine meant that even the morality and virtue of pagans, heretics, &c., is sin, his axiom is not only morose and repellent, Pharisaical and anti-scriptural, but historically, spiritually, and morally false.

emancipate himself from these scruples, however needless, and exhibits in his own conduct the same freedom in defiance of his scruples, then he stands self-condemned. Why? Because in that case he is acting falsely to that faith which is the ruling principle of his Christian life, and whatsoever is not of faith,—whatsoever involves the life of self, and not the life of Christ—is sin.[1]

The true principle, then, is that we ought not to please ourselves, even as Christ pleased not Himself, but to bear the infirmities of the weak, and aim at mutual edification. This is the lesson of Scripture, and he prays that the God of that patience and comfort which it is the object of Scripture to inspire, may give them mutual unanimity in Jesus Christ. And addressing alike the "weak" Judaizers and the "strong" Gentiles, he concludes his advice with the same general precept with which he began, "Wherefore take one another by the hand, as Christ also took us by the hand for the glory of God."[2]

And Christ had thus set His example of love and help to both the great divisions of the Church. He had become the minister of the circumcision on behalf of God's truth, to fulfil the promise made to the fathers; and to the Gentiles out of compassion. Christ therefore had shown kindness to both, and that the Gentiles were indeed embraced in this kindness—which, perhaps, in their pride of liberty they did not always feel inclined to extend to their weaker brethren—he further proves by an appeal to Deuteronomy, Isaiah, and the Psalms.[3] The last citation ends with the words "shall hope," and he closes this section with yet another prayer that the God of hope would fill them with all joy and peace in believing, that they might abound in hope in the power of the Holy Ghost.

But once more he takes up the pen to assure them of his confidence in them, and to apologise for the boldness of his letter. His plea is that he wished to fulfil to the utmost that ministry to the Gentiles which he here calls a priestly ministry, because he is as it were instrumental in presenting the Gentiles as an acceptable offering to God.[4] Of this Apostolate (giving all the glory to God)—of the signs by which it had been accompanied—of the width of its range, from Jerusalem to Illyricum—he may make a humble boast.

And he is still ambitious to preach in regions where Christ has not been named. He will not stay with them, because he has seen enough of the evil caused by those who built on a foundation which they had not laid; but he has often felt a strong desire to visit them on his way to Spain,[5] and after a partial enjoyment of their society,[6] to be furthered on his journey by their assistance. He has hitherto been prevented from taking that journey, but now—since for the present his duties in the East are over—he hopes to carry it out, and to gratify his earnest desire to see them. At present, however, he is about to start for Jerusalem, to accompany the deputies who are to convey to the poor saints there that temporal gift from the Christians of Macedonia and Achaia which is after all but a small recognition of the spiritual gifts which the Gentiles have received from them. When this task is over he will

[1] xiv. 22, 23. It is at this point that some MSS. place the doxology of xvi. 25—27; but this would be a most awkward break between the fourteenth and fifteenth chapters, and the reasons for regarding the fifteenth chapter as spurious seem to me to be wholly inconclusive.

[2] xv. 1—8. [3] Deut. xxxii. 43; Ps. xviii. 49; cxvii. 1; Isa. xi. 10.

[4] xv. 16, ἱερουργοῦντα. It is a ἅπ. λεγόμενον not due to any sacrificial conception of the Christian ministry (of which there is not in St. Paul so much as a single trace), but to the particular illustration which he here adopts.

[5] xv. 24 omit ἐλεύσομαι πρὸς ὑμᾶς with all the best MSS. "Having a desire for many years past to come to you whenever I journey into Spain."

[6] ἀπὸ μέρους "non quantum vellem sed quantum liceret" (Grot.).

turn his face towards Spain, and visit them on his way, and he is confident that he shall come in the fulness of the blessing of the Gospel of Jesus Christ. He, therefore, earnestly entreats their prayers that he may be rescued from the perils which he knows await him from the Jews in Jerusalem, and that the contribution due to his exertions may be favourably received by the saints, that so by God's will he may come to them in joy, and that they may mutually refresh each other.[1] "And the God of peace be with you all. Amen."[2]

There in all probability ended the Epistle to the Romans. I have already given abundant reason in support of the ingenious conjecture[3] that the greater part of the sixteenth chapter was addressed to the Ephesian Church.[4] Even a careless reader could scarcely help observing what we should not at all have conjectured from the earlier part of the Epistle that there were schisms and scandals (17—20) in the Roman Church, and teachers who deliberately fomented them, slaves of their own belly, and by their plausibility and flattery deceiving the hearts of the simple.[5] Nor, again, can any one miss the fact that the position of the Apostle towards his correspondents in verse 19 is far more severe, paternal, and authoritative than in the other chapters. If—as is surely an extremely reasonable supposition—St. Paul desired other Churches besides the stranger Church of Rome to reap the benefit of his ripest thoughts, and to read the maturest statement of the Gospel which he preached, then several copies of the main part of the Epistle must have been made by the amanuenses, of whom Tertius was one, and whose services the Apostle was at that moment so easily able to procure. In that case nothing is more likely than that the terminations of the various copies should have varied with the circumstances of the Churches, and nothing more possible than that in some one copy the various terminations should have been carefully preserved. We have at any rate in this hypothesis a simple explanation of the three final benedictions (20, 24, 27) which occur in this chapter alone.

The fullest of the Apostle's letters concludes with the most elaborate of his doxologies.[6]

[1] xv. 32, καὶ συναναπαύσωμαι ὑμῖν is omitted by B.

[2] xv. 9—33.

[3] First made by Schulz.

[4] We may be very thankful for its preservation, as it has a deep personal interest. On deaconesses see Bingham i. 334—366. Phœbe was probably a widow. Verse 4, ὑπέθηκαν, "laid their own necks under the axe," a probable allusion to some risk at Corinth (Acts xviii. 12; xix. 32). In verse 5 the true reading is Ἀσίας. Verse 7, συναιχμαλώτους—probably at Ephesus, ἐπίσημοι ἐν τοῖς ἀποστόλοις, "illustrious among the missionaries of the truth" (2 Cor. viii. 23; Acts xiv. 4), in the less restricted sense of the word. It is hardly conceivable that St. Paul would make it a merit that the Apostles knew them and thought highly of them (Gal. i. ii.)—verse 13. Rufus, perhaps one of the sons of Simon of Cyrene (Mark xv. 22)—verse 14. Hermas, not the author of *The Shepherd*, who could hardly have been born at this time. Verse 16, φίλημα ἅγιον, 1 Thess. v. 26; 1 Pet. v. 14; Luke vii. 45. The attempted identification of Tertius with Silas, because the Hebrew for Tertius (שְׁלִישִׁי) sounds like Silas, is one of the imbecilities of fanciful exegesis. On such names as Tryphæna and Tryphosa, voluptuous in sound and base in meaning, which may have suggested to St. Paul the κοπιώσας ἐν Κυρίῳ as a sort of noble *paronomasia*, see Merivale, *Hist.* vi. 260, and Wordsworth, *ad loc.*

[5] Phil. iii. 2, 18; 2 Cor. xi. 20.

[6] "Whether the Epistle proceeded in two forms from the Apostle's hands, the one closing with chapter xiv. and the doxology, the other extended by the addition of the two last chapters, or whether any other more satisfactory explanation can be offered of the

"Now to Him who is able to establish you according to my Gospel, and the preaching of Jesus Christ, according to the revelation of the mystery, buried in silence in eternal ages, but manifested now and made known by the prophetic Scriptures, according to the command of the Eternal God unto obedience to the faith to all nations:—To the only wise God, through Jesus Christ—to whom be the glory for ever. Amen."[1]

CHAPTER XL.

THE LAST JOURNEY TO JERUSALEM.

"Show me some one person formed according to the principles he professes. Show me one who is sick and happy; in danger and happy; dying and happy; exiled and happy; disgraced and happy."—EPICTETUS.

IT was now about the month of February, A.D. 58, and the work which St. Paul had set before him at Corinth was satisfactorily concluded. Having been nine months in Europe,[2] he was anxious to get to Jerusalem by the Passover, and intended to sail straight from Corinth to one of the ports of Palestine. Every preparation was made; it almost seems that he had got on board ship; when he was informed of a sudden[3] plot on the part of the Jews to murder him. As to all the details we are left in the dark. We know that the previous plot of the Jews, nearly five years earlier,[4] had been foiled by the contemptuous good sense of Gallio; but even if their revenge were otherwise likely to be laid aside, we cannot doubt that ample fuel had since been heaped upon the smouldering fire of their hatred. From every seaport of the Ægean, from the highlands of Asia Minor, from its populous shores, from Troas under the shadows of Mount Ida, to Athens under the shadow of Mount Pentelicus, they would hear rumours of that daring creed which seemed to trample on all their convictions, and fling to the Gentiles their most cherished hopes. The Jewish teachers who tried to hound the Judaising Christians against St. Paul would stand on perfectly good terms with them, and these Judaisers would take a pleasure in disseminating the deadliest misrepresentations of Paul's doctrine and career. But apart from all misrepresentation, his undeniable arguments were quite enough to madden them to frenzy. We

phenomenon of omission, repetition, transposition, authenticity, must be left for further investigation." Westcott (Vaughan's *Romans*, p. xxv.). One theory is that xii.—xiv. were substituted later for xv. xvi., and then both were accumulated in one copy with some modifications.

[1] Cf. Eph. iii. 20, 21. The text, as it stands, involves an anacoluthon, since the ᾧ should properly be ἐκείνῳ. Tholuck, &c., think that the Apostle was led by the parenthesis from a doxology to God to a doxology to Christ. It may be that he meant to insert the word χάρις, but lost sight of it in the length of the sentence. Here, as in Hab. iii. 6, the word αἰώνιος is used in two consecutive clauses, where in the first clause all are agreed that it *cannot* mean "endless" since it speaks of things which have already come to an end.

[2] He left Ephesus before the Pentecost of A.D. 57.

[3] Acts xx. 3, μέλλοντι ἀνάγεσθαι. γενομένης.

[4] A.D. 52.

may be sure that St. Paul taught as he wrote, and since we have noticed it as a characteristic of his intellect that he is haunted by *words* and expressions,[1] we might infer, *à priori*, even if it were not abundantly evident in his writings, that he is still more powerfully possessed and absorbed by any *thoughts* which might have been forced into immediate prominence. We may regard it as psychologically certain that his discourses at Corinth were the echo of the arguments which fill the two Epistles which he wrote at Corinth; and to the Jews the conclusions which they were meant to establish would be regarded as maddening blasphemies. "There is neither Jew nor Gentile"—where, then, is the covenant to Abraham and to his seed? "There is neither circumcision nor uncircumcision"—where, then, is Moses and all the splendour of Sinai? "Weak and beggarly elements"—are these the terms to apply to the inspired, sacred, eternal Thorah, in which God himself meditates, which is the glory of the world? We are not surprised that the Jews should get up a plot. Paul, under the ægis of Roman authority, might be safe in the city, but they would avenge themselves on him as soon as his ship had left the shore. The wealthy Jewish merchants of Corinth would find no difficulty in hearing of sailors and captains of country vessels who were sufficiently dependent on them to do any deed of violence for a small consideration.

How was the plot discovered? We do not know. Scenes of tumult, and hairbreadth escapes, and dangerous adventures, were so common in St. Paul's life, that neither he, nor any one else, has cared to record their details. We only know that, after sudden discussion, it was decided, that Paul, with an escort of the delegates, quite sufficiently numerous to protect him from ordinary dangers, should go round by Macedonia. The hope of reaching Jerusalem by the Passover had, of course, to be abandoned; the only chance left was to get there by Pentecost. It was doubtless overruled for good that it should be so, for if St. Paul had been in the Holy City at the Passover he would have been mixed up by his enemies with the riot and massacre which about that time marked the insane rising of the Egyptian impostor who called himself the Messiah.[2]

Of the seven converts[3] who accompanied St. Paul—Sosipater son of Pyrrhus,[4] a Berœan, Aristarchus and Secundus of Thessalonica, Gaius of Derbe, Timotheus of Lystra, Tychicus and Trophimus of Ephesus, and Luke—all except the latter left him apparently at Philippi, and went on to Troas to await him there.[5] St. Luke was closely connected with Philippi, where St.

[1] *V. supra*, pp. 273, 387, 407; *infra*, pp. 516, 698. [2] Verse 3, ἐγένετο γνώμη.

[3] In verse 4 the reading, ἀχρὶ τῆς Ἀσίας, is not quite certain, since it is omitted in ℵ, B, Coptic (both versions), and the Æthiopic. Some, at any rate, of the converts—Luke, Aristarchus, and Trophimus, if not others—accompanied him all the way to Jerusalem—xxi. 29, xxvii. 2, 1 Cor. xvi. 3, 4. How is it that there were no Corinthian delegates? Had the large promises of Corinth ended, after all, in words? or did they entrust their contributions to some of the other deputies?

[4] The Πύῤῥου was, perhaps, added to distinguish him from the Sosipater of Rom. xvi. 21, ℵ, A, B, D, E.

[5] Verse 5. If προσελθόντες (ℵ, A, B, E,) be the right reading, Tychicus and Trophimus must have met Paul at Troas.

Paul had left him on his first visit,[1] and the two stayed at the Roman colony to keep the Passover. Very happy, we may be sure, was that quiet time spent by St. Paul in the bosom of the Church which he loved best of all—amid the most blameless and the most warm-hearted of all his converts. Years must have elapsed before he again spent a Passover in circumstances so peaceful and happy.[2]

The eight days of the feast ended in that year on Monday, April 3, and on the next day they set sail. Detained by calms, or contrary winds, they took five days[3] to sail to Troas, and there they again stayed seven days.[4] The delay was singular, considering the haste with which the Apostle was pressing forward to make sure of being at Jerusalem by Pentecost. It was now about the 10th of April, and as the Pentecost of that year fell on May 17, St. Paul, dependent as he was on the extreme uncertainties of ancient navigation, had not a single day to spare. We may be quite sure that it was neither the splendour of the town, with its granite temples and massive gymnasium, that detained him, nor all the archaic and poetic associations of its neighbourhood, nor yet the loveliness of the groves and mountains and gleams of blue sea. Although his former visits had been twice cut short—once by the Macedonian vision, and once by his anxiety to meet Titus—it is even doubtful whether he would have been kept there by the interest which he must have necessarily felt in the young and flourishing Church of a town which was one of the very few in which he had not been subjected to persecution. The delay was therefore probably due to the difficulty of finding or chartering a vessel such as they required.[5]

Be that as it may, his week's sojourn was marked by a scene which is peculiarly interesting, as one of the few glimpses of ancient Christian worship which the New Testament affords. The wild disorders of vanity, fanaticism, and greed, which produced so strange a spectacle in the Church of Corinth, would give us, if we did not regard them as wholly exceptional, a most unfavourable conception of these Sunday assemblies. Very different, happily, is the scene to which we are presented on this April Sunday at Alexandria Troas, A.D. 58.[6]

It was an evening meeting. Whether at this period the Christians had already begun the custom of meeting twice—early in the morning, before dawn, to sing and pray, and late in the evening to partake of the Love Feast and the Lord's Supper, as they did some fifty years after this time in the neighbouring province of Bithynia[7]—we are not told. Great obscurity hangs over the observance of the Lord's day in the first century. The Jewish

[1] The first person plural is resumed in the narrative at xx. 5, having been abandoned at xvi. 17. It is now continued to the end of the Acts, and Luke seems to have remained with St. Paul to the last (2 Tim. iv. 11).

[2] Lewin, *Fasti Sacri*, § 1857.

[3] It had only taken them two days to sail from Troas to Neapolis, the port of Philippi, on a former occasion, xvi. 11.

[4] Compare xx. 6, xxi. 4, xxviii. 14.

[5] 2 Cor. ii. 13.

[6] It was early called Sunday, even by Christians. τῇ τοῦ Ἡλίου λεγομένῃ ἡμέρᾳ (Just. Mart. *Apol.* ii. 228).

[7] Plin. *Ep.* x. 96. "Quod essent soliti stato die *ante lucem* convenire . . . quibus

Christians doubtless continued to keep the Sabbath, but St. Paul reprobates the adoption of any such custom among the Gentiles; and, indeed, his language seems to show that he did not regard with favour any observance of times or seasons which savoured at all of Sabbatical scrupulosity.[1] All that we know is, that from the Resurrection onwards, the first day of the week was signalised by special Christian gatherings for religious purposes, and that on this particular Sunday evening the members of the Church of Troas were assembled, in accordance with their usual custom, to partake of the Love Feast, and to commemorate the death of Christ in the Holy Communion.[2]

The congregation may have been all the more numerous because it was known that on the next day the Apostle and his little company would leave the place. They were gathered in one of those upper rooms on the third storey, which are the coolest and pleasantest part of an Eastern house. The labours of the day were over, and the sun had set, and as three weeks had now elapsed since the full moon of the Passover, there was but a pale crescent to dispel the darkness. But the upper room was full of lamps,[3] and in the earnestness of his overflowing heart, Paul, knowing by many a mysterious intimation the dangers which were awaiting him, continued discoursing to them till midnight. On the broad sill of one of the open windows, of which the lattice or enclosing shutter had been flung wide open to catch the cool sea breeze, sat a boy named Eutychus.[4] The hour was very late, the discourse unusually long, the topics with which it dealt probably beyond his comprehension. Though he was sitting in the pleasantest place in the room, where he would enjoy all the air there was, yet the heat of a crowded meeting, and the glare of the many lamps, and the unbroken stream of the speaker's utterance,[5] sent the lad fast asleep. The graphic description of St. Luke might almost make us believe that he had been watching him, not liking, and perhaps not near enough to awaken him, and yet not wholly insensible of his danger, as first of all he began to nod, then his head gradually sank down on his breast, and, at last, he fell with a rush and cry from the third storey into the courtyard beneath.[6] We can imagine the alarm and excitement by which the voice of the speaker was suddenly interrupted, as some of the congregation ran down the outside staircase[7] to see what had happened. It was dark,[8] and the poor lad lay

peractis morem sibi discedendi fuisse rursusque coeundi ad capiendum cibum, promiscuum tamen et innoxium.

[1] Rom. xiv. 5; Gal. iv. 10; Col. ii. 16.

[2] This is implied by the expression συνηγμένων ἡμῶν κλάσαι ἄρτον. Cf. the word ἐπισυναγωγή, Heb. x. 25, and σύναξις.

[3] This is with St. Luke the casual incident mentioned by an eye-witness, on whose mind the scene was vividly impressed. The lamps are sufficiently accounted for by the darkness, but the mention of them is valuable, as showing how little of secrecy or disorder attended these late meetings. They had not as yet become subjects of suspicion, but it was not long before they did.

[4] It is a common slave name, but nothing more is known of him.

[5] Ver. 9, διαλεγομένου τοῦ Παύλου ἐπὶ πλεῖον.

[6] Ver. 9, καταφερόμενος ὕπνῳ βαθεῖ . . . κατενεχθεὶς ἀπὸ τοῦ ὕπνου ἔπεσεν. καταφέρεσθαι is a *vox solemnis de hâc re.* Aristot. *de Insomniis*, iii. &c.

[7] ἀναβαθμοί.

[8] Being now late at night, the crescent moon must have set.

senseless, and "was taken up dead."[1] A cry of horror and wailing rose from the bystanders; but Paul, going down-stairs, fell on him, and clasping his arms round him,[2] said, "Do not be alarmed, for his life is in him." After he had calmed the excitement by this remark, he left the lad to the effects of rest and quiet, and the kindly care, perhaps, of the deaconesses and other women who were present; for the narrative simply adds that the Apostle went up-stairs again, and after "breaking the bread,"[3]—words descriptive probably of the eucharistic consecration—and making a meal, which describes the subsequent Agapê, he continued in friendly intercourse with the congregation till the dawn of day, and then went out. By that time Eutychus had fully recovered. "They led the boy alive"—apparently into the upper chamber—"and were not a little comforted."

Next day the delegates—these "first Christian pilgrims to the Holy Land"—went down to their vessel to sail round Cape Lectum, while Paul went by land[4] across the base of the promontory to rejoin them at Assos. Whether he had friends to visit on the way, or whether he wished to walk those twenty miles through the pleasant oak-groves along the good Roman roads in silent commune with his own spirit, we do not know. Natures like his, however strong may be their yearning for sympathy, yet often feel an imperious necessity for solitude. If he had heard the witty application by Stratonicus, of Homer's line,

Ἄσσον ἴθ' ὥς κεν θᾶσσον ὀλέθρου πείραθ' ἵκηαι,

he might, while smiling at the gay jest directed against the precipitous descent from the town to the harbour, have thought that for him too—on his way to bonds and imprisonment, and perhaps to death itself—there was a melancholy meaning in the line.[5] Passing between the vast sarcophagi in the street of tombs, and through the ancient gate which still stands in ruin, he made his way down the steep descent to the port, and there found the vessel awaiting him. St. Luke, who was one of those on board, here gives a page of his diary, as the ship winged her way among the isles of Greece. The voyage seems to have been entirely prosperous. The north-west wind which prevails at that season would daily swell the great main-sail, and waft the vessel merrily through blue seas under the shadow of old poetic mountains, by famous cities, along the vernal shores. That same evening they arrived at Mitylene, the bright capital of Lesbos, the home of Sappho and Alcæus, and the cradle of lyric song. Here they anchored, because the moonless night rendered it unsafe to thread their course among the many intricacies of that sinuous coast. Next

[1] De Wette, Olshausen, Meyer, Ewald, and many others, take νεκρὸς to mean "as dead," "apparently dead," "in a dead swoon," interpreting this word by St. Paul's μὴ θορυβεῖσθε . . . γάρ, but the ἤγαγον . . . ζῶντα of vs. 12 seems to show St. Luke's meaning.

[2] ἐπιπεσὼν . . . συμπεριλαβὼν, 1 Kings xvii. 21; 2 Kings iv. 34.

[3] Ver. 11, κλάσας τὸν ἄρτον, καὶ γευσάμενος.

[4] πεζεύειν—possibly, but not necessarily, on foot.

[5] *Il.* vi. 143. The pun may be freely rendered "Go to Assos, if you want to meet your fate." The Vulgate, too, confuses the name Assos and the adverb *asson* ("near") in xxvii. 13.

day they anchored off rocky Chios, whose green fields were the fabled birth-place of Homer.[1] Next day they touched for a short time at Samos, and then sailed across the narrow channel to anchor for the night in the island-harbour of Trogyllium, under the ridge of Mycale, so famous for Conon's victory. Next day, sailing past the entrance of the harbour of Ephesus, they came to anchor at Miletus. St. Paul would gladly have visited Ephesus if time had permitted, but he was so anxious to do all in his power to reach Jerusalem by Pentecost, and therefore to avoid all delays, whether voluntary or accidental, that he resisted the temptation. At Miletus, however, the vessel had to stop, and Paul determined to utilise the brief delay. He had probably arrived about noon, and at once sent a messenger to the elders of the Church of Ephesus to come and see him.[2] It was but a distance of from thirty to forty miles along a well-kept road, and the elders[3] might easily be with him by the next day, which, reckoning from his departure at Troas, was probably a Sunday. He spent the day in their company, and before parting delivered them an address which abounds in his peculiar forms of expression, and gives a deeply interesting sketch of his work at Ephesus.

"Ye know," he said, "how from the first day on which I set foot in Asia I bore myself with you, serving the Lord with all lowly-mindedness, and tears, and trials that happened to me in the plots of the Jews;[4] how I reserved nothing that was profitable,[5] but preached to you, and taught you publicly, and from house to house, testifying both to Jews and Greeks repentance towards God and faith towards our Lord Jesus Christ. And now behold I, bound in the spirit,[6] am on my way to Jerusalem, not knowing what may happen to me there, save that in every city the Holy Spirit testifies to me, saying that bonds and tribulations await me. But I regard it as of no moment, nor do I hold my soul so precious to myself[7] as to finish my course,[8]

[1] τυφλὸς ἀνὴρ οἰκεῖ δὲ Χίῳ ἔνι παιπαλοέσσῃ (*ap.* Thuc. iii. 104).

[2] It is impossible to determine whether the vessel had been chartered by Paul and his companions, or whether they were dependent on its movements. Verse 16 is not decisive.

[3] It is of course known that the words "presbyter" and "bishop" are used interchangeably in the New Testament" (see ver. 28, where the E.V. has "overseers" for "bishops"). Ἐπισκόπους τοὺς πρεσβυτέρους καλεῖ· ἀμφότερα γὰρ εἶχεν κατ' ἐκεῖνον τὸν καιρὸν τὰ ὀνόματα (Theodor. *ad Phil.* i. 1).

[4] These are not mentioned in the narrative. This is one of the many casual indications that St. Luke knew many more particulars than it entered into his plan to detail.

[5] Ver. 20, ὑπεστειλάμην (lit. "reefed up"). The nautical word (cf. πληροφορία, Col. ii. 2, iv. 12; στελλόμενοι, 2 Thess. iii. 6; 2 Cor. viii. 20), so natural in a speaker who must have heard the word every day in his voyage, is very characteristic of St. Paul, who constantly draws his metaphors from the sights and circumstances immediately around him. He uses it again in ver. 27. These little peculiarities of style are quite inimitable, and, as Ewald says, "to doubt the genuineness of this speech is folly itself." Besides many other indications of authenticity, it contains at least a dozen phrases and constructions which are more or less exclusively Pauline.

[6] Ver. 22. Though the true order is δεδεμένος ἐγὼ, ℵ, A, B, C, E, the emphasis is best brought out in English, by putting "I" first.

[7] In the extreme varieties of the MSS. in this clause I follow ℵ, οὐδενὸς λόγου—οὐδὲ ἔχω. This is the very spirit of Luther on his way to Worms.

[8] Omit μετὰ χαρᾶς with ℵ, A, B, D. It is interpolated from Phil. i. 4; Col. i. 11; cf. 2 Tim. iv. 7.

and the ministry which I received from the Lord Jesus to testify[1] the Gospel of the grace of God. And now behold I know that ye shall never see my face again, all you among whom I passed proclaiming the kingdom.[2] Therefore, I call you to witness this very day that I am pure from the blood of all. For I reserved nothing, but preached to you the whole counsel of God. Take heed, then, to yourselves, and to all the flock over which the Holy Ghost appointed you bishops to feed the Church of the Lord[3] which He made His own by His own blood. I know that there shall come after my departure grievous wolves among you, not sparing the flock; and from your own selves[4] shall arise men speaking perverse things, so as to drag away disciples after them. Therefore be watchful, remembering that for three years, night and day,[5] I ceased not with tears[6] to admonish each one. And now I commend you to God, and to the word of His grace, who is able to build you up, and give you an inheritance among all the sanctified. No man's silver or gold or raiment did I covet. Yourselves know that to my needs, and to those with me, these hands"—and

[1] The third time that this verb has occurred in these few verses. It is quite true of St. Paul that "un mot l'obsède." This is an interesting sign of the genuineness of the speech.

[2] St. Paul speaks partly with a view to the dangers he is about to face, partly with reference to his intention to go to the far west. His οἶδα was not necessarily infallible (compare Phil. i. 25 with ii. 24), and in point of fact it is probable that he *did* visit Ephesus again (1 Tim. i. 3, iii. 14, iv. 12—20). But that was long afterwards, and it is quite certain that as a body (πάντες ὑμεῖς) the elders never saw him again.

[3] I accept the reading Κυρίου here with A, C, D, E, the Coptic, Sahidic, Armenian versions, Irenæus, Didymus, Cyril, Jerome, Augustine, &c., rather than Θεοῦ, the remarkable reading of ℵ, B, the Vulgate, Syriac, Chrysostom, Basil, Ambrose, &c., because "the blood of God" is an expression which, though adopted—perhaps from the variation of this very text—by some of the Fathers (Tert. *ad Uxor.* ii. 3), the Church has always avoided. Athanasius, indeed, distinctly says, οὐδαμοῦ δὲ αἷμα Θεοῦ δίχα σαρκὸς παραδεδώκασιν αἱ γραφαί. That St. Paul held in the most absolute sense the Divinity of the Eternal Son is certain; but he would never have said, and never has said, anything like "the blood of God," and I cannot but think it much more probable that he would have used the uncommon but perfectly natural expression "*Church of the Lord*," than seem to sanction the very startling "blood of God." I cannot attach much, if any, importance to the fact that "Church of the Lord" is a less usual combination than "Church of God;" for just in the same way St. Paul, in the Epistle to the Philippians, abandons his favourite expression of "the day of the Lord," and uses instead "day of Christ" (Phil. i. 10, ii. 16). If he had written Θεοῦ, it seems to me very improbable that the reading would have been early tampered with. Such a phrase would rank with terms like *Adelphotheos* and *Theotokos*, which are at once unscriptural and ecclesiastical, whereas, if St. Paul said Κυρίου, the *marginal* Θεοῦ of some pragmatic scribe might easily have obtruded itself into the text. Indeed, the very fact that "Church of the Lord" is not Paul's normal phrase may have suggested the gloss. If, however, Θεοῦ be the right reading, the nominative to περιεποιήσατο may simply have been suppressed by a grammatical inadvertency of the Apostle or his amanuensis. (See further, Scrivener, *Introd.* 540.) The mysterious doctrine of the περιχώρησις is one which the Apostle always treats with deepest reverence, and such a collocation as αἷμα Θεοῦ would have given at least *primâ facie* countenance to all kinds of Sabellian, Eutychian, and Patripassian heresies. (I have made some further remarks on this reading in the *Expositor*, May, 1879.)

[4] This sad prediction was but too soon fulfilled (1 Tim. i. 20; Rev. ii. 6; 1 John ii. 19).

[5] Undoubtedly this expression—though not meant to be taken *au pied de la lettre*—tells against the theory of a visit to Corinth during this period.

[6] Tears are thrice mentioned in this short passage—tears of suffering (19); of pastoral solicitude (31); and of personal affection (37). Monod, *Cinq Discours* (*Les Larmes de St. Paul*).

there he held up those thin, toilworn hands before them all—"these hands ministered. In all things I set you the example, that, thus labouring, you ought to support the weak, and to remember the words of the Lord Jesus, how He said, 'It is blessed rather to give than to receive.'"[1]

After these words, which so well describe the unwearied thoroughness, the deep humility, the perfect tenderness, of his Apostolic ministry, he knelt down with them all, and prayed. They were overpowered with the touching solemnity of the scene. He ended his prayer amidst a burst of weeping, and as they bade him farewell—anxious for his future, anxious for their own—they each laid their heads on his neck,[2] and passionately kissed him,[3] pained above all at his remark that never again should they gaze, as they had gazed so often,[4] on the dear face of the teacher who had borne so much for their sakes, and whom they loved so well. If Paul inspired intense hatreds, yet, with all disadvantages of person, he also inspired intense affection. He had—to use the strong expression[5] of St. Luke—to tear himself from them. Sadly, and with many forebodings, they went down with him to the vessel, which was by this time awaiting him; and we may be very sure that Paul was weeping bitterly as he stepped on board, and that sounds of weeping were long heard upon the shore, until the sails became a white speck on the horizon, and with heavy hearts the Elders of Ephesus turned away to face once more, with no hope of help from their spiritual father, the trials that awaited them in the city of Artemis.

The wind blew full in favour of the voyagers, and before the evening they had run with a straight course to Cos. Neither the wines, nor the purple, nor the perfumes of Cos, would have much interest for the little band;[6] but, if opportunity offered, we may be sure that "the beloved physician" would not miss the opportunity of seeing all that he could of the scientific memorials of the Asclepiadæ—the great medical school of the ancient world. Next day the little vessel rounded the promontory of Cnidus, and sped on for Rhodes, where, as they entered the harbour, they would admire the proverbial fertility of the sunny island of roses, and gaze with curiosity on the prostrate mass of its vast Colossus, of which two legs still stood on their pedestal,[7] though the huge mass of bronze had been hurled down by an earthquake, there to stay till, thirteen centuries later, they were broken up, and carried away on 900 camels, to be the ignoble spoil of a Jew.[8] The monstrous image—one of the wonders of the world—was a figure of the sun; and, with whatever lingering artistic sympathy it might have been regarded by the Gentile converts,

[1] The only "unwritten saying" (ἄγραφον δόγμα) of our Lord in the New Testament not preserved for us in the Gospels.

[2] cf. Gen. xlv. 14, xlvi. 29.

[3] κατεφίλουν, deosculabantur (cf. Matt. xxvi. 49).

[4] Ver. 38, θεωρεῖν. He had only said ὄψεσθε (cf. John xx. 5, 6). The word implies the feeling here alluded to.

[5] xxi. 1, ἀποσπασθέντας ἀπ' αὐτῶν (cf. Luke xxii. 41).

[6] Strab. xiv. 2; Hor. *Od.* IV. xiii. 13; Athen. x. 688 (Alf.).

[7] Plin. *H. N.* xxxiv. 18; Strab. xiv. 2.

[8] Cedrenus, *Hist.* p. 431.

St. Paul would perhaps think, with a smile, of Dagon, "when he fell flat, and shamed his worshippers," or point to it as a symbol of the coming day when all idols should be abolished at the returning dawn of the Sun of Righteousness. The empire of the sea, which this huge statue had been reared to commemorate, had not passed away more completely than the worship of Apollo should pass away; and to St. Paul the work of Chares of Lindos, spite of all its grace and beauty, was but a larger idol, to be regarded with pity, whereas the temple reared to that idol by the apostate Idumean usurper who had called himself king of the Jews could only be looked upon with righteous scorn.[1]

Next day, passing the seven capes which terminate the mountain ridge of "verdant Cragus," and the mouth of the yellow river which gave its name of Xanthus to the capital of Lycia, and so catching a far-off glimpse of temples rich with the marbles which now adorn our British Museum, the vessel which bore so much of the fortune of the future, turned her course eastward to Patara. Beneath the hill which towered over its amphitheatre rose also amid its palm-trees, the temple and oracle of Apollo Patareus. A single column, and a pit,—used possibly for some of the trickeries of superstition,—alone remain as a monument of its past splendour;[2] and it was due in no small measure to the life's work of the poor Jewish Apostle who now looked up at the vast world-famed shrine, that Christian poets would tell in later days how

> "The oracles are dumb,
> No voice nor hideous hum
> Runs through the arched roof in words deceiving;
> Apollo from his shrine
> Can no more divine,
> With hollow shriek the steep of Delphos leaving;
> No nightly trance or breathed spell
> Inspires the pale-eyed priest from the prophetic cell."

They could now no longer avail themselves of the vessel in which so far they had accomplished a prosperous, and, in spite of all misgivings, a happy voyage. Either its course ended there, or it would continue to coast along the shores of Pamphylia and Cilicia. But here they were fortunate enough to find another vessel bound straight for Phœnicia, and they at once went on board, and weighed anchor. Once more they were favoured by wind and wave. Sailing with unimpeded course—through sunlight and moonlight—at the rate of a hundred miles a day, they caught sight[3] at dawn of the snowy peaks of Cyprus, and passing by Paphos—where Paul would be reminded of Sergius Paulus and Elymas—in some four days, they put in at Tyre, where their ship was to unload its cargo. The Apostle must have ceased to feel anxiety about being at Jerusalem by Pentecost, since, owing to providential circumstances, he had now a full fortnight to spare. There were some disciples

[1] The Pythium. [2] Sprat and Forbes, i. 80; *ap.* C. and H. ii. 232.

[3] xxi. 3, ἀναφανέντες, cf. aperire (see Ps. Lucian, *Ver. Hist.* § 38, p. 687); the opposite technical term is, ἀποκρύπτειν, abscondere (Thuc. v. 65; Virg. *Æn.* iii. 275, 291).

at Tyre, and St. Paul may have seen them on previous occasions;[1] but in so populous and busy a town it required a little effort to find them.[2] With them Paul stayed his usual period of seven days, and they by the Spirit told him not to go to Jerusalem. He knew, however, all that they could tell him of impending danger, and he too was under the guidance of the same Spirit which urged him along—a fettered but willing captive. When the week was over[3] St. Paul left them; and so deeply in that brief period had he won their affections, that all the members of the little community, with their wives and children, started with him to conduct him on his way. Before they reached the vessel they knelt down side by side, men and women and little ones, somewhere on the surf-beat rocks[4] near which the vessel was moored, to pray together—he for them, and they for him—before they returned to their homes; and he went once more on board for the last stage of his voyage from Tyre to Ptolemais, the modern Acre. There they finally left their vessel, and went to greet the disciples, with whom they stayed for a single day, and then journeyed by land across the plain of Sharon—bright at that time with a thousand flowers of spring—the forty-four miles which separate Acre from Cæsarea. Here St. Paul lingered till the very eve of the feast. Ready to face danger when duty called, he had no desire to extend the period of it, or increase its certainty. At Cæsarea, therefore, he stayed with his companions for several days, and they were the last happy days of freedom which for a long time he was destined to spend. God graciously refreshed his spirit by this brief interval of delightful intercourse and rest. For at Cæsarea they were the guests of one who must have been bound to Paul by many ties of the deepest sympathy —Philip the Evangelist. A Hellenist like himself, and a liberal Hellenist, Philip, as Paul would have been most glad to recognise, had been the first to show the large sympathy and clear insight, without which Paul's own work would have been impossible. It was Philip who had evangelised the hated Samaritans; it was Philip who had had the courage to baptise the Ethiopian eunuch. The lots of these two noble workers had been closely intertwined. It was the furious persecution of Saul the Pharisee which had scattered the Church of Jerusalem, and thus rendered useless the organisation of the seven deacons. It was in flight from that persecution that the career of Philip had been

[1] Acts xxvi. 20; Gal. i. 21.

[2] xxi. 4, ἀνευρόντες τοὺς μαθητάς, "Seeking out the disciples," not as in E. V. "finding disciples."

[3] xxi. 5. ἐξαρτίσαι usually means "to refit," but here with ἡμέρας it seems to mean "complete." Hesychius makes it equivalent to τελειῶσαι, and so Theophylact and Œcumenius understood it. Meyer is probably mistaken in giving the word its first meaning here.

[4] Ver. 5, αἰγιαλὸν. Cf. xxvii. 39. There is, indeed, a long range of sandy shore between Tyre and Sidon, but near the city there are also rocky places. Dr. Hackett, *ad loc.*, quotes a strikingly parallel experience of an American missionary, Mr. Schneider, at Aintab, near Tarsus:—"More than a hundred converts accompanied us out of the city; and there, near the spot where one of our number had once been stoned, we halted, and a prayer was offered, amid tears. Between thirty and forty escorted us two hours farther . . . Then another prayer was offered, and with saddened countenances and with weeping they forcibly broke away from us. (Cf. ἀποσπασθέντας, ver. 1.) It really seemed as though they could not turn back."

changed. On the other hand, that new career had initiated the very line of conduct which was to occupy the life of Paul the Apostle. As Paul and Philip talked together in those few precious hours, there must have flourished up in their minds many a touching reminiscence of the days when the light of heaven, which had once shone on the face of Stephen upturned to heaven in the agony of martyrdom, had also flashed in burning apocalypse on the face of a young man whose name was Saul. And besides a community of thoughts and memories, the house of Philip was hallowed by the gentle ministries of four daughters who, looking for the coming of Christ, had devoted to the service of the Gospel their virgin lives.[1]

To this happy little band of believers came down from Judæa the Prophet Agabus, who, in the early days of St. Paul's work at Antioch, had warned the Church of the impending famine. Adopting the symbolic manner of the ancient prophets,[2] he came up to Paul, unbound the girdle which fastened his *cetôneth*, and tying with it his own feet and hands said, "Thus saith the Holy Spirit, Thus shall the Jews in Jerusalem bind the man whose girdle this is, and shall deliver him into the hands of the Gentiles." They had long been aware of the peril of the intended visit, but no intimation had been given them so definite as this, nor had they yet foreseen that a Jewish assault would necessarily end in a Roman imprisonment. On hearing it, St. Paul's companions earnestly entreated him to stay where he was, while they went to Jerusalem to convey the Gentile contribution; and the members of the Cæsarean Church joined their own tears and entreaties to those of his beloved companions. Why should he face a certain peril? Why should he endanger an invaluable life? Since the Spirit had given him so many warnings, might there not be even something of presumption in thus exposing himself in the very stronghold of his most embittered enemies? St. Paul was not insensible to their loving entreaties and arguments; there might have been an excuse, and something more than an excuse, for him had he decided that it was most unwise to persist in his intentions; but it was not so to be. His purpose was inflexible. No voices of even prophets should turn him aside from obedience to a call which he felt to be from God. A captive bound to Christ's triumphant chariot-wheel, what could he do? What could he do but thank God even if the Gospel, which was to some an aroma of life, became to him an aroma of earthly death? When the finger of God has pointed out the path to a noble soul, it will not swerve either to the right hand or the left. "What are ye doing, weeping and breaking my heart?" he said. "I am willing not only to go to Jerusalem to be bound, but even to die, for the name of the Lord Jesus." They saw that further importunity would be painful and useless—

"He saw a hand they could not see
Which beckoned him away,
He heard a voice they could not hear
Which would not let him stay."

[1] Cf. Plin. *Ep.* x. 96.

[2] Cf. 1 Kings xxii. 11; Isa. xx. 2; Jer. xiii. 1, &c.

They desisted and wiped away their tears, saying, "The Lord's will be done."

Too soon the happy days of rest and loving intercourse came to an end. It was seventy-five miles, an ordinary three days' journey, from Cæsarea to Jerusalem. That year the feast began at sunset on Wednesday, May 17.[1] The last day at Cæsarea was a Sunday. Next day they packed up their baggage[2]—and it was precious, for it contained the *chaluka*—and, accompanied by some of the Cæsarean converts, who, with multitudes of other Jews, were streaming up to Jerusalem on that last day before the feast began,[3] they started for the Holy City, with hearts on which rested an ever-deepening shadow. The crowd at these gatherings was so immense that the ordinary stranger might well fail to find accommodation, and be driven to some temporary booth outside the walls. But the brethren had taken care to secure for Paul and his delegates a shelter in the house of Mnason, a Cyprian, and one of the original disciples. St. Paul seems to have had a sister living at Jerusalem, but we do not know that she was a Christian, and in any case her house—which might be well known to many Tarsian Jews—would be an uncertain resting-place for an endangered man. And so for the fifth time since his conversion Paul re-entered Jerusalem. He had rarely entered it without some cause for anxiety, and there could have been scarcely one reminiscence which it awoke that was not infinitely painful. The school of Gamaliel, the Synagogue of the Libertines, the house where the High Priest had given him his commission to Damascus, the spot where the reddened grass had drunk the blood of Stephen must all have stirred painful memories. But never had he trod the streets of the Holy City with so deep a sadness as now that he entered it, avoiding notice as much as possible, in the little caravan of Cæsarean pilgrims and Gentile converts. He was going into a city where friends were few, and where well-nigh every one of the myriads among whom he moved was an actual or potential enemy, to whom the mere mention of his name might be enough to make the dagger flash from its scabbard, or to startle a cry of hatred which would be the signal for a furious outbreak. But he was the bearer of help, which was a tangible proof of his allegiance to the mother church, and the brethren whom he saw that evening at the house of Mnason gave him a joyous welcome. It may have cheered his heart for a moment, but it did not remove the deep sense that he was in that city which was the murderess of the Prophets. He knew too well the burning animosity which he kindled, because he remembered too well what had been his own, and that of his party, against the Christian Hellenists of old. The wrath which he had then felt was now a furnace heated sevenfold against himself.

The next day till sunset was marked by the ceremonies of the feast, and the

[1] *Fasti Sacri*, No. 1857.

[2] Verse 15. *Leg.* ἐπισκευασάμενοι, ℵ, A, B, E, G, and a mass of cursives. In the E. V. "carriages" means "baggage:" cf. Judges xviii. 21; 1 Sam. xvii. 22; Isa. x. 28. "We trussed up our fardeles," Genev. Vers.

[3] That St. Paul had only arrived on the very eve of the feast may be at once inferred from Acts xxiv. 11.

greater part of it was spent by St. Paul and his little company in an assembly of the elders, who met to receive him under the presidency of James.[1] The elders were already assembled when the visitors came in, and we may imagine that it was with something more than a thrill of curiosity—that it must have been with an almost painful shyness—that "timid provincial neophytes" like Timothy and Trophimus (the latter especially, an uncircumcised Gentile, whom his teacher had encouraged to regard himself as entirely emancipated from the Jewish law)—found themselves in the awful presence of James, the Lord's brother—James, the stern, white-robed, mysterious prophet, and the conclave of his but half-conciliated Judaic presbyters. No misgiving could assail them in their own free Asiatic or Hellenic homes; but here in Jerusalem, in "the Holy, the Noble city," under the very shadow of the Temple, face to face with zealots and Pharisees, it required nothing less than the genius of a Paul to claim without shadow of misgiving that divine freedom which was arraigned in the name of a history rich in miracles, and a whole literature of inspired books. That free spirit was a lesson which the Jews themselves as a body could not learn. It required, indeed, the earthquake shock which laid their temple in ruins, and scattered their nationality to the four winds of heaven, effectively to teach them the futility of the convictions to which they so passionately clung. They would have resisted without end the logic of argument had not God Himself in due time refuted their whole theology by the irresistible logic of facts. The destruction of Jerusalem did more to drive them from an immemorial "orthodoxy" than the Epistles of St. Paul himself.

As we read the narrative of the Acts in the light of the Epistles, it is difficult to resist the impression that the meeting between the Apostle and the Elders of Jerusalem was cold. It is, of course, certain that the first object of the meeting was the presentation of the contribution from which Paul had hoped so much. One by one he would call forward the beloved delegates, that they might with their own hands lay at the feet of James the sums of money which his Gentile Churches had contributed out of their deep poverty, and which in many and many a coin bore witness to weeks of generous self-denial. There lay all this money, a striking proof of the faithfulness with which Paul, at any rate, had carried out his share of the old compact at Jerusalem, when—almost by way of return for concessions which the Judaisers had done their best to render nugatory—the Three had begged him to be mindful of the poor. It must have been a far larger bounty than they had any reason to expect, and on this occasion, if ever, we might surely have looked for a little effusive sympathy, a little expansive warmth, on the part of the community which had received so tangible a proof of the Apostle's kindness. Yet we are not told about a word of thanks, and we see but too plainly that Paul's

[1] As none of the Twelve are mentioned, it is probable that none were present. The twelve years which, as tradition tells us, had been fixed by Christ for their stay in Jerusalem, had long elapsed, and they were scattered on their various missions to evangelise the world. St. Luke was aware of the contributions brought by St. Paul (xxiv. 17), though he does not mention them here.

hardly disguised misgiving as to the manner in which his gift would be accepted[1] was confirmed. Never in any age have the recipients of alms at Jerusalem been remarkable for gratitude.[2] Was the gratitude of the Zealots and Pharisees of the community extinguished in this instance by the fact that one of the bags of money was carried by the hands of an uncircumcised Gentile? Had it been otherwise, nothing would have lain more entirely in the scope of St. Luke's purpose to record. Though some at least of the brethren received Paul gladly, the Elders of the Church had not hurried on the previous evening to greet and welcome him, and subsequent events prove too clearly that his chief reward lay in the sense of having done and taught to his converts what was kind and right, and not in any softening of the heart of the Judaic Christians. Gratitude is not always won by considerateness. The collection for the saints occupies many a paragraph in St. Paul's Epistles, as it had occupied many a year of his thoughts. But there is little or no recorded recognition of his labour of love by the recipients of the bounty which but for him could never have been collected.

When the presentation was over, Paul narrated in full detail[3] the work he had done, and the Churches which he had confirmed or founded in that third journey, of which we have seen the outline. What love and exultation should such a narrative have excited! All that we are told is, that "they, on hearing it, glorified God, and said"—what? The repetition, the echo, of bitter and even deadly reproaches against St. Paul, coupled with a suggestion which, however necessary they may have deemed it, was none the less humiliating. "You observe, brother, how many myriads of the Jews there are that have embraced the faith, and they are all zealots of the Law." The expression is a startling one. Were there, indeed, at that early date "*many myriads*" of Jewish Christians, when we know how insignificant numerically were the Churches even at such places as Rome and Corinth, and when we learn how small was the body of Christians which, a decade later, took refuge at Pella from the impending ruin of Jerusalem? If we are to take the expression literally—if there were even as many as *two* myriads of Christians who were all zealous for the Law, it only shows how fatal was the risk that the Church would be absorbed into a mere slightly-differentiated synagogue. At any rate, the remark emphasised the extreme danger of the Apostle's position in that hotbed of raging fanaticism, especially when they added, "And they"—all these myriads who have embraced the faith and are zealots of the Law!—"have been studiously indoctrinated[4] with the belief about you, that you teach APOSTASY FROM MOSES, telling all THE JEWS of the dispersion not to circumcise their children, and not to walk in obedience to the customs. What then is the state of affairs? That a crowd will assemble is quite certain; for

[1] Rom. xv. 31.
[2] Witness the treatment in recent days of Sir M. Montefiore and Dr. Frankl, after conferring on them the largest pecuniary benefits.
[3] xxi. 19, καθ' ἓν ἕκαστον.
[4] Ver. 21, κατηχήθησαν. Very much stronger than the E. V., "they are informed."

they will hear that you have come. At once then do what we tell you. We have four men who have a vow upon them. Take them, be purified with them, and pay their expenses that they may get their heads shaved. All will then recognise that there is nothing in all which has been so carefully inculcated into them about you, but that you yourself also walk in observance of the Law. But as regards the *Gentiles* that have embraced the faith, we enjoined their exemption from everything of this kind, deciding only that they should keep themselves from meat offered to idols, and blood, and strangled, and fornication."

What did this proposal mean? It meant that the emancipation from the vow of the Nazarite could only take place at Jerusalem, and in the Temple, and that it was accompanied by offerings so costly that they were for a poor man impossible. A custom had therefore sprung up by which rich men undertook to defray the necessary expenses, and this was regarded as an act of charity and piety. The Jews, indeed, looked so favourably on a species of liberality which rendered it possible for the poor no less than the rich to make vows at moments of trial and danger, that when Agrippa I. paid his first visit to Jerusalem, he had paid the expenses which enabled a large number of Nazarites to shave their heads,[1] not only because he wished to give an ostentatious proof of his respect for the Levitical law, but also because he knew that this would be a sure method of acquiring popularity with the Pharisaic party. The person who thus defrayed the expenses was supposed so far to share the vow, that he was required to stay with the Nazarites during the entire week, which, as we gather from St. Luke, was the period which must elapse between the announcement to the priest of the termination of the vow, and his formal declaration that it had been legally completed.[2] For a week then, St. Paul, if he accepted the advice of James and the presbyters, would have to live with four paupers in the chamber of the Temple which was set apart for this purpose; and then to pay for sixteen sacrificial animals and the accompanying meat offerings; and to stand among these Nazarites while the priest offered four he-lambs of the first year without blemish for burnt offerings, and four ewe-lambs of the first year without blemish for sin offerings, and four rams without blemish for peace offerings; and then, to look on while the men's heads were being shaved and while they took their hair to burn it under the boiling cauldron of the peace offerings, and while the priest took four sodden shoulders of rams and four unleavened cakes out of the four baskets, and four unleavened wafers anointed with oil, and put them on the hands of the Nazarites, and waved them for a wave-offering before the Lord—which, with the wave-breads and the heave-shoulders, the priest afterwards took as his own perquisites. And he was to do all this, not only to disprove what was

[1] Jos. *Antt.* xix. 6, § 1, εἰς Ἱεροσόλυμα ἐλθὼν χαριστηρίους ἐξεπλήρωσε θυσίας οὐδὲν τῶν κατὰ νόμον ἀπολιπών. διὸ καὶ Ναζιραίων ξυρᾶσθαι διέταξε μάλα συχνούς.

[2] Neither the Talmud nor the Pentateuch mentions this circumstance. Numb. vi. 9, 10 refers only to the cases of accidental pollution during the period of the vow. It may have been on the analogy of this rule that a week was fixed as the period of purification.

undoubtedly a calumny if taken strictly—namely, that he had taught the Jews apostasy from Moses (as though his whole Gospel was this mere negation!)—but also to prove that there was no truth in the reports about him, but that he also was a regular observer of the Law.

That it was an expensive business was nothing. Paul, poor as he had now become, could not, of course, pay unless he had the money wherewith to pay it; and if there were any difficulty on this score, its removal rested with those who made the proposal. But *was* the charge against him false in spirit as well as in letter? Was it true that he valued, and—at any rate, with anything approaching to scrupulosity—still observed the Law? Would there not be in such conduct on his part something which might be dangerously misrepresented as an abandonment of principle? If those Judaisers on whom he did not spare to heap such titles as "false apostles," "false brethren," "deceitful workers," "dogs," "emissaries of Satan," "the concision,"[1] had shaken the allegiance of his converts by charging him with inconsistency before, would they not have far more ground to do so now? It is true that at the close of his second journey he had spontaneously taken on himself the vow of the Nazarite. But since that time circumstances had widely altered. At that time the animosity of those false brethren was in abeyance; they had not dogged his footsteps with slander; they had not beguiled his converts into legalism; they had not sent their adherents to undo his teaching and persuade his own churches to defy his authority. And if all these circumstances were changed, he too was changed since then. His faith had never been the stereotype of a shibboleth, or the benumbing repetition of a phrase. His life, like the life of every good and wise man, was a continual education. His views during the years in which he lived exclusively among Gentile churches and in great cities had been rendered clearer and more decided. Not to speak of the lucid principles which he had sketched in the Epistles to the Corinthians, he had written the Epistle to the Galatians, and had developed the arguments there enunciated in the Epistle to the Romans. It had been the very object of those Epistles to establish the nullity of the Law for all purposes of justification. The man who had written that the teaching of the Judaisers was a quite different gospel to his, and that any one who preached it was accursed[2]—who had openly charged Peter with tergiversation for living Judaically after having lived in Gentile fashion[3]—who had laid it down as his very thesis that "from works of Law no flesh shall be justified"[4]—who had said that to build again what he destroyed was to prove himself a positive transgressor[5]—who had talked of the Law as "a curse" from which Christ redeemed us, and declared that the Law could never bring righteousness[6]—who had even characterised that Law as a slavery to "weak and beggarly elements" comparable to the rituals of Cybele worship and Moon worship, and spoken of circumcision as being in itself no better than a contemptible mutilation[7]—who had talked

[1] 2 Cor. xi. 13; Gal. ii. 4; Phil. iii. 2; 2 Cor. xi. 13.
[2] Gal. i. 6–9.
[3] *Id.* ii. 14; *supra*, p. 250.
[4] *Id.* ii. 16.
[5] *Id.* ii. 18.
[6] Rom. iii. 20; Gal. ii. 16.
[7] Phil. iii. 2; Gal. v. 12.

again and again of being dead to the Law, and openly claimed fellowship rather with the Gentiles, who were the spiritual, than with the rejected and penally blinded Jews, who were but the physical descendants of Abraham—was this the man who could without creating false impressions avoid danger of death, which he had braved so often, by doing something to show how perfectly orthodox he was in the impugned respects? A modern writer has said that he could not do this without untruth; and that to suppose the author of the Epistles to the Romans and Galatians standing seven days, oil-cakes in hand, in the Temple vestibule, and submitting himself to all the manipulations with which Rabbinic pettiness had multiplied the Mosaic ceremonials which accompanied the completion of the Nazaritic vow—to suppose that, in the midst of unbelieving Priests and Levites, he should have patiently tolerated all the ritual nullities of the Temple service of that period, and so have brought the business to its tedious conclusion in the elaborate manner above described, "is just as credible as that Luther in his old age should have performed a pilgrimage to Einsiedeln with peas in his shoes, or that Calvin on his deathbed should have vowed a gold-embroidered gown to the Holy Mother of God."[1]

But the comparison is illusory. It may be true that the natural temperament of St. Paul—something also, it may be, in his Oriental character—inclined him to go much farther in the way of concession than either Luther or Calvin would have done; but apart from this his circumstances were widely different from theirs in almost every respect. We may well imagine that this unexpected proposal was distasteful to him in many ways; it is hardly possible that he should regard without a touch of impatience the tedious ceremonialisms of a system which he now knew to be in its last decadence, and doomed to speedy extinction. Still there were two great principles which he had thoroughly grasped, and on which he had consistently acted. One was acquiescence in things indifferent for the sake of charity, so that he gladly became as a Jew to Jews that he might save Jews; the other that, during the short time which remained, and under the stress of the present necessity, it was each man's duty to abide in the condition wherein he had been called. He was a Jew, and therefore to him the Jewish ceremonial was a part of national custom and established ordinance. For him it had, at the very lowest, a *civil* if not a religious validity. If the Jews misinterpreted his conduct into more than was meant, it would only be a misrepresentation like those which they gratuitously invented, and to which he was incessantly liable. Undoubtedly during his missionary journey he must again and again have broken the strict provisions of that Law to the honour and furtherance of which he had devoted his youth. But though he did not hold himself

[1] Hausrath (p. 453), who, however, erroneously imagines that Paul had himself on this occasion the vow of a Nazarite upon him. The person who paid the expense of the Nazarite had not, I imagine, to make offerings for himself—at least it is nowhere so stated—though we infer that he lived with the Nazarites during the period of their seclusion, and in some undefined way shared in their purification.

bound to do all that the Law and the Rabbis required, yet neither did he feel himself precluded from any observance which was not wrong. His objection to Levitism was not an objection to external conformity, but only to that substitution of externalism for faith to which conformity might lead. He did not so much object to ceremonies as to placing any *reliance* on them. He might have wished that things were otherwise, and that the course suggested to him involved a less painful sacrifice. He might have been gladder if the Elders had said to him, "Brother, you are detested here; at any moment the shout of a mob may rise against you, or the dagger of a Sicarius be plunged into your heart. We cannot under such circumstances be responsible for your life. You have given us this splendid proof of your own loyalty and of the Christian love of your converts. The feast is over.[1] Retire at once with safety, and with our prayers and our blessings continue your glorious work." Alas! such advice was only a "might have been." He accepted the suggestion they offered, and the very next day entered the Temple with these four Nazarites, went through whatever preliminary purification was deemed necessary by the Oral Law, and gave notice to the priests that from this time they must begin to count the seven days which must pass before the final offerings were brought and the vow concluded.[2]

If the Elders overrated the conciliatory effect of this act of conformity, they had certainly underrated the peril to which it would expose the great missionary who, more than they all, had done his utmost to fulfil that last command of Christ that they should go into all the world and preach the Gospel to every creature. The city was full of strangers from every region of the world, and the place where of all others they would delight to congregate would be the courts of the Temple. Even, therefore, if St. Paul, now that the storms of years had scarred his countenance and bent his frame, was so fortunate as to remain unrecognised by any hostile priest who had known him in former days, it was hardly possible that every one of the thousands whom he had met in scores of foreign cities should fail to identify that well-known face and figure. It would have been far safer, if anything compelled him to linger in the Holy City, to live unnoticed in the lowly house of Mnason. He might keep as quiet as he possibly could in that chamber of the Nazarites;

[1] The Pentecost only lasted one day.

[2] In some such way I understand the obscure and disputed expressions of ver. 26; but even with the Talmudic treatise *Nazir* beside us, we know too little of the details to be sure of the exact process gone through, or of the exact meaning of the expressions used. Some take ἁγνισθεὶς and ἁγνισμὸς to mean that St. Paul took on him the Nazarite vow with them (cf. Numb. vi. 3, 5, LXX.). This seems to be impossible, because thirty days is the shortest period mentioned by the Mishna for a temporary vow. Mr. Lewin and others have conjectured that he was himself a Nazarite, having taken the vow after his peril at Ephesus, as on the previous occasion after his peril at Corinth; and that this was the reason why he was so anxious to get to Jerusalem. But if so, why did not St. Luke mention the circumstance as he had done before? And if so, why was it necessary to pay the expenses of these four Nazarites when the fulfilment of his own personal vow would have been a sufficient and more striking proof of willingness to conform to Mosaism in his personal conduct? Moreover, the proposal of the Elders evidently came to St. Paul unexpectedly.

but even if, during those seven days of enforced idleness, he confined himself there to the utmost extent, and even if the other Nazarites abstained from divulging the secret of a name so famous, it was impossible that he should escape the eyes of the myriads who daily wandered through the Temple courts and took part in its multitudinous ceremonies.

For the Jews at that period were in a most inflammable state of mind, and the tremors of the earthquake were already felt which was soon to rend the earth under their feet, and shake their Temple and city into irretrievable ruin. On the death of Herod Agrippa I.,[1] Claudius, thinking that his son was too young to succeed to the government of so turbulent a people, kept him under his own eye at Rome, and appointed Cuspius Fadus to the Procuratorship of Judæa. To secure an additional hold upon the Jews, he ordered that the crown of Agrippa, and, what was of infinitely greater importance, the "golden robes" of the High Priest, should be locked up under the care of the Romans in the Tower of Antonia. So deep was the fury of the Jews at the thought that these holy vestments should be under the impure care of Gentiles, that the order could only be enforced by securing the presence at Jerusalem of C. Cassius Longinus, the Præfect of Syria, with an immense force. Claudius almost immediately afterwards cancelled the order, at the entreaty of a deputation from Jerusalem, supported by the influence of the young Agrippa. Claudius had owed to Agrippa's father his very empire, and since the youth inherited all the beauty, talent, and versatility of his family, he was a great favourite at the Imperial Court. Fadus had been succeeded by Tiberius Alexander, a nephew of Philo,[2] who was peculiarly hateful to the Jews because he was a renegade from their religion. He was superseded by Cumanus, and about the same time Agrippa II. was invested with the little kingdom of Chalcis, vacant by the death of his uncle Herod, and also with the functions of guarding the Temple and the Corban, and nominating to the High Priesthood.[3] The Procuratorship of Cumanus marked the commencement of terrible disturbances. At the very first Passover at which he was present an event occurred which was a terrible omen of the future. Just as at this day the Turkish soldiers are always prepared to pour down from the house of the Turkish Governor on the first occurrence of any discord between the Greek and Latin Churches, so it was the custom of the Roman commandant of the Tower of Antonia to post detachments of soldiers along the roof of the cloister which connected the fortress with the Temple area—ready at any moment to rush down the stairs and plunge into the very midst of the crowded worshippers. What occurred on this occasion was singularly characteristic. While standing there at guard, one of the Roman soldiers, weary of having nothing to do, and disgusted with watching what he despised as the mummeries of these hateful Jews, expressed his contempt for them by a gesture of the most insulting indecency.[4] Instantly the Jews were plunged into a paroxysm of fury. They cursed the new Procurator, and began to pelt

[1] A.D. 44. [2] Josephus calls him θαυμασιώτατος (*c. Ap.* i. 2).
[3] A.D. 49. [4] Jos. *B. J.* ii. 12, § 1; *Antt.* xx. 5, § 3.

the soldiers with stones, which seem to have been always ready to hand among this excitable race. Fearing that the Antonia detachment would be too weak to cope with so savage an onslaught, Cumanus marched his entire forces round from the Prætorium. At the clash of their footsteps, and the gleam of their swords, the wretched unarmed mass of pilgrims was struck with panic, and made a rush to escape. The gates of the Temple were choked up, and a multitude, variously stated at ten and at twenty thousand, was trampled and crushed to death.

This frightful disaster was followed by another tragedy. An imperial messenger was robbed by bandits at Bethhoron, not far from Jerusalem. Furious at such an insult, Cumanus made the neighbouring villages responsible, and in sacking one of them a Roman soldier got hold of a copy of the Scriptures, and burnt it before the villagers with open blasphemies. The horror of the insult consisted in the fact that the sacred roll contained in many places the awful and incommunicable Name. As they had done when Pilate put up the gilt votive shields in Jerusalem, and when Caligula had issued the order that his image should be placed in the Temple, the Jews poured in myriads to Cæsarea, and prostrated themselves before the tribunal of the Procurator. In this instance Cumanus thought it best to avert dangerous consequences by the cheap sacrifice of a common soldier, and the Jews were for the time appeased by the execution of the offender.

Then had followed a still more serious outbreak. The Samaritans, actuated by the old hatred to the Jews, had assassinated some Galilæan pilgrims to the Passover at En Gannim, the frontier village of Samaria which had repulsed our Lord.[1] Unable to obtain from Cumanus—whom the Samaritans had bribed—the punishment of the guilty village, the Jews, secretly countenanced by the High Priest Ananias, and his son Ananus, flew to arms, and, under the leadership of the bandit Eleazar, inflicted on the Samaritans a terrible vengeance. Cumanus, on hearing this, marched against them and routed them. A renewal of the contest was prevented by the entreaties of the chief men at Jerusalem, who, aware of the tremendous results at issue, hurried to the battle-field in sackcloth and ashes. Meanwhile the Præfect of Syria, Titus Ummidius Quadratus, appeared on the scene, and, after hearing both sides, found Cumanus and his tribune Celer guilty of having accepted a bribe, and sent them to Rome with Ananias and Ananus to be tried by the Emperor.[2] Jonathan, one of the very able ex-High Priests of the astute house of Annas, was sent to plead the cause of the Jews. At that time Agrippina was all-powerful with the Emperor, and the freedman Pallas all-powerful both with him and with Agrippina, who owed her elevation to his friendly offices. The supple Agrippa introduced Jonathan to Pallas, and it seems as if a little compact was struck between them, that Pallas should

[1] Luke ix. 53; Jos. *Antt.* xx. 6, § 1.

[2] The discrepancies in this story as told by Josephus in *B. J.* ii. 12, § 5, and *Antt.* xx. 6, § 2, are glaring, yet no one doubts either the honesty of Josephus or the general truth of the story. How scornfully would it have been rejected as a myth or an invention if it had occurred in the Gospels!

induce the Emperor to decide in favour of the Jews, and that Jonathan should petition him on behalf of the Jews to appoint to the lucrative Procuratorship his brother Felix. The plot succeeded. The Samaritans were condemned; their leaders executed; Cumanus banished; Celer sent to Jerusalem to be beheaded; Ananias and Ananus triumphantly acquitted; and A.D. 52, six years before St. Paul's last visit to Jerusalem, Felix—like his brother, an Arcadian slave—who had taken the name of Antonius in honour of his first mistress, and the name of Claudius in honour of his patron—became Procurator of Judæa.[1]

At first the new Procurator behaved with a little decent reserve, but it was not long before he began to show himself in his true colours, and with every sort of cruelty and licentiousness "to wield the power of a king with the temperament of a slave." After his emancipation he had been entrusted with a command in a troop of auxiliaries, and acting with the skill and promptitude of a soldier, he had performed a really useful task in extirpating the bandits. Yet even the Jews murmured at the shameless indifference with which this Borgia of the first century entrapped the chief bandit Eleazar into a friendly visit, on pretence of admiring his skill and valour, and instantly threw him into chains, and sent him as a prisoner to Rome. They were still more deeply scandalised by his intimacy with Simon Magus, who lived with him at Cæsarea as a guest, and by whose base devices this "husband or adulterer of three queens" succeeded in seducing Drusilla, the beautiful sister of Agrippa II.—who had now come as a king to Judæa—from her husband Aziz, King of Emesa. A crime of yet deeper and darker dye had taken place the very year before Paul's arrival. Jonathan, who was often bitterly reminded of his share in bringing upon his nation the affliction of a Procurator, who daily grew more infamous from his exactions and his savagery, thought that his high position and eminent services to Felix himself entitled him to expostulate. So far from taking warning, Felix so fiercely resented the interference that he bribed Doras, a friend of Jonathan's, to get rid of him. Doras hired the services of some bandits, who, armed with *sicae*, or short daggers, stabbed the priestly statesman at one of the yearly feasts. The success and the absolute impunity of the crime put a premium upon murder; assassinations became as frequent in Jerusalem as they were at Rome during the Papacy of Alexander VI. The very Temple was stained with blood. Any one who wanted to get rid of a public or private enemy found it a cheap and easy process to hire a murderer. It is now that the ominous term *sicarius* occurs for the first time in Jewish history.

This had happened in A.D. 57, and it was probably at the Passover of A.D. 58—only seven weeks before the time at which we have now arrived—that the Egyptian Pseudo-Messiah had succeeded in raising 30,000 followers, with no better pretensions than the promise that he would lead them to the Mount of Olives, and that the walls of Jerusalem should fall flat before him.

[1] A.D. 52.

Four thousand of these poor deluded wretches seem actually to have accompanied him to the Mount of Olives. There Felix fell upon them, routed them at the first onslaught, killed four hundred, took a multitude of prisoners, and brought the whole movement to an impotent conclusion. The Egyptian, however, had by some means or other made good his escape—was at this moment uncaptured—and, in fact, was never heard of any more. But the way in which followers had flocked in thousands to so poor an impostor showed the tension of men's minds.

Such was the condition of events—in so excited a state were the leaders and the multitude—at the very time that St. Paul was keeping himself as quiet as possible in the chambers of the Nazarites. Four days had already passed, and there seemed to be a hope that, as the number of pilgrims began to thin, he might be safe for three more days, after which there would be nothing to prevent him from carrying out his long-cherished wish to visit Rome, and from thence to preach the Gospel even as far as Spain. Alas! he was to visit Rome, but not as a free man.

For on the fifth day there were some Jews from Ephesus and other cities of Asia—perhaps Alexander the coppersmith was one of them—in the Court of the Women, and the glare of hatred suddenly shot into the eyes of one of these observers as he recognised the marked features of the hated Shaûl. He instantly attracted towards him the attention of some of the compatriots to whom Paul's teaching was so well known. The news ran in a moment through the passionate, restless, fanatical crowd. In one minute there arose one of those deadly cries which are the first beginnings of a sedition. These Asiatics sprang on Paul, and stirred up the vast throng of worshippers with the cry, "Israelites! help! This is the wretch who teaches all men everywhere against the people, and the Thorah, and the Temple. Ay, and besides that, he brought Greeks into the Temple, and hath polluted this holy place." Whether they really thought so or not we cannot tell, but they had no grounds for this mad charge beyond the fact that they had seen the Ephesian Trophimus walking about with Paul in the streets of Jerusalem, and supposed that Paul had taken him even into the holy precincts. To defile the Temple was what every enemy of the Jews tried to do. Antiochus, Heliodorus, Pompey, had profaned it; and very recently the Samaritans had been charged with deliberately polluting it by scattering dead men's bones over its precincts. Instantly the rumour flew from lip to lip that this was Shaûl, of whom they had heard—Paul, the *mesith*—Paul, one of the Galilæan *Minim*—one of the believers in "the Hung"—Paul, the renegade Rabbi, who taught and wrote that Gentiles were as good as Jews—the man who blasphemed the Thorah—the man whom the synagogues had scourged in vain—the man who went from place to place getting them into trouble with the Romans; and that he had been caught taking with him into the Temple a Gentile dog, an uncircumcised *ger*.[1] The

[1] Had he done this he would have incurred the censure in Ezek. xliv. 7; cf. Eph. ii. 14. The following remarkable passage of the Talmud is a self-condemnation by the Jewish teachers:—"What," it is asked, "was the cause of the destruction of the first Temple?

punishment for that crime was death—death by the full permission of the Romans themselves; death even against a Roman who should dare to set foot beyond the *Chêl*. They were now in the Court of the Women, but they only had to go through the Corinthian gate, and down the fifteen steps outside of it, to come to the *Chêl*—the "middle-wall of partition," that low stone balustrade with obelisks, on each of which was engraved on stone tablets the inscription in Greek and Latin that "No alien must set foot within that enclosure on pain of certain death."[1] Here, then, was a splendid opportunity for most just vengeance on the apostate who taught apostasy. A rush was made upon him, and the cry "To the rescue!" echoed on all sides through the streets.[2] To defend himself was impossible. What voice could be heard amid the wild roar of that momentarily increasing hubbub? Was this to be the end? Was he to be torn to pieces then and there in the very Temple precincts? If he had been in the court below, that would have been his inevitable fate, but the sacredness of the spot saved him. They began dragging him, vainly trying to resist, vainly trying to speak a word, through the great "Beautiful" gate of Corinthian brass, and down the fifteen steps, while the Levites and the Captain of the Temple, anxious to save the sacred enclosure from one more stain of blood, exerted all their strength to shut the ponderous gate behind the throng which surged after their victim.[3] But meanwhile the Roman centurion stationed under arms with his soldiers on the roof of the western cloisters, was aware that a wild commotion had suddenly sprung up. The outburst of fury in these Oriental mobs is like the scream of mingled sounds in a forest which sometimes suddenly startles the deep stillness of a tropic night. The rumour had spread in a moment from the Temple to the city, and streams of men were thronging from every direction into the vast area of the Court of the Gentiles. In another moment it was certain that those white pillars and that tessellated floor would be stained with blood. Without a moment's delay the centurion sent a message to Lysias, the commandant of Antonia, that the Jews had seized somebody in the Temple, and were trying to kill him. The Romans were accustomed to rapid movements, taught them by thousands of exigencies of their career in hostile countries,

The prevalence of idolatry, adultery, and murder. . . . But what was the cause of the destruction of the second Temple, *seeing that the age was characterised by study of the Law*, observance of its precepts, and the practice of benevolence? *It was groundless hatred; and it shows that groundless hatred is equal in heinousness to idolatry, adultery, and murder combined*" (*Joma*, f. 9, 2). As specimens of the groundless and boundless hatred of the Talmudists to Christians, see *Abhôda Zarah*, f. 26, 1, 2 (Amsterdam edition); Maimonides, *Hilch. Accum*, § 9.

[1] The חֵיל. (Jos. *B. J.* v. 5, § 2; vi. 2, § 4; *Antt.* xv. 11, § 5.) The discovery of one of these inscriptions by M. Clermont Ganneau—an inscription on which the eyes of our Lord Himself and of all His disciples must have often fallen—is very interesting. He found it built into the walls of a small mosque in the Via Dolorosa (*Palestine Exploration Fund Report*, 1871, p. 132). Paul had not indeed *actually* brought any Gentile inside the *Chêl*; but to do so *ideally* and *spiritually* had been the very purpose of his life. *V. infra, ad* Eph. ii. 14.

[2] xxi. 30, ἐκινήθη ἡ πόλις ὅλη, καὶ ἐγένετο συνδρομή.

[3] Jos. *B. J.* vi. 5, § 3; *c. Ap.* ii. 9.

but nowhere more essential than in a city which Præfect after Præfect and Procurator after Procurator had learnt to detest as the head-quarters of burning, senseless, and incomprehensible fanaticism. A single word was enough to surround Lysias with a well-disciplined contingent of centurions and soldiers, and he instantly dashed along the cloister roof and down the stairs into the Court of the Gentiles. The well-known clang of Roman arms arrested the attention of the mob. They had had some terrible warnings very lately. The memory of that awful day, when they trampled each other to death by thousands to escape the cohort of Cumanus, was still fresh in their memory. They did not dare to resist the mailed soldiery of their conquerors.

Lysias and his soldiers forced their way straight through the throng to the place where Paul was standing, and rescued him from his enraged opponents. When he had seized him, and had his arms bound to two soldiers by two chains, he asked the question, "Who the man might be, and what he had done?"[1] Nothing was to be learnt from the confused cries that rose in answer, and, in despair of arriving at anything definite in such a scene, Lysias ordered him to be marched into the barracks.[2] But no sooner had he got on the stairs which led up to the top of the cloister, and so into the fortress,[3] than the mob, afraid that they were going to be baulked of their vengeance, made another rush at him, with yells of "Kill him! kill him!"[4] and Paul, unable in his fettered condition to steady himself, was carried off his legs, and hurried along in the arms of the surrounding soldiers. He was saved from being torn to pieces chiefly by the fact that Lysias kept close by him; and, as the rescue-party was about to disappear into the barracks, Paul said to him in Greek, "May I speak a word to you?" "Can you speak Greek?" asked the commandant in surprise. "Are you not then really that Egyptian[5] who a little while ago made a disturbance,[6] and led out into the wilderness those 4,000 *sicarii*?"[7] "No," said Paul; "I am a Jew, a native of Tarsus, in Cilicia, a citizen of

[1] xxi. 33, τίς ἂν εἴη, καὶ τί ἐστιν πεποιηκώς.   [2] παρεμβολή

[3] Fort Antonia was a four-square tower, at the N.W. angle of the Temple area, with a smaller tower fifty cubits high at each corner except the southern, where the tower was seventy cubits high, with the express object of overlooking everything that went on in the Temple courts. Stairs from these towers communicated with the roofs of two porticoes, on which at intervals (διϊστάμενοι) stood armed Roman soldiers at the times of the great festivals, to prevent all seditious movements (Jos. *B. J.* v. 5, § 8; *Antt.* xx. 5, § 3).

[4] Cf. Luke xxiii. 18, and the cry of Pagan mobs, αἶρε τοὺς ἀθέους.

[5] Ver. 38, οὐκ ἄρα σὺ εἶ ὁ Αἰγύπτιος . . . ; One hardly sees why Lysias should have *inferred* that the Egyptian could not speak Greek, but he may have known that this was the fact. Since the Egyptian had only escaped a few months before, and the mass of the people—never favourable to him—would be exasperated at the detection of his imposture, the conjecture of Lysias was not surprising.

[6] ἀναστατώσας. Cf. xvii. 6; Gal. v. 12.

[7] Ver. 38, τοὺς τετρακισχιλίους ἄνδρας τῶν σικαρίων. Josephus (*Antt.* xx. 8, § 6) says that Felix, when he routed them, killed 400 and took 200 prisoners. In *B. J.* ii. 13, § 5, he says that he collected 30,000 followers, and led them to the Mount of Olives from the wilderness, and that the majority of them were massacred or taken prisoners. Most critics only attach importance to such discrepancies when they find or imagine them in the sacred writers. For the *sicarii*, see Jos. *B. J.* ii. 13, § 3. He says that they murdered people in broad day, and in the open streets, especially during the great feasts, and that they carried their daggers concealed under their robes.

no undistinguished city,[1] and, I entreat you, allow me to speak to the people."

It was an undaunted request to come from one whose life had just been rescued, and barely rescued, from that raging mob, and who was at that moment suffering from their rough treatment. Most men would have been in a state of such wild alarm as to desire nothing so much as to be hurried out of sight of the crowd. Not so with St. Paul. Snatched from his persecutors after imminent risk—barely delivered from that most terrifying of all forms of danger, the murderous fury of masses of his fellow-men—he asks leave not only to face, but even to turn round and address, the densely-thronging thousands, who were only kept from him by a little belt of Roman swords.[2]

Lysias gave him leave to speak, and apparently ordered one of his hands to be unfettered; and taking his stand on the stairs, Paul, with uplifted arm, made signals to the people that he wished to address them.[3] The mob became quiet, for in the East crowds are much more instantly swayed by their emotions than they are among us; and Paul, speaking in Syriac, the vernacular of Palestine, and noticing priests and Sanhedrists among the crowd, began—

"Brethren and Fathers,[4] listen to the defence I have now to make to you!"

The sound of their own language, showing that the speaker was at any rate no mere Hellenist, charmed their rage for the moment, and produced a still deeper silence. In that breathless hush Paul continued his speech. It was adapted to its object with that consummate skill which, even at the most exciting moments, seems never to have failed him. While he told them the truth, he yet omitted all facts which would be likely to irritate them, and which did not bear on his immediate object. That object was to show that he could entirely sympathise with them in this outburst of zeal, because he had once shared their state of mind, and that nothing short of divine revelations had altered the course of his religion and his life. He was, he told them, a Jew,[5] born indeed in Tarsus, yet trained from his earliest youth in Jerusalem, at the feet of no less a teacher than their great living Rabban Gamaliel; that he was not merely a Jew, but a Pharisee who had studied the inmost intricacy of the *Halacha*;[6] and was so like themselves in being a zealot for God, that he had persecuted "this way" to the very death,

[1] οὐκ ἀσήμου πόλεως (Eur. *Ion.* 8). It was αὐτόνομος, and a μητρόπολις, and had a famous university.

[2] Knox, who thought that Paul did wrong to take the vow, says, "He was brought into the most desperate danger, God designing to show thereby that we must not do evil that good may come."

[3] Ver. 40, κατέσεισε τῇ χειρὶ. Cf. xii. 17; xix. 33; xxi. 40. Cf. Pers. iv. 5, "Calidus fecisse silentia turbae Majestate manûs."

[4] See St. Stephen's exordium (vii. 2).

[5] xxii. 3, ἀνὴρ Ἰουδαῖος. To Lysias he had used the *general* expression ἄνθρωπος Ἰουδ. (xxi. 39).

[6] xxii. 3, κατὰ ἀκρίβειαν τοῦ πατρῴου νόμου. Cf. xxvi. 5; Jos. *B. J.* ii. 8, § 14. This "accuracy" corresponds to the Hebrew *tsedakah*, and the Talmudic *dikdukey* (דקדוקי).

haling to prison not only men, but even women; in proof of which he appealed to the testimony of the ex-High Priest Theophilus,[1] and many still surviving members of the Sanhedrin who had given him letters to Damascus. What, then, had changed the whole spirit of his life? Nothing less than a Divine vision of Jesus of Nazarath, which had stricken him blind to earth, and bidden him confer with Ananias.[2] He does not tell them that Ananias was a Christian, but—which was no less true—that he was an orthodox observer of the Law, for whom all the Jews of Damascus felt respect. Ananias had healed his blindness, and told him that it was "the God of our fathers," who foreordained him to know His will and see "the Just One,"[3] and hear the message from His lips, that he might be for Him "a witness to all men" of what he had heard and seen. He then mentions his baptism and return to Jerusalem, and, hurrying over all needless details, comes to the point that, while he was worshipping—now twenty years ago—in that very Temple, he had fallen into a trance, and again seen the risen Jesus, who bade him hurry with all speed out of Jerusalem, because there they would not receive his testimony. But so far from wishing to go, he had even pleaded with the heavenly vision that surely the utter change from Saul the raging persecutor—Saul who had imprisoned and beaten the believers throughout the synagogues—Saul at whose feet had been laid the clothes of them that slew His witness[4] Stephen—the change from such a man to Saul the Christian and the preacher of the Gospel of Jesus Christ—could not fail to win credence to his testimony. But He who spake to him would not suffer him to plead for a longer opportunity of appealing to his fellow-countrymen. Briefly but decisively came the answer which had been the turning-point for all his subsequent career—"Go, for I will send thee far away TO THE GENTILES!"

That fatal word, which hitherto he had carefully avoided, but which it was impossible for him to avoid any longer, was enough. Up to this point they had continued listening to him with the deepest attention. Many of them were not wholly unacquainted with the facts to which he appealed. His intense earnestness and mastery over the language which they loved charmed them all the more, because the soldiers who stood by could not understand a word of what he was saying, so that his speech bore the air of a confidential communication to Jews alone, to which the alien tyrants could only listen with vain curiosity and impatient suspicion. Who could tell but what some Messianic announcement might be hovering on his lips? Might not he who was thrilling them with the narrative of these visions and revelations have some new ecstasy to tell of, which should be the signal that now the supreme hour had come, and which should pour into their hearts a stream of fire so

[1] See p. 100.

[2] The narratives of St. Paul's conversion in ix., xxii., xxvi. are sufficiently considered and "harmonised"—not that they really need any harmonising—in pp. 107—112.

[3] "The Just One." See the speech of Stephen (vii. 52).

[4] μαρτὺς, not yet "martyr," as in Rev. xvii. 6. (Clem. *Ep.* 1 *Cor.* v.) But St. Paul would here have used the word *edh*, "witness."

intense, so kindling, that in the heat of it the iron chains of the Romans should be as tow? But was *this* to be the climax? Was a trance to be pleaded in defence of the apostasy of the renegade? Was this evil soul to be allowed to produce holy witness for his most flagrant offences? Were they to be told, forsooth, that a vision from heaven had bidden him preach to "sinners of the Gentiles," and fling open, as he had been doing, the hallowed privileges of the Jews to those dogs of the uncircumcision? All that strange multitude was as one; the same hatred shot at the same instant through all their hearts. That word "GENTILES," confirming all their worst suspicions, fell like a spark on the inflammable mass of their fanaticism. No sooner was it uttered[1] than they raised a simultaneous yell of "Away with such a wretch from the earth; he ought never to have lived!"[2]

Then began one of the most odious and despicable spectacles which the world can witness, the spectacle of an Oriental mob, hideous with impotent rage, howling, yelling, cursing, gnashing their teeth, flinging about their arms, waving and tossing their blue and red robes, casting dust into the air by handfuls, with all the furious gesticulations of an uncontrolled fanaticism.[3]

Happily Paul was out of the reach of their personal fury.[4] It might goad them to a courage sufficient to make them rend the air with their cries of frenzy, and make the court of the Temple look like the refuge for a throng of demoniacs; but it hardly prompted them to meet the points of those Roman broadswords. In great excitement, the commandant ordered the prisoner to be led into the barracks, and examined by scourging; for, being entirely ignorant of what Paul had been saying, he wanted to know what further he could have done to excite those furious yells. The soldiers at once tied his hands together, stripped his back bare, and bent him forward into the position for that horrid and often fatal examination by torture which, not far from that very spot, his Lord had undergone.[5] Thrice before, on that scarred back, had Paul felt the fasces of Roman lictors; five times the nine-and-thirty strokes of Jewish thongs; here was a new form of agony, the whip—the *horribile flagellum*—which the Romans employed to force by torture the confession of the truth.[6] But at this stage of the proceedings, Paul, self-possessed even in extremes, interposed with a quiet question. It had been useless before, it might be useless now, but it was worth trying, since both the soldiers and their officers seem already to have been prepossessed by his noble calm and self-control in

[1] xxii. 22, ἤκουον δὲ αὐτοῦ ἄχρι τούτου τοῦ λόγου, καὶ ἐπῆραν τὴν φωνὴν αὐτῶν λέγοντες, κ.τ.λ.

[2] Ver. 22, οὐ καθῆκεν. ℵ, A, B, C, D, E, G.

[3] xxii. 23. On the sudden excitability of Eastern mobs, and the sudden calm which often follows it, see *Palest. Explor. Fund* for April, 1879, p. 77.

[4] St. James had spoken of the "many myriads" (Acts xxi. 20) of Jews who, though zealots for the Law, had embraced the faith. How came it that not one of these "many myriads" lifted an arm cr raised a voice to liberate St. Paul from the perils into which he had been brought by religious hatred greedily adopting a lying accusation?

[5] xxii. 25, προέτεινεν αὐτὸν τοῖς ἱμᾶσιν—"stretched him forward with the thongs" to prepare him for examination by being scourged with μάστιγει. The word ἱμάντες seems never to mean a scourge.

[6] See *Life of Christ*, i. 187; ii. 380.

the midst of dangers so awful and so sudden. He therefore asked in a quiet voice, "Is it lawful for you to scourge a Roman who has not been tried?" The question was addressed to the centurion who was standing by to see that the torture was duly administered, and he was startled by the appeal. This was evidently no idle boaster; no man who would invent a privilege to escape pain or peril. Few under any circumstances would ever venture to invent the proud right of saying CIVIS ROMANUS SUM,[1] for the penalty of imposture was death;[2] and the centurion had seen enough to be quite sure that this prisoner, at any rate, was not the man to do so. He made the soldiers stop, went off to the commandant, and said to him, with something of Roman bluntness, "What are you about?[3] This man is a Roman." This was important. If he was a Roman, the Chiliarch had already twice broken the law which entitled him to protection; for he had both bound him and, in contravention of an express decree of Augustus, had given orders to begin his examination by putting him to the torture. Moreover, as being one who himself placed the highest possible value on the *jus civitatis*, he respected the claim. Hurrying to him, he said—

"Tell me, are *you* a Roman?"

"Yes."

But Lysias, as he looked at him, could not help having his doubts. He was himself a Greek or Syrian, who had bought the franchise, and thereupon assumed the prænomen Claudius, at a time when the privilege was very expensive.[4] Whether Paul was a Roman or not, he was clearly a Jew, and no less clearly a very poor one: how could *he* have got the franchise?

"*I* know how much it cost *me*[5] to get this citizenship," he remarked, in a dubious tone of voice.

"But I have been a citizen from my birth," was the calm answer to his unexpressed suspicion.

The claim could not be resisted. Paul was untied, and the soldiers dropped their scourges. But Lysias was not by any means free from anxiety as to the consequences of his illegal conduct.[6] Anxious to rid his hands of this awkward business in a city where the merest trifles were constantly leading to

[1] Cic. *in Verr.* v. 63.

[2] At any rate in certain cases. Suet. *Claud.* 25.

[3] Ver. 26, τί μέλλεις ποιεῖν; The ὅρα is omitted in ℵ, A, B, C, E.

[4] Some ten years before this time it had, however, become much cheaper. Messalina, the infamous wife of Claudius, who was put to death A.D. 48, openly sold it, first, at very high terms, but subsequently so cheap that Dion Cassius (lx. 17) says it could be bought for one or two broken glasses.

[5] Ver. 28, 'Εγὼ οἶδα πόσου, D. Though unsupported by evidence, the colloquialism sounds very genuine. Perhaps Lysias had bribed one of Claudius's freedmen, who made money in this way.

[6] Ver. 29. Theru is a little uncertainty as to what is meant by ἐφοβήθη . . ὅτι ἦν αὐτὸν δεδεκώς. If it means the chaining him with two chains (xxi. 33), Lysias did not at any rate think it necessary to *undo* what he had once done, for it is clear that Paul remained chained (xxii. 30, ἔλυσεν αὐτὸν). I therefore refer it to the binding with the thongs (ver. 25), by which Lysias seems to have broken two laws: (1) The Lex Porcia (Cic. *pro Rabirio*, 3; *in Verr.* v. 66); (2) "Non esse a tormentis incipiendum Div. Augustus constituit" (*Digest. Leg.* 48, tit. 18, c. 1).

most terrible consequences, he told the chief priests to summon next day a meeting of the Sanhedrin in order to try the prisoner.

The Sanhedrin met in full numbers. They no longer sat in the *Lishcath Haggassith*, the famous hall, with its tessellated pavement, which stood at the south side of the Court of the Priests.[1] Had they still been accustomed to meet there, Lysias and his soldiers would never have been suffered to obtrude their profane feet into a chamber which lay within the middle wall of partition —beyond which even a Procurator dare not even have set a step on pain of death. But at this period the Sanhedrin had probably begun their meetings in the *Chanujôth*, or "booths," the very existence of which was a proof of the power and prosperity of "the Serpent House of Hanan."[2] To this place Lysias led his prisoner, and placed him before them. The *Nasi*, or President, was, as usual, the High Priest.[3] The preliminary questions were asked, and then Paul, fixing on the assembly his earnest gaze,[4] began his defence with the words, "Brethren, my public life has been spent in all good conscience towards God till this day."[5] Something in these words jarred particularly on the mind of the High Priest. He may have disliked the use of the term "brethren," an address which implied a certain amount of equality, instead of one of those numerous expressions of servility which it was only fitting that a man like this should use to the great assembly of the wise. But Paul was no *Am-ha-arets*, on the contrary, he was as much a Rabbi, as much a *Chakam*, as the best "remover of mountains" among them all, and it may have been that he designedly used the term "brethren" instead of "fathers" because he too had been once a Sanhedrist. The bold assertion of perfect innocence further irritated the presiding *Nasi*, and he may have felt, somewhat painfully, that his own public life had not by any means been in all good conscience either towards God or towards man. This High Priest, Ananias, the son of Nebedoeus,[6] who had been appointed by Herod of Chalcis, was one of the worst, if not the very worst specimen of the worldly Sadducees of an age in which the leading hierarchs resembled the loosest of the Avignon cardinals, or of the preferment-hunting bishops in the dullest and deadest period of Charles the Second or George the First.[7] History records the revengeful un-

[1] See Lightfoot, *Hor. Hebr.* i. 1,105.

[2] *V. supra*, pp. 87, 94. *Life of Christ*, i. 77; ii. 337. Jost, *Gesch.* i. 145; Herzfeld, *Gesch.* i. 394. By this time, A.D. 58, the change had undoubtedly taken place.

[3] Endless mistakes have apparently arisen from confusing the President of the Sanhedrin with the President of the Schools. The subject is very obscure; but while undoubtedly the title of *Nasi*, or President of the Sanhedrin, was borne by great Rabbis like Hillel, Simeon, and Gamaliel, no less undoubtedly the High Priest—unless most flagrantly incompetent—presided as *Nasi* at the judicial meetings of the Sanhedrin, regarded as a governing body.

[4] xxiii. 1, ἀτενίσας. Cf. Luke iv. 20; Acts x. 4; xiii. 9.

[5] πεπολίτευμαι (Phil. i. 27; Jos. *Vit.* § 49; 2 Macc. vi. 1). Besides the general assertion of his innocence, he may mean that, whatever he had *taught* to the Gentiles, he had *lived* as a loyal Jew.

[6] On this man see Jos. *Antt.* xx. 5, § 2; 6, §§ 2, 3; 8, § 8; 9, § 2; *B. J.* ii. 17, § 9.

[7] No wonder that in these days there lay upon the Jews an abiding sense of the wrath of God against their race. No wonder that the Talmud records the legends how

wisdom of his conduct towards the Samaritans, and the far from noble means which he took to escape the consequences of his complicity in their massacre. The Talmud adds to our picture of him that he was a rapacious tyrant who, in his gluttony and greed, reduced the inferior priests almost to starvation by defrauding them of their tithes;[1] and that he was one of those who sent his creatures with bludgeons to the threshing-floors to seize the tithes by force.[2] He held the highpriesthood for a period which, in these bad days, was unusually long,[3] a term of office which had, however, been interrupted by his absence as a prisoner to answer for his misconduct at Rome. On this occasion, thanks to an actor and a concubine, he seems to have gained his cause,[4] but he was subsequently deposed to make room for Ishmael Ben Phabi, and few pitied him when he was dragged out of his hiding-place in a sewer to perish miserably by the daggers of the Sicarii, whom, in the days of his prosperity, he had not scrupled to sanction and employ.[5]

His conduct towards St. Paul gives us a specimen of his character. Scarcely had the Apostle uttered the first sentence of his defence when, with disgraceful illegality, Ananias ordered the officers of the court to smite him on the mouth.[6] Stung by an insult so flagrant, an outrage so undeserved, the naturally choleric temperament of Paul flamed into that sudden sense of anger which ought to be controlled, but which can hardly be wanting in a truly noble character. No character can be perfect which does not cherish in itself a deeply-seated, though perfectly generous and forbearing, indignation against intolerable wrong. Smarting from the blow, "God shall smite thee," he exclaimed, "thou white-washed wall![7] What! Dost thou sit there judging me according to the Law, and in violation of law biddest me to be smitten?"[8]

at this time the sacred light, which was to burn all night on the candlestick (*ner ma'arabi*), was often quenched before the daybreak; how the red tongue of cloth round the neck of the scapegoat on the Day of Atonement was no longer miraculously turned to white; how the huge brazen Nikanor-gate of the Temple, which required twenty Levites to shut it every evening, opened of its own accord; and how Johanan Ben Zacchai exclaimed, on hearing the portent, "Why wilt thou terrify us, O Temple? We know that thou art doomed to ruin."

[1] The Talmud tells us that when this person was High Priest the sacrifices were always eaten up, so that no fragments of them were left for the poorer priests (*Pesachîm*, 57, 1). (Grätz, iii. 279.)

[2] *Pesachîm, ubi supra.* St. Paul might well have asked him, ὁ βδελυσσόμενος τὰ εἴδωλα, ἱεροσυλεῖς (Rom. ii. 22; *v. supra*).

[3] From A. D. 48 to A.D. 59. The voyage as a prisoner to Rome was in A.D. 52.

[4] Wieseler *Chron. d. Ap. Zeit*, 76.

[5] Jos. *Antt.* xx. 9, § 2; *B. J.* ii. 17, § 9.

[6] To this style of argument the Jews seem to have been singularly prone (cf. Luke vi. 29; John xviii. 22; 2 Cor. xi. 20; 1 Tim. iii. 3; Tit. i. 7). This brutality illustrates the remark in *Joma*, 23, 1, *Sota*, 47, 2, that at that period no one cared for anything but externalism, and that Jews thought more of a pollution of the Temple than they did of assassination (Grätz, iii. 322).

[7] xxiii. 3, τοῖχε κεκονιαμένε. Cf. Matt. xxiii. 27, τάφοι κεκονιαμένοι. Dr. Plumptre compares Jeffreys' treatment of Baxter.

[8] For a Jew to order a Jew to be struck on the cheek was peculiarly offensive. "He that strikes the cheek of an Israelite strikes, as it were, the cheek of the Shechinah," for it is said (Prov. xx. 25), "He that strikes a man" (*i.e.*, an Israelite who alone deserves the name; Rashi quotes *Babha Metsia*, f. 114, col. 2), strikes the Holy One. *Sanhedr.* f. 58, col. 2, לע = *cheekbone*, and נקש, "to strike," in Syriac (*collidere*, cf. Dan. v. 6; Buxtorf, *Lex Chald. s. v.*), as well as to snare.

The language has been censured as unbecoming in its violence, and has been unfavourably compared with the meekness of Christ before the tribunal of his enemies. "Where," asks St. Jerome, "is that patience of the Saviour, who—as a lamb led to the slaughter opens not his mouth—so gently asks the smiter, 'If I have spoken evil, bear witness to the evil; but if well, why smitest thou me?' We are not detracting from the Apostle, but declaring the glory of God, who, suffering in the flesh, reigns above the wrong and frailty of the flesh."[1] Yet we need not remind the reader that not once or twice only did Christ give the rein to righteous anger, and blight hypocrisy and insolence with a flash of holy wrath. The bystanders seem to have been startled by the boldness of St. Paul's rebuke, for they said to him, "Dost thou revile the High Priest of God?" The Apostle's anger had expended itself in that one outburst, and he instantly apologised with exquisite urbanity and self-control. "I did not know," he said, "brethren, that he is the High Priest;" adding that, had he known this, he would not have addressed to him the opprobrious name of "whited wall," because he reverenced and acted upon the rule of Scripture, "Thou shalt not speak ill of a ruler of thy people."[2]

It has been thought very astonishing that St. Paul should not know that Ananias was the High Priest, and all sorts of explanations have consequently been foisted into his very simple words. These words cannot, however, mean that he was unable to recognise the validity of Ananias's title;[3] or that he had spoken for the moment without considering his office;[4] or that he could not be supposed to acknowledge a high priest in one who behaved with such illegal insolence.[5] Considering the disrepute and insignificance into which the high-priesthood had fallen during the dominance of men who would only, as a rule, take it for a short time in order to "pass the chair;"[6] considering that one of these worldly intruders took to wearing silk gloves that he might not soil his hands with the sacrifices; considering, too, that the Romans and the Herods were constantly setting up one and putting down another at their own caprice, and that the people often regarded some one as the *real* high priest, who was no longer invested with the actual office; considering, too, that in such ways the pontificate of these truckling Sadducees had sunk into a mere simulacrum of what once it was, and that the real allegiance of the people had been completely transferred to the more illustrious Rabbis—it is perfectly conceivable that St. Paul, after his long absence from Jerusalem,[7] had not,

[1] *Adv. Pelag.* iii. 1.

[2] Ex. xxii. 28, LXX. (cf. 2 Pet. ii. 10). Under the good breeding of the answer we notice the admirable skill which enabled Paul thus to show at once his knowledge of and his obedience to the Law, for the supposed apostasy from which he was impugned.

[3] Lightfoot, Schoettgen, Kuinoel, Baumgarten.

[4] Bengel (non veniebat mihi in mentem), Wetstein, Bp. Sanderson (non noveram, non satis attente consideravi), Bp. Wordsworth, &c.

[5] Calvin.

[6] The Jews themselves take this view of them. Grätz (iii. 322) refers to *Pesachim*, 57, 1, *Joma*, 23, 1, which speaks of their narrowness, envy, violence, love of precedence, &c.; Josephus (*Antt.* xx. 8, § 8, 9, § 4) speaks of their impudence and turbulence (see *Life of Christ*, ii. 329—342).

[7] This is the view of Chrysostom.

during the few and much occupied days which had elapsed since his return, given himself the trouble to inquire whether a Kamhit, or a Boethusian, or a Canthera was at that particular moment adorned with the empty title which he probably disgraced. He must, of course, have been aware that the high priest was the *Nasi* of the Sanhedrin, but in a crowded assembly he had not noticed who the speaker was. Owing to his weakened sight, all that he saw before him was a blurred white figure issuing a brutal order, and to this person, who in his external whiteness and inward worthlessness thus reminded him of the plastered wall of a sepulchre, he had addressed his indignant denunciation. That he should retract it on learning the hallowed position of the delinquent, was in accordance with that high breeding of the perfect gentleman which in all his demeanour he habitually displayed.

But while we can easily excuse any passing touch of human infirmity, if such there were, in his sudden vehemence, we cannot defend his subsequent conduct at that meeting. Surely it was more than pardonable if on that day he was a little unhinged, both morally and spiritually, by the wild and awful trials of the day before. In the discussion which was going on about his case, his knowledge of the Sanhedrin, of which he had been a member, enabled him easily to recognise that his judges were still mainly divided into two parties—the Sadducean priests and the Pharisaic elders and scribes. The latter were the more popular and numerous, the former were the more wealthy and powerful. Now St. Paul well knew that these two parties were separated from each other by an internecine enmity, which was only reconciled in the presence of common hatreds. He knew, too, that one main point of contention between them arose from questions about the Unseen World, and the life beyond the grave.[1] Seeing, therefore, that he would meet with neither justice nor mercy from that tribunal, he decided to throw among them the apple of discord, and cried out amid the Babel of tongues, "Brethren, I am a Pharisee, a son of Pharisees. I am being judged about the hope and resurrection of the dead." The plan showed great knowledge of character, and the diversion thus caused was for the time eminently successful; but was it worthy of St. Paul? Undoubtedly there were points in common between him and the Pharisees. "They taught a resurrection of the dead: so did he. They taught the coming of the Kingdom of God: so did he. They taught the Advent of the Messiah: so did he. They taught an intercourse of God with men by the medium of angels, dreams, and visions: so did he. He shared with the Pharisees exactly those doctrines, on account of which he was regarded by the Sadducees as a seducer of the people." This is true; but, on the other hand, his belief in the risen Messiah was *not* the point on which he was mainly being called in question.[2] That belief, had it stood alone, would

[1] Matt. xxii. 28; Jos. *B. J.* ii. 8, § 14; *Antt.* xviii. 1, § 4.

[2] Reuss, whose *Actes des Apôtres* I had not read till these pages were written, takes a very similar view, p. 218. Yet it is, of course, possible that St. Paul's exclamation *may* have been justified by some circumstances of the discussion which have not been preserved in the narrative.

have been passed over by the Sanhedrin as, at the worst, a harmless delusion. Nay, some of the Pharisaic Sanhedrists may even have been nominally Christians.[1] But the fury against St. Paul was kindled by the far more burning questions which arose out of his doctrine of the nullity of the Law, and the admission of the Gentiles to equal privileges with the seed of Abraham. Did not, then, the words of the Apostle suggest a false issue? And had he any right to inflame an existing animosity?[2] And could he worthily say, "I am a Pharisee?" Was he not in reality at variance with the Pharisees in every fundamental particular of their system? Is not the Pharisaic spirit in its very essence the antithesis of the Christian?[3] Did not the two greatest Epistles which he had written prove their whole theology, as such, to be false in every line? Was it not the very work of his life to pull down the legal prescriptions around which it was their one object to rear a hedge? Had not they been occupied—as none knew better than himself—in riveting the iron fetters of that yoke of bondage, which he was striving to shatter link by link? Was there not the least little touch of a *suggestio falsi* in what he said? Let us make every possible deduction and allowance for a venial infirmity; for a sudden and momentary "œconomy," far less serious than that into which his great brother-Apostle had swerved at Antioch; and let us further admit that there is a certain nationality in the chivalry of rigidly minute and scrupulously inflexible straightforwardness, which is, among Northern nations, and among the English in particular, the hereditary result of centuries of training. Let us also acknowledge, not without a blush of shame, that certain slight *managements* and *accommodations* of truth have in later ages been reckoned among Christian virtues. Yet, after all these qualifications, we cannot in this matter wholly see how St. Paul could say without qualification, in such an assembly, "I am a Pharisee." If we think him very little to blame for his stern rebuke of the High Priest; if, referring his conduct to that final court of appeal, which consists in comparing it with the precepts and example of his Lord, we can quite conceive that He who called Herod "a fox" would also have called Ananias "a whited wall;" on the other hand, we cannot but think that this creating of a division among common enemies on the grounds of a very partial and limited agreement with certain other tenets held by some of them, was hardly worthy of St. Paul; and knowing, as we do know, what the Pharisees were, we cannot imagine his Divine Master ever saying, under any circumstances, "I am a Pharisee." Moreover, the device, besides being questionable, was not even politic. It

[1] Acts xv. 5.
[2] Those who, in the teeth of all Scripture, will not believe that an Apostle can make a mistake, have built disastrous conclusions on this action of St. Paul's, quoting it to sanction the Machiavellian policy of the Romans, "Divide et impera." Corn. à Lapide, on this passage, says, "Bellum haereticorum est pax ecclesiae,"—a maxim on which the Romish Church has sometimes acted (see Wordsworth, *ad loc.*). On the other hand, Luther says, with his robust good sense, "Non mihi placet studium illud sanctos nimis efferendi et excusandi si sacræ scripturæ vim negat."
[3] Matt. xxiii. 25, 27; John xii. 43; Rom. ii.

added violence to a yet more infuriated reaction in men who felt that they had been the victims of a successful stratagem, and in the remark of St. Paul before the tribunal of Felix[1] I seem to see—though none have noticed it—a certain sense of compunction for the method in which he had extricated himself from a pressing danger.

But, as we have said, the stratagem was for the time almost magically successful. Paul's enemies were instantly at each other's throats. The High Priest, Ananias, was so singularly detested by the Pharisaic party that centuries afterwards the tradition still lingered of his violence and greed.[2] There rose a sudden uproar of angry voices, and the scribes, who sided with the Pharisees, started up in a body to declare that Paul was innocent. "We find the defendant not guilty; but if a spirit or angel spoke to him——?"[3] Again the Jews, even these distinguished Hierarchs and Rabbis, showed their utter incapacity for self-control. Even in the august precincts of the Sanhedrin the clamour was succeeded by a tumult so violent that Paul was once more in danger of being actually torn to pieces, this time by learned and venerable hands. Claudius Lysias, more and more amazed at the impracticability of these Jews, who first unanimously set upon Paul in the Temple, and half of whom in the Sanhedrin appeared to be now fighting in his defence, determined that his fellow-citizen should not at any rate suffer so ignoble a fate, and once more ordered the detachment of soldiers to go down to snatch him from the midst of them, and lead him to the one spot in Jerusalem where the greatest living Jew could alone find security—the barracks of foreign conquerors.

St. Paul might well be exhausted and depressed by the recurrence, on two consecutive days, of such exciting scenes, and even a courage so dauntless as his could not face unshaken this continual risk of sudden death. The next day was again to bring a fresh peril; but before it came, God in His mercy, who had ever encouraged His faithful servant at the worst and darkest crises, sent him a vision which saved him from all alarm as to his actual life for many a long and trying day. As at Jerusalem on his first visit, and as at Corinth, and as afterwards on the stormy sea, the Lord stood by him and said, "Cheer thee, Paul; for as thou didst bear witness respecting me at Jerusalem, so must thou also bear witness at Rome."

The dawn of the next day sufficed to prove that his manœuvre in the Sanhedrin had only won a temporary success at the cost of a deeper exasperation. So unquenchable was the fury against him, and so inflamed was the feeling of disappointment that Lysias should have snatched him away from their revenge, that in the morning no less than forty Jews bound

[1] Acts xxiv. 21, which I take to be a confession of his error on this occasion.

[2] Derenbourg, *Palest.* § 31.

[3] The expression is an aposiopesis, or suppression of the apodosis, not uncommon after εἰ, as suggesting an alternative. See my *Brief Greek Syntax*, § 309. The μὴ θεομαχῶμεν of the Received Text (omitted in א, A, B, C, E, the Æthiopic, the Coptic, &c.) is a gloss from chap. v. 39. Chrysostom fills up the sentence with ποῖον ἔγκλημα, "What sort of charge is that?"

themselves with a terrible *cherem* not to eat or drink till they had killed him.[1] The Jews, like some Christians in the worst days of Christendom, believed in the divine right of assassination as the means of getting rid of a tyrant or an apostate.[2] Their penal blindness had deceived them into the sanctification of religious murder. How dark a picture does it present to us of the state of Jewish thought at this period that, just as Judas had bargained with the chief priests for the blood-money of his Lord, so these forty *sicarii* went, not only without a blush, but with an evident sense of merit, to the hostile section of the Sanhedrin, to suggest to them the concoction of a lie for the facilitation of a murder. "We are bound under a curse not to touch food till we slay Paul. Do you then, and the Sanhedrin, give notice to the commandant to bring him down to you, under pretext of a more accurate inquiry into his case. We, before he gets near you, are prepared to slay him." So far from rejecting the suggestion with execration, as many a heathen would have done, these degenerate Jews and worldly priests agreed to it with avidity. But a secret known to forty conspirators, and requiring the complicity of an indefinite number more, is no secret at all. There were sure to be dark hints, ominous gestures, words of ill-concealed triumph, and, indeed, so unanimous among the orthodox Jews, and even, we fear, among some nominal Jewish Christians, was the detestation of the man who taught "apostasy from Moses," that in most circles there was no need for any pretence of concealment. When St. Peter had been in prison, and in peril of execution, the Christian community of Jerusalem had been in a ferment of alarm and sorrow, and prayer had been made day and night without ceasing to God for him; but St. Peter, and especially the St. Peter of that early period, was regarded with feelings very different from those with which the Judaic believers looked on the bold genius whose dangerous independence treated Mosaism and its essential covenant as a thing of the past for converted Gentiles. We hear of no prayer from any one of the Elders or the "many myriads" on behalf of St. Paul. He owed to a relative, and not to the Church, the watchful sympathy which alone rescued him from murder. He had a married sister living in Jerusalem, who, whether she agreed or not with the views of her brother—and the fact that neither she nor her family are elsewhere mentioned, and that St. Paul never seems to have put up at her house, makes it at least very doubtful—had yet enough natural affection to try to defeat a plot for his assassination. Most gladly would we have known something further about the details. All that we are told is, that the son of this lady, apparently a mere boy, on hearing of the intended ambuscade, went at once to the barracks of Fort Antonia, and gaining ready access to his uncle, who, as an untried Roman citizen, was only kept in *custodia militaris*, revealed to him the plot. The Apostle acted with his usual good sense and promptitude. Sending for one of the ten centurions of the garrison, he said

[1] For instances of a similar *cherem*, see 1 Sam. xiv. 24; Jos. *Antt.* 8, § 3, &c.
[2] *Sanhedr.* 9; Jos. *Antt.* xii. 6, § 2; Philo, *De Sacrif.* p. 855.

to him, "Lead this youth to the commandant, for he has something to tell him."[1] The centurion went immediately to Lysias, and said, "The prisoner Paul called me to him, and asked me to lead this youth to you, as he has something to say to you." There is a touch of very natural kindness in the way in which the Roman officer received the Jewish boy. Seeing, perhaps, that he was nervous and flustered, both from the peril to which he was subjecting himself by revealing this secret—since suspicion would naturally fall on him—and also by finding himself in the presence of the most powerful person in Jerusalem, the military delegate of the dreaded Procurator—Lysias took him by the hand, and walking with him to a place where they were out of earshot, began to ask him what his message was. The youth told him that he would immediately receive a request from the Sanhedrin to summon a meeting next day, and bring Paul once more before them to arrive at some more definite result; and that more than forty *sicarii* had agreed on time and place to murder his prisoner, so that the only way to defeat the plot was to refuse the request of the Sanhedrin. Lysias saw the importance of the secret, and instantly formed his plans. He told the youth not to mention to any one that he had given him information of the conspiracy, and, summoning two centurions, ordered them to equip two hundred legionaries, seventy cavalry soldiers, two hundred lancers,[2] with two spare horses, to be ready to escort Paul safely to Cæsarea that very evening at nine o'clock. He was extremely glad to get rid of a prisoner who created such excitement, and who was the object of an animosity so keen that it might at any moment lead to a riot. At that day, too, charges of bribery flew about in the most dangerous manner. Celer, a Roman knight of far higher rank than himself, had actually been dragged by Jews round the walls of Jerusalem, and finally beheaded, for receiving a bribe from the Samaritans.[3] Agrippa I. had been dismissed from Antioch; and no less a person than the Procurator Cumanus had been imprisoned and disgraced. So corrupt was the Roman administration in the hands of even the highest officials, that if Paul were murdered Lysias might easily have been charged with having accepted a bribe to induce him to connive at this nefarious conspiracy.[4] There was now sufficient pretext to send Paul away swiftly and secretly, and so get rid of an embarrassing responsibility. At nine that evening, when it was dark and when the streets would be deserted, the large escort of four hundred and seventy soldiers—an escort the necessity of which shows the dangerous condition of the country, and the extent of Lysias's alarm—stood ready at the gate of the barracks; and before the tramp of horse and foot began to startle the silent city, the commandant handed to

[1] The minuteness of the narrative, perhaps, indicates that St. Luke, who sought for information from all sources, had received the story from the youth himself.

[2] δεξιολαβοι, Vulg. *lancearii*. The only passage to throw light on the word is one adduced by Meyer from Constantine the Porphyrogenete, which proves nothing. A reads δεξιόβολοι. One explanation is *gens du train*—men who held a second horse by the right hand.

[3] Jos. *Antt.* xx. 6, § 3; *B. J.* ii. 12, § 7.

[4] One of the cursives (137) actually adds ἐφοβήθη γὰρ μηπότε ἁρπάσαντες αὐτὸν οἱ Ἰουδαῖοι ἀποκτείνωσι καὶ αὐτὸς μεταξὺ ἔγκλημα ἔχῃ ὡς χρήματα εἰληφώς.

the centurion in command a letter which, in its obvious genuineness, exhibits a very dexterous mixture of truth and falsehood, and by no means bears out the representation that Lysias was a stupid person. It was one of those abstracts of criminal charges called *elogia*, which it was the custom to write in submitting a prisoner to the cognisance of a superior judge; and it was ingeniously framed with a view to obviate beforehand any possible charge of illegal conduct towards a Roman citizen. The conduct of Lysias, though a little hasty at first, had however been, on the whole, both kind and honourable; and he would probably be assured by St. Paul that, so far as he was concerned, he might lay aside all anxiety as to any proceedings intended to vindicate the inalienable rights conferred by the citizenship.

The letter ran as follows:—

"Claudius Lysias to his Excellency the Procurator Felix, greeting.

"The prisoner whom I send to you is one who was seized by the Jews, and was on the point of being killed by them when I came down upon them with my forces, and rescued him on being informed that he was a Roman. As I wanted to know further the reason why they accused him, I took him down into their Sanhedrin, and found that he was being accused of questions of their law, but had against him no charge which deserved death or chains. But on receiving secret intimation of a plot which was to be put in force against him, I immediately sent him to you, at the same time giving notice to his accusers also to say all they had to say about him in your presence. Farewell!"

Paul was mounted on one of the horses provided for him, and the escort rode rapidly through the disturbed country, in the vicinity of Jerusalem, with a sharp look-out against any ambuscade. After that, being too numerous and well-armed to have any dread of mere brigands, they went at their ease along a Roman road, the thirty-five miles to Antipatris.[1] Here they rested for the remainder of the night. Next day the four hundred legionaries and lancers marched back to Jerusalem, while the mounted soldiers rode forward on the remaining twenty-five miles to Cæsarea. St. Paul thus entered Cæsarea with a pomp of attendance very unlike the humble guise in which he had left it, amid the little caravan of his fellow-Christians. They entered the town in broad daylight, and so large a body passing through the streets must have attracted many curious eyes. How must Philip and the other Christians of Cæsarea have been startled to recognise the rapid fulfilment of their forebodings as they saw the great teacher, from whom they had parted with so many tears, ride through the streets, with his right hand chained to the arm of a horseman, amid a throng of soldiers from the garrison of Antonia! That ride, in the midst of his Roman body-guard, was destined to be his last experience of air and exercise, till—after two years of imprisonment—his voyage to Rome began.

[1] Kefr Saba; Jos. *Antt.* xvi. 5, § 2.

The centurion and his prisoner were at once introduced into the presence of Felix. Felix read the letter of Lysias, and after briefly inquiring to what province Paul belonged, and being told he was a Cilician, he said, "I will hear out your case when your accusers have arrived."[1] He then handed Paul over to a soldier to be kept in one of the guard-rooms attached to the old Herodian palace which now formed the splendid residence of the Procurators of Judæa.

CHAPTER XLI.

PAUL AND FELIX.

"Antonius Felix, per omnem saevitiam et libidinem, jus regium servili ingenio exercuit."—TAC. *Hist.* v. 9.

"Jam pridem Judaeae impositus . . . et cuncta malefacta sibi impune ratus."—*Ann.* xii. 54.

A ROMAN judge to whom a prisoner had been sent with an *elogium* was bound, if possible, to try him within three days. Felix, however, had to send a message to Jerusalem, and fix a time for the case to come on, in order that the accusers might be present; and as the journey took nearly two days, it was the fifth day after St. Paul's arrival at Cæsarea that he was brought to trial. The momentary diversion in his favour, of which by this time the Pharisees were probably ashamed, had settled into an unanimous hatred, and the elders, probably of both parties, hurried down to accuse their adversary. Ananias in person accompanied them, eager for revenge against the man who had compared him to a plastered sepulchre. It must have been intensely disagreeable to these dignified personages to be forced to hurry on a fatiguing journey of some seventy miles from the religious to the political capital of Judæa, in order to induce a Gentile dog to give up an apostate *mesith* to their jurisdiction; but the Sanhedrists, smarting under defeat, would not be likely to leave any stone unturned which should bring the offender within reach of vengeance.

They wished to make sure of the extradition of their victim, and being little able to plead either in Greek or Latin, and more or less ignorant of the procedure in Roman courts, they gave their brief to a provincial barrister named Tertullus. Everything was done with due formality. They first lodged their complaint, and then the prisoner was confronted with them that he might hear, and if possible refute, their accusations. Tertullus was evidently a practised speaker, and St. Luke has faithfully preserved an outline of his voluble plausibility. Speaking with politic complaisance as though he were himself a Jew, he began by a fulsome compliment to Felix, which served as the usual *captatio benevolentiae*. Alluding to the early exertions of Felix against the banditti and the recent suppression of the Egyptian false Messiah,

[1] "Qui cum elogio mittantur ex integro audiendi sunt."

he began to assure his Excellency, with truly legal rotundity of verbiage, of the quite universal and uninterrupted gratitude of the Jews for the peace which he had secured to them, and for the many reforms[1] which had been initiated by his prudential wisdom. The real fact was that Felix was most peculiarly detested, and that though he had certainly suppressed some brigands, yet he had from the earliest times of his administration distinctly encouraged more,[2] and was even accused of having shared their spoils with Ventidius Cumanus when he had the separate charge of Samaria.[3] He then apologised for intruding ever so briefly on his Excellency's indulgent forbearance, but it was necessary to trouble him with three counts of indictment against the defendant—namely, that first, he was a public pest, who lived by exciting factions among all the Jews all over the world; secondly, that he was a ringleader of the Nazarenes; and thirdly, that he had attempted to profane the Temple. They had accordingly seized him, and wanted to judge him in accordance with their own law; but Lysias had intervened with much violence and taken him from their hands, ordering his accusers to come before the Procurator. By reference to Lysias[4] his Excellency might further ascertain the substantial truth of these charges. When the oration was over, since there were no regular witnesses, the Jews one after another "made a dead set" against Paul,[5] asseverating the truth of all that Tertullus had stated.

Then the Procurator, already impatient with the conviction that this was, as Lysias had informed him, some Jewish squabble about Mosaic minutiæ, flung a haughty nod to the prisoner, in intimation that he might speak. St. Paul's *captatio benevolentiae* was very different from that of Tertullus. It consisted simply in the perfectly true remark that he could defend himself all the more cheerfully before Felix from the knowledge that he had now been Procurator for an unusual time,[6] and could therefore, from his familiarity with Jewish affairs, easily ascertain that it was but twelve days[7] since the Pentecost, to which feast he had come, not only with no seditious purpose, but actually to worship in Jerusalem; and that during that time he had discoursed with no one, and had on no occasion attracted any crowd, or caused any disturbance, either in the Temple or in the Synagogues, or in any part of the city. He,

[1] xxiv. 2, διορθωμάτων, ℵ, A, B, E. The other reading κατορθωμάτων is a more general expression.

[2] Jos. *Antt.* xx. 8, § 5; *B. J.* ii. 13, § 2; Euseb. *H. E.* ii. 20—22.

[3] Jos. *Antt.* xx. 8, § 9; Tac. *Ann.* xii. 54, "*quies* provinciae reddita."

[4] This entire clause (Acts xxiv. 6—8) is omitted from καὶ κατὰ down to ἐπὶ σέ in ℵ, A, B, G, H, and in the Coptic, Sahidic, Latin, and other versions. If it be an interpolation, the παρ' οὗ must refer to Paul, but there are great difficulties either way, and verse 22 is in favour of their genuineness. On the other hand, if genuine, why should the passage have been omitted? D, which has so many additions, is here deficient.

[5] Ver. 9, συνεπέθεντο. ℵ, A, B, E, G, H.

[6] xxiv. 10, ἐκ πολλῶν ἐτῶν, since A.D. 52, *i.e.* six years. "Non ignoravit Paulus artem rhetorum *movere laudando.*" (Grot.)

[7] 1. Arrival. 2. Interview with James, &c. 3—7. Vow and arrest. 8. Sanhedrin. 9. Conspiracy. 10. Arrival at Cæsarea. 11, 12. In custody. 13. Trial.

therefore, met the first and third counts of the indictment with a positive contradiction, and challenged the Jews to produce any witnesses in confirmation of them. As to the second count, he was quite ready to admit that he belonged to what they called a sect; but it was no more an illegal sect than those to which they themselves belonged, since he worshipped the God whom, as a Jew, he had been always taught to worship—frankly accepted their entire Scriptures—and believed, exactly as the majority of themselves did, in a resurrection of the just and unjust. In this faith it had always been his aim to have a conscience void of offence towards God and towards man. He had now been five years absent from Jerusalem, and on returning with alms for the poor of his people, and offerings for the Temple, they found him in the Temple, a quiet and legally purified worshipper. For the riot which had ensued he was not responsible. It had been stirred up by certain Asiatic Jews, who ought to have been present as witnesses, and whose absence was a proof of the weakness of the case against him. But if their attendance could not be secured, he called upon his accusers themselves to state the result of their trial of him before the Sanhedrin, and whether they had a single fact against him, unless it were his exclamation as he stood before them, that he was being tried about a question of the resurrection of the dead.

The case had evidently broken down. St. Paul's statement of facts directly contradicted the only charge brought against him. The differences of doctrine between the Jews and himself were not in any way to the point, since they affected questions which had not been touched upon at all, and of which the Roman law could take no cognisance. It was no part of his duty to prove the doctrine of the Nazarenes, or justify himself for having embraced it, since at that time it had not been declared to be a *religio illicita*. Of this fact Felix was perfectly aware. He had a more accurate knowledge of "that way" than the Jews and their advocate supposed.[1] He was not going, therefore, to hand Paul over to the Sanhedrin, which might be dangerous, and would certainly be unjust; but at the same time he did not wish to offend these important personages. He therefore postponed the trial—*rem ampliavit*—on the ground of the absence of Lysias, who was a material witness, promising, however, to give a final decision whenever he came down to Cæsarea. Paul was remanded to the guard-room, but Felix gave particular instructions to the centurion[2] that his custody was not to be a severe one, and that his friends were to be permitted free access to his prison. St. Luke and Aristarchus certainly availed themselves of this permission, and doubtless the heavy hours were lightened by the visits of Philip the Evangelist, and other Christians of the little Cæsarean community to whom Paul was dear.[3]

[1] xxiv. 22, ἀκριβέστερον.

[2] Ver. 23, τῷ ἑκατοντάρχῃ—the centurion who was present at the trial; not at all necessarily, or even probably, the centurion who had escorted him from Antipatris to Cæsarea.

[3] It seems to have been about this time that Felix used the machinations of Simon Magus to induce Drusilla, the younger sister of Agrippa II., to elope from her husband

On his return to Cæsarea with his wife Drusilla, and apparently in order to gratify her curiosity to see and hear a person whose strange history and marvellous powers were so widely known, Felix once more summoned Paul into his presence, and bade him discourse to them about his beliefs. Right nobly did Paul use his opportunity. Felix was a Gentile, and was moreover his judge, and it was no part of St. Paul's duty to judge those that are without. Had he assumed such a function, his life must have become one incessant and useless protest. And yet, with perfect urbanity and respect for the powers that be, he spoke of the faith in Christ which he was bidden to explain, in a way that enabled him to touch on those virtues which were most needed by the guilty pair who listened to his words. The licentious princess must have blushed as he discoursed of continence; the rapacious and unjust governor as he spoke of righteousness—both of them as he reasoned of the judgment to come. Whatever may have been the thoughts of Drusilla, she locked them up in her own bosom; but Felix, less accustomed to such truths, was deeply agitated by them. As he glanced back over the stained and guilty past, he was afraid. He had been a slave, in the vilest of all positions, at the vilest of all epochs, in the vilest of all cities. He had crept with his brother Pallas into the position of a courtier at the most morally degraded of all courts. He had been an officer of those auxiliaries who were the worst of all troops. What secrets of lust and blood lay hidden in his earlier life we do not know; but ample and indisputable testimony, Jewish and Pagan, sacred and secular, reveals to us what he had been—how greedy, how savage, how treacherous, how unjust, how steeped with the blood of private murder and public massacre—during the eight years which he had now spent in the government, first of Samaria, then of Palestine. There were footsteps behind him; he began to feel as though "the earth were made of glass." He could not bear the novel sensation of terror which crept over him, or the reproaches of the blushing, shamefaced spirit which began to mutiny even in such a breast as his. He cut short the interview. "Go," he said, "for the present; I will take some future opportunity to summon you to a hearing." Even his remorse was not purely disinterested. Paul had indeed acquired over him some of that ascendency which could hardly fail to be won by so lofty a personality; and Felix, struck by his bearing, his genius, his

Aziz, and to become his wife. It was a strange thing, and one which must have required all the arts of Simon to effect, that this young and beautiful princess, who was at this time only twenty years old, should have abandoned all her Jewish prejudices, and risked the deadliest abhorrence of her race, by leaving a prince who loved her, and had even been induced to accept circumcision to gratify her national scruples, in order to form an adulterous connexion with a cruel and elderly profligate, who had been nothing better than a slave. Felix would never have dreamt for one moment of making for her sake the immense sacrifice which Aziz had accepted, and which her previous lover, the Prince of Commagene, had refused. Such, however, were the subtle arts of the Cyprian sorcerer, and such the Greek-like fascinations of the seducer, that he had gained his end, and how thus still further obliterated the memories of his servile origin by marrying a third princess. "Trium reginarum maritum aut adulterum" (Suet. *Claud.* 28). Another of his wives was also a Drusilla, daughter of Juba, King of Mauretania, and granddaughter of Antony and Cleopatra. The third is unknown.

moral force, sent for him not unfrequently to converse with him respecting his beliefs. But this apparent interest in religious subjects was, in reality, akin to that vein of superstition which made him the ready dupe of Simon Magus, and it did not exclude a certain hankering after a bribe, which he felt sure that Paul, who had brought considerable sums of money to Jerusalem, could either procure or give. He took care to drop hints which should leave no doubt as to his intentions. But Paul was innocent, and neither would he adopt any illicit method to secure his liberty, nor in any case would he burden the affection of his converts to contribute the ransom which he was too poor to offer. He did not wish by dubious human methods to interfere with God's plan respecting him, nor to set a questionable example to the future *libellatici*. He therefore declined to take the hints of Felix, and two years glided away, and he was still in prison.

Towards the end of that time he must have been startled by a terrible clamour in the streets of Cæsarea. Disputes, indeed, were constantly occurring in a city composed half of Jews and half of Greeks, or Syrians, between whom there was a perpetual feud for precedence. All the splendour of the place—its amphitheatre, its temples, its palace—was due to the passion for building which animated the first Herod. The Jewish population was large and wealthy, and since their king had done so much for the town, they claimed it as their own. It was quite true that, but for Herod, Cæsarea would never have been heard of in history. Its sole utility consisted in the harbour which he had constructed for it at enormous cost of money and labour, and which was extremely needed on that inhospitable coast. But the Greeks maintained that it was *their* town, seeing that it had been founded by Strato, and called Strato's Tower until Herod had altered the name in his usual spirit of flattery towards the Imperial House. Towards the close of Paul's imprisonment, the Greeks and Jews came to an open quarrel in the market-place, and the Greeks were being worsted in the combat by their enraged adversaries, when Felix appeared with his cohorts and ordered the Jews to disperse. As his command was not instantly obeyed by the victorious party, Felix, who like all the Romans sided with the Gentile faction, let loose his soldiers upon them. The soldiers were probably not Romans, but provincials.[1] They were therefore delighted to fall on the Jews, many of whom were instantly put to the sword. Not content with this, Felix, whose dislike to the whole race only deepened every year, allowed them to plunder the houses of the wealthier Jews.[2] This crowning act of injustice could not pass unnoticed. Felix, indeed, as Tacitus tells us, had so long learnt to rely on the overwhelming influence of Pallas over Claudius, that he began to think that he might commit any crime he liked without being called to question. But Claudius had now been dismissed

[1] There were no Jews among them, because no Jew could serve in the army without a constant necessity of breaking the rules of his religion, so that on this ground they were exempted from the liability to conscription.

[2] The scenes which took place on this occasion were analogous to those which happened at Alexandria under Flaccus.

to his *apotheosis* by the poisoned mushrooms of Agrippina, and the influence both of Pallas and Agrippina was on the wane. The Jews laid a formal impeachment against Felix for his conduct at Cæsarea, and he was recalled to answer their complaints. Accompanied by Drusilla and Simon Magus, who had by this time assumed the position of his domestic sorcerer, he sailed to Italy, and his very last act was one of flagrant injustice. He had already abused the power of a provincial governor by delaying the trial of Paul for two years. It was a defect in Roman law that, though it ordered the immediate trial of a prisoner sent to a superior court with an *elogium*, it laid down no rule as to the necessary termination of his trial, and thus put into the hands of an unjust Præfect a formidable instrument of torture. Paul had now languished for two full years in the Herodian palace, and Felix had not decided his case. Philo mentions a similar instance in which Flaccus kept Lampo for two years in prison at Alexandria[1] on a charge of *laesa majestas*, in hopes of breaking his heart by a punishment worse than death. Felix had no such object, for he seems to have felt for Paul a sincere respect; but since Paul would not offer a bribe, Felix would not set him free, and—more the slave of self-interest than he had ever been the slave of Antonia—he finally left him bound in order to gratify the malice of the Jews whom he thus strove, but quite vainly, to propitiate. He thought that he could, perhaps, settle some awkward items of their account against him by sacrificing to their religious hatreds a small scruple on the score of justice. Perhaps this was the last drop in the overflowing cup of his iniquity. How he closed his bad career we do not know. It required the utmost stretch of the waning influence of his brother Pallas to save him from the punishment which his crimes had deserved; and, although he was not put to death or banished, he had to disgorge the greater portion of his ill-gotten wealth. Drusilla had one son by her marriage with him, and this son, whose name was Agrippa, perished in the eruption of Vesuvius nineteen years after these events.[2] Felix himself vanishes henceforth into obscurity and disgrace.

CHAPTER XLII.

ST. PAUL BEFORE AGRIPPA II.

"When I consider this Apostle as appearing either before the witty Athenians, or before a Roman Court of Judicature, in the presence of their great men and ladies, I see how handsomely he accommodateth himself to the apprehension and temper of these politer people."—SHAFTESBURY, *Characteristics*, i. 30.

THE successor of Felix was Porcius Festus (A.D. 60),[3] who, though he too was probably of no higher rank than that of a freedman, was a far worthier and more honourable ruler. His Procuratorship was of very brief duration,

[1] Philo *in Flacc.* xvi.

[2] A.D. 79. Jos. *Antt.* xx. 7, § 2.

[3] This furnishes one of the few certain *points de repère* for the precise chronology of the Acts. He died the next year.

and he inherited the government of a country in which the wildest anarchy was triumphant, and internecine quarrels were carried on in the bloodiest spirit of revenge. Had he been Procurator for a longer time, difficult as was the task to hold in the leash the furious hatreds of Jews and Gentiles, he might have accomplished more memorable results. The sacred narrative displays him in a not unfavourable light, and he at any rate contrasts most favourably with his immediate predecessor and successor, in the fact that he tried to administer real justice, and did not stain his hands with bribes.[1]

His first movements show an active and energetic spirit. He arrived in Palestine about the month of August, and three days after his arrival at Cæsarea went direct to Jerusalem. One of the first questions which he had to face was the mode of dealing with St. Paul. Two years of deferred hope, and obstructed purposes, and dreary imprisonment had not quenched the deadly antipathy of the Jews to the man whose free offer of the Gospel to the Gentiles seemed to them one of the most fatal omens of their impending ruin. The terrible fight in the market-place between Jews and Syrian Greeks, which had caused the disgrace of Felix, had left behind it an unappeased exasperation, and the Jews of Cæsarea were unanimous[2] in demanding the immediate punishment of Paul. When Festus reached Jerusalem the same cry[3] met him, and the death of Paul was demanded, not only by the mob, but by deputations of all the chief personages in Jerusalem, headed by Ishmael Ben Phabi, the new High Priest.[4] We have seen already that the Jews, with great insight into human nature, eagerly seized the first opportunity of playing upon the inexperience of a newly-arrived official, and moulding, him if possible, while he was likely to be most plastic in his desire to create a favourable impression. But Festus was not one of the base and feeble Procurators who would commit a crime to win popularity. The Palestinian Jews soon found that they had to do with one who more resembled a Gallio than a Felix. The people and their priests begged him as an initial favour not to exempt Paul's case from their cognisance, but to bring him to Jerusalem, that he might once more be tried by the Sanhedrin, when they would take care that he should cause no second fiasco by turning their theologic jealousies against each other. Indeed, these sacerdotalists, who thought far less of murder than of a ceremonial pollution,[5] had taken care that if Festus once granted their petition, their hired assassins should get rid of Paul on the road "or ever he came near." Festus saw through them sufficiently to thwart their design under the guise of a courteous offer that, as Paul was now at Cæsarea, he would return thither almost immediately, and give a full and fair audience to their complaints. On their continued insistence Festus gave them the haughty and genuinely Roman reply that,

[1] Jos. *Antt.* xx. 8, § 9; 9, § 1; *B. J.* ii. 14, § 1.

[2] Acts xxv. 24, ἅπαν τὸ πλῆθος τῶν Ἰουδαίων . . . ἐνθάδε. [3] *Id.*, ἐπιβοῶντες.

[4] He had been appointed by Agrippa II., A.D. 59.

[5] See *Sota*, f. 47, 2; *Tosifta Sota*, c. 14; *Joma*, f. 23, 1; Jos. *B. J. passim.* (Grätz, iii. 321, *seqq.*)

whatever their Oriental notions of justice might be, it was not the custom of the Romans to grant any person's life to his accusers by way of doing a favour, but to place the accused and the accusers face to face, and to give the accused a full opportunity for self-defence. The High Priest and his fellow-conspirators, finding that they could not play either on the timidity of Festus or his complaisance, had to content themselves once more with organising a powerful deputation to carry out the accusation. Eight or ten days afterwards Festus returned to the palace at Cæsarea, and the very next day took his seat on the tribunal to hear the case. The Jews had not again hired a practised barrister to help them, and the trial degenerated into a scene of passionate clamour, in which St. Paul simply met the many accusations against him by calm denials. The Jews, tumultuously surrounding the tribunal, reiterated their accusations of heresy, sacrilege, and treason; but as not a single witness was forthcoming, Paul had no need to do more than to recount the facts. This time the Jews seem to have defined the old vague charge that Paul was a stirrer-up of sedition throughout the Diaspora, by trying to frighten Festus, as they had frightened Pilate, with the name of Cæsar;[1] but Festus had too thorough a knowledge of the Roman law not to see, through all this murky storm of rage, the two plain facts, that he was trying a false issue, since the inquiry really turned on matters which affected the arcana of Jewish theology; and that even if there was a grain of truth in the Jewish accusations, Paul had not been guilty of anything approaching to a capital crime. Wishing to put an end to the scene—for nothing was more odious to the dignity of a well-trained Roman than the scowling faces, and gleaming eyes, and screaming interpellations of despised Orientals—Festus asked Paul whether he was willing to go up to Jerusalem, and be tried before the Sanhedrin under his protection.[2] This was practically a proposal to transfer the question back from the Roman to the Jewish jurisdiction. But Paul knew very well that he had far more chance of justice at the hands of the Romans than at the hands of Jews, whose crimes were now dragging Jerusalem to her destruction. Jewish tribunals had invariably and even savagely condemned him; Gentile tribunals —Gallio, the Politarchs, the Asiarchs, Lysias, Felix, Festus, even the "Prætors," at Philippi, and at last even the monster Nero—always saw and proclaimed his innocence. But he was sick of these delays; sick of the fierce reiteration of calumnies which he had ten times refuted; sick of being made the bone of contention for mutual hatreds; sick of the arbitrary caprice of provincial governors. Terrible as the black dungeon of Machærus to the free soul of the Baptist, must have been the dreary barracks of Cæsarea to the ardent zeal of Paul. How he must have hated that palace, dripping with the blood of murdered Herods, and haunted by the worst memories of their crimes! How tired he must have been of the idleness and the ribaldries of

[1] Acts xxv. 8.

[2] This must be the meaning of ἐπ' ἐμοῦ, xxv. 9. There could be no conceivable object in taking Paul to Jerusalem, unless it were to have him once more tried by the Sanhedrin; but of course Festus could not preside at a meeting of the Sanhedrin, though he might be present (somewhat as Lysias was), and see that the accused received fair treatment.

provincial soldiers, and the tumultuous noises of collision between Jews and Gentiles which were constantly resounding in those ill-managed streets! Doubtless his imprisonment had been a period of deep inward calm and growth. He knew that his course was not yet over. He was awaiting the fulfilment of God's will. He saw that he had nothing more to hope for from High Priests or Procurators, and seized his opportunity. As a Roman citizen he had one special privilege—that right of appeal to Cæsar, which was still left as the venerable trophy of popular triumph in the struggles of centuries. He had only to pronounce the one word *Appello*, and every enemy would, for a time, be defeated, who was now thirsting for his blood.[1] He determined to exercise his privilege. The Procurator was but a shadow of the Cæsar. His offer sounded plausibly fair, but perhaps Paul saw through it. "I am standing," he said, "at Cæsar's tribunal. There, and not before the Sanhedrin, I ought to be judged. Even you, O Festus! knew full well that I never in any respect wronged the Jews. If I am an offender, and have committed any capital crime, it is not against them, but against the Empire; and if I am found guilty, I do not refuse to die. But if all the accusations which these bring against me are nothing, no one can sacrifice me to them as a favour." And then he suddenly exclaimed, "Caesarem appello!"

The appeal was a surprise; even Festus, who meant well and kindly, though perhaps with a touch of natural complaisance towards his new subjects, was a little offended by it. It was not agreeable to have his jurisdiction superseded by an "appeal" to a superior on the very first occasion that he took his seat on the tribunal. Paul had not yet had time to learn his character. He might doubtless have trusted him more, if he had known him better; but matters had fallen into a hopeless imbroglio, and perhaps Paul had some inward intimation that this, at last, was God's appointed way in which he was to visit Italy, and to bear witness at Rome.

The appeal at once put an end to all the proceedings of the court. Festus held a very brief consultation with his *consiliarii*—or council of his assessors—as to whether the appeal was legally admissible or not. The case was too clear to admit of much doubt under this head, and, after a moment's delay, Festus exclaimed, in words which, however brusquely spoken, must have thrilled the heart of more than one person in that assembly, and most of all the heart of the Apostle himself, "Caesarem appellasti; ad Caesarem ibis." Perhaps Festus avenged his momentarily wounded vanity by the thought, "You little knew what an appeal to Cæsar means!"

Of course some days must elapse before an opportunity would occur to send Paul from Cæsarea to Italy. A ship had to be provided, and other prisoners had to be tried whom it might be necessary to remand to the Emperor's decision. The delay was a providential one. It furnished Paul with a happy opportunity of proclaiming the truths and the arguments of Christianity in the presence of all the Jewish and Gentile magnates of the

[1] By the Lex Julia *De Appellatione*. Cf. Plin. *Epp*. x. 97.

capital and of the last scions of that Idumean house of brilliant adventurers who had allied themselves with the Asmonæan princes, and worn the title of Jewish kings.

For only a day or two had elapsed after the appeal, when Agrippa II., the last of the Herods, and his sister Berenice came down to Cæsarea to pay their respects to the new Procurator. It was a compliment which they could never safely omit, and we find that they paid similar visits to each Procurator in succession. The regal power of Agrippa, such as it was, depended on no popular support, but simply and solely on the will of the Emperor. As a breath had made him first king of Chalcis (A.D. 48), then of the tetrarchy of Philip (A.D. 52), and finally of various other cities (A.D. 55), so on any day a breath might unmake him. He was not, like his father, "the king of the Jews," and therefore St. Luke, with his usual accuracy in these details, only calls him "the king;" but as he had succeeded his uncle Herod of Chalcis in the guardianship of the Temple, with its sacred robes, and the right of nominations to the High-priesthood, he practically became a mere gilded instrument to keep order for the Romans, and it was essential for him to remain on good terms with them.[1] They in their turn found it desirable to flatter the harmless vanities of a phantom royalty.

During the visit of Agrippa and Berenice to Festus, he took the opportunity of referring to the perplexing case of the prisoner Paul. He told Agrippa of the fury which seemed to inspire the whole Jewish people at the mention of his name, and of the futile results of the trial just concluded. However much the Jews might try to misrepresent the real questions at issue, it was clear that they turned on Mosaic technicalities,[2] and "on one Jesus who was dead, whom Paul alleged to be alive"[3]—matters about which Festus had no jurisdiction, and could not be supposed to know anything. The prisoner, however, had refused to be tried again by the Sanhedrin, and had appealed to the decision of the Augustus.

"I should have liked myself also to hear this person," said Agrippa.[4] Festus eagerly closed with the wish, and fixed the next day for the gratification of the king's fancy.

It was not, as is commonly represented, a new trial. That would have been, on all grounds, impossible. Agrippa was without judicial functions, and the authority of the Procurator had been cut short by the appeal. It was more of the nature of a private or drawing-room audience—a sort of show occasion designed for the amusement of these princely guests, and the idle

[1] The Romans would have resented any neglect towards their representative, as much as we should resent the conduct of Scindiah or Holkar if they entered the district of one of our Indian Residents without paying their respects.

[2] xxv. 19. The use of the phrase, περὶ τῆς ἰδίας δεισιδαιμονίας, "about their own religious matters" (cf. xvii. 22), shows sufficiently that among Gentiles Agrippa was accustomed to speak of his religion quite in the tone of a man of the world.

[3] St. Luke and the early Christians were far too much in earnest in their belief to make them shrink in the least from recording the scorn with which it was spoken of.

[4] xxv. 22, Ἐβουλόμην καὶ αὐτὸς; cf. Gal. iv. 20. It might, however, mean, "I, too, was feeling a personal desire."

aristocracy of Cæsarea, both Jewish and Gentile. Festus ordered the auditorium to be prepared for the occasion, and invited all the chief officers of the army, and the principal inhabitants of the town. The Herods were fond of show, and Festus gratified their humour by a grand processional display. He would doubtless appear in his scarlet paludament, with his full attendance of lictors and body-guard, who would stand at arms behind the gilded chairs which were placed for himself and his distinguished visitors. We are expressly told that Agrippa and Berenice went in state to the Prætorium, she, doubtless, blazing with all her jewels, and he in his purple robes, and both with the golden circlets of royalty around their foreheads, and attended by a suite of followers in the most gorgeous apparel of Eastern pomp. It was a compliment to the new governor to visit him with as much splendour as possible, and both he and his guests were not sorry to furnish a spectacle which would at once illustrate their importance and their mutual cordiality. Did Agrippa think of his great-grandfather Herod, and the massacre of the innocents? of his great-uncle Antipas, and the murder of John the Baptist? of his father Agrippa I., and the execution of James the Elder? Did he recall the fact that they had each died or been disgraced, soon after, or in direct consequence of, those inflictions of martyrdom? Did he realise how closely, but unwittingly, the faith in that "one Jesus" had been linked with the destinies of his house? Did the pomp of to-day remind him of the pomp sixteen years earlier, when his much more powerful father had stood in the theatre, with the sunlight blazing on the tissued silver of his robe, and the people shouting that he was a god?[1] Did none of the dark memories of the place overshadow him as he entered that former palace of his race? It is very unlikely. Extreme vanity, gratified self-importance, far more probably absorbed the mind of this titular king, as, in all the pomp of phantom sovereignty, he swept along the large open hall, seated himself with his beautiful sister by the Procurator's side, and glanced with cold curiosity on the poor, worn, shackled prisoner—pale with sickness and long imprisonment—who was led in at his command.

Festus opened the proceedings in a short, complimentary speech, in which he found an excuse for the gathering, by saying that on the one hand the Jews were extremely infuriated against this man, and that on the other he was entirely innocent, so far as he could see, of any capital crime. Since, however, he was a Roman citizen, and had appealed to Cæsar, it was necessary to send to "the Lord"[2] some minute of the case, by way of *elogium*, and he was completely perplexed as to what he ought to say. He was, therefore, glad of the opportunity to bring the prisoner before this distinguished assembly, that they, and especially King Agrippa, might hear what he had to say for himself, and so, by forming some sort of preliminary judgment, relieve Festus from the ridiculous position of sending a prisoner without being able to state any definite crime with which he had been charged.

[1] A.D. 44. It was now A.D. 60.

[2] xxv. 26.

As no accusers were present, and this was not in any respect a judicial assembly, Agrippa, as the person for whom the whole scene was got up, told Paul that he was allowed to speak about himself. Had the Apostle been of a morose disposition he might have despised the hollowness of these mock proceedings. Had he been actuated by any motives lower than the highest, he might have seized the opportunity to flatter himself into favour in the absence of his enemies. But the predominant feature in his, as in the very greatest characters, was a continual seriousness and earnestness, and his only desire was to plead not his own cause, but that of his Master. Festus, with the Roman adulation, which in that age outran even the appetite of absolutism, had used that title of "the Lord," which the later Emperors seized with avidity, but which the earliest and ablest of them had contemptuously refused.[1] But Paul was neither imposed upon by these colossal titles of reverence, nor daunted by these pompous inanities of reflected power.

There is not a word of his address which does not prove how completely he was at his ease. The scarlet sagum of the Procurator, the fasces of the lictors, the swords of the legionaries, the gleaming armour of the Chiliarchs, did not for one moment daunt him,—they were a terror, not to good works, but to the evil; and he felt that his was a service which was above all sway.

Stretching out his hand in the manner familiar to the orators whom he had often heard in Tarsus or in Antioch,[2] he began by the sincere remark that he was particularly happy to make his defence before King Agrippa, not—which would have been false—for any special worth of his, but because the prince had received from his father—whose anxiety to conform to the Law, both written and oral, was well known—an elaborate training in all matters of Jewish religion and casuistry, which could not fail to interest him in a question of which he was so competent to judge. He begged, therefore, for a patient audience, and narrated once more the familiar story of his conversion from the standpoint of a rigid and bigoted Pharisee to a belief that the Messianic hopes of his nation had now been actually fulfilled in that Jesus of Nazareth, whose followers he had at first furiously persecuted, but who had won him, by a personal revelation of His glory, to the knowledge that He had risen from the dead. Why should that belief appear incredible to his hearers? It once had been so to himself; but how could he resist the eye-witness of a noonday vision? and how could he disobey the heavenly voice which sent him forth to open the eyes both of Jews and Gentiles, that they might turn from darkness to light, and the power of Satan unto God, that, by faith in Jesus, they might receive remission of sins and a lot among the sanctified? He had not been disobedient to it. In Damascus, in Jerusalem, throughout all Judæa, and subsequently among the Gentiles, he had been a preacher of repentance and conversion towards God, and a life consistent therewith. This was why the Jews had seized him in the Temple and tried to tear him

[1] Suet. *Oct.* 59; *Tiber.* 27; *Domit.* 13.
[2] Plut. *Caes.*, p. 729; Appul. *Metam.* ii., "porrigit dextram et ad instar oratorum conformat articulum."

to pieces; but in this and every danger God had helped him, and the testimony which he bore to small and great was no blasphemy, no apostasy, but simply a truth in direct accordance with the teachings of Moses and the Prophets, that the Messiah should be liable to suffering, and that from His resurrection from the dead a light should dawn to lighten both the Gentiles and His people.

Paul was now launched on the full tide of that sacred and impassioned oratory which was so powerful an agent in his mission work. He was delivering to kings and governors and chief captains that testimony which was the very object of his life. Whether on other topics his speech was as contemptible as his enemies chose to represent, we cannot say; but on this topic, at any rate, he spoke with the force of long familiarity, and the fire of intense conviction. He would probably have proceeded to develop the great thesis which he had just sketched in outline—but at this point he was stopped short. These facts and revelations were new to Festus. Though sufficiently familiar with true culture to recognise it even through these Oriental surroundings, he could only listen open-mouthed to this impassioned tale of visions, and revelations, and ancient prophecies, and of a Jewish Prophet who had been crucified, and yet had risen from the dead and was Divine, and who could forgive sins and lighten the darkness of Jews as well as of Gentiles. He had been getting more and more astonished, and the last remark was too much for him. He suddenly burst out with the loud and excited interruption, "You are mad, Paul;[1] those many writings are turning your brain." His startling ejaculation checked the majestic stream of the Apostle's eloquence, but did not otherwise ruffle his exquisite courtesy. "I am not mad," he exclaimed with calm modesty, giving to Festus his recognised title of "your Excellency;" "but I am uttering words of reality and soberness." But Festus was not the person whom he was mainly addressing, nor were these the reasonings which he would be likely to understand. It was different with Agrippa. He had read Moses and the Prophets, and had heard, from multitudes of witnesses, some at least of the facts to which Paul referred. To him, therefore, the Apostle appealed in proof of his perfect sanity. "The king," he said, "knows about these things, to whom it is even with confidence that I am addressing my remarks. I am sure that he is by no means unaware of any of these circumstances, for all that I say has not been done in a corner." And then, wishing to resume the thread of his argument at the point where it had been broken, and where it would be most striking to a Jew, he asked—

"King Agrippa, dost thou believe the Prophets? I know that thou believest."

But Agrippa did not choose to be entrapped into a discussion, still less into an assent. Not old in years, but accustomed from his boyhood to an atmosphere of cynicism and unbelief, he could only smile with the good-natured contempt of a man of the world at the enthusiastic earnestness which

[1] Wisd. v. 4; 2 Cor. v. 13. There is an iambic rhythm in Festus's interpellation which makes it sound like a quotation.

could even for a moment fancy that *he* would be converted to the heresy of the Nazarenes with their crucified Messiah! Yet he did not wish to be uncourteous. It was impossible not to admire the burning zeal which neither stripes nor prisons could quench—the clear-sighted faith which not even such a surrounding could for a moment dim.

"You are trying to persuade me offhand to be 'a Christian!'"[1] he said, with a half-suppressed smile; and this finished specimen of courtly *eutrapelia* was his bantering answer to St. Paul's appeal. Doubtless his polished remark on this compendious style of making converts sounded very witty to that distinguished company, and they would with difficulty suppress their laughter at the notion that Agrippa, favourite of Claudius, friend of Nero, King of Chalcis, Ituræa, Trachonitis, nominator of the High Priest, and supreme guardian of the Temple treasures, should succumb to the potency of this "short method with a Jew." That a Paul should make the king *a Christian* (!) would sound too ludicrous. But the laugh would be instantly suppressed in pity and admiration of the poor but noble prisoner, as with perfect dignity he took advantage of Agrippa's ambiguous expression, and said, with all the fervent sincerity of a loving heart, "I could pray to God that whether 'in little' or 'in much,'[2] not thou only, but even all who are listening to me to-day might become even such as I am—except," he added, as he raised his fettered hand—"except these bonds." They saw that this was indeed no common prisoner; one who could argue as he had argued, and speak as he had spoken; one who was so filled with the exaltation of an inspiring idea, so enriched with the happiness of a firm faith and a peaceful conscience, that he could tell them how he prayed that they all—all these princely and distinguished people—could be even such as he—and who yet in the spirit of entire forgiveness desired that the sharing in his faith might involve no share in his sorrows or misfortunes—must be such a one as they never yet had seen or known, either in the worlds of Jewry or of heathendom. But it was useless to prolong the scene. Curiosity was now sufficiently gratified, and it had become clearer than ever that though they might regard Paul the prisoner as an amiable enthusiast or an inspired fanatic, he was in no sense a legal criminal. The king, by rising from his seat, gave the signal for breaking up the meeting; Berenice and Festus, and their respective retinues, rose up at the same time, and as the distinguished assembly dispersed they were heard

[1] ἐν ὀλίγῳ, "in brief," "in few words" (cf. προέγραψα ἐν ὀλίγῳ, Eph. iii. 3), "*tout d'un coup.*" It cannot mean "almost," which would be πάρ' ὀλίγον, or ὀλίγου δεῖ. On the *conatus* involved in the present πείθεις, see my *Brief Greek Syntax*, § 136. But it is very doubtful whether we have got Agrippa's real remark. A reads πείθῃ (Lachm.), and perhaps πείθεις may have come from an original πείθει, "*you are persuading yourself*" (cf. οὐ πείθομαι, ver. 26); for instead of γενέσθαι, the reading of א, A, B is ποίησαι, which with πείθεις is unintelligible. From the confusion of readings we might almost conjecture that Agrippa ironically said, με χριστιανὸν ποιήσεις—"you'll soon be making me—a *Christian!*"

[2] St. Chrysostom thinks that St. Paul mistook Agrippa's meaning, and, from ignorance of colloquial Greek (?), supposed him to mean "almost." But Eph. iii. 3 is enough to disprove this.

remarking on all sides that Paul was undeserving of death, or even of imprisonment. He had made, in fact, a deeply favourable impression. Agrippa's decision was given entirely for his acquittal. "This person," he said to Festus, "might have been permanently set at liberty, if he had not appealed to Cæsar." Agrippa was far too little of a Pharisee, and far too much of a man of the world, not to see that mere freedom of thought could not be, and ought not to be, suppressed by external violence. The proceedings of that day probably saved St. Paul's life full two years afterwards. Festus, since his own opinion, on grounds of Roman justice, were so entirely confirmed from the Jewish point of view by the Protector of the Temple, could hardly fail to send to Nero an *elogium* which freely exonerated the prisoner from every legal charge; and even if Jewish intrigues were put in play against him, Nero could not condemn to death a man whom Felix, and Lysias, and Festus, and Agrippa, and even the Jewish Sanhedrin, in the only trial of the case which they had held, had united in pronouncing innocent of any capital crime.

CHAPTER XLIII.

THE VOYAGE AND SHIPWRECK.

> "Non vultus instantis tyranni
> Mente quatit solida, nec Auster
> Dux inquieti turbidus Adriae."—HOR. *Od.* iii. 3, 5.

> "The flattering wind that late with promised aid
> From Candia's bay the unwilling ship betrayed,
> No longer fawns, beneath the fair disguise,
> But like a ruffian on his quarry flies."
> FALCONER, *Shipwreck*, canto ii.

AT the earliest opportunity which offered, St. Paul, and such other prisoners[1] as were waiting the result of an appeal, were despatched to Italy under the charge of Julius, a centurion of an Augustan cohort. This Augustan cohort may either be some local troop of soldiers of that name stationed at Cæsarea, since the name "Augustan" was as common as "Royal" among us; or they may have belonged to the body of *Augustani*—veterans originally enrolled by Augustus as a body-guard;[2] or they may have been the Prætorian guards themselves, who occasionally, though not frequently, were sent out of Italy on imperial missions.[3] It is not, however, said that Julius was accompanied by his cohort, and it is not at all impossible that he may have been sent with a few of those chosen soldiers of the most distinguished Roman regiments

[1] xxvii. 1. *ἑτέρους* is not necessarily used with classical accuracy to denote "prisoners of a different class" (Luke viii. 3; Mark xv. 41).

[2] It certainly was not a cohort of "Sebasteni," *i.e.*, natives of Sebaste, the name which Herod had given to Samaria (Jos. *B. J.* ii. 12, § 5).

[3] Pliny, *H. N.* vi. 35. (Lewin, ii. 183.)

to give *éclat* to the arrival of Festus in one of the wealthiest but most disaffected of imperial provinces.[1] If this were the case, Julius may very well have been that Julius Priscus who afterwards rose to the splendid position of one of the two Præfects of the Prætorians, and committed suicide on the disgraceful overthrow of his patron.[2] We see enough of him during this voyage to lead us to believe that he was a sensible, honourable, and kindly man.

Roman soldiers were responsible with their own lives for the security of their prisoners, and this had originated the custom—so painful to the prisoners, and all the more painful because so necessarily irritating to the legionaries—of keeping the prisoners safe by chaining them with a long light chain by the right wrist to the left wrist of soldiers, who relieved each other in turn. It may be imagined how frightfully trying it must have been to have no moment and no movement free, and to be fettered in such horrible proximity to a man who would certainly have been an uneducated specimen of the lowest classes, and who, surrounded from boyhood upwards by rough and demoralising companionships, might be a coarse and loose provincial, or a morose and brutal peasant from the dregs of the Italian population. It is tolerably certain that ashore prisoners were not allowed to go anywhere without this galling protection, but we may hope that they were not always subject to it in the narrow fetid cribs and hatchways of the huge, rolling, unwieldy merchantmen in which their compulsory voyages had to be performed.

Since Festus had arrived in Palestine towards the end of June, it must now have been late in August, and the time was rapidly drawing on in which ancient navigation was closed for the year. Every day made the weather more uncertain and the voyage more perilous, and since time was pressing, Julius, to whom the commission was entrusted, embarked his prisoners on board a coasting merchantman of the Mysian town of Adramyttium. As the vessel would touch at the chief ports on the west of Asia, there was every possibility of their finding a ship at Ephesus, or at some nearer port, in which they could perform the rest of their voyage; but if not, Julius might, as a last resource, march his soldiers and their prisoners from Adramyttium to Troas, and thence sail to Neapolis, whence he could proceed along the great Egnatian Road, already so familiar to St. Paul, through Philippi and Thessalonica to Dyrrhachium. Dyrrhachium and Brundusium were to the Romans what Calais and Dover are to the English; and after crossing the Ægean, Julius would march along the Appian Road—in a reverse order through the scenes described with such lively humour by Horace in his *Iter ad Brundusium*—till his journey ended at Rome. This was the route traversed by St. Ignatius and his "ten leopards" who conducted him to his martyrdom, and in his disagreeable connexion with whom he says that he fought with wild beasts all the way. It is, however, most unlikely that a land journey entered into the immediate plans of Julius. As he had several prisoners under his charge, each of whom would require ten soldiers to relieve guard, such a journey

[1] More strictly Procuratorships. St. Luke, however, uses the general word ἐπαρχία.
[2] Tac. *Hist.* ii. 92: iv. 11. "Pudore magis quam necessitate."

would be inexpressibly tedious and extremely expensive; and Julius might rely with tolerable certainty on finding some vessel which was bound from one of the great emporiums of Asia for the capital of the world.

St. Paul was spared one at least of the circumstances which would have weighed most heavily on his spirits—he was not alone. Luke and Aristarchus accompanied him, and, whether such had been their original intention or not, both were at any rate driven by stress of circumstances to remain with him during great part of his Roman imprisonment. They, no doubt, were passengers, not prisoners, and they must either have paid their own expenses,[1] or have been provided with money for that purpose by Christians, who knew how necessary was some attendance for one so stricken with personal infirmities as their illustrious Apostle.

The voyage began happily and prosperously. The leading westerly wind was so far favourable that the day after they started they had accomplished the sixty-seven miles which lay between them and the harbour of Sidon. There they touched, and Julius, who can hardly have been absent from the brilliant throng who had listened to Paul's address before Agrippa, was so indulgently disposed towards him that he gave him leave—perhaps merely on parole—to land and see his friends who formed the little Christian community of that place. This kindness was invaluable to St. Paul. The two years' imprisonment must have told unfavourably upon his health, and he must have been but scantily provided with the requisites for a long voyage. The expression used by St. Luke that Julius allowed him to go to his friend and "be cared for,"[2] seems to imply that even during that one day's voyage he had suffered either from sea-sickness or from general infirmity. The day at Sidon was the one happy interlude which was to prepare him for many anxious, miserable, and storm-tossed weeks.

For from that day forward the entire voyage became a succession of delays and accidents, which, after two months of storm and danger, culminated in hopeless shipwreck. No sooner had they left the harbour of Sidon than they encountered the baffling Etesian winds, which blow steadily from the north-west. This was an unlooked-for hindrance, because the Etesians usually cease to blow towards the end of August, and are succeeded by south winds, on which the captain of the merchantman had doubtless relied to waft him back to his port of Adramyttium. His natural course would have been to sail straight across from Sidon to Patara, leaving Cyprus on the starboard; but the very winds which sped St. Paul so blithely along this course to his Cæsarean imprisonment more than two years before, were now against his return, and the vessel had to sail towards Cape Pedalium, the south-eastern promontory of Cyprus, hugging the shore under the lee of the island as far as Cape Dinaretum.[3] On rounding this cape they could beat to windward

[1] Luke, as a physician, might easily have procured a free passage.

[2] xxvii. 3, ἐπιμελείας τυχεῖν.

[3] ὑπεπλεύσαμεν, "we sailed under the lee of," *i.e.*, in this instance, "we left Cyprus on the left." Observe that in this narrative alone there are no less than thirteen different expressions for "sailing."

by the aid of land-breezes and westward currents right across the sea which washes the coasts of Cilicia and Pamphylia, until they dropped anchor in the mouth of the river Andriacus, opposite to a hill crowned with the magnificent buildings of Myra, the former capital of Lycia.[1]

Here they were fortunate—or, as it turned out, unfortunate—enough to find a large Alexandrian wheat-ship,[2] which had undergone the common fate of being driven out of the direct course by the same winds which had baffled the Adramyttian vessel, and which now intended to follow the usual alternative of creeping across the Ægean from island to island, northward of Crete, and so to the south of Cythera, and across to Syracuse.[3] This vessel, built for the purposes of the trade which supplied to all Italy the staff of life, could easily provide room for the centurion with his soldiers and prisoners, and such passengers as chose to accompany them. They were, therefore, shifted into this vessel, and sailed for Cnidus, the last point at which they could hope for any help from the protection of the shore with its breezes and currents. The distance between the two spots is only one hundred and thirty miles, and under favourable circumstances they might have got to their destination in twenty-four hours. But the baffling Etesians still continued with unseasonable steadiness, and to reach even to Cnidus occupied many weary and uncomfortable days. And when they got off the beautiful and commodious harbour they were destined to a fresh and bitter disappointment, for they could not enter it. Had they been able to do so the season was by this time so far advanced, and the wind was so steadily adverse, that we can hardly doubt that, unless they continued their journey by land, they would either have waited there for a more favourable breeze, or decided to winter in a port where there was every pleasant requisite at hand for the convenience of so large a vessel, and its numerous crew. Since, however, the wind would neither suffer them to put in at Cnidus,[4] nor to continue their direct voyage, which would have passed north of Crete, the only alternative left them was to make for Cape Salmone, at the eastern end of the island, and there sail under its lee. To get to Salmone was comparatively easy; but when they had rounded it they had the utmost difficulty in creeping along the weather shore until they came to a place called Fair Havens, a little to the east of Cape Matala, and not far from an obscure town of the name of Lasæa. While the wind remained in its present quarter it was useless to continue their voyage, for beyond Cape Matala the shore trends sharply to the north, and they would have been exposed to the whole force of the Etesians,

[1] Cf. Thuc. viii. 35.

[2] The Emperor Titus (Suet. *Tit.* 5) did the same on his return from Palestine (cf. Jos. *B. J.* vii. 2, § 1; Tac. *H.* iv. 81). At this period that part of the Mediterranean is almost always stormy (Falconer, *Dissert.*, p. 16).

[3] It will, of course, be borne in mind that (1) they had no compass; and (2) could not work to windward. The Cilician land breeze, which had helped the Adramyttian vessel to Myra, was quite local. Compare Socr. *H. E.* ii. 24; Sozomen, vi. 25 (speaking of the voyage of Athanasius from Alexandria to Rome). Wetst.

[4] xxvii. 7, μὴ προσεῶντος τοῦ ἀνέμου. It is not said that they got to Cnidus, but only that they got "opposite to" or "off" it, and that with difficulty.

with a lee shore on which they would inevitably have been dashed to pieces. At Fair Havens, therefore, they were obliged to put in, and wait for a change of wind. Time passed, and found them still windbound. It was now getting towards the close of September. At Fair Havens St. Paul and any Jewish Christians on board would probably keep the *Kippor*, or great day of Atonement,[1] the one fast in the Jewish calendar, which this year fell on September 24. The autumnal equinox passed. The Feast of Tabernacles passed, and perhaps some of the sailors regarded with superstitious terror the partial eclipse which occurred on that evening. The Jewish season for navigation was now over,[2] but the Gentiles did not regard the sea as closed until November 11.[3] Discussions took place as to whether they should winter where they were or choose the first favourable chance of pushing on round Cape Matala to Port Phœnix, which lay only thirty-four miles beyond it. St. Paul, whose remarkable ascendency had already displayed itself, was allowed to give his opinion, and he gave it emphatically in favour of staying where they were. "Sirs,"[4] he said, "I perceive that this voyage will certainly result in violent weather, and much loss not only of the cargo and of the ship, but even of our lives." His opinion was entitled to great weight, because his many voyages had made him thoroughly familiar with the winds and dangers of a sea in which he had thrice been shipwrecked, and had once floated for a night and a day. The captain, however, and the owner of the vessel gave their opinion the other way; and it must be admitted that they had much to urge. Fair Havens afforded a shelter from the norwester which had so long been prevalent, but it was entirely unprotected against east winds, and indeed lay open to most points of the compass. It would, therefore, be a dangerous haven in which to pass the winter, and it was further unsuitable because the place itself was a poor one, not quite close even to the town of Lassæa, and offering no means of employment or amusement for the soldiers and sailors. It would have been a serious matter to spend three or four months in a place so dreary and desolate, and it seemed worth while, if possible, to get to Port Phœnix. That town, the modern Lutro, which they could reach in a few hours' sail, enjoyed the advantage of the only harbour on the south of Crete which is safe in all weathers, and which was therefore a familiar resort of Alexandrian corn-ships. Its harbour was closed and protected by a little island, and was described by those who advocated its claims as "looking towards Libs and towards Caurus," or, as we should say, towards the south-west and the north-west. It has greatly puzzled commentators to account for this expression, seeing that the entrance to the harbour of Lutro (which is undoubtedly the ancient Phoenix) looks towards the east, and its two openings at the extremities of its sheltering island look precisely in the

[1] It was observed on the tenth of Tisri, which in this year (A.D. 60) fell at the autumnal equinox.

[2] Sept. 28. See Lewin, *Fasti Sacri*, § 1899; and *L'Art de vérifier les Dates*, iv., p. 51.

[3] See Schoettgen, *Hor. Hebr. ad loc.*; Plin. *H. N.* ii. 47; *Veget. De Re Milit.* v. 9.

[4] Ἄνδρες, "gentlemen," as in xiv. 15, xix. 25; not κύριοι, as in Acts xvi. 30.

opposite directions, namely, north-east and south-east. The explanation of this singular anomaly is not to be sought in grammatical illustrations, but in the subjectivity of the sailors, who simply regard the bearings of the harbour from the directions in which they sail into it, and might say, for instance, that a harbour "looked towards" the north, if they could only sail into it by turning their prow northward; just as farther on in the chapter they speak of "some land approaching them," when in reality they are approaching some land.[1] But besides the security of Port Phœnix, it was evidently a far more desirable place for nearly three hundred people to winter in than the comparatively obscure and lonely Fair Havens, and on both these grounds it seemed to be worth a slight risk to reach it. These arguments won the adhesion of the majority, and the centurion, with whom the decision rested, decided that this should be done. St. Paul claimed no inspiration for the solemn advice he gave,[2] and of course there was a fair chance of safely traversing so short a distance. Yet results proved that his advice was right. Fair Havens, though not a first-rate harbour, is yet partially protected by reefs and islets, and though it might not be wholly safe to winter there, yet the risk was much smaller than that which must be incurred by doubling Cape Matala, and so getting possibly seized in the grasp of one of the prevalent and sudden northerly gales, which would drive the ship into almost certain destruction. But there is a gambling element in human nature, and the centurion, at any rate, could hardly avoid following the opinion of the experts, whose interests were so deeply concerned, in preference to that of a prisoner, whose knowledge was not professional and who had so much less at stake.

It was not long before the wished-for opportunity occurred.[3] A soft south wind sprang up, and gladly weighing anchor, they hoisted the great mainsail, took their boat in tow, sailed close along the shore to the point of Cape Matala, and then gaily prepared for a delightful run of a few hours to the beautiful and hospitable harbour for which they were abandoning the dull, dreary Lasea. Now at last a little gleam of prosperity seemed to have shone on their tedious and unfortunate voyage. Perhaps they had a good-natured laugh against Paul the prisoner for advice which would have made them throw away a golden chance. But, alas! the gentle breathing of the south wind in the sails and cordage was but a siren song which had lured them to their destruction. They had not long passed the cape, when a tempestuous typhoon[4]—such as often in those latitudes succeeds a brief spell of the south wind—burst down from the Cretan Ida, and smote with terrible fury on the hapless vessel. The ancient name of this "Levanter," as it is now called, was probably Euroaquilo, a name

[1] See further, Smith, p. 49. [2] Ver. 10, θεωρῶ.

[3] Ver. 13, ἄραντες ἆσσον παρελέγοντο τὴν Κρήτην. The E.V. misses the exact force of the aorist ὑποπνεύσαντος.

[4] The word τυφωνικὸς describes the circular whirling of the clouds caused by the meeting of the S. and the E.N.E. winds. See Plin. *H. N.* ii. 48, "praecipua navigantum pestis;" A. Gell. xix. 1. This change of wind is exactly what might have been expected (Purdy, *Sailing Directory*, ii. 61; Smith, *Voy. and Shipwreck*, p. 412).

which exactly describes its direction, since we see from St. Luke's subsequent remarks that it must have been an east-north-easter, which, indeed, continued to blow during the remainder of their voyage.[1] From the first moment that this fatal blast rushed down from the hills and seized the wheat-ship in its grasp,[2] the condition of the vessel was practically hopeless. It was utterly impossible for her—it would have been impossible for the finest made vessel—to "look the wind in the face."[3] The suddenness and fury of the blow left the sailors not one moment to furl the mainsail, or to do anything but leave the ship to be driven madly forward before the gale,[4] until after a fearful run of twenty-three miles they neared the little island of Clanda,[5] and ran in under its lee. Happily the direction of the wind, and the fact—in which we see the clear hand of Providence—that the storm had burst on them soon after they had rounded Cape Matala, and not a little later on in their course, had saved them from being dashed upon the rocks and reefs, which lie more to the north-west between both Candia and Clanda; but their condition was, in other respects, already dangerous, if not quite desperate. The ships of the ancients had one main-mast and one mainsail; any other masts or rigging were comparatively small and insignificant. Hence the strain upon the vessel from the leverage of the mast was terrific, and it was impossible that the Alexandrian ship, however stoutly built, should have scudded with her huge sail set in the grasp of a typhoon, without her timbers starting. It is evident that she had already sprung a serious leak. There was no available harbour in the little island, and therefore the captain, who seems to have shown the best seamanship which was possible in his age, took advantage of the brief and partial lull which was afforded them by the shelter of the island to do the two things which were most immediately necessary—namely, first to secure the means of escape, for some at any rate of the crew, in case the vessel foundered, and next to put off that catastrophe as long as possible. He therefore gave orders at once to hoist the boat on board, and so secure it from being staved in. But this was a task

[1] Εὐρακύλων, A, B, Sahid., Copt., Smith, p. 59. It was thus a "point wind." If anything is to be said for the very ill-supported Εὐροκλύδων of the Syriac, we can only regard the word as *surfrappé* by Greek sailors (see *Language and Languages*, p. 119).

[2] Ver. 14, ἔβαλεν κατ' αὐτῆς may mean either "*struck against her*," the conception of a ship being in all languages feminine, and ναῦς being the prevalent substantive *in the mind* of the writer, though throughout the narrative he always uses τὸ πλοῖον, except in verse 41; or it may mean, no less correctly, "*down from it*," namely "Crete," which is the substantive immediately preceding. But that the former is the right translation in this instance is certain, because ἔβαλεν could not be used with nothing to follow it. The reader will more easily follow the details of the voyage, if he will compare the map with the directions indicated on this compass.

[3] ἀντοφθαλμεῖν. Eyes were painted on the prow (Eustath. *ad Il.* xiv. 717).

[4] One of the Cursives (137) adds συστείλαντες τὰ ἱστία.

[5] Clauda; B, Καυδᾶ; Plin. iv. 20; Gaudus, Gozzo.

by no means easy. The boat, which they had so securely towed astern in what they meant to be a sort of gala trip to Port Phœnix, had now been hurled after them through twenty miles of their swirling wake, and must therefore have been sorely battered, and perhaps half water-logged; and though they were now in slightly smoother water, yet such was the violence of the gale that it was difficult to perform the simplest duty. They managed, however—and Luke was one of those who lent a hand in doing it[1]—to heave the boat on board as a last resource in the moment of peril; and then the sailors proceeded to adopt the rough and clumsy method in use among the ancients to keep a vessel together. This consisted in undergirding, or, to use the modern and technical term for a practice which is now but rarely resorted to, in "*frapping*" it, by passing stout hawsers several times under the prow, and tying them as tightly as possible round the middle of the vessel.[2] They had thus met the two most pressing dangers, but a third remained. There was no place into which they could run for shelter, nor could they long avail themselves of the partial protection which they derived from the weather-shore of the little island, and they knew too well that the wind was driving them straight towards the Goodwin Sands of the Mediterranean—the dreaded bay of the Greater Syrtis.[3] There was only one way to save themselves, which was not, as the English Version most erroneously expresses it, to "strike sail and so be driven"—since this would be certain destruction—but to lie to, by rounding the prow of the vessel on the starboard tack as near to the wind as possible, to send down the topsail and cordage, lower the ponderous yard to such a height as would leave enough of the huge mainsail to steady the vessel,[4] set the *artemo*, or storm-sail, and so—having made all as snug as their circumstances permitted—let her drift on, broadside to leeward, at the mercy of wind and wave. This they did, and so ended the miserable day, which had begun with such soft breezes and presumptuous hopes.[5]

All night long the storm blew, and, in spite of the undergirding, the vessel still leaked. Next day, therefore, they kept throwing over from time to time everything that could possibly be spared to lighten the ship;[6] but even this was insufficient. The next night brought no relief; the vessel still leaked and leaked, and all labour at the pumps was in vain. The fate which most

[1] The narrative of St. Luke is admirably brief and pregnant, and yet we can at once trace in it the tasks in which he and St. Paul and other passengers or prisoners were able to take their share. They helped, for instance, in getting hold of the boat (ver. 16), and in lightening the vessel (ver. 19, *leg.* ἐῤῥίψαμεν); but they could not help in such technical tasks as frapping the vessel, heaving the lead, dropping the anchors, &c.

[2] ὑποζώματα, *mitrae*, Vitruv. x. 15, 6; Thuc. i. 29; Plato, *Rep.* x. 616; Hor. *Od.* i. 14, 6. "They [a Spanish man-of-war in a storm] were obliged to throw overboard all their upper-deck guns, and take six turns of the cable round the ship to prevent her opening" (Anson, *Voyage Round the World*). The *Albion* was frapped with iron chains after the battle of Navarino.

[3] Ver. 17, ἐκπέσωσι, not "fall into," but "be driven ashore on" (Hdt. viii. 13).

[4] χαλάσαντες τὸ σκεῦος, here "lowering the great yard" (Smith).

[5] Ver. 13, δόξαντες τῆς προθέσεως κεκρατηκέναι.

[6] Ver. 18, ἐκβολὴν ἐποιοῦντο, jacturam *faciebant*, whereas what they did the day after was an instantaneous act, ἐῤῥίψαμεν.

commonly befell ancient vessels—that of foundering at sea—was obviously imminent. On the third day, therefore, it became necessary to take some still more decisive step. This, in a modern vessel, would have been to cut down the masts by the board; in ancient vessels, of which the masts were of a less towering height, it consisted in heaving overboard the huge mainyard, which, as we see, was an act requiring the united assistance of all the active hands.[1] It fell over with a great splash, and the ship was indefinitely lightened. But now her violent rolling—all the more sensible from the loose nature of her cargo—was only counteracted by a trivial storm-sail. The typhoon, indeed, had become an ordinary gale, but the ship had now been reduced to the condition of a leaky and dismantled hulk, swept from stem to stern by the dashing spray, and drifting, no one knew whither, under leaden and moonless heavens. A gloomy apathy began to settle more and more upon those helpless three hundred souls. There were no means of cooking; no fire could be lighted; the caboose and utensils must long ago have been washed overboard; the provisions had probably been spoiled and sodden by the waves that broke over the ship; indeed, with death staring them in the face, no one cared to eat. They were famishing wretches in a fast-sinking ship, drifting, with hopes that diminished day by day, to what they regarded as an awful and a certain death.

But in that desperate crisis one man retained his calm and courage. It was Paul the prisoner, probably in physical health the weakest and the greatest sufferer of them all. But it is in such moments that the courage of the noblest souls shines with the purest lustre, and the soul of Paul was inwardly enlightened. As he prayed in all the peacefulness of a blameless conscience, it was revealed to him that God would fulfil the promised destiny which was to lead him to Rome, and that, with the preservation of his own life, God would also grant to him the lives of those unhappy sufferers, for whom, all unworthy as some of them soon proved to be, his human heart yearned with pity. While the rest were abandoning themselves to despair, Paul stood forth on the deck, and after gently reproaching them with having rejected the advice which would have saved them from all that buffeting and loss, he bade them cheer up, for though the ship should be lost, and they should be wrecked on some island, not one of them should lose his life. For they knew that he was a prisoner who had appealed to Cæsar; and that night an angel of the God, whose child and servant he was, had stood by him, and not only assured him that he should stand before Cæsar, but also that God had, as a sign of His grace, granted him

[1] Ver. 19, τὴν σκευὴν ἐῤῥίψαμεν. (This is the reading of G, H, most of the Cursives, both the Syriac versions, the Coptic, Æthiopic, &c. I agree with De Wette in thinking that the ἔῤῥιψαν of א, A, B, C, *Vulg.*, is a mistaken alteration, due to the ἐποιοῦντο of the previous verse.) The meaning of the expression is disputed, but it has been universally overlooked that the aorist requires *some single act*. Hence Alford's notion that ἡ σκευὴ means beds, furniture, spare rigging, &c., and Wetstein's, that it means the baggage of the passengers, fall to the ground, and Smith's suggestion that the main spar is intended is much strengthened. He observes that the effect would be much the same as that produced in modern vessels by heaving the guns overboard.

the lives of all on board. He bade them, therefore, to cheer up, and to share his own conviction that the vision should come true.

Who shall say how much those calm undoubting words were designed by God to help in bringing about their own fulfilment? Much had yet to be done; many a strong measure to avert destruction had yet to be taken; and God helps those only who will take the appointed means to help themselves. The proud words "Caesarem vehis"[1] may have inspired the frightened sailor to strenuous effort in the open boat on the coast of Illyria, and certainly it was Paul's undaunted encouragements which re-inspired these starving, fainting, despairing mariners to the exertions which ultimately secured their safety. For after they had drifted fourteen days, tossed up and down on the heaving waves of Adria,[2] a weltering plaything for the gale, suddenly on the fourteenth night the sailors, amid the sounds of the long-continued storm, fancied that they heard the roar of breakers through the midnight darkness. Suspecting that they were nearing some land, and perhaps even detecting that white phosphorescent gleam of a surf-beat shore which is visible so far through even the blackest night, they dropped the lead and found that they were in twenty fathom water. Sounding again, they found that they were in fifteen fathoms.[3] Their suspicions and fears were now turned to certainty, and here was the fresh danger of having their desolate hulk driven irresistibly upon some iron coast. In the face of this fresh peril the only thing to be done was to drop anchor. Had they anchored the vessel in the usual manner, from the prow,[4] the ship might have swung round against a reef; nor could they suppose, as they heard the extraordinary loudness of the surf beating upon the shore, that they were at that moment a quarter of a mile from land. So they dropped four anchors[5] through the hawse-holes in which the two great paddle-rudders ordinarily moved; since these—having long been useless as they drifted before the gale—had been half lifted out of the water, and lashed to the stern.[6] Having done this, they could only yearn with intense desire for the dawn of day. All through the remaining hours of that long wintry night, they stood face to face with the agony of death. In its present condition, the leak constantly gaining on them, the waves constantly deluging them with spray, the vessel might at any moment sink, even if the anchors held. But they did not know, what we know, that those anchors had dropped into clay of extraordinary

[1] Plut. *Caes.* 38; *De Fort. Rom.* 6; Florus, iv. 2; Dion Cass. xli. 46. "Et fortunam Caesaris" is a later addition.

[2] The Mediterranean between Greece, Italy, and Africa. Strabo, ii. 123. Ἰόνιον πέλαγος, ὁ νῦν Ἀδρίας (Hesych.). διαφερόμενον, "tossed hither and thither." So it would appear to those on board, but probably they drifted in the E.N. Easter, 477 miles in thirteen days at the natural rate of one mile and a half an hour. (See Smith, p. 101.)

[3] Mr. Smith says that Captain Stewart's soundings "would alone have furnished a conclusive test of the truth of this narrative" (p. ix.); and that we are enabled by these and similar investigations "to identify the locality of a shipwreck which took place eighteen centuries ago" (p. xiii.).

[4] "Anchora de prorâ jacitur" (Virg. *Æn.* iii. 277). Lord Nelson, reading this chapter just before the battle of Copenhagen, ordered our vessels to be anchored by the stern.

[5] Cf. Caes. *Bell. Civ.* i. 25.

[6] As appears from xxvii. 40.

tenacity, which, indeed, was the sole circumstance between them and hopeless wreck.

Gradually through the murky atmosphere of rain and tempest, the grim day began to dawn upon the miserable crew. Almost as soon as they could see the dim outlines of their own faces, haggard and ghastly with so much privation and so many fears, they observed that they were anchored off a low point, over which the sea was curling with a huge and most furious surf. Ignorant that this was Point Koura, on the north-east side of Malta,[1] and not recognising a single landmark on the featureless shore, the only thought of the selfish heathen sailors was to abandon the hulk and crew to their fate, while they saved themselves in the boat which they had with such trouble and danger hoisted on board. Pretending, therefore, that they could steady the pitching of the ship, and therefore make her hold together for a longer time, if they used more anchors, and laid them out at full length of the cables[2] instead of merely dropping them from the prow, they began to unlash the boat and lower her into the sea. Had they succeeded in their plot, they would probably have been swamped in the surf upon the point, and all on board would inevitably have perished from inability to handle the sinking vessel. From this danger alike the crew and the sailors were once more saved by the prompt energy and courage of St. Paul. Seeing through the base design, he quietly observed to Julius, who was the person of most authority on board, "If these sailors do not stay in the ship, ye cannot be saved." He says "ye," not "we." Strong in God's promise, he had no shadow of doubt respecting his own preservation, but the promise of safety to all the crew was conditional on their own performance of duty. The soldiers, crowded together in the vessel with their prisoners, heard the remark of Paul, and—since he alone at that wild moment of peril had kept calm, and was therefore the virtual captain—without the smallest scruple drew their swords and cut through the boat's ropes, letting her fall away in the trough of the sea. It is not likely that the sailors felt much resentment. Their plan was distinctly base, and it offered at the best a very forlorn and dubious hope of safety. But the daylight had now increased, and the hour was approaching in which everything would depend upon their skill and promptitude, and on the presence of mind of all on board. Once more, therefore, the Apostle encouraged them, and urged them all to take some food. "This is the fourteenth day," he said, "on which you are continuing foodless, in constant anxiety and vigilance, without taking anything. I entreat you, then, all to join in a meal, which is indeed essential to that preservation, of which I assure you with confidence, for not a hair of the head of any one of you shall perish." And having given them this encouragement, he himself set the example. Making of the simplest necessity of life a religious and eucharistic act, he took bread, gave thanks to God in the presence of them all, broke it, and began to eat. Catching the contagion of his cheerful trust, the drenched, miserable

[1] Where the English frigate *Lively* was wrecked in 1810.

[2] xxvii. 30, *ἐκτείνειν*, not "to cast out," as in E.V.

throng of 276 souls, who had so long been huddled together in their unspeakable wretchedness and discomfort, as their shattered vessel lay rolling and tossing under the dismal clouds, took fresh courage, and shared with him in a hearty meal. Knowing that this was the last meal they could ever take in the dismasted vessel, and also that it would be impossible to save the cargo, they lightened and righted the vessel by flinging overboard the wheat, which in the long drift of 476 miles from Clauda in the storm must have shifted much to one side and made the vessel heel over in a dangerous manner. When the full daylight enabled them to examine the shore, they saw no recognisable landmark—since the present Valetta, the harbour of Malta, at which ships often touched, was seven miles E.S.E. of the point where they were wrecked; but they saw a bay, at one extremity of which the cliffs sank down into a flat beach, and the only thing which they could hope to do was to thrust the ship out of her direct course, and strand her at this spot. To make a tack athwart the wind with a disabled ship was a manœuvre by no means easy, but it was worth attempting. They therefore cut away the anchors, letting the ropes drop into the sea,[1] unlashed and let down the paddle-rudders,[2] hoisted the *artemo*, or foresail[3]—which was all that was left them—to the wind, and steered straight for the beach. But their manœuvre, resolutely as it had been undertaken, was a failure. They had unconsciously anchored off Ras el Koura. The opposite point looked like another promontory, but was in reality the island of Salmonetta, separated from the mainland by a deep, narrow, and precipitous channel. Through this channel, about a hundred yards in width, ran a current, and in the stormy race where the waters of this current met the waters of the bay, the vessel[4] would not answer to the helm, and all they could do was to run her ashore. Happily for them she drove, not upon a rock, but deep into a bank of mud, such as still exists at that very spot. Here the prow stuck immovably fast, while the stern was free. The crew rushed to the prow, while the waves, which broke with fury over the unsupported stern, began instantly to batter it to pieces. Here, even at this extremity, there rose for Paul and the other prisoners a new, unexpected, and yet more terrible danger. It was the duty of the soldiers to be responsible with their own lives for their prisoners. The Roman law was stern, rigid, and unbending, nor did it admit of any extenuating plea. So long as death seemed imminent, and every hand on board might be useful in averting it, the prisoners must have been left unchained; but in such a crisis as this, what was there to prevent any one of them from taking a dive into the sea, and so escaping? It would have been a horrible thing that blood and butchery should stain the planks of a shipwrecked vessel at the very moment when safety seemed within reach, and that this human sacrifice of lives which God

[1] Ver. 40, ἀγκύρας περιελόντες εἴων εἰς τὴν θάλασσαν, *not* "when they had taken up the anchors, they committed *themselves* unto the sea," E.V.

[2] Eur. *Hel.* 1536.

[3] "Levato artemone," Vulg.; "a litil sail," Wycl.; "Vestibus extensis, et quod superaverat unum Velo prora suo," Juv. xii. 68, Artemone Solo. Sch.

[4] So διθάλασσος is used of the *Bosphorus* by Strabo, 124.

had rescued should be the only thanksgiving of the survivors. It was even more horrible that they who had fraternised with their fellows in the levelling communism of sympathy, as they huddled side by side, with death staring them in the face, should now thrust their swords into hearts with which their own had so long been beating in fearful sympathy. From this peril the prisoners were again indirectly saved by him whose counsel and encouragement had all along been the direct source of their preservation. If the prisoners were to be killed, equal justice, or injustice, must be dealt to all of them alike, and Julius felt that it would be dastardly ingratitude to butcher the man to whom, under God's providence, they all owed their rescued lives. He therefore forbade the design of the soldiers, and gave orders that every one who could swim should first fling himself overboard, and get to land.[1] The rest seized hold of planks and other fragments of the fast-dissolving wreck.[2] The wind threw them landwards, and at last by the aid of the swimmers all were saved, and—at a spot which, owing to the accurate fidelity of the narrative, can still be exactly identified—a motley group of nearly three hundred drenched, and shivering, and weather-beaten sailors and soldiers, and prisoners and passengers, stood on that chill and stormy November morning upon the desolate and surf-beat shore of the island of Malta. Some, we are sure, there were who joined with Paul in hearty thanks to the God who, though He had not made the storm to cease, so that the waves thereof were still, had yet brought them safe to land, through all the perils of that tempestuous month.

Book X.

ROME.

CHAPTER XLIV.

ST. PAUL'S ARRIVAL AT ROME.

"Paulus Romae, apex Evangelii."—BENGEL.

So ended St. Paul's fourth shipwreck. The sight of the vessel attracted the natives of the island,[3] a simple Punic race, mingled with Greek settlers, and under Roman dominion. There have been times far more recent, and coasts far nearer to the scenes of civilisation, in which the castaways of a

[1] Probably Paul was among these (2 Cor. xi. 25).

[2] Ver. 41, ἐλύετο, "was going to pieces." "Dissolutum navigium" (Cic. *Att.* xv. 11).

[3] The notion that the island on which they were wrecked was not Malta, but the little Adriatic island of Meleda, off the coast of Dalmatia, was started by Constantine the Porphyrogenite. It was founded on mistakes about Adria (xxvii. 27), barbarians (xxviii. 2), and vipers (*id.* 3), combined with various nautical considerations; and was supported by Georgi of Meleda, Jacob Bryant, and Dr. Falconer, and lastly by Dr. J. Mason Neale, in his *Notes on Dalmatia*, p. 161. All that can be said for it may be found in Falconer's *Dissertation* (3rd edit., with additional notes, 1872).

derelict would have been more likely to be robbed and murdered than received with hospitality and compassion; but these Maltese Phœnicians, nearly two millenniums ago, welcomed the rescued crew with unusual kindness. Heavy showers had come on, and the shipwrecked men were half-benumbed with fatigue and cold. Pitying their condition, the natives lit a huge fire of fagots and brushwood, that they might dry their clothes, and gave them in all respects a friendly welcome. Paul, with that indomitable activity and disregard of self which neither danger nor fatigue could check, was busy among the busiest collecting fuel. He had got together a large bundle of furze-roots,[1] and had just put it on the blazing fire, when a viper which had been lying torpid, being suddenly revived and irritated by the heat, darted out of the bundle and "fastened on Paul's hand." Seeing the creature hanging from his hand, and observing that he was a prisoner, the simple natives muttered to one another that he must be some murderer, rescued indeed from the waves, but pursued by just vengeance even on land. Paul, quite undisturbed, shook the creature off into the fire, and was none the worse.[2] The natives expected that he would suddenly drop dead.[3] For a long time they watched him with eager eyes, but when they observed that no unpleasant result of any kind followed, they, like the rude people of Lystra, gradually changed their minds, and said that he was a god.

For three months, until the beginning of February opened the sea to navigation, the crew lived in Malta; and during that time, owing once more to the influence of St. Paul, he and his associates received the utmost kindness. Not far from the scene of the shipwreck lay the town now called Alta Vecchia, the residence of Publius, the governor of the island, who was probably a legate of the Prætor of Sicily. Since Julius was a person of distinction, this Roman official, who bore the title of *Protos* ("First")—a local designation, the accuracy of which is supported by inscriptions[4]—offered to the centurion a genial hospitality, in which Paul and his friends were allowed to share. It happened that at that time the father of Publius was lying prostrated by feverish attacks complicated with dysentery. St. Luke was a physician, but his skill was less effectual than the agency of St. Paul, who went into the sick man's chamber, prayed by his bedside, laid his hands on him, and healed him. The rumour of the cure spread through the little island, and caused all the sick inhabitants to come for help and tendance. We may be sure that St. Paul, though we do not hear of his founding any Church, yet lost no opportunity of making known the Gospel. He produced a deep and most

[1] φρυγάνων (see Theophrast. *Hist. Plant.* 1, 4). Hence the objection that *Bosquetta*, some distance from St. Paul's Bay, is the only place where there is timber in Malta, drops to the ground, even if there were ever anything in it.

[2] The disappearance of the viper from Malta, if it *has* disappeared, is no more strange than its disappearance from Arran. There is a curious parallel to the incident in the Greek Anthology. (Ἔκτανε) λυγρὸς ἔχις σ'· οἱ μάταν πρὸς κύματ' ἐμόχθει τὴν ἐπὶ γῆς φεύγων μοῖραν ὀφειλομένην; (*Anthol.*)

[3] So when Charmian is bitten, "Trembling she stood, and on the sudden dropped," *Ant. and Cleop.* v. 2 (Humphry).

[4] Bochart, *Phaleg.* II. i. 26. Πρῶτος Μελιταίων, *Corp. Inscr. Græc.* 5754.

favourable impression, and was surrounded on all sides with respectful demonstrations. In the shipwreck the crew must have lost all, except what little money they could carry on their own persons; they were therefore in deep need of assistance,[1] and this they received abundantly from the love and gratitude of the islanders to whom their stay had caused so many benefits.

Another Alexandrian corn-ship, the *Castor and Pollux*—more fortunate than her shattered consort—had wintered in the harbour of Valetta; and when navigation was again possible, Julius and his soldiers embarked on board of her with their prisoners, and weighed anchor for Syracuse. It was but eighty miles distant, and during that day's voyage St. Paul would gaze for the first time on the giant cone of Etna, the first active volcano he had ever seen. At Syracuse they waited three days for a more favourable wind. Since it did not come, they made a circuitous tack,[2] which brought them to Rhegium. Here again they waited for a single day, and as a south wind then sprang up, which was exactly what they most desired, they sped swiftly through the Straits of Messina, between the chains of snow-clad hills, and after passing on their left the huge and ever-flashing cone of Stromboli, anchored the next day, after a splendid run of 180 miles, in the lovely Bay of Puteoli. The unfurled topsail which marked the Alexandrian corn-ship would give notice of her arrival to the idlers of the gay watering-place, who gathered in hundreds on the mole to welcome with their shouts the vessels which brought the staff of life to the granaries of Rome. Here Paul had the unexpected happiness to find a little Christian Church, and the brethren begged him to stay with them seven days. This enabled them to spend together a Sabbath and a Sunday, and the privilege was granted by the kindly and grateful Julius. Here, then, they rested, in one of the loveliest of earthly scenes, when Vesuvius was still a slumbering volcano, clad to its green summit with vines and gardens. Paul could not have looked unmoved on the luxury and magnificence of the neighbouring towns. There was Baiæ, where, to the indignation of Horace, the Roman nobles built out their palaces into the sea; and where the Cæsar before whose judgment-seat he was going to stand had enacted the hideous tragedy of his mother's murder, and had fled, pursued by her Furies, from place to place along the shore.[3] In sight was Pandataria, and the other distant rocky islets, dense with exiles of the noblest rank, where Agrippa Postumus, the last of the genuine Cæsars, had tried to stop the pangs of famine by gnawing the stuffing of his own mattress, and where the daughter of the great Augustus had ended, in unutterable wretchedness, her life of infamy. Close by was Cumæ, with its Sibylline fame, and Pausilypus, with Virgil's tomb, and Capreæ, where twenty-three years before Tiberius had dragged to the grave his miserable old age. And within easy distance were the little towns of Pompeii and Herculaneum, little dreaming as yet, in their

[1] τιμαῖς. Cf. Ecclus. xxxviii. 1; "honos," Cic. *ad Divv.* xvi. 9.

[2] xxviii. 13. περιελθόντες, "fetched a compass," 2 Sam. v. 23; 2 Kings iii. 9.

[3] A.D. 59. Διὸ καὶ ἄλλοσε ᾔει καὶ ἐπειδὴ κἀνταῦθα τὰ αὐτὰ αὐτῷ συνέβαινε, ἄλλοσε ἐμπλήκτως μεθίστατο. Dion, lxi. 13, 14; Tac. *Ann.* xiv. 8; Suet. *Nero*, 34.

Greek-like gaiety and many-coloured brilliance, how soon they would be buried by the neighbouring mountain in their total and sulphurous destruction.

Here, free and among brethren, Paul passed seven peaceful days. On the eighth they started for Rome, which was only distant a hundred and forty miles. News of their arrival had reached the brethren, and when they had gone about a hundred miles, past Capua, and through the rich vineyards of Italy, and then through the Pomptine Marshes, Paul and Luke and Aristarchus, among the bargees and hucksters who thronged Appii Forum,[1] caught sight of a body of Christians, who had come no less than forty miles to welcome them. Farther than this they could not have come, since there were two ways of reaching Rome from Appii Forum, and the centurion might have preferred the less fatiguing journey by the canal. Ten miles further on, at Tres Tabernæ, they found another group of brethren awaiting them. Though there were a few who loved him at Rome, Paul knew the power, the multitude, and the turbulence of the vast assemblage of synagogues in the great city, and on their favour or opposition much of his future destiny must, humanly speaking, depend. It was natural, therefore, that when he saw the little throng of Christians he should thank God, and take courage from this proof of their affection. Nothing cheered and inspired him so much as human sympathy, and the welcome of these brethren must have touched with the brightness of a happy omen his approach to a city which, greatly as he had longed to see it, he was now to enter under circumstances far more painful than he had ever had reason to expect.

And so through scenes of ever-deepening interest, and along a road more and more crowded with stately memorials, the humble triumph of the Lord's slave and prisoner swept on. St. Paul had seen many magnificent cities, but never one which was approached by a road so regular and so costly in construction. As they passed each well-known object, the warm-hearted brethren would point out to him the tombs of the Scipios and Cæcilia Metella, and the thousands of other tombs with all their architectural beauty, and striking bas-reliefs and touching inscriptions; and the low seats for the accommodation of travellers at every forty feet; and the numberless statues of the Dei Viales; and the roadside inns, and the endless streams of carriages for travellers of every rank—humble birotae and comfortable rhedae, and stately carpenta—and the lecticae or palanquins borne on the necks of slaves, from which the occupants looked luxuriously down on throngs of pedestrians passing to and from the mighty capital of the ancient world.

> "What conflux issuing forth or passing in;
> Prætors, Proconsuls to their provinces
> Hasting, or on return, in robes of state,
> Lictors and rods, the ensigns of their power,
> Legions and cohorts, turms of horse and wings;
> Or embassies from regions far remote,
> In various habits, on the Appian road . .
> Dusk faces with white silken turbans wreathed."

[1] Hor. *Sat.* I. v. 1.

How many a look of contemptuous curiosity would be darted at the chained prisoner and his Jewish friends as they passed along with their escort of soldiers! But Paul could bear all this while he felt that he would not be utterly lonely amid the vast and densely-crowded wilderness of human habitations, of which he first caught sight as he mounted the slope of the Alban hills.

Perhaps as they left the Alban hills on the right, the brethren would tell the Apostle the grim annals of the little temple which had been built beside

> ——"that dim lake which sleeps
> Beneath Aricia's trees,
> The trees in whose dim shadow
> The ghastly priest doth reign,
> The priest who slew the slayer
> And shall himself be slain."

And so through ever-lengthening rows of suburban villas, and ever-thickening throngs of people, they would reach the actual precincts of the city, catch sight of the Capitol and the imperial palace, pass through the grove and by the fountain of Egeria, with its colony of begging Jews,[1] march past the pyramid of C. Cestius, under the arch of Drusus, through the dripping Capenian gate,[2] leave the Circus Maximus on the left, and pass on amid temples, and statues, and triumphal arches, till they reached the *Excubitorium*, or barracks of that section of the Prætorian cohorts whose turn it was to keep immediate guard over the person of the Emperor. It was thus that the dream of Paul's life was accomplished, and thus that in March, A.D. 61, in the seventh year of the reign of Nero, under the consulship of Cæsennius Pætus and Petronius Turpilianus, he entered Rome.

Here the charge of the centurion Julius ended, though we can hardly suppose that he would entirely forget and neglect henceforth his noble prisoner, to whom in God's providence he owed his own life and the safety of the other prisoners entrusted to him. Officially, however, his connexion with them was closed when he had handed them over to the charge of the Præfect of the Prætorian guards. From this time forward, and indeed previously, there had always been two Praefecti Praetorio, but during this year a single person held the power of that great office, the honest and soldierly Afranius Burrus.[3] So far, Paul was fortunate, for Burrus, as an upright and humane officer, was not likely to treat with needless severity a prisoner who was accused of no comprehensible charge—of none at any rate which a Roman would consider worth mentioning—and who had won golden opinions both from the Procurators of Judæa and from the centurion who had conducted him from Jerusalem. A vulgar and careless tyrant might have jumped to the conclusion that he was some fanatical Sicarius, such as at that time swarmed throughout Judæa, and so have thrust him into a hopeless and intolerable captivity. But the good

[1] Juv. *Sat.* iii. 12.

[2] Porta di S. Sebastiano.

[3] Acts xxviii. 16, τῷ στρατοπεδάρχῃ. Trajan *ap.* Plin. *Epp.* x. 65, "Vinctus mitti ad *praefectos praetorii* mei debet."

word of Julius, and the kindly integrity of Burrus, were invaluable to him, and he was merely subjected to that kind of *custodia militaris* which was known as *observatio*. For the first three days he was hospitably received by some member of the Christian community,[1] and was afterwards allowed to hire a lodging of his own, with free leave to communicate with his friends both by letter and by personal intercourse. The trial of having a soldier chained to him indeed continued, but that was inevitable under the Roman system. It was in mitigation of this intolerable concomitant of his imprisonment that the goodwill of his Roman friends might be most beneficially exercised. At the best, it was an infliction which it required no little fortitude to endure, and for a Jew it would be far more painful than for a Gentile. Two Gentiles might have much in common; they would be interested in common topics, actuated by common principles; but a Jew and Gentile would be separated by mutual antipathies, and liable to the incessant friction of irritating peculiarities. That St. Paul deeply felt this annoyance may be seen from his allusions to his "bonds" or his "coupling-chain" in every Epistle of the Captivity. When the first Agrippa had been flung into prison by Tiberius, Antonia, out of friendship for his family, had bribed the Prætorian Prefect Macro to place him under the charge of a kind centurion, and to secure as far as possible that the soldiers coupled to him should be good-tempered men. Some small measure of similar consideration may have been extended to Paul; but the service was irksome, and there must have been some soldiers whose morose and sullen natures caused to their prisoner a terrible torture. Yet even over these coarse, uneducated Gentiles, the courtesy, the gentleness, the "sweet reasonableness" of the Apostle, asserted its humanising control. If he was chained to the soldier, the soldier was also chained to him, and during the dull hours until he was relieved, many a guardsman might be glad to hear from such lips, in all their immortal novelty, the high truths of the Christian faith. Out of his worst trials the Apostle's cheerful faith created the opportunities of his highest usefulness, and from the necessities of his long-continued imprisonment arose a diffusion of Gospel truths throughout the finest regiment of that army which less than a century later was to number among its contingents a "thundering legion," and in less than three centuries was to supplant the silver eagles of the empire by the then detested badge of a slave's torture and a murderer's punishment.

It was one of the earliest cares of the Apostle to summon together the leading members of the Roman Ghetto, and explain to them his position. Addressing them as "brethren," he assured them he had neither opposed his people nor contravened their hereditary institutions. In spite of this he had been seized at Jerusalem, and handed over to the Roman power. Yet the Romans, after examining him, had declared him entirely innocent, and would have been glad to liberate him had not the opposition of the Jews compelled him to appeal to Cæsar. But he was anxious to inform them that by this

[1] xxviii. 23, εἰς τὴν ξενίαν. Cf. Philem. 22; Acts xxi. 16.

appeal he did not intend in any way to set the Roman authorities against his own nation, and that the cause of the chain he wore was his belief in the fulfilment of that Messianic hope in which all Israel shared.

The reply of the Jews was very diplomatic. Differences within their own pale, connected as we have seen with the name of Christ, had kindled such anger and alarm against them, that less than ten years before this time they had suffered the ruinous indignity of being banished from Rome by an edict of Claudius. That edict had been tacitly permitted to fall into desuetude; but the Jews were anxious not to be again subjected to so degrading an infliction. They therefore returned a vague answer, declaring—whether truthfully or not we cannot say—that neither by letter nor by word of mouth had they received any charge against the Apostle's character. It was true that, if any Jews had been deputed to carry before Cæsar the accusation of the Sanhedrin, they could only have started at the same time as Julius, and would therefore have been delayed by the same storms. The Jews wished, however, to learn from Paul his particular opinions, for, as he was a professed Christian, they could only say that that *sect was everywhere spoken against*.[1] It is obvious that this answer was meant to say as little as possible. It is inconceivable that the Jews should never have heard anything said against St. Paul; but being keen observers of the political horizon, and seeing that Paul was favourably regarded by people of distinction, they did not choose to embroil themselves in any quarrel with him. Nor does their professed ignorance at all disprove the existence of a Christian community so important as that to which St. Paul had addressed his Epistle to the Romans.[2] The Jews could boast of one or two noble proselytes; and it is possible that Pomponia Græcina,[3] wife of Plautius, one of the conquerors of Britain, may have been a Christian. But if so she had long been driven into the deepest seclusion,[4] and the conversion of the Consular Flavius Clemens, and his wife, Flavia Domitilla, who were martyred by Domitian, did not take place till some time afterwards. The Christian Church was composed of the humblest elements, and probably its Jewish and Gentile members formed two almost distinct communities under separate presbyters.[5] Now, with uncircumcised Gentile Christians of the lowest rank

[1] This they might well say. See Tac. *Ann.* xv. 44; Suet. *Ner.* 16; and, doubtless, the *graffiti* of the catacombs are only successors of others still earlier, just as are the hideous calumnies against which the Christian apologists appeal (Tert. *Apol.* 16, &c.).

[2] In Rom. i. 8 St. Paul tells the Roman Christians that their faith is proclaimed in the whole world. No one familiar with his style would see more in this than the favourable mention of them in the scattered Christian Churches which he visited. To St. Paul, as to every one else, "the world" meant the world in the midst of which he lived, *i.e.*, the little Christian communities which he had founded. Renan remarks, that in reading Benjamin of Tudela, one would imagine that there was no one in the world but Jews; and in reading Ibn Batoutah that there was no one in the world but Moslim.

[3] On this lady see Tac. *Ann.* xiii. 32.

[4] She was privately tried by her husband, and acquitted, in A.D. 57.

[5] Lightfoot, *Philippians*, p. 219. It is at any rate a most remarkable fact that, when St. Paul wrote the Epistle to the Colossians, two only of the Judaic Christians showed him any countenance—namely, Mark and Jesus, whose surname of Justus, if it be intended as a translation of ὁ δίκαιος, shows that he, like "James the Just" was a faithful observer of the Law (Col. iv. 11).

the leading Jews would not be likely to hold any intercourse, even if they were aware of their existence. But is it remembered that Rome at this time was a city of more than two million inhabitants? Is there any improbability that, among so many myriads, a small and struggling sect might, to outsiders, remain utterly unknown? The immense weight of the Epistle to the Romans furnishes no proof that the Church to which it was addressed was one which the world would regard as of any importance. The Sandemanians or Glassites are a Christian body in London, and it is quite conceivable that some eminent member of their body, like the late Mr. Faraday, might address to them a letter of deep significance; would it be any sufficient reason to deny their existence if it was found that the Archdeacons and Rural Deans of London had barely so much as heard of their peculiar tenets?

Since, however, the Romish Jews professed a wish for further information, St. Paul begged them to fix their own day to hear what he had to set before them. They came to him in considerable numbers. That only the heads of their community can have been invited is clear. St. Paul's abode could only have accommodated an insignificant fraction of the Jewish residents, who at this time are believed to have amounted to 60,000. It is said that there were seven synagogues in Rome,[1] and the officers of these synagogues would probably be as many as Paul could hope to address at once. All day long, from dawn till evening, he set before them his personal testimony and his scriptural arguments. That they were not wholly unimpressed, appears from the length of the discussion; but while a few were convinced, others disbelieved. The debate acquired towards its conclusion a somewhat stormy emphasis; and before it broke up Paul addressed the dissentients with something of his old fiery energy, applying to them the passage of Isaiah once quoted by our Lord Himself, which said that they should not see nor hear because they *would* not, and that their blindness and deafness were a penal consequence of the grossness of their hearts. And then he sternly warned them that the salvation of God was now sent to the Gentiles, and that the Gentiles would listen to its gracious offer.[2]

Henceforth St. Paul took his own line, opening no further communication with his obstinate fellow-countrymen. For two whole years he remained in Rome, a fettered prisoner, but living in his own hired lodging,[3] and cheered by the visits of the fellow-workers who were truest and best beloved. The quiet and holy Timotheus perhaps acted as his amanuensis, and certainly showed him all the tenderness of a son;[4] the highly-cultivated Luke was his historiographer and his physician;[5] Aristarchus attended him so closely as to earn the designation of his "fellow-prisoner;"[6] Tychicus brought him news from Ephesus;[7] Epaphroditus warmed his heart by the contributions which showed the generous affection of Philippi;[8] Epaphras came to consult him

[1] Friedländer, iii. 510.

[2] Ver. 29 is not found in ℵ, A, B, E.

[3] Μίσθωμα, not "house," as in the E. V., but "lodging"—*meritorium conductum.*

[4] Phil. i. 1; ii. 19, *seqq.*; Col. i. 1; Philem. 1.

[5] Col. iv. 14; Philem. 24.

[6] Col. iv. 10; Philem. 24.

[7] Eph. vi. 21; Col. iv. 7.

[8] Phil. ii. 25; iv. 18.

about the heresies which were beginning to creep into the Churches of Laodicea, Hierapolis, and Colossæ;[1] Mark, dear to the Apostle as the cousin of Barnabas, more than made up for his former defection by his present constancy;[2] and Demas had not yet shaken the good opinion which he at first inspired.[3] Now and then some interesting episode of his ministry, like the visit and conversion of Onesimus, came to lighten the tedium of his confinement.[4] Nor was his time spent fruitlessly, as, in some measure, it had been at Cæsarea. Throughout the whole period he continued heralding the kingdom of God, and teaching about the Lord Jesus Christ with all openness of speech "unmolestedly."

With that one weighty word ἀκωλύτως, we lose the help of the Acts of the Apostles. From the Epistles of the imprisonment we learn that, chained though he was in one room, even the oral teaching of the Apostle won many converts, of whom some at least were in positions of influence; and that—as soldier after soldier enjoyed the inestimable privilege of being chained to him—not his bonds only, but also his Gospel, became known throughout the whole body of Prætorian guards. But besides this, God overruled these two years of imprisonment in Rome for the benefit of the whole world. Two imprisonments, away from books, away from all public opportunities for preaching, each of two years long, with only a terrible shipwreck interpolated between them—how sad an interruption to most minds would these have seemed to be! Yet in the first of these two imprisonments, if nothing else was achieved, we can perceive that his thoughts were ripening more and more in silent growth; and in that second imprisonment he wrote the letters which have enabled him to exercise a far wider influence on the Church of Christ throughout the world than though he had been all the while occupied in sermons in every synagogue and missionary journeys in every land.

CHAPTER XLV.

ST. PAUL'S SOJOURN IN ROME.

Πόλιν ἐπιτομὴν τῆς οἰκουμένης.—ATHEN. *Deipnos*, 1120.

"Fumum et opes strepitumque Romae."—HOR. *Carm.* iii. 29, 12.

ST. PAUL'S arrival at Rome was in many respects the culminating point of his Apostolic career, and as he continued to work there for so long a time, it is both important and interesting to ascertain the state of things with which he came in contact during that long stay.

Of the city itself it is probable that he saw little or nothing until he was

[1] Col. i. 7; iv. 12. [2] Col. iv. 10; Philem. 24; 2 Tim. iv. 11.
[3] Col. iv. 14; Philem. 24; 2 Tim. iv. 10. [4] Col. iv. 9; Philem. 10.

liberated, except such a glimpse of it as he may have caught on his way to his place of confinement. Although his friends had free access to him, he was not permitted to visit them, nor could a chained Jewish prisoner walk about with his guarding soldier. Yet on his way to the Prætorian barracks he must have seen something of the narrow and tortuous streets, as well as of the great open spaces of ancient Rome; something of the splendour of its public edifices, and the meanness of its lower purlieus; something of its appalling contrast between the ostentatious luxury of inexhaustible wealth, and the painful squalor of chronic pauperism.[1] And during his stay he must have seen or heard much of the dangers which beset those densely-crowded masses of human beings;[2] of men injured by the clumsy carrucae rumbling along with huge stones or swaying pieces of timber;[3] of the crashing fall of houses raised on weak foundations to storey after storey of dangerous height;[4] of women and children trampled down amid the rush of an idle populace to witness the horrid butcheries of the amphitheatre; of the violence of nightly marauders; of the irresistible fury of the many conflagrations.[5] It is obvious that he would not have been allowed to seek a lodging in the Jewish quarter beyond the Tiber, since he would be obliged to consult the convenience of the successions of soldiers whose duty it was to keep guard over him. It is indeed possible that he might have been located near the Excubitorium, but it seems more likely that the Prætorians who were settled there were too much occupied with the duties thrown on them by their attendance at the palace to leave them leisure to guard an indefinite number of prisoners. We infer, therefore, that Paul's "hired apartment" was within close range of the Prætorian camp. Among the prisoners there confined he might have seen the Jewish priests who had been sent to Rome by Felix, and who won from their nation so much approval by the abstinence which they endured in the determination that they would not be defiled by any form of unclean meat.[6] Here, too, he may have seen Caradoc, the British prince whose heroic resistance and simple dignity extorted praise even from Roman enemies.[7] The fact that he was not in the crowded city precincts would enable him at less cost to get a better room than the stifling garrets which Juvenal so feelingly describes as at once ruinously expensive and distressingly inconvenient. Considering that he was a prisoner, his life was not dull. If he had to suffer from deep discouragements, he could also thank God for many a happy alleviation of his lot. He had indeed to bear the sickness of hope deferred, and put up with the bitterness of "the law's delays." His trial was indefinitely postponed—perhaps by the loss, during shipwreck, of the *elogium* of Festus; by the non-appearance of his accusers; by their plea for time to procure the necessary witnesses; or by the frivolous and inhuman carelessness

[1] Juv. *Sat.* iii. 126--189.
[2] Juv. *Sat.* iii. 235; Tac. *Ann.* xv. 38.
[3] Juv. *Sat.* iii. 254—261; Mart. v. 22.
[4] Juv. iii. 197, *seq.*
[5] *Id.* 239, *seq.*, 190 - 231.
[6] Jos. *Vit.* 3.
[7] Tac. *Ann.* xii. 38; *H.* iii. 45.

of the miserable youth who was then the emperor of the world. He was saddened at the rejection of his teaching by his unconverted countrymen, and by the dislike and suspicion of Judaising Christians. He could not but feel disheartened that some should be preaching Christ with the base and contentious motive of adding affliction to his bonds.[1] His heart must have been sometimes dismayed by the growth of subtle heresies in the infant Church.[2] But, on the other hand, he was safe for the present from the incessant perils and tumults of the past twenty years; and he was deprived of the possibility, and therefore exempt from the hard necessity, of earning by incessant toil his daily bread. And again, if he was neglected by Jews and Judaisers, he was acceptable to many of the Gentiles; if his Gospel was mutilated by unworthy preachers, still Christ was preached; if his bonds were irksome, they inspired others with zeal and courage; if one form of activity had by God's will been restrained, others were still open to him, and while he was strengthening distant Churches by his letters and emissaries, he was making God's message known more and more widely in imperial Rome. He had preached with but small success in Athens, which had been pre-eminently the home of intellect; but he was daily reaping the fruit of his labours in the city of empire—the city which had snatched the sceptre from the decrepit hands of her elder sister—the capital of that race which represented the law, the order, and the grandeur of the world.

That many of the great or the noble resorted to his teaching is wholly improbable, nor is there a particle of truth in the tradition which, by the aid of spurious letters, endeavoured to represent the philosopher Seneca as one of his friends and correspondents. We have seen that Gallio prided himself on ignoring his very existence; and it is certain that Seneca would have shared, in this as in all other respects, the sentiments of his brother. In his voluminous writings he never so much as alludes to the Christians, and if he had done so he would have used exactly the same language as that so freely adopted many years later—and, therefore, when there was far less excuse for it—even by such enlightened spirits as Pliny, Tacitus, Epictetus, and M. Aurelius. Nothing can less resemble the inner spirit of Christianity than the pompous and empty vaunt of that dilettante Stoicism which Seneca professed in every letter and treatise, and which he belied by the whole tenor of his life. There were, indeed, some great moral principles which he was enabled to see, and to which he gave eloquent expression, but they belonged to the spirit of an age when Christianity was in the air, and when the loftiest natures, sick with disgust or with satiety of the universal vice, took refuge in the gathered experiences of the wise of every age. It is doubtful whether Seneca ever heard more than the mere name of the Christians; and of the Jews he only speaks with incurable disdain. The ordinary life of the wealthy and noble Roman of St. Paul's day was too much divided between abject terror and unspeakable depravity to be reached by anything short of a miraculous awakening.

[1] Phil. i. 16. [2] Later Epistles, *passim*.

"On that hard Pagan world disgust
And secret loathing fell;
Deep weariness and sated lust
Made human life a hell.

"In his cool hall, with haggard eyes,
The Roman noble lay;
He drove abroad in furious guise
Along the Appian Way.

"He made a feast, drank fast and fierce,
And crowned his hair with flowers—
No easier nor no quicker passed
The impracticable hours."

The condition of the lower classes rendered them more hopeful subjects for the ennobling influences of the faith of Christ. It is true that they also lived in the midst of abominations. But to them vice stood forth in all its bare and revolting hideousness, and there was no wealth to gild its anguishing reactions. Life and its temptations wore a very different aspect to the master who could lord it over the souls and bodies of a thousand helpless minions, and to the wretched slave who was the victim of his caprice and tyranny. As in every city where the slaves far outnumbered the free population, they had to be kept in subjection by laws of terrible severity. It it is no wonder that in writing to a Church of which so many members were in this sad condition, St. Paul had thought it necessary to warn them of the duty of obedience and honour towards the powers that be.[1] The house of a wealthy Roman contained slaves of every rank, of every nation, and of every accomplishment, who could be numbered not by scores, but by hundreds. The master might kill or torture his slaves with impunity, but if one of them, goaded to passionate revenge by intolerable wrong, ventured to raise a hand against his owner, the whole *familia*, with their wives and children, however innocent, were put to death.[2] The Roman lady looked lovely at the banquet, but the slave girl who arranged a curl wrong had been already branded with a hot iron.[3] The *triclinia* of a banquet might gleam with jewelled and myrrhine cups, but if a slave did but drop by accident one crystal vase he might be flung then and there to feed the lampreys in his master's fishpond. The senator and the knight might loll upon cushions in the amphitheatre, and look on luxuriously at the mad struggles of the gladiators, but to the gladiator this meant the endurance of all the detestable savagery of the *lanista*, and the taking of a horrible oath that, "like a genuine gladiator," he would allow himself to be bound, burned, beaten, or killed at his owner's will.[4]

[1] Rom. xiii., xiv.

[2] The necessity for this law had been openly argued in the Senate, and it was put in force during this very year, A.D. 61, when Pedanius Secundus, the prefect of the city, was murdered by one of his slaves (Tac. *Ann.* xiv. 42). In consequence of that murder—itself caused by dreadful depravities—no less than four hundred slaves had been executed, and it is far from impossible that there may have been some Christians among them. On their numbers see Juv. iii. 141; viii. 180; xiv. 305. Mancipiorum *legiones*, Plin. *H. N.* xxxiii. 6, § 26.

[3] Juv. xiv. 24; Becker, *Charicles*, ii. 53; *Gallus*, ii. 124.

[4] Petron. *Satyr.*, p. 117 (Sen. *Ep.* 7).

There were, doubtless, many kind masters at Rome; but the system of slavery was in itself irredeemably degrading, and we cannot wonder, but can only rejoice, that, from Cæsar's household downwards, there were many in this condition who found in Christian teaching a light and peace from heaven. However low their earthly lot, they thus attained to a faith so sure and so consolatory that in the very catacombs they surrounded the grim memorials of death with emblems of peace and beauty, and made the ill-spelt jargon of their quaint illiterate epitaphs the expression of a radiant happiness and an illimitable hope.

From the Roman aristocracy, then, Paul had little to expect and little to fear; their whole life—physical, moral, intellectual—moved on a different plane from his. It was among the masses of the populace that he mainly hoped for converts from the Gentiles, and it was from the Jews, on the one hand, and the Emperor, on the other, that he had most to dread. The first terrible blow which was aimed at any Church among the Gentiles was dealt by the Emperor, and the hand of the Emperor was not improbably guided by the secret malice of the Jews. That blow, indeed—the outburst of the Neronian persecution—St. Paul escaped for a time by the guiding Providence which liberated him from his imprisonment just before the great fire of Rome; but since he escaped it for a time only, and since it fell on many whom he had taught and loved, we will conclude this chapter by a glance at these two forces of Antichrist in the imperial city.

1. The importance of the Jews at Rome began, as we have seen, with the days of Pompeius.[1] Julius Cæsar—who, as Philo informs us, felt an undisguised admiration for the manly independence with which they held themselves aloof from that all but idolatrous adulation into which the degenerate Romans were so ready to plunge—allowed them to settle in a large district beyond the Tiber, and yearly to send deputies and temple-tribute to their holy city. From that time forward they were the incessant butt for the half-scornful, half-alarmed wit and wrath of the Roman writers. The district assigned to them—being in the neighbourhood of the wharfs where the barges from Ostia were accustomed to unlade—was particularly suitable for the retail trade in which they were mainly occupied.[2] They increased with almost incredible rapidity. Their wisp of hay and the basket, which were their sole belongings, and were adopted to secure them from the danger of unclean meats, were known in every quarter. Martial describes how Jewish hawkers broke his morning slumbers with their bawling, and Juvenal complains of the way in which their gipsy-like women got themselves smuggled into the boudoirs of rich and silly ladies to interpret their dreams.[3] Others of them, with a supple versatility which would have done credit to the Greeks them-

[1] Cic. *pro Flacc.* 28; Jos. *c. Apion.* i. 7; Tac. *Ann.* ii. 85; Philo, *Leg. ad Gaium*, p. 568.

[2] Jos. *Antt.* xvii. 11, § 1; Tac. *Ann.* ii. 85. See on the whole subject Friedländer, *Sittengesch. Roms*, iii. 500; Hausrath, p. 474, *seqq.*

[3] Mart. i. 41, 3; x. 5, 3; Juv. iv. 116; v. 8; xiv. 134.

selves, thrust themselves into every house and every profession, flung themselves with perfect shamelessness into the heathen vices, and became the useful tools of wealthy rascality, and the unscrupulous confidants of the "gilded youth."[1] Some became the favourites of the palace, and made nominal proselytes of noble ladies who, like Poppæa, had every gift except that of virtue.[2] But whatever their condition, they were equally detested by the mass of the population. If they were false to their religion they were flouted as renegades; if they were true to it, their Sabbaths, and their circumcision, and their hatred of pork, their form of oath, their lamp-lightings, and their solemn festivals were held up to angry ridicule,[3] as signs of the most abject superstition. If a Roman saw a knot of Jew beggars, he turned from them with a shudder of disgust; if he noticed the statue of a Jewish king or Alabarch, he frowned at it as a proof of the degradation of the age. Whether successful or unsuccessful—whether he was an Herodian prince or a match-selling pedlar—the Jew was to the Latin races an object of abhorrence and disdain. They were regarded with the same feelings as those with which a citizen of San Francisco looks on the Chinese immigrant—as intruders, whose competition was dangerous—as aliens, whose customs were offensive. And yet they made their presence tremendously felt. Rome, so tolerant and so indifferent in her own religious beliefs, was sometimes startled into amazement by the raging violence of their internal disputes. Cicero, one hundred and twenty years before this period, prided himself on his courage in defending Flaccus against their charges, and was obliged to deliver his speech in a low tone of voice, for fear of exciting a riot among the thousands of them who besieged the court to denounce their enemy. Sober Quirites had listened with astonishment to their wild wailing round the funeral pile of their patron Julius Cæsar.[4] Even poets and satirists imply that those who were attracted by feelings of superstition to adopt some of their customs were neither few in number nor insignificant in position.[5]

Under Augustus their condition was not materially altered. Tiberius, recognising them as a dangerous element in the population, made a ruthless attempt to keep down their numbers by conscriptions and deportations. Gaius, on the other hand, grossly as he behaved to their most venerable ambassadors, was so much attached to the elder Agrippa that he respected their religious and political immunities. The position of the Herodian princes in the imperial court was sufficient to protect them during the greater part of the reign of Claudius. During the reign of Nero, and therefore at the very time of St. Paul's Roman imprisonment, they enjoyed a secret influence of the most formidable kind, since Poppæa never hesitated to intercede for them, and had even given orders that after her death her body was—in accordance with the Jewish practice—to be buried and not burnt.

[1] Mart. xi. 94; vii. 30.
[2] Tac. *Ann.* xiii. 44, "Huic mulieri cuncta alia fuere praeter honestum animum."
[3] See Pers. v. 180; Hor. *Sat.* ii. 3, 288.
[4] Sueton. *Caes.* 84.
[5] Hor. *Sat.* 1, ix. 20.

2. If Paul had little to hope from the Jewish community at Rome, he had still less reason to place any confidence in the justice, or mercy, or even the ordinary discernment, of the Cæsar to whom he had appealed. The first three Cæsars had been statesmen and men of genius. For Gaius might have been urged the mitigating plea of congenital madness. Claudius was redeemed from contempt by a certain amount of learning and good-nature, But Nero was in some respects worse than any who had preceded him. Incurably vicious, incurably frivolous, with no result of all his education beyond a smattering of ridiculous or unworthy accomplishments, his selfishness had been so inflamed by unlimited autocracy that there was not a single crime of which he was incapable, or a single degradation to which he could not sink. The world never entrusted its imperial absolutism to a more despicable specimen of humanity. He was a tenth-rate actor entrusted with irresponsible power. In every noble mind he inspired a horror only alleviated by contempt. The first five years of his reign—that "golden quinquennium" which was regarded as an ideal of happy government—were a mere illusion.[1] Their external success and happiness had been due to the wise counsels exclusively of Burrus and Seneca, which Nero—who was but seventeen when his stepfather Claudius had been poisoned by his mother Agrippina—was too ignorant, too careless, and too bent on personal pleasure to dispute. Yet in all that concerned the *personal* conduct of himself and of Agrippina, even those five years had been thickly sown with atrocities and infamies, of which the worst are too atrocious and too infamous to be told. His very first year was marked not only by open ingratitude to his friends, but also by the assassination of Junius Silanus, and the poisoning of the young son of Claudius—Britannicus, a boy of fourteen, from whom he had usurped the throne. The second year was marked by the cowardly folly of his disguised nightly marauding among his peaceful subjects, after the fashion of the Mohawks in the reign of Queen Anne. From these he had descended through every abyss of vice and crime, to the murder of his mother, his public displays in the theatre,[2] the flight from place to place in the restless terrors of a haunted conscience, and finally to the most abandoned wickedness when he found that even such crimes as his had failed to sicken the adulation or to shake the allegiance of his people. He was further encouraged by this discovery to throw off all shadow of control. Shortly after Paul's arrival Burrus had died, not without suspicion of being poisoned by his imperial master. Nero seized this opportunity to disgrace Seneca from his high position. To fill up the vacancy created by the death of Burrus, he returned to the old plan of appointing two Prætorian Præfects. These were Fenius Rufus, a man of no personal weight, but popular from his benevolent disposi-

[1] Nero succeeded Claudius on October 13, A.D. 54.

[2] At the Juvenalia, which he instituted on the occasion of first shaving his beard, Gallio had to submit to the degradation of publicly announcing his appearance in the theatre, and Burrus and Seneca had to act as prompters and tutors, "with praises on their lips and anguish in their hearts" (Dion, lxi. 20, 19; Tac. *Ann.* xiv. 15).

tion,[1] and Sofonius Tigellinus, one of the worst characters of that bad age. Tigellinus was dear to Nero from the exceptional cruelty and infamy of his nature, and to him was practically entrusted the entire power.[2] The banishment and subsequent murder of Nero's wife Octavia, the unhappy daughter of Claudius, took place within a year of St. Paul's arrival at Rome.

Such are some of the events which must have been whispered to the Apostle from time to time by the Prætorians who guarded him; and if his condition was rendered less tolerable by the promotion of such a wretch as Tigellinus, he must also have felt that his hopes for the future had been rendered more precarious by the downfall of Seneca, and the now unchecked tyranny of the incestuous matricide before whose tribunal his appeal must soon be tried. But if deep fears as to the result of that appeal alternated with passing hopes, neither his natural fears nor his earthly hopes disturbed the serenity of his soul. He quietly continued the discharge of every duty which was still possible to him in his captivity, and for the rest he knew that his times were in God's hands, and that, whether life awaited him or death, all things were his, whether things present or things to come, and he was Christ's and Christ was God's. Alike on the stage of stormy publicity and in the solitude of his sad imprisonment, his life was hid with Christ in God.

CHAPTER XLVI.

EPISTLES OF THE CAPTIVITY.

"That man is very strong and powerful who has no more hopes for himself, who looks not to be loved any more, to be admired any more, to have any more honour or dignity, and who cares not for gratitude; but whose sole thought is for others, and who only lives on for them."—HELPS.

THE history of St. Paul's first imprisonment, as well as the thoughts by which he was then occupied, can only be derived from the "Epistles of the Captivity." The extant Epistles of St. Paul fall naturally into four connected groups, "separated from each other alike by chronological intervals and by internal characteristics." They are respectively the letters of the second missionary journey (1, 2 Thess.); those of the third missionary journey (1, 2 Cor., Gal., Rom.); those of the first imprisonment (Phil., Col., Philem., Eph.); and those of the second imprisonment (1, 2 Tim., Tit.). These groups may be respectively characterised as the Eschatological Epistles (1, 2 Thess.); the Epistles of the anti-Judaic controversy (1, 2 Cor., Gal., Rom.); the letters against incipient Gnosticism (Col., Eph.); and the Pastoral Epistles (1, 2 Tim.

[1] Tac. *Ann.* xiv. 51.

[2] "Validior Tigellinus in animo Principis et intimis libidinibus assumptus" (Tac. *l. c.*). Τιγελλῖνον δέ τινα Σωφόνιον ἀσελγείᾳ τε καὶ μιαιφονίᾳ πάντας τοὺς καθ' ἑαυτὸν ἀνθρώπους ὑπεραίροντα (Dion, lxii. 13).

Tit.). The Epistles to the Philippians and to Philemon stand in most respects, separate from the group to which they belong.

1. The two letters to the Thessalonians are the simplest of all in their matter and manner, and deal mainly (as we have seen) with the question of the shortly-expected return of Christ. They were written about A.D. 52.

2. The next great group of letters may be called in one of their aspects the letters of Judaic controversy. This group comprises the two Epistles to the Corinthians—which show St. Paul's method of dealing with questions of doctrine and discipline in a restless, intellectual, and partly disaffected Church; and those to the Galatians and Romans. They were written during the years A.D. 57 and A.D. 58, a period pre-eminently of storm and stress in the Apostle's life, of physical suffering and mental anxiety, which leave deep traces on his style.

Of these, the Epistles to the Corinthians are largely occupied with the personal question of Paul's Apostolate. His Jewish-Christian opponents had found it easier to impugn his position than to refute his arguments. It became a duty and a necessity to prove his claim to be a teacher of co-ordinate authority with the very chiefest of the Twelve.

The Epistles to the Galatians and the Romans contain the defence of his main position as regards the Law; a definition of the relations between Christianity and Judaism; and the statement and demonstration of the Gospel entrusted to him by special revelation. Of these, the latter is calmer, fuller, and more conciliatory in tone, and serves as the best commentary on the former.

The Epistle to the Philippians finds its main motive in an entirely different order of conceptions. In it we only hear the dying echoes of the great controversy, and if his one outburst of strong indignation against his opponents (ii. 3—6, 18) reminds us of the heat of the Epistle to the Galatians, on the other hand he here suppresses the natural sense of deep personal injuries, and even utters an expression of rejoicing that these very opponents, whatever may be their motives, are still preachers of the Gospel of Christ (i. 14—20).

3. The next two Epistles, those to the Colossians and Ephesians, mark the rise of a new phase of error. They are the controversy with incipient Gnosticism. Hence also they are the chief Christological and Ecclesiastical Epistles, the Epistles of Christian dogma, the Epistles of Catholicity. The idea and constitution of the Church of Christ was the destined bulwark against the prevalence of heresy, and the doctrine of Christ was the sole preservative against the victory of error. The dominant thought of the Colossians is Christ over all; that of the Ephesians, the Universal Church in Christ.

The Epistle to Philemon, a sort of appendix to the Colossians, stands alone as a letter addressed solely to an individual friend, though it involves the statement of an immortal principle.

4. In the last group stand the three Pastoral Epistles, containing, as we should have expected, the proof that there had been a development of the

Gnostic tendency on the one hand, and of Church organisation on the other. In the Second Epistle to Timothy we have the last words and thoughts of St. Paul before his martyrdom.[1]

May we go further, and attempt, in one or two words, a description of each separate Epistle, necessarily imperfect from its very brevity, and yet, perhaps, expressive of some one main characteristic? If so, we might perhaps say that the First Epistle to the Thessalonians is the Epistle of consolation in the hope of Christ's return; and the second, of the immediate hindrances to that return, and our duties with regard to it. The First Epistle to the Corinthians is the solution of practical problems in the light of eternal principles; the Second, an impassioned defence of the Apostle's impugned authority, his *Apologia pro vitâ suâ.* The Epistle to the Galatians is the Epistle of freedom from the bondage of the Law; that to the Romans, of justification by faith. The Epistle to the Philippians is the Epistle of Christian gratitude and Christian joy in sorrow; that to the Colossians, the Epistle of Christ the universal Lord; that to the Ephesians, so rich and many-sided, is the Epistle of "the heavenlies," the Epistle of grace, the Epistle of ascension with the ascended Christ, the Epistle of Christ in His One and Universal Church; that to Philemon, the Magna Charta of emancipation. The First Epistle to Timothy, and that to Titus, are the manuals of the Christian pastor; the Second Epistle to Timothy is the last message of a Christian ere his death.[2]

He must doubtless have written others besides these, but intense as would have been for us the theologic and psychologic interest of even the most trivial of his writings, we may assume, with absolute certainty, that those which we still possess have been preserved in accordance with God's special providence, and were by far the most precious and important of all that he wrote.

That the four letters which we shall now examine were written at Rome, and not, as some critics have imagined, at Cæsarea, may be regarded as absolutely certain. Although Rome is not mentioned in any of them, yet the facts to which they advert, and the allusions in which they abound, are such as exactly suit the ancient and unanimous tradition that they were penned during the Roman imprisonment,[3] while they agree far less with the novel and

[1] Other classifications have been attempted—*e.g.*, that of Baur, who divides them into ὁμολογούμενα (four), ἀντιλεγόμενα (six), and νόθα (three).

Similarly, M. Renan classes the Epistles as follows:—1. Incontestable—Gal., 1, 2 Cor., Rom. 2. Authentic, though disputed—1, 2 Thess., Phil. 3. Probably authentic, though open to serious objection—Col. and Philem. 4. Doubtful—Eph. 5. Spurious—The Pastoral Epistles. (*St. Paul*, v.)

Lange classes the Epistles as—1. Eschatological (1, 2 Thess.). 2. Soteriological (Gal., Rom). 3. Ecclesiastical (1 Cor., *polemically*; 2 Cor., *apologetically*). 4. Christological (Col., Eph.). 5. Ethical (Philipp.). 6. Pastoral (Philem., 1, 2 Tim., Tit.). (*Introd. to Romans.*)

Olshausen's classification of them under the heads of—1. Dogmatic; 2. Practical; 3. Friendly—is unsuccessful.

[2] See Excursus XXII., "Distinctive Words, Keynotes, and Characteristics of the Epistles."

[3] Chrys. *Proem ad Epist. ad Ephes.*; Jerome, *ad Eph.* iii. 1, iv. 1, vi. 20; Theodoret,

fantastic hypothesis that they were sent from Cæsarea.[1] If any confirmation for this certain tradition were required, it would be found, as far as the Epistle to the Philippians is concerned, in the salutation which St. Paul sends from the converts in "Cæsar's household." As regards the other three Epistles it is sufficient to say that internal evidence conclusively proves that all three were written at the same time, as they were despatched by the same messengers, and that whereas during his Cæsarean imprisonment St. Paul was looking forward to visit Rome,[2] he is, at the time of writing these letters, looking forward to visit, first Macedonia, then Colossæ.[3] Further than this, the allusions in these Epistles show that, prisoner though he was, he was enabled to exercise a powerful influence for the spread of the Gospel in a city of the highest importance.[4] Meyer, indeed—with that hypercritical ingenuity which, like vaulting ambition, so constantly overleaps itself and falls on the other side—argues that Onesimus is more likely to have fled from Colossæ to Cæsarea than to Rome; an argument of which we can only say that Cæsarea —a mere Procuratorial residence full of Jews—would be about the very last town which any one would naturally have dreamt of suggesting as a likely hiding-place for a runaway Asiatic slave. Meyer might as reasonably argue that a London pickpocket would be more likely to hide himself at Biarritz than at New York. His other arguments derived from the non-mention of the name of Onesimus in the Epistle to the Ephesians, and the incidental expression "you also" in that letter, are too trivial for serious discussion.

The question next arises, in what order these Epistles were written; and the *primâ facie* argument that the Epistle to the Philippians seems to have been written before the approaching crisis of his trial has been taken as a sufficient proof that it was written after the other three. On the other hand, there is the same expectation of approaching release in the Epistle to Philemon, so that on this circumstance no conclusion can be built. The notion that this Epistle shows traces of deeper depression than the others, and that this may be accounted for by the change wrought in his affairs through the influence of Tigellinus and Poppæa, is partly unsupported by fact, since a spirit of holy joy is the very key-note of the Epistle; and partly inconsistent with itself, since, if the hostile influences were at work at all appreciably, they were quite as much so within a few months after Paul's Roman imprisonment began, as they were at its close.[5] It is true that the letter could not have been

Proœm ad Epist. ad Eph., &c. If I do not mention Oeder's theory (?) that the Epistle to the Philippians was written from Corinth (see Schenkel, *Der Brief an die Philipper*, p. 110), it is because "it is not worth while," as Baur says, "to discuss vague hypotheses which have no support in history, and no coherence in themselves."

[1] I can only express my surprise that this theory should have commended itself not only to Schulz and Schneckenburger, but even to Holtzmann, Reuss, Schenkel, and Meyer.

[2] Acts xix. 21; xxiii. 11.

[3] Phil. ii. 24; Philem. 22.

[4] Eph. vi. 19, 20; Col. iv. 3, 4.

[5] The death of Burrus and the appointment of Tigellinus took place very early in A.D. 62, some nine months after St. Paul's arrival. Nero's marriage with Poppæa took place about the time, and indeed bears very little on the matter, since her influence as Nero's mistress was probably even greater than that which she enjoyed as his wife.

written during the earliest months of the captivity at Rome, because time must be allowed for the news of Paul's arrival there to have reached the Philippians; for the despatch of Epaphroditus with their contributions; for his illness at Rome; for the arrival of intelligence to that effect at Philippi; and for the return of their expressions of sorrow and sympathy.[1] Now a journey from Rome to Philippi—a distance of seven hundred miles—would, under ordinary circumstances, occupy about a month, and as we do not suppose that any of these letters were written during the first year of the imprisonment, ample time is allowed for these journeys, and no objection whatever to the traditional priority of the Epistle to the Philippians can be raised on this score.

Still less can any argument be urged from the absence of greetings from Luke and Aristarchus, or from the allusion to Timothy as the sole exception to the general selfishness which the Apostle was grieved to mark in those around him. The *presence* of particular names in the greetings of any letter may furnish a probable or even positive argument as to its date, but their *absence* is an indication of the most uncertain character. It needs no more than the commonest everyday experience to prove the utter fallaciousness of the "argument from silence;" and we know far too little of the incessant missions and movements, from church to church, and continent to continent, of the companions of St. Paul, to be able in any way to build upon the non-occurrence of the name of any one of them. Since, therefore, there are no adequate arguments *against* regarding the Epistle to the Philippians as the earliest of the four Epistles of the Captivity—although it may have been written only a few months before the other three—full weight may be given to the internal evidence, which is in favour of that supposition. That internal evidence consists in the general resemblance of this Epistle to those of the earlier group—especially to the Epistle to the Romans—which enables us to regard it as an intermediate link between the Epistles of the Captivity and those of the third Apostolic journey.[2] To the Epistle to the Romans it presents many and close parallels in thought and language, while its general tone and spirit, its

[1] Dr. Lightfoot (*Philipp.* p. 34) thinks that Aristarchus may have left St. Paul at Myra, and may have conveyed to Philippi the news of St. Paul's journey to Rome, as he was on his way home to Thessalonica; but I can see no sufficient reason for believing that Aristarchus, who was in some sense St. Paul's "fellow-prisoner" at Rome (Col. iv. 10), went home from Adramyttium (Acts xxvii. 2). In any case he could only have taken the news that St. Paul was *on his way* to Rome, not that he had arrived.

[2] Lightfoot, *Philippians*, pp. 40—45, *e.g.*—

Philippians.		Romans.	Philippians.			Romans.
i. 3, 4, 7, 8	...	i. 8—11	iii. 4, 5	...	...	xi. 1
i. 10 ...	...	ii. 18	iii. 9	...	...	x. 3
ii. 8, 9, 10, 11	...	xiv. 9, 11	iii. 21	...	...	viii. 29
ii. 4 ...	...	xii. 10	iii. 19	...	...	xvi. 18.

To these we may add Phil. iii. 3, Rom. xii. 1, and the use of φρονεῖν in Phil. i. 7, ii. 2, 5, iii. 15, with Rom. xii. 3, 16, xiv. 6. The Epistle also presents some interesting points of comparison with the last which he ever wrote:—Phil. i. 23, ἐπιθυμίαν ἔχων εἰς τὸ ἀναλῦσαι, 2 Tim. iv. 6, καιρὸς τῆς ἐμῆς ἀναλύσεως ἐφέστηκεν. Phil. ii. 17, εἰ καὶ σπένδομαι, 2 Tim. iv. 6, ἐγὼ γὰρ ἤδη σπένδομαι. Phil. iii. 14, κατὰ σκοπὸν διώκω ἐπὶ τὸ βραβεῖον, 2 Tim. iv. 7, 8, τὸν δρόμον τετέλεκα, ἀπόκειταί μοι ὁ τῆς δικαιοσύνης στέφανος.

comparative calmness, the spiritual joy which breathes through its holy resignation, the absence of impassioned appeal and impetuous reasoning, mark its affinity to the three by which it was immediately followed. Although not much more than four years had now elapsed since Paul, a free man and an active Apostle, elaborated at Corinth the great argument which he had addressed to the Gentiles and proselytes, who formed the bulk of the Church of Rome, his controversy with Judaism had to some extent faded into the background. Every Church that he had founded was now fully aware of his sentiments on the questions which were agitated between the advocates of Judaic rigour and Gospel freedom. In writing to the Philippians there was no need to dwell on these debates, for whatever dangers might yet await them—dangers sufficiently real to call forth one energetic outburst, which reminds us of his earlier tone—they had up to this time proved themselves faithful to his teaching, and were as yet unsophisticated by any tampering interference of emissaries from Jerusalem. The Judaisers of the party of James may have heard enough of the devotion of the Philippians for St. Paul to show them that it would be unadvisable to dog his footsteps through the Christian Churches of Macedonia. They might leave their view of the question with better policy in the hands of those unconverted Jews, who would never hesitate to use on its behalf the engines of persecution. Thus St. Paul had no need to enter on the debate which had so recently occupied the maturity of his powers; and in the Epistle to the Philippians we have only "the spent waves of this controversy." Nevertheless, as we have seen, his was a mind whose sensitive chords continued to quiver long after they had been struck by the plectrum of any particular emotion. He was reminded of past controversies by the coldness and neglect of a community in which some "preached Christ even of contention, supposing to add affliction to his bonds." If, then, he dwelt on doctrinal considerations at all in a letter of affectionate greetings to the community which was dearest to his heart, they would naturally be those on which he had last most deeply thought. By the time that he sat down to dictate the Epistle to the Colossians a fresh set of experiences had befallen him. His religious musings had been turned in an entirely different direction. The visit of Epaphras of Colossæ had made him aware of new errors, entirely different from those which he had already combated, and the Churches of Proconsular Asia evidently needed that his teaching should be directed to questions which lay far apart from the controversies of the last eight years. On the other hand, I regard it as psychologically certain that, had the Epistle to the Philippians been written, as so many critics believe, after those to the "Ephesians" and Colossians, it could not possibly have failed to bear upon its surface some traces of the controversy with that hybrid philosophy—that Judaic form of incipient Gnosticism—in which he had been so recently engaged. These considerations seem to me to have decided the true order of the Epistles of the Captivity, and to give its only importance to a question on which little would otherwise depend.

The Epistle to the Philippians[1] arose directly out of one of the few happy incidents which diversified the dreary uncertainties of St. Paul's captivity. This was the visit of Epaphroditus, a leading presbyter of the Church of Philippi, with the fourth pecuniary contribution by which that loving and generous Church had ministered to his necessities. At Rome, St. Paul was unable with his fettered hands to work for his livelihood, and it is possible that he found no opening for his special trade. One would have thought that the members of the Roman Church were sufficiently numerous and sufficiently wealthy to render it an easy matter for them to supply his necessities; but the unaccountable indifference which seems to have marked their relations to him, and of which he complains both in this and in his later imprisonment, shows that much could not be hoped from their affection, and strangely belied the zealous respect with which they had come thirty or forty miles to meet and greet him. It is, of course, possible that they may have been willing to help him, but that he declined an assistance respecting which he was sensitively careful. But the Phillippians knew and valued the privilege which had been accorded to them—and perhaps to them only—by their father in Christ—the privilege of helping him in his necessities. It was a custom throughout the Empire to alleviate by friendly presents the hard lot of prisoners,[2] and we may be sure that when once the Philippians had heard of his condition, friends like Lydia, and other converts who had means to spare, would seize the earliest opportunity to add to his comforts. Epaphroditus arrived about autumn, and flinging himself heartily into the service of the Gospel—which in a city like Rome must have required the fullest energies of every labourer—had succumbed to the unhealthiness of the season, and been prostrated by a dangerous and all but fatal sickness. The news of this illness had reached Philippi, and caused great solicitude to the Church.[3] Whatever gifts of healing were entrusted to the Apostles, they do not seem to have considered themselves at liberty to exercise them in their own immediate circle, or for any ends of personal happiness. No miracle was wrought, except one of those daily miracles which are granted to fervent prayer.[4] Paul had many trials to bear, and the death of "his brother, Epaphroditus," as he tenderly calls him, would have plunged him in yet deeper sadness. We can-

[1] The notion that the Epistle is really two and not one seems to have originated in Phil. iii. 1, and in a mistaken supposition that Polycarp, in his letter to the Philippians, mentions more than one letter of St. Paul to them (ὃς καὶ ἀπὼν ὑμῖν ἔγραψεν ἐπιστολάς, *ad Philipp.* c. 3). That 'Επιστολάς, however, may only differ from ἐπιστολὴ in being a more important term, is *conclusively* proved by Thuc. viii. 51; Jos. *Antt.* xii. 4, § 10. That St. Paul wrote other letters to the Philippians during the ten years which had elapsed since he visited them, and that he may have written other letters after this, is not only possible, but probable; but if any such letters had survived till the time of Polycarp, it is wholly improbable that they should not have been subsequently preserved.

[2] Thus, the friends of Agrippa had helped him by providing him with better fare and accommodation when he was imprisoned by Tiberius; and Lucian relates the warmth and open-handedness with which the Christians diminished the hardships, and even shared night after night the confinement of Peregrinus.

[3] Phil. ii. 26.

[4] Compare what Luther said of Melancthon's sickness and recovery.

not doubt that he pleaded with God for the life of his sick friend, and God had mercy on him. Epaphroditus recovered; and deeply as Paul in his loneliness and discouragement would have rejoiced to keep him by his side, he yielded with his usual unselfishness to the yearning of Epaphroditus for his home, and of the Christians of Philippi for their absent pastor. He therefore sent him back, and with him the letter, in which he expressed his thankfulness for that constant affection which had so greatly cheered his heart.

And thus it is that the Epistle to the Philippians is one of the least systematic, the least special in character, of all St. Paul's writings. But it is this which raises the genuineness of the letter, not indeed beyond cavil, but far beyond all reasonable dispute. The Tübingen school, in its earlier stages, attacked it with the monotonous arguments of its credulous scepticism. With those critics, if an Epistle touches on points which make it accord with the narrative of the Acts, it was forged to suit them; if it seems to disagree with them, the discrepancy shows that it is spurious. If the diction is Pauline, it stands forth as a proved imitation; if it is un-Pauline, it could not have proceeded from the Apostle. The notion that it was forged to introduce the name of Clement because he was confused with Flavius Clemens, and because Clement was a follow-worker of St. Peter, and it would look well to place him in connexion with Paul—and the notion that in Phil. ii. 6—8 the words *form* and *shape* express Gnostic conceptions, and that the verses refer to the Valentinian Æon Sophia, who aimed at an equality with God—are partly founded on total misinterpretations of the text, and are partly the perversity of a criticism which has strained its eyesight to such an extent as to become utterly purblind.[1] This Epistle is genuine beyond the faintest shadow or suspicion of doubt. The Philippian Church was eminently free from errors of doctrine and irregularities of practice. No schism seems to have divided it; no heresies had crept into its faith; no false teachers had perverted its allegiance. One fault, and one alone, seems to have needed correction, and this was of so personal and limited a character that, instead of denouncing it, Paul only needs to hint at it gently and with affectionate entreaty. This was a want of unity between some of its female members, especially Euodia and Syntyche, whom Paul begs to become reconciled to each other, and whose feud, and any partisanship which it may have entailed, he tacitly and considerately rebukes by the constant iteration of the word "all" to those whom he can only regard as one united body. In fact, we may say that disunion and despondency were the main dangers to which they were exposed; hence "all" and "rejoice" are the two leading words and thoughts. But this absence of any special object makes the letter less doctrinally distinctive than those which are more controversial in character. It would, indeed, be colourless if it did not receive a colouring from the rich hues of the writer's individuality. It is not, like the First Epistle to the Thessalonians, a

[1] Baur, *Paul.* ii. 50, *seqq.* Schwegler, *Nachapostol. Zeital.* ii. 133, *seqq.* The three arguments are: (1) Gnostic conceptions in ii. 6—9; (2) want of anything distinctively Pauline; (3) the questionableness of some of the historic data.

consolation to the afflicted, by reminding them of the near advent of their Lord;[1] or a series of replies to questions, like the greater part of the First Epistle to the Corinthians; nor a trumpet note of defiance to powerful and aggressive opponents, like the Epistle to the Galatians; nor a treatise of theology, like the Epistle to the Romans: but it is the warm, spontaneous outpouring of a loving heart expressing itself with unreserved gratitude and tenderness towards the favourite children of his ministry. If it exhibits to us somewhat less than other Epistles of St. Paul's peculiar teaching, it has this high source of interest that it shows to us more of his character and feelings. In this respect it somewhat resembles the Second Epistle to the Corinthians, except that in it St. Paul is writing to those who were kindest and most faithful to him, whereas towards the Corinthians he had little cause for gratitude, and much need of forbearance. Amid the trials and suspense of a galling imprisonment it reveals to us, not directly, but as it were unconsciously, the existence of an unquenchable happiness—a peace as of the inmost heart of the ocean under the agitation of its surface storms. It was dictated by a worn and fettered Jew, the victim of gross perjury, and the prey of contending enmities; dictated at a time when he was vexed by hundreds of opponents, and consoled but by few who cared for him; and yet the substance of it all may be summed up in two words—χαίρω, χαίρετε ("I rejoice; rejoice ye"). If any one compare the spirit of the best-known classic writers in their adversity with that which was habitual to the far deeper wrongs and far deadlier sufferings of St. Paul—if he will compare the Epistle to the Philippians with the "Tristia" of Ovid, the letters of Cicero from exile, or the treatise which Seneca dedicated to Polybius from his banishment in Corsica—he may see, if he will, the difference which Christianity has made in the happiness of man.

CHAPTER XLVII.

THE EPISTLE TO THE PHILIPPIANS.

"Summa Epistolae—gaudeo, gaudete."—BENGEL.

THE greeting is from "Paul and Timotheus, slaves of Jesus Christ, to all the saints who are in Christ Jesus in Philippi, with the bishops and deacons." Timothy is naturally associated with him as one who had laboured at Philippi, but so little is he supposed to have any share in the authorship that St. Paul afterwards proceeds to speak of him in the third person. The "bishops" (*i.e.*, the presbyters) and deacons are specially greeted, perhaps because they had taken an active part in the collection of the contribution. He does not

[1] The topic of "persecution" is prominent only in the Epistles to the Macedonian Churches. It had led the Philippians to despondency; the Thessalonians to a mistaken *form* of hope.

call himself an apostle, because to them no assertion of his authority was in any way needful.[1]

The thanksgiving which follows is unusually full. He tells them that he thanks God in *all* his remembrance of them, *always*, in *all* his supplication on behalf of them *all*, making his supplication with joy for their united work in furtherance of the Gospel from the first day when he had visited them—ten years ago—until now; and he is very sure that God, who began in them that sacred work of co-operation in a good cause, will carry it on to perfection until the day of Christ;[2] a conviction arising from his heartfelt sense that they were ALL of them partakers of the grace which God had granted to him, and which they had manifested by their sympathetic aid in his bondage, and in the defence and establishment of the Gospel. God knows how much he yearns for them in Christ; and his prayer for them is that their love may abound more and more in full knowledge of the truth, and all insight into its application, so that they may discriminate all that is best and highest,[3] and be pure towards God, and blameless towards men, for the day of Christ, having been filled with the fruit of a righteousness attainable not by their own works, but by Jesus Christ, for the glory and praise of God.[4]

They must not suppose, he tells them, that he is the Apostle of a ruined cause, or that his imprisonment is a sign that God's frown is on his work, and that it is coming to nought; on the contrary, he wants them to recognise that his misfortunes have been overruled by God to the direct furtherance of the Gospel. The necessity of his being coupled to guardsman after guardsman, day after day and night after night, had resulted in the notoriety of his condition as a prisoner for Christ among all the Prætorian cohorts,[5] and to everybody else; and the majority of the brethren had been stimulated by his bonds to a divine confidence, which had shown itself in a yet more courageous daring than before in preaching the word of God. Some of them preach Christ out of genuine good will, but some, alas! tell the story of Christ insincerely[6] out of

[1] Phil. i. 1, 2. This Epistle may be thus summarised:—i. 1, 2, Greeting; i. 3—11, Thanksgiving and prayer; 12—26, Personal details; i. 27—ii. 16, Exhortation to unity by the example of Christ; ii. 17—30, Personal details; iii. 1, 2, Last injunction suddenly broken off by a digression in which he denounces Judaism and Antinomianism; iii. 3—iv. 1, Exhortation to unity; iv. 2, 3, and to Christian joy; 4—9, Gratitude for their aid; iv. 10—20, Final greetings and benediction; 21—23, The unity of the Epistle (in spite of Heinrichs, Weisse, &c.) is generally admitted.

[2] "It is not God's way to do things by halves" (Neander).

[3] Ver. 10, δοκιμάζειν τὰ διαφέροντα, cf. Rom. ii. 18. "Non modo prae malis bona, sed ex bonis optima" (Bengel). "Ut probetis potiora" (Vulg.).

[4] i. 3—11.

[5] Ver. 13, ἐν ὅλῳ τῷ πραιτωρίῳ. The word, though used of royal residences in the provinces (Mark xv. 16; Acts xxiii. 35), was purposely avoided at Rome, where the ostentation of a military despotism was carefully kept out of sight (Merivale, vi. 268, *n.*). The use of *Prætorium* (properly "General's tent") for the house of the Emperor on the Palatine would have been an insult to the Romans. The contrast with τοῖς λοιποῖς πᾶσιν shows that *persons* are meant (Lightfoot, pp. 97—99; Schleusner, *s.v.*).

[6] i. 15, κηρύσσουσιν: 16, καταγγέλλουσιν. It is doubtful whether the change of word implies as much as Dean Blakesley seems to think (*Dict. of Bible*, *s.v.* Philippi). Ἐριθεία:—1, Working for hire; 2, Canvassing of hired partisans; 3, "Factiousness" Arist. *Polit.* v. 3).

mere envy and discord. The former are influenced by love to him, knowing that he is appointed for the defence of the Gospel; the latter announce Christ out of partisanship with base motives, thinking to make his bonds more galling.[1] Perhaps the day had been when Paul might have denounced them in tones of burning rebuke; but he is already Paul the prisoner, though not yet Paul the aged. He had learnt, he was learning more and more, that the wrath of man, even in a holy cause, worketh not the righteousness of God; he had risen, and was rising more and more, above every personal consideration. What mattered it whether these preachers meant only to insult him, and render his bondage yet more galling? After all, "in every way, whether with masked design or in sincerity, Christ is being preached, and therein I do—aye, and"—whatever angry feelings may try to rise within my heart—"I will rejoice."[2]

It is thus that the Apostle first tramples on the snake of any mere personal annoyance that may strive to hiss in his sad heart, and crushes it yet more vigorously with a determined effort if its hiss still tries to make itself heard. He has attained by this time to a holy resignation.

"For I know that this trouble will turn to salvation by means of your prayer, and the rich out-pouring[3] of the spirit of Jesus Christ, in accordance with my earnest desire[4] and hope that with all outspokenness, as always, so now"—he was going to say, "I may magnify Christ," but with his usual sensitive shrinking from any exaltation of himself, he substitutes the third person,[5] and says, "So now Christ shall be magnified in my body, whether by life or by death. For to me to live is Christ, and to die is gain.[6] But if life in the flesh means that I shall reap the fruit of labour . . . well, what to choose I cannot tell; but I am hard pressed by the alternatives. I desire to break up my earthly camp,[7] and be with Christ, for it is very far, far better;[8] but to abide by this earthly life is more necessary for your sakes. And I am confidently persuaded of this, that I shall bide and abide[9] with you all, for the advance and joy of your faith, that by a second stay of mine among you, you may have in me some further subject for your Christian glorying."[10]

Only in any case he bids them play worthily the part, not only of Roman, but of Christian citizens,[11] that, whether he came and saw their state, or only heard of it at a distance, he might know that they stood firm in one spirit, with one heart, fellow-wrestlers with the Faith in the Gospel, and not scared in anything by their adversaries—conduct which would be to those adversaries a proof of their ultimate perdition, and to themselves of salvation; an evidence

[1] *Leg.* ἐγείρειν (ℵ, A, B, D, F, G).

[2] i. 12—18. Perhaps the χαρήσομαι implies, "I shall in the long-run have good cause to rejoice; for," &c.

[3] Ver. 19, ἐπιχορηγία; Gal. iii. 5; 2 Cor. ix. 10; Eph. iv. 16; 2 Pet. i. 5.

[4] Ver. 20, ἀποκαραδοκίαν; Rom. viii. 19; ἐπιτεταμένη προσδοκία, Chrys. (See Jos. *B. J.* iii. 7, § 26, and Schleusner, *s.v.*)

[5] Lightfoot, *Phil.* i. 20.

[6] "Quicquid vivo, Christum vivo . . . In Paulo non Paulus vivit, sed Jesus Christus" (Bengel).

[7] 2 Cor. v. 1; iv. 6—8. On the intermediate state of the dead, see 1 Cor. xv. 51, 52.

[8] Ver. 23, πολλῷ μᾶλλον κρεῖσσον.

[9] μενῶ καὶ παραμενῶ (Lightfoot, *Phil.* i. 25).

[10] i. 19—26. καύχημα, "a ground of boasting."

[11] Ver. 27, πολιτεύεσθε.

from God Himself, since, thus, they were privileged not only to believe in Christ, but to suffer for Him, as sharers in a contest like that in which they saw Paul engaged when he was among them, and in which they knew by rumour that he was at that moment engaged.[1]

And this brings him to one main object of his letter, which was to urge on them this earnest entreaty:—

> "If, then, there be any appeal to you in Christ, if any persuasiveness in love, if any participation in the Spirit, if any one be heart and compassionateness,[2] complete my joy by thinking the same thing, having the same love, heart-united, thinking *one* thing. Nothing for partisanship, nor for empty personal vanity; but in lowliness of mind,[3] each of you thinking others his own superiors, not severally keeping your eye on your own interests, but, also severally, on the interests of others.[4]
>
> "Be of the same mind in yourselves as Christ Jesus was in Himself, who existing in the form (μορφῇ) of God, deemed not equality with God a thing for eager seizure,[5] but emptied Himself, taking the form of a slave, revealing Himself in human semblance, and being found in shape (σχήματι) as a man,[6] humbled Himself, showing Himself obedient even to death, aye, and that death—the death of the Cross."

Those words were the very climax; in striving to urge on the Philippians the example of humility and unselfishness as the only possible bases of unity, he sets before them the Divine lowliness which had descended step by step into the very abyss of degradation. He tells them of Christ's eternal possession of the attributes of God; His self-abnegation of any claim to that equality; His voluntary exinanition of His glory; His assumption of the essential attributes of a slave; His becoming a man in all external semblance; His display of obedience to His Father, even to death, and not only death, but —which might well thrill the heart of those who possessed the right of Roman citizenship, and were therefore exempt from the possibility of so frightful a degradation—death by crucifixion. Such were the elements of

[1] i. 27—30.

[2] ii. 1, εἴ τις σπλάγχνα καὶ οἰκτιρμοί. This reading of ℵ, A, B, C, D, E, F, G, K, has usually been treated as a mere barbarism. So it is grammatically; but the greatest writers, and those who most deeply stir the heart, constantly make grammar give way to the rhetoric of emotion; and if St. Paul in his eager rush of words really said it, the amanuensis did quite right to take it down. Possibly, too, the word σπλάγχνα had come to be used colloquially like a collective singular (cf. spoglia, dépouille, Bible, &c.). How entirely it had lost its first sense we may see from the daring ἐνδύσασθε . . σπλάγχνα of Col. iii. 12.

[3] A word redeemed from the catalogue of vices (Col. ii. 18; Plato, *Legg.* iv., p. 774; Epist. i. 3) into that of virtues.

[4] ii. 1—4, *leg.* σκοποῦντες (ℵ, A, B, F, G).

[5] This interpretation of the Greek Fathers is preferable to that of most of the Latin Fathers, followed by our E.V. It makes ἁρπαγμὸν ἡγεῖσθαι identical in meaning with the common phrase ἅρπαγμα ἡγ. = "to clutch at greedily." Besides, this sense is demanded by the whole context (μὴ τὰ ἑαυτῶν σκοπεῖν). This is the passage which is supposed to be borrowed from the conception of the Valentinian Æon *Sophia*, who showed an eccentric and passionate desire, προάλλεσθαι, "to dart forward;" κεκοινωνῆσθαι τῷ πατρὶ τῷ τελείῳ, "to be associated with the Perfect Father;" καταλαβεῖν τὸ μέγεθος αὐτοῦ, to grasp His greatness! (Iren. *Adv. Haer.* i. 2, 2).

[6] Baur sees Docetism here, as he saw Valentinianism in ver. 6 (*Paul.* ii. 15—21); μορφή, abiding substantial form (Rom. viii. 29; Gal. iv. 19); σχῆμα, outward transitory fashion (iii. 21; Rom. xii. 2; 1 Cor. vii. 31).

Christ's self-abasement! Yet that self-humiliation had purchased its own infinite reward, for—

"Because of it God also highly exalted Him, and freely granted Him the name above every name, that in the name of Jesus every knee should bend of heavenly and earthly and subterranean beings, and every tongue gratefully confess[1] that Jesus Christ is Lord, to the glory of the Father."[2]

Could they have a stronger incentive? In his absence, as in his presence, he exhorts them to maintain their obedience, and work out their own salvation with fear and trembling, since the will and the power to do so came alike from God.[3] Let them lay aside the murmurings and dissensions which were the main hindrance to their proving themselves blameless and sincere—children of God, uncensured in the midst of a crooked and distorted generation, among whom they appeared as stars,[4] holding forth the word of life, so as to secure to him for the day of Christ a subject of boast that he neither ran his race nor trained for his contest to no purpose.

"Nay, even if I am poured out as a libation over the sacrifice and free offering of your faith,[5] I rejoice and congratulate you all; and likewise rejoice ye too, and congratulate me."[6]

Perhaps, then, he might never come to them himself.

"But I hope in the Lord Jesus speedily to send Timothy to you, that he in turn may be cheered by a knowledge of your fortunes. For I have no emissary like him—no one who will care for your affairs with so genuine an earnestness. For," he sadly adds, "one and all seek their own interests, not those of Jesus Christ. But ye remember how *he* stood the test, since as a son for a father he slaved with me for the Gospel. Him then, at any rate, I hope to send—as soon as I get a glimpse of how it will go with me—at once. But I feel sure in the Lord that I myself too shall quickly come. I think it necessary, however, to send you Epaphroditus, my brother, and fellow-labourer, and fellow-soldier,[8] the messenger whom you sent to minister to my need, since he was ever yearning for you, and feeling despondent because you heard of his illness. Yes, he was indeed ill almost to death; but God pitied him, and not him only, but also me, that I may not have grief upon grief. With all the more eagerness, then, I send him, that you may once more rejoice on seeing him, and I may be less full of grief. Welcome him, then, in the Lord with all joy, and hold such as him in honour, because for the sake of the work he came

[1] ἐξομολογήσηται. Cf. Matt. xi. 25; Luke x. 21. [2] ii. 9—11.

[3] Vers. 12, 13, κατεργάζεσθε . . . ὁ Θεὸς γὰρ . . . Here we see the correlation of Divine grace and human effort. Cf. 1 Cor. ix. 24, τρέχετε, ἵνα καταλάβητε. Rom. ix. 16, οὐδὲ τοῦ τρέχοντος, ἀλλὰ τοῦ ἐλεοῦντος Θεοῦ.

[4] φωστῆρες. Gen. i. 14; Rev. xxi. 11. Bp. Wordsworth makes it mean "torches in the dark, narrow streets."

[5] Cf. 2 Tim. iv. 6. Compare the striking parallel in the death of Seneca, Tac. *Ann.* xv. 64. Some make ἐπὶ, not "over," but "in addition to," because Jewish libations were poured, not "on," but "round" the altar. (Jos. *Antt.* iii. 9, § 4.) But the allusion may be to Gentile customs.

[6] ii. 14—18. "We are reminded of the messenger who brought the tidings of the battle of Marathon expiring on the first threshold with these words on his lips: χαίρετε καὶ χαίρομεν (Plut. *Mor.*, p. 347)." (Lightfoot, *ad loc.*)

[7] ἀφίδω. [8] 2 Tim. ii. 3; Philem. 2.

near to death, playing the gambler with his life,[1] in order to fill up the necessary lack of your personal ministration towards me.[2]

"For the rest, my brethren, farewell, and indeed fare ye well in the Lord.[3] To write the same things to you is not irksome to *me*, and for *you* it is safe."[4]

Then came a sudden break.[5] It seems clear that the Apostle had intended at this point to close the letter, and to close it with a repetition of the oft-repeated exhortation—for which he half apologises—to greater peace and unity among themselves.[6] It is quite possible that these last words might have run on, as they do in the First Epistle to the Thessalonians, to a considerable length;[7] but here something occurred to break the sequence of the Apostle's thoughts. When he returned to his dictation he began a digression far more severe and agitated in its tone than the rest of his letter, and he does not resume the broken thread of his previous topic till the second verse of the fourth chapter, where, instead of any general exhortation, he makes a direct personal appeal.

As to the nature of the interruption we cannot even conjecture. It may have been merely a change of the soldier who was on guard; but in the exigencies of a life which, though that of a prisoner, was yet fully occupied, many circumstances may have caused a little delay before everything could be ready, and the amanuensis once more at his post. And meanwhile something had occurred which had ruffled the Apostle's soul—nay, rather which had disturbed it to its inmost depths. That something can only have been a conflict, in some form or other, with Judaising teachers. Something must either have thrown him in contact with, or brought to his notice, the character and doctrine of false Apostles, of the same class as he had encountered at Corinth, and heard of in the Churches of Galatia. Once more the thoughts and tone of the Epistle to the Galatians, the truths and arguments of the Epistle to the Romans, swept in a storm of emotion over his soul; and it is with a burst of indignation, stronger for the moment than he had ever before expressed, that, on once more continuing his letter, he bids Timothy write to the still uncontaminated Church:—

"Beware of the dogs![8] Beware of the bad workers![9] Beware of the concision party!"[10]

[1] παραβολευσάμενος (ℵ, A, B, D, E, F, G). It is used especially of one who endangers his life by attendance on the sick (*parabolani*). (Wetst. *ad loc.*)

[2] ii. 19—30.

[3] I have tried to keep up the two meanings of "farewell" and "rejoice."

[4] iii. 1.

[5] Ewald, *Sendschr.*, p. 438.

[6] This is the simplest and most reasonable explanation of τὰ αὐτὰ γράφειν, and accords with St. Paul's custom of a concluding warning (1 Cor. xvi. 22; Gal. vi. 15, &c.), or it may refer to the topic of joy (i. 18, 25; ii. 17; iv. 4). It has led to all sorts of hypotheses. St. Paul had doubtless written other letters to the Philippians (the natural though not the necessary inference from καὶ ἀπὼν ὑμῖν ἔγραψεν ἐπιστολάς—Polyc. *ad Phil.* 3), but these words do not show it. (*V. supra*, p. 594.)

[7] 1 Thess. iv. 1.

[8] Generally used of Gentiles and Hellenising Jews (Matt. xv. 26), involving a coarse shade of reproach (Deut. xxiii. 18; Rev. xxii. 15). We cannot be sure of the allusion here.

[9] Cf. 2 Cor. xi. 13; Matt. xxiii. 15.

[10] περιτομή, κατατομή would be in Latin "circumcisi," "decisi," (*Curti*, Hor. *Sat.* i.

The words are intensely severe. He implies, "They call us dogs, but they, not we, are the veritable dogs; and we, not they, are the true circumcision. Their circumcision is but concision—a mere mutilation of the flesh. We serve by the Spirit of God[1]—they serve ordinances; we boast in Christ Jesus—they do but trust in the flesh." And why should they put themselves into rivalry with him? If the external were anything in which to place confidence, he could claim it in even a greater degree than any one else. He had been circumcised when eight days old; he was an Israelite, and of one of the noblest tribes of Israel, and not a mere Hellenist, but a Hebrew—aye, and a Hebrew of Hebrews;[2] and—to pass from hereditary to personal topics of carnal boasting—as regards Law, he was a Pharisee; as regards Judaic enthusiasm, he had even persecuted the Church; as regards legal righteousness, he had proved himself above all reproach. Things like these were at one time the gains which he reckoned that life had brought him, but now for Christ's sake he had got to count them as a loss.

"Aye, and more than that, I even count all things to be a loss for the sake of the transcendence of the knowledge of Christ Jesus, my Lord, for whose sake I was mulcted of all things,[3] and I regard them as refuse flung to dogs,[4] that I may gain Christ, and may be found in Him, not having any righteousness of mine which is of Law, but that which is by means of faith in Christ, that which comes of God, which is based on faith,[5] that I may know Him, and the power of His resurrection, and the fellowship of His sufferings, being conformed to His death, if so be I may attain to the resurrection (I mean not the general resurrection, but the resurrection of those that are Christ's) from the dead."[6]

And yet, as he goes on to warn them—though he had all this pregnant ground for confidence in externalisms, though he had rejected it all for the sake of Christ as mere foul and worthless rubbish, though his whole trust was now in Christ's righteousness, and not in his own—so far was he even still from the secure and vaunting confidence of their adversaries, that he did not at all consider that he had grasped the prize, or had been already perfected:—

"But I press forward to see if I may even grasp—for which purpose[7] I too was grasped by Christ. Brothers, I do not reckon myself to have grasped; but one thing—forgetting the things behind, and leaning eagerly forward for the things before, I press forward to the goal for the prize of my heavenly calling of God in Christ Jesus."

He is like one of those eager charioteers of whom his guardsmen so often

9, 70); in German, *Beschnittene, Zerschnittene.* "Concision" means circumcision regarded as a mere mutilation. Cf. Acts vii. 51; Rom. iii. 25–29; Col. ii. 11; Ezek. xliv. 7; Deut. x. 16.

[1] iii. 3, λατρεύοντες, *intr.* Luke ii. 37; Acts xxvi. 7.

[2] iii. 5. A proselyte, son of a proselyte, was called a *Ger ben-ger*, but Paul was עברי בן עברי. (*Pirke Abhôth*, v.)

[3] May this refer to some sudden loss of all earthly means of living at his conversion?

[4] Ver. 8, σκύβαλα. In derivation perhaps from root σκωρ, but in usage = κυσίβαλα (Suid.). Some prefer the technical sense of the word = "excrementa" (Theodoret).

[5] Ver. 9, διὰ πίστεως . . . ἐκ Θεοῦ . . . ἐπὶ τῇ πίστει.

[6] iii. 2—11, *leg.* τὴν ἐκ νεκρῶν (א, A, B, D, E).

[7] ἐφ᾽ ᾧ may also mean "because" (2 Cor. v. 4); or there may be an ellipse of the accusative after καταλάβω, as in the R.V.

talked to him when they had returned from the contests in the Circus Maximus, and joined their shouts to those of the myriads who cheered their favourite colours—leading forward in his flying car, bending over the shaken rein and the goaded steed, forgetting everything—every peril, every competitor, every circling of the meta in the rear, as he pressed on for the goal by which sat the judges with the palm garlands that formed the prize.[1]

"Let all, then, of us who are full grown in spiritual privileges have this mind; then if in any other respect ye think otherwise[2] than ye should, this shall God reveal to you; only walk in the same path to the point whereunto we once reached."[3]

And as a yet further warning against any danger of their abusing the doctrine of the free gift of grace by antinomian practices, he adds—

"Show yourselves, brethren, imitators of me, and mark those who walk as ye have us for an example. For many walk about whom I often used to tell you, and now tell you even with tears—the enemies of the cross of Christ, whose end is destruction, whose god their belly, and their glory in their shame, men minding earthly things. For our real citizenship is in heaven, whence also we anxiously await as a Saviour the Lord Jesus Christ, who shall change the fashion of the body of our abasement so as to be conformable to the body of His glory,[4] according to the efficacy of His power to subject also every existing thing unto Himself. So, my brethren, beloved and longed for, my joy and crown, so stand ye firm in the Lord, beloved."[5]

Then after this long digression, which, beginning in strong indignation, calms itself down to pathetic appeal, he once more takes up the exhortation to unity with which he had intended to conclude. He entreats two ladies, Euodia and Syntyche, to unity of mind in Christ, and he also affectionately asks Syzygus[6]—on whose name of "yokefellow" he plays, by calling him a genuine yokefellow—a yokefellow in heart as well as in name[7]—to assist these ladies in making up their quarrel, which was all the more deplorable because of the worth of them both, seeing that they wrestled with him in the Gospel with Clement too, and the rest of his fellow-workers whose names are in the Book of Life.[8]

1 "Non progredi est regredi" (Aug.).

2 ἑτέρως, used euphemistically (= κακῶς, Od. i. 234, θάτερον = τὸ κακόν). So the Hebrew "acher." The meaning is, If you have the heart of the matter, God will enlighten you in non-essentials.

3 iii. 12—16, omit κανόνι, τὸ αὐτὸ φρονεῖν (א, A, B).

4 Ver. 21, μετασχηματίσει . . . σύμμορφον; ii. 6.

5 iii. 17—iv. 1.

6 iv. 3, γνήσιε Σύζυγε. Clement of Alexandria seems to have taken the word to mean Paul's *wife*, οὐκ ὀκνεῖ τὴν αὐτοῦ προσαγορεύειν σύζυγον ἣν οὐ περιεκόμιζεν (*Strom.* iii. 6, 53), cf. Euseb. *H. E.* iii. 30. Renan (p. 145) thinks it was Lydia. Why is she not saluted? If Lydia be merely a Gentilic name she may be one of those two ladies, or she may have been dead.

7 Schwegler thinks that this is intended to be taken as an allusion to the Apostle Peter! The play on names is quite in St. Paul's manner. The only difficulty is that Syzygus does not occur elsewhere as a name.

8 iv. 2, 3. Baur's wild conjecture (?) about Clement—that the whole story of his Romish Episcopate is invented to give respectability to the early Christians, by insinuating

"Fare ye well always; again I will say, fare ye well. Let your reasonableness be recognised by all men. Be anxious about nothing, but in everything, in your general and special prayers, with thanksgiving, let your requests be made known before God. Then shall the peace of God, which surpasseth all understanding, keep sentry over your hearts, and the devices of your hearts, in Christ Jesus.

"Finally, brethren, whatsoever things are real, whatsoever things are awful, whatsoever things are just, whatsoever things are pure, whatsoever things are amiable, whatsoever things are winning, if 'virtue,'[1] if 'honour,' have a real meaning for you, on these things meditate. The things which ye both learned and received, both heard and saw in me, these things do, and the God of peace shall be with you."[2]

Then comes the warm yet delicate expression of his heartfelt gratitude to them for the pecuniary contribution by which now, for the fourth time, they, and they only, had supplied the wants which he could no longer meet by manual labour.

"One word more:—I rejoiced in the Lord greatly, that now once more your thought on my behalf blossomed afresh.[3] In this matter ye were indeed bearing me in mind, but ye were without opportunity. Not that I speak with reference to deficiency, for I learnt to be always independent in existing circumstances. I know how both to be humiliated, and I know how to abound. In everything and in all things I have been initiated how both to be satisfied and to be hungry, both to abound and to be in need. I am strong for everything in Him who gives me power. Still ye did well in making yourselves partakers in my affliction. And ye know as well as I do, Philippians, that in the beginning of the Gospel, when I went forth from Macedonia, no Church communicated with me as regards giving and receiving, except ye only, for even in Thessalonica both once and twice ye sent to my need—not that I am on the look-out for the gift, but I am on the look-out for the fruit which abounds to your account. Now, however, I have all things to the full,[4] and I abound. I have been fulfilled by receiving from Epaphroditus the gifts you sent, an odour of sweet fragrance, a sacrifice acceptable, well-pleasing to God.[5] But my God shall fulfil all your need according to His riches, in glory, in Christ Jesus. Now to our God and Father be glory for ever and ever. Amen.[6]

"Salute every saint in Christ Jesus. The brethren with me salute you. All the saints salute you, and especially[7] those of Cæsar's household.[8]

"The grace of our Lord Jesus Christ be with your spirit."

his identity with the Consular Flavius Clemens, and that the whole of this Epistle is forged to lead up to this passing allusion—looks almost tame beside Volkmar's hypothesis (?) about Euodia and Syntyche—viz., that Euodia = "orthodoxy," the Petrine party, and Syntyche, "the partner" = the Pauline party! Clement, though a Philippian, *may possibly* be identical with "Clement of Rome" (Orig. *in Joann.* i. 29; Euseb. *H. E.* iii. 15, &c.); we cannot even say "probably," because the name is *exceedingly* common.

[1] iv. 8, ἀρετη, here alone in St. Paul.

[2] iv. 4—9.

[3] Ver. 10, ἀνεθάλετε, literally, "ye blossomed again to think on my behalf." Chrysostom says, ὅτι πρότερον ὄντες ἀνθηροὶ ἐξηράνθησαν, which is to touch the metaphor with an Ithuriel spear (*Repullulastis*, Aug.; *Refloruistis*, Vulg.).

[4] Ver. 18, ἀπέχω. (Matt. vi. 2.) The word is used for "giving receipt in full."

[5] Gen. viii. 21.

[6] iv. 10—20.

[7] Why especially? It is impossible to say.

[8] It should be borne in mind that these slaves would be counted by *thousands*—*atrienses*, *cubicularii*, *secretarii*, *lectores*, *introductores*, *nomenclatores*, *dispensatores*, *silentiarii* (to keep the others quiet), &c. &c., and even slaves to tell the master the names of his other slaves! We read of Romans who had 20,000 slaves. Four thousand was no very extraordinary number (Sen. *De Vit. Beat.* 17; Plin. *H. N.* xxxiii. 10; Athen. vi., p. 272).

No great future awaited the Philippian Church. Half a century later, Ignatius passed through Philippi with his "ten leopards," on his way to martyrdom; and Polycarp wrote to the Church a letter which, like that of St. Paul, is full of commendations. Little more is heard of it. Its site is still occupied by the wretched village of Filibidjek, but in spite of the fair promise of its birth, "the Church of Philippi has," in the inscrutable counsel of God, "lived without a history, and perished without a memorial."[1]

CHAPTER XLVIII.

GNOSTICISM IN THE GERM.

Οὐ, κάθαπερ ἄν τις εἰκάσειε, ἀνθρώποις ὑπηρέτην τινὰ πέμψας ἢ ἄγγελον ἀλλ' αὐτὸν τὸν τεχνίτην καὶ δημιουργὸν τῶν ὅλων.—Ep. ad Diognet. 7.

THE remaining three of the Epistles of the Captivity were written within a short time of each other, and were despatched by the same messengers. Tychicus was the bearer of those to the Ephesians and Colossians. Onesimus, who naturally took the letter to Philemon, was sent at the same time with him, as appears from the mention of his name in the Epistle to the Colossians. In both of these latter Epistles there is also a message for Archippus.

There is nothing but internal evidence to decide which of these letters was written first. The letter to Philemon was, however, a mere private appendage to the Epistle to the Colossians, which may have been written at any time. The letter to this Church must claim the priority over the circular Epistle which is generally known as the Epistle to the Ephesians. The reason for this opinion is obvious—the Epistle to the Colossians was called forth by a special need, the other Epistle was not. It is in exact psychological accordance with the peculiarities of St. Paul's mind and style that if, after writing a letter which was evoked by particular circumstances, and led to the development of particular truths, he utilised the opportunity of its despatch to send another letter, which had no such immediate object, the tones of the first letter would still vibrate in the second. When he had discharged his immediate duty to the Church of Colossæ, the topics dwelt upon in writing to the neighbouring Churches would be sure to bear a close resemblance to those which had most recently been occupying his thoughts. Even apart from special information, St. Paul may have seen the desirability of warning Ephesus and its dependencies against a peril which was infusing its subtle presence within so short a distance from them; and it was then natural that his language to them should be marked by the very differences which separate the Epistle to the Colossians from that to the Ephesians. The former is specific, concrete, and polemical; the latter is abstract, didactic, general. The same words and phrases predominate in both; but the resemblances are far more marked and numerous in the

[1] Lightfoot, p. 64.

practical exhortations than in the doctrinal statements. In the Epistle to the Colossians he is primarily occupied with the refutation of an error; in that to the Ephesians he is absorbed in the rapturous development of an exalted truth. The main theme of the Colossians is the Person of Christ; that of the Ephesians is the life of Christ manifested in the living energy of His Church.[1] In the former, Christ is the "Plenitude," the synthesis and totality of every attribute of God; in the latter, the ideal Church, as the body of Christ, is the Plenitude, the recipient of all the fulness of Him who filleth all things with all.[2] Christ's person is most prominent in the Colossians; Christ's body, the Church of Christ, in the Ephesians.

The genuineness of these two letters has been repeatedly and formidably assailed, and the grounds of the attack are not by any means so fantastic as those on which other letters have been rejected as spurious. To dwell at length on the external evidence is no part of my scheme, and the grounds on which the internal evidence seems to me decisive in their favour, even after the fullest and frankest admission of all counter-difficulties, will best appear when we have considered the events out of which they spring, and which at once shaped, and are sufficient to account for, the peculiarities by which they are marked.

Towards the close of St. Paul's Roman imprisonment, when his approaching liberation seemed so all but certain that he even requests Philemon to be getting a lodging in readiness for him, he received a visit from Epaphras of Colossæ. To him, perhaps, had been granted the distinguished honour of founding Churches not only in his native town, but also in Laodicea and Hierapolis, which lie within a distance of sixteen miles from each other in the valley of the Lycus. That remarkable stream resembles the Anio in clothing the country through which it flows with calcareous deposits; and in some parts of its course, especially near Colossæ, it flowed under natural bridges of gleaming travertine deposited by its own waters, the course of which was frequently modified by this peculiarity, and by the terrific earthquakes to which the valley has always been liable. The traveller who followed the course of the Lycus in a south-eastward direction from the valley of the Mæander into which it flows, would first observe on a plateau, which rises high above its northern bank, the vast and splendid city of Hierapolis, famous as the birthplace of him who in Nicopolis

> "Taught Arrian when Vespasian's brutal son
> Cleared Rome of what most shamed him"[3]—

and famous also for the miraculous properties of the mephitic spring whose exhalations could be breathed in safety by the priests of Cybele alone. About

[1] Col. ii. 19; Eph. iv. 16.

[2] Col. i. 19; ii. 9; Eph. i. 23; iii. 19; iv. 13. (John i. 14, 16.) German writers express the difference by saying that *Christlichkeit* is more prominent in the Colossians, *Kirchlichkeit* in the Ephesians.

[3] Epictetus was a contemporary of the Apostle. As to the Christian tinge of his Stoic speculations, see my *Seekers after God*.

six miles further, upon the southern bank of the river, he would see Laodicea, the populous and haughty metropolis of the "Cibyratic jurisdiction," which alone of the cities of proconsular Asia was wealthy and independent enough to rebuild its streets and temples out of its own resources, when, within a year of the time at which these letters were written, an earthquake had shaken it.[1] Passing up the valley about ten miles further, he might before sunset reach Colossæ, a town far more anciently famous than either, but which had fallen into comparative decay, and was now entirely eclipsed by its thriving and ambitious neighbours.[2]

This remarkable valley and these magnificent cities, St. Paul, strange to say, had never visited. Widely as the result of his preaching at Ephesus had been disseminated throughout Asia, his labours for the Ephesian Church had been so close and unremitting as to leave him no leisure for wider missionary enterprise.[3] And although Jews abounded in these cities, the divinely guided course of his previous travels had not brought him into this neighbourhood. It is true that St. Luke vaguely tells us that in the second missionary journey St. Paul had passed through "the Phrygian and Galatian country,"[4] and that in the shifting ethnological sense of the term the cities of the Lycus-valley might be regarded as Phrygian. But the expression seems rather to mean that the course of his journey lay on the ill-defined marches of these two districts, far to the north and east of the Lycus. In his third journey his natural route from the cities of Galatia to Ephesus would take him down the valleys of the Hermus and Cayster, and to the north of the mountain range of Messogis which separates them from the Lycus and Mæander. From St. Paul's own expression it seems probable that the Churches in these three cities had been founded by the labours of Epaphras, and that they had never "seen his face in the flesh" at the time when he wrote these Epistles, though it is not impossible that he subsequently visited them.[5]

And yet he could not but feel the deepest interest in their welfare, because, indirectly though not directly, he had been indeed their founder. Ephesus, as we have seen, was a centre of commerce, of worship, and of political procedure; and among the thousands, "both Jews and Greeks," "almost throughout all Asia," who heard through his preaching the word of the Lord,[6] must have been Philemon,[7] his son, Archippus, and Epaphras, and Nymphas, who were leading ministers of the Lycus Churches.[8]

And there was a special reason why St. Paul should write to the Colossian Christians. Philemon, who resided there, had a worthless slave named

[1] Tac. *Ann.* xiv. 27, "propriis opibus revaluit." Rev. iii. 14. Cicero, who resided there as Proconsul of Cilicia, frequently refers to it in his letters.

[2] Now Chonos. Dr. Lightfoot calls it "the least important Church to which any Epistle of St. Paul was addressed" (*Col.*, p. 16).

[3] Acts xx. 31.

[4] Acts xvi. 6. In Acts xviii. 23 the order is "the Galatian country and Phrygia." In the former instance he was travelling from Antioch in Pisidia to Troas; in the latter from Antioch in Syria to Ephesus.

[5] Col. i. 4, 6, 9; ii. 1.

[6] Acts xix. 10—26.

[7] Philem. 1, 2.

[8] Col. iv. 12, 13, 15.

Onesimus—a name which, under the circumstances, naturally lent itself to a satiric play of words; for instead of being "Beneficial," he had been very much the reverse, having first (apparently) robbed his master, and then run away from him. Rome was in ancient days the most likely place to furnish a secure refuge to a guilty fugitive, and thither, even more than to modern London, drifted inevitably the vice and misery of the world. Philemon was a Christian, and some access of wretchedness, or danger of starvation, may have driven the runaway slave to fling himself on the compassion of the Christian teacher, whom he may have heard and seen when he attended his master on some great gala-day at Ephesus. The kind heart of Paul was ever open; he had a deep and ready sympathy for the very lowest and poorest of the human race, because in the very lowest and poorest he saw those "for whom Christ died." His own sufferings, too, had taught him the luxury of aiding the sufferings of others, and he took the poor dishonest fugitive to his heart, and was the human instrument by which that change was wrought in him which converted the "*non tressis agaso*" into a brother beloved. But Onesimus was still legally the debtor and the slave of Philemon; and Paul, ever obedient to the law, felt it a duty to send him back. He placed him under the protecting care of Tychicus of Ephesus, and sent him with a letter which could not fail to ensure his pardon. It was necessary, therefore, for him to write to a citizen of Colossæ, and another circumstance determined him to write also to the Colossian Church.

This was the strange and sad intelligence which he heard from Epaphras. They had many opportunities for intercourse, for, either literally or metaphorically, Epaphras shared his captivity, and did not at once return to his native city. In his conversations with St. Paul he told him of an insidious form of error unlike any which the Apostle had hitherto encountered. The vineyard of the Lord's planting seemed, alas! to resemble the vineyards of earth in the multiplicity of perils which it had to overcome before it could bring forth its fruit. Now it was the little foxes that spoiled its vines; now the wild boar which broke down its hedge; and now, under the blighting influence of neglect and infertile soil, its unpruned branches only brought forth the clusters of Gomorrah. An erroneous tendency, as yet germinant and undeveloped, but one of which the prescient eye of St. Paul saw all the future deadliness, had insensibly crept into these youthful Churches, and, although they only knew the Apostle by name, he felt himself compelled to exert the whole force of his authority and reasoning to check so perilous an influence. Doubtless Epaphras had expressly sought him for the sake of advice and sympathy, and would urge the Apostle to meet with distinct warnings and clear refutation the novel speculations with which he may have felt himself incompetent to cope.

The new form of error was partly Judaic, for it made distinctions in meats, attached importance to new moons and sabbaths,[1] and insisted upon the value

[1] Col. ii. 16.

of circumcision, if not upon its actual necessity.[1] Yet it did not, as a whole, resemble the Galatian Judaism, nor did it emanate, like the opposition at Antioch, from a party in Jerusalem, nor was it complicated, like the Corinthian schisms, with personal hostility to the authority of St. Paul. Its character was Judaic, not so much essentially as virtually; not, that is, from any special sympathy with national and Levitical Hebraism, but rather because there were certain features of Judaism which were closely analogous to those of other Oriental religions, and which commanded a wide sympathy in the Eastern world.

We must judge of the distinctive colour of the dawning heresy quite as much from the truths by which St. Paul strives to check its progress, as by those of its tenets on which he directly touches.[2] In warning the Colossians respecting it, he bids them be on their guard against allowing themselves to be plundered by a particular teacher, whose so-called philosophy and empty deceit were more in accordance with human traditions and secular rudiments than with the truth of Christ. The hollow and misguiding system of this teacher, besides the importance which it attached to a ceremonialism which at the best was only valuable as a shadow of a symbol, tried further to rob its votaries of the prize of their Christian race by representing God as a Being so far removed from them that they could only approach Him through a series of angelic intermediates. It thus ignored the precious truth of Christ's sole mediatorial dignity, and turned humility itself into a vice by making it a cloak for inflated and carnal intellectualism. In fact, it was nothing more nor less than pride which was thus aping humility; and, in endeavouring to enforce an ignoble self-abrogation of that direct communion with God through Christ which is the Christian's most imperial privilege, it not only thrust all kinds of inferior agencies between the soul and Him, but also laid down a number of rules and dogmas which were but a set of new Mosaisms without the true Mosaic sanctions. Those rules were, from their very nature, false, transient, and trivial. They paraded a superfluous self-abasement, and insisted on a hard asceticism, but at the same time they dangerously flattered the soul with a semblance of complicated learning, while they were found to be in reality valueless as any remedy against self-indulgence. That these ascetic practices and dreamy imaginations were accompanied by a pride which arrogated to itself certain mysteries as an exclusive possession from which the vulgar intellect must be kept aloof; that, while professing belief in Christ, the Colossian mystic represented Him as one among many beings interposed between God and man; that he regarded matter in general and the body in particular as something in which evil was necessarily immanent,[3] seem to result from the Christology of the Epistle, which is more especially developed in one particular direction than

[1] Col. ii. 11.

[2] They were "Gnostic Ebionites," Baur; "Cerinthians," Mayerhoff; "Christian Essenism in its progress to Gnosticism," Lipsius; "A connecting link between Essenes and Cerinthians," Nitzsch; "Ascetics and Theosophists of the Essene school," Holtzmann; "Precursors of the Christian Essenes," Ritschl. (Pfleiderer, ii. 98.)

[3] So, too, Philo regarded the body as the Egypt of the soul. (*Ques. rer. div. haer.* 518.)

we find it to be in any of St. Paul's previous writings. Already, in writing to the Corinthians, he had said that "if he had ever known Christ after the flesh, from henceforth he knew Him no more," and in this Epistle the Person of our Lord as the Eternal Co-existent Son is represented in that divine aspect the apprehension of which is a boon infinitely more transcendent than a human and external knowledge of Jesus in His earthly humiliation. And yet—as though to obviate beforehand any Cerinthian attempt to distinguish between Jesus the man of sorrows and Christ the risen Lord, between Jesus the crucified and Christ the Eternal Word—he is, even in this Epistle, emphatic in the statement that these are one.[1] To say that there is any change in St. Paul's fundamental conception of Christ would be demonstrably false, since even the juxtaposition of our Lord Jesus Christ with God the Father as the source of all grace, and the declaration that all things, and we among them, exist solely through Him, are statements of His divinity in St. Paul's earliest Epistles[2] as strong as anything which could be subsequently added. But hitherto the Apostle had been led to speak of Him mainly as the Judge of the quick and dead, in the Epistles to the Thessalonians; as the invisible Head and Ruler of the Church in those to the Corinthians; as the Author of all spiritual freedom from ceremonial bondage, and the Redeemer of the world from the yoke of sin and death, as in those to the Romans and Galatians; as the Saviour, the Raiser from the dead, the Life of all life, the Source of all joy and peace, in that to the Philippians. A new phase of His majesty had now to be brought into prominence—one which was indeed involved in every doctrine which St. Paul had taught concerning Him as part of a Gospel which he had received by revelation, but which no external circumstance had ever yet led him to explain in all its clearness. This was the doctrine of Christ, as the Eternal, Preexisting, yet Incarnate Word. He had now to speak of Him as One in whom and by whom the Universe—and that not only its existing condition but its very matter and its substance—are divinely hallowed, so that there is nothing irredeemable, nothing inherently antagonistic to Holiness, either in matter or in the body of man; as One in whom dwells the "plenitude" of the divine perfections, so that no other angelic being can usurp any share of God which is not found in Him; as One who is the *only* Potentate, the *only* Mediator, the *only* Saviour, the Head of the Body which is the Church, and the Source of its life through every limb. And the expression of this truth was rendered necessary by error. The Colossian teachers were trying to supplement Christianity, theoretically by a deeper wisdom, practically by a more abstentious holiness. It was the beautiful method of St. Paul to combat false doctrine as little as possible by denunciation and controversy (though these two have at times their necessary place), and as much as possible by the presentation of the counter truth. We are able, therefore, to find the theological errors of

[1] i. 20, 22; ii. 6.

[2] 1 Thess. i. 1; v. 28; 1 Cor. viii. 6; 2 Cor. iv. 4; v. 19; Rom. ix. 5. Even Renan fully admit this (*St. Paul*, x. 274).

the Colossians reflected in the positive theology which is here developed in order to counteract them. In the moral and practical discussions of the Epistle we see the true substitute for that extravagant and inflating asceticism which had its origin partly in will-worship, ostentatious humility, and trust in works, and partly in mistaken conceptions as to the inherency of evil in the body of man. St. Paul points out to them that the deliverance from sin was to be found, not in dead rules and ascetic rigours, which have a fatal tendency to weaken the will, while they fix the imagination so intently on the very sins against which they are intended as a remedy, as too often to lend to those very sins a more fatal fascination—but in that death to sin which is necessarily involved in the life hid with Christ in God. From that new life—that resurrection from the death of sin—obedience to the moral laws of God, and faithfulness in common relations of life, result, not as difficult and meritorious acts, but as the natural energies of a living impulse in the heart which beats no longer with its own life but with the life of Christ.

Alike, then, from the distinct notices and the negative indications of the Epistle we can reproduce with tolerable clearness the features of the Colossian heresy, and we at once trace in it the influence of that Oriental theosophy, those mystical speculations, those shadowy cosmogonies and moral aberrations which marked the hydra-headed forms of the systems afterwards summed up in the one word Gnosticism. This very circumstance has been the main ground for impugning the genuineness of the Epistle. It is asserted that Gnosticism belongs to a generation later, and that these warnings are aimed at the followers of Cerinthus, who did not flourish until after Paul was dead, or even at those of Valentinus, the founder of a Gnostic system in the second century. In support of this view it is asserted that the Epistle abounds in un-Pauline phrases, in words which occur in no other Epistle, and in technical Gnostic expressions, such as plenitude, mystery, wisdom, knowledge, powers, light, darkness. Now, that Gnosticism as a well-developed system belongs to a later period is admitted; but the belief that the acceptance of the Epistle as genuine involves an anachronism, depends solely on the assumption that Gnostic expressions[1] may not have been prevalent, and Gnostic tendencies secretly at work, long before they were crystallised into formal heresies. As far as these expressions are concerned, some of them are not technical at all until a Gnostic meaning is read into them, and others, like "knowledge" (*gnôsis*), &c., "plenitude" (*plerôma*), though beginning to be technical, are used in a sense materially different from that which was afterwards attached to them. As for the asserted *traces* of doctrines distinctly and systematically Gnostic, it is a matter of *demonstration* that they are found, both isolated and combined, during the Apostolic age, and before it, as well as afterwards. The esoteric exclusiveness which jealously guarded the arcana of its mysteries

[1] The use of these expressions is admirably illustrated by some remarks of Tertullian, *Adv. Praxeam.*, 8. He has used the word προβολὴ, and anticipating the objection that the word is tainted with Valentinianism, he replies that Heresy has taken that word from Truth to mould it after its own likeness.

from general knowledge; the dualism which became almost Manichæan in the attempt to distinguish between the good and evil impulses; the notion that God's "plenitude" could only flow out in a multitude of imperfect emanations; the consequent tendency to exalt and worship a gradation of angelic hierarchies; the rules and purifications which were designed to minimise all infection from the inevitable contact with matter; the attempt to explain the inherency of evil in matter by vain and fanciful cosmogonies; the multiplication of observances; the reduction of food and drink to the barest elements, excluding all forms of animal life; the suspicious avoidance or grudging toleration of marriage as a pernicious and revolting necessity;—these are found in various Oriental religions, and may be traced in philosophies which originated among the Asiatic Greeks. They find a distinct expression in the doctrines of the Essenes.[1] Their appearance in the bosom of a Christian community was indeed new; but there was nothing new in their existence; nothing in them with which, as *extraneous* forms of error, St. Paul's Jewish and Gentile studies—were it only his knowledge of Essene tenets and Alexandrian speculations—had not made him perfectly familiar. That they should appear in a Phrygian Church, powerfully exposed to Jewish influences, and yet consisting of Gentiles trained amid the mysteries of a ceremonial nature worship, and accustomed to the utterances of a speculative philosophy[2] must have been painful to St. Paul, but could not have been surprising. The proof that these forms of heresy might have been expected to appear is rendered yet more cogent by the knowledge that, within a very short period of this time, they actually *did* appear in a definite and systematic form, in the heresy of Corinthus, with whom St. John himself is said to have come into personal collision.[3] And under these circumstances, so far from seeing a mark of spuriousness, we rather deduce an incidental argument in favour of the genuineness of the Epistle from the nature of the errors which we find that it is intended to denounce. Many critics have been eager to prove that St. Paul could not have written it, because they reject that fundamental doctrine of the Eternal Divinity of Christ, of which this group of Epistles is so impregnable a bulwark; yet this was so evidently the main article in the belief of St. Paul

[1] Neander (*Planting*, p. 323, *seq.*) points out the Phrygian propensity to the mystical and magical as indicated by the worship of Cybele, by Montanism, by the tendencies condemned at the council of Laodicea, and by the existence of Athinganians in the ninth century, &c. Perhaps the incipient heresies of Asia might be most briefly characterised as the germ of Gnosticism evolved by Essene and Oriental speculations on the origin of evil. These speculations led to baseless angelologies injurious to the supremacy of Christ; to esoteric exclusiveness injurious to the universality of the Gospel; and to mistaken asceticism injurious to Christian freedom. Cloudy theories generated unwise practices. It is interesting to observe that some at least of the same tendencies are traceable in St. John's rebukes to the seven Churches. Compare Rev. iii. 14 and Col. i. 15—18; Rev. iii. 21 and Col. iii. 1, Eph. ii. 6. Some interesting Zoroastrian parallels are quoted from Bleeck by the Rev. J. Ll. Davies in his essay on traces of foreign elements in these Epistles (*Ephes.* pp. 141—9). He says "the decay and mixture of old creeds in the Asiatic intellect had created a soil of 'loose fertility—a footfall there sufficing to upturn to the warm air half-germinating' theosophies."

[2] Lightfoot, *Col.* pp. 114—179.

[3] Neander, *Planting*, i. 325; *Ch. Hist.* ii. 42; Lightfoot, *Col.*, p. 107, *seq.*

that the proof of its being so would hardly be weakened, even if these Epistles could be banished from the canon to which hostile criticism has only succeeded in showing more conclusively that they must still be considered to belong.

The Christology, then, of these Epistles is nothing more than the systematic statement of that revelation respecting the nature of Jesus, which is implicitly contained in all that is written of Him in the New Testament;[1] and the so-called "Gnosticism" with which these Epistles deal is nothing more than a form of error—a phase of the crafty working of systematic deception—which is common to the intellectual, moral, and spiritual aberrations of all ages and countries. It is found in the Zend Avesta; it is found in Philo; it is found in Neoplatonism; it is found in the Kabbala; it is found in Valentinus. Abject sacerdotalism, superstitious ritual, extravagant asceticism, the faithlessness which leads men to abandon the privilege of immediate access to God, and to thrust between the soul and its One Mediator all sorts of human and celestial mediators; the ambition which builds upon the unmanly timidity of its votaries its own secure and tyrannous exaltation; the substitution of an easy externalism for the religion of the heart; the fancy that God cares for such barren self-denials as neither deepen our own spirituality nor benefit our neighbour; the elaboration of unreasonable systems which give the pompous name of Theology to vain and verbal speculations drawn by elaborate and untenable inferences from isolated expressions of which the antinomies are unfathomable, and of which the true exegetic history is deliberately ignored; the oscillating reactions which lead in the same sect and in even the same individual to the opposite extremes of rigid scrupulosity and antinomian licence:[2]—these are the germs not of one but of all the heresies; these are more or less the elements of nearly every false religion. The ponderous technicalities of the systematiser; the interested self-assertions of the priest; the dreamy speculations of the mystic; the Pharisaic conceit of the externalist; the polemical shibboleths of the sectarian; the spiritual pride and narrow one-sidedness of the self-tormentor; the ruinous identification of that saving faith which is a union with Christ and a participation of His life with the theoretic acceptance of a number of formulæ:—all these elements have from the earliest dawn of Christianity mingled in the tainted stream of heresy their elements of ignorance, self-interest, and error. In their dark features we detect a common resemblance.

"Facies non omnibus una
Nec diversa tamen, quales decet esse sororum."

There was Gnosticism in the days of St. Paul as there is Gnosticism now, though neither then nor now is it recognised under that specific name.

We may, therefore, pass to the study of the Epistle with the strongest

[1] "Les plus énergiques expressions de l'Epître aux Colossiens ne font qu'enchérir un peu sur celles des Epîtres antérieures" (Renan, *St. P.* x.).

[2] Clem. Alex. *Strom.* iii. 5; 2 Tim. iii. 1—7; Jude 8; Rev. ii. 14, 20—22.

conviction that there is no expression in it which, on these grounds at any rate, disproves its genuineness. None but Paul could have written it. To say that it is un-Pauline in doctrine is to make an arbitrary assertion, since it states no single truth which is not involved in his previous teachings. The fact that it is a splendid development of those teachings, or rather an expansion in the statement of them, in order to meet new exigencies, is simply in its favour. Nor do I see how any one familiar with the style and mind of St. Paul can fail to recognise his touch in this Epistle. That the style should lack the fire and passion—the "*meras flammas*"—of the Epistle to the Galatians, and the easy, fervent outflowing of thought and feeling in those to the Thessalonians, Corinthians, and Philippians, is perfectly natural. Of all the converts to whom St. Paul had written, the Colossians alone were entire strangers to him. He had not indeed visited the Church of Rome, but many members of that Church were personally known to him, and he was writing to them on a familiar theme which had for years been occupying his thoughts. The mere fact that he had already written on the same topic to the Galatians would make his thoughts flow more easily. But in writing to the Colossians he was handling a new theme, combating a recent error with which, among Christians, he had not come into personal contact, and of which he merely knew the special characteristics at secondhand. When, in the Epistle to the Ephesians, he reverts to the same range of conceptions,[1] his sentences run with far greater ease. The style of no man is stereotyped, and least of all is this the case with a man so many-sided, so emotional, so original as St. Paul. His manner, as we have repeatedly noticed, reflects to an unusual degree the impressions of the time, the place, the mood, in which he was writing. A thousand circumstances unknown to us may have given to this Epistle that rigid character, that want of spontaneity in the movement of its sentences, which led even Ewald into the improbable conjecture that the words were Timothy's, though the subject and the thoughts belong to St. Paul. But the difference of style between it and other Epistles is no greater than we find in the works of other authors at different periods of their lives, or than we daily observe in the writings and speeches of living men who deal with different topics in varying moods.

[1] *V. infra*, p. 630, *seq.* "These two letters are twins, singularly like one another in face, like also in character, but not so identical as to exclude a strongly-marked individuality" (J. Ll. Davies, *Eph. and Col.*, p. 7). He says that the style is laboured, but "the substance eminently genuine and strong." A forger would have copied phrases; who could copy the most "characteristic and inward conceptions of the Apostle?" Even critics who fail to admit the genuineness of the whole letter, see that its sentiments and much of its phraseology are so indisputably Pauline that they adopt the theory of interpolation (Hitzig, Weiss, Holtsman), or joint authorship of Paul and Timothy (Ewald).

CHAPTER XLIX.

THE EPISTLE TO THE COLOSSIANS.

"Per Me venitur, ad Me pervenitur, in Me permanetur."—Aug. *In Joann.* xii.

"Ἐν αὐτῷ περιπατεῖτε. In eo ambulate; in illo solo. Hic Epistolae scopus est." —Bengel.

"Viva, pressa, solida, nervis plena, mascula."—Böhmer, *Isag.* lx.

"Brevis Epistola, sed nucleum Evangelii continens."—Calvin.

After a brief greeting "to the saints and faithful brethren in Christ which are in Colossæ,"[1] he enters on the usual "thanksgiving," telling them how in his prayers he ever thanked God our Father[2] on their behalf, on hearing of their faith in Christ and love to all the saints, because of the hope stored up for them in heaven. Of that hope they had heard when the Gospel was first preached to them in its true genuineness; and as that Gospel grew and bore fruit[3] in all the world, so it was doing in them, from the day when they heard of the grace of God, and recognised it in all its fulness, from the teaching of Epaphras, the Apostle's beloved fellow-prisoner and their faithful pastor on the Apostle's behalf.[4] By Epaphras he has been informed of their spiritual charism of love, and from the day that he heard of their Christian graces it was his earnest and constant prayer that their knowledge of God's will might be fully completed in all spiritual wisdom and intelligence, in practical holiness, in fresh fruitfulness and growth, in increasing power to endure even suffering with joy, and in perpetual thanksgiving to God, who qualified us for our share in the heritage of the saints in light, and who rescued us from the power of darkness, and transferred us by baptism into the kingdom of the Son of His love, in whom we have our redemption, the remission of our sins.[5]

Of the nature of that Son of God, on whose redemption he has thus touched, he proceeds to speak in the next five verses. They form one of the two memorable passages which contain the theological essence of this Epistle. They are the full statement of those truths with respect to the person of Christ which were alone adequate to meet the errors, both of theory and practice, into which the Colossians were sliding under the influence of some

[1] Ver. 2, Κολοσσαῖς, ℵ, B, D, F, G, L; but probably πρὸς Κολασσαεῖς in the later superscription.

[2] This, if the reading of B, D, Origen, &c., be correct, is the only instance where God the Father stands alone in the opening benediction. The briefest summary of the Epistle is as follows:—I. Introduction: i. 1, 2, Greeting; i. 3—8, Thanksgiving; i. 9—13, Prayer. II. Doctrinal: the person and office of Christ, i. 13—ii. 3. III. Polemical: warnings against error, and practical deductions from the counter truths, ii. 4—iii. 4. IV. Practical: general precepts, iii. 5—17; special precepts, iii. 18—iv. 6. V. Personal messages and farewell, iv. 7—18.

[3] Ver. 6, καρποφορούμενον, "*spontaneously* bearing fruit" (ver. 10, καρποφοῦντες), and yet gaining progressive force in doing so (αὐξανόμενοι).

[4] Ver. 7, ὑπὲρ ἡμῶν, ℵ, A, B, D, F, G. This can only mean that Epaphras preached on St. Paul's behalf—*i.e.*, in his stead—and, if it be the right reading, furnishes another decisive proof that St. Paul had never himself preached in these Churches.

[5] i. 9—14. The "by His blood" of the E.V. is a reading interpolated from Eph. i. 7.

Essene teacher. The doctrine of Christ as the Divine Word,—the Likeness of God manifested to men—the Pre-existent Lord of the created world—could alone divert them from the dualism and ascetic rigour which their Phrygian mysticism and mental proclivities had led them to introduce into the system of Christianity. And therefore having spoken of Christ, he shows "His absolute supremacy in relation to the universe, the *natural* creation (15—17), and in relation to the Church, the new *moral* creation (ver. 18)."[1]

"Who is the Image of the Unseen God, the First-born of all Creation, since in Him all things were created[2] in the heavens and upon the earth, the things seen and the things unseen,—whether 'thrones' or 'dominations,' 'principalities' or 'powers':[3] all things have been created[4] by Him and unto Him: and HE IS[5] before all things, and in Him all things cohere; and He is the head of the body—the Church; who is the origin, the first-born from the dead, that He and none other may become the Presiding Power in all things; because in Him God thought good that the whole Plenitude[6] should permanently dwell,[7] and by Him to reconcile all things to Himself, making peace by the blood of His cross;—by Him; whether the things on the earth or the things in the heavens. And you, who once were alienated and enemies in your purpose, in the midst of wicked works,—yet now were ye

[1] Dr. Lightfoot, in his valuable note (p. 209), shows that Christ is spoken of *first* in relation to God—the word εἰκών involving the two ideas of Representation and Manifestation; and, *secondly*, in relation to created things—the words πρωτότοκος πάσης κτίσεως involving the idea of mediation between God and Creation, and πρωτότοκος being applied to the Logos by Philo, and to the Messiah in Ps. lxxxix. 27. It implies priority to, and sovereignty over, all creation. It seems as though there were already tendencies to find the cross an offence, and to distinguish between the crucified Jesus and the ascended Christ (i. 19, 20—22; ii. 6—9).

[2] Ver. 16, ἐκτίσθη, "created by one word."

[3] No definite angelology can be extracted from these words (cf. ii. 18; Eph. i. 21). The hierarchies of the pseudo-Dionysius are as entirely arbitrary as Milton's

"Thrones, dominations, virtues, princedoms, powers,
Warriors, the flower of heaven."

But to say that the passage is gnostic, &c., is absurd in the face of such passages as Rom. viii. 38; 1 Cor. xv. 24.

[4] Ver. 16, ἔκτισται, "have been created, and still continue."

[5] HE IS—ἔστιν, not ἐστιν (so Lightfoot), since the tense and the repetition of the pronouns imply pre-existence and personality (John viii. 58; Ex. iii. 14).

[6] This rendering "Plenitude"—in the sense of "completeness" and "completed fulfilment"—will be found to meet all the uses of the words in St. Paul, both in its ordinary sense (1 Cor. x. 26; Rom. xi. 12, 25; xiii. 10; xv. 29; Gal. iv. 4; Eph. i. 10), and in its later quasi-technical sense, as applied to the "totality of the Divine attributes and agencies" (Col. i. 19; ii. 9; Eph. i. 23; iii. 19; iv. 13). It is directly derived from the O.T. usage (Jer. viii. 16, &c.); and the later localised usage of Cerinthus and Valentinus is in turn derived from it. If it be derived from πληρόω, in the sense of "*fulfil*" rather than its sense to "fill," the difficulties of its usage by St. Paul are lessened; I cannot say that they disappear. Lightfoot, *Col.* 323—339. Those who wish to see other views may find them in Baur, *Paul.* ii. 93; Pfleiderer, ii. 172; Holtzmann, *Eph. Col.* 222, *seq.*; Fritzsche on Rom. x. 1. On the connexion of πλήρωμα with the Hebrew מקום there are some valuable remarks in Taylor's *Pirque Aboth*, p. 54. *Makom*, "place" = 186, and by Gematria was identified with Yehovah, because the squares of the letters of the Tetragrammaton ($10^2 + 5^2 + 6^2 + 5^2$) give the same result (Buxt. *Lex Chald.* 2001). So far from being exclusively gnostic, Philo had already said (*De Somniis*, I.) that the word has three meanings, of which the third is *God*. Hence the interesting Alexandrianism in the LXX. of Ex. xxiv. 10, εἶδον τὸν τόπον οὗ εἱστήκει ὁ θεός. "God," said a celebrated Jewish proverb, "is not in Ha-Makom [the "Place," the "Universe"], but all Ha-Makom is in God."

[7] Ver. 19, κατοικῆσαι, not a παροικία or transient, but a κατοικία or permanent abode. Cf. Gen. xxxvi. 44, LXX.; κατοικεῖν, ישב; παροικεῖν, גור, &c.

reconciled[1] in the body of His flesh by death, to present yourselves holy and unblemished and blameless before Him, if, that is, ye abide by the faith, founded and firm, and not being ever shifted from the hope of the Gospel which ye heard, which was proclaimed throughout this sublunary world—of which I became—I, Paul—a minister."[2]

The immense grandeur of this revelation, and the thought that it should have been entrusted to *his* ministry, at once exalts and humiliates him; and he characteristically[3] continues:—

"Now I rejoice in my sufferings on your behalf, and supplement the deficiencies of the afflictions of Christ in my flesh on behalf of His body, which is the Church,[4] of which I became a minister according to the stewardship of God granted to me to you-ward, to develop fully the word of God, the mystery[5] which has lain hidden from the ages and the generations, but is now manifested to His saints, to whom God willed to make known what is the wealth of the glory of this mystery among the Gentiles, which mystery is Christ in you the hope of glory; whom we preach" —not to chosen *mystae*, not with intellectual exclusiveness, not with esoteric reserves, but absolutely and universally—"warning *every* man, and teaching *every* man in *all* wisdom, that we may present *every* man 'perfect' in Christ.[6] For which end also I toil, contending according to His energy, which works in me in power.[7]

"For I wish you to know how severe a contest[8] I have on behalf of you, and those in Laodicea, and all who have not seen my face in the flesh, that their hearts may be confirmed, they being compacted[9] in love, and so brought to all wealth of the full assurance of intelligence, unto the full knowledge of that mystery of God, which is Christ,[10] in whom are all the treasures of wisdom and knowledge—hid treasures,"—yet, as the whole passage implies, hidden no longer, but now brought to light.[11] "This I say"—*i.e.*, I tell you of this possibility of full knowledge for you all, of this perfect yet open secret of wisdom in Christ—"that no man may sophisticate you by plausibility of speech. For even though personally absent, yet in my spirit I am with you, rejoicing in and observing your military array, and the solid front of your faith in Christ. As, then, ye received the Christ—Jesus the

[1] Ver. 21, ἀποκατηλλάγητε (B). The ἀπο, as in ἀπολαμβάνειν υἱοθεσίαν (Gal. iv. 5) and ἀποκατάστασις, points to the *restoration* of a lost condition.

[2] i. 15—23. At ver. 20 begins a sketch of Christ's work, first generally (20), then specially to the Colossians (21—23).

[3] Cf. Eph. iii. 2—9; 1 Tim. i. 11.

[4] τὰ ὑστερήματα. These latter words throw light on the former. Christ's sacrifice is, of course, "a full, perfect, and sufficient sacrifice, oblation, and satisfaction for the sins of the whole world," and the sufferings of saints *cannot*, therefore, be *vicarious*. But they *can* be *ministrative*, and *useful*—nay, even requisite for the continuance of Christ's work on earth; and in that sense St. Paul, and every "partaker of Christ's sufferings" (2 Cor. i. 7; Phil. iii. 10) can "personally supplement in Christ's stead (ἀνταναπληρῶ) what is lacking of Christ's afflictions on behalf of His body, the Church." Steiger, Maurice, Huth, &c., read "the sufferings of the Christ in my flesh;" but there can be no Χριστὸς in the σάρξ which Christ destroys.

[5] The mystery of the equal admission of the Gentiles (i. 27; iv. 3; Eph. i. 10; iii. 3, 8, and *passim*).

[6] The repetition of the πάντα is a clear warning against esoteric doctrines, and the exclusive arrogance of intellectual spiritualism which is a germ of many heresies. It is naturally a favourite word of the Apostle who had to proclaim the universality of the Gospel (1 Cor. x. 1; xii. 29, 30, &c.). Τέλειος was used of those initiated into the mysteries.

[7] i. 24—29.

[8] Ver. 1. ἀγῶνα, referring back to ἀγωνιζόμενος, i. 29.

[9] Read συμβιβασθέντες.

[10] Ver. 2. Read τοῦ Θεοῦ, Χριστοῦ. (Lightfoot, *Col.* p. 318.)

[11] Prov. ii. 4; Matt. xiii. 44; 1 Cor. ii. 7; iv. 5.

Lord—walk in Him, rooted, and being built up in Him.[1] and being confirmed by your faith, even as ye were taught, abounding in that faith with thanksgiving."[2]

He has thus given them a general warning against being dazzled by erroneous teaching. He has laid down for them, with firm hand and absolute definiteness, the truth that the Pleroma dwells permanently in Christ—the sole Lord of the created universe, and therefore the guarantee that there is in matter no inherent element of inextinguishable evil; the sole Head of the Church, the sole Redeemer of the world; the sole centre, and source, and revealer of wisdom to all alike, as they had all along been taught. But it is now time to come to more specific warnings—to the more immediate application of these great eternal principles; and he continues:—

"Look that there be no person [whom one might name][3] who is carrying you off as plunder by his 'philosophy,'[4] which is vain deceit in accordance with mere human traditions, and earthly rudiments,[5] and not in accordance with Christ. For in Him all the Plenitude of Godhead[6] has bodily its permanent abode, and ye are in Him, fulfilled with *His* Plenitude, who is the head of every 'principality' and 'power.'"[7]

From this great truth flow various practical consequences. For instance, the Essene mystic, who was making a prey of them by the empty and specious sophistry which he called philosophy, impressed on them the value of circumcision, though not, it would seem, with the same insistency as the Christian Pharisees who had intruded themselves into Galatia. But what possible good could circumcision do them? Their circumcision was spiritual, and had already been performed—not by human hands, but by Christ Himself; not as the partial mutilation of one member, but as the utter stripping away from them of the whole body of the flesh.[8] It was, in fact, their baptism, in which they had been buried with Christ, and also raised with Him through their faith in the power of God who raised Him from the dead.[9]

"You, too, dead by transgressions and the uncircumcision of your flesh, God quickened with Him, freely remitting to us all our transgressions, wiping out the bond which, by its decrees, was valid against us,[10] which was opposed to us—this bond He has taken away, nailing it to His cross. Stripping utterly away from Him

[1] Ver. 7. Notice the change from ἐρριζωμένοι, the permanent result of stability, to ἐποικοδομούμενοι, the continuous process of edification. Notice, too, the confusion of metaphor which is no confusion of thought: "walk," "rooted," "being built," "being strengthened."

[2] ii. 1—7.

[3] Ver 8, τις, indefinitely definite (cf. Gal. i. 7).

[4] Remarkable as being the only place where St. Paul uses the word "philosophy," just as he only uses "virtue" once (Phil. iv. 8). Both are superseded by loftier conceptions.

[5] See *supra*, p. 439. (Gal. iv. 3, 9.)

[6] θεότης, *deitas*; stronger than θειότης, *divinitas*.

[7] ii. 7—10.

[8] Ver. 11, ἀπέκδυσις.

[9] Cf. Phil. iii. 10.

[10] Deut. xxvii. 14—26; Gal. ii. 19, iv. 9; ὀφειλέτης. The "ordinances" are those of the Mosaic and the natural law. The δόγμασιν is difficult; the rendering 'consisting in ordinances' would seem to require ἐν, as in Eph. ii. 15. Also the Greek Fathers made it mean "wiping out *by the decrees of the Gospel.*"

the 'principalities' and 'powers' (of wickedness),[1] He made a show of them boldly, leading them in triumph on that cross"[2]—thus making the gibbet of the slave His *feretrum*, on which to carry the spoils of His triumph as an Eternal Conqueror, after deadly struggle with the clinging forces of spiritual wickedness.

Since, then, mere legal obligations are part of a dead compact, a torn and cancelled bond, which is now nailed to Christ's Cross—

"Let no one then judge you in eating and drinking,[3] and in the matter of a feast, or a new moon, or Sabbath,[4] which things are a shadow of things to be, but the substance is Christ's. Let no one then snatch your prize from you, by delighting in abjectness,[5] and service of the angels,[6] treading the emptiness of his own visions[7] in all the futile inflation of his mere carnal understanding, and not keeping hold of Him who is "the Head," from whom, supplied and compacted by its junctures and ligaments, the whole body grows the growth of God.[8] If ye died with Christ from mundane rudiments, why, as though living in the world, are ye ordinance-ridden with such rules as 'Do not handle,' 'Do not taste,' 'Do not even touch,' referring to things all of which are perishable in the mere consumption,[9] according to 'the commandments and teachings of men'? All these kinds of rules have a credit for wisdom in volunteered supererogation[10] and abasement—hard usage of the body—but have no sort of value as a remedy as regards the indulgence of the flesh."[11]

[1] Tearing himself free from the assaults of evil spirits, which would otherwise have invested Him as a robe (cf. 1 Pet. v. 5, ἐγκομβώσασθε; Heb. xii. 1, εὐπερίστατος; Isa. xi. 5, &c.), He carried away their spoils, as trophies, on His cross.

[2] ii. 11—15. For θριαμβεύσας, cf. 2 Cor. ii. 14, *infra*, p. 700.

[3] "This is the path of the Thorah. A morsel with salt shalt thou eat; thou shalt drink also water by measure" (*Perek*. R. Meir).

[4] If after nineteen centuries the Christian Church has not understood the sacred freedom of this language, we may imagine what insight it required to utter it in St. Paul's day, and how the Jews would gnash their teeth when they heard of it. When "the Emperor" asked R. Akibha how he recognised the Sabbath day, he said, "The river Sambatyon (the so-called 'Sabbatic river') proves it; the necromancer proves it (who can do nothing on the Sabbath); thy father's grave proves it (which smokes, to show that its tenant is in hell, except on the Sabbath, on which day even hell rests").—*Sanhedrin*, f. 65, 2. Myriads of passages might be quoted to show that it was the very keystone of the whole Judaic system: see *Babha Kama*, f. 82, 1; *Abhôda Zara*, f. 64, 2, &c. The law of the Sabbath, as our Lord strove so often to convince the Jews, is a law of holy freedom, not of petty bondage.

[5] θέλων ἐν, בְּ חָפֵץ, 1 Sam. xviii. 22, &c. See Aug., Beng., Olsh., Lightf.

[6] Angelology of the most developed description existed in the Jewish Church long before Gnosticism was heard of. See Gfrörer, *Jahr. des Heils*. i. 124, *seq*. I have collected some of the facts in a paper on Jewish Angelology and Demonology (*Life of Christ*, ii. 465, *seq*.). Neander refers to the κήρυγμα Πέτρου, and Clem. Alex. *Strom*. vi. 635. Theodoret (ii. 18) mentions that even in his day there were oratories to the Archangel Michael.

[7] ἃ ἑόρακεν (א, A, B, D). Dr. Lightfoot and others make the very simple conjectural emendation, ἃ ἑόρακεν κενεμβατεύων, *aut s. a.* This does not indeed occur in any MS., but its disappearance would be easily explained—(i.) by the homœoteleuton; (ii.) by the rare verb. The verb κενεμβατεύω (not unlike the ἀεροβατῶ καὶ περιφρονῶ τὸν ἥλιον, "I tread the air and circumspect the sun," of Arist. *Nub*. 225, and the αἰθεροβατεῖτε of Philo, i. 465) might conceivably have been suggested by one of the heretical theosophic terms, if κένωμα had ever been used by some incipient Gnostic of that day (as afterwards) by way of antithesis to Pleroma. But may not ἃ ἑώρακεν ἐμβατεύων be taken (metaphorically) to mean "*dwelling upon* what He has seen"?

[8] The accordance of the passage with the highest scientific range of that age is remarkable, and may be due to St. Luke.

[9] Mark vii. 1—23.

[10] Ver. 23, ἐθελοθρησκεία, a happy coinage of St. Paul's, which Epiphanius expands into ἐθελοπερισσοθρησκεία (*Haer*. i. 16).

[11] ii. 16—23. This remarkable passage, which is very obscure in the E. V., is an

The *true* remedy, he proceeds to imply, is very different :—

"If then ye were raised with Christ, seek the things above, where Christ is sitting on the right hand of God. Think of the things above, not the things on the earth. For ye died" (to sin in baptism), "and your life has been hidden with Christ in God. When Christ, our life, is manifested, then ye also with Him shall be manifested in glory. Kill then at a blow"—not by regulated asceticisms, but by this outburst of a new life, which is in Christ, which *is* Christ—"your members that are on the earth—fornication, uncleanness, passion, evil desire, and, above all, covetousness, for that is idolatry—because of which things cometh the wrath of God.[1] In which things ye also walked once, when ye were living in them; but now put ye away also *all* vices, anger, wrath, malice, railing, foul calumny, out of your mouths. Lie not one to another, since ye utterly stripped off the old man with his deeds, and put on the new man, which is being ever renewed to full knowledge, according to the image of his Creator, in a region wherein there is no room for Greek or Jew, circumcision or uncircumcision, barbarian, Scythian,[2] slave, free, but Christ is all things, and in all. Put on then, as elect of God, saints beloved, hearts of compassion, kindness, humbleness, meekness, long-suffering, forbearing one another, and forgiving one another, if any one have a complaint against any one. Even as the Lord forgave you, so also do ye. And over all these things put on love, for love is the girdle of perfection; and let the peace of Christ arbitrate in your hearts, unto which peace ye were even called in one body, and show yourselves thankful. Let the word of Christ dwell in you richly in all wisdom, teaching one another and admonishing one another in psalms, hymns,[3] spiritual songs in grace, singing in your hearts to God. And everything whatever ye do, in word or in deed, do all things in the name of the Lord Jesus, thanking God the Father by Him."[4]

Then follow various practical exhortations—to wives to love their husbands, as is eternally fit in the Lord;[5] to husbands to love their wives, and not behave bitterly towards them; to children to obey their parents; to fathers not to irritate their children, that they may not lose heart.[6] To slaves, of whose duties and position he must often have thought recently, from his interest in Onesimus, he gives the precept to obey earthly masters, working as ever in their Great Taskmaster's eye, looking for the reward of faithfulness to Him who would also send the retribution for wrong-doing. On masters he enjoins justice and equity towards their slaves, remarking that they too have a Lord in heaven.[7]

argument *against*, not *for*, the worrying scrupulosities of exaggerated asceticism—on the ground that they are useless for the end in view. St. Paul might have gone even further; for the lives of hermits and monks show us that the virulence of temptation is intensified into insupportable agony by the morbid introspection which results from mistaken means of combating it.

[1] Ver. 6, our ἐπὶ τοὺς υἱοὺς τῆς ἀπειθείας, introduced probably from Eph. v. 6.

[2] Ver. 11. The Scythians were the lowest type of barbarians (Gal. iii. 28).

[3] Christian hymnology began very early, though the hymns were not necessarily metrical (Rev. xv. 3; Acts xvi. 25; Eph. v. 19, 20; Plin. *Ep.* 97; *Mart. S. Ign.* vii. ᾠδαὶ ἀπ' ἀρχῆς ὑπὸ πιστῶν γραφεῖσαι, Euseb. *H. E.* v. 28. Rhythmic passages are Eph. v. 14; 1 Tim. iii. 16; vi. 15, 16; 2 Tim. ii. 11—13 (*Dict. Christ. Antt.* s. v. Hymns).

[4] iii. 1—17.

[5] ὡς ἀνῆκεν, "as ever *was*, and ever is fitting" (cf. Acts xxii. 22). (See my *Brief Greek Syntax*, § 140.)

[6] Notice the *rare* originality of the exhortation. Should we expect to find it in a forger?

[7] iii. 18—25. From such passages as these were drawn such noble warning rules of

Then he tells them to be constant in watchful prayer and thanksgiving, and asks their prayers that God would grant an opening for that ministry for which he was a prisoner. To the outer world he bids them walk in wisdom, buying up every opportunity, and addressing each one to whom they spoke with pleasant and wholesome words—"in grace seasoned with salt."[1]

He sends no personal news, because that will be conveyed by Tychicus, his beloved brother, and a faithful minister and fellow-slave in the Lord, whom he sends for that purpose[2] to strengthen their hearts, with Onesimus, their fellow-citizen, and *now* their faithful and beloved brother, whatever he may have been before. He sends them greetings from Aristarchus, his fellow-prisoner;[3] from Mark, the cousin of Barnabas,[4] about whose possible visit they had received special injunctions; and Jesus surnamed Justus—the only three Jewish Christians who worked with him to further God's kingdom, and so became a source of consolation to him. Epaphras, also one of themselves, greets them—a slave of Christ Jesus, ever contending on their behalf in his prayers that they may stand perfect and entire in all God's will, and one who was deeply interested in their Churches. Luke the physician, the beloved, greets them, and Demas.[5] He begs them to greet the Laodicean brethren, and Nymphas, and the church in the house of him and his friends.[6] He orders his Epistle to be publicly read, not only in the Colossian, but also in the Laodicean Church, and bids them read the circular letter which they could procure from Laodicea.[7] "And say to Archippus, Take heed to the ministry which thou receivedst in the Lord, that thou fulfil it."[8] The letter concludes with his own autograph salutation, to which he briefly adds, "Remember my bonds. Grace be with you."[9]

It is no part of my present task to trace the subsequent history of

feudalism as: "Entre toi vilain, et toi seigneur, il n'y a juge fors Dieu." "Le seigneur qui prend des droits injustes de son vilain, les prend au péril de son âme" (Beaumanoir). These humble practical rules might be all the more necessary for those who looked on outward family duties as vulgar, and obstructions to spiritual contemplation. (Maurice, *Unity*, 587.) How different this from οὐδὲ προσγελᾶν δούλοις Ἀριστοτέλης εἴα ποτε. (Clem. Alex. *Strom.* iii. 12, § 84.)

[1] iv. 1—6. [2] iv. 8, *leg.* ἵνα γνῶτε τὰ περὶ ἡμῶν (A, B, D, F, G).

[3] Ver. 10, συναιχμάλωτος. Properly, "a fellow-captive taken in war." So of Epaphras (Philem. 23), Andronicus, Junias (Rom. xvi. 7.) In none of these cases can we tell the exact allusion, or whether the word is literal or metaphorical.

[4] Barnabas was perhaps dead, and thus Mark would be free. Paul seems to have had a little misgiving about his reception.

[5] Perhaps Paul's insight into character is shown by his somewhat ominous silence about Demas. (2 Tim. iv. 10.)

[6] Ver. 15, αὐτῶν (א, A, C): αὐτῆς (B, Lachm.): αὐτοῦ (F, G, K, &c.).

[7] τὴν ἐκ Λαοδικείας, "written *to* Laodicea and coming to them from Thrace." Constructio praegnans. (*Brief Greek Syntax*, § 89; Winer, § lxvi. 6.) There can be little doubt that this was the Epistle to the "Ephesians." The apocryphal Epistle to Laodicea is a miserable cento. (See Lightfoot, *Col.* 340—366; Westcott, *Canon.* p. 542.)

[8] Archippus is believed to be a son of Philemon, and chief presbyter of Laodicea. If so, Tychicus would see him on his way to Colossæ. It is at least curious that the lukewarmness, the lack of zeal which seems here to be gently rebuked, is the distinguishing character of the Laodicean Church, as represented by its "angel" in Rev. iii. 15. (Trench, *Seven Churches*, 180.)

[9] This shorter form is characteristic of Paul's later Epistles—Col. i., 2 Tim., Tit. The longer form is found in all up to this date.

the Churches of the Lycus. The followers of Baur in Germany, and of Renan in France, have tried to represent that St. Paul's teaching in Asia was followed by a reaction in which his name was calumniated and his doctrines ignored. The theory is very dubious. The doctrines and the warnings of St. John to the Seven Churches are closely analogous to, sometimes almost verbally identical with, those of St. Paul; and the essence of the teaching of both Apostles on all the most important aspects of Christianity is almost exactly the same. An untenable inference has been drawn from the supposed silence of Papias about St. Paul, so far as we can judge from the references of Eusebius. It was the object of Papias to collect *traditional* testimonies from various Apostles and disciples, and of these St. Paul *could* not have been one. Papias was Bishop of Hierapolis, in which St. Paul may never have set his foot. Even if he did, his visit was brief, and had taken place long before Papias wrote, whereas after the destruction of Jerusalem St. John resided for many years at Ephesus, and there were gathered around him Andrew, Philip, Aristion, and others who had known the Lord. These were the authorities to which Papias referred for his somewhat loose and credulous traditions, and he may have quoted St. Paul, just as Polycarp does, without its at all occurring to Eusebius to mention the fact. Not only is there no proof of a general apostasy from Pauline principles, but in the decrees of the Council held at Laodicea about the middle of the fourth century, we read the very same warnings against angelolatry, Judaism, and Oriental speculation, which find a place in these Epistles of the Captivity. Colossæ itself—liable as it was to constant earthquakes, which were rendered more ruinous by the peculiarities of the Lycus with its petrifying waters—was gradually deserted, and the churches of Asia finally perished under the withering blight of Islam with its cruelties, its degradation, and its neglect.

CHAPTER L.

ST. PAUL AND ONESIMUS.

"Quasi vero curent divina de servis!"—MACROB. *Sat.* i. 11.

"In servos superbissimi, crudelissimi, contumeliosissimi sumus."—SEN. *Ep.* xlvii.

"Aequalitas naturae et fidei potior est quam differentia statuum."—BENGEL.

"Through the vista of history we see slavery and its Pagan theory of two races fall before the holy word of Jesus, 'All men are the children of God.'—MAZZINI, *Works*, vi. 99.

"'The story is too rare to be true.' Christian faith has answered that. 'It is too suggestive to be true.' Christian science has answered that."—LANGE, *Apostol. Zeitalt.* i. 134.

IN the Epistle to the Colossians St. Paul had sent no greeting to Philemon—who was a prominent member of that Church—because he purposed to write him a separate letter. A man like St. Paul, whose large and loving heart had won for him so many deeply-attached friends, must have often communicated with them by brief letters, but the Epistle to Philemon is the only private letter of this correspondence which has been preserved for us—the only private letter in the canon of the New Testament, with the exception of the brief letter of St. John to the well-beloved Gaius.[1] We cannot but regret the loss. Hundreds of letters of Cicero, of Seneca, and of Pliny, have come down to us, and, though some of them are models of grace and eloquence, how gladly would we resign them all for even one or two of those written by the Apostle! In style, indeed, his letter is quite careless and unpolished; but whereas the letters of the great Romans, with all their literary skill and finish, often leave on us an involuntary impression of the vanity, the insincerity, even in some instances the entire moral instability of their writers, on the other hand, this brief letter of St. Paul reveals to us yet another glimpse of a character worthy of the very noblest utterances which we find in his other Epistles. These few lines, at once so warmhearted and so dignified, which theological bigotry was once inclined to despise as insignificant, express principles of eternal applicability which even down to the latest times have had no small influence in the development of the world's history. With all the slightness of its texture, and the comparative triviality of the occasion which called it forth, the letter is yet a model of tact, of sympathy, and of high moral nobleness. This little "idyl of the progress of Christianity"[2] shows that under the worn and ragged gabardine of the wandering missionary there beat the heart of a true gentleman, whose high-bred manners would have done honour to any court.[3]

We have seen that during his imprisonment St. Paul was, by "that unseen Providence which men nickname Chance," brought into contact with a runaway slave from Colossæ, whose name was Onesimus, or "Profitable." He had fled to Rome—to Rome, the common *sentina* of the world[4]—to hide himself from the consequences of crimes for which a heathen master might without compunction have consigned him to the *ergastulum* or the cross; and in the basement of one of the huge Roman *insulae*, or in the hovel of some fellow-child of vice and misery in that seething mass of human wretchedness which weltered like gathered scum on the fringe of the glittering tide of civilisation, he was more secure than anywhere else of remaining undetected. What it was that rescued him from the degradations which were the sole possible outcome of such an ill-begun career we cannot tell. He would soon exhaust what he had stolen from his master; and as Rome was full to overflowing of slaves and idlers—as the openings for an honest maintenance even in the barest poverty were few—it is hard to see what resource was left to

[1] The "elect lady" of 2 John i. 1 is believed to be, not an individual, but a Church.

[2] Davies.

[3] Even Baur seems to blush for the necessity which made him declare this Epistle spurious. He only does so because it is more or less involved with the other three, and stands or falls with them. "What has criticism to do with this short, attractive, friendly, and graceful letter, inspired as it is by the noblest Christian feeling, and which has never yet been touched by the breath of suspicion?" (*Paul.* ii. 80.)

[4] Sall. *Cat.* xxxvii. 5.

him except a life of villany. Perhaps in this condition he was met by his fellow-Colossian, Epaphras, who as a Presbyter of Colossæ would be well known to Philemon. Perhaps Aristarchus, or any other of those who had been St. Paul's companions at Ephesus, had come across him, and recognised him as having been in attendance on Philemon at the time of his conversion by St. Paul. Perhaps he had himself been present at some of those daily addresses and discussions in the school of Tyrannus, which, though at the time they had not touched his heart, had at the least shown him the noble nature of the speaker, and revealed to the instinctive sense of one who belonged to an oppressed class, the presence of a soul which could sympathise with the suffering. How this may have been we do not know, but we do know that his hopes were not deceived. The Apostle received him kindly, sympathetically, even tenderly. The Rabbis said, "It is forbidden to teach a slave the Law."[1] "As though Heaven cared for slaves!" said the ordinary Pagan, with a sneer.[2] Not so thought St. Paul. In Christianity there is nothing esoteric, nothing exclusive. Onesimus became a Christian. The heart which was hard as a diamond against Pharisaism and tyranny, was yet tender as a mother's towards sorrow and repentant sin. Paul had learnt in the school of Him who suffered the penitent harlot to wash His feet with her tears and wipe them with the hair of her head; of Him who had said to the convicted adulteress, "Neither do I condemn thee; go, and sin no more." Paul in no wise shared the anti-Christian respect of persons which made some people in St. Jerome's days[3] argue that it was beneath his dignity to trouble himself about a runaway slave. He understood better than the Fathers that the religion of Christ is the Magna Charta of humanity. The drag-net of His "fishers of men" was dropped to the very depths of the social sea. Here was one whose position was the lowest that could be conceived. He was a slave; a slave of the country whose slaves were regarded as the worst there were; a slave who had first robbed a kind master, and then run away from him; a slave at whom current proverbs pointed as exceptionally worthless,[4] amenable only to blows, and none the better even for them.[5] In a word, he was a slave; a Phrygian slave; a thievish Asiatic runaway slave, who had no recognised rights, and towards whom no one had any recognised duties. He was a mere "live chattel;"[6] a mere "implement with a voice;"[7] a thing which had no rights, and towards which there were no duties. But St. Paul converted him, and the slave became a Christian, a brother beloved and serviceable, an heir of immortality, a son of the kingdom, one of a royal generation, of a holy priesthood. The satirist Persius speaks with utter scorn of the rapid process by which a slave became a freeman and a citizen:

[1] *Ketubhoth*, f. 28, 1.

[2] Macrob. *Saturn.* 11. The better Stoics furnish a noble exception to this tone.

[3] *In Ep. ad Philem.*

[4] Μυσῶν ἔσχατος. Menand. *Androg.* 7; Plat. *Theaet.* 209, B.

[5] Cic. *pro Flacc.* 27.

[6] Arist. *Pol.* i. 4, ἔμψυχον ὄργανον.

[7] Varro, *de Re Rust.* i. 17. "Instrumenti genus . . . vocale."

"There stands Dama—a twopenny stable-boy, and a pilfering scoundrel; the Prætor touches him with his wand, and twirls him round, and

> "Momento turbinis, exit
> Marcus Dama! . . . . Papae! Marco spondente recusas
> Credere tu nummos? Marco sub judice palles?"[1]

But the difference between Dama the worthless drudge and Marcus Dama the presumably worthy citizen was absolutely infinitesimal compared to the real and unsurpassable difference which separated Onesimus the good-for-nothing Phrygian fugitive from Onesimus the brother faithful and beloved.

And thus the Epistle to Philemon becomes the practical manifesto of Christianity against the horrors and iniquities of ancient and modern slavery.[2] From the very nature of the Christian Church—from the fact that it was "a kingdom not of this world"—it could not be revolutionary. It was never meant to prevail by physical violence, or to be promulgated by the sword. It was the revelation of eternal principles, not the elaboration of practical details. It did not interfere, or attempt to interfere, with the facts of the established order. Had it done so it must have perished in the storm of excitement which it would have inevitably raised. In revealing truth, in protesting against crime, it insured its own ultimate yet silent victory. It knew that where the Spirit of the Lord is there is liberty. It was loyal to the powers that be. It raised no voice, and refused no tribute even to a Gaius or a Nero. It did not denounce slavery, and preached no fatal and futile servile war. It did not inflame its Onesimi to play the parts of an Eunus or an Artemio. Yet it inspired a sense of freedom which has been in all ages the most invincible foe to tyranny, and it proclaimed a divine equality and brotherhood, which while it left untouched the ordinary social distinctions, left slavery impossible to enlightened Christian lands.[3]

This delicate relation to the existing structure of society is admirably illustrated by the Letter to Philemon. The tension always produced by the existence of a slave population, vastly preponderant in numbers, was at that moment exceptionally felt. Less than two years before St. Paul wrote to

[1] Pers. *Sat.* v. 76—80.

[2] "Omnia in servum licent" (Sen. *Clem.* i. 18). For an only too vivid sketch of what those horrors and iniquities were, see Döllinger, *Judenth. u. Heidenth.* ix. 1, § 2; Wallon, *Hist. de l'Esclavage dans l'Antiquité.* The difference between the wisdom which is of the world and the wisdom which is of God may be measured by the difference between the Epistle to Philemon and the sentiments of heathens even so enlightened as Aristotle (*Polit.* i. 3; *Eth. Nic.* viii. 13) and Plato (*Legg.* vi. 777, *seq.*; *Rep.* viii. 549). The difference between Christian morals and those of even such Pagans as passed for very models of virtue may be estimated by comparing the advice of St. Paul to Christian masters, and the detestable greed and cruelty of the elder Cato in his treatment of his slaves (Plut. *Cat. Maj.* x. 21; Plin. *H. N.* xviii. 8. 3). See too Plautus, *passim*; Sec. *Ep.* xlvii.; Juv. *Sat.* vi. 219, *seq.*; Tac. *Ann.* xiv. 42—45; and Plut. *Apophthegm.* vi. 778 (the story of Vedius Pollio).

[3] On the relation of Christianity to slavery see Lecky, *Hist. of Rationalism*, ii. 258; Troplong, *De l'Influence du Christ sur le Droit civil*, &c.; Gold. Smith, *Does the Bible sanction American Slavery?* De Broglie, *L'Eglise et L'Emp.* vi. 498, *seq.*; i. 162, 306; Wallon, *De l'Esclavage*, ii. *ad fin.*, &c. The feeling is indicated in Rev. xviii. 13.

Philemon, a Consular, a Præfect of the city, named Pedanius Secundus, had been murdered by a slave under circumstances of infamy which characterised that entire epoch. In spite of the pity of the people, the Senate had decided that the old ruthless law, re-established by the Silanian decree under Augustus, should be carried out, and the entire *familia* of slaves be put to death. Regardless of the menaces of the populace, Nero ordered the sentence to be executed by military force, and four hundred human beings of every age and of both sexes had been led through lines of soldiers to their slaughter in spite of the indubitable innocence of the vast majority. This horrible event, together with the thrilling debate to which it had given rise in the Senate, had made the subject of slavery a "burning question" at Rome, and deepened the general feeling which had long found proverbial expression, that "the more slaves the more enemies." In that memorable debate, it had been asserted by C. Cassius Longinus that the only way in which the rich could live in Rome—few amid multitudes, safe amid the terrified, or, at the worst, not unavenged among the guilty—would be by a rigid adherence to the old and sanguinary law.

Such then, was the state of things in which St. Paul sat down to write his letter of intercession for the Phrygian runaway. He could not denounce slavery; he could not even emancipate Onesimus; but just as Moses, "because of the hardness of your hearts,"[1] could not overthrow the *lex talionis*, or polygamy, or the existence of blood-feuds, but rendered them as nugatory as possible, and robbed them as far as he could of their fatal sting, by controlling and modifying influences, so St. Paul established the truths that rendered slavery endurable, and raised the slave to a dignity which made emancipation itself seem but a secondary and even trivial thing. A blow was struck at the very root of slavery when our Lord said, "Ye all are brethren." In a Christian community a slave might be a "bishop," and his master only a catechumen; and St. Paul writes to bid the Corinthians pay due respect and subjection to the household of Stephanas, though some of the Corinthians were people of good position, and these were slaves.[2] Onesimus repaid by gratitude, by affection, by active and cherished services to the aged prisoner, the inestimable boon of his deliverance from moral and spiritual death. Gladly would St. Paul, with so much to try him, with so few to tend him, have retained this warm-hearted youth about his person,—one whose qualities, however much they may have been perverted and led astray, were so naturally sweet and amiable, that St. Paul feels for him all the affection of a father towards a son.[3] And had he retained him, he felt sure that Philemon would not only have pardoned the liberty, but would even have rejoiced that one over whom he had some claim should discharge some of those kindly duties to the

[1] Matt. xix. 8.

[2] See Hausrath, *Neut. Zeitg.* ii. 405.

[3] It is not said in so many words that Onesimus was young, but the language used respecting him seems clearly to show that this was the case (Philem. 10, 12, &c.). The expression σπλάγχνα, like the Latin *viscera*, is used of sons—οἱ παῖδες σπλάγχνα λέγονται (Artemid. *Oneirocr.* i. 44; cf. v. 57).

Apostle in his affliction which he himself was unable to render.[1] But Paul was too much of a gentleman[2] to presume on the kindness of even a beloved convert. And besides this, a fault had been committed, and had not yet been condoned. It was necessary to show by example that, where it was possible, restitution should follow repentance, and that he who had been guilty of a great wrong should not be irregularly shielded from its legitimate consequences. Had Philemon been a heathen, to send Onesimus to him would have been to consign the poor slave to certain torture, to possible crucifixion.[3] He would, to a certainty, have become henceforth a "branded runaway," a *stigmatias*,[4] or have been turned into the slave-prison to work in chains. But Philemon was a Christian, and the "Gospel of Christ, by Christianising the master, emancipated the slave."[5] Paul felt quite sure that he was sending back the runaway—who had become his dear son, and from whom he could not part without a violent wrench—to forgiveness, to considerate kindness, in all probability to future freedom; and at any rate right was right, and he felt that he ought not to shrink from the personal sacrifice of parting with him. He therefore sent him back under the kind care of Tychicus, and—happily for us—with a "commendatory Epistle," which even Baur apologises for rejecting, and which all the world has valued and admired.[6] It has been compared by Grotius and others with the graceful and touching letter written by the younger Pliny to his friend Sabinianus to intercede for an offending freedman, who with many tears and entreaties had besought his aid. That exquisitely natural and beautifully-written letter does credit both to Pliny's heart and to his head, and yet polished as it is in style, while St. Paul's is written with a sort of noble carelessness of expression, it stands for beauty and value far below the letter to Philemon. In the first place, it is for a young freedman who had been deeply beloved, and not for a runaway slave. In the next place, it is purely individual, and wholly wanting in the large divine *principle* which underlies the letter of St. Paul. And there are other marked differences. Paul has no doubt whatever about the future good conduct of Onesimus; but

[1] Philem. 13, ἵνα ὑπὲρ σοῦ μοι διακονῇ. It is unlikely that διακονῶ here implies religious assistance.

[2] Many writers have felt that no word but "gentleman," in its old and truest sense, is suitable to describe the character which this letter reveals. (Stanley, *Cor.* 391; Newman, *Serm. on Various Occasions*, 133.) "The only fit commentator on Paul was Luther—not by any means such a *gentleman* as the Apostle was, but almost as great a genius" (Coleridge, *Table Talk*).

[3] Juv. *Sat.* vi. 219; Plin. *Ep.* ix. 21, "Ne torseris illum."

[4] δραπέτης ἐστιγμένος (Ar. *Av.* 759). (Becker, *Charikles*, p. 370.)

[5] Bp. Wordsworth.

[6] Baur's rejection of it is founded on un-Pauline expressions—*i.e.*, expressions which only occur in other Epistles which he rejects; on the assertion that the circumstances are improbable; and that the word σπλάγχνα—which he admits to be Pauline, and which might, he says, have occurred *twice*—is used *three* times! The Epistle is therefore to him an "*Embryo einer Christlichen Dichtung.*" *Admissi risum teneatis!* The "Vorwurf der Hyperkritik, eines übertriebenen Misstrauens, einer alles angreifenden Zweifelsucht" is, however, one which applies not only to his criticism of this Epistle, but to much of his general method; only in this instance, as Wiesinger says, it is not only *Hyperkritik* but *Unkritik*.

Pliny thinks that the young freedman may offend again. Pliny assumes that Sabinianus is and will be angry; Paul has no such fear about Philemon. Paul pleads on the broad ground of Humanity redeemed in Christ; Pliny pleads the youth and the tears of the freedman, and the affection which his master had once felt for him. Paul does not think it necessary to ask Philemon to spare punishment; Pliny has to beg his friend not to use torture. Paul has no reproaches for Onesimus; Pliny severely scolded his young suppliant, and told him—without meaning to keep his word—that he should never intercede for him again. The letter of Pliny is the letter of an excellent Pagan; but the differences which separate the Pagan from the Christian stand out in every line.[1]

CHAPTER LI.

THE EPISTLE TO PHILEMON.

"Servi sunt? immo conservi."—SEN.

"Evangelico decore conscripta est."—JER.

"Epistola familiaris, mire ἀστεῖος summae sapientiae praebitura specimen."—BENGEL.

"Ita modeste et suppliciter pro infimo homine se dimittit ut vix alibi usquam magis ad vivum sit expressa ingenii ejus mansuetudo."—CALVIN.

"PAUL, a prisoner of Christ Jesus, and Timothy the brother, to Philemon, our beloved and fellow-worker, and to Apphia the sister,[2] and to Archippus our fellow-soldier, and to the Church in thy house; grace to you, and peace from God our Father and the Lord Jesus Christ.

"I thank my God always, making mention of thee in my prayers—hearing thy love, and the faith thou hast towards the Lord Jesus and unto all the saints[3]—that the kindly exercise of thy faith may become effectual, in the full knowledge of every blessing we possess, unto Christ's glory. For I had much joy and consolation in thy love, because the hearts of the saints have been refreshed by thee, brother.

"Although, then, I feel much confidence in Christ to enjoin upon thee what is fitting, yet I rather entreat thee for love's sake, being such an one as Paul the aged,[4] and at this moment also a prisoner of Christ Jesus. I entreat thee about my child, whom I begot in my bonds—Onesimus—once to thee the reverse of his name—profit-

[1] A translation of Pliny's letter will be found in Excursus XXIII. (*Ep.* ix. 21.)

[2] The reading is uncertain, but ℵ, A, D, E, F, G (B is here deficient) read ἀδελφῇ, and we judge from Theodore of Mopsuestia that ἀγαπητῇ may in his age, and perhaps in the Apostle's, have given rise to coarse remarks from coarse minds.

[3] Ver. 5, πρὸς . . . εἰς.

[4] Ver. 9, τοιοῦτος ὢν ὡς is not unclassical, as Meyer asserts. (See instances in Lightfoot, *Col.*, p. 404.) St. Paul must at this time have been sixty years old, and people of that age, particularly when they have been battered, as he had been, by all the storms of life, naturally speak of themselves as old. I cannot think that this means "an ambassador" (Eph. vi. 20). To say nothing of the fact that the reading is πρεσβύτης, not πρεσβευτής, and allowing that the two might often have been confused (just as, indeed, πρέσβυς and πρεσβευτής interchange the meanings of their plurals), yet would Paul have said "an ambassador" without saying of whom?

less[1] not 'profitable,' and no Christian, but now truly profitable[2] and a good Christian—whom I send back to thee. Him that is the son of my bowels,[3] whom I should have preferred to retain about my own person that he may on thy behalf minister to me in the bonds of the Gospel—but without thy opinion I decided to do nothing, that thy kindly deed may not be a matter of compulsion, but voluntary. For perhaps on this account he was parted for a season, that thou mayst have him back for ever, no longer as a slave, but above a slave, a brother beloved, especially to me, but how far more to thee, both naturally and spiritually. If, then, thou holdest me as a comrade, receive him like myself. But if he wronged thee in any respect, or is in thy debt, set that down to me. I Paul write it with my own hand, I will repay it[4]—not to say to thee that thou owest me even thyself besides. Yes, brother, may I 'profit' by thee in the Lord.[5] Refresh my heart in Christ. Confiding in thy compliance I write to thee, knowing that even more than I say thou wilt do. But further than this, prepare for me a lodging, for I hope that by means of your prayers I shall be granted to you.

"There salute thee Epaphras, my fellow-prisoner in Christ Jesus, Marcus, Aristarchus, Demas, Luke, my fellow-labourers.

"The grace of the Lord Jesus Christ be with the spirit of you and yours."[6]

[1] ἀχρ. *Litotes;* erat enim noxius (Bengel).

[2] Ver. 11. There seems here, as Baur acutely observes, to be a *double* paronomasia, which I have endeavoured to indicate. For Χριστὸς and Χρηστὸς were confused with each other, and the Christians did not dislike this. Ἐκ τοῦ κατηγορουμένου ἡμῶν ὀνόματος χρηστότατοι ὑπάρχομεν χριστιανοὶ γὰρ εἶναι κατηγορούμεθα τὸν δὲ χρηστὸν μισεῖσθαι οὐ δίκαιον (Justin, *Apol.* i. 4). (Tert. *Apol.* 3.) *Supra*, p. 169.

[3] "Son of my bowels, Anselm!" (Browning, *The Bishop's Tomb.*) Σπλάγχνα = *corculum*, "my very heart;" "the very eyes of me;" רחמים. The elliptic form of the sentence, so characteristic of St. Paul, is filled up in some MSS. by Σὺ δὲ αὐτόν, τούτεστι τὰ ἐμὰ σπλάγχνα προσλαβοῦ.

[4] Ἀντὶ γραμματίου (a bond) τήνδε κατέχε τὴν ἐπιστολήν· πᾶσαν αὐτὴν γέγραφα (Theodoret). Some have supposed that Paul here took the pen from the amanuensis, and that this is the only autograph sentence. Oosterzee, &c., treat this as "a good-humoured jest;" and others think it unlike the delicacy which never once reminds the Judaisers of the *chaluka* which St. Paul had toiled to raise. But a slave was valuable, and something in the character of Philemon may have led to the remark. Bengel rightly says, "Vinctus scribit serio," as a father pays the debts of his son. Schrader, Lardner, Bleek, Hackett regard it as "no better than calumny" to say that Onesimus had stolen anything.

[5] Ver. 20, ὀναίμην. "I send you back an Onesimus now worthy of his name; will you be my Onesimus?" It is vain for critics to protest against these plays on names. They have been prevalent in all ages, and in all writers, and in all countries, as I have shown by multitudes of instances in *Chapters on Language*, ch. xxii. As a parallel to this play on Onesimus, compare Whitefield's personal appeal to the comedian Shuter, who had often played the character of Ramble—"And thou, poor Ramble, who hast so often rambled from Him . . . . Oh, end thy ramblings and come to Jesus."

[6] Paul had been trained as a Rabbi. To see what Christianity had taught him we have only to compare his teachings with those of his former masters. Contrast, for instance, the Rabbinic conception of a slave with that tender estimate of human worth —that high conception of the dignity of man as man—which stands out so beautifully in this brief letter. The Rabbis taught that on the death of a slave, whether male or female—and even of a Hebrew slave—the benediction was not to be repeated for the mourners, nor condolence offered to them. It happened that on one occasion a female slave of Rabbi Eliezer died, and when his disciples came to condole with him he retired from them from room to room, from upper chamber to hall, till at last he said to them, "I thought you would feel the effects of tepid water, but you are proof even against hot water. Have I not taught you that these signs of respect are *not* to be paid at the death of slaves?" "What, then," asked the disciples, "are pupils on such occasions to say to their masters?" "The same as is said when their oxen and asses die," answered the Rabbi—"May the Lord replenish thy loss." They were not even to be mourned for by their masters; Rabbi Jose only permitted a master to say—"Alas, a good and faithful man, and one who lived by his labour!" But even this was objected to as being too much (*Berachôth*, f. 16, 2; Maimonides, *Hilch. Aval.*, § 12; *Hal.* 12).

When Pliny interceded with Sabinianus for the offending freedman, he was able to write shortly afterwards, "You have done well in receiving back your freedman to your house and heart. This will give you pleasure, as it certainly gives me pleasure; first, because it shows me your self-control, and secondly, because you esteem me sufficiently to yield to my authority, and make a concession to my entreaties." What was the issue of St. Paul's letter we are not told, but we may feel quite sure that the confidence of one who was so skilful a reader of human character was not misplaced; that Philemon received his slave as kindly as Sabinianus received his freedman; that he forgave him, and not merely took him into favour, but did what St. Paul does not ask, but evidently desired, namely, set him free.[1] We may be sure, too, that if St. Paul was ever able to carry out his intended visit to Colossæ, it was no mere "lodging" that Philemon prepared for him, but a home under his own and Apphia's roof, where they and the somewhat slack Archippus, and the Church that assembled in their house, might enjoy his beloved society, and profit by his immortal words.

CHAPTER LII.

THE EPISTLE TO "THE EPHESIANS."

Τῇ Ἐκκλησίᾳ τῇ ἀξιομακαριστάτῳ τῇ οὔσῃ ἐν Ἐφέσῳ τῆς Ἀσίας.—IGNAT. *ad Eph.* i.

"Nulla Epistola Pauli tanta habet mysteria tam reconditis sensibus involuta."—JER. *in Eph.* iii.

Ἓν σῶμα καὶ ἓν πνεῦμα.—EPH. iv. 4.

THE polemical *speciality* of the Epistle to the Colossians, compared with the far more magnificent generality of the great truths which occupy the earlier chapters of the Epistle to "the Ephesians,"[2] seems (as we have already

[1] The ecclesiastical traditions about Philemon's episcopate, martyrdom, &c., are too late and worthless to deserve mention; and the same may be said of those respecting Onesimus. As far as dates are concerned, he *might* be the Onesimus, Bishop of Ephesus, mentioned forty-four years later by St. Ignatius. A postscript in two MSS. says that he was martyred at Rome by having his legs broken on the rack.

[2] That the Epistle was meant for the Ephesians, *among others*, is generally admitted, and Alford points out the suitableness of "the Epistle of the grace of God" to a church where Paul had specially preached "the Gospel of the grace of God" (Acts xx. 24, 32). And the pathetic appeal contained in the words ὁ δέσμιος (iii. 1; iv. 1) would come home to those who had heard the prophecy of Acts xx. 22. Other points of parallel between this Epistle and that to the Ephesian elders are the rare use of βουλή (i. 11; Acts xx. 27), of περιποίησις (i. 14; cf. Acts xx. 28), and of κληρονομία (i. 14, 18; v. 5; Acts xx. 32; and Maurice, *Unity*, 512—514). But without going at length into the often-repeated argument, the mere surface-phenomena of the Epistle—not by any means the mere omission of salutations, and of the name of Timothy—but the want of intimacy and speciality, the generality of the thanksgiving, the absence of the word "brethren" (see vi. 10), the distance, so to speak, in the entire tone of address, together with the twice-repeated εἴγε (iii. 2; iv. 21), and the constrained absence of strong personal appeal in iii. 2—4, would alone be inexplicable, even if there were no external grounds for doubting the authenticity of the words ἐν Ἐφέσῳ. But when we find these words omitted for no conceivable reason in ℵ, B, and know, on the testimony of Basil, that he had been traditionally informed of

observed) to furnish a decisive proof that the latter, to some extent, sprang out of the former, and that it was written because the Apostle desired to utilise the departure of Tychicus with the letter which had been evoked by the heresies of Colossæ.

Of the genuineness of the Epistle, in spite of all the arguments which have been brought against it, I cannot entertain the shadow of a doubt. I examine the question without any conscious bias. If the arguments against its Pauline authorship appeared valid, I am aware of no prepossession which would lead me to struggle against their force, nor would the deepest truths of the Epistle appear to me the less profound or sacred from the fact that tradition had erred in assigning its authorship.[1]

To the arguments which endeavoured to show that the Phaedo had not been written by Plato it was thought almost sufficient to reply—

εἴ με Πλάτων οὐ γράψε δύω ἐγένοντο Πλάτωνες.

Certainly if St. Paul did not write the Epistle to "the Ephesians," there must have been two St. Pauls. Baur speaks contemptuously of such an objection;[2] but can any one seriously believe that a forger capable of producing the Epistle to the Ephesians could have lived and died unheard of among the holy, but otherwise very ordinary, men and mediocre writers who attracted notice in the Church of the first century? It is true that De Wette, and his followers,[3] treat the Epistle *de haut en bas* as a verbose and colourless reproduction, quite inferior to St. Paul's genuine writings, and marked by poverty of ideas and redundance of words. We can only reply that this is a matter of taste. The colour red makes no impression on the colour-blind; and to some readers this Epistle has seemed as little colourless as is the body of heaven in

their omission, and found them omitted, ἐν τοῖς παλαιοῖς τῶν ἀντιγράφων, as also did Marcion, Tertullian, and Jerome, we are led to the unhesitating conclusion that the letter was not addressed exclusively to the Ephesians. The view which regards it as an encyclical, sent, among other places, to Laodicea, is highly probable (Col. iv. 16). In Eph. vi. 21, καὶ ὑμεῖς is most easily explicable, on the supposition that the letter was to go to different cities. In any case, the absence of greetings, &c., is a clear mark of genuineness, for a forger would certainly have put them in. The Epistle is by no means deficient in external evidence. Irenæus (*Haer.* v. 2, 3), Clement of Alexandria (*Strom.* iv. 8), Polycarp (*ad Phil.* i., xii.), Tertullian (*adv. Marc.* v. 1, 17), and perhaps even Ignatius (*ad Eph.* vi.), have either quoted or alluded to it; and it is mentioned in the Muratorian Canon. Impugners of its authenticity must account for its wide and early acceptance, no less than for the difficulty of its forgery. It is a simple fact that the Epistle was accepted as unquestionably Pauline from the days of Ignatius to those of Schleiermacher. Renan sums up the objections to its authenticity under the heads of (i.) Recurrent phrases and ἅπαξ λεγόμενα; (ii.) style weak, diffused, embarrassed; (iii.) traces of advanced Gnosticism; (iv.) developed conception of the Church as a living organism; (v.) un-Pauline exegesis; (vi.) the expression "holy Apostles;" (vii.) un-Pauline views of marriage. I hope to show that these objections are untenable.

[1] That the Epistle to the Hebrews was *not* written by the Apostle is now almost universally believed, yet this conviction has never led the Church to underrate its value as a part of the sacred canon of the New Testament Scriptures.

[2] *Paul.* ii. 2.

[3] Dr. Davidson, *Introd.* ii. 388. In his earlier edition, Dr. Davidson thought "nothing more groundless" than such assertions, and he then said, "The language is rich and copious, but it is everywhere pregnant with meaning." (Sea Gloag, *Introd.*, p. 313.)

its clearness. Chrysostom—no bad judge surely of style and rhetoric—spoke of the lofty sublimity of its sentiments. Theophylact dwells on the same characteristics as suitable to the Ephesians. Grotius says St. Paul here equals the sublimity of his thoughts with words more sublime than any human tongue has ever uttered. Luther reckoned it among the noblest books of the New Testament. Witsius calls it a divine Epistle glowing with the flame of Christian love, and the splendour of holy light, and flowing with fountains of living water. Coleridge said of it, "In this, the divinest composition of man, is every doctrine of Christianity: first, those doctrines peculiar to Christianity; and secondly, those precepts common to it with natural religion." Lastly, Alford calls it "the greatest and most heavenly work of one whose very imagination is peopled with things in the heavens, and even his fancy rapt into the visions of God." Pfleiderer, though he rejects the genuineness of the Epistle, yet says that "of all the forms which Paulinism went through in the course of its transition to Catholicism, that of the Epistle to the Ephesians is the most developed and the richest in dogma."

The close resemblance in expression, and in many of the thoughts, to the Epistle to the Colossians, when combined with the radical differences[1] which separate the two Epistles, appears to me an absolutely irresistible proof in favour of the authenticity of both, even if the external evidence were weaker than it is. Roughly speaking, we may say that the style of Colossians shows a "rich brevity;" that of Ephesians a diffuser fulness. Colossians is definite and logical; Ephesians is lyrical and Asiatic. In Colossians, St. Paul has the error more prominently in view; in Ephesians he has the counteracting truth. In Colossians he is the soldier; in Ephesians the builder. In Colossians he is arguing against a vain and deceitful philosophy; in Ephesians he is revealing a heavenly wisdom. Colossians is "his caution, his argument, his process, and his work-day toil;" Ephesians is instruction passing into prayer, a creed soaring into the loftiest of Evangelic Psalms. Alike the differences and the resemblances are stamped with an individuality of style which is completely beyond the reach of imitation.[2] A forger might indeed have sat down with the deliberate purpose of borrowing words and phrases and thoughts from the Epistle to the Colossians, but in that case it would have been wholly beyond his power to produce a letter which, in the midst of such resemblances, con-

[1] There is the *general* resemblance that in both (Col. iii.; Eph. iv. 1) the same transition leads to the same application—the humblest morality being based on the sublimest truths; and there are the *special* resemblances (α) in Christological views; (β) in phraseology—seventy-eight verses out of 155 being expressed in the same phrases in the two Epistles. On the other hand, there are marked differences—(α) there are ἅπαξ λεγόμενα in both; (β) the leading word τὰ ἐπουράνια is peculiar to Ephesians; (γ) Ephesians has deep thoughts and whole sections (i. 3—14; iv. 5—15; v. 7—14; 23—31; vi. 10—17) which are not found in Colossians; (δ) there are seven Old Testament allusions or quotations in Ephesians, and only one in Colossians (ii. 21).

[2] Hence the critics are quite unable to make up their minds whether the Epistles were written by two authors, or by one author; and whether St. Paul was in part the author of either or of neither; and whether the Colossians was an abstract of the Ephesians, or the Ephesians an amplification of the Colossians.

veyed so different an impression in a style so characteristic and so intensely emotional.[1] Even if we could regard it as probable that any one could have poured forth truths so exalted, and moral teaching so pure and profound, in an Epistle by which he deliberately intended to deceive the Church and the world,[2] it is *not* possible that one actuated by such a purpose should successfully imitate the glow and rush of feeling which marks the other writings of the Apostle, and expresses itself in the to-and-fro-conflicting eddies of thought, in the one great flow of utterance and purpose. The style of St. Paul may be compared to a great tide ever advancing irresistibly towards the destined shore, but broken and rippled over every wave of its broad expanse, and liable at any moment to mighty refluences as it foams and swells about opposing sandbank or rocky cape.[3] With even more exactness we might compare it to a river whose pure waters, at every interspace of calm, reflect as in a mirror the hues of heaven, but which is liable to the rushing influx of mountain torrents, and whose reflected images are only dimly discernible in ten thousand fragments of quivering colour, when its surface is swept by ruffling winds. If we make the difficult concession that any other mind than that of St. Paul could have originated the majestic statement of Christian truth which is enshrined in the doctrinal part of the Epistle, we may still safely assert, on literary grounds alone, that no writer, desirous to gain a hearing for such high revelations, could have so completely merged his own individuality in that of another as to imitate the involutions of parentheses, the digressions at a word, the superimposition of a minor current of feeling over another

[1] The similarity of expressions (Davidson, *Introd.* i. 384) often throws into more marked relief the *dissimilarity* in fundamental ideas. It is another amazing sign of the blindness which marred the keen insight of Baur in other directions, that he should say the contents of the Epistles "are so *essentially the same* that they cannot well be distinguished"! (*Paul.* ii. 6.) The metaphysical Christology, which is polemically dwelt upon in the Colossians, is only assumed and alluded to in the Ephesians; and the prominent conceptions of Predestination and Unity which mark the doctrinal part of the Ephesians find little or no place in the Colossians. The recurrence of any word ἥτις ἀειδόντεσσι νεωτάτη ἀμφιπέληται is a common literary phenomenon, and any careful student of Æschylus is aware that if he finds a startling word or metaphor he may find it again in the next hundred lines, even if it occurs in no other play. Nothing, therefore, was more natural than that there should be a close resemblance, especially of the moral parts of two Epistles, written perhaps within a few days of each other; and that even though the doctrinal parts had different objects, and were meant for different readers, we should find alternate expansions or abbreviations of the same thoughts and the repetition of phrases so pregnant as ὁ πλοῦτος τῆς δόξης (Eph. i. 18; Col. i. 27); τὸ πλήρωμα (Eph. i. 23; Col. i. 19); περιτομὴ ἀχειροποίητος (Eph. ii. 11; Col. ii. 11); and ὁ παλαιὸς ἄνθρωπος (Eph. iv. 22; Col. iii. 9). When Schneckenburger talks of "a *mechanical* use of materials" he is using one of those phrases which betray a strong bias, and render his results less plausible than they might otherwise seem. "How can he have overlooked the memorable fact, which all readers of the Epistle have noticed, that the idea of catholicity is here first raised to dogmatic definiteness and predominant significance?" (Pfleiderer, ii. 164.)

[2] iii. 1, 8, &c.

[3] "Every one must be conscious of an overflowing fulness in the style of this Epistle, as if the Apostle's mind could not contain the thoughts that were at work in him, as if each one that he uttered had a luminous train before it and behind it, from which it could not disengage itself" (Maurice, *Unity of the New Testament*, p. 535).

that is flowing steadily beneath it, the unconscious recurrence of haunting expressions, the struggle and strain to find a worthy utterance for thoughts and feelings which burst through the feeble bands of language, the dominance of the syllogism of emotion over the syllogism of grammar—the many other minute characteristics which stamp so ineffaceable an impress on the Apostle's undisputed works. This may, I think, be pronounced with some confidence to be a psychological impossibility. The intensity of the writer's feelings is betrayed in every sentence by the manner in which great truths interlace each other, and are yet subordinated to one main and grand perception. Mannerisms of style may be reproduced; but let any one attempt to simulate the language of genuine passion, and every reader will tell him how ludicrously he fails. Theorists respecting the spuriousness of some of the Pauline Epistles have, I think, entirely underrated the immense difficulty of palming upon the world an even tolerably successful imitation of a style the most living, the most nervously sensitive, which the world has ever known. The spirit in which a forger would have sat down to write is not the spirit which could have poured forth so grand a eucharistic hymn as the Epistle to the Ephesians.[1] Fervour, intensity, sublimity, the unifying—or, if I may use the expression, *esemplastic*—power of the imagination over the many subordinate truths which strive for utterance; the eagerness which hurries the Apostle to his main end in spite of deeply important thoughts which intrude themselves into long parentheses and almost interminable paragraphs—all these must, from the very nature of literary composition, have been far beyond the reach of one who could deliberately sit down with a lie in his right hand to write a false superscription, and boast with trembling humility of the unparalleled spiritual privileges entrusted to him as the Apostle of the Gentiles.

A strong bias of prejudice against the doctrines of the Epistle may perhaps, in some minds, have overborne the sense of literary possibilities. But is there in reality anything surprising in the developed Christology of St. Paul's later years? That his views respecting the supreme divinity of Christ never wavered will hardly, I think, be denied by any candid controversialist. They are as clearly, though more implicitly, present in the First Epistle to the Thessalonians as in the Second Epistle to Timothy. No human being can reasonably doubt the authenticity of the Epistle to the Romans; yet the Pauline evangel logically argued out in that Epistle is identical with that which is so triumphantly preached in this. They are not, as Reuss has observed, two systems, but two methods of exposition. In the Romans, Paul's point of view is *psychologic*, and his theology is built on moral facts—the universality of sin, and the insufficiency of man, and hence salvation by the grace of God, and union of the believer with the dead and risen Christ. But in the Ephesians the point of view is *theologic*—the idea of God's eternal plans realised in the course of ages, and the unity in Christ of redeemed humanity with the family of heaven. "The two great dogmatic teachers of

[1] J. Ll. Davies, *Eph.*, p. 19.

the sixteenth century, both essentially disciples of St. Paul, have both, so to speak, divided between them the inheritance of their master. The manual of Melancthon attaches itself to the Epistle to the Romans; the 'Institutes' of Calvin follow the direction marked out in that to the Ephesians; party spirit will alone be able to deny that, in spite of this difference of method, the system of the two writers has, after all, been one and the same."[1] Is there a word respecting Christ's exaltation in the Epistle to the Ephesians which implies a greater or diviner Being than Him of whom St. Paul has spoken as the Final Conqueror in the 15th chapter of the First Epistle to the Corinthians?

We can imagine that when he began to dictate this circular letter to the Churches of Asia, the one overwhelming thought in the mind of the Apostle was the ideal splendour and perfectness of the Church of Christ, and the consequent duty of holiness which was incumbent on all its members. The thought of Humanity regenerated in Christ by an eternal process, and the consequent duty of all to live in accordance with this divine enlightenment—these are the double wings which keep him in one line throughout his rapturous flight. Hence the Epistle naturally fell into two great divisions, doctrinal and practical; the idea and its realisation; pure theology and applied theology; the glorious unity of the Church in Christ its living head, and the moral exhortations which sprang with irresistible force of appeal from this divine mystery. But as he was in all his doctrine laying the foundations of practice, and throughout founded the rules of practice on doctrine, the two elements are not so sharply divided as not to intermingle and coalesce in the general design. The glory of the Christian's vocation is inseparably connected with the practical duties which result from it, and which it was directly intended to educe. Great principles find their proper issue in the faithful performance of little duties.

It is naturally in the first three chapters that St. Paul is most overpowered by the grandeur of his theme. Universal reconciliation in Christ as the central Being of the Universe is the leading thought both of the Ephesians and the Colossians, and it is a deeper and grander thought than that of the Epistle to the Hebrews, which only sees this unity in Christ's priesthood, or that of the Pseudo-Clementines, which sees it in Christ as the Prophet of Truth.[2] St. Paul is endeavouring to impress upon the minds of all Christians that they have entered upon a new *æon* of God's dispensations—the *æon* of God's ideal Church, which is to comprehend all things in heaven and on earth. Round this central conception, as round a nucleus of intense light, there radiate the considerations which he wishes them specially to bear in mind:—namely, that this perfected idea is the working out of a purpose eternally conceived; that the œconomy—*i.e.*, the Divine dispensation[3]—of all the past circumstances of history has been fore-ordained before all ages to tend to its completion; that it is a *mystery*—*i.e.*, a truth hidden from previous ages, but now revealed;

[1] Reuss, *Les Epitres Paulin.* ii. 146.
[2] Baur, *First Three Cent.* i. 126.
[3] *οἰκονομία*, Eph. i. 10; iii. 2.

that each Person of the Blessed Trinity has taken direct part therein; that this plan is the result of free grace; that it is unsurpassable in breadth and length, and height and depth, being the exhibition of a love of which the wealth is inexhaustible and passes knowledge; that the benefits of it extend alike to Jew and Gentile; that it centres in the person of the risen Christ; and that to the Apostle himself, unworthy as he is, is entrusted the awful responsibility of preaching it among the Gentiles.

The incessant recurrence of *leading words connected with these different thoughts* is a remarkable feature of the first three chapters.[1] Thus, in the endeavour to express that the whole great scheme of redemptive love is part of the Divine "Will" and "Purpose," those two words are frequently repeated. Grace (χάρις) is so prominent in the Apostle's mind that the word is used thirteen times, and may be regarded as the key-note of the entire Epistle.[2] The writer's thoughts are so completely with the risen and ascended Christ as the head, the centre, the life of the Church, that he six times uses the expression "the heavenlies" without any limitation of time or place.[3] He feels so deeply the necessity of spiritual insight to counteract the folly of fancied wisdom, that the work of the Spirit of God in the spirit of man is here peculiarly prominent.[4] The words "wealth,"[5] and "glory,"[6] and "mystery,"[7] and "plenitude,"[8] show also the dominant chords which are vibrating in his mind, while the frequent compounds in ὑπὲρ, πρὸ, and σὺν,[9] show how deeply he is impressed with the loftiness, the fore-ordainment, and the result of this Gospel in uniting the Jew and Gentile within one great spiritual Temple, of which the middle wall has been for ever broken down. "It would, indeed," says Mr. Maurice, "amply repay the longest study to examine the order in which these details are introduced, in what relation they stand to each other, how they are all referred to one ground, the good pleasure of His

[1] θέλημα, Eph. i. 1, 5, 9, 11 (v. 17; vi. 6); βουλὴ, i. 11; εὐδοκία, i. 9; πρόθεσις, iii. 11.

[2] χάρις, i. 2, 6 (*bis*), 7; ii. 5, 7, 8; iii. 2, 7, 8; iv. 7, 32; vi. 24.

[3] τὰ ἐπουράνια, i. 3, 20; ii. 6; iii. 10; vi. 12. "The Apostle carries us into '*the heavenlies*' (not 'the heavenly *places*,' as our translators render it, so perverting the idea of a sentence from which place and time are carefully excluded), into a region of voluntary beings, of spirits, standing by a spiritual law, capable of a spiritual blessing" (Maurice, *Unity of the New Testament*, p. 523).

[4] πνεῦμα and πνευματικὸς occurs thirteen times in this Epistle (i. 3, 13, 17; ii. 18, 22; iii. 5, 16; iv. 3, 4, 23, 30; v. 18; vi. 17, 18); and only once in the Colossians (i. 8, 9). (Baur, *Paul.* ii. 21.)

[5] πλοῦτος, πλούσιος, i. 7, 18; ii. 4, 7; iii. 8, 16. This word is only used in this sense by St. James (ii. 5). See Paley, *Horae Paulinae*, Ephes. ii. But see 2 Cor. viii. 9; Phil. ii. 7.

[6] δόξα, i. 6, 12, 14, 17, 18; iii. 16, 21, &c.

[7] μυστήριον, Eph. i. 9; iii. 3, 4, 9 (v. 32); vi. 19. In no other Epistle, except that to the Colossians and 1 Cor., does it occur more than twice.

[8] πλήρωμα, i. 23; iii. 19; iv. 10—13 (i. 10). In the quasi-technical sense it is only found in the Epistle to the Colossians, i. 19; ii. 9.

[9] ὑπέρβαλλον, i. 19; ὑπεράνω, 21. Cf. iii. 19, ὑπερεκπερισσοῦ; 20; iv. 10, &c. These compounds are characteristic of the emphatic energy of St. Paul's style.

Προορίσας, i. 5; προέθετο, i. 9; προητοίμασεν, ii. 10; πρόθεσις, iii. 11.

Συνεζωοποίησε, ii. 5; συνήγειρε, συνεκάθισεν, 6; συμπολῖται, ii. 19 (a late and bad word, Phryn., p. 172); συνοικοδομεῖσθε, 22; συγκληρόνομα, σύσσωμα, συμμέτοχα, iii. 6; σύνδεσμος, iv. 3; συμβιβαζόμενον, συναρμολογούμενον, 16.

will, and to one end, the gathering up of all things in Christ.[1] But however desirable the minute investigation is, after the road has been travelled frequently, the reader must allow the Apostle to carry him along at his own speed on his own wings, if he would know anything of the height from which he is descending and to which he is returning."[2]

After his usual salutation to the saints that are in —— (perhaps leaving a blank to be filled up by Tychicus at the places to which he carried a copy of the letter), he breaks into the rapturous sentence which is "not only the exordium of the letter, but also the enunciation of its design."

"Blessed be the God and Father of our Lord Jesus Christ, who blessed us with all spiritual blessings in the heavenlies in Christ, even as He chose us out in Him before the foundation of the world, that we should be holy and blameless before Him, in love; fore-ordaining us to adoption by Jesus Christ into Himself, according to the good pleasure of His will, *for the praise of the glory* of His grace wherewith He graced us in the beloved."[3]

This leads him to a passage in which the work of the Son in this great fore-ordained plan is mainly predominant.

"In whom we have our redemption through His blood, the remission of transgressions, according to the wealth of His grace, wherewith He abounded towards us, in all wisdom and discernment, making known to us the mystery of His will, according to His good pleasure which He purposed in Himself, with a view to the dispensation of the fulness of the seasons—to sum up all things in Christ, both the things in the heavens and the things on the earth—in *Him*. In whom we also were made an inheritance, being fore-ordained according to the purpose of Him who worketh all things according to the counsel of His will, that we should be *to the praise of His glory* who have before hoped in Christ."[4]

This repetition of the phrase "to the praise of His glory," introduces the work of the Third Person of the Blessed Trinity.

"In whom (Christ) ye also" (as well as the Jewish Christians who previously had hoped in Christ) "on hearing the word of truth, the Gospel of your salvation, in whom (I say), believing, ye too were sealed with the Holy Spirit of promise, who is the earnest of our inheritance, with a view to the redemption of the purchased possession *unto the praise of His glory*."[5]

Since, therefore, it is the fixed ordinance, from all eternity, of the Blessed God, that man should be adopted through the redemption of Christ to the praise of the glory of the Eternal Trinity, and should receive the seal of the

[1] The Epistle may be thus briefly summarised:—Salutation (i. 1, 2). Thanksgiving for the election of the Church, and the unity wrought by Christ's redemption and calling of both Jews and Gentiles (i. 3—14). Prayer for their growth into the full knowledge of Christ (15—23). Unity of mankind in the heavenlies in Christ (ii. 1—22). Fuller explanation of the mystery, with prayer for the full comprehension of it, and doxology (iii. 1—21). Exhortation to live worthily of the ideal unity of the Catholic Church in love (iv. 1—16). Exhortation to the practical duties of the new life, in the conquest over sin (iv. 17—v. 21), and in social relations (v. 22—vi. 9). The armour of God (vi. 10—17). Final requests and farewell (vi. 10—24).

[2] *Unity of the New Testament*, p. 525. See Excursus XXV., "Phraseology and Doctrines of the Epistle to the Ephesians."

[3] i. 3—6. Notice the marvellous compression and exhaustive fulness of this great outline of theology.

[4] i. 7—12.

[5] i. 13, 14.

Spirit as the pledge of full and final entrance into his heritage, St. Paul tells them that, hearing of their faith and love, he ceaselessly prayed that God—the God of our Lord Jesus Christ, the Father of the Glory—would grant them a full knowledge[1] of Himself, giving them "illuminated eyes in their hearts" to know what their calling means, and the wealth and glory of this heritage, and the surpassing greatness of the power which He had put forth in raising Christ from the dead, and seating Him at His right hand in the heavenlies, as the Supreme Ruler now and for ever of every spiritual and earthly power, and as the Head over all things to the Church,—which is His body, "the Pleroma" (*i.e.*, the filled continent, the brimmed receptacle) "of Him who filleth all things with all things."[2]

But for whom were these great privileges predestined, and how were they bestowed? The full answer is contained in the second chapter. They were intended for all, both Jews and Gentiles, and were bestowed by free grace. In this section the leading conception is the unity of mankind, in the heavenlies, in Christ. The Gentiles had been dead in transgressions and sins, absorbed in the temporal and the external,[3] showing by their disobedience the influence of the Prince of the power of the air; and the Jews, too, had been occupied with the desires of the flesh, doing the determinations of the flesh and the thoughts, and were by nature children of wrath[4] even as the rest; but God in His rich love and mercy quickened both Jews and Gentiles together, while still dead in their transgressions, and raised them together, and seated them together in the heavenlies in Christ Jesus—a name that occurs in verse after verse, being at the very heart of the Apostle's thoughts. The instrumental cause of this great salvation is solely free grace, applied by faith, that this grace might be manifested to the coming ages in all its surpassing wealth of kindness; and that we, thus created anew in Christ, and so prevented from any boast[5] that we achieved by good works our own salvation, might still walk in good works, to which God predestined us.[6] The Gentiles,

[1] Ἐπίγνωσις, i. 17; iv. 13. I have already alluded to the importance attached to true knowledge in these Epistles, written as it was to counteract the incipient but already baneful influence of a "knowledge falsely called." Hence we have also γνῶσις, iii. 19; σύνεσις, iii. 4; φρόνησις, i. 8; σοφία, *ib.*; ἀποκάλυψις, iii. 3; φωτίζειν, iii. 9; &c. &c.

[2] i. 15—23. See iv. 10. Cf. Xen. *Hell.* vi. 2, 14, τὰς ναῦς ἐπληροῦτο. On the different application of the word Pleroma here and in Col. i. 19, *v. supra.* The view that it here means "complement" like *parapleroma* seems to me much less probable. On the expression the "God of our Lord Jesus Christ," cf. ver. 3; John xx. 17. In the unique phrase, "the Father of the Glory," ὁ πατὴρ τῆς δόξης, Canon Barry sees an allusion to the Jewish identification of "the Word" with "the Shechinah." Compare the use of Δόξα in James ii. 1; Titus ii. 13; Heb. i. 3.

[3] ii. 2, κατὰ τὸν αἰῶνα τοῦ κόσμου τούτου.

[4] Mr. Maurice's rendering, "children *of impulse*," is untenable.

[5] ii. 9. The last appearance of the word "boast" in St. Paul.

[6] ii. 10. It is interesting to see how the epoch of *controversy* on the great topic of these verses is here assumed to be closed; ἐπ' ἔργοις ἀγαθοῖς, οἷς προητοίμασεν ὁ Θεὸς ἵνα ἐν αὐτοῖς περιπατήσωμεν. Certainly οἷς may be by attraction for ἅ; but it is surely a very awkward expression to say that "God created *good works* that we should walk in them," and although ἡμᾶς is not expressed, it is involved in περιπατήσωμεν. Alford, who adopts the E.V., compares it with John v. 36, which is, however, no parallel. Nowhere is the harmonising of good works with free grace more admirably illustrated than here. Good

then, were to remember that their former uncircumcision, so far as it was of any importance, was that spiritual uncircumcision which consisted in utter alienation from Christ, His kingdom, and His promises. But now in Christ, by the blood of Christ, the once afar have been made near. For He is our Peace; He has broken down the separating partition—the enmity between the two members of His great human family—by doing away with the law of ordinances and decrees,[1] that He might create the two—Jew and Gentile—into one fresh human being, making peace; and might reconcile them both in one body to God by the cross, slaying thereby the enmity between them both, and between them and God. The result, then, of His advent is peace to the far-off and to the nigh; for through Him we both have access by one Spirit to the Father. The Gentiles are no longer aliens, but fellow-citizens with the saints, built on the corner-stone of Christ which the Apostles and prophets laid—like stones compaginated[2] into the ever-growing walls of the one spiritual House of God.[3]

Then follows a chapter of parentheses, or rather of thoughts leading to thoughts, and linked together, as throughout the Epistle, by relatival connexions.[4] Resuming the prayer (i. 17) of which the thread had been broken by the full enunciation of the great truths in which he desired them to be enlightened: "For this cause," he says—namely, because of the whole blessed mystery which he has been expounding, and which results in their corporate union in Christ—"I, Paul, the prisoner of the Lord, on behalf of you Gentiles" —and there once more the prayer is broken by a parenthesis which lasts through thirteen verses. For, remembering that the letter is to be addressed not only to the Ephesians, of whom the majority were so well known to him, but also to other Asiatic Churches, some of which he had not even visited, and which barely knew more of him than his name,[5] he pauses to dwell on the exalted character of the mission entrusted to him, and to express at the same time his own sense of utter personal unworthiness. Having called himself "the prisoner of the Lord on behalf of you Gentiles," he breaks off to say—

"Assuming that you have heard of the dispensation of the grace of God given me towards you—that by revelation was made known to me the mystery [of the

works are here included in the predestined purpose of grace, so that they are not a condition of salvation, but an aim set before us, and rendered practicable by God's unconditional favour. (See Pfleiderer, ii. 189.)

[1] Cf. Col. i. 20—22. The application of the word is somewhat different; but it is exactly the kind of difference which might be made by an author dealing independently with his own expressions, and one on which a forger would not have ventured. The breaking down of the Chel, "the middle wall of partition," was that part of Christ's work which it fell mainly to St. Paul to continue. The charge that he had taken Trophimus into the Court of Israel, literally false, was ideally most true. And Paul the Apostle was the most effectual uprooter of the "hedge," which Saul the Pharisee thought it his chief work to make around the Law.

[2] This word, used by St. Jerome, may express the unusual συναρμολογουμένη.

[3] ii. 1—22.

[4] See Ellicott, *ad* iii. 5.

[5] Although undoubtedly the εἴγε ἠκούσατε, like the similar expression in iv. 21, Gal. iii. 4, &c., implies that the fact is *assumed*, yet it is certainly not an expression which would well accord with a letter addressed only to a church in which the writer had long laboured.

calling of the Gentiles], as I previously wrote to you in brief,[1] in accordance with which you can, as you read it, perceive my understanding in the mystery of Christ —a mystery which in other generations was not made known to the sons of men as it is now revealed to His holy Apostles[2] and prophets by the Spirit—(namely) that the Gentiles are[3] co-heirs, and concorporate, and comparticipant[4] of the promise in Christ Jesus by the Gospel, of which I became a minister, according to the gift of the grace of God given to me according to the working of His power. To me, the less-than-least[5] of all saints, was given this grace, to preach among the Gentiles the untrackable[6] wealth of Christ; and to enlighten all on the nature of the dispensation of the mystery that has been hidden from the ages in God, who created all things; that now to the principalities and the powers in the heavenlies may be made known by the Church the richly-variegated wisdom of God,[7] according to the prearrangement of the ages which He made in Christ Jesus our Lord, in whom we have our confidence and our access by faith in Him: wherefore I entreat you not to lose heart in my afflictions on your behalf, seeing that this is your glory. For this cause, then" (and here he resumes the thread of the prayer broken in the first verse) "I bend my knees to the Father,[8] from whom every fatherhood[9] in heaven and on earth derives its name, that He would give you, according to the wealth of His glory, to be strengthened by power through His Spirit into spiritual manhood,[10] that Christ may dwell in your hearts by faith—ye having been rooted and founded in love, that ye may have strength to grasp mentally with all saints what is the length and breadth and depth and height, and to know (spiritually) the knowledge-surpassing love of Christ, that ye may be filled up to all the plenitude of God."[11]

"Now to Him that is able above all things to do superabundantly above[12] all that we ask or think, according to the power [of the Holy Spirit] which worketh in us,

[1] i. 9 *seq.*; ii. 13 *seq.*

[2] Serious objections have been made to this phrase, as proving that it could not have been written by the pen that wrote Gal. ii. The objection is groundless. Assuming the ἁγίοις to be correct (though not found in every MS.; cf. Col. i. 26)—i. It is perfectly *generic*, not individual; cf. ver. 8 and ii. 20; 1 Cor. xvi. 1, 15. ii. Apostles and prophets are bracketed, and the epithet "holy" means "sanctified," a title which they share with all "saints." iii. "Apostles" does not here necessarily bear its *narrower* sense.

[3] Not "should be," as in A.V.

[4] iii. 6, συγκληρόνομα, σύσσωμα, συμμέτοχα. The two parts—Jews and Gentiles—are to become one body, the body of Christ, the Christian Church (ii. 16). The strange English words may perhaps correspond to the strange Greek words which St. Paul invented to express this newly-revealed mystery in the strongest possible form, as though no words could be too strong to express his dominant conception of the reunion in Christ of those who apart from Him are separate and divided.

[5] iii. 8, ἐλαχιστοτέρῳ. Would a forger have made St. Paul write thus? The expression has been compared to 1 Cor. xv. 9, but expresses a far deeper humility, because it is used when the writer is alluding to a far loftier exaltation. Those who criticise the phrase as exaggerated must be destitute of the deepest spiritual experiences. The confessions of the holiest are ever the most bitter and humble, because their very holiness enables them to take the due measure of the heinousness of sin. The self-condemnation of a Cowper or a Fénelon is far stronger than that of a Byron or a Voltaire. "The greatest sinner, the greatest saint, are equi-distant from the goal where the mind rests in satisfaction with itself. With the growth in goodness grows the sense of sin. One law fulfilled shows a thousand neglected" (Mozley, *Essays*, i. 327).

[6] iii. 8, ἀνεξιχνίαστον. Job v. 9, אֵין חֵקֶר. Cf. Rom. xi. 33, ἀνεξερεύνητα τὰ κρίματα αὐτοῦ καὶ ἀνεξιχνίαστοι αἱ ὁδοί.

[7] πολυποίκιλος. Cf. στέφανον π. ἀνθέων. Eubulus, *Ath.* xv. 7, p. 679.

[8] The addition "of our Lord Jesus Christ," however ancient, is probably spurious, as it is not found in א, A, B, C, the Coptic, the Æthiopic versions, &c.

[9] Not "the whole family," as in A.V.

[10] iii. 16, εἰς τὸν ἔσω ἄνθρωπον.

[11] iii. 1—19. In other words, "that ye may be filled with all the plenitude of goodness wherewith God is filled;" "omnes divinae naturae divitiae" (Fritzsche).

[12] Of twenty-eight compounds in ὑπὲρ in the New Testament, no less than twenty are found in St. Paul alone.

to Him be glory in the Church, in Christ Jesus, to all the generations of the age of the ages. Amen."[1]

With this prayer he closes the doctrinal part of the Epistle; the remaining half of it is strictly practical. St. Paul would have felt it no descent of thought to pass from the loftiest spiritual mysteries to the humblest moral duties. He knew that holiness was the essence of God's Being, and he saw in the holiness of Christians the beautiful result of that predestined purpose, which, after being wrought out to gradual completion in the dispensation of past *æons*, was now fully manifested and revealed in Christ. He knew that the loftiest principles were the necessary basis of the simplest acts of faithfulness, and that all which is most pure, lovely, and of good report, in the Christian life, is the sole result of all that is most sublime in the Christian's faith. The lustre of the planets may be faint and poor, but yet it is reflected from the common sun; and so the goodness of a redeemed man, however pale in lustre, is still sacred, because it is a reflexion from the Sun of righteousness. The reflected light of morality is nothing apart from the splendour of that religion from which it is derived. There is little which is admirable in the honesty which simply results from its being the best policy; or in the purity which is maintained solely by fear of punishment; or even in the virtue which is coldly adopted out of a calculation that it tends to the greatest happiness of the greatest number. It was not in this way that St. Paul regarded morality. Many of the precepts which he delivers in the practical sections of his Epistles might also have been delivered, and nobly delivered, by an Epictetus or a Marcus Aurelius; but that which places an immeasurable distance between the teachings of St. Paul and theirs, is the fact that in St. Paul's view holiness is not the imperfect result of rare self-discipline, but the natural outcome of a divine life, imparted by One who is the common Head of all the family of man, and in participation with whose plenitude the humblest act of self-sacrifice becomes invested with a sacred value and a sacred significance. And there are these further distinctions (among many others) between the lofty teachings of Stoicism and the divine exhortations of Christianity. Stoicism made its appeal only to the noble-hearted few, despising and despairing of the vulgar herd of mankind in all ranks, as incapable of philosophic training or moral elevation. Christianity, in the name of a God who was no respecter of persons, appealed to the very weakest and the very worst as being all redeemed in Christ. Again, Stoicism was dimmed and darkened to the very heart's core of its worthiest votaries by deep perplexity and incurable sadness; Christianity breathes into every utterance the joyous spirit of victory and hope. Even the best of the Stoics looked on the life of men around them with a detestation largely mingled with contempt, and this contempt weakened the sense of reciprocity, and fed the fumes of pride. But St. Paul addresses a revelation unspeakably more majestic, more profound, more spiritual, than any which Stoicism could offer, to men whom he well knows to have lived in

[1] iii. 20, 21.

the trammels of the vilest sins of heathendom, and barely even yet to have escaped out of the snare of the fowler. He confidently addresses exhortations of stainless purity and sensitive integrity to men who had been thieves and adulterers, and worse; and so far from any self-exaltation at his own moral superiority, he regards his own life as hid indeed with Christ in God, but as so little fit to inspire a feeling of satisfaction that he is lost in the conviction of his own unworthiness as contrasted with the wealth of God's compassion, and the unspeakable grandeur of the long-hidden mystery which now in due time he is commissioned to set forth. The mingled prayer and pæan of this magnificent Epistle is inspired throughout "by a sense of opposites—of the union of weakness and strength, of tribulation and glory, of all that had been and all that was to be, of the absolute love of God, of the discovery of that love to man in the Mediator, of the working of that love in man through the Spirit, of the fellowship of the poorest creature of flesh and blood on earth with the spirits in heaven, of a canopy of love above and an abyss of love beneath, which encompasses the whole creation." The Apostle would have delighted in the spirit of those words which a modern poet has learnt from the truths which it was his high mission to reveal:—

"I say to thee, do thou repeat
To the first man thou mayest meet
In lane, highway, or open street,
That he, and we, and all men move
Under a canopy of love
As broad as the blue sky above."[1]

"I then," continues the Apostle—and how much does that word "then" involve, referring as it does to all the mighty truths which he has been setting forth!—"I then, the prisoner in the Lord, exhort you to walk worthily of the calling in which ye were called." This is the keynote to all that follows. So little was earthly success or happiness worth even considering in comparison with the exceeding and eternal weight of glory which affliction was working out for them, that while he has urged them not to lose heart in his tribulations, he makes those very tribulations a ground of appeal, and feels that he can speak to them with all the stronger influence as "a prisoner in the Lord," and "an ambassador in a chain." And the worthy elevation to the grandeur of their calling was to be shown by virtues which, in their heathen condition, they would almost have ranked with abject vices—lowliness, meekness, endurance, the forbearance of mutual esteem. The furious quarrels, the mad jealousies, the cherished rancours, the frantic spirit of revenge which characterised their heathen condition, are to be fused by the heat of love into one great spiritual unity and peace. Oneness, the result of love, is the ruling thought of this section (iv. 3—13). "One body, and one spirit, even as also ye were called in one hope of your calling, one Lord, one Faith, one Baptism, one God and Father of all, who is above all, and through all, and in all."[2] Yet this unity is not a dead level of uniformity. Each has his separate

[1] Archbishop Trench. [2] Omit ἡμῖν, ℵ, A, B, C, &c.

measure of grace given by Him who, ascending in triumph, with Sin and Death bound to His chariot-wheels, "gave gifts for men,"[1] having first descended that by ascending "far above all heavens" He might fill all things. Apostles therefore, and Prophets, and Evangelists, and Pastors, and Teachers were all appointed by virtue of the gifts which He gave, with a view to perfect the saints, and so to build up the Church which is the body of Christ, until we all finally attain[2] to the unity of the faith, and the full knowledge of the Son of God, to perfect manhood, to the measure of the stature of the Plenitude of Christ." But to contribute to this perfect growth we must lay aside moral and spiritual childishness; we must keep the hand firmly on the helm that we may not be tossed like dismantled hulks by every wave and storm of doctrine, in that fraudful sleight and craft which many devote to further the deliberate system of error. To be true and to be loving is the secret of Christian growth.[3] Sincerity and charity are as the life-blood in the veins of that Church, of which Christ is the Head and Heart, "from whom the whole body being fitly framed and compacted by means of every joint of the vital supply, according to the proportional energy of each individual part, tends to the increase of the body, so as to build itself up in love."[4]

After this expansion of the duty of Unity, he returns to his exhortation; and, as before he had urged them to walk worthily of their vocation, he now urges them not to walk, as did the rest of the Gentiles, in the vanity of their mind, having been darkened in their understanding, and utterly alienated from the life of God because of their ignorance and the callosity of their hearts,[5] seeing that they, having lost all sense of shame or sorrow for sin,[6] abandoned themselves to wantonness for the working of all uncleanness, in inordinate desire:[7]—

> "But NOT so did *ye* learn Christ—assuming that ye heard Him, and were taught in Him as the truth is in Jesus,[8] that ye put off, as concerns your former conversation, the old man which is ever being corrupted according to the lusts of deceit, and undergo renewal by the spirit of your mind, and put on the new man which after God was created in righteousness and holiness of truth."[9]

Then follow the many practical applications which result from this clothing of the soul with the new-created humanity. Put away lying, because we are

[1] On this singular reference to Ps. lxviii., and the change of the ἔλαβες δόματα ἐν ἀνθρώποις, see Davies, p. 44. It is at least doubtful whether there is the slightest allusion to the descent into hell. The point is the *identity* of Him who came to earth (*i.e.*, the historic Jesus) and Him who ascended, *i.e.*, of the Eternal and the Incarnate Christ.

[2] The omision of ἂν marks the certain result.

[3] iv. 15, ἀληθεύοντες δὲ ἐν ἀγάπῃ—not merely "*speaking* the truth," but "*being* true."

[4] iv. 1—16.

[5] πῶρος, "tufa-stone," is used, secondarily, for a hard tumour, or *callus* at the end of injured bones.

[6] ἀπηλγηκότες. "Qui postquam peccaverint, non dolent." "A sin committed a second time does not seem a sin" (*Moed Katon*, f. 27, 2).

[7] πλεονεξία.

[8] The form of expression might seem to point to a warning against any incipient docetic tendency (cf. 1 John iv. 2, 3) to draw a distinction between Christ and Jesus, between the Eternal Christ and the human Jesus.

[9] iv. 17—24.

members of one another.[1] Let not just anger degenerate into chronic exasperation, neither give room to the devil. Let honest work, earning sufficient even for charity, replace thievishness. For corruption of speech[2] let there be such as is "good for edification of the need[3] that it may give grace to the hearers," since unwholesome impurity is a chronic grief to that Holy Spirit who has sealed you as His own to the day of redemption. Then, returning to his main subject of unity, he says:—

"Let all bitterness, and wrath, and anger, and clamour, and railing be put away from you with all malice, and become kind to one another, compassionate, freely forgiving one another, as God also in Christ[4] freely forgave you. Become, then, imitators of God as children beloved, and walk in love, even as Christ loved us and gave Himself for us an offering and sacrifice to God for a savour of sweet smell."[5]

Then, proceeding to other practical duties, he forbids every form of impurity or obscenity, in word or deed, with the worldly polish[6] which was often nearly akin to it, since they are unsuitable to the Christian character, and they who are addicted to such things have no inheritance in the kingdom of God, and whatever men may say, such things are the abiding source of God's wrath.[7] Let thanksgiving take the place of indecency of speech. For though they *were* darkness, they are now light in the Lord. Walk as children of light. For the fruit of light[8] is in all goodness, and righteousness, and truth. Light is the prevalent conception here, as love was in the last chapter.[9] Let them not participate in the unfruitful infamies of secret darkness, "but rather even convict them, for all things on being convicted are illumined by the light, for all that is being illumined is light."[10] And this is the spirit of what is perhaps a Christian hymn:—

[1] The necessity of the following moral exhortations will excite no astonishment in the minds of those who have studied the Epistle to the Corinthians, or who have sufficient knowledge of the human heart to be aware that the evil habits of a heathen lifetime were not likely to be cured in all converts by a moment of awakenment, or by an acceptance of Christian truths, which in many cases may have been mainly intellectual.

[2] iv. 29, σαπρὸς, "rotten" (Matt. vii. 17), the opposite of ὑγιής, "sound," in 2 Tim. i. 13, &c., and "seasoned with salt," Col. iv. 6.

[3] Not "for the use of edification," as in E.V., but for such edification as the occasion requires.

[4] iv. 32, ἐν Χριστῷ, not as in E.V., "for Christ's sake."

[5] iv. 25—v. 2.

[6] Ver. 4, εὐτραπελία Aristotle defines it as "cultivated impertinence" (*Rhet.* ii. 12), and places the polished worldling (εὐτράπελος, *facetus*) midway between the boor (ἄγροικος) and the low flatterer (βωμολόχος) (*Eth. N.* ii. 7). The mild word, τὰ οὐκ ἀνήκοντα, is due, not to the comparatively harmless "polish" which has been last mentioned, but to *litotes*—the use of a soft expression (like Virgil's [*Georg.* iii. 5] "*illaudati* Busiridis aras"), to be corrected by the indignant mental substitution of a more forcible word. (See *supra*, p. 694.)

[7] Ver. 6, ἔρχεται, is ever coming.

[8] This is the true reading (φωτὸς), not "fruit of the Spirit," as in the E.V. The reading was doubtless altered to soften the harshness of the metaphor; but St. Paul is as indifferent as Shakespeare himself to a mere verbal confusion of metaphors when the sense is clear. To see allusions here to Ormuzd and Ahriman is surely absurd.

[9] Paley (*Hor. Paul.*) says that St. Paul here "goes off" at the word light; but this is not nearly so good an instance of this literary peculiarity as iv. 8, "ascended."

[10] Deeds of darkness must cease to be deeds of darkness when the light shines on them. The light *kills* them. Everything on which light is poured *is* light, because it reflects light. φανερούμενον cannot mean "that maketh manifest," as in the E.V.

Ἔγειρε ὁ καθεύδων
Ἀνάστα ἐκ τῶν νεκρῶν
Ἐπιφαύσει σοι ὁ Χριστός.

("Awake thee, thou that sleepest,
And from the dead arise thou,
And Christ shall shine upon thee.")[1]

"Take heed, then, how ye walk carefully, not as unwise but as wise, buying up the opportunity because the days are evil. Do not prove yourselves senseless, but understanding what is the will of the Lord."[2]

Thus, mingling special exhortation with universal principles, he proceeds to warn them against drunkenness, and recalling perhaps the thrill of emotion with which he and they have joined in such stirring words as those he has just quoted, he bids them seek rather the spiritual exaltations of that holy enthusiasm which finds vent in the melodies of Christian hymnology, and in the eucharistic music of the heart, while at the same time all are mutually submissive to each other in the fear of God.[3]

The duty of submissiveness thus casually introduced is then illustrated and enforced in three great social relations.[4] Wives are to be submissive to their husbands, as the Church is to Christ; and husbands to love their wives, as Christ loved the Church, to sanctify it into stainless purity, and to cherish it as a part of Himself in inseparable union. Children are to obey their parents, and parents not to irritate their children. Slaves are to render sincere and conscientious service, as being the slaves of their unseen Master, Christ, and therefore bound to fulfil all the duties of the state of life in which He has placed them; and masters are to do their duty to their slaves, abandoning threats, remembering that they too have a Master in whose sight they all are equal.[5]

Having thus gone through the main duties of domestic and social life as contemplated in the light of Christ, he bids them finally "grow strong in the Lord and in the might of His strength."[6] The exhortation brings up the image of armour with which the worn and aged prisoner was but too familiar. Daily the coupling-chain which bound his right wrist to the left of a Roman legionary clashed as it touched some part of the soldier's arms. The baldric, the military boot, the oblong shield, the cuirass, the helmet, the sword of the Prætorian guardsman were among the few things which he daily saw. But

[1] Isa. lx. 1, 2. The versification is of the Hebrew type. On Christian hymnology, *v. supra*, on Col. iii. 16. Antiphonal congregational singing was very early introduced (Rev. xix. 1—4).

[2] Vers. 3—17. [3] Vers. 18—21.

[4] All commentators have felt a difficulty in seeing the connexion between singing and subjection. I believe that it lies in a reminiscence of the unseemly Babel of contentious vanities which St. Paul had heard of, perhaps even witnessed, at Corinth, where such disorder had been caused by the obtrusive vanity with which each person wished to display his or her particular χάρισμα. If so—or even if the association was something else—we have another inimitable mark of genuineness. No forger would dream of appending a most important section of his moral teaching to a purely accidental thought.

[5] Ver. 22—vi. 9.

[6] vi. 10. The ἀδελφοί is wanting in א, B, D, E, and does not occur in Eph. or Col.

we cannot doubt that, with his kindly human interest in life and youth, the Apostle, who knew that heathendom too was redeemed in Christ, whose boyhood had been passed in a heathen city, who loved man as man because he saw a vision of all humanity in God—would have talked often to the weary soldiers who guarded him; would have tried by wholesome and courteous and profitable words to dissipate their tedium, until we can well imagine that the legionaries who had to perform the disagreeable task would, in spite of intense national repugnances, prefer to be chained to Paul the Jewish prisoner than to any whom caprice, or justice, or tyranny consigned to their military charge. Doubtless the soldiers would tell him in what countries they had been stationed, what barbarians they had helped to subdue. He would ask them in what tumult they had got that fracture in the helmet, in what battle that dint upon the shield, by what blow they had made that hack in the sword.[1] They would tell him of the deadly wrestle with foes who grappled with them in the *mêlée*, and of the *falaricae*,[2] the darts wrapped round with flaming tow, from which their shields had saved them in the siege. And thinking of the sterner struggle against deadlier enemies, even against the world-rulers of this darkness, against the spiritual powers of wickedness in the heavenlies,[3] in which all God's children are anxiously engaged, he bids the Christian converts assume, not "the straw-armour of reason," but the panoply of God, that they may be able to withstand in the evil day. Let spiritual truth be their baldric or binding girdle;[4] moral righteousness their breastplate; zealous alacrity in the cause of the Gospel of Peace their *caligae* of war;[5] and in addition to these, let faith be taken up as their broad shield[6] against the darts of the evil one, however fiercely ignited. Their one weapon of offence is to be the sword of the Spirit, which is the Word of God.[7] Prayer and watchfulness is to be their constant attitude; and in their prayers for all saints he begs also for their prayers on his own behalf, not that his chains may be loosed, but that he may boldly and aptly make known the mystery of the Gospel, on behalf of

[1] The *pilum*, or heavy javelin, which a soldier would not bring with him to the guard-room, is omitted.

[2] Or *malleoli* (Ps. vii. 13).

[3] The Rabbinical קוסמוקרטור. Similarly, in 2 Cor. iv. 4, St. Paul goes so far as to call "the Prince of the power of the air," ὁ θεὸς τοῦ αἰῶνος τούτου. (Cf. 1 John v. 19; John xiv. 30; xvi. 11.) "The spirituals of wickedness in the heavenlies" are the *Geisterchaft* of iniquity in the regions of space; but one would expect ὑπουρανίοις. The E.V. conceals the difficulty by its "high places;" but if ἐπουρανίοις be right, it can only be in a physical sense. As for mortal enemies: "vasa sunt, alius utitur; organa sunt, alius jungit" (Aug.).

[4] "Veritas astringit hominem, mendaciorum magna est laxitas" (Grot.).

[5] Cf. Rom. iii. 16; x. 15; ἑτοιμασία may, however, mean "basis," "sole" (מָכוֹן, Ezra iii. 3; Ps. lxxxviii. 15, LXX.). The Gospel of *Peace* gives a secure foothold even in *war*.

[6] Faith, not merit, as in Wisd. v. 19. (Cf. Ps. xviii. 31, &c.) Notice the emphatic position of πεπυρωμένα.

[7] Dr. Davidson finds this a tedious and tasteless amplification of 1 Thess. v. 8, 2 Cor. x. 3, 4, and has many similar criticisms (*Introd.* i. 388, 390). It is impossible to argue against such criticisms as bearing on the question of genuineness. The general metaphor is not uncommon (Isa. lix. 16—19; 1 Thess. v. 8; Wisd. v. 17—20; Bleeck, *Zend Avesta*, p. 90; Davies, p. 61). (See the account of the arms in the Interpreter's House in *Pilgrim's Progress*, and Gurnall's *Christian Armour*.)

which he is an ambassador—not inviolable, not splendid, but—"an ambassador in a coupling-chain."[1]

He sends no news or personal salutations, because he is sending the faithful and beloved Tychicus, who will tell them, as well as other cities, all his affairs; but he concludes with a blessing of singular fulness:

"Peace to the brethren and love with faith from God the Father and the Lord Jesus Christ. Grace be with all who love our Lord Jesus Christ in incorruption."[2]

We have now examined all the Epistles of St. Paul except the last group of all—the three addressed to Timothy and Titus. These are usually known as the Pastoral Epistles, because they sketch the duties of the Christian Pastor. Of the Epistle to the Hebrews I have said nothing, because I hope to speak of it hereafter, and because, for reasons which appear to me absolutely convincing, I cannot regard it as a work of St. Paul's. But even if the Epistle to the Hebrews be accepted as having been written by the Apostle, it adds nothing to our knowledge of his history. But for the preservation of the Pastoral Epistles, we should not know a single additional fact about him, except such as we can glean from vague and wavering traditions.

The Acts of the Apostles ends with the statement that Paul remained a period of two whole years in his own hired lodging, and received all who came in to visit him, preaching the kingdom of God and teaching the things concerning the Lord Jesus Christ with all confidence unmolestedly.[3] The question why St. Luke deliberately ended his sketch of the Apostle at that point, is one which can never receive a decisive answer. He only related circumstances of which he was an eyewitness, or which he knew from trustworthy information, and for that reason his narrative, in spite of its marked *lacunae*, is far more valuable than if it had been constructed out of looser materials. It may, however, be safely asserted that since he had been with St. Paul during at least a part of the Roman imprisonment, he brought down his story to the period at which he first wrote his book. A thousand circumstances may have prevented any resumption of his work as a chronicler, but it is inconceivable that St. Paul should have died almost immediately afterwards, by a martyr's death, and St. Luke have been aware of it before his book was published, and yet that he should not have made the faintest allusion to the subject.[4] The conjecture that Theophilus knew all the rest, so that it was needless to commit it to writing, is entirely valueless, for whoever Theophilus

[1] vi. 10—20. In ver. 18 it is περὶ πάντων τῶν ἁγίων καὶ ὑπὲρ ἐμοῦ. "Paradoxon: mundus habet splendidos legatos" (Bengel).

[2] vi. 21—24.

[3] The cadence is expressive of stability; of motion succeeded by rest; of action settled in repose. "An emblem of the history of the Church of Christ, and of the life of every true believer in Him" (Bishop Wordsworth).

[4] So far as anything can be said to be probable in the midst of such uncertainties, the probability is that the leisure of his attendance on St. Paul during the Roman imprisonment had enabled St. Luke to draw up the main part of his work; that he concluded it exactly at the point at which St. Paul was expecting immediate liberation, and that he either published it at the first favourable opportunity after that time, or was prevented—it may be even by death—from ever continuing or completing his task.

may have been, it is clear that St. Luke was not writing for him alone. It is also, to say the least, a probable conjecture that soon after the close of those two whole years some remarkable change took place in the condition of the prisoner. That such a change *did* take place is the almost unanimous tradition of the Church. However slight may be the grounds of direct testimony, it has been generally believed in all ages that (about the beginning of the year A.D. 64) St. Paul was tried, acquitted, and liberated; and that after some two years of liberty, during which he continued to prosecute his missionary labours, he was once more arrested, and was, after a second imprisonment, put to death at Rome. This would, at least, accord with the anticipations expressed in his own undoubted Epistles. Although he was still a prisoner when he wrote the letter to the Philippians, his trial was near at hand, and while promising to send Timothy to inquire about their fortunes, he adds, "But I am confident in the Lord that I myself too shall come speedily;" and this is so far from being a *casual* hope that he even asks Philemon "to get a lodging ready for him, for he hopes that he shall be granted to them by their prayers." It is, of course, quite possible that St. Paul's sanguine expectations may have been frustrated,[1] but he certainly would not have expressed them so distinctly without good grounds for believing that powerful friends were at work in his favour. Whether Festus, and Agrippa, and Lysias, and Publius had used their influence on his behalf, or whether he had reason to rely on any favourable impression which he may have made among the Prætorian soldiers, or whether he had received intelligence that the Jews had seen reason to abandon a frivolous and groundless prosecution it is impossible to conjecture;[2] but his strong impression that he *would* be liberated at least helps to confirm the many arguments which lead us to believe that he actually was. If so, it must have been very soon after the close of that two years' confinement with which St. Luke so suddenly breaks off.

For in July, A.D. 64, there broke out that terrible persecution against the Christians, from which, had he been still at Rome, it is certain that he could

[1] For this reason I have not here laid any stress on his once-purposed visit to Spain (Rom. xv. 24, 28). It seems clear from Philem. 22 that he had either abandoned this intention, or at any rate postponed it till he had re-visited Asia.

[2] It is undesirable to multiply uncertain conjectures, but perhaps the Jews may have sent their documents, witnesses, &c., with Josephus when he went to Rome, A.D. 64. He tells us that, by the influence of the Jewish pantomimist Aliturus and of Poppæa, he was enabled to secure the release of some Jewish priests, friends of his own, whom Festus had, on grounds which Josephus calls trivial, sent bound to Rome. Josephus was doubtless one of a commission dispatched for this purpose, and it is conceivable that the prosecution of St. Paul's trial may have been a subordinate object of this commission, and that the trial may have broken down all the more completely from the loss of witnesses and evidence in the shipwreck which Josephus underwent. His vessel foundered on the voyage, and out of two hundred souls only eighty were picked up by a ship of Cyrene, after they had swum or floated all night in the waves. Josephus then proceeded to Puteoli in another ship. He makes little more than a dry allusion to these events (*Vit.* 3), which contrasts singularly with the vivid minuteness of St. Luke: but the general incidents so far resemble those of St. Paul's shipwreck that some have conjectured that the two events were identical. Chronology and other considerations render this impossible, nor is there any great reason to suppose that Josephus is here introducing embellishments from the story of St. Paul.

not have escaped. If, therefore, the Pastoral Epistles be forgeries, we have heard the last words of St. Paul, and at the last verse of the Acts the curtain rushes down in utter darkness upon the remainder of his life. Let us, then, consider what tradition says, and whether we can still accept as genuine the Epistles to Timothy and Titus. If the indications derived from these sources are in any degree trustworthy, we have still to hear some further thoughts and opinions of the Apostle. We catch at least a glimpse of his final movements, and attain to a sure knowledge of his state of mind up to the moment of his death. If tradition be mistaken, and if the Epistles are spurious, then we must acquiesce in the fact that we know nothing more of the Apostle, and that he perished among that "vast multitude" whom, in the year 64, the vilest of Emperors, nay, almost of human beings, sacrificed to the blind madness which had been instigated against them by a monstrous accusation. If, indeed, St. Paul perished amid that crowd of nameless martyrs, there is but little probability that any regard would have been paid to his claim as a Roman citizen. He may have perished, like them, by crucifixion; or have been covered, like them, in the skins of wild beasts, to be mangled by dogs; or, standing in his tunic of ignited pitch, may with his dying glance have caught sight of the wicked Emperor of triumphant Heathendom, as the living torch of hideous martyrdom cast a baleful glare across the gardens of the Golden House.[1] From all this, however, we may feel a firm conviction that, by the mercy of God, he was delivered for a time.[2]

It is true that, so far as direct evidence is concerned, we can only say that St. Paul's own words render it probable that he was liberated, and that this probability finds some slight support in a common tradition, endorsed by the authority of some of the Fathers. But this tradition goes little further than the bare fact. If we are to gain any further knowledge of the biography of St. Paul, it must be derived from the Pastoral Epistles, and from them alone. If they be not genuine, we know no single further particular respecting his fortunes.

Now, it must be admitted that a number of critics, formidable alike in their unanimity and their learning, have come to the conclusion that the Epistles to Timothy and Titus were not written by St. Paul.[3] Their arguments are entitled to respectful attention, and they undoubtedly suggest difficulties, which our ignorance of all details in the history of those early centuries renders it by no means easy to remove. Nevertheless, after carefully and impartially weighing all that they have urged—of which some account will be found in the Excursus at the end of the volume—I have come to the decided conviction that the Epistles are genuine, and that the first two of them were written during the two years which intervened between St. Paul's liberation and his martyrdom at Rome.

[1] Tac. *Ann.* xv. 44 (cf. Mart. x. 25; Juv. *Sat.* viii. 235); Sen. *Ep.* 14, 4; Schol. in *Juv.* i. 155; Tert. *Apol.* 15; *ad Nat.* i. 18; *ad Mart.* 5.

[2] See Excursus XXVI., "Evidence as to the Liberation of St. Paul."

[3] Schmidt, Schleiermacher, Eichhorn, Credner, De Wette, Baur, Zeller, Hilgenfeld, Schenkel, Ewald, Hausrath, Renan, Pfleiderer, Krenkel, Davidson, &c.

CHAPTER LIII.

THE FIRST EPISTLE TO TIMOTHY.

Ἐν ἀδήλῳ που σκότει φωλευόντων εἰσέτι τοτε τῶν, εἰ καί τινες ὑπῆρχον, παραφθείρειν ἐπιχειρούντων τὸν ὑγιῆ κανόνα τοῦ σωτηρίου κηρύγματος.—HEGESIPPUS *ap.* Euseb. *H.E.* iii. 32.

I SHALL not attempt, by more than a few sentences, to dispel the obscurity of that last stage of the Apostle's life which began at the termination of his Roman imprisonment. We feel that our knowledge of his movements is plunged in the deepest uncertainty the moment that we lose the guidance of St. Luke. I cannot myself believe that he was able to carry out his intention of visiting Spain. The indications of his travels in the two later Pastoral Epistles seem to leave no room for such a journey; nor, if it had really taken place, can we imagine that no shadow of a detail respecting it should have been preserved. But even if he did accomplish this new mission, we cannot so much as mention a single church which he founded, or a single port at which he touched. To speak of his work in Spain could only therefore leave a fallacious impression. If he went at all, it must have been immediately after his imprisonment, since his original object had been merely to visit Rome on his way to the "limit of the West." In writing to the Romans he had expressed a hope that he would be furthered on his journey by their assistance. Judging by the indifference with which they treated him in both of his imprisonments, there is too much reason to fear that this hope was in any case doomed to disappointment. The next trace of his existence is the First Epistle to Timothy. That Epistle is less organic—that is, it has less structural unity—than any other of St. Paul's Epistles. The time and place at which it was written are wholly uncertain, because the only historic indication which it contains is that "on his way to Macedonia Paul had begged Timothy to remain at Ephesus." [1]

"Paul, an Apostle of Jesus Christ, according to the commandment of God our Saviour,[2] and Christ Jesus our hope, to Timothy my true child in the faith; grace, mercy, and peace from God the Father[3] and Christ Jesus our Lord." [4]

This salutation is remarkable for the title "Saviour" applied to God the

[1] The general outline of the Epistle is as follows:—Salutation (i. 1, 2). The object of the letter to encourage Timothy to resist false teachers, and hold fast the faith (3—11, 18—20), with the Apostle's thanks to God for the mercy which had made him a minister of the Gospel (12—17). The duty of praying for rulers, with rules about the bearing of women in public worship (ii.). The qualifications of "bishops" (presbyters) and deacons (iii.). Fresh warnings respecting the false teachers, and the way in which Timothy is to deal with them (iv.). His relations to elders (v. 1, 2); to the order of "widows" (3—16); and to presbyters, with rules as to their selection (17—25). Directions concerning slaves, especially with reference to the false teachers; warnings against covetousness; with final exhortations and benediction (vi.).

[2] Not, of course, "a Saviour." The spread of Christianity is naturally marked by the increasing anarthrousness (omission of the article) of its commonest terms. We mark this fact in the word Christ, which is an appellative in the Gospels (almost always "*the* Christ"—*i.e.*, the Messiah), but has become, in the Epistles, a proper name.

[3] Omit ἡμῶν, ℵ, A, D, F, G (B, deficient).

[4] i. 1, 2.

Father, perhaps derived from some recent study of Psalm lxiii. 7, and continued throughout the Pastoral Epistles when once adopted; for the name "our Hope," applied to Christ, and not improbably borrowed from the same verse; and for the word "mercy" so naturally introduced by the worn and tried old man, between the usual greetings of "grace and peace."[1]

"As I begged thee to remain still in Ephesus, on my way to Macedonia, that thou mightest command some not to teach different doctrine, nor to give heed to myths and interminable genealogies,[2] seeing that these minister questions rather than the dispensation of God[3] which is in faith——"[4] The sentence, quite characteristically, remains unfinished; but St. Paul evidently meant to say, "I repeat the exhortation which then I gave."

In contrast with these false teachers he tells him that the purpose of the Gospel is love out of a pure heart, a good conscience, and faith unfeigned, failing of which some turned aside to vain jangling. They wanted to pass themselves off as teachers of the Jewish Law, but their teaching was mere confusion and ignorance.

The mention of the Law leads him to allude to its legitimate function.[5] To those who were justified by faith it was needless, being merged in the higher law of a life in unity with Christ; but its true function was to warn and restrain those who lived under the sway of mere passion in heathenish wickedness.[6] For these, though not for the regenerate, the thunders of Sinai are necessary, "according to the Gospel of the glory of the blessed God, wherewith I was entrusted."[7]

He then at once digresses into an expression of heartfelt gratitude to God for that grace which superabounded over his former ignorant faithlessness, a faithlessness which had led him to outrage and insult, such as only his ignorance could palliate.

"Faithful is the saying,[8] and worthy of all acceptation, that Christ Jesus came into the world to save sinners, of whom I am chief.[9] But on this account I gained mercy, that in me first and foremost Christ Jesus might manifest His entire long-suffering as a pattern for those who were hereafter to believe on Him to

[1] Cf. Gal. vi. 16.

[2] Though the Sephiroth of the Kabbala belong to a much later period, and the Zohar is probably a mediæval book, yet Judaic speculations of the same kind seem to have been the prototype of the Valentinian emanations with their successive intermarriages of *æons*.

[3] i. 4; *leg.* οἰκονομίαν (א, A, B, F, G, &c.). The questions do not further the divine scheme of God, which works, not in the sphere of misty uncertainties, but in the sphere of faith.

[4] 3, 4. For similar *anakolutha*, see Gal. ii. 4, 5; Rom. v. 12, &c.

[5] i. 8, 9, νόμος . . . νομίμως.

[6] For the true use of the Law, and the limitation to its validity, see Rom. vii. 12; Gal. iii. 19; Phil. iii. 9. It is idle to pretend that there is anything un-Pauline in this sentiment. With the list of crimes—which is, however, varied with perfect independence—cf. Rom. i. 29; 1 Cor. vi. 9; Gal. v. 19.

[7] i. 8—11.

[8] This arresting formula would naturally arise with the rise of Christian axioms; cf. "These words are faithful and true" (Rev. xxi. 5; xxii. 6).

[9] Cf. "God be merciful to me the sinner" (Luke xviii. 13; πρῶτος, "non tempore sed malignitate" (Aug. *in Ps.* lxxi. 1).

life eternal. Now to the King of the Ages,[1] the incorruptible, invisible, only God,[2] honour and glory unto the ages of the ages. Amen.[3]

"This charge I commit to thee, son Timothy, in accordance with the prophecies which in time past were prophesied of thee,[4] that thou in them mayest war the good warfare,[5] having faith and a good conscience, which some rejecting have been wrecked as regards the faith; of whom is Hymenæus and Alexander, whom I handed over to Satan, that they may be trained not to blaspheme."[6]

It will be seen that in this section he begins with the false teachers, and after two digressions—one suggested by the mention of the Law, the other by his personal commission to preach the Gospel—returns to them again.

The second chapter contains regulations for public worship, the duty of praying for those in authority, and the bearing and mutual relations of men and women in religious assemblies—broken by brief and natural digressions on the universality of God's offered grace, and on his own Apostolic office. He directs that

"Petitions, prayers, supplications, and thanksgivings[7] should be made for all, and especially for kings,[8] and those in authority, that we may spend a calm and quiet life in all godliness and gravity. This is fair and acceptable before our Saviour, God, who wills all men to be saved, and to come to full knowledge of the truth. For there is one God and one Mediator between God and men, the man Christ Jesus,[9] who gave Himself a ransom for all—the testimony in its own seasons. For which testimony I was appointed an herald and an Apostle (I speak the truth;[10] I lie not,[11]) in faith and truth."[12]

[1] Not here in its technical sense of "the *æons;*" cf. Ps. cxlv. 13, "a kingdom of all ages."

[2] Omit σοφῷ (א, A, D, F, G, &c.).

[3] For similar personal digressions, see Gal. i. 12; 1 Thess. ii. 4; 2 Cor. iii. 6; iv. 1, &c.; and for the doxology (Rom. xv. 33; xvi. 27; 2 Cor. ii. 14; ix. 15; Phil. iv. 20, &c. The passage is intensely individual, for "all Paul's theology is in ultimate analysis, the reflex of his personal experience" (Reuss, *Les Epîtres*, ii. 352).

[4] Perhaps a reference to his solemn ordination, as in iv. 14, when Silas, who was a prophet (Acts xv. 32), was present among others (Acts xiii. 3).

[5] στρατεία, not ἀγών, as in 2 Tim. iv. 7. It is St. Paul's favourite metaphor (Rom. xiii. 12; 2 Cor. x. 5; 1 Thess. v. 8, &c.).

[6] i. 12—20. It is impossible to know the exact circumstances referred to. For Hymenæus, see 2 Tim. ii. 17. For Alexander, 2 Tim. iv. 14; Acts xix. 33; but even the identifications are precarious. For "delivering to Satan," see 1 Cor. v. 5. Whether it was excommunication, or generally giving up from all Church influences, and leaving Satan to deal with them, or the delivery to præternatural corporal sufferings, the *intention*, we see, was merciful and disciplinary (παιδευθῶσι).

[7] The synonyms are mainly cumulative, though perhaps δεήσεις means special, προσευχὰς general, and ἐντεύξεις earnest prayers (see Phil. iv. 6).

[8] Baur sees in this plural an indication that the Epistle was written in the times of the Antonines, when Emperors took associates in the Empire. Can theorising be more baseless?—The word "kings" does not necessarily refer only to local viceroys, &c., like the Herods, but was in the provinces applied generically to the Emperors, as it constantly is in the Talmud. It was most important to both Jews and Christians that they should not be suspected of civic turbulence (Jos. *B. J.* ii. 10, § 4; Bingham, xv. 8, 14). Hence we see how baseless is the conjecture of Pfleiderer (*Protestanten bibel*) that it was written in the time of Hadrian, who befriended the Christians (Euseb. *H. E.* iv. 8, 9).

[9] The word μεσίτης as applied to Christ is new, but not the conception (Rom. v. 10; 2 Cor. v. 19). There may be a silent condemnation of incipient Docetism in ἄνθρωπος, as well as of the supposed mediation of angels in εἷς (Col. ii. 15, 18).

[10] Om. ἐν Χριστῷ (A, D, F, G, &c.).

[11] A natural reminiscence of the occasions when such asseverations had been so necessary that they had become habitual (2 Cor. xi. 31; Rom. xi. 1).

[12] ii. 1—7.

After this double digression he expresses his wish that the men[1] should pray in every place, "uplifting holy hands,[2] without wrath and doubting; and that women, with shamefastness and sobriety, should adorn themselves, not with plaits of hair, and gold or pearls, or costly raiment, but, in accordance with their Gospel profession, with good works." Let them be silent and submissive, not obtrusive and didactic. This rule he supports by the narrative of the Fall, as illustrative of *generic* differences between the sexes,[3] adding, however, that in spite of the greater liability to deception and sin, woman "shall be saved through motherhood, if they abide in faith and love and sanctification with sober-mindedness."[4]

The third chapter passes into the qualifications for office in the Church. It is introduced by a sort of Christian aphorism, "Faithful is the saying, If any man desires the office of the pastorate,[5] he desires a good work." The qualifications on which St. Paul insists are irreproachableness, faithful domestic life,[6] soberness, sobermindedness, decorousness, hospitable disposition, and aptitude to teach. He who is quarrelsome over wine, given to blows and covetousness, is unfit. Moderation, peacefulness, indifference to money, a well-ordered household, grave and obedient children, are signs that a man may aspire to the sacred work; but he must not be a neophyte,[7] that he

[1] τοὺς ἄνδρας (ii. 8).

[2] The ancient attitude of prayer (Bingham, *Antiq.* xiii. 8, 10; Ps. xxiv. 4; xxvi. 6); cf. Tennyson—

> "For what are men better than sheep or goats
> That nourish a blind life within the brain,
> If knowing God *they lift not hands* of prayer
> Both for themselves and those who call them friend?"

[3] This is quite independent of, yet exactly analogous to, his reasoning in 1 Cor. xi. 8, 9 (cf. 2 Cor. xi. 3; Wisd. xxv. 24).

[4] ii. 8—15. It will be seen that he is here looking at the question from a wholly different point of view to that in 1 Cor. vii., which applies not to the whole sex, but to a chosen few. So, too, in the previous verses, he is considering concrete facts, not the abstract abolition of all sexual distinctions in Christ (Gal. iii. 28). The ἡ τεκνογονία is probably not specific ("*the* child-bearing"—*i.e.*, the Incarnation—surely a most obscure allusion), but generic—*i.e.*, a holy married life, with the bearing and training of children, is, as a rule, the appointed path for women, and it will end in their salvation, in spite of their original weakness, if that path be humbly and faithfully pursued. Doubtless St. Paul was thinking of Gen. iii. 16.

[5] To translate this "the office of a bishop" is, as Alford says in his usual incisive way, "merely laying a trap for misunderstanding." Episcopacy proper was developed after the death of St. Paul, but before that of St. John, as a bulwark against heresy.

[6] I am not persuaded that μιᾶς γυναικὸς ἄνδρα really implies more than this, with reference to the prevalence of divorce, &c. The early prejudice against second marriages naturally inclined the ancient commentators to take it exclusively in one way; but the remark of Chrysostom, τὴν ἀμετρίαν κωλύει, seems to me to be nearest the truth. St. Paul's opinion was not in the least that of Athenagoras, that a second marriage is "specious adultery," since in some cases he even recommends it (v. 14; 1 Cor. vii. 39; Rom. vii., 2, 3), but he would possibly have held with Hermas (*Pastor.* ii. 4), that though a second marriage is no sin, it is a better and nobler thing to avoid it. It is as Gregory of Nazianzus says, "a concession" (συγχώρησις—*Orat.* xxxi.).

[7] The first occurrence of the word "neophyte"—"newly-*planted*"—a recent convert. For the metaphor, see 1 Cor. iii. 6. At Ephesus there must have been a choice of presbyters who were not "neophytes." Perhaps the reason why this qualification is omitted in Tit. i. 6 is that there would have been greater difficulty in carrying it out in the more recent Churches of Crete.

may not, through the cloudy fumes of pride, fall into the devil's judgment.[1] He must be well thought of by his Pagan neighbours, that he may not fall into disrepute, and the devil's snare which such loss of character involves.[2]

Deacons, too, must be grave, straightforward, sober, not avaricious, sound in faith, and pure of conscience; and their freedom from reproach must be tested before they are appointed.[3]

Deaconesses[4] must be grave, not slanderers, sober, faithful. The domestic relations of deacons and deaconesses must be irreproachable; for an honourable diaconate secures an honourable position,[5] and boldness in the faith.[6]

"These things I write to thee, though I hope to come to you unexpectedly soon;[7] but in order that, if I am delayed, thou mayest know how to bear thyself in the house of God—seeing that it is the Church of God—as a pillar and basis of the truth.[8]

"And confessedly great is the mystery of godliness—who was[9]

"Manifested in the flesh,
Justified in the Spirit,
Seen of angels,
Preached among the Gentiles,
Believed on in the world,
Taken up in glory."[10]

[1] These Epistles are peculiar in the use of the word "devil." Elsewhere St. Paul uses "Satan," except in Eph. iv. 27; vi. 11. It is impossible to say whether "the devil's judgment" means "that which he has incurred" or "that which he inflicts."

[2] iii. 1—7.

[3] iii. 8—10. Besides the "Seven," deacons properly so called may be referred to in 1 Cor. xii. 28; Rom. xii. 7; 1 Pet. iv. 11; as well as in Phil. i. 1.

[4] Γυναῖκας must mean "deaconesses" (Rom. xvi. 1. "Ancillae quae ministrae dicebantur"—Plin. ix. 27), because the wives of deacons were certainly not selected by the Church.

[5] iii. 11—13.

[6] καλὸς βαθμὸς can only mean "a fair standing-point," "an honourable position," from which to discharge nobly his Christian duties. The notion that it means "earning preferment" would be an immense anachronism. Cf. vi. 19: καλὸν θεμέλιον.

[7] τάχιον—an untranslatable ellipse. John xiii. 27; Heb. xiii. 23.

[8] Apart from the awkwardness of the Church being, in the same verse, the house of God and also a pillar and base of the truth, the expression is one of the most difficult and surprising—one of the least obviously Pauline—in the whole Epistle. The separate metaphors occur in Gal. ii. 9 and Eph. ii. 20, but only of *persons*. There is, therefore, much to be said for attaching them to ἀναστρέφεσθαι, and making them apply to Timothy, as I have done. (See Dean Stanley, *Sermons on the Apostolic Age*, p. 115.) The words are applied to the martyr Attalus in the Epistle of the Church of Lyons, c. 5. Others attach them to the next sentence—which they would turn into a most awkward and unnatural anti-climax. If, however, they are applied to the Church, the meaning is clear enough—namely, that apart from the Church the truth of the Gospel would be without that earthly institution on which, by Christ's ordinance, its stability and permanence depends.

[9] Ὃς is read by ℵ, A, C, F, G. (The reading of A was once supposed to be ΘC, but Bishop Ellicott testifies that the apparent line across the O was originally due to the *sagitta* of the ε in the word εὐσέβειαν on the other side of the page. See his *Pastoral Epistles*, p. 103.) Besides this, it is so unquestionably supported by every canon of criticism that it may now be regarded as a certain reading.

[10] iii. 14—16. These last phrases are so rhythmic in their introverted parallelism with the varied order of their triple antitheses, that they have, with much probability, been supposed (like Eph. v. 14) to belong to some ancient hymn or creed. The extreme antiquity of Christian hymns is proved by Eph. v. 19, and by Plin. *Epp.* x. 97. "Justi-

The true doctrine again recalls him to the subject of the false teachers. Beyond the present peril lies the prophecy of future apostasies, in which some shall give heed to deceitful spirits and doctrines of devils, by means of the hypocrisy of liars, whose consciences have been seared. This apostasy, partly present, partly future, is marked by dualistic tendencies. It hinders marriage,[1] and commands abstinence from meats,[2] forgetting that thankfulness and prayer sanctify everything. Another feature of the nascent heresy is a fondness for profane and anile myths. A third is mere bodily asceticism. This training may indeed have a partial advantage; but better is the gymnasium which trains for godliness, since godliness is profitable both for this life and the next ("faithful is the saying"): for with a view to this—because we have hope in the living God, who is the Saviour of all, specially of the faithful[3]—we are enabled to endure both toil and struggle.[4] These truths Timothy is to teach, showing himself an example to the faithful in speech, conversation, love, spirituality, faith, purity, so that none may despise his youth.[5] Till St. Paul arrives he is bidden to occupy himself in reading,[6] exhortation, teaching; securing progress by diligence, and not neglecting—which possibly Timothy, in his retiring character, was tempted to do—the grace which was solemnly bestowed on him at his ordination.[7]

Then he is advised how to behave towards various orders in his Church. He is not to use severe language to an elder, but to exhort them as fathers; the younger men as brothers; the elder women as mothers, the younger as sisters, in all purity.[8] Special directions are given about widows.[9] Those are true widows who rightly train their children or grandchildren, who do their duty to their parents, who devote themselves to constant prayer. But in a widow, a prurient, frivolous character is a living death; for, in a Christian, neglect of domestic duties and relations is worse than heathenism. No widow is therefore to be put on the list before sixty years of age, after one honourable marriage,[10] and after having acquired a character for motherliness, hospi-

fied in the Spirit" means that Christ was manifested to be the Son of God (Rom. i. 4) by the workings of His higher spiritual life; "seen of angels" refers to the various angelic witnesses of scenes of His earthly life.

[1] Not yet "forbids," but somewhat "discourages." Cf. Jos. *B. J.* ii. 8, 2, and 13.

[2] Cf. Rom. xiv. 1—4; 1 Cor. viii. 8; x. 20.

[3] The universalism of expression is here even more remarkable than in ii. 4.

[4] *Leg.* ἀγωνιζόμεθα, ℵ, A, F, C, G, K.

[5] The sneers that Timothy "seems to have been endowed by Christian legend with the gift of immortal youth" are very groundless. If he were converted in A.D. 45, at the age of sixteen, he would now (A.D. 66) be only thirty-seven—a very youthful age for so responsible a position. The aged rector of one who has now become a very exalted ecclesiastic, and is long past sixty, still says of his first curate, "I always told you that young man was very ambitious;" and when M. Thiers was Prime Minister of France, and called on his old schoolmaster, he found that he was only remembered as "the little Adolphus who played tricks."

[6] Perhaps the earliest allusion to the duty of reading Scripture.

[7] iv. 1—16. Acts xvi. 1, and 2 Tim. i. 6, where he receives a similar injunction.

[8] "Omnes puellas et virgines Christi aut aequaliter ignora aut aequaliter dilige" (Jer.). But how inferior to the direction of St. Paul!

[9] Acts ii. 44; vi. 1.

[10] Cf. Tit. i. 6. It is a remarkable sign of the position of widows in the Church that

tality, kindly service, succour to the afflicted, and continuance in every good work. But Timothy is to have nothing to say to younger widows who want to marry again when they begin to wax restive against the yoke of Christ—and so are convicted of setting at nought their first faith.[1] To avoid the danger of gadding idleness and unseemly gossiping, it is better that such should avoid all chance of creating scandal by quietly re-entering into married life. Hence all younger widows must be supported by their own relations, and not at the expense of the Church.[2]

Returning to the Presbyters, he quotes the passage of Deuteronomy, "Thou shalt not muzzle a threshing ox," and adds the maxim, "The labourer is worthy of his hire,"[3] to support his rule that "double honour" be paid to faithful and laborious pastors.[4] If they do wrong they must indeed be rebuked, but never on ill-supported accusations. "I solemnly charge thee before God, and the Lord Jesus Christ, and the elect angels,[5] to observe these rules without prejudice, and without doing anything by favour." He is not to ordain any one too hastily, lest he be involved in the responsibility for their sins; and this discrimination is the more necessary because there are flagrant sins which marshal men to judgment, and hidden sins which stealthily follow behind them; just as also there are some good works which are openly manifest, and others which are concealed, although ultimately all shall stand revealed in their true light.

In the very midst of these wise and serious directions are introduced two personal exhortations. One of them—"Keep thyself pure"—may naturally have been suggested by the passing thought that he whose duty it was to exercise so careful an oversight over others must be specially watchful to be himself free from every stain. The other, "Be no longer a water-drinker, but use a little wine because of thy stomach, and thy frequent infirmities,"[6] is so casual that, though we see at once how it may have occurred to St. Paul's

Polycarp calls them θυσιαστήριον Θεοῦ, "an altar of God" (*ad Phil.* 4). From the severity of some of St. Paul's remarks, Reuss thinks that he may have had in view the occasional second marriage of Christian widows with Pagans, which would be a disgraceful proceeding after they had received assistance from the Church. They might be "deaconesses" earlier than sixty, but not "widows."

[1] In their practical pledge not to marry again when they were placed on the official list of widows.

[2] v. 1—16.

[3] 1 Cor. ix. 9. Those who apply ἡ γραφὴ to both clauses must admit that the Gospel of St. Luke had been published, and had come to be regarded of Divine authority, before this Epistle (Luke x. 7). But the inference is most precarious, for our Lord often alluded to current proverbs, and ἡ γραφὴ may here only apply to the quotation from Deut. xxv. 4.

[4] διπλῆ τιμὴ is a perfectly general expression. The spirit of foolish literalism led to double rations for the Presbyters at the Agapæ.

[5] See 1 Cor. xi. 10; 1 Pet. i. 12. It is not possible to explain the exact shade of meaning in the word "elect." They are probably so called, as Calvin says, "excellentiae causâ." Cf. τοὺς ἱεροὺς ἀγγέλους in Agrippa's adjuration to the Jews not to rebel against Rome (Jos. *B. J.* ii. 16, § 4, and Tobit xii. 15).

[6] These "frequent infirmities" perhaps explain the timidity of Timothy's character (1 Cor. xvi. 10, 11). Some have seen a reflex of this in the reproaches addressed, in the midst of praise, "to the angel of the Church of Ephesus."

thoughts—since otherwise the former rule might have led to a self-denial still more rigid,[1] and even injurious to health—it is far too natural and spontaneous, too entirely disconnected from all that precedes and follows it, to have occurred to any imitator. An imitator, if capable of introducing the natural play of thought to which the precept "Keep thyself pure" is due, would have been far more likely to add—and especially in an Epistle which so scrupulously forbids indulgence in wine to all Church officials—"And, in order to promote this purity, take as little wine as possible, or avoid it altogether."[2]

He then passes to the duties of slaves.[3] Their conversion is not to be made a plea for upsetting the social order, and giving any excuse for abusing the Gospel. Christian masters are still to be treated as masters, and to be served all the more heartily "because all who are partakers of this kindly service are faithful and beloved." Here again he reverts to the false teachers—who had perhaps perverted the truth of Christian equality into the falsehood of socialism—to denounce their inflated ignorance and unwholesome loquacity as the source of the jealousies and squabbles of corrupt men, who look on religion as a source of gain.[4] A source of gain indeed it is when accompanied with the contentment[5] arising from the sense of the nakedness of our birth and death, and the fewness of our real needs,[6] whereas the desire of wealth breeds the numerous forms of foolish desire which plunge men into destruction and perdition. For all evils spring from the root of covetousness,[7] which has led many into heresy as well as into manifold miseries. The Apostle appeals to his son in the faith to flee these things: to pursue[8] righteousness, godliness, faith, love, endurance, gentleness; to strive the good strife of faith; to grasp eternal life, "to which also thou wert called, and didst confess the good confession before many witnesses." He most solemnly adjures him, by Christ and His good confession before Pontius Pilate,[9] to keep the commandment without spot, without reproach, till the manifestation of our Lord Jesus Christ, which He shall show in His own seasons, who is the blessed and only Potentate, the King of kings and Lord of lords, who alone hath immortality,

[1] Rom. xiv. 2. Plutarch speaks of an ἄοινος ἁγνεία (*De Isid. et Osir*, § 6).

[2] Ver. 17--23.

[3] Some have fancied, with very little probability, that the topic is suggested by the mention of those whose good works cannot be *finally* hid, but are little likely to be noticed in this world.

[4] Gal. iii. 28. The recognition of the existing basis of society is found throughout the Epistles (1 Cor. vii. 21; Col. iii. 22, &c.).

[5] αὐτάρκεια, self-sufficing independence (2 Cor. ix. 8; Phil. iv. 11). Cf. Prov. xiv. 14, "The good man shall be satisfied from himself."

[6] Phil. iv. 11—13.

[7] ῥίζα need not be rendered "*a* root," for it is a word which does not require the article; but St. Paul does not, of course, mean that it is the only root from which all evils spring, but the root from which all evils *may* spring. So Diogenes Laertius calls it "the metropolis of all evils" (*Vit. Diogen.* vi. 50; and Philo, *De Spec. Legg.* 346, calls it ὁρμητήριον πάντων παρανομημάτων (cf. Luke xii. 15—21).

[8] δίωκε, ἐπιλαβοῦ.

[9] There is an obvious allusion in the καλὴ ὁμολογία of Christ to that of the previous verse, but in the latter instance it seems to mean the faithful performance of the will of God even to death.

dwelling in light unapproachable, whom no man ever saw, or can see—to whom honour and eternal strength. Amen.[1]

With this majestic description of the Divine attributes it might well have been thought that the Epistle would close. A forger might naturally desire a climax; but St. Paul is never influenced by such considerations of style. Filled with the thought of the perils of wealth in a city like wealthy Ephesus, he once more, in a sort of postscript,[2] advises Timothy to warn the rich "not to be high-minded, nor to fix their hopes on the uncertainty of riches, but on the living God, who richly affords us all things for enjoyment," and to use their riches wisely and generously, "treasuring up for themselves a fair foundation for the future, that they may grasp that which is really life."[3]

Then, with one parting reference to the false teachers, the Epistle ends:—

> "O Timothy, guard the trust committed to thee, turning away from these profane babblings, and "antitheses" of the knowledge which usurps the name; which some professing have gone astray as regards the faith. Grace be with thee."[4]

The "Amen"[5] is probably a pious addition, and the various superscriptions which tell us that the Epistle was written from Laodicea, "which is the metropolis of Phyrgia Pacatiana," or "from Nicopolis," or "from Athens," "by the hands of his disciple Titus," or "from Macedonia," are idle guesses, of which the latter alone has any plausibility, though even this is only a precarious inference from the verse which suggested it.

CHAPTER LIV.

THE EPISTLE TO TITUS.

> "Lord Jesus, I am weary *in* Thy work, but not *of* Thy work. Let me go and speak for Thee once more . . . seal Thy truth, and then die."—WHITEFIELD.

FROM St. Paul's message to Philemon we infer that as speedily as possible after he was set free he visited Ephesus and the cities of the Lycus. Even if he deferred this visit till he had carried out his once-cherished plan of visiting Spain, we know that the moment his destiny was decided he sent Timothy to Philippi, with the intention of following him at no long interval.[6] Hence when Timothy rejoined him, probably at Ephesus, he left him there, as we have seen, to finish the task of setting the Church in order, and himself set out on his promised journey to Macedonia. It is not likely that he felt any desire to revive the gloomy reminiscences of Jerusalem, and to incur a second risk of being torn to pieces by infuriated Pharisees. In that unhappy city a fresh outburst of the spirit of persecution had ended the year before (A.D. 63) in

[1] vi. 1—16.
[2] Reuss, *Les Epîtres*, ii. 378.
[3] vi. 17—19. *Leg.* ὄντως, A, D, E, F, G.
[4] ℵ, A, F, G, read μεθ' ὑμῶν, as in 2 Tim. iv. 22; Tit. iii. 15.
[5] Omitted by ℵ, A, D, F, G.
[6] Phil. ii. 19—23.

the murder of James the Lord's brother.[1] Soon after the accession of Gessius Florus to the post of Procurator, there were violent disturbances throughout Judæa. The war which culminated in the total destruction of the Jewish polity did not indeed break out till A.D. 66, but the general spirit of turbulence, the deeply-seated discontent with the government of Agrippa II., and the threatening multiplication of the Sicarii, showed that everything was ripening for the final revolt.[2] We may be sure that when the ship of Adramyttium sailed from Tyre, St. Paul had seen his last of the Holy Land. From Macedonia he doubtless went to Corinth, and he may then have sailed with Titus to Crete.

On the southern shores of that legendary island he had involuntarily touched in the disastrous voyage from Myra, which ended in his shipwreck at Malta. But a prisoner on his way to trial, in a crowded Alexandrian corn-vessel which only awaited the earliest opportunity to sail, could have had but little opportunity to preach the gospel even at the Fair Havens and Lasæa, and we may at once reject the idle suggestion that the Church of Crete had then first been founded. It is probable that the first tidings of Christianity had been carried to the island by those Cretan Jews who had heard the thrilling words of St. Peter at Pentecost; and the insufficiency of knowledge in these Churches may be accounted for in part by these limited opportunities, as well as by the inherent defects of the Cretan character. The stormy shores of Crete, and the evil reputation of its inhabitants even from mythical days, may well have tended to deter the evangelising visits of the early preachers of Christianity; and the indication that the nascent faith of the converts was largely tainted with Jewish superstition is exactly what we should have expected. St. Paul's brief sojourn in the island with Titus was probably the first serious effort to consolidate the young, struggling, and imperilled Churches; and we can easily imagine that it was the necessity of completing an anxious work which reluctantly compelled the Apostle to leave his companion behind him. The task could not have been left in wiser or firmer hands than those of one who had already made his influence felt and his authority respected among the prating and conceited sophists of turbulent Corinth. Those who argue that, because Paul had but recently parted with Titus, the advice contained in the letter would be superfluous, are starting a purely imaginary difficulty, and one of which the futility is demonstrated by the commonest experiences of daily life. Objections of this kind are simply astonishing, and when we are told that the instructions given are too vague and commonplace to render them of any value, and that "the pointlessness of the directions must have made them all but worthless to an evangelist,"[3] we can only reply that the Christian Church in all ages, in spite of the incessant tendency to exalt dogma above simple practice, has yet accepted the Pastoral Epistles as a manual which has never been surpassed.

[1] Jos. *Antt.* xx. 9, §§ 1, 2; Acts xii. 1—11. [2] Jos. *B. J.* ii. 14, § 2.
[3] Davidson, *Introd.* ii. 129; Reuss, *Les Epîtres*, ii. 333.

From Crete, St. Paul may have returned by Ephesus and Troas to Macedonia, and thence to Dalmatia and Illyricum;[1] and we learn from the Epistle to Titus that he was accompanied by several friends, for whom he found the amplest employment in missions to various Churches. He intended to spend the winter at Nicopolis, which, beyond all question, must be the well-known and flourishing city of Epirus, built by Augustus to commemorate his victory at Actium. When he wrote the Epistle to Titus, he was about to send Artemas or Tychicus to him in Crete, to continue the work of organisation there, while Titus is directed to join the Apostle at Nicopolis before the winter comes on.

How little we really know about Titus will be best seen by the theories which attempt to identify him with Titus (or, Titius) Justus (Acts xviii. 7), with Silas, and even with Timothy! Though he is not mentioned in the Acts —probably because he never happened to be a companion of the Apostle at the same time that Luke was with him—he seems to have been one of the trustiest and most beloved members of the noble little band of St. Paul's friends and disciples. As he was a Greek by birth, St. Paul, whose convert he was, had chosen to take him to Jerusalem on that memorable visit, which ended in the recognition of Gentile emancipation from the yoke of Mosaism.[2] If we were right in the conjecture that the generous self-sacrifice of Titus on this occasion rescued Paul from a grievous struggle, if not from an immense peril, we may imagine how close would have been the personal bond between them. He had special connexions with Corinth, to which he had three times been sent by the Apostle during the troubles of that distracted Church.[3] The warm terms in which St. Paul always speaks of him as his brother, and associate, and fellow-labourer, and the yearning anxiety which made him utterly miserable when he failed to meet him in Troas, show that he was no ordinary man; and the absence from this Epistle of the personal warnings and exhortations which are found in those to Timothy, lead us to believe that Titus was the more deeply respected, even if Timothy were the more tenderly beloved. The last notice of him is his visit to Dalmatia during the second imprisonment, and we may feel the strongest confidence that this was undertaken as a special duty, and that he did not voluntarily desert his friend and teacher whom he had so long and faithfully served. The Epistle which St. Paul addresses to him goes over much the same ground as that to Timothy, but with additional particulars, and in a perfectly independent manner. It excited the warm admiration of Luther, who says of it: "This is a short Epistle, but yet such a quintessence of Christian doctrine, and composed in such a masterly manner, that it contains all that is needful for Christian knowledge and life." The subjects are touched upon in the same easy and natural order as in the other Pastoral Epistles, and the incidental mention of people so entirely unknown in the circle of the Apostle's friends as Artemas and Zenas, the lawyer, together with the marked variations in the initial and

[1] Rom. xv. 19. [2] Gal. ii. 3; Tit. i. 4. [3] 2 Cor. vii., viii.

final salutations, are among the many incidental circumstances which powerfully strengthen the argument in favour of its authenticity.

The greeting with which the Apostle opens is somewhat obscure and involved, owing to the uncertainty of the exact meaning of the various prepositions employed. It differs from all other salutations in the phrase "a slave of God," instead of a "a slave of Jesus Christ," and it is marked by the prominence of the title Saviour, which is applied throughout this Epistle both to God and to Christ.[1]

"Paul, a slave of God, but an Apostle of Jesus Christ for the faith of the elect of God and the full knowledge of the truth which is according to godliness, (based) on the hope of eternal life, which God, who cannot lie, promised before eternal times, but manifested His word in His own seasons in the preaching with which I was entrusted according to the commandment of God our Saviour—to Titus, my true son after the common faith, grace and peace, from God our Father, and the Lord Jesus Christ our Saviour."

After this solemn greeting he proceeds at once to the many practical directions which are the object of his writing. He left Titus in Crete to finish all necessary regulations, and especially to ordain presbyters in every city, who are to be men of irreproachable character, and well-ordered domestic positions, for a "bishop" must be blameless as God's steward, not self-willed, not passionate, and with the other positive and negative qualifications which he has already mentioned in the Epistle to Timothy—with the addition that he is to love what is good, and to hold fast the faithful word according to the instruction he has received that he may be able to exhort with healthy teaching and to refute the gainsayers.[2]

These opponents are described as being disorderly, prating, and self-deceiving Jewish Christians, who for the sake of filthy lucre turn whole families upside down. To these, as to the Cretans in general, St. Paul applies the stinging line of their fellow-countryman Epimenides—

"The Cretans are always liars, evil wild beasts, lazy gluttons,"[3]

—for which reason they must be sharply rebuked, that they may be healthy

[1] If the idea of God the Father as a Saviour had not occurred both in the Old Testament and elsewhere in St. Paul, the expression might fairly have been called un-Pauline. But the idea is distinctly found in 1 Cor. i. 21.

[2] i. 5—9.

[3] The line is an hexameter from the poem on "Oracles" by Epimenides, the Cretan poet and philosopher. It was quoted by Callimachus, *Hymn to Zeus*, 8, and well known in antiquity because it gave rise to the syllogistic catch known as "the Liar."

They were among the three very bad K's of antiquity.

Κρῆτες, Καππάδοκαι, Κίλικες, τρία κάππα κάκιστα.

As for their lying, κρητίζειν meant "to tell lies;" of their ferocity, gluttony, drunkenness, and sensuality, and above all of their greed, ample testimonies are quoted—"Cretenses spem pecuniae secuti" (Liv. xliv. 45); τοῖς χρήμασιν, ὥσπερ κηρίοις μέλιτται, προσλιπαροῦντες (Plut. *Paul. Æmil.* 23); Polyb. vi. 46, &c., and a remarkable epigram of Leonides—

Αἰεὶ λῃσταὶ καὶ ἁλιφθόροι οὔτε δίκαιοι
Κρῆτες· τίς Κρητῶν οἶδε δικαιοσύνην.

(See Meursius's Creta, and Wetstein *ad loc.*)

in the faith, ceasing to heed Jewish myths and the commandments of men who turn away from the truth.[1] Among these commandments there seem to have been many distinctions between things clean and unclean, all of which the Apostle sweeps aside in his clear decisive manner by the deep truth that to the pure all things are pure;—whereas nothing is or can be pure to men of defiled mind and conscience, such as these, who, professing knowledge of God, in deeds denied Him, being detestable, and disobedient, and to every good deed reprobate.[2]

"But speak thou the things which become the healthy teaching." The keynote of this wholesome teaching is sober-mindedness. *Aged men* are to be temperate, grave, sober-minded, sound in love, in faith, in endurance. *Aged women* are to show a sacred decorum in demeanour, free from slander and intemperance,[3] teachers of what is fair, that they may train the younger women, too, to be sober-minded, ennobling the estimate of their Christian profession by humble, diligent, submissive performance of their home duties. Titus must also exhort *young men* to be sober-minded, and in all respects he is to set them a pure example of dignity, and faithfulness to the truth. Slaves are to "adorn the doctrine of God our Saviour in all things," by silent obedience and cheerful honesty.

"For God's grace was manifested bringing salvation to all men, training us to the end that once for all rejecting impiety and all worldly desires, we should live in the present age soberly, and righteously, and godly, expecting the blessed hope and manifestation of the glory of the great God and our Saviour Jesus Christ,[4] who gave Himself for us, that He might ransom us from all lawlessness, and purify for Himself a peculiar people, zealous of good works. These things speak, and rebuke and exhort with all authority. Let no man despise thee."[5]

After this swift and perfect summary of the Christian life, alike in its earthly and spiritual aspects, he reverts to necessary subjects for practical exhortation. Naturally turbulent, the Cretans are to be constantly reminded of the duty of submission in all things right and good. Naturally ferocious, they are to be exhorted to meekness of word and deed towards all men. For even so God showed gentleness to us when we were living in foolish and disobedient error, the slaves of various passions, in a bitter atmosphere of

[1] Possibly Titus had tried to regard these "myths" as harmless.

[2] i. 10—16.

[3] ii 3, "Not enslaved by much wine." On the proverbial intemperance of women among the ancients, see *Antholog.* xi. 298; Aristoph. *Thesm.* 735 and *passim*; Athen. x. 57.

[4] The question as to whether these words should be rendered as in the text, or "*our great God and Saviour Jesus Christ*," is simply a critical question. The analogy of other passages throughout these and other Epistles (1 Tim. i. 1; v. 21; vi. 13; and, above all, ii. 3—5; 2 Peter i. 1; 2 Thess. i. 12; Jude 4, &c.), and the certainty that this translation is not required either by the anarthrous Σωτήρ, or by the word ἐπεφάνη, show that the view taken by our English Version, and the majority of Protestant and other versions, as well as by many of the ancient versions, is correct.

[5] Which of all the Fathers of the first or second century was in the smallest degree capable of writing so masterly a formula of Christian doctrine and practice as these verses (ii. 11—14), or the perfectly independent yet no less memorable presentation of Gospel truth—with a completeness only too many-sided for sects and parties—in iii.

reciprocal hatred. "But when"—and here follows another concentrated summary of Pauline doctrine unparalleled for beauty and completeness—

> "But when the kindness and love towards man of God our Saviour was manifested, not in consequence of works of righteousness which *we* did, but according to His mercy He saved us, by means of the laver of regeneration, and renewal by the Holy Ghost, which He poured upon us richly through Jesus Christ our Saviour, that being justified by His grace we might become heirs, according to hope, of eternal life."

Faithful is the saying[1]—and in accordance with it he desires Titus to teach with due insistence, that all who have believed may live up to their profession. This teaching is fair and beneficent, but foolish speculations and discussions,[2] and genealogies and legalist disputes are vain and useless. But if, after one or two admonitions, a man would not give up his own depraved and wilful perversities, then Titus is to have nothing more to say to him.[3]

The brief letter closes with a few personal messages. Titus may soon expect the arrival of Artemas or Tychicus,[4] and on the arrival of either, to take up his work, he is with all speed to join Paul at Nicopolis for the winter. He is also asked to do anything he can to further the journey and meet the requirements of Zenas the jurist,[5] and Apollos. And St. Paul hopes that all *our*

5—7? Will any one produce from Clemens, or Hermas, or Justin Martyr, or Ignatius, or Polycarp, or Irenæus—will any one even produce from Tertullian, or Chrysostom, or Basil, or Gregory of Nyssa—any single passage comparable for terseness, insight, and mastery to either of these? Only the inspired wisdom of the greatest of the Apostles could have traced so divine a summary with so unfaltering a hand. If the single chorus of Sophokles was sufficient to acquit him of senility—if the thin unerring line attested the presence of Apelles—if the flawless circle of Giotto, drawn with one single sweep of his hand, was sufficient to authenticate his workmanship and prove his power—surely such passages as these ought to be more than adequate to defend the Pastoral Epistles from the charge of vapidity. Would it not be somewhat strange if all the great Christian Fathers of three centuries were so far surpassed in power and eloquence by the supposed *falsarii* who wrote the Epistles of the First and Second Captivity of St. Paul?

[1] Π. ὁ λόγος here refers to what has gone before, and it is remarkable that this favourite formula is generally applied, as here, to expressions which have something solemn and almost rhythmic in the form of their expression (1 Tim. i. 15; iii. 1; 2 Tim. ii. 11—the analogous 1 Tim. iii. 16). Were the quotations from Lymus? The contrast between the regenerate present and the unregenerate past is common in St. Paul (1 Cor. vi. 11; Gal. iv. 3; Eph. ii. &c.). If any one were asked to fix on two passages which contained the essence of all Pauline theology he would surely select Rom. iii. 21—26 and Tit. iii. 5—7; and the latter, though less polemical, is in some respects more complete. Again I ask, Would it not be strange if the briefest yet fullest statement of his complete message should come from a spurious Epistle?

[2] St. Paul stigmatises these sophistic discussions as both κενοὶ and ματαιοὶ—*i.e.*, empty in their nature, and void of all results.

[3] αἱρέσεις only occurs in 1 Cor. xi. 19; Gal. v. 20, and means, not "heresies," but "ecclesiastical divisions."

[4] "Artemas *or* Tychicus." Who was Artemas, or Artemidorus? That he, like Trophimus and Tychicus (Acts xx. 4; xxi. 29), was an Ephesian, we may perhaps conjecture from his name, and Paul may have met with him in his recent visit to Ephesus; but what could possibly have induced a forger to insert a totally unknown name like that of Artemas? or to imagine any *uncertainty* in the mind of Paul as to which of the two he should send? (On Tychicus, see Col. iv. 7; Eph. vi. 21.)

[5] Does this mean "a lawyer" in the same sense as νομοδιδάσκαλος in Luke v. 17? Was he a Jewish scribe, or a Greek or Roman legist? It is quite impossible to say; and who was this Zenas, or Zenodorus? What should put such a name and such an allusion into a forger's mind?

people also will learn to follow the example of these kindly services to all who require them, that they may not be unfruitful. "All who are with me salute thee. Salute those who love us in the faith. God's grace with you all."

These last three greetings have several points of interest. They show us that Paul, who was soon to be so sadly and unworthily deserted, was still carrying on his manifold missionary activities as one in a band of devoted friends. The fact that they differ in expression from every other closing salutation is a mark of authenticity, because a forger would have been sure to confine himself to a servile and unsuspicious repetition of one of the forms which occur elsewhere. But what does St. Paul mean by the remarkable expression, "let *our people also* learn to be forward in good works"? It is usually explained to mean "the other believers as well as thou;" but this is obviously unsatisfactory. On the other hand, we have no sufficient data to interpret it of the existence of converts of Apollos forming a different body from those of Paul. Its very obscurity is a sign that the allusion is to some fact which was known to the correspondent, but is unknown to us.

Titus here disappears from Christian history. The rest of his biography evaporates into the misty outlines of late ecclesiastical conjecture scarcely to be dignified by the name of tradition.

CHAPTER LV.

THE CLOSING DAYS.

"Christianus etiam extra carcerem saeculo renuntiavit, in carcere autem etiam carceri. . . . Ipsam etiam conversationem saeculi et carceris comparemus, si non plus in carcere spiritus acquirit, quam caro amittit."—TERT. *ad Mart.* 2.

"In a free state Gaius would have found his way to Bedlam, and Nero to Tyburn."—FREEMAN, *Essays*, ii. 337.

SOME of those critics who have been most hostile to the genuineness of the Pastoral Epistles have felt and expressed a certain reluctance to set down the Second Epistle to Timothy as the work of a forger, and to rob the world of this supremely noble and tender testament of the dying soldier of Christ. And some who have rejected the two other Epistles have made an exception in favour of this. For myself I can only express my astonishment that any one who is sufficiently acquainted with the Christian literature of the first two centuries to see how few writers there were who showed a power even distantly capable of producing such a letter, can feel any hesitation as to its having been written by the hand of Paul. The Tübingen critics argue that the three Epistles must stand or fall together, and think that the First Epistle to Timothy shows signs of spuriousness, which drags the other two letters into the same condemnation. Accepting the close relationship which binds the three letters together, and seeing sufficient grounds in the First Epistle to Timothy and the Epistle to Titus to furnish at least a very strong probability of their genuineness, it seems to me that the probability is raised to certainty by the undoubted genuineness of the Second Epistle to Timothy. If, indeed, St. Paul was never liberated from his first Roman imprisonment, then the Pastoral Epistles must be forgeries; for the attempts of Wieseler and others to prove that they might have been written during any part of the period covered by the narrative of the Acts—during the three years' stay at Ephesus, for instance, or the stay of eighteen months at Corinth—sink to the ground not only under the weight of their own arbitrary hypotheses, but even more from the state both of the Church and of the mind and circumstances of the Apostle, which these letters so definitely manifest. But as the liberation and second imprisonment of St. Paul are decidedly favoured by tradition, and give a most easy and natural explanation to every allusion in these and in earlier Epistles, and as no single valid objection can be urged against this belief, I believe that there would never have been any attempt to disprove its possibility except from the hardly-concealed desire to get rid of these letters and the truths to which they bear emphatic witness.

The allusions in the Second Epistle, though too fragmentary and insignificant to have been imagined by an imitator, are only allusions, and it is quite possible that they may not supply us with sufficient data to enable us to arrive at any continuous narrative of events in the Apostle's history between his first and second imprisonment. To dwell on these events at any length would therefore be misleading; but it is perfectly allowable to construct an hypothesis which is simple in itself, and which fits in with every circumstance to which any reference is made. The probability of the hypothesis, and the natural manner in which it suits the little details to which St. Paul refers, is one more of the many indications that we are dealing here with genuine letters.

If, then, we piece together the personal notices of this Epistle, they enable us to trace the further fortunes of St. Paul after the winter which he spent at Nicopolis, in the society of Titus. At his age, and with his growing infirmities—conscious too, as he must have been, from those inward intimations which are rarely wanting, that his life was drawing to a close—it is most unlikely that he should have entered on new missions, and it is certain that he would have found more than sufficient scope for all his energies in the consolidation of the many Greek and Eastern Churches which he had founded, and in the endeavour to protect them from the subtle leaven of spreading heresies. The main part of his work was accomplished. At Jerusalem and at Antioch he had vindicated for ever the freedom of the Gentile from the yoke of the Levitic Law. In his letters to the Romans and Galatians he had proclaimed alike to Jew and Gentile that we are not under the Law, but under grace. He had rescued Christianity from the peril of dying away into a Jewish sect, only distinguishable from Judaism by the accepted fulfilment of Messianic hopes. Labouring as no other Apostle had laboured, he had preached the Gospel in the chief cities of the world, from Jerusalem to Rome, and perhaps even as far as Spain. During the short space of twenty years he had proclaimed Christ crucified to the simple

Pagans of Lycaonia, the fickle fanatics of Galatia, the dreamy mystics of Phrygia, the vigorous colonists of Macedonia, the superficial dilettanti of Athens, the sensual and self-satisfied traders of Corinth, the semi-barbarous natives of Dalmatia, the ill-reputed islanders of Crete, the slaves and soldiers and seething multitudes of Rome. He had created the terminology, he had formulated the truths of Christianity. It had been his rare blessedness to serve the Gospel at once as an active missionary and as a profound thinker. The main part of his work was done. There was no further danger to be apprehended from "them of the circumcision," or from "certain who came from James." New dangers were arising, but their worst developments lay far in the future.[1] As Karl the Great burst into tears when, after a life spent in subjugating Lombards and Saxons, he saw in the offing the barques of the pirate Norsemen, and knew that they would never give much trouble in his own days, but wept to think of the troubles which they would cause hereafter, so Paul felt the presentiment of future perils from the Essenic elements which were destined to ripen into Gnosticism, but he did not live to witness their full development. His desire would be, not to attempt the foundation of new Churches, but to forewarn and to strengthen the beloved Churches which he had already founded.

And therefore, after he left Nicopolis, he would naturally travel back to Berœa, Thessalonica, Philippi, and so by Neapolis to Troas, where he stayed in the house of a disciple named Carpus. Here it was that the final crisis of his fate seems to have overtaken him. It is at least a fair conjecture that he would not have left at the house of Carpus his precious books, and the cloak which was so necessary to him, unless his departure had been hasty and perhaps involuntary. His work and his success in that town had been sufficiently marked to attract general attention, and it was exactly the kind of town in which he might have been liable to sudden arrest. Since Nero's persecution of the Christians, they must have been more or less the objects of hatred and suspicion throughout the Empire, and especially in the provincial towns of Asia Minor, which were ever prone to flatter the Emperor, because their prosperity, and sometimes almost their existence, depended on his personal favour. Any officer eager to push himself into notice, any angry Jew, any designing Oriental, might have been the cause of the Apostle's arrest; and if it took place at Troas, especially if it were on some pretext suggested by Alexander the coppersmith, or connected with St. Paul's long and active work at Ephesus, he would, in the ordinary course of things, have been sent under guard to Ephesus to be judged by the Proconsul. While awaiting his trial there he would, of course, have been put in prison; and the fact that his place of imprisonment is still pointed out among the ruins of Ephesus, although no imprisonment at Ephesus is directly mentioned in Scripture, adds perhaps a slight additional probability to these conjectures. It was here that he experienced at the hands of Onesiphorus the kindness

[1] 2 Tim. iii. 1, ἐνστήσονται καιροὶ χαλεποί.

which was continued to him at Rome,[1] and to which he alludes with a gratitude all the more heartfelt, because very shortly afterwards Onesiphorus seems to have died.

From the trial at Ephesus, where his cause might have suffered from local prejudices, he may once more have found it necessary to appeal to Cæsar. Barea Soranus, the then Proconsul, may have been glad, as Pliny afterwards was in Bithynia, to refer the case to the highest tribunal. Timothy would naturally desire to accompany him, but at that time the Apostle—still sanguine, still accompanied by other friends, still inclined to believe that his life, which had long been valueless to himself, might be saved from human violence, however near might be its natural close—thought it necessary to leave his friend at Ephesus to brave the dangers, and fulfil the duties of that chief pastorate, respecting which he had recently received such earnest instructions. It was natural that they should part with deep emotion at a time so perilous and under circumstances so depressing. St. Paul, sitting in his dreary and desolate confinement at Rome, recalls with gratitude the streaming tears of that farewell, which proved how deeply his affection was requited by the son of his heart. In all his wanderings, in all his sickness, in all his persecutions, in all his imprisonments, in all his many and bitter disappointments, the one spot invariably bright, the one permanent consolation, the one touch of earthly happiness, had been the gentle companionship, the faithful attendance, the clinging affection of this Lycaonian youth. For St. Paul's sake, for the Gospel's sake, he had left his mother, and his home, and his father's friends, and had cheerfully accepted the trying life of a despised and hunted missionary. By birth a Greek, he had thrown in his lot by circumcision with the Jew, by faith with the Christian; and his high reward on earth had been, not the shadow of an immortal honour, but the substance of lofty service in the cause of the truth which was to subdue the world. The affection between him and the Apostle began in the spiritual sonship of conversion, and was cemented by community of hopes and perils until it had become one of the strongest ties in life. For troubled years they had cheered each other's sorrows in the midst of painful toils. The very difference in their age, the very dissimilarity of their characters, had but made their love for each other more sacred and more deep. The ardent, impetuous, dominant character and intense purpose of the one, found its complement and its repose in the timid, yielding, retiring, character of the other. What Melancthon was to Luther, whom Luther felt that he could not spare, and for whose life when all hope seemed over he stormed heaven with passionate and victorious supplication,[2]—that and more than that was the comparatively youthful Timothy to the more tried and lonely Paul.

[1] 2 Tim. i. 18, ὅσα ἐν Ἐφέσῳ διηκόνησε, "how many acts of service he rendered" to Paul and others. Wieseler's inference that Onesiphorus was a deacon is hardly supported by so general a verb.

[2] "Allda musste mir unser Herr Gott herhalten. Denn ich rieb Ihm die Ohren mit allen promissionibus exaudiendarum precum." (Luther.)

We may hope that the Apostle, now once more a prisoner, was not alone when he left Ephesus to cross the Mediterranean for the last time. Titus and Tychicus[1] had probably accompanied him from Nicopolis; Demas may have joined him at Thessalonica, Luke at Philippi; and Trophimus, undeterred by his past dangers at Jerusalem, volunteered to accompany him from the Ionian capital. But the kindly intentions of the latter were frustrated, for he fell ill at Miletus, and there the sad little band of Christians had to leave him when the vessel started.[2] Erastus, if he was with him at Ephesus, stayed behind when they reached his native Corinth.

Of the particulars of the voyage we know nothing. It may very possibly have been from Ephesus to Cenchreae, over the Diolkos to Lechaeum, and then along the Gulf of Corinth and across the Adriatic to Brundisium, whence the prisoner, his guards and his companions, would make their dreary way along the great Appian road to Rome. This time no disciples met them at the Appii Forum or the Three Taverns, nor could anything have well occurred to make Paul thank God and take courage. The horrible Neronian persecution had depressed, scattered, and perhaps decimated the little Christian community; and the Jews, who had received Paul at the time of his first imprisonment with an ostentatiously indifferent neutrality, had been transformed since then—partly, no doubt, by the rumours disseminated by emissaries from Jerusalem, and partly by the mutual recriminations after the fire of Rome—into the bitterest and most unscrupulous enemies. On the former occasion, after a short detention in the Prætorian camp, St. Paul had been allowed to live in his own lodging; and even if this had been in the humblest purlieus of the Trastevere, among the Jewish vendors of sulphur matches and cracked pottery,[3] it had still been his own, and had allowed him to continue, in a sphere however restricted, his efforts at evangelisation. But Christianity was now suspected of political designs, and was practically reduced to a *religio illicita*. This time he had no kindly-disposed Lysias to say a good word for him, no friendly testimonies of a Festus or an Agrippa to produce in his favour. The government of Nero, bad almost from the first, had deteriorated year by year with alarming rapidity, and at this moment it presented a spectacle of awful cruelty and abysmal degradation such as has been rarely witnessed by the civilised world. While an honest soldier like Burrus held the high

[1] Hence we infer that Artemas, and not Tychicus, had been sent to replace Titus at Crete; and the mention of the name Artemas first in Tit. iii. 12 is yet another of the numberless subtle traces of genuineness.

[2] This incidental allusion (*most* unlike a forger) throws a valuable light, as also does the almost fatal illness of Epaphroditus at Rome, on the limitation which the Apostles put on the exercise of any supernatural gift of healing. It is, further, an insuperable stumblingblock in the way of every possible theory which denies the second imprisonment. Some have suggested a desperate alteration of the text to Μελίτῃ, and Schrader is content with the preposterous fiction of a Miletus in Crete! But why should St. Paul tell Timothy that Trophimus was sick at Miletus? For the same reason that a person writing to London might, even in these days of rapid communication, tell a correspondent that their common friend was ill at Southend. Miletus was more then thirty miles from Ephesus, and Trophimus might be ill for months without Timothy knowing of it.

[3] But see *supra*, p. 582.

post of Prætorian Præfect, a political prisoner was at least sure that he would not be treated with wanton severity; but with a Tigellinus in that office—a Tigellinus whose foul hands were still dripping with Christian blood, and whose foul life was stained through and through with every form of detestable wickedness—what could be expected? We catch but one glance of this last imprisonment before the curtain falls, but that glimpse suffices to show how hard it was. Through the still blackened ruins of the city, and amid the squalid misery of its inhabitants—perhaps with many a fierce scowl turned on the hated Christian—Paul passed to his dungeon, and there, as the gate clanged upon him, he sat down, chained night and day, without further hope —a doomed man.

To visit him now was no longer to visit a man against whom nothing serious was charged, and who had produced a most favourable impression on the minds of all who had been thrown into relation with him. It was to visit the bearer of a name which the Emperor and his minions affected to detest; it was to visit the ringleader of those who were industriously maligned as the authors of a calamity more deadly than any which had afflicted the city since its destruction by the Gauls. Merely to be kind to such a man was regarded as infamous. No one could do it without rendering himself liable to the coarse insolence of the soldiers.[1] Nay, more, it was a service of direct political danger. Rome swarmed with spies who were ready to accuse any one of *laesa majestas* on the slightest possible occasion. Now who but a Christian would visit a Christian? What could any respectable citizen have to do with the most active propagandist of a faith which had at first been ignored as contemptible, but which even calm and cultivated men were beginning to regard as an outrage against humanity?[2] And if any Christian were charged with being a Christian on the ground of his having visited St. Paul, how could he deny the charge, and how, without denying it, could he be saved from incurring the extremest danger?

Under these circumstances the condition of the Apostle was very different from what it had been three years before. His friends had then the freest access to him, and he could teach Christ Jesus with all boldness undisturbed. Now there were few or no friends left to visit him; and to teach Jesus Christ was death. He knew the human heart too well to be unaware how natural it was that most men should blush to associate themselves with him and his chain. One by one his Asiatic friends deserted him.[3] The first to leave him were Phygellus and Hermogenes.[4] Then the temptations of the present course of things, the charm of free and unimperilled life, were too much for Demas, and he too—though he had long been his associate—now forsook him.

[1] See Juv. *Sat.* xvi. 8—12.

[2] "Odio generis humani convicti sunt." (Tac. *Ann.* xv. 44; cf. *H.* v. 5.)

[3] 2 Tim. i. 15.

[4] Nothing whatever is known of these two. In later days the Christians, under the stress of persecution, had learnt their lessons better, so that their tender faithfulness to one another in distress excited the envious astonishment of Pagans (Lucian, *De Morte Peregr.* § 13).

Crescens departed, perhaps on some necessary mission, to the Churches of Galatia, and Titus to those of Dalmatia. He had dispatched Tychicus to Ephesus shortly before he wrote this letter. One friend alone was with him —the beloved physician, the faithful, unobtrusive, cultivated Luke.[1] Of hardship Paul recked nothing; he had spent a life of endless hardship, and had learnt a complete independence of the outward elements of comfort; but to one situated as he was, and liable to constant pain, to be utterly companionless would have been a trial too hard to bear.

A single happy unexpected visit broke the continuity of his loneliness, and cheered him amid the sense of desertion. The good-hearted Ephesian Onesiphorus, who had already made himself conspicuous among the Christians of his native city by his active kindliness, came to Rome. He knew that St. Paul was somewhere in that city as a prisoner, and he rose above the timid selfishness of his fellow-countrymen. He set about searching for the captive Jew. In a city thronged with prisoners, and under a government rife with suspicions, upon which it acted with the most cynical unscrupulousness, it was by no means a safe or pleasant task to find an obscure, aged, and deeply implicated victim. Had Onesiphorus been less in earnest, it would have been easy for him to make an excuse to other Christians, and to his own conscience, that he had not known where Paul was, and that he had looked for him but could not find him. But he would not abandon his earnest search until it led him to the side of the Apostle.[2] Nor was he content with a single visit. Glad to face the shame and scorn of befriending one whose condition was now so abject, he came to the Apostle again and again, and refreshed his soul with that very consolation—the sense of human sympathy—for which most of all it yearned.[3] Probably the death of this true and warm-hearted Ephesian took place at Rome, for St. Paul utters a fervent wish that he may find mercy of the Lord in the great day, and in writing to Timothy he sends a greeting to his household, but not to him.[4] The tone of intense gratitude which breathes through the few verses in which the Apostle alludes to him makes us feel that the brave and loving friendliness of this true brother, contrasted as it was with the cowardly defection of the other Asiatics, was the brightest gleam of light which fell on the dense gloom of the second imprisonment.

At last the time came when the Apostle had to stand before the great Roman tribunal. What was called in Roman law the *prima actio* came on.[5] The Scriptures were written with other objects than to gratify our curiosity with the details of historic scenes, however memorable or however important.

[1] Where was Aristarchus (Acts xxvii. 2; Col. iv. 10; Phil. 24)? We cannot tell; but his name would not have been omitted by an ingenious imitator.

[2] 2 Tim. i 17, σπουδαιότερον ἐζήτησέν με καὶ εὗρεν.

[3] 2 Tim. i. 16, πολλάκις με ἀνέψυξεν.

[4] 2 Tim. iv. 19.

[5] Such certainly seems to be the natural meaning of πρώτη ἀπολογία (2 Tim. iv. 16), and it is not certain that this method of procedure and the *ampliatio* or *comperendinatio* had been entirely abandoned. In these matters the mere caprice of the Emperor was all that had to be consulted. It is, however, possible that the πρώτη ἀπολογία may refer to the first count of the indictment, since Nero had introduced the custom of hearing every count separately.

That which God has revealed to us in Scripture is rather the œconomy—the gradual unfolding and dispensation—of His eternal scheme for the salvation of mankind, than the full biography of those whose glory it was to be entrusted with the furtherance of His designs. Eagerly should we have desired to know the details of that trial, but St. Paul only tells us a single particular. His silence once more illustrates the immense difference between ancient and modern correspondence. A modern, in writing to a dear friend, would have been sure to give him some of the details, which could hardly fail to interest him. It may be said that these details might have been supplied by the bearer of the letter. It may be so; but if we judge St. Paul by his own writings, and by the analogy of other great and spiritually-minded men, we should infer that personal matters of this kind had but little interest for him. Accustomed to refer perpetually to his high spiritual privileges—digressing incessantly to the fact of his peculiar Apostolate—he yet speaks but little, and never in detail, of the outward incidents of his life. *They* did but belong to the world's passing show, to the things which were seen and evanescent. Two vivid touches alone reveal to us the nature of the occasion. One is the deplorable fact that not a single friend had the courage to stand by his side. He had to defend himself single-handed. No *patronus* would encourage him, no *advocatus* plead his cause, no *deprecator* say a word in his favour. "No man took his place by my side to help me; all abandoned me; God forgive them." The other is that even at that supreme moment, with the face of the threatening tyrant fixed loweringly upon him, and the axed fasces of the lictors gleaming before his eyes, his courage did not quail. If man forsook him, God strengthened him. If even Luke left him to face the court alone, the Lord Himself stood by him. He spoke, and spoke in a manner worthy of his cause. How much heathen literature would we freely sacrifice for even a brief sketch of that speech such as Luke could so well have given us had he only been present! How supreme would have been the interest of a defence uttered by St. Paul in the Roman forum, or in a Roman basilica! Alas! the echoes of his words have died away for ever. We only know what he who uttered it tells us of it. But he was satisfied with it. He felt that the Lord had strengthened him in order that, through his instrumentality, the preaching of the Gospel might be fulfilled to the uttermost, and that all the Gentiles might hear it. And he was successful—successful, we cannot doubt, not merely that he might prolong his days in useless and hopeless misery, but for some high design, and perhaps among other reasons that he might leave us his last precious thoughts in the Second Epistle to his dearest convert. But the danger had been imminent, and the too-certain result was only postponed. "I was rescued," he says, "out of the lion's mouth." Each juror received three voting tablets—one marked with A., for *Absolvo*; another with C., for *Condemno*; and a third with N.L., for *Non liquet*, or "not proven." The majority of votes had been of the third description, and the result had been the *ampliatio*, or postponement of the trial for the production of further evidence. But St. Paul was not deceived by any false hopes. "I was rescued out of the lion's mouth. The Lord shall deliver me"—not necessarily from death or danger, but—"from every evil work,[1] and shall save me unto His heavenly kingdom." Death by martyrdom was no such "evil work;"[2] from *that* he did not expect to be saved—nay, he knew, and probably even hoped, that through that narrow gate an entrance might be ministered unto him abundantly into Christ's heavenly kingdom. But he must have passed through perilous and exciting hours, or he would have hardly used that metaphor of the lion's mouth,[3] prompted perhaps by a reminiscence of the powerful image of the shepherd prophet, "As the shepherd tears out of the mouth of a lion two legs and the piece of an ear."[4]

But who was the lion? Was it Satan?[5] or Helius the Præfect of the city? or Nero?[6] or is the expression a merely general one? Even if so, it is not impossible that he may have pleaded his cause before Nero himself. The power of deciding causes had been one which the Roman Emperors had jealously kept in their own hands; and if the trial took place in the spring of A.D. 66, Nero had not yet started for Greece, and would have been almost certain to give personal attention to the case of one who had done more than any living man to spread the name of Christ. Nero had been intensely anxious to fix on the innocent Christians the stigma of that horrible conflagration, of which he himself had been dangerously suspected, and the mere suspicion of which, until averted into another channel, had gone far to shake even his imperial power. And now the greatest of the Christians—the very *coryphæus* of the hated sect—stood chained before him. He to whom popularity, forfeited in part by his enormous crimes, had become a matter of supreme importance, saw how cheaply it could be won by sacrificing a sick, deserted, aged, fettered prisoner, for whom no living soul would speak a word, and who was evidently regarded with intense hatred by Gentiles from Asia, by the dense rabble of the city, and by Jews from every quarter of the world. Cicero has preserved for us a graphic picture of the way in which, nearly a century and a half before this time, a screaming, scowling, gesticulating throng of Jews, undeterred by soldiers and lictors, surrounded with such threatening demonstrations the tribunal before which their oppressor, Flaccus, was being tried, that he, as his advocate, though he had been no less a person than a Roman Consul, and "father of his country," was obliged to plead in low tones for fear of their fury. If in B.C. 59 the Romish Jews could intimidate even a Cicero in

[1] From all that can be *really* called πονηρόν. "Liberabit me ne quid agam" (and we may add, *ne quid patiar*) "Christiano, ne quid Apostolo indignum" (Grot.).

[2] "Decollabitur? liberabitur, liberante Domino" (Bengel). It would be difficult for me to exaggerate my admiration for this truly great commentator. On the following words, "to whom be glory for ever and ever," he remarks, "Doxologiam parit spes, quanto majorem res."

[3] 2 Tim. iv. 17.

[4] Amos iii. 12. Cf. ἐνώπιον τοῦ λέοντος, referring to Xerxes (Apocr. Esth. xiv. 13).

[5] 1 Pet. v. 8.

[6] Λέοντα γὰρ τὸν Νέρωνά φησι διὰ τὸ θηριῶδες (Chrys.). τέθνηκεν ὁ λέων (of the death of Tiberius) (Jos. *Antt.* xviii. 6, § 10); but here λέοντος has no article. The metaphor is probably general, as in Ps. xxii. 21. Esther is said to have cried, "Save me from the lion's mouth," when she went to Ahasuerus (*Megillah*, f. 15, 2).

their hatred to a Flaccus, is it likely that they would have abstained from hostile demonstrations against an enemy so detested and so perfectly defenceless as St. Paul?

Paul before Nero! if indeed it was so, what a contrast does the juxtaposition of two such characters suggest—the one the vilest and most wicked, the other the best and noblest of mankind! Here, indeed, we see two races, two civilisations, two religions, two histories, two *æons* brought face to face. Nero summed up in his own person the might of legions apparently invincible; Paul personified that more irresistible weakness which shook the world. The one showed the very crown and flower of luxurious vice and guilty splendour; the other the earthly misery of the happiest saints of God. In the one we see the incarnate Nemesis of past degradation; in the other the glorious prophecy of Christian sainthood. The one was the deified autocrat of Paganism; the other the abject ambassador of Christ. The emperor's diadem was now confronted for the first time by the Cross of the Victim before which, ere three centuries were over, it was destined to succumb.

Nero, not yet thirty years of age, was stained through and through with every possible crime, and steeped to the very lips in every nameless degradation. Of all the black and damning iniquities against which, as St. Paul had often to remind his heathen converts, the wrath of God for ever burns, there was scarcely one of which Nero had not been guilty. A wholesale robber, a pitiless despot, an intriguer, a poisoner, a murderer, a matricide, a liar, a coward, a drunkard, a glutton, incestuous, unutterably depraved, his evil and debased nature—of which even Pagans had spoken as "a mixture of blood and mud"—had sought abnormal outlets to weary, if it could not sate, its insatiable proclivity to crime. He was that last worst specimen of human wickedness—a man who, not content with every existing form of vice and sin in which the taint of human nature had found a vent, had become "an inventor of evil things." He had usurped a throne; he had poisoned, under guise of affection, the noble boy who was its legitimate heir; he had married the sister of that boy, only to break her heart by his brutality, and finally to order her assassination; he had first planned the murder, then ordered the execution, of his own mother, who, however deep her guilt, had yet committed her many crimes for love of him; he had treacherously sacrificed the one great general whose victories gave any lustre to his reign; among other murders, too numerous to count, he had ordered the deaths of the brave soldier and the brilliant philosopher who had striven to guide his wayward and intolerable heart; he had disgraced imperial authority with every form of sickening and monstrous folly; he had dragged the charm of youth and the natural dignity of manhood through the very lowest mire; he had killed by a kick the worthless but beautiful woman whom he had torn from her own husband to be his second wife; he had reduced his own capital to ashes, and buffooned, and fiddled, and sung with his cracked voice in public theatres, regardless of the misery and starvation of thousands of its ruined citizens; he had charged his incendiarism upon the innocent Christians, and tortured them to death by hundreds in hideous martyrdoms; he had done his best to render infamous his rank, his country, his ancestors, the name of Roman—nay, even the very name of man.

And Paul had spent his whole life in the pursuit of truth and the practice of holiness. Even from boyhood a grave and earnest student of the Law of God, he surpassed in learning and faithfulness all the other "pupils of the wise" in the school of the greatest Doctor of the Law; and if the impetuous ardour of his nature, and that commonest infirmity of even noble minds—the pride of erroneous conviction which will not suffer itself to be convinced of error—had for a time plunged him into a course of violent intolerance, of which he afterwards repented with all the intensity of his nature, yet even this sin had been due to the blind fury of misdirected zeal in a cause which he took—or for a time thought that he took—to be the cause of God. Who shall throw the first stone at him? not even those learned and holy men whose daily lives shew how hard it is to abdicate the throne of infallible ignorance, and after lives of stereotyped error to go back as humble learners to the school of truth. But, if for a moment he erred, how grandly—by what a life of heroic self-sacrifice—had he atoned for his fault! Did ever man toil like this man? Did ever man rise to a nobler superiority over the vulgar objects of human desire? Did ever man more fully and unmurmuringly resign his whole life to God? Has it ever been granted to any other man, in spite of all trials, obstructions, persecutions, to force his way in the very teeth of "clenched antagonisms" to so full an achievement of the divine purpose which God had entrusted to his care? Shrinking from hatred with the sensitive warmth of a nature that ever craved for human love, he had yet braved hatreds of the most intense description—the hatred not only of enemies, but of friends; not only of individuals, but of entire factions; not only of aliens, but of his own countrymen; not only of Jews, but even of those who professed the same faith with himself.[1] Shrinking from pain with nervous sensibility, he yet endured for twenty years together every form of agony with a body weakened by incessant hardship. The many perils and miseries which we have recounted are but a fragment of what he had suffered. And what had he done? He had secured the triumph, he had established the universality, he had created the language, he had co-ordinated the doctrines, he had overthrown the obstacles of that Faith which is the one source of the hope, the love, the moral elevation of the world.

And now these two men were brought face to face—imperial power and abject weakness; youth cankered with guilt, and old age crowned with holiness; he whose whole life had consummated the degradation, and he whose life had achieved the enfranchisement of mankind. They stood face to face the representatives of two races—the Semitic in its richest glory, the Aryan in its extremest degradation: the representatives of two trainings—

[1] "They who hurt me most are my own dear children—my brethren—*fraterculi mei, aurei amiculi mei.*" (Luther, *Cochlearius*, 146.)

the life of utter self-sacrifice, and the life of unfathomable self-indulgence: the representatives of two religions—Christianity in its dawning brightness, Paganism in its effete despair: the representatives of two theories of life—the simplicity of self-denying endurance ready to give up life itself for the good of others, the luxury of shameless Hedonism which valued no consideration divine or human in comparison with a new sensation: the representatives of two spiritual powers—the slave of Christ and the incarnation of Antichrist. And their respective positions showed how much, at this time, the course of this world was under the control of the Prince of the Power of the Air—for incest and matricide were clothed in purple, and seated on the curule chair, amid the ensigns of splendour without limit and power beyond control; and he whose life had exhibited all that was great and noble in the heart of man stood in peril of execution, despised, hated, fettered, and in rags.

But Roman Law was still Roman Law, and, except where passions of unusual intensity interfered, some respect was still paid to the forms of justice. For the time, at any rate, Paul was rescued out of the lion's mouth. There was some flaw in the indictment, some deficiency in the evidence; and though St. Paul well knew that it was but a respite which was permitted him, for the time at any rate he was remanded to his prison. And Nero, if indeed he were "the lion" before whom this first defence had been pleaded, had no further door for repentance opened to him in this life. Had he too trembled, as Paul reasoned before him of temperance, righteousness, and the judgment to come? Had he too listened in alarm as Herod Antipas had listened to the Baptist? Had he too shown the hue of passing shame on those bloated features so deformed by the furrows of evil passion—as, at the Council of Constance, the Emperor Sigismund blushed when John Huss upbraided him with the breach of his pledged word? The Emperor, who stood nearest to Nero in abysmal depravity, and who, like him, being himself unutterably impure and bad, had the innermost conviction that all others were at heart the same, used to address grave men with the most insulting questions, and if the indignant blood mantled on their cheeks, he used to exclaim, "Erubuit, salva res est."[1] "He blushed; it is all right." But of Domitian we are expressly told that he *could not* blush; that his flushed cheeks were an impervious barrier against the access of any visible shame.[2] And in all probability Nero was infinitely too far gone to blush. It is far more probable that, like Gallio, he only listened to the defence of this worn and aged Jew with ill-concealed impatience and profound disdain. He would have regarded such a man as this as something more abject than the very dust beneath his feet. He would have supposed that Paul regarded it as the proudest honour of his life even to breathe the same atmosphere as the Emperor of Rome. His chance of hearing the words of truth returned no more. About this time he sailed on his frivolous expedition to Greece; and after outraging to an extent almost inconceivable the very name of Roman, by the public singings

[1] Heliogabalus. [2] Tac. *Agric.* 45; Suet. *Dom.* 18; Plin. *Paneg.* 48.

of his miserable doggrel, and the sham victories in which the supple and shameless Greeks fooled him to the very top of his bent, he returned to find that the revolt of Galba was making head, until he was forced to fly at night in disguise from his palace, to quench his thirst with ditch-water, to display a cowardice which made him contemptible to his meanest minions, and finally to let his trembling hand be helped by a slave to force a dagger into his throat.

But it is no wonder that when, over the ruins of streets which the fire had laid in ashes, St. Paul returned to his lonely prison, there was one earthly desire for the fulfilment of which he still yearned. It was once more to see the dear friend of earlier years—of those years in which, hard as were their sufferings, the hope of Christ's second coming in glory to judge the world seemed still so near, and in which the curtains of a neglected death and an apparently total failure had not yet been drawn so closely around his head. He yearned to see Timothy once more; to be refreshed by the young man's affectionate devotion; to be cheered and comforted by the familiar attendance of a true son in Christ, whose heart was wholly at one with his; who shared so fully in all his sympathies and hopes; who had learnt by long and familiar attendances how best to brighten his spirits and to supply his wants. It was this which made him write that second letter to Timothy, which is, as it were, his "cycnea oratio," and in which, amid many subjects of advice and exhortation, he urges his friend with reiterated earnestness to come, to come at once, to come before winter,[1] to come ere it is too late, and see him, and help him, and receive his blessing before he died.

CHAPTER LVI.

PAUL'S LAST LETTER.

Παῦλος δὲ ὁ τρισμακάριος τὴν κεφαλὴν ξίφει ἀπετμήθη ὁ ἀνεκδιήγητος ἄνθρωπος.—Ps. Chrys. *Orat. Enam.*

"Testamentum Pauli et cycnea cantio est haec Epistola."—Bengel.

"Hoc praestat carcer Christiano, quod eremus Prophetis."—Tert. *ad Mart.* 3.

"Mortem habebat Paulus ante oculos. . . . Quaecunque igitur hic legimus de Christi regno, de spe vitae aeternae, de Christianâ militiâ, de fiduciâ confessionis, de certitudine doctrinae, non tanquam atramento scripta, sed ipsius Pauli sanguine accipere convenit. . . . Proinde haec Epistola quasi solennis quaedam est subscriptio Paulinæ doctrinae, eaque ex repraesenti."—Calvin.

He began much in his usual form—

"Paul, an Apostle of Jesus Christ by the will of God,[2] according to the promise of the life which is in Christ Jesus, to Timothy my beloved son, grace, mercy, and

[1] 2 Tim. iv. 9, 21.

[2] διὰ θελήματος. The attempt to deduce some very special and recondite inference from the fact that he uses this phrase for the κατ' ἐπιταγὴν of the First Epistle, seems to me as arbitrary as Mack's argument that the use of ἀγαπητῷ for γνησίῳ in the next verse is a sign that this Epistle shows more affection but less confidence.

peace, from God our Father and Christ Jesus our Lord. I thank God, whom I serve from my forefathers in a pure conscience—as the remembrance which I have of thee night and day in my supplications is incessant, longing earnestly to see thee—remembering thy tears[1]—that I may be filled with joy.[2] [I thank God, I say] on being reminded[3] of the unfeigned faith which is in thee, which dwelt first in thy grandmother Lois, and in thy mother Eunice; yes, and I feel confident that it dwells also in thee."[4]

Perhaps the sadness of Timothy's heart—the tears for his absent and imprisoned teacher—had hindered the activity of his work, and plunged him in a too indolent despondency; and so Paul, remembering all the hopes which had inaugurated his youthful ministry, continues—

"For which cause[5] I remind thee to fan aflame the gift of God which is in thee by the imposition of my hands; for God gave us not the spirit of cowardice, but of power and of love, and of moral influence.[6] Be not then ashamed of the testimony of our Lord, nor of me His prisoner, but rather share my sufferings for the Gospel in accordance with the power of God, who saved us and called us with a holy calling, not according to our works, but according to His own plans and the grace given us in Christ Jesus before eternal times, but now manifested by the appearing of our Saviour Jesus Christ, who did away with death, and brought life and immortality to light by the Gospel, whereunto I was appointed a herald, and an Apostle, and teacher of the Gentiles, for which reason also I suffer these things; but *I* am not ashamed. For I know on whom I have believed, and I feel confident that he is able to preserve the trust committed to me till that day."[7]

Then—having ended the double digression on the word Gospel, which suggests to him first what that word implies (9, 10), and then recalls to him his own mission—he returns to his exhortation—

"As a pattern of wholesome teachings,[8] take those which thou heardest from me, in faith and the love which is in Christ Jesus. That fair trust preserve, through the Holy Spirit which dwelleth in us."[9]

Then he touches for a moment on the melancholy circumstances of which we have already spoken—his abandonment by the Asiatic converts,[10] and the

[1] Tears at parting. Cf. Acts xx. 37.

[2] Does not this involved sentence, with its tesselation of parenthetic thoughts, at once indicate the hand of Paul?

[3] How reminded? We do not know; but this is the proper meaning of ὑπόμνησις· ὅταν τις ὑφ' ἑτέρου εἰς μνήμην προαχθῇ.

[4] i. 1—5, πέπεισμαι δὲ. To make the δὲ imply "notwithstanding appearances," as Alford does, is too strong; but the adversative force of δὲ, though unnoticed by most commentators, and missed in many versions, does seem to imply that passing shade of hesitation about the fervour of the faith of Timothy—at any rate, as manifested in vigorous action—which I have tried to indicate in the "Yes, and I feel confident."

[5] This phrase—δι' ἣν αἰτίαν for διὸ—is peculiar to the Pastoral Epistles.

[6] σωφρονισμοῦ. The form of the word seems to imply not only "sobermindedness," but the teaching others to be sober-minded.

[7] i. 6—12.

[8] This seems to me the real meaning, though Alford has something to urge for his view that it should be rendered, "Have (in what I have just said to you) a pattern of sound words, which," &c.

[9] i. 13, 14.

[10] The expression οἱ ἐν τῇ Ἀσίᾳ πάντες, "all those *in* Asia," is difficult. It seems to imply that they had abandoned St. Paul in Rome, and had now returned to Asia, so that they would be "in Asia" by the time this letter arrived.

zealous refreshing kindness of Onesiphorus, for whom he breathes an earnest prayer.[1]

> "Thou therefore, my child, be strengthened in the grace which is in Christ Jesus, and the things which thou heardest from me in the presence of many witnesses, these things extend to faithful men who shall be adequate also to teach others. Share my sufferings as a fair soldier of Christ Jesus."[2]

The conditions of this soldiership he illustrates by three similes, drawn from the life of the soldier, the athlete, and the labourer, and doubtless meant to suggest to Timothy the qualities of which at that depressed period he stood most in need. The soldier must abandon all business entanglements, and strive to please his captain. The athlete, if he wants the crown, must keep the rules. The *toiling* husbandman has the first claim to a share of the harvest.[3] It was a delicate way of suggesting to Timothy the duties of increased single-heartedness, attention to the conditions of the Christian life, and strenuous labour; and that he might not miss the bearing of these similitudes he adds, "Consider what I say, for the Lord will give you[4] understanding in all things." By the example of his own sufferings he reminds him that the cardinal truths of the Gospel are ample to inspire toil and endurance.

> "Bear in mind," he says, "Jesus Christ, raised from the dead, of the seed of David, according to my Gospel—in the cause of which I suffer even to chains as a malefactor: but the word of God has not been chained. For this reason, for the sake of the elect, I am enduring all things, that they too may obtain the salvation which is in Christ Jesus with eternal glory. Faithful is the saying—
>
> 'If we died with, we shall also live with Him;[5]
> If we endure, we shall also reign with Him;
> If we deny, He also will deny us.
> If we are faithless, He abideth faithful,
> For He is not able to deny Himself.'"[6]

"These things call to their remembrance;" and from this verse to the end of the chapter he reverts to the false teachers among whom Timothy is labouring, and against whom he has warned him in the First Epistle, testifying to them before the Lord not to fight about "views"—a thing entirely useless—to the subversion of the hearers.[7] "Strive to present thyself approved to God, a workman unshamed, rightly dividing the word of truth."[8] He is to shun the vain babblings of men like Hymenæus and Philetus,[9] with their

[1] i. 15—18.

[2] The distinction between καλὸς and ἀγαθὸς can only be kept up by the old English word "fair," as in Tennyson's
"So that ye trust to our fair Father, Christ."

[3] ii. 1—6.

[4] ii. 7, *leg.* δώσει.

[5] Cf. 1 Cor. xv. 31; 2 Cor. iv. 18; Rom. vi. 8.

[6] ii. 7—13. The last words are rhythmical, perhaps liturgical.

[7] ii. 14. Logomachy is a sure mark of Sophistic teaching, and there is a resemblance of the Gnostics to the Sophists in several particulars.

[8] ὀρθοτομοῦντα, "rightly cutting," or "cutting straight." "Nihil praetermittere, nil adiicere, nil mutilare, discerpere, torquere" (Beza). But it is not clear whether the metaphor is from cutting roads, or victims, or furrows, or bread, or carpentry. It is better to regard it as general, "rightly handling," just as καινοτομεῖν came to mean merely "innovating." In patristic language ὀρθοτομία became another word for "orthodoxy."

[9] Nothing is known of them (1 Tim. i. 20).

ever-advancing impiety and the spreading cancer of their doctrine, which identified the resurrection with spiritual deliverance from the death of sin, and denied that there was any other resurrection,[1] to the ruinous unsettlement of some. Fruitlessly, however, for God's firm foundation stands impregnable with the double inscription on it,[2] "The Lord knoweth them that are His," and "Let every one who nameth the name of Christ stand aloof from unrighteousness."[3] Yet there should be no surprise that such errors spring up in the visible Church. It is like a great house in which are vessels of wood and earth, as well as of gold and silver, and alike for honourable and mean purposes. What each one had to do then was to purge himself from polluting connexion with the mean and vile vessels, and strive to be "a vessel for honour, sanctified, serviceable to the master, prepared for every good purpose."[4] He is therefore to "fly" from the desires of youth,[5] and in union with all who call on the Lord with a pure heart to pursue righteousness, faith, love, peace, having nothing to do with those foolish and illiterate questions which only breed strifes unworthy of the gentle, enduring meekness of a slave of the Lord, whose aim it should be to train opponents with all mildness,[6] in the hope that God may grant them repentance, so that they may come to full knowledge of the truth, and "awake to soberness out of the snare of the devil, after having been taken alive by him—to do God's will."[7]

The third chapter continues to speak of these evil teachers and their future developments in the hard times to come. A stern sad picture is drawn of what men shall then be in their selfishness, greed, conceit, ingratitude, lovelessness, treachery, besotted atheism, and reckless love of pleasure. He bids Timothy turn away from such teachers with their sham religion, their creeping intrigues, their prurient influence, their feminine conquests,[8] resisting the truth just as the old Egyptian sorcerers Jannes and Jambres[9]

[1] Since there is a trace of exactly the same heresy in 1 Cor. xv. 12, it is idle of Baur to assume any allusion to Marcion here. St. Paul's warning against thus making the resurrection a mere metaphor was all the more needful, because it was a distortion of his own expressions (Rom. vi. 4; Col. ii. 12, &c.).

[2] Cf. Rev. xxi. 14.

[3] See Numb. xvi. 5, 26.

[4] 2 Tim. ii. 21. The general meaning of the passage is clear, though it is indistinctly expressed; on ἐκκαθάρῃ Melancthon remarks, "Haec mundatio non est desertio congregationis, sed conversio ad Deum."

[5] ἐπιθυμίας, not exclusively sensual passions.

[6] See Matt. xii. 19, 20.

[7] ii. 14—26. The devil has taken them captive in a snare while they were drunk; awaking, they use their recovered soberness (ἀνανήψω, *crapulam excutio*) to break the snare, and return to obedience to God's will. αὐτοῦ probably refers to Satan, ἐκείνου to God, although this explanation is not absolutely necessary.

[8] Baur (*Pastoralbriefe*, p. 36) sees an allusion to the Gnostic prophetesses, Prisca, Maximilla, Quintilla, &c., and quotes Epiphan. *Haer.* xxvi. 11. But, on the one hand, these certainly did not deserve to be stigmatised as γυναικάρια (see Tert.), and on the other it is absurd to suppose that women would be any less susceptible to every phase of religious influence in the Apostle's days than they have been in all ages (cf. Jos. *Antt.* xvii. 2, § 4). Such a γυναικάριον was Helena whom Simon Magus took about with him (Justin, *Apol.* i. 26; Iren. *c. Haer.* i. 23). When Jerome speaks with such scorn and slander of Nicolas of Antioch (*choros duxit femineos*), Marcion and his female adherent, Apelles and Philumena, Arius and his sister, Donatus and Lucilla, Epidius and Agape, Priscillian and Galla, had he forgotten certain ladies called Paulla and Eustochium?

[9] Jannes and Jambres are mentioned by Origen, and even by Pliny (*H. N.* xxx 1),

did, and destined to have their emptiness equally *exposed*.[1] But Timothy—who has followed all that Paul has been in the teaching, the purpose, and the sufferings of his life, and well knows how the Lord saved him out of many trials and persecutions in his first journey[2]—must expect persecution, and be brave and faithful, making his life a contrast to that of these deceived deceivers, in accordance with that training which from a babe he had received in the Holy Scriptures, which were able to make him wise unto salvation through faith in Jesus Christ: since "every Scripture inspired by God is also profitable for teaching,[3] for reproof, for correction, for training in righteousness, that the man of God may be perfect, thoroughly equipped for every good work."[4]

The fourth chapter begins with a solemn appeal to him to do his duty as a pastor "in season, out of season,"[5] because the time would soon come when men would turn away from truth to the fantastic doctrines of teachers who would answer them according to their own lusts.

"Do *thou* then be sober in all things, endure sufferings. Do the work of an evangelist, fulfil thy ministry. For *I* am being already poured in libation, and the time of my departure[6] is close at hand. I have striven the good strife, I have finished my course, I have kept the faith. Henceforth there is laid up for me the crown of righteousness, which the Lord, the righteous Judge, shall give me in that day; and not to me only, but also to all who have loved His appearing."[7]

That is practically St. Paul's last word. The remainder of the letter is occupied with personal information, given in the natural, loose, accidental order of a letter, mingled with earnest entreaty to him that he would come at

who calls them Jannes and Jotapes, and Numenius (Orig. *c. Cels.* iv. 199). The names belong to the cycle of Jewish Hagadoth. They are mentioned in the Targum of Jonathan on Ex. vii. 11, and were said to be sons of Balaam.

[1] This is said to contradict ii. 16 and iii. 13. It only does so to an unintelligent literalism. Error will succeed, but its very success will end in its exposure. "Non proficient amplius, quamquam ipsi et eorum similes proficiant in ejus" (Bengel); or, as Chrysostom remarks, κἂν πρότερον ἀνθήσῃ τὰ τῆς πλάνης εἰς τέλος οὐ διαμενεῖ.

[2] It has been asked why he refers especially to these. Perhaps because they had come most heavily upon him, and affected him most severely as being the first of the kind which he had endured. Perhaps because Timothy was a Lycaonian, and Paul's memory of those old days is vividly awaked.

[3] This is almost certainly the true translation. It was so understood by Origen, Theodoret, by Erasmus and Grotius, by Whitby and Hammond, by Alford and Ellicott; is so translated in the Arabic, the Syriac, the Vulgate, Luther, the Dutch, and the Rhenish, and in the versions of Wiclif, Tyndale, Coverdale, and Cranmer. For the introduction of the predicate by καὶ see Gal. iv. 7, Luke i. 36, Rom. viii. 29, &c.

[4] iii. 1—17.

[5] iv. 2, εὐκαίρως, ἀκαίρως: "opportunè, importunè" (Aug.). The smallest element of literary sense is sufficient to save the verse from the fanatical abuse which has perverted so many passages of Scripture. If any antidote to its abuse is required, see Matt. vii. 6.

[6] ἀναλύσεως, "departure," not "dissolution" (Phil. i. 23). ἀναλύειν is "to set sail."

[7] iv. 1—8. "There is nothing better," says Chrysostom, "than this strife. There is no end to this crown. It is not a crown of price, nor is it assigned by any earthly arbiter, nor are men spectators of its bestowal; the theatre is filled with angel-witnesses." It is useless to argue with those who see a spirit of boasting here which contradicts 1 Cor. iv. 3; Phil. iii. 12; 1 Tim. i. 16. "Distingue tempora et concordabit Scriptura." The same man may, at different moments, in different moods, and from different stand-points, say, "I am the chief of sinners," and "I have striven the good strife."

once. "Do your best to come to me quickly." Demas, Crescens, Titus, are all absent from him; Erastus did not come with him farther than Corinth; Trophimus was taken ill at Miletus; Luke only is left. Mark is useful to him for service—perhaps because he knew Latin—and therefore Timothy is to take him up somewhere on the way, and bring him.[1] Tychicus is already on the way to Ephesus,[2] so that he can take Timothy's place when he arrives. Timothy is to be on his guard against the pronounced hostility of Alexander the coppersmith.[3] Then follows the touching allusion to his first trial and deliverance, on which we have already dwelt. Greetings are sent to Prisca, Aquila, and the house of Onesiphorus. Once more, "Do your best to come before winter;"—if he comes after that time he may be too late. "Eubulus greets thee, and Pudens, and Linus, and Claudia, and all the brethren. The Lord Jesus Christ be with thy spirit. Grace be with you."[4]

I have purposely omitted the one simple, touching message, introduced so incidentally, and with such inimitable naturalness. "When you come, bring with you the cloke that I left at Troas, at Carpus' house, and the books, especially the parchments."[5] The verse has been criticised as trivial, as

[1] Mark had been attached of late to the ministry of Peter. Perhaps—but all is here uncertain—St. Peter may have been already martyred. It is, at any rate, deeply interesting to observe how completely St. Mark had regained that high estimation in the mind of the Apostle which he had weakened by his early defection (Acts xv. 38).

[2] ἀπέστειλα. It is made a difficulty that St. Paul should mention this to Timothy, who is supposed to have been at Ephesus. But even if ἀπέστειλα cannot be an epistolary aorist, and so equivalent to "I am sending," Paul could not be sure that Timothy might not be visiting some of the neighbouring churches; and Tychicus may have gone by some longer route. Even apart from this, nothing is more common in letters than the mention of facts which must be perfectly well known to the person addressed; and, in any case, since Timothy could hardly leave without resigning his charge for a time into the hands of Tychicus, he might be glad of a personal assurance from Paul that he had sent him.

[3] The meaning of πολλά μοι κακὰ ἐνεδείξατο is not certain, but is probably nothing more than "exhibited very mischievous conduct towards me." The following words, "The Lord shall reward him (ἀποδώσει, ℵ, A, C, D, E, F, G), according to his works," have been rebuked as a malediction. But the μὴ αὐτοῖς λογισθείη of verse 16 is sufficient to show that this was not the mood of Paul; and it is no malediction to say of an enemy, "I must leave God to deal with him," since God is infinitely more merciful than man.

[4] iv. 9—22. Linus may be the traditional first Bishop of Rome (Iren. *c. Haer*. iii. 33; Euseb. *H. E.* iii. 4); but I am surprised that any one should accept the ingenious attempt to identify Pudens with the dissolute centurion of Martial's epigrams (iv. 13; xi. 53) and the Pudens who built a temple at Chichester to Neptune and Minerva; and Claudia with the British Claudia Rufina, whom he married, and with the daughter of the British king Cogidubnus or of Caractacus. The grounds of the identification were suggested by Archdeacon Williams in a pamphlet on Pudens and Claudia. No doubt the Pudens of Martial *may* be the Pudens of the Chichester inscription, since he married a British lady; and this Claudia *may* have been a daughter of Cogidubnus, and *may* have been sent to Rome as a hostage, or for education, and *may* have taken the name Rufina, because she *may* have been entrusted to the charge of Pomponia, the wife of Aulus Plautus, who had been a commander in Britain, and in whose family was a branch called Rufi. And it is possible that Pomponia *may* have been secretly a Christian (Tac. *Ann.* xiii. 32), and so this Claudia Rufina *may* have become a Christian too; but even if we grant the possibility of all these hypotheses, still nothing whatever remains to identify the Pudens and Claudia here separated from each other by another name with the Pudens and Claudia of whom we have been speaking. Claudia was the commonest of names, and the whole theory is an elaborate rope of sand.

[5] That φελόνης, if that be the true reading, means a cloak, seems to be nearly certain.

unworthy the dignity of inspiration. But men must take their notions of inspiration from facts, and not try to square the facts to their own theories. Even on these grounds the verse has its own value for all who would not obscure divine inspiration, nor obliterate the true meaning and sacredness of Scripture by substituting a dictated infallibility for the free play of human emotions in souls deeply stirred by the Holy Spirit of God. But even on other grounds how little could we spare this verse! What a light does it throw on the last sad days of the persecuted Apostle! The fact that these necessary possessions—perhaps the whole that the Apostle could call his own in this world—had been left at the house of Carpus, may, as we have seen, indicate his sudden arrest, either at Troas or on his way to it. A prisoner who is being hurried from place to place by unsympathising keepers is little able to look after his property. But now the Apostle is settled again, though his home is but a prison, and he feels that it will be his home for life. Winter is coming on, and winter in a Roman prison, as he knows by experience, may be very cold. He wants to get back his rough travelling cloak. It was one of those large sleeveless garments which we should call an "overall" or "dreadnought." Perhaps St. Paul had woven it himself of the black goat's hair of his native province. And, doubtless—for he was a poor man—it was an old companion—wetted many a time in the water-torrents of Asia, whitened with the dust of Roman roads, stained with the brine of shipwreck when Euroaquilo was driving the Adriatic into foam. He may have slept in its warm shelter on the chill Phrygian uplands, under the canopy of stars, or it may have covered his bruised and trembling limbs in the dungeon of Philippi. It is of little value; but now that the old man sits shivering in some gloomy cell under the palace or on the rocky floor of the Tullianum, and the winter nights are coming on, he bethinks him of the old cloak in the house of Carpus, and asks Timothy to bring it with him. "The cloke that I left at Troas with Carpus, bring with thee." "And the books, but especially the parchments."[1] The

It was the opinion of the Greek Fathers, who only mention alternatively the meaning γλωσσόκομον, or book-case. But had this been meant it would have been mentioned *after* the books, not before them. We may assume that the word is a transliteration of the Latin *poenula*, and meant a long thick cloak. The form of the transliteration might surprise us, but it is another incidental mark of genuineness, for it comes from the form which the work took in Syriac, פליון. Even if פליון be *pallium*, we see that in Syriac פ represents π. Modern ingenuity sees in it a sacrificial vestment—a chasuble!

[1] Many will recall the striking and pathetic parallel to this request in the letter written by the martyr William Tyndale, from the damp cells of Vilverde, in the winter before his death, asking, for Jesus' sake, for a warmer cap, and something to patch his leggings, and a woollen shirt, and, *above all, his Hebrew Bible, Grammar, and Dictionary*: "Quamobrem tuam dominationem rogatum habeo, idque per Dominum Jesum, ut si mihi per hiemen hic manendum sit, solicites apud dominum commissarium, si forte dignari velit, de rebus meis quas habet mittere calidiorem birethum. Frigus enim patior in capite nimium . . . calidiorem quoque tunicam, nam haec, quam habeo, admodum tenuis est. Item pannum ad caligas deficientias. *Duplois* (*sic*) *detrita est*, camiseae detritae sunt etiam. Camiseam laneam habet si mittere velit . . . Maxime autem omnium tuam clementiam rogo atque obsecro ut ex animo agere velit apud dominum commissarium quatenus dignari mihi velit *Bibl. Hebraicam, Grammaticam Hebraicam,*

biblia—the papyrus books—few we may be sure, but old friends. Perhaps he had bought them when he was a student in the school of Gamaliel at Jerusalem; or they may have been given him by his wealthier converts.[1] The papyrus books, then, let Timothy bring, but especially the parchments—the vellum rolls. What were those? Perhaps among them was the *diploma* of his Roman franchise; or were they precious rolls of Isaiah and the Psalms, and the lesser Prophets, which father or mother had given him as a life-long treasure in the far-off happy days when, little dreaming of all that would befall him, he played, a happy boy, in the dear old Tarsian home? Dreary and long are the days—the evenings longer and drearier still—in that Roman dungeon; and it will be a deep joy to read once more how David and Isaiah, in *their* deep troubles, learnt, as *he* had learnt, to suffer and be strong. A simple message, then, about an old cloak and some books, but very touching. They may add a little comfort, a little relief, to the long-drawn tedium of these last dreary days. Perhaps he thinks that he would like to give them, as his parting bequest, to Timothy himself, or to the modest and faithful Luke, that their true hearts may remember him when the sea of life flows smooth once more over the nameless grave. It would be like that sheepskin cloak which centuries afterwards the hermit Anthony bequeathed to the Archbishop Athanasius—a small gift, but all he had. Poor inventory of a saint's possessions! not worth a hundredth part of what a buffoon would get for one jest in Cæsar's palace, or an acrobat for a feat in the amphitheatre; but would he have exchanged them for the jewels of the adventurer Agrippa, or the purple of the unspeakable Nero? No, he is much more than content. His soul is joyful in God. If he has the cloak to keep him warm, and the books and parchments to teach and encourage him, and Mark to help him in various ways, and if, above all, Timothy will come himself, then life will have shed on him its last rays of sunshine; and in lesser things, as well as in all greater, he will wait with thankfulness, even with exultation, the pouring out in libation of those last few drops of his heart's blood, of which the rich full stream has for these long years been flowing forth upon God's altar in willing sacrifice.[2]

But there are no complaints, no murmurs—there is nothing querulous or depressed in these last words of St. Paul. If the Pastoral Epistles, and above all this one, were not genuine, they must have been written by one who not only possessed the most perfect literary skill, but who had also entered with consummate insight into the character and heart of Paul;—of Paul, but not of ordinary men, even of ordinary great men. The characteristic of waning life is disenchantment, a sense of inexorable weariness, a sense of inevitable

et *Vocabularium Hebraicum*, ut eo studio tempus conteram . . . W. Tindalus" (Life, by Demaus, p. 475).

[1] See Ewald, *Gesch.* iv. 626; vi. 391. Paul seems to have been a student all his life, as far as circumstances permitted. Acts xxvi. 24, τὰ πολλά σε γράμματα εἰς μανίαν περιτρέπει.

[2] Cf. Phil. ii. 17. Seneca, when dying, sprinkled the bystanders with his blood, saying, "*Libare* se liquorem illum Jovi Liberatori" (Tac. *Ann.* xv. 64). So, too, Thrasea, "Libemus, inquit, Jovi Liberatori" (*Id.* xvi. 35).

disappointment. We trace it in Elijah and John the Baptist; we trace it in Marcus Aurelius; we trace it in Francis of Assisi; we trace it in Roger Bacon; we trace it in Luther. All is vain! We have lived, humanly speaking, to little or no purpose. "We are not better than our fathers." "Art thou He that should come, or do we look for another?" "I shall die, and people will say, 'We are glad to get rid of this schoolmaster.'" "My order is more than I can manage." "Men are not worth the trouble I have taken for them." "We must take men as we find them, and cannot change their nature." To some such effect have all these great men, and many others, spoken. They have been utterly disillusioned; they have been inclined rather to check the zeal, to curb the enthusiasm, to darken with the shadows of experience the radiant hopes of their younger followers. If in any man such a sense of disappointment—such a conviction that life is too hard for us, and that we cannot shake off the crushing weight of its destinies—could have ever been excusable, it would have been so in St. Paul. What visible success had he achieved?—the founding of a few Churches of which the majority were already cold to him; in which he saw his efforts being slowly undermined by heretical teachers; which were being subjected to the fiery ordeal of terrible persecutions. To the faith of Christ he saw that the world was utterly hostile. It was arraying against the Cross all its intellect and all its power. The Christ returned not; and what could His doves do among serpents, His sheep among wolves? The very name "Christian" had now come to be regarded as synonymous with criminal; and Jew and Pagan—like "water with fire in ruin reconciled," amid some great storm—were united in common hostility to the truths he preached. And what had he personally gained? Wealth?—He is absolutely dependent on the chance gifts of others. Power?—At his worst need there had not been one friend to stand by his side. Love?—He had learnt by bitter experience how few there were who were not ashamed even to own him in his misery. And now after all—after all that he had suffered, after all that he had done—what was his condition? He was a lonely prisoner, awaiting a malefactor's end. What was the sum-total of earthly goods that the long disease, and the long labour of his life, had brought him in? An old cloak and some books. And yet in what spirit does he write to Timothy? Does he complain of his hardships? Does he regret his life? Does he damp the courage of his younger friend by telling him that almost every earthly hope is doomed to failure, and that to struggle against human wickedness is a fruitless fight? Not so. His last letter is far more of a *pæan* than a *miserere*. For himself the battle is over, the race run, the treasure safely guarded. The day's work in the Master's vineyard is well-nigh over now. When it is quite finished, when he has entered the Master's presence, then and there—not here or now—shall he receive the crown of righteousness and the unspeakable reward. And so his letter to Timothy is all joy and encouragement, even in the midst of natural sadness. It is the young man's heart, not the old man's, that has failed. It is Timotheus, not Paul, who is in danger of yielding to languor and timidity, and forgetting that the Spirit which God gave was one not of fear, but of power, and of love, and of a sound mind. "Bear, then, afflictions with me. Be strong in the grace of Jesus Christ. Fan up the flame in those whitening embers of zeal and courage. Be a good soldier, a true athlete, a diligent toiler. Do you think of my chains and of my hardships? They are nothing, not worth a word or a thought. Be brave. Be not ashamed. We are weak, and may be defeated; but nevertheless God's foundation-stone stands sure with the double legend upon it—one of comfort, one of exhortation. Be thou strong and faithful, my son Timothy, even unto death." So does he hand to the dear but timid racer the torch of truth which in his own grasp, through the long torch-race of his life, no cowardice had hidden, no carelessness had dimmed, no storm had quenched. "Glorious Apostle! would that every leader's voice could burst, as he falls, into such a trumpet-sound, thrilling the young hearts that pant in the good fight, and must never despair of final victory."[1] Yes, even so:

"Hopes have precarious life;
They are oft blighted, withered, snapped sheer off
In vigorous youth, and turned to rottenness;
But faithfulness can feed on suffering,
And knows no disappointment."[2]

CHAPTER LVII.

THE END.

"Bonum agonem subituri estis, in quo agonothetes Deus vivus est, xystarchos Spiritus Sanctus, corona aeternitatis, bravium angelicae substantiae, politia in coelis, gloria in saecula saeculorum."—TERT. *ad Mart.* 3.

"Qui desiderat dissolvi et esse cum Christo, patienter vivit et delectabiliter moritur."—AUG.

"Lieblich wie der Iris Farbenfeuer
Auf der Donnerwolke duft'gem Thau
Schimmert durch der Wehmuth düstern Schleier
Hier der Ruhe heitres Blau."—SCHILLER.

DID Paul ever get that cloak, and the papyri and the vellum rolls? Did Timothy ever reach him?[3] None can tell us. With the last verse of the Second Epistle to Timothy we have heard Paul's last word. In some Roman basilica, perhaps before Helius, the Emperor's freedman, in the presence of some dense, curious, hostile crowd of Jews and Pagans, he must have been heard once more, in his second defence, or on the second count of the indictment against him; and on this occasion the majority of the assessors must have dropped the tablet C—the tablet of condemnation—into the voting urn, and the presiding judge must have pronounced sentence of decapitation on

[1] Martineau, *Hours of Thought*, p. 89. [2] "Spanish Gypsy."

[3] That he did is a reasonable conjecture, and it not improbably led to that imprisonment the liberation from which is mentioned in the Epistle to the Hebrews (xiii. 23)

one who, though condemned of holding a dangerous and illegal superstition, was still a Roman citizen. Was he alone at his second trial as at his first? Did the Gentiles again hear of Jesus and the Resurrection? Did he to them, as to the Athenians, prove that the God whose Gospel he had been commissioned to proclaim was the same God after whom their fathers had ignorantly groped, if haply they might find him, in the permitted ages of ignorance, before yet, in the dispensation of the times, the shadow on the dial-plate of eternity had marked that the appointed hour had come? All such questions are asked in vain. Of this alone we may feel convinced—that he heard the sentence pronounced upon him with a feeling akin to joy—

> "For sure, no gladlier does the stranded wreck
> See, through the grey skirts of a lifting squall,
> The boat that bears the hope of life approach
> To save the life despaired of, than he saw
> Death dawning on him, and the end of all."

But neither respecting his bearing nor his fate do we possess any particulars. If any timid, disheartened, secret Christians stood listening in the crowded court—if through the ruined areas which marked the sites of what had once been shops and palaces before the conflagration had swept like a raging storm through the narrow ill-built streets—if from the poorest purlieus of the Trastevere or the gloomy haunts of the catacomb any converted slave or struggling Asiatic who believed in Jesus had ventured among the throng, no one has left a record, no one even told the story to his fellows so clearly as to leave behind him a floating tradition. We know nothing more. The last word has been spoken. The curtain has fallen on one of the noblest of human lives.

They who will may follow him in imagination to the possible scene of his martyrdom, but every detail must be borrowed from imagination alone. It may be that the legendary is also the real scene of his death. If so, accompanied by the centurion and the soldiers who were to see him executed, he left Rome by the gate now called by his name. Near that gate, close beside the English cemetery, stands the pyramid of C. Cestius, and under its shadow lie buried the mortal remains of Keats and Shelley, and of many who have left behind them beloved or famous names. Yet even amid those touching memorials the traveller will turn with deeper interest to the old pyramid, because it was one of the last objects on which rested the eyes of Paul. For nearly three miles the sad procession walked; and doubtless the dregs of the populace, who always delight in a scene of horror, gathered round them. About three miles from Rome, not far from the Ostian road, is a green and level spot, with low hills around it, known anciently as *Aquae Salviae*, and now as *Tre Fontane*. There the word of command to halt was given; the prisoner knelt down; the sword flashed, and the life of the greatest of the Apostles was shorn away.[1]

[1] I have not thought it desirable to trouble the reader with Mediæval legends of St. Paul's death, which may be seen, by those who list, in Fabricius, *Cod.* Apocr. iii. 632; Ordericus Vitalis, ii. 3.

"Dulce sonat æthere vox
Hiems transiit, occidit nox,
Imber abiit moestaque crux,
Lucet io perpetua lux."—BALDE.

Earthly favour could hardly have seemed more absolute. No blaze of glory shone on his last hours. No multitudes of admiring and almost adoring brethren surrounded his last days with the halo of martyrdom. Near the spot where he was martyred it is probable that they laid him in some nameless grave—in some spot remembered only by the one or two who knew and loved him. How little did they know, how little did even he understand, that the apparent earthly failure would in reality be the most infinite success! Who that watched that obscure and miserable end could have dreamed that Rome itself would not only adopt the Gospel of that poor outcast, but even derive from his martyrdom, and that of his fellow Apostle, her chief sanctity and glory in the eyes of a Christian world; that over his supposed remains should rise a church more splendid than any ancient basilica; and that over a greater city than Rome the golden cross should shine on the dome of a mighty cathedral dedicated to his name?

How little did men recognise his greatness! Here was one to whom no single man that has ever lived, before or since, can furnish a perfect parallel. If we look at him only as a writer, how immensely does he surpass, in his most casual Epistles, the greatest authors, whether Pagan or Christian, of his own and succeeding epochs. The younger Pliny was famous as a letter-writer, yet the younger Pliny never produced any letter so exquisite as that to Philemon. Seneca, as a moralist, stood almost unrivalled, yet not only is clay largely mixed with his gold, but even his finest moral aphorisms are inferior in breadth and intensity to the most casual of St. Paul's. Epictetus and Marcus Aurelius furnish us with the purest and noblest specimens of Stoic loftiness of thought, yet St. Paul's chapter on charity is worth more than all they ever wrote. If we look at the Christian world, the very greatest worker in each realm of Christian service does but present an inferior aspect of one phase only of Paul's many-sided pre-eminence. As a theologian, as one who formulated the doctrines of Christianity, we may compare him with St. Augustine or St. Thomas of Aquinum; yet how should we be shocked to find in him the fanciful rhetoric and dogmatic bitterness of the one, or the scholastic aridity of the other! If we look at him as a moral reformer, we may compare him with Savonarola; but in his practical control of even the most thrilling spiritual impulses—in making the spirit of the prophet subject to the prophet—how grand an exemplar might he not have furnished to the impassioned Florentine! If we consider him as a preacher we may compare him with St. Bernard; yet St. Paul would have been incapable of the unnatural ascetism and heresy-hunting hardness of the great Abbot of Clairvaux. As a reformer who altered the entire course of human history, Luther alone resembles him; yet how incomparably is the Apostle superior to Luther in insight, in courtesy, in humility, in dignity, in self-control! As a missionary we might compare him to Xavier, as a practical organiser to St. Gregory, as a fervent lover of souls to Whitefield, and to many other saints of God in many other of his endowments; but no saint of God has ever attained the same heights in so many capacities, or received the gifts of the Spirit in so rich an outpouring, or borne in his mortal body such evident brand-marks of the Lord. In his lifetime he was no whit behind the very chiefest of the Apostles, and he towers above the very greatest of all the saints who have since striven to follow the example of his devotion to his Lord.

"God buries his workmen, but carries on their work." It is not for any earthly rewards that God's heroes have sought—not even for the reward of hoping in the posthumous success of the cause to which they have sacrificed their lives. All questions of success or failure they have been content to leave in the hands of God. Their one desire has been to be utterly true to the best that they have known; their prayers have all been simplified to this alone—"Teach me to do the thing that pleaseth Thee, for Thou art my God; let Thy loving Spirit lead me into the land of righteousness." That God has seemed to be careless of their individual happiness they would be the last to complain; though He slay them, yet do they trust in Him. Failure was to St. Paul a word unknown. He knew that to fail—or seem to fail—in the cause of God, was to succeed beyond the dreams of earthly ambition.

His faith had never wavered amid life's severest trials, nor his hope grown dim amid its most bitter disappointments; and when he passed from the dungeon and the martyrdom to his crown of righteousness, he left the life which he had sown to be quickened by the power of God in the soil of the world's history, where it shall continue to bear fruit until the end of time, amid the ever-deepening gratitude of generations yet unborn. One who had lived with him, and knew his thoughts and hopes, and had himself preached the faith of Christ in days when to be a Christian was to suffer as a Christian, has written of God's heroes in words which St. Paul would have endorsed, and in which he would have delighted, "These all died in faith, not having received the promises, but having seen them afar off, and were persuaded of them, and embraced them, and confessed that they were strangers and pilgrims on the earth. For they that say such things declare plainly that they seek a country; and truly, if they had been mindful of that country whence they came out, they might have had opportunity to have returned. But now they desire a better country, that is, an heavenly; wherefore God is not ashamed to be called their God, for He hath prepared for them a city."

APPENDIX.

EXCURSUS I. (p. 15).

THE STYLE OF ST. PAUL AS ILLUSTRATIVE OF HIS CHARACTER.

THE reader may be interested to see collected a very few of the varying estimates of the style of the great Apostle :—

LONGINUS [Paul as master of the dogmatic style]—

> Κορωνὶς δ' ἔστω λόγου παντὸς καὶ φρονήματος
> Ἑλληνικοῦ Δημοσθένης κ. τ. λ. πρὸς τούτοις Παῦλος ὁ Ταρσεὺς
> ὅντινα καὶ πρῶτόν φημι προϊστάμενον δόγματος ἀναποδείκτου.

ST. CHRYSOSTOM [Paul a champion, and his Epistles a wall of adamant round the Church]—

> ὥσπερ γὰρ τεῖχος ἐξ ἀδάμαντος κατασκευασθὲν οὕτω τὰς
> πανταχοῦ τῆς οἰκουμένης ἐκκλησίας τὰ τούτου τειχίζει γράμματα· καὶ
> καθάπερ τις ἀριστεὺς γενναιότατος ἕστηκε, κ. τ. λ. (quoting 2 Cor. x. 5).
>
> *De Sacerdotio*, 1, iv. 7.

ST. JEROME [Paul's words thunders].—"Paulum proferam quem quotiescunque lego, video mihi *non verba audire sed tonitrua* . . . Videntur quidem verba simplicis et quasi innocentis hominis et rusticani et qui nec facere nec declinare noverit insidias, *sed quocunque respexeris fulmina sunt.* Haeret in causâ ; capit omne quod tetigerit ; tergum vertit ut superet ; fugam simulat ut occidat" (*Ep. ad Pammach.* 68, 13).

DANTE—

> "Vidi due vecchi in abito dispari
> Ma pari in atto, ognuno onesto e sodo.
> L' un[1] si monstrava alcun de famigliari
> Di quel sommo Ippocrate, che natura
> Agli animali fe' ch' ella ha piu cari.
> Monstrava l' altro[2] la contraria cura
> Con una spada lucida ed acuta[3]
> Tal che di qua dal rio mi fe' paura.
>
> *Purgatorio*, xxix. 134.
>
> Andovvi poi lo *Vas d' elezione*[4]
> Per recarne conforto a quella Fede
> Ch' è principio alla via di salvazione.
>
> *Inferno*, ii. 28.

LUTHER.—"Paulus meras flammas loquitur tamque vehementer ardet ut incipiat etiam quasi Angelis maledicere" (*in Gal.* i.).

"In S. Paulo und Johanne ist eine sonderliche fürtreffliche Gewissheit und *Plerophoria ;* sie reden davon als sey es schon allbereit vor Augen" (*Tischreden*, iv. 399 ; ed. Forstemann).

Bishop HERBERT DE LOSINGA.—"Certe, fratres, verba Pauli, non verba hominis, sed aetheris tonitrua esse videntur" (*Life and Sermons*, ii. 309).

ERASMUS [Paul's style like a thunderstorm].—"Non est cujusvis hominis Paulinum pectus effingere ; tonat, fulgurat, meras flammas loquitur Paulus" (*ad Col.* iv. 16).

[1] St. Luke, "the beloved *physician.*" [2] St. Paul. [3] The Epistles.
[4] σκεῦος ἐκλογῆς (Acts ix. 15). For other allusions see *Parad.* xviii. 131, xxi. 119.

And again [Paul's rhetorical skill like the course of a stream]—"Sudatur ab eruditissimis viris in explicandis poetarum ac rhetorum consiliis, at in hoc rhetore longe plus sudoris est ut deprehendas quid agat, quo tendat, quid velit; adeo stropharum plenus est undique, absit invidia verbis. Tanta vafrities est, non credas eundem hominem loqui. Nunc ut turbidus quidam fons sensim ebullit, mox torrentis in morem ingenti fragore devolvitur, multa obiter secum rapiens, nunc placide leniterque fluit, nunc late velut in lacum diffusus exspatiatur. Rursum alicubi se condit ac diverso loco subitus emicat; cum visum est miris maeandris nunc has nunc illas lambit ripas, aliquoties procul digressus, reciprocato flexu in sese redit" (Id. *Paraph.* Dedicat.).

CASAUBON.—"Ille solus ex omnibus scriptoribus non mihi videtur digitis, calamo, et atramento scripsisse, verum ipso corde, ipso affectu, et denudatis visceribus" (*Adversaria, ap.* Wolf., p. 135).

On the other hand, CALVIN, after alluding to his anakolutha, ellipses, &c., adds—"Quae sunt quidem orationis vitia sed quibus nihil majestati decedit caelestis sapientiae quae nobis per apostolum traditur. Quin potius singulari Dei providentia factum est, ut *sub contemptibili verborum humilitate* altissima haec mysteria nobis traderentur, ut non humanae eloquentiae potentia, sed solâ spiritus efficaciâ niteretur nostra fides."

HEMSTERHUSIUS [Character of St. Paul's flowers of speech].—"Eloquentia ejus non in flosculis verborum et rationis calamistratae pigmentis . . . sed indolis excelsae notis et pondere rerum. . . . In ejus epistolis nullae non exstant oratorum figurae, non illae quidem e rhetorum loculis et myrotheciis depromptae . . . Verum affectus animi coelesti ardore inflammatus haec scriptionis lumina sponte sub manum praevenientia pergignebat."[1]

REUSS.—"Ordinairement il débute par des phrases on ne peut plus embarrassées. . . . Mais dès qu'il a trouvé la bonne veine, combien son style n'est-il pas le fidèle miroir de son individualité ! Il n'est ni correct, ni classique ; il lui manque la cadence sonore. Des antithèses paradoxales, des gradations pleines d'effet, des questions pressantes, des exclamations passionnées, des ironies qui terrassent l'opposition, une vivacité, enfin, qui ne permet aucun repos au lecteur, tout cela alterne avec des épanchements naïfs et touchants, qui achèvent de gagner le cœur" (*Théol. Chrét.* ii. 11).

R. H. HUTTON.—"Who that has studied St. Paul at all has not noticed the bold soaring dialectic with which he rises from the forms of our finite and earthly thought to the infinite and the spiritual life embodied in them? What ease and swiftness and power of wing in this indignant upward flight from the petty conflicts of the Corinthian Church; the upward flight which does not cease till the poor subjects of contention, though he himself was one of them, seem lost like grains of sand beneath the bending sky! . . . The all but reckless prodigality of nature which made St. Paul now and then use a stratagem, and now and then launch a thunderbolt, in the fervour of his preaching, is the spring of all his finest touches, as when he wishes himself accursed from Christ if it could save his Jewish brethren" (*Essays*, 321—330).

The AUTHOR of "Saul of Tarsus."—"If he staggers under the greatness of his subject, if he is distracted by the infinity of the interests which he treats, if every word which rises to his lips suggests a host of profound and large associations, if the care of all the Churches, gives all the facts a varied but a real significance. . . . Human speech must be blamed for its poverty; human experience, which has developed speech, for its narrowness. His life was ever in his hand, his heart was on his lips. The heart was often too great for the speech" (p. 229).

MARTINEAU.—"What can be more free and buoyant, with all their variety, than his writings? Brilliant, broken, impetuous as the mountain torrent freshly filled, never smooth and calm but on the eve of some bold leap, never vehement but to fill some receptacle of clearest peace, they present everywhere the image of a vigorous joy.

[1] See next Excursus.

Beneath the forms of their theosophic reasonings, and their hints of deep philosophy, there may be heard a secret lyric strain of glorious praise, bursting at times into open utterance, and asking others to join the chorus. . . . His life was a battle from which in intervals of the good fight, his words arose as the song of victory" (*Hours of Th.ught*, p. 156).

PROF. JOWETT speaks of him as teaching his great doctrines "in broken words and hesitating form of speech, with no beauty or comeliness of style."

BAUR, after pointing out how the style is filled to overflowing with the forms and elements of thought, and that thoughts not only follow hard on thoughts, but that those thoughts succeed each other as determinations and *momenta* of some one conception that is greater than all of them, so that the thought unfolds itself, as it were, out of its own depths, and determines itself by taking up its own *momenta*, adds:—"Hence the peculiar stamp of the Apostle's language: it is distinguished on the one hand for precision and compression; on the other hand it is marked by a harshness and roughness which suggests that the thought is far too weighty for the language, and can scarcely find fit form for the superabundant matter it would fairly express" (*Paul.* ii. 281).

HAUSRATH.—"Es ist schwer diese Individualität zu charakterisiren in der sich christliche Liebesfülle, rabbinischer Scharfsinn, und antike Willenskraft so wunderbar mischen. Wie wogt strömt, drängt alles in seinen Briefen. Welch ein Wechsel glühender Ergüsse und spitzer Beweisführungen! Hier überwindet er das Heidenthum mit der Liebesfülle Jesu. Dort knebelt er das Judenthum, mit dessen eigenen Gürtel rabbinischer Schriftbeweise. Am wenigsten hat die Phantasie Antheil an seiner innern Welt. Die Sprache ist oft hart und herb weil nur die Gedanke sie geboren hat. Die Bilder die er braucht sind meistens farblos. . . . Das ist die Schranke seines Geisteslebens. Darin blieb er stets ein Rabbi" (*Der Apostel Paulus*, 502).

RENAN [Paul's style like a conversation].—"Le style épistolaire de Paul est le plus personnel qu'il y ait jamais eu; la langue y est, si j'ose le dire, broyée; pas une phrase suivie. Il est impossible de violer plus audacieusement, je ne dis pas le génie de la langue grecque, mais la logique du langage humain; on dirait une rapide conversation sténographiée et reproduite sans corrections. . . . Un mot l'obsède. . . . Ce n'est pas de la stérilité; c'est de la contention de l'esprit et une complète insouciance de la correction du style" (*St. Paul*, p. 232).

The less favourable of the above estimates shelter themselves in part under the assertion that St. Paul recognised the popular and vulgar character of his own style. But such passages as 2 Cor. xi. 6 do not bear out these remarks. His language was not indeed of a class which would have gained applause from pedantic purists and Atticising professors; it bears about the same relation to the Greek of Plato as the Latin of Milton does to that of Cicero. But this fact constitutes its very life. It is a style far too vivid, far too swayed and penetrated by personal emotion, to have admitted of being polished into conformity with the artificial standards and accuracies of the schools. It more closely resembles the style of Thucydides than that of any other great writer of antiquity.[1] That many defects in it can be pointed out is certain; but then in one important point of view these defects are better than any beauties, because they are due to Paul's individuality. In whole sections of his Epistles his very want of style is his style. His style, like that of every great man, has the defects of its qualities. "Le style," said Buffon, not (as he is usually quoted) *c'est l'homme*, but "c'est de l'homme."[2]

[1] See some good remarks of Baur:—"Such passages as 1 Cor. iv. 12, 13; vii. 29—31; 2 Cor. vi. 9, 10, have the true ring of Thucydides, not only in expression, but in the style of the thought. The genuine dialectic spirit appears in both, *in the love of antithesis and contrast, rising not unfrequently to paradox*. . . . With both these men the ties of national particularism give way before the generalising tendency of their thought, and cosmopolitanism takes the place of nationalism" (*Paul.* ii. 281). He refers to Bauer's *Philologia Thucydideo-Paulina*, 1773, which I have not seen.

[2] D'Alembert, *Œuvres*, vi. 13. The "de" in Buffon's phrase occurs in later editions.

He has, as every great writer has, "le style de sa pensée:" he has the style of genius, if he has not the genius of style.[1]

After quoting such remarkable and varied testimonies, it is needless for me to write an essay on the Apostle's style. That he could when he chose wield a style of remarkable finish and eloquence without diminishing his natural intensity, is proved by the incessant assonances and balances of clauses and expressions (parechesis, parisosis, paromoiosis) in such passages as 2 Cor. vi. 3—11. And yet such is his noble carelessness of outward graces of style, and his complete subordination of mere elegance of expression to the purpose of expressing his exact thought, that he never shrinks, even in his grandest outbursts of rhythmic eloquence, from the use of a word, however colloquial, which expresses his exact shade of meaning.[2]

All that has been written of the peculiarities of St. Paul's style may, I think, be summed up in two words—Intense Individuality. His style is himself. His natural temperament, and the circumstances under which that temperament found its daily sphere of action; his training, both Judaic and Hellenistic; his conversion and sanctification, permeating his whole life and thoughts—these united make up the Paul we know. And each of these has exercised a marked influence on his style.

1. The absorption in the one thought before him, which makes him state without any qualification truths which, taken in the whole extent of his words, seem mutually irreconcilable; the dramatic, rapid, overwhelming series of questions, which show that in his controversial passages he is always mentally face to face with an objection;[3] the *centrifugal* force of mental activity, which drives him into incessant digressions and goings off at a word, due to his vivid power of realisation; the *centripetal* force of imagination, which keeps all these digressions under the control of one dominant thought;[4] the grand confusions of metaphor;[5] the vehemence which makes him love the most emphatic compounds;[6] the irony[7] and sarcasm;[8] the chivalrously delicate courtesy;[9] the overflowing sympathy with the Jew, the Pagan, the barbarian—with saint and sinner, king and slave, man and woman, young and old;[10] the passion, which now makes his voice ring with indignation[11] and now break with sobs;[12] the accumulation and variation of words, from a desire to set forth the truths which he is proclaiming in every possible light;[13] the emotional emphasis and personal references of his style;[14] the depressed humility passing into boundless exultation;[15]—all these are due to his *natural temperament*, and the atmosphere of controversy and opposition on the one hand, and deep affection on the other, in which he worked.

2. The rhetorical figures, play of words, assonances, oxymora, antitheses, of his style, which are fully examined in the next Excursus; the constant widening of his horizon;[16] the traceable influence of cities, and even of personal companions, upon his vocabulary;[17] the references to Hellenic life;[18] the method of quoting Scripture; the Rabbinic style of exegesis, which have been already examined[19]—these are due to his training at Tarsus and Jerusalem, his life at Corinth, Ephesus, and Rome.

3. The daring faith which never dreads a difficulty;[20] the unsolved antinomies, which, though unsolved, do not trouble him;[21] "the bold soaring dialectics with which he rises

[1] Grimm, *Corresp.*, 1788.

[2] *E.g.*, φυσιόω and περπερεύεται in 1 Cor. xiii. 3, 4; κατενάρκησα, 2 Cor. xi. 8; ἀποκόψονται, Gal. v. 12.

[3] Rom. x.; 2 Cor. vi., xi., and *passim*.

[4] 2 Cor. ii. 14—16; xii. 1—3, 12—16; Eph. iv. 8—11; v. 12—15; and Paley, *Hor. Paulinae*, vi. 3.

[5] 2 Cor. iii. 1; Col. ii. 6.

[6] Especially compounds in ὑπέρ. *Supra*, p. 344.

[7] 1 Cor. iv. 8; 2 Cor. xi. 16—20, and *passim*.

[8] Phil. iii. 2; Gal. iv. 17; v. 12, and *passim*.

[9] 1 Cor. i.—iii.; Philem. and Phil. *passim*; Acts xxvi. 29, &c.

[10] Rom. i., iv., and all the Epistles *passim*.

[11] Galatians, Corinthians, Phil., 2 Tim., *passim*.

[12] All the Epistles *passim*.

[13] All the Epistles *passim*.

[14] All the Epistles *passim*.

[15] 2 Cor. ii. 14; Rom. vii. 25, &c.

[16] "Eo (ordine Epistolarum chronologico) constituto . . . incrementum Apostoli spirituale cognoscitur" (Bengel, *ad Rom.* i. 1).

[17] *V. supra*, pp. 273, 691.

[18] See Excursus III.

[19] See Excursus IV.

[20] See Ep. to Romans, *passim*.

[21] See Excursus XXI., "The Antinomies of St. Paul."

from the forms of one finite and earthly thought to the infinite and spiritual life embodied in them;" the "language of ecstasy," which was to him, as he meant it to be to his converts, the language of the work-day world; that "transcendental-absurd," as it seems to the world, which was the very life both of his conscience and intellect, and made him what he was; the way in which, as with one powerful sweep of the wing, he passes from the pettiest earthly contentions to the spiritual and the infinite; the "shrinking infirmity and self-contempt, hidden in a sort of aureole of revelation, abundant beyond measure"[1]—this was due to the fact that his citizenship was in heaven, his life hid with Christ in God.

EXCURSUS II. (p. 15).

Rhetoric of St. Paul.

M. Renan, in describing the Greek of St. Paul as Hellenistic Greek charged with Hebraisms and Syriacisms which would be scarcely intelligible to a cultivated reader of that period, says that if the Apostle had ever received even elementary lessons in grammar or rhetoric at Tarsus, it is inconceivable that he would have written in the *bizarre*, incorrect, and non-Hellenic style of his letters.

Now, I do not think that St. Paul would have made about his own knowledge of Greek the same remarks as Josephus does, who tells us that he had taken great pains to master the learning of the Greeks and the elements of the Greek language. St. Paul had picked up Greek quite naturally in a Greek city, and I think that I have decisively proved that he could not have possessed more than a partial and superficial acquaintance with Greek literature. But I have little doubt that he, like Josephus, would have said that he had so long accustomed himself to speak Syriac that he could not pronounce Greek with sufficient exactness, and that the Jews did not encourage the careful endeavour to obtain a polished Greek style, which they looked on as an accomplishment of slaves and freedmen.[2] Yet, after reading the subjoined list of specimens from the *syntaxis ornata* of St. Paul, few, I think, will be able to resist the conviction that he had attended, while at Tarsus, some elementary class of Greek rhetoric. I will here content myself with brief references; if the reader should feel interested in the subject, I have gone further into it in the *Expositor* for 1879.

Figures (σχήματα) are divided by Greek and Latin rhetoricians into Figures of Language (*figurae verborum, elocutionis*, λέξεως), and Figures of Thought (*sententiae*, διανοίας). They drew this distinction between them—that figures of language disappear, for the most part, when the words and their order are changed; whereas figures of thought still survive.[3] The distinction is superficial and unsatisfactory, and it would perhaps be more to the point to divide figures into :—1. Those of *colour*, dependent on the imagination; as metaphor, simile, allegory, personifications, metonyms, catachresis, &c. 2. Those of *form*, ranging over an immense field, from the natural expression of passions, such as irony, aposiopesis, erotesis, &c., down to mere elegancies of verbal ornament, and variations of style (such as zeugma, &c.) or of order (such as chiasmos, hysteron-proteron, &c.). 3. Those of *sound*, dependent on analogies of words, resemblance of sounds, unconscious associations of ideas, &c., such as alliteration, parisosis, paromoiosis, parechesis, paronomasia, oxymoron, plays on names, &c.

1. On figures of *Colour* I have already touched.[4] As specimens of the two other classes in St. Paul's Epistles we may take the following—referring to my *Brief Greek Syntax*, or to other books, for an explanation of the technical terms:—

[1] See 2 Cor. x.—xiii. *passim*, and some excellent remarks in Hutton's *Essays*, i. 325—330.

[2] Jos. *Antt.* xx. 11, § 2.

[3] So Aquila, Rutilius, &c., following Cic. *De Orat.* 3. See Voss, *Instt. Orat.* v. 1; Glass, *Philologia Sacra*, p. 953, &c.

[4] *Supra*, pp. 10—12.

2. Figures of *Form*.

Chiasmus—a crosswise arrangement of words or clauses, as in Rom. ii. 6, 10. (This figure is much more common in the Epistle to the Hebrews.) A good instance is—

1 Cor. iii. 17, εἴ τις τον ναὸν τοῦ Θεοῦ φθείρει, φθερεῖ αὐτὸν ὁ Θεός.

Euphemism.

1 Cor. v. 1, 2, ἔχειν . . . ὁ τὸ ἔργον τοῦτο ποιήσας.

2 Cor. vii. 11, ἐν τῷ πράγματι.

1 Thess. iv. 6, *supra*, p. 334.

Litotes.

Rom. i. 28, ποιεῖν τὰ μὴ καθήκοντα.

Eph. v. 4, τὰ οὐκ ἀνήκοντα.

1 Cor. xi. 22, ἐπαινέσω ὑμᾶς ἐν τούτῳ; οὐκ ἐπαινῶ.

Philem. 18, εἰ δέ τι ἠδίκησέ σε ἢ ὀφείλει.

Philem. 11, τόν ποτέ σοι ἄχρηστον.

Meiosis.[1] Rom. iii. 9, οὐ πάντως (comp. 1 Cor. xvi. 12).

1 Cor. i. 29, ὅπως μὴ καυχήσηται πᾶσα σάρξ.

Rom. iii. 20, ἐξ ἔργων νόμου οὐ δικαιωθήσεται πᾶσα σάρξ.

Antithesis, Parisosis, Paromoiosis,[2] *Paradox, Alliteration, Erotesis, Epexergasia*—all exhibited in such passages of deep emotion as 2 Cor. vi. 3—16; xi. 22—28; 1 Cor. iv. 8—11.

Epanaphora.

Phil. iv. 8, ὅσα . . . ὅσα . . . κ. τ. λ. εἴ τις, κ. τ. λ.

Phil. ii. 1, εἴ τις . . . εἴ τι . . . κ. τ. λ.

2 Cor. vii. 11, ἀλλὰ . . . ἀλλὰ . . . κ. τ. λ.

Aposiopesis.

2 Thess. ii., *vide supra*, p. 346.

Proparaitesis, Protherapeia, Captatio Benevolentiae, &c.

The Thanksgiving at the beginning of every Epistle except the "Galatians."

Rom. ix. 1—5.

Acts xxiv. 10 (before Felix), and xxvi. 2, 3, before Agrippa.

Paraleipsis (*praeterita*).

Philem. 19, ἵνα μὴ λέγω σοι.

1 Thess. iv. 9, οὐ χρείαν ἔχετε ὑμῖν γράφεσθαι (cf. v. 1; 2 Cor. ix. 1).

Intentional *Anakoluthon*.

Gal. ii. 6, ἀπὸ δὲ τῶν δοκούντων εἶναί τι . . .

2 Thess. ii. 3, ὅτι ἐὰν μὴ ἔλθῃ ἡ ἀποστασία πρῶτον . . .

2 Thess. ii. 7, μόνον ὁ κατέχων ἄρτι . . .

(The Anakolutha of mere inadvertence, due to the eager rapidity of thought, are incessant in St. Paul, as in Rom. ii. 17—21; xvi. 25—27, &c., &c.)

Climax.

Rom. v. 3—5.

Rom. viii. 29, 30.

Rom. x. 14, 15, &c.

Zeugma.

1 Cor. iii. 2, γάλα ὑμᾶς ἐπότισα καὶ οὐ βρῶμα.

1 Tim. iv. 3, κωλυόντων γαμεῖν, ἀπέχεσθαι βρωμάτων.

Oxymoron.

2 Cor. vi. 9, θανατούμενοι καὶ ἰδοὺ ζῶμεν (being slain, yet behold we live).

1 Tim. v. 6, ζῶσα τέθνηκεν (living she is dead).

Rom. i. 20, τὰ ἀόρατα αὐτοῦ . . . καθορᾶται (His unseen things are clearly seen).

Rom. xii. 11, τῇ σπουδῇ μὴ ὀκνηροὶ (in *haste* not sluggish).

[1] These usages are, however, idiomatic (Winer, § 26).

[2] See Arist. *Rhet.* iii. 9, 9.

1 Thess. iv. 11, φιλοτιμεῖσθαι ἡσυχάζειν (be *ambitious* to be *quiet*).

1 Thess. i. 6, ἐν θλίψει πολλῇ μετὰ χαρᾶς (joyous affliction).

1 Cor. viii. 10, οἰκοδομηθήσεται (ruinous edification).

Rom. i. 22, φάσκοντες εἶναι σοφοὶ ἐμωράνθησαν.

Eph. vi. 15, Gospel of *peace* part of panoply of *war*.

2 Cor. viii. 2, deep *poverty* abounding to *wealth* of liberality.

2 Cor. xii. 10, "When I am weak, then I am strong."

It will be sufficient to make the merest reference to *Anadiplosis* (Rom. ix. 30; Phil. ii. 8); *Epanodos* (Gal. ii. 16); *Epanorthosis* (Rom. viii. 34; Gal. ii. 20; iii. 4, &c.); *Asyndeton* (1 Cor. xv. 43; 1 Tim. i. 17; 2 Tim. iii, 2—5, 10, 11, &c.); *Antiptosis* (Col. iv. 17; Gal. vi. 1; iv. 11); *Hyperbaton* (2 Thess. ii. 5, &c.); *Alliteration* (1 Cor. ii. 13; 2 Cor. viii. 22; ix. 8, &c.); *Constructio praegnans* (2 Thess. ii. 4, &c.); and many minor figures.

3. Coming to figures of the third division—*Sound*—we find that St. Paul makes most remarkable and frequent use of paronomasia.

E.g. (α) Paronomasia, dependent on the change of one or two letters[1] :—

Rom. i. 29, πορνείᾳ πονηρίᾳ . . . φθόνου, φόνου.

Rom. i. 30, ἀσυνέτους, ἀσυνθέτους.

Rom. xi. 17, τινες τῶν κλάδων ἐξεκλάσθησαν.

Cf. Heb. v. 8, ἔμαθεν ἀφ' ὧν ἔπαθεν.

(β) Paronomasia, dependent on a play of words of similar sound or derivation.[2] This is St. Paul's most frequent rhetorical figure :—

2 Cor. iii. 2, γινωσκομένη καὶ ἀναγινωσκομένη.[3]

Rom. i. 28, οὐκ ἐδοκίμασαν (they *refused*) . . . ἀδόκιμον νοῦν (a *refuse* mind).

Phil. iii. 2, 3, κατατομὴ (*concision*) . . . περιτομὴ (*circumcision*).

Rom. ii. 1, κρίνεις . . . κατακρίνεις.

1 Cor. xi. 29, *seq.*, διάκρισις . . . κρίμα . . . κατάκριμα.

Rom. xii. 3, "Not to be high-*minded* (ὑπερφρονεῖν) above what we ought to be minded (φρονεῖν), but to be *minded* so as to be sober-minded" (σωφρονεῖν). Cf. Thuc. ii. 62, οὐ φρονήματι μόνον ἀλλὰ καὶ καταφρονήματι.

1 Cor. vii. 31, χρώμενοι . . . καταχρώμενοι.

2 Cor. vi. 10; ἔχοντες . . . κατέχοντες.

2 Cor. iv. 8, ἀπορούμενοι . . . ἐξαπορούμενοι.

2 Tim. iii. 4, φιλήδονοι . . . φιλόθεοι.

2 Thess. iii. 11, not *busy* (ἐργαζομένους) but busybodies (περιεργαζομένους).[4]

1 Tim. v. 13, οὐ μόνον δὲ ἀργαὶ, ἀλλὰ καὶ περίεργοι (female toilers in the school of idleness).

Cornelius à Lapide and others have imagined a latent paronomasia in 1 Cor. i. 23, 24. If St. Paul thought in Syriac it might be "To the Jews a *micsol*, and to the Greeks a *mashcal*, but to those that are called—Christ the *secel* of God." But this is probably a mere ingenious fancy.[5]

(γ) A third class of paronomasias consists in plays on names, of which we find three in St. Paul :—

Philem. 11, Ὀνήσιμον . . . ἄχρηστον.[6]

Philem. 20, Ναὶ, ἐγώ σου ὀναίμην.

[1] See Cic. *De Orat.* ii. 63; Auct. *ad Herenn.* iv. 24; Quint. *Instt. Orat.* ix. 3, 66, &c. An instance in our Prayer Book is—"among all the changes and chances of this mortal life."

[2] A curious instance occurs in our E. V. of James i. 6, "He that *wavereth* is like a *wave* of the sea," where it does not occur in the original.

[3] Compare Acts viii. 30, and Basil's remark to the Emperor Julian, ἀνέγνως οὐκ ἔγνως, εἰ γὰρ ἔγνως οὐκ ἂν κατέγνως.

[4] So Domitius Afer, "Non agentes sed satagentes" (Quint. vi. 3, 54).

[5] Glass, *Philolog. Sacra*, p. 959.

[6] *V. supra, ad loc.*, where I have noticed the possible second paronomasia in ἄχρηστον, εὔχρηστον

Phil. iv. 3, Σύζυγε γνήσιε, "yoke-fellow by name and yoke-fellow by nature."[1] St. Jerome imagines another in Gal. i. 6, where he thinks that "ye are being removed" (μετατίθεσθε) is a play on the name Galatæ and the Hebrew *Galal*, "to roll."

Since, then, we find upwards of fifty specimens of upwards of thirty Greek rhetorical figures in St. Paul, and since they are far more abundant in his Epistles than in other parts of the New Testament, and some are found in him alone, may we not conclude that as a boy in Tarsus he had attended some elementary class in Greek rhetoric, perhaps as a part of his education in the grammatical knowledge of the language? Professional rhetoricians abounded in Tarsus, and if Paul's father, seeing the brilliant capacity of his son, meant him for the school of Gamaliel, he may have thought that an elementary initiation into Greek rhetoric might help to pave the way for his future distinction among the Hillelites of Jerusalem; since, as we see from the Talmud, this kind of knowledge opened to some Rabbis a career of ambition. If so, the lessons which the young Saul learnt were not thrown away, though they were turned to very different objects than had been dreamt of by one who intended his boy to be, like himself, a Pharisee of Pharisees and a Hebrew of Hebrews.

EXCURSUS III. (p. 23).

The Classic Quotations and Allusions of St. Paul.

1. Those who maintain the advanced classic culture of St. Paul, rely on the fact that he quotes from and alludes to Greek and Roman writers.

Three quotations are incessantly adduced. One is the hexameter written by the Cretan poet Epimenides in such stern and contemptuous depreciation of the character of his own countrymen—

Κρῆτες ἀεὶ ψεῦσται, κακὰ θηρία, γαστέρες ἀργαί.[2]
("Liars the Cretans aye, ill monsters, gluttonous idlers.")

Another is the half-hexameter in which he reminds his audience, in the speech on the Areopagus, that certain also of their native poets had said—

Τοῦ γὰρ καὶ γένος ἐσμέν.[3]
("For we are also his offspring.")

A third is the moral warning to the Corinthians—

Φθείρουσιν ἤθη χρηστὰ ὁμιλίαι κακαί[4]
("Evil communications corrupt good manners;")

or it may, perhaps, be more correctly rendered, "Evil associations destroy excellent characters."

Now, if we look a little closer at these quotations, we shall see how very little proof they furnish of anything more than the most superficial acquaintance with Greek writers. The first of them is just such a current national characterisation[5] as might pass everywhere from mouth to mouth, and which St. Paul might very well repeat without having read a line of the poem of Epimenides on *Oracles*, or Callimachus's *Hymn to Zeus*, in both of which it occurs.[6] The second is a recognised commonplace of heathen insight, to which many parallels might be quoted, but which is found in Cleanthes,[7] nearly in the form in which St. Paul quotes it. The actual quotation is from one of those tedious

[1] *V. supra, ad loc.* [2] Tit. i. 12. [3] Acts xvii. 28. [4] 1 Cor. xv. 33.

[5] See, as to the Cretans, Leonidas, *Anthol.* iii., p. 369; Polyb. vi. 47; Diod. Sic. xxxi. Fr.; Wetst. *ad loc.*

[6] Callim. *Hymn. in Jov.* 8. Κρῆτες ἀεὶ ψεῦσται, καὶ γὰρ, τάφον ὦ ἄνα σεῖο Κρῆτες ἐτεκτήναντο. See Chrysostom and Jerome *ad* Tit. i. 12. Moreover, the line had originated one of the commonest syllogistic puzzles, called "the Liars." "Epimenides said that the Cretans were liars; but Epimenides was a Cretan; therefore Epimenides was a liar; therefore the Cretans were not liars; therefore Epimenides was not a liar," &c. &c. (Diog. Laert. ii. 108.) It was invented by Eubulides; cf. Cic. *Div.* ii. 4. "mentiens."

[7] Cleanthes, *Hymn. in Jov.* 5.

poems which were most in vogue at this period, the *Phænomena* of Aratus.[1] With the writings of this poet St. Paul may have become acquainted, both because they are entirely harmless—which is more than can be said of almost any other Pagan production which was popular at that time—and because Aratus was a Cilician, and very probably a Tarsian.[2] The third was one of those common sententious pieces of morality which had passed into a proverb, and which in all probability Menander, in his *Thais*, had appropriated from some lost tragedy of Euripides. St. Paul is far more likely to have heard it used in common parlance, or to have seen it inscribed on one of the Hermæ at Tarsus or Athens, than to have read it in Menander, or even—as Socrates[3] and Chrysostom seem to think—in one of the Greek tragedians. It is further remarkable about these quotations, first, that *all three* of them were so current, they are found in at least two poets each; and next, that two of them occur at the very beginning of *Hymns to Zeus*. If any collection of *Hymns to Zeus* was to be found on any bookstall at Athens, it is exactly the kind of book into which St. Paul's human sympathies may have induced him to dip in support of his liberal and enlightened view that God had revealed Himself even to the heathen, to a degree sufficient for their happiness and their salvation, had they chosen to make use of the light they had.[4] A third very remarkable point is that in the quotation from Menander or Euripides, whichever it may have been, the great majority of the best MSS. read χρηστὰ, not χρῆσθ'[5]—a reading which may therefore be regarded as certainly genuine, since no one would have dreamt of altering the correct metre, if it had been given in the original manuscript. Now if such be the case, it seems to indicate that the ear of St. Paul was unfamiliar with—or, which comes to the same thing, was indifferent to—even so common a rhythm as that of the iambic verse. Our conclusion, therefore, is that St. Paul's isolated quotations no more prove a study of Greek literature than the quotation of such a national epigram as

> "Inglese italianato, Diavolo incarnato,"

or of such a line as

> "Lasciate ogni speranza voi ch' entrate,"

would necessarily prove that an English writer was a proficient in the literature of Italy, or had read the poems of Dante. St. Paul was a man of remarkable receptivity, and, as we have seen, an habitual quoter. Except in Epistles intended for readers to whom Old Testament quotations would have been unintelligible, he can hardly write five sentences in succession without a Biblical reference. The utter absence of any similar use of even the noblest of the classic writers, is a proof either that he had intentionally neglected them, or that, at any rate, they had left little or no mark on an intellect so sensitive to every cognate influence. For that it was not only the Scriptures of the Jewish canon which thus clung to his retentive memory, is apparent from the free use which he makes of the Book of Wisdom, and perhaps of other books of the Jewish Apocrypha.[6] It is also

[1] Aratus flourished about B.C. 270. His poems, considering that they only bear a sort of dull resemblance to Thomson's *Seasons*, acquired astonishing popularity. They were translated, among others, by Cicero, and by Cæsar Germanicus.

[2] Buhle, *Aratus*, ii. 429. [3] *Hist. Ecc.* iii. 16. [4] Acts xiv. 17; xvii. 27; Rom. i. 20.

[5] ℵ, A, B, D, E, F, G, &c., ἰαμβείῳ τραγικῷ. Clem. Alex. *Strom.* i. 14, 59; Meineke, *Fr. Com.*, p. 75.

[6] See Hausrath, p. 23. He compares 1 Cor. vi. 2 with Wisd. iii. 8, the image of the Christian armour with Wisd. v. 17, the metaphor of the potter making one vessel to honour and another to dishonour with Wisd. xv. 7. The memorable thrice-repeated saying, "Neither circumcision is anything, nor uncircumcision" (Gal. v. 6; vi. 15; 1 Cor. vii. 19), is by Photius, Syncellus, and others said to be a quotation from "Revelation of Moses." Dr. Lightfoot (on Gal. vi. 17) shows that there is some reason to doubt this, and says that "a sentiment which is the very foundation of St. Paul's teaching was most unlikely to have been expressed in any earlier Jewish writing; and if it really occurred in the apocryphal work in question, this work must have been either written or interpolated after St. Paul's time (See Lücke, *Offenb. d. Johan.* i., p. 232)." The same must be said of the Book of Wisdom on the ingenious hypothesis that it was written by Apollos (Plumptre, *Expositor*, i. 422, *sq.*).

traceable in the extent to which he is constantly haunted by a word,[1] and in the new and often rare expressions which are found in every one of the Epistles,[2] and which show us a mind keenly susceptible to impressions derived from the circumstances around him, and from the intercourse of those among whom he was habitually thrown.

2. But though the Greek culture of Tarsus had little or no influence on the current of the Apostle's thoughts, it would be a mistake to suppose that it produced no influence at all on his life or on his style. Besides the direct quotations, there is more than one isolated passage which may be the distant echo of classical reminiscences. Such, for instance, is the apologue of the self-asserting members in 1 Cor. xii., which reminds us at once of the ingenious fable of Menenius Agrippa;[3] and the fearful metaphor of Rom. vii. 24, which has less probably been held to refer to a true story of the family of Regulus.[4] And it is far from improbable that it was in some "class of rhetoric" at Tarsus that the Apostle acquired the germs, at any rate, of that argumentative habit of mind, that gift of ready extempore utterance, and that fondness for chiasmus, paronomasia, paraleipsis, oxymoron, litotes, and other rhetorical figures, which characterise his style.[5] It was there, too, that he may have learnt that ready versatility, that social courtesy, that large comprehensiveness, that wide experience and capacity for dealing with varied interests and intricate matters of business, which made him, in the high and good sense of the word, a true gentleman, a Christian man of the world. He was, in heart and feeling, an ideal specimen of what the Greeks call the *καλὸς κἀγαθός*—"fair and good"—and his intercourse with polished Greeks may have tended to brighten that spirit of "entirely genuine Attic urbanity"[6]—a spirit more flexible and more charming than natural Semitic dignity—which breathes in every line of the Epistle to Philemon.

3. It is a remarkable proof of this natural liberality that, in spite of the burning hatred of idolatry which we have already noticed, he is yet capable of looking with sympathy, and even admiration, on some of those nobler and more innocent aspects of heathen life which his countrymen indiscriminately condemned.[7] The hallowing of heathen symbols, the use of metaphors derived from heathen life for the illustration of Christian truths and Christian duties, is a very remarkable feature of the style of St. Paul. There were few of the crimes of Herod which the strict Pharisees had regarded with more undisguised horror and hatred than his construction of a theatre at Cæsarea; yet St. Paul quite freely, and without misgiving, adopting a metaphor which would have caused a shudder to any Palestinian Pharisee, compares the transient fashion of the world to the passing scene of a theatrical display, and in other places turns the whole Universe into a theatre, on the stage of which were displayed the sufferings of the Apostles as a spectacle to angels and to men.[8] We recognise, too, the more liberal son of the Disper-

[1] *e.g.* *γινομαι* in 1 Thess. i.; *τὰ ἐπουράνια* in Eph. i.; *χαίρω* and *χάρις* in Phil.; *μὴ γένοιτο* in Rom.; *φυσιόω* in 1 Cor. iv.; *καυχᾶσθαι* in 2 Cor. xi.; *παρακαλέω* in 2 Cor. i.; *λύπη* in 2 Cor. ii., &c.

[2] As, for instance, *καταναρκάω* and *ἡμέρα* in 1 Cor.; *πλήρωμα* in the Epistles of the Captivity; *ὑγιής* in the Pastoral Epistles, &c.

[3] Liv. ii. 32. There is also a remarkable parallel in Sen. *De Irâ*, ii. 31.

[4] The *ἐκ* is against this supposed reference. On the other hand, the "*perikatharmata*" and *peripsema* of 1 Cor. iv. 13 *may* be an allusion to ancient piacular offerings (*v. supra, ad loc.*).

[5] *E.g.*, *Chiasmus*, Rom. ii. 7—10; *Paronomasia*, 2 Thess. iii. 11 (*supra, ad loc.*); *Paraleipsis*, 1 Thess. iv. 9, v. 1; *Oxymoron*, Rom. i. 20, Philem. 11; *Litotes*, 1 Cor. xi. 22, &c. (See Excursus II., "The Rhetoric of St. Paul."

[6] Krenkel, p. 12. See Arist. *M. Mor.* ii. 9, 2.

[7] The Talmud abounds in passages which utter nothing but unmixed scorn of the Gentiles, even of their very virtues. In *Babha Bathra*, f. 10, 2, there is a notable discussion on Prov. xiv. 34. It is rendered, "Righteousness exalteth a nation, and *the goodness of nations is sin*." R. Eleazar explained it to mean, "Righteousness exalts Israel; but the goodness of other nations is sin, being only due to their self-exaltation." Rabban Gamaliel said, "They were only good in order to heap reproach on the shortcomings of Israel;" and Rabbi Nechunya Ben Hakanah punctuated the verse, "Righteousness exalteth a nation (Israel) and goodness: but the nations, a sin-offering." This explanation was adopted by Rabban Johanan Ben Zakkai.

[8] 1 Cor. vii. 31, *παράγει τὸ σχῆμα τοῦ κόσμου*. 1 Cor. iv. 9, *θέατρον ἐγενήθημεν*. (Cf. Heb. x. 33, *θεατριζόμενοι*.)

sion—the man whose thoughts have been enlarged by travel and by intercourse with men of other training and other race—in the apparently vivid sympathy with which St. Paul draws some of his favourite metaphors from the vigorous contests of the Grecian games.[1] Those games constituted the brightest, the most innocently attractive feature of Hellenic life. During his long stay at Ephesus and at Corinth he had doubtless witnessed those wrestling bouts, these highly-skilled encounters of pugilism, those swift races to win the fading garlands of laurel or pine, which, for some of his heathen converts, and particularly for the younger among them, could not at once have lost their charm. We can well imagine how some young Ephesian or Corinthian might have pressed St. Paul to come with him and see the struggle and the race; and how, for one whose sympathies were so vividly human, there would have been a thrilling interest in the spectacle of those many myriads assembled in the vast stadium—in the straining eyes and eager countenances and beating hearts—in the breathless hush with which they listened to the proclamations of the herald—in the wild-eyed charioteers bending over their steeds, with the hair blown back from their glowing faces—in the resounding acclamations with which they greeted the youthful victor as he stepped forward with a blush to receive his prize. Would these fair youths do so much, and suffer so much, to win a poor withering chaplet of pine and parsley, whose greenness had faded before the sun had set, and would they use *no* effort, make *no* struggle, to win a crown of amaranth, a crown of righteousness which could not fade away? And that, too, when here the victory of one was the shame and disappointment of all the rest, while, in that other contest, each and all might equally be victors, and the victory of each be a fresh glory to all who were striving for the same high prize.[2] And as such thoughts passed through his mind there was no Judaic narrowness, but a genial sympathy in his soul, and a readiness to admire whatever was innocent and beautiful in human customs, when he wrote to his converts of Corinth—"Know ye not that they which run in a stadium run all, but one receiveth the prize? So run that ye may grasp.[3] Now every one that striveth is temperate in all things; they, however, that they may receive a corruptible crown, but we an incorruptible. I, then, so run, not as uncertainly; so box I, as one who beateth not the air; but I bruise my body with blows and enslave it, lest perchance, after making proclamation to others, I myself should prove to be a rejected combatant."[4]

4. But it was not only with Greek customs that St. Paul became familiar during his residence at Tarsus. It is clear that he must also have possessed some knowledge of Roman law. His thoughts often have a juridical form. He speaks of the "earnest-money" of the Spirit; of the laws of inheritance; of legal minority; of the rights of wives and daughters.[5] The privileges and the *prestige* conferred upon him by his rights of *Civitas* would have inevitably turned his thoughts in this direction. The Laws of the Twelve Tables had defined the authority which might be exercised by fathers over sons even after they have come of age (*patria potestas*) in a manner which Gaius tells us was peculiar to Roman jurisprudence, with the single exception that it also existed among the *Galatæ*. If this means the Galatians it would give peculiar significance to the illustration in Gal. iv. 1, which in any case proves St. Paul's familiarity with Roman institutions which had no existence among the Jews. So, too, we are told by Sir H. Maine that "a true power of testation" was nowhere provided for in the Jewish Code of Laws, and that the Romans "invented the will." Yet to the rules of testamentary bequests, and their irrevocability in certain cases, St. Paul seems to make an express allusion (Gal.

[1] 1 Cor. ix. 24; Phil. iii. 14; 1 Tim. vi. 12; 2 Tim. iv. 8; ii. 5; 1 Thess. ii. 19.

[2] See a close parallel in Sen. *Ep. Mor.* lxxviii. 16.

[3] *καταλάβητε*. Cf. Phil. iii. 12—14, *κατὰ σκοπὸν . . . ἐπὶ τὸ βραβεῖον*.

[4] 1 Cor. ix. 24—27. *ἀδόκιμος, vocabulum agonisticum* (Beng.; Philo, *de Cherub.* § 22). On the temperate training of competitors, see Hor. *A. P.* 412; Epict. *Enchir.* 35; *Dissert.* iii. 15; Tert. *ad Mart.* 3. *ἀέρα δέρειν* is to fight a *σκιαμαχία* (*i.e.*, make mere feints), (Eustath. *ad Il.* xx. 446; Athen. 154, A, &c.; Virg. *Æn.* v. 376). Κηρύξας, perhaps "heralding the laws of the contest" (Æsch. *Eum.* 566).

[5] Gal. iii. 17, 18; iv. 1, 2; Rom. vii. 2, &c.

iii. 15). Again, he gives prominence to the Roman idea of artificial "adoption," even to the extent of making an apparent reference to the fact that a son, fully adopted, abandoned the domestic rites (*sacra*) of his own family, and attached himself to those of his new parent (Gal. iv. 5; Eph. i. 5).[1]

5. We may select one more passage—though in this case it involves no admiration or sympathy—to show how accurately the customs of the Pagan life had been observed by St. Paul in that varied experience which made him, in the best sense, a citizen of the world. It is a passage which, from the absence of this knowledge, has often been entirely misunderstood. It occurs in 2 Cor. ii. 14—16: "Now thanks be to God, who always leadeth us everywhere in triumph[2] in Christ, and who by us maketh manifest the odour of the knowledge of Him in every place. For we are to God a sweet odour of Christ among those who are being saved, and among those who are perishing. To the latter we are an odour of death to death, to the former an odour of life to life."

Here, though the details of the metaphor are intricately involved, the general conception which was in the thoughts of the Apostle, and swayed his expression, is derived from the customs of a Roman triumph. It was one main feature of such "insulting vanities" that the chief captives were paraded before the victor's path, and sweet odours were burnt in the streets while his car climbed the Capitol.[3] But when he reached the foot of the Capitoline hill there was a fatal halt, which, in the utter deadness of all sense of pity, might be a moment of fresh exultation to the conqueror, but which was death to the captive; for at that spot the captives ceased to form any part of the procession, but were led aside into the rocky vaults of the Tullianum, and strangled by the executioner in those black and fetid depths. And thus the sweet odours, which to the victor—a Marius or a Julius Cæsar—and to the spectators were a symbol of glory and success and happiness, were to the wretched victims—a Jugurtha or a Vercingetorix—an odour of death. Reminded of this by his use of the words "leadeth us in triumph," St. Paul for an instant fancies himself a captive before the chariot of God—a captive in connection with Christ; and then another passing fancy strikes him. The preachers of Christ are like that burning incense whose perfume filled the triumphant streets,[4] but they were not an odour of life and hope to all. As light is light yet pains the diseased eye, as honey is honey yet palls on the sated taste,[5] so the odour retained its natural fragrance, although to many—through their own sins and wilfulness—it might only breathe of death. The tidings of salvation were glad tidings, but to the guiltily hardened and the wilfully impenitent they might prove to be tidings of wrath and doom.[6]

Little, perhaps, did it occur to St. Paul as he wrote those words, that the triumph of God, in which he was being led along from place to place as a willing victim, might end for him also in the vaults of that very Tullianum[7]—the description of which must have

[1] These instances are pointed out by Dean Merivale, *Boyle Lectures*, and in *St. Paul at Rome*, pp. 172—180. The passages of Gaius referred to are *Instt.* i. 55 (cf. Cæsar, *B. G.* vi. 19) and 189; *Digests*, xxvi. 8; but I cannot pretend to say that the conclusions formed are indisputable.

[2] The rendering of the E. V., "which always *causes us to triumph* in Christ," is both philologically impossible (cf. Col. ii. 15), and confuses the metaphor to such an extent as to render it entirely unintelligible. St. Paul may well have heard of the famous triumph of Claudius over the Britons a few years before (A.D. 51), in which Caractacus had walked as a prisoner (θριαμβευθείς), but "had passed from the ranks of the 'lost' to those of the 'saved'" (Tac. *Ann.* xiii. 36). (See Dr. Plumptre, *ad loc.*) Cleopatra had proudly said, οὐ θριαμβευθήσομαι.

[3] Dion Cass. lxxiv.; Hor. *Od.* IV. ii. 50; Plut. *Æmil.* p. 272.

[4] St. Paul rises superior to the vulgar prejudice of the Rabbis, who said that "a man is a sinner who while walking in a part of a town inhabited by idolaters inhales purposely the odour of incense offered up by them" (*Berachôth*, f. 53, 1).

[5] See Theophyl. *ad loc.*

[6] Similarly the Rabbis spoke of the law as an "aroma of life" to those who walk on the right, an "aroma of death" to those on the left (*Shabbath*, f. 88, 2).

[7] The Tullianum is, according to old tradition, the scene of the last imprisonment, before martyrdom, both of St. Peter and St. Paul. It was the rock-hewn lower dungeon added by Servius Tullius to the *carcer* of Ancus Martius. Excavations within the last few months prove that it was much larger than has been hitherto supposed.

been mingled in his thoughts with the other details of the Roman pomp—and that if not from the Mamertine, yet from some other Roman prison he would only be dragged forth to die.

EXCURSUS IV. (p. 33).

ST. PAUL A HAGADIST: ST. PAUL AND PHILO.

THERE are two large divisions of Rabbinic lore, which may be classed under the heads of *Hagadôth*, or unrecorded legends, and *Halachôth*, or rules and precedents in explanation of dubious or undefined points of legal observance.[1] It is natural that there should be but few traces of the latter in the writings of one whose express object it was to deliver the Gentiles from the intolerable burden of legal Judaism. But though there is little trace of them in his writings, he himself expressly tells us that he had once been enthusiastic in their observance.[2] "I was making," he says to the Galatians, "continuous advance in Judaism above many who were my equals in age in my own race, being very exceedingly a zealot for the traditions handed down from my fathers."[3] And there are in the Epistles abundant signs that with the *Hagadôth* he was extremely familiar, and that he constantly refers to them in thought. Thus in 2 Tim. iii. 8 he traditionally names Jannes and Jambres, two of the Egyptian magicians who withstood Moses. He adopted the current Jewish chronologies in Acts iii. 20, 21. He alludes to the notion that the Adam of Gen. i. is the ideal or spiritual, the Adam of Gen. ii. the concrete and sinful Adam.[4] The conception of the last trumpet,[5] of the giving of the Law at Sinai by angels,[6] of Satan as the god of this world and the prince of the power of the air,[7] and of the celestial and infernal hierarchies,[8] are all recurrent in Talmudic writings. When, in 1 Cor. xi. 10, he says that "a woman ought to have a veil[9] on her head because of the angels," there can, I think, be no shadow of doubt in the unprejudiced mind of any reader who is familiar with those Jewish views of the subject, in which St. Paul had been trained, that he is referring to the common Rabbinic interpretations of Gen. vi. 2 (LXX. Cod. A, "the angels"), where the Targum, and, indeed, all Jewish authorities down to the author of the Book of Enoch (quoted in the Epistle of Jude),[10] attribute the Fall of the Angels to their guilty love for earthly women. St. Paul could not have been unaware of a notion which for many ages seems to have been engrained in the Jewish mind[11]—a notion which is found over and over again in the

[1] I have tried fully to explain the nature of the *Halachah* and the *Hagadah* in the *Expositor*, October, 1877. The former dealt mainly with the Pentateuch, the latter with the Hagiographa. Dr. Deutsch (Smith's *Dict.* s. v. "Versions") says, "If the Halachah used the Scriptural word as a last and most awful resort against which there was no further appeal, the Hagadah used it as the golden nail on which to hang its gorgeous tapestry. If the former was the iron bulwark round the nationality of Israel, the latter was a maze of flowery walks within those fortress walls."

[2] Gal. i. 14.

[3] The παράδοσις did not mean the written Law, but the Oral Law, the πάτρια ἔθη of which Josephus speaks so much; the germ, in fact, of the *Halachôth* of the Mishna and Gemara.

[4] 1 Cor. xv. 47. This is also found in Philo, *De Opif. Mund.* i. 32.

[5] 1 Cor. xv. 52; 1 Thess. iv. 16. [6] Gal. iii. 19. [7] Eph. ii. 2.

[8] Eph. i. 21; iii. 10; vi. 12; Col. i. 16; ii. 15.

[9] Such, however arrived at, or whatever be the special shade of thought about the use of the word—which may be a mere provincialism—is the obvious meaning of ἐξουσία in 1 Cor. xi. 10. St. Paul gives three reasons for this rule—(1) our instinctive sense that an uncovered head, like a shaven head, is a dishonour to a woman, whose hair is a glory to her; (2) the fact that woman's hair indicates her subordinate position towards man, as man's covered head denotes his subordination to God; (3) "because of the angels." [10] 2 Pet. ii. 4; Jude 6, 14.

[11] The argument that οἱ ἄγγελοι is never used in the New Testament except for good angels is quite valueless, for the fallen angels were supposed to have been good angels until they fell, and, if they had fallen thus, there was nothing to show the impossibility that others might similarly fall. This interpretation is given quite unhesitatingly by Tertullian, *de Virg. Vel.* 7, "propter angelos, scilicet quos legimus a Deo et coelo excidisse ob concupiscentiam feminarum." I have thoroughly examined this point in a paper in the *Homiletic Quarterly* of 1878, and quoted many Rabbinic illustrations. (*Tanchuma*, f. 51, 4; *Abhôth* of Rabbi Nathan, c. 34.)

Talmud, and which is still so prevalent among Oriental Jews, as also among Mohammedans,[1] that they never allow their women to be unveiled in public lest the *Shedim*, or evil spirits, should injure them and others.[2] To this very day, for this very reason, Jewish women in some Eastern cities wear an inconceivably hideous headdress, called the *khalebí*, so managed as to entirely conceal the hair. It exposes them to derision and inconvenience, but is worn as a religious duty, "because of the spirits."

Again, in Rom. iv. 5, 13, Paul evidently accepts the tradition, also referred to by St. Stephen, that Abraham had been an uncircumcised idolater when he first obeyed the call of God, and that he then received a promise—unknown to the text of Scripture—"that he should be the heir of the world."[3] In Rom. ix. 9 it has been supposed, from the form of his quotation, that he is alluding to the Rabbinic notion that Isaac was created in the womb by a fiat of God; in Gal. iv. 29 to the Hagadah that Ishmael not only laughed, but jeered, insulted, and mis-treated Isaac;[4] and in 2 Cor. xi. 14 to the notion that the angel who wrestled with Jacob was an evil angel assuming the semblance of an Angel of Light. These three latter instances are slight and dubious; but there is a remarkable allusion to the smitten rock in the wilderness, which in 1 Cor. x. 4 is called "a spiritual *following* rock." The expression can have but one meaning. Among the many marvellous fancies which have been evolved from the thoughts of Jewish teachers, occupied for centuries in the adoring and exclusive study of their sacred books, was one to which they repeatedly recur, that the rock, from which the water flowed, was round and like a swarm of bees, and rolled itself up and went with them in their journeys. When the Tabernacle was pitched, the rock came and settled in its vestibule. Then came the princes, and standing near it exclaimed, "Spring up, O well; sing ye unto it,"[5] and it sprang up. How are we to regard these strange legends? Can we suppose that wise and sensible Rabbis like Hillel and Gamaliel took them literally? There is no ground whatever for supposing—indeed, it is essentially impossible—that any one could have accepted, *au pied de la lettre*, all the fables of the Talmud, which are in many instances both senseless and contradictory. Many of them were doubtless regarded as mere plays of pious fancy—mere ingenious exercises of loving inference. Others were only an Oriental way of suggesting mystic truths—were, in fact, intentional allegories. Others, in their broad outlines, were national traditions, which may often have corresponded with fact, and which, at any rate, had passed into general and unquestioned credence in ages little troubled by the spirit of historical criticism.[6] Though St. Paul might quite naturally glance at, allude to, or even make use of some of these latter, it would be an utter mistake to assume that he necessarily attached to them any objective importance. If he alludes to the simplest and most reasonable of them, he does so ornamentally, incidentally, illustratively, and might in all probability have attributed to them no value

[1] See the very remarkable story of Khadijah, who discovers that it is really Gabriel who has appeared to Mohammed by his flying away directly she takes off her veil, "knowing from Waraka that a good angel must fly before the face of an unveiled woman" (Weil, *Mohamed*, 48). (See Dean Stanley's exhaustive note, *Cor.* p. 187.)

[2] See *Berachôth*, f. 6, 1: "Abba Benjamin says that if we had been suffered to see them, no one would stand before the hurtful demons. Rav Huna that each of us has 1,000 at his left and 10,000 at his right hand (Ps. xci. 7)," &c. &c. The reason why Solomon's bed was guarded by sixty valiant men with drawn swords was "because of fear in the night" (Cant. iii. 7, 8). "Walk not alone at night, because Egrath, daughter of Machlath, walks about—she and 180,000 destroying angels, and every one of them individually has permission to destroy" (*Pesachim*, 112, 2). They are called *ruchin, shedim, lilin, tiharim*, &c. (Hamburger, *s.v.* "Gespenster"). The only other view of the passage which seems to me even possible (historically) is that of St. Chrysostom, "because good angels present at Christian worship rejoice to see all things done decently and in good order."

[3] Rom. iv. 13. Cf. Josh. xxiv. 15. [4] *Sanhedr.* f. 89, 2. [5] Num. xxi. 17.

[6] The Rabbis themselves draw a distinction between passages which are to be accepted literally (לפי פשוטו) and those which are meant to be "hyperbolical," in ordinary Oriental fashion (לשון הבאי). (Reland, *Antt. Hebr.*, p. 140). It must further be remembered that much of the Talmud consists of cryptographs which designedly concealed meanings *φωνᾶντα συνετοῖσιν* from "persecutors" and heretics." Space prevents any further treatment of these subjects here, but I may refer those who are interested in them to my papers on the Halacha and the Hagada, Talmudic cryptographs, &c., in the *Expositor* for 1877.

beyond their connexion with loving reminiscences of the things which he had learnt in the lecture-hall of Gamaliel, or in his old paternal home. In this very passage of the Corinthians the word "following" (ἀκολουθούσης) is only a graceful allusion to the least fantastic element of a legend capable of a spiritual meaning; and St. Paul, in the instant addition of the words "and this rock was Christ," shews how slight and casual is the reference to the purely *Hagadistic* elements which, in the national consciousness, had got mingled up with the great story of the wanderings in the wilderness.[1] Meanwhile—since it is the spiritual and not the material rock which is prominent in the thoughts of St. Paul—is there any one who holds so slavish and unscriptural a view of inspiration as to think that such a transient allusion either demands our literal acceptance of the fact alluded to, or, if we reject it, weakens the weight of apostolic authority? If a modern religious writer glanced allusively at some current legend of our own or of ancient history, would it be at once assumed that he meant to support its historical certainty? If he quotes Milton's line about Aaron's breastplate "ardent with gems oracular," is he held to pledge himself to the Rabbinic theory of the light which moved upon them? Does any one think himself bound to a literal belief in seven heavens, because St. Paul, in direct accordance with Jewish notions, tells us that he was caught up into Paradise as far as the third?[2]

There is one respect in which these traces of Judaic training are specially interesting. They show the masterly good sense of the Apostle, and they show his inspired superiority to the influences of his training. That he should sometimes resort to allegory is reasonable and interesting; but when we study the use which he makes of the allegorising method in the case of Sarah and Hagar, we see at once its immense superiority to the fantastic handling of the same facts by the learned Philo. How much more soberly does St. Paul deal with the human and historic elements of the story; and how far more simple and natural are the conclusions which he derives from it! Again, when he alludes to the legends and traditions of his nation, how rational and how purely incidental is his way of treating them! Compare St. Paul with Philo, with the Talmudists, with any of the Fathers in the first three centuries, and we can then more clearly recognise the chasm which separates the Apostle from the very greatest writers both of his own nation and of the early Christian Church.

The question as to whether St. Paul had or had not read Philo is not easy to answer. Gfrörer's work on Philo might seem a decisive proof that he had done so. Undoubtedly many passages may be adduced from the voluminous pamphlets of the eloquent Alexandrian which might lead us to repeat the old remark that "either Paul Philonises, or Philo is a Christian." Philo, like St. Paul, speaks of the Word of God as the antitype of the manna, and the smitten rock, and the pillar of cloud and fire; and as a Mediator, and as begotten before the worlds, and as the Heavenly Man. He speaks of the strife between the fleshly and the rational soul; of the assisting grace of God; of the milk of doctrine; of seeing God as through a mirror; of the true riches; and of the faith of Abraham. And, besides agreement in isolated phrases, Philo resembles St. Paul in his appeal to overwhelming revelations,[3] in modes of citing and interpreting Scripture, in his use of allegory, in the importance which he attaches to the spiritual over the carnal meaning of ordinances, and in many other particulars. But when we look closer we see that many of these expressions and points of view were not peculiar to Philo. They were, so to speak, in the air. They fall under the same category as the resemblances to Christian sentiments which may be adduced from the writings of Seneca,

[1] Seven such current national traditions are alluded to in St. Stephen's speech. (See *supra*, p. 92.)

[2] 2 Cor. xii. 2, 4; Eph. iv. 10. Many other passages and expressions of St. Paul find their illustration from the Talmud—*e.g.*, 1 Cor. xv. 37, 45, γυμνὸν κόκκον; Eph. ii. 14 (the *Chel*); 1 Cor. v. 2 (*ardtsôth*, "other lands"); 2 Cor. ii. 16, ὀσμὴ θανάτου; 2 Cor. v. 2, ἐπενδύσασθαι, &c. (See Meyer on these passages.)

[3] *De Cherubim*, i. 443.

Epictetus, and Marcus Aurelius, and may therefore be explained as having been due rather to the prevalent currents of moral and religious sentiment, than to any imitation or conscious interchange of thought. And side by side with these resemblances, the differences between Paul and Philo are immense. The cardinal conception of Philo is that of the Logos, and it is one which, in *this* sense, is never used by St. Paul. St. Paul makes but one or two distant and slighting allusions to the ancient Greek philosophy, which Philo regarded as of transcendent importance. St. Paul makes but the most subordinate use of the allegoric method, which with Philo is all in all. To Philo the Patriarchs become mere idealised virtues; to St. Paul they are living men. Philo addresses his esoteric eclecticism to the illuminated few; St. Paul regards all alike as the equal children of a God who is no respecter of persons. Philo clings to the Jewish ritualisms, though he gives them a mystic significance; St. Paul regards them as abrogated for Gentiles, and non-essential even for Jews. Philo still holds to the absolute superiority of the Jew over the Gentile; St. Paul teaches that in Christ Jesus there is neither Jew nor Gentile. In Philo we see the impotence of Hellenising rationalism; in St. Paul the power of spiritual truth. Philo explains and philosophises in every direction; St. Paul never recoils before a paradox, and leaves antinomies unsolved side by side. Philo, like St. Paul, speaks much of faith; but the "faith" of Philo is something far short of a transforming principle,[1] while that of St. Paul is a regeneration of the whole nature through mystic union with Christ. The writings of Philo are a collection of cold abstractions, those of St. Paul a living spring of spiritual wisdom. "Philo," says Professor Jowett, "was a Jew, St. Paul a Christian. Philo an eclectic, St. Paul spoke as the Spirit gave him utterance. Philo was an Eastern mystic, St. Paul preached the resurrection of the body. Philo was an idealiser, St. Paul a spiritualiser of the Old Testament. Philo was a philosopher, St. Paul a preacher; the one taught a system for the Jews, the other a universal religion. The one may have guided a few more solitaries to the rocks of the Nile, the other has changed the world. The one is a dead, unmeaning literature, lingering amid the progress of mankind; the other has been a principle of life to the intellect as well as to the heart. While the one has ceased to exist, the other has survived, without decay, the changes in government and the revolutions in thought of 1,800 years."[2]

Of the Apocryphal books there was one at least with which St. Paul was almost certainly acquainted—namely, the Book of Wisdom. No one, I think, will question this who compares his views of idolatry, and the manner in which he expresses them, with the chapters in which that eloquent book pursues the worship of heathenism with a concentrated scorn hardly inferior to that of Isaiah; or who will compare together the passages to which I have referred in a former note. If the books for which St. Paul wrote from his last imprisonment were any but sacred books, we may feel a tolerable confidence that the Book of Wisdom was among their number.[3]

EXCURSUS V. (p. 64).

GAMALIEL AND THE SCHOOL OF TÜBINGEN.

I SHALL not often turn aside to meet what seem to me to be baseless objections; but as the name of Gamaliel will always be associated with that of St. Paul, it may be worth while to do so for a moment in this instance. It seems, then, to me that this accusation

[1] Philo's highest definition of faith is "a bettering in all things of the soul, which has cast itself for support on the Author of all things" (*De Abraham*, ii. 39). [2] *Romans*, i. 416.

[3] Comp. Rom. v. 12; xi. 32; 1 Cor. vi. 2; 2 Cor. v. 4, &c., respectively, with Wisd. ii. 24; xi. 23—26; iii. 8; ix. 15, &c. But see *supra*, p. 97.

of St. Luke is founded on a mass of errors.[1] Gamaliel, like St. Paul, was a Pharisee, the son of Pharisees, and it was doubtless his nobleness and candour of disposition which impressed the Apostle with the better elements of Pharisaism. The fiery zeal of a youthful Tarsian may have led him for a time to adopt the more violent tone of the school of Shammai, and yet might have been very far from obliterating the effects of previous teaching. But, in point of fact, even a Hillel and a Gamaliel, in spite of their general mildness, would have described themselves without hesitation as "exceedingly zealous for the traditions of the fathers." Their concessions to expediency were either concessions in their conduct to the heathen, or concessions to necessity and the general interest.[2] The difference between the two Pharisaic schools was not nearly so wide as that between the two great Jewish sects. The Pharisees were beyond all question allied to the Zealots in political sympathies, while the Sadducees had natural affinities with the Herodians. In what we know of Gamaliel, we trace a spirit, a tone, a point of view, which eminently resembles that of his far greater pupil. His decision that soldiers in war time, and all people engaged in works of mercy, duty, or necessity, might be exempted from the more stringent Sabbatical traditions; his concession of rights of gleaning to the poorer brethren;[3] his direction that the "Peace be with you" should be addressed even to pagans on their feast days[4]—are all exactly analogous to the known sentiments of the Apostle; while the just, humane, and liberal regulations which he laid down to prevent the unfairness of husbands towards divorced wives, and of disobedient children towards their mothers, are identical in spirit to those which St. Paul applies to similar subjects. The story that he bathed in a bath at Ptolemais which was adorned with a statue of Aphrodite, and answered the reproaches of a *min* with the remark that the statue had evidently been made for the bath, and not the bath for the statue, belongs not to him but to his grandson, with whom he is perpetually confused.[5] To the latter is also due the wise and kindly rule of burying the dead in simple white linen, instead of in costly robes. Yet so close was the unity of doctrine which bound together the successive hereditary presidents of the school of Hillel, that we may look on any anecdote of the younger Gamaliel as fairly illustrative of the views of the elder; and the argument of Gamaliel II., that, if he were to be excluded from the enjoyment of every place which had been defiled by the rights of idolatry, he would not be able to find any place to live in at all, reminds us of more than one passage in St. Paul's argument about meats offered to idols. We may therefore regard it as a significant fact that, in spite of these liberal principles, Gamaliel of Jabne sanctioned the use of the "curse against heretics,"[6]

[1] The precept of Gamaliel, "Get thee a teacher, eschew that which is doubtful, and do not multiply uncertain tithes" (*Pirke Abhôth*,1,15), might have emanated from Shammai himself. In fact, the difference between the two schools existed far more in infinitesimal details than in fundamental principles.

[2] מפני תיקון העולם, "for the good order of the world," *Gittin*, v. 5. (Derenbourg, *Palestine*, p. 189.) It is difficult, however, to account for Gamaliel I. having a figure engraved on his seal if that story belongs to him.

[3] See Dr. Ginsburg, s. v., in Kitto's *Cycl.*, and Grätz, *Gesch. d. Juden*, iii. 274, sq.; Jost, *Gesch. d. Judenthums*, i. 281; Frankel, *Hodegetica in Mischnam*, 57; Derenbourg, *Palestine*, 239, sq.

[4] In *Jer. Berachôth*, ix. (Schwab, p. 159), there is a story that meeting a beautiful Pagan woman he uttered to her the *Shalôm alaikh*. "Is it possible?" is the amazed remark of the Gemara. "Did not R. Zeira say, on the authority of R. Josê bar R. Hanina, and R. Ba or R. Hiya, on the authority of R. Jochanan, that one ought not to express admiration for Pagans?" (a rule based on a sort of *jeu des mots* derived from Deut. vii. 3). The answer is that Gamaliel only admired her as he might have admired a beautiful horse or camel, exclaiming that Jehovah had made beautiful things in the universe. The Talmudist then proceeds to excuse Gamaliel for the enormity of looking at a woman, on the ground that it could only have been unexpectedly in a narrow street.

[5] *Abhôda Zara*, f. 44, 2. Conybeare and Howson, Krenkel, Lewin, and others, confuse the anecdotes of this Gamaliel (*Ha-zaken*, or "the Elder") and Gamaliel II., as also does Otho, *Lex. Rabb.*, s. v. (Etheridge, *Hebr. Lit.*, p. 45).

[6] ברכת המינים, *Berachôth*, f. 28, 2. Its first sentence is, "Let there be no hope to them that apostatize from the true religion; and let heretics (*minim*), how many soever they be, all perish as in a moment." The actual author of this prayer was Samuel the Little (*Ha-katôn*). (Grätz, iv. 105,

which is given twelfth in order in the *Shemone Esre*.[1] It is probable that his grandfather, who was equally liberal in many of his sentiments, would yet have been perfectly willing to authorise a similar prayer. His sense of expediency was so little identical with any indifference to pure Mosaism, that when he died it was said that the purity and righteousness of Pharisaism was removed, and the glory of the Law ceased.[2] Neither, then, in St. Paul's original zeal for the oral and written Law, nor in the liberality of his subsequent views and decisions about Mosaic observances, do we find any reason whatever to doubt the statement of his relation to Gamaliel, but on the contrary we find it confirmed by many minute and, at first sight, counter indications. And as far as the speech of Gamaliel is concerned, it seems probable that his toleration would have had decided limits. As it is by no means clear that he did not *afterwards* sanction the attempt to suppress the Christians, so it is by no means improbable that up to this time even Saul of Tarsus, had he been present at the debate, might have coincided with the half-tolerant, but also half-contemptuous, views of his great teacher. Although the Pharisees, in their deadly opposition to the Sadducees, were always ready to look with satisfaction on that one part of Christianity which rested on the belief in the Resurrection, the events of the next few months greatly altered the general relations of the Church, not only towards them, but also towards the entire body of the Jewish people, of whom, up to this time, a great multitude had welcomed its early manifestations with astonishment and joy.

EXCURSUS VI. (p. 93).

Capital Punishments: The Stoning of St. Stephen.

Generally speaking the Sanhedrin were not a sanguinary tribunal. They shuddered at the necessity of bloodshed, and tried to obviate its necessity by innumerable regulations. So great was their horror at putting an Israelite to death, that any means of avoiding it seemed desirable. Simeon Ben Shatach is the only conspicuous Rabbi who, for his cruelty in deciding causes, is said "to have had hot hands." Josephus expressly marks it as disgraceful to the Sadducees that, unlike the rest of their nation, they were savage in their punishments. We are told that if even once in seven years—Rabbi Eleazar Ben Asariah went so far as to say that if once in seventy years—a Sanhedrin inflicted capital punishment it deserved the opprobrious title of "sanguinary."[3] The migration of the Sanhedrin forty years before the destruction of Jerusalem, from their

434.) The notion that this Samuel the Less (for his name is, perhaps, given to distinguish him from the prophet Samuel: cf. ὁ μέγας, as the title of Herod, *Life of Christ*, i., p. 48, *n.*) has anything to do with Saul (Shaûl being a contraction of Shamuel, and Paulus being supposed to mean *the little*; Alting, *Schilo*, iv. 28; Basnage, Bk. III. i., pp. 12, 13) is an absurdity hardly worthy of passing notice. (Eisenmeng. *Entd. Judenth.* ii. 107; Buxtorf, *Lex. Talm.*, 1,201, 2,662; Wolf, *Bibl. Hebr.*, i. 1,119.)

[1] In point of fact, there is a considerable amount of obscurity about this prayer. The *Shemone-esre* or *amida* is a prayer recited after the *Shema*. It is named from the "eighteen blessings," or sections, of which it is composed, and is recited three times a day, or oftener on feast days. It *actually* contains nineteen sections, the 12th, which is numbered 11 *bis*, being the celebrated *Birkath ha-Minim*, or prayer against the *minim*, or heretics. Now, in *Jer. Berachôth*, ch. iv., § 3, we are expressly told that this prayer was added to the *Amida* at Jabne, and therefore by Gamaliel II. in the second century, long after the destruction of Jerusalem (Cahen, *Hist. de la Prière*, p. 30, sq.; and *Megillah*, f. 17, 2). How this can be reconciled with the asserted death of Samuel the Little, before the destruction of Jerusalem, is only one of the confusions and contradictions which meet us in every stage of Talmudic literature. Hallel (quoted by Schwab) says that the prayer is sometimes called "the *blessing* (by euphemism) of the Sadducees," and is intended as a protest of the Pharisees against the mixture of temporising and severity by which the Sadducees ruined their country. Chronology shows this to be futile.

[2] *Sotah*, f. 49, 1. He, or his grandson, are cited with high respect for various minute decisions in the *Berachôth*. (See Schwab's *Traité des Berachôth*, pp. 1, 11, 12, &c.)

[3] חובלנית. *Maccoth*, f. 7, 1; Derenbourg, p. 201.

"Hall of Squares," which was beside the great Court of the Temple to the Chanujôth or "shops" which were under two cedars on the Mount of Olives, is expressly stated to have been due to their desire to get to a greater distance from the sacred precincts, in order that they might not feel it so sternly incumbent upon them to inflict the strict punishments of the Law.[1] But if, after strict and solemn voting, a man was condemned to any of the four capital punishments, the utmost care was taken to remove from the punishment all semblance of vindictive haste. In the case of a convicted blasphemer the death assigned by the Law was stoning, and in Leviticus it is ordained that the witnesses should lay their hands upon his head, and all the congregation should stone him.[2] In Deuteronomy we read the further regulations that the hand of the witnesses was first to be upon him[3]—and this horrible duty was one of the deterrents from false or frivolous accusation. But if we may accept the authority of the *Mishna*, the process was an elaborate one. On pronunciation of the sentence the condemned was handed over to the *Shoterîm* or Lictors of the Sanhedrin, and led to the place of execution. An official stood at the door of the Judgment Hall[4] holding in his hand a handkerchief; a second on horseback was stationed just in sight of the first, and if, even at the last moment, any witness could testify to the innocence of the condemned, the first shook his handkerchief, and the second galloped at full speed to bring back the accused, who was himself allowed to be led back as many as four or five times if he could adduce a single solid proof in his own favour. Failing this he was led on with a herald preceding him, who proclaimed his name, his crime, and the witnesses on whose testimony he had been condemned. At ten paces' distance from the place of death he was bidden to confess, because Jewish no less than Roman law valued the certainty derived from the "confitentem reum," and the Jews deduced from the story of Achan that his punishment would be, as regards the future world, a sufficiently complete expiation of his crime.[5] A bitter draught containing a grain of frankincense was then given him to stupefy his senses and take away the edge of terror. At four cubits' distance from the fatal spot he was stripped bare of his upper garments, and according to the older and simpler plan of procedure was then stoned, the witnesses simultaneously hurling the first stones.[6] But the later custom seems to have been more elaborate. The place of execution[7] was twelve feet high, and one of the witnesses flung the criminal down, back foremost, from the top, the other immediately hurling a heavy stone upon his chest. If this failed to produce death, all who were present joined in stoning him, and his body was subsequently hung by the hands on a tree until the fall of evening.[8]

We may be quite sure that none of these elaborate prescriptions were followed in the martyrdom of Stephen. He was murdered in one of those sudden outbursts of fury to which on more than one occasion the life of our Lord had been nearly sacrificed.

EXCURSUS VII. (p. 94).

THE POWER OF THE SANHEDRIN TO INFLICT DEATH.

A QUESTION has often been raised how the Sanhedrin at this time had the power of inflicting death at all? The well-known passage of St. John, "It is not lawful for us

[1] The *Dinî Kenasôth* or punitive decisions (*Abhôda Zara*, f. 8, 2; *Shabbath*, f. 15, 1). Rashi inferred from Deut. xvii. 10, that minor Sanhedrins outside Jerusalem could not pronounce capital sentences (*Dinî Nephashôth*) unless the greater Sanhedrin was seated on the Temple Mount.

[2] Lev. xxiv. 14.

[3] Deut. xvii. 7.

[4] All these particulars, except when otherwise stated, I derive from the tract *Sanhedrin* of the Mishna, cap. vi. (Surenhus. ii., p. 234, seqq.)

[5] *Tanchuma*, f. 39, § 3; Schöttg. *Hor. Hebr. ad* Acts vii. 58.

[6] *Tanchuma*, *ubi supr.*; Deut. xvii. 7.

[7] Called בית הסקלה

[8] Deut. xxi. 22, 23.

to put any man to death," has been asserted to be in direct contradiction to the narrative. The explanation of that passage to mean "it is not lawful at the time of the feast" is both philologically and historically untenable, and there seems to be little doubt that there is truth in the statement of the Talmud that about forty years—a well-known vague term in Jewish writers—before the fall of Jerusalem, the Sanhedrin had relinquished—it would be truer to say, had been deprived of—the power of death.[1] That deprivation was due to the direct interference of the Romans, who would not extend the highest judicial functions to men so likely to abuse them for seditious ends. It is, perhaps, only an attempt of the Rabbis to veil their national humiliation, when they attribute the diminished glories of their "House of Judgment" to their own leniency; to their reluctance to shed the blood of a descendant of Abraham; to the consequent increase of crimes; and to the migration from the Hall of Squares to the "Shops" of the Beni Hanan. But, on the other hand, we know the astute connivance which the Romans were always ready to extend to acts which were due to religious excitement and not to civil rebellion.[2] They rarely interfered with national superstitions. Even Pilate, though by no means void of a sense of justice, had been quite willing to hand over Jesus to any extreme of ecclesiastical vengeance, provided only that the direct responsibility did not fall upon himself. Further than this, there is every reason to believe that St. Stephen's martyrdom finds its counterpart in the murder of James, the Lord's brother. That was brought about by the younger Hanan during a High Priesthood of only three months' duration, in which he seized his opportunity, and availed himself of a brief interregnum which followed on the death of Festus, and preceded the arrival of his successor Albinus. It was at just such an interregnum that the death of Stephen is believed to have taken place. Pontius Pilate had been sent to Rome by his official chief, Vitellius, the Præfect of Syria, to answer to the Emperor for the complaints of cruelty and insult brought against him by the inhabitants of every division of his Procuratorship. Before his arrival the Emperor Tiberius died. An event of this magnitude relaxed the sternness of government in every province of the Empire,[3] and though Vitellius appointed Marcellus as a brief temporary *locum tenens* until the arrival of Marullus, who was appointed Procurator by Gaius,[4] the Sanhedrin may have met while there was no Procurator at all, and in any case would have found it easy to persuade a substitute like Marcellus, or a new-comer like Marullus, that it would be useless to inquire into a mere riot which had ended in the richly deserved punishment of a blaspheming Hellenist. In short, we find that the possibility of tumultuous outbreaks which might end in a death by stoning is constantly recognised in the New Testament;[5] and it would have been easy for the Sanhedrin to represent the stoning of St. Stephen in such a light.

EXCURSUS VIII. (p. 101).

DAMASCUS UNDER HARETH.

HARETH was the father-in-law of Herod Antipas, and from the day when the weakness of that miserable prince had beguiled him into his connexion, at once adulterous and

[1] *Abhôda Zara*, f. 8, 2.

[2] The policy of Rome towards her Oriental subjects was a policy of contemptuous tolerance in all matters that affected the local cult.

[3] That there was at this very time a special desire to conciliate the Jews, who had been so much exasperated by the cruelties of Pilate, is clear from the circumstance that Vitellius, after a magnificent reception at Jerusalem, had just restored to the Jews the custody of the pontifical vestments, which since the days of Herod the Great had been kept in the Tower of Antonia (Jos. *Antt.* xv. 11, § 4; xviii. 4, § 2). The privilege was again forfeited, and again restored to them by Claudius, at the request of Agrippa II. (*id.* xx. 1, § 2). The power of inflicting *minor* punishments seems always to have rested with the Jews, as it does with many religious communities of *raïas*, even under the tyranny of Turkish misrule (Renan, *Les Apôtres*, p. 144).

[4] Jos. *Antt.* xviii. 6, § 10 (cf. 4, § 2).

[5] John viii. 59; x. 31—33; Matt. xxiii. 37; Acts v. 26. See Orig. *ad African.* § 14, *apud* Wordsworth.

incestuous, with Herodias, his brother Philip's wife, Hareth had been the implacable foe of the Tetrarch of Galilee. Their quarrel had ended in a battle, in which the troops of Hareth won a signal victory. After this defeat, in which the Jews saw a retribution for the murder of John the Baptist,[1] Antipas applied to the Emperor Tiberius, who sent Vitellius to chastise the audacious Emir who had dared to defeat an ally of Rome. But when Vitellius had reached Jerusalem, he heard the news of the death of Tiberius. The death of a Roman emperor often involved so immense a change of policy, that Vitellius did not venture, without fresh instructions, to renew the war. The details of what followed have not been preserved. That Hareth ventured to seize Damascus is improbable. Vitellius was too vigorous a legate, and the Arab had too wholesome a dread of imperial Rome, to venture on so daring an act of rebellion. On the other hand, it is not impossible that the Emperor Gaius—who was fond of distributing kingdoms among princes whom he favoured,[2] and whose mind was poisoned against Antipas by his friend and minion Agrippa I.—should have given back to Hareth a town which in old days had belonged to the Nabathæan dynasty.[3] The conjecture receives some independent confirmation. Coins of Damascus are found which bear the image of Augustus, of Tiberius, and again of Nero, but none which bear that of Gaius or of Claudius. This would lead us to infer that during these reigns Damascus was subject to a local sway.[4]

EXCURSUS IX. (p. 120).

SAUL IN ARABIA.

Few geographical terms are more vaguely used by ancient writers than "Arabia," and some have seen the explanation of St. Luke's silence about the retirement of St. Paul, in the possibility that he may scarcely have gone beyond the immediate region of Damascus. Justin Martyr challenges Trypho to deny that Damascus "belongs and did belong to Arabia, though now it has been assigned to what is called Syrophœnicia." Some shadow of probability may be, perhaps, given to the view that St. Paul did not travel far from Syria, because the Arabic translator of the Epistle to the Galatians renders the clause in Gal. i. 17, &c., "Immediately I went to *El Belka;*" and in Gal. iv. 25, mistaking the meaning of the word συστοιχεῖ (which means "answers to," "corresponds with," "falls under the same row with"), he says that "Mount Sinai or El Belka is contiguous to Jerusalem."[5] But since Sinai is certainly not in the El Belka with which alone we have any acquaintance—namely, the region to the north and east of the Dead Sea—this curious version does not seem worthy of any further notice. Doubtless, in the then disturbed and fluctuating relations between the Roman Empire and the various Eastern principalities, St. Paul might have found himself far beyond the range of interruption by taking but a short journey from the neighbourhood of Damascus.

But is it not more probable that when St. Paul speaks of his visit to Arabia, he means Arabia in that Hebrew sense in which the word would be understood by the majority of his readers? We cannot, indeed, accept the proof of his familiarity with these regions which is derived from the reading of our Received text, "for this Hagar is Mount Sinai in Arabia," and from the supposition that Hagar was a local name for the mountain itself.[6]

[1] Jos. *Antt.* xviii. 5, §§ 1, 2.

[2] Thus in A.D. 38 he gave Ituræa to Sohcym; Lesser Armenia to Cotys; part of Thrace to Rhœmetalces; Pontius, &c., to Polemo II. (Dion Cass. lix. 12). Keim thinks that Aretas may have had a sort of *partial* jurisdiction in Damascus.

[3] Jos. *Antt.* xiii. 5, §§ 2, 3; Wieseler, *Chron. des Apost. Zeitalt.* 174.

[4] Wieseler, in his article on Aretas in Herzog's *Encycl.*, refers to Mionnet, p. 204, as his authority for the existence of a coin of Aretas, which bears the date 101 (A.D.). Now, if this date refer to the Pompeian era, the coin would belong to A.D. 37—38, about the very time in which Saul's mission to Damascus took place.

[5] Lightfoot, *Galatians*, p. 81.

[6] Gal. iv. 25.

For the true reading of that verse seems to be, "for Sinai is a mountain in Arabia;" and, as Dr. Lightfoot has shown, there is no adequate authority for the assertion—perhaps originally a mistake of St. Chrysostom—that Mount Sinai was ever called Hagar. Moreover, it is doubtful whether, even by way of allegoric paronomasia, St. Paul would have identified *Hagar*, "a wanderer," with *chadjar*, "a stone;" especially since Philo, who also has an allegory about Hagar and Sarah, had already extracted a moral meaning from the correct derivation. But setting this ancient argument aside, nothing can seem more natural than that St. Paul, possibly already something of a fugitive, almost certainly a sufferer in health and mind, driven by an imperious instinct to seek for solitude, should have turned his lonely steps to a region where he would at once be safe, and unburdened, and alone with God.

EXCURSUS X. (p. 125).

St. Paul's "Stake in the Flesh."

THERE are two main passages on which our inferences about the "stake in the flesh" must be founded, and the impression which they leave is only strengthened by more isolated allusions. These two passages, to give them in their chronological order, are: 2 Cor. xii. 1—10 [1] and Gal. iv.; [2] and I translate them in all their ruggedness, and the interchanges of thought which render it almost impossible to explain the rapid transition of their causal connexions.

i. The first of them runs as follows:—After showing that, however weak and unworthy he may be, he has yet laboured and suffered more than "the super-pre-eminent Apostles,"—a boastfulness the very semblance of which he loathes, but which, again and again, he says has been forced upon him by the intrigues and slanders of interested opponents—he mentions his perilous escape from Damascus, which had made a deep impression on his memory, and then continues: "Boasting, evidently, is not expedient for me; for I will come to visions and revelations of the Lord.[3] I know a man in Christ fourteen years ago—(whether in the body I know not, or whether out of the body I know not: God knoweth)—caught up, such a one as far as the third heaven. And I know such a man—(whether in the body, or apart [4] from the body, I know not: God knoweth) —that he was caught up into Paradise and heard unutterable things which it is not lawful for man to speak. About such a one I will boast; but about myself I will not boast except in mine infirmities. For if I should wish to boast, I shall not be a fool, for I shall speak the truth; but I forbear, that no one may reckon about me more than what he seeth me or heareth anything from me. And, that I may not be puffed up by this abundance of revelations, there was given me a stake in the flesh an angel of Satan [5] that it may buffet me that I may not be puffed up. For this, thrice did I entreat the Lord that it might depart from me. And He hath said to me: My grace sufficeth for thee; for power is being perfected in weakness.[6] Most gladly, then, rather will I boast in my infirmities, that the power of Christ may spread its tent over me. Therefore, I am content in infirmities, in insults, in necessities, in persecutions, in distresses, for Christ's sake, for when I am weak then I am powerful." [7]

ii. The other passage is Gal. iv. 12—16. St. Paul has been vehemently urging the Galatians not to sink to the low level of their previous bondage from the freedom of the Gospel, and in the midst of his reasonings and exhortations he inserts this tender appeal:—

[1] Written not earlier than the autumn of A.D. 57.

[2] Written perhaps in the spring of A.D. 58.

[3] The reading of this verse is extremely doubtful; *v. supra, ad loc.*

[4] χωρίς, B, D, E, which is more likely to have been altered into the ἐκτὸς of the previous verse (א, F, G).

[5] Cf. 1 Cor. v. 5.

[6] Omit μου (א, A, B, D, F, G).

[7] 2 Cor. xii. 1—10.

"Become as I am, for I too have become as you, brethren, I beseech you. In no respect did ye wrong me. Yea, ye know that because of infirmity of the flesh I preached to you the first time, and your temptation in my flesh[1] ye despised not nor loathed, but as an angel of God ye received me, as Christ Jesus. What, then, was your self-congratulation? For I bear you witness that, if possible, ye dug out your eyes[2] and gave them me. So, have I become your enemy by telling you the truth?"

iii. The most prominent *allusions* to the same bodily affliction are—Gal. vi. 17: "Henceforth let no man trouble me, for I carry in my body the brands of Jesus;"[3] 2 Cor. iv. 10: "Always bearing about in the body the putting to death of the Lord Jesus;" and perhaps indirectly, Col. i. 24: "Now I rejoice[4] in my sufferings for you, and I supplement in Christ's stead the deficiences of the afflictions of Christ in my flesh for His body which is the Church." When, too, we remember that the word for "stake" is only a more contemptuous form of the word for "cross,"[5] there may be a further allusion to this special trial in the words, "I have been crucified with Christ."[6]

α. Now, from the first of these passages we see that St. Paul, so far from boasting of exceptional revelations, will only mention them because they are connected with infirmities so painful as to render it ridiculous as well as sinful for him to boast at all, unless he might boast that his very weakness was but a more signal proof of that strength of Christ which had enabled him to do and to suffer more than the very chiefest Apostles.

β. We gather that his trial was something agonising, or it would not be called a stake in the flesh;[7] mysterious in its nature, or it would not be described as an angel of Satan; intermittent, as is implied in the word "buffet," and as is also apparent from various special paroxysms to which St. Paul alludes; and a direct consequence of, or at any rate intimately connected with, his most exalted moments of revelation and ecstasy.

γ. From the second passage, we have the additional particulars, that it was in consequence of some sharp attack of his malady that he had been detained in Galatia; that this malady was of such a nature as to form an actual trial to the Galatians, and naturally dispose them to look on him with contempt, if not with positive loathing; but that they had so completely triumphed over this feeling as to receive him with almost divine respect, and that they had so congratulated themselves on his visit as to have been ready, had it been possible, to dig out their very eyes and give them to their suffering teacher.

δ. The other references confirm these conclusions. In one of them we learn that St. Paul looked on his physical infirmities as sacred stigmata by which Jesus had marked him out as His slave, that he might be secured from molestation;[8] and in the others that he regarded his living death as a sort of continuation of his Lord's crucifixion, and a supplement to those sufferings for the sake of His Church, in which Christ allowed His servants to participate by taking up their cross and following after Him for the service of mankind.[9]

Now these passages at once exclude nine-tenths of the conjectures which have been so freely hazarded, and which could not have been hazarded at all by those who had carefully considered the conditions of the question. Many of these conjectures would not have even deserved a passing mention if they had not, on the one hand, possessed a certain archæological interest as belonging to the history of exegesis, and on the other

[1] The true reading is *τὸν πειρασμὸν ὑμῶν ἐν τῇ σαρκί μου.*

[2] The omission of the *ἂν* (cf. John xix. 11; Matt. xxvi. 28) gives far more vividness to the expression. (See my *Brief Greek Syntax*, § 137.)

[3] *Leg.* τοῦ Ἰησοῦ (all but uncials).

[4] *Leg.* Νῦν χαίρω (A, B, C).

[5] Lipsius, *De Cruce*, i. 4. Hence σκολοπίζω = σταυρόω (cf. *stipes*).

[6] Gal. ii. 20, Χριστῷ συνεσταύρωμαι. This epistle is full of the "cross," and was written with vivid reminiscence (at least) of the "stake." The allusion of 1 Thess. ii. 18, "but Satan hindered us," is too vague to be referred with any special probability to this affliction.

[7] Ἄκανθαι καὶ σκόλοπες ὀδύνας σημαίνουσι διὰ τὸ ὀξὺ (Artemid. iii. 33, Meyer); (cf. Num. xxxiii. 55; Josh. xxiii. 13; Ezek. xxviii. 24; σκόλοψ πικρίας, Hos. ii. 6: LXX.). Hence perhaps the rendering "thorn."

[8] Gal. vi. 17.

[9] 2 Cor. iv. 10; Col. i. 24; Phil. iii. 10; Gal. ii. 20.

brought to light some fragments of old tradition, or pointed to certain features in the character of the Apostle.

1. It is, for instance, abundantly clear that the stake in the flesh was nothing of a spiritual nature. If we find such men as Jean Gerson,[1] and Luther, and Calvin more or less confidently deciding that the expression alludes to *high spiritual temptations*, such as shrinking from his duties as an Apostle, tormenting doubts, and stings of conscience for the past, the decision is only interesting as a proof that these great and holy men could so well sympathise with these painful hindrances. Yet such an explanation is wholly impossible. It is excluded at once by the references to the infirmity as being of a physical description. It is excluded also by St. Paul's character, and by the circumstances of his life. There is much in his Epistles about weariness and sorrow, about fightings without and fears within, but there is not the faintest trace that the fire of zeal burnt low, even at his moments of deepest discouragement, on the altar of his heart. Nor could tormenting doubts have had much reality in the soul of one who had seen the risen Christ, and to whom were constantly vouchsafed the vivid revelations which not only solved the problems, but even guided the movements of his life.[2]

2. And while we reject this view of some great Reformers, we must reject quite as decidedly the fixed opinion of the most eminent Roman Catholics. Vague expressions in St. Jerome, St. Augustine, and Gregory the Great seem to have led to an opinion that the stake in the flesh was *some form of carnal temptation*.[3] This view, repeated by the Venerable Bede, has been continued through Aquinas, Bellarmine, Cornelius à Lapide, and other Roman Catholic writers down to Van Est in the sixteenth century, till it has become almost a stereotyped part of the exegesis of the Roman Catholic Church. It is due to the ambiguous rendering of "stake in the flesh," by *stimulus carnis* in the Vulgate translation. Now, in this case also—though we may observe with sorrowful interest that the struggles of ascetics to subdue by unwise methods their carnal passions made them glad to believe that even in the case of St. Paul such an infirmity was never wholly removed—we are nevertheless obliged on every ground to reject the explanation. It in no way satisfies the general tenor of St. Paul's expressions. It is not an infirmity of which by any possibility he could boast. We cannot conceive so revolting a stain on the character of the Apostle as that which would be involved in the supposition that such tendencies, if he had been cursed with them, should have so manifested themselves as to be a hindrance to his ministry, and a source of loathing to those who heard him. It is still more outrageous to imagine that such criminal concupiscence would have been implanted or strengthened in him as a counterpoise to the spiritual pride which might otherwise have resulted from special revelations. But besides all this, it fixes on the memory of the Apostle a weakness from which we may well believe that he was most exceptionally free. It is true that in the Epistle to the Romans he describes, in language of intense emotion, the struggle in the soul between the good and the evil impulse—the *Yetser ha-tôbh* and *Yetser ha-râ* of which he had heard so much in the Beth Midrash of his education. But it is idle to imagine that a strife so multiform must be referred to one only of its manifestations. And we judge that St. Paul had very early subdued every motion of rebellious sensuality, not only because no man who ever lived has uttered words of loftier purity; not only because upon his principles more than upon those of any human moralist have been founded the very bases of Christian abstinence; not only because, to an extent unparalleled in literature, he has the high gift of being able to brand the shamelessness of impurity without wounding the delicacy of Christian thought;[4] but more than this, because he is able to appeal to others that they should learn by his example how possible it was to live by the rule of a holy continence. Ad-

[1] Perhaps the author, or part author, of the *Imitatio Christi*. (See *Companions of the Devout Life*, p. 8, *sq.*)

[2] See Acts xvi. 7; xxi. 4; xxii. 17; Gal. ii. 2, &c.

[3] Greg. *Moral.* x. 8, 315. See the authorities in Tillemont, i. 222 (ed. 1693).

[4] Rom. i.; Eph. v., &c.

mitting as he does to the Corinthians that it is better once for all to marry than to be consumed by the slow inward fires of concupiscence,[1] he yet says to the unmarried, "it is good for them to abide even as I," and that "he would that all men were even as he himself."[2] There would be hypocrisy, and something worse than hypocrisy, in such language if the "stake in the flesh," which was still unremoved when he wrote the Second Epistle, were that which this long succession of commentators have supposed it to be.[3]

3. It may, then, be regarded as certain that the stake in the flesh was some physical malady; for the fancy first mentioned by Chrysostom and adopted by the Greek fathers, as well as by Hilary and Augustine, that it means the *opposition and persecution* with which St. Paul met at the hands of Judaists, and perhaps especially of one leader among them who was "a thorn in his side,"[4] is too entirely at variance with the conditions of the question to deserve further notice. But when, in our anxiety to understand and sympathise as far as possible with the Apostle's personality, we still ask what was this malady, we are left in uncertainty. To omit the more futile conjectures, neither attacks of headache nor earache mentioned traditionally by Tertullian and Jerome, nor the stone which is the conjecture of Aquinas, present those features of external repulsiveness to which the Apostle evidently alludes as the concomitants of his trial. The only conjectures which have much intrinsic probability are those which suppose him to have suffered from epilepsy or from ophthalmia.

4. There is something to be said in favour of the view that it was *Epilepsy*. It is painful; it is recurrent; it opposes an immense difficulty to all exertion; it may at any time cause a temporary suspension of work; it is intensely humiliating to the person who suffers from it; it exercises a repellent effect on those who witness its distressing manifestations. Moreover, it was regarded in ancient days as supernatural in its character, was surrounded with superstitious fancies, and was directly connected by the Jews with demoniacal possession.[5] Further, St. Paul himself connects his infirmity with his trances and visions, and the soul of man is so constituted that any direct intercourse with the unseen world—even, in a lower order, any deep absorption in religious thought, or paroxysms of religious feeling—does tend to a violent disturbance of the nervous organism.[6] It would be specially certain to act in this way in the case of one whose temperament was so emotional as was that of St. Paul. It is not impossible that the prostration which followed his conversion may have been induced by the shock which his system received from his miraculous conversion on the road to Damascus; and that the recurrence of this shock, involving a chronic liability to its attacks, accompanied that second trance in the Temple, which determined his future career as the Apostle of the Gentiles. His third ecstasy happened fourteen years[7] before he wrote the Second

[1] 1 Cor. vii. 9, *κρεῖσσον γαμῆσαι ἢ πυροῦσθαι.* [2] 1 Cor. vii. 7, 8.

[3] It is difficult to believe that 2 Cor. vii. 2; xi. 8; and 1 Thess. ii. 3 are intended to refute charges which had been even brought against Paul himself. They may be intended to contrast his own conduct with that of other teachers, and indeed the first two passages do not necessarily refer to unchastity at all. The *ἀκαθαρσία* of 1 Thess. ii. 3 is explained, even by Chrysostom, of vile and juggling arts; and Olshausen, Lünemann, Alford, Ellicott, and others all suppose it to refer primarily to *αἰσχροκέρδεια* and similar impure motives.

[4] A special person may be indicated in 2 Cor. x. 7, 10, 11, 18; xi. 4, 20; and in Gal. i. 9; iii. 1; vi. 7, 12.

[5] *Morbus Comitialis*, Dion Cass. xlvi. 33; Gell. xix, 2. In Welsh it is called *gwialen Christi*, "the rod of Christ," and *eledyt bendigaid*, "blessed disease." A curious Celtic tradition to this effect is preserved in the old Irish name for epilepsy, *in galar Poil* (Stokes, *Old Irish Glossary*, p. 120; *Anc. Laws of Ireland*, iii. 506). Krenkel, in Hilgenfeld's *Zeitschr.* xvi. (ii.) 233—244, notices the curious fact that the evil omen of epilepsy was averted by *spitting*. Hence Plautus calls it the "morbus *qui sputatur*" (*Captiv.* iii. 4, 15; cf. Plin. *H. N.* x. 23, 33; xxviii. 4, 7). He connects this with *ἐξεπτύσατε* (as though it meant "neither did ye spit") of Gal. iv. 14.

[6] The trances of Socrates, the fits of Mohammed, accompanied by foaming at the mouth, and followed by the sleep of exhaustion, the faintings and ecstasies of St. Bernard, St. Francis, and St. Catherine of Siena, have been adduced as parallels (Hausrath, pp. 52—56). We may add the cases of George Fox, of Jacob Boehme, of Swedenborg, &c. [7] The "about" in the E. V. is interpolated.

Epistle to the Corinthians, and therefore at some period during his second residence in Tarsus. If we take the words, "thrice I besought the Lord," literally, we may ther further believe that it was at each of these recurrences of anguish upon the renewals of special revelations that he had made his most earnest entreaty to be delivered from the buffets of this angel of Satan; and that it was only during, or after, his third and most memorable vision that his Lord pointed out to him the meaning of the trial, and told him that, though it could not be removed, he should be strengthened with grace sufficient to enable him to bear it.[1]

5. But even if this was the actual "stake in the flesh," there is the strongest reason to believe that St. Paul suffered further from *acute Ophthalmia*, which also fulfils in every particular the conditions of the problem. This, too, would have the advantage of following the analogy of God's dealings, by being a trial not arbitrarily inflicted, but one which might have resulted naturally—or, to use the more exact term, let us say, providentially —from the circumstances through which Paul had passed. We know that he was physically blinded by the glare of light which surrounded him when he saw the risen Lord. The whole circumstances of that event—the noonday journey under the fierce Syrian sun, the blaze of light which outshone even that noonday brightness, and the blindness which followed it—would have been most likely to leave his eyes inflamed and weak. His stay in the desert and in Damascus—regions notorious for the prevalence of this disease—would have tended to develop the mischief when it had once been set up; and though we are never told in so many words that the Apostle suffered from defective sight, there are yet so many undesigned coincidences of allusion all pointing in this direction, that we may regard it as an ascertained fact. Apart from the initial probability that eyes which had once been so seriously affected would be liable to subsequent attacks of disease, we have the following indications:—(i.) When speaking of his infirmity to the Galatians, St. Paul implies that it might well have rendered him an object of loathing; and this is pre-eminently the case with acute ophthalmia. The most distressing objects, next to the lepers, which the traveller will ever see in the East—those who will most make him inclined to turn away his face with a shudder of pity and almost involuntary disgust—are precisely those who are the victims of this disease.[2] (ii.) And this would give a deeper pathos and meaning to the Apostle's testimony that the Galatians in the first flush of their Gospel joy, when they looked on the preacher of those good tidings as an angel of God, would, had it been possible, *have dug out their eyes* in order to place them at the sufferer's service. (iii.) The term, "a stake in the flesh," would be most appropriate to such a malady, because all who have been attacked with it know that the image which it recalls most naturally is that of a sharp splinter run into the eye.[3] (iv.) Moreover, it would be extremely likely to cause epileptic or other symptoms, since in severe attacks it is often accompanied by cerebral disturbance. (v.) In spite of the doubt which has been recently thrown on the commonly accepted meaning of the expression which St. Paul uses to the Galatians, "Ye see in what large letters I write to you with my own hand," it must at any rate be admitted that it suits well with the hypothesis of a condition which rendered it painful and difficult to write at all. That this was St. Paul's normal condition seems to result from his almost invariable practice of employing an amanuensis, and only adding in autograph the few last words of greeting or blessing, which were necessary for the identification of his letters in an age in which religious forgeries were by no means unknown. (vi.) It is obvious, too, that an ocular deformity, caused as this had been, might well be compared to the brand fixed by

[1] Compare the interesting parallels of Alfred and of St. Bernard.

[2] When Dr. Lightfoot, who rejects this theory, says that "St. Paul's language implies some more *striking* complaint," he is probably thinking of the milder forms of ophthalmia with which alone we are familiar in England, and not of those virulent attacks which are but too common in Syria, and which make such terrible havoc of the human countenance.

[3] Alford's remark that ophthalmic disorders are not usually painful is singularly mistaken.

a master on his slave. (vii.) Lastly, there is no other reasonable explanation of the circumstance that, when St. Paul had uttered an indignant answer to the High Priest, and had been rebuked for it, he at once frankly offered his apology by saying that "he had not recognised the speaker to have been the High Priest." Now, considering the position of the High Priest as *Nasi* of the Sanhedrin, seated at the end of the hall, with the *Ab Beth Din* on one side of him, and the *Chacham* on the other,[1] it is almost inconceivable that Paul should not have been aware of his rank if he had not suffered from defective sight. All that his blurred vision took in was a white figure, nor did he see this figure with sufficient clearness to be able to distinguish that the overbearing tyrant was no less a person than the High Priest himself.[2]

But if these conjectures are correct—and to me they seem to be almost certain—how immensely do they add to our conception of Paul's heroism; how much do they heighten the astonishment and admiration which we feel at all that he endured and all that he accomplished! This man, who almost single-handed carried the Gospel of Christ from Damascus to Rome, was so great a sufferer from inflammation of the eyes that he was often pitiable to look upon; was unable to write except with pain, and in large letters; was liable to attacks of severe agony, accompanied at times with loss of consciousness. He was so weak and ailing that under circumstances of danger he was personally helpless; that be had to be passively conducted from place to place; that it was almost impossible for him, I will not say only to preach, but even to get through the ordinary routine of life without companions to guide, and protect, and lead him by the hand.[3] We can then see how indispensable it was that St. Paul should have some "that ministered unto him;" how strongly he would feel the necessity of being always accompanied upon his missions by faithful friends;[4] how much anguish might lie in his remark that in his strong affection for the Thessalonians he was even ready for their sakes to part with his beloved Timotheus, and to be left at Athens *alone*.[5] How close, then, and how tender would be the bond of mutual gratitude and affection which would inevitably grow up under such circumstances between himself and the little band of disciples by whom he was usually accompanied! With what deepened bitterness would he feel the cruelty of neglect and ingratitude when, at his first answer, no man stood with him, but all forsook him![6]

EXCURSUS XI. (p. 127).

ON JEWISH SCOURGINGS.

EVEN a single Jewish scourging might well entitle any man to be regarded as a martyr. Thirty-nine blows were inflicted, unless, indeed, it was found that the strength of the patient was too much exhausted to admit of his receiving the full number. Both of his hands were tied to what is sometimes called a column, but which was in reality a stake a

[1] Acts xxiii. 5. It is possible that the presence of Roman officials disturbed this order.

[2] The expression "fixing an earnest gaze" (ἀτενίσας) has often been adduced as yet another sign that St. Paul's eyesight was weak, and therefore that he had acquired the intent stare so common in short-sighted people. This argument is, however, untenable, since the word is a favourite one with St. Luke (Acts xiii. 9; xxiii. 1) and is applied not only to St. Paul, but also to St. Peter, St. Stephen, and even to whole bodies of men (Luke iv. 20; xxii. 56; Acts i. 10; iii. 2—4; vi. 15; vii. 55).

[3] Acts xvii. 14, τὸν Παῦλον ἐξαπέστειλαν οἱ ἀδελφοί; 15, οἱ δὲ καθιστάνοντες (καθιστῶντες, E, G, H), τὸν Παῦλον ἤγαγον ἕως Ἀθηνῶν. These phrases seem more specific than those in Gen. xviii. 16; Rom. xv. 24 (προπεμφθῆναι).

[4] Mr. Lewin (*St. Paul*, i. 189, third edition) was, I believe, the earliest to point out that these passages bear on the question. They are not in themselves conclusive; but when we find the same words used in Acts ix. 30 (to which Mr. Lewin does not refer), when we may well suppose that a fresh attack had followed a fresh revelation, they not improbably point to some such state of things as that which I have inferred.

[5] 1 Thess. iii. 1.

[6] 2 Tim. iv. 16.

cubit and a half high.[1] The public officer then tore down his robe until his breast was laid bare. The executioner stood on a stone behind the criminal. The scourge consisted of two thongs, one of which was composed of four strands of calf-skin, and one of two strands of ass's-skin, which passed through a hole in a handle. The executioner, who was ordinarily the *Chazzan* of the synagogue, could thus shorten or lengthen them at will, so as not to strike too low.[2] The prisoner bent to receive the blows, which were inflicted with one hand, but with all the force of the striker, thirteen on the breast, thirteen on the right, and thirteen on the left shoulder. While the punishment was going on, the chief judge read aloud Deut. xxviii. 58, 59, "If thou wilt not observe to do all the words of this law that are written in this book, that thou mayest fear this glorious and fearful name, the Lord thy God; then the Lord will make thy plagues wonderful, and the plagues of thy seed." He then read Deut. xxix. 9, "Keep therefore the words of this covenant, and do them, that ye may prosper in all ye do;" and lastly, Ps. lxxviii. 38, 39, "But He, being full of compassion, forgave their iniquity, and destroyed them not: yea, many a time turned He His anger away, and did not stir up all His wrath." If the punishment was not over by the time that these three passages were read, they were again repeated, and so timed as to end exactly with the punishment itself. Meanwhile a second judge numbered the blows, and a third before each blow exclaimed "*Hakkehu*" (strike him). All these particulars I take from the Treatise on Punishments (מכות, *Makkôth*) in the Mishna.[3] The severity of the pain may best be estimated by the brief addition: "*If the criminal die under the infliction*, the executioner is not accounted guilty unless he gives by mistake a single blow too many, in which case he is banished."

These facts have an interest far deeper than archæological. They not only show how awful were the trials which St. Paul had to endure, if such as these were hardly counted worthy of narration amongst them, but also they illustrate to a singular degree the minute scrupulosity which reigned through all Jewish observances. If, for instance, only thirty-nine blows were inflicted instead of forty, it was not only, as is usually stated, to avoid the possibility of error in the counting, but also (such at least is the reason assigned by Maimonides[4]) because the Law says, "in number, forty,"[5] not "forty in number;" whence they concluded that they might assign a smaller but not a larger number; and, perhaps, also because the word "thy brother" (אחיך) stands by Gematria for thirty-nine.[6] Another assigned reason is that the passage of the Psalm (lxxviii. 38, 39) which was recited on the occasion ends at verse 39. The scourge was made partly of ox-hide, partly of ass's-hide, for the astounding reasons that immediately after the passage in Deuteronomy which orders the infliction of scourging follows the verse, "Thou shalt not muzzle the ox when he treadeth out the corn;"[7] and that in Isa. i. 3 we find, "The ox knoweth his owner, and the ass his master's crib; but Israel doth not know, my people doth not consider." And thus it was thought right that those who do know should punish him who does not know![8] The criminal was to receive only thirteen blows on his breast, but twenty-six on his shoulders, because it was inferred from Deut. xxv. 2 that it was only on the back that he was to be beaten,[9] "according to his fault," so that the back

[1] Marble "columns," traditionally assigned to this purpose, are shown among the relics of Roman Catholic churches; *e.g.*, the column of the flagellation in the Church of the Holy Sepulchre; that of the scourging of St. Paul in *S. Paolo fuori de' Muri* at Rome, &c.

[2] This was not strictly in accordance with Deut. xxv. 2; but it is strange to see how traditional laxity was mingled by the Jews with unintelligent literalism.

[3] See Surenhusius, *Mishna*, vol. iv., p. 286, seqq.

[4] Maimon. *Sanhedr.* 17.

[5] במספר ארבעים.

[6] *Gematria* (Geometria) was one of the Kabbalistic methods of drawing interpretations from the numerical value of letters. I have given many instances in *Rabbinic Exegesis* (*Expositor*, May, 1877). Thus because both *Mashiach* and *nachash*, "serpent," numerically represent 358, they inferred that it was the Messiah who would bruise the serpent's head, &c.

[7] Deut. xxv. 4.

[8] So Maimonides and R. Ob. de Bartenora, *ap.* Surenhus. *l. c.*

[9] Buxtorf, *Synag.*, p. 523. See also *Praef. Libr. de Abbreviaturis.* This was one of the numerous instances in which the Jews were more legal than the Law itself. Similarly they extended the Sabbath into a Little Sabbath, an hour before and an hour after the true Sabbath. They were for-

received a double number of blows. The duty of reading aloud while the scourging continued was also a minute inference from the words of Scripture.[1]

A person was liable to this penalty if he wilfully violated any of the negative precepts of the Law, and inadvertently any of those which, if deliberately transgressed, involved the threat of excision from among the people,[2] or "death by the visitation of God."[3] Under which of the numerous offences for which this punishment was assigned Paul five times suffered, is by no means easy to say. Looking through them all as enumerated in the treatise *Makkôth*,[4] and as expanded by Maimonides,[5] I cannot find any of which the Apostle could possibly have been guilty. Where, however, the will to punish him existed, the pretext would not long be wanting. His flagellation must have been that minor but still terrible punishment which was called "the legal scourging" or the "scourging of forty,"[6] because the yet deadlier flagellation with rods, which was called the Rabbinic, or the flagellation of contumacy,[7] was never inflicted within the limits of the Holy Land, and is expressly stated to have been a beating to death.

When once an offender had been scourged this punishment was considered to remove the danger of "cutting off,"[8] and not only so, but it was regarded as leaving no ignominy behind it. The humane expression of Moses that forty stripes were not to be exceeded "lest thy brother seem vile unto thee," was interpreted to mean that when the punishment was over the sufferer was "restored to his integrity." So completely was this the case that even the High Priest himself might be thus scourged, and afterwards be "restored to his majesty." But although it was assumed that he would suffer no ulterior injury, but rather be sure to win an inheritance in the future, yet, of course, if he again offended he was again scourged.[9] It was even possible that for one offence, if it involved the disobedience to several negative precepts, he might incur several consecutive scourgings, care being only taken that he had sufficiently recovered from the first before the next was inflicted. It is, therefore, by no means impossible, or even improbable, that during those "many days" which Paul spent in Damascus in trying to convince these passionate disputants, he may have incurred this torture several times.

To have refused to undergo it by sheltering himself under the privilege of his Roman citizenship would have been to incur excommunication, and finally to have cut himself off from admission into the synagogues.

EXCURSUS XII. (p. 141).

Apotheosis of Roman Emperors.

The early Emperors rather discouraged than stimulated this tendency to flatter them by a premature apotheosis. If temples had been built to them in their lifetime, they had always been to their "genius," or had at least been associated—as at Athens—with the divinity of Rome.[10] Augustus, with these restrictions, had yielded to the earnest

bidden to have leaven in their houses during the Passover, and they abstained from even using the word. Being forbidden swine's flesh, they avoid the word pig altogether, and call the pig דָּבָר אַחֵר, *dabhar acheer*, "the other thing," &c. (Godwyn, *Moses and Aaron*, viii. 12.) These are specimens of the "*hedge* of the Law."

[1] Deut. xxv. 4, בקרת תהיה, "hinc colligimus plagas infigi debere inter legendum" (R. Ob. de Bartenora, *ap.* Surenhus. *Mishna*, iv. 290).

[2] כרת.

[3] מיתה בידי שמים.

[4] III., 1, 2, 3, 4.

[5] *Hilkoth Sanhedr.* xviii., xix.

[6] *Malkooth*, דאורייתא, or ארבעים.

[7] מרדות. See Carpzov. *App. Crit.*, p. 589. The Greek τυμπανισμός.

[8] 2 Macc. iii. 35.

[9] They quoted Lev. xviii. 29; 2 Macc. iii. 15.

[10] Dion Cass. li. 20; Suet. *Aug.* 52. Though he knew that even Proconsuls had in the provinces been honoured with temples, yet in "nullâ provinciâ, *nisi communi suo Romaeque nomine* recepit." See the excellent chapter on "L'Apothéose Impériale," in Boissier, *La Religion Romaine*, i. 123—205.

entreaties of the people of Pergamos and Nicomedia, but had expressly forbidden the Romans to take any part in this new cult. The base example spread rapidly in the provinces, and though it is probable that in secret Augustus was not displeased at so astonishing a proof of his own power, he affected to smile at it as a man of the world.[1] In the frenzy of flattery, which is the disease of despotisms, it was but too likely that this deification of a living man would creep from the provinces into Italy, and, in spite of the assertion of Dion Cassius, that in Italy no one ventured to worship Augustus, it is certain from the *Corpus Inscriptionum* that at his death there had sprung up, either by his permission or without his interference, priests of Augustus at Pompeii, flamens at Præneste, an Augusteum at Pisa, and a Cæsareum at Puteoli; and this—though it was due far more to the religious degradation of the age than to the phrenetic pride of the autocrat—was made a source of bitter blame against him when he was dead. Even at Rome,[2] though no temple rose to him till he was dead, yet we need go no further than the poetry of Virgil, Horace, and Ovid,[3] to show that he was commonly addressed as a deity (*numen*) and a god, and that sacrifices were offered either to him or in his name; and, as appears from inscriptions, even at Rome, if they did not worship him directly, they did so indirectly, by rearing altars to his virtues and his laws, and by inserting his name among those of ancient deities in the songs of the Arval brothers. After his death the worship was extended without limit. He was known universally as the Divine Augustus, a phrase which became as common as *feu le roi*.[4]

Tiberius, for political reasons, patronised, and even to a certain extent enforced, this new worship, but he also discouraged the extravagance which endeavoured to extend divine honours to his *living self*, and by doing so he at once gratified his undisguised cynicism and showed his strong good sense. But the tendency to apotheosis was in his time firmly established. He was, as a matter of course, deified after his death, and his panegyrist, Velleius Paterculus, tells us a story that when he was in the midst of a campaign among the Chauci, a barbarian chief obtained permission to see him, and after crossing the river in order to do so, gazed at him for a long time in silence, and exclaiming that he had now seen the gods,[5] asked to touch his hand, and then pushed off his boat towards the opposite shore, gazing to the last on the living deity. So rapidly did the disease of adulation grow that, according to Suetonius, Domitian actually used to begin his letters with the words "Dominus et Deus noster sic fieri jubet"—"Thus orders our Lord and God, Domitian!"[6]

EXCURSUS XIII. (p. 165).

BURDENS LAID ON PROSELYTES.

WE are told in the Talmud that if a Gentile wished to become a proselyte he was asked his reasons for the wish, and informed that Israel is now afflicted, persecuted, and cast down with all kinds of sufferings. If he replies that he knows it, and is not worthy to share in their sufferings, he is admitted, but is told enough of the "light" and the

[1] Quintil. *Instt. Orat.* vi. 3, 77.

[2] Tac. *Ann.* i. 10, "Nihil deorum honoribus relictum, cum se templis et effigie numinum per flamines et sacerdotes coli vellet;" Aurel. Vict. *de Cæsar.* 1, "Huicque, uti Deo, Romae provinciisque omnibus, per urbes celeberrimas vivo mortuoque templa sacerdotes et collegia sacravere." This seems, however, to be a positive mistake, though Pliny, *Nat. Hist.* xii. 19, mentions a temple which Livia erected to him after his death (Divo) on the Palatine. Suetonius, a very high authority on such a subject, says that he most obstinately refused this honour at Rome when it was pressed upon him (*Aug.* 52, "In urbe quidem pertinacissime abstinuit hoc honore").

[3] See Bentley's note on Hor. *Epp.* II. i. 16; Virg. *Ecl.* i. 7; *Georg.* i. 42; Hor. *Od.* i. 2, 41; iii. 5, 1; iv. 5, 16; Ov. *Trist.* ii. 8, 9; iv. 9, 111. (Boissier, i. 153.)

[4] Tac. *Ann.* i, 73, "Caelum decretum."

[5] Vell. Paterc. ii. 107, "Quos ante audiebam hodie vidi deos."

[6] Suet. *Domit.* 13.

"heavy" precepts to warn him to desist in time if he is not sincere, since, as Rabh Chelbo said, "proselytes are as injurious to Israel as a scab." He is told about the rules respecting gleaning, and tithes, and the penalties attached to any transgression of the Law, and is informed that henceforth if he desecrates the Sabbath he is liable to death by stoning. If he submits he is circumcised, and even circumcised a second time, if there were any neglect or carelessness in the first performance of the rite. After his recovery he is immersed without delay by way of baptism, and two "disciples of the wise" stand by him, repeating some of the "light" and "heavy" precepts.[1] In fact, a Gentile could only become a proselyte by submitting himself to the whole yoke of Rabbinism, the tyranny of archaic, puerile, and wearisome *halachôth* which year by year was laid more heavily on Jewish shoulders by the pedantry of their theologic schools. It was the fault of the Jews that the Gentiles usually concentrated their attention on mere transient Jewish *rites*, and not on the eternal *principles* which God had revealed to them. Can we be surprised at this when we find R. Eleasar Ben Chasmah saying that the rules about birds' nests (*kinim*), and the "uncleanliness" of women (*niddah*) are *essentials* of the Law?[2]

EXCURSUS XIV. (p. 186).

Hatred of the Jews in Classical Antiquity.

It is at once curious and painful to perceive how strange was the mixture of curiosity, disgust, and contempt, with which the Jews were regarded in pagan antiquity. From Manetho the Egyptian priest, with whom seems to have originated the calumny that they were a nation of lepers,[3] down to Annæus Florus, who brands them as an impious race,[4] the references to them in secular literature are a tissue of absurd calumnies or biting sarcasms. Chæremon alludes to them as unclean and polluted;[5] Lysimachus, as diseased and unsocial;[6] Diodorus Siculus, as addicted to strange rites, and hostile to strangers;[7] Apollonius Molon, a Greek rhetorician of the time of Cicero, as "godless and misanthropical;"[8] Cicero heaps scorn and indignation upon them in his Oration for the extortionate and tyrannous Flaccus,[9] and in that on the consular provinces calls them "a race born for slavery;"[10] Horace sneers at their proselytism, and their circumcision, and their Sabbaths;[11] Seneca calls them "a most abandoned race;"[12] Martial, besides odious allusions to their national rite, pours his contempt on their poverty, their mendicancy, their religion, and their low trade of selling sulphur matches and buying broken glass, and he seems to be the first to originate the slander repeated by Sir Thomas Browne in his "Popular Errors;"[13] Quintilian, gentle as he was, yet admits a very bitter remark against the Jews and Moses;[14] Lucan alludes to their "uncertain Deity;"[15] Petronius Arbiter seems to think, as did many of the ancients, that the Jews did not abhor, but actually worshipped the pig;[16] Tacitus, in his History,

[1] *Yebhamôth*, f. 47, 1.

[2] *Pirke Abhôth*, iii. 28. In partial defence of the Jews it may be said that some were inclined to become proselytes to avoid military service (Tac. *Ann.* ii. 35; Suet. *Tib.* 36; Jos. *Antt.* xviii. 3, § 5), others were *Shechemite* proselytes—*i.e.*, to marry rich Jewesses (*id.* xvi. 7, § 5; xx. 7, §§ 2, 3), others were "*lion*-proselytes"—*i.e.*, out of fear (2 Kings xvii. 26; Jos. *B. J.* ii. 17, § 10). Herzog, *Real-Enc.*, s. v.

[3] *Ap.* Jos. *c. Ap.* i. 26.

[4] Speaking of Pompey, Florus says, "Et vidit illud grande impiae gentis arcanum."

[5] Jos. *c. Ap.* i. 32.

[6] *Id.* i. 34.

[7] Diod. Sic. xl.

[8] Jos. *c. Ap.* ii. 14.

[9] Cic. *pro Flacco*, xxviii.

[10] *De Prov. Cons.* v.

[11] Hor. *Sat.* i. iv. 143; v. 100; ix. 69.

[12] *Ap.* Aug. *De Civ. Dei*, vii. 36, "Usque eo sceleratissimae gentis consuetudo convaluit [the Sabbath] ut," &c.

[13] Mart. *Ep.* i. 42; xii. 30, 85, 57; iv. 4; vii. 82; xi. 94, i. 4. Cf. Stat. *Silv.* i. 6. The relation of the Herods to the Cæsars had attracted a large share of attention to the Jews in the Imperial epoch. Pers. v. 179—184; Juv. vi. 157.

[14] *De Instt. Orat.* iii. 7.

[15] *Pharsal.* ii. 593, "incerti Judaea Dei."

[16] *Satiric.* Büchler, p. 221, "Judaeus licet et *porcinum* numen, adoret," &c. (Cf. Plut. *Symp.* iv. 5.)

reproaches them with gross sensuality, low cunning, and strong hatred of all nations but their own, and gives at full length, and with all gravity, the preposterous story about their veneration for the ass.[1] In his Annals he speaks with equal horror and equal ignorance of Jews and Christians, and considers that if the thousands of Jews who were deported to Sardinia died it would be a cheap loss;[2] Juvenal flings scornful allusion at their squalor, beggary, turbulence, superstition, cheatery, and idleness;[3] Celsus abused them as jugglers and vagabonds;[4] Ammianus Marcellinus as "disgusting and noisy;"[5] Rutilius Numatianus closes the long line of angry slanderers by a burst of abuse, in which he characterises Judæa as a "lying slave-cage."[6] Jeremiah had bidden the Jews to seek the peace of, and to pray for, the city of their captivity, "for in the peace thereof shall ye have peace."[7] Better had it been for the ancient Jews if they had lived in the spirit of that large advice. But the Gentiles were well aware that in the Jewish synagogues there was an exception to the dead uniformity of the Romish Empire, and that they and their customs were there treated with open and bitter scorn, which they repaid tenfold.[8]

EXCURSUS XV. (p. 186).

JUDGMENTS OF EARLY PAGAN WRITERS ON CHRISTIANITY.

SUETONIUS (died circ. A.D. 110).

"Judaeos impulsore Chresto assidue tumultuantes Româ expulit" (*Claud.* 25).[9]

"Afflicti suppliciis Christiani genus hominum superstitionis novae et maleficae" (*Nero*, 16).

"Percrebuerat Oriente toto vetus et constans opinio, esse in fatis, ut eo tempore Judaea profecti rerum potirentur" (*Vesp.* 4).

TACITUS (Consul suffectus, A.D. 97).

"Ergo abolendo rumori Nero subdidit reos, et quaesitissimis poenis affecit, quos per flagitia invisos vulgus Christianos appellabat. Auctor ejus nominis Christus Tiberio imperitante per procuratorem Pont. Pilatum supplicio affectus est; repressaque in praesens exitiabilis superstitio rursum erumpebat non modo per Judaeam originem ejus mali, sed per urbem etiam quo cuncta undique atrocia aut pudenda confluunt celebranturque. Igitur primum correpti qui fatebantur, deinde indicio eorum multitudo ingens, haud perinde in crimine incendii quam odio generis humani convicti sunt. Et pereuntibus addita ludibria, ut ferarum tergis contecti laniatu canum interirent, aut crucibus affixi aut flammandi, atque ubi defecisset dies, in usum nocturni luminis urerentur . . . unde quamquam adversus sontes et novissima exempla meritos miseratio oriebatur tamquam non utilitate publicâ sed in saevitiam unius absumerentur" (*Ann.* xv. 44).

Gentiles in the Letter of the Churches of Vienne and Lyons complain, *ξένην τινα καὶ καινὴν ἡμῖν εἰσάγουσι θρησκείαν* (*ap.* Euseb. *H. E.* v. 1).

[1] Tac. *Hist.* v. 2—5; Diod. Sic. i. 28; Plut. *Synop.* iv. 5. On this story see Geiger, *Juden und Judenthum*, *Illustr. Monatsch. d. Judenth.*, Oct., 1865.

[2] *Ann.* xv. 44; ii. 85, "si ob gravitatem caeli interissent, vile damnum." (Cf. Suet. *Tib.* 36; Jos. *Antt.* xviii. 3, § 5; Philo, *Leg.* 24.)

[3] *Sat.* vi. 542—547, 156—160; xiv. 96—107. See, for other allusions, *id.* iii. 13, 296.

[4] *Ap.* Orig. *c. Cels.* i. 33, *γοήτων*.

[5] Ammian. Marc. xxii. 5, "fetentes Judaei." (See "Gentiles" in Kitto.)

[6] *Itinerar.* i. 3, 89. In the above quotations and references I have made free use (with certain additions) of Dr. Gill's *Notices of the Jews by Classic Authors* (see also Meier's *Judaica*, and the article of Geiger, above quoted).

[7] Jer. xxix. 7.

[8] Ps. Heraclit. *Ep.* vii.; Hausrath, *N. T. Gesch.* ii. 79. Specimens of this scorn may be seen in Jos. *c. Ap.* ii. 34, 35.

[9] According to Sulpic. Severus (*Hist. Sacr.* ii. 30), Titus decided that the Temple should be destroyed that Christianity and Judaism might be eradicated together. "Quippe has religiones, licet contrarias sibi, iisdem tamen auctoribus profectas; Christianos ex Judaeis exstitisse; radice sublatâ, stirpem facile perituram." This is believed by Bernays to be a quotation from Tacitus.

PLINY THE YOUNGER (died circ. A.D. 117).

His famous letter to Trajan is too long for insertion. He asks whether he is to punish persons for simply being Christians, or for crimes involved in the charge of being so (*nomen ipsum, si flagitiis careat, an flagitia cohaerentia nomini*). He says that he has punished those who, after threat of punishment, still declared themselves Christians, because he considers that in any case their "inflexible obstinacy" should be punished. Others equally infatuated (*similis amentiae*) he determined to send to Rome, being Roman citizens. Having received an anonymous accusation which inculpated many, he tested them, if they denied the charge of being Christians, by making them call on the gods, and offer incense and wine to the Emperor's image, and curse Christ. If they did this he dismissed them, because he was told that no true Christian would ever do it. Some said that they had long abjured Christianity, but declared that the head and front of their "fault" or "error" had simply been the custom of meeting before dawn, and singing antiphons to Christ as a God, and binding themselves with an oath [1] not to steal, rob, commit adultery, break their word, or deny the trust committed to them; after which they separated, meeting again for a harmless meal—a custom which they had dropped after Pliny's edict forbidding guilds. Scarcely crediting this strange account of their innocent life, he had put two deaconesses (ex duabus ancillis quae *ministrae* dicebantur) to the torture, but discovered nothing beyond perverted and immoderate superstition (*pravam, immodicam*). He therefore consults Trajan, because of the multitude of the accused, who were of every age, rank, and sex, both in the city and in the country. So widely had "the contagion of that wretched superstition" spread that the temples were almost deserted, and there was scarcely any one to buy the victims (*Ep.* x. 97).

To this letter Trajan briefly replies that the Christians are to be punished if convicted, but not to be sought out; to be pardoned if they sacrifice, and not to be tried on anonymous accusations.

EPICTETUS (died A.D. 117).

"Then through madness it is possible for a man to be so disposed towards these things" (*i.e.*, to be indifferent to the world), "and the Galilæans through habit" (*Dissert.* iv. 7).

M. AURELIUS ANTONINUS (died A.D. 180).

Speaking of readiness to die, he says that it is noble, "so that it comes from a man's own judgment, not from mere obstinacy (διὰ ψιλὴν παράταξιν), as with the Christians, but considerately, and with dignity" (*Eucheir.* xi. 3).

LUCIAN (died circ. A.D. 200).

His sneers and parodies of what he calls the θαυμαστὴ σοφία of the Christians are to be found in the *Ver. Historia*, I. 12, 30; II. 4, 11—12 (*Alexand.* (Pseudomantis) xxv. 38). The *Philopatris* is not by Lucian, but a hundred years later.

GALEN, the great writer on Physic (died A.D. 200).

In his book, *De different. pulsuum*, he alludes twice to the obstinacy of Christians.

EXCURSUS XVI. (p. 197).

THE PROCONSULATE OF SERGIUS PAULUS.

THE title of "Proconsul" [2] given to this insular governor is one of those minute touches of accuracy which occur on every page of the Acts of the Apostles.

It might have been a serious difficulty that the name of Sergius Paulus does not occur in the *Fasti* of the Consuls till long after this period,[3] but the difficulty vanishes when

[1] Interesting as the earliest Christian application of the word "Sacrament" (Waterland, *On the Eucharist*, i.).

[2] E. V. "Deputy."

[3] Serg. Paulus, consul suffectus, A.D. 21, and another, Consul, A.D. 168.

we find that the title of Proconsul was given to the Governor of a senatorial province, whatever may have been his previous rank.[1] But another and more serious difficulty was once urged. There were two kinds of provinces, the imperial and the senatorial, both of which were called Eparchies (ἐπαρχίαι). The imperial were those to which the governors were sent by the Emperor, because their circumstances involved the necessity of military command. Augustus, under pretence of relieving the Senate from the burden of the more disturbed provinces, had astutely reserved for his personal administration those regions of the empire where the presence of an army was required. As the title Praetor (in Greek, Στρατηγὸς, or general) still retained some shadow of its old military significance, the Governors of these provinces were called Propraetors, or Ἀντιστράτηγοι, for which, in the New Testament, the more general term Ἡγεμὼν is often used. This Greek word for "Governor" serves as an equivalent both for "Procurator" and also for *Praeses* or *Legatus*, which was, for instance, the ordinary designation of the Governor of Syria. These *Praesides*, *Legati*, or *Propraetors* held their commands at the Emperor's pleasure, and, especially in the reign of Tiberius, were often left for years undisturbed in their tenure of office. The Proconsuls, or Ἀνθύπατοι, on the other hand, who were appointed by the Senate, only held their posts for a single year. Now it appears from Strabo that when, in B.C. 27, Augustus divided the provinces between himself and the Senate, Cyprus was reserved as one of the imperial districts (στρατηγικὴ ἐπαρχία), and with this Dion Cassius agrees.[2] Consequently even eminent writers like Grotius thought that St. Luke had here fallen into an error; and Baronius supposes that Cyprus must at this time have been an honorary adjunct to the Proconsulship of Cilicia, while Grotius suggests that Greek flattery might have often given to a Propraetor the more distinguished title of Proconsul, and that St. Luke might have used it in accordance with the common parlance. But a little more research has resulted in the discovery that though Cyprus originally was an imperial province, and ultimately reverted to the same condition, yet Augustus restored both it and Gallia Narbonensis to the Senate in exchange for Dalmatia, because he found that they did not need the presence of many soldiers.[3] And to set the matter finally at rest, copper coins and inscriptions of this very epoch have been found at Curium and Citium in which the title of Proconsul is given to Cominius Proclus, Julius Cordus, and L. Annus Bassus, who must have been immediate predecessors or successors of Sergius Paulus.[4]

The name Sergius Paulus is itself interesting. Of this particular Proconsul, indeed, we know nothing beyond the eulogy of the sacred historian that he was a man of sense,[5] and that he was deeply impressed by the teaching of St. Paul. But Pliny the Elder, in his Natural History, three times refers to a Sergius Paulus as a person interested in intelligent researches; and it is not impossible that this Sergius Paulus may be none other than our Cyprian Proconsul.[6] If so, the character given him in one passing word by St. Luke will be confirmed, and we feel additional pleasure in tracing similar characteristics in others of the same name who may well have been his descendants; for instance, in the Sergius Paulus who, more than a hundred years afterwards, receives the encomium of the physician Galen for his eminence both as a theoretic and a practical philosopher.[7]

[1] Dion Cass. liii. 13, καὶ ἀνθυπάτους καλεῖσθαι μὴ ὅτι τοὺς δύο τοὺς ὑπατευκότας (ex-Consuls) ἀλλὰ καὶ τοὺς ἄλλους τῶν ἐστρατηγηκότων (ex-Praetors), κ. τ. λ.

[2] Dion Cass. liii. 12; Strabo, xiv. 685; Suet. *Aug.* 47.

[3] Dion Cass. liii. 13, τὴν Κύπρον . . . τῷ δήμῳ ἀπέδωκεν: liv. 4, καὶ οὕτω ἀνθύπατοι καὶ ἐς ἐκεῖνα τα ἔθνη πέμπεσθαι ἤρξαντο.

[4] Eckhel, iii. 84; Akerman, *Numism. Illustr.*, pp. 39, 42; Boeckh, *Corp. Inscr.* 2631, 2632.

[5] Acts xiii. 7, ἀνδρὶ συνετῷ. The name of a Proconsul Paulus has been found on an inscription at Soli (Cesnola, *Cyprus*, p. 425).

[6] Plin. *H. N.* i. Pliny is writing only twenty years after this period.

[7] Renan, *St. Paul*, p. 15, who refers to Orelli, 2414, 4938. Galen, *De Anatom.* 1 (*apud* Wetstein), ἀνδρὸς τὰ πάντα πρωτεύοντος ἔργοις τε καὶ λόγοις τοῖς ἐν φιλοσοφίᾳ.

EXCURSUS XVII. (p. 249).

St. John and St. Paul.

Of the three "seeming pillars," John appears to have taken no part in the synod at Jerusalem, or if he did it was not sufficiently decisive to be recorded. He belonged, it is clear, at this time to the Church of the Circumcision, and, so far as we know, this was the only occasion on which he was thrown into the society of St. Paul. But we have St. Paul's express testimony—in the only passage in which he is mentioned in the Epistles—that he recognised his apostolate; and the Apocalypse, his earliest writing, so far from showing that irreconcilable hatred to the doctrines of St. Paul which has been assumed on grounds inconceivably frivolous, and repeated subsequently with extraordinary recklessness, offers a close parallelism to St. Paul's Epistles in thoughts and principles, which is all the more striking from the marked differences of tone and expression. We are calmly assured, without even the condescension of an attempted proof, that the "false Jew," the "false Apostle," the "false prophet," the "Balaam," the "Jezebel," the "Nicolas," the "chief of the synagogue of Satan," alluded to in the Apocalypse,[1] are as indubitably intended for St. Paul as are the savage allusions covertly made to him under the name of Simon the Magician in the Pseudo-Clementines. Now, on what basis is this conclusion founded? Simply on the resemblance in tone of a spurious Ebionite romance (the Clementines) to the phrases, "those which say they are Apostles and are not," "those which say they are Jews and are not," and the allusions to some who held the doctrine of Balaam, and of "that woman Jezebel," who taught people "to commit fornication, and to eat things sacrificed unto idols." It is true that there were Judaisers who attacked St. Paul's claim to be an Apostle; but to assert that St. John was one of them is to give the direct lie to St. Paul, while to class St. Paul with them "that say they are Jews and are not" is to falsify the most notorious facts concerning one who was a Pharisee of Pharisees, and a Hebrew of the Hebrews. Again, to assert boldly that St. Paul ever taught people to eat things offered to idols, or anything which could be so described without the grossest calumny, is a distinct contradiction of his own words, since he expressly warned his converts *not* to do this, and assigns for his warning the very reason that to do so would be "to cast a stumbling-block before the children of Israel."[2] In fact, though St. Paul would have denied that to eat them was *wrong in itself*, his concessions on this point went very little beyond those which are sanctioned in the Talmud itself.[3] Once more, what conceivable excuse could there be for saying that St. Paul ever taught men "to commit fornication"?—a sin against which, whether literally or metaphorically understood, he has urged considerations more deeply seated, more likely to touch the heart, more likely to bind the conscience, than all the other writers in the New Testament put together. That even in earliest days there did spring up antinomian sects which were guilty of such accursed teaching, we know from Church history, and find traces even in the sacred writers; and it is therefore probable that the allusions of the Apocalypse are as literal as the Old Testament analogies to which St. John no less than St. Paul refers.[4] That "the fornication" of the Apocalypse means "mixed marriages" there is not even a shadow of reason to believe, nor if it did would there be

[1] Rev. ii. 2, 6, 9, 14, 15, 20, 34; iii. 9. (See Renan, *St. P.*, 302—305, who quietly asserts this as if it were indisputable.) Yet St. Paul himself was the first to use this very comparison with Balaam (1 Cor. x. 7, 8), and to denounce the extreme wickedness of putting a stumbling-block before others (Rom. xiv. 21; 2 Cor. xi. 29).

[2] 1 Cor. viii. 13 (cf. x. 32).

[3] *Ketubhôth.* f. 15. 1. which, almost in the very language of St. Paul, lays down the rule that if a man has bought meat, and is doubtful whether it is legally clean, he must not eat it; but if he lights upon it accidentally, he may eat it without further inquiry. Meat declared to be legally clean (*tâhor*) is stamped with a leaden seal, on which is the word *kashar* ("lawful," *καθαρὸν*). (I. D'Israeli, *Genius of Judaism*, p. 154.)

[4] 1 Cor. x. 7, 8. (See some excellent remarks in Lightfoot's *Gal.*, pp. 290, 335.)

any ground for saying that St. Paul encouraged them. Though he used, on that as on all such topics, the language of wisdom and of charity, the whole tendency of his teaching is to discourage them.[1] Moreover, if Paul had been aimed at, and if St. John, the Apostle of Love, really had been the slanderous and rabid Judaiser which these allusions would then imply, it is inconceivable that no word should be said about the points respecting which, to a Judaiser, he must have seemed infinitely more assailable—namely, St. Paul's very low estimate of circumcision, and his declared conviction that by the works of the Law no man can be justified in God's sight. Now, in the Apocalypse neither circumcision, nor the Law, nor Moses, nor oral tradition are scarcely so much as mentioned or alluded to, while redemption by the blood of the Lamb, and the universality of that redemption as extending to "every kindred and tongue and people and nation,"[3] are asserted as absolutely and unconditionally as they could have been by Paul himself. Further, it needs but a casual study of St. John and St. Paul to see that "Jesus Christ" is in both of them the divine secret and the fundamental conception of all Christianity. St. John at this time was the more contemplative, the less prominently active, St. John of the Gospels. "The hidden fires of his nature" had not yet "burst out into a flame." Two incidents preserved for us in the Gospels had indeed shown that those fires were there;[4] but it was not till James the Lord's brother, and Peter, and Paul himself had passed away that he became the bold and uncompromising leader whose counsels were as oracles to the Asian Church. Nevertheless, we may be sure that St. John was *not* found among the opponents of St. Paul. That opposition is always connected with the adherents and the influence of James. During the lifetime of Jesus James had not fully accepted His mission, and seems only to have been converted by the Resurrection. He had not therefore lived, as the other Apostles had lived, in daily contact with the mind and influence of Jesus, and was in consequence more deeply imbued with the beliefs of his early Jewish training, and less entirely permeated in intellect by the breath of the new life. But Peter and John, more than any living men, must have known what was the mind of Christ. We know that they were one in heart, and we may be sure that they who had gone together to visit and confirm the detested Samaritans and witness their participation in the gifts of the Holy Ghost, would be little likely to look with rabid jealousy on the equal freedom of a yet wider extension of the Kingdom of God.

EXCURSUS XVIII. (p. 254).

The Attacks on St. Paul in the Clementines.

That Paul, in consequence of the death-blow which he gave to Jewish Pharisaism, was pursued by a particular section of the Judæo-Christian Church with unrelenting opposition, is a matter of history. It needs no further proof than the large sections in his Epistles which are occupied with arguments against Pharisaic or Gnostic Judaism, such as had invaded the Churches of Corinth, Galatia, Colossæ, and Crete. But true though it is that he was obliged to contend in lifelong struggle with a *party*, it is not true that he remained long unrecognised by the Church at large. The supposition that he was, has merely originated from the exceptional literary activity of a single section of Christian Ebionites. Dr. Lightfoot, in his essay on "St. Paul and the Three," has shown, by patient and entirely candid investigation, that even the Church of Judæa was not exclusively anti-Pauline, and that the anti-Pauline faction within it, so far from representing the tendencies of the whole Christian Church, did not even represent the Christians of Palestine. The Christian Jews of the Holy Land naturally continued, as a

[1] See especially 2 Cor. vi. 14.
[2] Which will be explained by Rev. xv. 3.
[3] Rev. v. 9; vii. 9.
[4] Luke ix. 54; Matt. xx. 21.

body, to observe the Mosaic Law—as was done by St. Paul himself so far as he could do so without compromising the emancipation of the Gentiles—until the fall of Jerusalem rendered all such observance a mere mockery and sham.[1] If the Passover, the very central ordinance of Mosaism, was rendered simply impossible, God had Himself demonstrated that the *aeon* of the Law was closed. The withdrawal of the Church to Pella, caused by a recollection of the warnings of Jesus, would look to the Jews like an unpatriotic desertion of their cause; and the frantic denunciations of the *Mins*, which date from this epoch, were but signs of the gathering detestation of Jew for Christian which culminated in the savage massacres by Bar-cochba of those Christians who refused to apostatise and blaspheme. When the name of Jerusalem had given way to that of Ælia Capitolina, and Christians were allowed to live where no Jew might set his foot, the Church of the new city became predominantly Gentile, and was for the first time governed by a Gentile bishop.[2] It is not till after this period that we hear of two sects, distinct from each other, but often confused. These were the Nazarenes and the Ebionites. The NAZARENES were not in any way hostile to the work and memory of Paul, and they differed from other Christians only in holding that the Law was still binding on Jewish converts. "The Testaments of the Twelve Patriarchs"—a book which, whether written by a Nazarene or not, expresses their general tenets so far as we can gather them—not only does not oppose the doctrines of St. Paul, but, though written from the Judæo-Christian standpoint, puts into the mouth of Benjamin a splendid eulogy of Paul, as one who is to arise from that tribe "beloved of the Lord, listening to His voice, enlightening all the Gentiles with new knowledge." The EBIONITES, on the other hand—a powerful and zealous sect—breathed the exact spirit of Paul's Judaising enemies, and the views of many of them became deeply tinged with the Gnostic tendencies of the more advanced Essenes. To this section of the Ebionites we owe the forgeries known as the Clementine Homilies, the Clementine Recognitions, extant in a Latin paraphrase of Rufinus,[3] and a spurious letter of Peter to James. In the Homilies St. Paul is surreptitiously attacked in the guise of Simon Magus.[4] The allusion to his reproof of St. Peter at Antioch is too plain to be overlooked, and discredit is thrown on his doctrine, his revelations, and his independent attitude towards James. In the letter of St. Peter he is still more severely, though still covertly slandered, as "the enemy" whose teaching was antinomian and absurd, and who calumniously asserted that St. Peter held one view and sanctioned another. In the Recognitions these attacks do not appear, but "the enemy" sent by Caiaphas to arrest St. Peter at Antioch, and who throws St. James down the Temple steps, is evidently meant for St. Paul, and this notable story is believed to have been borrowed from a prating fiction called the "Ascents of James," which is also the source of the venomous calumny that Paul was a Gentile who had accepted circumcision in hopes of marrying the High Priest's daughter, and had only apostatised from Mosaism when his hopes were disappointed.[5]

It is on trash of this kind, at once feeble and virulent, at once baseless and malignant, that some have based the belief that there was deadly opposition between Paul and the Twelve, and that his work was not fully recognised till the close of the second century. The fact, however, is that these Ebionite slanders and forgeries are representative of none but an isolated sect. Justin lived in Samaria in the earlier half of the second century, and shows no trace of these views. Hegesippus was a Jewish Christian who travelled to Rome in the middle of the second century, visiting many Christian Churches; and

[1] Grätz, *Gesch. d. Juden*, iv. 112. [2] Marcus, B.C. 132. Just. Mart. *Apol.* i. 31, p. 72.
[3] And partly in Syriac.
[4] The English reader may see these passages translated in Baur's *First Three Centuries*, i. pp. 89—98.
[5] Epiphan. *Haeres.* xxx. 16. Renan also refers to Massechta *Gérim*, 1, ed. Kirchheim.

Eusebius, who knew his writings, vouches for his perfect orthodoxy.[1] Such being the case, it is hardly even necessary to prove that the other churches of the second century were in no sense anti-Pauline. It may be true that for a short time there were two sections—a Jewish and a Gentile—in the Church of Rome, and even that each section had its own bishop, the possible successors respectively of the Apostles of the circumcision and of the uncircumcision.[2] But if so, these two sections were, at the close of the first century, united under the gentle and orthodox Clement; and even on the doubtful hypothesis that the Clementines had a Roman origin, their indirectness—the cautious, subterranean, timid sort of way in which they attack the great Apostle—is alone a decisive proof that the forger *could by no means rely on the general sympathy of the readers into whose hands his writings fell.* And yet on this very attenuated apex is built the huge inverted pyramid of inference, which finally declares the Epistle of St. Jude to be a specimen of one of the letters, breathing sanguinary hatred and atrocious falsehood, which are supposed to have been despatched from Jerusalem in the name of the Apostles, and in the composition of which, "since James and Jude probably could not speak Greek," they probably employed Greek secretaries![3] Let any one read the Epistle of St. Jude, and consider, verse by verse, how it could be possibly applied to St. Paul, and how absolutely such a theory contradicts every really authentic fact of his relation to the Apostles, as well as the character and bearing of the Apostles themselves, and he will be able to estimate the validity of the criticism which calmly represents as reasonable history this darkening fume of inferences from the narrow aperture of a worthless forgery.

EXCURSUS XIX. (p. 351).

The Man of Sin; or, "The Lawless."

"Ego prorsus quid dixerit fateor me ignorare."—S. Aug.

The various conjectures as to the "Man of Sin," and "that which withholdeth," may be classed under three heads—(i.) the nearly contemporary, (ii.) the distantly prophetic, and (iii.) the subjectively general. And in each of these classes the suggested antitypes are either (α) general and impersonal, or (β) individual and special.

(i.) The opinion adopted will, of course, depend greatly on the extent to which the destruction of Judaism in the overthrow of Jerusalem can be regarded as "a coming of the Lord." Those who, in accordance with most of the definite temporal prophecies of Scripture, think that St. Paul must have been alluding to something *nearly contemporary*—something which already loomed on the horizon, and therefore to something which would alone have a direct bearing on the lives of contemporary Christians, explain the Apostasy and the Man of Sin to represent, (α) generally, the Pharisees, or Gnosticism, or

[1] It is no disproof of this that he borrows the Ebionite account of St. James; and his supposed condemnation of St. Paul for using the expression "Eye hath not seen," &c., seems to rest on an entire misapprehension (Lightfoot, *Gal.*, p. 311).

[2] Some such fact may lie behind the remark of Tertullian that Clement was ordained bishop by St. Peter, whereas Irenæus places Linus and Anencletus before him.

[3] Renan, *St. Paul*, p. 300. "En quittant Antioche les agents du parti hiérosolomyte jurèrent de bouleverser les fondations de Paul, de détruire les Eglises, de renverser ce qu'il avait édifié avec tant de labeurs. Il semble qu'à cette occasion de nouvelles lettres furent expédiées de Jérusalem, au nom des apôtres. Il se peut même qu'un exemplaire de ces lettres haineuses nous ait été conservé dans l'Epitre de Jude, frère de Jacques, et comme lui 'frère du Seigneur,' qui fait partie du canon," &c. The apparent array of authorities quoted in support of such inferences has no real bearing on them, and upon examination dwindles into the narrow limits indicated below. Nor does M. Renan adduce a single proof, or anything remotely resembling a proof, that by πορνεία the Apocalypse and the Epistle of Jude imply the doctrine of St. Paul (*id.* p. 300), or that the relative moderation of Michael (Jude 9) is contrasted with the impertinence of St. Paul (!), or, in fact, any other of the utterly wild conclusions into which he has exaggerated the perverted ingenuity of Tübingen theorists. See further the Excursus on St. John and St. Paul.

the growth of heresy; or (β) individually, Nero, or some Roman Emperor, Simon Magus, or Simon the son of Gioras; and they see "the check" generally in the Roman Emperor, or the Jewish Law, or spiritual gifts,[1] or the time appointed by God;[2] or individually in some Emperor (*e.g.*, Claudius=qui claudit=ὁ κατέχει),[3] or James the Just,[4] or—in St. Paul himself!

(ii.) Those who have taken the *distantly prophetical* view of the passage explain the Apostasy of the Man of Sin to be, (α) generally, the Papacy, or the Reformation, or Rationalism, or something as yet undeveloped; or (β) individually, Mahomet, or Luther, or Napoleon, or some future personal Antichrist; while they see "the check" either, as above, in the Roman Empire, or in the German Empire, or, more generally still, in the fabric of human polity.

(iii.) Finally, those who take an entirely broad and subjective view of the passage, see in it only a vague forecast of that which finds its fulfilment in all Christian, and, indeed, in all secular, history, of the counter working of two opposing forces, good and evil, Christ and Antichrist, the *Jetser tôbh* and the *Jetser-ha-râ*, a lawless violence and a restraining power.

Now, of all these interpretations one alone can be regarded as reasonably certain—namely, that which views "the check" as the Roman Empire,[5] and "the checker" as the Roman Emperor. This may be regarded as fairly established, and has received the widest acceptance, first, because it fulfils the conditions of being something present and intelligible; secondly, because we see an obvious reason why it should have been only hinted at, since to express it would have been a positive danger both to the writer and the community;[6] and, thirdly, because, as Bishop Wordsworth has pointed out, the Epistle was from the first publicly read, and the Thessalonians must have attached a meaning to it, and that meaning has been handed down to us traditionally from the earliest times.[7] Whatever may have been the wild vagaries of theological rancour, expressing itself in the form of Biblical commentary, the early Fathers, at least, were almost unanimous in regarding "the restraining power" as being the Roman Empire,[8] and the "restrainer" as being some Roman Emperor.[9] And it seems obvious that one main feature in the blasphemous self-exaltation and opposition to God which is to be a mark of the Man of Sin is suggested by the insane and sacrilegious enormities of Caligula (A.D. 40) thirteen years earlier, as well as by the persecutions of Antiochus Epiphanes. Other traits may have been suggested by the pretensions and sorceries of Simon Magus

[1] Chrysostom.

[2] Theodoret (ὁ τοῦ Θεοῦ ὅρος).

[3] Hitzig—very precariously.

[4] Wieseler, *Chron.* 268—273.

[5] "Quis nisi Romanus status?" (Tert. *De Resurr. Carn.* 24). "Clausulam saeculi acerbitates horrendas comminentem Romani imperii commeatu scimus retardari" (id. *Apol.* 32). This was all the more natural, because the Roman Empire was regarded as the Fourth Kingdom of Daniel. Prof. Jowett objects (1) that he could not have expected it to be so soon swept away; and (2) that it is not *in pari materiâ*. But for (1) see 1 Thess. i. 10; v. 4; 1 Cor. xvi. 22, &c.; and (2) St. Paul daily saw the bearing of the Empire on the spread and position of Christianity.

[6] St. Paul had already found this by experience, even though his conversation with the Thessalonians had been comparatively private. But when the Church grew, and heathens dropped not unfrequently into its meetings, it would have been most compromising to them to speak of the destruction of the Roman Empire contemplated as a near event.

[7] The Rabbis held a similar view. One of them said, "The Messiah will not come till the world *has become all white with leprosy* (Lev. xiii. 13) by the Roman Empire embracing Christianity." *Sanhedrin*, f. 97, 1; Sotah, f. 49, 2; (Amsterd. ed.).

[8] So Tert. *De Resurr. Carnis*, 24; Iren. v. 25, 26; Aug. *De Civ. Dei*, xx. 19; Jer. Qu. xi. *ad Algas*; Lact. vii. 15, &c.

[9] Claudius was Emperor when the Epistle was written, early in A.D. 54. Whether there is any allusion to his name in the word κατέχω I am not prepared to say. Kern believes that Nero is intended by "the Lawless," and therefore (seeing that the first five years of Nero were that "golden quinquennium," which Roman writers so highly praise) concludes that the Epistle is spurious. Rev. xvii. 10, 11, refers to a later time, and possibly to the strangely prevalent notion that Nero was not really dead, but would in due time re-appear. The expressions used are evidently coloured by the picture of Antiochus Epiphanes in Dan. xi. He is called "a man of sin" (ἀνὴρ ἁμαρτωλός) in 1 Macc. ii. 48, 62.

and similar widely-accredited impostors. Nero became to the Christian Church some years afterwards the very impersonation of their ideal Antichrist.

But to form any conception as to St. Paul's meaning, besides being guided by his belief of the probable nearness of the Advent, and by the necessity that what he said should have some meaning and value to his hearers, we must consider (α) the views of the age; (β) the symbols he uses; and (γ) his own subsequent language when he alludes to any similar topic.

Turning, then, to these, we find that (α) St. Paul was fully aware that, in the then present dispensation, the triumph of Christ was not to be final or complete. He may well have heard of Christ's solemn question, "Nevertheless, when the Son of Man cometh, shall he find faith on the earth?"[1] Even thus early in his career his prescient eye may have observed the traces of that Judaic and Antichristian faction which was to undo so much of his work, and embitter so many years of his life, and to whom he applies the sternest language. Already he may have noticed the germs of the various forms of Gnosticism, of which, in his Epistle to Timothy, he describes the "devilish doctrines" in language which recalls some of his expressions in this place.[2] And the views of the early Christians, as expressed by other Apostles, were all founded on warnings which Christ had uttered, and all pointed in the same direction.[3] That St. Paul should have thrown his forebodings into the concrete was natural to one so familiar with Old Testament prophecy,[4] so given to personification, and so trained to the expectation of a Messiah who should be the personal victor over all iniquity in the person of the Arch-foe, the *Rashâ*, the Antichrist. That this personification should also in part have taken its colour from the monstrous wickedness and blasphemous follies of emperors like Tiberius and Caligula, was exactly what we should have expected; and, indeed, the hopes and fears of the Jews had acted on the world of heathendom, which in its turn reacted upon them. It is a most interesting confirmation of this fact that the Jews gave to Antichrist the name of *Armillus* (ארמילוס). Thus, in the Targum of Jonathan on Isa. xi. 4, we find, "With the breath of His lips shall He destroy the wicked Armillus;" and in the Jerusalem Targum on Numb. xi. 26, and Deut. xxxiv. 2, we are told of Armalgus the Impious. This seems to be an allusion to the bracelets (*armillæ*) which, with utter defiance of all public dignity, were worn in public by Caligula.[5] We see, then, what St. Paul's anticipations at this moment were. He thought that ere long the Roman Empire, so far at any rate as it was represented by the reigning Emperor, would be swept away; that thereupon the existing tendencies of iniquity and apostasy, whether in Judaism or in the Church itself, would be concentrated in the person of one terrible opponent, and that the destruction of this opponent would be caused by the personal Advent of the Lord. At this time portents and presages of the most direful character were in the air. The hideous secrets of the Imperial Court were darkly whispered among the people. There were rumours of monstrous births, of rains of blood, of unnatural omens.[6] Though Claudius had been the last to learn the infamous orgies of his wife Messalina, and perhaps the last to suspect the murderous designs of his wife and niece Agrippina, yet by this time even he was not unaware that his life hung on a thread. Little was as yet known of Nero in the provinces, but it might have been anticipated, before the illusive promise of the early part of his reign, that the son of such a father and such a mother could only turn out to be the monster which his father expected, and which he *did* ultimately turn out to be. If St. Paul anticipated that the present condition of the

[1] Luke xviii. 8.

[2] 1 Tim. iv. 1–3 (cf. 2 Tim. i. 15; iii. 1—9; Col. ii. 8, 16—19; Acts xx. 29).

[3] Luke xviii. 8; 1 John iv. 3; 2 Pet. ii. 1, 2; iii. 3; Rev. xiii. and *passim*; and the Epistle of Jude.

[4] Ezek. xxxviii. 16, 17.

[5] Suet. *Calig.* 52, "*Armillatus* in publicum processit" (Hitzig., *Gesch. Is.* 583). The anniversary of his death was observed as a festival (Derenbourg, *Palest.* 208). Others, however, connect *Armillus* with ἐρημόλαος, or "Romulus" (Hamburger, *Talm. Wörterb.* s. v.).

[6] Tac. *Ann.* xii. 64; Suet. *Claud.* 43; Dion Cass. lx. 34, 35.

government would perish with Claudius, the reigning Emperor, and that his successor would be the Man of Sin, his anticipation was fulfilled. If he further anticipated that this representative of lawless and already working opposition to God and His Christ would be destroyed by the second Advent, he was then absolutely right so far as its Judaic elements were concerned, and so far as the second Advent was foreshadowed by the destruction of Jerusalem; and his anticipations were only mistaken *on a point respecting which all knowledge was confessedly withheld*—only in that ante-dating of the personal second Advent which was common to him with all Christians in the first century of Christianity. Nor need it be surprising to any one that he should mingle Jewish and heathen elements in the colours with which he painted the coming Antichrist. In doing this he was in full accord with that which must be the case, and with the dim expectations of paganism no less than with Rabbinic notions respecting the rival of the Messiah.[1] —Further than this we cannot go; and since we cannot—since all attempts at nearer indication have failed—since by God's express and declared Providence we are as far as the Thessalonians could have been from any accurate conception as to the times and seasons of the coming of Christ—it is clear that we lose no *vital* truth of the Gospel by our inability to find the exact interpretation of an enigma which has been hitherto insoluble, and of which, had it been necessary for us, the exact explanation would not have been withheld.[2]

[1] It was but a few years after this time that Balbillus, the Ephesian Jew, who professed a knowledge of astrology, used the prophecies of the Old Testament to assure Nero that he should be King at Jerusalem.

[2] The Thessalonians, says St. Augustine, knew what St. Paul meant, we do not. "Nos qui nescimus quod illi sciebant pervenire labore ad id quod sensit Apostolus cupimus, nec valemus."

EXCURSUS XX.—Chief Uncial Manuscripts

—	Century.	Acts of the Apostles.	Romans.	1 Cor.	2 Cor.
ℵ, Sinaiticus, at Petersburg (Imp. Library)	IV.	All.	All.	All.	All.
A, Alexandrinus, at British Museum ...	V.	All.	All.	All.	(i. 1 to iv. 13) (xii. 7 to end)
B, Vaticanus, at Rome (Vatican Library) ...	IV.	All.	All.	All.	All.
C, Ephraemi, at Paris (Imperial Library), a Palimpsest MS. ...	V.	(i. 2 to iv. 3) (v. 35—x. 43) (xiii. 1—xvi. 37) (xx. 10—xxi. 31) (xxii. 21—xxiii. 18) (xxiv. 15—xxvi. 19) (xxvii. 17-xxviii. 5)	(i. 1—ii. 5) (iii. 21—ix. 6) (x. 15—xi. 31) (xiii. 10—end)	(i. 1—vii. 18) (ix. 7—xiii. 8) (xv. 40—end)	(i. 2—x. 8)
D_1, Bezae, at Cambridge (Univ. Library) ...	VI.	(i. 1—viii. 29) (x. 14—xxi. 2) (xxi. 10—16) (xxi. 18—xxii. 10) (xxii. 20—29)	......	......	......
D_2, Claromontanus, Paris (Imp. Lib.) ...	VI.	......	(i. 7—end)	All.	All.
E_2, Laudianus, Oxford (Bodleian)...	VI.	(i. 1—xxvi. 29) (xxviii. 26—end)	......	......	......
E_3, Sangermanensis, Petersburg (Imperial Lib.). A transcript of D_2, mutilated ...	X.	......	......	......	......
F_2, Augiensis, Trinity College, Cambridge...	IX.	......	(iii. 19—to end)	(i. 1—iii. 8) (iii. 16—vi. 7) (vi. 16—end)	All.
F_a, Coislinianus, Paris	VII.	......	Some fragments of the Epistles found in		
G_2, Angelicus, Rome (August. Monks) ...	IX.	(viii. 10—end) Same as L_2. See below.	The *Epistles of St. Paul* in this MS. are known as L_2.		
G_3, Boernerianus, Dresden (Royal Library)	IX.	......	(i. 1—onward)	This is a sister MS. to F_2.	
H_2, Mutinensis, Modena (Grand Ducal Library)	IX.	(v. 28—ix. 39) (x. 19—xiii. 36) (xiv. 3—xxvii. 4)	......	......	......
H_3, Coislinianus (twelve leaves at Paris, two leaves at Petersburg)	VI.	......	......	(x. 23—29) (xi. 9—17)	......
I, Fragmenta, Palimpsesta Tischendorfiana. They are seven fragments, at Petersburg	V.—VII.	(ii. 6—17) (xxvi. 7—18) (xxviii. 8—17)	......	(xv. 53—xvi. 9)	......
K_2, Mosquensis, at Moscow	IX.	......	(i. 1—x. 18)	(i. 13—viii. 7) (viii. 12—end)	All.
L_2, Angelicus, Rome. Same as G_2	IX.	(viii. 10—end) See G_2 above.	All.	All.	All.
M_2, Ruber. Fragments at Hamburg and at British Museum ...	X.	......	......	(xv. 52—end)	(i. 1—15) (x. 13—xii. 6)
P, Porphyrianus. Published by Tischendorf. Monumenta sacra inedita. (See Alford, vol. 2.) ...	IX.	(ii. 14—end)	......	(i. 1—xii. 23) (xiii. 6—xiv. 23) (xiv. 39—end)	All.

This Table has kindly been drawn up for

[The general reader should notice (i.) that D and E mean different MSS. for the Acts and for the

(iii.) that F (Augiensis) is in most instances

OF THE ACTS, AND EPISTLES OF ST. PAUL.

Gal.	Eph.	Philip.	Colos.	1 Thess.	2 Thess.	1 Tim.	2 Tim.	Titus.	Philem.
All.	All.	All.	All.	All.	All.	All.	All.	All.	All.
All.	All.	All.	All.	All.	All.	All.	All.	All.	All.
All.	All.	All.	All.	All.	All.	......	......	......	......
(i. 21—end)	(ii. 18-iv. 17)	(i. 22-iii. 5)	(i. 2—end)	(i. 2—ii. 9)	......	(iii. 9-v. 20)	(i. 3—end)	(i. 4—end)	(3 to end)
......	......	......	......	......	......	......	......	......	......
All.	All.	All.	All.	All.	All.	All.	All.	All.	All.
......	......	......	......	......	......	......	......	......	......
......	......	......	......	......	......	......	......	......	......
All.	All.	All.	{ (i. 1—ii. 1) (ii. 8—end) }	All.	All.	All.	All.	All.	(1—21)

marginal notes to the great Septuagint Octateuch known as Cod. Çoislinianus I.

supplying the commencement of Romans, *not* other deficiencies. It is considerably mutilated.

Gal.	Eph.	Philip.	Colos.	1 Thess.	2 Thess.	1 Tim.	2 Tim.	Titus.	Philem.
......	......	......	......	......	......	......	......	......	......
{ (i. 4—10) (ii. 9—14) }	......	......	......	......	......	(iii. 7—14)	......	{ (i. 1) (i. 15—ii. 5) (iii. 13 to end) }	...
......	......	......	......	......	......	......	......	(i. 1—13)	......
All.	All.	All.	All.	All.	All.	All.	All.	All.	All.
All.	All.	All.	All.	All.	All.	All.	All.	All.	All.
......	......	......	......	......	......	......	......	......	......
All.	All.	All.	{ (i. 1—iii. 16) (iv. 8—end)	(i. 1—iii. 5) (iv. 17—end) }	All.	All.	All.	All.	All.

me by the Rev. J. S. Northcote.

Epistles; (ii.) that E (Sangermanensis) is a copy of the third corrector of D (Claromontanus); almost identical with G (Boernerianus).]

EXCURSUS XXI. (p. 398).

Theology and Antinomies of St. Paul.

I HAVE treated so fully of the main outlines of St. Paul's theology in the sketch of the Epistle to the Romans that I need not here enter upon it, but it may be convenient to the reader to see at one glance two of his own most pregnant summaries of it. These are Rom. iii. 21—26; Tit. iii. 3—7, for further explanation of which I must refer to pp. 472, *seq.*, 663.

Rom. iii. 21—26: "But now apart from Law, God's righteousness has been manifested, being witnessed to by the Law and the Prophets—even God's righteousness (I say) by means of faith in Jesus Christ unto all and upon all believers; for there is no difference. For all sinned and are falling short of the glory of God, being made righteous freely by His grace, by the means of the redemption which is in Christ Jesus, whom God set forth as "a propitiary" by means of faith in His blood for the manifestation of His righteousness, because of the praetermission of past sins by the long-suffering of God—with a view (I say) to the manifestation of His righteousness in the present season, so that He may be righteous and the giver of righteousness to him who is of faith in Jesus."

Tit. iii. 3—7: "For we were once ourselves also foolish, disobedient, wandering slaves to various lusts and pleasures, living in malice and envy, hateful, hating one another. But when the kindness and the love to man of our Saviour God appeared, not by works of righteousness which we did, but according to His mercy He saved us by means of the laver of regeneration and renewal of the Holy Ghost, which He poured forth upon us richly by means of Jesus Christ our Saviour, that being justified by His grace we should become heirs of eternal life according to hope."

By "antinomies" I mean the apparent contradictoriness to human reason of divine facts. Such antinomies must arise when Reason seeks to know something of the absolute, stepping beyond the limits of experience.

Among the apparent antinomies left without any attempt—because there is no possibility—of their reconciliation to our finite reason in the writings of St. Paul, are—

1.	Predestination (Absolute dependence).	Rom. ix. (as explaining the rejection of Israel from the objective and theological point of view).
	Free Will (Moral self-determination).	Rom. ix. 30—x. 21 (as explaining the rejection of Israel from the moral and anthropological point of view).

2. Sin through Adam's fall; Rom. v. 12—21.
   Sin as inherent in the flesh; 1 Cor. xv. 50, *seq.*
3. Christ judging *all Christians* at His Advent; Rom. ii. 16; xiv. 10; 1 Cor. iii. 13; 2 Cor. v. 10.
   God finally judging *all men* through Christ; 1 Cor. iv. 5 (xv. 24, 25).
4. Recompense for ALL according to works; Rom. ii. 6—10; 2 Cor. v. 10.
   Free forgiveness of the redeemed; Rom. iv. 4; ix. 11; xi. 6.
5. Universal Restoration and Blessedness; Rom. viii. 19—23; xi. 30—36.
   A twofold end; Rom. ii. 5—12. "The perishing;" 2 Cor. ii. 15, &c.
6. Necessity of human effort; 1 Cor. ix. 24. "So run that ye may obtain."
   Ineffectualness of human effort; Rom. ix. 16, "It is not of him that willeth, nor of him that runneth."
   The two are brought together in Phil. ii. 12, 13, "Work out your own salvation . . . For it is God which worketh in you."

To these others might perhaps be added, but none of them causes, or need cause, any trouble to the Christian. On the one hand, we know that *omnia exeunt in mysterium*, and that we cannot think for five minutes on any subject connected with the spiritual life without reaching a point at which the wings of the soul beat in vain as against a wall of adamant. On the other hand, we must bear in mind that Paul almost created the language of Christian theology; that he often enshrines in a single word a whole world of ideas; and that he always refuses to pursue the great saving truths of religion into mere speculative extremes. If we cannot live as yet in the realms of perfect and universal light, we have at any rate a lamp which throws a circle of radiance around our daily steps.

> "Lead thou me on. I do not ask to see
> The distant scene; one step enough for me."

EXCURSUS XXII. (p. 590).

DISTINCTIVE WORDS, KEY-NOTES, AND CHARACTERISTICS OF THE EPISTLES.

IT may perhaps serve to call attention to the individuality of the Epistles if I endeavour to point out how some of them may be roughly characterised by leading words or conceptions.

I.—The Eschatological Group.

1 THESSALONIANS.—This Epistle is marked by the extreme sweetness of its tone. Its key-note is Hope. Its leading words, *παρουσία, θλίψις*. Its main theme is Consolation from the near hope of the Second Advent, iv. 17, 18, *ἡμεῖς οἱ ζῶντες ἁρπαγησόμεθα, κ. τ. λ. παρακαλεῖτε ἀλλήλους ἐν τοῖς λόγοις τούτοις.*[1]

2 THESSALONIANS.—The key-note is ii. 1, 2, *μὴ τάχεως σαλευθῆναι . . . ὡς ὅτι ἐνέστηκεν ἡ ἡμέρα τοῦ κυρίου.* Peculiar doctrinal section on the Man of Sin.

II.—The Anti-Judaic Group.

1 CORINTHIANS.—Love and unity amid divergent opinions. Little details decided by great principles. Life *in* the world but not *of* it.

2 CORINTHIANS.—The Apostle's *Apologia pro vitâ suâ*. The leading words of i.—vi. "tribulation" and "consolation." In viii.—end, the leading conception "boasting not on merits but in infirmities."

GALATIANS.—The Apostle's independent authority. Christian liberty from the yoke of the Law. Circumcision nothing, and uncircumcision nothing, but——

ROMANS.—The Universality of sin, and the Universality of grace (*πᾶς* a leading word). Justification by faith. This Epistle is the sum of St. Paul's theology, and Rom. i. 16, 17 is the sum of the Epistle.

III.—The Christological or Anti-Gnostic Group.

PHILIPPIANS.—Joy in sorrow. "Summa Epistolæ, *gaudeo, gaudete*" (Bengel).

COLOSSIANS.—Christ all in all. The Pleroma. Leading conception, ii. 6, *ἐν αὐτῷ περιπατεῖτε.* "Hic epistolae scopus est" (Bengel).

PHILEMON.—Can a Christian master treat a brother as a slave? Leading conception, 12, *προσλαβοῦ αὐτόν.*

EPHESIANS.—Christ in His Church. The Epistle of the Ascension. The leading words are *χάρις, τὰ ἐπούρανια, ἐν Χριστῷ.*

[1] "Habet haec epistola meram quandam dulcedinem, quae lectori dulcibus affectibus non assueto minus sapit quam ceterae severitate quadam palatum stringentes" (Bengel). "Im Ganzen ist es ein Trostbrief" (Hausrath, p. 299).

IV.—The Pastoral Group.

1 TIMOTHY TITUS	Manuals of the Christian pastor's dealing with the faithful and with false teachers. Leading conceptions, *sobriety* of conduct, *soundness* of faith.

2 TIMOTHY.—Last words. Be brave and faithful, as I have tried to be. Come quickly, come before winter; come before I die. iv. 6, ἐγὼ γὰρ ἤδη σπένδομαι.

EXCURSUS XXIII. (p. 628).

LETTER OF PLINY TO SABINIANUS ON BEHALF OF AN OFFENDING FREEDMAN.

"C. Plinius Sabiniano suo S.

"Libertus tuus, cui succensere te dixeras, venit ad me advolutusque pedibus meis tanquam tuis haesit. Flevit multum, multum rogavit, multum etiam tacuit, in summa fecit mihi fidem paenitentiae. Vere credo emendatum, quia deliquisse se sentit. Irasceris, scio, et irasceris merito, id quoque scio: sed tunc praecipua mansuetudinus laus, cum irae caussa iustissima est. Amasti hominem et, spero, amabis: interim sufficit ut exorari te sinas. Licebit rursus irasci, si meruerit, quod exoratus excusatius facies. Remitte aliquid adulescentiae ipsius, remitte lacrimis, remitte indulgentiae tuae: ne torseris illum, ne torseris etiam te. Torqueris enim, cum tam lenis irasceris. Vereor ne videar non rogare, sed cogere, si precibus eius meas iunxero. Jungam tamen tanto plenius et effusius, quanto ipsum acrius severiusque corripui, districte minatus numquam me postea rogaturum. Hoc illi, quem terreri oportebat; tibi non idem. Nam fortasse iterum rogabo, impetrabo iterum: sit modo tale ut rogare me, ut praestare te deceat. Vale!"

TRANSLATION.

"C. Plinius to his Sabinianus, greeting:—

"Your freedman, with whom, as you had told me, you were vexed, came to me, and, flinging himself at my feet, clung to them as though they had been yours. He wept much, entreated much, yet at the same time left much unsaid, and, in short, convinced me that he was sincerely sorry. I believe that he is really reformed, because he is conscious of his delinquency. You are angry, I know; justly angry, that too I know; but gentleness is most praiseworthy exactly where anger is most justifiable. You loved the poor fellow, and I hope will love him again; meanwhile, it is enough to yield to intercession. Should he ever deserve it you may be angry again, and all the more excusably by yielding now. Make some allowance for his youth, for his tears, for your own kindly disposition. Do not torture him, lest you torture yourself as well, for it is a torture to you when one of your kindly nature is angry. I fear you will think that I am not asking but forcing you if I join my prayers to his; I will, however, do so, and all the more fully and unreservedly in proportion to the sharpness and severity with which I took him to task, sternly threatening that I would never say a word for him again. *That* I said to him because he needed to be well frightened; but I do not say it to you, for perhaps I shall say a word for him again, and again gain my point; provided only my request be such as it becomes me to ask and you to grant. Farewell!"

EXCURSUS XXIV. (pp. 175, 556).

THE HERODS IN THE ACTS.

IF there be sufficient ground for the plausible conjecture which identifies Agrippa I. and Cypros with the king and queen who figure in the two following anecdotes of the Talmud, we shall see that the part he had to play was not always an easy one, and even led to serious complications.

i. The Talmud relates that on one occasion, at a festival, a lizard was found in the royal kitchen. It appeared to be dead, and if so the whole banquet would have become ceremonially unclean. The king referred the question to the queen, and the queen to Rabban Gamaliel. He asked whether it had been found in a warm or a cold place. "In a warm place," they said. "Then pour cold water over it." They did so. The lizard revived, and the banquet was pronounced clean. So that, the writer complacently adds, the fortune of the entire festival depended ultimately on Rabban Gamaliel.[1]

ii. The other story is more serious. It appears that at a certain Passover the king and queen were informed by their attendants that two kinds of victims—a lamb and a kid—either of which was legal—had been killed for them, and they were in doubt as to which of the two was to be regarded as preferable. The king, who considered that the kid was preferable, and was less devoted to the Pharisees than his wife, sent to ask the high priest Issachar of Kephar-Barchaï, thinking that since he daily sacrificed victims, he would be sure to know. Issachar, who was of the same haughty, violent, luxurious temperament as all the numerous Sadducean high priests of the day, made a most contemptuous gesture in the king's face, and said that, if the kid was preferable, the lamb would not have been ordained for use in the daily sacrifice. Indignant at his rudeness, the king ordered his right hand to be cut off. Issachar, however, bribed the executioner and got him to cut off the left hand. The king, on discovering the fraud, had the right hand cut off also.[2] It is thus that the story runs in the *Pesachim*, and further on it is said that when the doubt arose the king sent to the queen, and the queen to the Rabban Gamaliel, who gave the perfectly sensible answer that as either victim was legal, and as the king and queen had been perfectly indifferent in giving the order for the Paschal victims to be slain, they could eat of the one which had been first killed.[3]

As this story was not very creditable to Agrippa I., we find a sufficient reason for the silence of Josephus in passing over the name of Issachar in his notices of the High Priests.[4] His was not a name which could have sounded very agreeable in the ears of Agrippa II. The elder Agrippa seems to have been tempted in this instance into a violence which was not unnatural in one who had lived in the court of Tiberius, but which was a rude interruption of his plan of pleasing the priestly party, while Cypros took the Pharisees under her special patronage. Issachar seems to have come between Theophilus, son of Hanan, and Simon, son of Kanthera the Boethusian.[5] Whatever may have been the tendencies of Cypros, and his own proclivities, it was important to Agrippa that he should retain the support of the sacerdotal aristocrats; and they were well pleased to enjoy, in rapid succession, and as the appanage of half-a-dozen families, the burdensome dignity of Aaron's successor.

The Pharisees, on the other hand, recounted with pleasure the fact that no sooner had Agrippa arrived at Jerusalem than he caused to be suspended on the columns of the *oulam*, or Temple portico, the chain of massive gold which he had received from Gaius as an indemnification for his captivity;[6] that he was most munificent in his presents to the nation; that he was a daily attendant at the Temple sacrifice; that he had called the attention of the Legate Petronius to the decrees of Claudius in favour of Jewish privileges, and had thereby procured the reprimand and punishment of the inhabitants

[1] *Pesachim*, f. 88, 2.

[2] *Pesachim*, f. 57, 1. In *Keritôth*, f. 28, 2, it is told with some variations, and the king is called Jannæus. It is, however, a fashion of the Talmud to give this name to Asmonæan kings (Derenbourg, p. 211). May this wild story have been suggested by the indignation of the Jews against the first High Priest who wore gloves to prevent his hands from being soiled?

[3] *Id.* 88 *b*. When I was present at the Samaritan passover on the summit of Mount Gerizim, six lambs and one kid were sacrificed.

[4] *Antt.* xx. 10, § 1.

[5] Herod the Great had married a daughter of Boethus.

[6] *Middôth*, iii. 7. Josephus (*Antt.* xix. 6, § 1) says that it was hung "over the treasury."

of Dor,[1] who had insulted the Jews by erecting in their synagogue a statue of the emperor. They had also told with applause that he carried his basket of first-fruits to the Temple like any ordinary Israelite;[2] and that although every one had to give way in the streets to the king and his suite, yet Agrippa always yielded the right of road to a marriage or funeral procession.[3] There were two stories on which they dwelt with peculiar pleasure. One was that on a single day—perhaps that of his arrival at Jerusalem—he offered a thousand holocausts, and that when they had been offered, a poor man came with two pigeons. The priest refused this sacrifice, on the pretext that on that day he had been bidden to offer none but royal victims; but he yielded to the poor man's earnest solicitation on being told that the pigeons were brought in fulfilment of a vow that he would daily offer half the produce of his day's work; and Agrippa warmly approved of this disobedience of his orders.[4] On another occasion, at the Feast of Tabernacles, he received from the hands of the High Priest the roll of the Law, and without seating himself, read the Lesson for the day, which was Deuteronomy xvii. 14—20. When he came to the words, "Thou mayest not set a stranger over thee which is not thy brother," the thought of his own Idumæan origin flashed across his mind, and he burst into tears. But the cry arose on all sides, "Fear not, Agrippa; thou art our brother, thou art our brother."[5]

There were other tendencies which would win for Agrippa the approval of the people no less than that of the Pharisees. Such, for instance, were his early abolition of a house-tax in Jerusalem, which had been felt to be particularly burdensome; and his construction of a new quarter of the Holy City, which was called Bezetha.[6] The Rabbis, indeed, refused to accord to the new district the sanctity of the old, because it had not been inaugurated by the presence of a king, a prophet, the Urim and Thummim, a Sanhedrin of seventy-one, two processions, and a choir.[7] It is far from improbable that this addition to Jerusalem was mainly intended to strengthen its natural defences, and that Agrippa had formed the secret intention of making himself independent of Rome. If so, his plans were thwarted by the watchful jealousy of Vibius Marsus,[8] who had succeeded Petronius as Praefect of Syria. He wrote and informed the Emperor of the suspicious proceedings of Agrippa, and an Imperial rescript commanded the suspension of these building operations. Petronius had been on terms of intimacy with Agrippa, but Marsus distrusted and bitterly offended him.[9] After the completion of the magnificent theatre, and other buildings which he had presented to Berytus, he was visited by a number of neighbouring princes—Antiochus, King of Commagene, Sampsigeramus of Emesa, Cotys of Lesser Armenia, Polemo of Pontus, and his brother Herod, King of Chalcis. It is probable that these royal visits were not of a purely complimentary character, but may have been the nucleus of a plot against the Roman power. If so, their machinations were scattered to the winds by the contemptuous energy of the Praefect, who felt a truly Roman indifference for the gilded impotence of these Oriental vassals. As the gathering took place at Tiberias, he went thither, and Agrippa,

[1] Jos. *Antt.* xix. 6, § 3.
[2] *Bikkurim*, iii. 4; Derenbourg, p. 217.
[3] *Bab. Kethubhôth*, f. 17, 1; Munk, *Palest.* p. 571.
[4] *Vayyikra-rabba*, iii.
[5] *Sota*, f. 41, 1, 2. But, as Derenbourg points out, there were not wanting some stern Rabbis who unhesitatingly condemned this "flattery of the king." (See, too, Jost, *Gesch. d. Judenthums*, 420. It is not certain that the anecdote may not refer to Agrippa II.) In continuation of the story about Babha Ben Buta's advice to Herod the Great to rebuild the Temple, the Talmud adds that the Romans were by no means willing, but that the task was half done before the return of the messenger, who had been purposely told to spend three years in his mission. Among other things the Romans said, "If thou hast succeeded by violence at home, we have the genealogy here. *Thou art neither a king, nor the son of a king, but a liberated slave*" (*Babha Bathra*, f. 3, 2).
[6] Josephus (*B. J.* v. 4, § 2) says that this word means "New City"; but elsewhere (*Antt.* xii. 10, § 2; 11, § 1) he writes it *Bêth-Zêtho*, or "House of Olive-trees." In the Syriac version of Acts i. 12, *ἐλαιών, olive-yard*, is rendered *Bêth-Zêtho*; and in *B. J.* ii. 19, § 4, Josephus seems to draw a distinction between Bezetha and the New City (Munk, *Palest.*, p. 45). Derenbourg, however, holds that Bezetha is a transliteration of the Chaldaic *Beth Hadta*, and that Josephus is right (*Palest.*, p. 218).
[7] *Jer. Sanhedr.* i. 3; Jos. *B. J.* v. 4, § 2.
[8] Jos. *B. J.* ii. 11, § 6.
[9] Jos. *Antt.* xix. 7, § 2.

in whose character, as in that of all his family, there was a large vein of ostentation,[1] went seven furlongs out of the city to meet him, with the five other kings in his chariot. Marsus did not like the look of this combination, and sent his servants to the kings with the cool order that they were all to make the best of their way at once to their respective homes. It was in consequence of this deliberate insult that, after the death of Agrippa, Claudius, in respect to his memory, and in consequence of a request which he had received from him, displaced Marsus, and sent C. Cassius Longinus in his place.[2]

Agrippa and Berenice.

Not a spark of true patriotism seems ever to have been kindled in the breast of Agrippa II. He was as complete a renegade as his friend Josephus,[3] but without his versatility and genius. He had passed all his early years in the poisoned atmosphere of such courts as those of Gaius and Claudius, and was now on excellent terms with Nero. The mere fact that he should have been a favourite with the Messallinas, and Agrippinas, and Poppæas, of a palace rife with the basest intrigues, is sufficient to condemn him. His appointments to the High-priesthood were as bad as those of his predecessors, and he incurred the displeasure of the Jews by the arbitrary rapidity of the constant changes which he made. Almost the only specific event which marked his period of royalty was a dispute about a view from a window. In a thoroughly unpatriotic and irreverent spirit he had built a banquet-hall in Herod's palace at Jerusalem, which overlooked the Temple courts. It was designed to serve the double purpose of gratifying the indolent curiosity of his guests as they lay at table, by giving them the spectacle of the Temple worship in its most sacred details, and also of maintaining a certain espionage over the movements of the worshippers, which would at any moment enable him to give notice to the Roman soldiers if he wished them to interfere. Indignant at this instance of contemptible curiosity and contemptible treachery, the Jews built up a counter wall to exclude his view. Agrippa, powerless to do anything himself, invoked the aid of the Procurator. The wall of the Jews excluded not only the view of Agrippa, but also that of the commandant in the tower of Antonia, and Festus ordered them to pull it down. The Jews resisted this demand with their usual determined fury, and Festus so far gave way that he allowed them to send an embassy to Rome to await the decision of the Cæsar. The Jews sent Ishmael Ben Phabi the high priest, Helkias the treasurer, and other distinguished ambassadors, and astutely gaining the ear of Poppæa —who is believed to have been a proselyte, but if so, was a proselyte of whom the Jews ought to have been heartily ashamed—obtained a decision in their favour. Women like Poppæa, pantomimists like Aliturus--such were in these days the defenders of the Temple for the Jews against their hybrid kings! We hear little more of Agrippa II. till the breaking out of the war which ended in the destruction of Jerusalem. As might have been expected, he, like Josephus, like Tiberius Alexander, and other eminent renegades, was found in the ranks of the Roman invaders, waging war on the Holy City. He probably saw the Temple sink amid its consuming fires. Like Josephus he may have watched from a Roman window the gorgeous procession in which the victor paraded the sacred spoils of the Temple, while the wretched captives of his countrymen—

> "Swelled, slow-pacing, by the car's tall side,
> The Stoic tyrant's philosophic pride."

After that he fell into merited obscurity, and ended a frivolous life by a dishonoured old age.

[1] Thus on a coin, engraved by Akerman, *Numism. Illustr.*, he is called βασιλεὺς μέγας.

[2] Jos. *Antt.* xix. 8, § 1.

[3] For instance, he changed the name of Cæsarea Philippi to Neronias; stripped Judæa to ornament Berytus; and even stooped to take the surname *Marcus*, which is found on one of his coins (Jos. *Antt.* xx. 9, § 4; Eckhel, *Doct. Num. Vet.* iii. 493).

Such was the prince who came to salute Festus, and he was accompanied by his sister, who was unhappily notorious even among the too notorious ladies of rank in that evil time. Berenice was the Lucrezia Borgia of the Herodian family. She was beautiful, like all the princesses of her house. Before the age of sixteen she had been married to her uncle Herod of Chalcis, and being left a widow before she was twenty, went to live in Rome with her equally youthful brother. Her beauty, her rank, the splendour of her jewels, the interest and curiosity attaching to her race and her house, made her a prominent figure in the society of the capital; and a diamond, however lustrous and valuable, was enhanced in price if it was known that it had once sparkled on the finger of Berenice, and had been a present to her from her brother.[1] The relations between the two gave rise to the darkest rumours, which gained credence, because there was nothing to contradict them in the bearing or character of the defamed persons. So rife indeed did these stories become, that Berenice looked out for a new marriage. She contracted an alliance with Polemo II., King of Cilicia, insisting, however, that he should save her from any violation of the Jewish law by submitting to the rite of circumcision.[2] Circumcision, not conversion, was all that she required. So true is the charge brought alike by St. Paul in his Epistles, and by the writers of the Talmud, that the reason why the Jews insisted upon circumcision was only that they might have whereof to glory in the flesh.[3] The lowering of the Gentile fasces in token of external respect was all that they cared for, and when that was done, the Ger might go his own vile way—not improbably to Gehenna.[4] Circumcision to them was greater than all affirmative precepts, and was therefore exalted above love to God or love to our neighbour.[5] No doubt it cost Polemo something to accept concision, in order to satisfy the orthodox scrupulosity of an abandoned Jewess; but her wealth was an inducement too powerful to resist. It was hardly likely that such a marriage could last. It was broken off very rapidly by the elopement of Berenice, after which Polemo immediately repudiated every shadow and semblance of allegiance to the Jewish religion, and Berenice returned to the house of her brother, until her well-preserved but elderly beauty, added to the munificence of her presents, first won the old Vespasian, and then his son Titus.[6] The conqueror of Judæa was so infatuated by his love for its dishonoured princess that he took her with him to Rome, and seriously contemplated making her a partner of his imperial throne.[7] But this was more than the Romans could stand, far gone as they were in servitude and adulation. The murmurs which the rumoured match stirred up were so wrathful in their indignation, that Titus saw how unsafe it would be to wed a Jewess whose name had been dragged through the worst infamy. He dismissed her—*invitus invitam*—and we hear of her no more. Thus in the fifth generation did the sun of the Herodian house set in obscure darkness, as it had dawned in blood; and with it set also the older and purer splendour of the Asmonæan princes. They had mingled the honourable blood of Judas the Maccabee with that of Idumæan adventurers, and the inheritors of the grandest traditions of Jewish patriotism were involved in a common extinction with the representatives of the basest intrigues of Jewish degradation.

1 "Adamas notissimus, et Berenices
In digito factus pretiosior; hunc dedit olim
Barbarus incestae, dedit hunc Agrippa sorori."
Juv. *Sat.* vi. 156; Jos. *Antt.* xx. 6, § 3.

2 Jos. *Antt.* xx. 7, § 3.

3 Gal. vi. 13. It was, of course, a Judaic triumph to make a king not only a *Ger Thoshab*, or a proselyte of the gate (Ex. xx. 14), but even a *Ger hatsedek*, "a proselyte of righteousness," or "of the Covenant." These latter were despised alike by Jews and Gentiles (Suet. *Claud.* 25; *Domit.* 12; *Yebhamôth*, xlvii. 4; see Wetstein on Matt. xxiii. 15).

4 See McCaul, *Old Paths*, pp. 63 *seqq.*

5 *Nedarîm*, f. 32, c. 2.

6 Jos. *Antt.* xx. 7, § 3.

7 Suet. *Tit.* 7; Tac. *H.* ii. 2.

EXCURSUS XXV. (p. 637).

PHRASEOLOGY AND DOCTRINES OF THE EPISTLE TO THE EPHESIANS.

IT is admitted that there are some new and rare expressions in this Epistle;[1] but they are sufficiently accounted for by the idiosyncrasy of the writer, and the peculiarity of the subjects with which he had to deal. It is monstrous to assume that, in the case of one so fresh and eager as St. Paul, the vocabulary would not widely vary in writings extending over nearly twenty years, and written under every possible variety of circumstances, to very different communities, and in consequence of very different controversies. The wide range of dissimilarity in thought and expression between Epistles of *admitted* authenticity ought sufficiently to demonstrate the futility of overlooking broad probabilities and almost universal testimony, because of peculiarities of which many are only discoverable by a minute analysis. It must be remembered that at this period the phraseology of Christianity was still in a plastic, it might almost be said in a fluid, condition. No Apostle, no writer of any kind, contributed one tithe so much to its ultimate cohesion and rigidity as St. Paul. Are we then to reject this Epistle, and that to the Colossians, on grounds so flimsy as the fact that in them for the first time he speaks of the remission (*ἄφεσιν*, Eph. i. 7; Col. i. 14) instead of the pretermission (*πάρεσιν*, Rom. iii. 25) of sins; or that, writing to a Church predominantly Gentile, he says "Greeks and Jews" (Col. iii. 11) instead of "Jews and Greeks" (Rom. i. 16, &c.); or that he uses the word "Church" in a more abstract and generic sense than in his former writings; or that he uses the rhetorical expression that the Gospel has been preached in all the world (Col. i. 6, 23)? By a similar mode of reasoning it would be possible to prove in the case of almost every voluminous author in the world that half the works attributed to him have been written by some one else. Such arguments only encumber with useless *débris* the field of criticism. There is indeed one very unusual expression, the peculiarity of which has been freely admitted by all fair controversialists. It is the remark that the mystery of Christ is now revealed "to the holy Apostles and Prophets" (iii. 5). The Prophets (as in ii. 20; iv. 11) are doubtless those of the New Testament—those who had received from the Spirit His special gifts of illumination; but the epithet is unexpected. It can only be accounted for by the general dignity and fulness (the *σεμνότης*) of the style in which the Epistle is written; and the epithet, if genuine, is, it need hardly be said, official and impersonal.

It would be much more to the purpose if the adverse critics could produce even one decided instance of un-Pauline theology. The demonology of the Epistle is identical with that of Paul's Rabbinic training.[2] The doctrine of original sin, even if it were by any means necessarily deducible from Eph. ii. 3—which is not the case, since the word *φύσει* is not identical with "by birth"—is quite as clearly involved in the Epistles to the Romans and Galatians. The descent of Christ into Hades is not necessarily implied in iv. 8; and even if it were, the fact that St. Paul has not elsewhere alluded to it furnishes no shadow of a proof that he did not hold it. The method of quoting Scripture is that of all Jewish writers in the age of Paul, and the reminiscences of the Old Testament in iv. 8 and v. 14 (if the latter be a reminiscence) are scarcely more purely verbal than others which occur in the Epistles of which no doubt has ever been entertained. On the other hand, it is frankly admitted that in all essential particulars the views of the Epistle are distinctly Pauline. The relations of Christianity to Judaism; the universality of human corruption through sin; the merging of heathenism and Judaism in the higher unity of Christianity; the prominence given to faith and love; the unconditional freedom of

[1] Such *ἅπαξ λεγόμενα*, or unusual expressions, as *τὰ ἐπουράνια, κοσμοκράτορες πολυποίκιλος, περιποίησις, ἀφθαρσία, διάβολος*.

[2] *Thacksiphis*—an association of demons, and *Isbalganith* (see *Berachôth*, f. 51, 1).

grace; the unserviceableness and yet the moral necessity of good works; are in absolute accordance with the most fundamental conceptions of St. Paul's acknowledged writings. If some of these great truths of theology here receive a richer, more mature, and more original development, this is only what we should expect from the power of a mind which never ceased to grow in grace and wisdom, and which regarded growth in grace and wisdom as the natural privilege of a Christian soul. On the other hand, we might well be amazed if the first hundred years after the death of Christ produced a totally unknown writer who, assuming the name of Paul, treats the mystery which it was given him to reveal with a masterly power which the Apostle himself rarely equalled, and most certainly never surpassed. Let any one study the remains of the Apostolic Fathers, and he may well be surprised at the facility with which writers of the Tübingen school, and their successors, assume the existence of Pauls who lived unheard of and died unknown, though they were intellectually and spiritually the equals, if not the superiors, of St. Paul himself! In no single Epistle is the point of view so clear, so supreme, so final—in no other Epistle of the Homologoumena is the doctrine so obviously the outcome and issue of truths which before had been less fully and profoundly enunciated—so undeniably the full consummate flower from germs of which we have, as it were, witnessed the planting. At supreme epochs of human enlightenment whole centuries of thought seem to separate the writings of a few years. The questions which occupy the Apostle in the Thessalonians and Galatians seem to lie indefinitely far behind the goal which his thoughts have now attained. In earlier Epistles he was occupied in maintaining the freedom of the Gentiles from the tyrannous narrowness of Jewish sacerdotalism; here, on the other hand, he is dwelling on the predestined grandeur of the equal and universal Church. In the Epistles to the Romans and the Galatians he has founded the claims of Christianity on "a philosophy of the history of religion," by showing that Christ is the Second Adam, and the promised seed of Abraham; here he contemplates a scheme predestined before the ages of earth began, and running through them as an increasing purpose, so that æon after æon revealed new forms and hues of the richly-varied wisdom, and the Gentiles (καὶ ὑμεῖς, i. 13) as well as the Jews are included in the predestined election (ἐκληρώθημεν, προορισθέντες, i. 11) to the purchased possession (περιποίησις, 14). And not to exhaust, which would be indeed impossible, the manifold aspects of this so-called "colourless" Epistle, the manner in which it expresses the conception of the quickening of spiritual death by union with the Risen Christ (ii. 1—6); the present realisation, the immanent consciousness of communion with God; the all-pervading supremacy of God in Christ; the importance of pure spiritual knowledge; the dignity given to the Church as the house (ii. 20—22), the body (iv. 12—16) and the bride (v. 25—27) of Christ,—all mark it out as the most sublime, the most profound, and, if I may use the expression, the most advanced and final utterance of that mystery of the Gospel which it was given to St. Paul for the first time to proclaim in all its fulness to the Gentile world.[1] It is not surprising that when these truths had once found utterance they should have had their influence on the teachings of the author of the Epistle to the Hebrews and upon St. Peter and St. John; nor is this any ground whatever, but rather the reverse, for looking with suspicion on the authenticity of the Epistle.[2]

[1] Entirely as I disagree with Pfleiderer, I have received great help from his *Paulinismus* (E. T. ii. 162—193) in the study of this Epistle.

[2] See 1 Pet. i. 14 (Eph. iv. 14); 1 Pet. i. 20 (Eph. i. 4); 1 Pet. i. 7 (Eph. i. 6); i. 5 (Eph. iii. 5); ii. 9 (Eph. i. 14); i. 8 (Eph. i. 17); ii. 11 (Eph. ii. 3); iii. 7 (Eph. iii. 6); v. 10 (Eph. iv. 2), &c. See Weiss, *Petrinisch. Lehrbegr.* 434.

EXCURSUS XXVI. (p. 649).

Evidence as to the Liberation of St. Paul.

The chief passages on the remaining life of St. Paul which have much historic importance are the following:—

I. Clemens Romanus, possibly a personal friend and fellow-worker of St. Paul, if he be the Clement mentioned in Phil. iv. 3,[1] but certainly a Bishop of Rome, and a writer of the first century, says that:—

"Because of envy, Paul also obtained the prize of endurance, having seven times borne chains, having been exiled, and having been stoned. After he had preached the Gospel both in the East and in the West, he won the noble renown of his faith, having taught righteousness to the whole world, and having come to the limit of the West, and borne witness[2] before the rulers. Thus he was freed from the world, and went into the holy place, having shown himself a pre-eminent example of endurance."[3]

II. The fragment of the Muratorian Canon (about A.D. 170), though obscure and corrupt, and only capable of uncertain conjectural emendation and interpretation, yet seems on the whole to imply the fact of "Paul's setting forth from the city on his way to Spain."[4]

III. Eusebius, in the fourth century, says:—

"Then, after his defence, there is a tradition that the Apostle again set forth to the ministry of his preaching, and having a second time entered the same city [Rome], was perfected by his martyrdom before him [Nero]."[5]

IV. Chrysostom (died A.D. 407) says:—

"After he had been in Rome, he again went into Spain. But whether he thence returned into those regions [the East] we do not know."[6]

V. St. Jerome (died A.D. 420) says that "Paul was dismissed by Nero, that he might preach Christ's Gospel also in the regions of the West."[7]

I take no notice of the inscription supposed to have been found in Spain (Gruter, pp. 238—9), which gratefully records that Nero has purged the province of brigands, and of the votaries of a new superstition, because even on the assumption that it is genuine it has no necessary bearing on the question. Nor does any other writer of the least authority make any important contribution to the question, since it cannot be regarded as adding one iota of probability to the decision to quote the general assertions of Cyril of Jerusalem and Theodoret that St. Paul visited Spain; nor can it be taken as a counter-evidence that Origen does not mention Spain when he remarks "that he carried the Gospel from Jerusalem to Illyricum, and was afterwards martyred in Rome in the

[1] We can only say that this is an ancient and not impossible tradition (see Lightfoot, *Philippians*, pp. 166—169).

[2] The word at this period did not *necessarily* mean "suffered martyrdom," but probably connoted it.

[3] *Δια ζῆλον [καὶ ὁ] Παῦλος ὑπομονῆς βραβεῖον ὑπεσχεν, ἑπτάκις δεσμὰ φορέσας, φυγαδευθεὶς, λιθασθείς, κῆρυξ γενόμενος ἔν τε τῇ ἀνατολῇ καὶ [τῇ] δύσει, τὸ γενναῖον τῆς πίστεως αὐτοῦ κλέος ἔλαβεν, δικαιοσύνην διδάξας ὅλῳ τῷ κόσμῳ καὶ ἐπὶ τὸ τέρμα τῆς δύσεως ἐλθὼν, καὶ μαρτυρήσας ἐπὶ τῶν ἡγουμένων οὕτως ἀπηλλάγη τοῦ κόσμου καὶ εἰς τὸν ἅγιον τόπον ἐπορεύθη, ὑπομονῆς γενόμενος μέγιστος ὑπογραμμός.* —*Ep.* 1 *ad Cor.* 5 (see Lightfoot, *Epistles of Clement*, pp. 46—52).

[4] "Lucas obtime Theophile comprindit quia sub praesentia ejus singula gerebantur, sicuti et remote passionem Petri evidenter declarat, sed profectionem Pauli ab urbe ad Spaniam proficiscentis . . . ."

[5] *τότε μὲν οὖν ἀπολογησάμενον, αὖθις ἐπὶ τὴν τοῦ κηρύγματος διακονίαν λόγος ἔχει στείλασθαι τὸν ἀπόστολον, δεύτερον δ' ἐπιβάντα τῇ αὐτῇ πόλει τῷ κατ' αὐτὸν (Νέρωνα) τελειωθῆναι μαρτυρίῳ* (Euseb. *H. E.* ii. 22, 25). He quotes Dionysius of Corinth to show that Peter and Paul had both been at Rome (*id. ib.* 25), which is also stated by Ignatius (*ad Rom.* iv.).

[6] *Μετὰ τὸ γένεσθαι ἐν Ρωμῇ πάλιν εἰς τὴν Σπανίαν ἀπῆλθεν· εἰ δὲ ἐκεῖθεν πάλιν εἰς ταῦτα τὰ μέρη οὐκ ἴσμεν* (Chrys. *ad* 2 *Tim.* iv. 20).

[7] "Sciendum est. . . . Paulum a Nerone dimissum ut evangelium Christi in occidentis quoque partibus praedicaret" (Jer. *Catal. Scrip.*). See also Tert. *Scorp.* 15, *De Praescr.* 36; Lactant. *De Mort. Persec.* 2.

time of Nero." Even as late as the fourth century, no writer ventures to do more than allude distantly to the supposed fact in a manner which shows that not a single detail on the subject existed, and that tradition had nothing tangible to add to the data furnished by the New Testament, or the inferences to which it led. On the other hand, the testimony of the pseudo-Dionysius (A.D. 170) that St. Peter and St. Paul, after founding the Church of Corinth, went to Italy—apparently together (ὁμόσε)—and were there martyred about the same time, is, so far as it goes, somewhat unfavourable to the Spanish journey, and at any rate proves that even in the second century tradition had buried its ignorance in the shifting sand of erroneous generalities.

If we be asked what is the *historic value* of this evidence, we must answer that it is very small indeed. The testimony of Clement, assuming it to be genuine, would be important from his early date if it were not so entirely vague. It is a purely rhetorical passage, in which it seems not impossible that he means to compare St. Paul to the sun rising in the east and setting in the west. The expression that "he taught righteousness to the whole world" shows that we are here dealing with enthusiastic phrases rather than rigid facts. The expression "having *come* to the limit of the West" is unfavourable to a Spanish journey. "The limit of the West," though undoubtedly it would mean Spain to an author who was writing from Rome, if he were speaking in plain and lucid prose, has not necessarily any such meaning in a glowing comparison, least of all on the hypothesis that the native place of the writer was Philippi. If, however, Spain is intended, and if the word "bearing witness" (μαρτυρήσας) means martyrdom, then the author, taken *literally*, would imply that St. Paul perished in Spain. The argument that "before the rulers" must be a reference to Helius and Polycletus, or Tigellinus and Nymphidius Sabinus, or two other presidents left to act as regents during Nero's absence in Greece, is a mere gossamer thread of attenuated inference. The authority of St. Clement, then, must be set aside as too uncertain to be of decisive value.[1]

Nor is the sentence in the second-century Canon discovered by Muratori at Milan of any great value. The verb which is essential to the meaning has to be supplied, and it is even possible that the writer may have intended to quote Luke's silence as to any Spanish journey to prove that the tradition respecting it—which would have been naturally suggested by Rom. xv. 24—had no authority in its favour.

Eusebius, indeed, is more explicit, but, on the one hand, he lived so late that his testimony, unless supported by reference to more ancient authorities, is of no importance; and on the other hand, he is so far from following his usual habit of quoting any authority for his assertion, that he distinctly ascribes it to tradition. He merely observes that "it is said," and then proceeds to support the probability of this tradition by an extraordinary misconception of 2 Tim. iv. 16, 17, in which he founds an argument for the Apostle's second imprisonment on the grounds that he spoke of deliverance from the first when he said, "I was saved from the mouth of the lion." His testimony is rendered the more worthless because in his *Chronicon* he misdates by nearly ten years the time of the first imprisonment, and his erroneous inference from 2 Tim. seems to show that the floating rumour was founded on a mere hypothesis suggested by the Epistles themselves.[2] The real proofs of St. Paul's liberation are, as we have seen, of a different character.

[1] See however Döllinger, *First Age*, 78, *seq.*; Westcott, *Hist. of Canon*, p. 470; and Lightfoot, *Ep. of Clement*, p. 508, who quotes Strabo, ii. 1, Vell. Paterc. i. 2, to show that Spain is probably meant.

[2] He makes Paul arrive at Rome A.D. 55.

EXCURSUS XXVII. (p. 649).

The Genuineness of the Pastoral Epistles.

As our knowledge of the life of St. Paul, after his first imprisonment, depends entirely on the decision as to the authenticity of the Pastoral Epistles, I will here briefly examine the evidences.

I. Turning first to the external evidence in their favour, we find an almost indisputable allusion to the First Epistle to Timothy in Clement of Rome.[1] That they were universally accepted by the Church in the second century is certain, since they are found in the Peshito Syriac, mentioned in the Muratorian Canon, and quoted by Ignatius, Polycarp, Hegesippus, Athenagoras, Irenæus, Clemens of Alexandria, Theophilus of Antioch, and perhaps by Justin Martyr. After the second century the testimonies are unhesitating and unbroken, and Eusebius, in the fourth century, reckons them among the homologomena or acknowledged writings of St. Paul. With the exception of Marcion, and Tatian, who rejected the two Epistles to Timothy, there seems to have been no doubt as to their genuineness from the first century down to the days of Schmidt and Schleiermacher. On what grounds Marcion rejected them we are not informed. It is possible that Baur may be right in the supposition that he was not aware of their existence.[2] But this would be no decisive argument against them, since the preservation and dissemination of purely private letters, addressed to single persons, must have been much more precarious and slow than that of letters addressed to entire Churches. But in such a case Marcion's authority is of small value. He dealt with the Scriptures on purely subjective grounds. His rejection of the Old Testament, and of all the New Testament except ten Epistles of St. Paul, and a mutilated Gospel of St. Luke, shows that he made no sort of scruple about excluding from his canon any book that militated against his peculiar dogmas. Nor is Tatian's authority of more weight. The only reason why he accepted as genuine the Epistle of Titus while he rejected those of Timothy, is conjectured to have been that, in the Epistle to Titus the phase of incipient Gnosticism which meets with the condemnation of the Apostle is more distinctly identified with Jewish teaching.[3]

But perhaps it may be argued that the Pastoral Epistles were forged in the second century, and that the earlier passages which are regarded as allusions to them, or quotations from them, are in reality borrowed from Clemens, Polycarp, and Hegesippus, by the writer, who wished to enlist the supposed authority of St. Paul in condemnation of the spreading Gnosticism of the second century. No one would argue that there is a merely *accidental* connexion between, "Avoiding profane and vain babblings, and oppositions [or antitheses] of the knowledge [Gnosis] which is falsely so called" in 1 Tim. vi. 20, and "the combination of impious error arose by the fraud of false teachers [ἑτεροδιδασκάλων, comp. 1 Tim. i. 3, ἑτεροδιδασκαλεῖν] who henceforth attempted to preach their science falsely so called" in Hegesippus.[4] But Baur argues that the forger of the Epistle stole the term from Hegesippus, and that it was aimed at the Marcionites, who are especially indicated in the word "Antitheses," which is the name of a book written by Marcion to point out the contradiction between the Old and New Testament, and between those parts of the New Testament which he rejected and those which he retained.[5] Now, "Antitheses" may mean simply "oppositions," as it is rendered in our version, and the injunction is explained by Chrysostom and Theophylact, and even by

[1] "Let us then approach Him in holiness of soul, lifting to Him pure and unstained hands."—*Ep.* 1, *ad Cor.* 29; *cf.* 1 Tim. ii. 8.

[2] Baur, *Pastoralbriefe*, p. 138.

[3] Tit. i. 10, 14; iii. 9. Tatian founded a sect of Gnostic Encratites towards the close of the second century.

[4] *Ap.* Euseb. *H. E.* iii. 32.

[5] Tert. Adv. *Marc.* i. 19; iv. &c. Baur also (*Paul.* ii. 111) dwells on the use of the word ὑγιής, "sound," "wholesome," by Hegesippus and in 1 Tim. i. 10.

De Wette, to mean that Timothy is not to embroil himself in idle and fruitless controversies. But even, supposing that "antilogies" are meant, what shadow of proof is there that nothing of the kind existed among the "vain babblings" of Essenian speculation? "Hegesippus," says Baur,[1] "considering his Ebionite views, can scarcely have drawn from an Epistle supposed to be by Paul." It is difficult to believe that this remark is perfectly serious;[2] but if it be, I would ask, Is it not indefinitely more improbable that the *falsarius*[3] would instantly condemn his own work as spurious by interpolating marked passages from Clemens, Polycarp, and Hegesippus, which his instructed readers would be sure to recognise, and which would then be absolutely fatal to the success of his design?

II. Let us, then, pass to the internal evidence. It is argued that these three Epistles cannot have been written by St. Paul—(1) Because "they stand far below the originality, the wealth of thought, and the whole spiritual substance and value of the authentic Epistles;"[4] (2) Because they abound in un-Pauline words and phrases; (3) Because their theology differs from that of the Apostle; (4) Because they deal with conditions of ecclesiastical organisation which had no existence till long after the age of the Apostles; (5) Because they betray allusions to later developments of Gnostic heresy: and these objections we will briefly consider.

(1) Now as to the style of these Epistles, we admit at once that it is inferior to that of St. Paul's greatest productions. For eloquence, compression, depth, passion, and logical power, they cannot for one moment be compared to the letters to the Corinthians, Romans, Galatians, or Ephesians. St. Paul is not here at his best or greatest. "His restless energies," says Alford,[5] "are still at work; but those energies have changed their complexion; they have passed from the dialectic character of his earlier Epistles, from the wonderful capacity of intricate combined rationalism of his subsequent Epistles, to the urging, and repeating, and dilating upon truths which have been the food of his life; there is a resting on former conclusions, a constant citation of the *temporis acti*, which lets us into a most interesting phase of the character of the great Apostle. We see here rather the succession of brilliant sparks than the steady flame; burning words indeed and deep pathos, but not the flower of his firmness as in his discipline of the Galatians; not the noon of his bright, warm eloquence, as in the inimitable Psalm of Love."[6]

But in what way does this invalidate their authenticity? We entirely dissent from Baur's exaggerated depreciation of their value; if we admitted that they were as meagre of contents, as colourless in treatment, as deficient in motive and connexion, as full of monotony, repetition, and dependence, as he asserts—what then? Must a writer be always at his greatest? Does not the smallest knowledge of literary history prove at once that writers are liable to extraordinary variations of literary capacity? Do not their shorter and less important works offer in many cases a most singular contrast to their more elaborate compositions? Are all the works of Plato of equal value? Do we find in the *Epinomis* the grandeur and profundity which mark the *Phaedo* and the *Theaetetus*? Is the *Leges* as rich in style as the *Phaedrus*? Is there no difference in manner between the *Annals of Tacitus* and the dialogue *De Oratoribus*? Was it the same hand which wrote

[1] *Paul.* ii. 101.

[2] Davidson freely admits that "there is no great difficulty in supposing that he read the Pastoral Epistles written in Paul's name, and remembered some of their expressions" (*Introd.* ii. 181).

[3] Admitting that "pseudonymity and literary deception" were regarded in antiquity as very different things, I would willingly avoid the word "forger" if there were any other convenient word which could be substituted for it. I quite concede to De Wette, Schleiermacher, Baur, &c., that the word connotes much more than it ought to do, as applied to a writer of the first two centuries, and that "the forging of such Epistles must not be judged according to the modern standard of literary honesty, but according to the spirit of antiquity, which attached no such definite value as we do to literary property, and regarded the *thing* much more than the person" (Baur, *Paul.* ii. 110).

[4] Baur, *Paul.* ii. 106.

[5] *Greek Test.* iii. 83.

[6] 1 Cor. xiii.

Love's Labour's Lost and *Hamlet?* Would any one who read the more prosaic parts of the *Paradise Regained* recognise the poet of the first or sixth books of the *Paradise Lost?* Is the style of Burke in the *Essay on the Sublime and Beautiful* the same as his style in the *Essay on the French Revolution?* It would be quite superfluous to multiply instances. If it be asserted that the Pastoral Epistles are valueless, or unworthy of their author, we at once join issue with the objectors, and, independently of our own judgment, we say that, in that case, they would not have deceived the critical intuition of centuries of thinkers, of whom many were consummate masters of literary expression. If, on the other hand, it be merely contended that the style lacks the *verve* and passion of the earlier Epistles, we reply that this is exactly what we should expect. Granted that "it is not the object of this, as of preceding Epistles, to develop fully some essentially Pauline idea which has still to vindicate itself, and on which the Christian consciousness and life are to be formed, but rather to apply the contents of Christian doctrine to practical life in its varying circumstances," we reply that nothing could be more natural. Granted that, unlike all the other Epistles, they have no true organic development; that they do not proceed from one root-idea which penetrates the whole contents, and binds all the inner parts in an inner unity, because the deeper relations pervade the outward disconnectedness; that no one creative thought determines their contents and structure; that they exhibit no genuine dialectic movement in which the thought possesses sufficient inherent force to originate all the stages of its development;[1] granted, I say—and it is a needlessly large concession—that this depth of conception, this methodical development, this dialectic progress, are wanting in these three letters, we entirely refuse to admit that this want of structural growth belies their Pauline origin. It is little short of absurd to suppose that every one of St. Paul's letters—however brief, however casual, however private—must have been marked by the same features as the Epistles to the Romans or the Galatians. I venture to say that every objection of this kind falls at once to the ground before the simple observation of the fact that these were not grand and solemn compositions dealing with the great problems which were rending the peace of the assembled Churches before which they would be read, but ordinary private letters, addressed by an elder and a superior to friends whom he had probably known from early boyhood, and who were absolutely familiar with the great main features of his teaching and belief. Add the three circumstances that one of them was written during the cruel imprisonment in which his life was drawing to its close; that they were probably written by his own hand, and not with the accustomed aid of an amanuensis;[2] and that they were certainly written in old age,—and we shall at once see how much there is which explains the general peculiarities of their style, especially in its want of cohesion and compression. There are in these Epistles inimitable indications that we are reading the words of an old man. There is neither senility nor garrulity, but there is the dignity and experience which marks the *jucunda senectus*.[3] The digressiveness becomes more diffuse, the generalities more frequent, the repetitions more observable.[4] Formulæ are reiterated with an emphasis which belongs less to the necessities of the present than to the reminiscences of the past. Divergences into personal matters, when he is writing to Timothy, who had so long been his bosom companion, become more numerous and normal.[5] And yet it is impossible not to feel that a

[1] Baur, *Paul.* ii. 107.

[2] The Epistle to the Galatians and the concluding doxology of the Epistle to the Romans were also autographic; and Dean Alford—than whom few men have ever been more closely acquainted with the style of the Apostle in all its peculiarities—has pointed out a series of resemblances between these writings and the Pastoral Epistles (*Greek Test.* iii. 86).

[3] Even when he wrote the Epistle to Philemon he calls himself Paul the Aged, and he had gone through much since then. Supposing him to have been converted at the age of thirty, he would now have been nearly sixty, and could hardly have seemed otherwise than aged, considering the illnesses and trials which had shattered a weak and nervous frame.

[4] 1 Tim. i. 15; ii. 4—6; iii. 16, &c.; 2 Tim. i. 9; ii. 11—13; Tit. i. 1[?]; ii. 11; iii. 3, &c. &c.

[5] 1 Tim. i. 11, *seqq.*; 2 Tim. i. 11, *seqq.*; 15, *seqq.*; iv. 6, *seqq.*

Paul is still the writer. There are flashes of the deepest feeling, outbursts of the most intense expression. There is rhythmic movement and excellent majesty in the doxologies, and the ideal of a Christian pastor is drawn not only with an unfaltering hand, but with a beauty, fulness, and simplicity, which a thousand years of subsequent experience have enabled no one to equal, much less to surpass. In these Epistles direct logical controversy is to a great extent neglected as needless. All that the Apostle had to say in the way of such reasoning had probably been said to his correspondents, in one form or other, again and again. For them, as entrusted with the supervision of important Christian communities, it was needless to develop doctrines with which they were familiar. It was far more necessary to warn them respecting the fatal moral tendencies in which heresies originated, and the fatal moral aberrations in which they too often issued.

And while we are on this subject of style, how much is there which we must at once see to be favourable to the authenticity of these writings! Take the First Epistle to Timothy alone, which is more seriously attacked than the other two, and which is supposed to drag down its companions by the evidence of its spuriousness. Do we not find in it abundant traces of a familiar style? Is it even conceivable that a forger would have actually begun with an *anakoluthon* or unfinished construction? Such sentences abound in the style of St. Paul, and to imitate them with perfect naturalness would be no easy task. But even supposing the possibility of imitation, would a forger have started off with one? Again, it would be very easy to caricature or clumsily imitate the digressive manner which we have attributed to familiarity and age; but to reproduce it so simply and naturally as it here appears would require supreme literary accomplishment. Would an imitator have purposely diverged from St. Paul's invariable salutation by the insertion of "mercy" between "grace" and "peace"? It is easy to understand on psychological grounds that St. Paul might call himself "the chief of sinners" (i. 15); but would a devoted follower have thus written of him? Would he *purposely* and *continually* have lost the main thread of his subject as at ii. 3, 7? A writer with a firm grasp of truths which he knows to be complementary to each other would never hesitate at any merely apparent contradiction of his previous opinions; still less would he hesitate to modify those opinions in accordance with circumstances; but would a forger have been so bold as apparently to contradict in ii. 15 what St. Paul had taught in 1 Cor. vii.? Would he be skilful enough to imitate the simple and natural manner in which, more than once, the Apostle has resumed his Epistle after seeming to be on the point of ending it, as at iii. 14, 15? St. Paul, like most supremely noble writers, is quite indifferent to confusion of metaphors; but would an imitator be likely to follow him with such lordly indifference as at vi. 19? In writing to familiar friends, nothing is more natural than the perfectly casual introduction of minute and unimportant particulars. There is nothing like this in St. Paul's other letters, not even in that to Philemon, and therefore a forger would have had no model to copy. How great a literary artist, then, must have been the forger who—writing with some theory of inspiration, and under the shadow of a great name, and with special objects in view—could furnish accidental minutiæ so natural, so interesting, and even so pathetic as that in 1 Tim. v. 23, or introduce, by way of precaution, such particulars—"unexampled in the Apostle's other writings, founded on no incident, tending to no result"—as the direction to Timothy to bring with him to Rome "the cloak which I left at Troas with Carpus, and the books, especially the parchments." It seems to me that forgery, even under the dominant influence of one impressive personality and one supreme idea, is by no means the extraordinarily easy and simple thing which it appears to be to the adherents of the Tübingen criticism. It is a comparatively simple matter to pass off imitations of a Clemens Romanus or an Ignatius, but it is hardly likely that the world would be long deceived by writings palmed off upon it as those of a Milton—still less of a St. Paul.

(2) It is said they abound in unusual, isolated, and un-Pauline expressions. Among these are "It is a faithful saying,"[1] "piety," and "piously" (*εὐσέβεια, εὐσεβῶς*), found eight times in these Epistles, and nowhere else except in 2 Pet.;[2] the metaphor of "wholesomeness" (*ὑγιής, ὑγιαίνειν*), applied to doctrines nine times in these Epistles, and not elsewhere;[3] the use of *δεσπότης* "Lord" for *κύριος* "master";[4] the use of *ἀρνεῖσθαι* "to deny" for the renunciation of true doctrine; and of *παραιτεῖσθαι* "to avoid," of which the latter is, however, used by Paul in his speech before Festus, and which, as well as *προσέχειν*, with a dative in the sense of "attend to," he very probably picked up in intercourse with St. Lake, to whom both words are familiar.[5] No one, I think, will be seriously startled by these unusual phrases, nor will they shake our belief in the genuineness of the Epistles when we recall that there is not a single Epistle of St. Paul in which these *hapax legomena*, or isolated expressions, do not abound. Critics who have searched minutely into the comparative terminology of the New Testament Scriptures, tell us there are no less than 111 peculiar terms in the Epistle to the Romans, 186 in the two Epistles to the Corinthians, 57 and 54 respectively in the short Epistles to the Galatians and Philippians, 6 even in the few paragraphs addressed to Philemon. It is not therefore in the least degree surprising that there should be 74 in the First Epistle to Timothy, 67 in the Second, and 13 in that to Titus. Still less shall we be surprised when we examine them. St. Paul, it must be remembered, was the main creator of theological language. In the Pastoral Epistles he is dealing with new circumstances, and new circumstances would inevitably necessitate new terms. Any one who reads the list of unusual expressions in the Epistles to Timothy will see at once that the large majority of them are directly connected with the new form of error with which St. Paul had recently been called upon to deal. Men who are gifted with a vivid power of realisation are peculiarly liable to seize upon fresh phrases which embody their own thoughts and convictions, and these phrases are certain to occur frequently at particular periods of their lives, and to be varied from time to time.[6] This is simply a matter of psychological observation, and is quite sufficient to account for the expressions we have mentioned, and many more. We can have little conception of the plasticity of language at its creative epoch, and we must never forget that St. Paul had to find the correct and adequate expression for conceptions which as yet were extremely unfamiliar. Every year would add to the vocabulary, which must at first have been more or less tentative, and the harvest of new expressions would always be most rich where truths, already familiar, were brought into collision with heresies altogether new. The list of *hapax legomena* in the note[7] are all due, not to the difference of authorship, but to the exigencies of the times.

(3) It would be a much more serious—it would indeed be an all but fatal—objection to the authenticity of these Epistles, if it could be proved that their theology differs from that of Paul. But a very little examination will show that there is no such contradiction

[1] Tim. i. 15; iii. 1; iv. 9; 2 Tim. ii. 11; Tit. iii. 8.

[2] 1 Tim. ii. 2; iii. 16; iv. 7; vi. 11; 2 Tim. iii. 5, 12; Tit. i. 1; ii. 12. Pfleiderer suggests that this word *εὐσέβεια* may have been taken as the fundamental idea of the Christian holy life as the word "faith" became gradually externalised.

[3] 1 Tim. i. 10; vi. 3, 4; 2 Tim. i. 13; iv. 3; Tit. i. 9, 13; ii. 1, 8. And, as a natural antithesis, *γάγγραινα* and *νοσεῖν* are applied to false doctrine.

[4] 1 Tim. vi. 1, 2; 2 Tim. ii. 21; Tit. ii. 9.

[5] Alford, *l.c.* Can the use of *δεσπότης* instead of *κύριος* be due to the literary inconvenience which was gradually felt to arise from the fact that the latter word was more and more incessantly employed as the title of our Lord Jesus Christ?

[6] I feel convinced that the Tübingen methods applied to the writings of Mr. Carlyle (for instance) or Mr. Ruskin, would prove in the most triumphant manner that some of their writings were forgeries (α) from their resemblance to, (β) from their dissimilarity from, their other writings. But as Dean Alford happily says, "In a fresh and vigorous style there will ever be (so to speak) *vibrations* over any rigid limits of habitude which can be assigned; and such are to be judged of, not by their mere occurrence or number, but by their subjective character being or not being in accordance with the writer's well-known characteristics" (*Test.* iii. 54).

[7] *γενεαλογίαι*, 1 Tim. i. 4, Tit. iii. 9; *ματαιόλογος*, 1 Tim. i. 6, Tit. i. 10; *κενοφωνίαι*, 1 Tim. vi. 20, 2 Tim. ii. 16; *λογομαχίαι, παραθήκη, βέβηλος, ἀστοχεῖν, τυφοῦσθαι*: &c.

—nothing beyond the varying expression of truths which complement but do not contradict each other. Some, indeed, of the alleged discrepancies are too shadowy to grasp. If Christianity be described as "the doctrine," and as "sound doctrine";[1] if the word "faith" has acquired a more objective significance, so as sometimes almost to imply a body of truths as opposed to heresy;[2] if the name "Saviour"—rare in St. Paul—be applied to God, and not to Christ;[3] if "Palingenesia" (regeneration) occurs only in the Epistle to Titus;[4] these are peculiarities of language, not differences of theology. There is a dominant practical tendency in these Epistles;—so there is, we reply, in all St. Paul's Epistles. The value and blessedness of good works is incessantly insisted on;[5]—is this, then, to be stigmatised as "utilitarianism and religious eudæmonism," and a decided pietistic attenuation of the Pauline doctrine? Are they not, then, insisted on even in the Epistles to the Romans and Galatians, though there he is developing a theory, and here he is professedly occupied with moral instructions? Will any one attempt to prove that St. Paul, either in these Epistles or elsewhere, held any other view of good works than this—that they are profitless to obtain salvation, but are morally indispensable?[6] De Wette's further objection, that St. Paul here makes an apology for the Law (1 Tim. i. 8), and his attempt to draw a subtle distinction between the universalism of these Epistles and of the other Pauline writings, deserve no serious refutation. St. Paul's method and object are here wholly unlike those of his Epistles to Churches composed of heterogeneous and often of hostile elements; but it may be asserted, beyond all fear of contradiction, that, bearing in mind the non-theoretical treatment of the points on which he here touches, and the fact that he is writing to friends and disciples already absolutely convinced of the main truths of his theology, there is not one word in these Epistles which either contradicts or seriously differs from the fundamental ideas of St. Paul. Even Baur—candid, with all his hypercritical prejudices—only sees in them "a certain *something* of the specific Pauline doctrine with a dominant practical tendency," an "applying of the contents of Christian doctrine to the various circumstances of practical life."[7]

(4) It is not, however, on the above grounds that the Pastoral Epistles have been most seriously attacked. The considerations which we have here seen to be untenable are really due to after-thoughts; and the assaults on the genuineness of the Epistles have mainly risen from the belief that they are "tendency-writings," meant to serve the twofold object of magnifying ecclesiastical organisation and of covertly attacking a Gnosticism which was not prevalent till long after the Apostle's time. The two subjects are by no means disconnected. The Gnostics, it is said—as the first heretics properly so called—gave occasion for the episcopal constitution of the Church; and if there were no such heretics at that time, then those ecclesiastical arrangements will be devoid of any historical occasion or connexion! I have sought the strongest and fullest statements of these objections, and shall try to express the reasons why they appear to me to be most absolutely groundless. I quite freely admit that there are some remarkable peculiarities in these Epistles; I do not deny that they suggest some difficulties of which we can give no adequate explanation; I cannot go so far as to say that the objections brought against them are "not adequate even to raise a *doubt* on the subject of their authenticity;" but for these very reasons I can say, with all the deeper sincerity, that, whatever minor

[1] 1 Tim. i. 10; vi. 1.

[2] 1 Tim. i. 19; ii. 7; iii. 9; iv. 1—6; vi. 10, 21. Pfleiderer, *Paulinism*, ii. 201.

[3] Pfleiderer says that in Tit. ii. 13 Christ is called "our great God and Saviour," and that "this goes beyond all the previous Christology of St. Paul." But there can be no doubt that the phrase is applied to God in this place, as also in 1 Tim. i. 1; ii. 3; iv. 10; Tit. i. 3; ii. 10. The anarthrousness of Σωτὴρ is no valid grammatical objection.

[4] Tit. iii. 5.

[5] Baur, *Paul.* ii. 106; De Wette, *Pastoralbr.* 117, c.; Pfleiderer, *Paulinism*, 210; Reuss, *Les Epîtres*, ii. 314.

[6] Rom. ii. 6—10; xiii. 3; Gal. v. 6, &c.; Eph. ii. 8—10, &c.

[7] *Paul.* ii. 107. It is the view of some hostile critics that the Asiatic Epistles (Eph. and Col.) are Pauline with un-Pauline interpolations; and the Pastoral Epistles un-Pauline, yet containing Pauline matter.

hesitations and doubts may remain unremoved, the main arguments of those who reject the Epistles have—even without regard to other elements of external testimony and internal evidence in their favour—been fairly met and fairly defeated all along the line.

(a) Let us first consider the question of ecclesiastical organisation. And here we are at once met with the preliminary and fundamental objection of Baur, that in the Epistles which supply us with the surest standard of St. Paul's principles he never betrays the slightest interest in ecclesiastical institutions, not even when they might be thought to lie directly in his way; and that this want of interest in such things is not merely accidental, but founded deep in the whole spirit and character of Pauline Christianity.

But this form of statement is invidious, and will not stand a moment's examination. In the minutiæ of ecclesiastical institutions, as affected by mere sectarian disputes, St. Paul would have felt no interest; and to that exaltation of human ministers which has received the name of sacerdotalism—feeling as he did the supreme sufficiency of one Mediator—he would have been utterly opposed. It is very probable that he would have treated the differences between Presbyterianism and Episcopacy as very secondary questions—questions of expediency, of which the settlement might lawfully differ in different countries and different times. But to say that he would have considered it superfluous to give directions about the consolidation of nascent Churches, and would have had no opinion to offer about the duties and qualifications of ministers, is surely preposterous. It is, moreover, contradicted by historic facts. His tours to confirm the Churches, his solemn appointment of presbyters with prayers and fastings in his very first missionary journey,[1] and his summons to the Ephesian presbyters, that they might receive his last advice and farewell, would be alone sufficient to prove that such matters did—as it was absolutely necessary that they should—occupy a large part of his attention. Are we to suppose that he gave no pastoral instructions to Timothy when he sent him to the Churches of Macedonia, or to Titus when he appointed him a sort of commissioner to regulate the disorders of the Church of Corinth?

It is true that the pseudo-Clementines, the Apostolical constitutions, parts of the letters of Ignatius, and in all probability other early writings, were forged, with the express object of giving early and lofty sanction to later ecclesiastical development, and above all to the supposed primacy of Rome. But what could be more unlike such developments than the perfectly simple and unostentatious arrangements of the Pastoral Epistles? In the rapid growth of the Christian Church, and the counter-growth of error, the establishment of discipline and government would almost from the first become a matter of pressing exigency. Even in the Epistles to the Corinthians and Romans we find terms that imply the existence of deacons, deaconesses, teachers, prophets, apostles, rulers, overseers or presbyters, and evangelists; and a comparison of the passages referred to will show that all these names, with the exception of the first,[2] were used vaguely, and to a certain extent even synonymously, or as only descriptive of different aspects of the same office.[3] If the imposition of hands is alluded to in the Epistles to Timothy, so it is in the Acts.[4] The notion that a formal profession of faith was required at ordination so little results from 2 Tim. i. 13 that the very next verse is sufficient to disprove such a meaning. If the Pastoral Epistles contained a clear defence of the episcopal system of the second century, this alone would be sufficient to prove their spuriousness; but the total absence of anything resembling it is one of the strongest proofs that they belong to the Apostolic age. Bishop and presbyter are still synonyms,

[1] Acts xiv. 23.

[2] 1 Cor. xii. 28; xvi. 15; Rom. xii. 7; xvi. 1; Phil. i. 1; 1 Thess. v. 12; Eph. iv. 11; Acts xx 17, 28.

[3] To a certain extent, indeed, the overseers, presbyters, and deacons, in their purely official aspect, corresponded to the *Sheliach*, the *Rosh ha-Keneseth*, the *Chazzan* of the synagogue.

[4] 1 Tim. iv. 14; v. 22; Acts vi. 6; viii. 17.

as they are throughout the New Testament.[1] If ἐπίσκοπος, "overseer," or "bishop" be used in the singular, this is partly an accident of language in the common generic use of the Greek article, and partly arises from the very nature of things as a transitional stage to the ultimate meaning of the word—since, even in a presbytery, it is inevitable that some one presbyter should take the lead. Timothy and Titus exercise functions which would be now called episcopal; but they are not called "bishops"; their functions were temporary; and they simply act as authoritative delegates of the Apostle of the Gentiles.[2] Nor is there any trace of exalted pretensions in the overseers whom they appoint. The qualifications required of them are almost exclusively moral. The directions given are "ethical, not hierarchical." And yet it is asserted that one main object of the First Epistle to Timothy is "to establish the primacy of the bishops as against the presbyters"![3] A more arbitrary statement could hardly be formulated. Let any one turn from the Epistle to the letters of St. Ignatius,[4] where he will read, "Give heed to the bishop, that God also may give heed to you;" to the pseudo-Ignatius,[5] who tells us that "he who doeth anything without the knowledge of the bishop serveth the devil"; to the pseudo-Clementines, which say that "the bishop occupies the seat of Christ, and must be honoured as the image of God;"[6] and he will see how glaring is the anachronism of supposing that it was written towards the middle of the second century to oppose the Marcionites; and how utterly different is the mild and natural authority which the Apostle assigns to a representative presbyterate from that "crushing despotism" of irresponsible authority for which the writers of the second century were willing to betray their Christian liberty.

We will consider the minor objections on this head when we come to the actual passages to which exception is taken, and especially the difficult expression in which the Church is apparently called "a pillar and ground of the truth."[7] But another ground of objection is the rules about widows, which, as Baur asserts, "can only be successfully explained out of the ecclesiastical vocabulary of the second century," in which the term χῆραι is applied to an order consisting not only of bereaved persons but even of young virgins.[8] That this use of the word did not arise in the Apostle's time may be fairly assumed, but if there be not one single fact in the passage referred to which makes this necessary, the objection falls to the ground. Baur's only argument is that if χῆραι be actual widows, the Apostle gives two directly contradictory precepts about them, bidding the younger widows to marry again (1 Tim. v. 11—14), and yet ordering that a second marriage is to exclude them, should they again become widows, from the *viduatus* of the Church. But where is the contradiction? We learn from the Acts that the Church continued the merciful and, indeed, essential custom, which it had learnt from the synagogue, of maintaining those widows, who from the circumstances of Eastern and ancient society were its most destitute members, and whose helpless condition constituted a special appeal to pity. But it was only natural that each Church should try as far as

[1] Thus in 1 Tim. iii. St. Paul passes at once from "bishops" (1—7) to "deacons" (8—13), and afterwards speaks of these same bishops as "presbyters" (v. 17—19), and in Tit. i. 5—7 the identification is indisputable. No one is ignorant that "bishops" and "presbyters" are in the New Testament identical (Acts xx. 17—28; Phil. i. 1; 1 Pet. v. 2). The fact was well known to the Fathers, οἱ πρεσβύτεροι τὸ παλαιὸν ἐκαλοῦντο ἐπίσκοποι . . . καὶ οἱ ἐπίσκοποι πρεσβύτεροι (Chrys. *ad Phil.* i. 1; Jer. *ad Tit.* i. 5). The more marked distinction of the two is first found in Ignatius *ad Polyc.* 6.

[2] 1 Tim. i. 3; iii. 14; 2 Tim. iv. 9, 21; Tit. i. 5; iii. 12.

[3] Pfleiderer, *Paulinism*, ii. 205. Yet he admits (p. 203) that in the second Epistle the remarks addressed to Timothy are "very far removed from the later conceptions of the exalted condition of a bishop," and that even in the first Epistle "the difference between bishops and presbyters does not appear to be any fixed difference of officers."

[4] *Ad Polyc.* 6. If the shorter form of the seven Ignatian Epistles be genuine, they show that even at the beginning of the second century, the ecclesiastical development was so far in advance of the Pastoral Epistles as almost to demonstrate the genuineness of the latter.

[5] *Ad Smyrn.* 9.

[6] Clem. *Hom.* iii. 62, 66, 70. For these and other quotations see Dr. Lightfoot's essay on the Christian ministry (*Philippians*, p. 209, *seqq.*).

[7] 1 Tim. iii. 15.

[8] τὰς παρθένους τὰς λεγομένας χήρας (Ign. *ad Smyrn.* 13). The genuineness of the passage is far from certain.

possible to utilise this institution, and that the widows should themselves desire to be serviceable to the brethren to whom they owed their livelihood. Hence "the widows" became a recognised order, and acquired a semi-religious position. Into this order St. Paul wisely forbids the admission of widows who are still of an age to marry again. Of the female character in general and in the abstract he does not ordinarily speak in very exalted terms; and in this respect he only resembles most ancient writers, although, in spite of surrounding conditions of society, he sees the moral elevation of the entire sex in Christ. He regarded it as almost inevitable that the religious duties of the "order of widows," although they involved a sort of consecration to celibacy for the remainder of their lives, would never serve as a sufficient barrier to their wish to marry again; and he thought that moral degeneracy and outward scandal would follow from the intrusion of such motives into the fulfilment of sacred functions. There is here no contradiction, and not the shadow of a proof that in the language of the Epistle there must be any identification of widows with an order of female celibates or youthful nuns.[1]

(β) We now come to the last objection, which is by far the strongest and most persistent, as it is also the earliest. The spuriousness of the Pastoral Epistles is mainly asserted on the ground that they indicate the existence of a Gnosticism which was not fully developed till after the death of St. Paul. A more extensive theory was never built on a more unstable foundation.[2] The one word *antitheseis* in 1 Tim. vi. 20, seems to Baur a clear proof that the First Epistle to Timothy is a covert polemic against Marcion in the middle of the second century. To an hypothesis so extravagant it is a more than sufficient answer that the heretical tendencies of the false teachers were distinctly Judaic, whereas there was not a single Gnostic system which did not regard Judaism as either imperfect or pernicious. Objections of this kind can only be regarded as fantastic until some proof be offered (1) that the germs of Gnosticism did not exist in the apostolic age; and (2) that the phrases of Gnosticism were not borrowed from the New Testament, nor those of the New Testament from the Gnostic systems. Knowing as we do that "Æon" was thus borrowed by Valentinus,[3] and that "Gnosis" was beginning to acquire a technical meaning even when St. Paul wrote his Epistle to the Corinthians,[4] we see that on the one hand Gnostic terms are no proof of allusion to Gnostic tenets, and on the other, that Gnostic tendencies existed undeveloped from the earliest epoch of the Christian Church. It would be far truer to say that the absence of anything like definite allusion to the really distinctive elements of Marcionite or Valentinian teaching is a decisive proof that these Epistles belong to a far earlier epoch, than to say that they are an attempt to use the great name of Paul to discountenance those subtle heresies. In the Epistle to the Colossians St. Paul had dealt formally with the pretended philosophy and vaunted insight, the incipient dualism, the baseless angelology, and the exaggerated asceticism of local heretics whose theosophic fancies were already prevalent.[5] In these Epistles he merely touches on them, because in private letters to beloved fellow-workers there was no need to enter into any direct controversy with their erroneous teachings. But he alludes to these elements with the distinct statement that they were of Judaic origin. Valentinus rejected the Mosaic law; Marcion was Antinomian; but these Ephesian and Cretan teachers, although their dualism is revealed by their ascetic discouragement of marriage, their denial of the resurrection, and their interminable "genealogies" and myths,[6] are not only Jews, but founded their subtleties and specula-

[1] 1 Cor. xiv. 34; 1 Tim. ii. 12—14; 2 Tim. iii. 6; &c.

[2] Apparently the use of the word ἑτεροδιδασκαλεῖν in 1 Tim. i. 3 as compared with ἑτεροδιδάσκαλοι in Hegesippus first led Schleiermacher to doubt the genuineness of the First Epistle.

[3] Hippolytus (*R. H.* vi. 20) tells us that Valentinus gave the name of Æons to the emanations which Simon Magus had called Roots.

[4] 1 Cor. viii. 1. The adjective "Gnostic" is ascribed to the Ophites, or to Carpocrates. (Iren. *Haer.* i. 25; Euseb. *H. E.* iv. 7, 9.)

[5] See Col. ii. 16, 17; ii. 8, 18; and Mansel, *The Gnostic Heresies*, p. 54.

[6] 1 Tim. i. 4; iv. 4; 2 Tim. ii. 18.

tions on the Mosaic law.[1] In dealing with these Paul has left far behind him the epoch of his struggle with the Pharisaic legalists of Jerusalem. Thought moves with vast rapidity; systems are developed into ever-varying combinations in an amazingly short space of time, at epochs of intense religious excitement, and as the incipient Gnosticism of the apostolic age shows many of the elements which would hereafter be ripened into later development, so it already shows the ominous tendency of restless speculation to degenerate into impious pride, and of over-strained asceticism to link itself with intolerable license.[2] These are speculations and tendencies which belong to no one country and no one age. Systems and ideas closely akin to Gnosticism are found in the religions and philosophies of Greece, Persia, India, China, Egypt, Phœnicia; they are found in Plato, in Zoroaster, in the Vedas, in the writings of the Buddhists, in Philo, in neo-Platonism, and in the Jewish Kabbalah. In all ages and all countries they have produced the same intellectual combinations and the same moral results. A writer of the second century could have had no possible object in penning a forgery which in his day was far too vague to be polemically effective.[3] On the other hand, an apostle of the year 65 or 66, familiar with Essene and Oriental speculations, a contemporary of Simon Magus the reputed founder of all Gnosticism, and of Cerinthus, its earliest heresiarch, might have had reason—even apart from divine guidance and prophetic inspiration—to warn the disciples to whom he was entrusting the care and constitution of his Churches against tendencies which are never long dormant, and which were already beginning to display a dangerous activity and exercise a dangerous fascination. If there is scarcely a warning which would not apply to the later Gnostics, it is equally true that there is not a warning which would not equally apply to errors distinctly reprobated in the Epistles to the Philippians, Corinthians, and Colossians, as well as to the Churches addressed by St. Peter, St. Jude, and St. John.[4] Greek subtleties, Eastern imagination, Jewish mysticism—in one word, the inherent curiosity and the inherent Manicheism of unregenerate human nature—began from the very first to eat like a canker into the opening bud of Christian faith.

Those who wish to see every possible argument which can be adduced against the Pauline authorship of these Epistles, may find them marshalled together by Dr. Davidson in the latter editions of his "Introduction to the Study of the New Testament."[5] To answer them point by point would be tedious, for many of them are exceedingly minute;[6] nor would it be convincing, for critics will make up their minds on the question on the broader and larger grounds which I have just examined. But to sum up, I would say that, although we cannot be as absolutely *certain* of their authenticity as we are of that of the earlier Epistles, yet that scarcely any difficulty in accepting their authenticity will remain if we bear in mind the following considerations. (1) In times like those of early Christianity, systems were developed and institutions consolidated with extraordinary rapidity. (2) These letters were written, not with the object

[1] 1 Tim. i. 7; Tit. i. 10, 14; iii. 9.

[2] 1 Tim. i. 7, 19; iv. 2; 2 Tim. ii. 17; iii. 1—7; Tit. i. 11, 15, 16.

[3] The vagueness is due to the still wavering outlines of the heretical teachings. The "Gnosticism" aimed at has been by various critics identified with Kabbalism (Baumgarten); with Pharisaism (Wiesinger); with Essenism (Mangold); with Marcionism (Baur)—

> "If shape it could be called which shape had none
> Distinguishable in vesture, joint, or limb."

But whether Gnosticism be regarded as theological speculation (Gieseler), or an aristocratic and exclusive philosophy of religion (Neander), or allegorising dualism (Baur), if "it is still an accomplished task to seize amidst so much that is indefinite, vague, merely circumlocutory and only partly true, those points that furnish a clear conception of it," then it is clearly idle to say that its undeveloped genius cannot have existed in the days of the Apostles.

[4] Phil. iii. 18; 1 Cor. xv.

[5] Vol. ii., pp. 137—195.

[6] I shall, however, touch on some of these in speaking of the Epistles separately. It has been said that Paley uses the discrepancies between the Acts and the Epistles to prove their independence, and the agreements to establish their truthfulness. It may certainly be said that the Tübingen school adduces un-Pauline expressions to prove non-authenticity, and Pauline expressions to prove forgery.

of entering into direct controversy, but to guide the general conduct of those on whom that duty had devolved, and who were already aware of that fixed body of truth which formed the staple of the apostolic teaching. (3) They abound in unusual expressions, because new forms of error required new methods of stating truth. (4) Their unity is less marked and their style less logical, because they are the private and informal letters of an elder, written with the waning powers of a life which was rapidly passing beyond the sphere of earthly controversies. Pauline in much of their phraseology, Pauline in their fundamental doctrines, Pauline in their dignity and holiness of tone, Pauline alike in their tenderness and severity, Pauline in the digressions, the constructions, and the personality of their style, we may accept two of them with an absolute conviction of their authenticity, and the third—the First Epistle to Timothy, which is more open to doubt than the others—with at least a strong belief that in reading it we are reading the words of the greatest of the Apostles.[1]

EXCURSUS XXVIII.

Chronology of the Life and Epistles of St. Paul.

To enter fully into the chronology of this period would require a separate volume, and although there is now an increasing tendency to unanimity on the subject, yet some of the dates can only be regarded as approximate. As few definite chronological indications are furnished in the Acts or the Epistles, we can only frame our system by working backwards and forwards, with the aid of data which are often vague, from the few points where the sacred narrative refers to some distinct event in secular history. These, which furnish us with our *points de repère*, are—

The Death of Herod Agrippa I., A.D. 44.
The Expulsion of the Jews from Rome, A.D. 52.
The Arrival of Festus as Procurator, A.D. 60.
The Neronian Persecution, A.D. 64.

How widely different have been the schemes adopted by different chronologers may be seen from the subjoined table, founded on that given by Meyer.

[1] Even Usteri, Lücke, Neander, and Bleek are unconvinced of the authenticity of the First Epistle. Otto, Wieseler, and Reuss have said all that is to be said in favour of a single captivity; but on the assumption that the Pastoral Epistles are genuine, such a theory forces us into a mass of impossibilities. The conviction at which I have arrived may be summed up thus:—If St. Paul was put to death at the end of his first imprisonment, the Pastoral Epistles must certainly be spurious. But there is the strongest possible evidence that two of them at least are genuine, and great probability in favour of the other. They therefore furnish us with a proof of the current tradition that his trial, as he had anticipated, ended in an acquittal, and that a period of about two years elapsed between his liberation and his subsequent arrest, imprisonment, and death.

EVENTS.	[H. A. W. Meyer].	Eusebius.	Jerome.	Chronicon Paschale.	Baronius.	Petavius.	Usher.	Spanheim.	Pearson.	Tillemont.	Basnage.
Ascension of Christ	31	33	33	31	32	31	33	33	33	33	33
Stephen stoned	33 or 34	...	...	a. Claud. I.	32	31	33	38?	34	33	37
Paul's conversion	35	...	33	a. Claud. II.	34	33	35	40	35	34	37
Paul's first journey to Jerusalem	38	...	...	a. Claud. III.	37	36	38	43	38	37	40
Paul's arrival at Antioch	43	...	...	a. Claud. III.	41	40	43	43?	42	43	40
Death of James	44	...	...	...	42	41	44	...	44	44	44
The famine	44	41	44	...	42	42	44	44	44	44	42
Paul's second journey to Jerusalem	44	...	...	46	42	41	44	44	44	44	42
Paul's first missionary journey	45 to 51	...	...	a. Claud. V.	44 to 47	42	45 to 48	...	44 to 47	44 to 46	45 to 47
Paul's third journey to Jerusalem, to the Apostolic convention	52	...	...	...	49	49	52	53	49	51	50
Paul commences the second missionary journey	52	...	...	...	49	49	53	...	50	51	50
Banishment of the Jews from Rome	52	...	49	...	49	49	54	...	52	49 to 52	51
Paul arrives at Corinth ...	53	...	...	...	50	50	54	54?	52	52	51
Paul's fourth journey to Jerusalem (*al.* Cæsarea) and third miss. journey	55	...	...	...	52 Cæs	52	56	54?	54	54	53
Paul's abode at Ephesus ...	56 to 58	...	...	...	53 to 55	52 to 54	56 to 59	56 to 58	54 to 57	54 to 57	53 to 55
Paul's fifth journey to Jerusalem, and imprisonment	59	...	...	53 or 54	56	55	60	59	58	58	56
Paul is removed from Cæsarea to Rome ...	61	55	57	under Nero.	56	56	62	60	60	60	59
Paul's imprisonment of two years in Rome ...	62 or 64	...	to a Ner. IV.	...	57 to 59	...	63 to 65	61 to 63	61 to 63	61 to 63	60 to 62

Bengel.	Michaelis.	Eichhorn.	Kuinoel.	Winer.	De Wette.	Schrader.	Olshausen.	Anger.	Sanclemente and Ideler.	Wieseler.	Ewald.	Lechler.	Wordsworth.	Alford.
30	33	32	33	30?	...	35	33	31	29 Id.	30	33	...	30	30
30	...	37	37 or 38	37?	...	35	...	37	...	39?	38	...	33	37
31	37?	37 or 38	40	38?	37 or 38	39	36	38	35 or 38	40	38	between 37 and 41	34	37
33	...	40 or 41	43	41	40 or 41	42	38	41	38 or 41	43	41	...	37	40
39	...	42	...	...	43 or 44	43	41	43 or 44 or 45?	...	44	44	...	43	41
42	about 44	44	43 or 44	44	44	44	...	43 or 44	...	44	44	...	...	44
44	44	44 or 45	44	44	...	...	...	{44 or 45 or 46?}	...	45	45 to 46	between 44 and 45	44	44
44 to 44	44	44	44	45	44 or 45	44	44		44	45	45 to 46	...	44	44
45 to 46	...	45 ff.	...	...	...	44 to 46	to 49	to about 48	...	45 to 47	48 to 51	46 to 48	45	45
47	...	52	52	51	50 or 51	47	52	51	52	about 50	52	...	49 to 50	50
47	...	53	...	...	51 or 52	47	52	51	...	about 50	52	...	51	51
...	54?	54?	52	52	between 52 and 54	49	...	51 or 52	...	52	52	...	...	...
48	54?	about 54	52	52	52 or 53	49	53	52	...	52	53	...	53	53
49	...	56	Cæs	54	53 or 54	51	55	54	56	54	55	54 or 55	54	54
50 to 52	...	57 to 59	...	55 to 57	54 or 55ff.	51 ff	56 and 57	54 to 57	...	54 to 57	to 58	55 to 57	54 to 57	55
53	60	60	57	58	58 or 59	59	60	58	60	58	59	58	58	58
55	62	62	59	60	60 or 61	61	62	60	62	60	61	60	61	61
56 to 58	63 to 65	63 to 65	60 to 62	61 to 63	62 to 64	62 to 64	63 to 65	61 to 63	63 to 65	61 to 64	62 to 64	62 to 64	61 to 63	61 to 63

I subjoin a separate list of the dates of the Epistles adopted in this volume. The reasons are stated *in loco*, but the reader will understand that the dates in some instances can only be *approximate*.

DATES OF THE EPISTLES.

EPISTLE.	WRITTEN AT	A.D.
1 Thessalonians.	Corinth.	52.
2 Thessalonians.	Corinth.	52.
1 Corinthians.	Ephesus.	57.
2 Corinthians.	Philippi (?).	58 (early).
Galatians.	Corinth.	58.
Romans.	Corinth.	58.
Philippians.	Rome.	61 or 62.
Colossians } Philemon }	Rome.	63.
Ephesians.	Rome.	63.
1 Timothy.	Macedonia (?).	65 or 66.
Titus.	Macedonia (?).	66.
2 Timothy.	Rome.	67.

The subjoined table will give the probable dates of the chief events in the Apostle's life, with those of the events in secular history with which they synchronised.

TABLE OF CONTEMPORARY RULERS, ETC.

	EMPERORS.	PROCURATORS.	LEGATES OF SYRIA.	KINGS.	HIGH PRIESTS.	EVENTS IN LIFE OF ST. PAUL.
14	TIBERIUS (sole Emperor).					
25	......	......	......	......	Caiaphas.	
26	......	Pontius Pilatus.				
29						
30						
31						
32	Retires to Capreæ					
33						
34	A Phœnix said to have been seen in Egypt.	......	Vitellius.			
35						
36						
37	GAIUS (Caligula) (March 16).	Marullus (Ἱππάρχης).	......	......	Jonathan	Martyrdom of Stephen. St. Paul's Conversion.
38	......	......	......	......	Theophilus.	
39	......	......	Petronius Turpilianus.	Herod Agrippa I.	......	First Visit to Jerusalem.
40	Orders his statue to be placed in the Temple. Embassy of Philo.	......	......	......	......	At Tarsus.
41	CLAUDIUS (Jan. 24).	......	......	......	Simon Kanthera.	At Antioch.
42	Disciples called Christians at Antioch.	......	Vibuis Marsus.	Herod Agrippa I. (dominion extended).	Matthias.	
43	......	......	......	......	Elionæus, son of Kanthera.	

TABLE OF CONTEMPORARY RULERS, ETC.—*continued.*

	EMPERORS.	PROCURATORS.	LEGATES OF SYRIA.	KINGS.	HIGH PRIESTS.	EVENTS IN LIFE OF ST. PAUL.
44	Famine (Jos. *Antt.* xx. 5, § 2).	Cuspius Fadus	Cassius Longinus.	Death of Herod Agrippa I.	......	Second Visit to Jerusalem.
45	......	......	......	......	Joseph Ben Kamhit.	First Mission Journey.
46	......	Tiberius Alexander.				
47	......	......	......	......	Ananias, son of Nebedæus.	
48	......	Ventidius Cumanus.	Ummidius Quadratus.			
49	Expulsion of Jews from Rome.	......	......	Agrippa II., King of Chalcis.		
50	Caractacus taken to Rome.					
51	......	......	......	......	......	Third Visit to Jerusalem, and Synod. At Corinth.
52	......	......	......	Agrippa II. (Batanæa and Trachonitis).	Ishmael Ben Phabi.	1, 2 Thess.
53	......	Claudius Felix	......	......	......	Fourth Visit to Jerusalem.
54	NERO (Oct. 13)					
55						
56	Birth of Trajan.					
57	Trial of Pomponia Græcina (as a Christian?).	......	......	......	......	Paul at Eph. 1 Cor.
58	......	......	......	......	......	Second Ep. to Corinthians. Epistle to Galatians.
59	Murder of Agrippina.					
60	......	Porcius Festus	Corbulo			
61	Revolt of Boadicea.	......	......	......	Joseph Cabi	At Rome.
62	Deaths of Burrus, Octavia, and Pallas. Nero marries Poppæa.	Albinus	......	......	Ananus	Epistle to Philippians.
63	Power of Tigellinus.	......	......	......	Jesus, son of Damnæus.	Ep. to Colossians, Philemon, and Ephesus. Paul liberated
64	Great Fire of Rome. Persecution of Christians.					
65	Death of Seneca	Gessius Florus	......	......	......	First Epistle to Timothy. Ep. to Titus.
66	Beginnings of Jewish War. Nero in Greece.					
67	Siege of Jotapata	......	......	......	......	Second Epistle to Timothy. Martyrdom
68	Suicide of Nero (June). GALBA.	Vespasian takes Jericho.	......	......	......	

EXCURSUS XXIX.

TRADITIONAL ACCOUNTS OF ST. PAUL'S PERSONAL APPEARANCE.

THE traditional accounts of the personal appearance of the great Apostle are too late to have any independent value, but it is far from improbable that where they coincide they preserve with accuracy a few particulars. Such as they are, the reader may perhaps care to see them translated; but he must bear in mind the sad probability that there were periods of St. Paul's career at which, owing to the disfigurement wrought by the ravages of his affliction, we should not have liked to gaze upon his face.

In the sixth century John of Antioch, commonly called Malala,[1] writes that "Paul was in person round-shouldered (τῇ ἡλικίᾳ κονδοειδής), with a sprinkling of grey on his head and beard, with an aquiline nose, greyish eyes, meeting eyebrows,[2] with a mixture of pale and red in his complexion, and an ample beard. With a genial expression of countenance, he was sensible, earnest, easily accessible, sweet, and inspired with the Holy Spirit."

Nicephorus,[3] writing in the fifteenth century, says, "Paul was short, and dwarfish in stature, and, as it were, crooked in person and slightly bent. His face was pale, his aspect winning. He was bald-headed, and his eyes were bright. His nose was prominent and aquiline, his beard thick and tolerably long, and both this and his head were sprinkled with white hairs."

In the Acts of Paul and Thekla, a romance of the third century, he is described as "short, bald, bow-legged, with meeting eyebrows, hook-nosed, full of grace."[4]

Lastly, in the Philopatris of the pseudo-Lucian,[5] a forgery of the fourth century,[6] he is contemptuously alluded to as "the bald-headed, hook-nosed Galilæan who trod the air into the third heaven, and learnt the most beautiful things."

The reader must judge whether any rill of truth may have trickled into these accounts through centuries of tradition. As they do not contradict, but are rather confirmed by, the earliest portraits which have been preserved to us, we may perhaps assume from them thus much, that St. Paul was short—a fact also mentioned by the pseudo-Chrysostom,[7] and to which he may himself allude with somewhat bitter touches of irony in his Second Epistle to the Corinthians[8]—that he had a slight stoop, if not a positive bend, in the shoulders; that his nose was aquiline, and that his thin hair was early "sable-silvered." We may also conjecture from these notices that his face was pale, and liable to a quick flush and change of expression, and that when he was not absolutely disfigured by his malady, or when he was able to throw off the painful self-consciousness by which it was accompanied, the grace and sweetness of his address, the dignity and fire of his bearing, entirely removed the first unfavourable impression caused by the insignificance of his aspect. We may conclude that this was the case from many of the circumstances of his intercourse with men and churches, and also from the fact that the rude inhabitants of Lystra take him—before he had yet attained to middle age, and before his body had been so rudely battered as it was by many subsequent miseries—for an incarnation of the young and eloquent Hermes.

[1] X. 257.

[2] This συνοφρύωμα, and the expression ἀτενίσας, may be the sole ground for fancying that the eyes of St. Paul were grey and bright.

[3] *H. E.* ii. 37.

[4] I can make nothing of the εὔκνημος following the ἀγκύλος ταῖς κνήμαις.

[5] *Philopatr.* 12.

[6] Such is the opinion of Gesner in his dissertation *De Aetate et Auctore Philopatridis.*

[7] ὁ τρίπηχυς ἄνθρωπος.

[8] 2 Cor. x. 10—16, especially verse 14.

INDEX.

D.

E.

H.

I.

J.

K.

L.

M.

N.

R.

S.

T.

U.

V.

W.

Y.

Z.

PASSAGES OF SCRIPTURE

QUOTED OR REFERRED TO.

THE END.

CASSELL & COMPANY, LIMITED, BELLE SAUVAGE WORKS, LONDON, E.C.

50,981

BY THE SAME AUTHOR.

THE LIFE OF CHRIST.

By the Ven. ARCHDEACON FARRAR, D.D., F.R.S.,

LIBRARY EDITION. *Thirty-first Edition.* Two Vols., demy 8vo. cloth, 24s.; morocco, £2 2s.; tree calf, £2 5s.

ILLUSTRATED EDITION. With about 300 Original Illustrations, Coloured Map, and Steel Title. Extra crown 4to, cloth, gilt edges, 21s.; morocco or calf, 42s.

POPULAR EDITION. One Volume crown 8vo, cloth, 6s.; gilt edges, 7s. 6d.; Persian morocco, 10s. 6d.; tree calf, 15s.

BIJOU EDITION. Five Vols., cloth, in case, 10s. 6d.; or, in French morocco, 21s.

"Dr. Farrar's qualifications for this great work are in many respects eminent. No thoughtful mind will rise from the perusal of this book without feeling that it reveals a beautiful and an harmonious conception. It will serve to raise the mind from mere objections in detail to a comprehensive view of the whole subject, and it will at the least assist candid objectors to do justice to the Christian tradition." —*Times.*

"Dr. Farrar has not spent in vain the years he has devoted to the researches of his predecessors, or the labour of his own investigations in the Holy Land; and the light he has thus been enabled to throw, often by a few explanatory words, sometimes by the turn of a phrase, sometimes by the more accurate translation of a verse, raises the most familiar sentences to new significance, and gives to his most interesting book more than the value of bulky commentaries."—*Daily News.*

"Space does not permit us to notice as they deserve the abounding notes which show the brilliant scholarship of their author, and present on almost every page matter for study and reflection to the cultivated reader."—*Daily Telegraph.*

"Regard the book from what point of view we may, it stands almost alone as a Life of Christ, both in beauty of style and in completeness."—*Standard.*

"Dr. Farrar may certainly be congratulated upon a literary success to which the annals of English theology present no parallel."—*Quarterly Review.*

"We have in every page the result of an intimate acquaintance with the literature bearing upon this great subject."—*Guardian.*

"We value Dr. Farrar's work as an able exposition of the mass of critical information which has been collected by the labours of learned men, whether friendly or unfriendly to revelation, during recent years."—*Record.*

"A scholarly yet popular Life of Christ was much wanted by the thousands who teach in our schools, and by the tens of thousands who now read and study the Gospels for themselves. This want has been met, fully and admirably, by the Life now before us."—*Nonconformist.*

"We do not hesitate to say that the amount of illustrative matter thus accumulated is by far the richest that has been hitherto offered to the English public."—*Academy.*

"The book is rendered far more useful, as well as extremely beautiful and attractive, by the magnificent series of pictorial illustrations with which it is now supplied in the present edition."—*Illustrated London News.*

"In scholarship, in criticism, in learning, it is abreast with our time. But it stands among modern lives alone for its deep piety, its reverent spirit, and especially its wealth of illustration and splendour of rhetoric."—*New York Church Journal.*

CASSELL & COMPANY, LIMITED, LUDGATE HILL, LONDON.

BY THE SAME AUTHOR.

THE EARLY DAYS OF CHRISTIANITY.

By the Ven. ARCHDEACON FARRAR, D.D., F.R.S.

LIBRARY EDITION. *Ninth Edition.* Two Vols., demy 8vo, cloth, price 24s.; or in morocco, £2 2s.

POPULAR EDITION. One Vol., cloth, 6s.; cloth, gilt edges, 7s. 6d.; Persian morocco, 10s. 6d.; tree calf, 15s.

"These volumes are the result of wide reading and independent thinking. All the talents of the author come out in them prominently."—*Athenæum.*

"Of the six bulky octavos, averaging nearly 600 pages apiece, exclusive of tables, contents, and indexes, devoted to what we may call 'the Origins of Christianity,' given to the world during the last eight years by the unwearied industry of Dr. Farrar's facile pen, the two last are decidedly the best."—*Guardian.*

"After all that can be said on points assailable by stern criticism, Dr. Farrar's book remains a powerful and brilliant performance. He writes with unflagging energy; he never fails for effective language."—*British Quarterly Review.*

"The English readers whom he addresses will feel that the charm exerted on them by the 'Life of Christ' and the 'Life of St. Paul' is still kept up in these volumes, which deal with controversies less familiar to the general public, and with the most important but, in some respects, the most obscure period in the history of the Christian Church. . . . The part of the second volume which deals with the life of St. John, and especially the second section of the twenty-seventh chapter, will take many 'English readers' over new ground. They will everywhere find in Canon Farrar a most eloquent and interesting guide, and will rise from the reading of these volumes with a vivid picture of the 'Early Days of Christianity' in their minds."—*Daily News.*

"Presents us with a picture of the 'Church and Society' in the first century of the Christian era, lively, graphic, and interesting. . . . Dr. Farrar has borrowed from contemporary history all the light which it is capable of throwing on the writings of the Apostles."—*Standard.*

"It needs but a glance through the two substantial volumes in which Canon Farrar has, as he tells us, embodied the results of twelve years' leisure hours devoted to the work, to see that this will probably be the book of the season. . . . That this book will have numerous and deeply-interested readers it is impossible to doubt. It contains many passages of exceeding power and beauty which may well tend to edification."—*Rock.*

"Its object is to furnish English readers with a companion, partly historic and partly expository, to the whole of the New Testament, and when we say that it fully answers this purpose, and that it is quite equal to the Canon's former works, we have said enough to commend it to the attention of our readers, many of whom will peruse and study it for themselves."—*Watchman.*

"It displays in a marked degree the skill of the author in presenting old religious questions in a new and vivid historic light."—*Scotsman.*

"The author sets forth with remarkable clearness of statement and fulness of knowledge the distinctive characteristics of the work and the writings of St. Peter, St. James, St. Jude, St. John, and the Author of the Epistle to the Hebrews, in combination with vigorously-drawn narrative portraits and powerful sketches of the manners, customs, and faiths of the times in which they lived."—*Edinburgh Daily Review.*

CASSELL & COMPANY, LIMITED, LUDGATE HILL, LONDON.

SELECTIONS FROM

CASSELL & COMPANY'S Publications.

The Early Days of Christianity. By the Ven. Archdeacon FARRAR, D.D., F.R.S.

LIBRARY EDITION. (*Ninth Thousand.*) Two Vols., demy 8vo, cloth, 24*s.*; or morocco, £2 2*s.*

POPULAR EDITION, cloth, 6*s.*; cloth gilt, 7*s.* 6*d.*; Persian morocco, 10*s.* 6*d.*; tree-calf, 15*s.*

The Life and Work of St. Paul. By the Ven. Archdeacon FARRAR, D.D., F.R.S.

LIBRARY EDITION. (*Nineteenth Thousand.*) Two volumes, demy 8vo, cloth, 24*s.*; or bound in morocco, £2 2*s.*

ILLUSTRATED EDITION. With about 300 Illustrations. £1 1*s.*; or bound in morocco, £2 2*s.*

POPULAR EDITION, cloth, 6*s.*; cloth gilt, 7*s.* 6*d.*; Persian morocco, 10*s.* 6*d.*; tree-calf, 15*s.*

The Life of Christ. By the Ven. Archdeacon FARRAR, D.D., F.R.S.

LIBRARY EDITION. (*Twenty-ninth Edition.*) Two Vols., demy 8vo, cloth, 24*s.*; or morocco, £2 2*s.*

ILLUSTRATED EDITION. With about 300 Original Illustrations. 4to, cloth, gilt edges, 21*s.*; calf or morocco, £2 2*s.*

BIJOU EDITION. Five Vols., cloth, in box, 10*s.* 6*d.* the set; or French morocco, 21*s.*

POPULAR EDITION, in One Vol., cloth, 6*s.*; cloth, gilt edges, 7*s.* 6*d.*; Persian morocco, 10*s.* 6*d.*; tree-calf, 15*s.*

THE NEW BIBLE COMMENTARY.

The Old Testament Commentary for English Readers. Edited by the Right Rev. C. J. ELLICOTT, D.D., Lord Bishop of Gloucester and Bristol. Five Volumes, price 21*s.* each.

Volume I., price 21*s.*, *contains*—GENESIS TO NUMBERS.
Volume II., price 21*s.*, *contains*—DEUTERONOMY TO II. SAMUEL.
Volume III., price 21*s.*, *contains*—I. KINGS TO ESTHER.
Volume IV., price 21*s.*, *contains*—JOB TO ISAIAH.
Volume V., price 21*s.*, *contains*—JEREMIAH TO MALACHI.

The New Testament Commentary for English Readers. Edited by the Right Rev. C. J. ELLICOTT, D.D., Lord Bishop of Gloucester and Bristol. Complete in Three Volumes. Extra crown 4to, 21*s.* each; or in half morocco, £4 14*s.* 6*d.* the set.

Volume I., price 21*s.*, *contains*—ST. MATTHEW TO ST. JOHN.
Volume II., price 21*s.*, *contains*—THE ACTS OF THE APOSTLES TO GALATIANS.
Volume III., price 21*s.*, *contains*—EPHESIANS TO THE REVELATION.

Sermons Preached at Westminster Abbey. By ALFRED BARRY, D.D., D.C.L., Bishop of Sydney, Metropolitan of New South Wales, and Primate of Australia. 5*s.*

Cassell & Company, Limited: Ludgate Hill, London: Paris; and New York.

L. Ch.—8.84

A Commentary on the Revised Version of the New Testament for English Readers. By Prebendary HUMPHRY, B.D., Member of the Company of Revisers of the New Testament. 7*s.* 6*d.*

The Bible of Christ and His Apostles. By Professor ALEXANDER ROBERTS, D.D. Cloth, 7*s.* 6*d.*

Secular Life, The Gospel of the. Sermons preached at Oxford. By the Hon. W. H. FREMANTLE, Canon of Canterbury. Price 5*s.*

The Child's Life of Christ. Complete in One handsome Volume, with nearly 300 Original Illustrations. 21*s.*

The Child's Bible. With 200 ORIGINAL ILLUSTRATIONS. Being a Selection from the Holy Bible, in the Words of the Authorised Version. Cloth, gilt edges, £1 1*s.* *Cheap Edition*, 7*s.* 6*d.*

Roberts's Holy Land. THREE DIVISIONS. Containing 120 Tinted Plates. 18*s.* each.

Cassell's Bible Dictionary. With nearly 600 Illustrations. Crown 4to, 1,159 pages. *Cheap Edition.* Cloth, 7*s.* 6*d.*; half morocco, 10*s.* 6*d.*

The Bible Educator. Edited by the Very Rev. Dean PLUMPTRE, D.D. Containing about 400 Illustrations. Complete in Four Vols., cloth, 6*s.* each.

The Doré Bible. ROYAL 4TO EDITION. Complete in Two Vols., with 220 Illustrations by GUSTAVE DORÉ. Cloth, £2 10*s.*; Persian morocco, £3 10*s.*

The Family Bible. With 900 ILLUSTRATIONS. Printed on Fine Toned Paper. Leather, gilt edges, £2 10*s.*

Cassell's Illustrated Bible. With 900 ILLUSTRATIONS. Royal 4to, 1,476 pages. Persian morocco, gilt edges; or in leather, with corners and clasps.

The Crown Illustrated Bible. With 900 Original Illustrations, executed specially for this Edition. Crown 4to, cloth, 7*s.* 6*d.* *Can also be had in Leather Bindings in great variety.*

The History of Protestantism. By the Rev. J. A. WYLIE, LL.D. Three Vols., with 600 ILLUSTRATIONS. 27*s.*

Moses and Geology; or, The Harmony of the Bible with Science. By SAMUEL KINNS, Ph.D., &c. *Seventh Edition.* With 110 Illustrations. Cloth, 10*s.* 6*d.*; cloth, gilt edges, 12*s.* 6*d.*

The Church at Home. A Series of Short Sermons, with Collect and Scripture for Sundays, Saints' Days, and Special Occasions. By the Right Rev. ROWLEY HILL, D.D., Lord Bishop of Sodor and Man. 5*s.*

Glories of the Man of Sorrows, The. Sermons preached at St. James's, Piccadilly. By the Rev. H. G. BONAVIA HUNT, Warden and Chaplain of Trinity College, London. Cloth, 2*s.* 6*d.*

Simon Peter: His Life, Times, and Friends. By EDWIN HODDER, Author of "Heroes of Britain," &c. Crown 8vo, 352 pages, cloth, 5*s.*

The Quiver. An Illustrated Religious Magazine. Yearly Volumes, 7*s.* 6*d.*; also Monthly Parts, 6*d.*

The History of the English Bible. By the Rev. W. F. MOULTON, M.A., D.D. 2*s.* 6*d.*

The Family Prayer Book. *Cheap Edition.* Edited by the Rev. Canon GARBETT, M.A., and the Rev. SAMUEL MARTIN. Extra crown 4to, 398 pages, cloth, gilt edges, 5*s.*

Shortened Church Services and Hymns, suitable for use at Children's Services. Compiled by the Rev. T. TEIGNMOUTH SHORE, M.A., Chaplain in Ordinary to the Queen. *Enlarged Edition.* 1*s.*

Some Difficulties of Belief. By the Rev. T. TEIGNMOUTH SHORE, M.A. *Cheap Edition.* 2*s.* 6*d.*

St. George for England, and other Sermons preached to Children. By the Rev. T. TEIGNMOUTH SHORE, M.A. *Fourth Edition.* Cloth, gilt edges, 5*s.*

Day-Dawn in Dark Places; or, Wanderings and Work in Bechwanaland, South Africa. By the Rev. JOHN MACKENZIE. Illustrated throughout. Cloth, 3*s.* 6*d.*

Martin Luther the Reformer. By Professor JULIUS KOESTLIN. With Portrait. Stiff paper wrapper, 1*s.*; cloth gilt, 2*s.*

The Near and Heavenly Horizons. By the Countess DE GASPARIN. *30th Thousand.* 8vo, stiff paper covers, 1*s.*; cloth, 2*s.*

"Heart Chords." Consisting of Little Books by Eminent Divines, having for their object the stimulating, guiding, and strengthening the Christian Life. Appropriately bound in cloth, red edges, price 1*s.* each.

My Work for God. By the Right Rev. Bishop Cotterill.

My Object in Life. By the Ven. Archdeacon Farrar, D.D.

My Body. By the Rev. Prof. W. G. Blaikie, D.D.

My Growth in Divine Life. By the Rev. Prebendary Reynolds, M.A.

My Emotional Life By the Rev. Preb. Chadwick, D.D.

My Aspirations. By the Rev. Geo. Matheson, D.D.

My Aids to the Divine Life. By the Very Rev. Dean Boyle.

My Place in Creation. By the Rev. Hugh Macmillan, D.D.

My Bible. By the Right Rev. Boyd Carpenter, Bishop of Ripon.

My Soul. By the Rev. P. B. Power, M.A.

My Hereafter. By the Very Rev. Dean Bickersteth.

My Walk with God. By the Very Rev. Dean Montgomery.

My Sources of Strength. By the Rev. E. E. Jenkins, M.A., Secretary of Wesleyan Missionary Society.

My Father. By the Right Rev. Ashton Oxenden, late Bishop of Montreal.

Bunyan's Pilgrim's Progress. With 100 Illustrations by Selous and Priolo. Cloth, 7*s.* 6*d.* *Cheap Edition*, 3*s.* 6*d.*

Bunyan's Holy War. With 100 Illustrations by Selous and Priolo. Cloth, 7*s.* 6*d.*

The Young Man in the Battle of Life. By Rev. W. Landels, D.D. *Cheap Edition*, 1*s.*; cloth gilt, 2*s.*; cloth gilt, gilt edges, 2*s.* 6*d.*

The Marriage Ring. A Gift-Book for the Newly Married, and for those Contemplating Marriage. By the Rev. William Landels, D.D. White leatherette, gilt edges, in box, 6*s.*

The Patriarchs. By the late Rev. W. Hanna, D.D., and the Ven. Archdeacon Norris. *Cheap Edition.* Cloth, 2*s.* 6*d.*

The Music of the Bible. By John Stainer, M.A., Mus. Doc. *Cheap Edition.* Cloth, 2*s.* 6*d.*

History of the Waldenses. By the Rev. J. A. Wylie, LL.D. With Illustrations. 2*s.* 6*d.*

The Voice of Time. By John Stroud. Cloth gilt, 1*s.*

Shall We Know One Another? By the Right Rev. J. C. Ryle, Lord Bishop of Liverpool. 1*s.*

☞ COMPLETE CATALOGUES OF CASSELL & COMPANY'S PUBLICATIONS, *containing a List of Several Hundred Volumes, together with a Synopsis of their numerous* Illustrated Serial Publications, *sent post fre application to* Cassell & Company, Limited, *Ludgate Hill, London.*

Breinigsville, PA USA
05 October 2010

246791BV00002B/3/P